# Lecture Notes in Computer Science 3118

Klaus Miesenberger Joachim Klaus
Wolfgang Zagler Dominique Burger (Eds.)

# Computers Helping People with Special Needs

9th International Conference, ICCHP 2004
Paris, France, July 7-9, 2004
Proceedings

Springer

Volume Editors

Klaus Miesenberger
University of Linz, Institut „integriert studieren"
Altenberger Strasse 69, 4040, Linz, Austria
E-mail: klaus.miesenberger@jku.at

Joachim Klaus
Universität Karlsruhe (TH)
Study Centre for Blind and Partially Sighted Students (SZS)
Engesserstr. 4, 76128 Karlsruhe, Germany
E-mail: klaus@szs.uni-karlsruhe.de

Wolfgang Zagler
Technische Universität, Institut für Elektronik und Materialwissenschaften
Favoritenstr. 11/366-1B, 1040 Wien, Austria
E-mail: zagler@fortec.tuwien.ac.at

Dominique Burger
BrailleNet, INSERM U483, UPMC B23
9, quai Saint Bernard, 75252 Paris cedex 5, France
E-mail: Dominique.Burger@snv.jussieu.fr

Library of Congress Control Number: 2004108218

CR Subject Classification (1998): H.5.2, H.5.3, H.3, H.4, K.4, K.3

ISSN 0302-9743
ISBN 3-540-22334-7 Springer-Verlag Berlin Heidelberg New York



Springer-Verlag is a part of Springer Science+Business Media

springeronline.com


Printed in Germany

Typesetting: Camera-ready by author, data conversion by Olgun Computergrafik
Printed on acid-free paper SPIN: 11015048 06/3142 5 4 3 2 1 0

# Preface

The introduction to the 1st International Conference on Computers for Handicapped Persons (Vienna, 1989) by A Min Tjoa (University of Vienna) and Roland Wagner (University of Linz) finished with the following mission statement on the "Future Direction on Computers for Handicapped Persons":

"The different themes show that a lot of problems are solved by the usage of computer technology for helping handicapped persons, for instance for the blind and visually handicapped. A consequence of the discussed themes there are two directions which should be done in the next years. One direction is obvious. The tools must be improved and research and development work should be extended to all groups of handicapped (even if they are numerically not so large as for instance the blind or visually handicapped persons). On the other side in the area of social implications there is an increasing demand on social science studies on overall computer use among disabled persons. Because sources are in principle missing today about disabled persons work tasks, research in this field must begin by trying to survey this aspect. Particular attention should be paid to the extent and character of computer use among the handicapped in work life. There are a lot of questions, which should be answered during the next years for reaching the aim of rehabilitation."

Fifteen years later the 9th International Conference on Computers Helping People with Special Needs (Paris, 2004) offered a comprehensive and deepened view on general awareness, special research and individual applications concerning disabled people and their participation in our society.

Remarkable changes are to be registered:

- Besides blindness and visual impairment, deafness and hearing impairment, mobility impairment, cognitive, speed and learning impairment will be focused on.
- Increased research and special training should be dedicated to elderly people and their disabilities.
- The early years' mission towards assistive technology for disabled individuals has changed over to a holistic approach towards accessibility in the whole environment. Smart houses, designs for all, and the transition from human interfaces to humane interfaces characterize accessibility and the new generation of Web development tools.
  Does this summary mean success, fulfillness and the realization of those topics evoked by the pioneers from 1989?
  Concerning people with disabilities – and their right to equal education and adequate jobs – are the above topics being realized?
- Has their daily discrimination finished?
- Are adapted living conditions and partnerships via democratic society solved?
  Surely not. Looking around, we have to confess that, despite a lot of progress, the new challenges demand continuity, consequent action and persistence.

The European Union declared 2003 to be the "European Year of People with Disabilities" in order to raise awareness about the situation of its millions of disabled citizens. The feedback from this initiative – gathered in a EU barometer – was the following:

- 38 million citizens of the EU (10%) suffer from a disability;
- 97% of Europeans express their opinion that it is still very difficult for people with disabilities to participate in social life and that further activities are necessary to improve their integration;
- 93% demand more money to overcome barriers in public buildings;
- 76% register that physical access to public buildings and institutions (for example public service buildings, universities, schools) is far from being acceptable, although 57% confess a remarkable improvement in the last decade.

Continuing the biannual conferences, ICCHP 2004 took over this comprehensive responsibility and brought together a community from around the world to share their thoughts at the various presentation and communication opportunities. ICCHP 2004 took place under the high patronage of Mr. Jacques Chirac, President of the French Republic, and was sponsored by the European Union as well as by private and public companies and institutions. Our thanks go to:

- The General ICCHP 2004 Chair, H.J. Murphy (Founder and Former Director of the Centre on Disabilities, California State University, Northridge, USA and International Ambassador, Pulsedata International)
- The Programme Chairs:
  - A. Karshmer (University of South Florida at Tampa, USA)
  - A.M. Tjoa (Technical University of Vienna, Austria)
  - R. Vollmar (Universitaet Karlsruhe (TH), Germany)
  - R. Wagner (University of Linz, Austria)
- The Programme Committee:

| | | |
|---|---|---|
| Alquie, G. | Université Pierre et Marie Curie | France |
| Andrich, R. | SIVA Fondazione Don Carlo Gnocchi Onlus | Italy |
| Arató, A. | Hungarian Academy of Science | Hungary |
| Arató P. | TU Budapest | Hungary |
| Archambault, D. | Université Pierre et Marie Curie | France |
| Azevedo, L. | Instituto Superior Tecnico | Portugal |
| Batusic, M. | University of Linz | Austria |
| Bidaud, P. | Université Pierre et Marie Curie | France |
| Blenkhorn, P. | University of Manchester Institute of Science and Technology | United Kingdom |
| Bothe, H.-H. | Technical University of Denmark | Denmark |
| Bühler, C. | Forschungsinstitut Technologie-Behindertenhilfe | Germany |

| | | |
|---|---|---|
| Burnod, Y. | Institut National de la Santé et de la Recherche Médicale | France |
| Busby, G. | EASAMS Ltd. | United Kingdom |
| Charlier, J. | Metrovision | France |
| Dotter, F. | University of Klagenfurt | Austria |
| Edwards, A. | University of York | United Kingdom |
| Ekberg, J. | Stakes | Finland |
| Emiliani, P.L. | Istituto di Fisica Applicata "Nello CARRARA" | Italy |
| Engelen, J. | Katholieke Universiteit Leuven | Belgium |
| Freitas, D. | University of Porto | Portugal |
| Gardner, J. | Oregon State University | USA |
| Gupta, G. | University of Texas at Dallas | USA |
| Hara, S. | Tsukuba College of Technology | Japan |
| Helle, K.M. | Work Research Institute | Norway |
| Holzinger, A. | Graz University Hospital | Austria |
| Horlait, E. | Université Pierre et Marie Curie | France |
| Kowalik, R. | Technical University of Gdansk | Poland |
| Kremser, W. | Austrian Computer Society | Austria |
| Lauruska, V. | Siauliai University | Lithuania |
| Lindström, J.-I. | Telia AB | Sweden |
| Mariani, J. | Université Pierre et Marie Curie (Paris VI) | France |
| Mendelova, E. | Comenius University of Bratislava | Slovak Republic |
| Mokhtari, M. | INST | France |
| Neveryd, H. | Lund University | Sweden |
| Nussbaum, G. | KI-I | Austria |
| Ortner, D. | University of Linz | Austria |
| Oussik, V. | Logos | Russia |
| Panek, P. | Technical University of Vienna | Austria |
| Penaz, P. | University of Brno | Czech Republic |
| Petrie, H. | University of Hertfordshire | United Kingdom |
| Ponteli, E. | New Mexico State University | USA |
| Pühretmair, F. | KI-I | Austria |
| Quirchmayr, G. | University of Vienna | Austria |
| Soede, T. | iRv | The Netherlands |
| Stephanidis, C. | ICS-Forth | Greece |
| Stöger, B. | University of Linz | Austria |
| Strauss, Ch. | University of Vienna | Austria |
| Svensson, H. | National Institute for Special Needs Education | Sweden |
| Tabeling, P. | CNRS | France |
| Traunmüller, R. | University of Linz | Austria |
| Trehin, P. | World Autism Organisation | Belgium |
| Vaspöri, T. | Hungarian Academy of Science | Hungary |
| Velasco, C. | Fraunhofer Institute for Applied Information Technology (FIT) | Germany |
| Wagner, I. | Technical University of Vienna | Austria |
| Wünschmann, W. | TU Dresden | Germany |

– The Organizing Committee:

| University of Linz | Université Pierre et Marie Curie | INSERM/BrailleNet |
|---|---|---|
| Arrer, B. | Békefi, B. | Burger, D. |
| Batusic, M. | Bigot, R. | Pinto, S. |
| Feichtenschlager, P. | Lafont, R. | |
| Herramhof, S. | Merle, D. | |
| Köttstorfer, M. | Poutier, C. | |
| Miesenberger, K. | | |
| Ortner, D. | | |
| Petz, A. | | |
| Schüler, C. | | |
| Stöger, B. | | |

We thank the Austrian Computer Society for announcing and sponsoring the *Roland Wagner Award on Computers Helping People with Special Needs.*

The Austrian Computer Society decided in September 2001 to endow this award in honour of Prof. Dr. Roland Wagner, the founder of ICCHP. He is the founder and head of the Institute of the Austrian-wide institute of "integrated study" offering services for print-disabled students at Austrian universities. He is the founder of the working group "ICT for/with People with Disabilities" of the Austrian Computer Society, the group that established the ICCHP conference as an outstanding international event.

Prof. Wagner is one of the pioneers in ICT for people with disabilities in Austria and has been pushing the field forward for years. His early visionary understanding of the role of ICT to change the perspectives of people with special needs and his dedication to fighting for equal rights for this target group has had important impacts on awareness and on beginning changes in society. This award should give further incentives and should support the important work which has been the passion of Prof. Wagner over decades.

The Roland Wagner Award is a biannual award and will be in the range of 3000 Euros. It will be handed over at the ICCHP conferences.

Award winners:

- Award 0 was handed over to Prof. Dr. Roland Wagner on the occasion of his 50th birthday.
- Award 1 was won by WAI-W3C. It was handed over to Judy Brewer at ICCHP 2002.
- Special Award 2003; A special award was handed over to Prof. Dr. A Min Tjoa, one of the founders of ICCHP, on the occasion of his 50th birthday in 2003.

Altogether we feel a common responsibility to advance a global understanding of human partnership and the inclusion of all human beings and providing for their personal fulfillment and welfare.

July 2004

Joachim Klaus, Klaus Miesenberger,
Dominique Burger,and Wolfgang Zagler *(Publishing Chairs)*

# Table of Contents

## Design for All in IST – Co-operation in Europe



## Personalization of Interactive Systems

## e-Learning and Accessibility



## Making Music Accessible

## Accessible Games and Entertainment



## Accessible Tourism



## Accessibility and the Next Generation of Web Development Tools

## Elderly and Disabled People: Therapy and Care

## Blind and Visually Impaired People: Orientation and Mobility

## Blind People: Braille Interfaces



## Blind and Visually Impaired People: Access to Documents and Information

## Blind and Visually Impaired People: Education and Training



## Blind People: Access to Mathematics

## Blind People: Access to Graphics and Haptic Interfaces

## Mobility Impaired People: HCI

## Mobility Impaired People: Rehabilitaiton and Health Care

## Smart Environments for All

## People with Cognitive, Speech and Learning Impairment: Autism



## People with Cognitive, Speech and Learning Impairment: Software Accessibility



## People with Cognitive, Speech and Learning Impairment: Education and Training

## Deaf People: Sign Language and Digital Media

## Deaf and Hearing Impaired People: ICT and AT

# We Are All Blind: Cognetics and the Designing of Interfaces for Accessibility

## *Introduction to the Special Thematic Session*

Jef Raskin

Adjunct Professor of Computer Science
University of Chicago
jef@jefraskin.com

**Abstract:** Today's GUIs and their familiar methods are far from optimal for typical users, wasting time, causing unnecessary errors, exacerbating repetitive stress injuries, and inducing frustration and annoyance. These problems are often amplified when standard interface methods are used in systems for less-abled users. We must not be distracted from good interface design by the strait-jackets of present paradigms. To this end we employ insight, ingenuity, and testing – but they are not enough. Cognetic tools, which are quantitative and objective instead of being based on heuristics and subjective judgment, can play an important role in increasing accessibility, even where we use existing hardware.

## 1 Introduction

In a very real way, even a person with superb visual acuity is as handicapped as the unseeing when using present computer interfaces. Let me give an example. If you have a computer, its keyboard probably has a "Caps Lock" key, which when tapped puts the keyboard into a mode where any letter you type subsequently is appears as a upper case instead of a lowercase letter. In this state, a light illuminates to show you that the Caps Lock mode is engaged.

It sometimes happens that we hit the Caps Lock key accidentally. We are then surprised, and often annoyed, when our typing suddenly appears in all caps. Upon catching this, we have to erase and retype some portion of whatever we were typing. The light doesn't help us: in fact, we almost never notice it in these situations, even though it is plainly visible. Anybody who types a lot does not look at the keyboard: we are blind to an indicator on the keyboard when looking at the computer's display. A similar event happens when a dialog box appears on the display you are not looking at when using a dual-screen computer: Apparently, the computer has frozen. Even indicators on the screen we are using are often missed.

A similar, and even more important, blindness occurs when we are paying attention to something; we can be blind (and deaf) to many events, depending on our degree of absorption in our task. Elizabeth Loftus [1] has written eloquently on this topic and a number of examples are given in [2].

This is a blindness that can affect any of us, regardless of physical conditions, and we must design our interfaces to allow us to work in spite of this universal human handicap. The field of cognetics and its results can help us avoid this and other inter-

K. Miesenberger et al. (Eds.): ICCHP 2004, LNCS 3118, pp. 1–5, 2004.

face design traps. Cognetics is the engineering of products to accommodate human mental abilities and limitations; it is an analog of ergonomics, which guides the design of products to match human physical attributes.

Enormous energy is being put into devices for the blind and to compensate for other physical and mental differences that take individuals away from center of the ergonomic and cognetic bell curves. This effort is both noble and necessary, but it also needs to be paralleled with a solution to more basic problems with human-computer interaction that make using technology more difficult than it need be for all humans. It is only a half-solution to make a system for, say, a blind person, work as well as it does for a sighted person when the system doesn't work all that well for the sighted person in the first place.

Douglas Adams, in his delightful “Hitchhiker's Guide to the Galaxy” spoke about his imaginary “Sirius Cybernetics Corporation” but was clearly describing today's systems when he said, “This is the rock-solid principle on which the whole of the Corporation's success is founded – their fundamental design flaws are completely hidden by their superficial design flaws.” My point is that we are so taken with fixing the superficial flaws in creating systems for people with special needs that we are missing the essential need to fix some deeper design flaws that handicap all of us. These pervasive problems constitute a double burden on the disabled.

For example, a user who must type one character at a time with a stylus held in the mouth wants to use the minimum number of characters conceivable in order to perform a task. In their case, it is obvious that the cost of wasted user actions is very high. But wasted actions are a cost to all of us. The wasted effort required by present software designs is enormous, but goes largely unnoticed. The problem is that when designing software, we tend to use the familiar paradigms we grew up with as we learned to use computer technology. If those paradigms are faulty, so will anything we build using them. But because they are familiar, they seem inevitable, natural, and obvious. Any change can be upsetting, even if it is a change for the much better.

In general people with physical disabilities have the same mental faculties as those who do not. This leads to the conclusion that if some aspect of a computer interface that is not affected by the disability is difficult for a fully-abled person, then that same aspect will be difficult for the disabled. This seems obvious, but the implication is that where present interfaces are troublesome for the majority of users, they are at least as troublesome – and possibly much more troublesome – for those who have physical impediments to using computers. We need but one more fact: today's interfaces, such as Windows or the Mac OS, are full of major design errors that increase error rates, cause and exacerbate repetitive stress injuries, and require far more effort (in terms of time, keystrokes, and mouse moves and clicks) than is necessary to complete almost any of the tasks we do with them.

Building software or an apparatus that makes it easier to deal with, say, Microsoft Windows, is a useful endeavor, but providing an environment that is far more efficient and pleasant can have even greater returns in terms of usability.

## 2 About Efficiency

Efficiency is defined as how much work needs to be done divided by the amount of work that is actually done. It is always a number between 0 and 1. If a system has an efficiency of 0.5, then you are doing twice as much work as necessary. For anybody, interfaces with low efficiency wastes their time and effort. For a person who finds physically interacting with computers difficult, a high degree efficiency can make the difference between a usable and an unusable system.

Efficiency of an interface can be precisely measured, allowing you to judge the quality of an interface design even before it has been implemented. The definition of efficiency of an interface is identical to that of efficiency in thermodynamics, as Claude Shannon discovered [2, 3].

An example of extreme loss of efficiency is in the desktop model of present GUIs [4]. If the task is, for example, to edit a memo, one must start in the desktop, navigate to the memo, and then "launch" the memo (or, in cruder systems, launch the word processor and "open" the memo). When done editing, one must "save" the memo and often you have to give it a name. None of this effort adds to the content of the memo and is wasted (it is also technically unnecessary). The historical reasons that the desktop model came about are clear, but irrelevant. We can and should do better now, especially for those for whom operating a computer is physically challenging. More efficient approaches are available but as that is in itself a book-length topic [2], it cannot be discussed in the space allotted for this paper.

## 3 About Time

It is also possible to predict the time it will take a user to achieve a goal with a given interface. This can be done based on the specifications of the interface, before it is built. While not all design decisions can be made without building and testing actual software and hardware, the use of these tools can greatly speed development and help the developer to avoid numerous difficulties. The work of Card, Moran, and Newell was the first major exploration of this, and their GOMS model [5] and its more recent extensions [6] are well validated.

While the constants in these models sometimes have to be adjusted experimentally for individuals with special needs, they are well established for the majority of the population.

Classic laws of psychology that yield numerical results include Fitts's law which relates time to make a gesture to the overall size of the gesture and the size of the target toward which the gesture is aimed.

Screen layout can often be optimized by applying Fitts's law. Hick's law gives a measure of the time it takes to make a sequence of decisions. For example, when deciding between an interface modeled as a deep tree with few branches at each node or as a broad tree with few nodes but many branches, this law comes into play. These laws have been discussed widely [2, 5].

## 4 About Habituation

Habituation is a universal property of humans (and many other organisms). In humans it can be characterized by a shift, caused by near-identical repetition of a task, from having to do the task with conscious attention to being able to do it without conscious attention. Learning to juggle three balls is a typical example. At first it seems nearly impossible and requires your full attention; any distraction will cause the beginner to lose control of the balls. With practice, the juggler can walk, talk, and perform other tasks while juggling. An expert can nearly forget that he or she is juggling: it has become automatic, a habit has been formed.

Humans can pay conscious attention to only one task at a time (though we can sometimes switch between tasks quickly). This key property of cognition has been largely ignored in interface design. It should be central in every interface designer's mind. Only a very severe head injury or disease can affect habituation, so designing interfaces to take account of habituation applies to almost any class of user, whether able-bodied or not.

To work effectively, we must form habits, and thus protect our attention from being distracted from the content of our task by what should be routine operations.

Habituation can take place only in a stable environment, where the same gesture always produces the same results. Unfortunately, this is not a characteristic of most computer systems. Without getting into technical detail (discussed in [2]), we can observe that present computer software has modes. A mode is where the same gesture (such as typing a "control-C") has one meaning (for example, to "cut" the selection from the text), but in another mode of the system that same gesture can mean to adjust the contrast of an image. Another way that systems frustrate habit formation is by having the same task done in two ways. In one application "N" might mean to create a "New" document, in another application "G" might mean to "Get" a new document.

The user, concentrating on his or her task, if both applications are frequently used, will not be able to form a habit. If one application is used more than the other, they might form the habit of using, say, "N" automatically, and thus give the wrong command when in the other application. This is the principle that underlies the usual search for the somewhat ill-defined concept of "consistency".

We must design systems which, unlike those available today, allow users to form safe, helpful habits.

If we do not they will either (1) not form habits and thus be distracted from their tasks or (2) they will form habits that will cause them to make errors, which also distract them from what they are doing. This is true for both able-bodied and disabled users. In other words, present interfaces don't work properly for anybody.

## Overuse of the Mouse

One of the difficulties facing many of the disabled is the use of pointing devices. Whether it is due to the tremor of Parkinson's disease or a lack of clarity of vision, a graphic input device (GID) presents difficulties.

Less well known is that GIDs also cause difficulties for the fully-able user. Studies have shown that most repetitive stress injuries from computer use are associated with GID use and not with keyboard use [7]. Lastly, use of a GID is slower for nearly all users in applications such as choosing menu items, clicking at on-screen buttons and palettes, and pointing in text. GIDs are appropriate and necessary for those situations where true graphic input is necessary (as when drawing in a drawing program) and where a person cannot physically use a keyboard. Methods for avoiding GID use while maintaining or improving usability are in reference [2].

Overuse of the mouse has led to overuse of icons, which are symbols that are often universally incomprehensible. This is why many programs have words that pop up when you point at an icon. Notice that icons are not used to explain words. The logical conclusion is that buttons should be labeled with words and not with icons. This does make internationalization of software more difficult for the group producing it, but it makes using the software easier for the end user. The ethical question is: which is more damaging, causing a few days or weeks of additional effort for a small development group or causing years of additional effort for a large group of users?

## 5 The Need for Better Development Systems

It is my belief that, having made the honorable choice of working to increase the accessibility of technology, we should apply all that we know to the task. It is very difficult to do so, as the development tools that are widely available reinforce some very poor interface methods. Worse, they often prevent or make it very difficult to do things in new and better ways. In developing The Humane Interface (THE) [8], we ran into this difficulty time after time. For example, in one design it would have been advantageous to be able to detect the shift keys independently. We found that every operating system mapped both to the same code, and had to abandon that interface design.

Designing for accessibility requires the utmost in flexibility from software and hardware systems. While USB is a far better electronic interface in many ways than the old parallel ports, it is much harder to write software for.

If you are designing an electromechanical device to solve an individual's needs, you will have it working much sooner from a parallel port than from a USB port. Even if you use a commercial USB-to-parallel port electronic interface, the software will be more complex.

Similarly, if you wish to avoid the multitude of methods you need to control windows because you wish to offer the user the full screen, today's operating systems will try to force you to work within windows anyway.

If computer companies are truly interested in accessibility, it is not enough to provide add-on applications, they must give developers the ability to do whatever they wish with the hardware and software and keep it open source so that we can change what needs to be changed to help people with special needs.

## References


1. Loftus, E.F., *Eyewitness Testimony*. 1979, Cambridge (MA): Harvard University Press.
2. Raskin, J., *The Humane Interface: New Directions for Designing Interactive Systems*. 2000, Boston (MA): Addison-Wesley-Longman.
3. Shannon, C.E. and W. Weaver, *The Mathematical Theory of Communication*. 1949, Urbana (IL): University of Illinois Press.
4. Microsoft, *The Windows Interface Guidelines for Software Design*. 1995, Redmond (WA): Microsoft Press.
5. Card, S.K., T.P. Moran, and A. Newell, *The psychology of Human-Computer Interaction*. 1983, Hillsdale (NJ): Erlbaum.
6. John, B.E., *Why GOMS?* interactions, 1995. **2**(4): p. 80-89.
7. Anderson, J.H., Thomsen, J. F., Overgaard, E., Lassen, C.F., Brandt, L.P.A., Vilstrup, I., Kryger, A.I., Mikkelsen, S., *Computer Use and Carpal Tunnel Syndrome: A 1-Year Follow-up Study*. JAMA, 2003. **289**(22): p. 2963.
8. www.jefraskin.com, last access: April, 15, 2004

# The Design Question of Development of Multimedia Educational Software for Aphasia Patients

Cecília Sik Lányi [1], Erzsébet Bacsa[1], Rita Mátrai[1], Zsolt Kosztyán[1], and Ilona Pataky[2]

[1] Department of Image Processing and Neourocumputing, University of Veszprém
H-8200 Veszprém, Egyetem u. 10., Hungary
lanyi@almos.vein.hu, erzsebet.bacsa@freemail.hu
ritka@primposta.hu, kzst@vision.vein.hu
[2] National Centre of Brain Vein Diseases OPNI
H-1021 Budapest, Hűvösvölgyi u 116, Hungary
pataky@opni.hu

**Abstract.** Aphasia is an impairment of language, affecting the production or comprehension of speech and the ability to read or write. Most common cause of aphasia is – about 23–40 % of stroke survivors - acquired aphasia. The rehabilitation of aphasia is a medical, special treatment (speech therapy), which is the task of a psychologist. It needs long and intensive therapy. More detailed information about therapy can be found in [2,6]. In this paper we present our implementation or realization of interactive multimedia educational software to develop readiness of speech for helping the therapy within the frame of youth scientific and MSc thesis works. The first program was developed in Flash, the second in Macromedia Director. The goal of our software is to teach the most important everyday words. The software will be a useful device in the education of children with heavy mental deficiencies. Reading the program you can learn how it works and what current results we have achieved.

## 1 What Is Aphasia?

Aphasia is an impairment of language. An acquired communication disorder that impairs a person's ability to process language, but does not affect intelligence. It also impairs ability to speak and understand others and most people with aphasia experience difficulty in reading and writing. While aphasia is most common among older people, it can occur in people of all ages, races, nationalities and gender. Further information about Aphasia can be found in [5].

### 1.1 Types of Aphasia [8]

Global Aphasia is the most severe form. Patients with this type of aphasia produce only few recognizable words, can understand little or no spoken speech at all and they can neither read nor write. These symptoms can usually be seen after a patient has suffered a stroke and they may rapidly improve if the damage has not been too extensive and there has not been greater brain damage or more severe and lasting disability.

K. Miesenberger et al. (Eds.): ICCHP 2004, LNCS 3118, pp. 6–13, 2004.

Broca's Aphasia means that speech output is severely reduced limited mainly to short utterances of less than four words. As a result vocabulary access is limited, the formation of the sounds is often laborious and clumsy. Patients with Broca's aphasia may understand speech and be able to read but the quality of speech is halting and effortful. Furthermore, they are very limited in writing.

Mixed non fluent aphasia means sparse and effortful speech resembling Broca's aphasia. Patients of this illness are limited in comprehension of speech and they do not read or write beyond elementary level.

In case of Anomic Aphasia persons are left with a persistent inability to supply words for the things that they want to talk about. Mainly they have problems with nouns and verbs. However they can understand speech well and in most cases they can read adequately. Unfortunately they have poor writing ability.

## 1.2 What Causes Aphasia?

Most common cause of aphasia – about 23–40 % of stroke survivors acquire aphasia. It can also result from head injury, brain tumour or other neurological causes. It is estimated that about one million people in the United States have acquired aphasia, or 1 in every 250 people.

More common than Parkinson's Disease, cerebral palsy or muscular dystrophy. About 1/3rd of severely head-injured persons have aphasia. However, most people have never heard of it.

## 1.3 Recovery from Aphasia

After stroke – If symptoms last longer than two or three months, complete recovery is unlikely. However, it is important to note that some people continue to improve over a period of years and even decades. Improvement is a slow process that usually involves both helping the individual and the family understand the nature of aphasia and learning compensatory strategies for communicating.

How do you communicate with a person with aphasia? Communication Do's and Don'ts. First and foremost, a person with aphasia has to be considered as a normal human being, so talk to them as an adult not as a child. Minimizing or eliminating background noises helps a lot in understanding. Before starting communication make sure you have the person's attention. To make them feel confident encourage them all the time. Use all modes of communication: speech, writing, drawing and yes-or-no responses to avoid being boring during studying. Give them enough time to talk and permit a reasonable amount of time to respond as well. It is essential that you should accept all communication attempts. Keep your own communication simple but adult-like. It is better to use simplified sentence structures and keep in mind to reduce your rate of speech. Keep your voice at a normal level and do emphasize key words. If it is possible, use a lot of gestures and aids during communication. Do not hesitate to repeat any statement when it is necessary but never ever attempt to finish the patients' statements for them.

# 2 Software Development

## 2.1 Developing Environment

The first program was developed in Flash MX, the second in Macromedia Director.

The Flash MX has more useful tools, which helped programming the subtasks. The Flash MX is suitable to develop interactive multimedia programs, too, in contrast with other programming languages. As a matter of fact, the Flash MX is an animated software which supports the vector graphical and "raster" based pictures. This is a development environment constructing interactive programs by means of its ability to be programmed. With the help of the animated software called Flash MX interactive programs including extremely fast and spectacular multimedia elements can be created. Further information about Macromedia Flash MX can be found in [9].

The Macromedia Director alloys efficacy of a high-level programming language with the spectacle of animation studios. Macromedia Director is a widely used multimedia developing environment, which combines the effectiveness of high level programming languages with the show of animation studios. This developing interactive multimedia program is considerably complicated and takes a lot of time with conventional programming languages, such as Pascal or C++, but with the help of Director these applications can be written more easily and quickly. Further information about Macromedia Director can be found in [9].

We will make a comparison between both developing pieces of software so that the user can decide which one has more advantages for them and is worth further development. The major characteristic feature of the program developed in Flash MX is its extraordinary quickness that can be achieved with not using much memory. Due to the low number of kbytes it can be used through the Internet very easily. What helps the Aphasic patients the most is that they do not need to study in rehabilitation centres but owing to the flexibility of the program they can also practise in their homes. Though they need the guidance of a teacher in every case. The comparison and analysis of developing environments is not the theme of this article.

## 2.2 Progress of Development

First of all, I got acquainted with the topic through several books my consulant offered me. Naturally, after immersing in studying the disease itself I consulted with the therapists in the school a couple of times. Their confirmations meant an essential step during the process of developing of the program since from their feedback I knew that the main idea of the program functioned smoothly, it just needed some polishing at certain parts. The basis of the multimedia software are the books "Everyday tasks" by Jacqueline Stark [4] and "Speak without fear" by Takácsné Csór Marianna [7]. The second book has more exercises becoming more and more difficult through the whole book. After collecting the tasks into several groups we designed the main menu. We took the following items into account: simplicity, easy to survey, easy to use, do not distract the attention.

The programming was started after the searching for simple figures and illustrations easy to survey. At the beginning we had to consider that there were a lot of similar exercises. The program had to be terminable. The number of the visible pictures on the screen is not the same in every task therefore we had to watch out for their sizes. The order of the cast members on the stage was also important. The pictures are randomly arranged in every skill level of the program. In this way protection against monotony is assured. By using the interactivity of our software the computer informs the user about the right or wrong solution. Both cases are marked with adequate figure and sound.

## 3 The Introduction of the Software

The application of an educational software can have difficulties in Hungarian schools and rehabilitation institutes because of the low number and quality of the computers. Unfortunately the situation is the same with the equipment of the psychologist and special teachers who take care of the aphasia patients. It was an important point of view that the programs should also run easily on an average computer to avoid any difficulties. Considering these factors we have chosen programming on HTML basis because of its being modular and having a small size. The Microsoft Windows operating system is generally installed on school computers. The objects and their interactivities were made with Flash MX which does not need a compiler and building large executable files, only the downloading of the Flash Player 6.

We can direct the interactive objects of the film in the Director, as a fictive director. The action is taking place on the stage and it is visible for the user. The cast members are pictures, video clips, music and all of the buttons and tools. Events can be added to the objects and with them we can handle the information received by the computer.

The program starts in both cases with choosing one of the tasks. The user may not be able to use the software alone in this phase of the rehabilitation, so a teacher or a therapist's guidance is inevitable. Answering the questions does not happen in a fixed order, so it is possible to begin the practice from his (or her) own skill level.

We take care of the interactive participation using the possibilities of the manipulation technique in every task. The number of the right answers isn't displayed with points but only with illustrating animations. The programs are user friendly, they do not require special knowledge and everybody is able to acquire how to use them in a few seconds. Requirements: Pentium class or equivalent CPU, SVGA display with 800*600 resolution, Windows operating system with included Internet Explorer WEB browser, Mouse, Macromedia Flash Player 6.

### 3.1 The Structure of the Menus

There are two pictures in the main menu of the first program (Fig. 1). Here the patient or the teacher can choose from the house or the city with a mouse click. The second program shows only the objects of the house. The main menu of the second program starts with a user's guide (Fig. 2).

Fig. 1. Main menu (Flash version)

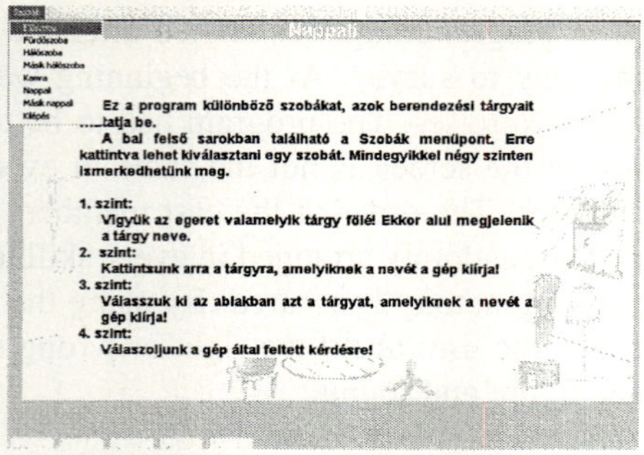


Fig. 2. Main menu (Director version)

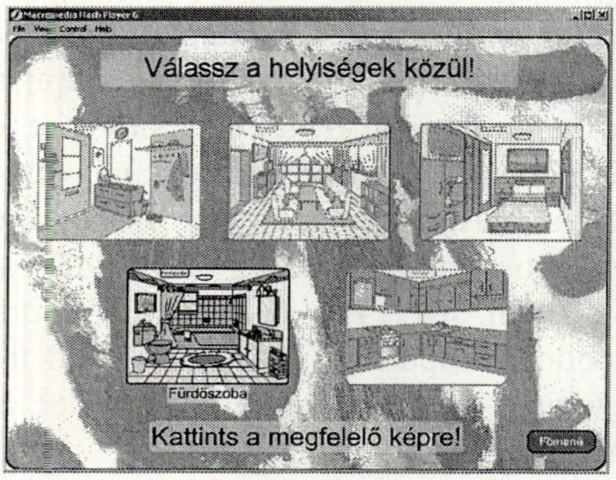


Fig. 3. The rooms – submenu (Flash)

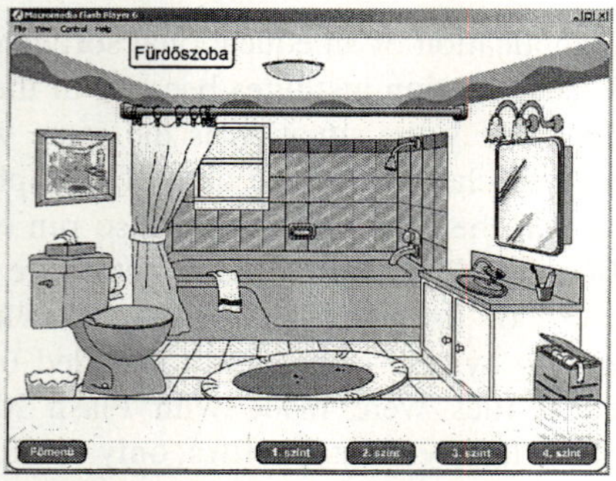


Fig. 4. The task level in a room (Flash)

In the first program, after the first choice there is a second choice from the premises of the house if the user choose the house earlier. (Fig. 3) (This choice is the first step of the first program.) This is in a pop-up window on the left up corner. (Fig. 2)

If the city was chosen in the first program, the patient can practise the orientation in the street for example in a post office, in a hospital, etc. The back function to the main menu works from every submenus, and then one can choose another task too.

### 3.2 The User Interface Design

The good arrangement and the harmony of the colours were important view-points at the design of the user interface. The sizes, colours and elaboration of the pictures have to be taken into consideration, but it should not distract the user's attention from the task. That is why too strong colours are not used in the program.

## 4 The Tasks

The main task of both pieces of software is to teach the everyday words of the house or of the environment near the house. (Fig. 4) In every submenu there are 4 skill levels.

The first level makes the user acquainted with the objects of the room. (Fig. 5 and Fig. 6) If the user points with the mouse to an object, the name of the object appears on the screen and it can be read. This first skill level trains the user's memory power.

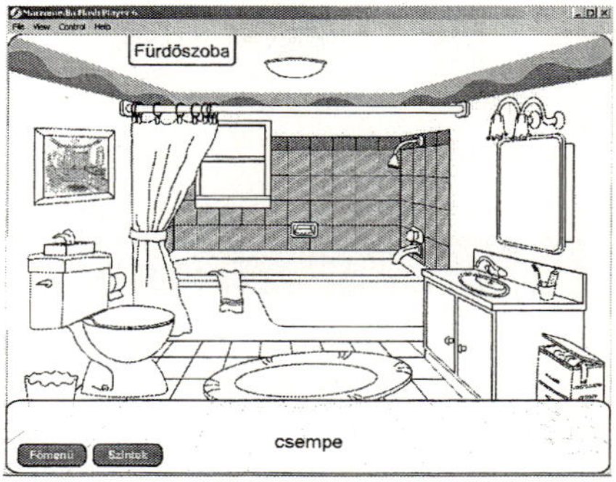


**Fig. 5.** 1st skill level (Flash)

**Fig. 6.** 1st skill level (Director)

The second level shows an uncoloured picture. The program asks the user to show the named objects. (Fig. 7 and Fig. 8) If the user manages to find the asked object, that turns into a coloured one. In this way the user can make the whole picture colourful. If the user is unsuccessful, the program sends an error message and the user can continue.

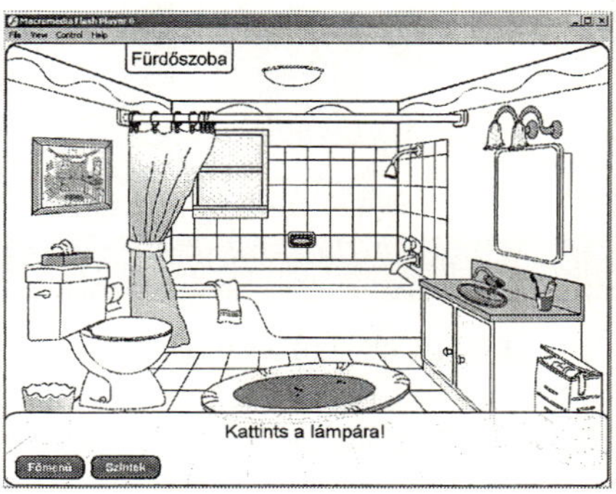


**Fig. 7.** 2nd skill level (Flash)

**Fig. 8.** 2nd skill level (Director)

The user's ability is also controlled on the third level. The earlier learned room is in the background, but it is pale. (Fig. 9 and Fig. 10) The program shows three figures randomly and the user has to choose one with answering a question. This is essential because the user cannot recall its name but only its place properly. The real knowledge is examined at this level.

If the user could not answer, the program sends an error picture and asks a new question. This third level asks questions as long as the user or the teacher does not choose another skill level.

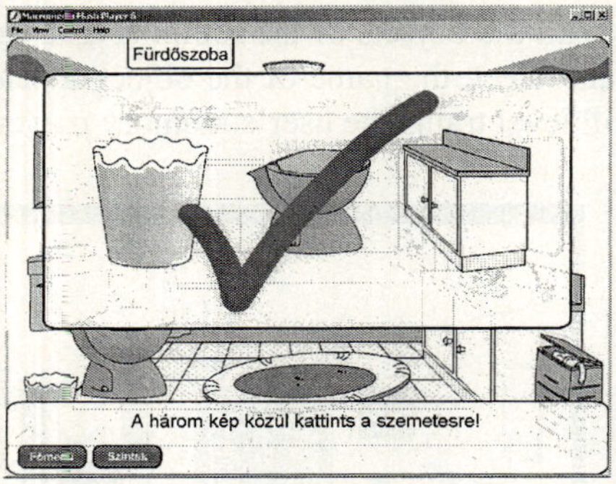


**Fig. 9.** 3rd skill level by right answer (Flash) (Which is the bin?)

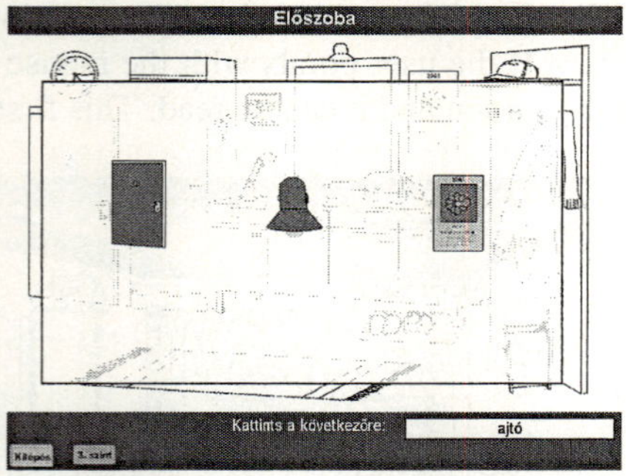


**Fig. 10.** The question of 3rd skill level (Director) (Show the door!)

The fourth level asks more difficult questions than the third level. The questions deal with the handling of the objects. (Fig. 11 and Fig. 12) If the user can find the object, the program asks its name and the user has to write it into an input row on the screen. After the right answer the program asks a new question.

**Fig. 11.** 4th skill level (Flash)

**Fig. 12.** 4th skill level (Director)

The starting level and the tasks are chosen by the therapist. It can be used with the therapist's assistance.

## 5 Summary

Within the frame of youth scientific and MSc thesis works we have prepared interactive multimedia educational pieces of software to develop the readiness of speech for helping the therapies. The software package contains two programs. The first program was developed in Flash, the second in Macromedia Director. The goal of our software is to teach the most important everyday words. We made the first tests in the Kozmutza Flora Special Primary School and Talent Developing / Training Collage.

We have tested only the user interface design so far. In the second step during second term in the 2003/2004 academic year we are going to make the efficiency examination not only in this school but in the National Centre of Brain Vein Diseases too. We will report on the result of the efficiency examinations during the conference.

One result of the first test is that the software is a useful device not only in the education of aphasic but heavy mental deficient children too. Moreover, it can be used easily by both the children and the teachers themselves. Considering the advice of the teachers helping us during the program the children needs some motivating animation reassuring the right answer and increasing their interests for the oncoming items. On the contrary, adults do not require such motivating exercises or tasks. The English and German versions and the audio confirmation of the words are being developed at present.

## Acknowledgements

Hereby, I, the constructor of the program, express my thanks for the enormous help I received from the teachers of the Kozmutza Flora Special Primary School and Talent Developing / Training Collage.

The authors would like to thank for the assistance of NKFP 2/052/2001 project.

## References

1. Cseh Katalin – Hegyi Ágnes: Exercises for the cognitive therapy of Aphasia, Gyakorlatok az afázia kognitív nyelvi terápiájához, Nemzeti Tankönyvkiadó, Bp. 1995
2. Engl E.M., Kotten A., Ohlendorf J., Poser E.: Exercises for the Aphasia Therapy, Gyakorlatok az afázia terápiájához, Medician, Bp. 1990
3. Hegyi Ágnes: Aphasia Therapies: Proposal for the cognitive lingual therapy of Aphasia, Afáziaterápiák: Javaslat az afázia kognitív nyelvi terápiájára, Nemzeti Tankönyvkiadó, Bp. 1995
4. Jacqueline Stark: Everyday tasks Handbook, (Mindennapi tevékenységek kézikönyv), CIE, Wien, 1992
5. Leel – Őssy Lóránt: The paralysed man, A megbénult ember, Statisztikai Kiadó, Bp. 1988
6. Subosits I: Collection book of selected passages of the clinical disturbance in speaking, Educational Publisher Bp, 1986, Szemelvénygyűjtemény a klinikai beszédzavarok köréből, Tankönyvkiadó Bp. 1986
7. Takácsné Csór Marianna: Speak without fear! Exercise Book for the therapy of Aphasia, Beszélj bátran Feladatgyűjtemény az afázia terápiához, Tankönyvkiadó Bp. 1986
8. The National Aphasia Association's website http://www.aphasia.org/
9. The national Macromedia website http://www.macromedia.com

# Multimedia Programs for Children with Hearing Difficulties

Cecília Sik Lányi[1], Ágnes Váry[2], András Sik[3], András Nemetz[1], and Zoltán Geiszt[1]

[1] Department of Image Processing and Neourocumputing , University of Veszprém
8200 Veszprém, Egyetem u. 10, Hungary
lanyi@almos.vein.hu
http://www.knt.vein.hu

[2] Török Béla Kindergarten, Elementary School and Special Trade School, Budapest
1142 Budapest, Rákospatak u. 101, Hungary
varyagnes@yahoo.com

[3] Padányi Bíró Márton High School, Veszprém
8200 Veszprém, Szeglethy u. 14, Hungary
sikandras24@freemail.hu

**Abstract.** Two multimodal speech teaching and training programs have been developed for 6-10 years old hearing handicapped children. The first program is "Now I know already what its name is". The main menu has eight topics. For example school, Christmas, Eastern, garden, summer, in the hospital and so on. In the sub menu of a topic there are two other sub menus. The painting and the talking sub menus. Every talking submenu has a cartoon like presentation. The second program has been developed during the last school year and has been prepared to increase the vocabulary of the school children. The main menu has five sub-menus: vocabulary, one item that is not in place, a fairy-tale, painting, and a short description for the teacher how to use the program. The task of both multimedia software is to teach the everyday words.

## 1 Introduction

In Hungary there are more then 300 thousand hearing impaired people. It is more then 3% of the population of Hungary. The most difficult task is to teach a child with severe hearing problems how to articulate the words. The problem is that we learn to speak by imitating the persons in our environment. The deaf – or nearly deaf child does not hear the voice of the grown-up, and thus does not learn to speak. But to be able to communicate with other persons and to be integrated into the society, deaf children have to learn to speak too. Without being able to speak they would have extra difficulties in learning. But simple everyday tasks, as buying something, discussing a problem in an office, just to be able to have a job would be very difficult for somebody who can not speak.

The main task in the kindergarten for the 3 to 6 years old deaf children is to learn to speak. They have almost no time for other occupations. Even during the school years, between 6 and 16 years of age the teaching of speaking continues. They have to deal with this subject besides of their normal school subjects. In Hungary deaf children have special schools, where much emphasis is given to teach them to speak. This

K. Miesenberger et al. (Eds.): ICCHP 2004, LNCS 3118, pp. 14–21, 2004.

special task continuous beside of the general educational subjects and the teaching of vocational subjects during the years between 16 and 19 years of age. From all this you can see that deaf children have much less time for other activities, to play or to make physical exercises then healthy children. If we can help them to learn to speak and increase their vocabulary by playing with the computer, it will be a big help for them.

Teachers of deaf children have special tasks not occurring in this form with healthy children:

- To increase listening comprehension,
- Differentiated improvement of talents,
- Increasing the vocabulary,
- Increasing their ability to express themselves,

Naturally these are tasks also in normal schools, only with deaf children the communication with them is different and more complicated then with healthy children.

In this paper I show you two programs we have developed for children with severe hearing difficulties (almost completely deaf children), who are in their lower school grades.

We developed two multimedia programs to help these children to learn the most important every day words.

The deficiencies of the auditory sense in the hearing-impaired raises the question: to what extent does this deficiency affect their cognitive and intellectual skills. Researchers have found, that in regard with reasoning, particularly when the process of induction is required, hearing-impaired children usually have some difficulties [6]. Although it may seem that hearing-impaired people are similar to normal hearing people in the structure of their thoughts and in their cognitive capabilities, auditory and language deficiencies may lead to lower verbal functioning and an overall lack of appropriate experience. The consequence, it is suggested, can be lower results in Conclusive Thinking and in reaching reasoned conclusion using inductive processing [4], [6]. Researchers studied the ability of hearing-impaired children to think flexibly both verbally and in terms of shapes. This study relates solely to non-verbal ability [8]. Also King and Quigley [7] claim that hearing children surpass deaf, and hard-of-hearing children in creative ability. In recent years, however, there have been growing efforts for intervening in the cognitive capabilities of the deaf children to improve intellectual functioning, but the base of these tasks is to teach the meaning of the words for these children.

Obviously, it is not a simple task to assess the effectiveness of a multimedia teaching system. There are some organizations, which published techniques for the evaluation of multimedia teaching software [10], [3]. For example the Evaluation Outline Team (Evalutech) [3] is very good, giving detailed questionnaires about the Installation, Content, Design and Navigation, Easy of use, Special needs, Courseware etc. These questionnaires are very important, and the answers help the software development, but they are too general and usually concern the usage or outward appearance. In recent years many software were developed in Hungary too [2], [5], [9]. Our goal was to develop not only educational software, but games too. There can be used easily without any informatics knowledge.

## 2 The Software

The first program is "Now I know already what its name is". The main menu has eight topics. For example school, Christmas, Eastern, garden, summer, in the hospital and so on (Fig. 1).

**Fig. 1.** The main menu of the first program. (The mouse is pointing to the school sub menu).

**Fig. 2.** One of the sub menus of the first program.

If you click on a picture, you can go into a sub menu. In the sub menu of a topic there are two other sub menus. The painting and the talking sub menus (Fig. 2). Every talking submenu has a cartoon like presentation, (Fig. 3) because we saw, when we were in the special school for deaf children that they like to read cartoons. Why? Because it has a lot of pictures and not so much sentences. The painting sub menu is the real task for the children. The picture shows a scene, where objects are shown only in black and white. The program asks a question, written below the picture. For example – Show where is the cake? (Fig. 4) If the child clicks on the right place in the screen, it will be coloured. If she or he can identify every object, all of them will be coloured.

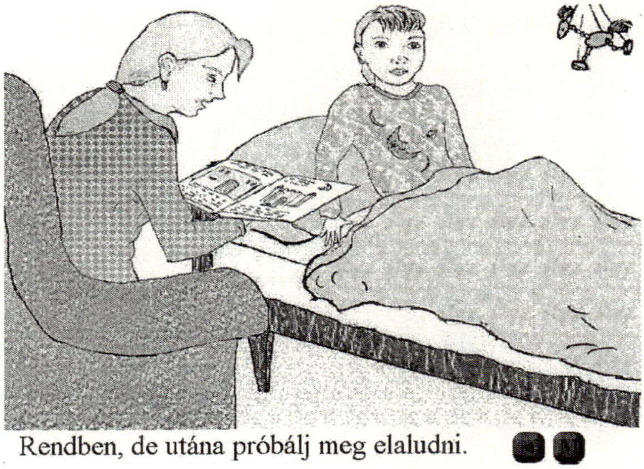


**Fig. 3.** One figure from the talking submenus.

**Fig. 4.** One figure from the painting submenus.

Based on the good reception of this first program we started a second one. The second program has been developed during the last school year and has been prepared to increase the vocabulary of the school children. The main menu has five sub-menus: vocabulary, one item that is not in place, a fairy-tale, painting, and a short description for the teacher how to use the program (Fig. 5). The vocabulary sub-menu contains in 14 sections the most important words of our everyday life (Fig. 6).

These are grouped into the following sections: animals, the parts of the human body, seasons, fruits, the house, domestic animals, verbs, school, traffic, at the doctor, clothing, sports, flowers, vegetables. In the next part of the program we test whether the child has learned the name of the objects correctly: Several objects are shown, and the sentence at the bottom of the page asks the child to show one item in the picture (Fig. 7). The child has to point on the item with the mouse. Deaf children might have difficulty with this identification. In addition there are tales and colouring submenus. In the tale submenu there are well known tales (Fig. 8). The tale is depicted in 4 to 5

**Fig. 5.** The main menu of the 2nd program.

**Fig. 6.** One page from the vocabulary submenu.

**Fig. 7.** One item that is not in place submenu.

slides, with the tale itself written at the bottom of the slide, and above the text there is a picture showing an episode from the tale. In the colouring submenu an episode becomes seen with a question. Below the picture there is a question, e.g. asking the child to point onto an object in the picture. If the child points with the cursor to the correct object the black and white part of the picture turns into colour, and a new question is seen under the picture (Fig. 9).

**Fig. 8.** The tale submenu.

**Fig. 9.** The painting submenu of the second program.

## 3 Efficiency Test

The efficiency test of both software were performed in the Török Béla Kindergarten, Elementary School and Special Trade School in Budapest. The students of this school have various type and intensity hearing difficulties. This test was performed with children in the age group of 5-7 years. These children had normal mental ability. It would be interesting to make the test in the mentally handicapped population too.

Both softwares were very popular in the 5-7 years age group. They were used in the individual and sensitive training of the mother language classes. Both softwares develop primarily the active and passive vocabulary. At the same time they have more possibilities. They can be used for the development of reading- and hearing skills. These help together the speech learning.

The advantages of the software are the easy navigation and easy tasks. The children understood the tasks very quickly. They worked in pairs together, but they can solve the tasks alone too. Learning the use of the next and the back button was very easy. Accordingly the motivation of the children was dynamic. The first attempt is very important for every child and the success is an affirmation.

The topics of the first "Now I know it's name" software suit to the mother language curriculum of this age group. Accordingly the children selected easily the tasks and orientated themselves well in the main menu.

As regard the figures, Firstly we used here very simple pictures, because the design of the pictures they have used preciously were overcrowded, and therefore the navigation in them was difficult. The children did not missed the overcrowded and very coloured figures. The simple figures, like children-drawings were reassuring for the children, therefore they could easily and bravely navigate in the simple figures. In every topic there were 3 or 4 words that have not got into in the children's vocabulary yet. They followed the learning way accurately, and in this way at the third or fourth time many of children could find the questioned objects. After the painting submenu, if every object was coloured, and the written name of the objects vanished, the task was an ear-training, i.e. they had to find the details leaning only on their auditive channel, excluding lip-reading.

After that there was a speech training, the children had to recite the name of the objects. In this developing period the main goal was the correct articulation.

Children enjoyed especially the school, beach, Christmas and at the doctor's topics.

The second software offered different possibilities to the expansion of the vocabulary, explanation of the words, their auditive differentiation, the training based on hearing. Children could easily orient themselves in the menu. To find the odd words caused difficulty only for the children with heavy impairments, but for them it provided further new knowledge. The influence of the rewarding with the animations was very typical, the success was so big, that the children in most cases jumped and in front of the mirror they imitated the movement and dancing of the animals. (The dancing animals were the reward.)

## 4 Conclusion

The teachers gave a summarised opinion about our software. The general experiences of the teachers are the following:

- Children can use both softwares by themselves very easily and they use it with enjoyment, which is a very important factor from the point of view of efficiency.
- The system is a useful tool for teachers in the individual linguistic training. It gives possibility to train in small groups too and pupils can use the system themselves and practice alone.

- The simple drawings like children drawings are more favourable, than the professional figures.
- The most hearing impaired children require the sounds too.

To sum up the children used the software with pleasure and success, they wish more software were like these software in the school.

## References


1. American Society for Curriculum Development ("Only the Best", List, http://www.ascd.org/services/newotb/eval.html)
2. Beszédmester: http://www.inf.u-szeged.hu.beszedmester
3. EvaluTech (Software Evaulation Organisation of SREB in US). http://www.evalutech.sreb.org/
4. Friedman, J. (1985) Classification Skills in Normally Hearing and Oral Deaf Preschoolers. A Study in Language and Conceptual Thought. In Martin D.S. (ed.) *Cognition, Education and Deafness.* Washington: Gallaudet University Press (pp. 70-72).
5. Hallástréning: http://alfa.tmit.bme.hu/speech/ht
6. Hilleyeist, E., Epstein, K., (1991) Interactions between Language and Mathematics with Deaf Students: Defining the "Language-Mathematics" Equation. In D. S. Martin (ed.), *Advances in Cognition Education and Deafness.* Washington: Gallaudet University Press (pp. 302-307).
7. King, C.M., Quigley, S.P. (1985) *Reading and Deafness.* California: College–Hill Press.
8. Saraev, S.A., Koslov, V.P. (1993) Characteristics of Pathological Personality Development in Deaf Children. *Journal of Russian and East European Psychiatry*, Vol.26 (1), 54-60.
9. Vicsi, K., Váry, Á. (2002) Distinctive training methods and evaluation of a multilingual, multimodal speech training system. *The 4th International Conference on Disability, Virtual Reality and Associated Technologies Proceedings*, Veszprém (pp. 47-52).
10. Wallace, L.. at al. (1998) Applications of Speech Recognition in the Primary School Classroom *ESCA – Still 98 Workshop Proceedings*, Marholmen, (pp. 21-24).

# Multimedia and Virtual Reality in the Rehabilitation of Autistic Children

Cecília Sik Lányi and Ádám Tilinger

Department of Image Processing and Neurocomputing, University of Veszprém
H-8200 Veszprém Egyetem u. 10. Hungary
tilinger@vision.vein.hu

**Abstract.** At present autism is beyond recovery, thus the only way that autistic children can adapt themselves to grown-up life is rehabilitation. As the application of computers becomes more and more general in teaching healthy children so does it in teaching children with learning disabilities. Thence a multimedia and virtual reality software package was designed for the rehabilitation of autistic children. This paper presents the developed programs and the results of their usability test.

## 1 Introduction

Autism is a sever aberration of mental activity, which affects the elementary areas of development and is perpetual. It occurs in lack of social behaviour, communication, imaginational functioning and flexible logic.

The cause of autism is unknown yet, but according to several researchers' opinion it can be traced back to the smaller size of the cerebellum. Thus, this mental disorder is not curable, and although it can be compensated, it lasts a life long. That is why rehabilitation is so important, a way that children should be able to adapt themselves into grown-up life to become independent and should be able to work. Autistic people are abnormally self-centred, introverted; their contact to others is weak or missing. They lack social acquaintance and show dim or no response for social signals.

The range of autism is wide. It ranges from serious deficiency to mild social disability. The most acute symptoms can be observed in the ages three to five. Their approach to the environment and adaptation skill can be improved however the basic problem still remains. Only five percent of autistic children become self-sustaining, independent adults these days, and thirty of hundred can be significantly improved [9].

One of the hypotheses of the phenomenology of autism is that the cause of the symptoms is the lack of coherence in processing new information [4]. This and the fragmentation of their perception results that they seem to live in a virtual world, with special rules. Therefore it is possible that a properly designed virtual environment has the potential to support their rehabilitation.

Using multimedia and virtual reality in teaching healthy children is getting more and more general. Along with this the application of computers for teaching children with learning disabilities is also getting started. Some primary advantages of these technologies can be deduced based on former applications and other studies in this domain. An interactive computer program encourages the users to active participation and gives them the experience of control over the learning process [5]. This is espe-

K. Miesenberger et al. (Eds.): ICCHP 2004, LNCS 3118, pp. 22–28, 2004.

cially important in the case of children with learning disabilities, because they are susceptible to passive behaviour.

Thence a multimedia and virtual reality software package (a virtual environment helping to learn shopping, and two interactive multimedia software for teaching clothing and public transport) was designed at the University of Veszprém that can be used in rehabilitation and can help the work in the school, but can also be applied at home. These programs were created to help autistic children to acquire the habits of everyday life.

## 2 Computer Aided Education of Everyday Life

Other virtual reality applications were prepared before for the purpose of teaching integration for autistic children and people with learning disabilities [1]. Some primary advantages of the technology can be deducted based on these projects and other studies in this domain. Cromby (1996) and Stricland (1997) identified the main characteristics that confirm the right of virtual environments in the education [7], [8], [3]:

- Immersing into the computer created environment can exclude the annoying surroundings, helping the child to focus on the task.
- Virtual reality can teach rules and concepts without the use of language or symbol-systems. The function of an object can be discovered by direct interaction. It may ease the understanding of concepts by practice, without abstract thinking or combining.
- The complexity of a virtual world is controllable.
- It allows the guided and successive adjustment of the scene, which supports generalisation of activities.
- These environments allow the child to learn from his or her mistakes without suffering the humiliating or even dangerous consequences of them. These scenes can be much more tolerant but similarly realistic.
- The thought patterns of autistic children are mostly visual, which can be effectively exploited by virtual reality.
- The vision and hearing of autistic children are very effective in understanding abstract concepts, and actual virtual environment technologies are concentrating on the visual and auditory stimuli instead of the haptic or other ones.
- The system can be adjusted according to the behaviour and response of the autistic user. Since many of them never succeed to learn how to communicate, a system with these characteristics may have the possibility of interaction with the environment without the verbal support of the educator.

By developing the software package we pursued these benefits of computer education.

## 3 The Software Package

The software package consists of a virtual environment based on DirectX API, and two multimedia applications. These programs aim the improvement of regions that are elemental and necessary for grown-up life. These are: shopping, clothing and public transport.

### 3.1 Virtual Shop Scenario

The Virtual Shop scenario is teaching the process of shopping to autistic children. A main characteristic of autism is the special, uneven development of psychological skills, which occurs in unusual weaknesses and advantages. Our educational software builds on these advantages aiming the improvement of weak points.

The scenario is a virtual reality program with simplified navigation and interaction interface. It applies the most general control devices that are available at the special schools with adjustable settings. The users can practice shopping in a virtual environment without suffering the dangerous consequences of their mistakes.

The verbal communication with autistic children is limited. They do not comprehend spoken language or do not pay attention to the words. Therefore the teaching of everyday life is not solvable with simple dialogs.

This fact leads to the evolution of an alternative communication system, which combines the verbal communication with an advanced skill of the autistic children. One such major ability is the visual perception [1]. In this respect the application of symbol-cards proved to be useful in practice. These cards may provide solution when spoken language cannot support learning.

**Fig. 1.** An application of symbol-cards in the scenario.

According to these, the Virtual Shop project aims their visual perception, applying symbol-cards (Fig. 1) and an audio-visual virtual environment. The goal of preparing the software was to produce a serviceable support for the education. The application is designed to be used in the teaching process or even at home - with the help of a monitoring person - as a playful way of learning.

Based on the advice of teachers educating autistic children, the software uses speech in guidance of the user with the combination of visual support, aiming the amelioration of verbal comprehension and communication.

Throughout the development of the virtual environment we paid special attention to make it open to improvement. It is possible to create all new shops only by altering external files.

This is important because the exercises could become boring, or in worse case the children could con the solution, and the tasks will not work their thinking. Besides that, practising shopping in different situations enhances their generalising skill. The possibility to change the language of the program makes the software accessible for a larger audience.

## 3.2 Clothing and Public Transport Scenarios

Communication between autistic people and their environment is often limited. Autistic children frighten, discourage the people trying to communicate with them, because they cannot adjust themselves to their customs, requirements and they seldom break their sphere of interest. Important consequences of these are learning difficulties even in basic every-day activities like clothing or bathing. Parts of the software package are two multimedia programs, with the purpose of teaching two of these basic activities: clothing and public transport. These programs are to improve skills needed in every-day life in a playful manner.

The application of colours and the continuous movement of the graphical elements serve the purpose of sustaining the interest (Fig. 2.). The animation of the characters plays a great role in demonstrating chronological order and dependence of an effect upon a case. The autistic child becomes immediate response to his action, thus he doesn't lose his tune and élan for solving the exercises. Like in the Virtual Shop scenario the user obtains positive confirmation, praise for his correct solutions.

**Fig. 2.** The Clothing scenario.

Besides that, there are several other features implemented with teaching nature at the suggestion of the teachers caring about autistic children. One of these is for example the motion of the head of the characters, which gets the child on focusing on the human face, what is essential in real life.

## 4 Investigation of Usability

At present we are investigating the usability of the software. The observation of the test persons and discussions with teachers and some autistic users help us to adjust the scene to reach the accessible efficiency.

The analysis of the software focuses on the following four domains [6]:

- Usability, the options of interaction with the computer generated environment.
- Enjoyment, the motivation of the autistic children to use the software.
- Learning, the understanding of skills.
- Transfer of skills learnt from the virtual reality to the real world [2].

### 4.1 Evaluation of the Virtual Shop Scenario

The tasks to be carried out by the children consist of three types of subtasks; these are the understanding of the exercise, the navigation and the interaction with the virtual environment.

The comprehension of the task is supported by verbal guidance and the cards mentioned above, minimising the role of the monitoring teacher.

The group of autistic children testing the software was very wide from the point of acquaintance and handling a computer. Thence the control of the completed program had to be adjustable. Therefore it uses the controlling devices generally used in schools (keyboard, mouse and joystick) with variable sensitivity.

Interaction with the virtual environment is simplified to such a degree, that it doesn't need more support from the monitoring teacher than it could require in the real world scenario. We kept the number of controlling keys low; as a matter of fact the software offers the interaction to the user (Fig. 3), so he or she needs to use only one key.

Motivating children to use the software is in cases limited by the original aversion towards computer, but the playful way of application eases this antipathy.

The target of our work, the evaluation of transferring the skills learnt from the virtual environment to the real world scenario requires a long-term study, at present we are investigating this problem but have no particular result yet.

The software was handed to several special schools in Hungary that are teaching children with learning disabilities. We are improving the programs relying on the opinion of these teachers. After some filled out inquiry forms and case studies sent back by them, we can say that the reaction of the teachers is positive, they found the package useful.

**Fig. 3.** Realisation of interactivity.

## 5 Conclusion

As a result of our work we developed a multimedia and virtual reality software package for rehabilitation of autistic children. We have also investigated the special design requirements and guidelines of these kinds of educational applications. With these in mind we produced a program that can be amended according to the changing demands.

Teachers of children with learning disabilities confirm the usefulness of the package, and it can be a practical resort for further investigations in computer education of autistic children.

We hope that multimedia and virtual reality will become a part of rehabilitation of autistic people in the near future.

## References


1. Charitos, D., Karadanos, G-Sereti, E., Trintafillou, S., Koukouvinou, S., Martakos, D.: Employing virtual reality for aiding the organisation of autistic children behaviour in everyday tasks, Paper presented at The 3rd International Conference on Disability, Virtual Reality an Associated Technologies, Alghero, Sardinia, Italy (2000) 147-152
2. Cobb, S. V. G., Neale, H. R., Reynolds, H.: Evaluation of virtual learning environments, Paper presented at The 2nd European Conference on Disability, Virtual Reality an Associated Technologies, Skovde, Sweden (1998)
3. Cromby, J. J., Standen, P. J., Brown, D. J.: The potentials of virtual environments in the aducation and training of people with learning disabilities, Journal of Intellectual Disability Research, 40 (1996) 489-501
4. Frith, U.: Autism Explaining the Enigma, Oxford, Blackwell (1989)
5. Neale, H. R., Cobb, S. V. G., Wilson, J. R.: Designing virtual learning environments for people with learning disabilities: usability issues, Paper presented at The 3rd International Conference on Disability, Virtual Reality an Associated Technologies, Alghero, Sardinia, Italy (2000) 265-270

6. Pantelidis, V. S.: Virtual reality in the classroom, Educational Technology, April: 23-27 (1993)
7. Strickland, D.: Virtual Reality for the Treatment of Autism, Virtual Reality in Neuro-Psicho-Psichiology, Ed. G. Riva, IOS Press (1997) 81-86
8. Strickland, D., Marcus, L., Hogan, K., Mesibov, G., McAlister, D.: Using Virtual Reality as a Learning Aid for Autistic Children, Autisme et Informatique, 3e congres International Autisme France, Nice Acropolis (1995) 119-132
9. Takács, I.: Titokzatos autizmus, Népszava 2000. október 21. (2000) http //www.kunsagi.com/kunsagi/autizmus/autizmus.html

# Mobile Phone Based User Interface Concept for Health Data Acquisition at Home

Günter Schreier[1], Alexander Kollmann[1], Martin Kramer[1], Jürgen Messmer[1], Andreas Hochgatterer[2], and Peter Kastner[1]

[1] ARC Seibersdorf research GmbH, Biosignal Processing and Telemedicine, Graz, Austria
schreier.guenter@arcs.ac.at
[2] ARC Seibersdorf research GmbH, Rehabilitation & Integration, Wiener Neustadt, Austria

**Abstract.** The availability of mobile information and communication technologies is increasing rapidly and provides huge opportunities for home monitoring applications. This paper presents a new human-computer interface concept which is based on digital camera enabled mobile phones. Only two keystrokes are necessary to take a photo of a medical measurement device, for example a blood pressure meter, and to send the photo to a remote monitoring centre where specifically designed algorithms extract the numeric values from the photo and store them to a database for further processing. The results of a feasibility study indicates the potential of this new method to give people access to mobile phone based, autonomous recording and documentation of health parameters at home.

## 1 Introduction

Chronic diseases like hypertension, heart failure or diabetes are common among the elderly. Patients suffering from those and other diseases face a reduced quality of life and a high risk for severe events like myocardial infarction or stroke. Such events often lead to severe disabilities and dramatically change the lives of the affected persons [1]. To prevent or at least postpone such events, methods are needed which allow to optimise the therapy of chronic diseases. Ideally, such methods give patients' the means to participate in and to contribute to the management of their chronic diseases.

### 1.1 The Role of the Patient in Managing Chronic Diseases

Patients suffering from chronic diseases have to be active participants in the treatment because they are inevitably responsible for their own day-to-day-care.

Nowadays patients are asked to track their key measures like blood pressure, pulse, diabetes relevant data or events by daily writing them down onto a piece of paper – called a health data or diabetes diary. The captured data are expected to show trends in the illness patterns and to help the doctor in guiding the patient to the best possible health status.

K. Miesenberger et al. (Eds.): ICCHP 2004, LNCS 3118, pp. 29–36, 2004.

However, patients' compliance using the conventional method in self-management is often poor and so are data representation and feedback. This is hardly surprising if patients are confronted with complex documents and instructions [2]. Therefore an easy-to-use and home based data acquisition system would be helpful to guide the patient through data capturing and the complex process of self management.

Particularly elderly or disabled patients are asked to capture their health data continuously to avoid an aggravation in their illness patterns and to ensure appropriate medical decisions at the earliest possible stage. Therefore and because these patients are often very unskilled an easy-to-use system for data acquisition at home is urgently required.

## 1.2 Management of Chronic Diseases Utilizing Information Technologies

Home monitoring using information and communication technologies is particularly suitable for managing chronic diseases since it permits observing patient's health parameters in regular intervals using standard measuring devices like blood glucose meters, blood pressure meters or scales in conjunction with a telecommunication system [3, 4]. The basic idea is to track the patient's personal health status using a home monitoring terminal (HMT) to send the data to a remote monitoring centre (Fig. 1). An automated monitoring process checks the values and gives feedback in order to guide the patient through the self managing process and to turn the doctor's or other caregivers' attention to the patient when necessary by means of notifications and alerts.

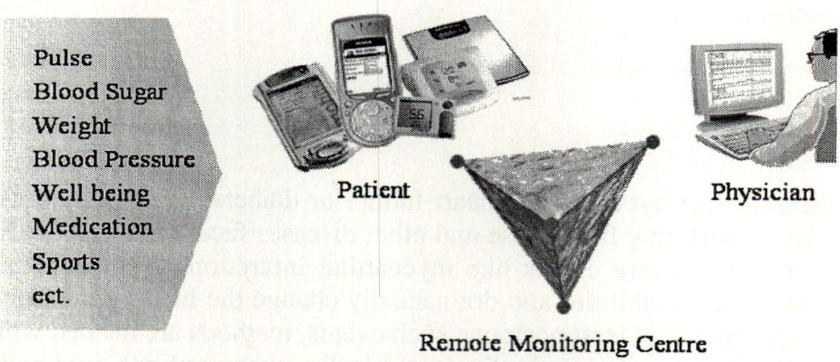


**Fig. 1.** Overview of a home monitoring system facilitating an additional way of communication between patients and physicians by means of a remote monitoring centre.

Today, wireless telecommunication services like GSM (Global System for Mobile Communications), GPRS (General Packet Radio Service) and UMTS (Universal Mobile Telecommunications Systems) are or will soon be ubiquitously available. The possibility to use the mobile phone for standard voice communication as well as transmission of a variety of multimedia information like text, audio, images and video, makes it the HMT of choice for home based interactive communication applications. Recent statistics [5] on the in-home availability of devices with the potential to serve as HMT in the general population indicate that - with an availability of 75% - the mobile phone is second only to TV sets (94%) and beats the PC (49%) and Internet Access (36%) by huge margins (Fig. 2).

The objective of this paper has been to present a unique mobile phone based human-computer interface concept and to compare this to other such technologies considered for the broad usage as HMT, in particular for elderly or disabled patients. This concept is based on digital camera enabled mobile phones and Multimedia Messaging Service (MMS) and is called "MoniCam" – Monitoring Camera.

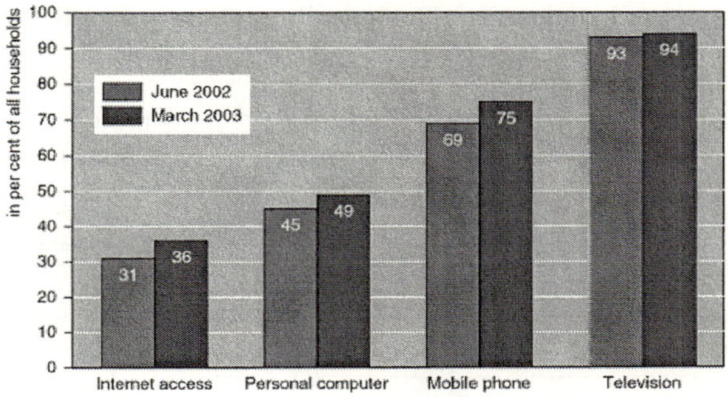


**Fig. 2.** Availability of devices with the potential to serve as home monitoring terminal in the general population (Source: STATISTICS AUSTRIA, European Survey on ICT usage in households 2003).

# 2 Methods

## 2.1 Health Data Management System

We developed a person centred health data management concept for regular and home based measurement and transmission of health parameters like blood pressure, body weight, symptoms, medication, etc. as shown in Fig. 1. The system has been built using mostly standard components and state-of-the-art Internet technology and comprises of:

- *medical measurement devices* - to measure health parameters (blood pressure measuring device, glucose meter, weight scale, etc.),
- *patient terminal* – mobile phone based human computer interface featuring various methods to record and transmit the health data to a health monitoring centre,
- *health monitoring centre* – 24/7 accessible server system to receive and store the data and to provide those data to the caregivers in a standardised and easily comprehensible format,
- *caregiver terminal* - a web-based user interface which gives authorized persons access to the health data,
- *data processing and alert system* - to analyse incoming data, to check for alert conditions and to send automatic notification and reminder messages if necessary.

## 2.2 The MoniCam Principle

The general workflow of the MoniCam based data acquisition process is depicted in Fig. 3. The patient uses his/her blood pressure meter (BPM) to measure systolic and diastolic blood pressure as well as the heart rate. The measured values show up on the display of the BPM. Next the patient uses the camera of the mobile phone to take a photo of the display. This photo is automatically sent to the health monitoring centre via MMS.

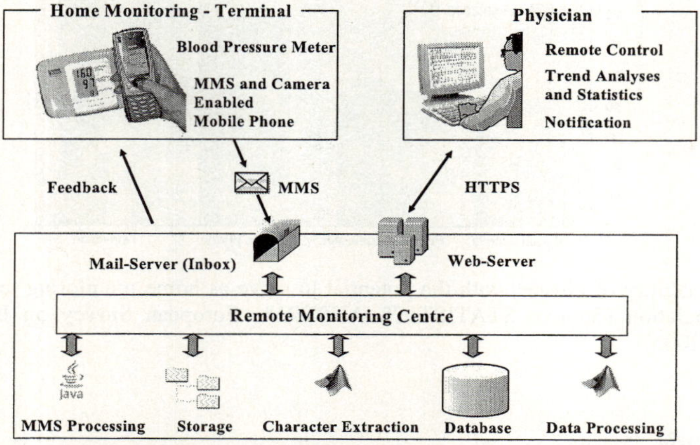


**Fig. 3.** General workflow of the MoniCam based home monitoring procedure

A special Symbian [6] based software, running on the mobile phone, helps the user to handle this data acquisition process in the easiest possible way. The picture section which eventually will be represented at the photo is marked with a red rectangle in order to help the user to navigate the camera (Fig. 4). Once the display of the BPM fits the rectangle the photo can be taken and sent to the monitoring centre via MMS with only two keystrokes. After the first keystroke a preview of the resulting photo is shown on the mobile phone's display. The user can decide to send this picture by a second key press or to take a new photo in case of bad contrast or reflections.

Thus, there is no need to enter an email address, telephone number or being familiar with sending MMS at all. All necessary configurations are made by the program automatically. If an online connection to the data carrier service (GPRS, UMTS) at a given location and time is not available, the mobile phone repeatedly tries to send the data until the message has been sent successfully.

At the monitoring centre the MMS arrives as a photo attached to an email. The subject of this email contains the IMEI (International Mobile Station Equipment Identity) of the mobile phone. Thus, the photo can unambiguously be assigned to a patient. Other important parameters like capturing date and time are also stored within the email.

A Java based application, running on the web server, fetches the email available on the mail server, extracts the photo and moves it to the local file system. Subsequently, the incoming photo is registered to the database and assigned to the corresponding patient.

A special character extraction algorithm starts to process the photo in order to extract the numerical values. In case of successful character extraction the values are also stored to the database and the report processing unit is started. Graphs and trends are generated and limit checks are performed. Finally, all information is made accessible via the web-interface to authorised users. In case of unsuccessful character extraction or failed plausibility check the user may receives a message via SMS (Short Message Service) to repeat the measurement.

### 2.3 Character Extraction Algorithm

This complex process can be divided into two tasks:

*Display identification process* - After grey value conversion of the image, the mobile phone specific lens distortion is corrected. A median filter is applied to suppress small details before the image undergoes canny edge detection. By means of the radon transformation the six strongest vertical and horizontal lines are identified. These lines are combined in the right way to compose the borders of the assumed display. This method allows the detection of displays, even if they are distorted by perspective projection. This gives the user more flexibility in the picture acquisition process but has to be corrected prior to the succeeding character recognition process.

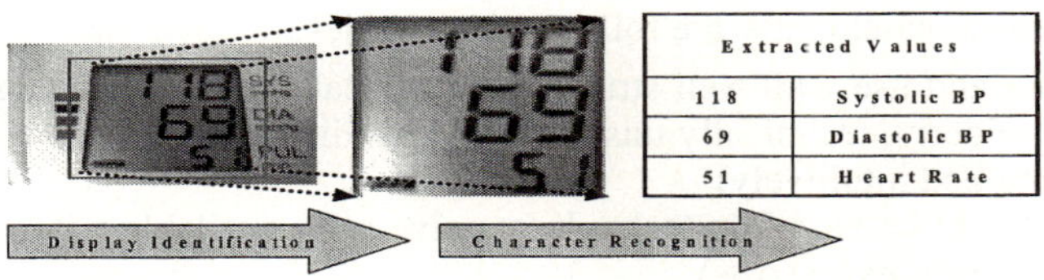


**Fig. 4.** The two subsequent stages of the character extraction algorithm: display identification and character recognition.

*Character recognition* – Once the image of the display is identified and corrected, further pre-processing is done to improve contrast. Then the values are recognised by 2D correlation. The respective correlation templates are stored within the file system and have to be predefined.

An second algorithm seeks for rapid changes of the grey value along certain lines and serves as a plausibility measure in the decision process.

## 3 Results

After the algorithms had been developed based on an initial series of images, we asked five test users with four different blood pressure devices and two different camera enabled mobile phones to use the system and to document a number of blood pressure recordings. The MMS based transmissions succeeded in all cases.

Table 1 gives an overview on the outcome of the automated value extraction process at the remote monitoring centre.

**Table 1.** Results of the feasibility study using two different mobile phones and five different blood pressure recording devices.

| Blood Pressure Device | omronM5 | bosoC | bosoP | bosoPC | bosoPC |
|---|---|---|---|---|---|
| Mobile Phone | Nokia 7650 | | | | Nokia 7250 |
| Number of Images | 47 | 86 | 103 | 393 | 176 |
| Display Found [%] | 100 | 100 | 98,1 | 100 | 100 |
| Systolic Value Correct [%] | 76,6 | 87,2 | 66,0 | 94,3 | 95,2 |
| Diastolic Value Correct [%] | 89,4 | 93,0 | 56,3 | 97,2 | 98,2 |

The results in Table 1 indicate that the rate of correct value extraction varied considerably with respect to the type of the BPM device but was comparable for the two different mobile phone types. For two types of BPM devices the method was capable to determine the correct values in well above 90% of the cases.

## 4 Discussion

Many of the components necessary for home-based health monitoring application are readily available or can be designed and developed based on standard state-of-the-art Internet technology. The most challenging part still is the HMT, i.e. to provide the user with a method to enter the measured data into the system. Ideally, this human computer interface would have the following properties:

1. easy to learn and use with well structured graphical design (metaphoric), intuitive navigation (elderly, technically unskilled and handicapped persons should be able to use the method intuitively)
2. low-cost (should be based on technology universally available without significant set-up expenses or extra costs)
3. error-resistant (allowing source data verification or leave no room for data transcription errors)

A major focus of our research activities has been to develop and test new ways to utilize mobile phones for home based health data acquisition. Basically, mobile phones provide several technical possibilities for the usage as HMT:

- WAP (Wireless Application Protocol): The WAP browser prompts the user to enter data into an input template generated by WML (Wireless Markup Language) syntax in order to be sent to the remote monitoring centre.
- HTTP (Hyper Text Transfer Protocol): The input template is generated by HTML (Hyper Text Markup Language) syntax whereby a mobile phone based WEB browser, e.g. Opera 6.1, is necessary. If supported, it is also possible to run Java or Symbian based data acquisition software on mobile phones. For data transmission to the remote monitoring centre a HTTP connection is initiated by the application automatically.
- SMS (Short Message Service): Data are entered by editing a predefined character template using the numeric keypad. The resulting character string is sent to the remote monitoring centre via SMS-Gateway.
- MMS (Multimedia Messaging Service): Recent mobile phones provide a build in camera in order to send taken pictures to other (mobile) subscribers. This technology is used for data acquisition in the presented MoniCam application.

**Table 2.** Comparison of major aspects of different technologies for the usage in mobile phone based home monitoring terminals that we considered in the present and previous projects. Usability is classified as good, ok, and poor. (* available on recent mobile phones, ** developed, but not yet in use).

| Technology | Input | Usability | Transmission Protocol | Requirements | Offline Data Acquisition |
|---|---|---|---|---|---|
| WAP/WML | text | ok | WAP | GSM, GPRS | no |
| Mobile Application (J2ME, Symbian) | text | good | HTTP, MMS, SMS | GPRS, J2ME, Symbian support * | yes |
| MoniCam (Symbian) | picture | good | MMS | GPRS, Symbian support * | yes |
| WEB-Browser ** (Opera 6.1) | text | ok | HTTP | GPRS, Symbian support * | no |
| SMS ** | text | poor | SMS | GSM | yes |

Two previous studies [7, 8] had been performed utilising WAP/WML and HTTP combined with Java 2 Platform, Micro Edition (J2ME) as graphical user interface (GUI) technologies.

Although - in contrast to WML - Java based GUI allowed the use of graphical elements (metaphoric, colourful) and the design of intuitive menu items and input fields both technologies required basic knowledge in handling a mobile phone and using the numeric keypad which some - in particular elderly - people did not have. Thus type errors, missing or incompletely inputs were common.

Because of these limitations we developed a camera and MMS technology based data acquisition method to provide particularly unskilled patients an easy and comfortable way to capture their health data.

Table 2 indicates that the MoniCam method offers advantages with respect to usability and is less affected by temporary lack of network availability. It is unique since it provides source data verification based on inspection of the images of the measurement device displays. The proposed method is actually very intuitive and easy-to-use, given that most people are used to take photos. In the future - if the current trend persists - an increasing number of mobile phones will have the necessary technical features required to perform this procedure at no extra costs.

Of course, there is still a lot of work to be done to improve the flexibility with respect to different measuring devices (BPM, glucose meter, weight scale, ect.) from different manufacturers. Furthermore the character extraction algorithm has to be continuously improved regarding the resolution and colour depth of the cameras of upcoming mobile phones. Nevertheless, the results of our feasibility study indicate that there is a good chance to improve the algorithms to a point where the automated value extraction process reaches a sufficiently high percentage of success. Correct values in about 19 out of 20 cases could be considered to be sufficiently high for routine application and has already been achieved for two types of BPM.

## 5 Conclusion

If the results obtained in the present feasibility study for particular blood pressure measuring devices can be confirmed in a representative group of patients this concept may develop into an easy-to-use, in-expensive and readily available method. This gives people access to mobile phone based, autonomous recording and documentation of health parameters and could improve the treatment not only for patients suffering from hypertension but also from other chronic diseases like diabetes or congestive heart failure.

## References

1. Holman, H., Lorig, K.: Patients as partners in managing chronic diseases. British Medical Journal, Vol. 320. (2002) 526 - 527
2. Celler, B., Lovell, N., Basilakis, J.: Using information technology to improve the management of chronic diseases. Medical Journal of Australia, Vol. 179. (2003) 242 – 246
3. Louis, A. et al.: A systematic review of telemonitoring for the management of heart failure: The European Journal of Heart Failure Vol. 5. (2003) 583 - 590
4. Roine, R., Ohinmaa, A., Hailey, D.: Assessing telemedicine: a systematic review of the literature. Canadian Medical Association Journal, Vol. 165(6). (2001) 765 - 771
5. Statistik Austria, European Survey on ICT usage in households in Austria http://www.statistik.at/englisch/results/vgr/ict_txt.shtml (2003)
6. Wiley, J. (ed.): Programming for the Series 60 Platform and Symbian OS: Digital Information Architects Inc., Helsinki Finland (2003)
7. Kastner P, Kollmann A, Pusch W, Riedl M, Ludvik B, Schreier G.: Diab-Memory: Ein mobilfunk-gestütztes Datenservice zur Unterstützung der funktionellen Insulintherapie. In: Gell G, Gabler G, Holzinger A (eds.) a-telmed 2003 Telemedizin - Von der Wissenschaft zur Realität. Österreichische Computer Gesellschaft, Wien (2003) 141-152
8. Kastner P, Schreier G, Pusch W, Scherr D, Fruhwald FM, Zweiker R, Klein W. Ein Telemonitoring-System für Patienten mit Herzinsuffizienz. In: Boenick, U., Bolz, A. (eds.): Biomedizinische Technik Vol. 48. (2003) 136-137

# Multi-parameter Data Acquisition on Interface Devices for the Development of Adaptive Input Systems

Stefan Mina[1], Andreas Hochgatterer[1], Barbara Prazak[1], Sten Hanke[2], and Günter Schreier[1]

[1] ARC Seibersdorf research GmbH, Rehabilitation & Inclusion Research Group, Viktor Kaplan Str. 2/1, A-2700 Wiener Neustadt, Austria
{stefan.mina,andreas.hochgatterer, barbara.prazak,guenter.schreier}@arcsmed.at
http://www.arcsmed.at

[2] Technische Universität Dresden, Institut f. Biomedizinische Technik, Georg-Schumann-Str. 9, 01062 Dresden, Germany
{sten.hanke}@arcsmed.at

**Abstract.** Since the amount of special input devices on the assisitive technology market is growing the selection of the right device for an individual user becomes more and more difficult. Once a device is selected and seems to be suitable it may be possible that it cannot be operated any more after a certain time due to changing user needs as result of a progressive disease. A system for the assessment of the user interaction with input devices under certain conditions and the possible usage of the resulting data for further evaluation and for the development and simulation of adaptive input systems will be described by the authors.

## 1 Background

The assistive technology market provides an amount of different alternative input devices for people with disabilities to operate the computer or other equipment. Very often the user chooses the device that seems to be the most comfortable or a device suggested by another person.

In some cases the device works well but in other cases the user is not able to interact successfully in practice or after a certain time a progressive disease necessitates a new alternative.

The latter case leads to strive for new solutions and investigate the development of adaptive devices that adjust automatically to the user needs. Before contemplating the development of such systems we have to be aware that there is a lack of detailed information in rehabilitation technology research about how users operate alternative input devices, and that the problems and coping strategies developed by the user must be clarified first.

The presented research work intends to identify methods to gain the requested basic data and to objectify the interaction between user and input device.

K. Miesenberger et al. (Eds.): ICCHP 2004, LNCS 3118, pp. 37–44, 2004.

## 2 Methods

For the evaluation of the usage of pointing devices users have to fulfil a set of different tasks. These tasks must contain common procedures that are usually required for the operation of a personal computer but may also contain other, more difficult tasks that require an increased ability in handling the input device and may reflect difficulties operating the device over a longer period of time.

It was decided to develop an assessment software which is able to provide test batteries for navigating the cursor to a target which is either static or dynamic and has a variable size. These batteries should be similar to the normal computer operation tasks. For additional testing of long term tasks a target tracking task appeared to be appropriate.

**Table 1.** Tasks

| Task | Target | Variations |
|---|---|---|
| Point / Point & Click – Static Target | Positioned randomly on the screen | - different target size<br>- click on target required or not required |
| Point / Point & Click – Dynamic Target | Target moving on the screen – initial position randomly generated | - different target size<br>- different target speed<br>- click on target required or not required |
| Track | Target moving on the screen – cursor has to be kept within the target for a defined time | - different target size<br>- different target speed |

During all tasks the current position of the target (i.e. a square) and of the mouse cursor is recorded for data analysis.

Pointing and point & click tasks will result in the movement of the cursor from the origin (centre of screen) to the target and the length and speed of the cursor motion being calculated. To allow a comparison the index of difficulty (ID) according to Fitts' law (1) [1, 2] is calculated. This equation describes the ID as a function of the target width (W) and the distance from the origin to the target (A).

$$ID=\log2(A/W+1) \tag{1}$$

For tracking tasks the percentage of the cursor staying on track, the total time and the orthogonal index (OI) are processed. The target moves with an angle of 45 degrees (equivalent increment of X and Y coordinates), it can be expected that the cursor movement also shows a similar angle. As a calculate measure of performance of this 45 degree motion the orthogonal index figures out the percentage of cursor movements that occur only parallel to the X or Y axis (corresponding 0 or 90 degrees).

To obtain more specific information to support the interpretation of the recorded sessions it was decided to additionally record electrophysiological data like ECG, EMG and EOG. The ECG was recorded with disposable Ag-AgCl electrodes attached to the right arm (RA), left leg (LL) and right leg (RL) resulting in ECG lead II ac-

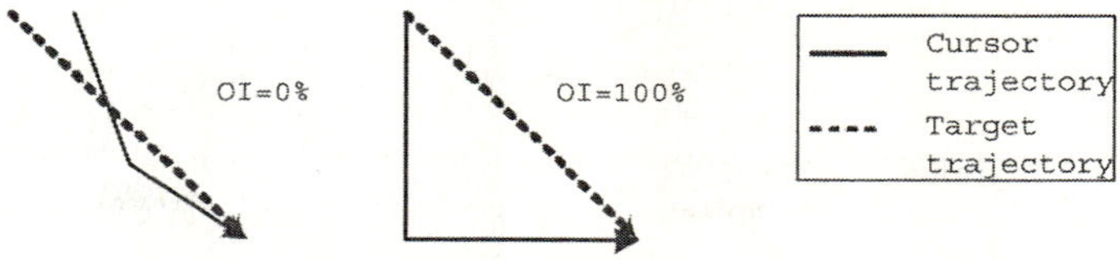


**Fig. 1.** Orthogonal Index

cording to Eindhoven's triangle [3]. The ECG signal was primarily used to calculate the heart rate (HR). This calculation was done with a QRS detector to figure out the R waves of the electrocardiogram and to calculate the inter-beat-interval (IBI) between them [4].

For detection of muscle activities while operating the input device two EMG channels were derived from the left and right m. trapezius and a third channel measured the EMG from the m. frontalis. Many psychophysiological studies, especially biofeedback applications, use the EMG derived from the m. frontalis, which may be used to generalize muscle tonus of the whole body. In conjunction with the additional measurement of the heart a detection of activation [5, 6] is possible. To make the changes in the EMG channels more evident a moving average filter was applied to every EMG signal after recording, delivering the envelope of the signal.

Longitudinal and transversal electrooculography (EOG) were used to track eye movements.

For EMG and EOG recording gold cup electrodes with conductive paste were used which are smaller than the disposable Ag-AgCl electrodes and can be applied more precisely on the correct anatomical locations without disturbing the user.

A short questionnaire was used to get the users subjective impression about the difficulty of the different tasks with the various input devices. The difficulty of pointing, clicking and tracking had to be ranked between 1 (very easy) and 5 (very difficult).

All data except the electrophysiological records were statistically evaluated regarding mean, standard deviation and standard error.

## 3 Results

The resulting test environment is shown in figure 2 and 3. It consists of two PC workstations, a data acquisition system and a biopotential amplifier system. The PC 2 workstation applies the visualization of the tasks and PC 1 managed session control and data acquisition. The interchange of data and controlling commands is realized via TCP and UDP protocols.

The general user information such as user name, date of birth, gender and additional session parameters are stored with the name of the corresponding data files in an xml file. For the analysis of the user habits the x and y coordinates of cursor and target as well as the information of the mouse buttons are recorded with the software and written in a data file.

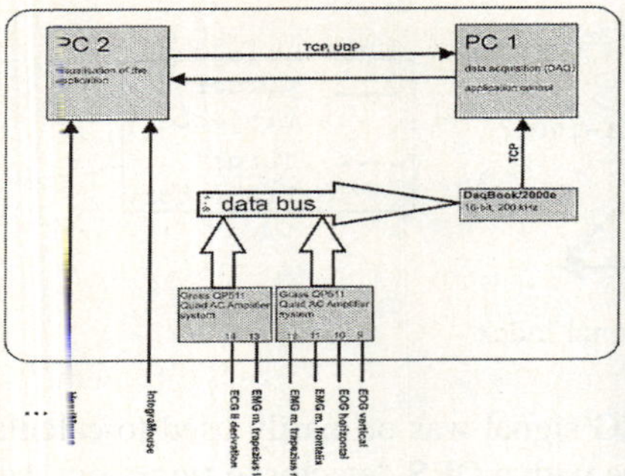


**Fig. 2.** Test environment diagram

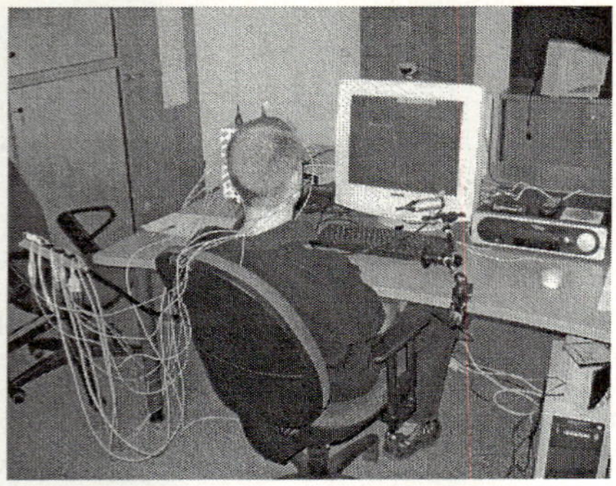

**Fig. 3.** Test environment

Two special pointing devices were analyzed in the presented work: the first one is the LifeTool IntegraMouse® [7], a mouth operated mouse, and the second one is the SmartNAV™ AT headmouse. In case of the IntegraMouse® a special research version was used that allowed measuring forces applied to the mouthpiece and the sip and puff pressure. Both devices are alternatives to the standard computer mouse for people with no or very limited upper extremity control; e.g. for people with conditions such as spinal cord injury, multiple sclerosis or amyotrophic lateral sclerosis(ALS). Since both devices operate as standard mouse the operating system mouse settings were not changed during trials.

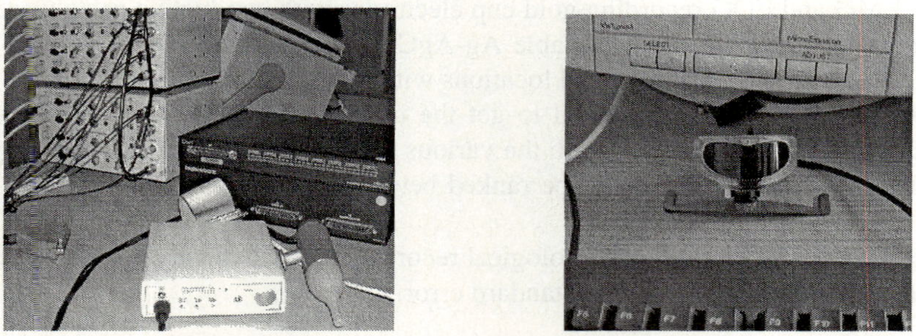

**Fig. 4.** IntegraMouse® research version with biopotential amplifiers and DAQ (left), SmartNAV™ (right)

For data acquisition of these forces and the electrophysiological signals from the biopotential amplifiers an IOtech DaqBook/2000E was used which provides Ethernet connectivity.

Two quad channel biopotential amplifiers from Grass Instruments (QP511) were chosen for EMG, EOG and ECG recording, the amplifier parameters are shown in table 2.

The sample frequency for the cursor coordinates was 100 samples per second and for all channels of the data acquisition system (forces, pressures and biopotentials) 5000 samples per second. To test the whole system data from five test people were acquired where 4 of them had used neither the IntegraMouse® nor the headmouse.

**Table 2.** Biopotential amplifier configuration

| Recording Signal | Low Pass | High Pass | Gain | Notch Filter (50Hz) |
|---|---|---|---|---|
| EMG | 1kHz | 10Hz | 10,000 | Off |
| EOG | 100Hz | 0.1Hz | 10,000 | On |
| ECG | 100Hz | 0.3Hz | 5,000 | On |

Processing of raw data and graphical representation was performed with Matlab 6.5.1 and the processed data was statistically evaluated with SPSS 8.0. All tasks were presented on a 21 inch CRT monitor with a resolution of 800x600 pixel. The distance between the monitor and the users head was set to 75cm for sessions using the IntegraMouse® and to 60cm for sessions with the headmouse.

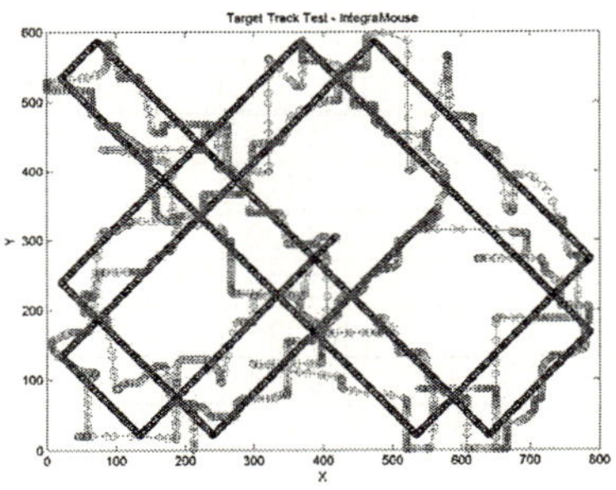


**Fig. 5.** X/Y Representation of a tracking task

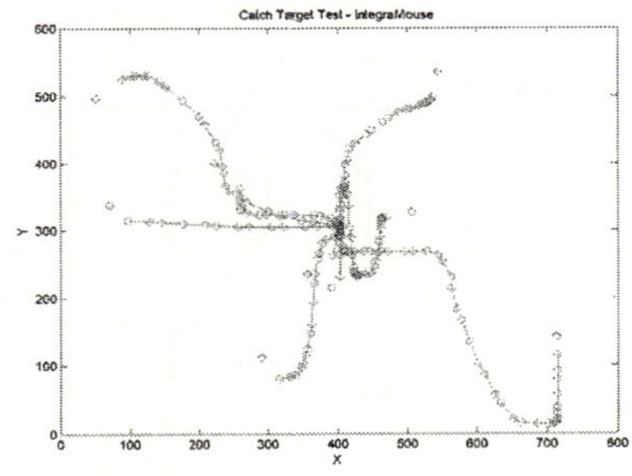


**Fig. 6.**X/Y Representation of point&click task

Figures 5 and 6 show an example of tracking and click and point tasks. In figure 5 the regular track presented by the system that the user should follow and the deviating cursor movements of the user are shown.

**Table 3.** Evaluation of tracking tasks

| Test Group | Parameter | Mean | STD | STD ERR |
|---|---|---|---|---|
| Tracking Task IntegraMouse Novice User N=2 | On Track [%] | 54.8416 | 7.1855 | 5.0810 |
| | Off Track [%] | 45.1585 | 7.1855 | 5.0810 |
| | OI [%] | 65.3411 | 1.9754 | 1.3968 |
| | Total Time [s] | 581.7500 | 92.9845 | 65.7500 |
| Tracking Task IntegraMouse Expert User N=5 | On Track [%] | 86.8493 | 7.8059 | 3.4909 |
| | Off Track [%] | 13.1507 | 7.8059 | 3.4909 |
| | OI [%] | 43.3468 | 5.0985 | 2.2801 |
| | Total Time [s] | 170.9400 | 168.1628 | 75.2047 |
| Tracking Task Headmouse Novice User N=17 | On Track [%] | 87.1876 | 4.8604 | 1.1788 |
| | Off Track [%] | 12.8124 | 4.8604 | 1.1788 |
| | OI [%] | 25.8808 | 5.6690 | 1.3749 |
| | Total Time [s] | 63.3412 | 65.1161 | 15.7930 |

**Table 4.** Evaluation of point / point & click tasks

| Test Group | Parameter | Mean | STD | STD ERR |
|---|---|---|---|---|
| IntegraMouse W=80 User A3 N=7 | Way to Target [% of shortest possible way] | 128.3923 | 31.2240 | 11.8016 |
| | Speed [pixel per sec] | 49.7296 | 12.5665 | 4.7497 |
| | ID | 2.1596 | .4231 | 1.599 |
| | Total Time [s] | 2.8429 | 1.3302 | .5028 |
| Headmouse W=80 User A3 N=7 | Way to Target [% of shortest possible way] | 124.8937 | 34.8023 | 13.1540 |
| | Speed [pixel per sec] | 49.0379 | 10.3438 | 3.9096 |
| | ID | 2.4014 | .2405 | .0909 |
| | Total Time [s] | 2.6571 | .9502 | .3591 |

**Table 5.** Evaluation of user questionnaires

| Pointing Device | Task | Mean | STD | STD ERR |
|---|---|---|---|---|
| IntegraMouse | Point (N=4) | 2.5 | .5774 | .2887 |
| | Click (N=4) | 3.25 | .9574 | .4787 |
| | Track (N=4) | 4.75 | .5000 | .2500 |
| Headmouse | Point (N=4) | 1.5 | .5774 | .2887 |
| | Click (N=3) | 2.33 | 1.5275 | .8819 |
| | Track (N=4) | 1.75 | .9574 | .4787 |

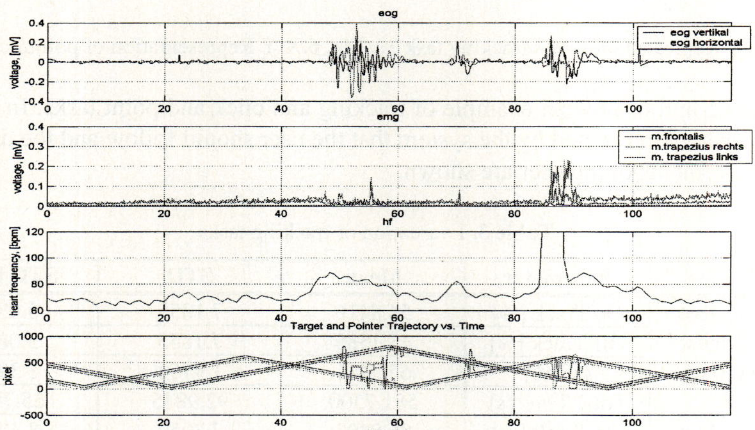


**Fig. 7.** Graphical representation of electrophysiological data

## 4 Discussion

At this moment all data have been acquired with able-bodied users just to demonstrate and proove the functionality of the test environment and of the data processing and evaluation methods and to draw first conclusions. Even if the data may not relevant for some specific diseases some interesting effects could be noticed while analyzing the results of the tests. Almost every novice user performing tracking tasks with the LifeTool-IntegraMouse® showed a high orthogonal index and had problems keeping the cursor on track from the defined time of 10 seconds. With the current mouse settings applied the headmouse delivered better results for tracking tasks and the novice users subjective impression about the difficulty was less than with the IntegraMouse® (compare with table 5.). Also within the electrophysiological data interesting results could be found, e.g. increasing EMG activities during the session until the user made a mistake whilst tracking the target, an increasing heart rate and correlation between EOG channels, EMG channels and tracking errors (see figure 7.).

In general the system appears to be an excellent tool to gain data and information about how users operate pointing devices, how pathological components affect this operation and how input devices can be adjusted to the user.

If enough data is available it may be used for the development of a decision support system which input device is the best choice for a user depending on disease symptoms and specific needs and for the future development of adaptive input systems. Since a progressive disease or even a bad daily constitution may impede the operation of assistive technology or other equipment the parameters of the input device are in most cases static.

An adaptive input device should 'learn' how it is operated by the user and could adjust its parameters automatically. Using data acquired during trials with the introduced system for the development of algorithms for adaptive input systems and testing of them may have several advantages. The dynamic force processing input strategy exemplified on a shear force sensor plate may be considered as a first step in this direction [8]. In future the database will provide trial data of different user groups with different age, education and diseases so that developers have enough possibilities to test their models with real life data without stressing the users. Of course this should not reduce the importance of user involvement but it should avoid disturbing users too frequently at a very early stage and to raise expectations that the user will get the 'perfect' input device to early. Reliable adaptive input devices depend on reliable knowledge concerning the interaction of users with input devices. Therefore future work will concentrate on data acquisition on people with disabilities, on the evaluation of short and long-term effects like fatigue and/or familiarisation and on the evaluation in real-life tasks and environments. This will then allow conclusions to be drawn on "performance" (linking recorded/calculated data on "performance").

## References

1. Fitts P.M.: The information capacity of the human motor system in controlling the amplitude of movement. Journal of Experimental Psychology 47 (1954) 381-391
2. MacKenzie I.S.: Movement time prediction in human-computer interfaces. In: Kaufmann (ed.) Readings in human-computer interaction.Los Altos. CA (1995) 483-493
3. Webster J.G.: Medical Instrumentation – Application and Design. Wiley. NY (1998) 235-239

4. Tompkins W.J. (1993): Biomedical Digital Signal Processing, Prentice Hall, NJ
5. Duffy E.: Activation. In: Greenfield N.S., Sternbach R.A. (eds.): Handbook of Psychophysiology. Holt. New York (1972) 577-622
6. Duffy E.: The psychological significance of the concept of arousal or activation. Psychol. Rev. 64 (1957) 265-275
7. Fugger E., Asslaber M., Hochgatterer A.: Mouth-controlled interface for Human-Machine Interaction in education & training. In: Marincek Č. (eds.): Assistive Technology – Added Value to the Quality of Life. Proceedings of the AAATE 2001. IOS Press. Amsterdam (2001) 379-383
8. Mina S., Prazak B., Hochgatterer A.: Dynamic Force Processing Input Strategy. In:Keates S, Clarkson P.J., Langdon P., Robinson P. (eds.) Proceedings of the 2nd Cambridge Workshop on Universal Access and Assistive Technology. Cambridge. (2004) 25-33

# How Governments Can Use Technology to Promote Employment of People with Disabilities

Dinah F.B. Cohen[1] and Ilene R. Zeitzer[2]

[1] Computer/Electronic Accommodations Program
U. S. Department of Defense
5111 Leesburg Pike, Suite 810
Falls Church, VA 22041, USA
Dinah.cohen@tma.osd.mil
[2] Disability Policy Solutions
1525 Q Street NW, #11
Washington, DC 20009, USA
Ilenezdc@yahoo.com

**Abstract.** The increasing use of technology in workplaces all over the world has resulted in unprecedented opportunities for people with disabilities to remain in, or enter the work force. Technology can be the key that levels the playing field for individuals with disabilities if their needs are met through the proper assistive or adaptive accommodations. Governments are in a unique position to harness this prospect and promote the increased employment of people with disabilities. This employment promotion can be achieved through a number of policies, programs and strategies that are both overt and subtle. Governments can develop various policies and initiatives to impact their own hiring, retention and promotion of individuals with disabilities. Governments can also use their purchasing power to influence the private sector to do more to hire and retain workers with disabilities. This paper explores how governments can use technology to improve employment outcomes for individuals with disabilities.

## 1 Overview: Comparisons of the Labor Market Situation of People with Disabilities

Governments, whether of industrialized or developing countries, are in a unique position to promote the employment of people with disabilities. This employment promotion can be achieved through a number of policies, programs and strategies that are both overt and subtle. In the first example, governments themselves can develop various policies and initiatives in their role as employers to hire, retain and promote individuals with disabilities in the public sector. In a more subtle way, governments can also use their enormous purchasing power to influence the private sector to do more to hire and retain workers with disabilities. This paper will explore both means of achieving these outcomes and will especially explore how governments can and are using technology to improve employment outcomes for individuals with disabilities both as employers and as purchasers of goods and services.

K. Miesenberger et al. (Eds.): ICCHP 2004, LNCS 3118, pp. 45–51, 2004.

Some governments attempt to achieve employment goals through mandatory quota systems that impose fines or levies on employers if they fail to meet the required percentage level of employees with disabilities. Quota systems are controversial in that: (1) it is not clear that in most countries who use them, quotas meet the goals of promoting hiring of new disabled workers; (2) some argue that they are easily manipulated through reporting existing personnel with minor impairments; (3) they may have an unintended dampening effect in that they may persuade employers that disabled workers are inferior workers who need this extra help to compensate for their productivity shortcomings; and, (4) disabled individuals themselves may resent quotas for the reasons mentioned in (3).

Another way some governments promote employment of people with disabilities is through paying supplements to employers who hire or employ disabled workers. In essence, the employer is subsidized for each disabled worker that is employed. Arguments against this practice resemble those that surround the use of quotas, i.e., it assumes disabled workers are less productive than non-disabled ones. Furthermore, many countries are still relying on sheltered work environments for at least some employment promotion efforts for individuals with disabilities. In fact, in some countries such as the Netherlands, sheltered work accounts for the vast majority of labor force involvement of disabled workers. As can be imagined, similar criticism exists against the use of sheltered work as a usual or common strategy for most individuals with disabilities especially, if it is used as other than a means of transitioning to open employment. Finally, the practice in many industrialized countries is for people to work under strong labor contracts that require the employer to hold the job, typically for at least a year and often for two or more years, should a worker develop a disabling condition. During that time, the worker receives anywhere from 70 to 100 percent of his or her former salary, paid either fully by the employer or for an initial period after which the social insurance or sick leave system picks up the payment.

The labor market situation with regard to disability, as described above, is quite different from that in the United States. First, there is no quota/levy system. U.S. employers would highly object to them and most disability advocates would also, though for very different reasons. Equally there are no supplements paid to employers who hire disabled workers to offset their payroll costs. Moreover, there are virtually no set-aside job sectors anymore, although some small programs started about 50 years ago for blind individuals and veterans still provide jobs running newsstands in public buildings and making products for the government. Finally, a small and increasingly diminishing number of people work under labor contracts and with few exceptions, employers have the right to dismiss workers who develop chronic or disabling conditions and without any obligations to continue to pay their salaries. In short, the labor atmosphere for job retention and hiring of disabled workers is far tougher in many ways in the United States.

Given this situation, one might well wonder what positive factors exist to help job promotion and retention among U.S. workers with disabilities. High among the positive factors is that the U.S. has a strong civil rights underpinning. In 1990, the Americans with Disabilities Act (ADA) was passed that mandates civil rights for people with disabilities across a wide spectrum of areas including employment, public access, transportation, and telecommunications. The law not only outlaws discrimination, but also requires reasonable accommodations to help level the playing field. In other words, it is not enough for an employer to say he does not discriminate against employees with disabilities, he must make reasonable accommodations unless doing so would prove an undue hardship. The burden of proof concerning undue hardship is on the employer. A federal agency is responsible for administering the law and investigating charges brought by workers who feel they have been discriminated against because of a disability. Cases that cannot be resolved through education or mediation can be brought to the court system.

Although the ADA is the most recent and most powerful piece of civil rights legislation for people with disabilities, it is by no means the first. There were several precedent pieces of legislation, most notably, Section 504 of the Rehabilitation Act of 1973 that made it unlawful for any federal agency, public university, defense or other type of federal contractor, or any other institution or activity that receives federal funds to discriminate against anyone because of disability. Another strong point in the US is that, particularly thanks to the ADA, the societal infrastructure is quite accessible and that includes public transportation. In fact, opinion polls have demonstrated that most people with disabilities no longer view physical barriers as among the major impediments to employment.

In addition, the U.S. labor economy has become heavily reliant on information technology (IT) to carry out its work and that in turn has prompted a growth in development of assistive technology. Both factors are contributing to great improvement in the integration of today's assistive technology products with current electronic and information technology. Finally, without a doubt, one of the major positive aspects of the US situation for employment of disabled people is the subject of this paper, namely the role that the government itself plays in promoting the hiring and retention of disabled workers. As a model employer, the government not only directly improves the employment picture for disabled workers, but it is also seen as practicing what it preaches and thereby can subtly accustom the rest of society to the idea of disabled workers as part of the mainstream labor force.

In addition to promoting employment of individuals with disabilities through actually employing them, governments can also use their enormous purchasing power to influence the hiring, retention and promotion of people with disabilities in the private sector. One tool that helps governments to achieve both types of influence is through the use of technology.

## 1.1 The Role of Technology

The increasing use of technology in workplaces all over the world has resulted in unprecedented opportunities for people with disabilities to remain in, or enter the work force. Technology can be the key that helps level the playing field for individuals with disabilities if their needs are met through the proper assistive or adaptive accommodations. Moreover, many individuals with disabilities have good familiarity with computers and software programs because they often need to rely on them more than do non-disabled individuals in order to communicate. Finally, in this information age, governments are increasingly relying on technology to carry out the business of government, so they have an increased need for trained and skilled workers, thus presenting new opportunities to hire individuals with disabilities who possess those abilities.

## 2 Government as an Employer: The U.S. Model

As mentioned, there are no quotas in the United States for hiring or retention of disabled workers. Nevertheless, the U.S. Government has long set the tone in promoting hiring, retention and career advancement of individuals with disabilities as part of the federal workforce. More recently, State and local governments have more actively recruited individuals with disabilities as they have realized the need to demonstrate greater diversity in their workforces. For the last several years, workers with disabilities make up between 7.1 and 7.2 percent of the 1.8 million federal workforce. About half of these employees are individuals with severe disabilities, such as paraplegia, quadriplegia, blindness and deafness. An Executive Order signed in 2000, directed federal agencies to come up with hiring plans to bring another 100,000 employees with disabilities on board over the following five years. The Office of Personnel Management (OPM) was to monitor how well agencies were doing in meeting that goal. In Fiscal Year 2002, OPM reported that 15,592 people with disabilities were hired, representing 5.7 percent of all new hires.

### 2.1 How the Government Promotes Hiring of Workers with Disabilities

As the federal government's employment and personnel agency, OPM does a great deal to help promote the hiring, retention and career advancement of disabled workers. For example, most federal jobs are competitive appointments but for people with disabilities, there are hiring options called excepted service appointing authorities. This special authority is known as Schedule A, which permits federal employers to appoint individuals with severe physical, cognitive or psychiatric disabilities or those who have a history of such disabilities, to positions for up to two years. These individuals must gain initial certification typically through the state Vocational Rehabilitation system. At the end of the two-year period, if the individual has performed satisfactorily, he or she may convert to competitive service status. In addition, federal employers may use Schedule A authority to hire readers, interpreters or other personal assistants for employees with severe disabilities. Disabled veterans with at least a 30 percent disability also can be hired under special authorities. OPM has additional information on all the disability programs on their website www.opm.gov/disability.

The Workforce Recruitment Program (WRP) is coordinated by the U. S. Department of Labor's Office of Disability Employment Policy (ODEP) and the Department of Defense. WRP aims to provide summer work experience, and in some cases full-time employment, for college students with disabilities. The program develops partnerships with other Federal agencies, each of whom makes a commitment to provide summer jobs and a staff recruiter. Each year, recruiters interview about 1,800 students with disabilities at over 200 colleges and university campuses across the nation, and develop a database listing the qualifications of each student. This program serves as an excellent opportunity for disabled college students to get some work experience. Historically, approximately 50% of the WRP students that have graduated are offered to remain in their summer position as a permanent employee.

## 3 Government as a Purchaser of Technology

The U.S. federal government is the largest buyer of electronic and information technology in the country. This buying power enables the government to leverage its position to influence the direction and focus of the marketplace. The impact the federal government has on the economy is a powerful component that all sectors must realize and understand. From a disability and technology perspective, it is critical to understand that the federal government is both a powerful economic force and also the leader in employing people with disabilities.

In 1998, Congress amended the Rehabilitation Act to require Federal agencies to make their electronic and information technology accessible to people with disabilities. Inaccessible technology interferes with an individual's ability to obtain and use information quickly and easily. Section 508 was enacted to eliminate barriers in information technology, to make available new opportunities for people with disabilities, and to encourage development of technologies that will help achieve these goals. The law applies to all Federal agencies when they develop, procure, maintain, or use electronic and information technology.

The U.S. Access Board, an independent federal agency, provided the standards that established a minimum level of accessibility. The provisions cover the following types of technologies: software applications an operating systems; web-based information; telecommunication products; video and multimedia products; self contained products (copiers) and desktop and portable computers. The impact on the electronic and information technology market is extremely large.

The Access Board published an online tool to assist programmers and developers in understanding the accessibility provision of Section 508. The Guide to the Standards (http://www.access-board.gov/sec508/guide/index.htm) has details for each item and provides best practices. This tool has been used by federal agencies and vendors to ensure their respective conformance and compliance.

Furthermore, the United States General Services Administration, in conjunction with other federal agencies, created the www.section508.gov website as a portal to Section 508 information and training. One key feature of the site is Buy Accessible. Buy Accessible represents a partnership between government and industry to provide a service to federal procurement staff. It assists government personnel in completing market research necessary to ensure that they are buying the most accessible electronic and information technology products and services available in order to conform to Section 508.

The implementation of Section 508 has created some real improvements in the design and development of web site and standard office equipment and technology. For example, Section 508 requires that all computers sold to the federal government must have the "on/off" button in the front of the computer processing unit. This simple requirement has been adopted by industry (whether they sell to the government or not) as a better design for all users. However, real success lies in the ability of the federal government to hire more employees with disabilities who will be more productive because the information technology was designed with them in mind. The federal government strives to improve the connection between system accessibility (Section 508) and individual accommodation (Section 501/504 of the Rehabilitation Act) as it realizes more ways to create a more user-friendly environment.

## 3.1 How the Government Uses Technology to Increase Employment

As recruiting, hiring, and retaining people with disabilities is a federal focus, so are the reasonable accommodation process and procedures. The Department of Defense (DoD) established the Computer/Electronic Accommodations Program (CAP) in 1990 to eliminate employment barriers for employees with disabilities. As the government's centrally-funded program to provide assistive technology for employees with disabilities, CAP provides the tools for employees to access the fast-changing electronic and information technology environment. Since the program's inception, CAP's mission and role has been to provide real solutions for real needs.

CAP provides the latest assistive technology and accommodation services to ensure people with disabilities have equal access to the information environment and employment opportunities within the U.S. Federal government. Currently, CAP provides services to DoD and 58 Federal partner agencies and has provided over 40,000 accommodations to Federal employees with disabilities. In support of the U.S. Federal legislation, CAP provides assistive technology free of charge for individuals with visual, hearing, dexterity and cognitive disabilities that best meets the needs of the employee. By removing the cost and management of the assistive technology, CAP has leveled the playing field for employees with disabilities.

CAP also serves as the U.S. Federal government's largest buyer of assistive technology with annual procurements of approximately $3,000,000. With the growing number of requests for assistive technology due to increase employment opportunities and the aging workforce, the assistive technology vendors are working hard to keep pace with the demands of its customers and the changes in the federal workplace. Making the match between the employees with disabilities and the appropriate assistive technology is CAP's responsibility.

The reality of these trends mean that CAP has an increased role in moving employment issues forward throughout the federal government. It also means that CAP works to ensure its vendors and service providers recognize the links between individual accommodation, system accessibility, and how the changing environment will impact federal employees with disabilities.

Recognizing this interconnectedness and the changing environment will enable government, industry, and people with disabilities to determine the requirements for a more accessible future. The following is a list of roles/actions/discussions taking place in the United States:

- U.S. Federal government's role with mainstream electronic, information technology and accessibility via Section 508
- U.S. Federal government's role and partnership with assistive technology vendors
- Customers' needs for assistive technology services, delivery, installation, integration, and training
- Integration of assistive technology capabilities to create more flexible, usable products
- Incorporation of assistive technology attributes into mainstream technologies
- Improved processor speeds and engines to improve assistive technology performance
- Movement from individual applications to enterprise-wide solutions

In conclusion, it should be recognized that the role of the U.S. Government in promoting employment, job retention and advancement for disabled workers is not and need not be unique. All governments are similarly able to affect such changes if they have the will. For example, in Brazil, the centers for independent living (CILs) serve as personnel agencies, recruiting, training and placing disabled individuals in public sector jobs. The independent living centers have the sole right to provide the Brazilian government with highly skilled and trained workers. Thus, the CILs not only promote employment for disabled people but also ensure their own financial sustainability. Given the very high proportion of disabled people around the world who have no employment, it's time that governments recognize their responsibilities in this regard and understand that doing so is a win/win situation for all concerned.

# Influence of Accessibility Related Activities on the Usability of Business Software

Rakesh Jani and Martin Schrepp

SAP AG, Neurottstraße 16, 69190 Walldorf, Germany
{rakesh.jani,martin.schrepp}@sap.com

**Abstract.** To make business software accessible to users with disabilities is often seen by software developers as an additional burden, which is only beneficial for a small group of users. We will argue in this paper that this perception is not correct. Our experience from several projects shows that often the general usability of an application improves significantly when it is made accessible for disabled users. Especially expert users of the application profit often directly from the enhancements made for accessibility. This results from the fact that their special needs are in many aspects identical to the special needs of disabled users. We will discuss and explain this observation from a theoretical point of view. In addition we will demonstrate several examples, which show that following the existing guidelines for accessibility will also generate a benefit for non-disabled users of a software product.

## 1 Introduction

The importance of software is still increasing in our daily life. More and more jobs require the ability to interact with software products. Such computerized workplaces offer disabled persons often a good opportunity for a job, which is not in conflict with their disability. A necessary condition for that is that the design of the used software products takes the special needs of disabled users into account and allows disabled people to work efficiently with it.

Accessibility refers to the ability of every person, especially people with sensory or mobility impairments, to access and use products, e.g., business software. Different assistive technologies, such as screen reading software, Braille displays, special keyboards, or screen magnifiers enable software users with physical impairments to work with a software product, if this product is properly designed for accessibility. This means that the design of the software product considers already that some of its users may rely on assistive technology to access its user interface. Therefore, the software design must organize the information on the user interface in a way that allows assistive technology to interpret it correctly.

For example, to allow blind users to work with an application with the help of a screen reader, each non-textual element on the user interface (like icons, graphics, etc.) which carries important information must have in addition a hidden textual description which explains its meaning. The screen reader spells out this hidden textual description when the user sets the focus on this element.

K. Miesenberger et al. (Eds.): ICCHP 2004, LNCS 3118, pp. 52–59, 2004.

The accessibility of business software is a prerequisite to give persons with disabilities adequate chances on the labour market. If a company introduces new business software, it is extremely important that this software is accessible; otherwise disabled employees may not be able to do their jobs as before and are thus forced to move to other (often less attractive) jobs inside the company.

Several countries have already implemented or preparing legal requirements to force software vendors to make their products accessible. The best-known example for such legal requirements is Section 508 [1] of the Federal Rehabilitation Act in the United States. Section 508 requires that Federal agencies' electronic and information technology is accessible to people with disabilities. This law formulates a set of basic properties for a software product to be accessible. All the products to be purchased by US federal government agencies require to be compliant with those requested properties.

Other countries, for example Germany (Barrierefreie Informationstechnik-Verordnung [2]) or Japan (Accessibility Guidelines for Use of Computers by People with Disabilities and Elderly [3]) have similar guidelines or regulations.

On the other hand it is often very difficult to build in accessibility features into already existing software packages. This requires often a redesign of basic functionality or at least large enhancements to the already existing functionality. But under restricted budgets and time pressure in software development, it is often difficult to get the necessary resources. Often the argument is raised that the added accessibility features will be of use only for a small population of potential users. We will show in this paper that this argument is not valid. Making a product accessible usually improves also its general usability.

## 2 What Does It Mean to Make Business Software Accessible?

Since early 1990, the Graphical User Interface (GUI) is the dominant concept for building user interfaces. The main design paradigm in a GUI is a rich visual representation of the available information and functions and the possibility of direct manipulation (i.e. pointing and clicking on graphical elements with the mouse or usage of concepts like drag & drop).

Many of today's accessibility problems result from the current GUI paradigm. From today's perspective more primitive command or text based interfaces are nearly equally accessible by disabled (especially blind) and non-disabled users, since the sequential text contents of the interface accurately conveyed all necessary information. For a GUI we have to explicitly add some extra information, which allows the assistive technology to convert the content of the graphical display in a form that a blind user can understand.

To make a software product accessible, several guidelines are available. Well-known examples are the Section 508 guidelines [1], the Web Content Accessibility Guidelines [4] from the W3C's Web Accessibility Initiative, the technical specification ISO TS 16071 [5] from the International Organization of Standardization (ISO), and internal accessibility guidelines or standards from companies like SAP [6] or IBM [7].

In general, these guidelines consist of a number of checkpoints which describe properties which an accessible Web Site or Application must have. The checkpoints are oriented on the special needs of people with sensory (like the different forms of colour blindness or even total blindness), mobility (e.g. arthritis or total paralysis) or even cognitive impairments. To make business software accessible, the following categories of checkpoints are of interest[1].

### 2.1 Guidelines Concerning Colour and Font Setting

These guidelines are especially important for people with low vision or colour deficiencies. The most important points covered in this set of guidelines are:

- It must be possible for the user to define the font size, so that users with low vision can switch to font sizes that are comfortable for them.
- Colour should not be used as the only way to provide information. Thus, colour must always go together with a redundant additional attribute that is also visible for colour-blind users.
- The application must provide (or the user must be enabled to set) sufficient contrast levels between different elements of the user interface, for example background and text.

### 2.2 Guidelines Concerning Text Equivalents for Non-textual Elements

This set of requirements is especially important for blind users who rely on a screen reader or a Braille display to access the information displayed on the screen. The most important guidelines from this category are:

- It is required to provide text equivalents for every relevant interface element, like for example icons, graphics, etc. These text equivalents are then spelled out by the screen reading software or can be accessed over the Braille display when the user sets the focus on the element.
- The structure of tabular information must be made explicit. Row and column headers must be identified for tables.
- Screen areas, for example frames, sub-screens, or group boxes must have a clear and understandable title, which facilitates identification and navigation on the screen.

### 2.3 Guidelines Concerning Keyboard Support

Since many disabled users are not able to use the mouse, it is necessary to provide unlimited keyboard access for the application. This is vital for blind users, since the keyboard is for them only available input medium. There are also many users who are not able to work efficiently with the mouse, because their tactile skills are restricted. The most important guidelines concerning keyboard support are:

---

[1] Guidelines regarding the display of multimedia files or concerning audio files are ignored here, since they play only a minor role in business software.

- Each and every part of the interface that carries information (for example buttons, editable fields and non-editable fields, links, icons, etc.) must be reachable by keyboard actions.
- All actions on the interface (pressing buttons, clicking links, etc.) must be supported over the keyboard, for example it must be possible to start functions with the SPACE or ENTER key.
- To allow an efficient work for a user who cannot use the mouse it is more or less mandatory to provide keyboard shortcuts at least for the most frequently used functions.
- The current input focus must be clearly visible. Additionally, the current focus must be exposed so that assistive technology can track focus changes.

## 3 A Comparison of the Needs of Disabled Users and Power Users

Users of a software product are novices, experts or something in between. The expectations a user has towards the user interface of a software product change with the degree of expertise he or she has reached [8]. For novice users the most important usability aspect is that it is easy to learn the basic functions of the software. When the user gets more experienced the need to work as efficiently as possible with the software increases.

A method to allow novice and expert users to work efficiently with the same user interface is to add *accelerators* [9] for expert users to this interface. Accelerators are user interface elements that allow the user to perform frequent tasks quickly, even though the same tasks can also be performed in a more general and possibly slower way. It includes function keys or command keys that trigger an event by a single key press.

Several studies in cognitive psychology show that experts in an area do not only know more than novices, but even their knowledge structures are organized differently compared to the knowledge structures of novices [10, 11]. Expert users have high-level concepts that allow them to characterize and solve new problems quickly and efficiently. When using a software program, experts can quickly transform their goals into sequences of actions [12, 13] to achieve these goals. Their major need is to reduce their interactions with the system and thus to speed up their actions. They want a highly efficient interface.

Accordingly, [8, 14] the experts ask for possibilities to automate action sequences, want keyboard shortcuts nearly for everything (since working with keyboard shortcuts is much faster than working with the mouse) and need extended possibilities to personalize the interface to their desired working style. This need for efficiency is also covered by the common definition of usability given in the ISO-Norm 9241 (Part 11) [15] where usability is defined as the extent to which a product can be used by specified users to achieve specified goals with *effectiveness*, *efficiency* and *satisfaction* in a specified context of use.

If we compare the special needs of an expert to the guidelines described in the previous section we directly see that the expert users will directly profit from the full keyboard support added because of the accessibility guidelines.

Also personalization features, like adjusting the font size, are highly beneficial to expert users. For example, it can be important for them to choose a smaller font size, so that more information fits on the screen and they are thus able to avoid time consuming scrolling operations.

## 4 Examples

Call center software is a typical example for business software. A call center is a centralized workplace that handles the incoming phone calls from customers. The persons working in call centers are called call center agents. Two types of calls exist: Inbound calls and outbound calls. Inbound calls are the calls initiated by a customer to obtain information or ask for help. Outbound calls are the calls initiated by the call center agent aimed at selling a product or offer a service to a customer. The call center agents are a typical example for expert users who interact most of their working time with the call center software.

The agents need to be quick and efficient. They have to satisfy the customer as fast as possible. The time needed per call is limited, as the agent has to handle huge number of calls per day. In addition, the caller has, in general, a dedicated request and do not want to stay longer on the phone. So it is important that the call center agent does not spend unnecessary time for his or her interactions with the software. A call center agent has two different tasks, one to talk with the caller on the phone and other to enter the relevant data into the system. Thus, the mental load of the agent is quite high. So the interface of the software must be as simple as possible.

Accessibility was not considered during the initial design of the call center software. When special features for accessibility were added to the first prototype the general impression was that these features improved the overall usability of the software considerably. Following are few examples to illustrate this effect:

- Removing Complex Control – A channel selector control as shown in figure 1 automatically changes to the channel the agent is working on. If the agent is having a call or writing a mail or chatting with the customer then the control automatically switches to phone, mail or chat icon respectively. Change of communication channel also changes the toolbar functions. During the accessibility check it was found that the control was not accessible. The possible solution was to remove the control and replace it with the drop-down list box. Making the control accessible also improved the usability because for a normal user it is easy to recognize the channels in drop-down list box then to think about meaning of each icon.

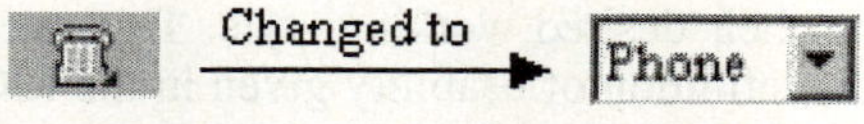


**Fig. 1.** Selector control changed to drop-down list box

- Focus Setting – There were two problems concerning the focus. First problem was that the cursor focus was lost after each server roundtrip (the interface exchanges information with the database server in the background) and secondly, it was not possible to set the focus on the value in the text box with keyboard. Now after the accessibility check, it is possible for the user to continue from the field he left be-

**Fig. 2.** Focus is set on the whole value in text box

fore roundtrip. Figure 2 shows the solution for the second problem. The focus is set to the value in the text box, thus letting the disabled user know the entered value in the text box. As the focus is set on the whole text in the text box, the user does not have to explicitly mark the text e.g. if he wants to remove the text. Thus, the solution is beneficial not only for visually handicapped user but also for a normal user working with keyboard.

- Keyboard Shortcut – The call center agent has to perform multiple tasks efficiently. So it is necessary to provide him with keyboard shortcuts or accelerators for the frequently used functions. Figure 3 shows one of the functions called Scratch Pad. A Scratch Pad is used by the agent to note down the most important information that can be used at later stage while talking with the customer. As the scratch pad is a frequently used function, a keyboard shortcut was provided so that the agent can open it quickly.

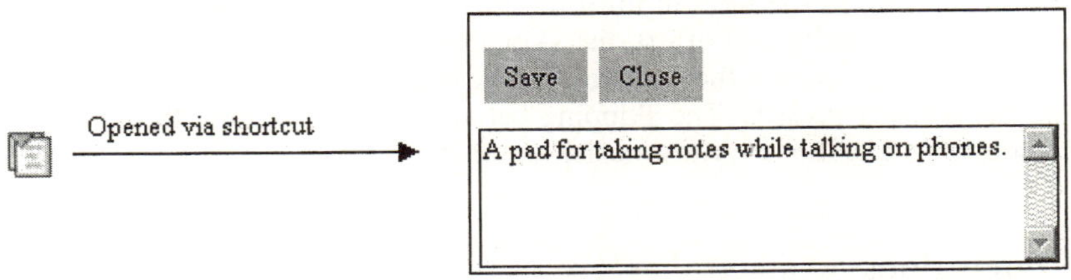


**Fig. 3.** A pad that can be opened with a keyboard shortcut

We performed a GOMS analysis [16, 17] to illustrate the difference between the handling of the scratch pad over the mouse and the handling over the keyboard shortcut. With the mouse the agent has to perform the following actions: position the cursor on the icon, click on the icon, position the cursor in the text area, type the text (we assume for the analysis a text with 20 characters), position the cursor on the Save-Button, click the Save-Button. Accordingly to the GOMS analysis an experienced user will need around 11 seconds for this action chain. With the introduction of keyboard shortcuts this action chain becomes much simpler. The user has to press the keyboard shortcut, the cursor is then automatically positioned in the text area, the user has to type the text, and to close the scratch pad he or she has to use a second shortcut. The GOMS analysis shows that the user will need around 6 seconds to perform this action chain.

- Meaningful Labels – When the customer calls for the service of the product, then the agent has to look for related documents of the customer. To search for documents quickly, the search functionality must be easy to understand. During the accessibility check, we encountered that the labels (date fields) as shown in figure 4 were very confusing, and does not tell the user what type of data to enter. So we came up with a solution (figure 5) of having precise and meaningful labels conveying the field type to the user.

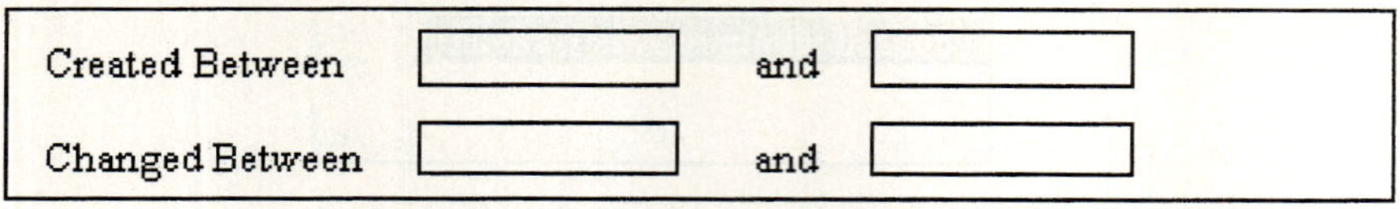


**Fig. 4.** Labels before Accessibility Check

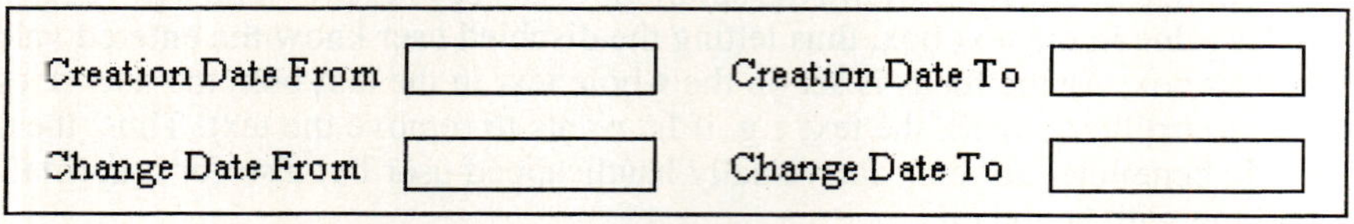


**Fig. 5.** Labels after Accessibility Check

- Simple and Consistent Layout – The layout is kept clear and simple to avoid scrolling and visual noise on the screen. It is also necessary to have consistency throughout the application. Consistent and structured navigation was considered to navigate easily and quickly within the application. The interface was divided into small parts called tiles. The problem was that if the user wants to jump from the field in first tile to the field in third tile then, he has to tab through each field. To achieve the task with less effort, the skipping mechanism was implemented. Skipping mechanism allows the user to skip or jump from one area (e.g. tiles) to another in few key presses. The skipping behavior was consistent throughout the application to make the workflow easier and faster.

## 5 Conclusions

We have tried to show that the needs of disabled users, especially blind users or handicapped users who are not able to use the mouse, are in many aspects similar to the needs of expert users. Thus, an effort to make a software product accessible to disabled users pays off not only for this intended target group, but is in addition also beneficial to expert users of the software.

Thus, the argument that an accessibility action is only of use for a small fraction of possible users is in our opinion not valid. A software product properly designed to meet the needs of expert users will already contain a huge amount of features that are mandatory for accessibility. Thus, it is in each case a good investment to consider the accessibility needs early during interface design.

## References

1. US Department of Justice. Section 508 of the Federal Rehabilitation Act. Available online under http://www.section508.gov/
2. Bundesministerium des Innern (2002). Verordnung zur Schaffung barrierefreier Informationstechniken nach dem Behindertengleichstellungsgesetz (Barrierefreie Informationstechnik-Verordnung – BITV). Available online under http://bundesrecht.juris.de/bundesrecht/bitv/gesamt.pdf

3. Ministry of International Trade and Industry. Notification No.362 (2002). Accessibility Guidelines for Use of Computers by People with Disabilities and Elderly. Available online under http://www.kokoroweb.org/guide/guideE.html
4. Chrisholm, W., Vanderheiden, G., Jacobs, I. (1999): Web Content Accessibility Guidelines 1.0. Available online under http://www.w3c.org/TR/WCAG10/
5. ISO/TS 16071 (2003). Ergonomics of human-system interaction -- Guidance on accessibility for human-computer interfaces. Genf: International Organization for Standardization
6. SAP Accessibility Guidelines. Available online under http://www.saplabs.com/accessibility/guide_eval/guides_checks.htm
7. IBM Accessibility Guidelines. Available online under http://www-306.ibm.com/able/ guidelines/software/accesssoftware.html
8. Cooper, A. (1995). About Face: The essentials of User Interface Design. IDG Books, Foster City, CA
9. Wu, J. (2000). Accommodating both Experts and Novices in one Interface. In: Browne, H., Carver, J. & Kolatch, E. (Eds.), UUGuide – Practical Design Guidelines for Universal Usability. University of Maryland. Available online under http://otal.umd.edu/UUGuide/
10. Chase, W.G. & Simon, H.A. (1973). The mind's Eye in Chess. In: Chase, W.G. (Ed.), Visual Information Processing. New York, Academic Press
11. Shneiderman, B. (1976). Exploratory Experiments in Programmer Behaviour. International Journal of Computer and Information Services 5, pp. 123-143
12. Rector, A. L., Newton, P. D., and Marsden, P. H. (1985). What kind of system does an expert need? People and Computers: Designing the interface. Cambridge: Cambridge University Press. pp.239-247
13. Nielsen, J. (1993). Usability Engineering. Academic Press
14. Nielsen, J. (2000). Novice vs. Expert Users. In: Useit.com - Usable Information Technology. Available online under http://www.useit.com/alertbox/20000206.html
15. ISO 9241-11 (1998). Ergonomic requirements for office work with visual display terminals - Part 11: Guidance on usability. Genf: International Organization for Standardization
16. John, D. & Kieras, D. E. (1996). The GOMS family of user interface analysis techniques: Comparison and Contrast. ACM Transactions on Computer-Human Interaction 3, 4, pp. 320-351
17. Wandmacher, J. (2002). GOMS Analysen mit GOMSED. Available online under: http://www.tu-darmstadt.de/fb/fb3/psy/kogpsy/

# Data Entry in Application-Independent Voice Interfaces

Frankie James[1], Jeff Roelands[2], and Rama Gurram[1]

[1] Corporate Research Center, SAP Labs, LLC, 3410 Hillview, Palo Alto, CA 94304
{frankie.james,rama.gurram}@sap.com
[2] Voice Development Center, Advanced Software Development, Inc.,
540 North Santa Cruz Avenue #257, Los Gatos, CA 95030
jeff@advancedswdev.com

**Abstract.** Complex graphical portals present multiple applications to users in a single display. However, portal interfaces are heavily mouse and keyboard intensive, making them inaccessible to users with physical disabilities. We are investigating the design of application-independent voice interfaces to add accessibility for physically disabled users to pre-existing applications. This paper describes a user study comparing voice data entry to keyboard and mouse, to assess efficiency and user satisfaction. Feedback and results show voice data entry to be useful, although some performance issues still remain.

## 1 Introduction

Complex graphical user interfaces (GUIs) are prevalent in business today. Portals, used by SAP, Plumtree, and even Yahoo, present multiple applications and information sources in a single display, and allow efficient access to several applications and services simultaneously. However, portals are mouse and keyboard intensive, and thus problematic for many people.

Many groups have difficulty using standard keyboards and mice, including mobile users with inadequately sized devices and factory workers with busy hands. In addition, physically disabled users often cannot use standard input devices at all. Voice interfaces can provide portal access for all of these groups.

This paper presents a user study comparing an application-independent voice interface called the Voice-Enabled Portal (VEP [4]) to keyboard and mouse for entering time sheet data, to evaluate comparative efficiency and user satisfaction. The study also compares voice usage by disabled and non-disabled users to identify differences between the groups. Our ultimate aim with VEP is to develop a commercially viable voice interface to a web-based portal that can be used as an alternative to keyboard and mouse.

VEP is an application-independent interface that uses voice as an accessibility tool for pre-existing applications. Users interact with screen elements (hyperlinks, text boxes, etc.) directly. Although VEP is less conversational than some voice interfaces, we feel that the benefits of application-independence outweigh other limitations.

The study presented here compares data entry using VEP to keyboard and mouse. VEP data entry begins with selection of the desired screen element, either by name, or, when there are no names (as with the text boxes in Figure 1), by type (e.g., "text

K. Miesenberger et al. (Eds.): ICCHP 2004, LNCS 3118, pp. 60–68, 2004.

box"). RESOLV[1] icons (see Figure 2) are automatically overlaid on matching targets when an ambiguous command is given; the desired target is selected by number. The benefits of RESOLV over similar systems are described in more detail in [4].

VEP allows data entry to most GUI elements. Selected elements display a blue border to indicate that input is expected. The border disappears upon completion.

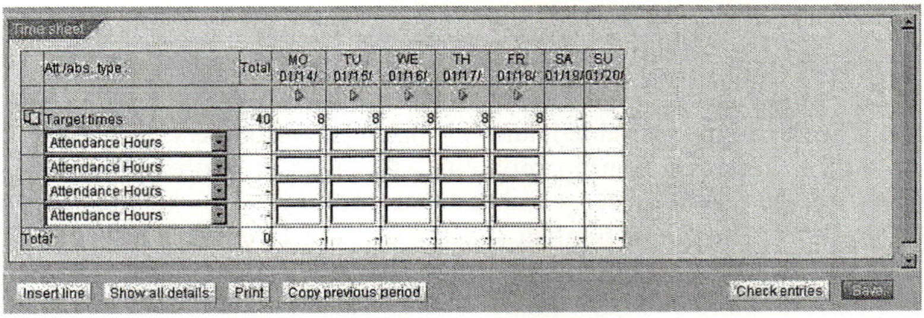


**Fig. 1.** Cross-Application Time Sheet (CATS) application used in study

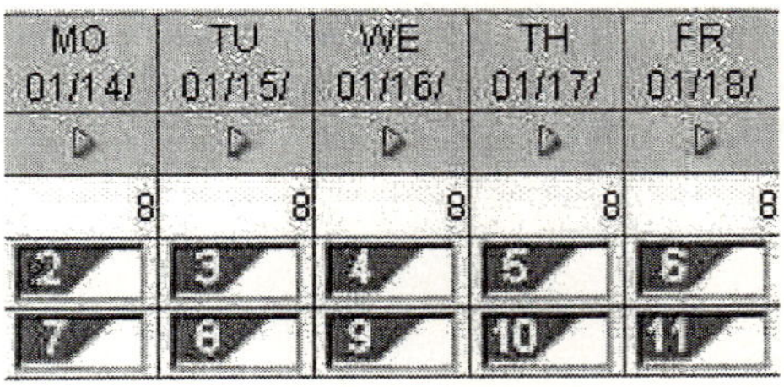


**Fig. 2.** RESOLV icons appear when user says "text box"

### 1.1 Minimizing Recognition Errors through Grammar Assignment

To improve recognition quality in this study and to allow users to focus on the VEP interaction style, data entry to short-response boxes was supported through specialized recognition grammars. Grammars were manually associated with text boxes.

### 1.2 Interacting with GUI Widgets

When an icon, button, radio button, or check box is selected, VEP behaves as though the item has been clicked with a mouse. Otherwise, a blue border highlights the item and the interaction proceeds. Text boxes expect the user to enter a value. Combo boxes display the associated drop-down list and allow users to scroll the list or select an entry.

---

1 Representational Enumerated Semi-transparent Overlaid Labels for Voice.

## 2 Experiment Outline

In previous user studies, we tested various interaction styles for voice navigation. [4] This study tests voice data entry, and compares it to a baseline of keyboard and mouse.

### 2.1 Participants

Participants were 24 non-disabled and 11 disabled volunteers. All were English speakers with no reported hearing problems. Although it is preferable to test with native speakers, the disabled user population was too limited to exclude non-native or accented speakers. Therefore, English fluency was our baseline for all groups. Self-reported experience with computers and time sheets was comparable for all participants.

Non-disabled participants were randomly assigned to use VEP or keyboard/mouse (KB/M). Disabled participants, who were selected based on limitations using KB/M, all used VEP. Of the disabled participants, 7 regularly used speech to access computers, 1 a mouth pointer, and 3 used keyboard and pointing device, with limited functionality. Disabled and non-disabled participants had comparable voice interface experience. Participants were paid $50; disabled participants received an additional $10 travel stipend.

### 2.2 Procedure

Test users participated one at a time in a room equipped with a scan converter and microphone. Consent for recording was obtained prior to testing. Users received a general instruction sheet, instructions about the Cross-Application Time sheet (CATS; see Figure 1), and (for VEP users) a description of the available commands. Users were encouraged to keep the command sheet available for later reference.

Users entered five scenarios of time sheet data (one at a time) using CATS. Each scenario required users to enter one week of data. Users were able to take notes and ask questions. For questions about which command to use, the user was referred to the command sheet. After completing all five scenarios, users answered a Likert-scale questionnaire about various interface features. An experimental session lasted about one hour.

### 2.3 Measures

Both objective and subjective data were evaluated. Measures involving all three groups were compared with one-way ANOVA with planned comparisons, so that non-disabled VEP users were compared independently with KB/M and disabled VEP users. Measures applicable only to voice compared VEP groups with independent sample t-tests.

### 2.3.1 Objective Data

Objective data was collected using video tapes from the experiment, which were transcribed to yield measures related to time and, for the voice users, recognition accuracy.

**Task Completion Time.** Task completion time was the elapsed time from the start of the user's first action (utterance or KB/M action) until the end of the last system action. VEP occasionally crashed and required a system restart. Modified completion times used in our analysis start from the first command given after the last restart. This restart occurred for 12 task scenarios out of a total of 88 for VEP, and affected 10 users.

**Task Interaction Time.** Interaction time includes user action time and system reaction time to update the GUI. For KB/M, user action and system reaction times were combined into KB/M time, because GUI response was nearly instantaneous. For VEP, interaction time included utterance time, system reaction time, and a delay time, during which VEP processed and recognized the utterance (see Figure 3).

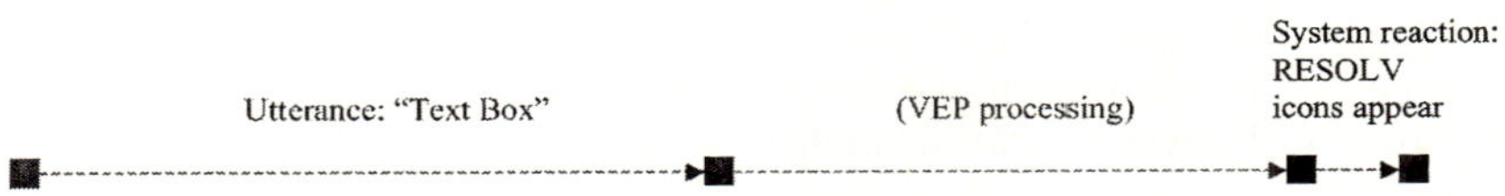


**Fig. 3.** Interaction time for VEP actions

**Task Interaction Steps.** In addition to examining the interaction time, we also calculated the number of steps taken to complete tasks. This allowed us to determine whether the voice interface requires more (or fewer) steps than keyboard and mouse.

**Error Rates.** Recognition data was collected for correct recognition, misrecognition, out-of-grammar, and mode error rates. Mode errors are commands given when the microphone is in sleep mode, or side comments made while the microphone is listening.

### 2.3.2 Subjective Data

The main factor of interest from our questionnaire was General Satisfaction. In addition, single question measures were compared for Likelihood of Future Use, Perceived Efficiency, Perceived Naturalness, and Perceived Recognition Quality. Details regarding all measures can be found below.

## 3 Results and Discussion

This user study compared user reactions and performance along two dimensions:

1. Differences between VEP and keyboard/mouse (KB/M); and
2. Differences between disabled and non-disabled users of voice interfaces

Although there are clear accessibility benefits to voice, it is important to understand the differences between standard input tools (keyboard and mouse) and voice. In addition, a clearer understanding of the differing needs of disabled and non-disabled users can help us to create more usable voice interfaces for both groups.

### 3.1 Comparing VEP to Keyboard and Mouse

Previous studies have compared voice to mouse interaction. Karl et al. [5] substituted voice for mouse in word processing, and found reduced task times for formatting. This arises from voice's ability to bypass hierarchies: whereas a GUI will be too complex if all commands are available as toolbar actions, voice can have essentially unlimited one-step actions. If navigation alternatives are provided for novices, experienced users can quickly activate commands otherwise hidden in a complex hierarchy. Christian, et al. [1] compared voice and mouse in a test that required hierarchical menu navigation for both modalities. Because voice often introduces recognition delays, its performance tends to be poorer than mouse in such tasks. However, a non-hierarchical map-based task in the same study showed no performance difference between mouse and voice.

These studies show that voice can be comparable to and, in some cases, more efficient than mouse-based interfaces, when voice's advantages are exploited. Our study extends this work to compare voice not only to mouse, but also to keyboard-based tasks. In our study, planned-comparison ANOVA tests allowed us to compare disabled and non-disabled VEP users, and then non-disabled VEP and KB/M. Because no differences were found for the following measures between disabled and non-disabled VEP users, we can generalize the results to both VEP groups, in comparison to KB/M.

#### 3.1.1 Objective Measures

Objective measures comparing VEP to KB/M were task completion time, task interaction time, and task interaction steps. Interaction step comparison showed no difference between groups, therefore, time differences may be attributed to the time taken per step. Task completion time was significantly higher for VEP than KB/M ($p = .002$; $F(1, 13.567) = 15.547$). As seen in Figure 4, completion time consisted of user/system interaction time, VEP processing time, and idle time. Interaction time (VEP processing *plus* user/system interaction) was also significantly higher ($p < .001$; $F(1, 12.884) = 32.17$) for VEP. A further comparison excluding the VEP processing delay showed *no* difference between groups, allowing us to attribute interaction time difference to this delay.

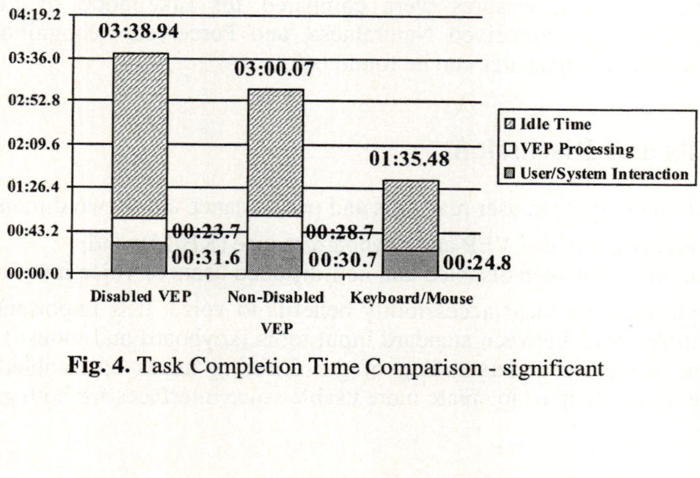


**Fig. 4.** Task Completion Time Comparison - significant

The rest of the completion time difference can be attributed to idle time, when the user is deciding what to do next. This additional time is likely due to reduced interface experience for VEP users compared to KB/M, and may decrease with experience.

### 3.1.2 Subjective Measures

Subjective comparisons between VEP and KB/M showed few differences. The combined factor General Satisfaction showed no difference (see Figure 5). Likelihood of Future Use is also comparable for VEP and KB/M (see Figure 6). The only difference in the subjective data was in Perceived Efficiency, where VEP was rated as being significantly less efficient than KB/M ($p = .031$; $F(1,31) = 5.12$, see Figure 6).

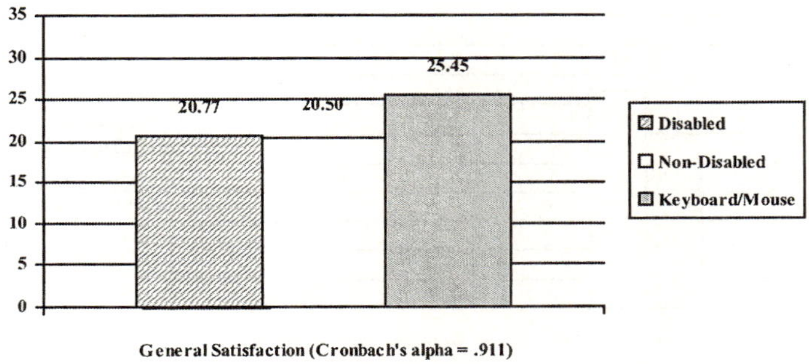


**Fig. 5.** General Satisfaction (liked very much-7/did not like at all-1, helpful-7/not helpful-1, easy-7/difficult-1, enjoyable-7/annoying-1, efficient-7/time consuming-1) - no difference

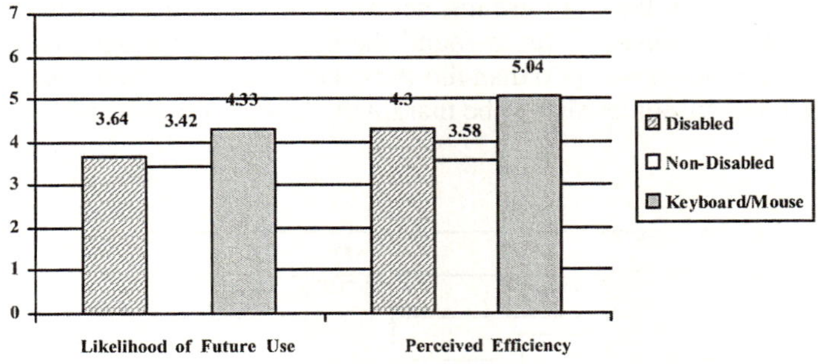


**Fig. 6.** Likelihood of Future Use (very likely-5/not likely at all-1) – no difference; Perceived Efficiency (efficient-7/time consuming-1) - significant

## 3.2 Comparing Disabled and Non-disabled VEP Users

Disabled and non-disabled users often have different opinions of non-standard interfaces (see James [3]), which do not necessarily coincide with objective differences. The likely reason is that non-disabled users exposed to non-standard technologies have an inherent prejudice that pre-existing standards must be better because they are more familiar. Technology acceptance failure, described by Cohen and McGee [2], is less often found in disabled users, who rely on non-standard technologies to access computers.

Our present findings confirm the technology acceptance failure in non-disabled users. In our comparisons of the two VEP groups, no differences were found in objective measures. Utterance time, VEP processing, and system reaction time were comparable. Referring back to Figure 3 illustrating interaction time, each VEP interaction step consisted of roughly 49% utterance time, 43% processing time, and 8% system reaction time. The (relatively) large amount of time required for VEP processing should drop as recognition software gains efficiency, thereby improving the system's performance. Recognition error rates were also comparable for the two voice groups (see Figure 7).

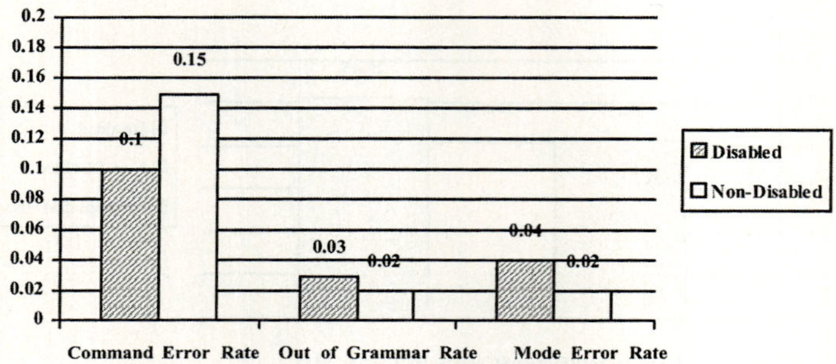


**Fig. 7.** Error Rates for VEP Users - no differences

Interestingly, while there are no differences in objective recognition quality or performance between the VEP groups, certain subjective questions related do differ (see Figure 8). Non-disabled users found the command language significantly less natural ($p = .026$; $t(21) = 2.393$) than did the disabled users. In addition, non-disabled users judged recognition quality to be marginally lower ($p = .091$; $t(21) = 1.774$) than disabled users.

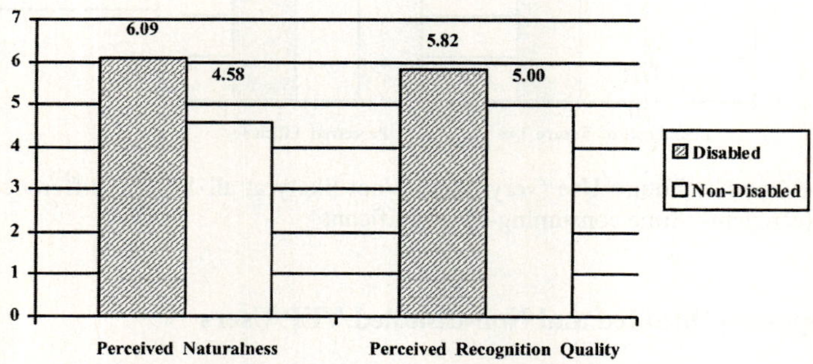


**Fig. 8.** Perceived Naturalness (natural-7/artificial-1) – significant; Perceived Recognition Quality (understood me most of the time-7/hardly understood me at all-1) – marginal

# 4 Expanding VEP

The results of this study suggest that VEP is a reasonable alternative to keyboard and mouse, particularly for physically disabled users. Since this study, we have made several improvements to the interface and expanded the functionality.

## 4.1 Improved Recognizer Efficiency

VEP uses third-party speech recognition technologies, such as developed by Microsoft and IBM. Recently, we have focused on increasing interaction efficiency between VEP and third-party recognizers to reduce the processing time required. Informal evidence suggests that newer versions of VEP are more efficient in processing commands.

## 4.2 Advanced Data Entry

The version of VEP described in this study supports basic data entry. To increase VEP's commercial value, we are working to extend the data entry capabilities of the system.

### 4.2.1 Sticky Grammars for Text Boxes

Grammar-based recognition performance is, in general, better than free dictation. However, determining which grammar to assign to a text box is a huge challenge, especially for a system such as VEP that allows voice access to almost any web page.

VEP allows users to make grammar assignments at run-time, using a technique called "sticky grammars." On the initial visit to a text box, the user selects from a list of available grammars (e.g., date, time, number). On subsequent visits, VEP remembers whether a grammar has already been assigned and if so, labels the text box with the grammar's name. The user may then enter data or change the grammar to be used.

### 4.2.2 Dictation and Multi-select Data Entry

Supporting both data entry and navigation in a voice interface requires determining when data entry is completed. For most simple items, such as combo boxes, completion detection is straightforward. For multi-select items, the end of interaction is flexible and dependent on the number of items selected. Similarly, dictation can continue indefinitely. We therefore refer to dictation boxes and multi-select items as "open interaction elements," to indicate that the end of interaction with such elements is not constrained.

In a recent study, we explored various methods for determining completion with open interaction elements. Our results show that a combination of explicit and "implicit" exit commands (i.e., a navigation command after a selection) appears to work well. Current efforts involve integrating the new findings into VEP's interaction style to create a consistent exit model that handles both open and "closed" interaction elements.

## 5 Conclusion

Application-independent voice interfaces are a valuable accessibility tool. Although they may seem less natural than conversational interfaces, the benefits gained by not requiring changes to underlying applications produce a valuable trade-off. The user study described here shows that data entry using one application-independent voice interface, VEP, is acceptable to users, although some work is needed to improve the efficiency.

Based on our user studies, we feel that VEP can be a commercially viable accessibility solution. We currently seek to test VEP with experienced users in an environment where the interface is integral to completing real work. Field-test users will likely have different requirements and opinions. Their feedback will be vital to making further improvements to support productivity with this application-independent voice interface.

## References

1. Christian, K., Kules, B., et al., A comparison of voice controlled and mouse controlled web browsing. *ASSETS '00*, (Arlington, VA, 2000), ACM, 72-79.
2. Cohen, P.R. and McGee, D.R. Tangible Multimodal Interfaces for Safety-Critical Applications. *Communications of the ACM*, *47* (1). 41-46.
3. James, F. *Representing Structured Information in Audio Interfaces: A Framework for Selecting Audio Marking Techniques to Represent Document Structure*. Ph.D. Thesis, Stanford University, Department of Computer Science. Stanford, CA, 1998.
4. James, F. and Roelands, J., Voice over Workplace (VoWP): Voice Navigation in a Complex Business GUI. *ASSETS 2002*, (Edinburgh, Scotland, 2002), ACM Press, 197-204.
5. Karl, L.R., Pettey, M. and Shneiderman, B. Speech versus mouse commands for word processing: An empirical evaluation. *International Journal of Man-Machine Studies*, *39* (4). 667-687.

# Designing User Interfaces Tailored to the Current User's Requirements in Real Time

Martín González Rodríguez, J. Ramón Pérez Pérez, and M. Puerto Paule Ruíz

The Human Communication and Interaction Research Group (HCI-RG)
Department of Computer Science, University of Oviedo, Asturias
{martin,jrpp,paule}@lsi.uniovi.es
http://www.hci.uniovi.es

**Abstract.** Traditional design of user interfaces is based on a perfect knowledge of the user's interaction requirements for the target audience. This approach leads to user interfaces designed for a generic ideal user who doesn't exist at all. As a result, every user or the interface has to adapt his/her own user's interaction requirements to those of this ideal user. In a ideal scenario, there should be as many versions of the user interface as final users. Each of those versions would be designed to satisfy the user's interaction requirements of a single user. Under this approach, we have designed GADEA, a user interface management system able to design different versions of a user interface, on the fly, depending on the cognitive, perceptive and motive skills of each user of the application. This system observes the users as they perform common tasks, analyzing their behavior in order to determine their interaction requirements.

## 1 Introduction

Traditional design of user centered interfaces is based on the identification and definition of the target audience of the application under development. Several design guidelines include the identification and understanding of the target audience as the most important steps to start the design of a product [1, pp. 13; 2] [6–8]. The idea is that once the target audience has been defined; an interface that effectively satisfies their needs can be designed.

However, the quest for the typical user is opposite to the individuality and diversity that makes up some much of our identity. If the design of the interaction mechanisms of an application aims to make interfaces accessible and appealing to all users, it shouldn't rely on an abstract generalization [9]. In the design of applications targeted to a wide range of users, it is almost impossible to determine the typical user without falling in serious misconceptions. For example, is it possible to describe the typical user of Microsoft Office? Is it possible to describe the typical user of Google?

At the design stage of a generic user interface, it is completely impossible to determine the specific cognitive, perceptive and motor skills of each of its target users. The uncertainty about the interaction requirements of real user makes any decision at the design stage completely useless at run time. To illustrate this fact, we might con-

K. Miesenberger et al. (Eds.): ICCHP 2004, LNCS 3118, pp. 69–75, 2004.

sider the design of the syntactical level for the user interface of a simple web site. Whenever the designers decide to include buttons on the navigation bar, they will get in trouble as soon as they try to define the size of these widgets. Considering that small buttons will be difficult to be used by elderly users or people with visual disabilities (short-sighted people, for example), while big buttons will look ugly for people with average perceptive systems, there is not a unique-size-fits all button.

As the user interface of computer applications should be usable and must be accessible by any kind of users (independently of the accuracy of their perceptive system), each design decision should be taken at execution time, once the interaction requirements of the current target user are finally known. As designers are not present during execution time, the user interface should be able to play the role of the human designer, creating the user interface on the fly.

Following this design goal we have developed GADEA, a User Interface Management Expert System (UIMES) able to generate dynamic versions of the syntactical level of a user interface on the fly at execution time. These interactive dialogs are specially designed to comply with the interaction requirements of the current user of the application. This UIMES has been designed to provide universal access to the interactive dialogs, supporting the interaction requirements of users with different degrees of physical, visual or hearing disabilities.

## 2 An Overview of GADEA

The UIMES GADEA provides full support to java-based and web-based applications, creating the interactive dialogs required to interchange information between the user and those applications dynamically. This system is able to provide support for several host applications simultaneously.

GADEA tries to emulate the behavior of a human expert in Human-Computer Interaction (HCI) being in charge of the design of a set of interactive dialogs for a specific user. Those dialogs are designed bye mean multimodal-based communication channels [13] (visual and auditory communication channels). In this scenario, a human expert would select the most suitable interaction style available for the target platform (the web or standalone applications) depending on the unique cognitive, perceptive and motive requirements of the target user, adapting the appearance, contents and access mode of every widget included in the dialog to the user's interaction requirements. That's what GADEA tries to do dynamically.

The architecture of GADEA relies on three independent components which has been specially designed to cope with the main three goals that the we wanted to achieved with the development of this system. Those components are DEVA, ANTS and Codex (see Fig. 1) and they try to address the following issues:

- Creation of user-tailored interactive dialogs at real time (DEVA module).
- Constant actualization of the user model for each user of every application hosted by GADEA (ANTS module).
- Effective and automatic separation of the user interface from the functionality of the application (Codex module).

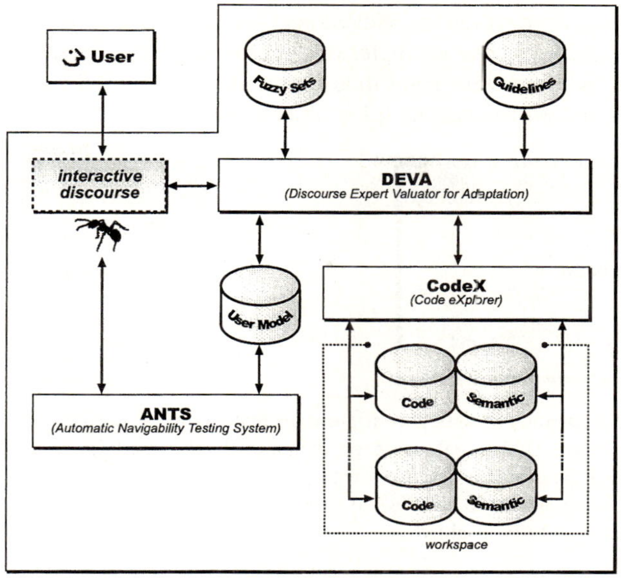


**Fig. 1.** The design of GADEA is made up of three modules: *CodeX, DEVA and, ANTS.* The first one is the UIMS's back-end, being in charge of the communications with the host application. The second one is the GADEA's front-end, converting the application's interaction request into interactive dialogs with the user. Finally, the third one is in charge of observing and recording the user's behavior while they interact with the application, updating the corresponding user model.

### 2.1 DEVA (Dialog Expert Valuator for Adaptation)

The interaction requests sent by the application through the CodeX module must be converted into interactive dialogs in order to establish communication with the user. DEVA is the module responsible for the creation of those interactive dialogs, checking and validating the information provided by the user, before sending it to the application for further processing.

The first task performed by DEVA to convert the interaction requests of the application into interactive dialogs is the identification and assignment of specific widgets (buttons, text fields, etc.) needed to fill every single piece of data (text strings, arrays of numbers, etc.) required by the application to perform a specific task. The same applies when the application has to show information to the user (the information provided by the application to the user in terms of data structures must be converted into widgets before being displayed in the user interface).

The assignation of every widget to each piece of data depends on the semantics of the data as well as on the interaction requirements of the current user. During this process DEVA selects every widget suitable to be used to fill a specific data structure, evaluating it according to cognitive criteria. This valuating task is performed by mean of a usability rating algorithm that provides higher scores for the current's user favorite widgets and lower scores for widgets that the user doesn't like or can't use due to disabilities constraints. For example, this scoring algorithm might favor the use of popup menus for users with good mouse pointing skills and the use of text field for users with better performance in typing tasks (see Fig 2.).

**Fig. 2.** Different interactive dialog configuration that might be used by DEVA to obtain the user's favorite color. Dialog left has been dynamically designed for users with good typing skills. Dialog right is designed for users who prefer the use of a pointing device. Widgets are numbered (in reverse style) to be selected using the keyboard, making them accessible to motive disable and/or visually disabled users.

The scoring algorithm is based on the 'Keystroke Model' developed by Card et al. [2] whose original intended use was the prediction of the time required to perform simple computer tasks by average user. In the original keystroke model, each of the parameters employed in the prediction functions was an estimation of the time required by an average user to execute any basic user interface task (pointing tasks, clicking task, decision tasks, etc). However, as GADEA has constantly updated report of the real time consumed by the current user in every task, the results obtained are not only more accurate by also tailored to the performance of each user of the application. The actualization of the timed required by individual user to perform every basic task is performed by the ANTS module (described later in this paper).

Once DEVA has selected the appropriate widgets to be employed in the design of an interactive dialog, the module will define the layout for the interactive dialog. This module makes use of orientation metaphors [5] (cited in [6]) mapping the vertical attribute of any location of the visual space to the 'up is more' and 'down is less' metaphors [6], so whenever it is possible, DEVA distributes visual objects following a vertical orientation, locating relevant objects values upwards in the visual space of the user interface. Objects aligned to the left or to the right depend on the writing system of the language employed by the current user. In GADEA, Roman languages (written from left to right) are aligned to the left, while Semitic languages must be aligned to the right [1, pp. 19-24].

DEVA makes a clear distinction between visual objects, whose unique task is restricted to provide visual information to the user (labels for example) and interactive objects which are employed by the user to interact with the application (buttons for example). While the formers are aligned following the horizontal orientation strategy, the interactive objects are aligned depending on the current user's laterality (interactive widgets are left aligned when the user is left handed and right aligned when the user is right handed).

The next step in the design of the interactive dialog is the configuration of the selected widgets in size, shape, color and any other parameter. DEVA makes use again of the current user model to determine these values, depending on the requirements of the perceptive and motive system of the current user. While the size of visual objects depends exclusively on the user visual capacity, the size of interactive objects might depend on user's motive skills too.

The following example represents one of the dozens of fuzzy logic rules used by the inference engine of DEVA to determine the size of an interactive object. Clicking on a widget with a pointing device is a task that requires a high visual and motive accuracy. If a user has a low motive accuracy (motor disable users, for example), the clicking target area is increased to facilitate the pointing task.

```
If Motor Accuracy of User is Low AND Visual Accuracy of
User is High then width of Interactive Object is Big
```

The use of a fuzzy logic engine in DEVA facilitates the incorporation of new rules designed by experts in human-computer interaction. It also avoids dramatic changes in the user interface as the system learns from the user behavior.

In our experiments, once the system has obtained basic knowledge about the user behavior (visual accuracy, motor accuracy, laterality, etc.) the representation of any interactive dialog thorough the system changes very little, and many times it is inappreciable by the user. Anyway, the user has the option to disable to constant adaptation of the user interface, applying changes to the interface only when he/she desires it of from time to time.

## 2.2 ANTS (Automatic Navigability Testing System)

ANTS is the module in charge for keeping the current user model updated. The information required is obtained by a small army of data gathering agents, who keep track of the user behavior at execution time.

The design metaphor of ANTS is based on the life of a community of ants. The ants (agents) depart from their anthill (a server) looking for food (the information) in every picnic available (interactive dialogs). Once the ant has got the food, it comes back to the anthill and stores it carefully in one of the anthill's data warehouses (a data base).

Whenever an interactive dialog is created, the ant is downloaded from the anthill (the ANTS server) being inserted inside the dialog or web page generated by DEVA. Once the dialog is displayed to the user, the ant establishes a communication channel with the anthill, which is used to send the data collected. An ant-assistant object located in the server-side maintains the communication channel alive during the interactive dialog's cycle of life, collecting the information sent by the ant, classifying it, and sending it to the warehouse object commissioned to store it in the proper user model.

DEVA can include different kind on agents inside every dialog. Every agent class in ANTS is specialized in gathering a specific kind of data. For each parameter needed to adapt the user interface, there will be a specific class of agents. So ANTS have specific agents to gather information related the user's perception system accuracy (tactile, visual, auditory, etc.), the user's motive system accuracy, the user's reaction and decision time, etc.

The agents keep track of every action performed by the user in every user process, crating an abstract navigation model similar to those employed by the Object Oriented Hypermedia Design Model (OOHDM) [10]. This abstract navigation is used to determine the landmarks, routes and mental models [11] employed by the users when they make use of each user process of the application. This information can e used to determine the user's expertise degree in the use of the application [12].

### 2.3 CodeX (Code eXplorer)

CodeX represents the interface between GADEA and the host applications that run under the control of this UIMES. The module converts user interaction requests into runtime calls to specific methods inside the application's domain workspace. CodeX is also in charge of the actualization of every single piece information displayed by the user interface, keeping track of possible changes done by the application in the value of public variables and data structures associated to the interface. All this information is obtained automatically inspecting the application's code by mean of the structural reflection mechanisms provided by the Java platform.

CodeX automatically inspects the binary code of each application at execution time; looking for any user process defined by the programmers during the design of the application. CodeX consider a 'user process' as those methods designed to satisfy a specific user's interaction request and will represent them as options or commands in the respective application user interface.

CodeX provide a programming API 100% compatible with Java 1.0. This API allows programmers to select and include different data objects inside interaction request components. Whenever it is required, programmers can force the interaction requests to be displayed in the active communication channel. CodeX will send the interactive request component to DEVA which will convert the request into an interactive dialog displayed to the user.

Programmers using CodeX don't need to use any kind of widgets in their code as they will picked up at execution time by DEVA. The only thing programmers need to do is to define the data structures required to provide information to the user (strings objects, integer objects, etc.) as well as the data structure required to store the information provided by the users in the scope of those interactive dialogs.

This automatic code exploring system allows an easy adaptation of the low-level aspects of a user interface with little or almost no programming effort.

## 3 Conclusions

The use of an expert system responsible for taking every decision concerning with the design of the interface In the GADEA development model, the interactive dialogs are designed by humans in terms of data flows, defining which kind of data must be owned by every interactive dialog. However, decisions about how the data must be displayed by the user are taken at execution time by this system, tailoring the interactive dialogs to the cognitive, perceptive and motor skills of the current user.

This approach guarantees a strong internal and external consistency in the user interface as well as support for standard accessibility and usability guidelines, which are adapted to the unique interaction requirements of every single user.

## References


1. APPLE COMPUTER INC; (1992) Macintosh Human Interface Guidelines. Addison-Wesley Publishing Company. ISBN 0-201-62216-562216.
2. CARD, Stuart K.; MORAN, Thomas P.; NEWELL, Allen; The Psychology of Human-Computer Interaction. Lawrence Erlbaum Associates, 1983.
3. JUL, S.; FURNAS, G. W.; (1997). Navigation in Electronic Worlds: a CHI'97 Workshop. SIGCHI Bulletin Vol. 29, No. 4, October 1997, ACM Press.
4. KARN S., Keith; PERRY, Thomas J.; KROLCZYK, Marc. J.; (1997) Testing for Power Usability: a CHI 97 Workshop. ACM SIGCHI Bulletin Vol . 29, No. 4, October 1997. www.acm.org/sigchi/bulletin/1997.4/karn.htm
5. LAKOFF, G.; JOHNSON, M.; (1980). Metaphors We Live By. Chicago: University of Chicago Press.
6. LYNCH, J.; HORTON, S.; (2000) Yale Centre for Advanced Media (WWW Style Manual). http://info.med.yale.edu/ caim/manual/ages/editorial_style.htm.
7. MICROSOFT, INC. (1998) The Windows Interface Guidelines for Software Design. http://www.microsoft.com/win32dev/uiguide/default.htm.
8. NIELSEN, J.; (2004) Alertbox. http://www.useit.com/alertbox.
9. REYNOLDS, C.; (1997) A Critical Examination of Separable User Interface Management Systems: Constructs for Individualisation. ACM SIGCHI. 29(3).
10. SCHWABE, D.; ROSSI, G.; (1995). Abstraction, Composition and Lay-Out Definition Mechanism in OOHDM. Proceedings of the ACM Workshop on Effective Abstractions in Multimedia. San Francisco, California.
11. SHULZ, E.; VAN ALPHEN M.; RASNAKE W. 1997. Discovering User-generated Metaphors through Usability Testing. Proceedings of the Second International Conference on Cognitive Technology. Aizu, Japan.
12. SULLIVAN, Joseph W.; TYLER, W. Sherman (Eds.) Intelligent User Interfaces. Frontier Series. ACM Press.
13. WAHLSTER, Wolfgang; (1991) User and Dialog Models for Multimodal Communication.

# Evaluating Accessibility of Public Information Kiosks

Seongil Lee[1] and Joo Eun Cho[2]

[1] Sungkyunkwan University, School of Systems Management Engineering,
440-746 Suwon, Korea
silee@yurim.skku.ac.kr

[2] ITthinknet, 159-1 Samsung-Dong, Seoul
june@itnit.org

**Abstract.** An accessibility assessment model was developed for calculating an accessibility index for public information kiosks. The model consists of eight terms to be considered in kiosk design and its operation. Taking into account the level of importance among the terms included in the model and the possibility of realization with current levels of technology for the terms, an index was organized to quantitatively assess the accessibility of public kiosks. It is expected that through this study, the current level of accessibility of public information kiosks can be objectively assessed and enhanced in the future.

## 1 Introduction

The privileges of information are not available to everyone, which is the core problem of digital divide, where some people lack access to information or cannot adequately utilize that information. More and more services in public places are now provided through information kiosks, and the classes marginalized from informatization are now discriminated in receiving these services, too. Public information kiosk is defined as a light, open-fronted booth or cubicle in which foods, newspapers, tickets, etc. are sold. But more recently, it also refers to 'an unmanned information search system or unmanned automatic information system that can provide information, and promote and sell products simultaneously through screens, audios and visuals such as printers, touch screens, computers with embedded sound cards or graphic cards'. Among the various types of information and communication products and services, public information kiosks should be considered foremost in light of accessibility due to its nature and importance in public services.

This study has developed a method to assess the accessibility of public information kiosks operated by central or regional governments and other public agencies in Korea to evaluate the level of accessibility. This study intends to develop a quantitative method to assess the accessibility of public information kiosks by producing an accessibility index from existing accessibility guidelines and surveys with experts. It is expected that through this study, the current level of accessibility of public information kiosks can be objectively assessed and enhanced in the future.

K. Miesenberger et al. (Eds.): ICCHP 2004, LNCS 3118, pp. 76–79, 2004.

## 2 Background

Accessibility is defined as 'physical access to equipment in sufficient quality, in appropriate places in convenient times '[1], or 'a general demand of users with different abilities, skills, needs, signs, environments and contents to access certain objects'.

Without compliance to any accessibility guidelines published for general use, public information and communications products and services would be problematic to the disabled and elderly users. To be inclusive, public information kiosks must be designed to cater for those with limited skills or experience, or with physical and cognitive impairments, and should be supportive towards those who are inhibited in interacting with them in a public area [4].

Kearsley[3] listed structure, location, materials, operation, maintenance, and integration as general kiosk design considerations. For handicapped access to public kiosks, three guidelines were suggested: providing as much redundancy as possible in system operation; allowing as much user control of the system as possible; and keeping all screen displays and control options very simple, minimizing any potential confusion or complications for translation to other modalities. Maguire[4] well documented the user-interface design guidelines for information kiosk systems for general public. The design guidelines cover all the aspects and issues of kiosk usage such as physical access, I/O methods, navigation, language, and even the privacy. The design guidelines, however, were intended for general users, thus not dealing the accessibility issues extensively for impaired users, even though the author pointed out the importance of considering and including elderly and disabled users in design process throughout the paper.

## 3 Building an Accessibility Assessment Model

The method in technically building a model for accessibility assessment in the current information and communication environment can be very diverse. Normally, the basic framework of a model to evaluate the accessibility of public information kiosks is divided into physical and functional aspects, and the functional aspect can again be divided into operational and cognitive aspects [2]. The physical aspect refers to the physical access such as the location, size, and arrangement of the controls and I/O devices. The accessibility of the operational aspect can be acquired through providing a function or instrument that substitutes the limits of operation or control due to handicaps in utilizing information and communication products and services. The accessibility of the cognitive aspect refers to the providing of instruments or functions that reduces mental burden so that the user of information and communication products and services can easily perceive and understand the commands, control methods and results.

This study has developed a model that assesses the accessibility by evaluating the level of importance for the term that decides the accessibility of public information kiosks, assigning a weight according to the level of importance and technology status (Table 1), and finally calculating an accessibility index as a whole.

**Table 1.** Content of assessment model concerning accessibility of public information kiosks. Each term is weighted for use in calculation of public kiosk accessibility index

| Term | Content | Weight |
|---|---|---|
| Provision of physical accessibility | To provide public information kiosk services that are easily accessible to the disabled and elderly in physical dimension such as location, height, and ports for assistive equipments | 0.106 |
| Supplementing hand and arm movements | Public information kiosk services should be able to be accessed without hand and arm movement requirements using alternative methods. | 0.184 |
| Supplementing reaction time | Public information kiosk services with functions of reacting or printing within a certain limit of time are recommended to provide supplementary methods | 0.053 |
| Supplementing and substituting sight | Public information kiosk services that require sight are recommended to provide supplementary devices or alternative options | 0.131 |
| Supplementing color differentiation | Public information kiosk services that require color differentiation are recommended to provide alternative options for grey-scale presentation | 0.114 |
| Supplementing hearing | Public information kiosk services that require hearing or communicate through sound are recommended to provide supplementary devices or alternative options | 0.151 |
| Substituting voice input | Public information kiosk services that require voice input are recommended to provide alternative input methods | 0.016 |
| Supplementing cognitive ability | To provide an independent method so that a user with cognitive limitations is not confused | 0.245 |
| Total | | 1.000 |

When assessing the accessibility of public information kiosks, two important concepts should be considered in using a model. The priority of the terms consisting of the model must be reflected by considering the level of importance. A prime example of this would be the Web Content Accessibility Guidelines of W3C, in which guidelines are prioritized in three levels according to their importance. It is also important to reflect in the model how realizable each term would be based on current technology status. For example, substituting voice input for the blind users may be a very important and desirable method. However, current technology level has limits in applying those methods in commercial information and communications products.

More specifically, producing the accessibility index was processed into two steps. In the first step, the level of importance of each term in the model was evaluated. For this process, a survey with accessibility experts was made for subjectively rating the importance of the terms in the model. The level of importance is graded in 3 levels and points are given according to the importance: P1 (5 points) for the terms with a great importance, P2 (3 points) for the terms with an average importance, and P3 (1 point) for the terms with lesser importance. In the second step, the possibility of realization with current technology levels for each term was graded with the same scale.

This was evaluated with a survey with technology experts, mostly professors in rehabilitation, engineering, and special education fields. The two points were combined to calculate an aggregated sum, which was later normalized to make a total of 1.

## 4 Conclusion

In order to develop an accessibility assessment method, this study has developed a model for calculating an accessibility index for public information kiosks, taking into account the level of importance among the terms included in the model and the possibility of realization with current levels of technology for the terms. Using the model, the accessibility index of public information kiosks in Korea, particularly for the kiosks located at public sites and institutes in metropolitan Seoul area, has been calculated, which was measured at 46.7 out of 100. Among the accessibility terms consisting of the model, 'supplementing cognitive ability' was rather satisfactory, but 'supplementing reaction time' was very poor.

There can be many influencing factors contributing to the public information kiosks' accessibility, but the most important factor mst be the provision of a 'kiosk design standard' established by the government. There are currently two such standards in Korea, 'Guidelines in Actualizing Unmanned Information Terminal (kiosk)'(1999), the standard for information and communications producer and service provider groups, and 'Standard for Unmanned Civil Petitions Issuing Machines(kiosk) for Information Processing in Administration'(2000), the standard for administration. These two standards include items that guarantee accessibility, and estimate to satisfy 46.4% of the terms included in the accessibility assessment model. For example, 'voice recognition' and 'voice synthesizing' are offered as options for the disabled in the system demands for users by both guidelines, and both guidelines clearly state that information messages in the screen be provided through sound in the 'keypad for the blind'. Enforcing manufacturers and providers to follow these guidelines in design and operation would make lots of public information kiosks more accessible.

## References

1. Benyon, D., Crerar, A., Wilkinson, S.: Individual Differences and Inclusive Design. In: Stephanidis, C., (ed.): User Interfaces for All. Lawrence Erlbaum Assoc. London (2001) 21–46
2. Fain, W. B., Folds, D.: Accessibility Evaluation Methodology. A technical report, Information Technology Technical Assistance and Training Center, GTRI (2001)
3. Kearsley, G.: Public Access Systems. Alex Publishing Corporation, Norwood New Jersey (1994)
4. Maguire, M.C.: A review of user-interface design guidelines for public information kiosk systems International Journal of Human-Computer Studies, Vol. 50. (1999) 263-286

# European Co-operation Activities Promoting Design for All in Information Society Technologies

## *Introduction to the Special Thematic Session*

Christian Bühler[1] and Constantine Stephanidis[2]

[1] FTB, Germany
Grundschöttelerstr.40 58300 Wetter, Germany
ch.buehler@ftb-volmarstein.de
[2] ICS-FORTH, Greece
Science and Technology Park of Crete, Heraklion, Crete, GR - 71110 Greece
cs@ics.forth.gr

**Abstract.** Design for All (DfA), sometimes addressed as Universal Design, Barrier Free Design, Inclusive Design is seen as an important complement to Assistive Technology. The basic idea is to produce products and services in a way that as many people as possible can use it directly or with the help of Assistive Technology. This concept is of particular importance in a quickly changing world, in order to keep pace with innovation. A concept to adapt all products and services for those who cannot operate it is costly, time consuming and may lead to discrimination. It is further a more economic strategy to design and produce for as many as possible. Information Society Technologies (IST) are an important and interesting field in Design for All that have the potential to ensure access to products and services for all citizens and can help overcome traditional barriers that a number of population groups in the use of technology in their everyday life.

## 1 Design for All – An Introduction

In recent years, the need to address accessibility as a problem pending a generic solution has created a substantial literature concerned with the meaning and scope of the term "accessibility" and the potential design philosophies, which could contribute towards a widely acceptable frame of reference. Specifically, terms such as accessible design, barrier-free design, universal design, DfA, inclusive design, have all come about to provide a means for understanding the various aspects of accessibility. Although consensus is still lacking, it is perhaps worthwhile pointing out the different DfA connotations frequently associated with these terms. Some individuals consider that these terms refer to a new, politically correct approach and effort to introduce "special features" for "special users" in the design of a product. To others, these terms point to a deeply meaningful and rich notion of design, which elevates what designers often call "good user-based design" to a more encompassing concept of addressing the needs of all potential users, including persons with special needs (e.g., disabled and elderly). Accordingly, DfA, or *universal design* or *inclusive design*, are all in-

K. Miesenberger et al. (Eds.): ICCHP 2004, LNCS 3118, pp. 80–87, 2004.

tended to reflect a new concept or philosophy for design that recognises, respects, values and attempts to accommodate the broadest possible range of human abilities, requirements and preferences in the design of all computer-based products and environments. Thus, it promotes a design perspective that eliminates the need for "special features" and fosters individualisation and end-user acceptability.

In the present document, we adopt a broad definition of the term. For this purpose, we provide a contextual definition in the context of the eEurope initiative. Specifically, one of the objectives of the eEurope action plan is the integration of older people and people with disabilities into the information society. It is claimed that this will only come about as a result of designing mainstream products and services to be accessible and usable by as broad a range of users as possible. This approach is termed "DfA" or inclusive design (the two terms are used interchangeably), and consists of three principal strategies:

- Design of IST products, services and applications, which are demonstrably suitable for most of the potential users without any modifications.
- Design of products which are easily adaptable to different users (e.g., by incorporating adaptable or customisable user interfaces).
- Design of products, which have standardized interfaces, capable of being accessed by specialised user interaction devices.

From the above, it follows that DfA, in the present context, is interpreted as either subsuming or as being a synonym of other terms such as accessible design, inclusive design, barrier-free design, universal design, etc., respecting the fact that each of them may be highlighting different aspects of the notion. Finally, it is important to point out that although DfA could cover a very wide range of products[1], the work described in the present project will focus mainly on information society products and services, as indeed does the referenced eEurope initiative.

Given the above broad connotation, the context of the proposed work is the eEurope 2005 action plan, and in particular some of the eEurope 2005 targets. The proposed work seeks to promote and facilitate the commitment of the eEurope plan towards an inclusive Information Society, by fostering the creation of tight links between academia, industry, non-market institutions, governmental agencies, etc., in the area of DfA, through networking. Such networking will bring together representatives of all member states. The ultimate objective is to facilitate knowledge transfer, information sharing and the exchange of experience in the designated area of DfA, in the context of the information society.

## 2 DfA in the Information Society – European Initiatives

The *e*Europe 2002 and *e*Europe 2005 action plans, recognise the compelling need for "an information society for all" and point out four lines of action, namely policy measures, dissemination of good practices, benchmarking indicators to monitor progress, and overall coordination activities, as primary means to achieve the designated targets.

---

[1] Examples of the application of *design for all* are reported by (Mueller, 1998) for interior and workplace design, and (Mace, 1998) for housing.

DfA in the context of the IST sector is increasingly motivated by the globalisation of the market, the ageing of the population and the progressively increasing number of people experiencing permanent or temporal loss of functional ability. Such loss, in turn, impacts independent living, mobility, education and access to information. In the past, the case of accessibility for disabled and elderly people was mainly addressed through a posteriori adaptations of interactive software. This represented a reactive approach, whereby Assistive Technology experts attempted to react to contemporary technological developments by building accessibility features into interactive applications, as a result of specific user requirements. The disadvantage of this approach stems directly from the shortcomings of adaptations. In particular, with rapid technological change, each new wave of technology introduces a new generation of access problems. By the time suitable adaptations have been devised, the technology is substituted by a subsequent generation, thus introducing the same problem all over again. In consequence, a posteriori adaptations provide solutions that lag behind, at least one technological trajectory.

From the above, it becomes evident that the reactive paradigm to accessible products and services does not suffice to cope with the rapid technological change and the evolving human requirements. Instead, proactive strategies are needed that will lead the fields involved towards a research and practice agenda based on the principle of shared social responsibility and on actual and emerging human requirements. The real challenge of the proactive approach is how to design systems that facilitate systematic and cost-effective approaches to accommodating the requirements of all users (Mueller et al., 1997; Ellis 2003). DfA, as considered in the present context, advocates such a proactive approach towards products and environments that can be accessible and usable by the broadest possible end-user population, without the need for additional adaptations or specialised (re-)design. Moreover, advancing such a perspective towards the design of IST products requires multidisciplinary consideration, which forms the basis of the approach followed by EDeAN and D4ALLnet (see below).

## 3 EDeAN

The European Design for All e-Accessibility Network (EDeAN) was established by the European Commission and the Member States in July 2002 as one of the specific goals of the eEurope 2002 Action Plan. The goal of this network is to raise the profile of Design for All (DfA) and emphasize its importance in achieving greater accessibility to the

EDeAN
European Design for All
e-Accessibility Network

**Fig. 1.** Logo of EDeAN

Information Society for as many people as possible. EDeAN was set-up to provide support to *e*Europe objectives, a European forum for Design for All issues, awareness raising in the public and private sectors, input for European curricula on Design for All as well as links to appropriate educational channels to incorporate Design for All in new curricula (Bühler 2002). EDeAN is supported by two EC funded projects: IDCnet and D4ALLNet.

### 3.1 EDeAN NCCs

National Contact Centers (NCCs) have been appointed in 15 European countries. They are working with Design for All, e-Accessibility and Assistive Technology issues as contact points of the EDeAN network:

- Austria: Universität Linz
- Belgium: Toegankelijkheidsbureau
- Denmark: Danish Center
- Finland: STAKES
- France: IRIT
- Germany: DfA-Deutschland
- Greece: ICS-FORTH
- Ireland: CRC
- Italy: CNR-IFAC
- Netherlands: IRV
- Norway: Telenor
- Portugal: SNRIPD
- Spain: CEAPAT
- Sweden: Handicap Institutet
- United Kingdom: HCID

(More information about EDeAN and contact details for the NCCs are available through the EDeAN website at www.e-accessibility.org.)

### 3.2 EDeAN National Networks

Each NCC is responsible for liasing with the EDeAN secretariat and members in its own country. These NCCs contribute to and share EDeAN information. There are already more than 120 organizations represented in EDeAN. New members are still welcome to join.

### 3.3 EDeAN Special Interest Groups

The exchange and interaction in the EDeAN network is largely organised by topics in special interest groups (SIGs). Five EDeAN SIGS have been up and running since mid 2003:

- Policy and legislation - moderated by Jan Ekberg (Finland)
- Standardisation - moderated by Jan Engelen (Belgium)
- Curricula on DfA - moderated by Yngve Sundblad (Sweden)
- Benchmarking - moderated by Christian Bühler (Germany)
- Proactive Assessment - moderated by Pier-Luigi Emiliani (Italy)

Most of the networking is performed virtually, through HERMES, the virtual working platform of EDeAN. HERMES is available at http://www.edean.org .

### 3.4 EDeAN Sectretariat

For the central network coordination the EDeAN secretariat has been established, and is managed on a yearly rotating basis, by selected NCCs. The initial term (7.2002-12.2003) was taken by the Danish Centre, followed by iRv in the Netherlands (2004) and ICS-FORTH in Greece (2005).

### 3.5 Support Projects

The **Inclusive Design Curriculum Network** is a Thematic Network funded by the Information Society Technologies programme of the European Commission (IST-2001-38786 – IDCnet). The project concentrates on curricula in Design for All for Information and Communication Products, Systems and Services. The objectives of IDCnet are to:

- produce recommendations on the content of DfA curricula
- integrate relevant information
- identify core knowledge sets and skills
- integrate support products for DfA in design and education
- influence education and research policies
- mainstreaming DfA in the education sector.

Another EDeAN-supported project is the **Design for All network of excellence**, also an IST-funded thematic network (IST-2001-38833-D4ALLnet). D4ALLnet actively supports the operation and the networking activities of EDeAN, as it provides HERMES, the virtual networking platform and communication tool for the network. In that way, the project provides the necessary infrastructure to enable systematic cooperation amongst EDeAN members. Based on the HERMES platform, D4ALLnet aims to promote and stimulate online discussions related to Design for All and eAccessibility. The D4ALLnet approach comprises an effective and complementary mix of expertise, skills and competencies, which guarantee the quality of the project's outcomes and the support of EDeAN.

### 3.6 EDeAN Contribution to the Information Society in Europe

EDeAN builds on the notion of policy measures (particularly legislation and standardization) at national and European levels to streamline member states actions towards the adoption of DfA practices. To this effect, there is an explicit focus on consensus creation (through networking) on a range of topics, including DfA benchmarking indicators, good DfA practices, DfA curricula, etc., so as to compile a validated "knowledge base on DfA". This "knowledge base on DfA" will form the baseline of a "DfA Resource Centre" in an effort to establish and promote a public resource on DfA and a reference point for industry, academia, government agencies and non-governmental organisations interested in the adoption and implementation of DfA.

A strong connection exists to the IST programme Key Action I – Systems and Services for the citizen, grants the supporting projects. The priority for KA I is to enable European users (citizens, businesses, public authorities) to take advantage of the recent advances in ubiquitous computing, ubiquitous communication and intelligent interfaces to improve access to, and delivery of, general interest services. This implies the creation of the next generation of interoperable, general interest application systems capable of meeting user demands for flexible access, for everybody, from anywhere, at any time (examples of such likely developments are included in the ISTAG scenarios on ambient intelligence[2]).

As market competition intensifies, those design codes will prevail, which are capable of accommodating diversity in users abilities, skills and preferences, but also the variety of contexts of use, in the increasing availability and diversification of information, and in the proliferation of technological platforms. DfA holds a special promise for Europe in this respect. Therefore, the EDeAN network aims to substantially contribute towards:

- increasing awareness about DfA
- promoting the diffusion and adoption of DfA approaches and practices making appropriate resources and benchmarking instruments available to the European IST community
- facilitating education and training in all issues related *to* DfA at a European level and
- stipulating policy recommendations on pre-standardisation, legislation and public procurement.

## 3.7 Stakeholder Benefits

Specifically, for industry, the expected benefit amounts to accessing, through the EDeAN web portal and the participation in SIGs, the network's on-going activities, as well as the accumulated and consolidated body of knowledge on DfA, which includes principles, examples of good practice, benchmarking tools (e.g., criteria and heuristics for assessing products and services), information on national and European policy, procurement guidelines, etc. Access to such information is expected to have multiple effects on industry, including appreciation of the benefits of DfA, improved innovation capability, new capacity to diversify, alternative market windows, wider customer bases and customer loyalty.

The academic community will benefit through the joint effort to promote DfA curriculum at the university level. It is considered important to organise such courses as joint activities between different National Contact Centres, whereby competent professionals from different institutions are invited to organise and deliver designated

[2] ftp://ftp.cordis.lu/pub/ist/docs/istagscenarios2010.pdf

parts of the course. This will foster, amongst other things, closer collaboration between National Contact Centres and a stronger sense of DfA community membership.

End users' (citizens') benefits include the articulation of a demand for DfA to industries, thereby facilitating improved quality, usability and satisfaction in the use of advanced IST-based products and services.

Finally, for non-market institutions such as regional governments, public procurement organizations, and for end user communities, the benefits amount to greater ability to influence the development of technology through assessing adherence and compliance of emerging solutions to a prescribed code of universal design.

## 4 Introduction to the STS

In the STS during ICCHP 2004 an overview of the cooperation of EDeAN will be presented. After an introduction of the STS, the content work of the special interest groups will be reported. Next the Hermes virtual networking platform will be introduced and the status of the development of curricula in DfA will be presented. The DfA resource centre as central information pool and its mechanisms will be reported. Finally, the new activity of EC on the DfA-Award 2004 will be introduced to the session. Participants are invited to contribute with own experiences during the discussions.

## References


1. Mace, R. 1998. *Universal Design in Housing*. Assistive Technology, vol. 10, pp. 21-28.
2. Mueller, J. 1998. Assistive Technology and Universal Design in the Workplace. Assistive Technology, vol. 10, pp. 37-43.
3. Ellis, G. 2003. *From Information Age to Inclusive Age ;The Economic Concept of Inclusion*. AT Research Series 11, pp.19-24, IOS Press (ISBN 1 5863 373 5).
4. Perlick, O. e.a. (2003) *A Context-Sensitive Word Prediction in a Public Terminal.* AT Research Series 11, pp.673-677, IOS Press (ISBN 1 5863 373 5).
5. Bühler, C. (2002) *eEurope – Accessibility – User Participation; Participation of People with Disabilities and Older People in the Information Society.* ICCHP 2002 Springer Verlag pp. 3-5.
6. Preiser, W.F.E.,Ostroff, E. (Eds) (2001) *Universal Design Handbook,* McGraw-Hill (ISBN 0-07-137605-4).
7. Stephanidis, C. (Ed.). (2001). *User Interfaces for All - Concepts, Methods, and Tools.* Mahwah, NJ: Lawrence Erlbaum Associates (ISBN 0-8058-2967-9, 760 pages).
8. Stephanidis C. (Ed.), Salvendy, G., Akoumianakis, D., Bevan, N., Brewer, J., Emiliani, P.L., Galetsas, A., Haataja, S., Iakovidis, I., Jacko, J., Jenkins, P., Karshmer, A., Korn, P., Marcus, A., Murphy, H., Stary, C., Vanderheiden, G., Weber, G., & Ziegler, J. (1998). Toward an Information Society for All: An International R&D Agenda. *International Journal of Human - Computer Interaction*, 10 (2), 107-134. [On-line]. Available: http://www.ics.forth.gr/hci/html/files/white_paper_1998.pdf
9. Stephanidis, C. (Ed.), Salvendy, G., Akoumianakis, D., Arnold, A., Bevan, N., Dardailler, D., Emiliani, P.L., Iakovidis, I., Jenkins, P., Karshmer, A., Korn, P., Marcus, A., Murphy, H., Oppermann, C., Stary, C., Tamura, H., Tscheligi, M., Ueda, H., Weber, G., & Ziegler, J. (1999). Toward an Information Society for All: HCI challenges and R&D recommendations. *International Journal of Human - Computer Interaction*, 11 (1), 1-28. [On-line]. Available: http://www.ics.forth.gr/hci/html/files/white_paper_1999.pdf

10. Stephanidis , C. (Ed.) (2001). International Journal Universal Access in the Information Society. 1(1). [On-line]. Available:
http://link.springer-ny.com/link/service/journals/10209/tocs/t1001001.htm
11. Bühler, C.; Knops, H. (Eds.) (1999). *Assistive Technology at the Threshold of the New Millennium.* AT Research Series Vol 6. IOS Press (ISBN 1 58603 001 9).
12. Stephanidis, C., & Emiliani, P.L. (1999). Connecting to the Information Society: a European Perspective. *Technology and Disability Journal*, 10 (1), 21-44. [On-line]. Available: http://www.ics.forth.gr/hci/html/files/TDJ_paper.PDF

# A Special Design Approach for Special People

Mary Zajicek

Department of Computing, School of Technology,
Oxford Brookes University, Wheatley Campus, Oxford OX33 1HX, UK
{Hofmann,Beyer,Kramer,mzajicek}@brookes.ac.uk
http://www.brookes.ac.uk/speech

**Abstract.** Those designing software for older adults and disabled people often have little knowledge of their interactional needs. Additionally the usual method of ensuring optimal interaction, User Centred Design, is particularly difficult to employ with these users. This paper proposes the use of interface design patterns, which enable researchers to present design knowledge gained through experimentation with our special users and pass on instances of successful design to inexperienced mainstream IT applications builders.

## 1 Introduction

With the introduction in the UK of the Special Educational Needs and Disability Act (SENDA, 2001) and many other initiatives, mainstream software designers are becoming increasingly aware of the need to design for our special user group of older and disabled people. This paper explore the special characteristics of this group which makes design for them more complex and difficult than for other users and sets out the reasons why standard User Centered Design methodologies become unsuitable.

It then explores the way in which research-based design knowledge is made available to inexperienced software developers commonly through the use of guidelines, which are then analysed for their effectiveness. The concept of interface design patterns as a means for passing on instances of good design is proposed, and an example set of patterns for speech systems for older adults is presented. Finally the argument is made that the patterns for a special user group represent good design for all.

## 2 Our Special User Group

Older and disabled people experience a wide range of impairments including loss of vision, hearing, memory, cognitive ability and mobility, the combined effects of which mean that they cannot use a computer interface in the same way as the standard computer user who is assumed to be able to see small icons and text, move the mouse quickly, handle complex multi-tasking applications and build robust conceptual models for systems they have never met before.

K. Miesenberger et al. (Eds.): ICCHP 2004, LNCS 3118, pp. 88–95, 2004.

The impairments found in our special group vary widely between people and also over time due to a variety of causes including illness, blood sugar levels and just plain tiredness. This presents a fundamental problem for the designers of interfaces to computing systems, whether they be generic systems for use by all, or specific systems to compensate for loss of function. User Centered Design outlined by Nielsen (Nielsen, 1993) and widely used for human computer interface design tends to rely upon homogeneous groups for requirements gathering and user testing in order to focus on design decisions. The ´typical user` of standard systems is assumed to have abilities which are broadly similar for everybody, and are perceived to remain static over time, and current software design typically produces an artifact which is static and which has no, or very limited, means of adapting to the changing needs of users as their abilities change. The interface development tools and methods we currently use are therefore not effective in meeting the needs of diverse user groups or addressing the dynamic nature of diversity. Newell and Gregor (Newell & Gregor, 2000) first proposed the need for a new form of design for dynamic diversity and the case for its use is provided in (Gregor et al, 2002).

Designing for our special group of users is complex. Standard interface design is based upon active user involvement for requirements capture and user testing to establish workable design. It has been found that for example focus groups used for requirements capture must be adapted for older people. Auditory impairment affects older people' attention and the ability to follow a discussion. Lines and Hone (Lines & Hone, 2002) report that smaller numbers in sessions were preferable, allowing everybody time to contribute and those who appeared nervous to be drawn into the discussion more easily by the moderators.

Gathering interface requirements from older and disabled people therefore requires considerable skill and understanding of the user group. Newell and Gregor also proposed (Gregor et al, 2000) that standard user centered design techniques, which rely on relatively homogeneous user groups for user testing, should be replaced by User Sensitive Inclusive Design, which seeks out diversity, in order to ensure that systems are truly usable by older and disabled people and demands a more sensitive approach to the user's role in system development. These comments highlight the challenges involved in defining systems requirements from, in this case, older people's experience and perspectives. It is therefore particularly important that instances of design that work well for older people should be carefully documented and passed on for other less experienced designers to use.

## 3 Passing Researched Design Knowledge to Designers

Interface design knowledge derived from experimental research with our special user group is traditionally passed on as design guidelines in the form of simple statements that provide the interface designer with rather a diluted version of the knowledge generated by the original experimental work. In the particular the 'Why' part of the information which may be based on theoretical knowledge, or may derive from observation during experimentation or the experimental results themselves, has been lost. For example the guideline 'Keep speech output messages for older adults as short as possible' derived from experimentation which found that older people were confused by long messages and actually remembered less than they did from short messages, and moreover this phenomena was not found with younger people (Zajicek & Morrissey, 2001). The guideline is concerned with memory loss and how it affects older people' information retention, useful information which can unfortunately, be lost when generalizing experimental knowledge to craft simple guidelines.

Simple guidelines therefore, do not adequately reflect the body of information they seek to encapsulate. Some researchers have sought to include more detail in their guidelines. For example the W3C, Web Access Initiative, Web Authoring Guidelines (Web Authoring Guidelines, 1999) developed for Web designers to help them create more accessible Web pages for non-standard users, are accompanied by the reasons for the guidelines, to make the Web designer more aware of who she or he is excluding by not following the guidelines. However this introduces a new level of complexity and can distance the designer even further from the original concepts from which the guidelines were generated. Interestingly, in order to reduce the complexity of their formal guidelines the Web Access Initiative have also created a set of ten Quick Tips to be used as a quick checklist for accessibility. Quick Tips are actually a set of simpler guidelines derived from the more detailed guidelines because they were complex for new designers to apply. The ambivalence demonstrated by the Web Access Initiative exemplifies the dilemma inherent in the use of guidelines. One contains detailed information but is difficult to access and the other is easy to access but doesn't contain enough information. Academic papers also exist describing the experiments from which the guideline was distilled, but these usually contain more information than the designer requires.

We can see from the detailed guideline versus Quick Tips approach adopted by the Web Access Initiative that neither form of encapsulated 'knowledge' is completely satisfactory. One contains detailed information but is difficult to access and the other is easy to access but doesn't contain enough information. If the guideline comes with the 'reason' attached together with an example of the use of the guideline, and is set out in a structured manner so that each component is recognizable and easy to access, the designer is a stronger position to utilize the information. Designers therefore, especially those designing systems for older and disabled people, would benefit from access to the information, experimental or otherwise relevant to good design practice that gave rise to the guideline, presented in an easily accessible way i.e. in pattern form.

## 4 Patterns for Interface Design for Our Special User Group

The concept of patterns and pattern language originated in the domain of architecture; with the publication of Christopher Alexander's book *The Timeless Way of Building* (Alexander, 1979). A pattern describes an element of design possibly together with how and why you would achieve it. Alexander for example created patterns that describe ways of placing windows in a room. There already exists a range of interface design pattern forms that can be found at Sally Fincher's *Pattern Form Gallery* (Fincher, 2003a), and to introduce uniformity of form a workshop entitled 'Perspectives on HCI Patterns: Concepts and tools' was held at CHI 2003, where participants formulated the generic Pattern Language Markup Language (PLML) (Fincher, 2003b).

Interface designers are rarely older or disabled people themselves and therefore have little concept of how it would feel to access a computer when you are experiencing the combined effects of memory, sight, and mobility loss coupled with reduced confidence that comes with slower processing of visual, spatial and verbal information. Furthermore, dynamic diversity of ability in our special user group poses particular challenges for interface designers who are not experienced in this field.

Therefore it is particularly important that those designing systems for use by our special user group are able to consult a robust set of design patterns that enable them to access best practice and help them to create sympathetic and successful designs. Importantly the patterns reflect the experience of our special user group through experimentation and observation, which the designers themselves lack. The use of patterns will also nurture good design and provide a framework for analysis and discussion within which poor design is less likely to occur. It is important to establish interface design patterns for systems for use by our special user group because their design needs are more complex as a result of their dynamic diversity and because it is more difficult to include our special user group in a user centered design process.

## 5 An Interface Design Pattern Set

By way of example, a set of patterns for speech systems designed for use by older adults is presented. They include special output messages that support memory loss and lack of confidence. They can be found at (Zajicek, 2003) and form part of the pattern set in PLML form at the CHI 2004 workshop 'Human-Computer-Human Interaction Patterns: on the human role in HCI Patterns' (Workshop, 2004). The patterns concern dialogue structure and the nature and occurrence of output messages. The pattern **Error Recovery Loop**, which is concerned with dialogue structure, is presented in its complete PLML form as follows:

**Pattern ID:** 7-ERL-SPST-OP-MPZ

**Pattern Name:** Error Recovery Loop

**Problem:** Errors and error recovery represent the primary usability problem for speech systems. Standard menu driven systems often start with a long set of instructions in a bid to avoid errors happening. Older users are not able to remember these messages, which also slow down the dialogue, rendering them useless. The pattern described here directs designers to embed instructions in an error recovery loop: in effect to wait for the error to happen and then try to recover it.

**Context:** This approach is most useful in dialogues which are used mostly by experienced users who are unlikely to require any instruction and will if they use the dialogue successfully never have to listen to an error recovery message. Use when errors in data input are likely to occur. This form of error recovery does not prepare the user in advance for possible errors, as they have to create the error before it is invoked. The trade-off is against providing long instructions before the user embarks on a task.

**Forces:** Different people have different tendencies to make errors. Providing different levels of error recovery ensures support for those who make many errors but does not delay those who make few errors.

**Solution:** Count how many times a data input occurs and on each count invoke an increasingly detailed error recovery message. In the examples below Example (1) simply gives instructions for efficient input, but the more detailed Example (2) provides information about which might help the user work better with the system.

**Synopsis:** Error Recovery Loop provides increasing levels of information as more errors occur.

**Evidence:** The Error Recovery Loop pattern was successfully applied in the Voice Access Booking System (Zajicek et al, 2003).

**Example:** (1) "Your name has not been recognized. Please speak slowly and clearly into the telephone.

(2) "The system is trying to match your name against the names it holds in the database. Please try to speak your name in the same way that you did when you registered for the Voice activated Booking System.

**Rationale:** Because older people cannot remember lengthy preliminary spoken instructions about data input. It is best to let them try to input data and if it goes wrong invoke an error recovery message.

**Confidence:** 50%

**Literature:** Zajicek M., Wales, R., Lee, A., 2003, Towards VoiceXML Dialogue Design for Older Adults, In Palanque P., Johnson P., O'Neill E (eds) *Design for Society*. Proceedings of HCI 2003

**Related Patterns:** This pattern is a member of the Pattern Group (3) – **'Reducing Input Errors patterns'** consisting of three patterns that offer different solutions to reduce the errors associated with speech data input.

**(3) Default Input Message Pattern** (3-DIM-SPO-OP-MPZ)
**(7) Error Recovery Loop Pattern** (7-CM-SPST-OP-MPZ)
**(8) Partitioned Input Message Pattern** (8-PIM-SPST-OP-MPZ)

Pattern **(4) Context Sensitive Help Message Pattern** (4-CSHM-SPO-OP-MPZ) can be used as part of pattern **(7) Error Recovery Loop Pattern** (7-CM-SPST-OP-MPZ)

**Author:** Mary Zajicek
**Creation Date:** 7th January 2004
**Revision Number:** 1
**Last Modified:** 7th January 2004

We see that each pattern has its own unique identifying code. It also includes a description of the problem that it seeks to solve, the context in which it would be used and the way in which it can be achieved with examples. Some headings perhaps are not so intuitive. 'Forces' refers to existing circumstances that force the need for the pattern. The confidence level is set at 50% because the pattern has as yet been used in only one system. This will increase as the pattern is used successfully in further systems. Other patterns in this pattern set are:

**Confirmatory Message** (1-CM-SPO-OP-MPZ) – suggests (with examples) providing confirmatory messages at certain points in the dialogue to boost users confidence.

**Menu Choice Message** (2-MCM-SPO-OP-MPZ) – suggests that menu choices should be limited and provides examples for setting them up.

**Default Input Message** (3-DIM-SPO-OP-MPZ) – suggests (with examples) ways of setting up default input when errors in speech input have occurred.

**Context Sensitive Help Message** (4-CSHM-SPO-OP-MPZ) – suggests (with examples) providing help messages at particular points in the dialogue to help those who are lost.

**Talk Through Message Pattern** (5-TTM-SPO-OP-MPZ) – suggests (with examples) output messages that talk the user through their interaction telling the user where they are in their interaction and what they can do next.

**Explanation Message Pattern** (6-EM-SPO-OP-MPZ) – suggests (with examples) that explanation messages can be useful at points in the dialogue which might not be easy to understand.

**Partitioned Input Pattern** (8-PIM-SPST-OP-MPZ) – suggests (with examples), as an alternative to speech input, how to arrive at an element of ordered input data by successively halving the search area.

Here we see that **Partitioned Input Pattern** together with **Error Recovery Loop** described above in PLML are the two dialogue structure patterns in the set, while the others are all speech output message type patterns. They can be found in their entire PLML form at (Workshop, 2004) and are intended for discussion and can be replaced, enhanced or discarded at any time as better solutions are found.

## 6 Good Design for the Special Group Is Good Design for All

Patterns have been used successfully by Christopher Alexander in architecture and by the software engineering community. However in these domains the proposed patterns were useful for everybody not simply a small section of society. At first glance it appears that the patterns listed in this paper are specially designed and useful only for older people, and would not help the more standard computer user, and even that the suggested designs could make speech interfaces complicated and slow for the standard user who requires less support. However everybody to a greater or lesser extent experiences, for example, problems remembering aspects of their computer interaction and can therefore benefit from memory supporting patterns.

Although there is insufficient space to set out the full pattern set in detail, it can be shown that all but one of the patterns represents good design for all users. Patterns **Menu Choice Message**, **Explanation Message** and **Confirmatory Message** represent standard good practice in interface design. **Partitioned Input**, **Default Input Message** and **Error Recovery Loop** sensitise designers to the difficulties users experience with poor speech recognition, and offer solutions. However, all users experience speech recognition problems at some time and would benefit from these patterns. **Default Input Message**, **Context Sensitive Help** and **Error Recovery Loop** are invoked only when difficulties arise, thus ensuring that people who do not experience recognition problems would be unaware that they exist. It could be argued that the pattern **Talk Through Message** could make interaction tiresome for people who don't require the support, if the system were frequently telling the user where they are in the dialogue and what they can do next. The solution here is to provide for the talk through option to be either on or off, or invoked as the user starts to display a non-optimum interaction.

These patterns therefore provide a strong argument for universal design, where designing for our special user group can help all users who might otherwise be expected to be flexible and adapt to poor speech interaction design. Dulude (Dulude, 2002) showed that performance on interactive voice response systems was worse for older people than younger users, simply because older people were responding more negatively to design problems that made their interaction difficult whereas younger people were more flexible and able to work around the problem. The inference here is that features that are specially designed to make interaction easier for our user group will be useful for everybody. Taking the argument one step further, we should therefore seek out and design for our special user group to promote the design of systems that are easier for everybody to use.

Just as we have shown that all users benefit from the designs encapsulated in the above patterns, and in most cases are not aware that extra support for age related disabilities was built into the speech dialogue, so the dynamic diversity found in our special user group is accommodated by these patterns. *The Error Recovery Loop* in particular accommodates diversity dynamically as error messages are linked to the number of mistakes that a user makes, which will be a function of their abilities.

## 7 Conclusions

The pattern set provides a powerful and acceptable means of presenting knowledge concerning the design requirements of, in this case, older people, where examples of good design and reasons for using it are presented in an accessible form. Alexander's work also encourages a design community to find their own patterns and use them selectively for individual problems. Their purpose is to educate, and to stimulate discussion between designers and ideally users as well. The CHI 2004 workshop 'Human-Computer-Human Interaction Patterns: on the human role in HCI Patterns' specifically addresses the issue of user involvement in interface design patterns (Workshop, 2004). Extending the concept of patterns to encompass user participation involves particular challenges when working with our special user group. Simply because communication proved challenging in the past, does not mean that it need always be. Lines and Hone (Lines & Hone, 2002) have made a start with recommendations on interview procedure, and Newell and Gregor (Newell & Gregor, 2000) have outlined a new design methodology, User Sensitive Inclusive Design with more emphasis on the characteristics of the user. The future challenge is to find a fluent means of communication that will enable our special user group to provide effective input to interface design.

## References


1. Alexander, C., 1979, The Timeless Way of Building, Oxford University Press.
2. Dulude L., 2002, Automated telephone answering systems and aging. Behaviour Information Technology 21(3), (2002) 171-184.
3. Fincher, S., 2003a, HCI Pattern-Form Gallery, http://www.cs.ukc.ac.uk/people/staff/saf/patterns/gallery.html, (last accessed 27.12.3).
4. Fincher, S., 2003b, CHI 2003 Workshop Report, *Interfaces* No. 56, Journal of the BCS HCI Group.
5. Gregor, P., Newell, A., Zajicek, M., 2002, Designing for Dynamic Diversity – interfaces for older people, Proceedings of 5th ACM/SIGAPH Conf. on Assistive Technologies.
6. Lines, L., Hone, K., 2002, Research Methods for Older Adults, Presented at the workshop 'A new research agenda for older adults' at HCI 2002.
7. Newell A.F. & Gregor P., 2000, User Sensitive Inclusive Design – in search of a new paradigm, Proc A.C.M. Conference on Universal Usability, Washington, DC Nov. 2000, pp. 39-44.
8. Nielsen, J., 1993, Usability Engineering, London Academic Press.
9. SENDA, 2001, Special Educational Needs and Disabilities Act, http://www.hmso.gov.uk/acts/acts2001/20010010.htm (last accessed 25.1.4)
10. Web Authoring Guidelines, 1999, http://www.w3.org/TR/WCAG10/, (last accessed 27.12.3).
11. Workshop, 2004, Human-Computer-Human Interaction Patterns, http://media.informatik.rwth-aachen.de/patterns//tiki/tiki-index.php?page=CHI2004Workshop (last accessed 15.1.4)
12. Zajicek, M., 2003, Patterns For Speech Dialogues For Older Adults, http://cms.brookes.ac.uk/computing/speech/index.php?id=61 (last accessed 25.1.4
13. Zajicek, M., Wales, R., Lee, A., 2003, Towards VoiceXML Dialogue Design for Older Adults, In Palanque P., Johnson P., O'Neill E (eds) *Design for Society.* Proceedings of HCI 2003.

# Accessibility from Scratch: How an Open Focus Contributes to Inclusive Design

David Crombie, Roger Lenoir, and Neil McKenzie

FNB Netherlands, accessible information for people with a print impairment
Molenpad 2, 1016 GM Amsterdam, The Netherlands
projects@fnb.nl
http://projects.fnb.nl/

**Abstract.** When attempting to solve the riddle of the planets, Pythagoras the mathematician applied his 'philosophy of numbers' to the available information on the dynamics of the solar system. Having also studied music as science, he called the unity he found the *Harmony of the Spheres,* believing that the divine could hear a hum created by the perfect harmonies in the oscillations caused by celestial bodies. This paper concerns the provision of music for people who are blind or otherwise print impaired. Our experience has shown that by considering *accessibility from scratch* we can establish some fundamental harmonies which can be achieved by taking a more 'openfocus' to inclusive design. No divine hum perhaps, but we can help people to whistle a good tune.

## 1 Introduction

### 1.1 Design for All

The Design For All approach [1] is now a very familiar one and most designers are aware of the basic tenets. Despite this, one has to look very hard indeed to find concrete examples of the successful implementation of this approach. If we are fundamentally to examine the different aspects of designing a more inclusive world, we must also consider the education of software designers and innovators to think about an inclusive world. This activity cannot be performed in isolation, as there is a parallel need to educate consumers to make their demands more explicit.

We must also provide software designers and innovators with a clear insight of the fundamental impact of the Design For All approach. This can be achieved through educating software designers who in turn will educate consumers. The products from these designers should raise public awareness of Design For All through demonstrably useful products. These products will have a built-in software interface that enables a dialogue between the developers and consumers and it is this dialogue that forms the basis for favourably influencing public opinion. In this way, the emerging results of this educational process would be a far wider and more 'openfocus' within design processes. It would then be more likely that inter-operable software (and hardware) will emerge and a more inclusive world can begin to take shape.

K. Miesenberger et al. (Eds.): ICCHP 2004, LNCS 3118, pp. 96–103, 2004.

### 1.2 Open Focus

Designing a more inclusive world requires a more *Open Focus*. This 'openfocus' can be achieved through an interplay of practical solutions conceived by greater co-operation between science and philosophy; technology and industry; and community and education. The traditional route to solving a problem requires that 'expert knowledge' is built onto the subject at hand before the problem is tackled. This layered knowledge is built upon until the expert points of view are focused almost exclusively on the solution. However, incorrect or inappropriate knowledge may lead to an intellectual dead-end. The solution to this dead-end is to take a step back, or in structural terms to move to a perspective with a higher level of abstraction. This can be described as an 'openfocus'.

In order to model user requirements central to the users' needs rather than relying on existing tools, a change of focus is required. This may often seem to be counter-intuitive, apparently undermining the focused concentration usually associated with such fundamental problems. This 'openfocus' requires thinking in a non-standard abstraction layer, and can actually be very easy if the mind is trained to overlook fundamental beliefs. The 'openfocus' approach refers to a generalisation of the problem by looking at the bigger picture, which may involve considering different perspectives. These perspectives are often far removed from the perceived core of the problem, such as user requirements or product aesthetics, but they can lead to generic and robust solutions. Under 'openfocus', abstraction leads to a better understanding of the situation by contributing information from multiple viewpoints. Mathematics has, after all, improved our understanding of music.

### 1.3 Accessibility, Technology and Science

We may find science fascinating. We may even find technology fascinating. Providing useful services to people in need is not quite as fascinating, but sustaining the provision of useful services and meaningful accessible content can be considered vital to the growth of the information society as a whole. Combining the above presents a considerable challenge. When designing, specifying and building applications and infrastructures to store accessible content, several apparently unrelated issues arise. How do we describe the knowledge and capabilities we possess and capture the repository of resources we can use to implement these capabilities? How do we describe the questions and problems of end users and content providers? How do we marry both within manageable and consistent frameworks? How do we re-apply this knowledge and combine these resources with new insights to solve new problems? How can we accelerate the process described above?

When providing accessible media for print impaired users, many of these issues must be examined in a more *extreme* context. Creating accessible media requires a whole range of processing stages and involves many different people and tasks. Given the need to provide reliable content transformations to end users, which can involve diverse materials ranging from mathematics and physics to musical scores, a great deal of additional effort is needed for researching production tools and representation techniques that keep these specific requirements in mind.

One part of the challenge described above is to provide end users with a sense of freedom. This means actively pursuing a strategy that merges accessible media with 'normal' media. While adhering to the principle that all original information is also provided in alternative format materials, key choices regarding the structure of these adaptive materials remain. As content producers, a great deal of effort is invested in production procedures and researching innovative applications that help our customers as well as, for example, the library community, computer community or the production community. This represents a wide range of overlapping (and highly specialist) requirements. If content providers in general, with no specialist knowledge of these issues, are to have greater integration in production processes, it is incumbent upon us to explain the ways in which sustainable accessible information provision can benefit them directly. This paper will illustrate some of these issues by examining a research project in the area of accessible music production. This project aimed to bring all these different requirements and procedures together within an open framework, one which would enable us to re-use the similarities in requirements of all of the individuals involved in the production and consumption of accessible music.

## 2 Establishing the Right Perspective

The traditional approach taken to the provision of music for the visually impaired has been largely concerned with Braille Music, building on a system first developed in the middle of the 19th century. Braille Music is presented as a Braille description of a single voice or a single bar of music. This Braille description is 'coded' using the standard Braille signs according to an internationally defined grammar [2]. However, reading Braille Music is a complex task and for those people who become impaired beyond the age of twenty, it is extremely difficult to learn Braille.

Talking Music is presented as a played fragment of music, a few bars long, with a spoken description of the example. The musical example is there to provide the user with a context for the spoken material, making it easier to understand and play. The format was automated and standardised in the Accessible Music Software project which uses the plug-in environment available in Finale® music notation software [3].

One of the most important requirements for musical presentation in Braille or Talking Music formats for impaired users is understanding the context of the musical material [4]. This means that important information regarding context deduction must be clearly perceivable: that is, the end user must be able to distinguish their location in the musical material and so be able to understand the functions of the musical material at hand. The end user must not be overloaded with redundant information, but at the same time be provided with enough musical material to be able to deduce its function.

Given these requirements, we considered whether or not there was a way to merge consumer and producer requirements using new technologies. Most of the requirements for the consumers of accessible music are the same as those for the producers of accessible music. If the effort involved in creating accessible production tools is combined with the effort for producing accessible consumption tools, a more harmonic relationship between the two is guaranteed.

When examining the similarities between consumer and producer requirements, the role of structure appears to be very important [5,6,7,8]. Visually impaired people have difficulties with the simultaneous perception of the attributes visualised in a graphical musical score, so the visually impaired musician cannot gain a perspective on the musical score in one glance. Playing music and reading music are two distinct but inter-related processes. We can mimic this integration of the senses by providing assistive mechanisms that help retrieve the consistency in the information being presented; what we would call *well-formed information,* a term borrowed from the HTML/XML internet technology lexicon. In both transcription methods (Braille Music and Talking Music), it is very important to preserve as much information from the original music score as possible, but not too much. The end user must be able to assimilate the separate musical attributes and thus be able to understand the music described in Braille or spoken using Talking Music. This also means that the end user must, in one way or another, be given the chance to control the quantity of information. The real challenge in providing these kinds of features to the end user as well as the producer lies in keeping the representation and presentation structures consistent on *all* processing levels.

## 3 Widening the Focus

At the development stage of the Accessible Music Software project, we considered very carefully what needed to be present in a system that aims to service various requirements, preferences and specialisations. This raised a number of philosophical issues rarely addressed in software and hardware design for inclusive computing.

New products tend to be used as a de facto reference for future research, but if these new products have been designed with a short-term view, they will only solve short-term problems and they will severely limit any ability to step over the boundary of application. Fragmented short term solutions for accessibility problems might provide only inflexible boundaries to the solutions we can come up with to address the needs of all users involved in the design process. We are all familiar with the oversized, one-off 'prototype accessibility application' which gathers dust in the corner of the research lab.

Requirements never stay the same over time: requirements change for all users of any service. The end user's sight or other senses might deteriorate over time, their needs being met with appropriate features in accessible media. The differentiation of user requirements in general might grow, forcing the system to deal with a broader variety of processing possibilities with which it cannot cope. The processing system *itself* might in due time signal changes in memory requirements. The consumer base might be expanded to cater not only for visually impaired users, but also for dyslexic users. How can we anticipate fundamental changes like this?

### 3.1 Building Harmonic Relationships

**Design Goals.** Through previous development experience, and with the objectives outlined above, several accessible production tools were created. These tools were built within the 'openfocus' paradigm and this created a robust and extensible framework upon which to build outcomes. This is evident in the ability of the software packages to personalise the needs of both consumers and producers, a key concept of 'Design for All'. This in turn provided several transparent requirements for implementation goals. The tools under development had to be based on very clear and very simple design decisions. The models that we require to be able to represent and model content are not aimed at achieving an 'ultimate' representation. Rather they are modularised and open to expansion. This modularisation takes into account notions from the Human-Computer Interaction domain [10]. This notion of expansion and the accessibility of this expansion is a fundamental design decision [8,9]. This fundamental design decision might also be called *accessibility from scratch* (see Figure 1 below).

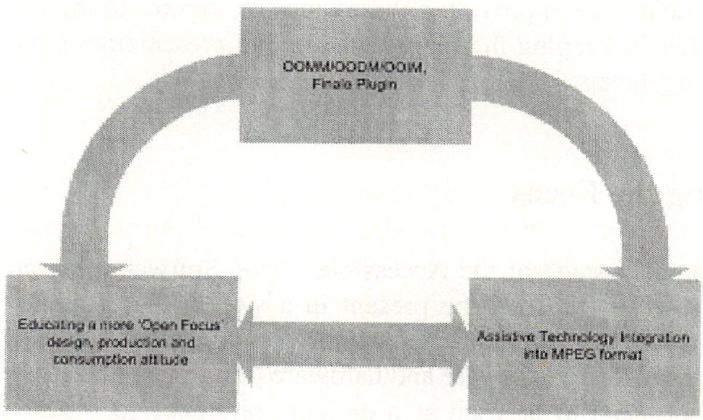


**Fig. 1.** Relations between design goals. The grey arrows indicate exchange and re-use of knowledge and experience in both design and application

All of the designs and modules are based on the Object Oriented Modelling paradigm and can be documented in existing modelling languages, such as UML. This provides a strong distribution base for the knowledge required to implement accessibility notions from scratch. This provides an advanced user-configurability, giving control over preferences to the end user without destructive consequences in system design. Because of the object oriented nature of the paradigm, there is a high level of configurability from the developers' perspective. Next to the production capabilities of this initiative, the shared modelling environment enables a level of communication between the consumer and producer of accessible music. The learning experience provides valuable information on how to enhance the understanding of the services we can provide to the print impaired users.

**Domains and Users.** Most of the music provided to print impaired consumers is based on Western Music Notation (WMN), a notation scheme for music based on bars, lines and notes. As most music nowadays is available in this form, it is therefore available for accessibility processing. There also exists a lot of music that is *not* available in WMN, but WMN can be used to transcribe this un-notated music. Prior to the transcription of a piece of music, we must consider this piece of music to be completely inaccessible for any print impaired user. A lot of new experimental music or existing ethnic music is completely missing from the repertoire that this category of users is able to learn from and enjoy.

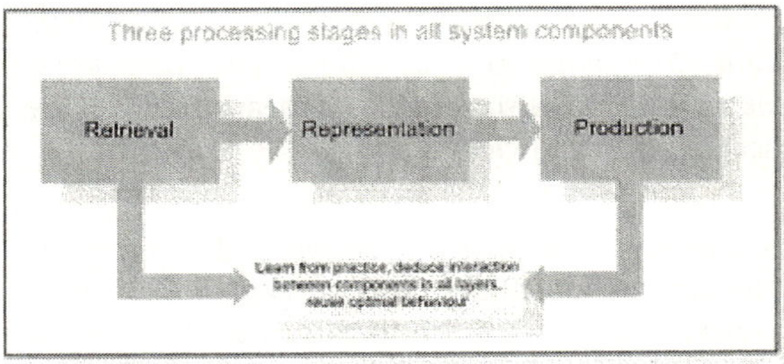


**Fig. 2.** Separation of system components in three layers. These layers are used to classify processes involved in producing and consuming accessible music

The use of Western Music Notation for music provision in the broadest sense is a very fundamental choice. WMN provides a wealth of primitive building blocks for constructing a detailed description of the music. However, it also lacks many fundamental building blocks that are of vital importance when trying to achieve *naturally* accessible music notation. Producing and consuming accessible music involves processes of a multimedia nature. The representation of processes is not explicitly available in WMN and explicitness is what we consider *the* fundamental aspect that is required to 'open up' digital information sources for the target audience. Every composer and transcriber has preferences based on professional choices or taste. Every user and consumer has preferences, also based on profession and taste; or on limitations in perceptual abilities, understanding or even mobility. Most people can adapt to the rigidity enforced by WMN: they just have to learn to read the notation. However, some people are not able to learn or are not willing to learn because of their physical or mental limitations or because of the limitations inherent in WMN itself.

As a result of all these preferences and all the translations and modifications these additional requirements will have on the music that is processed, it is important to represent this behaviour in a system that is going to model this process. A layered design is required that permits runtime modelling of relations between various kinds of actors, entities and requirements. This layered design must also incorporate a representation model of the content.

**Interpersonal Perspective Taking.** This raises more questions than it answers. What would *that* person think of *this* content which *another* person created and which *I* collected and which *I* think is vital to *this* endeavour? How can we understand the wishes of the person at the receiving end of the communication line? How do we learn what *is* important for the employees in department Y and how can we communicate the fact that we respect their requirements – be they personal or corporate? How do we gain a level of trust in our technological and scientific effort with our colleagues, employees, customers, clients and so forth? The ability to see one another's requirements without too much destructive filtering is called *interpersonal perspective taking* [11]. How do we *represent* interpersonal perspective taking in a manageable framework that not only incorporates diverse wishes, but also locates these wishes within an organisational structure? The framework used to implement the Accessible Music software also provides a means to collect requirements such as these alongside accessibility knowledge.

**Implementation.** Given the similarities between the producer and consumer requirements and the various modelling tasks at hand, we examined the possibility of merging these requirements using existing software. However, the various complex output formats meant that we needed a flexible model for the representation of music (and modelling of the transformations of this representation), as well as very basic navigational capabilities. A more detailed description of this work has been published elsewhere [12].

The Object Oriented Music Model used as a backbone for the transcription of Finale® formatted music into various output formats, should be as flexible as possible. The model should provide abstract means of describing various styles of music. Moreover, it should provide a means of structuring the musical information in more than one representation, preferably simultaneously. When coupled to a Document model that can handle the modifications of the output format, this provides a framework within which the key objectives can be met. In this way, the open abstract music representation model provides a level of abstraction and decoupling between the various components that enable specialisation of musical classes. This serves as a foundation for future work, making all parts of any score accessible.

## 4 Conclusion

This paper has examined aspects of inclusive design and has argued that by taking a more fundamental approach, we can help designers to incorporate *accessibility from scratch*. Designing a more inclusive world requires a more *Open Focus*. In order to model user requirements central to the users' needs rather than relying on existing tools, a change of focus is required. The 'openfocus' approach refers to a generalisation of the problem by looking at the bigger picture, which may involve considering different perspectives. Under 'openfocus', abstraction leads to a better understanding of the situation by contributing information from multiple viewpoints.

This paper has sought to illustrate these issues by examining a research project in the area of accessible music production. By combining current expertise in the domain of accessible multimedia music production, accessible text production and the fundamental approach outlined above, a production and consumption environment that integrates software, hardware and fundamental design notions was established. It was argued that the changing nature of requirements - and with that the potential design of *any* system - is a fundamental issue in the design of a more inclusive world.

## References


1. See `http://www.design-for-all.org` or `http://www.e-accessibility.org`
2. Krolick, B (1996), "New International Manual of Braille Music Notation", World Blind Union, FNB, Amsterdam
3. `http://www.finalemusic.com`
4. Crombie, D., Dijkstra, S., Lindsay, N & Schut, E (2002), "Spoken Music: enhancing access to music for the print disabled", Lecture Notes in Computer Science, Vol 2398. Springer-Verlag, Berlin Heidelberg New York
5. Crombie, D, Lenoir, R, & McKenzie, N, (2003) "Producing Accessible Multimedia Music" in Proceedings 2nd International Conference on Web Delivering of Music, IEEE
6. Ballard, D.H. and C.M. Brown (1982), "Computer Vision", Prentice Hall, Inc. Englewood Cliffs, New Jersey
7. Dodge, C., Jerse, T.A. (1985) "Computer Music – Synthesis, Composition and Performance", Schirmer Books
8. Cope, D (1991), "Computers and Musical Style", Oxford University Press, Oxford
9. Desain, P., Honing, H. (1992) "Music, Mind and Machine", Thesis Publishers Amsterdam
10. Winograd, T. (2001), "Interaction Spaces for 21st Century Computing", in John Carroll (ed.), Human-Computer Interaction in the New Millennium, Addison-Wesley, 2001.
11. Parks Daloz, L A, Keen, C H, Keen, J P, Parks, S D (1996) "Common Fire", Beacon Press, Boston
12. Crombie, D., Lenoir, R., & McKenzie, N., (2004) "Integrating music representations within MPEG environments" in Proceedings 4th International Conference on Web Delivering of Music, Barcelona, IEEE (forthcoming)

# Design for All: Experience-Based Strategies for User Involvement in IST Research Projects

Tony Verelst

ISdAC International Association, c/o IGL, Boddenveldweg 11,
B-3520 Zonhoven, Belgium
chairman@isdac.org

**Abstract.** Ever since 1998, ISdAC International Association has been actively promoting a Design for All approach with regard to IST applications, as well as supporting several initiatives in this regard. It is ISdAC's belief that Design for All starts with active user involvement in the earliest stage of the product development process. Therefore, part of our activities focused on gathering information on disabled people's experiences with existing products, as well as on creating an inventory of the difficulties encountered when becoming active online. We have been able to put together a group of disabled experts online, who can act as a user test bed for several research projects in this regard. Recently we have been involved in three IST research projects. This paper will present in detail the user requirements capture strategies and experiences, mainly in the scope of the IPCA project. Furthermore I will formulate some conclusions and recommendations in the field of an IST DfA approach based on our experiences.

## 1 Introduction

Over the years, the importance of a Design for All approach has been growing. Nowadays almost everyone acknowledges the need for and benefits of user centered design, incorporating the needs of specific target groups in the design process in order to obtain a better end product with a wider market audience. Several methodologies and guidelines have been developed in order to facilitate this (e.g. USERfit [1], INUSE[1]), and EU funding has been made available to explore further what needs to be done in order to incorporate the DfA concept in the product development process as well as education (DfA curricula[2]).

This field is also of interest to ISdAC[3]. Founded in 1998 as a European organisation of and for People with Disabilities (PwD), we have a two-fold mission:

- Challenging Europe and its nations to make the Information Society fully accessible to people with disabilities
- Challenging people with disabilities to express their possibilities and to demonstrate their abilities in the context of ICT

[1] http://www.ejeisa.com/nectar/inuse/6.2/contents.htm
[2] IDCNET Project (IST-2001-38786), http://www.idcnet.info
[3] http://www.isdac.org/

K. Miesenberger et al. (Eds.): ICCHP 2004, LNCS 3118, pp. 104–109, 2004.

The members of the ISdAC team form a strong virtual unity with a common vision. They extensively use Information and Communication Technologies to interact with each other, and are therefore very aware of the necessity of direct user involvement in the design process as early as possible.

Over the years, ISdAC has evolved more and more in the direction of a European user organization, rather than a political lobbying group, although both are equally important and we will remain active on both fronts. Our involvement as a user group within several EC funded projects, has given us the opportunity to build up expertise in the field of user modeling. I would like to present one of these experiences in detail, and discuss our user requirements capture and user feedback strategies, as well as highlight some of the results and formulate some recommendations that can be of use to anyone thinking about a DfA approach.

## 2 The IPCA Project

IPCA[4] aims to develop a new intelligent interaction mechanism that will enable people with severe motor and speech disabilities to control standard, and especially web-based, applications. The system will be based on a flexible combination of existing non-invasive sensors and encoders able to control different physiological parameters, and a set of software tools that will allow the user to interact with existing computer applications, in order to facilitate user interaction with different Internet applications and services.

Given the aims of the project and the developed product, the main target user group is people with severe physical and/or speech impairments.

### 2.1 User Requirements' Capture

Let us now take a look at the strategies used to recruit the test users and guide them throughout the tests. For gathering the user needs regarding the hardware components of the system (Multichannel Monitoring System, MMS), the actual test as well as the user recruitment has been coordinated by our project partner IBV[5], whereas the software components testing (Ambient Navigation Toolkit, ANT) has been coordinated by ISdAC. What follows is not a discussion of technical issues concerning IPCA, but an analysis of the process from the user's standpoint.

### 2.2 User Recruitment

With regards to finding test users, a slightly different approach has been taken by both IBV and ISdAC. For the recruitment of the test users of the MMS, IBV has cooperated with user associations in Valencia, as well as the Neurological Service of the "Hospital General Universitario", where some of the patients took part in the tests. The contacts with the users always took place through these intermediary organizations.

ISdAC has taken on a slightly different approach, using an 'online recruitment procedure'. This was done by building up an Internet presence through active involve-

[4] IPCA project (IST-2001-37370), http://www.ipca.info

[5] http://www.ibv.org/

ment is several online news- and interest groups on relevant topics (e.g. disability newsgroups). Simultaneously, relevant organizations that were present online were also contacted. Through these existing channels a standard message was spread, introducing IPCA and the forming of a user test bed, inviting interested individuals to join and apply as a test user online by means of a form that already gathered some basic information about the user and his specific disability. That way, a first selection could already be made based on this information.

This approach had the advantage that the targeted users were individuals (home users), and already had some internet expertise, which was relevant for the test scenario. In most cases Assistive Technology was used to allow them to access the World Wide Web. The next step was then a close follow-up, initially by e-mail and telephone, followed by a personal visit at the user's home or a neutral location if desired. That way we could already get a general idea about the user's specific situation, the current tools used for accessing the PC, and specific difficulties being encountered in doing so. Based on this information, the best possible candidates for the ANT test were selected.

Evidently, the latter approach involves some ethical issues regarding anonymity and privacy of the individual test users. This was overcome by signing an anonymity agreement stating that ISdAC would not pass this information on to third parties. Furthermore, privacy was ensured by only stating the user's age, sex and location in any external communication and reporting. All users taking part in the ISdAC test receive a lump sum payment by means of a cost statement to compensate for their time, effort and sharing of expertise.

### 2.3 The Actual Tests

The tests were aimed at obtaining user feedback on the needs and requirements in the early stage of the project, so that they can be taken into account during the next development phase of the product.

The test coordinated by IBV was on the possibilities and requirements regarding the sensors that will be used to allow the user to control the mouse. Two possible sensors were tested: an EMG sensor, measuring muscle activity by detecting and amplifying the tiny electrical impulses that are generated by muscle fibers when they contract, and a tilt sensor that registers horizontal as well as vertical inclination. In both cases, additional software was used in order to 'translate' the sensor signals into mouse movement on the screen. An interview procedure was used to obtain the user's comments and feedback about the systems being tested.

The ANT toolkit test was focusing on gaining insight in obstacles the layout and design of a Web site or standard application may cause when using a mouse emulation system. Usability issues due to information overload, misleading links and etc. were neglected during the test. This approach was chosen because in later stages of the project, mouse emulation will be controlled by biofeedback sensors which may be the only means of accessing a computer system for people with severe physical handicaps and speech impairments. The tests were coordinated by the Competence Center BIKA from the Fraunhofer Institute of Applied Information Technology (FIT[6]). The scientific results of the tests are presented in a separate paper.

[6] http://access.fit.fraunhofer.de/

# 3 Recommendations

Through the experience of ISdAC with setting up and maintaining a user test bed within the scope of IPCA as well as the IRIS[7] project, we have obtained a good view on the difficulties being faced when choosing a User Centered Design approach. Based on our experiences we can formulate some recommendations that might facilitate this process.

## 3.1 General Recommendations

The following recommendations are applicable for test scenario's of web pages and standard applications, regardless whether the tests will be guided by an instructor, who will be observing during the test (face to face interaction) or the complete test environment (including questionnaires) is fully available online, and the user needs to perform it individually at its own pace.

- In order to find the needed users, promote the potential product/service at relevant user forums and newsgroups, also indicating that you are looking for test users.
- Provide a short (online) template for registration in order to get some basic information about the user. This will allow you to check whether the user fits the 'tester profile', and choose the best possible candidates for the test based upon this information in case the number of participants is limited. This way you will also have some possible 'backup users' if needed later on during the test (for this kind of tests, drop rates are usually high). If necessary, visit the users in their home environment to get a good view on their current situation and the Assistive technology being used.
- Try to provide an 'interesting' test environment. This can be done e.g. by creating test scenarios within the specific context of the internet service that are as close as possible to the user's field of interest and his daily life sphere. Try to highlight the potential benefit of the application for the user during the test.
- Ensure the protection of the users' privacy by clearly stating that no personal information will be passed on to third parties. Make sure that in all reports, presentations etc. the users remain anonymous.
- User requirements regarding accessibility and usability issues are often very individual, based on one's preferences regarding presentation of the information and the type of Assistive Technology being used. Therefore, try observing the user while performing the test, taking notes on protocol sheets. Furthermore, try to separate the user feedback resulting from personal preferences, from the one that is related to the examined web page or application.
- Make sure that all the activities are logged. Going through the logfiles might bring up possible problem areas within the test environment (e.g. if the user seems to be browsing through the internet application without a pattern, it might indicate that a specific functionality is not 'as easily found as you thought').
- Arrange some kind of reimbursement to compensate for the users' time and effort and sharing of his expertise, as well as his willingness to take part.

---

[7] http://www.iris-design4all.org/

– After the tests, keep the user involved about the results and the further development of the project, so they keep an interest and are available for additional tests in the future.

### 3.2 Recommendations for Online Test Environments

In case of a full online test environment, where the user has to perform the activities by herself, with only email or phone support from the instructor in case of difficulties, the following things should be kept in mind:

– With regards to personal preferences and the Assistive Technology being used, try working as individual as possible, building up close and active communication with the users (e.g. by email), but leaving room for conversation outside the strict test-related working area. Very often, in the case of a 'distant test environment' normal social interaction brings up interesting facts about the user's specific requirements, that can not be captured within a test scenario, but are nevertheless important in order to realize the user's needs and preferences, and to be able to properly respond to them in the design phase.
– Create a single contact point the user can turn to in case of difficulties performing the test. If the user 'gets stuck' at a specific point within the test scenario (e.g. problem finding a specific functionality or button within an internet service), try to give him some 'pointers' to help him in the right direction, rather than just providing him with the solution. If this has no effect, clearly state in the result processing at which point you provided the solution, so that you know at least the 'problem areas' within your internet service. Otherwise this will affect the credibility of the obtained information.
– In the case of questionnaires, avoid too much textual input, e.g. by using multiple choice questions whenever possible. However, leave enough room for the user's personal comments and feedback.
– If possible, provide the test environment and questionnaires in the mother tongue of the user.
– Closely follow up on the test user's progress so that you can identify possible problem cases (e.g. dropouts) as early as possible, and replace them if necessary.

## 4 Conclusions

As you can see, most of these recommendations require a close follow-up and prompt response, as well as some background about the disabled user's specific requirements, preferences, living situation, etc. This expertise might not always be available at hand within the organization that designs the product. Also, communication between e.g. a designer or researcher and the end user might be complicated because of the 'different angle' when looking at the product.

In order to allow a maximum user support and minimize the efforts recruiting the disabled test users with the right 'disability profile' to test the specific internet service, one can think about involving an intermediary organization with close contacts to the targeted test user group (e.g. user organization, organization with background on specific problems/user requirements) to take care of these issues. In many cases they have the right test users easily available, or at least know where to find them. This way the intermediate organisation can take care of following up on the tests and the processing of the results, while the designer can focus on designing and implementing enhancements to the product, based on the user's feedback.

In this regard, ISdAC has already proven its added value and expertise within the framework of the IPCA and IRIS project, and is this way building up expertise in the area of user modeling. The fact that ISdAC is actively involved in several online discussion groups on different subjects and has established contact with several user organizations and individuals as part of its outreach actions, makes our organization a valuable partner for any manufacturer wanting to test the usability and accessibility of his internet service, web page or standard application. Furthermore, we are currently working on setting up a user database online, where disabled people that are potentially interested to take part as a test participant, can register without any further obligation. This way it will be easier to select and approach suitable candidates according to specific user profiles required for future test environments.

This approach is a win-win situation for both parties: the designer is sure to get the 'right users' without too much effort, and the intermediate organization (and thus the disabled user himself) gets involved in the design process and can build up a 'reputation' in this regard towards the disabled community. When both parties bring their specific expertise together, the result will be an IST environment with a maximum usability for all, this way making the potential market share as big as possible from the part of the designer, and ensuring that the product/service will be usable and accessible based on 'expert feedback', which already in itself might be an argument for the users to purchase it.

ISdAC commits itself to assist anyone interested in Design for All, by the necessary experts in order to achieve this goal. It is part of our mission to ensure a maximum integration of People with Disabilities in the Information Society, and we are convinced that a user centered design approach is one of the major drivers that can positively influence and speed up this process.

## Acknowledgements

Parts of this work have been undertaken in the framework of the project IPCA – IST–2001–37370, partly funded by the IST Programme of the European Commission. The author would like to acknowledge the contributions of their colleagues from the Fraunhofer Institute for Applied Information Technology (FIT), Mind Media BV, the Institute of Biomechanics of Valencia (IBV) and ISdAC International Association.

## References

1. Poulson, D. (Ed): (1996) USERfit. A practical handbook on user-centred design for Assistive Technology. European Commission, DGXIII TIDE Project 1062

# IDCnet: Inclusive Design Curriculum Network – First Results

Carlos A. Velasco[1], Jan Engelen[2], Christophe Strobbe[2], Jenny Darzentas[3], Päivi Tahkokallio[4], Colette Nicolle[5], and Rafael Romero[6]

[1] Fraunhofer-Institut für Angewandte Informationstechnik (FIT), Schloss Birlinghoven, D53757 Sankt Augustin, Germany
Carlos.Velasco@fit.fraunhofer.de
[2] Katholieke Universiteit Leuven, Kasteelpark Arenberg 10, B3001 Heverlee-Leuven, Belgium
{jan.engelen,christophe.strobbe}@esat.kuleuven.ac.be
[3] University of the Aegean, Voulgaraktonou 30, GR11472 Exarchia, Athens, Greece
jennyd@aegean.gr
[4] STAKES, P.O. Box 220, FIN-00531 Helsinki, Finland
Paivi.Tahkokallio@stakes.fi
[5] Loughborough University, Holywell Building, Holywell Way, LE11 3UZ Loughborough, United Kingdom
C.A.Nicolle@lboro.ac.uk
[6] Universitat de Valencia, C/ Blasco Ibáñez 21, E46010 Valencia, Spain
Rafael.Romero@uv.es

**Abstract.** This paper presents the preliminary results of the IDCnet Thematic Network in regard to the development of curriculum recommendations for Higher Education institutions in the area of ICT that include Design for All. These recommendations are based upon discussion with relevant actors in industry and academia to identify core knowledge sets and skills.

## 1 Introduction

IDCnet[1] is a Thematic Network funded under the IST Thematic Priority of the 5th Framework Programme from the European Commission. The activities of IDCnet are aimed at supporting the objectives of eEurope[2] and the European Design for All e-Accessibility Network (EDeAN[3]) in regard to the development of curriculum recommendations in the area of Design for All (DfA) in ICT.

The strategic goal of IDCnet is to integrate information and identify core knowledge sets and skills for model curricula in Design for All for Information and Communication Products, Systems and Services. We situate our activities in the multidisciplinary area of design, especially design for, and supported by, information and communication technologies.

---

[1] Inclusive Design Curriculum Network, IST–2001–38786, http://www.idcnet.info/

[2] http //europa.eu.int/information_society/eeurope/

[3] http://www.e-accessibility.org/

K. Miesenberger et al. (Eds.): ICCHP 2004, LNCS 3118, pp. 110–116, 2004.

The objectives of IDCnet are to:

- Integrate relevant information to understand the ICT design education culture and the industry needs in Europe.
- Identify knowledge sets and skills that should be part of a curriculum for DfA in ICT.
- Integrate R&D products that contribute to DfA in design and learning processes.
- Influence education and research policies.
- The mainstreaming DfA in the education sector.

The activities of the project are focused on gathering relevant information and exchanging experiences with relevant actors. To that end, the Consortium members have organized two workshops (Helsinki, Feb 2003; and Sankt Augustin, January 2004), and participated in several conferences.

This paper will present briefly some of the major outcomes of the project, and will outline some of the future recommendations.

## 2 The Needs of Industry and the Optimal Graduate Profile

It is a known fact that a high percentage of European universities' curricula do not reflect the needs of industry. Therefore, we tried to focus our work in a context that could identify first those needs, and then introduce recommendations dealing with Universal Access [5].

There are several technological landscapes in the area of ICT that can be affected by the incorporation of DfA:

- Accessibility guidelines and APIs;
- Device independence;
- User and device profiling;
- Semantic Web and metadata; and
- Multi-modality.

A number of big industry players are already working on DfA or accessibility, but they face a number of barriers. Software engineers are not taught about accessibility at the university, so they need to be retrained. For Web developers, the situation is even worse, because they have often no formal training.

The drive for DfA is usually top-down, not driven by the knowledge or training of the developer. Accessible products are developed by companies where senior management understands the value of accessibility. Similarly, large accessibility initiatives in the Open Source community are usually supported by big industry players (IBM, Sun) instead of grassroots initiatives.

Many companies have misconceptions about DfA, and think that it is only design for the elderly and disabled, or that it means 'one size fits all'. Many also consider anything that costs more than the able-bodied version as an 'undue burden'. Existing guidelines, for example the Web Content Accessibility Guidelines, are sometimes seen as too complex and too detailed. There have been surveys on what would be good incentives to incorporate accessibility: profits or increase in Web site traffic always come out on top, while legislation and policy are the least popular incentives.

Industry also wants closer ties with organisations that perform research on DfA, easier access to research results and exemplars of good design as sources of inspiration. They also would like more support from the outside. Companies who start out in this area want to know how to implement DfA in their organisation.

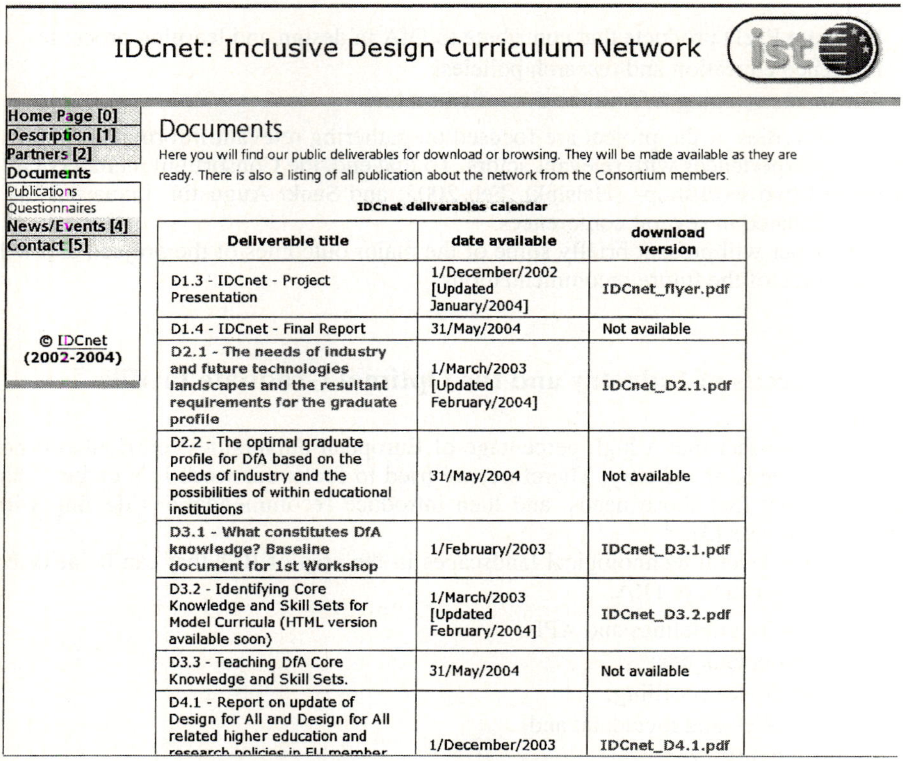


**Fig. 1.** IDCnet Web site (http://www.idcnet.info/).

There are few sources on the ideal graduate profile for designers and engineers with regard to DfA, so it was necessary to extrapolate from recommendations from related fields (HCI and ergonomics). Some examples gathered from the HCI area state that:

- There is a greater need for HCI experts than for methods and tools.
- The industry prefers pragmatic knowledge and hands-on advice on guidelines to perfectionism.
- People should be trained to become sensitive to good and bad design.
- Learning on the job and using your skills and expertise in projects is one of the best ways of learning.
- Inviting guest lecturers from companies can increase credibility.
- There is a need for HCI education for people who end up in supervisory or decision making positions.
- There might be a greater need for soft skills than knowledge.

The Consortium is actively pursuing the definition of the optimal graduate profile, which will be made publicly available at the end of May (before the camera-ready paper was sent to the publisher; further information will be available in the project's Web site).

## 3 Identifying Core Knowledge and Skill Sets for Model Curricula

In order to work towards curricula recommendations, it is also necessary to understand what constitutes the knowledge and skill sets that form the body of knowledge about DfA. Defining and understanding this body of knowledge or 'discipline area' forms a basic task of most curriculum studies [1]. It may be argued that DfA is more of a philosophy than a discipline in its own right. This argument is taken up and refuted in [2], and a taxonomy of knowledge and skill sets that can be said to be distinct to DfA has been proposed.

This taxonomy has undergone some refinement, both as a result of peer review and of the actual teaching process, but remains fundamentally the same as it was first proposed [3,4]:

- **Design for All Awareness**
  This knowledge category serves most often as an introduction to DfA. By various means students are encouraged to think of users in a wider category than just mirror images of themselves, to understand how barriers are unintentionally put up when user needs are not sufficiently understood, and to understand that DfA does not mean design for disabled, but for diversity of users and contexts.
- **Why Design for All? Ethical, Legal and Commercial Considerations**
  As part of ethical considerations, students learn about the history of DfA, the move from segregation to integration, from specialized solutions to inclusive solutions and equal opportunities for all.
  As part of legal considerations, students learn about various pieces of legislation, how they have come about, their impact, and what is set to happen in the future.
  As part of commercial considerations, students are introduced to the commercial benefit of DfA, and various supporting arguments, such as demographics, the problem of retro-fitting design, etc. Other requirements, such as the importance of making sure that products appeal to all and do not carry stigma are re-iterated since the 'specialised solution' design that is non-aesthetic is often rejected, even though it may fulfill its functional requirements.
- **Recommendations**
  This knowledge category is a 'catch all' for work such as Principles, Guidelines, Standards, Recommendations, and Specifications that have a bearing on DfA. Students are made aware that such bodies of knowledge exist. They should be encouraged to search for such work and consult the relevant ones as a first step. At the same time, it is acknowledged and explained (and illustrated) that these are not always easy to find, and rarely in a format that is easy for them to use and implement in specific contexts. The 'jargon' of each type of recommendation is also a consideration.

– **Interpersonal Skills for Teamwork**
  This category is slightly different from the preceding ones because it centers on skills rather than on knowledge. However, it can be stressed to students that behavioral skills such as team work, communication skills, information representation, information retrieval, etc. are very important to design work practice in general and to Design for All in particular. This is because DfA is not widely understood or accepted as yet. Designers with DfA knowledge may find themselves the only person in the team. They will have to work to convince their co-workers, at many different areas within the organization of its importance.
  For this area, the actual teaching strategies are the most useful way to give students the opportunity to learn these skills, by organizing team work, presentations and critical evaluations (critiques). In particular students who are to work as agents of change for DfA, should be able to demonstrate their skills to convince with sound argument and efficient persuasion.
– **Accessible Content: Knowledge about Documents and Multimedia**
  In this category the emphasis is on making sure that 'content' (mostly information and interactive Web pages) is accessible and usable. Students develop the ability to understand when content is problematic and why. They learn about current methods and techniques to produce accessible content, or to convert content. Depending upon type of student/course, they may develop the ability to produce accessible content/convert content.
– **Accessible Interaction: Input and Output**
  This category deals with hardware and software enablers of interaction, but abstracted from human users. It includes:
  • Knowledge about assistive and adaptive devices that enable alternative input and output, e.g. speech synthesizers, screen reader software, screen magnifiers, alternative keyboards, etc., as well as different types of browsers and operating systems that allow different manipulation of the content, etc.
  • Knowledge about different types of modalities: speech, haptics, gesture, sketch, force feedback, scanning, bio-sensors, etc.
  • Knowledge about different bandwidths, device capabilities, etc.
– **New Paradigms of Interaction**
  The justification for the creation of this category was to be a place for the work that is mostly in research state currently, but within the next five years –the typical time span of an undergraduate+master's university education– could breakthrough into mainstream development. Topics that can be distinguished are affective and social computing, a range of smart computing applications, smart homes, clothes, cars, ambient intelligence, etc.
– **User-Centered Design**
  Into this category go all the human, user, usability/accessibility philosophies, methodologies, techniques that apply to requirements and evaluation phases of design, etc. Many of these are routinely taught as part of HCI courses, but as they are currently used they do not always include diversity in users and situations.

The objective of drawing up this taxonomy is to have a framework in which to place the disparate information about DfA and to give it a classification. In this way, it forms both a way of dealing with present-day knowledge as well as having somewhere to 'pigeon-hole' new results and work, be they to do with standards, or applications, or whatever. It helps map out the area both for prospective students, as well as for prospective teachers. This is not to say, or course, that every category will be used to the same degree, this will depend very much on the background of the instructors, the students, and the type of course they are doing. Thus it is up to each instructor to decide upon what breadth and depth is appropriate for his students. It should be noted that the categories of the taxonomy group the knowledge and organize it, but do not discuss in any detailed fashion how to teach the knowledge. This will be in part documented in the work on the IDCnet teaching pilots.

### 3.1 IDCnet Pilots

Some Consortium members have started or will start several pilots to demonstrate our results and to implement in actual curricula, the taxonomy categories identified in the previous section. These pilots have proven to be very useful, and have helped us to:

- Refine the knowledge and skill sets classification;
- Provide auxiliary materials, like questionnaires for lecturers and students, which can help us to measure the impact of including DfA in the courses.
- Exchange peer information with researchers as well as teachers that can be of mutual benefit. For instance, applications such as e-learning have made great progress in research for design for all. These results can both be used as exemplars for students, as well as indicating research themes that warrant pursuing.

This work will be reported on in deliverable 3.3 in May 2004, and will be available in the IDCnet website.

## 4 Recommendations for Higher Education and Research Policies

One of the goals of the IDCnet project is to influence Design for All related education and research policies and strategies in Europe. To reach this, a survey of the state-of-the-art of education and research policies and strategies in EU countries has been made. Policies and strategies have been analyzed at the EU level, at the national level and at the level of individual universities to provide an understanding of to what extent DfA approach is at present included. The European situation is also reflected against the situation in USA.

The desk research of policy and strategy documents is supported and complemented by identification of a group of experts in all levels mentioned, to come up with recommendations of how education and research policies and strategies could be encouraged to support Design for All curriculum development.

The work completed shows that differences in education and research systems and support structures in EU countries will also affect how recommendations on DfA related education and research policies could be implemented. A challenge therefore is recognized that recommendations produced as the final outcome of the IDCnet project in May 2004, should be realistic and applicable in a variety of education and research policy and strategy contexts.

## 5 Conclusions and Future Work

It is clear to us that at the macro level, the impact of our recommendations still depends greatly on national and international policies, and to a greater extent, in the pressure received by the higher education institutions from industry to satisfy its demands for future designers and engineers.

However, at the micro level, progress has been made in both documenting and classifying a body of knowledge for DfA that educators and researchers may draw upon and use as a basis for their work. It is our belief that this will be of help both in the fleshing out of the recommendations, as well as giving practical assistance to those involved at grass roots level in getting acceptance for the incorporation of the subject matter within curricula. When there is a sizeable body of recognizable DfA knowledge fuelled by lively research in the area, it will be easier for industry and policy makers to understand the importance of including DfA in their agenda.

## Acknowledgements

This work has been undertaken in the framework of the project IDCnet – IST–2001–38786, funded by the IST Programme of the European Commission. The authors would like to acknowledge the contributions of their colleagues from the Fraunhofer Institute for Applied Information Technology, Department of Product and Systems Design Engineering of the University of the Aegean, DocArch, Katholieke Universiteit Leuven Research & Development, Ergonomics and Safety Research Institute, Loughborough University, the Universitat de València Estudi General (Research Unit ACCESO), STAKES (National Research and Development Centre for Welfare and Health), ISdAC International Association, The Royal National Institute of the Blind, Central Remedial Clinic, University of Linz "integriert studieren - integrated study" (i3s3), Hypermedia - L'École de Design Nantes Atlantique, Multimedia Campus Kiel and the School of Informatics of City University London.

## References

1. ACM curricula work can be seen at: http://www.acm.org/education/curricula.html
2. Darzentas, J S, Darzentas, J (2003). Design for All Key Knowledge and Skill Sets for Information and Communication Products, Services and Systems. In: Stephanidis, C (ed), Universal Access in HCI, Inclusive Design in the Information Society (Volume 4, Proceedings of the 2nd International Conference on Universal Access in Human – Computer Interaction, 22–27 June, Crete, Greece), pp. 53–57. New Jersey: Lawrence Erlbaum Associates.
3. Darzentas, J S (ed) (2003). What constitutes DfA Knowledge? Identification of a range of work that contributes to DfA. IDCnet, IST-2001-38786, deliverable D3.1. Available at: http //www.idcnet.info/documents
4. Darzentas, J S (ed) (2003). Identifying Core Knowledge and Skill Sets for Model Curricula. IDCnet, IST-2001-38786, deliverable D3.2. Available at: http://www.idcnet.info/documents
5. Strobbe, C (ed) (2004). The Needs of Industry and Future Technologies Landscapes and the Resultant Requirements for the Graduate Profile. IDCnet, IST-2001-38786, deliverable D2.1. Available at: http://www.idcnet.info/documents

# Personalization of Interactive Systems

## *Introduction to the Special Thematic Session*

Helen Petrie[1] and Gerhard Weber[2]

[1] City University, Centre for Human Computer Interaction Design
City University, Northampton Square, London EC1V 0HB, Great Britain
h.l.petrie@city.ac.uk
[2] University of Kiel – Multimedia Campus Kiel
Theodor Heuss Ring 140, 24143 Kiel, Germany
g.weber@mmc-kiel.com

**Abstract.** User interfaces and specially those based on internet technologies must met high expectations for usability. The evaluation of usability features competes with approaches to algorithmically measure accessibility. In this session on personalisation of interactive systems we demonstrate how customisation of interactive systems supports accessibility but is still dependent on the usability of assistive devices. Limitations of customisations exist for transforming browsing techniques and for time-dependent media.

## 1 Introduction

The quality of interactive systems is determined by their usability. User centered design process principles (ISO13407 - Human centered design process for interactive systems) improve the usability. Still, it is unclear which properties of usable interactive systems can be determined by algorithms and which properties require empiric approaches.

Support tools can automatically apply Algorithms if machine readable languages such as XHTML or XFORMS [2] specify the user interface. Both of these languages have been created for web-based user interfaces and can be processed with industry standard parsers on a variety of different computers. Validation of user interfaces according to the language definition is a standard technique. By interpretation of user interface specifications using appropriate algorithms it is possible to generate feedback to designers which supports them in creating more usable interaction techniques.

ISO 9241 (Ergonomic requirements for Office work with visual display terminals) describes in part 11 the general process of how to determine usability of a interactive system with a visual display unit. In part 10 of ISO 9241 criteria for design features of usable interactive systems are listed.

Some features directly support the accessibility of an interactive system. The Venn diagram in Fig. 1 explains that accessibility features are seen as a subset of usability features.

In this context we refer to accessibility as it is done by ISO 16071 (Ergonomics of human system interaction – Guidance on accessibility for human-computer inter-

K. Miesenberger et al. (Eds.): ICCHP 2004, LNCS 3118, pp. 117–120, 2004.

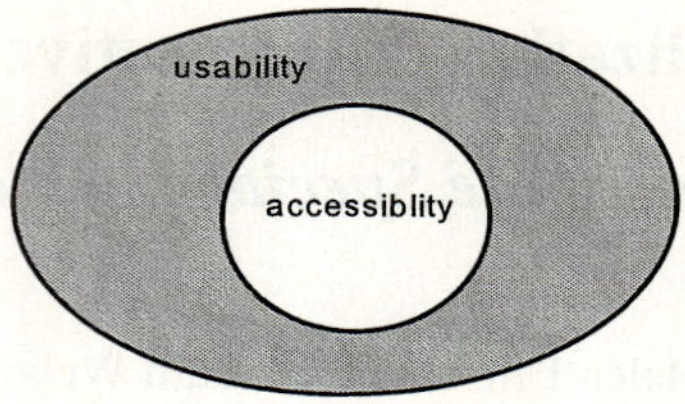


**Fig. 1.** Usability vs. accessibility

faces). Accessibility includes (a) task-appropriateness, which requires for formal processing further analysis and specification work, (b) individualized user instruction and training, and (c) methods for customisation of the user interface. In this session on personalisation of interactive systems we are interested especially in the ability for customisation of user interfaces aiming at diverse user requirements ranging from visual impairment, restrictions in controlling limbs and mental impairments.

## 2 Supporting Customisation

Customisation as a designed feature of a user interface appears in many different ways and requires a considerable amount of implementation work. Moreover it is difficult to evaluate [3]. A key usability feature according to ISO 9241 is self-explanatoriness, as it requires to make information explicit which in turn implies multiple, redundant descriptions of the same contents using possibly different media. If the contents is described explicitly the user interface can be made accessible to users with special reading needs such as blind and visually impaired people. Based on the encoding of data explaining the screen contents a transformation process may generate Braille or synthetic speech or the presentation is replaced by a more suitable layout for example using a larger font size.

Controllability is also an important feature requested by ISO 9241. Some industry guidelines extend this request and require alternatively control by keyboard or a mouse in order to address people's preferences. Several types on handicaps require further customisation of input techniques such as one-handedness, tremor, etc. Use of assistive devices such as a scanner implies to create a different method for control of single keystrokes. In general, however, this implies prolonged interaction techniques. Better customisation of the user interface could be achieved if multiple steps in the interaction could be customised according to these users.

While the first example makes clear that accessibility can be assessed by checking the ability to transform the content for presentations, the later example makes clear that the features of devices used for interaction cause great differences in the usability.

Both examples of usability features make clear that design guidelines already address users with special needs if designers are aware of the limitations implied by their own design work [4]. As a hypothesis one can assume that designers are not aware of all user's requirements. However if a design is still expressing the intension of the author, after some considerable customisation has been applied, its accessibility can be better ensured. As a consequence, customisation needs to be challenging with respect to the media and methods used for input and output.

In this session the authors discuss customisation of interactive systems by addressing two or more user groups with heterogeneous requirements at the same time and addressing each with their own preferred presentation or input technique.

People with communication needs are challenged by web sites containing long text. Transforming such pages into a simper language can be beneficial according to Nicolle's contribution. Simple expression might be achieved for example by a summary or even require to support symbolic and iconic notations such as BLISS.

Velasco discusses how biofeedback sensors work for people having some lack of control of manual devices. Customisation appears in this application not only as adaptation but as adaptivity within different interaction techniques. Through adaptivity the efficiency of the dialogue is improved compared to elongation by computer-driven menu presentation and binary selection techniques.

Transformation of contents which includes already multiple media is detailed on a technical level by Weiman and Weber. Through XML technologies and on the basis of the user's profile the adaptation of user interfaces takes place. These authors refer to more then four different user groups.

A mixture of interaction techniques using voice and keyboard is discussed also by Stobbe in the application domain of eLearning units. Ensuring inclusive usability for quizzes is an important objective as inaccessibility prevents disabled students from participation in assessments such as for example the TOEFL test.

Encelle and Baptiste-Jessel describe their approach to capture all user requirement in machine readable format based on XML. They propose "individual policies" which address the customisation of different aspects of the user interface. Thereby they make clear that customisation is a method to be designed for user interfaces but aims first of all at the personalisation of the user interface for a particular user.

## 3 Current Limitations for Personalisation

There are limitations to personalisation of arsing from time-dependencies in user interfaces. For time-independent presentation media W3C has developed already through the web content authoring guidelines [5] for HTML criteria which even can be used to check this aspect of accessibility which is related to self-explanatoriness.

Surfing as the major interaction technique in the web is only sometimes easy to transform and personalize, as this requires an NP-complete algorithm [6]. Personalisation of navigation techniques hence can cause major performance problems, especially if the hypertext consists of non-linear, circular structures. For example, to designers it is often unclear how long it takes a blind user to reach the "important" parts of a web page unless they are aware of functionalities of screen readers. Figure 2 details how accessibility is dependent also to the particular devices used for interaction. Moreover only some aspects of the ergonomics of devices are related to accessibility. Unless browsing techniques (such as scrolling, following skip links, etc.) are specified, it is difficult to quantify the intersection between accessibility features and features of devices (including assistive devices). In other words if usability is degraded to people with special needs it is difficult to pinpoint whether this is a consequence from lack of accessibility or lack of functionality of the assistive device to support interaction.

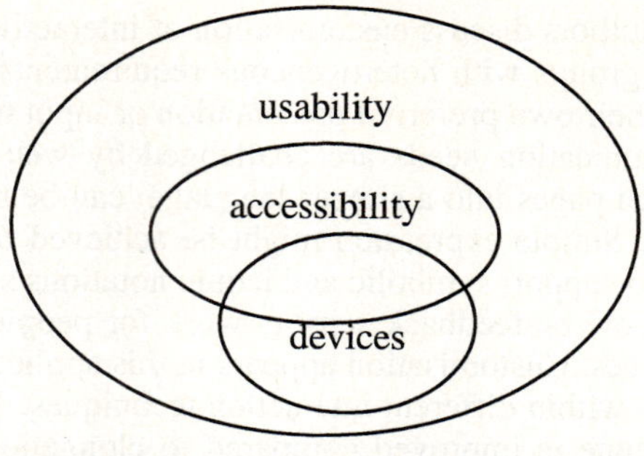


**Fig. 2.** Usability of assistive devices may affect accessibility or usability

Both the time design of input and the time design of output may implicitly challenge further on which level of granularity customisation takes. It is not acceptable to ask for completely different user interfaces most of the time as social exclusion is to be avoided. For time-dependend media such as movies however personalisation options rely on a granularity that cover several seconds, for example for subtitling or audio description. Below this level personalisation cannot easily be achieved or only with considerable increase in the author's work.

Finally, multimodal interaction techniques which includes multiple input facilities such as speech and pointing are addressed by VoiceML and XForms. Their customisation is planned and future work will show guidelines can be developed that support designers appropriately.

## References

1. Hill, R.D. (1986). Supporting concurrency, communication, and synchronization in human-computer interaction – the Sassafras UIMS, ACM Transactions on Graphics, Volume 5 , Issue 3 (July 1986) , pp. 179–210.
2. World Wide Web Consortium (W3C), http://www.w3.org/ (21.4.2004).
3. Edwards, A. (1996). An approach to the evaluation of assistive technology, In: Proceedings of the second international ACM conference on Assistive Technologies ASSETS'96, (Marina del Rey, CA: April 15-17, 1998), pp. 54–71, ACM: New York.
4. Shackel, B. (2001). Foreword, In: Nicolle, C.; Abscal, J. (eds.) Inclusive Design Guidelines for HCI, Taylor&Francis: London, p.xv.
5. Web Content Accessibility Guidelines 2.0, http://www.w3.org/TR/WCAG20/ (21.4.2004).
6. Levene, M. and Loizou, G. (1999). Navigation in Hypertext is easy only sometimes. SIAM Journal on Computing, 29, pp. 728–760.

# Learning from Internet Requirements of People with Communication Needs

Colette Nicolle[1], Zaheer Osman[1], Katharine Black[2], and Andrew Lysley[2]

[1] Ergonomics and Safety Research Institute (ESRI), Loughborough University,
Holywell Building, Holywell Way,
Loughborough, Leics. LE11 3UZ, United Kingdom
{c.a.nicolle,z.osman}@lboro.ac.uk

[2] ACE Centre Advisory Trust, 92 Windmill Road, Headington,
Oxford OX3 7DR, United Kingdom
{black,lysley}@ace-centre.org.uk

**Abstract.** A supportive Web browser, developed by the EU WWAAC project, aims to make the Internet easier to use by people with complex communication needs who use graphic symbol-based augmentative and alternative communication. Further user consultations with older users, people with aphasia and people with learning disabilities, specifically with dyslexia, have demonstrated that the ability to personalise Internet software (for example, through the provision of simple summaries of content and the ability to configure the interface to suit individual needs) can potentially provide more accessible and usable interfaces for other user groups.

## 1 Introduction

The goal of the EU WWAAC project (World Wide Augmentative and Alternative Communication) is to make the electronic highway more accessible and usable for people who have complex communication difficulties and who use graphic symbol-based augmentative and alternative communication (AAC) [1]. Despite advances in commercially available assistive technologies, people using AAC have commented on continuing difficulty and frustration in physical access to technology and subsequent reliance on non-disabled partners [2, 3]. Therefore, one of the key objectives and evaluation criteria of the WWAAC project is to enable a higher degree of independent access for people with complex communication needs.

A number of research and development activities have been taking place since the project began in January 2001, including the development of an adapted Web browser, email package, and supportive writing software, all tailored to the needs of people who use graphic-symbol based AAC. These developments have been informed and refined through an iterative design and evaluation process, beginning with a survey of the requirements of end-users and their facilitators, followed by simulator studies, and alpha, beta and longitudinal evaluations with people who use AAC.

This paper will consider just the development and evaluation of the supportive Web browser, built upon Internet Explorer, which includes the following key features:

K. Miesenberger et al. (Eds.): ICCHP 2004, LNCS 3118, pp. 121–128, 2004.

- Integrated Speech Output, accompanied by a customisable visual focus to highlight the text being read
- Graphical Favourites Page, capturing a screen shot of the Web page to facilitate recognition. The facilitator is able to replace this with an alternative image if required
- Summary Function, whereby the end-user is able to view a summary of the current Web page based upon the page title, the meta tags, the html headings and the links contained within the page
- Alternative Access, enabling access by one or two switches for those who cannot use a mouse, as well as access by a standard or adapted keyboard or on-screen keyboard emulator
- Selection Set, which can be used to input data into online fields, as well as inputting symbol supported items into a search engine
- Layout Editor, enabling the browser's toolbars and buttons to be fully configurable, allowing functionality to be gradually introduced, and the ability to personalise the appearance of the browser to meet the needs of individuals
- Concept Coding Aware, enabling symbol-to-symbol and text-to-symbol conversion, provided that the Web page has been developed to add concept codes to the text. A Dreamweaver extension has been developed in the project to facilitate this process.

Some of these Web browsing features are available from other commercial products. In addition, other systems under research and development, such as the AVANTI Web browser [4] and BrookesTalk [5], are exploring ways of providing more adaptable and usable interaction for people with disabilities.

Currently, the needs of symbol users are not adequately being considered in much research and development work. The ALDICT project (Access for Persons with Learning Disability to Information and Communication Technologies), however, has made significant impact in this area. Its email software, Inter_Comm, enables symbol users to compose, send and receive email messages in his/her own symbol set and language, using Widgit's software 'Writing with Symbols' [6, 7]. Following on from ALDICT's work, Widgit Software Ltd. has developed new software called Communicate Webwise. This software can process most Web pages, apart from complicated ones with Java or Flash components, as either symbols, plain text in any font size, or as spoken words. It is necessary to consider, however, whether symbol support for the entire page is needed or desired by end-users, or if a symbol-embellished summary of the Web page or site would be more appropriate. Allowing the user to choose is really the answer.

In the area of symbol support, however, the WWAAC project will be providing a more unique contribution. A communication infrastructure and protocol have been developed to support symbol-based communication on the Web, based upon *open-sourced* concept coding. With concept coding, instead of images and symbols having to be transferred from one computer to another, it is possible to share a unique code designating the meaning of the symbol needing to be transferred, and the code can then be displayed as a PCS symbol, Picto symbol, Bliss symbol, etc., depending on the requirements of the end-user. By making this open-sourced, it could enable symbol users to communicate across different email packages and utilise a range of browser applications. Using this infrastructure, work is also in progress to develop a Web authoring tool which will enable Web developers to embellish their Web pages with symbols using the on-line concept coding database. This optional symbol support can then be displayed by concept-coding-aware browsers, like that developed by the WWAAC project.

## 2 From User Requirements to Beta Software

The primary target population of end-users defined by the project are people between the ages of 12 and 25 years who use graphic symbol-based AAC in face-to-face interaction, and who are professionally supported in their use of AAC and the Internet within school/college or receiving non-professional support at home.

The results of the survey of users' requirements with both users and experts [3, 8, 9] not only testified that access to the Internet is problematic for people who use AAC, but also fed into the development of the WWAAC software. The first stage of the development work included a simulated off-line Web browser to test out design ideas, first with experts, and then with end-users. These results then informed the development of the alpha and beta versions of the browser, which were evaluated with end-users, their facilitators, and other experts working in the area of AAC. Some of these results are yet to be publicly available [9].

In each of the trials, the Web browser was perceived to be much better than other Web browsers for the primary target population due to its flexibility. Using the Layout Editor, the most important functions can be made available to the user, with the potential of adding further buttons later on. Figure 1 illustrates the Favourites Page and browser layout for a particular switch user with Cerebral Palsy, after some additional functionality had been added. This flexibility may well be applicable to a broader range of groups who may benefit from easier access to the Internet, such as people with learning disabilities who use symbols as aids to literacy, people with aphasia, and the elderly. The final stages of the project aimed to explore these possibilities.

## 3 Further User Consultations

The purpose of further user consultations was to explore whether or not the ability to personalise Internet software (for example, through the provision of simple summaries of content and the ability to configure the interface to suit individual needs) can potentially provide more accessible and usable interfaces for other user groups. Even though the BBC found that only a very small percentage of users want to personalise services, usually the most experienced users [10], personalisation is likely to be the only way that some users are able to access the Internet.

These investigations were meant to be more informal than the alpha or beta trials, collecting qualitative information from different user groups to assess to what extent the software met their needs. As work is currently still in progress, only a selection of the results are presented and discussed below.

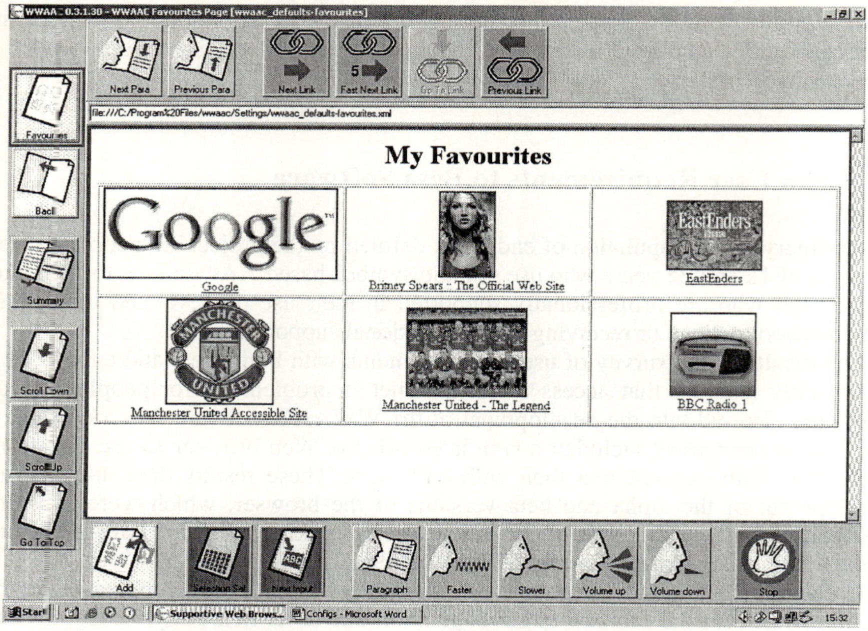


**Fig. 1.** Sample Favourites Page used with AAC users

### 3.1 Older Users

These consultations took place in the UK with 4 older users: 1 user aged between 46-55 with no functional disability; 2 users between 66-75, both with no functional disability over and above the normal course of ageing; and 1 user who was 84 years of age with vision in only one eye.

Their usage of the Internet (World Wide Web and email) had begun under a shared scheme, whereby training had been provided in the use of the Care-on-Line information service provided by social services [11]. A computer was made available in the Manager's office, which the residents were able to use on a regular basis if they did not have their own. Frequency of use varied, and ranged from no recent usage since being in hospital, to 2-3 times a week, to use at home on a daily basis. All 4 persons used a mouse and used the computer and the Internet independently, with Internet Explorer and Outlook Express as their usual software.

The browser software was first demonstrated to the group, and then the users worked in pairs, with a researcher supporting and observing the interactions. Differences in the layout from Figure 1 were: to include 'Zoom in/Zoom out' buttons for older eyes, to remove the 'Next Link' and 'Select Link' buttons for literate mouse users, and to include the 'Stop/Reload' buttons for more regular Internet users.

Some of the advantages of the WWAAC browser were felt to be the following:

- Favourites page as the home page, with images for favourite Web sites
- Very clear and simple
- Easy to see and select the large buttons
- Easy to zoom in and out.

However, compared to conventional browsers, the users felt that the WWAAC browser has lost some functionality which would be useful for people without communication impairments or more advanced users; for example, auto-saving last few addresses visited, auto-complete of previous address entered again, history of Web sites visited, and being able to open more than one window at a time (e.g., when wanting to listen to radio over the net while surfing).

### 3.2 People with Dyslexia

Dyslexia describes a pattern of difficulties people may experience in learning. It commonly affects memory, organisational skills and the acquisition and use of language. During the evaluation of the simulated Web browser (ISAAC Workshop, Odense, 13 August 2002), comments from a user with dyslexia suggested that the WWAAC browser could be very useful to support people with reading difficulties. Although this particular user could read, he suggested that the speech support could help him improve his reading comprehension and confidence, and also the summary was a useful feature to extract important information like a description of the page and key words.

Further investigations provided additional food for thought. This user was an expert in educational technology for people with dyslexia and also dyslexic himself. The WWAAC browser and email software was demonstrated and the following comments were made.

**Outline around the Text.** According to Beacham et al [12], dyslexic students should be allowed to use active reading and learning strategies while performing particular tasks. Based on his research, this expert's advice for the speech output of the WWAAC browser was to remove the line around the words as they are spoken, as the outline may inhibit the ability of people with dyslexia to understand what is being read to them. The reader needs to be able to concentrate on the meaning of what he or she hears, rather than the word that he or she is seeing. What is seen and what is heard are 2 different tasks to a person with dyslexia, and therefore, the combination of the media (movement of the line around the text and the spoken word) is unhelpful and could distract the reader from the task at hand, i.e., understanding the content. In contrast, if the task were proofreading, and the task were to read word by word, then the line around the word would be acceptable in order to help focus on the individual word rather than the meaning of the full text.

**Choice of Colour.** Most users prefer dark print on a pale background, but users should be able to set their own choice of font style and size, as well as background and print colours [13]. A simple technique for providing choice of background colour was suggested. Provided by the Dyscalculia and Dyslexia Interest Group (DDIG) at Loughborough University (`http://ddig.lboro.ac.uk`), the cursor hovers over a background colour grid, and the user is able to visualise the preferred background colour to suit individual needs, thus enabling this colour to be chosen for the entire DDIG Web site. This is an easy tool that could have wider application through supportive Web browser software. The Layout Editor of the WWAAC browser could, for example, enable the user to see the change in background colours in a preview. Then the colour could be saved in the user's preferences.

### 3.3 People with Aphasia

Aphasia is a communication disability that affects the language system. It may be acquired following cerebral vascular accident (stroke), head injury, or other neurological condition, causing difficulties with comprehension, reading, spoken language and/or written communication. The first workshop took place in the Netherlands with 5 people with aphasia, 2 men and 3 women, with 2 volunteers assisting. Aged between mid-40s and 75 years of age, all but 1 user had used the Internet before this evaluation, and 1 person was an experienced Internet user.

A second workshop was held in the UK with 4 people with aphasia, as well as related professionals. All the users had had aphasia for at least a few years, and all were over the age of 55. Each of the end-users had participated in a regular computer group that was run by one of the professionals involved in the workshop. Many commented on the fact that they had now forgotten what they had learnt in this group, and none use the computer independently at the current time. The professional involved stressed the fact that when working with people with aphasia, maintenance of skills is a key issue. Having simplified software is helpful, but it needs to be in conjunction with proper support structures. Support is needed first to teach people with aphasia how to use the software and then to enable them to maintain those skills over time.

From both these workshops, some of the advantages of the WWAAC browser were:

- Favourites page
- Use of buttons rather than the mouse when tired or having a bad day
- Speech output, with easy access and lines around words and sentences
- Flexibility, through the Layout Editor
- Large text through the use of Zoom-in button.

However, more flexibility was desired, e.g., by allowing only text, and not icons, on the buttons; as well as the ability to change the size and colour of font on the favourites page. It was also evident that the one experienced user of the Internet did not see advantages over existing software, which indicates that, as in the case of the older users, the software's functionality must compare well with conventional browsers in order for it to be accepted by a wider range of user groups.

### 3.4 Younger Users

Younger than the target users of the project, this boy, age 11 with Cerebral Palsy, was experienced in accessing his communication aid via a single switch. His main interest was football, but unfortunately this caused some problems as every football site visited proved to be inaccessible. We then tried a Simpson's site, but it was not very interesting to him. He lost interest, the session was terminated, and no interview was conducted.

This appears at first glance to be data not worth reporting; however, it emphasises the fact that all the personalisation in the world is not going to help a user when Web sites are not designed to be accessible and usable. Therefore, it is vital that Web developers apply best practice in usability into their Web sites, and also follow the Web Content Accessibility Guidelines, as proposed by World Wide Web Consortium's Web Accessibility Initiative (W3C–WAI) [14].

## 4 Conclusion

Consultations with a range of user groups, over and above the target users of the project, have demonstrated that the ability to personalise Internet software can potentially provide more accessible and usable interfaces for a wide range of users. The diverse requirements and preferences of different users emphasise the importance of flexibility in configuring not just the WWAAC browser, but software and hardware in general. Further research is still needed, however, in order to decide the most appropriate default configurations for different user groups, while still providing flexibility for individual choice and preferences.

This valuable and unique insight into the needs of people with complex communication needs should provide guidance for all Web content and browser developers through the Web Content Accessibility Guidelines [9, 14, 15]. Whilst it will not be possible to provide general guidelines that encompass all disability groups in the most optimal way, it is a desirable objective to try and maximise the numbers and range of users that can access Web sites for use by the general public. It is also important, as much as possible, to try to go beyond minimum adherence to best practice and policy, which will help to ensure quality and inclusiveness for all [10].

## Acknowledgements

The authors are grateful to the European Commission for the funding received within the Information Society Technologies (IST) Programme and also wish to thank the entire WWAAC Consortium for their comments and contributions to this work, including Handicom (The Netherlands); The ACE Centre Advisory Trust (United Kingdom); Loughborough University (United Kindgom); Dundee University (United Kingdom); DART Regional Children's Habilitation, Sahlgrenska University Hospital (Sweden); Department of Speech, Music and Hearing, Kungl Tekniska Hogskölan (Sweden); Modemo (Finland); MITC (Denmark); and Femtio Procent Data (Sweden). The authors would also like to thank the users and experts who participated in all the evaluation activities, and especially Eelke Verschuur for conducting workshops with people with aphasia and learning disabilities.

## References

1. WWAAC (World Wide Augmentative and Augmentative Communication) project Web site. Available at `http://wwaac.org`
2. Murphy, J., Markova, I., Collins, S. and Moodie, E. (1996). AAC Systems: Obstacles to Effective Use. European Journal of Disorders of Communication, **31**, 31-44.
3. Clarke, M., Lysley, A., Nicolle, C. and Poulson, D. (2002). World Wide AAC: Developing Internet Services for People using AAC. In: Proceedings of ISAAC 2002 10th Biennial Conference of the International Society for Augmentative and Alternative Communication, 10-15 August 2002, Odense, Denmark.
4. Stephanidis, C., Paramythis, A., Sfyrakis, M. and Savidis, A. (2001). A Case Study in Unified User Interface Development: the AVANTI Web Browser. In: Stephanidis, C. (ed.) User Interfaces for All–concepts, methods and tools. New Jersey: Lawrence Erlbaum, 525-568.

5. Zajicek, M. and Morrissey, W. (2001). Speech Output for Older Visually Impaired Adults. In: Proceedings of IHM-HCI Conference, Lille, 503-513.
6. ALDICT project DE 4201 (Access for Persons with Learning Disability to Information and Communication Technologies). Available at www.inclusion-europe.org/aldict
7. Pereira, L., Saragoça, E., Loura, L. and Espadinha, C., (2003). An e-mail programme for mentally impaired persons. Technology and Disability, **15** 4, 217-222.
8. Clarke, M., Nicolle, C. and Poulson, D. (2001). User Requirements Document, EU IST WWAAC project (Deliverable No. 2). Available at www.wwaac.org
9. Nicolle, C., Black, K., Lysley, A., Poulson, D. and Hekstra, D. (2004). An AAC-Enabled Internet: From User Requirements to Guidelines. In: Keates, S., Clarkson, J., Langdon, P. and Robinson, P. (eds.), Designing a More Inclusive World. Proceedings of CWUAAT (2nd Cambridge Workshop on Universal Access and Assistive Technology), Fitzwilliam College, University of Cambridge, 22nd-24th March, 2004.
10. Office of the E-envoy, (2003). Quality Framework for UK Government Website Design: Usability issues for government websites, and Guidelines for UK Government Websites Available at http://www.e-envoy.gov.uk/webguidelines.htm
11. Leicestershire CareOnLine. Available at https://www.leicscareonline.org/uk/careonline/default.asp
12. Beacham, N., Szumko, J. and Alty, J. eds. (2003). An initial study of computer-based media effects on learners who have dyslexia, the Media Effects on Dyslexic Individuals in Academia (MEDIA) Project, Final Report. Available at http://www.techdis.ac.uk/
13. British Dyslexia Association's Dyslexia Style Guide. Available at http://www.bda-dyslexia.org.uk/main/home/index.asp
14. World Wide Web Consortium–Web Accessibility Initiative (2004). Web Content Accessibility Guidelines 2.0, working draft. Available at http://www.w3.org/TR/WCAG20/
15. Poulson, D. and Nicolle, C. (2004). Making the Internet Accessible by People with Cognitive and Communication Impairments. In: Gulliken, J., Harker, S. and Vanderheiden, G. (eds.) Universal Access in the Information Society, **3** 1, 48-56.

# IPCA:
# Adaptive Interfaces Based upon Biofeedback Sensors


Carlos A. Velasco[1], Yehya Mohamad[1], Dirk Stegemann[1], Henrike Gappa[1], Gaby Nordbrock[1], Erwin Hartsuiker[2], Javier Sánchez-Lacuesta[3], and Juan M. Belda[3]

[1] Fraunhofer-Institut für Angewandte Informationstechnik FIT, Schloss Birlinghoven, D53757 Sankt Augustin, Germany
{Carlos.Velasco,Yehya.Mohamad,Dirk.Stegemann}@fit.fraunhofer.de
{Henrike.Gappa,Gaby.Nordbrock}@fit.fraunhofer.de

[2] Mind Media B.V., Postfach 251, NL 6100AG Echt, The Netherlands
info@mindmedia.nl

[3] Instituto de Biomecánica de Valencia, IBV, Universidad Politécnica de Valencia Edificio 9C, Camino de Vera s/n, E46022 Valencia, Spain
{jslacues,jmbelda}@ibv.upv.es



**Abstract.** This paper presents some preliminary results of the IPCA project, targeted to the development adaptive interfaces for people with severe motor and speech impairments based upon biofeedback sensors. We will introduce the results of the user requirements capture and their influence in the project prototype being developed at the moment.


## 1 Introduction

IPCA[1] is a research project funded under the IST Thematic Priority of the 5th Framework Programme from the European Commission. IPCA is targeted to the development of interfaces that can enable people with severe motor and speech impairments to control standard, and especially Web-based, applications. IPCA tries to support a user group for which the existing market products are posing a lot of usability/affordability problems, as proved via thorough tests conducted in the labs of the Consortium members with different user organizations.

The system is based on a flexible combination of existing non-invasive sensors and encoders that monitor different physiological parameters, and a set of software tools that will enable the user to interact with existing computer applications. The physiological parameters used to control the applications are based upon a combination of electromyogram (EMG) and tilt sensors, together with skin conductance and blood pressure sensors that support the adaptivity of the system, based upon the user's affective states [3,5,6].

The Consortium evaluated at the beginning of the project the possibility of using non-invasive electroencephalogram (EEG) sensors as an additional control interface[2].

---

1 Intelligent Physiological Navigation and Control of web-based Applications, IST–2001–37370, http://www.ipca.info/

2 There are at the moment ongoing activities in the area of invasive brain-computer interfaces [1,4] that lay outside the scope of the project.


K. Miesenberger et al. (Eds.): ICCHP 2004, LNCS 3118, pp. 129–134, 2004.

Detailed testing carried out with the user organization participating in the Consortium (ISdAC) did not bring adequate results, and therefore the Consortium discarded this approach.

IPCA has two main components:

- The hardware part, called the Multi-channel Monitoring System (MMS) that encompasses sensors and encoders. The sensor electronics is directly connected to the MMS through a flexible cable and acquire the physiological signals from the user. These signals, such as the electromyographic signal and the positioning of the sensor, are filtered to minimize artifacts and noise. The internal firmware of the device adjusts and calibrates itself to the individual user by acquiring and computing personal settings in the proper range and sensitivity. After its initial calibration, the minimal physiological control the user is able to exercise is translated into digital commands that are sent to the computer via the PS2 port, and are used to operate the ANT system. While operating, the device continuously adjusts its settings, in order to compensate for factors such as muscle fatigue and movement artifacts.
- The software part, called the Ambient Navigation Toolkit (ANT) that interfaces between the MMS and standard software applications, by providing keyboard and/or mouse emulation functions. Its components are: a Web browser with the interface optimized to the MMS, a training system, a personal profile manager, an on-screen keyboard with scanning and word prediction capabilities and the Emotional Response Monitoring System (ERMS).

## 2 User Requirements Analysis

The Consortium focused the analysis of the user requirements separating hardware and software components. This option was selected because it was not feasible to produce a rapid prototype to test the joint system (MMS and ANT). All the tests were conducted in collaboration with different users in Belgium and Spain.

Users were selected to cover a wide range of disabilities within the target group: quadriplegia, cerebral palsy, multiple sclerosis, spinal muscular atrophy and amyotrophic lateral sclerosis, for whom other input systems such as speech, joysticks, etc. were not feasible.

Hardware tests were focused on evaluating the feasibility of using EMG and tilt sensors as input and control systems, and to verify the reliability of the system for these users. Other factors affecting performance, such as fatigue, were analyzed as well. Results have shown the viability of our approach to use the sensors as control systems, and users were able to control its behavior very accurately [7]. As a result of the tests, two configurations will be initially implemented in the system:

- Single channel mode (1 EMG sensor).
- Dual channel mode (1 EMG sensor, 1 tilt sensor).

The requirements' capture process for software components was focused on two points:

- Analysis of accessibility and usability issues of existing commercial mouse/keyboard emulation systems related to application and operating system control.

– Accessibility issues for these user groups when using standard Internet application and services, from the user agent point of view, i.e., how can the browser facilitate typical online standard tasks. For this evaluation exercise, the Consortium designed an application called User's Design Workspace (UDW), where test participants could tweak the design and layout of different Web sites, as well as extract relevant information.

The results of the tests provided us with feedback on the expected user agent behavior. Many of the ideas collected are not reflected in the current version of the User Agent Accessibility Guidelines [1], probably due to the demanding personalization requirements [7] that can only implemented via a user profiling framework [8]. Summarizing the results, users demand:

– Simplified navigation via link lists, thematic grouping and stored personal preferences.
– Form-filling support via separate presentation, and easy manipulation of stored personal data.
– Enhanced search capabilities in the browser, when the provided search mechanisms of the Website do not provide an adequate interface. That requires from the user agent indexing capabilities, combined with crawling mechanisms in the background.
– Look and feel personalization of the Website, to be ported throughout the same domain, and become available in subsequent sessions. Due to the lack of semantic capabilities of actual versions of (X)HTML, this functionality will be implemented by advanced statistical methods that will allow the comparison of DOM (Document Object Model) trees, and the identification of common structures.

In the initial prototyping phases, it is expected that emotional modeling mechanisms will be only implemented in the training components of the system, based upon previous experiences of the authors [3].

## 3 Preliminary Implementations

When preparing the camera-ready version of this paper, the Consortium is actively working on the first prototypes of the MMS and the ANT system. Efforts are concentrated on the single channel mode and the mouse and keyboard emulation.

The mouse emulation system (see Figure 1) is envisioned as a on-screen application that provides visual feedback to the user on the active mode of the mouse (e.g., click-mode, displacement-mode, etc.) in combination with the mouse cursor. All parameters, including GUI scanning speed, mouse speed and acceleration, GUI transparency, size and position are configurable for every user.

The on-screen keyboard (or soft-keyboard) is offering different layouts to the user, starting with some language-specific distribution of keys like QWERTY (English) or QWERTZ (German). However, these layouts are very inefficient for sequential access [9]. Therefore, we are implementing layouts based upon letter frequencies in the languages of countries where tests are going to be carried out with end users.

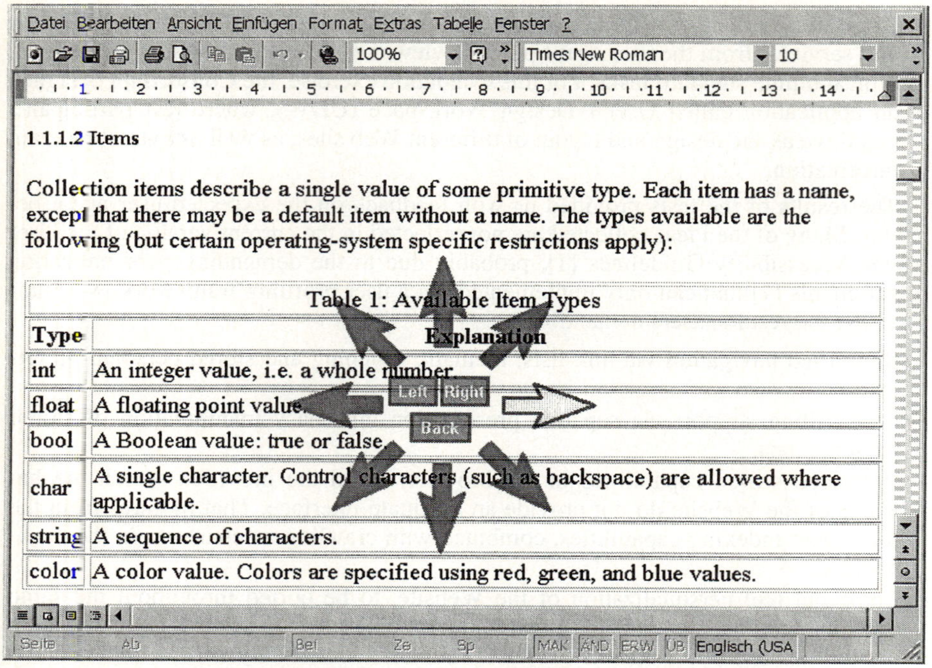


**Fig. 1.** ANT mouse emulation system in transparency mode.

## 4 Conclusions and Future Work

The Consortium is actively working in the preparation of the prototype[3] and is confident in the viability of the concept, based upon the preliminary evaluation results. We are also preparing thorough user testing scenarios that will help us to identify and refine the interface and the adaptivity of the system [2]. As mentioned earlier, there is also a need to extend previous work of the authors in the area of user and device modeling [8] to include issues related to biofeedback sensors.

The authors are also investigating further applications of the system, especially in the area of ubiquitous computing and multimodal interfaces, where the opportunities of interaction for this target user group will be greatly enhanced via the use of wireless sensors and roaming profiles.

## Acknowledgements

This work has been undertaken in the framework of the project IPCA – IST–2001–37370 partly funded by the IST Programme of the European Commission. The authors would like to acknowledge the contributions of their colleagues from the Fraunhofer-Institut für Angewandte Informationstechnik (FIT), Mind Media B.V., the Institute of Biomechanics of Valencia (IBV) and ISdAC International Association.

[3] To be demonstrated at the conference.

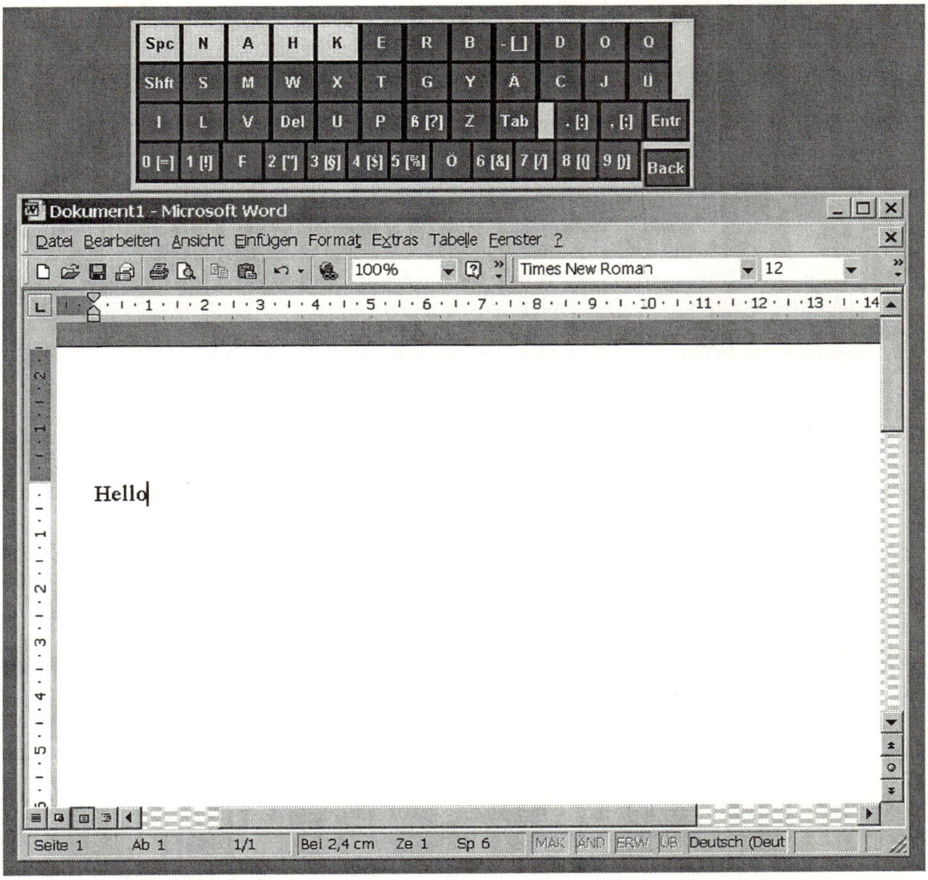


**Fig. 2.** ANT on-screen keyboard. Layout based-upon letter-frequency for the German language.

## References

1. Jacobs, I., Gunderson, J., Hansen, E. (eds): User Agent Accessibility Guidelines 1.0, W3C Recommendation 17 December 2002. World Wide Web Consortium. Available at: http://www.w3.org/TR/UAAG10/ (2002)
2. Mason, S.G., Bozorgzadeh, Z., Birch, G.E.: The LF-ASD brain computer interface: on-line identification of imagined finger flexions in subjects with spinal cord injuries. In: Proceedings. of the fourth international ACM conference on Assistive Technologies (ASSETS'00, November 13-15, 2000, Arlington, VA), New York: ACM Press (2000) 109-113
3. Mohamad, Y., Velasco, C.A., Tebarth, H., Berlage, T.: Building Adaptive Training and Therapeutic Systems by Considering the User's Affective States. In: Stephanidis C (ed), Universal Access in HCI, Inclusive Design in the Information Society (Volume 4, Proceedings of the 2nd International Conference on Universal Access in Human - Computer Interaction, 22-27 June, Crete, Greece), New Jersey: Lawrence Erlbaum Associates (2003) 572-576

4. Moore, M.M., Kennedy, P.R.: Human Factors Issues in the Neural Signals Direct Brain-Computer Interface. In: Proceedings of the fourth international ACM conference on Assistive Technologies (ASSETS'00, November 13-15, 2000, Arlington, VA), New York: ACM Press (2000) 114–120
5. Picard, R.: Affective computing. The MIT Press. (1997)
6. Picard, R.: IBM Systems Journal, Volume 39, Numbers 3 & 4, MIT Media Laboratory. (2000)
7. de la Torre, F.J. (ed): User Requirements Analysis and Preliminary Evaluation Criteria. IPCA, IST–2001–37370, Deliverable D0402. Available at: http://www.ipca.info/ (2003)
8. Velasco, C.A., Mohamad, Y., Gilman, A.S., Viorres, N., Vlachogiannis, E., Arnellos, A., Darzentas, J.S.: Universal Access to Information Services - the Need for User Information and its Relationship to Device Profiles. Universal Access in the Information Society, to appear. (2004)
9. Venkatagiri, H.: Efficient Keyboard Layouts for Sequential Access. AAC, 15(2) (1999) 126-128

# Adaptation of Multimedia Browsing Techniques

Kurt Weimann[1], Ine Langer[2], and Gerhard Weber[1]

[1] University of Kiel - Multimedia Campus Kiel, Theodor Heuss Ring 140,
24143 Kiel, Germany
{k.weimannn,g.weber}@mmc-kiel.com
[2] University of Applied Studies, Friedrichstr. 57-59,
38855 Wernigerode, Germany
ilanger@hs-harz.de

**Abstract.** Documents become more accessible if they are enriched with alternative media. The paradigm of "one document for all" is challenged by the needs of heterogeneous reader groups when reading multimedia documents. The user interface to allow browsing is to be adapted through assistive devices such as screen readers, but in time-dependant presentations adaptation is required to suit each user group. Some criteria and approaches implemented in the MultiReader system are being discussed.

## 1 Introduction

Adaptation of user interfaces for users with different needs has been demonstrated together with the development of screen readers and screen magnification tools for the blind and visually impaired [1]. An off-screen model allows describing the contents of windows in an acoustic or tactile way. Dynamic tracking of changes enables users to interact with a multitude of applications in graphical user interfaces of Java Swing, MS Windows, X Windows, and Gnome. By these GUIs, the generation of the off-screen model is supported in different degrees of fidelity, and directly implies the degree of accessibility to an individual application. In other words, making an unusable application accessible cannot be achieved by a screen reader's adaptation of the GUI. For designers of graphical user interfaces, little support is provided to understand how usable their visual system is, while working as a blind user with a screen reader, although some efforts have been undertaken [2].

HTML explicitly provides an off-screen model (document object model, DOM) for time-independent media such as text and graphics. Screen readers and other assistive devices cooperating with the user agent can adapt the presentation according to the syntactic elements such as headline, paragraphs, links, and table cells.

With the development of mark-up techniques for time-dependent contents, such as for encyclopaedias, cookbooks, and other multimedia documents the need to be able to ensure both, accessibility and usability has emerged again. While screen readers do not try to make these kinds of presentations accessible, it has become feasible to read and control animations, videos, as well as multiple and parallel operating layers of audio contents and other single media objects (SMOs) through mark-up languages such as SMIL or SVG.

K. Miesenberger et al. (Eds.): ICCHP 2004, LNCS 3118, pp. 135–142, 2004.

To ensure accessibility, both WCAG 1.0 and 2.0 [3] ask for the ability to control the temporal duration of time-dependent media within a wide range. Enrichment features have been embedded into some mark-up languages explicitly. Our working hypothesis is that for control of the duration of time-dependent media by the reader, adaptation of both, the user interface with its interactive elements, as well as the contents of documents is required. This can be achieved only by modifying the presentation of contents more dynamically and by adapting it to the users needs.

The MultiReader project has identified several heterogeneous user groups, such as blind, visually impaired, and deaf, or hard of hearing people, for which different renderings are being produced at reading time.

In the following, we describe the process of adapting documents and their temporal outline using XSLT on a technical level. Documents contain beside XHTML mark-up, SVG, and SMIL (TIME). We describe why authors may follow the standard WAI guidelines for making these documents accessible. If only some additional mark-up is provided, then temporal control of multimedia contents by very different users can be improved as evaluations within the MultiReader project have shown.

## 2 MultiReader Document Generation and Processing

The MultiReader (file-based) backend [4] processes several XSL [5] files to personalize a book written in chapter files and to create navigation aids such as a table of contents and an index. This kind of processing is a common procedure for most Content Management Systems. Fig. 1 shows which files are used in which processing step.

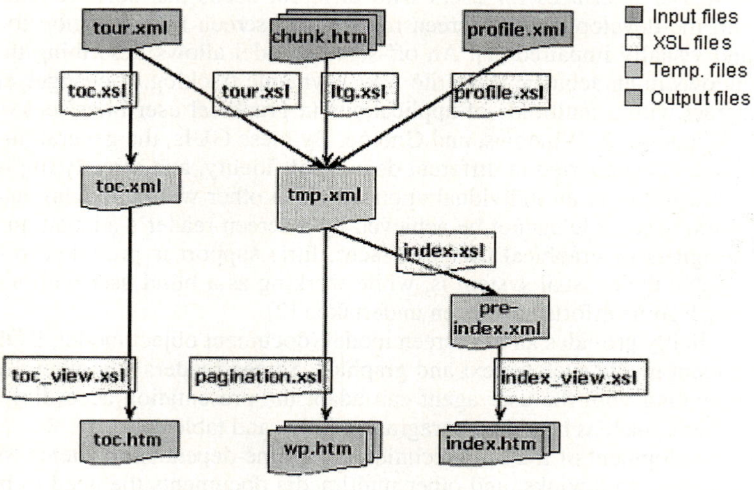


**Fig. 1.** Files involved in the personalization process

The file toc.xml is the basis for the table of contents. Via a parameter to toc_view.xsl, the presentation format of the table of contents can be changed. This results either in a tree view or in a static list of links.

The main transformation process creates the file tmp.xml. It contains all the information from the source files which is relevant to the user (user preferences are indicated through profile.xml) in the appropriate order (specified by tour.xml). The pagination process splits the content into separate files and adds navigation information.

The file tmp.xml also serves as the basis for the index process. This ensures that only those terms which are really contained in the personalized book are listed in the index. Indexes are items in alphabetical order, topic based, or media based. The main transformation process (which results in tmp.xml) deserves further explanation:

The source files contain special `<span>` elements, so called containers. They are described in detail in the following section. The class attribute of such a container indicates what kind of media it contains, for example, the following class "cvideo" denotes a video clip:

```
<span class="cvideo">...</span>
```

In this container, there would be the mark-up referring to the video file and its enrichments such as audio tracks, a long description, and subtitles. The following is the XSL template which is called when the parser encounters an element as the one above:

```
<xsl:template match="*[@class='cvideo']">
 <xsl:if test="$videoEnabled">
  <xsl:copy>
   <xsl:attribute name="id">
    <xsl:value-of select="generate-id()"/>
   </xsl:attribute>
   <xsl:apply-templates select="@*|node()"/>
  </xsl:copy>
 </xsl:if>
</xsl:template>
```

The `<xsl:if>` instruction is used to check whether the user preference includes video clips (see also section 3). The variable `$videoEnabled` holds the Boolean value obtained from profile.xml. If it is set to `'true'` the `<xsl:copy>` element and its children are evaluated. `<xsl:copy>` creates a copy of the current node which is the `<span>` node. An additional attribute is appended to that node, the id attribute. Its value is generated not by the author but by the generate-id() function which ensures that this value is unique and can be used to serialize all required containers. For example the video container is identified by id in order to play, pause, or stop it. Finally, the processing of the `<span>`'s child nodes is triggered by the instruction `<xsl:apply-templates>`. A very general template copies any element, for example the `<t:video>` element. Other containers (`<span>`) are handled similar to the above example.

## 3 Document Container

The MultiReader document containers are storing redundant presentation alternatives for one fragment of information. One MultiReader node consists of a couple of document containers. Document containers are logical units for presenting a main single media object (SMO) for heterogeneous users with print disabilities. This is done by providing redundant presentations of the main SMO by other SMOs. A text paragraph would be presented to a deaf reader by SMOs like sign video and text highlighting. To a dyslexic reader could be delivered the same text with speech tracks as audio representation. The selection of additional SMOs is done by user specific profiles. MultiReader documents contain presentational SMOs for blind, partially sighted, dyslexic, deaf, or mainstream users. The bundle of first and second level SMOs is arranged in containers. The information about the selection of additional representational SMOs for each main SMO is based on user preferences [6].

## 4 Rendering Document Containers

Time dependent media need to be synchronized carefully and therefore require special attention when documents are being created through rendering. The XHTML+SMIL source code assigns a first presentation order, simply because of the fact that visual elements in XHTML documents are rendered from left to right and from top to bottom (by default). This presentation order can be overridden by CSS style sheets. The following is a sample MultiReader node, showing a document generated by a deaf reader's sample profile as displayed in Fig. 2.

It becomes clear that the sign language video is displayed to the right of the headlines, even though it precedes them in the source code. At this level it is the author's task to create the layout in such a way, that elements which belong together are displayed next to each other. This is important for both screen and screen reader users. Differences in the requirements of those two user groups need to be considered and often point out the limitations of XHTML and CSS layout (and their current implementations in web browsers). Partially sighted users may set a large font and large line spacing, so that only a few words can be seen without scrolling. This leaves no room for a picture or video clip which needs to be enlarged, too.

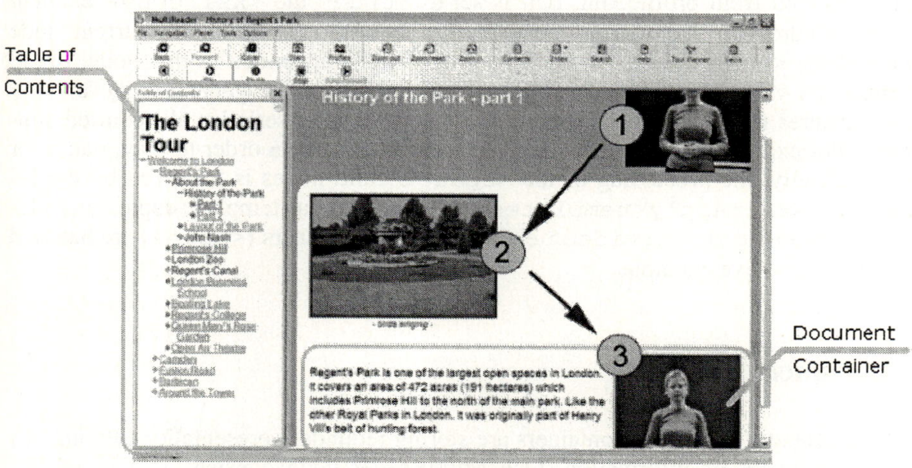


**Fig. 2.** Temporal ordering of content

On the other hand, screen readers usually stick to the order of elements in the source code. Therefore, it is important to arrange the code elements properly. For example, the long description of a picture must be right above or below the image tag, without any other document text in between. Otherwise the screen reader would announce the picture, read the other text and then read the description of the picture – although the visual display might show the description right next to the picture.

The order of elements in the source code also affects the playback order of time-dependent media.

MultiReader documents contain a `<par>` element as parent of other content elements. This means that all media would start playing at once when the document is opened. This behaviour can be overridden for serialization. It is the author's task to define a reasonable playing order. Usually, it will follow the reading flow from top to bottom.

When the documents are rather long and require scrolling, media elements further down the page should not start playing immediately, because the user would start reading at the top of the page and get confused by sounds coming from a video clip he/she can't see.

The playing order can be defined using a combination of SMIL attributes and JavaScript functions [7]. When the page is opened, the parent `<par>` starts playing. This event can be captured and used to start preloading the media elements:

```
<t:par id="oMedia" onbegin="m1.beginElement()">
```

In the example above, this causes the sign language video ① to play. The sign language video is placed in a time container identified by "m1". The triggered event "onbegin" in this container is used to preload the second media element (video clip ② in the example).

```
<span class="time" timeContainer="par"
begin="indefinite" id="m1"
onbegin="m2.beginElement();m2.pauseElement()"
onend="m2.resumeElement()" fill="freeze">
```

The second video starts playing and is paused immediately. This freezes the first frame. When the first video clip ends, its last frame freezes, and the second video clip is resumed. This technique is applied to all media elements in the document to enforce serialisation. It is then quite easy to change the playing order, simply by changing the condition on which a certain element is resumed.

## 5 Timelines and Relations between Document Containers

The document containers are presented in human reading order as mentioned above. Document containers have their own timelines internally. This timeline consists of single timelines for each presented single model object. Since redundant user dependant presentation of content might differ in length, and redundant content (SMO) is presented in a parallel manner, the resulting container timeline is equal to the timeline of the largest SMO's timeline (end sync, see Fig. 2). It is also permitted to split alternative SMOs into smaller chunks, e.g. for timed highlighting of text sentence by sentence. The corresponding timeline length is the sum of all highlighted sentences, since they are presented in a sequential order.

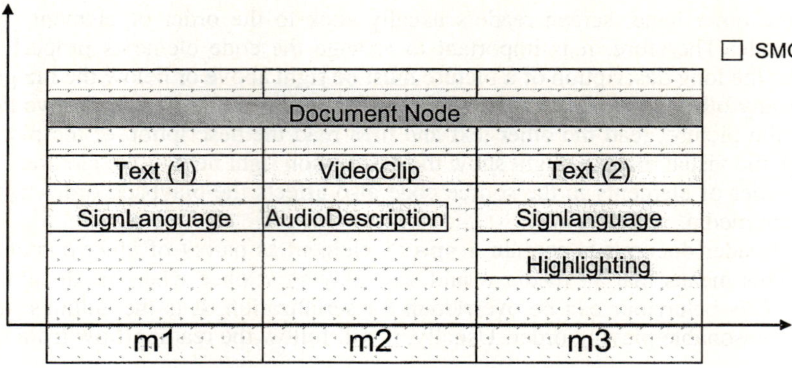


**Fig. 3.** Document Containers consist of parallel SMOs

*Corresponding source code:*

```
<t:par id="oMedia" fill="freeze">
<span class="time" timeContainer="par" SPEED="1.0"
id="m1">
<pseudoTag1/>
<pseudoTag2/>
...
</span>
<span class="time" timeContainer="par" SPEED="1.0"
id="m2">
...
</span>
<span class="time" timeContainer="par" SPEED="1.0"
id="m3">
...
</span>
</t:par>
```

In the above code snippet, the SMO tags are considered as placeholders for redundant presentations inside a document container. Unique container ids are built during the document generation process. They are results of the generate-id() function and have values from $m_1$ to $m_n$. These ids make it possible to address containers directly, as shown in Section 4. Instead of controlling the start sequence of the containers, it is also possible to change the presentation speed by changing the speed attribute during run-time through JavaScript [7]. If no speed attribute is specified, the speed value defaults to 1.0. By specifying a value of 0.5, the container will run at half speed. The value will also affect the child elements of the container. The container speed will be changed by applying the following JavaScript to the container:

```
m1.speed(speed)
```

To influence the speed of the text highlighting, it is only necessary to change the speed attribute of the container m3. Besides the text highlighting, the sign language video is also affected (see Fig. 4). By this approach it is possible to change the presentation speed without loosing the synchronization between the SMOs of containers.

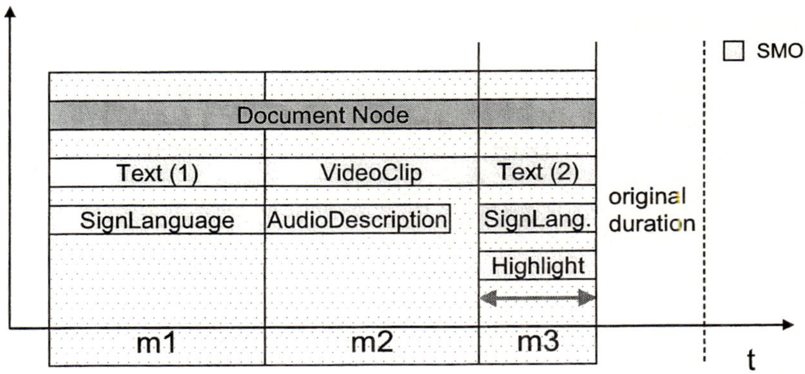


**Fig. 4.** Stretching or Reducing a Container's Timeline

Changing the timeline of one container will also stretch or expand the node's timeline. By specifying the speed attributes it is to make them persistent [6].

The advantages which were reached by using this mechanism are that the effect is easy to understand for users since the document or parts of it are acting like an every day multimedia device, e.g. cd/dvd player. Moreover, a kind of inside node navigation is provided by fast forwarding. And the most important advantage is that the SMOs are still synchronized and the whole MultiReader node remains valid in sense of time design. Since most screen readers are not capable of reading SMIL documents (screen readers read text, independent from any modal information), MultiReader nodes are optionally self-voicing. This is reached by providing generated synthetic speech tracks, which are adjusted for stretching timelines. However, this level of temporal granularity might produce unwanted results in the form of too fast, or too slow speech samples.

Containers which benefit from the adaptation of the timeline are text, video, and animation. The alternative representations for text are sign language, speech, and text highlighting. Videos are intended to be displayed alternatively by narrations and long audio descriptions. Animations are constructed out of sequential pictures and enriched by long descriptions plus audio presentations for e.g. blind readers.

## 6 Outlook

One of the main recommendations brought up by the users of the MultiReader documents was to manipulate the presentation speed of time dependant media. We have shown above that additional markup through classes enables for such a temporal control. Future work will address integration of time dependant SMOs with interaction techniques such as following links in videos and filling out forms. One scenario as possibly required in interactive TV could be a link which will lead outside the current document node. This link has a validity of 5s which would be for some users too short to figure out as navigation possibility. If the user has the option to slow down the presentation to half speed he/she would be able to react inside a time frame of 10s. It is easy to understand that this could increase the usability dramatically.

## Acknowledgements

The MultiReader Project (IST-2000-27513) is supported by the IST Programme of the Commission of the European Communities (Project IST-2000-27513). The Consortium consists of the City University London (UK), the Electrotechnical Engineering Department (ESAT) of the Katholieke Universiteit Leuven (Belgium), the Royal National Institute for the Blind (UK), the Federation of Dutch Libraries for the Blind (the Netherlands), the Harz University of Applied Studies (Germany), and Multimedia Campus Kiel (Germany).

## References

1. Mynatt, B., Weber, G. (1994) "Nonvisual Presentation of graphical user interfaces: contrasting two approaches", in Proceedings of CHI 1994 (Boston, MA, USA, April 24-28, 1994), ACM, New York, pp. 166-172
2. Weber, G.: "Programming for Usability in Nonvisual User Interfaces", Proceedings of ASSETS'98, (Marina del Rey, CA: April 15-17, 1998), ACM: New York, pp. 46-48
3. Web Content Accessibility Guidelines 2.0, April 13 2004, `http://www.w3.org/TR/WCAG20/`
4. Langer, I., Weber, G., Petrie, H.: "Multimediale Präsentationen für Menschen mit Behinderungen", Stanke, G.; Hemsley, J. (eds.) Proc. Electronic Imaging & the Visual Arts, EVA 2002 Berlin, Gesellschaft zur Förderung angewandter Informatik e.V.: Berlin, pp.61-67
5. World Wide Web Consortium (W3C), April 13 2004, `http://www.w3.org/`
6. Weimann, K.: "Modeling Users with Special Reading Needs", Proceedings of Universal Access in HCI 2003, (Crete, GR,: June 22-27, 2003), LEA, New Jersey, pp. 1487-1491
7. HTML+TIME 2.0 Reference, April 13 2004, `http://msdn.microsoft.com/library/default.asp?url=/workshop/author/behaviors/reference/time2/htime_overviews_entry.asp`

# Adapting Presentation and Interaction with XML Documents to User Preferences

Benoît Encelle and Nadine Baptiste-Jessel

IRIT - Université Paul Sabatier
118, route de Narbonne
31062 Toulouse Cedex 4, France
encelle@irit.fr

**Abstract.** In this paper, we introduce the concept of "user policies". The objective of policies is to specify user preferences in terms of presentation and interaction with information. Using this concept, the presentation/interaction with information will be adapted to user's needs, making information more accessible. We define several kinds of policies (navigation, exploration, presentation, etc.). The concepts of "presentation policies" and "navigation policies" are studied in this article. As XML is the standard for encoding electronic information, we will apply the concept of policies to the browsing of XML Documents.

## 1 Introduction

Today, more and more people have an Internet access, having an ever-growing volume of information at their disposal. However, with the most used Web browsers, the presentation and generally speaking, the interaction with information, remains identical, whatever the user. The problem is that each user has different physical and/or cognitive capacities, preferring to interact with the information in such or such a way. Consequently, the goal is to develop tools or interfaces able to fit each user's needs - personalizing the presentation of information and the interaction with information. Such tools (i.e. interfaces) are mandatory for people with disabilities that physically are not able to use "standard" tools. As a consequence, the objective of our works is to define a method for specifying user preferences that results in a user-tailored presentation/interaction with information. In this way, the first part deals with existing solutions for making accessible/personalizing information to the user (State of the Art). In a second part, we introduce the concept of "user policies" and its applications. In the third part, we propose a model for specifying user policies. Finally, we will conclude by suggesting possible further developments with this approach.

## 2 State of the Art

As the Web is today the biggest source of information, we will firstly study initiatives taken to make Web information more accessible. Secondly, we will

K. Miesenberger et al. (Eds.): ICCHP 2004, LNCS 3118, pp. 143–150, 2004.

focus our attention on a research domain that adapts (i.e. personalizes) the information to the user: Adaptive Hypermedia. Finally, possible adaptations of information highly depend on information representation (encoding language) that is used: we will explain why HTML is not suitable to user information adaptation and why XML, its successor, overcomes HTML drawbacks.

### 2.1 Web Information Accessibility

In order to make Web information accessible, transformations (i.e. adaptations) of information must be performed. We distinguish two kinds of adaptations: adaptation performed at authoring-time (i.e. during the writing of documents) and adaptation performed at run-time (i.e. during documents consultation).

Authoring-time adaptation results in a set of "accessibility" rules that authors of Web documents have to follow. In this way, the Web Accessibility Initiative (WAI) from the W3C wrote a document entitled "Web Content Accessibility Guidelines"[1] containing these accessibility rules. For instance, one of these rules consists in giving a textual alternative to each picture embedded in a Web document.

The second kind of adaptations (Run-Time Adaptation) results in the development of dedicated Web browsers. These browsers use non-common input/output devices (i.e. media) to compensate a given disability. For instance, several dedicated browsers for blind people exist[2]: IBM HomePage Reader, Braillesurf, pwWebspeack, Internet Explorer (using the Jaws screen reader), etc. Most of these browsers use, in an alternative or cumulative way, a vocal synthesis and a Braille display for transmitting information.

**Our Approach**
Concerning authoring-time adaptation, authors have to add extra accessibility information in their documents. We do not base our work on this approach: Making Web companies develop content accessible to people with disabilities remains a monumental task. Moreover, in order to have all Internet content accessible, all existing content should be modified. As a consequence, we have to develop some principles that result in a run-time adaptation of information.

Like with dedicated browsers, the users - with our approach - must have the possibility to use several media (devices) for the presentation of information and for the interaction with information. However, difference with dedicated browser - with our approach - is that user preferences have to be highly (deeply) customizable. Indeed, due to the fact that this kind of software is already "dedicated" to a well specialized group of users, the personalization or customization aspect (i.e. the adaptation to each user's needs) is often a bit limited. An interesting research area focused on the personalization of presentation and interaction with information is Adaptive Hypermedia.

### 2.2 Information Personalization

According to Brusilovsky, Adaptive Hypermedia (AH) is one of the most promising application areas for user modeling and user-adapted interaction techniques [3]. AH systems (AHS) build a model of the context in which they are used. For instance, information concerning the user (goals, knowledge, preferences), the environment (available devices), is included in this context model. Adaptive means that the system permanently collates information about the user into the model and automatically applies it for customizing the presentation of information and the interaction with information. The taxonomy of adaptive hypermedia technologies[4], distinguishes two categories of adaptation: adapting the presentation (what information must be shown to the user) and adapting the navigation support (where the user can go) in order to guide the user through several elements of information. Concerning disabled people, AHS have been developed for special purposes (e.g. the AVANTI project[5]).

**Our Approach**
Mostly AHS adaptation techniques are based on system assumptions concerning user knowledge and goals. In our point of view, adaptation performed by AHS is more a customization of informational content rather than a customization of presentation of information or interaction with information.

Moreover, due to the lack of semantic information in HTML, most of AHS includes directly accessibility rules inside their informational content (documents). As a result, authors have to mix, inside documents, accessibility rules and informational content. We do not want to have some kind of "dedicated" systems where documents are in advance written with accessibility problems in mind. We want an approach that can be more easily generalized.

### 2.3 Information Encoding Languages

The HTML Language, used to "present" and interact with information, is basically a language used for formatting the information graphically. As a result, HTML is adapted to the representation of textual information but is not adapted to the representation of other types of information (for instance, mathematical or musical information). The meta-language XML[6] comes in response to HTML drawbacks. XML languages model various types of information. For instance, there are languages for representing mathematical information (MathML), musical information (MusicXML) and many other information fields. XML philosophy is to separate the informational contents (the semantics) from its presentation (graphical, using sounds...). As a result, several ways can be used to present a same XML document, depending on what media are in use. With XML documents, it is possible to provide a user-adapted presentation of information and interaction with information.

**Our Approach**
As XML is the standard for encoding information, we will suppose that information that must be presented is XML-conformant. Several applications or standards, designed for people with disabilities, take advantages of XML-conformant information. For instance, in the context of Digital Talking Books (i.e. DTB), the Daisy Consortium has written a standard[7] for specifying digital talking books,

gathering advantages of several XML applications (SMIL[8] for choreographing a multimedia content, DTBook for markup of the textual content files of books and other publications presented in digital talking book format, etc.). Like the DAISY standard for DTB information, we want to develop some principles that result in a multimedia presentation/interaction of any kind of XML information.

## 3 The Concept of Policy

In order to describe the user's needs, we will separate his preferences in terms of presentation and interaction. We will use the concept of policy for describing his preferences. A user preferences model (profile) will be made up of several policies: Presentation policies and interaction policies. A policy indicates the system's reaction according to a given user event. For instance, a presentation policy specifies how the system must present such or such information. As a kind of interaction policy, navigation policies indicate for a user action in a given context what are the targeted information elements. In this paper we only develop the concepts of presentation and navigation policies but others kinds of policies can be considered (for instance exploration policies - giving overviews concerning the structure of a document). The idea is to give to the user more adapted possibilities concerning the presentation of information and interaction with information. A policy must be able to be laid down by the user: we can thus use the term of user policy.

### 3.1 Presentation Policies

Our objective – to present information in a user-adapted manner – has led us directly to the idea of a presentation policy. We will study the components of such a policy. First of all, information must be transmitted by one or more channels of diffusion (or media), in order to be communicated to the user. Currently, most information is presented graphically. However, disabled users (blind or visual impaired people) cannot access this information. These users, because of their handicap, receive information through other media (sound or tactile). As a result, a presentation policy must specify which media will present which information, the order of presentation and the way in which information will be adapted to the media. The visual channel is able to communicate a large amount of information in a very short time : For blind users, information must be transmitted on other channels with much narrower "band-width". So, the idea of filtering information, i.e. to start by presenting only the information deemed essential by the user (the user can subsequently access detailed information), the idea of being able to go from a general view to a specific one, means the user will not be lost in the mass of information obtained.

Information must be converted into a media-readable format to be transmitted. This transformation describes the logic for adapting information to the media. This adaptation logic does not really belong to the user profile (model), but rather to a "media profile". A presentation policy thus describes for each "type" of information (XML elements):

1. Which information parts (XML elements) must be presented: User profile
2. Which media present these information parts (link between the part and the media) and description of the presentation order in time: User profile
3. How information is adapted to the media: Media profile

These three points will be illustrated in section 4 - Modeling a Presentation Policy. As an example, we will consider a document that describes an address book, indexing information on people (last name, first name, address, mobile phone number, e-mail). The name of the root element of these address book documents is "address_book". This element has several children (i.e. these children are "person" elements). Each "person" element is made up of the last name, first name, phone number of a person, etc.

At consultation time, the system will firstly present the root element of the document, namely the element "address_book". Several manners for presenting this element can be imagined - resulting in several different presentation policies.

**Example:** Presentation policies for the "address_book" element.

- A first presentation policy for this element can be "*to present using a voice synthesis the first name and last name of each person in the address book.*"
- An other example can be "*to present alphabetically the first and last names of each person using voice synthesis while his phone number is displayed on the Braille line.*"

### 3.2 Navigation Policies

As we said, the goal of navigation policies is to indicate for a user action in a given context what are the targeted information elements. A user action is for instance a key pressed event, a mouse click, a sentence pronounced by the user, etc. The context represents the information element (i.e. XML element) the user was consulting before his action. Context notion is essential for delimiting the number and the meaning of possible user actions. Indeed, a given action can be possible in a particular context (information element) but cannot be possible in an other context (an other information element). In the same way, the same action – according to the courant context (XML element) – can result in different system's reactions. We use the XPath language[9] for targeting the information elements corresponding to the user action. In other terms, a navigation policy describes for each "type" of information (XML elements):

- What actions of navigation the user can perform on this element
- For each action, an XPath expression - targeting elements - is provided

We will keep the example of the address book document in order to illustrate the notion of navigation policies.

**Example:** Navigation policies for the "address_book" element.

*When the user pronounces the last name of a given person in the address book, the targeted element ready to be presented is the corresponding person element (i.e. the parent element of the pronounced last name element).*

## 4 Implementation of the Concept of Policy

We choose XML for modeling policies. We developed a rudimentary schema (DTD) for specifying policies content.

```
<!ELEMENT Policies (Type*)>
<!ELEMENT Type (Policy*)>
<!ATTLIST Type id (presentation|exploration|navigation) #REQUIRED>
<!ELEMENT Policy ANY>
<!ATTLIST Policy id CDATA #REQUIRED>
```

**Fig. 1.** Policies Schema

Here is an instance of this schema:

```
<Policies>                    <- Type of policies : presentation, navigation, ...
 <Type id="presentation">     <- Policy identifier : URI of the
  <Policy id="address_book">     namespace used in the document
   ...                        <- (1) XSLT templates that describe transformation
  </Policy>                      rules to apply to XML elements.(address_book, ...)
 </Type>
</Policies>
```

**Fig. 2.** Instance of the "Policies" Schema

### Modeling Presentation Policy

The application of a presentation policy to an XML element can be represented as a transformation of this element. XML Technologies benefit from a transformation language for an XML document which is called XSLT[10] (XML Stylesheet Language Transformation). A presentation policy will be defined as a transformation process. The transformation result will be another XML document, describing the multimedia presentation to be carried out. Specific features of SMIL – taken from the "SMIL Timing and Synchronization Modules" – will be used to describe the multimedia presentation. These modules define a powerful way of choreographing multimedia content.

**Example:** XML implementations of the first example of presentation policy.

User profile part:

```
<xsl:template match="address_book">
 <xsl:element name="SEQ">  <-------- SMIL Information of "choreography"
  <xsl:element name="MEDIA"> <- Media used for presentation (Text-To-Speech)
   <xsl:attribute name="name">TTS</xsl:attribute>
   <xsl:element name=" address_book">
    <xsl:for-each select="person">
     <xsl:element name="person">
      <xsl:copy-of select="lastname"/>
      <xsl:copy-of select="firstname"/>
     </xsl:element>
    </xsl:for-each>
   </xsl:element>
  </xsl:element>
 </xsl:element>
</xsl:template>
```

Second point of a presentation policy specification: *Media and choreography information*

First point of a presentation policy specification: *Which information parts (XML Elements) must be presented.*

**Fig. 3.** XSLT Templates (1) for the two first points of the presentation policy.

Media profile part:

```
<xsl:template match="address_book">
  <xsl:element name="SENT">
    <xsl:for-each select="person">
      <xsl:value-of select="lastname"/>
      <xsl:text> </xsl:text>
      <xsl:value-of select="firstname"/>
      <xsl:element name="BREAK"/>
    </xsl:for-each>
  </xsl:element>
</xsl:template>
```

Third point of a presentation policy specification:
Java Speech Markup Langage tags[11]
*How information is adapted to the media.*

**Fig. 4.** XSLT Templates (1) describing the third point of the presentation policy.

Concerning navigation policies, we also use the "policies" schema for specifying them. Because modeling a navigation policy is quite similar to modeling a presentation policy, we will not give more details concerning this topic.

## 5 Conclusion and Future Work

In this article, we introduce the concept of policy (user policy). The goal of these policies is to improve information accessibility for a given user. This concept results in the specification of user preferences in terms of presentation and interaction with information. We adapt, on one hand, this concept to the presentation of information (presentation policy) and, on the other hand, to the navigation through informational content (navigation policy).

Personalizing presentation and interaction using multimedia possibilities can be very interesting for disabled people (like blind or visually impaired people) that are not able to use common devices for accessing information (for blind or visually impaired people: screen and mouse). Presentation policy generates, according to user preferences, a multimedia presentation from textual XML information. Navigation policy specifies what kind of navigation actions a user can perform on a given information element and - according to the performed action - the targeted information elements.

We illustrate how a presentation policy and navigation policy can be implemented by indicating some elements of modeling using XML technologies.

The objective is to integrate the user policies in a more complete user model (i.e. profile). User models, gathering information about the user (system assumptions concerning user goals, knowledge, etc.), already exist. These models are used to give an adapted informational content to the user. Presentation policies, navigation policies and etc. can be integrated to this kind of models in order to have a user-adapted informational content and also a user-adapted presentation/interaction with information.

Presentation and navigation policies given in examples were purposefully "simples" for teaching reasons, using most of time only one medium. However, several media can be used in order to have a richer multimedia presentation. In this case, user profile construction, including various policies, quickly becomes tiresome.

Tools facilitating the edition of profiles, the construction of policies, must be developed. The ideal framework would be to develop a multimedia browser of XML documents, taking into account all features of these policies.

In this article, only the concepts of presentation policy and navigation policy have been studied but others kinds of policy - like exploration policy (giving overviews concerning the structure of a document) - must also be studied in-depth.

Finally, we have to study the impact, in terms of cognitive and ergonomic load and generally speaking in terms of user performance, of the tools implementing these concepts. We will propose a test protocol studying, in a comparative way, the behavior of disabled users: on one hand facing of a multimedia (X)HTML documents browser (implementing user policies concepts), on the other hand facing of a dedicated Web browser.

## References


1. Web Accessibility Initiative
   W3C - http://www.w3.org/WAI/
2. Alternative Web Browsing, Browsers specifically designed for people with disabilities. W3C - Web Accessibility Initiative
   http://www.w3.org/WAI/References/Browsing.html#1
3. Brusilovsky, P.: Adaptive hypermedia: the state of the art. In Proc.of MHVR'94 Multimedia, Hypermedia and Virtual Reality (Moscow, Sep. 14-16, 1994), ICSTI, 24-29
4. Brusilovsky, P.: Adaptive hypermedia User Modeling and User-Adapted Interaction Volume 11, Issue 1-2, 2001, 87-110 Kluwer Academic Publishers
   http://ipsapp008.kluweronline.com/content/getfile/5219/12/3/fulltext.pdf
5. Fink, J., Kobsa, A. and Nill, A.: Adaptable and Adaptive Information. Provision for All Users, Including Disabled and Elderly People.
   The New Review of Hypermedia and Multimedia Volume 4 (1998), 163-188
   http://www.ics.uci.edu/ kobsa/papers/1998-NRHM-kobsa.pdf
6. W3C, Extensible Markup Language (XML) 1.0 (Second Edition)
   http://www.w3.org/TR/REC-xml
7. DAISY 3, ANSI/NISO Z39.86-2002 standard
   http://www.niso.org/standards/resources/Z39-86-2002.html
8. W3C, Synchronized Multimedia Integration Language (SMIL 2.0)
   http://www.w3.org/TR/smil20/
9. XML Path Language (XPath) http://www.w3.org/TR/xpath
10. W3C, XSL Transformations (XSLT) Version 1.0 http://www.w3.org/TR/xslt
11. Sun Microsystems, Inc., Java Speech API Markup Language Specification
    http://java.sun.com/products/java-media/speech/forDevelopers/JSML/

# Living, Teaching and Learning at Any Time and at Any Place. e-Learning – Opportunities and Barriers for Visually Impaired Students

Joachim Klaus

Study Center for Blind and Partially Sighted Students
Universität Karlsruhe (TH) Germany
klaus@szs.uni-karlsruhe.de
www.szs.uni-karlsruhe.de

**Abstract.** e-Learning as a new integrative and ubiquitous environment in academic teaching and learning opens new opportunities for students with disabilities. At the same time there are new barriers just overcome in electronic communication and interaction. The Notebook University – a model project at the Universitaet Karlsruhe (TH) experiences the different parts of a comprehensive wireless teaching and learning surrounding. The Study Center for Blind and Partially Sighted Students – as a micro project in between – focuses on the special opportunities and barriers for visually impaired students. Personal experiences, case studies and tests of assistive technology result in documentations, final recommendations and an open cooperative homepage.

The information technology is characterized by a tremendous change and a half-time of knowledge. To be able to follow or to contribute to these developments demands a continuous willingness and preparedness – a life long learning attitude. Being involved in this learning process means socialization – social competence and personal communication skills. Regarding the ubiquity of the computer world, the process of penetration of our private and professional life is unstoppable – and there was and still is the promise that a linked global society leads to further democratization and more social justice. The internet is an important medium, but

- who is controlling or is it still possible to be a transparent system for the individual end user and
- is it realistic to think of a global democratically entitled institution to guarantee peace, social justice and welfare – confronted with powerful interests and their representatives?

Society and informatics have to oppose these challenges of a well understood assessment and structuring of the effects of the technology regarding a world with a human face.

Everybody of us – being a responsible partner in our society – has to put these questions and add his/her competence and involvement.

If we regard – in this context – the situation of people with disabilities we have to realize a vast gap of inclusion and exclusion, an assistive technology developed and

K. Miesenberger et al. (Eds.): ICCHP 2004, LNCS 3118, pp. 151–156, 2004.

progressing regardless the individual necessities: accessibility, availability, affordability, awareness and appropriateness are the key words, if we want to realize an information society for all like proclaimed by the European Commission.

e-Europe demands a dominating role of education in order to be able to bridge the gap.

Concerning the Higher Education level the German Ministry of Education and Research sponsored 22 notebook universities toward the development of new didactic concepts, educational inclusions of teacher and learner and correspondent organizational environments. Mobile devices are to open permanent connections to modern teaching software, networks and databases.

Guaranteed access to modern learning technology – disregarding social or financial barriers – that's the Governments' mission!

The Universitaet Karlsruhe (TH) was one of these sponsored universities – intending to enrich daily education by introducing the modern organisational form of "Notebook University".

The characteristics of the Notebook University will become an integral part of living, researching and especially of teaching and learning at the university.

The aim of the project comprises in addition to the creation of organisation and management structures for a notebook university, which are presently being realised, also the development of application specific basic services. These basic services will support the production of ubiquitous e-learning applications. Furthermore, the place and time independent utilisation of various teaching materials and information - provided by different institutions as well as students and staff of the university - will be coordinated by basic services and adjusted to personal or location-dependent requirements.

In addition to the basic services, another objective is the realisation of numerous ubiquitous e-learning application scenarios from different domains of the university, in order to develop an exemplary Notebook University environment. The expected early and continuous gleaning of pedagogic and didactic experience, in the context of the Notebook University, will be reused towards the constant improvement of organisational structures, curricula and media competence. Furthermore there will be many other interesting insights, experience and perspectives which are presently not foreseeable.

The Universitaet Karlsruhe (TH) sees four main foci in the coming years with regard to the integration of this organisational form into university education:

- Organisation, Production and Utilisation – Coordination and management of the organisational form Notebook University
- Ubiquitous e-Learning and Knowledge Transfer Applications – Teaching material, presentations, simulations, exercises etc. in multimedia form by the faculties, institutes and members of the university
- Ubiquitous Support Services – Support by application-specific, quality-increasing and cost-reducing basic services for the production and utilisation of ubiquitous e-learning and knowledge transfer applications
- Infrastructure and Environment for ubiquitous access – To operate the most modern available communications networks, support different access methods and utilisation possibilities.

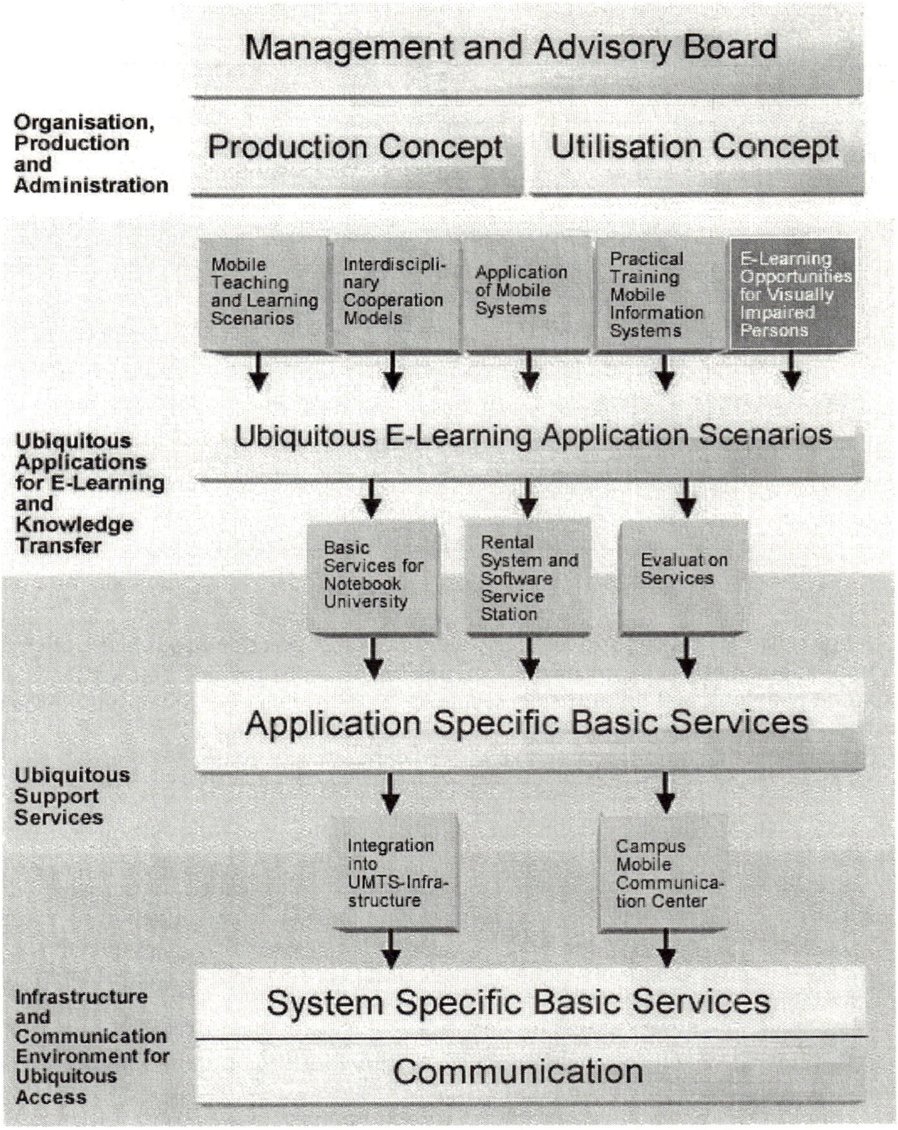


**Fig. 1.** Notebook University Universitaet Karlsruhe (TH)

The Study Centre for Blind and Partially Sighted Students was involved into this programme dedicated to the special questions:

- Do these new developments offer new opportunities for this group of students with disabilities or
- are there new barriers which in a first step have to be recognized and determined in their personal, social and educational consequences?

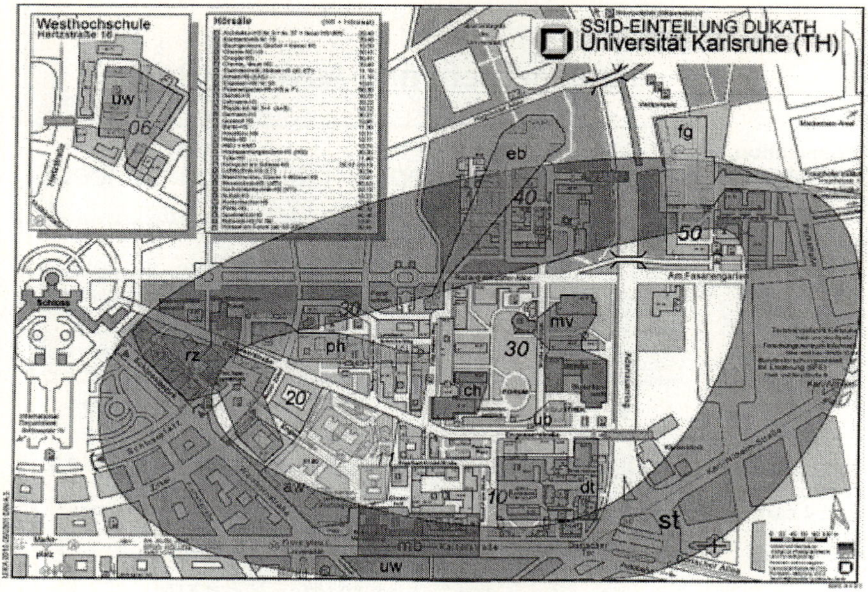


**Fig. 2.** Wireless Network

In this sense the project had an important transversal function towards the other e-learning application scenarios of the participating faculties besides its own focus on visual impairment and information technology. This bilateral dimension opened methods of participatory research and the inclusion of our students.

The conflict situation in processing with our project was the fact of generalization on the basis of few visually impaired students involved.

1. The Practical Training "Mobile Information Systems" was followed by one blind student.
   How to use his personal remarks as a feedback for this lecture and in which dimension to transfer into the general mission of the Notebook University?
2. The special scenarios of the SZS were supported and answered by some ten students – blind and partially sighted – depending on their special interest and time available.
   Is it justifiable to take their presentations as a version that can be generalised to inform the peer students and to train the teaching staff to promote a higher sensibility of the university community?

If you consider the social disability research you find a strong discussion on inclusion vs. exclusion of disabled people. Mainstream research is seen as failing disabled people.

"Disabled people have come to see research as a violation of their experience, as irrelevant to their needs and as failing to improve their material circumstances and quality of life"[1] and correspondant the comments of Barnes: "The social model of

[1] Oliver, M. 1992: Changing the social relations of research production in: Disability, Handicap and Society, 7 (2), 105.

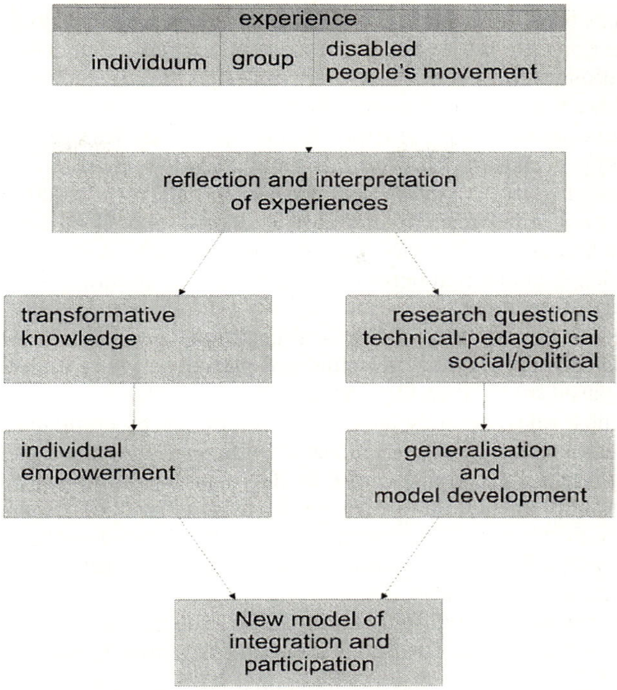


**Fig. 3.** From Experience to Standardization

disability represents nothing more complicated than a focus on the economic, environmental and cultural barriers encountered by people viewed by others as having some form of impairment."[2]

The philosophy of the SZS – based up the starting phase in 1987 on electronic communication, interaction and learning – is to regard visually impaired students as qualified as their non-disabled peers with the same educational surroundings and their demands, getting their degrees like the others. They get an equal competence for integrating into the labour market and taking correspondent positions.

Consequently, a team of staff members of the SZS and visually impaired students applied themselves to the following fields:

1. Blind students at work.
   Course selection – Preparing for a course – technical aids – communication and interaction.
2. Partially sighted students at work.
   The importance of the viewing field – Optical aids – Computers with magnification software and speech output – Mobile and stationary camera systems – A healthy mix.

---

[2] Barnes, C. 2003: What a difference a decade makes: reflections on doing, emancipatory' research.
Disability and Society, 18 (1), 9.

3. File formats used in Higher Education - barriers for visually impaired students.
   Via a questionnaire the different file formats were tested and evaluated and recommendations were given for lecturers to design their materials in such way that barriers were removed or at least reduced.
4. Use of multimedia - the presentation forms and barrier-free versions.
   Via learning scenarios the working group developed, experienced and documented the methods of interaction during al lecture (interaction between students, interaction between lecturers and students) as well as the communication and interaction during the work process before and after a lecture (interaction between students, interaction between students and lecturers).
5. Availability of documents.
   The different presentation forms – illustrations and texts – were evaluated concerning their accessibility for blind and partially sighted students.
6. Study aids used by blind and by partially sighted students.
   Here the most relevant study aids were – supported by companies who produce those assistive technology – tested and documented. In this way the SZS became something like a competence centre for German and European producers. Concerning the implementation of their products into the higher educational process there is a high interest of the companies, which can be of profit for both sides – users and companies – and in addition for technical counsellors.
7. Acoustic and light conditions.
   Finally there were as well discussed topics like the acoustic of audience and lecture rooms and their light conditions including situations in open air lecturing.

All these scenarios, results and recommendations are to be found in the SZS-homepage (both English and German version):
`http://elba.szs.uni-karlsruhe.de`

# Accessibility for e-Learning Environments

Mari Luz Guenaga[1], Dominique Burger[2], and Javier Oliver[1]

[1] Grupo MIRA. Facultad de Ingeniería-ESIDE, Universidad de Deusto
Avda. de las Universidades, 24, Bilbao
{mlguenag,oliver}@eside.deusto.es
[2] Association BrailleNet
INSERM U483 – UPMC B23
9, quay Saint Bernard
75252 Paris cedex 05
Dominique.Burger@snv.jussieu.fr

**Abstract.** All entities involved in creating, managing and using e-Learning content and tools have a great challenge making it accessible for students and instructors with disabilities. Current accessibility guidelines have to be concreted and adapted to this context, so they can find the way to make learning process accessible and usable without too much additional work. There are complex elements, concepts and structures in e-Learning, difficult to transmit to people with disabilities and that are out of the scope of current guidelines.

## 1 Introduction

Internet has contributed in a very significant way to the construction of the Information Society we enjoy nowadays; it provides services and content anytime to all people who can connect anywhere. One of the important uses of the Internet in particular, and the information and communication technologies (ICT) in general is education, the so called e-Learning. Teachers, instructional designers, engineers and all entities involved in the process of providing e-Learning have been working more than 20 years in creating the tools, platforms, methodologies, content and services to provide high quality learning experiences to all kind of target students.

Learning management system (LMS) providers have developed very good and broadly used products like WebCT, Blackboard, Macromedia e-Learning Suite or Docent Enterprise Suite. They provide all the functionality an educational institution may need. A new challenge for them will be to provide these services for all, which means that people with disabilities should be able to use, as a teacher or as a student, all the services, content and tools included in the LMS.

Being aware of the opportunities that ICT and e-Learning offers to people with disabilities is the responsibility of all entities involved in the creation, development and providing of e-Learning to facilitate the access at a moderate cost and to promote its use [6]. Now that many teaching innovations are being made, the needs of students with disabilities must be taking into account [9], otherwise they will be excluded. For achieving this aim, there is no need of different versions of all educational resources and tools for each group of target users, but a *design for all* methodology has to be adopted.

In this paper we will analyze the accessibility problems faced by different user profiles involved in eLearning experiences when they use the set of tools included in

K. Miesenberger et al. (Eds.): ICCHP 2004, LNCS 3118, pp. 157–163, 2004.

LMSs. Although guidelines and specifications are being provided everyday, they can not cover all the aspects for a correct application to eLearning context, due to some difficulties we will expose. Many institutions and organizations are working in the specification of the features and techniques needed by present and future accessible eLearning tools, like design-for-all methodologies, usability, user-centered design or adaptability to different user.

## 2 Accessibility

Web Accessibility Initiative (WAI) guidelines are the result of the compromise that the World Wide Web Consortium (W3C) adopted to promote the use of ICT for people with disabilities. Collaborating with organizations all over the world, they are making a great effort to promote accessibility, mainly for the Internet, through five main areas of work and R&D, which are technology, guidelines, tools, education and contact. Their best result is the published and broadly used guidelines [11]:

- Web Content Accessibility Guidelines 1.0. (WCAG) Explains in detail how to make a Web site accessible for people with a variety of disabilities.
- Authoring Tool Accessibility Guidelines 1.0. (ATAG) For software developers, explains how to make a variety of authoring tools support the production of accessible Web content, and also how to make the software itself accessible.
- User Agent Accessibility Guidelines 1.0. (UAAG) For software developers, explains how to make accessible browsers, multimedia players, and assistive technologies that interface with these.
- XML Accessibility Guidelines. (XMLAG) For developers of XML-based applications, explains how to ensure that XML-based applications support accessibility.

IMS Global Learning Consortium [4] has published specific guidelines for developing accessible learning applications and content. They have provided specifications to organize learner information (IMS Profiles and enterprise system), interchange content and assessments with any LMS (IMS Content Packaging and IMS Question & Test Interoperability) and describe learning resources created and used in different LMS (IMS Learning Resources Meta-Data).

## 3 e-Learning

Different technologies have been used in the different eras of e-Learning, and as new technologies emerge they are applied and used in e-Learning. These changes have promoted the several names that have been given to e-Learning styles and tools during the years, for example Computer Based Training (CBT), Computer Managed Instruction (CMI), Distributed Online Learning (DOL), Learning Management System (LMS) or Learning Virtual Environment (LVE). Finally, they are a set of tools, more or less complex, to be used by three main user profiles: system administrators, teachers and students.

Many and good LMSs have been developed, in which you can find all the functionality you may need. The problem they faced some years ago was that they worked with proprietary formats, so if users wanted to share educational content or change the LMS, they have to rewrite all the content in the new format, this makes them be attached to the provider. They see the need of creating specification and standards to avoid these problems. Many organizations like IEEE, IMS, ADL or AICC worked to create standards like SCORM [7], IMS Global Learning Consortium specifications [3] or IEEE LTSC Learning Object Metadata standard [5]. This makes educational content interoperable, reusable, flexible and durable, so authors can develop educational content from previously developed chunks of information, reusing it when needed and running it in any LMS that conforms the same standard.

Content and tools included in the LMS should also be accessible, that means that people with disabilities should be able to use and access all the information provided for the learning experience, regardless the type or degree of disability they suffer. Later we will see the accessibility problems of current e-Learning environments.

As well as accessible, the LMS and educational content has to be usable. "Usability is the quality of a system that makes it easy to learn, easy to use, easy to remember, error tolerant, and subjectively pleasing" [10] Nowadays, designers and developers are creating user-centered interfaces, customizable, easily internationalizable and personalizable, in this way, target teachers and students would have an efficient and satisfactory usage of ICT.

Leporini [1] proposes 16 criteria to improve the usability of accessible web pages read by screen-readers. These criteria are classified in presentation guidelines, how the interface provides information to the user, and dialogue, describes how the actions made by the user and by the system can be sequencialized.

TechDis proposes seven precepts of usability and accessibility [8]. Some of these precepts are closely related to WAI ATAG 1.0 accessibility guidelines, others go beyond, in order to improve the navigation mechanism and structure, content structure, organization and design.

In the technologies world the future is focused in mobile devices, that as well as the desired features of a computer (multimedia capabilities, data input/output devices, connectivity...) they offer good price and very small size. These devices have to become accessible for people with disabilities, because they are very valuable and useful for them.

After analyzing several e-Learning platforms, tools, LMS and virtual campus you can determine what the functionality is they offer, what kind of content they generate or the target users of each part of the system. We will briefly classify the services included in most of the e-Learning systems, the tools provided, the actions each user can do and the accessibility problems they have to overcome.

### 3.1 Educational Content Authoring Tool

It is one of the most complex tools of LMSs; it has to enable the teacher the edition of complete educational content from scratch, the linking or insertion of external objects and media, as well as the linking of internal parts of the course.

The complexity of authoring tools can vary very much depending on the capability for creating media and composing it to create educational content, or if they are more integrating tools of external media. If media can be created with the LMS their level of accessibility can be controlled more easily than if it integrates external media, in this case, accessibility is more difficult to assure, because it relies mainly in the knowledge and responsibility of the instructor. The systems should provide the author all the guidelines, techniques, information and tools needed to know how to make this external media accessible.

The LMS should help and encourage teachers to create accessible content in a natural way, not only providing guidelines to be followed by instructors, like many current systems do, but assuring that these are followed, providing an automatic control and way to conform of guidelines. For example, the system should ask for alternative media to make it accessible for all target users, emulators and additional tools can help authors to understand how users will perceive the content (text only browser, voice browser, black and white screens, disability of the mouse...), accessible templates could be provided to create all kind of contents or assessments, tools for synchronizing text, speech, sound and images would improve the equivalency of formats, and so on. These kinds of tools would improve in a perceivable way the accessibility of educational experiences.

All tools provided to create, check and validate educational content should be accessible for teachers and system administrators with disabilities. This checking should be personalized by the author, so he / she can control the level of accessibility to be reached, the moment of checking (during the editing process or on-demand), the guidelines to be followed or the kind of report he / she wants to get.

e-Learning path and tracking of learner's activity are elements difficult to understand and overview for people with disabilities. Users have to be able to create and manage the mental structure of the learning experience they are taking or creating, and know which part of the content has been visited or which assessment has been done. The LMS should provide different and personalizable styles of giving this information, with different levels of detail and transmitting the connection between educational pieces of content, assessment or resources.

## 3.2 Asynchronous Communication and Collaboration Tools

Tools like shared workspaces, document repositories, discussion forums, organizers, schedulers and bulletin boards are available anytime for teachers and students.

The system administrator is responsible of managing the permissions of different users. Teachers can manage the permissions of students or students' groups, add, modify or remove resources uploaded in shared workspaces or messages from forums or bulletin boards, moderate discussions and manage forum categories.

Finally, students are the target of all this information. Depending on their privileges they are also able to upload resources or participate actively in discussion forums and put messages on the bulletin board.

All users of asynchronous tools have to be able to locate and scan items easily, follow the thread and flow of discussions and post responses or messages.

## 3.3 Synchronous Communication and Collaboration Tools

The most common and broadly used synchronous tool is the chat or instant messenger. It is a very appropriate tool for online tutoring, problem solving between students and teacher, and promotes an active participation of students in their learning process. Many of these tools allow the sharing of files, whiteboards or applications, which is very useful in collaborative work.

Other synchronous tools are audio/video-conferencing, which transmits audio and video instead of plain text, and Multi-user Domain Object Oriented Environments (MOOs), virtual worlds where users are represented and interact like avatars.

In these kinds of tools, system administrators manage permission of users and chat rooms, teachers moderate the discussion and do the necessary actions for a normal flow of events, while students are the main characters of the process, and participate asking and answering questions and problems or topics proposed by the teacher.

The main accessibility problems faced in synchronous tools are the difficulties in following the flow and rhythm of events and communication, the need to convert text-to-speech and speech-to-text in real time, the necessary description of images and virtual environments in real time. Users who communicate slowly have more problems with these tools and special care has to be taken, especially if the group is formed by heterogeneous users.

In these kind of tools the instructor or administrator has a very important role, because he / she has to assure that all students are able to follow the flow of events, and take the necessary decisions if it is not like this. The system has to provide tools to stop messaging, slow down the flow or modify user's priority.

### 3.4 Testing and Assessment. Students' Progress and Reporting

Testing and assessment usually includes the most common tools to manage multiple choice like exercises, fill in the blank or relate items activities, which are easily evaluable by the LMS. The results of these exercises have to be recorded and reported to teachers and students, so they can see individual or collective progress, difficulties or problems in any of the educational content, and teachers should also be able to modify the learning path, activities or style, if needed.

All accessibility problems mentioned before apply also to testing and assessment, as well as those derived from the importance of testing.

You have to distinguish between formative assessment, that has not serious consequences in the student's activity, and high-stake assessment, like the test to register on a given course, that has serious consequences for them. Several times accessibility features conflict with assessment validity, which is why e-Learning providers and instructors who design assessments have to be especially careful and assure that no group of students has advantage over the others.

## 4 Accessibility of Current LMS

Accessibility guidelines and specifications described before do not cover all the needs of accessible e-Learning. As guidelines, they are very general and try to cover the most contexts, usages and target users as possible, so when they have to be applied to a concrete context, it is difficult to find the way to do it. For example, one of the guidelines provided by the ATAG says "Ensure that the authoring tool is accessible to authors with disabilities". This affirmation is obvious, but the problem is how to make it real.

On the other hand, most guidelines focus on content, presentation and media, but e-Learning is much more than this, it includes the edition and visualization of the e-Learning path, synchronous and asynchronous communication and collaboration tools, assessments, exercises, interaction, tracking...so developers find a lack of guidelines to make these basic elements of e-Learning accessible.

Other devices besides personal computers are being used to provide and receive e-Learning, for example Pocket PC, Personal Digital Assistants or Tablet PCs. These also should be accessible to be used by people with disabilities.

Recent developments in speech technology have led to improvements in quality and accuracy and a reduction in prices. This is important for people with disabilities since speech technology can be used for communication, access to information and control of the environment [2]. Speech synthesis is a stable technology, but speech recognition is still inadequate when compared with human capabilities.

For many software vendors, user-friendly computer interfaces is directly applied as GUIs (graphical user interfaces). This means a need of training and many problems in the speed of use of these systems for people with disabilities.

Most broadly used LMSs do not include tools and advanced systems to provide accessibility on the content they generate, authors have guidelines, documentation and help to know how to make content accessible, for example: "you have to provide alternative media for disabled people", "you have to synchronize text and speech", "you have to assure that tables linearize correctly" or "you have to use headline markups for titles". It should not be responsibility of the author to know how to apply all these recommendations, he / she has to create and design educational content and guide learners in their experience, he / she has not to become an expert on accessibility to become an e-Learning instructor.

## 5 Conclusions

Accessible e-Learning gives the opportunity to many students and instructors with disabilities to use ICT as a tool to study or work. These technologies have great advantages over other methods used before, their multimodal capabilities makes it easier to provide equivalent information and services in different formats.

Content and LMS providers could think of creating different versions of the products for each kind of target users, but they have to realize that this is useless, because the number of different users can be extremely high. A design for all has to be made, and then provide interfaces and tools to personalizable and adapt to different users or contexts.

Designers do not have to forget usability, it is not enough the conformance all accessibility guidelines, and the application or content can remain useless if users are not satisfied with the experience.

The LMS, as well as the tools needed to create the e-Learning experience, has to provide personalizable tools to automatically check and repair accessibility and usability problems. Following the clear and concrete instructions of the LMS the author should be able to create accessible educational content in a natural way, from the beginning of the process and without adding special complexity.

Finally, educational standards and specifications, like SCORM, and standard formats and technologies, like XML or XHTML, should be used to assure accessibility and interoperability of tools and content.

## References


1. Leporini, B., Paternò, F.: "Criteria for Usability of Accessible Web Sites", Proceedings 4th Edition User Interface for All, Springer Verlag.
2. Dr John Gill. Royal National Institution for the Blind. The Design of Man-Machine Interfaces for Use by Visually Disabled People. http://www.tiresias.org
3. IMS Global Learning Consortium. Open specifications for Interoperable Learning Technology. http://www.imsglobal.org
4. IMS Guidelines for Developing Accessible Learning Applications. http://www.imsglobal.org/accessibility
5. Learning Object Metadata. IEEE Learning Technology Standard Committee (LTSC). http://ltsc.ieee.org
6. Multimedia technologies and the Internet for education, training and lifelong learning in Europe. ElearningEuropa.info. http://www.elearningeuropa.info
7. Shareable Content Object Reference Model. Advanced Distributed Learning (ADL) Initiative. http://www.adlnet.org
8. Techdis Website. Seven precepts of Usability and Accessibility: http://www.techdis.ac.uk/index.html
9. The Joint Information System Committee. Accessibility: making ICT available to everyone. http://www.jisc.ac.uk
10. Usable Information Technology. Useit.com: Jakob Nielsen's Website: http://www.useit.com
11. W3C Web Accessibility Initiative. http://www.w3c.org/wai

# ECDL-PD: International Co-operation to Keep the Syllabus and MQTB Open for Everybody

Klaus Miesenberger[1], Martin Morandell[1], Andrea Petz[1], and Denise Leahy[2]

[1] "integriert studieren/integrated study" University of Linz
Altenbergerstraße 69, A-4040 Linz, Austria
Tel: +43-(0)732-2468 9232, Fax: +43–(0)732–2468 9322
morandell@gmx.at
{klaus.miesenberger,andrea.petz}@jku.at
[2] Department of Computer Science, Trinity College
Dublin 2, Ireland
denise.leahy@cs.tcd.ie

**Abstract.** The ECDL, a world wide accepted standard certificate on the basic skills in using computers, offers opportunities for people with disabilities to support their vocational integration. By focusing on the accessibility of the certificate for four target groups of people with disability, the ECDL-PD project will create a forum for all involved in ECDL to understand the needs, issues and solutions in order to accommodate people with disabilities to achieve the certification without changing the standard.

## 1 ECDL

The European Computer Driving Licence (ECDL is an internationally recognized computer skills certification programme. ECDL was launched in August 1996 and it was planned that it should try to gain Europe wide acceptance as soon as possible.[1] It now has almost 4 million participants in more than 130 countries. This industry standard is promoted by the ECDL Foundation. Outside Europe, ECDL is known as ICDL (International Computer Driving Licence)[1]. It is exactly the same certification, with the same syllabus and procedures.

ECDL is accepted as a standard of core computer literacy. In order to maintain this standard, much work has been done in the areas of validation of tests, quality of tests, testing methods and procedures. ECDL certifies that the holder has knowledge of the essential concepts of IT and is able to use a personal computer and common professional computer application at a recognised level of competence.

ECDL is run within its member countries by a network of Test Centres which are managed by a local ECDL licensee. This licensee is usually, although not always, the local Informatics or Computer Society. [2]

[1] All references to ECDL includes ICDL.

K. Miesenberger et al. (Eds.): ICCHP 2004, LNCS 3118, pp. 164–170, 2004.

## 2 ECDL as a Standard

ECDL is created by an international panel of subject matter experts with input from the ECDL community, from members of computer societies world wide and from test centres, teachers and trainers.

The ECDL syllabus is open to the public and published on the ECDL web site [www.ecdl.com]. The ECDL tests are confidential and are available only to members of the ECDL community.

Strict quality control procedures are in place. Tests may be run using manual test evaluation or automated test evaluation. The manual tests are developed by the ECDL Foundation expert group and are translated for each country. The automated tests consist of test engine, test database and administration modules. These have to be approved by the expert team at the ECDL Foundation. Standards for the duration of tests, content to be examined and methods have been defined. The ECDL Foundation has created a Characterisation Test Template (CTT) which defines the requirements for each test. [3]

Procedures for approving Test Centres and for running tests are defined. These are followed by all countries. Quality audits are carried out at national and international level. At national level the test centres are visited and reviewed on a regular basis by the local licensee. Internationally, a team of auditors visits each country to review all the procedures. These are representatives from an international panel of auditors managed by the Quality Assurance Committee of the ECDL Foundation. [4]

## 3 ECDL-PD

The ECDL for people with disabilities (ECDL-PD) is a Leonardo Da Vinci Project, which aims at adapting the widespread and well-known ECDL certificate to the needs of people with disabilities. It is important that ECDL-PD does not create a special or reduced ECDL. The standard must be maintained while addressing the needs identified in the ECDL-PD project. The findings from the project will be validated according to ECDL standards. The ECDL should not only become a tool for people with disabilities, but also for the increasing number of under-represented people on the labour market (e. g. elderly people, people with poor education, people from a poorer social background, immigrants ...).

*The basic philosophy of ECDL-PD is to keep the certificate untouched.* The focus is on accessibility of the Syllabus and the MQTB (Manual Question and Test Base) as well as better training, teaching and learning.

ECDL should become a tool to foster the vocational integration of people with disabilities. It should also help training providers to improve the quality of their training as well as higher the attractively of their programs by orienting towards and international business standard.

The main advantages of the ECDL for people with special needs are the product independence and that testing is independent from training. ECDL is open to everyone, regardless of age, education, experience or background. ECDL is basically very flexible towards the organisation of testing; this allows flexibility with regards to accessibility. ECDL believes it is its mission to address all people including those with disabilities [4].

## 4 Accessibility Evaluation of the Syllabus and the MQTB [5,6,7] by Making Use of a Dynamic Internet Tool

"Evaluation" must not be understood as working on changes to the standard. Evaluation means providing clarification of how test items and other issues should be addressed to meet the needs of the candidate. Evaluation searches for examples and best practice on how to overcome critical aspects in the Syllabus and the MQTB. As the ECDL Foundation is involved and hosting this forum in the long run by an ECDL Foundation working group, serious problems which need further clarification and perhaps adaptations of the Syllabus or the MQTB will be fed into the relevant channels of the Foundation. Only after checking the compliance with the standard and passing the quality assurance procedures such alternatives might be used.

Based on the fact that the Syllabus is open to everyone, but the MQTB just to authorized persons, the evaluation tools are also separated in an open part ("Syllabus") and the strictly secured part for the "MQTB".

### 4.1 Syllabus

The syllabus is the curriculum of the ECDL. It specifies all skills, which should be known for each of the 7 modules:

1. Basic Concepts of Information Technology
2. Using a Computer and Managing Files
3. Word Processing
4. Spreadsheets
5. Database
6. Presentation
7. Information and Communication

It is designed and regularly updated by a panel of international experts to ensure its relevance to the working world and the advances in technologies and practices.

**Syllabus Accessibility.** ECDL PD evaluates the ECDL Syllabus for people with disabilities in order to find barriers for different groups of people with disabilities in the description of the content and the definition how the different tasks have to be fulfilled. Based on this analysis, proposals of methodologies, techniques and arrangements to overcome these barriers are made and presented to the ECDL Foundation. These proposals for solutions have to be evaluated by the ECDL Foundation so that the proposals are in accordance with the general guidelines and the level of ECDL. Only if in accordance with the general ECDL Quality requirements, these solutions are collected and presented as so called "Syllabus accessibility evaluation tool".

**Dynamic Syllabus Accessibility Evaluation Tool.** This section will specify how the Syllabus accessibility work should be done after the end of the project and how users and experts at international level should get involved by making use of an Internet based system.

These solutions are the recommendations of the project team and will be presented to the ECDL Foundation at the end of the project.

The evaluation tool scheme consists of three main parts:

- The tool itself: Provides information about the Syllabus Modules, their barriers for the specific target groups and possible solutions, techniques and methodologies to overcome them.
- The Open Forum: an open place to discuss barriers, problems and their solutions, specific to ECDL. For every Syllabus Module an additional FAQ-section should be provided.
- The Expert Forum: There should be an Expert Forum where members can address issues. The ECDL Foundation group should discuss submitted solutions and proposals, which should be added to Syllabus accessibility evaluation tool.

The page is kept very simple and clear. It has to be easy to use for everyone, and accessible for the specific target groups. The Evaluations are divided into the different target groups, the 7 Modules and major known categorized problems. They can be accessed by filling in a form of three questions.

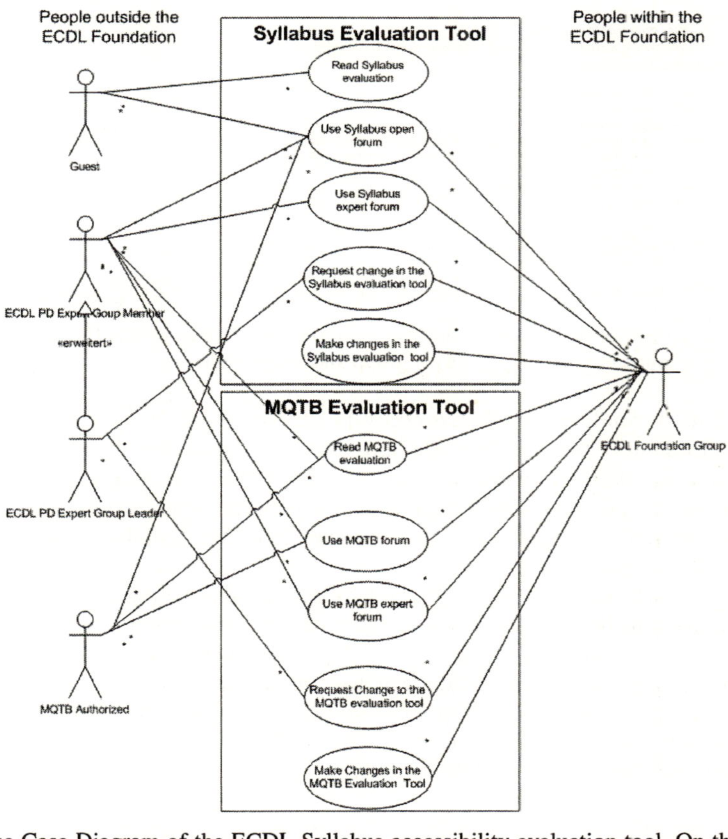


**Fig. 1.** Use Case Diagram of the ECDL Syllabus accessibility evaluation tool. On the left side are the users who don't have to be members of the ECDL Foundation. In the middle are the tasks, divided into the Syllabus Evaluation Tool and the MQTB Evaluation Tool.. On the right side, are the users who are members of the ECDL Foundation group.

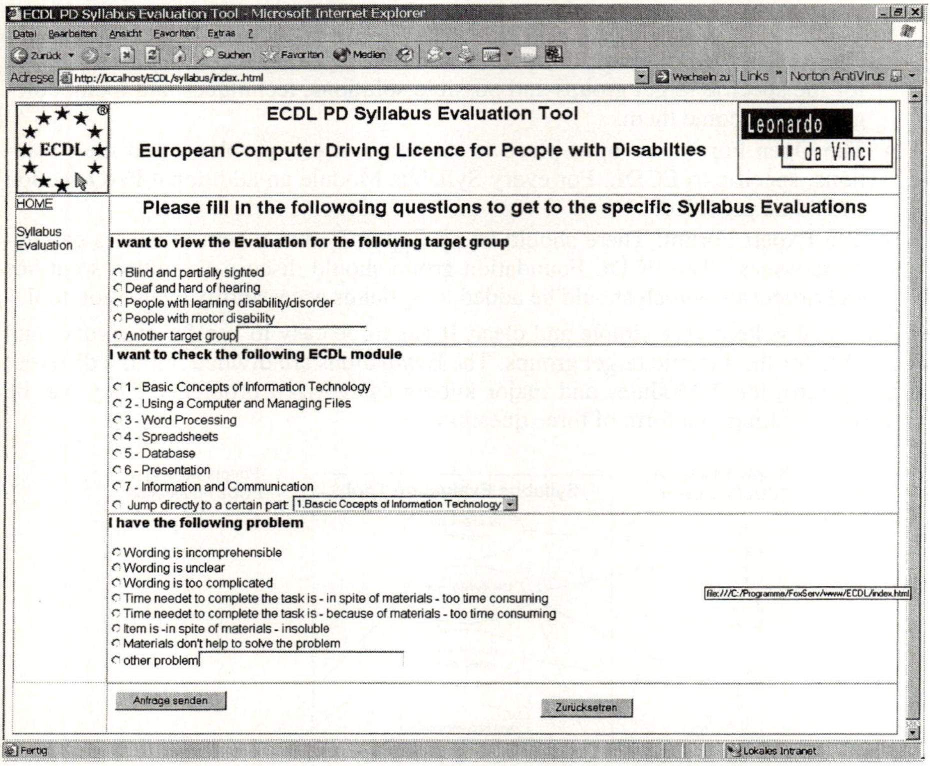


**Fig. 2.** Screenshot of Syllabus accessibility evaluation tool. Filling in this form, the users gets directly to the wanted evaluations of target group and the module.

Afterwards a window split horizontally is shown, at the top the actual Syllabus Module and its (sub) chapters. By selecting a chapter, in the lower frame the notes – the "Evaluations" to this specific question - can be found in the bottom frame.

In case the needed information cannot be found in the actual evaluation, an "Open Forum" is provided, which is also structured like the ECDL Syllabus. There the topics can be discussed by everyone.

The "ECDL-PD Expert Forum" should follow the discussion in the open forum. Topics that seem to be relevant for the evaluation will be discussed in the "ECDL-PD Expert Forum". To make a change to the ECDL PD evaluation tool the Expert Team has to make a suggestion to the ECDL Foundation Group, who, after assuring that the wanted "evaluation" still fits all principles of the ECDL Foundation, makes the changes to the Syllabus evaluation tool. The ECDL Foundation group should also participate in the discussions in both forums.

## 4.2 The MQTB

The Manual Question and Test Base (MQTB) is the catalogue of exam questions. While Syllabus is public domain, the MQTB is confidential. This section will outline

- the structure of the MQTB
- the workflow of updating to new versions and how the evaluation work should be integrated into this procedures

**Accessibility Work.** ECDL PD evaluates the exam questions and provides MQTB clarifications. Again it has to be guaranteed that the level remains unchanged. All materials are evaluated by general ECDL authorities. In addition ECDL-PD also does some evaluation work on automated testing tools and their accessibility and usability for the target groups.

**Dynamic MQTB Accessibility Tool.** This tool specifies how the MQTB accessibility work should be done after the end of the project and how users and experts at international level should get involved by making use of an Internet based system.

Due to the confidentiality of the MQTB, the strict security and access rules have to be guaranteed also for the evaluation reports.

Basically the MQTB tool is structured in accordance to the Syllabus tool, just that the MQTB Forum and the MQTB accessibility evaluation tools cannot be accessed by unauthorized users.

The MQTB evaluations should help the ECDL Test centers to get information how to deal with certain questions resulting from servicing a specific target group.

## 5 Summary

This structure should help to get a very open but serious, versatile platform for all users to develop the concepts of the ECDL-PD project. Additionally, people interested in the ECDL PD will be able to understand how ECDL tests can be made accessible or are already accessible for their specific needs. ECDL candidates will find help available for specific issues and problems. Trainers and Training Centers will get information on how to deal with applicants with special needs and build up effective procedures and strategies for servicing and preparing their clientele in the best way.

By implementing these procedures and tools, people with disabilities, trainers and test centres should get the possibility to find solutions for the training and the test situation for specific target groups and individuals. Based on the pool of experiences, examples of best practice, guidelines and recommendations, people should find a place where they can search for solutions to their problems. At the minimum they will have a forum where they can fill in their comments, questions or solutions to a certain items of the Syllabus Open Forum, or, of course only authorized people, to the MQTB. The goal of this is to address the problems of accessibility for the different target groups of ECDL-PD. The ECDL Foundation group has to make sure that these questions, examples and/or recommendations are taken into account and implemented to improve the accessibility and usability of the certificate for people with disabilities.

At the moment the specification for these evaluation tools is finished. A first prototype will be available at the end of April. A first test version will be available to be presented at the ICCHP conference.

## Acknowledgement

The ECDL PD project is funded by the Leonardo da Vinci program of the European Commission.

## References

1. Carpenter D, Dolan D, Leahy D, Sherwood-Smith M:, ECDL/ICDL: a global computer literacy initiative, in 16th IFIP Congress (ICEUT200, educational uses of information and communication technologies), Beijing, China, August 2000
2. www.ecdl.com
3. Characterisation Test Template, ECDL Foundation, 2003. This is not a public document
4. ECDL Quality Assurance system, EDCL Foundation, 2003. This is not a public document
5. Miesenberger, K.: ECDL/PD European Computer Driving Licence for People with Disabilities in: Vollmar,R., Wagner, R., Computer Helping People with Special Needs, ICCHP '00
6. Petz, A., Miesenberger, K.: ECDL PD Using a Well Known Standard to Lift Barriers on the Labour Market in : Miesenberger, K., Klaus J., Zagler, W.(eds) Computers Helping People with Special Needs, 8th International Conference, ICCHP, Linz, Austria, July, 2002, Springer 2002
7. People with Disabilities, Compendium of Projects 2000 – 2002, LEONARDO DA VINCI, National Agency Austria

# Essential Competencies of Special Educator in Integrating Assistive Technology into the Curriculum

Ming-Chung Chen[1], Ting-Fang Wu[2], and Chi-Nung Chu[3]

[1] Department of Special Education, National Chiayi University
300 University Rd., Chiayi, 600 Taiwan, R.O.C.
ming@chen.twmail.cc
[2] Department of Occupational Therapist, Chung Gung University
259 Weng Hwa 1st Rd., Kweishan, 333 Taoyuan , Taiwan, R.O.C.
tfwu@mail.cgu.edu.tw
[3] Department of Management Information Systems, Chung Cuo Institute of Technology
56 Sec. 1 Shinglung Rd., 116 Taipei, R.O.C.
nung@mail.ckitc.edu.tw

**Abstract.** This study addresses the essential competencies of special educator in integrating assistive technology (AT) into the curriculum. Researchers identified ten categories of skills required to integrate assistive technology, after viewing deliberate literature. Fourteen professionals in special education, rehabilitation and assistive technology formed as a web-based Delphi panel and reviewed the importance of the competencies. Following three rounds of a web-based Delphi survey, 51 statements were determined to be important or very important to AT integration.

## 1 Introduction

Assistive technology (AT) has been regarded as an equalizer for students with disabilities enabling them to access the general educational curriculum, and facilitating their fulfilling potential. However, AT must be integrated into learning activities to enable the benefits of assistive technology to be exploited [3]. Most in the field acknowledge about the importance of the integration of AT into the curriculum and instruction. However, some barriers prevent effective integration of AT into learning activities. One of the most important obstructions is the inadequate training of special education teachers [10].

Following the Special Education Act of 1997 in Taiwan, AT has been considered to be an important service for providing special education to students with disabilities [9]. Educational authorities in Taiwan have implemented numerous training programs related to AT, such as introducing AT and elucidating the manipulation of AT devices, to help special education teachers. Researchers and educational authorities have recently paid more attention to integrating AT into classroom activities and curricula, because of innovations in general education that related to the integration of information technology into instructional activities [1]. However, comprehensive indicators of AT integration are lacking, and are required to help educational authorities evaluate a special education teacher's competencies and organize systematically AT integration training programs.

K. Miesenberger et al. (Eds.): ICCHP 2004, LNCS 3118, pp. 171–177, 2004.

Some professional associations and educational authorities have developed various assistive technology competencies to prepare qualified teachers of special education with AT literacy. Technology and Medial, a division of the Council for Exceptional Children (CEC), has developed 51 statements of important AT competencies based on the CEC's format of Professional Standards. They were developed by AT experts from the U. S. A. through a three-round of Delphi survey [6].

AT competency is not only used to qualify educators, but is also adopted to develop competency-based pre-service AT courses or in-service AT training programs. For instance, the National Association of State Directors of Special Education in the U. S. A. (1998) developed "*Recommended Competencies for Professional Staff Members in the Area of Assistive Technology*" and used these competencies to establish objectives for in-service training programs [8].

AT competency, especially that associated with integrating AT into instructional activities, covers a set of essential skills to be acquired by special educators to enable them to provide the benefits of AT devices to their students with special educational needs. Educational authorities must be aware of the AT skills possessed by special education teachers before setting in-service AT training programs. Therefore, it is necessary to frame a group of representative AT competencies.

Accordingly, the major purpose of this work, funded by the National Science Council of Republic of China, is to develop the essential assistive technology integration competencies that teachers of special education should possess in Taiwan.

## 2 Method

### 2.1 Research Design

A web-based Delphi survey was conducted to collect the experts' opinions through questionnaires. Consistent expert opinions were elicited following numerous rounds of the survey. Some studies with similar goals have also used Delphi surveys [4], [6]. In these studies, a Delphi survey is conducted by mailing a printed questionnaire to experts and processing the data manually after the questionnaires have been returned. However, the delivery of the questionnaires and the processing of data collection are time-consuming. This work adopted a web-based Delphi survey that sent notice to experts via electronic mail and asking them to fill out the questionnaire on a web site using an identifying code and password. The web-based Delphi survey system automatically collected the individual responses after the expert had completed the questionnaire. It then generated a table of all of the experts' responses to each item.

Fourteen professionals from Taiwan in the areas of assistive technology, special education, and rehabilitation constituted an on-line Delphi panel to evaluate the importance of various statements of AT competencies. They discussed each statement in a blind iterative process until they reached agreement.

### 2.2 Tool Development

This study developed two tools for conducting the on-line Delphi survey. One is a statement of AT integration competencies taken from related literature on AT competencies [5], [6] and AT integration [1], [[2], [3]. The other is a web-based Delphi survey system that was developed in HTML and ASP collocated responses with the SQL server. Experts had to login to the system using their code and password before they could fill out the questionnaire.

The frame of AT integration competencies, as shown in Fig. 1, presents two steps. One is *basic competencies*, which fall into three categories - (a) philosophy and law, (b) AT devices and (c) AT service. The other is *integrating competencies*, which fall into seven categories - (a) concepts of AT integration, (b) assessment, (c) selection and acquisition, (d) training, (e) instruction accommodation, (f) implementation and management, (g) resources and support. Based on the definitions of literacy, competency of AT integration is measured on three dimensions: *knowledge* specifies the understanding of the concepts, philosophy and advantages of AT; *skills* represents the capacity to operate AT devices and demonstrate the integration of AT devices during instructional activities; *Dispositions* represents the values and commitment that affect the AT-related behaviors of teachers [7].

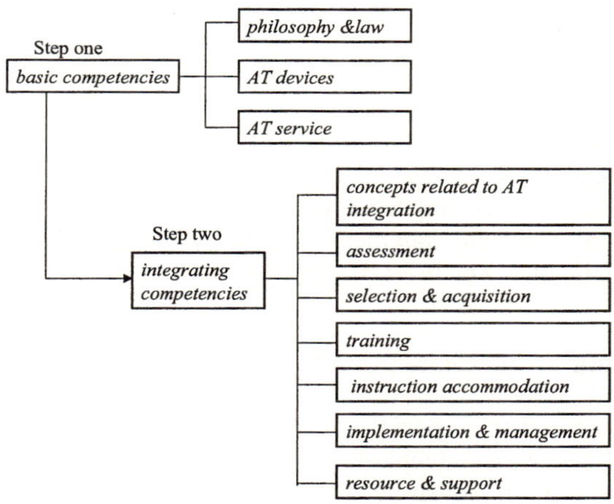


**Fig. 1.** The frame of essential assistive technology integrated competencies.

Researchers developed 55 essential statements after an extensive review of the literature. These 55 statements were the items used in the first-round of the Delphi survey. Each expert reviewed and rated each statement as "very important", "important", "general", "unimportant" or "very unimportant" on the website. The statement was revised or deleted in the following round according to the experts' responses.

### 2.3 Survey Procedure

Researchers found potential experts in assistive technology, special education and rehabilitation and invited them to participate in this study. Fourteen professionals finally participated and sat on the panel of experts. Researchers informed them by e-mail of the procedure for filling out the questionnaire on the website when prior to the first round of the survey. The researchers revised or deleted the statements in response to the qualitative opinions and then undertook the second round survey. The experts received by email a report of their ratings and comments after each round of the survey, and used it as a reference for rating statements in the following round.

Researchers analyzed the consistency of the responses to each statement across the first two rounds of the survey after the second round survey has been completed. The statements with inconsistent responses were e-mailed to the experts with the results of the second round survey. The experts filled out the questionnaire and mailed it back to the first researcher. The survey involved a total of three rounds.

### 2.4 Data Analysis

The experts' responses to each statement were transferred from SQL database into a Microsoft Excel file and analyzed. The mean was used to decide the importance of each statement. The median and mode were determined central location to characterize the experts' responses. Moreover, quartile deviation (QD) was used as measures of variation of the responses.

## 3 Results

The experts reached agreement at the third round of the Delphi survey. The final number of the statements regarding AT integration was 51. These 51 statements were regarded as very important or important competencies of AT integration for teachers of special education. The final statements retained the original frame of AT integration mentioned in Fig. one. The brief descriptions are below:

### 3.1 Philosophy and Laws Related to AT

The professionals agreed that special educators must understand the legislation and regulations related to assistive technology used in special education in Taiwan, and that they must be able to demonstrate the advantages of AT to the lives, learning and vocation of individuals with disabilities. They also claimed that educators should exhibit a positive disposition toward the use of AT devices to help students with disabilities to participate in the general curriculum and demonstrate their capabilities.

### 3.2 *AT* Devices

The experts felt that the educators should be familiar with the features of the various categories of AT devices and operate the devices generally employed in the classroom, as well as Internet or computer information technology. Although teachers of special education were not expected to be AT specialists, human resources in the classroom are limited, so teachers should take the responsibility of demonstrating and using specific devices.

### 3.3 AT Service

AT service is an important issue related to the successful and effective use of AT devices. Teamwork guarantees the provision of proper AT services. However, effective teamwork training of professionals in related disciplines is lacking. Teachers of special education are not supposed to provide the AT service without support. Therefore, knowledge of AT service was highlighted in this category.

Special educators are expected to demonstrate an understanding of AT service. As members of a team to provide AT service, teachers must display knowledge of the role of each team member, procedures for applying and obtaining funding for AT devices, the methods used to evaluate the effects of the AT intervention, the AT resource center and its services, and the procedure and models using to assess the need of AT using.

### 3.4 Concepts Related to AT Integration

Concepts related to the integration of AT devices into the curriculum are prerequisites to successful AT integration. However, this category contains only three statements. Special educators are expected to identify the parts of learning activities for which AT applications are suitable in the classroom. The panelists also agreed that teachers should demonstrate understanding of the process of integrating AT devices into the curriculum, as well as an intent to do so.

### 3.5 Assessment

This category concerns the assessment of AT integration. As a member of a team, a special education teacher should demonstrate skills in assessment. He or she must be able to assess the client's abilities in the areas of cognition and communication as well as his or her adaptive skills. They must be able to provide related information to other members of the team. Additionally, they must be able to refer the client to the resource center according to the required AT devices. Teachers must be able to identify the AT devices required for particular learning activities.

### 3.6 Selection and Acquisition

In the selection of devices, teachers are expected to use skills of collaborating with other professionals and parents, to evaluate the AT devices, select proper devices and determine the objectives of AT intervention. They must also be able to find responsible agencies or third-party organizations from which to acquire AT devices, by either borrowing or purchasing.

### 3.7 Training

To integrate AT devices into learning activities, not only clients, but also their teachers and parents, must be familiar with the devices they use. Educators must be able to teach clients and their parents to manipulate any device adopted by the client. Not every teachers needs to be an AT expert, but teachers should be able to perform sample tasks, such as operating digital communicators, or maintaining devices.

### 3.8 Instruction Accommodation

The instructional environment must be made to be able to integrate AT devices. Educators must demonstrate their skills related in implementing learning materials (such as editing electronic material), instructional strategies, methods of engagement (such as replacing handwriting with typing in writing class) and an appropriate physical environment (such as by reorganizing the layout of seats to suit students with wheelchairs).

### 3.9 Implementation and Management

Human resources for helping teachers in the classroom are limited, so educators must take responsibility for planning AT integration and evaluating its effectiveness during implementation. Rather than performing these tasks by themselves, teachers are encouraged to cooperate with other professionals in a dynamic process.

### 3.10 Resources and Support

Being a member of a team that provides special education services, special educators are expected to act as a resource person who could provide related supports for the general educators. They should also participate in AT-related professional education programs and actively seek assistance from other professionals.

## 4 Conclusions

The process of integrating AT into the curriculum is dynamic and ongoing. Teachers of Special education need training and support in integrating AT. These 51 items related to competencies in integrating AT, specified herein, are important indicators for qualifying special education teachers.

The items identified in this work can be used to examine the literacy of special educators in integrating AT. Researchers can also evaluate the support required by teachers, and develop competency-based AT in-service training programs.

## Acknowledgement

The authors would like to thank the National Science Council of the Republic of China for financially supporting this research under Contract No. NSC 92-2614-H-415-001-F20.

## References

1. Chen, M. C., & Lai, C. Y.: A Project-Based Assistive Technology Inservice Training Program. Proceeding of 2003 Special Education Conference at Chiayi University. Special Education Center, Chiayi Taiwan (2003), 31-50

2. Church, G., & Glennen, S.: The Handbook of Assistive Technology. Singular Publishing Group, San Diego (1992)
3. Gardner, J. M., & Edyburn, D. L.: Integrating Technology to Support Effective Instruction. In J. D. Lindsey (Ed.), Technology and Exceptional Individuals. 3rd edn. Pro-ed, Austin Texas (2000) 191-240
4. Gaskin, C. J., Obrien, A. P, & Hardy, D. J.: The Development of a Professional Practice Audit Questionnaire for Mental Health Nursing in Aotearoa/ New Zealand. International Journal of Mental Health Nursing, Vol. 12. (2003) 259-270
5. Jane, M. W.: A Study on the Assistive Technology Literacy of Special Education Teachers in Junior High Schools. Unpublished Master dissertation, Taiwan Normal University, Taipei Taiwan (2002)
6. Lahm, E. A, & Nickels, B. L.: Assistive Technology Competencies for Special Educators. Teaching Exceptional Children, Vol. 32(1). (1999) 56-63
7. Michaels, C. A. & McDermott, J.: Assistive Technology Integration in Special Education Teacher Preparation: Program Coordinators' Perceptions of Current Attainment and Importance. Journal of Special Education Technology, Vol. 18(3). (2003) 29-44
8. National Association of State Directors of Special Education.: Recommended Competencies for Professional Staff Members in the Area of Assistive Technology http://www.cde.ca.gov/spbranch/sed/atstaff.htm (1998)
9. Wu, T. F., & Chen, M. C.: Policy of Assistive Technology for Special Education in Taiwan. Bulletin of Special Education, Vol. 20. (2000) 47-68
10. York, M. A.: Assistive Technology as Viewed by Special Education Teachers in Kansas, Unpublished doctoral dissertation, Kansas State University, Manhattan Kansas (1999)

# Web Adaptation of Learning Objects for Special Access WALOSA

Carole Salis[1], Cristian Lai[1], and Claude Moulin[2]

[1] Centro di Ricerca Studi Superiori e Sviluppo in Sardegna, Italy
{calis,clai}@crs4.it
http://www.crs4.it

[2] UMR CNRS 6599 HeuDiaSyc – Université de Compiègne, France
claude.moulin@utc.fr
http://www.utc.fr

**Abstract.** Diversity in learning style represents an obstacle teachers have to deal with. In the case of pupils with visual perception troubles, teachers cannot propose to students with difficult vision the same online material they propose to peers. Currently we are attempting to diminish the major obstacles this problem arises with the development within CRS4 of a system prototype that introduces two main characteristics: the teacher's pedagogical support with the search of didactic resources over the Internet adapted to objects which have been predefined for others and the adaptation of these resources to the personal characteristics of end user, in this case both students with and without trouble of visual perception.

## 1 Introduction

The activities of object decomposition from an online didactical material are being studied respecting the objective parameters presented from medical diagnoses and through materials teachers may retrieve online. New organizational editing object will allow students to manage their own digital visual space at their best; the graphical disposition of visual elements as well as key words represent samples of what a student will control by himself for a personal representation. The prototype will contribute to the following operations: the sending of demands via Internet to the material elaboration centre, the research and the progressive interactive adaptation of the material through the manipulation of important parameters for the visual perception.

## 2 Pedagogical Objective

The main characteristics of the prototype regard both the methodological and technological functions. The pedagogical function will allow the following procedure from the system interface for special requests: teachers will indicate in related fields (fields that respect determined taxonomies like categories of ability, instructional strategies,

K. Miesenberger et al. (Eds.): ICCHP 2004, LNCS 3118, pp. 178–182, 2004.

support of media.) the instructional objective, the nature of the didactic elements useful to the attainment of objectives, the level of complexity of the didactic object according to age and grade, the nature of the discipline, etc. During this very first phase, teachers will select some parameters extracted from the category of the diseases (Cim-10 1998) regarding: visual acuity, field of vision, centered vision and peripheral vision. Each category of visual deficiency introduces a particular object representation, perception of the contours, the shapes, the contrasts, the light, details, etc, which we must bear in mind at the moment of the adaptation phase of the didactic material we will supply the end user with.

## 3 The System

The system consists of several modules each dedicated to a specific role. Operatively speaking ,the first step is the request of the educational materials. The searching is performed by experts in the specific argument. Documents are decomposed in "learning objects" the system recognizes. Speaking of "learning objects" we mean elements or parts of content related to the definition contained in the standardization work of the Institute of Electrical and Electronic Engineers (IEEE). The end user will be able to adapt the obtained objects within presentation schemes called templates, depending on the needs and on his/her sight capabilities. To pursuit this goal the system provides several templates related to the different presentations concerning the disability categories. The described features implicate the adoption of a technology based on the Web client-server paradigm. We can point out two levels of action:

- the expert receives the request, looks for the materials, and performs the decomposition in "learning objects";
- the user gets the retrieved materials presented within the most suitable template; using the authoring tools he can modify the properties.

### 3.1 Meta Data and Learning Objects

The term "learning objects" has been the source of some confusion. In the field of Instructional Design it is a term that describes shareable "chunks" of content; in computer engineering it is an extension of "object oriented" programming to the field of learning management; among educators it can describe both content and processes. In the context of e-learning or Web-based teaching [6], learning objects are becoming accepted as the building blocks of course design. The IEEE originally defined a Learning Object very loosely as: "any entity, digital or non digital, that can be used for learning, education or training"; however in practice learning objects are normally digital, discrete units of instruction that are distributed via a computer network as components of a web-based learning management system. XML metadata has become the de-facto standard for indexing, defining and searching learning objects and all of the repositories mentioned above use metadata standards developed under the IEEE's Learning Object Metadata (LOM) project. Standard formats include IMS,

Dublin Core, CanCore and associated projects, such as the Cnn/ISSS European vocabularies initiatives (for multilingual indexing). The LOM differs from library catalogue systems in that it incorporates data relevant to curriculum design and teaching methodology in addition to descriptions of content and authorship. We think it is interesting to deal with the decomposition of the document into objects identified as learning assistants, such as the elements we can find within an electronic document and/or a web page. Samples of interesting information are: author, bibliography, but the most important decomposable elements are titles, images, tables, definitions, samples, key words, etc.; the system is able to locate thanks of a hybrid automatic and manual process the known objects and to produce the internal representation based on Java Bean technology. The obtained objects are flexible in that they can be adapted to more training situations in the field of partial sightedness.

### 3.2 Templates

The display of the learning objects depends on the user's needs, and only the user can decide their final organization. The objects are initially positioned within pre-created graphical pages, called templates. The most important feature of templates is the possibility to modify the initial organization. In fact, templates are general presentation models, empty documents with anonymous content at definition time. Only at runtime the elements will be placed within the template and the adaptation will be performed. Furthermore templates are reusable elements which, once they are defined, can be applied several times. The system defines a set of basic templates based on general user needs (related to the disability).

### 3.3 The Architecture

The client-server system is composed of three main modules:

- service request
- searching and decomposition of the material
- presentation and adaptation

The user entry point consists of a web page located within a portal for the service.

### 3.4 The Request

The service is requested through an HTML page placed within the portal. The user is requested to provide the basic information related to the documents needed and he will be invited to define the category of learning goal end users should reach and/or the nature of capabilities teachers want students will develop. Moreover it is necessary to clarify how the nature of the disability, in order to make the initial presentation possible. Choices can be made within a set of possibilities which concern, for example, position of key words, menu, schema, abstract, title, font, size, interline, contrast, position of the image on the page, etc.

### 3.5 The Decomposition

The decomposition module is developed in Java because of its main feature of object oriented and multi platform language. It is mainly a stand alone application devised for the expert in the retrieving of the didactic documents. Starting from an electronic document based on the XHTML format, the application allows to obtain the learning objects the system recognizes. An algorithm which transforms XHTML tags into Java Bean objects will be used; for example <TABLE> XHTML elements correspond to TABLE learning object. At the end of the process all learning objects will be available for the next step.

### 3.6 The Adaptation

The adaptation is the last step of the process. At the highest level, people are clearly interested in interacting with the information contained within the document [4]. Learning objects are positioned within the template which better meets the user's needs. Now the user is able to make the most of the document modifying and adapting it. The interaction is allowed by an authoring tool provided within the portal. It is mainly a Java Applet. The user helped by an expert (for example the teacher) can move, enlarge, resize the objects contained within the document. Every object allows a set of adaptations which depends on the features of the object itself. For example TEXT object allows to modify the font, the size, the position on the page, etc.

## 4 Methodology

Successively to the research already started on the parameters specific for each typology of visual deficiency and on the nature of the pedagogic data the requests will have to present, developmental activities will be started, with the participation of experts in the fields of ophthalmology, tiflology, school support, instructional technology and computer engineering in order to establish which flexible parameters will be presented in the platform. At the end of the development of the prototype platform the experimentation phase of the service will begin, with a particular emphasis on the exploration of the actions more frequently detected from the web stations of each institute taking part in the experimentation. This stage of the research will occur only after a period of training on the utilization of the prototype and the services it supplies. Either the educational institutes or the vocational schools will present coeducational classes in which students with a normal or a lower visual acuity coexist. The gathering of objective data (manipulation of parameters) will be activated through the screen reader. Two different types of semi-structured interviews will be proposed to teachers (normal classes teachers, support teachers, specialized educators) and partially sighted pupils. The spreading of the experimentation activities and the publication of the results will be effected through a number of actions such as seminars, newsletters and description of the project in specific sites of interest (associations and institutes for partially sighted people).

## 5 Conclusion

The project results from several interactions, specialist seminars and meetings with local realities on the problems of blindness and partial sight (Istituto per Ciechi in Cagliari and Unione Italiana Ciechi) as well as the cues suggested by the European project Vickie [5] which has reached its last year of activity. Such referential pattern has led us, first of all, to verify the level of participation of the protagonists in the sector of specialist education and the assent of support teachers strongly interested in combining the telematic aids currently used in teaching and partial sight support aids. The combining of the professional profiles within the research-development team is a feature fundamental for the path of this cross-curricular project and it is important to intervene since the beginning with the co-partnership of de sectors directly involved. One of the original features of the system is to automate a mechanical procedure, such as the adaptation of didactic support, often applied to one single class of partially sighted people (low visual acuity) with high costs and without the opportunity to reiterate the process since the moment when the product is issued in printed form. The two main functions of the service will lead teachers, on the one hand, to benefit from a pedagogic service adaptable to the special context; on the other hand, they will carry out the necessary interaction that the end user – the partially sighted person – will have to experiment with daily, in order to overcome the effects of his/her diversity and perceptive unrest.

## References


1. Brodsky, Mark W.: Making Sense of Self-Service E-learning Simulations: Fun or Functional?. Learning & Training Innovations Magazine, (January 2003)
2. Cheese, P.: What Keeps Universities from Embracing e-Learning?, E-Learning and Training Innovation Magazine., (November 2003)
3. Holbrook, Cay M. (a cura di): Il bambino con disabilità visiva. Guida per i genitori, Biblioteca Italiana per i Ciechi "Regina Margherita", (2000)
4. Kottapally, K.,Ngo, C., Reddy, R., Pontelli, E., Son, T.C., Gillan, D.: Towards the creation of accessibility agents for non-visual navigation of the web. ACM Conference on Universal Usability, Vancouver, British Columbia, Canada, (2002), 132-141
5. Moulin, C., Giroux, S., Archambault, D., Carboni, D., Burger, D.: A Distributed Document Oriented Architecture for Rendering Services to Visually Impaired Students. In K. Miesenberger, J. Klaus, and W. Zagler, editors, Computer Helping People with Special Needs. Volume 2398 of Lecture Notes in Computer Science. Springer Verlag, Wien, (2002), 329-336
6. Petrucco, C.,: Le prospettive didattiche del Semantic Web. Didamatica 2003, Italy, (2003), 168-176
7. Romagnoli, A.: I minorati della vista. Storia e metodi delle scuole speciali. Ceppi E. Armando Editore, Roma, (1994)
8. Updating the International Classification of Diseases, Tenth Revision in Epidemiological Bulletin Pan American Health Organization. Vol.24, No. 2, (June 2003)

# Postgraduate Course on Accessible Web Design

Daniela Ortner, Mario Batušić, and Klaus Miesenberger

Universität Linz, Institut "integriert studieren"
Altenbergerstrasse 69
A-4040 Linz, Austria
{daniela.ortner,mario.batusic,klaus.miesenberger}@jku.at
http://www.integriert-studieren.jku.at

**Abstract.** Due to the successful endeavour of raising awareness towards accessibility in the last years, there is a high and increasing demand towards knowledge in this field. The path from theory towards practice should be supported by an easy access to knowledge in this field. This short paper reports on the work in a project which will try to close the gap between theory and practice in a specific field of accessibility: accessible web design. The organisational framework, the modularised curriculum, the planned content as well as the e-Learning system that will be adapted to fit the project's requirements will be presented. As an open platform the project invites to benefit from the content as well as it invites for contributions.

## 1 Introduction

The last years' endeavour to establish awareness towards the need to design and keep the Internet based on its basic principle of openness towards all users has shown impact all over the world. Web designers more and more get aware of this basic necessity. The public sector advocates that public information has to be accessible to all citizens and launched accessibility legislation accordingly. Industry and business also learn how design for all supports the general usability and thereby has a positive impact on reaching their goals.

Due to that, an increasing demand for education, consulting and support in design for all can be seen. Several US univerities such as the university of Illinois [1] or the university of Wisconsin-Madison [2] offer basic web accessibility courses for some years already. But there is not yet any complete teaching offer including web accessibility in depth as well as related topics such as the basics of software accessibility, usability, assistive technologies and deeper studies of various specific needs according to different disabilities.

In Austria the situation is the same. No complete courses are available. This motivated us to start working towards establishing a new educational offer. We report on a project to establish a postgraduate course named "Barrierefreies Webdesign" – "Accessible Web Design". The course will be offered as an online e-Learning application with a minimum of mandatory attendance hours.

K. Miesenberger et al. (Eds.): ICCHP 2004, LNCS 3118, pp. 183–186, 2004.

The participants of the course will be recruited from a rather large target group:

- Persons living in the border regions of Austria
- Parents who have to take care of their children
- Web designers
- University students and graduates
- People with disabilitite
- People trying to achieve reengagement

As people with disabilities should be able to attend the course without problems, all learning materials are planned to be fully accessible electronic documents available over an accessible online distance learning system. Some of the learning materials already exist from previoes lectures offered by the institute, the other materials will be developed within the project through strong co-operation of lecturers and computer science students.

The duration of the studies totals four terms (two years). The first course will start in the summer term 2005. The course language will be German. Subject to approval by the university of Linz, the course graduates will get an academic degree such as "Academic Web Accessibility Engineer".

## 2 Curriculum

The curriculum of the postgraduate course is composed of six modules:

1. Web Accessibility
2. Assistive Technologies
3. Software Accessibility
4. Usability
5. Legal Requirements
6. Preparation of materials for print disabled people

Each of the modules contains several lectures belonging to the specific field. For example, the main module Web Accessibility contains seminars on HTML, CSS, Evaluation and Repair Tools, Flash, SMIL [7], XML and a seminar on applications such as e-Government, e-Commerce, e-Banking etc.

Besides mandatory seminars, the curriculum will also envisage a number of elective ones. Thus students will be able to take a certain amount of lectures regarding to their personal interest and to immerse themselves into a special topic.

The modular approach enables us to easily adapt the curriculum so as to fit different educational settings. Single seminars taken form the curriculum could for example be used

- to provide training for interested companies and organisations
- to push vocational integration
- to offer introductory seminars to raise awareness or
- to be integrated into the regular studies at Austrian universities.

So the development of the curriculum is based on the principle that splitting the seminars into different levels of complexity and offering different layers can be reached very easily.

## 3 e-Learning System

As mentioned earlier, the course will get by with a minimum of mandatory attendance hours. All other lessons will be offered using an online e-Learning system.

As the postgraduate course should be open for all interested people regardless of a possible disability, accessibility issues have to be strongly taken into account when choosing such a system. Additionally, as not to price ourselves out of the market, the system should be purchasable at a low cost.

As a fully accessible system is not to be found on the market, the first step within the project is to adapt an existing system. The decision fell out in favour of a system called "Moodle" [3], as a first accessibility evaluation following the Web Content Accessibility Guidelines [4] published by the Web Accessibility Initiative [5] showed rather good results.

Moodle is an e-Learning system designed to help educators create quality online courses. Such e-Learning systems are sometimes also called course management systems (CMS), Learning Management Systems (LMS) or Virtual Learning Environments (VLE).

One of the main advantages of Moodle over other systems is a strong grounding in social constructionist pedagogy. Moodle offers different formats for the management of courses (weekly, topic and social format), also different features within a single lecture are available, for example:

**Assignment**
Teachers can give homework assignments that the students have to hand in.

**Forum**
Students and teachers can discuss specific topics.

**Quiz**
Teachers can review the student's standard of knowledge.

**Resource**
Teachers can provide scripts, slides, videos etc. supporting their lecture.

**Survey**
Students can evaluate single courses.

As Moodle is an open source system, our intention within the project is also to pass our adaptations of the system regarding accessibility issues on to the development community such that future users of this open source system can also profit from our work.

## 4 Materials

As stated in the previous chapter, course materials can be provided online using the Resource feature of Moodle. As the intention of the project is to continuously implement the design for all approach, all materials have to be accessible themselves. Therefore, special attention has to be paid on the structure of documents and the formats used. As one of the main tasks of our institute is to support print disabled students, we have more than ten years of experience in this field.

Beneath scripts and slides, the learning process will also be supported by multimedia applications such as video and audio. To ensure accessibility for people with disabilities, appropriate synchronisation is necessary. For example, following the recommendations of the W3C [6], SMIL [7] will be used for video captioning and synchronisation.

## 5 Impact

The postgraduate course "Accessible Web Design" should be a contribution of the Johannes Kepler University of Linz towards the current worldwide efforts to make the global and local public information available for all citizens, independent of their social status or disability. The more web designers have consolidated knowledge about accessibility issues and the ways of overcoming them, the better the inclusion situation for people with disabilities and the bigger the chance of an independent living. The graduation of this course offers a new vocational field where especially disabled graduates can scoop out their experience and propose new, better solutions.

Last but not least we hope that our project is also going to bring a portion of awareness in this area at universities. This would cause by and by that – in the field of web and software design – one or another seminar or even a whole module of our course becomes part of the university's regular studies.

## References

1. University of Illinois – Designing Universally Accessible WWW Resources for People with Disabilities
http://cita.rehab.uiuc.edu/courses/
2. University of Wisconsin-Madison – Web Accessibility 101
http://www.doit.wisc.edu/accessibility/online-course/index.htm
3. Moodle – an open source e-Learning system
http://www.moodle.org
4. WCAG 1.0 – Web Content Accessibility Guidelines 1.0
http://www.w3.org/TR/WAI-WEBCONTENT/
5. WAI – Web Accessibility Initiative of the W3C
http://www.w3.org/WAI/
6. W3C – World Wide Web Consortium
http://www.w3.org/
7. SMIL – Synchronized Multimedia Integration Language
http://www.w3.org/AudioVideo/

# Cognitive Training with Animated Pedagogical Agents (TAPA) in Children with Learning Disabilities

Yehya Mohamad[1], Carlos A. Velasco[1], Sylvia Damm[2], and Holger Tebarth[2]

[1] Fraunhofer Institute for Applied Information Technology (FIT)
Schloss Birlinghoven, D53757 Sankt Augustin, Germany
{Yehya.Mohamad,Carlos.Velasco}@fit.fraunhofer.de

[2] Klinik am Schlossgarten, Schlossgarten 1
48249 Duelmen, Germany
Holger.Tebath@web.de

**Abstract.** Adaptive User Interfaces are seen as a critical success factor in the development of training and learning systems. Adaptive interfaces have been based on an approach consisting of user and device profiles. Recently, personality and mental states have been added and are used in research projects to expand the reliability and context awareness of such systems. This approach enhances adaptive usage of training and therapeutic systems. The developed system effectively combines biofeedback sensors and a set of software algorithms to estimate the current motivation/frustration level of the user. Based on this concept, it will be possible to develop narrative training and therapeutic systems, which could adapt to the motivation level of the user and focus her attention on the fulfilment of the current task.

## 1 Introduction

Important factors in *human-human* interaction are also relevant in *human-computer* interaction [10]. In human-human interaction, it has been argued that skills of “emotional intelligence” are more important than traditional mathematical and verbal skills of intelligence [2]. These skills include the ability to recognize the emotions of another and to respond appropriately to them. It is clear that these skills are important in human-human interaction, and when they are missing, interaction is more likely to be perceived as frustrating and not very intelligent. Until now the mechanisms of the emotional intelligence, the expression and recognition of emotions by humans are not yet fully understood; therefore it is not an easy task to do it through computers.

In the Design of the **TAPA** system we have effectively combined biofeedback sensors and a set of software algorithms to estimate the current motivation/frustration level of the user. Based on this concept, and integrating it with interface agents, it was possible to develop narrative training and therapeutic systems which can adapt to the motivation level of the user and focus her attention on the fulfillment of the current task [6].

K. Miesenberger et al. (Eds.): ICCHP 2004, LNCS 3118, pp. 187–193, 2004.

The agents in a virtual world have their *artificial* emotional states conditioned to the status of their environment and to the goals they want to achieve. The goals of the agents depend mainly on the training units, the user's preferences and her *natural* emotional status.

Emotion recognition through the combination of non-intrusive biofeedback sensors and stochastic algorithms has increased the chances for the development of new advanced systems in many areas like e-learning and entertainment. The use of this technology improves Human-Computer Interaction by complementing existing interaction models. The research area of recognition and integration of emotions into computer systems is an interdisciplinary topic. In particular, we foresee an impact on interface agents, story-telling systems, neuropsychological emotion theory, e-learning, user profiling techniques, sensors and biofeedback systems.

The topic of emotional systems is increasingly attracting the attention of several research groups. The most prominent applied cognitive models are the OCC model [7] and the agent personality model FFM [3]. According to the OCC model, emotions are simply classes of emotion-eliciting conditions such as the agent's beliefs, goals, standards, and attitudes. An interesting set of emotions is crucially dependent on the agent's attitudes. The agent might be happy for its interlocutor if the agent likes the interlocutor and experiences joy over a state of affairs that it presumes to be desirable for the interlocutor. Otherwise, if the agent dislikes the interlocutor, it might resent its interlocutor for the same reason. [11].

The Training by Animated Pedagogical Agents paradigm has been developed in recent years and is one of the current main research topics in Human-Computer-Interaction (HCI). Animated Pedagogical Agents have life-like, animated personas and represent a type of autonomous agents. They can be employed to attract the user's focus of attention and are capable of pursuing goals in complex environments and adapting their behaviour as needed in response to unexpected events. Their typical environment is an educational simulation, together with the learner and other interacting agents. Animated Pedagogical Agents may seek to achieve pedagogical goals (e.g., to help a student to learn about a topic), communicative goals (e.g., to acknowledge a learner's action), and task goals (e.g., to help the learner solve some particular problems).

Agents can respond to the learner with a human-like combination of verbal communication and non-verbal gestures such as gaze, pointing, body stance, and head nods. And finally they are able to convey emotions such as surprise, approval, or disappointment. HCI research showed that – taken these capabilities together – Animated Pedagogical Agents can interact with learners in a manner that is close to face-to-face collaborative learning [12].

## 2 Architecture of Emotional Systems

The generic architecture of emotional systems according to [1] contains, in addition to recognition and response to users' emotions, other aspects of affective computing, such as the use of emotion-like mechanisms within the machine to help it make decisions, adjust perceptions, and influence learning (see Fig. 1).

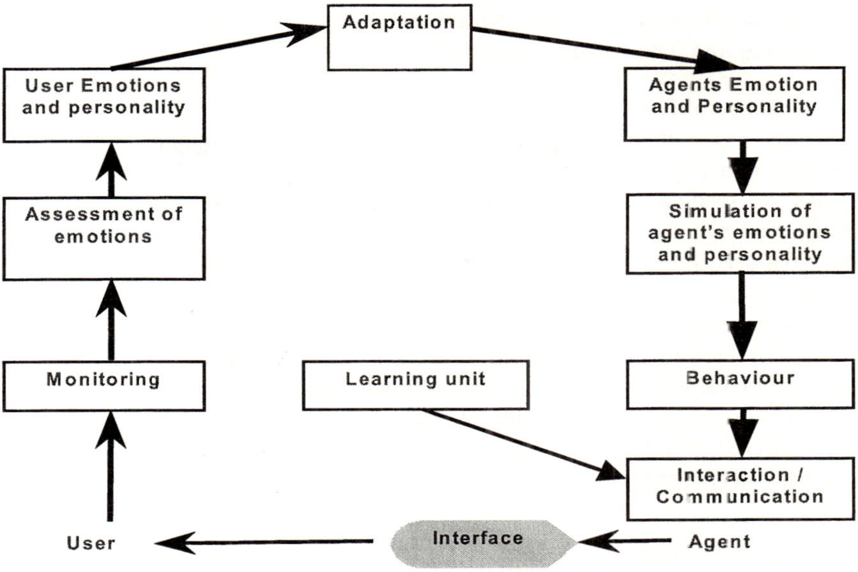


**Fig. 1.** Architecture of an emotional computer system.

The main components of an emotional system are:

- Biofeedback sensors to measure physiological parameters, such as skin conductance, heart-rate or blood pressure, known to be good parameters for measuring emotional excitement.
- Pattern recognition of emotions.
- Models of human emotions where computer systems get the ability to recognize them [9].
- Functionalities to simulate emotions and to build an interface, which is able to express emotions, e.g. through Interface Agents.

### Methods and Devices for the Measurement of User's Emotions

In this regard, the **TAPA System** is based upon the concepts of Animated Pedagogical Agents (APA) and adaptive user interfaces, and opens up new perspectives in realizing individual intervention for memory improvement in children.

There are different methods and sensors that can be used to obtain values for the assessment of the emotional states of users. For our work, we have used skin conductance sensors. The sensors are connected to the skin surface with two electrodes; any weak signals could be then recognized by the sensors. The skin conductance measures in the first line the activity of the respiratory glands. If sweat is produced, then the ability to conduct electricity will increase, and a higher skin conductance can be measured.

### A Conceptual Model to Integrate Emotions into Training and Therapeutic Systems

Under the scope of our projects (TAPA and IPCA[1]), we have developed an approach to recognize user's emotions, integrating and using them together with other parameters to personalize training units. The main focus was on the development of a model to assess the recognized emotions and to combine them with other parameters to adapt the training units to the actual user's motivational level and the context of use.

We have used Interface Agents in the user interface to complement the emotional system as described in the previous section and to convey emotional expressions to the user. Furthermore, they can play a role in increasing the motivation level of the user. The interface adaptation can be enhanced using the described emotional system. In our framework we have evaluated the following input technologies: touch-screen, speech recognition, mouse, keyboard, skin conductivity sensors, diverse virtual input options via GUI buttons, questions through the interface agents (generally from the user interface), and behavioural monitoring through a psychologist.

### Description of the Assessment Algorithm

To achieve the recognition of the arousal state of the user we have used many input variables. All these parameters are based on the measuring of skin conductance signals in a training session. These parameters are used in a stochastic algorithm to detect if the user is positively or negatively aroused and her arousal level (see Fig. 2).

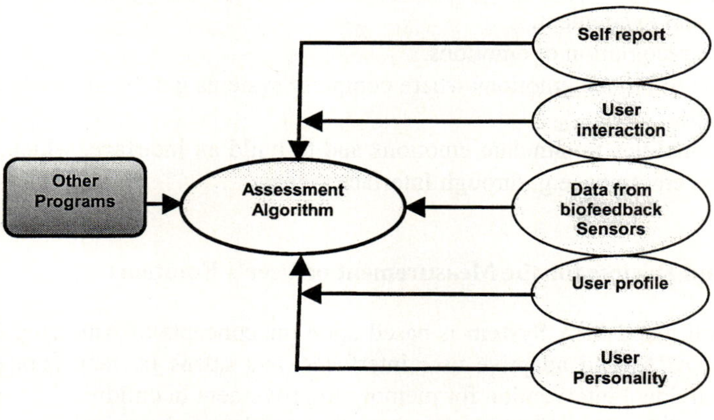


**Fig. 2.** Components of the emotion assessment algorithm.

To develop adaptive training units that consider the motivational level of the user, input from many other parameters as mentioned above must be integrated into the system.

---

[1] Intelligent Physiological Navigation and Control of web-based Applications, IST–2001–37370, `http://www.ipca.info/`

The output of the algorithm is a parameter to adjust the training. We have identified two possible sources for errors, named $\alpha$ and $\beta$. The first one ($\alpha$) corresponds to the case that a motivational change was assumed, but no change occurred, and the second one ($\beta$) corresponds to the case that no motivational change was assumed, but a change occurred. These uncertainties can also be considered in the stochastic algorithm used for the calculation.

**Therapeutic System as a Story in an Animated World (TAPA)**

Virtual environments such as training simulators and video games do an impressive job at modeling the dynamics of the physical world, but fall short when modeling the social dynamics of anything but the most impoverished human encounters. However, the social dimension is at least as important as graphics for creating engaging games or effective training tools.

The presented framework has been implemented in a prototype, considering the aforementioned social awareness with the following components:

- Pedagogical interface agents [4];
- A story played in an animated world, where the training units are encapsulated;
- Emotional monitoring and response components.

The prototype has the following characteristics:

- **Task/goal oriented:** e.g., if the agent wants to give a reward to the user, it would not be very helpful to display sadness but to display happiness.
- **Environment influence:** e.g., if something happens suddenly it would be suitable to be surprised and to show an appropriate behaviour reaction.
- **Personality:** every agent has its own character, so the emotions should follow an individual personality concept.
- **Time:** synchronization is a very important issue, since we are dealing with many agents simultaneously; the behavior of each agent must be adequate to the behaviour of all others at that moment [6].

## 3 Prototype Evaluation

The developed software **T**raining with **A**nimated **P**edagogical **A**gents (**TAPA**) [9] presents a special training environment for children with cognitive impairments.

We involved in this study 71 students between 9 and 14 years at a special school for learning disabled children, comparing a TAPA-treated group with a non-treated control group. The intention was to examine the effectiveness of the training as well as the functionality of the bi-directional communication process between the agent and the user. The main aspect of the cognitive training is to impart a special meta-memory strategy which is called "categorical organisation". It is known that this memory strategy as one of many, is spontaneously shown in the age between 9-11 years in "normal" cognitive development. If world-knowledge and ability to think in abstract terms increases, then children begin to recognize the possibility of categori-

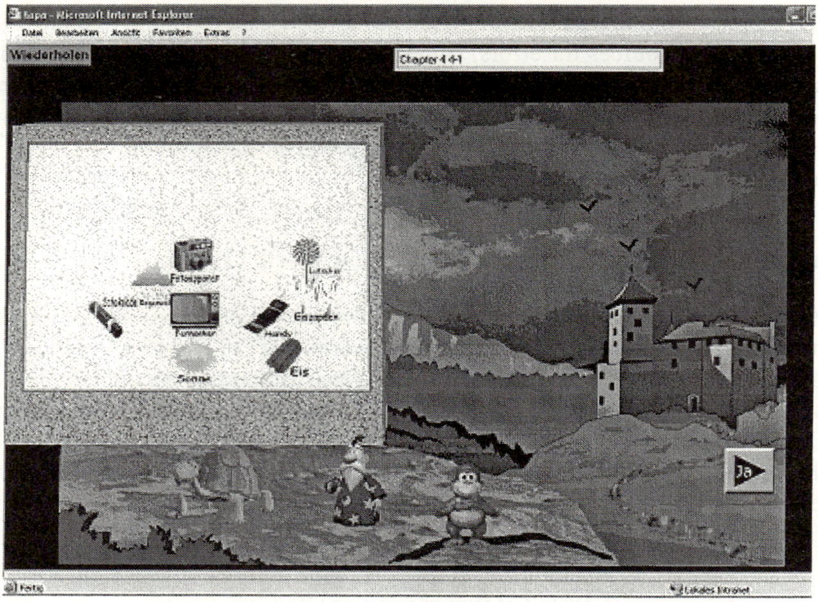


**Fig. 3.** TAPA GUI screenshot.

zation of objects. This ability belongs to the so-called meta-cognitive performance and is used instinctively in different learning situations. Children with learning disabilities do not develop these strategies in time and that is one reason why they are often affected by memory impairment.

Psychological research has shown that it is basically possible to coach these children effectively and to give them a chance to improve their learning situation. But to be successful, it is especially important for disabled children to give them an individual motivational support.

Considering these requirements, we combined measurement of skin conductance with self-report-tools and learning performance of the user to define several algorithms expressing the child's motivational situation and deriving TAPA's reaction. Measurement of the skin conductance shows the user's psycho-physiological arousal status, and allows to conclude indirectly the effectiveness of the learning process. It can be postulated that a status of relatively medium arousal is ideal for learning situations. Over and under medium arousal should be avoided. Self-report-tools ask the child for the fun or pleasure it has felt while fulfilling the tasks and allow to start a 'repair'-communication in the case of variant input data.

The TAPA system's reaction is basically in two different directions: 1. tasks difficulty decrease or increase in three ways (number of objects and categories, clearness of categories) and 2. the agent's behaviour. Following the individual algorithm the agent intervention is used to influence the child, regarding psycho-physiological arousal and motivational situation. For this purpose the little life-like characters are equipped with several emotions expressing behaviour sequences and natural speech engines.

Results of the study give as a whole an interesting idea of the possibilities of animated agents as special pedagogical support. Next to the successful teaching of a meta-memory strategy to teach disabled children, it could be shown that it is possible to influence the user's motivation status via agent's behaviour. The study results allow to conclude that animated pedagogical agents can play a valuable job in future assistive technology.

## 4 Conclusions

Although these results seem to be very promising for the developed approach, further and more complex evaluations are planned to strengthen the technical integration of physiological emotion measuring. We are planning to conduct more evaluation rounds with an enhanced system. Further examination appears necessary to clear the precise role of agent's motivational support in the learning process. The authors are working as well on the development of an advanced interface system called IPCA, to help users with severe motor and speech impairments to browse the Internet with the help of an input system based on biofeedback sensors. Here we intend to use the emotional response of the user to adapt the interaction of the system to the needs of the user, as well as for the training module.

## References


1. Ball, G., Breese, J. (2000) Emotion and Personality in a Conversational Agent. pages 189–217
2. D. Goleman, Emotional Intelligence, (1995). Bantam Books, New York
3. McCrae, R., John, O. (1992) An introduction to the five-factor model and its implication. Journal of Personality, pages 175–215
4. Microsoft Agent Software Development Kit (1999). USA, Redmond Washington
5. Mohamad, Y., Tebarth, H. (2001) Evaluation in the Development of a tele-medical Training System. Universal Access in HCI: Towards an Information Society for All. Volume 3 of the Proceedings of HCI International 2001. New Orleans: Lawrence Erlbaum Associates
6. Mohamad, Y., Hammer, S., Haverkamp, F., Nöker, M., Tebarth, H. 2002 Evaluational Study: Training with Animated Pedagogical Agents. ICCHP 2002: 117-124
7. Ortony, A, Clore, GL, Colins, A. (1988) The Cognitive Structure of Emotions. Cambridge: Cambridge University Press
8. PERLETH, C. (1992) Strategienutzung, Metagedächtnis und intellektuelle Begabung. (Dissertationschrift). München: LMU
9. Picard, R. (1997). Affective computing. The MIT Press
10. Picard, R. (2000). IBM Systems Journal, Volume 39, Numbers 3 & 4, MIT Media Laboratory
11. Prendinger, H., Ishizuka, M. (2002). Evolving social relationships with animate characters. Symposium of the AISB-2 Convention on "Animating Expressive
12. Shaw, E, Ganeshan, R, Johnson, W.L., et al. (1999). Building a Case for Agent-Assisted Learning as a Catalyst for Curriculum Reform in Medical Education. In: Proceedings of the International Conference on Artificial Intelligence in Education. Marina del Rey (California/USA): University of Southern California, Center for Advanced Research in Technology for Education (CARTE)

# A Concept Map_Based Adaptive Tutoring System Supporting Learning Diagnosis for Students with Learning Disability

Sook-Young Choi

Dept. of Computer Education, Woosuk University
490 Hujong-ri Samrae-up Wanju-kun Chonbuk 565-701, Korea
sychoi@core.woosuk.ac.kr

**Abstract.** One of the effective instruction methods for students with learning ability is to check precedent knowledge of students before learning and to supplement it when want of precedent knowledge is found. In this paper, we propose an adaptive tutoring system, which analyzes learning characteristics of students with leaning disability, diagnoses learning problems of them, and then provides proper advice accordingly. The system uses concept map to represent relationships among learning concepts and to diagnose the learning problems of students.

## 1 Introduction

Learning disability is a general term that describes specific kinds of learning problems. A learning disability can cause a student to have trouble learning and using certain skills. To help a student with Learning disability, first, accurate diagnosis for him/her, after that proper instruction methods for it are required. One of the effective instruction methods for students with learning ability is to check precedent knowledge of students before learning and to supplement it when want of precedent knowledge is found[1]. The adaptive instruction system is capable of adapting to the individual, which could provide learners with adaptable learning methods and learning materials considering the learning characteristics of each learner such as learning environment, learning goal and degree of previous learning[5].

In this paper, we propose an adaptive tutoring system, which analyzes learning characteristics of students with leaning disability, subject materials, and test items, diagnoses learning problems of them, and then provides proper advice accordingly. In the system, learning materials are constructed using concept map. A concept map is a graphical representation where nodes represent concepts, and links represent the relationships between concepts[3]. The concept map can be used to assess students' achievement by misconception and missing concepts and to reinforce students' understanding and learning for key concepts. Like this, concept map can be used for several purposes in instruction process.

Our work considers that constructing concept maps for subjects, teachers use them to check the problems in learning process for students with learning ability, and

K. Miesenberger et al. (Eds.): ICCHP 2004, LNCS 3118, pp. 194–201, 2004.

which is based on Ausubel's theory of meaningful learning which stresses that learning new knowledge is dependent on what is already known[8]. That is, it means that precedent concepts should be thoroughly learned to comprehend new concepts. Grasping the learning state of students with learning disability for precedent concepts to be required before learning new concepts, our system provides proper learning materials for want of them, and diagnoses the concepts which students have trouble to understand in the learning process. It reflects the weight value of difficulty degree and learning frequency and time as the features of test items and students' learning for effective diagnosing. As the suggestions after diagnosis, concepts to require supplementary learning are presented in the paths of concept map-based graph. Thus, the learning problems of each student are then identified based on these relationships.

## 2 Related Notions

### 2.1 Concept Map Model

Concept map, developed by Prof. Joseph D. Novack of Cornell University, is a technique for visually representing the structure of information - how concepts within a domain are interrelated[3]. A concept map is a graphical representation where nodes represent concepts, and links represent the relationships between concepts. The links between the concepts can be one-way, two-way, or non-directional. The concepts and the links may be categorized. The concept map can be used to assess students' achievement by misconception and missing concepts and to reinforce students' understanding and learning for key concepts. There are several uses for concept mapping, such as idea generation, design support, communication enhancement, learning enhancement, and assessment. A wide range of computer software for concept mapping is now available for most of the popular computers used in education.

### 2.2 Learning Disabilities

Students with learning disabilities have difficulty acquiring basic skills or academic content. Learning disabilities are characterized by intra-individual differences, usually in the form of a discrepancy between a student's ability and his or her achievement in areas such as reading, writing, mathematics, or speaking[6]. Intra-individual differences are differences within a student across academic areas. For example, a student with a learning disability may be quite successful in math computation and listening comprehension but may read poorly. Other students with learning disabilities may read and speak well but differently expressing their thoughts in writing. While a learning disability cannot be "cured," its impact can be lessened through instructional intervention and compensatory strategies. In general, a variety of instructional modes enhance learning for students with learning disabilities. In working with a student with a learning disability, the faculty member should try to identify the nature of the disability of the individual student to determine the kind of strategies that the student may need to compensate.

## 3 Learning Diagnosis Using Concept Map

During tutoring, students learn new concepts and new relationships among previously learned concepts, and this knowledge can be represented as a concept map. The following presents the concept map-based graph to represent relationships among learning concepts, learning diagnosis process using the concept map, and the structure of the system.

### 3.1 Knowledge Structure Based on Concept Map for Learning Diagnosis

The relationships among learning concepts are represented on concept map. The structure of concept map offers not only an overall cognition of subject contents but also the relationship to indicate the effect of learning one concept on the learning of other concepts. That is, the relationship shows prerequisite concepts to be learned before new concept. For example, if a student fails to learn the concept "Division", this may be because he/she did not learn the concept "Subtraction" and "Multiplication" well. In this case, we would suggest that the student should study "Subtraction" and "Multiplication" more thoroughly before attempting "Division". When the relationships among concepts are defined, it is possible to check the learning state of each student with learning disability for prerequisite concepts before learning a concept and to determine learning problems of them after learning thus to provide suggestions.

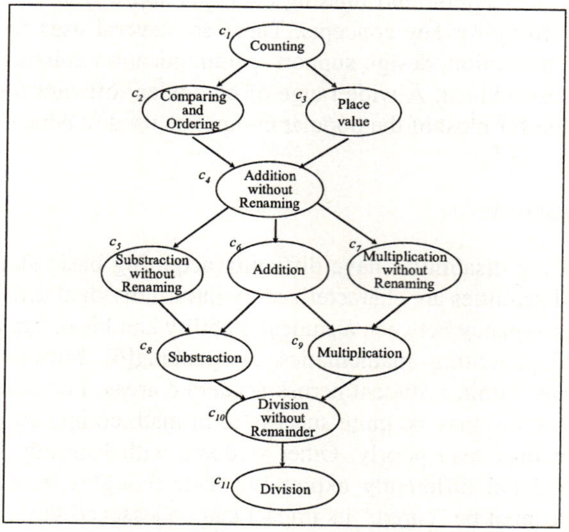


**Fig. 1.** Concept map-based graph.

To model these relationships among concepts, considering two concepts $C_i$ and $C_j$, we define that if $C_i$ is prerequisite concept of $C_j$, a relationship $C_i \ldots C_j$ exists. A single concept may have multiple prerequisite concepts, and multiple concepts come from a prerequisite concept. Fig.1. shows the concept map-based graph representing the relationships among concepts for the subject unit "number operations". The relationships of concepts in a concept map-based graph can be represented by a two-dimensional table like Table 1. In Table 1, if ($C_i$ ,$C_j$) = 1, it means that $C_i$ is one of the prerequisites of $C_{j.}$

**Table 1.** Table for concept map-based graph of Fig.1.

| $C_j$ \ Prerequisite $C_i$ | $C_1$ | $C_2$ | $C_3$ | $C_4$ | $C_5$ | $C_6$ | $C_7$ | $C_8$ | $C_9$ | $C_{10}$ | $C_{11}$ |
|---|---|---|---|---|---|---|---|---|---|---|---|
| $C_1$ | 0 | 0 | 0 | 0 | 0 | 0 | 0 | 0 | 0 | 0 | 0 |
| $C_2$ | 1 | 0 | 0 | 0 | 0 | 0 | 0 | 0 | 0 | 0 | 0 |
| $C_3$ | 1 | 0 | 0 | 0 | 0 | 0 | 0 | 0 | 0 | 0 | 0 |
| $C_4$ | 0 | 1 | 1 | 0 | 0 | 0 | 0 | 0 | 0 | 0 | 0 |
| $C_5$ | 0 | 0 | 0 | 1 | 0 | 0 | 0 | 0 | 0 | 0 | 0 |
| $C_6$ | 0 | 0 | 0 | 1 | 0 | 0 | 0 | 0 | 0 | 0 | 0 |
| $C_7$ | 0 | 0 | 0 | 1 | 0 | 0 | 0 | 0 | 0 | 0 | 0 |
| $C_8$ | 0 | 0 | 0 | 0 | 1 | 1 | 0 | 0 | 0 | 0 | 0 |
| $C_9$ | 0 | 0 | 0 | 0 | 0 | 1 | 1 | 0 | 0 | 0 | 0 |
| $C_{10}$ | 0 | 0 | 0 | 0 | 0 | 0 | 0 | 1 | 1 | 0 | 0 |
| $C_{11}$ | 0 | 0 | 0 | 0 | 0 | 0 | 0 | 0 | 0 | 1 | 0 |

### 3.2 Learning Diagnosis

Table 2 displays a test item relation table for a test sheet containing 10 test items($Q_1$, $Q_2$,..., $Q_{10}$ ) on a learning unit for a subject involving the concepts illustrated in Fig.1. Each value of table, raging 0 to 1, represents the relationship between test item $Q_i$ and the concept $C_{j.}$

Analyzing the learning state of students with disability using the relationships between test items and the subject concepts, inferring the want of learning concepts, learning diagnosis module suggests the concepts to require supplementary learning. When the concepts for supplementary learning is given, rather the concepts inferred intelligently through concept map than only fragmentary concepts related to failed test items are systematically suggested.

The process for learning diagnosis is as follow. First, get the union set of concepts related to incorrect test items. Assuming that the student fails to answer $Q_2$, $Q_3$, $Q_6$, and $Q_7$, then the union set of concepts related to incorrect test items are as follows.

$$Q_2 \cup Q_3 \cup Q_6 \cup Q_7 = \{ C_1, C_2, C_4, C_5 C_7, C_9, C_{10}, C_{11} \}$$

Second, to determine the concepts for supplementary learning in the union set, seek inversely the relation degrees of incorrect test items($R_{incor}$) and the relation degrees of correct test items($R_{cor}$) for each concept. As the example, the relation degrees of incorrect test items and correct test items for $C_1$ are as follows.

**Table 2.** Relationship table for concepts and test items.

| | $C_1$ | $C_2$ | $C_3$ | $C_4$ | $C_5$ | $C_6$ | $C_7$ | $C_8$ | $C_9$ | $C_{10}$ | $C_{11}$ |
|---|---|---|---|---|---|---|---|---|---|---|---|
| $Q_1$ | 0.4 | 0 | 0.9 | 0 | 0 | 0 | 0 | 0 | 0 | 0 | 0 |
| $Q_2$ | 0.2 | 0 | 0 | 0.9 | 0 | 0 | 0 | 0 | 0 | 0 | 0 |
| $Q_3$ | 0 | 0 .5 | 0 | 0 | 0.6 | 0 | 0.8 | 0 | 0 | 0 | 0 |
| $Q_4$ | 0 | 0 | 0.6 | 0 | 0 | 0.9 | 0 | 0 | 0 | 0 | 0 |
| $Q_5$ | 0 | 0 | 0 | 0.3 | 0 | 0 | 0 | 0.8 | 0 | 0 | 0.5 |
| $Q_6$ | 0 | 0 | 0 | 0 | 0 | 0.5 | 0 | 0 | 0 | 0.8 | 0.7 |
| $Q_7$ | 0 | 0 | 0 | 0 | 0 | 0 | 0.5 | 0 | 0.6 | 0.9 | 0 |
| $Q_8$ | 0 | 0.5 | 0 | 0 | 0 | 0 | 0 | 0 | 0 | 0 | 0 |
| $Q_9$ | 0.5 | 0 | 0.8 | 0 | 0 | 0 | 0 | 0 | 0 | 0 | 0 |
| $Q_{10}$ | 0 | 0 | 0.5 | 0.5 | 0 | 0 | 0.6 | 0.6 | 0 | 0 | 0 |

$$R_{cor} : \{ 0.4\,(Q_1), 0.5(Q_9) \} \quad R_{incor} : 0.2\,(Q_2)$$

Third, considering the relation degrees between test items and the concepts, answer results of test items, and the difficulty degree of test items($D$), the inference process checks whether students with learning disability understood each concept in the union set or not. For this, multiply each the relation degrees of incorrect test items and correct test items by the difficulty degree of test items then compare the two values as the following. Assume that the difficulty degrees of related test items are 0.2 ($Q_1$), 0.7($Q_9$) and 0.3 ($Q_2$).

$$\Sigma\, C_1(R_{cor} \times D) = ((0.4 \times 0.2) + (0.5 \times 0.7)) = 0.43$$
$$\Sigma\, C_1(R_{incor} \times D) = (0.2 \times 0.3) = 0.06$$
$$\Sigma\, C_1(R_{cor} \times D) > \Sigma\, C_1(R_{incor} \times D)$$

As above, the value of incorrect test items(0.06) is smaller than the value of correct test items(0.43). Therefore, inferring that the student may understand the concept($C_1$), the system doesn't include $C_1$ in the concept list for supplementary learning. If the final concept list for supplementary learning through this process is determined as { $C_9$, $C_{10}$, $C_{11}$}, the learning paths based on concept map are suggested to the students with learning disability as following.

**Learning path:** Multiplication □ Division without remainder □ Division

### 3.3 Structure of the System

The system comprises user interface, learning-information-collection module, learning -materials-generation module, and learning-diagnosis module. The user interface is classified into two parts for students and teachers. Through the user interface, students can take a test and an explanation of the test result is presented to guide them in further learning. Teachers can identify the relationships between subject concepts and test items on the user interface. Monitoring the information such as learning path, learning frequency, and learning time, learning-information-collection module trans-

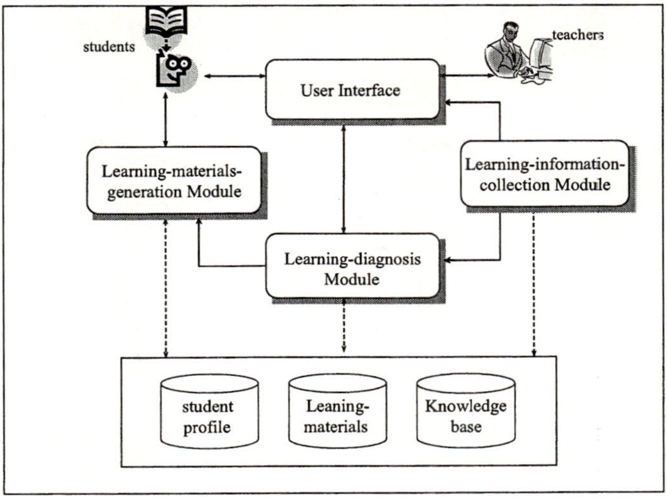


**Fig. 2.** Components and interactions of the system.

fers it to learning-diagnosis module. Learning-materials-generation module provides learning materials and test items according to students' learning state and level. Learning-diagnosis module performs learning analysis and guidance as described in previous chapter.

## 4 Development of an Adaptive Tutoring System Supporting Learning Diagnosis

Our system was implemented with Java on a Windows NT platform. To evaluate the efficiency of our approach, an experiment was conducted on math to students with learning disability at the elementary school. The experimental result reveals that the group of students who received the learning guidance generated by our tutoring system made significant progress.

Fig. 3 shows the graphical user interface for constructing the concept map-based graph. After learning and tests of students, the learning diagnosis module presents learning guidance to students as shown Fig. 4.

## 5 Conclusion

In this paper, we presented a web-based adaptive tutoring system based on concept-map for students with learning disabilities. It is important to provide adaptable learning methods and learning materials considering the learning characteristics of each one for students with learning disability. The system can provide personalized suggestions for each student by analyzing student answers and the relationships among the subject concepts and test items. That is, analyzing the learning state of the student,

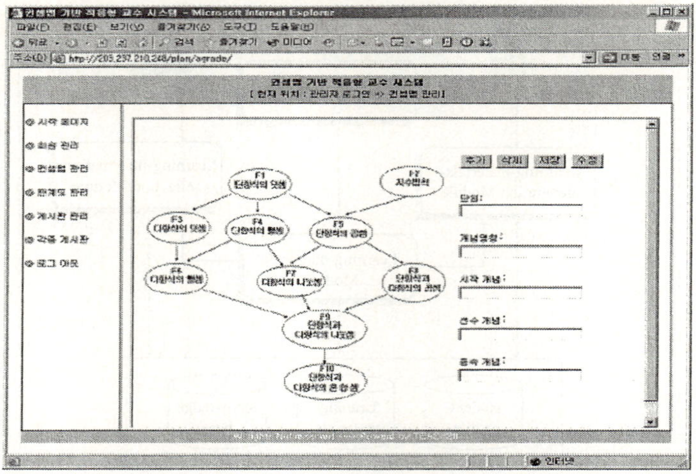

**Fig. 3.** Graphical user interface for constructing the concept map-based graph.

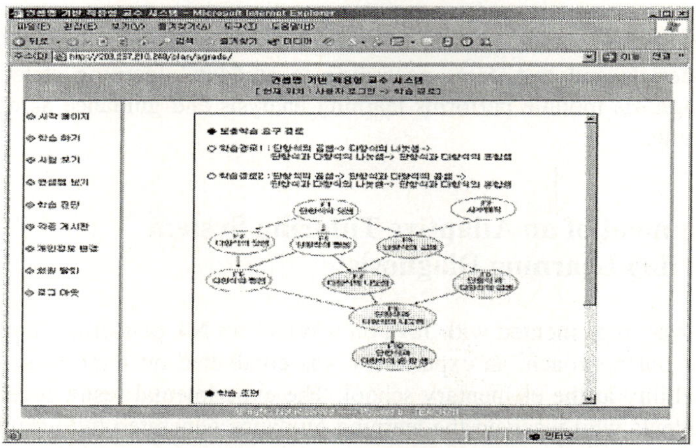

**Fig. 4.** Learning guidance presented by the system.

the system diagnoses the misunderstood concepts and suggests the concepts to require supplementary learning. When the concepts for supplementary learning is given, rather the concepts in relation to prior concepts on concept map than only fragmentary concepts related to failed test items are suggested.

Experiments have been conducted to evaluate the behavior of the proposed model in adapting the lesson of a course. The result has been obtained using educational materials developed for a chapter of mathematic of elementary school. The performance of the proposed approach has been evaluated by students and teachers in elementary school and has been characterized as reliable.

## References


1. Bender, W. N.: Learning disabilities : Characteristics, identification and teaching strategies. Needham Heighrs, MA :Allyn and Bacon (1992).
2. Gwo-Jen, H.: A Concept map model for developing intelligent tutoring systems. Computers & Education 40 (2000) 217-235.
3. Novak, J. D., et al.: The use of concept mapping and knowledge mapping with junior high school science students. Science Education 67 (1983) 625-645.
4. Jonassen, D. H. : Computers in the classroom: Mindtools for critical thinking. Eaglewoods, NJ: Merill/Prentice Hall (1996).
5. Brusilovsky, P. : Adaptive Educational System on the World Web: A Review of Available Technologies. http://www-aml.cs.umassedu/stern/websits/itsworkshop/ brusilovsky.html
6. Siegel, L.S.: Issues in the definition and diagnosis of learning disabilities. 32 (1999) 304-319.
7. Yoshikawa, A. et al.: Intelligent tutoring system for electric circuit exercising. IEEE Transaction on Education 35(2) (2000) 222-225.
8. Ausubel, D.: Educational psychology: A cognitive view. New York. Holt, Rinehart, and Winston. (1968).
9. Papanikolaou, K.A. et al.: INSPIRE: an Intelligent system for personalized instruction in a remote environment. In the proc. of 3rd workshop on Adaptive Hypertext and Hypermedia. (2001).

# Tutor Informatico: Increasing the Selfteaching in Down Syndrome People

Eduardo Campos, Ana Granados, Sergio Jiménez, and Javier Garrido

Departamento de Ingeniería Informática, E. P. S. Universidad Autónoma de Madrid
Ctra Colmenar Viejo km15, 28049 Madrid, Spain
eduardo.campos@ii.uam.es

**Abstract.** The Tutor Informatico System provides a new tool based on the new mobile technologies to Down syndrome people. This system is not intended to be a solution to the Down syndrome handicap, but a useful support that helps users to overcome the obstacles this handicap implies and to advance in this process towards self-sufficiency. For this purpose web technologies, data transmission technologies like GPRS and location technologies like GPS will be combined to offer a small terminal that works like a tutor, reminding and showing the user the daily tasks that he must accomplish. In addition a global positioning system provides the user with a certain degree of mobility.

## 1 Introduction

The system is a tool which attempts to increase personal autonomy and to improve abilities such as self-control. The system offers the Down syndrome (DS) people more chances of taking decisions, making their cognitive process easier, and apart from that, tries to improve their connections with themselves, with others and with the environment. It would certainly improve their quality of life balancing the limitations that prevent them from developing their daily life's activities. This tool, integrated in a small PDA system, will accompany the user and helps him to remember his daily tasks, advises him in these displacements, allows making telephone calls in a very simple way, etc.

The system tries to stimulate the user self teaching by means of assistance in his daily tasks scheduling, and helping him to establish links with his particular environment. This support can be taken to different phases from learning within the daily life of the user and can be made without the presence of another person. It offers services such as the routing aid or monitoring from a control centre. The information can be controlled and stored with the evolution of the user. Other advantages that the system offers are: better quality communication interactions, increase of the amount of communication interaction, cognitive processes improvement, better integration in different contexts and new or hypothetic situations anticipations. We are conscious of the difficulties in the project (specially the price of the PDA devices), but we think that it's interesting to measure in what degree new technologies can be applied to the handicap field and more precisely to the Down syndrome area.

K. Miesenberger et al. (Eds.): ICCHP 2004, LNCS 3118, pp. 202–205, 2004.

## 2 The System

The system tries to improve the processes of learning in the user through the involvement of three human groups: the users, the family and the professional tutors, with them we were building a notion of autonomy and independence.

From this exposition the tutor has been elaborated, like an instrument that facilitates support activities in diverse areas: the home, the community, the use, the security... In order to carry out this purpose, they have been selected and designed a series of representative tasks of different areas and activities from support, prioritized tasks that include an ample fan of activities of the daily life within the denominated instrumental abilities. Starting off of these, it is tried that the TUTOR facilitates the access to learning that the person with DS previously has acquired for the putting in practice of conceptual abilities as much social. The following step was to make a revision of the characteristics: sensorial and motor, perceptive, cognitive and communicative that presents/displays the people with DS, analyzing the present regulations and legislations on design for the accessibility of the people with handicap and determining the characteristics that must have the interface of use of the tutor for finally makes a selection and adaptation of the representational level of the information (written, spoken language, icons, etc.) to the interface of the system.

Due to the different levels of skills of the people with Down syndrome, it's necessary to make an evaluation of the possible users of the system. That is why was made a selection of standardized tests and an elaboration of specific tests with the suitable evaluation to be able to identify the possible users of the system. At the same time, we made a specification of software and hardware that the TUTOR needs for the terminal and for the Attention Centre.

We designed and implemented the platform of the attention centre, creating its structure, a Web server, relational databases and services (oriented to provide aid in emergency situations). Thus, we designed a Story Board of the real tasks previous to implementation of the system as a first form to observe the tasks by the experts. In this manner, psychological and technical aspects were introduced that enormously enriched the final quality of the tasks. These revised tasks were used during the field studies, with the end users of the system. Finally we are now in the first stage of the field studies, thanks to which we could obtain the first evaluation of the system. This serves us to improve some aspects of the system to be able to develop the TUTOR INFORMATICO System completely.

### 2.1 The System Architecture

TUTOR INFORMATICO System modules are: a Control Centre (composed of information manager servers, Data Bases, geographic information servers and a call centre), PDA's (mobile terminals that give more portability to the system), and a Web Portal.

### 2.2 The Mobile Terminals

We need a terminal with the following features: small size, transportable, multimedia, provided with a wireless communications system, allowing GPS location. These requirements took us to use a PDA which only inconvenience is its high price.

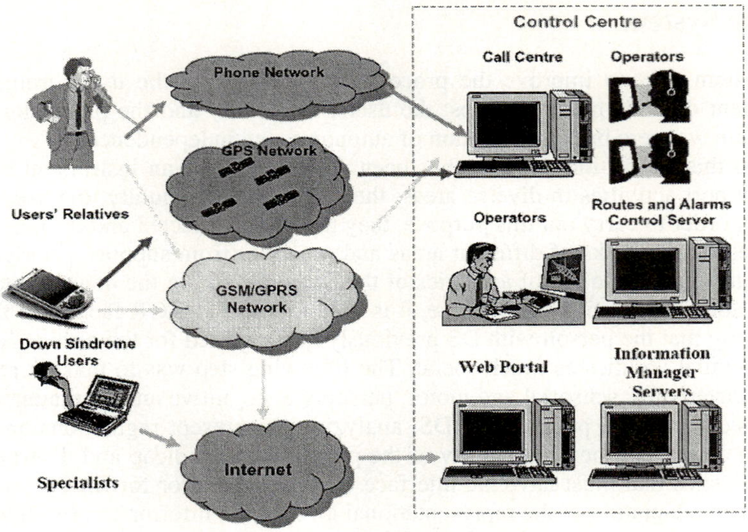


**Fig. 1.** The system architecture.

Development was made using visual C ++ under embedded Visual Microsoft C++ and FLASH technology under Macromedia Flash MX. The power of the C within Windows CE for PDA's allows the control of a GPS and a MODEM GPRS connected to the PDA.

### 2.3 The Control Centre

The Control Centre is the "brain" of the system. It has a module that is connected with the PDA and is continuously transmitting the information obtained to the other modules: Data Base Server, GIS Server and Operator Server. Telephone lines give support for the incoming calls from users, relatives, and tutors. It is run by a team formed by telephone operators, Down syndrome specialists and computer technicians that assure the good operation of the system.

### 2.4 The Web Portal

The Web Portal is a common web site. It allows to configure and to interact with certain modules of the system from any computer connected to the Internet.

## 3 Experiments

The current phase of the project is focused on the following two tasks: to make a shopping list and to do the shopping. For the first task, the user must access the Tutor-web in which he was previously registered. By means of a friendly interface the user will choose items from different categories to make his own shopping list. If it was necessary, at the beginning, the Down people learn how to navigate the web with the help of his tutor or his family.

## 4 Conclusions

Nowadays some tools based on the new communication technologies, help thousands of handicapped people in their daily life. In this project we present one of these tools oriented to improve Down syndrome people's autonomy. Many functionalities could be implemented using this platform, oriented to DS collective but also to other kind of handicapped people. In this project we designed and built a pilot to demonstrate the potentiality of the idea. At the moment a physiologist study is in progress in order to detect the benefits of the tool in a Down's collective. There are still some problems to surpass related to costs and portability. It has been observed that the system is adapted perfectly to the daily situation of a user with Down syndrome.

## Acknowledgments

This project has been developed in collaboration with the Applied Psychology Centre (CPA) of the Universidad Autónoma de Madrid (UAM) and the Spanish Federation of Down's Syndrome (FEISD). This work has been financed by the IMSERSO.

## References

1. Abascal, J. Aplicaciones de la Informática para las Personas con Limitaciones Cognitivas. *Actas del 6º Congreso Mundial sobre el Síndrome de Down* . Madrid: FEISD. (1997)
2. Alcantud, F. y otros Estudio sobre el impacto de las nuevas tecnologías en las personas con discapacidad. *Poibea, 49* (p.4-6). (2001)
3. Bermingham,J.,Conway, M. Los Deficientes Mentales y las Nuevas Tecnologías. *Siglo Cero, 115 (p. 34-37).*Centro para el Diseño Universal. www.design.ncsu.edu/cud(1988)
4. Ekberg, J., Proyecto INCLUDE. Inclusión de personas con discapacidad y mayores en telemática. www.stakes.fi/INCLUDE
5. González Rus, G.,López, Torrecilla, M. Las Nuevas Tecnologías en el ámbito de la Discapacidad y las NEE. Su Aplicación en el Síndrome de Down. *Polibea , 58 (p. 51-57).* (2001)
6. González, G. y López, M. Las Nuevas Tecnologías en el Ámbito de la Discapacidad y las NEE(II). Su Aplicación en el Síndrome de Down. *Polibea, 59 (p. 51-58)* . (2001) (2001)

# The Effect of Assistive Technology on Educational Costs: Two Case Studies

Amy Gips[1], Philip A. DiMattia[2], and James Gips[3]

[1] Carroll School of Management, Boston College, Chestnut Hill, MA 02467, USA
amy.gips@bc.edu
[2] Lynch School of Education, Boston College, Chestnut Hill, MA 02467, USA
philip.dimattia@bc.edu
[3] Computer Science Department, CSOM, Boston College, Chestnut Hill, MA 02467, USA
james.gips@bc.edu

**Abstract.** Until recently children with very profound disabilities–children who cannot speak and can move only their eyes or head–could be made comfortable, but by and large could not be educated. Assistive technologies now enable them to communicate and to be educated alongside their non-disabled peers. This is a wonderful development. But what is the financial cost? In this paper we look in detail at the costs associated with the education of two children who have used assistive technologies developed at our university and compare them with the educational costs had they not started using the assistive technologies. For these two children the costs of the technologies and special teachers hired are offset by savings from the tuition and transportation of sending them to special schools.

## 1 Introduction

Over the past ten years we have developed and deployed two new technologies (EagleEyes and Camera Mouse) to enable children with severe physical disabilities to use the computer. The technologies have helped children advance their education and interact with teachers, parents, and peers. The development of new technologies holds the hope and promise of helping many people with disabilities live much fuller lives and participate and contribute to society.

The technologies are not inexpensive. There is the initial cost of the equipment and the ongoing costs of training people to use the system and adapting curricular materials appropriately. The question often arises about whether using assistive technologies greatly increases the costs of educating students with disabilities. In this paper we examine in detail the costs of educating two children who have adopted technologies developed in our lab. Working with personnel at the schools of the children, we also look at what the costs of educating the children would have been without the assistive technologies. We conclude that in these two cases the technologies roughly paid for themselves as they allowed the children to stop attending expensive special schools for children with disabilities and begin attending regular schools with the other children in their town.

K. Miesenberger et al. (Eds.): ICCHP 2004, LNCS 3118, pp. 206–213, 2004.

## 2 Background

Education for children in the U.S. is controlled and financed mainly at the town and city level with increasing regulations and some funding from the state and federal governments. Under the Individuals with Disabilities Education Act (IDEA) of 1990 all children in the U.S. must be provided with a "free appropriate public education" (FAPE) in the least restrictive environment. IDEA requires that "to the maximum extent appropriate, children with disabilities ... are educated with children who are not disabled. And that special classes, separate schooling, or other removal of children with disabilities from the regular educational environment occurs only when the nature or severity of the disability of a child is such that education in regular classes with the use of supplementary aids and services cannot be achieved satisfactorily." In 1999-2000 the total spending to provide education services for students with disabilities in the United States was $77.3 billion, an average of $12,474 per student. Expenditures of educating students with disabilities represent over 21% of the spending on all elementary and secondary education in the United States. [1]

In order to be provided with a "free appropriate public education," children with disabilities can be placed in several different types of educational settings. These include: hospital-based schools for children with the most severe disabilities, separate residential schools, private separate daytime schools where the children live at home, public collaborative day schools where neighboring towns collaborate in establishing day schools for children with special needs, and various programs within the regular public school. These settings are listed roughly in order of decreasing restrictive environment and decreasing cost.

As a brief example, consider the town of Hudson, Massachusetts, a town with a population of 17,233 and an area of 30 $kms^2$ located 45 kms west of Boston. In 2003-04 the town had 2,806 students with a total education budget of $23,200,000 for an average cost of $8,268 per student. Of the 2,806 total student enrollment, 569 students have Individual Education Programs (IEPs), meaning they have special needs of some type, of whom 32 receive out of district services. These include 7 children in residential schools costing $954,270 for an average of $136,324 per student, 13 children in private day schools costing $509,065 for an average of $39,159 per student, and 12 special needs students in public collaborative schools part-time or full-time costing $220,628 for an average of $18,386 per student. Like other towns and cities in Massachusetts, Hudson funds its schools largely through property taxes on the families and businesses that reside in the town.

## 3 Assistive Technologies

At Boston College we have developed two technologies to enable people who cannot speak and can move only their eyes or head to access the computer. EagleEyes [2,3] uses five electrodes placed on the head, around the eyes, to detect eye movements. As the person moves his or her eyes, the mouse pointer on the screen moves accordingly. Camera Mouse [4] uses a video camera to track head movements and then control the mouse pointer accordingly. Camera Mouse is easier than EagleEyes for people to use, but they must have voluntary head control.

The families and schools of children with severe physical disabilities learn about our technologies in various ways. Anyone can try the technologies for free. If one of the technologies works for a child between the ages of 3 and 22, then it is usually up to the school district to obtain the technology for the child to enable the child's free and appropriate education. For EagleEyes this involves signing a use license with the university. We then send a list of hardware for the school to purchase directly from the vendors. The cost is approximately $6,000 plus a computer. We will send a student to set up the system and provide initial training. For Camera Mouse the technology has been licensed by the university to a start-up company in Texas. The family or school needs to purchase a USB camera for approximately $100. A 30 day free trial of the software is available at www.cameramouse.com. In either case, the school might well decide to contract with the Campus School at Boston College to provide services in training teachers how to use the technology in a class and how to adapt the curriculum to work with the technology. If the child lives in the greater Boston area, he or she might use the technology at Boston College on a regular basis.

Special Education expenses are a controversial part of school budgets. The question always arises "What is adopting the assistive technology really going to cost us in educating this child?" That is the question we are seeking to answer in this study. Our approach is to look in detail at two students who have successfully used EagleEyes and Camera Mouse in their education. With the help of personnel at their local school districts, we try to determine the total costs of educating the students with the assistive technology and what the costs would have been without the assistive technology.

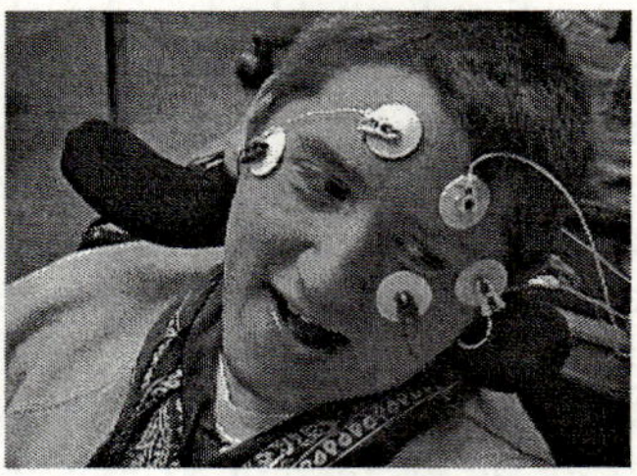

**Fig. 1.** Michael Nash using EagleEyes.

## 4 Case Study: Michael Nash and EagleEyes

Michael Nash (see Figure 1) was born in 1981 with spastic quadriplegic cerebral palsy. Michael cannot speak and can voluntarily move only his eyes. On three separate evaluations, Michael was diagnosed as having the mental age of 18 months. As a youth he was sent to special schools for children with disabilities. In 1994 Michael lived in Marshfield, MA and attended school at a separate day program at Reads Collaborative. His mother saw a television program on EagleEyes and called Boston College for information on the system. Michael tried the EagleEyes electrodes system and was able to communicate for the first time. His parents brought special education personnel from the Marshfield Public School system up to the Campus School at Boston College and they arranged to begin sending Michael for educational sessions on EagleEyes at the Campus School. In addition, Michael's parents obtained an EagleEyes system for Michael to use at home. The next year, in 1995, the superintendent of the Marshfield Public School systems saw Michael using EagleEyes and decided that Michael had the cognitive and communicative ability to be mainstreamed into a regular classroom. In June 2003 Michael completed his studies at Marshfield Public High School.

In 1994-95 tuition at Reads was $31,000. In 1995-96 when Michael was placed in the regular Marshfield Public School (MPS) they hired a special Teacher Aide for Michael for $28,859 and contracted with the Campus School at Boston College for $14,000 to continue to provide services including several afternoons a week at Boston College using EagleEyes. Actual costs for Michael are shown in Table 1. Professional Services include Occupational Therapy, Physical Therapy, and Evaluation.

**Table 1.** Annual educational costs for Michael Nash attending Marshfield public schools (MPS) with EagleEyes and using EagleEyes at the Campus School of Boston College. In $ US.

| School | Reads | MPS | MPS | MPS | MPS | MPS | MPS | MPS | MPS |
|---|---|---|---|---|---|---|---|---|---|
| | 94-95 | 95-96 | 96-97 | 97-98 | 98-99 | 99-00 | 00-01 | 01-02 | 02-03 |
| Reads Tuition | 31,000 | | | | | | | | |
| EagleEyes | 10,000 | 14,000 | 13,000 | 12,000 | 15,000 | 16,000 | 18,700 | 17,600 | 27,400 |
| Teacher Aide | 1,684 | 28,859 | 32,303 | 35,327 | 38,690 | 41,310 | 42,770 | 48,159 | 53,340 |
| Tutor | 11,000 | | | | | | | | |
| Transportation | 6,200 | 6,800 | 7,200 | 7,800 | 8,438 | 9,000 | 9,500 | 15,400 | 15,400 |
| Prof. Services | 4,000 | 4,500 | 4,700 | 4,900 | 5,100 | 5,320 | 5,750 | 7,400 | 8,250 |
| Total | 63,884 | 54,159 | 57,203 | 60,027 | 67,228 | 71,630 | 76,720 | 88,559 | 104,390 |

**Table 2.** Estimated hypothetical educational costs for Michael Nash at Reads Collaborative without EagleEyes.

| School | Reads | Reads | Reads | Reads | Reads | Reads | Reads | Reads | Reads |
|---|---|---|---|---|---|---|---|---|---|
| | 94-95 | 95-96 | 96-97 | 97-98 | 98-99 | 99-00 | 00-01 | 01-02 | 02-03 |
| Reads Tuition | 31,000 | 34,592 | 34,592 | 39,472 | 38,472 | 38,452 | 38,452 | 46,512 | 46,512 |
| EagleEyes | | | | | | | | | |
| Teacher Aide | 1,684 | 1,852 | 2,038 | 2,241 | 2,466 | 2,712 | 2,983 | 3,282 | 3,610 |
| Tutor | 11,000 | 12,100 | 13,310 | 14,641 | 16,105 | 17,716 | 19,487 | 21,436 | 23,579 |
| Transportation | 6,200 | 6,800 | 7,200 | 7,800 | 8,438 | 9,000 | 9,500 | 15,400 | 15,400 |
| Prof. Services | 4,000 | 4,500 | 4,700 | 4,900 | 5,100 | 5,320 | 5,750 | 7,400 | 8,250 |
| Total | 53,884 | 59,844 | 61,840 | 69,054 | 70,581 | 73,200 | 76,172 | 94,030 | 97,351 |

In Table 2 we estimate the costs for Michael if he had never used EagleEyes and stayed at Reads. The actual educational costs with EagleEyes show a slight overall savings compared to the estimated costs without EagleEyes (see Table 3). The cost of hiring a special Teacher Aide for Michael and sending him several days a week to Boston College was more than made up for by the savings of not sending him to Reads.

**Table 3.** Actual educational costs for Michael Nash with EagleEyes (EE) versus estimated educational costs (hypothetical) without EagleEyes.

| | 94-95 | 95-96 | 96-97 | 97-98 | 98-99 | 99-00 | 00-01 | 01-02 | 02-03 |
|---|---|---|---|---|---|---|---|---|---|
| Actual with EE | 63,884 | 54,159 | 57,203 | 60,027 | 67,228 | 71,630 | 76,720 | 88,559 | 104,390 |
| Without EE | 53,884 | 59,844 | 61,840 | 69,054 | 70,581 | 73,200 | 76,172 | 94,030 | 97,351 |
| Difference | 10,000 | (5,685) | (4,637) | (9,027) | (3,353) | (1,570) | 548 | (5,471) | 7,039 |
| (Negative numbers represent estimated cost savings from using EagleEyes) | | | | | | | | | |
| Difference as % of Actual | 15.7% | -10.5% | -8.1% | -15.0% | -5.0% | -2.2% | 0.7% | -6.2% | 6.7% |

**Fig. 2.** Amanda and a message she spelled out using Camera Mouse.

## 5 Case Study: Amanda Anastasia and Camera Mouse

Amanda Anastasia (please see Figure 2) is a ten-year old who lives in Hopatcong, NJ. She has a severe, undiagnosed neurological condition that leaves her without speech and with very limited voluntary muscle control. She can move her head.

From preschool until summer 2002 Amanda attended The Children's Center, a private special educational facility located in Morris County, NJ, near her home. While attending The Children's Center, Amanda tried several assistive technology devices with varying degrees of success. In 2001 the Hopatcong Boroughs School system bought a switch-based PowerBook system for Amanda. Not completely satisfied with the system, educational staff members along with Amanda's parents continued to search for other systems. Later that year people from Hopatcong Schools discovered the Camera Mouse system. Amanda and her parents traveled 400 kms to the Campus School at Boston College to try out the system. It was decided that the Camera Mouse system was the right assistive technology system for Amanda. The school district purchased a system for Amanda to use at school, and another system was donated for Amanda to use in her home. Amanda continued to practice and become more proficient with the technology. Her parents supplemented her education at home so that she could catch up with her peers. In September 2002 Amanda entered a second grade classroom at her local public school. Amanda had a special education teacher and aide assigned to provide support in the classroom. The Campus School has been working with Hopatcong to adapt the curriculum and help integrate the Camera Mouse into Amanda's education. Amanda has learned to read and write using the Camera Mouse and is being educated with the other children in her town.

Costs for Amanda's education are shown in Table 4. 1998-99 was a partial year of education. Amanda attended The Children's Center full-time for the next three years. The tuition and transportation costs for Amanda to attend The Children's Center as well as all education-related services were paid by her local school system, the Hopatcong Borough School system. In mainstreaming Amanda into the public school Hopatcong hired an Aide and then a full-time private Teacher for Amanda and contracted with the Campus School to provide consulting and training services on the use of the Camera Mouse. Beginning in 2002 they no longer needed to pay tuition or transportation costs for Amanda to attend The Children's Center. The Services entries in the table include Occupational Therapy, Physical Therapy, Speech and Language, and also extended school expenses for each summer. The figures for 2003-04 are the best estimates as of March 2004.

**Table 4.** Annual educational costs for Amanda Anastasia attending the private Children's Center (CC) and then obtaining Camera Mouse and attending Hopatcong public schools (HPS).

| School | CC | CC | CC | CC | HPS | HPS |
|---|---|---|---|---|---|---|
| | 98-99 | 99-00 | 00-01 | 01-02 | 02-03 | 03-04 |
| CC Tuition | 11,799 | 30,500 | 31,000 | 34,500 | | |
| Camera Mouse | | | | 5,040 | 2,316 | 2,548 |
| Aide | | | | | 15,044 | 16,548 |
| Teacher | | | | | 23,535 | 52,580 |
| Transportation | 958 | 18,358 | 22,279 | 21,328 | | |
| Services | | | 5,166 | 5,750 | 14,053 | 14,833 |
| Supplies | | | | 1,714 | 4,327 | 2,770 |
| Total | 12,757 | 48,858 | 58,445 | 68,332 | 59,275 | 89,279 |

Estimates of the costs if Amanda had not adopted Camera Mouse and had stayed at the private Children's Center are shown in Table 5. School system personnel told us they would have hired an Aide for Amanda but not a special Teacher to adapt the curriculum for her.

In Table 6 the actual educational costs with Camera Mouse are compared with the estimated hypothetical costs if Amanda did not use Camera Mouse and stayed at The Children's Center. The difference in 2001-02 is the $5,040 cost involved in obtaining and installing a Camera Mouse and the personal computer on which it runs. Amanda used a prototype system; the cost now is significantly lower. The savings of 2002-03 are the result of Hopatcong not having to pay tuition and transportation for Amanda to attend The Children's Center offset by a half-time Teacher salary. In 2003-04 the school system decided to hire a full-time teacher just for Amanda to supplement the regular classroom teacher, but the total still was slightly less than placement in The Children's Center would have cost.

**Table 5.** Estimated educational costs if Amanda Anastasia had not adopted Camera Mouse in 2001-02 and had continued to attend the Children's Center (CC).

| School | CC | CC | CC | CC | CC | CC |
|---|---|---|---|---|---|---|
| | 98-99 | 99-00 | 00-01 | 01-02 | 02-03 | 03-04 |
| CC Tuition | 11,799 | 30,500 | 31,000 | 34,500 | 37,950 | 41,745 |
| Camera Mouse | | | | | | |
| Aide | | | | | 15,044 | 16,548 |
| Teacher | | | | | | |
| Transportation | 958 | 18,358 | 22,279 | 21,328 | 23,461 | 25,807 |
| Services | | | 5,166 | 5,750 | 6,325 | 6,958 |
| Supplies | | | | 1,714 | 2,692 | 2,770 |
| Total | 12,757 | 48,858 | 58,445 | 63,292 | 85,472 | 93,828 |

**Table 6.** Actual educational costs for Amanda Anastasia with Camera Mouse (CM) versus estimated educational costs (hypothetical) without Camera Mouse.

| | 98-99 | 99-00 | 00-01 | 01-02 | 02-03 | 03-04 |
|---|---|---|---|---|---|---|
| Actual with CM | 12,757 | 48,858 | 58,445 | 68,332 | 59,275 | 89,279 |
| Without CM | 12,757 | 48,858 | 58,445 | 63,292 | 85,472 | 93,828 |
| Difference | | | | 5,040 | (26,197) | (4,549) |
| (Negative numbers represent estimated cost savings from using Camera Mouse) | | | | | | |
| Difference as % of Actual | | | | 7.4% | -44.2% | -5.1% |

# 6 Conclusion

The use of assistive technologies allowed Michael and Amanda to move from special placements into their neighborhood public schools. This not only fulfills federal law (IDEA) but makes sense educationally. Michael completed his studies at Marshfield High School in June 2003. Amanda is now keeping up with her peers academically. Their local towns needed to hire special aides and teachers for them and spent money for the assistive technology and training and curriculum adaptation. Roughly speaking these costs were offset by tuition and transportation savings, though allocating and estimating costs especially in hypothetical situations necessarily is inexact. Still, we conclude that the assistive technologies allowed the school districts to provide a much better education for Michael and Amanda in the least restrictive environment at roughly no additional financial cost.

## Acknowledgments

Our most sincere thanks to: the school districts of Hudson MA, Marshfield MA, and Hopatcong NJ; the Nash family and Anastasia family for allowing us to work with their children and make this information public; Prof. Hassan Tehranian and Prof. Alan Marcus of the Finance Department at Boston College; Kathy Gips of Adaptive Environments.

Note that James Gips has a minor financial interest in the company that licenses and sells Camera Mouse.

## References

1. Chambers, J., Parrish, T., Harr, J.: What Are We Spending on Special Education Services in the United States, 1999-2000? Special Education Expenditure Project, United States Department of Education, Office of Special Education Programs (2002). See http://csef.air.org/publications/seep/national/AdvRpt1.PDF.
2. Gips, J., Olivieri, C.P., Tecce, J.: Direct Control of the Computer through Electrodes Placed Around the Eyes. In: Smith, N., Salvendy, G. (eds.): Human-Computer Interaction: Applications and Case Studies. Elsevier Amsterdam (1993) 630-635. See http://www.bc.edu/eagleeyes.
3. DiMattia, P., Curran, F.X., Gips, J.: An Eye Control Teaching Device for Students Without Language Expressive Capacity: EagleEyes. Edwin Mellen Press Lewiston, NY (2001).
4. Betke, M., Gips, J., Fleming, P.: The Camera Mouse: Visual Tracking of Body Features to Provide Computer Access for People with Severe Disabilities. IEEE Transactions on Neural Systems and Rehabilitation Engineering 10 (2002) 1-10. See http://www.bc.edu/schools/csom/eagleeyes/cameramouse.

# Making Music Accessible

## *Introduction to the Special Thematic Session*

David Crombie[1], Roger Lenoir[1], Neil McKenzie[1], and Ben Challis[2]

[1] FNB Netherlands, accessible information for people with a print impairment
Molenpad 2, 1016 GM Amsterdam, The Netherlands
projects@fnb.nl
http://projects.fnb.nl/

[2] Leeds Metropolitan University, School of Technology
Leeds, LS1 3HE
b.challis@leedsmet.ac.uk
http://www.leedsmet.ac.uk/

**Abstract.** Musical material is a very rich corpus of data. Data with all kinds of features, entities, relations and a potentially endless number of abstraction levels on all these perspectives. It is therefore important to establish which set of elements we are going to use for the preservation, processing and provision of music; which features are redundant; which building blocks are mandatory; and how many can be shared amongst all of them. These considerations hold especially true for the community that is dependent on the accessibility of music. The area of music encoding is moving towards greater unification and co-ordination of effort and it is important that accessibility requirements are built into design processes. This also requires organisations working in this area to make their requirements clear and to participate in emerging standards.

## 1 Introduction

In the field of accessible music, the primary technology over the last century has been Braille Music [1], but the increasing use of computers for creating and using music scores opens up new possibilities for addressing the needs of print impaired people. Of course, many people have by-passed music notation and become successful performers, creators and users of music without the need for access to music scores. The problem of music encoding for print impaired people is similar to that for many accessibility solutions: the accessible market is a niche market and solutions are designed with the mainstream market in mind. The solution at this stage is very often a *piggyback* solution, failing to incorporate the basic ideals of Design For All. The original software is usually designed with very robust and modern design methodologies, yet a quick solution is designed for the niche markets. If the original solution incorporates extensibility and questions how the solution can be adapted beyond the primary user needs, then the solution can become available to a wider market. The main task within accessible design is to encourage just this type of thinking and design, despite the fact that the rewards are rarely reaped in the short term.

K. Miesenberger et al. (Eds.): ICCHP 2004, LNCS 3118, pp. 214–217, 2004.

## 2 Existing Approaches

### 2.1 Braille Music

One area of access to music that is still a huge problem is the unavailability of Braille scores. This is largely due to the expensive nature of music Braille production. The main factors governing the current price of Braille scores are costly manufacturing materials and transcription time. Transcribers must have an extensive knowledge of print music and be equally familiar with Braille music code [2]. Very often the transcription process for Braille Music is manual. The Braille transcription is then checked against the print score. There is a clear need for systems that eliminate the potential for human error and reduce the length of the process. Currently there are a variety of methods available to produce Braille music, including:

- Scanning print music and converting using digital transcribers
- Inputting music through a MIDI device (playing in or using MIDI file) and translating to Braille code
- Inputting a notated music file, transcribing to Braille (Dancing Dots [5])
- Inputting note-for-note with a software editor
- Using a print to Braille notation editor (such as Toccata [6] or BMK [7])
- Using tactile overlays (such as Weasel [8])

We can therefore surmise that to cut the cost of Braille music production, we must cut the time taken to transcribe the music; lessen the need for only specially trained transcribers; and reduce the cost of materials. This is precisely what is being attempted by some of the software and hardware that has been developed in recent years.

The need for one system that can be used to both notate print scores and perform Braille conversions has become greater. Current Braille transcription processes are extremely time consuming. Automation of the transcription processes would immediately reduce the need to check and correct transcriptions. Furthermore, a system should input and output a variety of file formats. It would also be desirable to have a system that can be used by the print-impaired themselves. However, there is no system capable of satisfying all of these requirements at the same time. The most suitable alternative in common use is a professional quality print notation editor and a separate Braille transcription programme, ensuring a higher quality product.

### 2.2 Spoken Music

Spoken Music provides a spoken description of the elements of the score. These spoken descriptions are provided in such a way that the information is compressed as much as possible to ensure the spoken elements provide usable information but also that the descriptions do not become unwieldy [3,4]. The format is proving very popular with print impaired users, who in the past have either had no access to scores, or have had to be content with the logistic problems of traditional production methods associated with Braille Music. Spoken Music has therefore become valuable to many users as both a learning tool for music and a means of obtaining a score that can be used in much the same way as a traditional score is used by non-impaired users.

### 2.3 Other Formats and Solutions

In widening the scope of accessible formats, it is important to consider that many of the users in this market are not actually blind. Many people have a partial sight deficiency. A format which has received some interest in this field is that of large print music notation. Some organisations produce large print music using commercially available software. This is not simply a matter of enlarging the page to assist the partially sighted, as that tends to produce a score that is difficult to manipulate. In the large print version of the music score, the software enlarges the music staff within the standard page size turning a piece with, for example, six bars to a line into one with as few as one bar to a line. The copy can in effect be tailored to the needs of individual clients. Interesting solutions would be possible if modern extensible methods were used and incorporated at the graphic rendering stage of the music notation production. One possibility in this field would be the use of SVG (Scalable Vector Graphics) [9], where an XML based description of the graphic is used and, because it is vector based, the representation can in theory be used to increase the size of the rendering to any level.

## 3 Recent Initiatives

In recent years a number of initiatives (e.g. CANTATE [10], HARMONICA [11] and WEDELMUSIC [12]) have opened up new opportunities in the field of interactive multimedia music. The area of music encoding is moving towards greater unification and co-ordination of effort with the activities and strategies being pursued by the Music Network [13]. For print impaired people this offers the exciting challenge of bringing together several disparate activities and building a far stronger future for coding activities in this field.

Given the ever-changing requirements of music representation, the interfacing with accessibility tools is constantly set back. With every modification of the models that are used for music analysis, representation and synthesis, additional effort has to be invested to synchronise the consumption and production opportunities for print impaired users with those of the average end user. If we were able to incorporate the 'changing' nature of music representations in the model itself, we would have a means to integrate the volatile nature of music representation. In this respect the work being undertaken by the Music Network with the MPEG ad-hoc group on Symbolic Music Recognition is encouraging [14]. Integration of accessibility notions into the MPEG family will provide previously unavailable opportunities in the provision of accessible multimedia information systems. It will open up modern information services and provide them to all types and levels of users both in the software domain and the hardware domain. In particular, the work being undertaken by MPEG will provide access to multimedia content to print impaired users. Additionally, new devices and environments can be addressed from this platform, such as information on mobile devices with additional speech assistance.

## 4 Conclusion

Recent research suggests that music representation should be based on extensible music representation models. There is a need to integrate such an approach within existing and new DRM systems and thereby satisfying commercial needs. There is a need to integrate such an approach with future alternative presentations. Every representation of musical material has its own specialised properties, attributes and requirements. It is highly unlikely that we can foresee which musical entities will be needed for specialised representations that will become needed in the (near) future. The representation requirements do not solely depend on technological representation possibilities. We must also consider user preferences, cultural preferences and scientific needs. Naturally, these preferences and requirements will evolve over time and force us to consider only extensible solutions, but the still greater challenge lies in making these preferences coherent for the wider development community.

## References


1. Krolick, B. (1996), "New International Manual of Braille Music Notation", World Blind Union, FNB, Amsterdam
2. Crombie, D., Lenoir, R., and McKenzie, N., (2003) "Producing accessible multimedia music" in Proceedings 3rd International Conference on Web Delivering of Music, Leeds, IEEE
3. Crombie, D., Lenoir, R, McKenzie, N,, Ng, K. (2003) "Finding the Right Note: Making Multimedia Music Visible" in Proceedings Electronic Arts & Visual Imaging (EVA2003), Institute of Archaeology, London, UK
4. Crombie, D., Lenoir, R., and McKenzie, N. (2003) Bridging the Gap: Music and Communication, Proceedings Rencontres Internationales des Technologies pour la Musique (Resonances 2003), IRCAM, Paris
5. http://www.dancingdots.com
6. http://members.optusnet.com.au/~terryk/toccata.htm
7. Project PLAY, http://www.dodiesis.com/
8. Challis, B.P. and Edwards, A.D.N. (2000) "Weasel: A System for the Non-Visual Presentation of Music Notation", in proceedings of ICCHP 2000, OCG
9. http://www.w3.org/TR/SVG/
10. http://projects.fnb.nl/cantate/default.htm
11. http://projects.fnb.nl/harmonica/default.htm
12. http://www.wedelmusic.org
13. http://www.interactivemusicnetwork.org
14. http://www.interactivemusicnetwork.org/mpeg-ahg/

# The Design of Spoken Music Web Browser for Teaching Learning-Disabled Children: A Chevé System Approach to Music Notation

Chi-Nung Chu[1] and Yu Ting Huang[2]

[1] National Taiwan Normal University, Information & Computer Education, 162, Sec. 1 Hoping East Rd., Taipei, 106 Taiwan
nung@mail.ckitc.edy.tw
[2] Shih Chien University, Department of Music, 70 Ta-Chih Street Chung-Shan District,Taipei, Taiwan, R.O.C.
cnchu@sinamail.com

**Abstract.** Reading music notation is a specialized skill and a key to get into the music. Traditionally, the very complexity of music notation is taught in abstract way. It is hard for the learning-disabled children to comprehend and memorize the abstract concepts. We have developed a Spoken Music Web Browser which incorporates Chevé system, a system of musical notation with the idea of indicating notes by numbers, to bridge the gap between the cognition of learning-disabled children and music notation. In addition to providing functions of melody and solmization for the Chevé system, this design of Spoken Music web browser could also analyze each note of Chevé system on the web page and automatically provide corresponding stave notation and vocal descriptions about its clef, pitch name, meter and beat as needed. This new interactive Spoken Music web browser would supply an opportunity for the learning-disabled children to learning music through the Internet.

## 1 Introduction

The function of music is beyond the language and it is widely believed that the benefit for children is beyond the realm of music as well. Musical training can especially facilitate cognitive skills, including reading, abstract spatial abilities and creativity for the learning-disabled children [7, 8].

Reading music notation is a specialized skill and a key to get into the music. Traditionally, the very complexity of music notation is taught in abstract way. It is hard for the learning-disabled children, including mental retardation, to comprehend and memorize the abstract concepts [9]. As the information technology implemented on the Internet is attaining to maturity. The web-based learning henceforth has become an important platform for the education renovation [10]. Music notation is presently transmitted over the Web in graphic formats (PDF, GIF, etc.). The musical information retrieval is difficult for people who use screen readers, Braille displays or text to speech systems, this means that the graphic information cannot be read or processed further by these software applications. There are two popular file formats for music notation to make it accessible on the web with computer mark-up language. One is the NIFF (Notation Interchange File Format) which is a standard digital format for the

K. Miesenberger et al. (Eds.): ICCHP 2004, LNCS 3118, pp. 218–223, 2004.

representation of standard musical notation [5]. The format is flexible enough to allow simple implementations with minimal graphical information and descriptions about associated midi data and custom symbols. Another popular file format developed by the CERL research group, at the University of Illinois, is an extensible music notation format called TILIA [4]. Although today's MusicXML software modeled on W3C can convert between several very different music formats, including Finale, SharpEye, Sibelius, TaBazar, Virtual Composer, and MuseData [2][3]. However there are no further utility to translate these file formats to meet the learning-disabled children's special needs.

Invented by a French physician E. Chevé, there is a Chevé system which represents musical notation with the idea of indicating notes by numbers for teaching purposes. The figures 1 to 7 are used instead of do, re, mi fa, sol, la, ti to locate their position on the stave. Musical notations can be therefore shown with proper numerical alignment in easy recognition way. The Talking Music concept provides a useful preliminary example of accessible music. One of the guiding principles of FNB is that print impaired people should have access to the same information as sighted people. That means everything on the page of a music score must be represented in a spoken format [6]. Spoken Music may become one of the good ways for the learning-disabled children to retrieve music information.

The goal of this design is to find a solution to bridge the gap between the cognition of learning-disabled children and music notation. That means to allow the music notation to be transformed from Chevé system, including vocal descriptions, solmization and melody. We also have designed a Chevé system authoring tool to create the HTML file which can be posted on the web. As a result, this integrated system facilitates the music notation learning and teaching for the learning-disabled children and their instructors on the web.

## 2 Spoken Music Web Browser

The design of Spoken Music web browser (Fig. 1) is based on the Microsoft Internet Explorer engine running on the Windows platform. In order to build the foundation of aural skills for the learning-disabled children, the Spoken Music web browser provides the function of solmization•5th button from the left of tool bar•and melody (4th button from the left of tool bar•for Chevé system as needed. It coordinates the Chinese text-to-speech engine of IBM ViaVoice as a solmization producer. It also connects with the on-board synthesizer on the PC sound card. The synthesizer on PC sound card can act like any other MIDI device as a source of melody. Each note of Chevé system on the web page can be explicitly taught from the Spoken Music web browser. Children can scaffold through the Spoken Music web browser by watching the stave notation, listening to music notation description; rhythm syllables. That would encourage them to make their own mental model for the music notation. The integrated Spoken Music web browser software is installed at the client side. This design not only reduces the overload of server computation and network traffic, but also avoids the redesigning of the existing web sites for the children's special needs. The major features of Spoken Music web browser are described below.

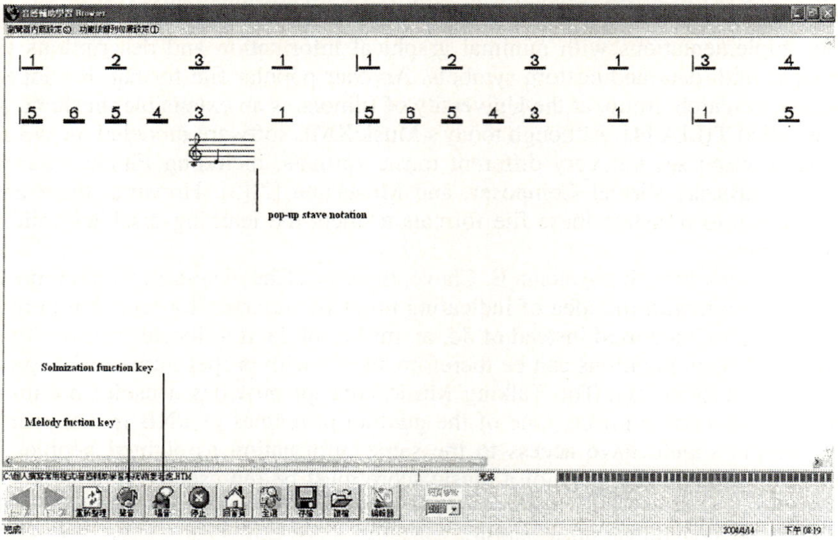


**Fig. 1.** Spoken Music web browser.

## 2.1 Stave Notation

Each note of Chevé system on the web page is an independent character. As children move mouse over a specific note on the web page, Spoken Music web browser will recognize it and automatically pop-up the corresponding stave note picture near it (Fig. 1). Thus children can try to make their own mind map related to the pointed music notation. The Spoken Music web browser is bundled with a stave note picture database for each symbol in Chevé system. This number symbol of Chevé system is transformed into stave notation to assist children in reading music notation.

## 2.2 Vocal Descriptions

The Spoken Music web browser could retrieve music information from the Chevé system on a web page. As children moves mouse to one specific note of Chevé system, they can click the right button of the mouse to trigger the Spoken Music web browser speaking out its corresponding clef, pitch name, meter and beat. As a result children could understand the musical information of the note more in depth.

## 2.3 Solmization

The Spoken Music web browser integrates the technologies of Chinese text-to-speech engine to provide the solmization for Chevé system. It is a system of syllables - do, re, mi, fa, sol, la, ti with respect to keynote in Chevé system. In addition, children can practice ear-training, sight-reading and rhythm perception to form a foundation of aural skills. Children can use the Spoken Music web browser to play single note, measure, phrase and even whole piece from the highlighted notes of Chevé system on the web page.

### 2.4 Melody

Similar to the solmization, children may practice the ear-training, sight-reading and rhythm perception from the melody of Chevé system on the web page. The Spoken Music web browser links the MIDI synthesizer on the sound card of each computer. And the melody can be played in the sound of piano, violin, trumpet, flute, and so on for the children. Children can try to sing the music notation and say the rhythm with the Spoken Music web browser at the same time. It could help make music notation more concrete for the learning-disabled children.

### 2.5 Adaptive Interface

For considering the children's cognition abilities, the toolbar of Spoken Music web browse provides only graphic icons that are used frequently. Reducing the amount of options makes the learning-disabled children to manipulate it much more easily [1]. Furthermore, there is voice description for each button that can help children to understand its function better. According to users' habit or motor capabilities, the toolbar of Spoken Music web browser could be located to different positions such as the topside, the bottom, the right side, and the left side of the window. For people with sight problem, the Spoken Music web browser prepares the use of magnifier for surfing.

## 3 Chevé System Authoring Tool

The Chevé system combines the principle of the movable notes – do re mi, with the old idea of indicating notes by figures. The figures from 1 to 7 represent the tones of the scale (in any given key); lower or higher octaves are indicated by a dot under or above the figures (Fig. 4). A rest is indicated by 0.

The design of Chevé system authoring tool is base on Chevé system principles. And it is integrated into the Spoken Music web browser. Instructors can compose the Chevé system directly to the World Wide Web through playing the connected keyboard or clicking the mouse.

The Chevé system authoring tool provides two kinds of manipulating interfaces (Fig. 2, Fig. 3) for both the instructors and children to compose Chevé system notes. It offers 128 most common patch types from pianos to gunshots through the synthesizer on the sound card. The learning-disabled children can play the virtual instruments to promote the learning interest and motivation for music notation.

## 4 Preliminary Experiment

This case study involves five 6$^{th}$ grade students with moderate mental retardation. Three are females and two are males. They all study in a special school for the mentally retarded. The subjects selected can recognize the numbers from one to nine, but can not read the music notation even once taught. In order to avoid the familiarity

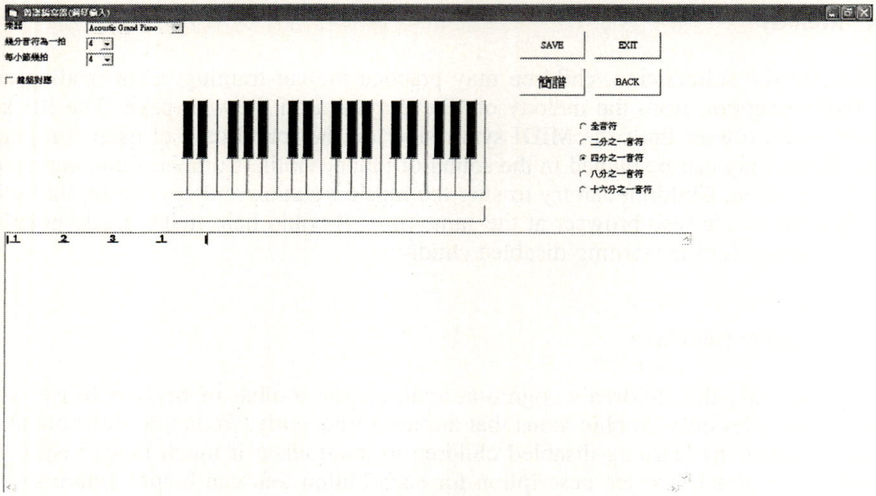


**Fig. 2.** Piano interface of the Chevé system authoring tool.

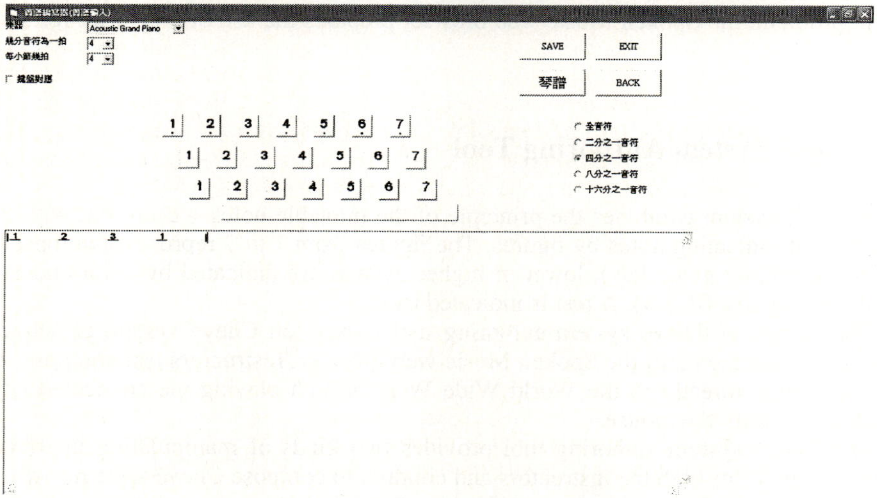


**Fig. 3.** Single note interface of the Chevé system authoring tool.

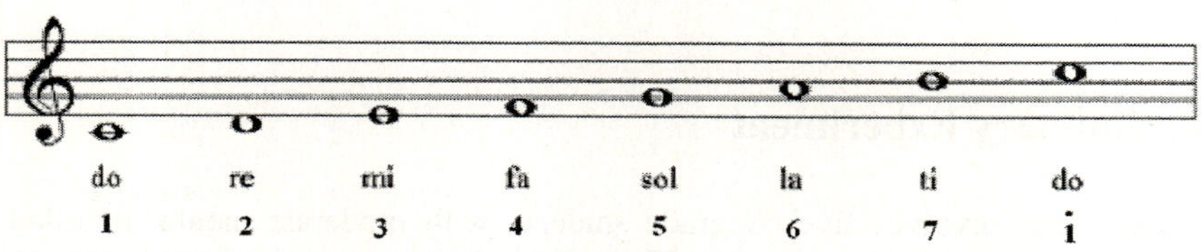


**Fig. 4.** Example of the Chevé system.

effect of the experimental materials, we composed the unknown pieces of melody for them to read. The result indicates that they all can identify the range of music notation from do to ti. And interestingly, at the same time they are trying to sing the pitch name with rhythm when they read the music notation. All the five students said that it is more fun to learn music notation with the Spoken Music web browser. They can play the Chevé system by themselves in the multi-sensory forms of vocal description, melody, solmization and even diverse sound of instruments.

## 5 Conclusion and Future Work

The goal of this study is to find an efficient solution on the World Wide Web that would allow transformation of music notation through Chevé system. It is great for children to have opportunity to aurally identify what they see on a Chevé system when they start to learn the music on notation. It links the sound and mark on Chevé system and helps to present a more complicated music notation related to a specific sound. With scaffolding stave notation figure, vocal descriptions, melody and solmization, the learning-disabled children can build the foundation of reading music notation by themselves. Children may require a lot of learning support for this but this is where our design comes in extremely handy.

As a future project, we plan a long term study to give children more time to become accustomed to the Spoken Music web browser. We hope to train and test children on dictation (ear training) for listening intelligently to music and sight singing for rhythmic reading. For the children with special needs, music does not presented on scores. To bring it to life there must be an instrument that can sing, an ear that can hear, and an emotion that can sing and hear in their minds.

## References


1. Chu, C.N., Chen, M.C., Li, T.Y.: A study on the design and evaluation of an adaptive web browser for students with reading difficulties. International Conference on Computers in Education (2002)
2. David, C., Dijkstra, S., Schut, E., Lindsay, N.: Spoken Music: Enhancing Access to Music for the Printed Disabled. Lecture Notes in Computer Science, 2398 (2002) 667-674
3. `http://nide.snow.utoronto.ca/music/index_old2.html`
4. `http://www.musicxml.com/xml.html`
5. `http://www.musique.umontreal.ca/personnel/Belkin/NIFF.doc.html`
6. `http://www.w3.org/TR/xag`
7. Hurwitz, I., Wolff, P.H., Bortnick, B.D., Kokas, K.: Nonmusical effects of the Kodaly music curriculum in primary grade children. Journal of Learning Disabilities, 8, (1975) 45-51
8. Lamb, S.J., Gregory, A.H.: The relationship between music and reading in beginning readers. Educational Psychology, 13, (1993) 19-26.
9. Ormrod, J.E.: Educational psychology: Developing learners. (3rd ed). New Jersey: Prentice-Hall, Inc. (2000)
10. Web-based Education Commission (WBEC). The power of the Internet for learning: Moving from promise to practice (Report). Washington, DC: U.S. Department of Education (2000) 17-49

# DaCapo, a Project on Transforming Ink Printed to Braille Notes Semi-automatically

## The Project's Current State

Thomas Kahlisch, Matthias Leopold, and Christian Waldvogel

Deutsche Zentralbücherei für Blinde zu Leipzig
http://www.dzb.de

## 1 Introduction

DaCapo is a working group as well as a project of the German Central Library for the Blind (DZB). The project is financed by the Federal Ministry of Health and Social Security (BMGS) and started in the summer of 2003. The project's members are translating ink printed notes to Braille notes by order.

At the same time software is being developed that will help to make the translation more efficient and of higher quality. Commercial note scanning programs shall be integrated into the operating process. The output of these programs is going to be used as the input for the further interactive translation of ink printed notes to Braille notes. Although the scanned ink printed notes have to be postprocessed we hope to increase the Braille note production rate preserving at least the same quality.

Furthermore there are great quantities of Braille notes in different libraries for the blind. An automatic transformation from Braille to ink printed notes can reveal the quality of these notes more easily. One could also consider making some limited automatic corrections to them. Thus old writing standards can be substituted by modern ones more quickly.

## 2 The Project's Goals

The project DaCapo aims at developing a software package, that will allow to translate ink printed notes to Braille notes and vice versa. The former shall be an interactive, semi-automatic process. The basic idea is to keep the software as general as possible so that it can be extended and adapted for different tasks needed. For the sake of generality, we need to allow different kinds of input.

Of course a completely automatic translation process has to be the goal. But the existence of countless exceptions and special situations forces the translation to be interactive. Thus we do not intend to implement a fully automatic transformation of Braille notes. Rather the translation shall be interactive to combine the best possible results of automatic calculations with the expert knowledge of our note translators. The former is planned to minimize translation errors and maximize the efficiency, the latter to guarantee the overall quality by supporting direct interventions providing best possible readability for the blind.

K. Miesenberger et al. (Eds.): ICCHP 2004, LNCS 3118, pp. 224–227, 2004.

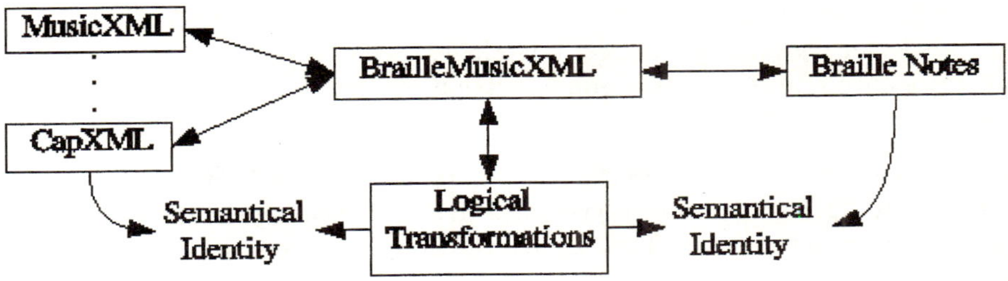


**Fig. 1.** Overview over the DaCapo project.

## 3 The Project's Framework

The software will work in three independent stages (see Figure 1):

1. ink printed note's source access and unification of it's representation,
2. logical transformation of ink printed notes to Braille notes and
3. the Braille note's setting.

### 3.1 Accessing Ink Printed Notes

Many different sources of ink printed notes should be permitted as input to our program. Therefore we do not want to restrict ourselves to using one special scanning program like *capellaScan* or *Finale*. This would be problematic with regard to future developments. In one or two years *capellaScan* could be surpassed by another program, so that we might want to use this for our purposes. Keeping this in mind, we are developing interfaces to two different ink printed note sources so far:

1. CapXML, XML-format used by the note setting and note scanning software *Capella* and *capellaScan* and
2. MusicXML an independent format used by *Finale* (note setting), *SharpEye* (note scanning) and others.

The format of the sources must not influence the process of logically transforming the idea of ink printed notes to the idea of Braille notes. To achieve this, the different XML sources (MusicXML or CapXML) are translated into an intermediate XML-Format, that we defined ourselves. This format, called BrailleMusicXML, is developed in a joint venture with the Swiss Library for the Blind and Visually Impaired (SBS, http://www.sbs-online.ch).

BrailleMusicXML will have to include all aspects of ink printed notes as well as all aspects of Braille notes. For now, such a format is not provided by a third party.

The transformation from ink printed notes to Braille notes has to perform the following tasks (they are at most CapXML specific):

1. Identify and differentiate slurs and ties,
2. unspecific assignment of "free" fingerings,
3. recognition, interpretation and allocation of "free" texts,
4. rhythmical controls etc.

The goal of this transformation step is to transform ink printed notes, represented by XML into BrailleMusicXML, that is describing the notes at least as exact as ink printed notes. This means, the note's representation in BrailleMusicXML at this point is not complete. Imagine fingering in ink printed notes: it mainly consists of numbers being somehow assigned to notes. If there are two notes of a chord and one finger (i.e. one number is given), you have to find out to which of those two notes the finger belongs. Despite of its lack of information this non-specific description is correct according to the rules of ink printed notes. This problem will have to be processed in the following stage.

### 3.2 Logical Transformations

The ink printed notes, that are represented by BrailleMusicXML, are now logically translated to Braille notes. The Braille notes contain lots of elements in short-written form helping the blind to read and learn the notes.

Special attention has to be directed to:

1. short written forms of accidentals (staccati, tenuti, etc.),
2. compressing of measure parts or whole measures (simile, parallel shifts, Braille segno),
3. automatic interpretation of voice fragmentations (full voice or part voice) and of switching intervals,
4. marking of positions, where slurs or ties are changing voices or systems,
5. relating fingering to corresponding notes ...

At this point of progress, the professional translator controls the further process to influence the note setting. For example, there can be situations that make a Simile compression seem appropriate, others that should be handled by using short-written forms of elements like staccati etc. It is not always possible to automatically find the right solution.

At the end of this stage, the former ink printed notes are logically represented as Braille notes in BrailleMusicXML.

### 3.3 Setting Braille Notes

Because of Braille notes being "difficult to understand" for machines, (especially the representation of texts causes many problems) BrailleMusicXML aims at bringing them into machine-readable form whilst exactly preserving their basic structure and setting.

At the end of the BrailleMusicXML internal translating process the note's representation has to be Braille notes in XML. For example, BrailleMusicXML will have to support both forms of chord's representation, the one in intervals used by Braille notes and the one in stem connected note heads used by ink printed notes. Now coming from BrailleMusicXML, an optimal setting and formatting of Braille notes can be calculated and achieved. The optimal setting depends on some parameters,that shall control the Braille note setting, that have to be a compromise with respect to the requirements of form ("appearance"), legibility, space economy etc.

## 4 Current State

At the moment, both data formats – MusicXML and CapXML – are being translated to BrailleMusicXML. CapXML causes many problems regarding to the translation process. For MusicXML, much less preparation is needed. But because the note scanning software *capellaScan* is presently offering the best compromise between scanning quality and usability (time of postprocessing), we have to deal with the suboptimal data format CapXML. The present note scanning software supporting MusicXML is not sufficiently accurate for the requirements of an economic note translation.

We have not yet started working on the reverse process (translating BrailleMusicXML to MusicXML to allow ink printed note setting via *Finale*).

The works on the second stage (logical transformations between ink printed notes and Braille notes within BrailleMusicXML) have not yet started.

At this moment, there is only a rudimentary work on transforming BrailleMusicXML to Braille. Furthermore we developed a program that is able to transform Braille notes to BrailleMusicXML based on statistical, lexical and syntactical knowledge.

## 5 Future Work and Assurances for the Future

A first important step to get the programs for ink printed note access and setting of Braille notes running so that we can soon provide a bridge between ink printed notes and Braille notes. This will ensure the note's transcription.

After establishing the bridge, it will be extended by and by to enable the high amount of Braille note specific setting options, thus increasing the quality of the basic translation.

We use well-known tools to keep the project general for future developments. The independence of input, i.e. of note scanning software, is guaranteed by transforming the producer-specific formats (MusicXML, CapXML etc.) to BrailleMusicXML. The project is based on XML, a well accepted standard of representations that is both simple and powerful. The recognition of Braille notes is programmed in Perland the XML internal transformation in SWI-PrologBoth are system independent, important standards handling the problems adequately.

# Using SVG and a Force Feedback Mouse to Enable Blind People to Access "Graphical" Web Based Documents

Nadine Baptiste-Jessel, Bertrand Tornil, and Benoit Encelle

IRIT, Université Paul Sabatier
118, Route de Narbonne
31062 Toulouse Cedex 4
France
{baptiste,tornil,encelle}@irit.fr
http://www.irit.fr

**Abstract.** We present a system that enables a blind user to access 2D WEB based "graphical" documents. After introducing the SVG format and the Force Feedback Mouse, we present how, in a WEB browser application, we associate force, voice and sound feedback.
Our approach is applied with two kinds of graphical information: geographical and musical information. In both application, after a training phase of the mouse handling, the user can make his own mental construction of displayed data. When the user knows the relative position of different elements, he can move the mouse pointer towards the region he wants.

## 1 Introduction

In a classical situation, a blind user uses to handle a keyboard to operate a computer. The machine answers him by a voice synthesis and/or a braille display. The text reading is adapted to these methods. When browsing the WEB, a blind user will have accessibility problems with graphical documents. The W3C has proposed guidelines [1] for web authors to design their WEB sites. For instance, graphical data have to be linked with a textual description. So, a graphic document may be presented to him by long and tiresome descriptions, when they are available.

The force feedback devices are used within the context of the accessibility for the blind users because they enable a more direct interaction based on sensory capacities.

Many works [2–7] aim at using a force feedback device to make a haptic feedback to the visual elements displayed on the screen. For example, passing of the pointer of the force feedback mouse on an icon will cause a small jolt in the user hand. Moreover, Dufresne showed the interest of the audio-haptic bimodality for blind users [8].

We will first set the main definitions of the haptic perception. We propose a specific context of use for these devices: relative localization. We will show some

K. Miesenberger et al. (Eds.): ICCHP 2004, LNCS 3118, pp. 228–235, 2004.

technical precisions about our system. Then we will present two prototypes that enable blind people to access geographical and musical documents in a web context. Lastly, we will conclude by presenting the outlooks which we consider.

## 2 Definitions of Haptic Context: Relative Localization

The tactilo-kinesthetic or "haptic" [9] system is the synthesis of the movements of exploration of the motor system and of perceptions of the tactile system. The haptic sense is thus both effector and receptor. It consists of:

1. the cutaneous sense: it is the touch sense. It allows to feel the temperature, the pressure or the pain, and is relayed by sensory receptors located under the skin.
2. the kinesthetic sense: it is the sense related on the position and the movements of the body. It enables us for example to know the weight of an object we're handling and its position. It is relayed by receptors based in the muscles, the tendons and the articulations.

The handling of force feedback pointing devices as a mouse is based on the kinesthetic perception of the arm. This perception enables us to visualize the position of the hand in space. Thus, if an haptic event, like a vibration or a shock, occurs during a move of the arm, we can mentally represent the position that the hand had when the event occurred.

Associated with a voice or sound synthesis, and thanks to the sensory memory, this approach will allow the rebuilding of a mental image of an object from the relative positions of the elements of this object.

The two applications which we will present are founded on this context.

## 3 Technical Aspects

### 3.1 SVG Format

We use the SVG format (Scalable Vector Graphic [10]), which is an application of XML (eXtended Markup Language). A SVG file is coded in marked-up plain text and is read by the client computer as a text file. Indeed, its contents can be indexed by search engines and it can be generated. Moreover, SVG supports the DOM (Document Object Model) and can react to the user events via a script programming. SVG files can be displayed on an Internet browser with the plugin from Adobe [11].

In our applications, the graphical elements are defined explicitly in SVG file as lists of coordinates. It is a real advantage compared to the image bitmap formats.

Thanks to its features, the SVG format is yet used in an accessibility context [12] [13].

### 3.2 Wingman Forces Feedback Mouse(r)

This force feedback mouse (figure 1), was created by Immersion Corporation [14] and marketed by Logitech.

The mouse is interdependent of its base. The effective surface of work is of 1.9 X 2.5 cm and the forces can reach 1N in peak. The Wingman® formerly was a game device, but its use was diverted toward research on the accessibility [2] [4] [3] [12] [13].

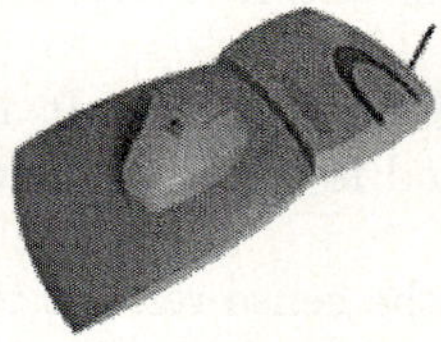

**Fig. 1.** Wingman force Feedback Mouse.

Immersion Corporation proposes a plugin for the Internet navigators, which gives the possibility to control a force feedback device, via the script programming contained in a HTML page [15].

### 3.3 Architecture of our Applications

In a WEB context, the architecture we use is a Client-Server Scheme on a Local Area Network (Figure 2).

On the server side, we have the SVG files and the sound files. By now, the SVG files are stored on the server or generated on the client via an ECMAScript programming. We plan to generate all SVG files on the server via perl programming language, accessing to databases. For the sound files, in this first prototype,

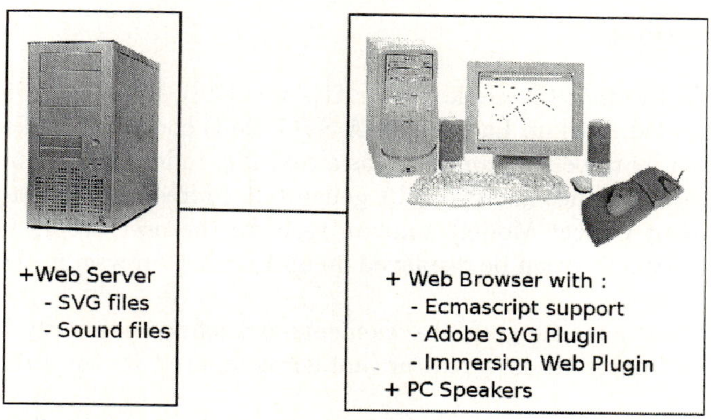


**Fig. 2.** System architecture.

we use a speech and sound synthesis on the server to generate them. That may avoid any conflict. Indeed, in a general case, a blind user use his own screen reader and his own speech synthesis.

The client browser must have downloaded from the server the different plugins that enable our system to work: the "Immersion Web Plugin" [15] for the force feedback and the "Adobe SVG Viewer Plugin" [11] in order to display the SVG files.

## 4 Description of the Geographical Application

In our application (figure 3), a map is displaying the USA, showing the states. A blind user uses the force feedback mouse to explore the surface of the screen. The mouse can have two different behaviors. When the pointer of the mouse:

1. goes out of the map area, the user feels a texture effect in his hand.
2. pass on a region, it is "magnetized" towards its center.

A sound feedback gives the name of the state, via a screen reader and a voice synthesis. Now, when the user has his mouse pointer toward a region, he has to force to quit the state and either

1. falls into a region bordering.
2. leaves the map, and then feels an effect of texture

The study of geography is well adapted to the use of the mouse, as it may require a transfer of information from the computer to the user, via the mouse.

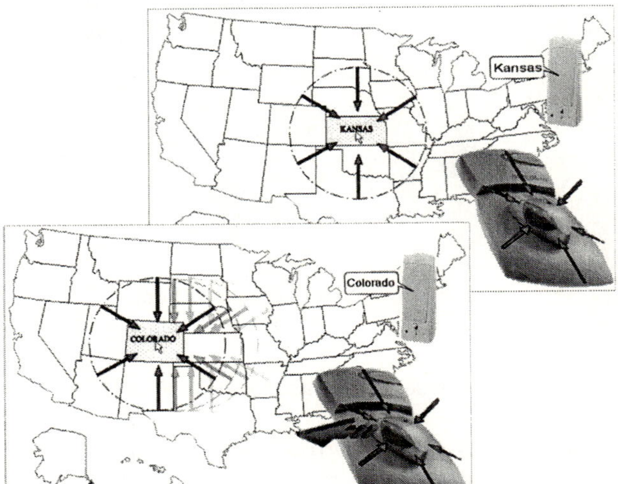


**Fig. 3.** Geographical Application.

With HTML tags and bitmap pictures, the blind user could only "reach" the links name through the screen reader with no logical order, with the TAB key. Using a force feedback mouse enables them to apprehend the layout of the links, and thus the layout of the regions.

## 5 Description of the Musical Application

In order to use the same approach in music, we needed a spatial view of musical data. Jean Marc Chouvel has showed a torus-shaped hexagonal representation of a musical score [16]. This representation provides some nice harmonic characteristics.

### 5.1 Hexagonal Representation of Musical Data

It is a instantaneous representation of the score. Notes are showed independently from eighth interval. They are displayed on an hexagonal lattice, showing on figure 4. It is also a torus representation: it loops horizontally and vertically.

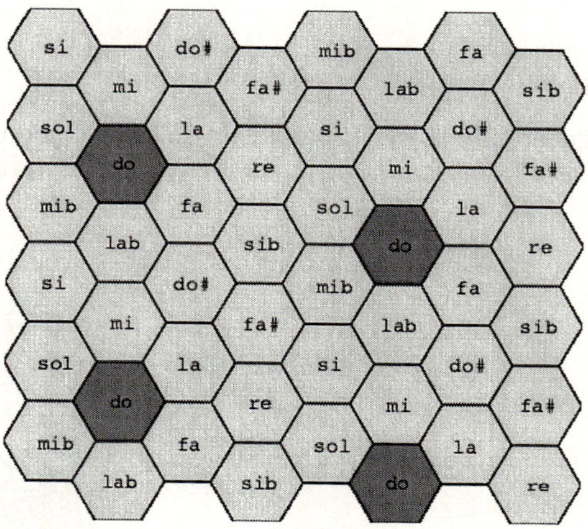


**Fig. 4.** Hexagonal Representation.

Main features of this representation are described in [17]:

1. Vertical axis is made by major thirds. The cycle is long of 3.
2. Axis from the left bottom to the right top is made by minor thirds. It is 4 cells long cycle.
3. Last axis (from the right bottom to the left top) is made by fifths. This axis has got every notes and its long is 12.

4. From a note, its neighbors in the representation are notes with a strong harmonic relationship (third or fifth).
5. Close chromatic notes (half tone and tone) are separate by one line between 2 hexagons.
6. When two shapes are identical, it is the same chord.

### 5.2 Implementation

In our prototype, we use the hexagonal representation in order to present the different chords to the user.

We have implemented the simplest chords: major, minor, augmented and diminished fifth, dominated, major, minor and diminished seventh. Thanks to the hexagonal representation, each chord has got a specific shape (Figure 5).

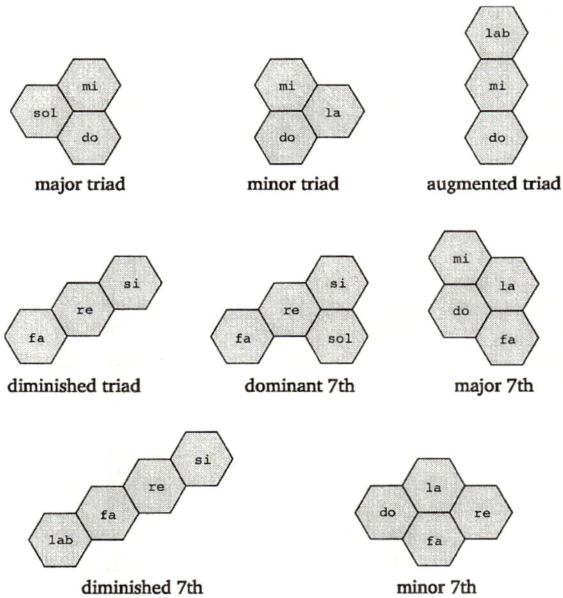


**Fig. 5.** Simple Accords.

### 5.3 Haptic Feedback and Usability

When using our prototype, a blind user is able to explore the hexagonal draughtboard. Each note is materialized via the mouse by magnetizing the cursor on the center of the hexagon, while a sound synthesis play the note. In any moment, the user can build one of the chord available by pressing a key.

Once a chord created, haptic feedback changes. Then, user can recognize the specific shape of the chord.

## 6 Conclusion and Outlooks

In our approach, the layout of graphic elements is displayed thanks to a force and sound feedback. This enables blind users to access graphical information.

We plan to prepare a test protocol, to estimate how our applications can really improve the ability for blind users to access geographical or musical documents. However, for the geographical experience we have already tested our system with two blind users, and they admit that our system enables them to create a mental representation of a geographical map; that is very useful in a pedagogic situation.

For the musical application, we are about to extend the usability of our prototype. By now, only an explorative mode is available. Next, we plan to add a listening mode, in order to access and analyze harmonic scheme in a music. We will add also an editing mode. Some features of the hexagonal representation hadn't been used, such as spatial animation of cadences (an authentic cadence is a translation of a triangle by one cell).

Finally, we are working on a more general approach of our architecture. We are developing a software framework to create easier any haptic-SVG WEB applications. And we are still testing other speech and sound synthesis and SVG generation scripting methods.

## References


1. World Wide Web Consortium: Web Accessibility Initiative (WAI). http://www.w3.org/WAI/ (2004)
2. Sile O'Modhrain, M., Guillepsie, R.: The moose: A haptic user interface for blind persons. In: Procedings of the Third WWW6 Conference, Santa Clara, California. (1996)
3. Offen, D., Thomlinson, B.: Good vibrations: Using a tactile mouse to convey page layout information to visually impaired computer users. In: Proceedings of CSUN'S Sixteenth Annual International Conference: "Technology and Persons with Disabilities", Los Angeles. (2001)
4. Wies, E., Gardner, J., O'Modhrain, M., Hasser, C., Bulatov, V.: Web-based touch display for accessible science education. Haptic Human-Computer Interaction **LNCS 2052** (2001) 52–60
5. Colwell, C., Petrie, H., Kornbrot, D., Hardwick, A., Furner, S.: Use of a haptic device by blind and sighted people: perception of virtual textures and objects. In: Improving the quality of life for the European citizen: technology for inclusive design and equality. I. placencia-porrero and e. ballabio edn. Amsterdam: IOS Press (1998)
6. Ramstein, C., Martial, O., Dufresne, A., Carignan, M., Chassé, P., Mabilleau, P.: Touching and Hearing GUIs: Design issues for the PC-Access System. In: ASSET'96, ACM/SIGCAPH. In 2nd Annual ACM Conference on Assistive Technologies, Vancouver, BC, Canada. (1996) 2–9
7. Magnusson, C., Rassmus-Gröhn, K., Sjöström, C., Danielsson, H.: Navigation and recognition in complex haptic virtual environments – reports from an extensive study with blind users. http://www.english.certec.lth.se/staff/kirre/#publ (2002)

8. Dufresne, A., Martial, O., Ramstein, C.: Multimodal user interface system for blind and 'visually occupied' users: Ergonomic evaluation of the haptic and auditive dimensions. In: Proceedings of IFIP International Conference Interaction'95, Lillehammer, Norway. (1995) 163–168
9. Revesz, G.: Psychology an art of the blind. New York: Longmans (1950)
10. World Wide Web Consortium: the SVG format. www.w3.org/Graphics /SVG/Overview.htm8 (2001)
11. Adobe: Adobe svg viewer. http://www.adobe.com/svg/viewer/install/main.html (2004)
12. Gardner, J., Bulatov, V.: Smart figures, svg, and accessible web graphics. In: Proceedings of Technology And Persons With Disabilities Conference 2001, Los Angeles. (2001)
13. Campin, B., Brunet, L.L., McCurdy, W.A., Siekierska, E.M.: Svg mapping for people with visual impairment. In: Proceedings of SVG Open 2003. (2003)
14. Immersion: Touchsense devices. http://www.immersion.com/developer/technology /devices/index.php (2003)
15. Immersion: Immersion web plugin. http://www.immersion.com/plugins/ (2002)
16. Chouvel, J.M., Assayag, G., Cholleton, J.P.: La représentation hexagonale toroïdale, application à l'analyse harmonique de la musique d'hermeto pascoal. Séminaire MaMux 2002 (2002)
17. Mathieu, B.: Outils informatiques d'analyse musicale. http://www.ircam.fr/equipes/repmus/Rapports/mathieu2002/outils-analyse-BM-2002.pdf (2002)

# Modified Stave Notation – An Approach to Making Stave Notation More Accessible to Users Who Are Partially Sighted

Sally-Anne Zimmermann

Music Education and Employment Adviser
Royal National Institute of the Blind
105 Judd Street
London WC1H 9NE
sally.zimmermann@rnib.org.uk

**Abstract.** Stave notation is a complex code with more variety in symbol appearance and usage than alphabetical language. To parallel work on making information accessible, the Royal National Institute of the Blind is compiling benchmarks for producing Modified Stave Notation. Modifications are quickly executed using music score-writing packages. By reducing the extremes of symbol size, removing redundant space, placing symbols in consistent positions and providing verbal description to support the musical text, the notation is clearer than mere photo-enlargement. Two examples of this process are discussed, based on small-scale surveys of musicians who are partially sighted.

Stave notation makes great demands on users, greater than those involved in everyday reading and writing. Music symbols come in a wide variety of shapes, sizes and relative positions. Certain symbols have different meanings in different contexts: the dot, for example, can shorten or increase a note depending on whether it is placed above or below the note head, or following it. The shapes of musical symbols may vary, just as there are different fonts in standard print. That performers, having read the symbols, then have to convert them into sounds accurately, and in sequence, adds to the cognitive complexity of music literacy.

In 2001, the Royal National Institute of the Blind produced guidelines called "See it Right" for making information accessible for blind and partially sighted people. The checklist for large print contains areas where there are comparable issues in stave notation. For example:

| RNIB's large print checklist | Link to stave notation |
|---|---|
| Is the typeface at least 16 points or above? | Are the main signs – staves, notes, rests, etc. – at least of a size comparable with 16 point typeface? |
| Is there enough space between each line of type? | Is there sufficient space between each instrumental/vocal part and a sufficient gap between systems on the page? |

K. Miesenberger et al. (Eds.): ICCHP 2004, LNCS 3118, pp. 236–239, 2004.

| | |
|---|---|
| Is the typeface either roman, semi-bold or bold? | Is the typeface for text sans serif, semi-bold or bold? Are the musical notes as "unfussy" as possible? |
| Are the numerals clear? | Are page and bar numbers, rehearsal figures and fingering all sufficiently large and consistently placed? |
| Does the text follow easily from column to column? | Does the music follow easily from system to system with convenient places for page turns? |
| If there are images, are they clearly defined and easy to read? | If any unconventional or very small signs are used, are these explained and their location listed in a footnote? |
| Can the document be flattened, so it can be placed under a scanner or screen magnifier? | Can the document be flattened, so it can be placed under a scanner or screen magnifier? |
| [Taylor (2001) See It Right: Large Print, pages 11, 12] | |

In altering printed scores, the overall aim is to give the reader a more consistent copy than is often the case in the huge variety of music layouts produced. The individual user may then of course extend the modification manually or electronically.

In addition to clear printing of the symbols and general enlargement, the aims in producing Modified Stave Notation are generally to even out symbol size and density, reduce redundant space, place symbols consistently (putting non-pitch and rhythm signs around, rather than on, the stave) and describe in words the location of sporadic or unusual symbols.

In 2001, RNIB set up a working party to revise "Music in Large Print" [Ockelford, 1994], mainly because of the increasing ease with which altered stave notation can be produced using current software. A large part of this work has been in defining benchmarks and orders of precedence in the music notation itself. Samples of piano music and vocal music have been analysed by musicians who are partially sighted, and detailed interviews carried out seeking their preferences. New guidelines will be produced which will also consider other issues such as binding and colour of paper, as well as lighting, multimedia possibilities, and reading and memorising techniques.

Fig. 1 shows an extract from a Novello edition of Handel's "Messiah", from the alto part in the final chorus, and Fig. 2 is the Modified Stave Notation version, pro-

**Fig. 1.**

duced using Sibelius™1.4. The general dimensions of the extract have been increased by altering the staff size to 9mm. To even out the symbol size and density the thicknesses of barlines, note beams and leger lines were increased; the stem thickness, staff line width and size of duration dots were increased; the text was set in Arial font; and the broken text line was replaced with a continuous line.

(A note would be supplied at the opening of the work to indicate that slurs used for more than one syllable have been removed, and to state that hyphens --- between words had been replaced with continuous underlining _____.)

**Fig. 2.**

Redundant space was reduced by increasing the number of bars per system to take up only slightly more space horizontally than in the original. Care was taken to keep the bars reasonably evenly spaced in length and to keep beams moving in the direction of the pitch movement, though in the examples sent out for comment some had beams parallel to the stave. In this example one further subtle change was made by moving the second tie out of the stave. The original has one feature not maintained by Sibelius™ that may be helpful for readers – the straight tails to single quavers.

Taking a more complicated example, the views of fifteen partially-sighted stave notation readers were sought on the appearance of five versions of a short but complex piano piece. Whilst each version used a 14mm stave size, some musical symbols were altered in size or in location, and the overall layout of the bars on the page varied. Considerations included whether articulation marks should follow the pitch contour or lie in a horizontal line, and whether they should be next to note heads or next to stems; whether slurs should be especially thickened or not; whether dynamic letters should be in italic Opus text or Arial non-italic; and whether hairpins, stave lines and barlines should be thickened or not. Different approaches to the indication of fingering were tried, with the numbers variously following the melodic shape or being horizontal, lying outside or inside cleared parts of staves, or, overriding all other priorities, placed as close to the notes as possible.

All participants appreciated the modification as being a great improvement on the unmodified or photo-enlarged music they currently use. With individual variables, however, there was little agreement. Overall, preferences showed a desire to even out the extremes of size and contrast in musical symbols. These preferences were tempered by the degree of interest in the feature concerned for each reader.

In the future, it is hoped to carry out more small-scale surveys with a choice of modification of the same piece. While such research is complicated to evaluate, as priorities are as much due to usage as ease of reading, it is important that potential consumers inform the benchmarking suggestions. In Modified Stave Notation, additional notes will state verbally where deviation from the text has occurred. Some composers or editors shower their pieces with detail, or compress music with many repeat signs, whilst others leave the music largely as pitch and rhythm. This variety will remain. The aim of Modified Stave Notation is just to make the symbols chosen by the composer, arranger or editor easier to read.

Music notation is, like all languages, evolving. Modified Stave Notation, by reducing contrast and placing symbols consistently, hopefully enables more attention to be paid to the visual perception of this "space-bound vocabulary of symbols created for the ear but accessible only through the eye" [Read, 1979, page vii]. Score-writing computer packages now make the production of Modified Stave Notation quick, enabling the desired consistency to be achieved cheaply and accurately. The reader of Modified Stave Notation is hopefully able to read more fluently and with greater confidence.

## References

1. Ockelford, A. (1994) "Music in Large Print" London: RNIB
2. Read, G. (1979) "Music Notation: a Manual of Modern Practice" New York: Crescendo
3. Taylor (2001) "See It Right: Large Print" London: RNIB
4. www.sibelius.com

# Entertaining Software for Young Persons with Disabilities

Morten Tollefsen and Magne Lunde

Tangerudbakken 2D, N-0982 Oslo, Norway
{morten,magne}@medialt.no
http://www.medialt.no/

**Abstract.** Leisure time activities that are exciting, fun and entertaining are important for everyone, also disabled people. Computer games have become part of everyday life for many people. There are however few entertaining computer games which are accessible for disabled users. Research and development in the field of IT and the disabled has focused on education rather than leisure. The aim of the UPS project is therefore untraditional: "to make entertaining software accessible". The setting up of guidelines for development of new products is important both for standard software and products designed especially for disabled users. Young people with disabilities wish to use the popular computer games used by friends and family. The complexity and speed of standard computer games and the input requirements often prevent this. The project is focusing on standard products. However the variation in the level and type of disability means that not all can use standard products, and one activity is to develop new software. The project will also establish a web site for disabled users, parents, teachers and assistants.

## 1 Introduction

Exciting, fun computer games and multimedia products for young people with complex learning disabilities, are these available? This question was discussed in the UPS pre-project (01.04.2002 - 30.11.2002). The most important conclusion from the pre-project is that it is difficult to find entertaining software for people with severe disabilities.

The target group in the pre-project was similar to the target group in the main project: *Persons with mental disabilities, or persons with a combination of severe motor handicaps and perceptual losses.*

Many young people with disabilities wish to use the popular computer games and entertaining multimedia products used by friends and family. There is a need for these multimedia products to be adapted to suit the special needs of disabled users, but it is also essential to develop special software. However specially developed products should contain the best aspects of entertainment products for the general population, so that family and friends and disabled young people can enjoy these products together.

It is not surprising that disabled users want to use computer games. The game industry realized about 6 billion Euros in Europe (2001), and 9 out of 10 in the age 9-16 are playing computer games in Norway (www.forskning.no). Computer games are not necessarily a one-man occupation. Network based entertainment is important for a lot

K. Miesenberger et al. (Eds.): ICCHP 2004, LNCS 3118, pp. 240–247, 2004.

of people [1]. For some people RL (real life) is less important than their life in cyberspace. This observation is frightening, and computer games are of course not only positive. Computer games have however become part of our society, and disabled persons should not be excluded from participation.

The application for a main project was accepted in 2003. This paper describes the most important activities in the project as well as the results from the pre-project. UPS is funded by the Norwegian research council, Microsoft, Electronic Arts and endowment funds.

## 2 The UPS Project

The main project started in October 2003 and will run over a three-year period. The main goal is to:

*adapt and develop entertaining software for young persons with disabilities, which is inclusive.*

Based on the results from the pre-project, the main goal is divided into three sub goals:

1. Adapt standard software. It is important to develop tools and/or types of co-operation that make such adaptations possible.
2. Develop software based on the needs of the target group.
3. Establish a web with information and a database with free, digital materials. The user interface is an important challenge: the target group of the project, experts, helpers, ... should all be able to use the site.

As a basis for both our adaptations and development activities, we have made a set of guidelines for software development. These guidelines are described before discussing the three sub goals.

## 3 Guidelines for Software Development

The pre-project was focused on mapping user needs. The methods used were case studies and interviews with users and helpers. Based on the pre-project results, literature and experts in this field, a set of guidelines for usable software has been developed. These guidelines will be used both in our development activities and when evaluating/testing standard products. We will also use the guidelines to influence the standard game industry.

The guidelines cover five main aspects:

1. Level/progression
2. Input
3. Graphics
4. Sound
5. Installation and adaptations

The five categories are briefly discussed below. An English version of the guidelines can be found at:

http://www.medialt.no/rapport/entertainment_guidelines/index.htm.

### 3.1 Level/Progression

It is important to offer differing degrees of difficulty in computer games and other entertaining software. This can be done as a progression from easy to difficult and/or to offer options that influence complexity, speed, language etc. Most commercial computer games use various kinds of progression, but the "easiest level" is often too fast or complicated. The practice mode found in some games is very helpful, especially if the player is "immortal".

In games composed of several tasks, it should be possible to select each task directly (this is also the case for so called secret rooms). A disabled user can enjoy individual tasks, but he/she is perhaps not able to reach this activity because it is necessary to follow a particular path in the game. Direct choice of individual tasks can be simulated if the game includes functionality to save status. This solution however requires that helpers are willing to spend time using the product.

Additional products dealing with the same main theme as a computer game, e.g. videos, books, toys or stickers may be helpful for some disabled users. This is the case for many persons with Down's syndrome.

The language (both verbal and written) is also very important. Products should be translated into local languages, and the usage should be as simple as possible. Some games use what can be called a cult language, and this can be particularly hard for disabled users.

### 3.2 Input

Entertaining software should allow for different input devices. In most standard software for PCs it is possible to use keyboard, mouse and joystick. More specialized devices like steering wheels and pedals are also common. One of the main problems for our target group is that most standard software requires too many different commands (about 10 buttons/mouse movements are typical in car, sports and action games).

Qualified training is very important to utilize the users potential for controlling the computer. Perhaps computer games are the best applications to motivate the users to go through with this training? A thorough and methodical training scheme is described by Brænde and Halvorsen [2].

Games cannot generally be fully controlled using one or two switches, and scanning techniques are also difficult to implement (e. g. because of speed). Specialized input devices for the disabled can often be used with entertaining software, but the number of commands are too few. It is therefore important to allow for the use of several different input devices simultaneously. A group of users can then work together to manage the different functions.

It is usually not possible to adjust sensitivity, fault tolerance, speed and size of pointers (or other interactive controls) in standard computer games. This functionality is desirable both for users with motor handicaps and sight disturbances. Entertaining software does not often use standard pointers found in the operating system (where appropriate choices are available). Implementing suitable functionality should not be very complicated because games already support a wide range of input devices and the calibration of these devices.

### 3.3 Graphics

Modern computer games use advanced graphics. Even if this is impressing, it should be possible to adjust resolution, size, details, colours, contrast etc. The speed in videos and animations should also be adjustable.

Graphic presentations often include less important elements (e. g. decorations), and it should be possible to turn these elements on/off. Visual disturbances are common in the target group, and simpler graphics increases the number of possible users.

When a task is solved, it is important to use explicit visual feedback and reward. Explicit visual (and auditory) feedback is of vital importance if persons with severe learning disabilities should maintain the dialogue with an application. As skills increase, the result of the users actions is motivating by itself, and the value of response from an application will, to a greater degree, be associated with informative feedback.

### 3.4 Sound

It is important to offer different choices for speed, length, voices, volume etc. Furthermore it should be possible to turn off different sound elements, e.g. background music and effects. Repetition is very helpful for spoken messages, and the user should be able to start/stop these messages.

Different options for sounds are more common than for graphic elements. The main reason for this is probably that graphics are essential for using the game while sound may just make the experience more fun or realistic.

When a task is solved, it is important to use explicit auditory feedback and reward.

### 3.5 Installation and Options

Simple installations are essential, and it is important not to change system files. If system files are changed, assistive devices sometimes do not work correctly after the installation.

Use a wizard or another simple interface to set software options. It should be possible to save these settings (perhaps in different profiles). The user/helper also should be able to save the current game. This will make it possible to go directly to particular tasks/positions.

Use a standard procedure for exiting the application (e. g. Alt+F4 in Windows).

## 4 The Adaptation of Standard Software

As mentioned in the introduction, young persons with disabilities want to use standard software for entertainment. Different adaptations are possible: alternative input devices, built in adjustments etc. For many users practice in using assistive devices is also essential.

It is often very difficult to make standard computer games and multimedia products usable for our target group. This is still the case if appropriate assistive devices are available, and the person has accomplished qualified training programs. If different assumptions and needs had been addressed in the software development process, adaptations would be much easier.

Even if a computer game is too complex or fast for a disabled person, parts of the game could be fun and usable. Typical examples of this are products with a demo or trial mode. In products made up of small tasks, some of the tasks can be applicable. In other products, e.g. in car and snowboard games, the player may be immortal, and the game is fun, even if the player does not win.

User tests are important in the UPS project. We want to find out if standard products are fun for our target group. It is quite obvious that not all persons are able to use all games, and therefore we want to pick usable products for each of the test persons. Our main methods for selecting games are expert evaluation and interviews with disabled persons and/or helpers.

### 4.1 Expert Evaluation

About 30 standard computer games, of different types and from different producers, will be evaluated in the project. A set of test criteria based on the guidelines is developed. The evaluation will be used to pick out about 10 products for user testing.

A typical test scenario for PC games is as follows:

1. Previewing handbooks
2. Product installation
3. Playing with the game for about one hour (possibly more if this is necessary)
4. Testing different standard input devices (including keyboard)
5. Map options (sound, graphics, input devices etc.)
6. Try to find hidden options (e. g. registry settings)
7. Complete the evaluation outline

PC is the most important platform in the UPS project. Xbox and PS2 are also used, and the expert tests are more or less similar. The tests are more detailed than the guidelines, e.g. concerning alternative input. The evaluation outline may also be used for other applications.

The expert evaluations can be used as references for parents and helpers, and the results will be stored in a database (available on the web).

### 4.2 User Tests

As mentioned above our goal is to select usable games for the test persons. Five persons will test about 10 games each. In addition we collaborate with Haukåsen School for the disabled, Trøndelag Centre of competence and other institutions. Our goal is to test several games in these environments as well.

We have two main goals with the user tests:

1. Evaluate the guidelines for software development
2. Determine if standard computer games, whole or parts, can be adapted to meet the target group needs

The first step is to test games without adaptations (except for assistive devices or software). Tests will be documented using video, and we have developed an interview scheme. Both testers and eventually helpers will be interviewed.

After the completion of all user tests we will select one of the games. This game will be adapted to meet as many user needs as possible. The same test group will try the product after the adaptation.

### 4.3 Standard Product Adaptation

The adaptation method is not obvious at this point. Our first step is to analyse the test results. The next step is to pick one of the games, and to suggest and implement necessary changes.

Possible work includes:

1. New interfaces for assistive devices (hardware or software)
2. Development of system software (e. g. to slow down computers)
3. Modifications and/or add ons to the program code

Microsoft and/or Electronic Arts have to assist in implementing these changes, and a game from one of these publishers probably will be selected.

## 5 Specially Designed Software

Even if some standard software can be adapted, specially designed products are necessary. Persons in the target group have very different assumptions and needs, and the persons with the most severe disabilities will not be able to use standard games. It is however very important to use successful design rules from standard software. The goal is that the specially developed software should also be fun for friends and siblings.

### 5.1 Suggestions for Possible Applications

The UPS project has completed two brainstorming sessions on possible products. The proposals are very different, and we have started work to select one of the ideas. One of the most important dividing lines is between applications that can be implemented using presentation tools for the disabled, and those that have to be developed from scratch.

The main advantage of using a presentation tool is that alternative input (switches, scanning etc.) is already implemented. The disadvantage is limitations in this type of software (usually not developed to design entertaining software, but to develop educational applications).

Examples of suggested applications from the brain storming session are quoted in the table below.

The suggestions above are all examples of entertaining software. It is however not possible to implement typical computer games using the accessible presentation tools. A collective term for these applications could be "searching different environments". An accessible media player is neither a computer game, but e.g. listening to music is entertainment! Using computers as an interface to other devices is also suggested, e.g. to trains or a robot. Of course this is entertainment! A robot could for example be used to search other environments than an electric wheelchair. In other words: "The computer can be used as an interface to entertaining activities, not only as a platform for computer games".

**Table 1.** Examples of suggested applications.

| Accessible presentation tools | Standard programming tools |
|---|---|
| Nature experience | Controlling physical trains using PC |
| Farm | Controlling a robot (with a built in camera) |
| Search a house | Platform game |
| Search a CD shop | Winter sports or car game |
| Media player | Wheelchair madness |

Sport and car games are very popular. Sport games include: football, snowboard, golf, … Car games include everything from rally to car races. These games usually require very good eye-hand control. A specially designed winter sports or car game were suggested, also because these games are used by friends and family.

### 5.2 Testing the Specially Designed Software

The specially designed software will be based on the design guidelines. A test group consisting of at least 5 persons will be selected.

The most important goals with these user tests are:

1. Are the users able to use the product?
2. Do the users have fun?

The users may be able to use the product without having fun, but the opposite is probably not true. A statement identified in the pre-project summarizes the challenge when developing entertaining software for the target group: "Simple but not childish and slow but with speedy excitement!"

## 6 Web Site

A web site will be associated with the project. The goal is to provide for management also after the project period. Important contents will include:

- Information about adaptations and entertaining software
- Discussion groups
- A database with free multimedia contents

Pictures, videos, sounds etc. can be used in different tool kits, e. g. in the Norwegian software package Programsnekker (application joiner). A database with free multimedia content was demanded in the pre-project. We will also test if it is possible to include finished applications in the database (or file system). This is dependent on different aspects, but most important is the installation procedure. Basic functionality is already implemented in "Programsnekker".

To design a suitable user interface is not trivial. We want to include information/services for different users, including our target group. The use of symbols, assistive devices/software (e. g. scanning) and navigation for visually impaired users are examples of the challenges.

We will try to develop the web site in collaboration with other Scandinavian projects and institutions. A Swedish project, Interagera, also want to establish a site, and these sites have several similar goals.

## References

1. Turkle, Sherry.Life on the Screen: Identity in the Age of the Internet . Simon and Schuster, New York (1995)
2. Brænde, E. and Halvorsen, A.K.: Fra vilje til uttrykk - Metodikk for utprøving av betjeningsutstyr for barn med omfattende motoriske vansker Kommuneforlaget, Oslo (2003)

# The TiM Project: Overview of Results

Dominique Archambault

Université Pierre et Marie Curie, Inserm U483/INOVA,
9 quai Saint Bernard, 75252 Paris cedex 5, France

**Abstract.** The TiM project, funded by the European commission intended to develop and to adapt computer games for blind children and for partially sighted children who need specific graphical display settings that fit to their visual possibilities. A game engine has been developed that allows to design modality-adaptable multimedia games. These games can be played using various modalities according to the specific devices needed by the player. A set of such adapted games was developed and used to study the adaptation of game interaction situations and the potential of such games with respect to Education, Learning and Therapy, and to demonstrate the possibilities of the game engine. Additionally a new relief deposit method was created, a Braille device programming library was developed, and a juridical study about adaptation of existing contents was carried out. This paper summarises the results of the project.

## 1 The TiM Project

The overall aim of the TiM Project [1] is to provide young visually impaired children, with or without additional disabilities, with multimedia computer games they can access independently, that is without the assistance of a sighted person.

Currently, hundreds of computer games are available to sighted children, that they can use to play and learn without the assistance of an adult. Many of these games would be of great interest for blind children because their contents include a large amount of audio resources with coherent educational and ludic content. These games are usually based on an 'exclusive' graphical interface, that is the only way to interact with the games is to use a mouse. Then, blind children cannot access them in an autonomous way. More widely visually impaired children experience difficulties with those games, depending on to the level of their visual possibilities.

The use of access technology for visually impaired people, like screen readers (software allowing blind and partially impaired users to access to computer contents), is often impossible with games, because of technical incompatibilities. Moreover in the rare case where standard access software would be compatible, the result would hardly be called a game, as we will see in section 1.3.

K. Miesenberger et al. (Eds.): ICCHP 2004, LNCS 3118, pp. 248–256, 2004.

The operational objectives of the project were:

- To develop tools facilitating the design of games intended to visually impaired children;
- To study the adaptation of game interaction situations to non visual interfaces;
- To develop a set of working games, adapted to visually impaired children, and corresponding to various game situations;
- To evaluate these games with visually impaired children;
- To study the potential of these games for visually impaired children, from an educational, a learning and a therapeutic points of view;
- To study legal questions raised by the adaptation of existing multimedia product;
- To study the conditions to ensure effective diffusion of those kind of games towards visually impaired children.

### 1.1 Users Group

The main group of children currently concerned is composed of children who cannot use ordinary graphical interfaces because of a visual disability: blind children and partially sighted children whose vision is rated less than 0.05.

We focus on ages from 3 to 10 years old. The games can be used by older children, especially in case of children with additional disabilities.

### 1.2 Specific Modalities

To reach the specific needs of these children, the games should be adaptable to the visual possibilities of each of them, according to the specific modalities he/she can use. In the case of blind children, only tactile-based (Braille, tactile boards) and audio-based (stereo sounds, surround sounds, speech synthesis) modalities are available.

A visual modality is accessible to partially sighted children, that as been called "Customisable Graphical Display". It uses an graphical equipment and the software must allow a large variety of settings: scalable font prints, adjustable colours and contrast...

Additionally a graphical view is always available and should be attractive to sighted people like parents, brothers and sisters or school mates.

A very important issue is to supply the support for all existing models of each category of device, as well as being able to add drivers easily when a new model comes on the market. Indeed specialised devices are usually very expensive (Braille displays starting at $ 5,000). So it is necessary that the games can run with any models that children might have access to.

### 1.3 Usability

The adapted games have to be considered by children as real games. In some rare case, access technology would be compatible, but it would result in a very complex interface, and the result would hardly be called a game.

Adults accept to make concessions in order to be able to use the same tools as their sighted peers via Assistive technology. Usually this requires a long and difficult learning, and a lot of fastidious operations. For instance when using a word-processor with a screen reader, to check if a word is in bold face in a paragraph, it is necessary to select this word, to open the dialog box corresponding to the characters attributes, and then to seek in this box if the attribute "bold" is checked or not. This can hardly be accepted by children, especially when they play.

## 2 The Game Development Platform

The main goal of the project was to develop a programming tool that allows to easily design games adapted to our target group.

The approach chosen by the TiM project has been to design games using a modality-independent model [2]. A game development platform [3] was developed as an API for designing the game scenarios using Python[1] scripts. This platform allows to design computer games able to manage different kinds of special devices corresponding to various modalities (tactile, audio, large screen displays).

The most important feature of this platform is the separation between the game scenario and the multimodal and multilingual resources:

### 2.1 Game Scenarii

Game scenarii are implemented independently of the devices and of the language. A game scenario is a Python script that uses the TiM Platform API components. Those components are preexisting functionalities that are provided to the game designer to simplify game design. Given TiM's objective of adaptive games, components are very high level objects completely independent of the representation they will have on the different devices. 3 kinds of components are available.

- Fundamental components are the basic elements of each game situation:
  - *widget* is a generic component that can be a label or a button, used to display any information or picture.
  - *source* is a component allowing to handle surround enabled sound sources and to play sound files on these sources.
  - *timer* is a component allowing to start a function after a given delay.
- High level components include facilities that are often necessary in a computer game:
  - *player* is a component that represents the main character of a game.
  - *navigator* may be used to control a character as well as to move in a menu. It can handle keyboard input as well as joystick or game pads.
- Scenario components are used to describe the different time sequences of the game:

[1] The Python language: http://www.python.org

- *scene* correspond to a part of a game taking place in a rather constant environment. It is a way to divide a game in many small sequences, like in a movie.
- *game* is the main component of a game and includes all the scenes.

Each component manipulated in the scenario is an abstract element, that is there are no reference to any resource files there.

### 2.2 XML Stylesheets

Each game scenario is associated to a style sheet that contains all the necessary resources that are needed to render each component using each modality, and when it is relevant in each language. This style sheet is an XML document with a specific DTD that was designed to fit our needs.

For instance the resources available for a widget component may include text, pictures, alternative text for Braille displays, alternative pictures for the Customisable Graphical Display, graphical information like position on the screen, colours and fonts to use for the prints, etc.

Additionally each widget may have several "states" allowing to define various contents and layout for the same element depending on the situation in the game.

## 3 Programming Libraries

Each kind of user device is managed using external an external libraries. We used existing software libraries when it was possible: OpenAL[2] is used to play sounds, as well in stereo and localised in a surround environment; and SDL[3] is used to access to the graphic frame-buffer, audio devices, keyboards and joysticks.

Then we developed the programming libraries that were necessary in specific cases like Braille or tactile board devices (see below). The architecture allows to easily update those modules or add a new one corresponding to a new kind of device.

Two programming libraries were developed within the framework of the project:

**libbraille** is a programming library to access braille displays [4, 5].
This library is responsible for all the low level interactions with Braille displays. It allows:
- to write a text string on the display;
- to raise Braille dots independently;
- to use any Braille table in order to be usable in any language — the user can also use a personalised table;
- to get the keys that have been pressed by a user, depending of the availability on each model:

[2] OpenAL: the Open Audio Library, http://www.openal.org
[3] SDL: Simple DirectMedia Layer, http://libsdl.org

  - function keys;
  - Braille keyboard;
  - chords (combination of space bar and Braille keys);
  - cursor routing keys.

**libboard** is to tactile boards what libbraille is to braille displays. Since Tactile boards are much more simple devices as Braille Terminals, this is a light library. It allows to get the number of the cell pressed on a tactile device.

Currently the game platform does not support speech output. Actually it was observed that young children have difficulties to understand synthetic speech. Then in the TiM games the texts were recorded by actors. Anyway the development of a libspeech library, that will have the same philosophy as libbraille and libboard, was started and is planned to be included in the platform in the future.

## 4 Tactile Overlay Production

Research have been carried to produce tactile overlays that respect two important constraints:

- they need to be tacitly attractive for the children
- they need to be very solid, since it is game interfaces that the players may use for a long time, they have to press on it (this is different from tactile books where each page is touched during a shorter period, and not pressed).

Actually a new relief deposit technology was developed, that give the possibilities of textures, black print, and relief print as Braille, diagrams, or weft. This technology allows to put Braille on any kind of support (plastic, CD, metal, etc).

## 5 Theoretical Results

### 5.1 Game Analysis

During the project an important knowledge was acquired about development of game for visually impaired children, particularly about adaptation of game situations, and the use of various input and output modalities. By using some of the TiM games as case studies, it was possible to point out some challenges and possible solutions. Then a set of guidelines concerning design of specific games or adaptation of game situations for non visual interaction was developed.

### 5.2 Potential of Games

TiM project has been exploring possibilities to design or re-design conventional game activities as sound only applications for blind and visually impaired children. The seven developed games allow direct interaction in meaningful sound environments.

The potential for education, learning and therapy was evaluated with respect to the special needs of blind and visually impaired children at primary school age. The educational potential lays mainly in modes of interactions which mirror or complement a variety of classroom interactions.

For the process of individual learning TiM games mainly contribute to autonomous learning, the development of listening skills and audio-tactile coordination. Game interactions are highly motivating for children and are a good shared focus for guided learning for young blind children.

The therapeutic potential was analysed with respect to a number of behavioural problems often met by blind and visually impaired children: the attention span, listening skills, the sense of achievement and communication. Additionally we explored the possible contribution of audio-graphical interfaces which could be tailored to different visual impairments and which would allow systematic training of the use and integration of both senses.

### 5.3 Ergonomic Studies

A study of game adaptation, from an ergonomic point of view was carried out [6]. The ergonomics's approach studies the accountancy between human people and the product. The aim is to understand the human behaviour concerning the product in order to improve its accessibility and usability. This discipline is described as a factor of innovation and safety.

### 5.4 Juridical Studies

The process of adapting existing games in the manner suggested by the TIM project raises a number of issues never encountered before. Some challenging legal work is needed with the objective of sourcing appropriate negotiating partners to secure the right to adapt the existing multimedia works to specific audiences. First, it is necessary to identify the exploitation right holders, then, it is necessary to build a contractual framework which will enable the utilisation and the adaptation of multimedia works. The juridical studies carried out during the project aimed at study the relations between the owner of an original multimedia product (publisher) and the designer of an adaptation (adapter). A contract signed with the company owning one of the games that was adapted during the project was used as a case study. A model of contract was proposed.

## 6 TiM Games

A set of games was developed using the Blindstation within the framework of the TiM project. These games were the basis for 2 kind of studies:

- to study adaptation of game interaction for visually impaired children
- to demonstrate the kind of games that can be developed using the TiM platform

**Mudsplat** is an arcade like game where the player has to shoot on everything he can ear. Using stereo, the objects are on a line in front of the player and he can move left and right.

**X-Tune** is a musical construction game where the player can sequence and play with different sound environments.

**Reader Rabbit's: Toddler** is an adaptation of a mainstream discovery game designed for very young children.

**Magic Dictation** is a educational game for learning reading and writing. A set of activities are proposed: spelling, recognise words, hangman, etc. It can be played with the screen (scalable fonts) and the Braille display, but also only on the audio modality, with a reduced set of activities (because some are not possible without reading).

**Tactile/Audio Discovery** is a very simple game for very young children or children with additional disabilities to to associate sounds and pictures on the screen or tactile information of a tactile board.

**Hide and Seek** is a game where the player as to reach animals localised by a sound in a simple surround sound environment.

**Tim Journey** is an exploration game. The player solves a mystery in real-time: he has to explore a complex surround sound environment, divided in various scenes (beach, forest, harbour, etc...) and to solve puzzles to collect evidences that will allow him to solve the mystery.

## 7 Distribution of Software

**TiM Game Engine**
The TiM game engine will be released as opensource, with the GNU LGPL license[4].

**libbraille**
libbraille was released as an opensource librairie, with the GNU LGPL license and is available at: `http://libbraille.sourceforge.net`

**TiM Games**
Some of the games that were developed within the project will be soon available (like Mudsplat and XTune for instance), while others are still working prototypes that can be used to play with children. Then the last one (TiM journey) is a prototype version of a very ambitious game idea intended to show the possibilities of the platform and to setup the navigation in a surround environment.
Information about the dissemination of games will be available on the timgames website: `http://www.timgames.org`

[4] GNU Lesser General Public License, http://www.gnu.org/copyleft/lesser.html

## Acknowledgements

The **TiM** project is are funded by the European Commission[5], on the program IST 2000 (FP5/IST/Systems and Services for the Citizen/Persons with special needs), under the references IST-2000-25298.

The TiM project participants are: *Inserm U483 INOVA, Université Pierre et Marie Curie* (France), co-ordinator, *Les Doigts Qui Rêvent* (France), *Université du Havre* (France), *Association BrailleNet* (France), *Royal Institute of Technology* (Sweden), *Sunderland University* (United Kingdom), *Swedish Institute for Special Needs Education* (Sweden) and *Virtua Ltd* (United Kingdom).

We thank the company *'Mindscape'* for allowing the adaptation of the game *"Reader rabbit's: Toddler"*.

## References

1. Archambault, D., Burger, D., Sablé, S.: The TiM Project: Tactile Interactive Multimedia computer games for blind and visually impaired children. In Črt Marinček, Bühler, C., Knops, H., Andrich, R., eds.: Assistive Technology – Added Value to the Quality of Life, Proceedings of the AAATE'01 Conference, Ljubljana, Slovenia, Amsterdam, The Netherlands, IOS Press (2001) 359–363
2. Archambault, D., Burger, D.: From Multimodality to Multimodalities: the need for independent models. In Stephanidis, C., ed.: Proceedings of the UAHCI'01 conference — Universal Access in Human-Computer Interaction (joint with 9th International Conference on Human-Computer Interaction) — Towards an Informatino Society for All, New-Orleans, Louisiana, USA, Lawrence Erlbaum Associates (2001) 227 – 231
3. Sablé, S., Archambault, D.: Blindstation: a Game platform adapted to visually impaired children. In Craddock, G., McCormack, L., Reilly, R., Knops, H., eds.: Assistive Technology – Shaping the future, Proceedings of the AAATE'03 Conference, Dublin, Ireland, Amsterdam, The Netherlands, IOS Press (2003) 232 – 236
4. Sablé, S., Archambault, D.: Libbraille: A portable library to easily access braille displays. In Miesenberger, K., Klaus, J., Zagler, W., eds.: Proc. ICCHP 2002 (International Conference on Computers Helping People with Special Needs). Volume 2398 of LNCS., Linz, Austria, Springer (2002) 345 – 352
5. Sablé, S., Archambault, D.: libbraille: a programming library for easy access to Braille displays. In Craddock, G., McCormack, L., Reilly, R., Knops, H., eds.: Assistive Technology – Shaping the future, Proceedings of the AAATE'03 Conference, Dublin, Ireland, Amsterdam, The Netherlands, IOS Press (2003) 435 – 440
6. Buaud, A., Archambault, D., Roussel, B.: Ergonomic evaluation of computer games for visually impaired children. In Stephanidis, C., ed.: Universal Access in HCI – Inclusive Design in the Information Society. Volume 4., Mahwah, New Jersey, USA, Lea (2003) 1265 – 1269
7. Archambault, D.: The tim computer games for visually impaired children. In: Proc. CSUN'04 (19th Annual Conference "Technology and Persons with Disabilities"), Los Angeles, California, USA (2004)

[5] The contents of this paper is the sole responsibility of the authors an in no way represents the views of the European Commission or its services.

8. van Leeuwen, L., Power, A., Ellis, P.: Choosing methods for prototype testing of inclusive computer games. In Klaus, J., Miesenberger, K., Zagler, W., Burger, D., eds.: Proc. ICCHP 2004 in Paris (International Conference on Computers Helping People with Special Needs). LNCS, Linz, Austria, Springer (2004)
9. Hildén, A., Svensson, H.: Can all young disabled children play at the computer. In Miesenberger, K., Klaus, J., Zagler, W., eds.: Proc. ICCHP 2002 (International Conference on Computers Helping People with Special Needs). Volume 2398 of LNCS., Linz, Austria, Springer (2002)

# 3D Shooting Games, Multimodal Games, Sound Games and More Working Examples of the Future of Games for the Blind

Eric Velleman, Richard van Tol, Sander Huiberts, and Hugo Verwey

Accessibility Foundation,
Utrechtseweg 84, 3702AD Zeist, Netherlands
www.accessibility.nl
www.soundsupport.net

**Abstract.** Blind people shooting virtual monsters on a real football field. Is that possible? The European Media Master of Arts-program of the Utrecht School of the Arts (Arts, Media & Technology) and the Bartiméus Accessibility Foundation in Zeist have developed a curriculum for accessible game and program development together. Within this curriculum already many spectacular games have been developed like Drive, The Curb Game, Hall of Sound, Powerchords, Wow, Demor and others. The games include the use of user panels and extensive user testing and present the future possibilities of gaming.

## 1 Introduction

The European Media Master of Arts-program of the Utrecht School of the Arts (Arts, Media & Technology) and the Bartiméus Accessibility Foundation in Zeist have developed a curriculum for accessible game and program development together. Within this curriculum already many spectacular games have been developed like Drive, The Curb Game, Hall of Sound, Powerchords, Wow, Demor and others.

These games are all examples of the valuable collaboration between the Utrecht School of the Arts (HKU) and the Accessibility Foundation. The HKU-students have the technological skills while the Accessibility Foundation offers the necessary expertise in the field of accessibility and a forms a direct link to the target group. With the availability of the right resources and the right knowledge there is the possibility of producing high-quality prototypes in a very short amount of time. Together with the pupils of the Bartiméus School the prototypes can be adjusted to fit their wishes and needs. These prototypes are not only proof of concepts but many of them can be further developed into high-quality products. At the moment the curriculum is being exported to other institutes like the University of Twente and involve stakeholders like disability organizations, web design companies, government agencies, publishers etc.

K. Miesenberger et al. (Eds.): ICCHP 2004, LNCS 3118, pp. 257–263, 2004.

## 2 Drive, Racing Game for the Blind

The Drive-project was one of the first projects in the collaboration between Bartiméus Accessibility and the Utrecht School of the Arts. The goal of the Drive project was to create a (non-visual) computer game that resembles the same level of accessibility and fun as a game with visual output. The game had to be as exciting and challenging as visual games. It is designed for blind children of the age of 10 to 14. The game is programmed by Sander Huiberts, Hugo Verwey and Richard van Tol, is available on CD-rom and can be ordered at www.accessibility.nl and/or downloaded at www.soundsupport.net

Although most people like the game, it is the research behind it that gives an enormous amount of information about sound and games. The research gives us more insight into the emotional aspects of a game and focuses not on translation of visual information to sound but takes sound as the starting point to produce a game. The game has been downloaded from the site more than 50.000 times.

Development: September 2001-january 2002.

### 2.1 Project Goals

Drive originated from the fact that there was a huge and unexplored gap between the present computer games at that time and games for visually impaired users. While seeing gamers ventured into 3D gaming worlds such as 'Myst' and 'Final Fantasy', blind gamers were forced to play yet another game of Blackjack, Battleship or Memory.

Several attempts to create a game that is as exciting as a game for the seeing had failed because they consisted of translating (read: 'sonifying') the visual content of existing games. Unfortunately, various aspects of what makes the game fun to play get neglected in this process, because these other aspects are not translated into the audio-domain. This means that real important aspects of the game play disappear.

During the concept phase all visual terminology was eliminated to avoid visual terminology in the game.

This project was the first step in researching the possibilities of using sound as the main fundamental throughout a design process. The research illustrated that
Drive focuses on sonifying the essence of a game instead of the visual output. In this case, the essence of a racing game is not steering but the sense of speed (compare which one is more fun: steering but travelling with 5 mph or no steering but travelling with 700 mph). To really focus on the challenge of expressing speed using only sound, Drive leaves out steering completely.

Extra time was also put into the design of the audio menu, preceding the actual game. It works on two levels, one for new users and one for regular users. The new user will go through the menu listening slowly at each spoken option, while regular users can browse through the menu listening to short beep-sounds which vary in pitch and are placed just before the spoken option. This menu and game intro are also very important for transferring the gamer into the right atmosphere and mood.

## 2.2 Game Description

*Drive* is an audio-racing game. In the game the player is chosen to test a newly developed 'shuttle', which travels over land on a fixed track. The goal of the game is to try and reach the highest speed possible. This is done by picking up 'boosters' which are basically temporary gear-extensions. Boosters are spread along the track and they can be picked up using the left cursor key. Then the booster is activated, by pressing the right cursor key. It might seem easy at first but as the player gains speed, the boosters get harder to catch, due to the change of speed. The game lasts 3 minutes after which the player gets points for picked up boosters and for the distance he has reached (measured by checkpoints). If an internet connection is present, this score is checked with the Drive-website to see if the player has reached a hi-score. If that is the case he is asked to type his name, which is then uploaded to the website.

*Drive* is completely based on sound and aims to exceed existing audio games through several ways (some of which were never used in an audio game before). First, there's Bob. Bob is the co-pilot and he reacts to the way the gamer handles the shuttle. If the player is doing bad Bob persuades to go faster.

Drive features adaptive music which reacts to the speed of the shuttle. When the player is moving slowly the music is a little easy but if he accelerates, the composition will get more stimulating and rewarding. This way it amplifies the sensation of speed. The music will also develop in theme and roughness while the player moves further and further over the track.

During the game the player will hear a variety of Doppler sounds passing his shuttle, like helicopters and sirens. The theory behind this is called 'force-focusing' which basically means that different sounds are intentionally breaking the concentration of a listener by adding new sounds to an existing soundscape (this changes the focus). In the game high quality sounds and studio-recorded voice-actors are used, in contrast to the existing games, which mostly feature self-voicing speech synthesizers, which do not sound stimulating.

## 2.3 Project Results

Drive can be downloaded for free at the Drive-website. More than 50.000 people have downloaded the game. The project has attracted a lot of media attention and appeared in television programs, radio shows, newspapers, news sites and magazines. Many blind and seeing gamers and have played the game and appeared in the hi-score hall of fame.

Drive is playtested with a large (blind) audience and the overall opinion was that Drive is an exciting and accessible game. The blind users could handle the game just as good as the seeing users. In general, blind users are capable of reaching higher scores than seeing users. This shows Drive is a game in which the blind gamer is not handicapped at all. Several seeing users joked they felt handicapped themselves, because they were used to receiving visual feedback.

Because of the sonification of every element of the essence from racing games, both the accessibility-factor and the fun-factor become clear during concept phase. This shows that 'Drive' is a good example of a design-process purely based on sound, one of the aims of the project. It also illustrates that accessible does not mean 'an adapted original' but 'a re-designed original based on the essence'.

During research phase, much effort has been put into the relationship between sound and emotion in a game environment and into meta-gaming elements. Competition is very important for blind gamers and especially competition with their seeing friends. Drive makes this competition possible by offering a central website where players can meet and compare their scores and leave messages in the guestbook.

The Drive project was the first step into the development of prototypes for the blind target group. The enthusiastic reactions of the gamers prove that the development of a game is a valuable step into the creation of more stimulating games for the blind.

## 3 Curb Game, Cross the Street

Life isn't really exciting when you're a hedge-hog living on a curb. But life is what you make of it! So get your quills moving because there's bound to be some excitement waiting in the place all hedge-hogs know as... The Other Curb!

Development: May 2002 – June 2002.

### 3.1 Project Goals

The Curb Game is developed by the same team as Drive (Richard van Tol, Sander Huiberts and Hugo Verweij). The game is an attempt to create an accessible online game, similar to the massive amount of online (Shockwave) games for sighted gamers.

With this game we research the possibilities of designing a game which is fully based on sound (like Drive) in combination with a graphic layer. Since sound is used as the fundamental element in the game's design, accessibility for visually impaired gamers comes natural. By adding a graphic layer on top of this audiogame, the game not only becomes more attractive for sighted gamers but also accessible for users with hearing impairments. During the game the player is able to turn off the graphics and continue to play on sound alone!

We deliberately chose the theme for this game, "crossing the road", for several reasons. First, the tension of crossing the road while not being able to see the traffic is something most blind people have experienced in real life. It is this tension that we wanted to use in a game. The second reason is that we wanted to present seeing people (since we were making a hybrid game) with a situation blind people face everyday.

### 3.2 Game Description

In The Curb Game you are a small hedge-hog living on a city curb, which isn't really that exciting. So, as a hedge-hog, you get your thrills from crossing the road as many times possible! Not an easy task because you may either end up as road kill or die from boredom if you stay on your curb.

### 3.3 Project Results

The final demo product is an online shockwave game that can be accessed through. So far The Curb Game has been played 142.818 times. That's an average of almost 200 times a day for two years. The Curb Game is played by a mixed crowd of gamers with and without a visual handicap. We received a lot of positive feedback from surprised sighted players, saying that they "thought they were playing simple shockwave game like any other".

## 4 Demor, 3D Shooting Game for the Blind

Demor is a location based 3D audio shooter. Demor does not only focus on the entertainment aspect of computer gaming, but also attempts to contribute to the emancipation and mobility of the blind and visually impaired people in order to enhance their integration with the 'sighted' world. It is a proof of concept developed on the basis of theoretical and practical research. The game information, sound samples and more can be downloaded at: http://demor.hku.nl. KMT-HKU Project leader of the project and leading a multidisciplinary team of 9 students: Arnout Hulskamp.

Development: September 2003 – February 2004.

### 4.1 Project Goals

The main goal of the project was to explore the possibilities of a location-based game for visually impaired users. The emphasis lay on the development of an innovative concept for a product that could contribute to the emancipation of the blind and visually impaired people in order to enhance their integration within the 'sighted' society. It is a proof of concept developed on the basis of theoretical and practical research. The final game would not be for commercial but for research purposes only. If the proof of concept would fail then all the gathered research would still be documented in a thorough research report. The final game, if achieved, should be equally playable by both blind and sighted players and should provide entertainment.

### 4.2 Game Description

Demor is a 3D audio first person shooter (FPS). The game play consists of navigating through a 3D audio environment. This environment contains loads of environmental sounds but also ... the bad guys! The goal then, of course, is to shoot as many bad guys without getting shot and receiving the highest score.

The game takes place in 2066. Misshapen and deformed creatures now walk the earth, hating mankind for their creation. They therefore try to change every place on Earth into bare and empty wastelands in order to extinguish humanity.

Of course, there's human resistance and that's where the player comes in. The player's character is asked to take over one of the creatures' settlements in order to regain a healthy earth. The settlement is divided in 4 segments, each with their own soundtrack, environmental sounds and enemies. These represent 4 different zones: a breeding ground for new monsters, a swamp-like environment caused by industrial pollution, an monster transport site and a barren wasteland.

Demor is a "location based" game. Simply said, it means that the player physically takes part in the game and that he or she controls the game with physical actions. The player carries a laptop in a backpack, wears a headphone and holds on simple joystick input device in his hand. The game is played on a big empty outdoor space, like a soccer field for instance. A simple portable head tracking device is attached to the headphone. The laptop is connected to a GPS module. The Global Positioning System (GPS) is a satellite-based navigation system made up of a network of 24 satellites placed into orbit by the U.S. Department of Defence. GPS was originally intended for military applications, but in the 1980s, the government made the system available for civilian use. GPS works in any weather conditions, anywhere in the world, 24 hours a day. There are no subscription fees or setup charges to use GPS.

The system works with a zero-point. The player basically stands in the middle of the open area and presses the joystick once. The system will initialise itself from where the player is standing (the zero point) and the 3D auditory environment will unfold itself around him. The player is now standing in the exact middle of the game. When he moves around the GPS satellites will keep track of the location of the player and communicate that to the laptop, which will then adjust the audio landscape.

It co-operates with the simple head tracking device. When the player turns his head, you will actually hear the soundscape turn around as well. This means that the whole audio game environment will adjust itself to what the player is doing. Whenever the player hears an enemy somewhere he has to turn his head in that direction and pull the trigger on the joystick. If the player aimed right he will have shot the enemy. The computer tracks the aim very precisely. If the player aims very well he will receive more points for shooting the monster than if he aimed less well. This makes the game a whole lot more repayable and realistic as well.

### 4.3 Project Results

A working demo of Demor has been developed. The game has been received very well by the blind and sighted audience. The primary objective, creating entertainment, has been received. The technology used in this project is still a bit expensive but it has set a clear example for future systems. The game is not only groundbreaking for combining audio games with GPS technology, but also for using 3D sound in combination with a head tracker at the same time.

The concept of using a wearable 3D audio system for navigating could be used for applications other than entertainment applications like games. Examples are navigating in the real world, as well as audio augmented workstations. New technology, such as the Ultra Wide Band (UWB) standard for wireless communication could be used to improve the system.

## 5 Conclusion

The games described above all proved to be successful. As Drive was one of the first games totally based on sound which could be compared to current visual games, Demor is already experimenting with the newest technologies. But there is still a lot of research to be done. Subjects like 'sound interfaces', 'audio guiding' and 'immersion through sound' are still to be researched. And as technology keeps developing there will be new possibilities to be discovered.

## 6 More Information

www.soundsupport.net
The number one site about sound based games. With the results of the research and downloadable demo's of the games named in this paper.

www.accessibility.nl
Homepage of the Accessibility Foundation

www.hku-kmt.nl
Homepage of the European Media Master of Arts-program of the Utrecht School of the Arts (Arts, Media & Technology)

demor.hku.nl
Homepage of the Demor project (until end of 2004)

# Choosing Methods for Prototype Testing of Inclusive Computer Games

Lieselotte van Leeuwen, Aoife Power, and Phil Ellis

Department of Arts, Design, Media and Culture
University of Sunderland
Bede Tower Ryhope Road
Sunderland SR2 7EG England
Lieselotte.van-leeuwen@sunderland.ac.uk

**Abstract.** A range of methods used in the development of computer games for young blind and visually impaired children demonstrates how depending on the stage and focus of a design process different ways of working with children allow to identify relevant information. It is also shown how methods help to create mutual understanding between special needs children and a design team.

## 1 Introduction

Developing methods for the evaluation of prototype computer games with children is a field which slowly gains more attention. In the area of usability testing progress has been made in applying methods developed for adult users to testing with child users [1,2]. However, testing e.g. the appeal of content or the fun children have is still not very far developed with respect to a) the measurability and b) the way results of testing can be made effective for the design process.

When working with children with sensory disabilities, again re-thinking of methods is required in order to ensure mutual understanding between the children and the design team. In the following we will use the development of one computer game for blind and visually impaired children as a case study to demonstrate possibilities and problems in identifying and using a range of evaluation methods.

The TiM project [3], funded by the European commission within the 'Information Society Technologies' (IST) programme was dedicated to providing blind and visually impaired children with autonomous access to computer games. The goal of the project was to develop software tools which allow a) the development of audio-tactile game contents and b) the adaptation of existing commercial games. Within the project we worked together with 72 visually impaired and blind children in order to explore potentially useful and enjoyable computer-based game-interactions.

## 2 User Needs Analysis

In the idea development phase two approaches to identify user needs were chosen. One was a questionnaire investigating the availability and use of computers, special-

K. Miesenberger et al. (Eds.): ICCHP 2004, LNCS 3118, pp. 264–271, 2004.

ised hardware and software and the familiarity with game and educational software in the home environment. The relationship of computer use to severity of visual impairment, age, gender and country were analysed.

The second approach was dedicated to the needs and requirements for play and learning experienced by the children themselves. The chosen methodologies focused on the abilities of the children more than on the compensation for disability. In the following some examples of results will be shown. The data are part of the final report of the TiM project [3].

### 2.1 Questionnaire

A total of 76 questionnaires were retuned by parents and carers in France (26), Sweden (23) and the UK (27). Of the children 49 are in the age range 3 to 12 years, 27 children where between 13 and 18 years of age. 43 were boys and 33 girls.

The Tim project aimed at blind or severely visually impaired children. The questionnaire therefore was designed to explore the effect these impairments have on the accessibility of computer games. A comparison with less severe visual impairment (acuity higher than 0.01) was chosen in order to highlight differences between the groups. Note, that the distributions shown in Table 1 are not representative for the general population of people with visual impairments but were chosen to allow comparisons of the three groups.

The degree of visual impairment was coded in three categories - blind (no vision), visual acuity below 0.01 and acuity better than 0.01. A person with a visual acuity below 0.01 has some residual vision but must in most cases rely on tactile (Braille) or spoken output to be able to use a computer. Table 1 shows the distribution of visual impairment.

**Table 1.** Degree of visual impairment for n=76 children.

| Visual Impairment | Number of children | Percentage |
|---|---|---|
| Blind | 27 | 35.5 |
| <0.01 | 26 | 34.2 |
| >0.01 | 23 | 30.3 |
| Total | 76 | 100 |

*Example of results 1.*

<u>The Availability of Computers in Home Environments</u>
Results of the questionnaire show the availability of computers as well as the degree of specialized assistive technology in the home environments of blind and visually impaired children.

The majority of the questioned families (59%) in all three countries do have standard PCs with operating systems Windows 95 or higher at home. 20% have special computers and 13% of the families did not have a computer at home. Standard monitors with or without synthetic speech were the most used in home environments. In France and Sweden Braille & synthetic speech outputs were available to small groups of children at home, but not in the UK.

The Need for Support in Using Computers

The need for support from sighted peers or adults in using the computer is influenced by age as well as the degree of visual impairment. 69% of younger children as well as 61% of children who are blind or have an acuity below 0.01 require some or full support when using the computer compared to 34% of older and 45 % of children with an acuity higher than 0.01.

### 2.2 Sessions with Children

**Semi-structured Interviews.** We met individual or small groups of blind and visually impaired children in their school context. After introducing the TiM project to them we asked a series of questions about problems the children meet playing in schools and at home. When asked about what would be most important to be changed in order to solve those problems, 12 children between 8 and 11 years old agreed about the following points:

*Example of Results 2:* The understanding of sighted children about what it means to be blind/VI.

- The need to have to ask for help so often and not be able to do things autonomously.
- The feeling to be locked out of the fun their sighted peers are engaging in, especially the world of computer games and teenage magazines.
- The inability to communicate to others who they really are.

**Observations.** Observations took place in everyday school life within and outside lessons.

*Example of Results 3.* Observing the use of Desk top computers with keyboards, mouse or tactile input devices like IntelliKeys we found

- A lack of continuous control interfaces (only key/button/area of touch on/off control mechanisms).
- The use of sound is predominantly indirect, i.e. descriptive of objects/events rather than direct.
- There is no direct manipulation of sound, only of graphics.
- The performance of control actions is based on graphics with more or less specific audio-feedback. There is no audio-guidance of navigation on the screen.

## 3 Scenario Development

The results of the user needs analysis were one factor influencing the development of a series of scenarios. Out of a number of game scenarios developed in the TiM project we chose 'Mudsplat' as case study to demonstrate how user needs information was integrated in the design of game prototypes.

Mudsplat is an Arcade game based scenario with several levels in which monsters who try to cover a city in mud need to be splashed with water in order to disappear. The player is the hero who can free the city from the monsters. This game was developed for short-term play, giving the children access to the kind of game play and fun their sighted peers are engaged in. The design goal was to support autonomous use of the game by blind and visually impaired children. Table 2 summarizes how user needs were incorporated in the game scenario.

**Table 2.** Design features of Mudsplat integrating a number of requirements resulting from the user needs analysis.

| User needs | Mudsplat Design features |
|---|---|
| Standard PC | Arcade game with relatively low system requirements including stereo or surround sound. |
| Standard keyboard or specialized interfaces | A minimum of 4 clearly distinctive keys (return, arrow keys and space bar) are sufficient to play the game. |
| Sound as direct medium of interaction | Monsters are specified through different non-human voices; Feedback for navigation and splashing monsters are action sounds; The position of the monsters is specified through changing left/right position of the voices in stereo or surround sound acoustic environments. |
| Continuous control | The movement of monsters as well as the navigation of the player are continuous. In absence of continuous control devices such as joy sticks the repetitive pressing of arrow keys fulfill this function. |
| Use of the game after installation is independent of vision | Direct game interaction; navigation through and use of menu options can be performed through audio interaction. A manual is available in audio as well as Braille print. |
| Increasing complexity | Levels of difficulty are introduced increasing complexity and speed of interaction in order to allow players at different age and/or experience level to play the game and stay motivated for a longer period of time. |

## 4 Prototype Development

Iterative evaluation of prototypes occurred in three phases. Phase 1 was a peer review of the first prototype. From Prototype 2 on evaluation sessions were performed with 70 blind and visually impaired children in France, Sweden and the UK. The focus of evaluation changed from mainly content in the earlier stages to mainly usability for the late stages of game development.

### 4.1 Peer Review

All game prototypes were first evaluated by minimally two members of the project team who where not involved in the direct concept and programming work. The peers concentrated on the evaluation from a user perspective, taking into account the result of the user needs analysis. Aspects for evaluation were:

- Interface (comprehension, navigation, control);
- Content (suitability for certain age groups, complexity of possible interactions, expectation of motivation/excitement);
- Quality of sound (e.g. identifying and differentiating sounds);
- Quality of interaction (e.g. interactive vs. passive sounds).

The goal of the peer review was to ensure the basic handling and understanding of the game by children. This step prevents frustrating experiences for the children and unnecessary delays in creating design-relevant information. After every iteration a short peer evaluation took place in order to review the changes as solutions to the problems which were raised. From the peer review also resulted the awareness of potential problems concerning content and usability of the game which required exploration with the children.

For effective use of the peer review results by the game developers they were presented specifically for aspect(s) of design adjustments. Table 3 shows in case of the 'Mudsplat' game results of the peer review would be presented to the design team.

*Example of Results 4.*

**Table 3.** Peer review results ordered by design aspect.

| Design Aspect | Mudsplat Peer review |
|---|---|
| Programming | Left/right navigation: should be only available with left/right arrow key, not also with up/down ones. |
| Content | The introductory story gives no information about how to play. Story teller could introduce relevant sounds e.g. by telling while trying to hide from and hit monsters. |
| Sound quality | Differentiation between different monsters is difficult. |
| Input devices | Movement mapping: Joystick moves too fast, keys too slow. |

## 4.2 Game Evaluation with Children

Prototype evaluation with children includes two approaches of working towards design-relevant results. One concerns questions raised by the designers (top-down approach), and the other concerns problems found when children actually use prototypes (bottom up approach). Identifying the content and methods for a session requires to translate the questions of the designers into for children relevant terms and, it requires the translation of children's answers and suggestions back into terms which are directly usable for the respective partners in the design team being e.g. interface designers or concept developers [4, 5] . In our view, when working with disabled children, facilitating mutual understanding between children and designers means facilitating perspective taking and re-experiencing the perception of action possibilities along shared abilities. In the case of blind and visually impaired children this has been proven a challenge to the design team in the visually dominated area of computer game designs.

Evaluating software requires analyzing the inter-relationship between interface and game content topics. Not being able to fulfill a task can in principle be caused by either usability problems, problems concerning the meaning or goal of activities or a combination of both. Therefore, in order to provide results which can be directly incorporated in design, testing has not only to identify a problem but also its source.

Whenever possible, users should be involved in finding solutions to clearly identified problems. Children are known for their pragmatic and often unconventional way of approaching problems and therefore may expand the potential for solutions. Especially in the case of disabled users, their experience and insight in problems related to their disability makes them the experts the design team might need for efficient problem solving. In cases of big structural changes in a design, mocking up and discussing possible solution with the children before implementing them can prevent mistakes and save time.

In the following the methods used for testing the evolving Mudsplat game prototypes will be described and discussed. Examples of respective results and their use in the design will be given.

### 4.3 Methods for Prototype Testing

- Observation in free exploration of the prototype (solitary and pair use);
- Observation in guided activities with the prototype (solitary and pair use);
- Observation in guided activities *not* involving the prototype (solitary and small groups);
- Interviews;
- Brainstorming sessions.

**Observations of Free Exploration** are used for an initial overview of problem areas the children meet, or in a later phase of development in order to capture the variety of ways children choose to relate to a certain product. This method reveals the problems children find in using a prototype without being prompted.

*Example of Results 5.* Silent gaps in which no information is given about how to proceed at points 1-n in the game.

- Audio feedback for successful entering a name for the safe file needs to be added.

**Observation in Guided Activities** is focused on certain aspects of design such as e.g. the understanding of a task or the effectiveness of navigation. A series of those activities can be set up in order to isolate the source(s) of certain problems or test possible solutions. This method is the main strategy chosen in evaluating the usability of a product. Methods, which are available for adults can become adapted for children, but a scientific approach to those adaptations has only just been started [1].

Using observational methods as well as **interviews** for the same question has been useful as it helps us to become aware of possible discrepancies between the results of both methods. The comparison highlights the difference between the verbalized experience of children (interview) and interpretations of observations.

*Example of Results 6. Repetitive failing to finish a level was seen by an observer as a serious problem while the children experience it as an inherent part of starting to play a computer game.*

**Observation in Guided Activities *Not* Involving the Prototype** is mainly used for two reasons: One is the attempt to isolate the source of a problem which is impossible through the integration of aspects in the prototype. The other is the need to gather information before a prototype is functioning well enough to start testing it.

The use of already existing products which allow the exploration of a certain aspect of the new design, (e.g. the comparison of different navigation methods) is a very efficient way to create relevant information for the design team at an early enough stage to be effective.

*Example of Results 6.* The children between 6 and 8 years seemed to randomly use the arrow keys in order to navigate towards or away from a monster sound. We needed to identify if the problem was a) due to left/right discrimination of the sound source; b) the delay between key pressing and sound change or c) the understanding of the game functionality.

a) Children were standing in the middle between two loudspeakers with the same distance as in Mudsplat playing. A monster sound or another sound was played at different positions in the left/right plain. The children were asked to first point and then go to the position of the sound. Identifying the direction and position of the sound source was not a problem.
b) In the same setup as in a) we played one sound and asked the children which of the two cardboard keys they had to press in order to go to or away from that stationary sound. Again, it was no problem for them to do so.
c) We played different sounds from the game and asked children which of them were monster sounds and which were others. The young children had difficulties in discriminating them. From this result we decided to change the introduction of sounds and the volume difference between interactive and non-interactive games. As a result young children felt more under control.

## 5 Conclusion

The methods used for the evaluation of Mudsplat, a computer game for blind and visually impaired children, demonstrate the diversity of approaches required in order to understand children's needs on one side and produce information which can be directly used by a design team at the other. A systematic analysis of the potential and effectiveness of a wide range of methods used with children related to the kind, stage and focus of a design process is required in order to provide product developers with a tool box of methods which give children a clear voice in the design of products for them.

## References

1. Kesteren, v I., Bekker, M.M., Vermeeren, A.,& P. Llyod: Assessing usability evaluation methods on their effectiveness to elicit verbal comments from children subjects. IDC 2003 Conference Proceedings, The Association for Computing Machinery, Inc., New York (2003) pp.41-49.
2. Markopoulos, P., Bekker, M.M., How to compare usability testing methods with children participants, IDC 2002 Conference Proceedings. Eindhoven, The Netherlands, (2002) pp. 153-158.
3. TiM Project EU IST grant 2000-25298. www.http://inova.snv.jussieu.fr/tim.
4. Van Leeuwen, L. How children contribute to the design of technology for them. In: Siraj-Blatchford (Ed.) Developing new technologies for children. Trendham Books, London. To be published June 2004.
5. Druin, A. (Ed.) The design of children's technology. Morgan Kaufmann Publishers, San Francisco. 1999.

# It's Time to Make eTourism Accessible

Franz Pühretmair

Competence network information technology
to support the integration of people with disabilities (KI-I)
Hauptstraße 119, Hagenberg i. M., Austria
fp@ki-i.at

**Abstract.** *"Nearly half of all handicapped people would travel more frequently, if there were more barrier-free offers. And about 40 percent have already renounced a travel because adequate offers were missing" (Max Stich, ADAC vice-president for tourism, 2003).* So far the tourism industry still has hardly recognized the potential and the value of barrier-free tourism. As long as the tourism industry will not identify that barrier-free tourism is an indicator for quality, a trademark and a competitive advantage they will not attract its considerable market-share. Often the lack of not supporting barrier-free tourism is a combination of missing offers and inadequate or missing information presentation.

## 1 Introduction

The European Union estimates that currently 15-20% of the population are affected by a disability from temporary to permanent nature [1]. The types of disability range from visual, hearing and mobility impairment to mental and cognitive impairment and comprise also elderly people. Currently the population in Europe is continuously aging. The fact, that older people share many of the access barriers faced by people with disabilities, demonstrates that a tourism industry that addresses these issues can attract significantly more customers [2].

Tourism information providers who consider the needs of "Accessible Tourism" or "Tourism for All" do not concentrate on a small market niche, they try to take advantage of a remarkable market segment. Good accessibility does not only improve the accessibility and usability for people with disabilities but make tourism in general more accessible especially for elderly people and a wide range of the population.

To be able to assess the market potential of people with disabilities, the share of the population is not the only significant parameter but also the intention for travelling. Scientific studies have shown that the intensity of people with disabilities travelling in general is only a little below average, while the intensity of travelling in the native country is clearly above average [3]. Therefore it is recognizable, that people with disabilities don't travel less and they represent under this point of view also an attractive target group. Furthermore it is widely recognized that people with disabilities frequently travel accompanied by people without disabilities like parents, friends or other companions. For the tourism industry this fact causes a multiplier effect that enlarges the potential of the market segment. However, the possibility of taking advantage depends on how the tourism industry will address the issue of accessible tourism.

K. Miesenberger et al. (Eds.): ICCHP 2004, LNCS 3118, pp. 272–279, 2004.

The paper is organized as follows: Section 2 gives an overview on the accessibility of official tourism Web-sites in the European Union, which constitutes the basis to present information about accessible services and products to potential customers. Section 3 explains the traditional ways to present tourism information and outlines a concept to make eTourism accessible. Section 4 and 5 conclude the paper with an outlook on the current legislation followed by a short conclusion.

## 2 Accessibility of Tourism Web-Sites

To discover the current status regarding accessibility of tourism Web-sites the institute of Future Studies and Technology Assessment (IZT) [4] has carried out a study that evaluates the 16 National official tourism Web-sites of the European Union.

The study used the 14 Web Content Accessibility Guidelines (WCAG) 1.0 [5] as a basis to analyze the degree of accessibility and to identify the bandwidth regarding the implementation of accessible Web-Design. The WCAG-guidelines consist of 14 guidelines which each includes checkpoints for three priority levels. The priority level identifies the checkpoint's impact on accessibility.

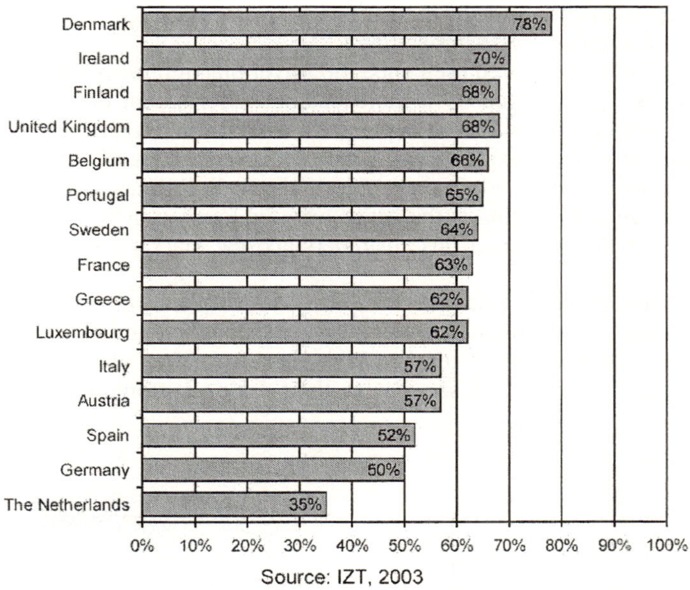


**Fig. 1.** Ranking of Accessibility Evaluation of European tourism Web-sites [6].

The study was curried out with respect to the first priority level which represents the basic requirement for some user groups to be able to use Web documents (Conformance Level "A"). The English Web site of 16 National official tourism Web-sites were analyzed and 59 criteria were evaluated.

Fig. 1 gives an overview on the results of the study [6]. If a Web-site meets all priority 1 checkpoints of WCAG 1.0, the site received 100 percent. The analysis of the

European Web-sites points out that at present some accessibility guidelines are reflected but the issue of Web accessibility in tourism is still at the beginning.

The study has shown a bandwidth of fulfilling the criteria that ranges from 78 to 34 percent. Therefore the main result of the analysis [6] is that in summer 2003 none of the checked official National Tourism Web-sites complied with all priority 1 checkpoints of the 14 WCAG guidelines. None of these Web-sites support accessibility in a way to reach at least a minimum of accessibility that is reflected in a level "A" conformance [5].

## 3 Tourism and Accessibility

When travelling, people with disabilities and older people have special needs like accessibility of transportation, accommodation, sights, restaurants, streets, parks, communication infrastructure, etc. An accessible infrastructure is the basis to support Tourism for All. The strategic planning of travels does not start at the holiday location, information on the accessible infrastructure influence the whole booking and decision making process.

To improve the quality of services for people with disabilities and to cope with their needs the tourism industry has to support tourists in an appropriate way in both stages travel planning as well as travelling.

Because of their special requirements, the travel planning of people with disabilities normally is characterized by a more detailed information enquiry than known from people without disabilities. People with disabilities require information with respect to their individual special need, which is often significantly different from the information usually requested from people without disabilities. Frequently the unavailability of this information is the cause why the tourism industry and their products and services do not attract this customers and the market potential remains untapped.

Fig.2. explains the traditional way to present tourism information in the Internet. Such information representation can be found on state-of-the-art destination management systems as wells on single tourism Web-sites. A tourism object like a hotel or a sight presents its products and services to their online customers. Frequently such

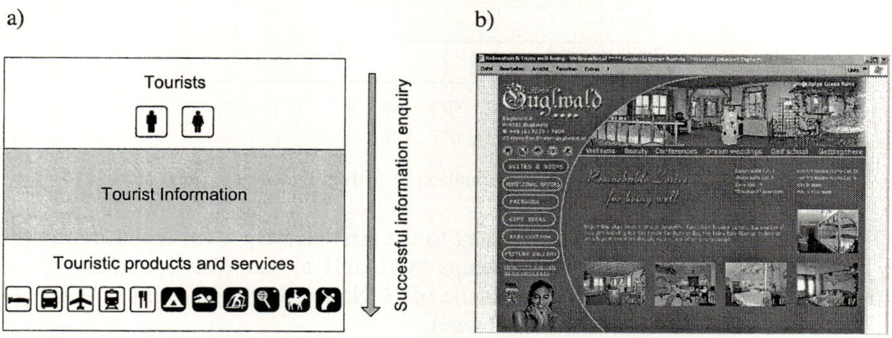


**Fig. 2.** Traditional representation of tourism information a) the concept – b) an example: Hotel Guglwald (http://www.hotel-guglwald.at).

Web-sites are not implemented as accessible Web-sites and are therefore not accessible for people with disabilities and moreover contain no information about the availability of accessibility features.

If a tourism object contains information on accessibility features these features are often consolidated on a single page or in a separated area. This is convenient if the tourist is looking for a summary but it's often hard to find and therefore hard to access. This fact is aggravated if the Web-pages are not designed as accessible Web-pages. Furthermore Fig.2 and Fig.3 demonstrate the differences in information inquiry and booking process of tourists without (Fig.2) and with disabilities (Fig.3).

a) b)

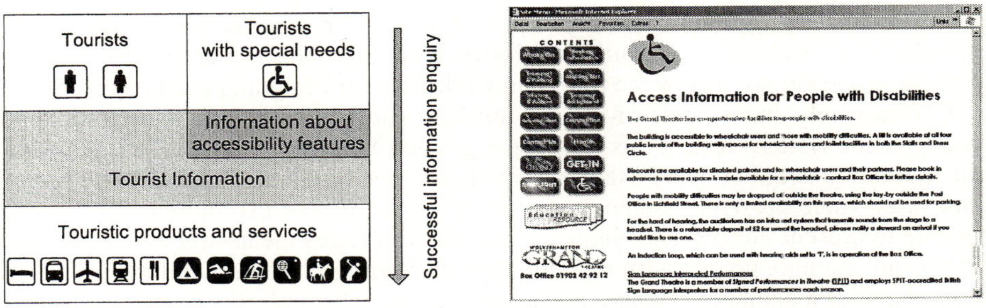


**Fig. 3.** Traditional representation of tourism information extended with accessibility information a) the concept - b) an example: Wolverhampton Grand Theatre (http://www.grandtheatre.co.uk).

Tourists look for certain information according to their interests, to book different touristic products and services like accommodations, transports, events, wellness activities, etc. Tourists with disabilities also look for certain information according to their interests. Additionally this group of tourists has the need to check different accessibility information before booking touristic products or services to ensure that during their travel condign attention will be given to their special needs like appropriate accommodation, accessible transportation as well as an accessible infrastructure and events.

The information mostly required is information regarding access. Access varies depending on the kind of disability. [1] characterizes access from three main dimensions:

*Physical access*: people with mobility impairment like people using wheel-chairs, they require information on accessible hotel rooms, lifts, ramps, etc.

*Sensory access*: people with hearing or visual impairment, need tactile markings or hearing augmentation.

*Communication access*: people who have difficulties with written word, vision, speech, and language problems.

A detailed summary and description of touristic quality criterions to cope with these requirements for people with disabilities and elderly people has been published in [7].

The physical support of accessibility is the basis to make touristic products and services attractive to people with disabilities and elderly people. For a successful marketing of tourism products and services just the existence isn't sufficient, it is very important to communicate this information to potential customers. People with disabilities have a clear need to receive information on accessible facilities. Such accessibility information is a quality criterion that will influence the tourist's decision making and booking process.

The Internet as an information medium offers impressing possibilities for people with disabilities. The Internet opens the access to information which is otherwise hard to obtain. Especially tourism information systems and destination management systems are one of the most frequently accessed information sources in the Internet. However people with disabilities often hit barriers when surfing the Web. Usually, this is not caused by their disability – people with special needs use assistive technologies that compensate disabilities. Mostly Web pages are not accessible because Web designers do not follow the rules and guidelines for designing such pages [5].

Unfortunately many state-of-the art tourism information pages and destination management systems reflect this lack [6], e.g. often Web pages include images without alternative text, but many users cannot see images. Some are blind and use screen readers or voice browsers, others have turned off images or use mobile devices not capable to present images. Designing accessible Web pages means to build Web Sites that do not exclude people with mobility, visual, hearing or cognitive impairments to reach the widest audience possible and to leave nobody behind [8].

In principle there are two different ways for a successful support of accessible eTourism. The first concept is an accessible version of the traditional approach which is extended with accessibility information (Fig.3). It offers tourism information with accessibility information for people with disabilities and elderly people added in an additional section or respectively on additional Web-pages. The whole information representation is implemented as accessible Web-pages and therefore accessible for all tourists (Fig.4).

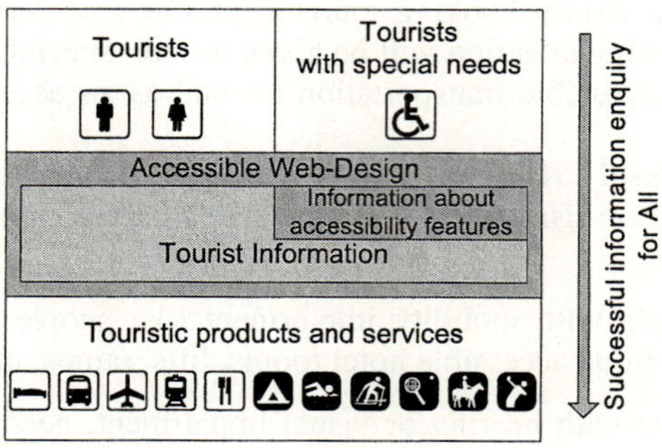


**Fig. 4.** Accessible eTourism with accessibility information added on additional Web-pages.

This approach inherits the advantages and disadvantages of the traditional approach (Fig.3). It offers the user a compact overview on accessibility information, but lacks because the accessibility information is separated from the service or product description.

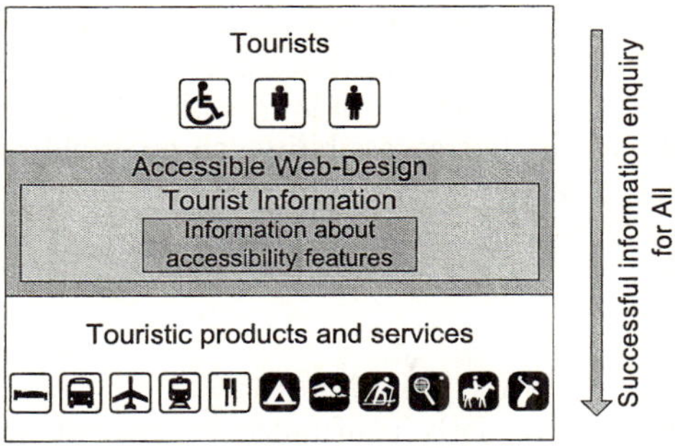


**Fig. 5.** Accessible eTourism with omnipresent accessibility information.

To overcome this lack, the accessibility information has to be integrated into the original product or service description (Fig. 5). In this way accessibility information is omnipresent and therefore easy to retrieve. For people with disabilities this means that no additional information enquiry is necessary.

For successful destination marketing the presentation of information on accessible environments via accessible media like accessible Web-pages is by far the most important area of concern to make barrier-free tourism a success story. In many cases tourism information provider lack in communicating and marketing accessible services [9]. Information on accessible environments is the basis to attract people with disabilities, to make the destination interesting for the tourists, to influence the tourist's decision making and to accomplish to welcome them as guests.

## 4 Accessibility and the Legislation

The accessibility of Web-sites for people with disabilities is one specific target of the eEurope Action plan [10]. The last years process to implement these target in the legislation of the members of the European Union has been started. All member states have committed to integrate the WAI guidelines [5] into national law. Starting with official public Web-pages on an European and National level, which will later be extended to Regional and Local sites [6].

Increasingly, there is a growing body of national laws and policies which address accessibility of Information and Communications Technology (ICT), including the Internet. These legislations provide and aggravate the need for organizations to pay attention to accessibility issues.

The approaches among these laws and policies differ from country to country: Some establish a human or civil right to ICT, or define that any ICT purchased by the government must be accessible, while others issue that ICT sold in a given market must be accessible [11].

The United States with the "Americans with Disabilities Act (ADA)" which was passed as a law in 1990 was a precursor in this area. Other countries like Australia ("Disability Discrimination Act"), Canada ("Common Look and Feel for the Internet"), United Kingdom ("The Disability Discrimination Act 1995") or Germany ("Barrierefreie Informationstechnik Verordnung (BITV)") [12] followed with their regulatory and legal requirements. As enforceable law the ADA shows effects not only in daily life - "If you take a walk around your state or local government complex, school or library, you'll see new ramps, wider doorways, new elevators and Braille signs where needed" [10], but also in the accessibility of public Web pages. With such legal and regulatory activities accessibility can be established as a civil right of all citizens.

## 5 Conclusion

People with disabilities are regularly confronted by environment, economic, social and attitudinal barriers when travelling as tourists [2]. Physical barriers include inaccessible accommodations, restaurants, sights, visitor attractions and inadequate transport as well as inaccessible Web-based information and lack of adequate or appropriate assistance [2].

Increasingly there is a growing body of national laws and policies which address accessibility including ICT and the Internet. These legislations provide and aggregate the need for organisations to pay attention to accessibility issues. Barrier-free tourism is therefore not only an indicator for quality and an image forming factor but also a competitive advantage if the information provider undertakes the work necessary for "tourism for all" early.

If the tourism industry wants a successful access to this market potential, they must understand the needs involved and learn to respond to the challenges for the benefit of both parties.

It is a fact that accessible tourism has a huge economic potential with a lot of space for increase [9]. By improving the quality of information and services for people with disabilities, the tourism industry would also improve the quality of information and services for all customers. But often a lack of promoting and communicating information on accessible services causes an untapped potential.

## References

1. National Disability Authority Udaras Naisiunta Michumais (NDA), Accessibility and Tourism – Submission to Tourism Policy Review Group, Dublin, Irland (2003)
2. European Disability Forum (EDF), EDF Position Paper on Tourism: Framing the Future of European Tourism, Doc. EDF 01/13 EN, Brussels, Belgium (2001)
3. Neumann, P., Barrierefreier Tourismus – Vom Tourismus für Menschen mit Behinderung zum Tourismus für Alle, Universität Paderborn, Germany (2002)
4. Institute for Futures Studies and Technology Assessment (IZT), online available on http://www.izt.de/ (03.03.2004)
5. World Wide Web Consortium, Web Accessibility Initiative (WAI), online available on http://www.w3c.org/wai (22.01.2004)
6. Oertel, B., Hasse, C., Scheermesser, M., Thio, S. L., Feil, T., Accessibility of Tourism Web sites within the European Union, Proceedings of the 11th International Conference on Information and Communication Technologies in Tourism (ENTER 2004), ISBN 3-211-20669-8, Springer Verlag, pp. 358 - 368, Cairo, Egypt (2004)
7. Berdel, D., Gödl, D., Schoibl, H., Institut für soziales Design, Entwicklung und Forschung – IST, Studie im Auftrag des Bundesministeriums für soziale Sicherheit und Generationen, Vienna, Austria (2002)

8. Puehretmair, F., Designing inclusive Web Sites, International Symposia Vision Plus 10: Tourist Information de Luxe for All - , Lech/Arlberg, Austria (2003)
9. Bundesministerium für Wirtschaft und Arbeit – Referat Kommunikation und Internet, Ökonomische Impulse eines barrierefreien Tourismus für alle, Münster and Berlin, Germany (2003)
10. eEurope 2002 – An Information Society for All, Communication on a Commission Initiative for the Special European Council of Lisbon, p. 18, 23rd and 24th of March 2000
11. World Wide Web Consortium (W3C), Policies Relating to Web Accessibility, online available on http://www.w3.org/WAI/Policy/ (04.03.2004)
12. Bühler, C., Application of Barrier free Internet in German Legislation, Proceedings of the 10th International Conference on Human-Computer Interaction (HCI 2003) – Universal Access in HCI, Volume 4, ISBN 0-8-8058-4933-5, Lawrence Erlbaum Associates, pp. 930 - 934, Crete (2003)

# Tourism Information Systems Promoting Barrier-Free Tourism for People with Disabilities

Hildegard Rumetshofer and Wolfram Wöß

Institute for Applied Knowledge Processing (FAW)
Johannes Kepler University Linz, Austria
{hrumetshofer,wwoess}@faw.uni-linz.ac.at

**Abstract.** Providing comprehensive accessibility is the major challenge for tourism service providers to address people with disabilities (and older people) as growing consumer groups. Information about accessibility of tourism objects (accommodation, sights, streets, parks, etc.) is equally important as barrier-free tourism information systems to support the booking and decision making process.

Consequently, this paper introduces the extension of tourism information systems in a twofold way. First, each tourism object is provided with information about its accessibility realized by additional meta data information. Second, based on user profiles content presentation and user interface navigation are dynamically adapted to the user's individual needs in order to support appropriate search as well as presentation features.

**Keywords:** Tourism information systems (TIS), accessibility, people with disabilities, barrier-free tourism, eTourism.

## 1 Introduction

During the last years a broad spectrum of different Web-based tourism information systems (TIS) has been established. The acceptance and consequently the competitiveness of a TIS is mainly determined by the quantity and quality of data it provides. Therefore most existing TIS already try to fulfill the tourists' request for an extensive data collection.

Tourism industry now realized the potential of people with disabilities (and older people) as growing consumer groups, thus representing a growing market segment. A main topic in this context is *accessibility*, one important aspect to improve the quality of a TIS. Accessibility covers several sub-topics like

- accessibility of transportation, accommodation, sights, restaurants, infrastructure, signs, medical support, access guides, etc. (barrier-free tourism)
- spreading of the products accessibility information
- accessibility information in tourism information systems
- accessible tourism Web-sites and accessible tourism information systems

In order to provide technologies and applications supporting accessible tourism in this paper *usability* of Web-based tourism information systems as well as *accessibility information* about tourism objects (transportation, accommodation, etc.) are mainly focused.

K. Miesenberger et al. (Eds.): ICCHP 2004, LNCS 3118, pp. 280–286, 2004.

People with disabilities have very special requirements concerning the usability of Web-based tourism information systems. This is explained by the heterogeneity of their disabilities (visual, speech, hearing, physical, etc.). But sometimes different disabilities require similar accommodations. For instance, someone who is blind and someone who cannot use his or her hands both require full keyboard equivalents for mouse commands in browsers and authoring tools, since they both have difficulty using a mouse but can use assistive technologies to activate commands supported by a standard keyboard interface [1]. To meet these requirements for each user an individually adapted (personalized) user interface is suggested.

Accessible tourism information systems are only the first step towards barrier-free tourism and must therefore be followed by comprehensive offers of information about the accessibility of tourism objects.

Taking implementation costs into account and at the same time increasing the usability of the concept the presented approach proposes the extension of existing tourism information systems instead of expensive adaptation processes. Tourism objects within existing systems are extended with both presentation and accessibility meta information, thus enabling a dynamic adaptation of a tourism information system's layout, navigation and its content corresponding to individual user profiles.

The paper is organized as follows: Section 2 gives an overview of related work in the field of accessibility. In Section 3 the concept of the intelligent accessibility extension for TIS is introduced. The presented approach only considers software extensions and does not discuss the possibilities of other assistive technologies (e.g. hardware used by people with disabilities to help accomplish tasks that they cannot accomplish otherwise or could not do easily otherwise). Chapter 4 concludes the paper and describes further research activities.

## 2 Related Work

In May 2001 the world health organization (WHO) initiated the international classification of functioning, disability and health (ICF). This initiative was the consequence of previous classifications to harmonize empirical studies in the field of medical diseases. ICF complements ICD-10 (international statistical classification of diseases and related health problems) and therefore is looking beyond mortality and disease. The improved classification strengthens the fact that people with disabilities are mainly influenced by their environment because environmental factors provoke sequences starting from a person's impairment over handicap, and finally, it gets the disability. Briefly mentioned with respect to this classification there are visual, hearing, motor, intellectual or psychological disabilities [2].

Although, the classification of disabilities is available in medicine there exists no similar standardization in the context of Web usage. However, the Web accessibility initiative (WAI) provides a set of scenarios that illustrates how people with disabilities use the Web and how they can be supported. The working group outlines different disabilities that can affect Web accessibility such as blindness, deafness, hard of hearing, dyslexia or aging-related conditions. For all those disabilities the group describes barriers that people may encounter on the Web and proposes assistive technology and adaptive strategies to overcome those limitations [1]. Assistive technologies are products used by people with disabilities to help accomplish tasks that they cannot accomplish otherwise or could not do easily otherwise. When used with computers, assistive technologies are also referred to as adaptive software. Some assistive technologies rely on output of other user agents, such as graphical desktop browsers, text browsers, voice browsers, multimedia players, plug-ins. Adaptive strategies may be techniques that people with disabilities use, with or without assistive technologies, to assist in navigating Web pages.

Additionally, the Web accessibility initiative (WAI) initiated by the W3C recommends a set of guidelines that helps designers of Web pages to improve design and navigational handling. Generally, those guidelines aim to ameliorate Web accessibility for all people. Especially, for those who operate in specific contexts because of some kind disability. The design guidelines cover two general topics: (i) ensuring graceful transformation, and (ii) making content understandable and navigable [3]. In total, there are fourteen recommendations of how to provide accessible design solutions such as "do not rely on color alone" or "ensure that documents are clear and simple". Those guidelines are easy to understand and even easy to implement. Unfortunately, the existing bottleneck is their missing promotion for a simple implementation.

At the European online market the tourism information system TIScover [4] is one of most important and successful ones. Within one month more than 34 Mio Web users access the system for searching, planning and finally booking holidays or business trips. The sophisticated technology provides a meta data framework that supports tourism providers such as tourist offices, agencies and hoteliers to present and administrate their individual tourism products by using one common extranet. This meta data concept provides ideal pre-conditions for introducing and realizing accessibility in multiple facets. Additional information required for barrier-free tourism, accessible tourism objects, and accessible system features may be represented through additional meta layers, which are semantically interpreted through an intelligent extension or add-on of the existing system.

## 3 Intelligent Accessibility Extension

To meet the special requirements of people with disabilities and older people extensions concerning the usability of Web-based TIS as well as the accessibility information about tourism objects are necessary.

The presented approach aims to provide an appropriate adaptation process based on *user profiles*. Such a profile is specified by each individual user and contains information about the user's special requirements. For example, to use the Web many people who are deaf rely on captions for audio content. When browsing a Web page they are allowed to toggle the captions on an audio file on/off. In contrast to a deaf person a blind person normally will prefer audio files. Attributes such as name, address, gender or preferences for interests, which are actually state of the art in common user profiles, are also helpful in context of accessible tourism information systems. However, for individualization purposes in terms of respecting requirements of people with disabilities the proposed system contains information about the kind of disability according to the ICF standard [2]. The configuration of individual user profiles can be regarded as multi-step process, whereby the system assumes a default profile in an initial stage and updates it incrementally depending on the user's input and actions over time. The result is in any case represented by an XML structure and serves as decision-maker for personalization and adaptation.

To enable the introduced personalization and adaptation features existing tourism objects are extended with meta data concerning four different levels (i-iv), whereby the goal is to decide which objects are individually relevant for a user and how this information should be presented in order to optimize Web usage, navigation, and information gathering.

(i) content such as hotel accessibility or room equipment,
(ii) tourism offers according to the user's individual interests,
(iii) layout to provide barrier-free Web accessibility, e.g. audio for blind, and
(iv) specific information to provide accessible electronic tourism guides, e.g. interactive tourist maps while traveling in both audio or graphical mode.

For the implementation it is sufficient to reduce these four levels of meta data to two groups. First, *ta* representing information about tourism object accessibility (i-ii) and second, *wa* representing Web accessibility and usability (iii-iv) (see Figure 1). Looking at (educational) hypermedia systems, the concept proposed in this paper supports a comparable threefold adaptation of content, navigation, and layout (presentation) [5] [6].

The introduced intelligent accessibility add-on (Figure 2) is divided into a personalization (first-level control) and an adaptation (second-level control) module. After a user request (Figure 2, User A or User B) the personalization module filters appropriate tourism objects (Figure 2, ①-A, ①-B, ②-A, ②-B). For example, depending on both the specification within the user profile as well as tourism object accessibility meta data (ta) a tourism object "canyoning " is not selected for persons in wheelchairs. In the next step, the adaptation mechanism module prepares each tourism object for the individual presentation on the user's client application of the TIS. For this adaptation the corresponding user profile and Web accessibility meta data (wa) of the tourism object are used (Figure 2, ③-A, ③-B).

The *personalization mechanism* is implemented based on topic maps which are quite suitable and convenient to handle huge amount of (meta) data in a structured form and especially, to reproduce relationships among those data [7]. With respect to accessible tourism information systems this technology enables representation of tourism objects accessibility information, user profile information and any aspects relevant for managing the system environment in concise and navigational style. For example, it allows consideration of the ICF standard to define which disability has which impact on the kind of selected objects or the WAI scenarios to describe which Web presentation techniques are relevant for which kind of disabilities.

In the presented approach topics represent user profile characteristics and its implications on the selection of tourism objects. A certain user profile (Figure 2, User (Profile) A, User (Profile) B) represented by an XML structure is compared with and mapped against the general topic map of the personalization module which covers information about all possible and supported disabilities (e.g. corresponding to ICF and WAI). In topic map terms this means that specific "topics" are visited and its associations to implications are followed. The result of the personalization mechanism is a set of user selected tourism objects which are pre-selected corresponding to the user's disabilities. The resulting XML structure builds the basis for the following adaptation process.

```
<accommodation>
      <name>Hotel Europa</name>
      <category>
            <accotype>hotel</accotype>
            <accocategory>5-stars</accocategory>
      </category>
      <tourism_object_accessibility short="ta">
      <content>
            <nearto>
                  <citycentre>yes</citycentre>
            </nearto>
            <equipment>
                  <bathtub>yes</bathtub>
                  <elevator>yes</elevator>
                  <shower>no</shower>
            </equipment>
            <convenient>
                  <wheelchairs>yes</wheelchairs>
                  <seniors>yes</seniors>
                  <children>yes</children>
            </convenient>
      </content>
      </tourism_object_accessibility>
      <web_accessibility short="wa">
      <layout>
            <style>…/guidelines/personal.css</style>
            <multimedia>
             <text>
              <language code="en">Hotel Europe is …</language>
              <language code="de">Das Hotel liegt …</language>
              <language code="fr">L'hotel se trouve …</language>
             </text>
             <audio>
              <file code="en">…/audio/en/description.wav</file>
              <file code="de">…/audio/de/beschreibung.mp3</file>
              <file code="fr"> …/audio/fr/descr.mp3</file>
             </audio>
             <video></video>
             <image>
              <file>…/img/europa.gif</file>
              <size code="normal" width="250px" height="200px"/>
              <size code="large" width="400px" height="300px"/>
              <size code="extralarge" width="700px" height="500px"/>
              <alt code="en">The hotel is situated in …</alt>
              <alt code="de">Das Hotel befindet sich …</alt>
              <alt code="fr"> L'hotel se trouve …</alt>
             </image>
            </multimedia>
      </layout>
      <navigation>
            <context>
             <language code="en">
              Austria / Tyrol / Innsbruck / Accommodations
             </language>
             <language code="de">…</language>
             <language code="fr"> …</language>
            </context>
      </navigation>
      </web_accessibility>
</accommodation>
```

**Fig. 1.** Example of a tourism object's meta data extension.

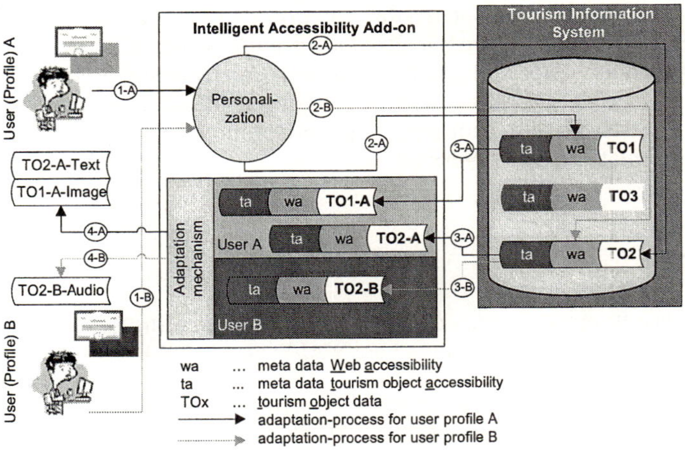


**Fig. 2.** User profile based presentation and content adaptation processes.

The *adaptation process* is responsible for defining how selected objects are presented (visualized/made audible) by a Web browser or any other target device such as a PDA (personal digital assistant). Knowledge provided by WAI guidelines that represent characteristics of user profiles and its impact on navigation and layout are relevant for this second-level control mechanism, as well represented by topic maps. Adaptive navigation support helps users to find the most relevant path in the hyperspace. Adaptation of layout (visible/audible) supports alternative forms of how to present the content, navigational links, or the Web page as a whole.

The appropriate transformation technology, especially when considering standard initiatives, is obviously XSL transformation (XSLT). XSLT is an effective way to produce adopted output in form of HTML (hypertext markup language), WML (wireless markup language), XML or any other target language. Rule-based stylesheets form the essence of the XSLT language and build an optimal basis for the introduced adaptation mechanism. They are most useful when processing source documents whose structure is flexible or unpredictable and are very useful when the same repertoire of elements can appear in many different document structures. Finally, personalization and adaptation mechanisms provide users personalized and individually adapted tourism information (Figure 2, ④-A, ④-B).

## 4 Conclusions and Future Work

This paper introduces an approach to provide intelligent accessibility based on personalization mechanisms as convenient add-on to existing tourism information systems with the aim to enable barrier-free tourism in several facets.

Existing tourism information systems are extended in a twofold way. First, each tourism object is extended with information about its accessibility realized by additional meta data information. Second, based on user profiles content presentation and user interface navigation are dynamically adapted to the user's individual needs (disabilities) in order to support appropriate search as well as presentation features.

Future work will focus on accessible electronic tourism guides to support people with disabilities not only before but also during and after traveling with individual and adapted information. Especially, in the context of barrier-free tourism user acceptance is the key to success. Therefore, usability and user-interface evaluations and studies have to be done to prove the concept. The tourism information system TIScover provides the ideal platform for those activities.

## References

1. W3C – The World Wide Web Consortium: How People with Disabilities Use the Web, W3C Working Draft, http://www.w3.org/WAI/EO/Drafts/PWD-Use-Web/20010104.html (2004)
2. World Health Organization: International Classification of Functioning (ICF), Disability and Health, October 2001, http://www3.who.int/icf/icftemplate.cfm, (2004)
3. W3C – The World Wide Web Consortium: Web Content Accessibility Guidelines 1.0, W3C Recommendation 5-May-1999, http://www.w3.org/TR/WAI-WEBCONTENT (2004)
4. TIS AG Innsbruck, FAW Hagenberg: TIScover, http://www.tiscover.com (2004)
5. Brusilovsky, P.: Adaptive Hypermedia, User Modeling and User-Adapted Interaction 11, pp. 87-110 (2001)
6. Papanikolaou, K., Grigoriadou, M., Magoulas, G., Kornilakis, H.: Towards new forms of knowledge communication: the adaptive dimension of a web-based learning environment, Computer & Education 39, pp. 333-360 (2002)
7. Liongosari, E.S., Dempski, K.L., Swaminathan, K.S.: In Search of A New Generation of Knowledge Management Applications, ACM SIGGROUP Bulletin, Vol. 20, No. 2, August (1999), pp. 60-63

# AccesSights – A Multimodal Location-Aware Mobile Tourist Information System

Palle Klante[1], Jens Krösche[1], and Susanne Boll[2]

[1] OFFIS Research Institute, Escherweg 2, D-26121 Oldenburg, Germany
{klante,kroesche}@offis.de,
http://www.offis.de

[2] University of Oldenburg, Escherweg 2, D-26121 Oldenburg, Germany
susanne.boll@uni-oldenburg.de,
http://mmit.informatik.uni-oldenburg.de

**Abstract.** Through recent developments in the segment of mobile devices like personal digital assistants (PDA) the usage of mobile applications in different areas of our normal life increases. New applications support mobile users with location-aware information. But today's systems are not usable for all: there still exist various barriers for blind and visually impaired people. This user group does not receives the same information as normally sighted users. AccesSights overcomes these barriers by supporting both user groups with the same information. Meeting the different user requirements we designed a multimodal user interface to support different user groups – each in their suitable fashion. The introduced AccesSights system is based on our highly flexible and modular Niccimon platform.

## 1 Introduction

When visiting cities or gardens as tourists most users share the same goal: they intend to explore the area and find interesting information. Even though the tasks are the same for all user groups, the means to find and receive tourist information are typically laid out for sighted users. Consequently, most of the information is not accessible for people with special needs, like blind tourists. Modern technologies and mobile computers can help to overcome these barriers and allow for *Acces*sible *Sights*eeing.

Together with the growing availability and variety of wireless networks, like Global System for Mobile Communication (GSM), General Packet Radio Service (GPRS), Wireless LAN (WLAN), and the expected Universal Mobile Telecommunication Systems (UMTS), users are able to communicate everywhere, to connect to servers, and share information even in mobile scenarios. Consequently, today's mobile systems enable the users to carry around these devices with the respective software and information to be used both online and offline, e. g., when traveling. Localisation techniques such as the Global Positioning System (GPS) complement these technologies providing the basis for location-aware services and information. Hence, by locating the tourist one can provide interesting

K. Miesenberger et al. (Eds.): ICCHP 2004, LNCS 3118, pp. 287–294, 2004.

information and services about the local spot or the surrounding. This development helps to counteract one of the basic problems for tourists: when visiting cities and sights so far they do not necessarily find satisfactory information on the spot. In addition, some sights of interest might be missed due to missing signs, incorrect description, wrong language, or too small letters. Let alone that there is any support for people with special needs, such as blind. With the development of our proposed multimodal location-aware mobile tourist information system – AccesSights – we meet the needs of different user groups by exploiting modern technology. The focus of this work is to support both blind users and sighted users at the same time with the same tourist content but for each user group in their preferred modality. Therefore, we analysed the typical demands in mobile tourism and extracted three main phases for tourists during their visit: an *orientation phase*, a *movement phase*, and an *information* perception *phase*. In each of these phases we support different modalities which we identified necessary for the different user groups and their needs in our AccesSights system. With AccesSights we contribute to modern tourist information systems that allows to share the same tourism experience for all users.

### 1.1 State of the Art

One of the first projects to enhance the mobility situation of "visitors" to present further information while on the move was Cyberguide [1, 2]. Cyberguide supports visitors when exploring a Lab. Main element of the system's user interface is a map on which a visitor can see his or her actual position. The map shows a floor plan, containing the location of the different projects. A visitor can walk to the different locations and receive a description in form of hypertext documents on an Apple Newton. Later approaches like for instance LoL@ [3, 4] integrated the usage of modern positioning services like GPS and communication technologies like UMTS in such a scenario.

Further projects started to enable the blind and visually impaired to receive the same tourist information as normally sighted users, e. g. the MoBIC project [5]. MoBIC concentrates on the overall enhancement of mobility for blind people. It addresses the known problem that blind people do not get sufficient information when planning their route and about the location they wish to travel. They developed a commercial product, the Trekker [6]. It uses speech output to inform the user about his or her location, which streets are crossed, and generates a list of orientation points for the route. The MoBIC system mainly uses speech output and the user always has to ask for the needed information. Speech output, however, is very distracting and presents the information only in a serial manner; so the output tends to be very long. Humans, however, are able to perceive information also in a parallel manner. Therefore, an information flow should be ambient in order to allow other information sources to be perceived. To support the idea of permanently presented information the AudioGPS [7] project uses non-speech sound. The main purpose of the project is to help the user navigate through the real world whereas the actual position of the user is acquired through GPS. AudioGPS supports the user in answering the following questions: Where am I? How far is my target away? In which direction do I have to move? The target object is enhanced by a special sound which presents the current position of the target. The known problem to distinguish a sound playing in front of the user or behind – when using headphones – is solved by using different sounds.

In our approach we aim at a combination of both concepts, speech output to receive further information and an ambient auditory environment for navigation, supports the blind visitors and at the same time enables them to receive the same tourism information as normally sighted visitors. In this paper, we present a concept and implementation for such an approach. We identified three typical phases for a tourist when visiting a park and developed the AccesSights system which supports the blind tourist in all three phases.

## 2 Requirements for Blind and Sighted Users

In order to design a mobile tourist guide that is suitable for blind and sighted users, it is necessary to analyse the user characteristics, the tasks they have to solve, and to describe the context in which the users interact with the system. We analysed the occurring tasks when visiting a park like the Royal Herrenhausen Gardens in our project mobiDENK [8]. In this first field test, we identified three main phases: orientation, movement, and information. These main phases, presented in the following, are the same for both user groups. However, the means with which these phases are processed differ much in the distinguished user groups.

### 2.1 Interaction Phases of a Tourist Information System

When tourists visit a park for the first time, they typically start by orientating themselves. Afterwards, they walk around, finally reach a point of interest (POI), and try to get more detailed information about this POI. A short task and context description explains the general requirements of each of these phases:

- In the orientation phase the tourists are often making themselves familiar with the area. Normally, in a calm environment the visitors will spend some time to identify interesting areas or POIs in the garden and then set of to explore the area.
- While moving around the visitors either strolls through the gardens or try to find POIs. In this phase the tourists rely on navigation information and at the same time have to watch their steps, not to run into other visitors or obstacles (e. g., a rake), to be careful at dangerous places (e. g., a crossing), and not to leave the narrow path. Therefore, the tourists need to pay full attention on their movement tasks.
- In the information phase the visitors have reached the desired destination and spend some time to receive information about the local spot.

All three tasks have their different challenges and demand different attention from the visitors. In order to offer a barrier free access in these three phases a multimodal support is essential for blind and sighted users.

### 2.2 Multimodal Support for Different User Groups

To support blind and normally sighted persons one has to regard the suitable modalities of these user groups to let them both share the same experience. The primary form of perception for normally sighted people is the visual sense whereas blind persons mainly use the auditory sense. We consider these special needs to differentiate the modality in each phase.

- In the orientation phase the normally sighted person can use the visual display to find out about the area, the paths, and the location of POIs. As this is typically done while standing still there is nothing that draws the attention of the visitor away from his or her task. Correspondingly, for blind visitors this information needs to be presented in auditory fashion.
- In the movement phase, the normally sighted visitor uses both visual and auditory senses to navigate, watch out for other visitors, find signs, etc. The blind visitor has to solve this task relying only on the auditory sense. But here we find the most barriers, as most of information is only visually perceivable such as, signs, obstacles, or other visitors, and are therefore not accessible for the blind.
- In the information phase at a certain POI, for sighted people both auditory and visual information can be helpful. Blind people have to rely on auditive information only.

With regards to the aforementioned requirements and the possible multimodal information support in the different phases we now present the concrete design of the AccesSights system.

## 3 AccesSights' Multimodality Design

Our multimodal mobile tourist information system supports both user groups in each of the different phases. The data concerning the visited area is transformed and presented so that it suits the modality the tourist needs. For each information object in the tourist information system we aim at providing both a graphical and acoustical presentation. The basis for this information presentation is the multimedia content of the mobile tourist information system. In the following, we are looking into the multimodal information presentation and the user interaction with the system in more detail.

### 3.1 Supporting Multimodal Orientation

In the orientation phase normally sighted tourists use a graphical map of the park to find POIs as shown in Fig. 1(a) and plan the route to get there. The visitors can see their own position and the positions of the POIs and infer the distance to the designated POIs. Additionally, different types of POIs can be distinguished by different iconic representations. For the blind users auditory information allows them to build a mental model of the area: Each of the sightseeing POIs is represented by a distinct and unique sound, a so called Hearcon.

Through the Hearcons a representation of the real world with various POIs is mapped onto a virtual auditory environment around the user. The distance between the own position and each POI is mapped directly onto the loudness of the Hearcons in the scene as shown in Fig. 1(b). The result is a weakly intrusive virtual auditory map of the garden. Using different sound families for different types of auditive information, the sources can be distinguished.

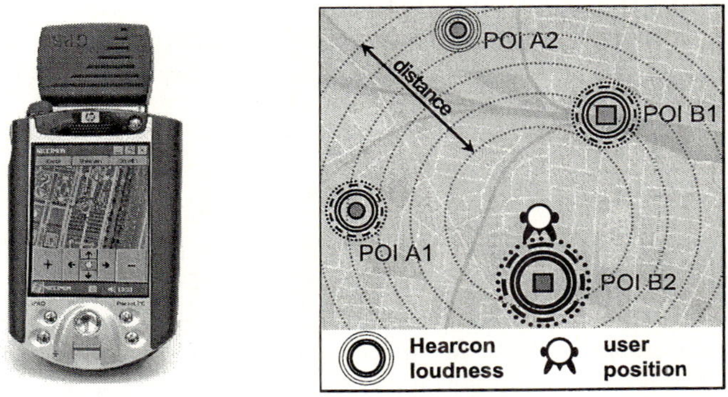


(a) Map Interface (b) Ambient auditory navigation

**Fig. 1.** The AccesSights system

### 3.2 Supporting Multimodal Movement

While moving around the tourists need information about distance to and location of the POIs. They try to find the beforehand identified POIs or stroll around in the park without no special destination. For the normally sighted users auditory support like sounds to identify POIs or speech output is an additional help enhancing and extending the visual information, enabling them to look at the digital map only from time to time. For the blind the central sense to carry out navigation in the park is the auditory sense. They need their auditory sense to orientate themselves in their surrounding and are not able to perceive multiple system information in auditory fashion at the same time. Therefore, the blind user must be able to explicitly decide, when to hear the virtual auditory map. By this the information presentation will not overlap with the real world auditory information which is most important to them.

Additionally, we aim to overcome a common problem for blind people to notice obstacles on their way. With our system a visitor is able to mark a location as dangerous when he or she finds an obstacle there. Afterwards, other visitors receive a warning message when they get close to that location. Obstacles are presented through other auditory cues then monuments, to easily distinguish dangerous artifacts from the monuments in the park. The system must support a mechanism to dynamically remove these "virtual" obstacles after a predefined time limit or other visitors must be able to remove them, when they later notice that there is no problem anymore.

### 3.3 Supporting Multimodal Information Presentation

When a visitor reaches a POI, the location-aware system signals that the user can now receive more detailed information and the system switches from movement phase to information phase. Both, the blind and normally sighted user can select the desired information from the multimodal system. The presented information is adapted to the user's actual location. While the system presents pictures and text to the sighted users it generates an auditive version of the content via speech output to the blind user. Through the hardware-buttons on the hand held computer the user navigates through the information space. The normally sighted user can also interact with the visual display and select the desired information with a graphical user interface.

## 4 AccesSights System Platform

The basis for our multimodal mobile tourist guide is the *Niccimon platform* which has been developed in our Research Center of Excellence of Lower Saxony for Mobile Applications (Niccimon) [9], Germany. This platform provides different autonomous modules for map visualisation, POI definition, location sensing, etc. A mediator realises the cooperation between those modules. Additionally, the Niccimon platform offers live cycle control, visualisation, auditory support, network communication, and inter-component communication through specific interfaces. Using these modules and interfaces, the rapid development of innovative mobile applications can be achieved by reusing existing modules and implementing the applications particular tasks on top of these, as shown in Figure 2. This platform has been successfully employed in different application domains, such as location-aware games [10] or location-aware tourist guides [8].

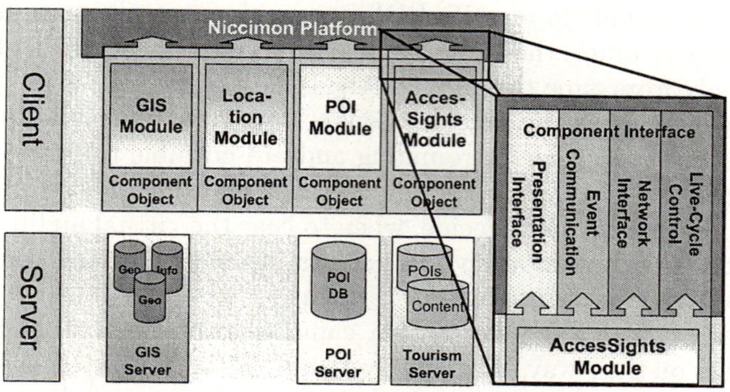


**Fig. 2.** Modules of the Niccimon platform

### 4.1 Multimodal Information Presentation

To realise multimodal requirements mentioned in Section 3, we integrated auditory support into the Niccimon platform with our AIR3DSound framework (auditory interaction realm three dimensional sound package). This framework combines the definition of virtual sound scenes, different digital sound standards, and various output devices (headphones, Quad loudspeakers, and loudspeaker arrays). By integrating this sound framework we gain the advantage of a seamless combination of visual and auditory elements in our application. Objects such as POIs and Danger-Areas are presented as graphical icons as well as sound sources, through Hearcons. In respect to the auditory "dimension", all these objects are used to create an ambient background sound which provides support for orientation, movement, and information for the user, on command.

AIR3DSound has initially been developed in the context of providing web pages to blind users [11]. The extended version of this framework allows us to generate a mobile auditory environment, which is represented by a 2D/3D scene with an associated geometry. Within this auditory scene the application can place Hearcons, which augment/represent objects and information in the real world. To distinguish diverse objects, different types of information are realised by different sounds. So each of this non-intrusive sounds represents a distinct information source in the application. Besides the additional objects and information, the user (listener) has to be part of this auditory scene; his or her location is mapped into the auditory scene and forms the reference point for the overall sound generation. The sounds produced by the different Hearcons in the scene are mixed in a manner that gives the listener the impression of actually standing in the auditory scene. Through this we are able to create a virtual auditory environment that augments the real world with additional auditory information.

### 4.2 Modality Independent Content Modeling in XML

Looking at the World Wide Web for example, content presentation is typically built and structured for sighted users using desktop PCs. Therefore the existing user interfaces are not usable for visually impaired persons, in general. This leads to an information gap excluding users with special needs. To overcome this information gap we modeled the content in a modality independent fashion so that it can be easily transformed matching different modalities and/or different platforms. In our AccesSights system we support blind as well as sighted users, interacting with standard mobile hardware (PDA) in their role as tourists visiting a park. We define modality-independent content by the usage of XML and encapsulate tourist information in XML-Files. Through the combination of XML and user/hardware profiles we are able to dynamically create content matching the users needs considering also the device characteristics. The XML document structure itself is exploited to provide both sighted and blind users suitable visual or auditive navigation structure. The XML based content is transformed into an appropriate visual and/or auditive presentation exploiting transformation languages such as XSLT and text to speech mechanisms.

## 5 Conclusion

In this paper, we introduced the general phases for the usage of mobile tourist information systems. From the different user groups we want to address, we derived the modality requirements for experiencing mobile, location-aware tourist information. With our system design, we share the same content in different modalities with these two user groups. Blind users and sighted users can experience the tourism space on their own, but can also cooperate with each other as they are able to receive the same information. The Niccimon platform together with the AIR3DSound framework and XML content modeling provides the basis for the development of the AccesSights system. In future user studies we will test and evaluate the system with the two user groups and receive feedback for further development of the system.

## References

1. Long, S., Kooper, R., Abowd, G.D., Atkeson, C.G.: Rapid Prototyping of Mobile Context-Aware Applications: The Cyberguide Case Study. In: 2th ACM Interantional Conference on Mobile Computing And Networking, Rye, New York, USA (1996) 97–107
2. Abowd, G.D., Atkeson, C.G., Hong, J., Long, S., Kooper, R., Pinkerton, M.: Cyberguide: A Mobile Context-Aware Tour Guide. ACM Wireless Networks **3** (1997) 421–433
3. Pospischil, G., Kunczier, H., Kuchar, A.: LoL@: a UMTS location based service. In: International Symposion on 3rd Generation Infrastructure and Services, Athen, Greece (2001)
4. Uhlirz, S., Lechthaler, M.: LoL@ - City Guide. Prototyp einer kartenbasierten UMTS-Applikation. Geowissenschaftliche Mitteilungen, Schriftenreihe der Studienrichtung Vermessungswesen und Geoinformation TU Wien **58** (2002) 171–182
5. Fritz, S., Michel, R., Petrie, H., Raab, A., Strothotte, T.: MoBIC: User Needs and Preliminary Design for a Mobility Aid for Blind and Elderly Travellers. In Placencia-Porrero, I., Puig de la Bellacasa, R., eds.: The European Context for Assistive Technology, Amsterdam, Netherlands, IOS Press (1995) 348–351
6. http://www.papenmeier.de/reha/products/trekker/trekker.htm.
7. Holland S., M.D.: AudioGPS: Spatial Audio in a minimal attention interface. Proceedings of Human Computer Interaction with Mobile Devices (2001) 28–33
8. Krösche, J., Boll, S., Baldzer, J.: MobiDENK – Mobile Multimedia in Monument Conservation. IEEE MultiMedia **11** (2004) 72–77
9. Competence Center of Lower Saxony for Information Systems for Mobile Usage (Niccimon), www.niccimon.de.
10. Boll, S., Krösche, J., Wegener, C.: Paper chase revisited – a real world game meets hypermedia. In: The fourteenth conference on Hypertext and Hypermedia, Nottingham, UK (2003)
11. Donker, H., Klante, P., Gorny, P.: The design of auditory user interfaces for blind users. In: NordiCHI '02, ACM Press (2002)

# Accessibility and the Next Generation of Web Development Tools

## *Introduction to the Special Thematic Session*

Carlos A. Velasco

Fraunhofer-Institut für Angewandte Informationstechnik (FIT), Schloss Birlinghoven
D53757 Sankt Augustin (Germany)
Carlos.Velasco@fit.fraunhofer.de

**Abstract.** This session introduces a series of papers that present new perspectives to support the industry in its quest to support a wider variety of users. Through them, we will learn how different research groups are approaching the topic, and will try to understand whether the research arena is tackling in a supportive way the needs of the industry.

The World Wide Web is offering content in a wide variety of media and formats that is difficult to compare to the technological landscape of a few years ago. Authoring and publishing processes must be able to deal with a diversity of devices. Furthermore, portals as content aggregators are becoming commonplace.

It is also noticeable that despite the wide corpus of research on the topic available to the industry, together with the set of guidelines published by the Web Accessibility Initiative (WAI[1]) of the World Wide Web Consortium (W3C[2]), which cover Web content, user agents and authoring tools, Web accessibility for people with special needs has not drastically improved over the last years[3].

The sessions is targeted to challenge academia and industry to come together and find out how research work can truly support industry needs in the nearer future, where mobile and ubiquitous computing will be omnipresent in our lives.

The session will try to display current advances in the area of authoring, and evaluation and repair tools, that support private and public online service providers in the development of accessible portals and intranets of commercial dimensions (in the order of thousands of pages). The papers tackle not only technical aspects, but issues related to the support given to the involved actors by the implementation of reliable quality assurance, standards compliance and monitoring methodologies.

We want to open new doors to Web accessibility by integrating it within standard software development processes. Only when these developments become available, the uptake of guidelines and recommendations by the industry will grow, and it will allow their cross-validation and improvement, thus making feasible an Information Society accessible to All.

---

1 http://www.w3.org/WAI/

2 http://www.w3.org/

3 See, for example, "The Web. Access and Inclusion for Disabled People A formal investigation conducted the Disability Rights Commission (London, 2004)". Available online at: http://www.drc.org.uk/publicationsandreports/report.asp

K. Miesenberger et al. (Eds.): ICCHP 2004, LNCS 3118, p. 295, 2004.

# Preferences of People with Disabilities to Improve Information Presentation and Information Retrieval Inside Internet Services – Results of a User Study

Henrike Gappa, Gabriele Nordbrock, Yehya Mohamad, and Carlos A. Velasco

Fraunhofer-Institut für Angewandte Informationstechnik (FIT), Schloss Birlinghoven
D53757 Sankt Augustin, Germany
{Henrike.Gappa,Gaby.Nordbrock,Yehya.Mohamad,Carlos.Velasco}
@fit.fraunhofer.de

**Abstract.** A part of a larger user study conducted within the scope of the EU project IRIS was to investigate the preferences of people with disabilities in regard to interface design of Web applications. User requirements of online help and search engines were also in the focus of this study, since the target user group depends heavily upon powerful tools to support them in the process of seeking information. The results showed that user preferences for information presentation vary a great deal, which could be solved by comprehensive user profiling. However, the functionalities of online help and search functions, as presented in the Internet today, need to be enhanced so they can be used more flexibly and be adjusted to the users' mental representation of problems and information needs to help them fulfill their tasks.

## 1 Introduction

Improving orientation and navigation, adding mechanisms to support information retrieval, and coping with the structure of a Web site is a pressing issue in designing accessible and usable Web sites [4,6,7,8]. We conducted a user study within the scope of the EU-funded project IRIS[1] to research these issues more closely. The collection of data aimed at enhancing results of another user study previously carried out in the beginning of the project, to evaluate the needs of disabled people in regard to appropriate information presentation to prevent information overload, and functionalities facilitating accessibility and usability of a Web site among other issues [6]. The main objective of the user study reported in this paper was to evaluate accessibility and usability issues of two upgraded Internet services, a Web-based collaborative environment and an e-shop generator for B2B applications. The data baseline for our work was a detailed questionnaire administered in addition to the core test scenario.

## 2 Methodology

The test sample consisted of 18 people with different disabilities. In accordance to the primary disability of the test participants, they were categorized in the group of per-

[1] Incorporating Requirements of People with Special Needs or Impairments in Internet-based Services (IST-2000-26211): `http://www.iris-design4all.org/`

K. Miesenberger et al. (Eds.): ICCHP 2004, LNCS 3118, pp. 296–301, 2004.

sons with motor impairments (6 people), deafness (5 people) and vision impairments (7 people). They used different types of assistive technologies like Braille-lines, screen readers, text-to-sign software, speech recognition software and mouse emulation. Since test participants needed at least some background in Internet usage, to answer some of the questions, no novice user participated in the study. There was one short-term user; however, the rest of the test participants were middle-term users (5) and long-term users (12). All test participants were using the Internet since more than one year and accessed the Internet at least four days a week with a minimum 2.5 hours per week.

Since it was the main goal of the user study to evaluate two upgraded Internet services, a test scenario was designed comprising a standard task reflecting typical user activities when utilizing such services. To facilitate our analysis log files were recorded. The users had to fill 3 questionnaires. In the first questionnaire, we collected data about the personal, educational and professional background, as well as prior computer and Internet usage of the test participants. The use of assistive technology was also determined. More relevant for our user study was the third questionnaire, which explored the preferences and needs of the test participants in regard to information presentation, color-schemes, and required functionalities of an efficient online help system and search function. The questionnaire consisted of 25 structured questions, many times accompanied by an enhanced checklist, which means that several options were provided for response. Whenever feasible, all checklists offered an "other" option accounting for the fact that not all possible replies might have been considered.

## 3 Results

Appropriate information arrangement plays an important role, because it is a constituting factor of orientation and can ease navigation on a Web page. Particularly for people with motor impairments it is crucial to be able to reach a navigation link with a minimum effort. Test participants were asked about their preferences on placement of navigation information like main menu bar, section links and in-site functionalities such as help and search. Most of the test participants (35%) agreed that the main menu bar should be placed on top of the viewport. 18% voted for showing it on the left side of the viewport, whereas 12% preferred to have the main menu bar on the bottom of the viewport. Sub-section commands should be found on the left of the viewport according to 18% of the test participants. 30% of the test participants agreed to place less relevant information on the right side.

It seems that the placement of navigation information most test participants agreed on complies with the quasi-standard in the Internet, where the main menu bar is most often placed on top of the screen, sub-section commands are on the left side and the right side is left for additional information like advertisement or log-in facilities for registered users. However, the results show also, that user preferences vary and a large group of test participants preferred a different design.

Since information overload is a usability issue often mentioned by Internet users in general, but in particular by people with special needs, an option was suggested to allow the user to transfer menus or navigation links from a Web page into a list the user may access any time if wanted. 47% of the test participants would make use of such an option, and considered it helpful to enhance accessibility and usability of a Web site[2].

To support orientation and information comprehension on Web pages, color cues are often mentioned as important tools. Therefore, test participants were asked about their preferences on coloring for menu links, embedded text links, visited links, etc. It could be seen that in all instances, except for the color of embedded text links, where 60% voted for blue, 30%–40% of the test participants agreed on the same color. The rest of the test group was divided in groups of 10%–20% favoring different color-combinations or was indifferent. For instance, for section titles, 30% of the test participants preferred black, but 10% voted for yellow, 10% for dark red, 10% for green, 10% for blue, 10% for orange, 10% for light blue and 10% were indifferent. In regard to menu links, 40% of the test participants were in favor of black, yet also 40% preferred blue. In summary, the colors selected by most of the test participants were: blue for embedded text links (60%), red for visited text links (40%), blue when hovering links (30%), black for section titles (30%), red for visited sections (30%) and black for keywords (30%). However, it cannot be underestimated that the group of test participants preferring different color-combinations was all together in most cases larger and split up in groups with differing preferences. Therefore, this study acknowledges that user preferences seem to vary a great deal in regard to color-schemes.

User preferences in regard to formatting were also researched, because it is also a tool for highlighting and organizing information. It was suggested by most of the test participants that bold typeface should be used for titles (40%) and keywords (20%), usage of different typefaces should be avoided according to 30%, underlining should be used for links (30%) and titles (10%), 25% would prefer if lists are numbered and suggest continuous numbering of all titles.

As it could be observed in several user studies, disabled and older people are not very keen to experiment in order to find information [8], probably because they are afraid to get lost on a Web site or trigger a harmful process. Therefore, it is very important for this user group to provide reliable means to help them getting around on a Web site and support them in using functionalities of an Internet service they are interested in. Provision of a flexible online help function is a powerful tool to assist users in this respect. First of all, it is important that the online help is designed with the questions prospective users will have in mind, so a problem-oriented approach should be taken, also allowing for cross-referencing [5]. The help function should be context-sensitive and guide the user step-by-step in how to fulfill the action required, with illustrative examples, whenever appropriate. Very stressed by the test participants, the wording of the online help must be easy to understand and technical terms should be avoided, or at least explained in a glossary. It was also suggested that the online help function must be flexible in use, meaning that forward and backward navigation should be possible, and that the user should always be informed where she is within the help system [9,9]. According to the test participants, the most important functionalities a help system should provide are: bookmarking of visited help sections (35%), print function (50%), indexing (70%), list of topics covered in the help system (80%), and a facility to search it (100%). Thus, a comprehensive list of keywords with synonyms should be incorporated in the help system. The latter finding underlines

---

[2] Option already incorporated in some modern browser versions like Opera 7.x (`http://www.opera.com/`).

again the importance of offering powerful search facilities to enable people with disabilities to find the information sought [4,6,8]. For this user group, skimming through chapters of irrelevant information in regard to their request is extremely discouraging, because navigating with assistive technologies takes in most cases a lot of effort and the probability of losing context is high.

To improve the accessibility and usability of an Internet service, powerful search facilities are not only relevant for the online help function, but for successful information retrieval on the whole site. Much work has been done in regard to representation of data in search facilities to support the users individual search strategy [11,11]. 60% of the test participants stated that they prefer to use a search function when looking for information, instead of skimming menus or following links. As it could be seen in another user study [8], 100% of the group of learning disabled people used the search function for finding information. One reason might be that reading text takes a lot of effort for people with a learning disability. However, reading on a computer screen is very fatiguing for the eyes of every computer user, and for some people like motor impaired or blind people, it is very important to get to the information sought for in the most direct way saving "clicks" as much as possible. Test participants were asked what kind of information they think should be retrievable and prioritized within a search function. 50% mentioned that it should be possible to find services offered on a Web site; 50% selected that they would like to be able to find links and headers via the search function; 60% found helpful if sub-sections could be searched for; and 70% decided that main sections need to be highly ranked.

In regard to how to formulate a successful search query, it is important to keep in mind that most of the times people have a question or expression in mind when looking for information. Therefore words might be used for input in a conjugated or declined from which should be accounted for according to 50% of the test participants by enabling the search function to derive the root of a word. 50% of the participants considered important that a search function can compensate for misspelled words. 80% of the test participants would like to be able to search for possible keywords. In case a search query was not successful, 60% would like to get a list of synonyms for the entered keyword(s). 90% of the test participants considered helpful to refine a search query with the help of a list of keyword(s) somehow related to the entered search term(s). In regard to how the test participants would prefer to state a search query, results show different approaches: 20% thought a search function should be able to process natural language questions; 40% would like to type in a word phrase; and 90% chose to type in one or several keywords. Most search engines today are designed to handle one or several keywords to start a search query. However, facilities to react upon unsuccessful search queries are most often lacking, e.g. the possibility to search in a list of possible keywords is normally not available.

## 4 Conclusions

Comparing the test results in regard to information presentation with standards prevalent in the Web, e.g., indicating links by underlining, marking visited links as red, it can be stated that a considerable group of the test participants (at least 30% in most cases) seem to have adopted those standards. The majority of the test participants, however, preferred completely different solutions. This can partly be attributed to differences in personal taste, but in most cases it is due to special needs caused by a disability. Therefore, the further development of quasi layout and design standards to support orientation and navigation on a Web site is not of much help for the majority of disabled people. For this user group, accessibility and usability of a Web site is influenced significantly by the possibility to determine their personal style of information presentation, according to their needs as part of their user profile.

The issue of personalizing Internet services and applications via user and device profiles is the subject of ongoing research (see, e.g., [13] and references therein). When sites are properly designed separating content and presentation, as described in, e.g., the Web Content Accessibility Guidelines 1.0 [1,2,3], users can make use of their own stylesheets overriding author preferences. This functionality is available in the recent versions of common browsers. However, the design of such stylesheets is beyond the skills of the average Internet user.

Since the efficient use of a Web site is related to the problem of finding the information sought for, and being able to handle its available functionalities, it is very important to provide a comprehensive online help and a powerful search function. Information on accessibility features like `accesskeys` must be part of the help function and should be easily accessible. The user study showed that it is crucial for both functionalities to support different strategies to search for information and alternative problem representation. For disabled people, particularly with cognitive impairments, non-native language speakers and novice users, it is sometimes difficult to circumscribe their problem with the appropriate keyword(s). Therefore, support is very important in case the appropriate section could not be found in the online help or the search query was not successful. For instance, provision of synonyms for keyword(s) can alleviate these problems, thus the likelihood that a search query is successful can be increased. Furthermore, search functions particularly on complex Web sites rarely rank properly their own content, which means that main or sub-sections, and services offered on the own Web site cannot be retrieved via the search function. Since most users are more likely to keep a title or keyword in mind, rather than the navigation path leading to this information, it is to the benefit of all users to provide a powerful tool to retrieve this information. Beyond information retrieval, we want to stress that the search function also provides an important means to ease navigation, because the starting point is always the same and the user is lead directly to the appropriate place, which is a favorable solution for all users. Since the online help and the search function provide the most important means to support the user in making good use of a Web site, the effort is worth to improve it with the mentioned functionalities.

## Acknowledgements

Parts of this work have been undertaken in the framework of the project IRIS IST-2000-26211, which was partly funded by the European Commission. The authors would like to acknowledge the contributions of their colleagues from European Dynamics S.A., the University of the Aegean, the University of the Basque Country and ISdAC (Information Society disAbilities Challenge) International Association.

## References


1. Caldwell, B., Chisholm, W., Vanderheiden, G., White, J. (eds) (2002). Web Content Accessibility Guidelines 2.0, W3C Working Draft 11 March 2004. World Wide Web Consortium. Available at: http://www.w3.org/TR/WCAG20/
2. Chisholm, W., Vanderheiden, G., and Jacobs, I. (eds) (1999). Web Content Accessibility Guidelines 1.0, W3C Recommendation 5-May-1999. World Wide Web Consortium. Available at: http://www.w3.org/TR/WCAG10/
3. Chisholm, D., Vanderheiden, G., and Jacobs, I. (Eds) (2000). HTML Techniques for Web Content Accessibility Guidelines 1.0, W3C Note 6 November 2000. World Wide Web Consortium. Available at: http://www.w3.org/TR/WCAG10-HTML-TECHS/
4. Coyne, K.P., Nielsen, J. (2001). Beyond ALT Text: Making the Web Easy to Use for Users with Disabilities. Design Guidelines for Websites and Intranets Based on Usability Studies with People Using Assistive Technology. Fremont, CA: Nielsen Norman Group
5. Duffy, T.M., Palmer, J.E., Mehlenbacher, B. (1992). Online Help: Design and Evaluation. Norwood NJ: Ablex Publishing Corporation
6. Gappa, H., Nordbrock, G., Mohamad, Y., Velasco, C.A., et al. (2001). Requirements analysis for enabling people with special needs to access Internet-based services. IRIS Consortium, IST-2000-26211
7. Gappa, H., Nordbrock, G., Mohamad, Y., Velasco, C.A., et al. (2003).User Evaluation of Enhanced Internet Services. IRIS Consortium, IST-2000-26211
8. Gappa, H., Nordbrock, G. (2004). Applying Web Accessibility to Internet Portals. Universal Access in the Information Society, to appear
9. McCathieNevile, C. (2001). Accessibility (Web-Based) Help Systems. Available at: http://www.w3.org/2001/Talks/0329-help/
10. Reed, W., Yankee, E., Fornoff, W. (2003). Guidelines for Writing Accessible Online Help. Available at: http://www.stcsig.org/usability/newsletter/0304-help.html
11. Russell, J. (2002). Find What I Mean: Exploring New Kinds of Search Results. In: Proceedings of the 20th annual international conference on Computer documentation (SIGDOC'02, Toronto, Ontario, Canada), pp. 179–185
12. Shneiderman, B., Byrd, D., Bruce, W. (1997). Clarifying Search. A User-Interface Framework for Text Searches. D-Lib Magazine, January 1997. ISSN 1082-9873
13. Velasco, C.A., Mohamad, Y., Gilman, A.S., Viorres, N., Vlachogiannis, E., Arnellos, A., Darzentas, J.S. (2004). Universal Access to Information Services - the Need for User Information and its Relationship to Device Profiles. In: Gulliksen, J, Harker, S, Vanderheiden, G (eds), Special issue on guidelines, standards, methods and processes for software accessibility. Universal Access in the Information Society, 3, pp. 88–95

# Web Accessibility through Adaptation

Chrisoula Alexandraki[1], Alexandros Paramythis[1], Napoleon Maou[1], and Constantine Stephanidis[1,2]

[1] Foundation for Research and Technology – Hellas (FORTH)
cs@ics.forth.gr
[2] University of Crete, Department of Computer Science

**Abstract.** This paper presents the e*AccessibilityEngine* tool, which employs adaptation techniques to automatically render web pages accessible by users with different types of disabilities. Specifically, the e*AccessibilityEngine* is capable of automatically transforming web pages to attain AAA-level conformance to the W3C WAI Web Content Accessibility Guidelines and to "Section 508" of the US Rehabilitation Act. The proposed tool is intended for use as a web-based service and can be applied to any existing web site.

## 1 Introduction

It is widely acknowledged that people who are faced with difficulties in exploiting the capabilities of the Internet may experience social exclusion. Nevertheless, most web sites are currently partially or entirely inaccessible to people with disabilities [4]. Thus far, the majority of initiatives for promoting web accessibility are oriented towards the design of accessible web sites. These efforts include, for example, guidelines for web design, accessibility evaluation software for checking web page compliance with guidelines, etc.[1] Although this "proactive" approach to ensuring accessibility is, arguably, the most promising long-term strategy, there is a pressing need to re-design existing, non-accessible sites, rendering them accessible in a fully- or semi-automated way.

This paper presents a tool, called e*AccessibilityEngine*, which can automatically introduce web accessibility enhancements in existing web sites. The e*AccessibilityEngine* transforms non-accessible web pages into accessible forms; the actual "output" of the tool can vary in accordance with specific user needs, and the assistive software and hardware available to the user for accessing the web. The primary motivation driving the development of this tool has been to facilitate "reactive" approaches to introducing e-accessibility support in existing web sites. Development to date has focused on supporting, primarily, the "Web Content Accessibility Guidelines 1.0"[2] and the provisions made in "Section 508" of the US Rehabilitation Act[3].

[1] A thorough review of existing technologies and tools can be found in "Evaluation, Repair, and Transformation Tools for Web Content Accessibility", available at: http://www.w3.org/WAI/ER/existingtools.html.

[2] W3C – WAI, Web Content Accessibility Guidelines 1.0: http://www.w3.org/TR/WCAG10/.

[3] Section 508: http://www.section508.gov.

K. Miesenberger et al. (Eds.): ICCHP 2004, LNCS 3118, pp. 302–309, 2004.

The e*AccessibilityEngine* is based on concepts and techniques derived from the field of user-adaptable systems [5]. Specifically, the tool maintains user profiles and uses them to decide upon the type of adaptations to be applied to a document, in order to render it accessible to a particular user. The tool does not engage in active interaction monitoring during run-time, nor does it modify the user model automatically. The later is modified / maintained directly by the users.

The rest of the paper is organised as follows. The next section "Related Work" presents other relevant systems and technologies, while the following one provides an outline of the main operational principles of the tool, its architecture, and the way in which users interact with it. The paper is concluded with a brief overview of ongoing and future work on the tool.

## 2 Related Work

In recent years, research efforts have focused on design and development tools facilitating the construction of accessible user interfaces for applications and services [6]. Additionally, efforts have been directed towards tools such as Betsie[4], or the Web Access Gateway[5] that can be installed "on top" of specific web sites with the purpose of providing equivalent but more accessible forms of their pages. However, such tools mainly address the requirements of users with visual disabilities (i.e., colour impairment, low-vision, etc). As a result, their role is typically restricted to removing graphics from web pages, and providing text-only versions, with very limited control and configuration capabilities offered to the user.

A significant body of related work has also been presented in the literature recently, under the general title of "accessibility-oriented transcoding". Although a full review of the area is beyond the scope of this paper, the rest of this section examines a few representative examples for the purpose of pointing out potential limitations or gaps, which the e*AccessibilityEngine* aspires to address.

"Aurora" [2] is an example of a system that uses a semantic-approach to web content transcoding, with the intention of identifying and facilitating multi-step, goal-oriented transactions. The system uses XML-transcoding technologies to extract from web content and present for user interaction only the data relevant to execute these transactions. Aurora, like other tools in this category, provides good results in terms of e-accessibility, but cannot be considered a comprehensive solution that can be applied to a web site as a whole.

At the other end of the spectrum, the framework presented in [1] does represent a comprehensive solution, based on a so-called "ability driven" approach to accessibility-oriented transcoding. Nevertheless, it is not obvious whether users can control the transformation behaviour of the system. Furthermore, several assumptions are made about the way in which the framework is integrated with existing web-based systems, which suggest a rather "intrusive" approach that may not be easily applied to existing web sites.

---

[4] Betsie: http://www.bbc.co.uk/education/betsie/about.html.

[5] Web Access Gateway: http://www.flatline.org.uk/~silas/access.html.

Another line of work in the field is related to annotation-based transcoding of web documents[6]. External annotations of documents and document transcoding on the basis of these annotations, is a quite powerful approach that can also be used to address accessibility. The downside is that, where existing sites are involved, applying the approach would require not only the integration of a transcoding "engine", but also the creation and maintenance of the external annotations, which may prove impractical as an entry-level solution.

## 3 An Adaptation-Based Approach to Web Accessibility

### 3.1 Principles of Operation

The e*AccessibilityEngine* is based on an approach to web accessibility targeted towards addressing physical or perceptual disabilities, or combinations thereof. Disabilities are modeled using stereotypes [3], and each stereotype is associated with a set of accessibility transformations that adapt web pages according to the needs of the respective group of users. An individual user model may comprise of one or more stereotypes (one or more stereotypes may be active for a given user). Users may have full control over the creation of their individual user models, i.e., they can both inspect and manipulate. It should also be noted that the e*AccessibilityEngine* is designed so that new disability stereotypes can easily be introduced and associated with appropriate web document transformations.

The accessibility transformations associated with specific stereotypes are sequences (or "chains") of elementary transformations (Transformation Processing Units, or TPUs for short). TPUs can perform modifications both at the physical level of interaction (e.g., fonts and colours), and at the syntactic level of interaction (i.e., restructuring) of web documents. TPU functionality is based, to a large extent, on the ability to "recognise" and address patterns of inaccessibility in web pages (e.g., HTML tables used for page layout).

For the majority of disability stereotypes, a web page undergoes a first transformation process, which aims at providing Level AAA accessibility according to the W3C - WAI standard. Fig. 1 illustrates the result of an AAA accessibility transformation. Besides complying with the AAA level standard, this initial transformation is designed to have the following supplementary features:

- The resulting page is rendered linearly, in a top-down manner. Any tables used for page layout are removed at this stage.
- "Tab" browsing is supported. A tab index is assigned to every active element of the page (links and form elements), making it possible for the user to navigate through them in a sequential manner using the "Tab" key.
- HTML anchor elements are added to demarcate specific sections of the HTML document (e.g., top of the page, navigation bar, core content of the page, bottom of the page). Additionally, each of these anchors is associated with a specific access key (in effect, a key which acts as a "shortcut" to the anchor). This enables users to jump to these sections with a single key press.

[6] W3C, "Annotation of Web Content for Transcoding": http://www.w3.org/1999/07/NOTE-annot-19990710/

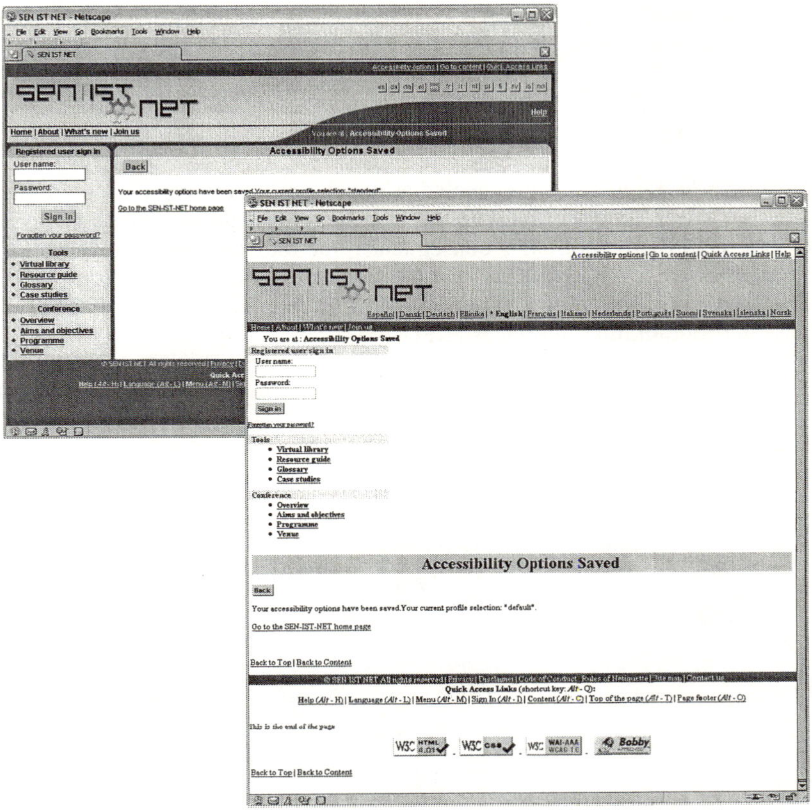


**Fig. 1.** Transformation of a web page to an AAA-WAI conformant version.

- Icons are added to indicate conformance to standards and specifications (AAA-WAI conformance icon[7], Valid HTML 4.01 icon[8], Valid CSS icon[9], Bobby approved icon[10]).

Usually, the TPU chains defined for certain disability stereotypes perform additional modifications to the AAA-WAI conformant version of the web document. For example, a stereotype profile for blind users could begin from the AAA-WAI conformant version and add, as an extra transformation, the replacement of images by their alternative text. However, certain disability stereotypes do not need to provide AAA accessibility. Consider for example, a user with dexterity impairment. In this case, the full graphic layout of the page may be retained, and the active elements of the page (links and form elements) can simply be enlarged, so as to provide easier interaction to the particular user. The described approach therefore adopts the per-

---

[7] Level Triple-A conformance to Web Content Accessibility Guidelines: http://www.w3.org/WAI/WCAG1AAA-Conformance.

[8] W3C Markup Validation Service: http://validator.w3.org/check/referer.

[9] W3C CSS Validation Service: http://jigsaw.w3.org/css-validator.

[10] Bobby: http://www.cast.org/bobby.

spective that interface adaptation is a fundamental mechanism towards achieving optimal accessibility for target user groups with diverse needs and requirements [7].

### 3.2 Architecture

The e*AccessibilityEngine* is implemented as a web-based service. The communication with the user's web browser and with the web server that delivers the content is done through the HTTP protocol. As a consequence, the tool may be deployed on a separate machine than the web server. The software itself is implemented using the Java™ Platform in conjunction with a variety of XML technologies (XSLT, XPATH), and Application Programming Interfaces (API).

The overall architecture of the e*AccessibilityEngine* (see Fig. 2) comprises of three main components: the Communication Component (CC), the Profile Managing Component (PMC), and the TPU Managing Component (TPUMC). The adaptation process is as follows:

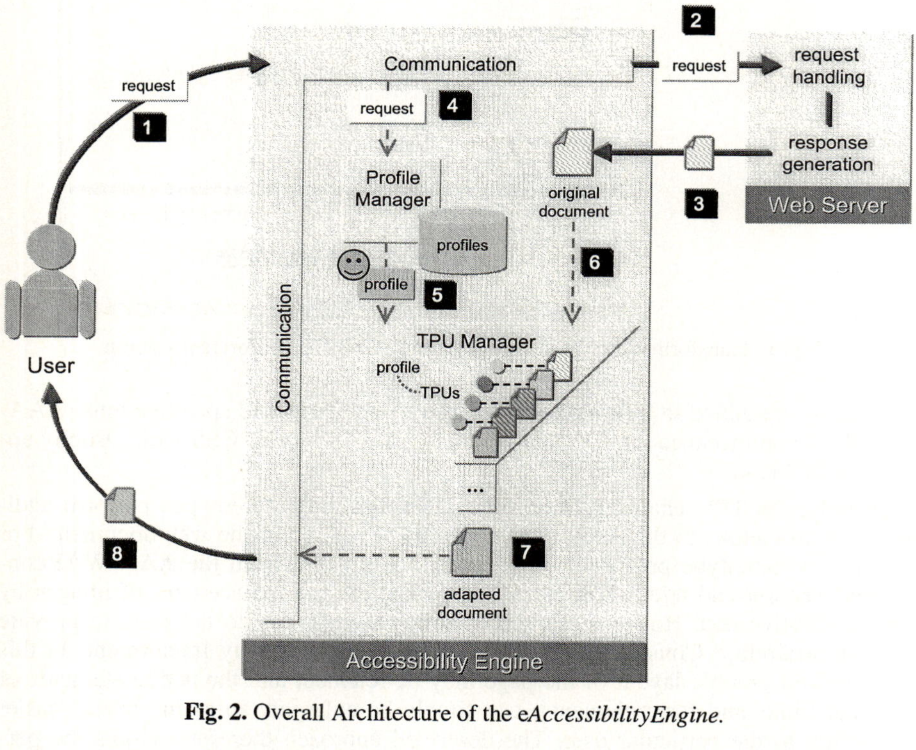


**Fig. 2.** Overall Architecture of the e*AccessibilityEngine*.

The CC receives a request for a web page, located on a remote web server, from the user's web browser (Fig. 2, (1)), and forwards the complete request (including HTTP headers and parameters) to the remote web server (Fig. 2, (2)). Upon receiving the page (Fig. 2, (3)), the CC forwards the HTTP request headers to the PMC (Fig. 2, (4)). The PMC identifies the user, and transmits the corresponding user profile to the

TPUMC (Fig. 2, (5)). Concurrently, the web server transmits to the TPUMC the page to be adapted (Fig. 2, (6)). The TPUMC selects the TPUs to apply on the document, on the basis of the user profile. The result of this selection process is a TPU chain, which is sequentially applied to the document. The result of the step-wise transformation process is a document that has been adapted for accessibility, in accordance with the user profile (Fig. 2, (7)). The adapted document is provided as a response to the client, along with the HTTP response headers previously received from the web server (Fig. 2, (8)).

Integrating the e*AccessibilityEngine* with an existing web site involves typically the following steps:

- The e*AccessibilityEngine* is installed as a stand-alone web application (installation can be at the same server as the web site is served from, or at a different one). The tool can be deployed as J2EE web application, using any of the available application servers (e.g., Apache Tomcat[11]).
- Links are added to the existing web pages, through which the e*AccessibilityEngine* can be invoked. Basically, these links "point" to the corresponding web application and pass the URL of the existing page as a parameter. Using these links users can retrieve the "accessible versions" of pages.
- Pages served through the e*AccessibilityEngine* have a one-to-one correspondence to the pages in the original web site. The adapted pages also contain additional links that enable users to interact directly with the e*AccessibilityEngine*, as described in the following section.

It is important to note that the e*AccessibilityEngine* does not pose requirements to the original web site / system, other that the ones outlined above, for its basic operation. It does, however, provide additional facilities that can be integrated on a need-to-have basis. Such facilities enable, for instance, the manipulation of user models / profiles directly on the associated web system, the configuration of operating parameters of the tool (e.g., caching of adapted documents), the configuration of presentation parameters of the tool (e.g., style sheets, which provide the accessible pages with the same look-and-feel as that of the site), introduce site-specific transformation possibilities (e.g., by defining the standard structural elements of pages), etc.

### 3.3 User Interaction

Users are not necessarily aware of the presence of the e*AccessibilityEngine*. In fact, if users do not wish to modify their initial selection of an "accessibility profile" (see below), they need to directly interact with the tool only once.

More specifically, the first time the tool is invoked for a particular user, the user is prompted to choose one, or a combination of, the available disability profiles (each corresponding to a stereotype). Invocation of the tool, in this context, is simply achieved by following a link to the "accessible version" of a page.

The user's choice is stored as an individual default profile. Individual profiles may be controlled and refined by the user, by fine-tuning parameters of the transformations that apply for the chosen disability stereotype. For example, a user with vision impairment may choose the preferred font size and colour contrast for viewing the web

[11] Apache Tomcat: http://jakarta.apache.org/tomcat/index.html.

site (achieved by modifying the options provided by default in the low vision stereotype), or may even define the preferred position for the navigation bar at the top or at the bottom of the page.

## 4 On-going and Future Work

The e*AccessibilityEngine* is a working prototype system currently under user evaluation. The tool has been successfully employed to provide accessibility support to the SEN-IST-NET[12] web portal (see also acknowledgements).

The main limitation of the current implementation is that accessibility transformations need to be applied to a specific context. In order to register web sites with the e*AccessibilityEngine*, some minimum requirements regarding the content of the pages must be fulfilled. Such requirements include the validity of the markup language (currently HTML, and XHTML) and the use of CSS style sheets. To take advantage of some of the more advanced capabilities of the tool, the "tagging" of the different sections in the web document may be required in some cases (e.g., in order to indicate items of the navigation bar).

Our main objective, which largely defines our ongoing work on the tool, is to build additional facilities into the system, so that comparable levels of functionality can be achieved, without enforcing the aforementioned requirements on the target system. This involves the development of algorithms that can intelligently "tag" or annotate pages at run-time, as well as the integration of functionality that would enable the tool to break down pages and serve their individual components to the users (e.g., by utilising a document cache in the system).

## Acknowledgements

The SEN-IST-NET project (IST-2000-26449) has been partly funded by the Information Society Technologies Programme of the European Commission – DG Information Society. The partners in the SEN-IST-NET consortium are: European Agency for Development in Special Needs Education – Project Co-ordinator; Department of Education, University of Innsbruck (Austria); Institute of Computer Science – FORTH (Greece); GIUNTI Interactive labs Srl., Sestri Levante (Italy); European Disability Forum (Belgium); Swedish Institute for Special Needs Education (Sweden).

## References

1. Balasubramanian, V., & Venkatasubramanian, N.: Server Transcoding of Multimedia Information for Cross Disability Access. ACM/SPIE Conference on Multimedia Computing and Networking (MMCN 2003). Electronically available at: http://www.ics.uci.edu/~dsm/suga/servertrans-mmcn.pdf (2003)

---

[12] SEN-IST-NET: http://www.senist.net.

2. Huang, A., Sundaresan, N.: Aurora: A Transaction-Based Approach to Web Accessibility. In Poster Proceedings of the 9th International World Wide Web Conference (WWW9) (2000)
3. Kay, J.: User Modeling for Adaptation. In: Stephanidis, C. (ed.): User Interfaces for All - Concepts, Methods, and Tools. Lawrence Erlbaum Associates, Mahwah NJ (2001) 271-294
4. Lazar, J., Beere, P., Greenidge, K-D, Nagappa, Y.: Web accessibility in the Mid-Atlantic United States: a study of 50 homepages. Universal Access in the Information Society, 2 (4) (2003) 331 – 341
5. Stephanidis, C.: Adaptive techniques for Universal Access. In: User Modelling and User Adapted Interaction International Journal, 11 (1/2) (2001) 159-179
6. Stephanidis, C. (ed.): User Interfaces for All - Concepts, Methods, and Tools. Lawrence Erlbaum Associates, Mahwah NJ (2001)
7. Stephanidis, C.: User Interfaces for All: New perspectives into Human-Computer Interaction. In: Stephanidis, C. (ed.): User Interfaces for All - Concepts, Methods, and Tools. Lawrence Erlbaum Associates, Mahwah NJ (2001) 3-17

# imergo: Supporting Accessibility and Web Standards to Meet the Needs of the Industry via Process-Oriented Software Tools

Yehya Mohamad, Dirk Stegemann, Johannes Koch, and Carlos A. Velasco

Fraunhofer-Institut für Angewandte Informationstechnik FIT*, Schloss Birlinghoven
D53757 Sankt Augustin Germany
{Yehya.Mohamad,Dirk.Stegeman,Johannes.Koch,Carlos.Velasco}
@fit.fraunhofer.de

**Abstract.** Although the legal requirements for Web accessibility are spreading world-wide, and mobile devices are common-place nowadays, support to standards and accessibility by the mainstream industry is still sloppy. This paper analyzes the limitations of existing evaluation and repair tools and presents a new tool developed by the authors to overcome existing limitations and support the industry by the implementation of quality assurance processes that include accessibility.

## 1 Introduction

The Web Content Accessibility Guidelines 1.0 [2] are close to its fifth anniversary, and despite the growing number of countries that are introducing policies related to ICT accessibility, its uptake by the mainstream industry is still very slow. This low acceptance might be partially due to the strong technological focus of the first version of the document, appropriate when the recommendation was issued, but which is difficult to apply to the wide variety of media and formats that populate the Web today.

The Web Accessibility Initiative from the World Wide Web Consortium is aware of this fact, and is working towards a second version of the document to address this concern, among others [1]. However, the main issue is the lack of support to authoring and publishing processes of big Web sites and portals that include accessibility and usability, by the existing commercial evaluation and repair tools.

This fact coincides in time with a growing concern from the industry with Web standards to be able to support a variety of mobile devices and user agents that are far from the times of the browsers war at the end of the nineties.

In this paper, we will present a brief analysis of the limitations of existing tools, and how the authors have tried to overcome these barriers by developing a tool suite that can support the industry in the coming challenges of the mobile Internet and accessibility. The paper reflects our experiences with real commercial projects in the public and private sector.

---

* http://access.fit.fraunhofer.de/

K. Miesenberger et al. (Eds.): ICCHP 2004, LNCS 3118, pp. 310–316, 2004.

## 2 Why Web Standards?

The Web industry was unique in its beginnings, and an inherent dose of amateurism populated many Web sites due to lack of understanding of the technical complexity of the new media, combined with the easiness to produce content with simple WYSIWYG tools. As sites grew in complexity, portals became commonplace in the Internet and the public demanded more quality, it became clear the need to implement development processes, similar to those of the software industry.

However, the absence of a wide variety of user agents to access content led to some stagnation of the industry that was basically producing content for the two dominant browsers in the market. It has not been until recent years, with the appearance of mobile devices, and a wider offer of alternative browsers, when it became clear that it was impossible to produce ad-hoc content and design for every specific platform.

Therefore, big media companies like ESPN or Wired News, among many others, have already migrated to sites strictly compliant Web-sites. In general, the benefits of using Web standards are (see, e.g. [4,5,7]):

- **Lower Costs.** It becomes much easier to manage a site-wide look and feel due to the separation of content and presentation. The development and deployment processes are simplified, and rendering differences become minimal across browsers. Furthermore, page sizes are reduced, and they render faster in browsers. The speed is increased by the browser caching mechanism of CSS, combined with faster rendering speed of browser engines in standards-compliance mode.
- **Future-Proof.** Standardized code is more portable across devices, and allows its reuse, without giving room to less compelling designs. It also allows extensibility to other XML-based languages like SVG, SMIL or MathML, that can be easily rendered in new browsers. It also avoids being locked to a particular tool, browser or even a particular developer, that created code-forkings compatible with different browsers.
- **Wider Customer Base.** Better search engine rankings are obtained because separating presentation from content augments the information/markup ratio.

In this context, accessibility must be seen as another important issue linked to a standards conformity process that brings along a wider customer base. In our opinion, linking accessibility only to policy compliance might difficult the adoption of accessibility by the mainstream Internet industry.

## 3 Limitations of Current Evaluation and Repair Tools

As stated earlier, the industry needs a set of tools that support them in the process of implementing accessibility within the overall scope of their Content Management System. An analysis performed by the authors in the early phases of developing the **imergo** platform[1], allowed us to identify the following limitations in existing tools:

[1] imergo is the medieval Latin word for "I dive in" or "I plunge into."

– Limited crawling capabilities for very large Web sites. This is also very important for the public sector, especially for ministries and local governments that have to maintain several Internet portals with actual topics.
– Most of them do not support properly project handling. That includes not only a robust database backend, but also versioning capabilities and a monitoring system that allows to check only modified pages. That is also important when implementing Quality Assurance methods.
– Lack of validation against published grammars (particularly complex for SGML parsers) and Cascading Style Sheets. This is again critical for browsers running in mobile devices, which have much lower processing capabilities, therefore requiring valid documents to parse them efficiently. These user agents are less fault-tolerant than many known desktop browsers. Large scale validation for the monitoring of big portals is also inexistent.
– Poor or inexistent support for other languages. That includes not only localization issues related to the GUI, but also adaptation to the different policy frameworks that are emerging in Europe. This issue is particularly relevant to the EU, where the knowledge of English is not in general good enough to allow the average developer to understand and interpret complex evaluation reports.
– Low quality components to analyze and repair DOM (Document Object Models) trees [5]. A surprisingly high number of applications do not implement DOM parsers to verify the accessibility rules that can be automatically tested, and are using sophisticated text parsers that are however not adequate for this task, thus leaving to manual verification tests that could be easily automated.
– Undocumented lists of carried tests and existing limitations for their customers.
– Fragmentation, i.e., lack of integration between different tests, that require, for instance, the use of several tools (e.g., validation, color contrast, etc.).
– No capability to perform color-blindness simulations.
– No support to the development of in-house tests, related to, e.g., corporate image checks, etc. via plug-ins.
– Very limited filtering capabilities in regard to errors, warnings, etc. Also they are focused on producing technical reports, but not in producing reports for different audiences: management, customers, etc.

But the most important deficiency is the lack of integration with Content Managements Systems. Only very small Web sites are produced now with any of the well-known Web design tools, or are only used in the conception phase. Web portals are produced with different teams, and content is aggregated via CMS. CMS are in most cases based upon XML templates derived from some proprietary DTD or Schema, which also demands from the tools the possibility to realize on the fly XSLT transformation and aggregations to be able to evaluate accessibility issues.

## 4 imergo Architecture and Characteristics

Bearing in mind the limitations of existing tools, as described in the previous section, we saw a gap where a new type of application could be developed to adequately support accessibility and standards compliance. It was also a key issue that the underlying architecture could adapt itself to different development environments. The appli-

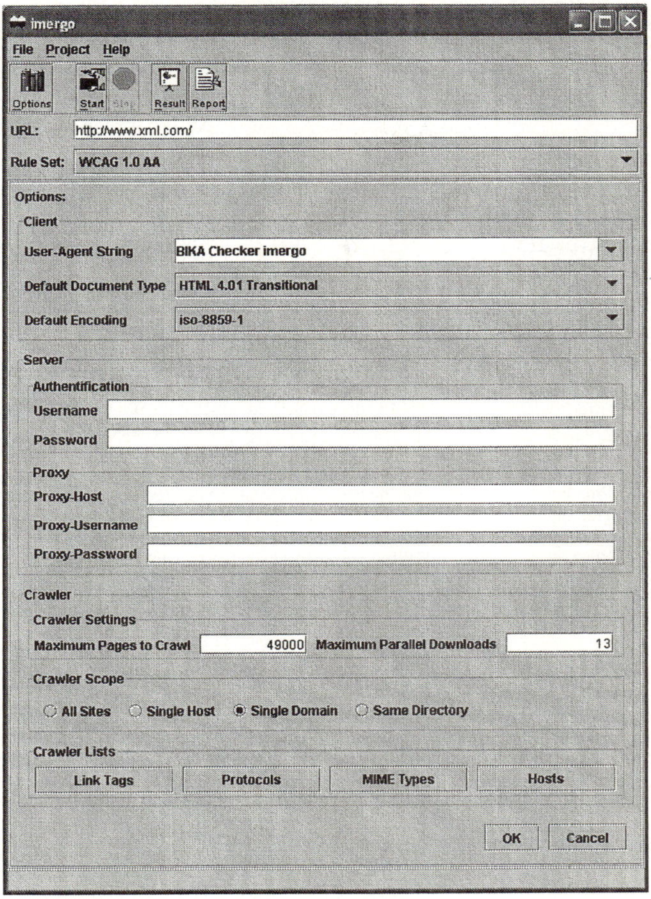


**Fig. 1. imergo** Graphical User Interface: configuration options.

cation is designed to provide three interfaces: a command-line interface, a Web Services interface, and a multiplatform GUI interface. It is obvious that for the type of application we mainly targeted, batch processing was the more important issue, combined with powerful post-processing of results.

The architecture of the suite includes:

- An XML-database back-end compatible with any XML:DB[2]-compliant commercial or Open Source database.
- A localizable interface, implemented via a flexible and accessible Java [7] GUI framework. The localization includes the reporting system as well.
- A powerful multi-threaded and configurable crawler able to process many different document types (including authentication and proxy support).
- A flexible reporting and project management system, targeting different audiences: Web developers, management, etc.

[2] http://www.xmldb.org/

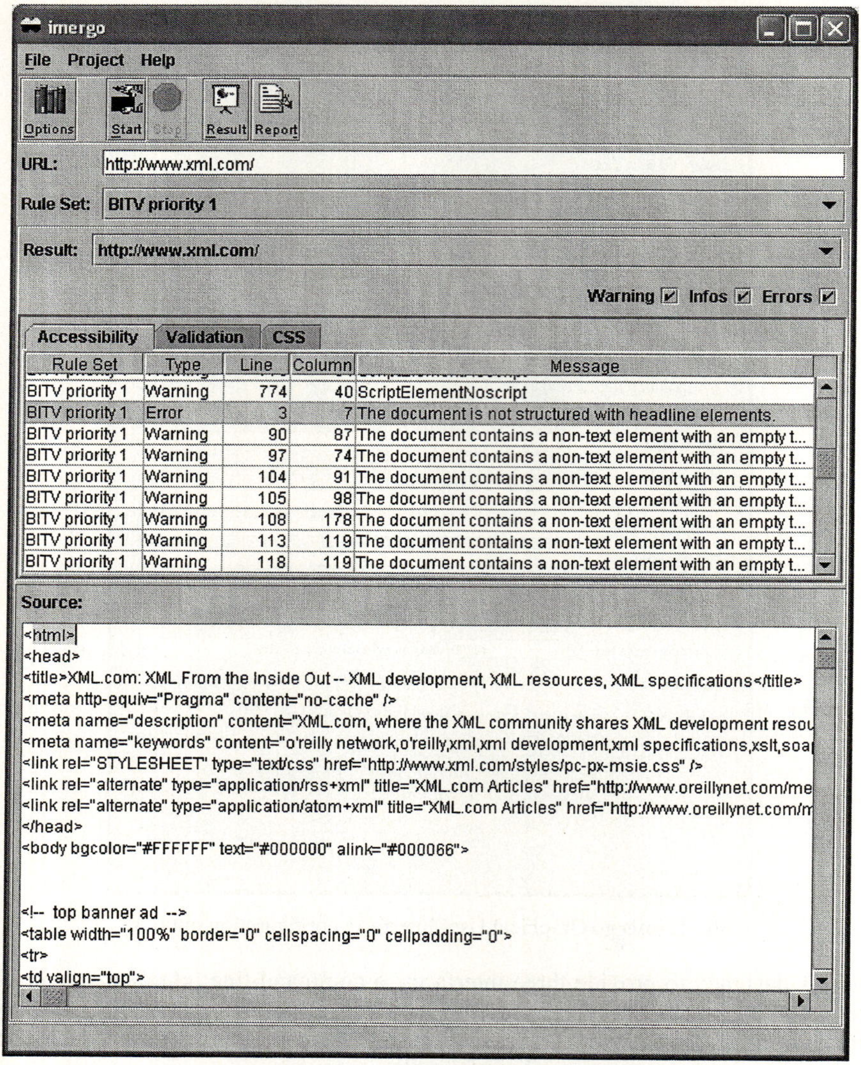


**Fig. 2. imergo** Graphical User Interface.

**imergo** offers as well a flexible and customizable definition of validation rules, both for accessibility and document validation (standards compliance). To our knowledge, **imergo** is the only tool in the market supporting pure SGML/HTML, as well as XML, validation of complete Internet portals (including XHTML, XML, XSLT, XLink, and any other XML application). From the accessibility standpoint, it offers off-the-shelf support for:

- Web Content Accessibility Guidelines 1.0.[3]
- Section 508.[4]
- German Accessibility decree.[5]

Initial benchmarking comparisons with other known tools in the market, demonstrated a superior performance in:

- Number of documents found, stored and checked.
- Reliability and speed for big Internet portals.
- Number of checkpoint items identified and implemented.
- Monitoring capabilities and project management.

## 5 Conclusions and Future Work

**imergo** has been successfully tested in the last year with several big portals in Germany in both the public and the private sector. It has helped to the Internet providers that use it to establish realistic monitoring procedures in combination with Quality Assurance methods to deploy accessible solutions within their Internet presence. Of course, this tool is a complement to expert evaluation and it is never intended to replace manual checks, but to support the experts in their tasks by offering a single tool with different solutions integrated.

We want also to highlight that this tool is not intended for certification purposes, as it is totally unrealistic to pretend that huge Web sites (in the order of several tens of thousands of pages) can be absolutely accessible. In the authors' opinion, certification is being preached by people lacking the technical awareness about the complexity of the technical processes involved in the development of Web applications with continuously updated content. However, adequate tools can support industry efforts to implement reliable **Quality Assurance** methods and help to make the Internet more accessible to all.

The tool is being further enhanced with several new functionalities that include different WYSIWYG views of analysis, support for manual tests, and in-site analysis of DOM structures via statistical methods to identify issues like navigation consistency, etc.

## References

1. Caldwell, B, Chisholm, W, White, J, and Vanderheiden, G (eds) (2003). Web Content Accessibility Guidelines 2.0, W3C Working Draft 24 June 2003. World Wide Web Consortium. Available at: http://www.w3.org/TR/WCAG20/

---

[3] http://www.w3.org/TR/WCAG10/

[4] http://www.section508.gov/

[5] Verordnung zur Schaffung barrierefreier Informationstechnik nach dem Behindertengleichstellungsgesetz (Barrierefreie Informationstechnik-Verordnung – BITV): http://www.behindertenbeauftragter.de/gesetzgebung/behindertengleichstellungsgesetz/rechtsverordnung/rvo11bgg

2. Chisholm, W, Vanderheiden, G, and Jacobs, I (eds) (1999). Web Content Accessibility Guidelines 1.0, W3C Recommendation 5-May-1999. World Wide Web Consortium. Available at: http://www.w3.org/TR/WCAG10/
3. Harrison L, O'Grady (2004). Web accessibility validation and repair: which tool and why?. Library Hi Tech. 21(4), pp. 463-470.
4. Hazaël-Massieux, D (ed) (2002). Buy standards compliant Web sites. World Wide Web Consortium. Available at: http://www.w3.org/QA/2002/07/WebAgency-Requirements
5. Le Hors, A, Le Hégaret, P, Wood, L, Nicol, G, Robie, J, Champion, M, Byrne S (eds) (2000). Document Object Model (DOM), Level 2 Core Specification, Version 1.0, W3C Recommendation 13 November, 2000. World Wide Web Consortium. Available at: http://www.w3.org/TR/DOM-Level-2-Core/
6. Nonnenmacher, F (2003). Web Standards for Business (Translated from the original French version "Les standards web pour l'entreprise"). The Web Standards Project. Available at: http://www.webstandards.org/learn/reference/web_standards_for_business.html
7. Schwerdtfeger, R S (2000). IBM Guidelines for Writing Accessible Applications Using 100% Pure Java, Version 2.1. IBM Accessibility Center. Available at: http://www-3.ibm.com/able/guidelines/java/snsjavag.html
8. Zeldman, J (2003). Designing With Web Standards. Indianapolis, USA: New Riders.

# Evaluation Methodology and Quality Mark for Web Accessibility

Eric Velleman

Accessibility Foundation
Utrechtseweg 84, 3702AD Zeist - Netherlands
www.accessibility.nl

**Abstract.** How can you be sure that your website complies with the W3C guidelines. Research shows that many websites use the W3C Accessibility logo's on their site. Research has also shown that most of the sites that use the logo's do not comply with the guidelines at all. Because there is no control over the quality of the logo except by the public and the evaluation and interpretation of the checkpoints leave space for discussion, the Netherlands government together with stakeholder organisation and companies have set up a transparant evaluation scheme and a controlled conformance logo. This paper describes the project and the results of the feasability study.

## 1 Introduction

In many countries, web accessibility and building accessible websites is not mandatory. However, many organizations and web designers make an intentional effort to aim for accessibility. The final results are not always checked according to the Web Content Accessibility Guidelines (WCAG) of the W3C and an increasing number of websites prove to be non-compliant. The same situation occurs more or less in countries where accessibility is mandatory. Because of the multi interpretable nature of the first generation guidelines (WCAG1.0) it is not so easy to objectively evaluate compliance without adding extra objective and measurable criteria. This problem will be solved by the guidelines Working Group in the next version by providing clear criteria. The Euroaccessibility project that combines the experience of more than 24 members in 12 countries will be setting up a European scheme for evaluation and certification that is based on a clarification of the criteria and best-practice in all the countries. The organisation and scheme used in this European project is based largely on the project described in this paper.

Many organizations ask for a way to ensure that their websites comply with the guidelines. Many websites use the W3C Accessibility logo's on their site. Research has shown that most of the sites that use the logo's do not comply with the guidelines at all. Because there is no control over the quality of the logo except by the public and the evaluation and interpretation of the checkpoints leave space for discussion, the Netherlands government together with stakeholder organisation and companies have expressed the need for a transparant evaluation scheme and for a controlled conformance logo. Based on research and experience from the Design4all Evaluation and

K. Miesenberger et al. (Eds.): ICCHP 2004, LNCS 3118, pp. 317–322, 2004.

the Dutch Drempels Weg-project, it appears that organizations, when it comes to a quality mark, are in need of:

- External testing of the website for accessibility;
- Accordance with international law and regulations. This means access to and anticipation on developments in the US and Europe;
- A way of showing that they have delivered an accessible website, which meets a certified quality mark that is also recognized by the government;
- Development of objective measurable criteria;
- Regular inspection of the website in order to see if it is still in accordance with the quality mark, and additional rights and obligations.

The Drempelvrij project (Barrier Free) is developing a Quality Mark based on these needs together with all stakeholders in the Netherlands. The project has developed objective measurable criteria for web content accessibility, which can be used to review websites. The criteria are in full accordance with the Web Content Accessibility Guidelines priority 1 (16 checkpoints) and can be used for evaluation and validation of website accessibility.

The results of the project are used as input into the new W3C guidelines and the EuroAccessibility project. Websites that comply with the criteria are allowed to use the quality mark that is controlled by the project.

The project is funded by the Dutch government. The project results will be available to other countries directly and through EuroAccessibility and the EDeAN network.

This paper first describes the work done in the feasability study and then the development of a clarification of the web accessibility guidelines with evalution criteria. This clarification is a prerequisite for a quality mark and for objective evaluation results.

## 2 Feasability Study

In the exploring phase, a feasibility study has been carried out on the social support for a quality mark regulation.

In order to involve experts and other parties concerned, from the very beginning, a supervisory committee has been formed. After a short presentation of the supervisory committee we will discuss the feasability study.

### 2.1 Supervisory Committee

The supervisory committee is constructed in such a manner that all interested parties (stakeholders) are involved from the very first beginning. Participation in the supervisory committee is guaranteed on the basis of expertise of the parties. For the time being, the following parties take a seat in the supervisory committee: The Bartimeus Accessibility Foundation (www.accessibility.nl); Nederland~ICT (FENIT); De Nederlandse Thuiswinkel Organisatie (the Dutch home shopping organisation); VNO-NCW (Confederation of Netherlands Industry and Employers), also on behalf of

SMEs; Advies.overheid.nl; Ministry of the Interior and Kingdom Relations; Ministry of Health, Welfare and Sport; Dutch Council of the Chronically Ill and the Disabled (CG-Raad); Federation of organisations of people with intellectual disabilities and their parents (FvO); Federation for the Interests of the Visually Impaired and the Blind; Seniorweb; National Accessibility Agency (LBT).

## 2.2 Feasability Study

The feasibility of the quality mark regulation depends on a minimum of two elements. First of all there should be a market for a quality mark regulation. This means that a sufficient number of organizations should take an interest in applying and using the quality mark. Moreover, these organizations should be willing to pay for the quality mark.

Secondly the regulation needs a broad social support in order to have a distinctive effect on the market. Both aspects have been tested.

The feasibility study revolves around four central aspects of quality mark regulation:

- Demands of the market;
- Expectations of parties concerned;
- Affordability;
- Initiation by the government (subsidy and to make it mandatory).

The potential scale of acceptance of the quality regulation in the market has been registered by interviewing several relevant parties. In total 10 interviews where conducted. When selecting stakeholders for the interviews, care was taken to ensure that potential certificate holders from the private and public sectors on the one hand and Internet users with disabilities on the other were represented to an equal extent.

First of all, interviews have been held with (multi) national organizations to check if the quality mark can count on acceptance by a substantial group of organizations. Also by interviewing, an inventory of expectations and wishes has been drawn up to establish how much support and approval the quality mark can rely upon from the side of interest groups and parties concerned. Also the possible acceptation of the quality mark regulation among local and central authorities has been tested.

Finally, by way of an extensive digital survey all stakeholders have been involved in the feasibility study.

The digital survey was brought to the attention of about 1,355 potential certificate holders through the cooperation of the stakeholder organisations. Additionally when selecting stakeholders for the digital survey, care was taken to include representatives of consumer organisations, web builders and government agencies. Several different representative organisations of each group of interested parties were asked to cooperate by circulating the link to the digital survey amongst their members.

Consumer organisations: 115
Web builders and Internet providers: 491
Government agencies: 73
Others: 676

### 2.3 Results of the Feasability Study

The full report can be ordered on the website of http://www.accessibility.nl. On the basis of the findings from the interviews with the representative organisations and the results of the digital survey among website providers, the following can be concluded:

1. There is broad social support for the development of a quality mark, as the interviews reveal that the organisations representing the business sector, the public sector and people with disabilities all want to support the development and implementation of the quality mark. Most of the respondents in the digital survey indicated that they are willing to make their own websites accessible and to have them monitored in order to obtain the quality mark.
2. The willingness of the people concerned to contribute to the development of the quality mark has different motives dictated by their specific interests. The interviews reveal that, depending on the position of the people concerned, these interests may relate to product development, market potential, image improvement, pressure from interest organisations and taking social responsibility.
3. The digital survey did not reveal a lack of willingness on the part of potential certificate holders to obtain the quality mark, as a large number of respondents indicated that they:
   - are aware of the problem of digital accessibility;
   - need more objective and verifiable criteria;
   - want to realise or improve the accessibility of their own websites;
   - want the accessibility of their own websites to be checked;
   - want to draw web builders' attention to digital accessibility;
   - ask their web builders to build digitally accessible sites.
4. Despite their willingness to obtain the quality mark, the digital survey reveals that many of the respondents are not willing to pay much for monitoring. They are willing to invest in digital accessibility if the emphasis is not on the monitoring but on actually improving the website.
5. The study reveals that the majority of people involved in the study find the quality mark a suitable method of achieving digital accessibility. Furthermore, the following preconditions were expressly given with regard to the decision as to whether to introduce the quality mark:
   - The quality requirements must be market-oriented and easy to apply;
   - The quality requirements must be reasonable in terms of preserving the layout, the functionality and the flexibility of a website;
   - The quality requirements should not stand in the way of the technological development of a website;
   - Monitoring costs should be set at an acceptable level;
   - The credibility of the scheme must be guaranteed.
6. It has emerged that the parties involved need a number of supporting activities that also reinforce the quality mark and improve digital accessibility in general. The suggestions for parallel activities from the parties involved are developing

the knowledge needed to create digitally accessible websites, providing supporting resources for the quality requirements, such as a manual, providing standard contracts which include requirements for digital accessibility, development of tools and more.

7. Potential certificate holders would derive value-added from the quality mark mainly in that it reinforces the image of the website holder and identifies the fact that it is accessible to people with disabilities. The digital survey reveals that these aspects were the most important reasons for the respondents rating the quality mark positively. The interviews with representative organisations in the public sector reveal that a positive assessment of the quality mark is mainly based on taking social responsibility and on aspects of image. To business sector interest organisations, the commercial impetus is the most important aspect, and image and the differentiating role are of secondary importance.
8. The interviews reveal that website providers find that there should be no formal obligation to obtain the quality mark. Providers in both the private sector and the public sector expressly indicate that they would prefer the quality mark to be voluntary. Conversely, representatives of Internet users with disabilities have indicated that they would prefer the quality mark to be obligatory for government agencies and businesses with an important social function.
9. The study reveals that awareness of the problem of digital accessibility positively influences the willingness to pay for obtaining an accessible site and a quality mark. Most of the organisations interviewed pointed out the importance of communication by providing information on the subject and giving examples of digital accessibility.

## 3 Developing Objective Evaluation Criteria

The development of the criteria follows the W3C Web Content Accessibility Guidelines. Starting point is the priority 1 checkpoints (16 checkpoints) of the current WCAG1.0. Research has enabled the translation of this document into a normative document by adding objective measurable criteria and points of verification, with a major and minor non-conformance level caesura. Additionally, a digital tool is manufactured to help people perform a multi-step tool assisted manual evaluation of a website following the normative document.

Also research has been done to find out which regulations, issuing of rules and lawmaking rules by the authorities stipulate the draft of the quality mark as well as the testing criteria. An example is the legislation on accessibility in the UK, the Netherlands and Germany. In order to do so research has been done into similar quality mark regulations from other (international) authorities. Both researches lead to an accurate determination of the institutional framework and policy plans.

To develop the quality mark a committee was installed. In this committee ICT-companies, social organizations, central and local bodies and consumer organizations participate. Based on the W3C Web Content Accessibility Guidelines, the committee has, in an iterative process, determined the testing criteria according to a jointly arranged procedure leading to a quality mark regulation that meets all legal demands and conditions on a national, European and international level. This should result in the validation of the regulation. The current normative accessibility evaluation document can be downloaded from the Accessibility.nl website.

## 4 More Information

More information about the Quality Mark project can be found on the following websites and pages:

http://www.accessibility.nl
Dutch site about accessibility. The documents produced in the Quality Mark project can be found in English:

http://www.accessibility.nl/en/qualitymark/
On this page you can order a copy of the feasability study including detailed results.

http://www.accessibility.nl/en/qualitymark/normdoc.php
Last version of the normative document for the Quality Mark. Also available as a Word document.

http://www.design4all.org
Website of the design4all evaluation (also available in English) and of the Quality Mark when ready. The site offers ongoing evaluation of a website.

www.euroaccessibility.org
The home of the EuroAccessibility consortium. This is an open consortium that focuses on a common European evaluation methodology and a certification scheme.

http://www.gebruikersonderzoek.nl
Dutch website where organisations can find user testing and user supported evaluation protocols that have been specially designed for testing websites with people with disabilities by the University of Twente, the Accessibility Foundation and other stakeholders.

http://www.drempelsweg.nl
The website of the Drempels Weg Project. A project funded by the Dutch government that aims to help more people with disabilities on the internet and make the internet more accessible. The project produced a scheme for the ongoing monitoring of websites and also a Logo that is protected. This scheme is placed on a seperate website www.design4all.org.

Brochure about the Accessibility guidelines ('access all WWW areas')
A special brochure has been produced that explains the guidelines, the rationale behind them, gives examples of accessible code and helps evaluate a website. The brochure is primarily intended for designers and builders of websites.

Brochure about Accessibility for policy makers
A brochure focusing on policy makers to help them understand about accessibility and make them aware of the businesscase, the policy implications, the ease of implementation and the way to test the results.

# A Cost-Benefit Approach for Accessible Web Presence

Valeska Heerdt and Christine Strauss

University of Vienna, Department of Business Studies,
Bruenner Str. 72, A-1210 Vienna, Austria
christine.strauss@univie.ac.at

**Abstract.** Providing an accessible Web presence is often regarded as an ethical or social obligation. Profit-oriented enterprises in particular tend to interpret the implementation of "barrier-free" access to their websites as a cost-intensive technological gimmick rather than as a business opportunity. This paper provides systematic insight into the cost and benefit drivers that might determine a purely rational management decision on Web presence that takes accessibility into consideration. The relative price for one percentage point of audience increase ("reach") combines cost-benefit aspects, and provides the basis for a quantitative, scenario-based, general approach that reveals possible savings for enterprises of various sizes under differing cost assumptions and provides a viable, easy-to-use framework for individual use cases.

## 1 Introduction

"The Web has become a commodity that everyone has to have and everyone needs to use because it is built upon the most important commodity of the net millennium: information." [15]. The issue of full Web accessibility to this most important of commodities has become a controversial subject on which a wide spectrum of differing notions exist. However, there is still only limited awareness of those people who are excluded from this important source of information and means of communication. In this context, "full access" refers to Web content that is made available to all users, whatever user agent they are using (e. g., desktop browser, voice browser, mobile phone) or constraints they may be operating under (e. g., noisy surroundings, under- or over-illuminated rooms, or in a hands-free environment) ([21], p. 5). Reducing the issue of accessibility to a matter of assistive technology is a widely held approach that is nevertheless both misleading and hampering – in fact, accessibility is a question of appropriate compliance to Web design basics [18].

Given the large pent-up demand represented by the large size of this group of deprived persons, the number of websites truly providing full access to the Web appears almost diminutive at this time. The discrepancy between demand and supply is even more obvious, considering that nearly half of all European enterprises (46 %) already operated a corporate website in 2000. However, a notable gap exists between large companies on the one hand and small and

K. Miesenberger et al. (Eds.): ICCHP 2004, LNCS 3118, pp. 323–330, 2004.

medium-sized enterprises (SME) on the other: 80 % of the large companies are present on the Web, compared to only 44 % of SME's ([5], p. 2). By 2002, 55 % of all companies had created a presence on the Web ([14], p. 1). These trends imply that a large percentage of companies will launch their own website in the near future. They, together with those companies pondering a relaunch of their existing website, will thus have to consider the accessibility issue on the basis of cost-benefit criteria. The fact that most cost-benefit-factors are difficult, if not impossible, to quantify represents an important barrier hampering the implementation of accessible websites.

The lack of fully-accessible websites is largely attributable to ill-considered cost considerations and to a widespread unawareness of the beneficial consequences of providing such access [4, 12]. Therefore, this paper outlines the benefits of integrating accessibility into the website design process and identifies the determining cost factors involved. As the size of an enterprise usually determines the Web design costs, we provide a rough estimate for the dimension of these costs based on expert statements for each category of enterprise size. We evaluate three different cost scenarios (*facile*, *normal*, and *complex*) for five different sizes of enterprises (from *micro* to *very large*) to reflect the rough market-potential and the fact that the approach presented is meant to serve as a general method applicable to individual sectors. The scheme presented in this paper is based on a comparison of classic costs for advertising in print media and the expected gains realized by increasing the number of potential customers reached. Combining a classic yardstick ("reach") with the estimated costs for an accessible website provides an application-independent measurement of the economic impact for an enterprise.

Section 2 provides an insight into the beneficial business impacts of Web accessibility (such as corporate image), highlights the risks involved in ignoring customers with special needs (such as legal liabilities), and addresses the dynamic developments expected in the future. Section 3 defines categories for enterprises and website costs and develops a quantitative framework. Section 4 provides concluding remarks as well as an outlook on future work.

## 2 Impacts and Benefits of Web Accessibility

### 2.1 Image

The increasing relevance and public awareness of accessibility-related issues might have significant impacts on a company's reputation. Non-conformance may result in a negative media attention, unfavorable publicity, or a potential loss of business. Considering that a major motivation for Web presence lies in improving the corporate identity and reputation ([11], p. 9), it may turn out to be highly contradictory if the website does not conform to accessibility requirements. In contrast, accessible websites provide brand enhancement, increased goodwill and positive public perception to an ever growing extent. Analogous to the legal aspects, the repercussions to image issues are highly case-dependent and therefore go beyond the scope of this paper.

### 2.2 Legal Liability

A higher legal exposure due to national and international laws and regulations must be taken into account to a greater extent when operating a website that is not fully accessible: lawsuits and litigation expenses, fines, and penalties are more likely to accrue over time [19, 17]. Very few legal cases concerning Web accessibility exist, and in most cases, the parties agreed on a settlement; 'NFB (National Federation of the Blind) v. AOL (America Online, Inc)' provides a useful example. On the other hand, the case 'Maguire v. SOCOG' (Sydney Organizing Committee for the Olympic Games), in which SOCOG was fined A$20,000, is often quoted as a precedent for cases worldwide. The potential occurrence of such losses and the associated risk should also be part of the decision-making process. As there is not enough evidence to provide a sound basis for a general estimation, only a case-specific risk analysis would provide some indicators of the associated costs; therefore, this factor is omitted in the basic application-independent approach.

### 2.3 Audience

One of the most frequently mentioned reasons for considering accessibility lies in increasing the website's potential audience size, as accessible websites accommodate a wider range of users in a wider range of access conditions [19]. These new potential customers consist of disabled people, senior citizens, and users with reduced bandwidth or technically obsolete devices, as well as people with situational constraints (e. g., hands-free environment) or using different user agents (e. g., mobile phone or PDA).

The share of the general population with disabilities has always been viewed as a niche market, but about 15 % of the EU-population in the age group 16 to 64 years have a disability ([10], p. 8). Additionally, 20 % of the population in Europe presently consists of people older than 60, who are far more likely to have reduced physical abilities (e. g., arthritis, visual impairments etc.) that hamper Web access or make it even impossible. Although the older generation represents about 20 % of the population, only 5 % of marketing budgets are spent on them on the average [6]. This fact neglects that the actual and future senior citizens have an above-average living standard and dispose over an income higher than that of the younger generation (cf. [6]).

Because of the barriers to accessing the Web, people with disabilities and elderly are under-represented among Internet users: recent studies state that about 30 % [13] of disabled and 20 % ([9], p. 24) of the generation 55+ use the Internet, compared to the 53 % of the total EU-population ([9], p. 25).

Most companies underestimate the potential sales growth that this development implies. Sales are rising either in a direct (i. e., through Internet sales) or an indirect way (i. e., where customers just pick information before purchasing via conventional ways in a shop) [2].

### 2.4 Time Dynamics

Because all of these effects are not static, one might have also to analyze their development over time. These days, the initial costs of creating an accessible website are higher than those incurred in creating a standard, but non-compliant website. Cost reduction is the motivation for profit-oriented enterprises to use appropriate standard markup language, content management systems or style sheets, when creating a new website. As these measures greatly support accessibility as a side effect, they promote the spread of accessible sites, leading the cost gap between conventional and accessible websites to be leveled out. Over time, the regulative authorities throughout the world will have enacted stricter laws and regulations that require websites to be fully accessible. As a consequence, lawsuits and the degree of penalties are likely to increase. Furthermore, at the moment there is less awareness in Europe than in the USA concerning on accessibility [3]. The image loss or gain will change as the consciousness of this subject matter rises. The demographic development will be characterized by declining birth rates and rising life expectancy. The fastest growing demographic segment in Europe includes people over the age of 50. By the year 2050 it is expected that the relative ratio of people over 60 increases from 20 % to over 37 % within the European Union [20].

## 3 A Scenario-Based Cost-Benefit Approach

In the following section, we first develop a pure cost approach that makes it possible to estimate the additional costs incurred by creating an accessible Web presence. An enhanced approach integrates benefits by estimating the size of the additional audience that can be addressed through an accessible Web presence.

### 3.1 Cost Analysis

The choice of business scenarios for a generally applicable framework was driven by the goal of keeping the approach relevant to all potential industries and sectors. Therefore, five basic business scenarios provide the basic pattern for a comparison of different approaches that focus on set-up costs for a Web presence. We distinguish five categories of enterprises on the basis of their size (*micro*, *small*, *medium*, *large* and *very large* (cf. [8])) as determined by their turnover (0.2, 3, 25, 100, 400 million Euros (cf. [7], p. 11)).

Furthermore, we assume that accessibility is implemented during the initial phase of designing a new website and therefore that an entirely new Web presence and a complete relaunch are equivalent in terms of costs. Retrofitting an existing site always involves higher relative additional costs, whose extent depends on a variety of factors, including the size and complexity of the existent site and its original coding. Initially, we compare the costs of designing an accessible website from scratch with the costs incurred when accessibility is ignored. The mean costs for such a standard website depend the enterprise's size and are assumed to be 2,500, 10,000, 20,000, 40,000, or 150,000 Euros (cf. [1], p. 7) in the case of a micro, small, medium, large, or very large enterprise.

Because the topic of accessibility is relatively new, there are as yet no studies reporting on the costs that may arise when a site is made accessible. Consequently, experts have widely differing opinions, ranging from negligible additional costs to extra costs of up to 25 % [4]. It can be assumed that a website's degree of complexity determines the design costs and, as a consequence, the relative extra costs for providing full accessibility (e. g., a website with online-shopping and associated payment functions is more complex and as such requires higher relative additional costs than a plain static homepage).

Therefore, in order to calculate the resulting absolute total costs, the cost scenarios distinguish between facile, normal and complex implementation, which imply an estimated cost increase of 2 %, 10 %, and 25 %, respectively. To provide rough relative total costs these absolute values are placed in context of the respective mean turnovers. Covering the whole spectrum of enterprise sizes and various website complexities requires several simplifying assumptions: mean turnover per size-category, mean website costs per size-category, and selected representative ratios for the effort to implement full accessibility. Table 1 shows the derived absolute total costs for accessible Web pages for each enterprise size as well as the relative total costs, which depend on turnover.

**Table 1.** Estimated Absolute and Relative Total Accessibility Costs (values in Euros)

| enterprise size | facile implementation | | normal implementation | | complex implementation | |
|---|---|---|---|---|---|---|
| | abs. | rel. | abs. | rel. | abs. | rel. |
| micro | 2,550 | (1.28 %) | 2,750 | (1.38 %) | 3,125 | (1.56 %) |
| small | 10,200 | (0.34 %) | 11,000 | (0.37 %) | 12,500 | (0.42 %) |
| medium | 20,400 | (0.08 %) | 22,000 | (0.09 %) | 25,000 | (0.10 %) |
| large | 40,800 | (0.04 %) | 44,000 | (0.04 %) | 50,000 | (0.05 %) |
| very large | 153,000 | (0.04 %) | 165,000 | (0.04 %) | 187,500 | (0.05 %) |

Table 1 makes clear that the investment costs involved are relatively small in relation to turnover (usually less than 0.5 % of an average size-specific turnover, except for micro enterprises, for whom the relative cost might extend to 1.56 % due to the relatively low total turnover). For each cost-scenario, the ratio of the costs relative to turnover for the accessible Web costs decreases as the size of enterprise increases. While the total relative costs range from 0.04 % of turnover for large firms to 1.56 % for a micro enterprise, the actual cost increase incurred by providing full accessibility is very small and varies between 0.3 % and 0.001 % of turnover. Our general cost analysis reveals that the costs for accessible Web presence are lower than commonly assumed (cf. [4]). Table 1 may be used as an initial guide for decision-makers who are considering their first Web presence or a relaunch of their existing website. For a specific application-case, a more detailed cost analysis based on the actual parameters needs to be performed in a next step in order to provide the basis for a sound management decision.

### 3.2 A Cost-Benefit Approach

To provide a key figure that effectively combines the costs and benefits of accessibility, we introduce the yearly average costs for one single percentage point of the so-called "reach". This common marketing measure denotes the relative ratio of persons that can be reached by a specific media (e. g., Web, print, television). Associating the reach with the estimated absolute costs determined in Section 3.1 provides the cost for one single percentage point of reach. This key figure represents the relationship between the number of persons reached by a certain website relative to the investment for this Web presence. Furthermore, for accessible websites, this figure includes the costs adjusted by those factors determined in the previous cost analysis. The increase in audience is estimated based on statistics (cf. Section 2.3) as well as by relying on surveys, which establish that the consolidated number of disabled and seniors in the EU lies at roughly 25 % of the general public [16]. Given that the target audience of users facing difficulties online lies at 10 % to 25 % of the general public and assuming that only one-third of this potential audience is actually present on the Web [9, 13], one can identify three scenarios 7 %, 12 %, and 18 % for the estimated *low*, *medium*, and *high* increase in actual audience. Due to the lean and flexible design of accessible websites, we further assume that the website's operating time can be extended by 30 %.

Table 2 shows the numerical evaluation of the entire set of nine outlined scenarios. Each scenario combines the relevant additional costs for accessibility (for each implementation type) with the potential audience-increase and presents the possible relative savings based on the reach.

**Table 2.** Estimated Relative Savings for Accessible Websites

| | implementation type | | |
|---|---|---|---|
| audience increase | facile implementation | normal implementation | complex implementation |
| low | 29 % | 23 % | 12 % |
| medium | 32 % | 26 % | 16 % |
| high | 35 % | 30 % | 21 % |

Given the outlined assumptions concerning augmentation of audience, website costs, operating time, and the enterprises' characteristics, the possible relative savings may vary between 12 % and 35 % of the website costs per reach point. These global estimates are independent from the size of the enterprise and from the business sectors. For a stop-or-go decision upon accessibility in a certain context, Table 2 and the underlying approach will support the decision-maker by providing basic aspects and some statistical material. Considering, that a recent study ([12], p. 13) establishes that 30 % of the responsible managers state that accessible Web pages were not (yet) implemented for cost reasons and another 75 % state lack of information as the reason for their inaction, our approach provides some of the missing information and substantiates that costs are likely to be dominated by benefits.

## 4 Summary and Perspective

Web accessibility is a topic of increasing concern to organizations for a variety of reasons, including financial, moral and legal considerations. This paper addresses major business aspects of the accessibility issue and discusses various business advantages that can be achieved by adding accessibility to the website development process: improving an enterprise's public image, increasing the number of potential customers, preventing litigation, conforming to laws and regulations, and accruing cost savings. Because business executives require hard facts to support them in making better decisions regarding the online channel, this paper provides a framework for a cost analysis approach based on statistics. A very general quantitative approach combines cost with benefits in terms of the additional audience and potential customers that can be reached by providing an accessible Web presence.

As such, a sector-independent approach can only provide rough values for orientation; individual applications require that adaptations be performed and case-specific constraints be taken into consideration. One possible direction for future work would include case studies about real-world applications, which allow a more detailed benefit view (e. g., websites with ordering function will immediately experience an increase in sales). Because the relevant legislation is relatively new or not yet enacted, another direction of impact should use risk analysis to analyze the effects of lawsuits and litigation costs. Similarly, the scope of image loss and gain should be investigated, with market analyses of the impact of unfavorable publicity, as well as of the business lost in the event that the needs of persons requiring fully accessible websites are ignored. The result of our general cost-benefit approach may be interpreted as an indicator that improving the accessibility of a website is an easy-to-attain, cost-effective business opportunity. Not only is it a wise business decision to improve accessibility of a Web presence, as the Internet as a whole is still growing, the information and communication technology continues to progress and we, the consumers, are growing older.

## References

1. Bundesministerium für Wirtschaft und Arbeit, Referat Kommunikation und Internet (ed.): "Unternehmenspräsentation im Internet". In: *e-f@cts: Informationen zum E-Business*, Iss. **11**. Berlin (2002)
2. Bundesministerium für Wirtschaft und Arbeit, Referat Kommunikation und Internet (ed.): "E-Business im Handel 2003". In: *e-f@cts: Informationen zum E-Business*, Iss. **14**. Berlin (2003)

3. Chamberlain, H.: "Opening Doors to Information Technology – Section 508 of the US Rehabilitation Act of 1973". In: *Miesenberger, K., Klaus, J., and Zagler, W. (eds.): 8th International Conference on Computers Helping People with Special Needs.* LNCS, Vol. **2398**, Springer, Berlin (2002) 686–691
4. Clark, J.: *Building Accessible Websites.* New Riders, Indianapolis (2002)
5. Deiss, R.: "E-commerce in Europe". In: *Statistics in focus, Theme 4*, Vol. **12**. Luxembourg (2002)
6. Economist: "Over 60 and overlooked: Marketing to the old". In: *The Economist (UK-edition)*, Vol. 364, No. **8285** (Aug 10th, 2002)
7. European Communities (ed.): "SMEs in Europe, including a first glance at EU Candidate Countries". In: *Observatory of European SMEs 2002*, No **2**. Belgium (2002).
8. European Commission (ed.): "SME Definition: Commission Recommendation of 06 May 2003 concerning the definition of micro, small and medium-sized enterprises". In: *Official Journal of the European Union (OJ)* **L124** (2003).
9. European Commission (ed.): "Flash Eurobarometer 135 'Internet and the public at large'", (2002). `<http://europa.eu.int/comm/public_opinion/flash/fl135_ en.pdf>`
10. European Commission, Eurostat (ed.): "Disability and social participation in Europe". Theme 3. Luxembourg (2001)
11. IBM: "Internet- und E-Business-Einsatz im bundesdeutschen Mittelstand 2003". (2003). `<http://www-5.ibm.com/de/mittelstand/download/ebi_praesentation.pdf>`
12. Icomedias and University of Graz: "Studie: Barrierefreies Internet in Österreich". Graz (2003). `<http://icomedias.com/cms/dokumente/10003397/7306dba5/studie_barrierefreiheit.pdf>`
13. Lenhart, A.: "The ever shifting internet population: A new look at Internet access and the digital divide". In: *PEW Internet & American Life Project.* Washington (2003). `<http://www.pewinternet.org/reports/toc.asp?Report=88>`
14. Ottens, M.: "Statistics on the information society in Europe". In: *Statistics in focus, Theme 4*, Vol. **38**. Luxembourg (2003)
15. Paciello, M. G.: *Web Accessibility for People With Disabilities.* CMP Books, Lawrence (2000)
16. Sandhu, J.: "Demography trends and issues". In: *Besson, R. (ed.): Proceedings of the 5th COST 219 Conference on Trends in technologies for disabled and elderly.* Gummerus printing, Jyväskylä (1995)
17. Sierkowski, B.: "Achieving web accessibility". In: *Proceedings of the 30th annual ACM SIGUCCS conference on User services.* ACM Press, Providence (2002) 288–291
18. Slatin, J. M., and Rush, S.: *Maximum Accessibility: Making Your Web Site More Usable for Everyone.* Addison-Wesley, Boston (2002)
19. Thatcher, J., Bohman, P., Burks, M., Henry, S., Regan, B., Swierenga, S., Urban, M., and Waddell, C.: *Constructing Accessible Web Sites.* Glasshaus, Birmingham (2002)
20. United Nations, Population Division, Department of Economic and Social Affairs (ed.): Population Ageing 2002. New York, USA (2002). `<http://www.un.org/esa/ population/publications/ageing/Graph.pdf>`
21. The Web Accessibility Initiative (WAI), W3C WAI Education and Outreach Working Group (EOWG): "Presenting the Case for Web Accessibility". `<http://www. w3.org/WAI/EO/Drafts/bcase/Overview.html>`

# The Use of Current Content Management Systems for Accessibility

Laura Burzagli, Marco Billi, Francesco Gabbanini, Paolo Graziani, and Enrico Palchetti

Italian National Research Council Institute for Applied Physics "Nello Carrara", Via Panciatichi, 64 50127 Firenze, Italy
{L.Burzagli,M.Billi,F.Gabbanini,P.Graziani,E.Palchetti}
@ifac.cnr.it
http://www.ifac.cnr.it

**Abstract.** Accessibility tries to avoid introducing in web pages any kind of barriers that might prevent their being understood by disabled users. Content Management Systems are a widespread class of products that enable the creation, archiving and publishing of information on web. This paper discusses how to relate accessibility with CMS, starting from some key functions of this family of products. This requires analysing some aspects which are sometimes very remote from a technological perspective, but closer and more related to the environment in which they are used. Many of them are suggested by experience, and need to be correctly reformulated in order to be included in the life cycle of a CMS.

## 1 Introduction: The Problem of Accessibility. Theory and Practice

"Accessibility" is a key characteristic for modern web pages. This characteristic tries to avoid the introduction in web pages of any kind of barriers that might prevent their being understood by disabled users. In recent years, many countries have introduced specific laws regarding the accessibility of electronic services.

In Italy, for example, a law called "Provisions to support the access to information technologies for the disabled" has been adopted since the beginning of this year.

The problem has just been faced by the international community, and several sets of guidelines have been created by W3C Web Accessibility Initiative [3]. The most important ones are entitled"Web Content Accessibility Guidelines 1.0, W3C Recommendation, 5 May 1999", generally referred to with the acronym WCAG 1.0.

These guidelines represent a basic aspect in the design of accessible web pages.

In principle, writing an accessible web page should involve adopting only the above cited guidelines when coding the page, using an appropriate language, such as HTML or XHTML. For instance, the guidelines specify that a number of redundant contents must be included, such as alternative text for images, and different and clear browsing paths have to be offered to users. This implies an in-depth knowledge of languages and of accessibility options. For example, if an author uses HTML 4, a set of tags and options is made available to follow this low level approach, so that the author can use these facilities when accessibility problems are to be considered during the design process of a page.

K. Miesenberger et al. (Eds.): ICCHP 2004, LNCS 3118, pp. 331–338, 2004.

Experience has shown that this particular application of accessibility principles is feasible only for web sites with a limited number of pages. In practice, when a company has to build and maintain a large web site, made up of hundreds of pages and the contents of which change dynamically over time, a different kind of approach has to be used. The adoption of particular instruments is necessary, such as Content Management System (CMS) that are able to support the creation, management and publishing of web information. Since CMS also include authoring tool functions, another set of guidelines published by WAI is eligible for considering and improving their accessibility: "Authoring Tool Accessibility Guidelines 1.0 W3C Recommendation 3 February 2000".

In the next section, an overview of CMS will be presented. Next, the relations between CMS and accessibility will be discussed, starting not from technical requirements, but from some key functions that are common to most CMS.

## 2 An Overview of Content Management System (CMS)

A Content Management System makes it possible to create, archive, search, control and publish information from within a flexible and integrated environment. A wide variety of implementations is offered for this kind of product, the technical characteristics of which are often very different, because they are developed for different market sectors [1,2].

By means of the use of a CMS, the process of creating web pages basically consists of manually entering their text or dynamically fitting their content into a preformatted page template that has a predetermined layout.

The CMS then takes care of every aspect related to a graphical presentation of information to users. This provides a non technical way of creating web pages: knowledge of HTML XHTML, or any other specific language, is not required, because, with a CMS, users will seldom (if ever) have to code pages directly. Furthermore, because a CMS automatically applies style and layout during publishing, another benefit is that pages are consistent across the site and have a uniform appearance.

Now, how does the process of publishing web pages using a CMS relate to accessibility?

Undoubtedly significant changes of perspective have to be adopted when facing the problem of accessibility for CMS-generated pages, and this is what we will try to clarify in the rest of this discussion.

## 3 CMS and Accessibility

Studying the relations between CMS and accessibility is not an easy task. Basically, at least two different approaches could be followed.

The aim of the one is to develop totally new products, redesigning them while having accessibility in mind, with a publishing engine that is capable of generating pages that fully conform to a given set of accessibility guidelines. Of course this is a difficult task and considerable efforts in terms of human and financial resources are required in order to develop a new product.

A less ambitious, but still very important, approach can be to study the process that current CMS available on the market follow for generating pages and highlighting the main points where possible difficulties related to accessibility could arise.

In this paper, we will mainly follow this second approach, i.e. the intelligent use of already existing CMS. However this will lead us to locate a few aspects that could possibly prove to be helpful during the design process of new-generation CMS.

This discussion will not focus on the different technical requirements of each product, but, starting from a specific experience carried out by the authors as Public Administration consultants, will try to identify certain key functions to be found in most products, and to analyze if and how the correct use of each of these functions can contribute to achieving accessibility in the final documents.

In other words, operating systems, databases, languages and hardware and software requirements will not be dealt with, because these are not directly involved in accessibility and, moreover, because a huge number of different CMS is available, all having their own technical characteristics and software/hardware requirements.

To begin the discussion on CMS and accessibility, it is useful to focus on the following four main functions of a CMS.

### 3.1 Content Creation

Content creation includes all the functionalities required by authors to produce contents using the CMS. For example, one of these functionalities could be the presence of an integrated authoring environment with, perhaps, an editor with a visual WYSIWYG interface.

This is a crucial point for accessibility, even if it is not the only one, as will be explained in the rest of the paper.

It must be clear that pages created with a visual editor will be accessible only if the translation process from visual to mark up, which is performed by the editor itself, complies with accessibility rules. Moreover, the editor must include the possibility of specifying all elements and attributes relevant to accessibility, in particular those related to alternative contents.

For example, when inserting an image, the editor must prompt or at least allow the user to insert alternative text, without having to edit the source code for the page. This is particularly important when the CMS stores page directly in a repository, because, once entered, page sources can no longer be edited.

Another common situation is when editors allow entering a page directly coding its source. An example of this situation may be experienced when using PostNuke CMS [2].

If the author is not an accessibility expert, s/he could unintentionally introduce accessibility barriers into the page.

To avoid this, an additional step is necessary before the page is actually published, i.e. validation of the page by means of a validation tool. This action avoids including accessibility barriers in an otherwise accessibly-designed site.

### 3.2 Content Management

In general, the content management phase does not directly concern accessibility, because its function is only to store previously-entered contents in a common repository.

However, it has been found that the integration process for documents coming from external systems is often included in this step.

When a web site with hundreds of page is designed and maintained, since the contents are generally distributed among several different systems, it may sometimes be necessary to import pre-existing documents into the site.

From the perspective of accessibility, it is important to consider that importing external documents without first checking them with validation software could possibly introduce potential sources of inaccessibility.

This happens, for example, when an external page includes an image without an alternative text or a link with a title that is anything but descriptive, such as "click here".

When the validation program returns a negative report, different strategies can be adopted. The first one is to let the program automatically repair the page, if technically possible.

Otherwise, users should be allowed to fix any accessibility problem reported by the validation program. Of course, this requires users to have a good knowledge of the markup language used to code pages and, also, of accessibility guidelines.

### 3.3 Publishing

During the publishing phase, the CMS takes the content stored in the repository and automatically generates the final pages.

The first key feature of the publishing step is the use of page templates.

Templates completely characterize the overall structure of a web page. It is important that they be designed according to accessibility requirements, because they will act as a common container for anything that was entered in the CMS during the content creation step. If a template does not meet accessibility requirements, any attempt at generating accessible documents will undoubtedly have no results.

If templates are well designed and the content creation process is strictly controlled for accessibility, the web site produced by the CMS is likely to meet excellent accessibility standards, and the problem of electronic barriers is solved, with good stability and reliability over time.

If templates contain sources of inaccessibility, users will meet barriers when browsing the page. For example, it is common to encounter templates structured so to convey contents in a succession of deeply-nested tables, a situation that is discouraged by accessibility guidelines.

In this case, accessibility problems arise from page structure rather than from the specific information that it contains. But, again, the result will be that electronic obstacles will prevent disabled users from accessing the page.

The publishing phase is also the time when page stylesheets are created to give the page its final graphical appearance. For example, they take care of colors, font families and font size, and, clearly, have an influence on accessibility.

It is then particularly important that templates and stylesheets be designed by a well-trained group of professional web designers (perhaps belonging to the company that produces the CMS), who have some knowledge in the field of accessibility.

The best thing would be to have an expert in accessibility among them, in order to also keep up with legal regulations that may well differ from country to country throughout the world.

This is also important because templates and stylesheets are not likely to change frequently over time, and CMS final users often have little or no control over them - even if the possibility of customizing at least stylesheets would be a great bonus for a CMS.

### 3.4 Documentation and Training

This phase includes various different aspects, such as training, documentation and maintenance. At first sight, they might seem (and often are considered) completely unrelated to accessibility, because the latter is considered to be connected only to technical and implementation issues.

As with any other software product, good training should clearly be offered by the producer in order to illustrate the various CMS features to users (in this case, content creators). This point is even more important if the CMS has to produce pages that conform to accessibility requirements.

In this case, the training process should include the fundamentals of accessibility, in order to properly educate content creators, especially if the CMS lets them enter pages directly code them in an appropriate markup language (see point 1). This does not mean that authors need to become experts, but only that the training process will clearly provide a few key principles of accessibility.

During this phase, different training paths should be set up by the CMS producer, who should customize them to match the different needs that each role may have. This concept will be clarified in section 5.

The same argument applies for documentation, which should contain a brief tutorial on how to design accessible web pages.

## 4 Evaluation and Repair Instruments

An important factor that should act as a guideline in choosing or designing an accessible CMS is the presence of an integrated evaluation and repair system.

Until now, complete and exhaustive automatic software to evaluate accessibility has not yet been engineered. However, very good results can be achieved with the correct use of special tools which are often offered as plug-ins in many web authoring tools. A complete list of evaluation and repair instruments can be found on the WAI web site at the following page: http://www.w3.org/WAI/ER/existingtools.html.

## 5 Roles

The previous discussion was focused on the general key features of a CMS, as a software product. Because a CMS is unquestionably a complex application, to completely examine and judge carefully all the CMS-related accessibility issues, one has to critically observe what roles are involved during the process of choosing, setting up and using a CMS.

It is useful to identify three roles: the customer, the contractor and the author.

1. The customer is usually the person who requests the development of a web site and defines the requirements of the final product.
2. The contractor, or the technological partner, is a person or a group of skilled persons with an adequate technical background, who design and implement the CMS.
3. The author is the person, or group, who introduces and updates information in the web site. This group could itself be divided into subgroups in which authors have different rights with respect to the introduction and editing of information.

Of course, this does not mean that it is always possible to identify three different persons or groups, but that it is possible to identify three different main roles.

This scheme is convenient, because CMS are not yet capable of automatically producing fully accessible web sites. It is important, therefore, to study what kind of knowledge regarding accessibility each role must have, and what kind of interaction it must have with the application in order to achieve the maximum level of accessibility from existing CMS.

### 5.1 Contractor

The first actor, i.e. the contractor, is mainly active during the first phase of product development. This is not a technical role and its main function is to decide what the accessibility requirements should be. It is thus the starting point of the entire accessibility process.

The contractor must be informed on the level of accessibility required for the product, and so must have an adequate knowledge of this field.

Moreover, in some important sectors, such as the Public Administration, the contractor must also follow a set of specific governmental regulations, and all the relevant information must then be included in the contract.

For example, in Italy, all Public Administration web sites have to comply with the Italian law about accessibility, and, thus, it is the contractor's legal responsibility to observe this law.

### 5.2 Technological Partner

In response to the contractor's request, the technological partner has the task of implementing a product with the appropriate requirements, or choosing and appropriately customizing an existing product.

A technological partner may be part of the same company as the contractor (if it is big enough and has the necessary skills), or from an external company.

In any case, this partner is characterised by the highest level of technical skills within the lifecycle of a CMS, because it is the responsible for translating the contractor's requirements in technical terms.

With respect to the content creation process, when a new CMS is designed, this partner must design and implement an editor to be used to enter contents in the CMS.

Otherwise, if an existing editor is adopted, it must clearly define how to use the built-in editor. In any case, this aspect, with regard to all the remarks in section 3.1 should be considered.

This partner should also define how the author has to interact with the editor, choose how much freedom to leave up to the author and, as a consequence of this, set up all the appropriate controls. For example, an author might be left free to edit the source code. In this case, however, a validator software must be included as a plug-in in the editing module (see section 4).

In the content management phase, the technological partner has to design the interaction appropriately with external documents (see section 3.2).

This partner then has to face the problem of setting up templates in the publishing phase (see section 3.3), by editing any existing ones or writing new ones from scratch.

This partner also has to train CMS users in accessibility, according to the strategies adopted during the development phase. He has to produce the appropriate documentation.

This does not mean that a complete knowledge of accessibility must be provided, but an exhaustive set of rules on how to use the CMS in order to get accessible web pages must be made available.

### 5.3 Author

An author is responsible for entering contents, and does not take part in the development of the CMS.

He must receive appropriate training in how to introduce and edit information, in order to use the CMS correctly.

As pointed out before, this only requires that an author be aware of an exhaustive set of rules on how to use the CMS in order to obtain accessible web pages.

## 6 Conclusions

To conclude, due to the complex nature of a CMS, dealing with accessibility requires analysing certain aspects that, at times, are very remote from a technological perspective, but are closer and more related to the environment in which they are used.

Many of them are suggested by experience, and have to be correctly reformulated in order to be included in the life cycle of a CMS.

Future developments might consist of giving a more accurate classification of functions and roles, taking into account both new real-world experiences and new products tested in the laboratory, but keeping in mind that the fundamental idea is to translate a set of very general guidelines into an actual context and real world practice.

By starting from the point of view that has been sketched in this discussion, it could also be possible to develop new conceptual solutions for a more correct and more effective use of CMS as regards accessibility.

## References

1. CMS Watch website, http://www.cmswatch.com
2. PostNuke website, http://www.postnuke.com
3. Robertson, J.: So, what is a content management system? StepTwo Designs, June 2003, http://www.steptwo.com.au/papers/kmc_what/index.html
4. W3C Web Accessibility Initiative (WAI), http://www.w3.org/wai

# Accessing Documents via Audio: An Extensible Transcoder for HTML to VoiceXML Conversion*

Narayan Annamalai, Gopal Gupta, and B. Prabhakaran

Department of Computer Science
University of Texas at Dallas
{narayan,gupta,praba}@utdallas.edu

**Abstract.** Increasing proliferation of hand-held devices as well as the need for delivering information to visually impaired persons have caused the need for transcoding web information into documents that can be delivered as audio. Web information is typically represented as HTML (Hyper Text Mark-up Language) documents. Audio delivery of web documents is done using VoiceXML. Due to this difference in mark-up notation, much of the web is inaccessible via audio. One way to solve this accessibility problem is to *automatically transcode* HTML documents to VoiceXML. In this paper, we describe such an automatic transcoder that converts HTML into VoiceXML. The transcoder is *compositional* and is realized in two phases: The parsing phase where the input HTML file is converted to HTML node tree, and the semantic mapping phase where each node in the HTML tree is *compositionally* mapped to its equivalent VoiceXML node. Our transcoder is extensible in the sense that: (i) it can be upgraded easily by users to accommodate modifications to and extensions of HTML; (ii) it provides means for the user to modify the translation logic while dealing with certain HTML tags. The translator is being publicly distributed.

## 1 Introduction

The World Wide Web (WWW) has seen tremendous growth in the recent years and has become the primary source of information all over the world. The major drawback of the existing web infrastructure is that it requires users to visually look at the information displayed. Thus it cannot be used in situations where constant visual attention of the user is required, e.g., while driving an automobile. In such situations, a good solution to interactively access documents on the web is through audio and voice.

VoiceXML [10] is a standard mark-up language created by the VoiceXML forum and the W3C consortium to make Internet content and information accessible via voice and audio. VoiceXML documents can be *aurally* browsed on a desktop computer with microphone and speakers or over the phone. Just as a

* Authors partially supported by grants from the National Science Foundation and the Department of Education.

K. Miesenberger et al. (Eds.): ICCHP 2004, LNCS 3118, pp. 339–346, 2004.

web browser renders HTML documents visually, a VoiceXML interpreter (or a voice browser) renders VoiceXML documents *aurally*.

One solution to this accessibility problem is to maintain different versions of the same web site that provides content: formatted in HTML for visual browsers and in VoiceXML for voice browsers. From the web server's perspective, maintaining two versions of the same web site is labor intensive and expensive. Thus the only effective option is to maintain the information in HTML format and develop an application that automatically converts an HTML document on the web to a VoiceXML document.

In this paper we report on the development of a *transcoder* that can automatically translate HTML documents to VoiceXML documents on the fly. The transcoder is extensible in that its behavior can be customized according to the user's preference. The user can influence the system's behavior via a user *interface sheet*. The user can also adapt the transcoder to handle new tags that may get added to HTML in the future.

The World Wide Web Consortium (W3C) has developed an official XML transformation language, XSLT (XSL Transformations) [1], for the purpose of facilitating transforming documents from one XML format to another. One could argue that XSLT would be the easy and natural choice for building HTML to VoiceXML transcoder. However, recent research [2, 3] has highlighted XSLT's drawbacks in handling the task of generic HTML to VoiceXML transcoding. These drawbacks include XSLT's poor syntax (XSLT programs are so verbose that they become unreadable, even for simple XMLs), lack of facilities for "nuts and bolts" programming [2], its poor interface with other languages, and the difficulty in transforming XSLT documents themselves.

## 2 Related Work

VoiceXML is a relatively recent phenomenon, and its popularity for aural navigation of the web has still not caught on (primarily due to the lack of the number of documents available in VoiceXML as well as the fact that it is still a new technology). Telecom companies, however, have widely adopted it and have developed numerous applications (especially for automated call handling) that make use of VoiceXML.

Currently, computer screens and the web are auralized through software applications called *screen readers*. *Screen readers* [4], such as *Jaws for Windows*, *Windoweyes*, and *Webspeak* [7], capture the text present in a web page and employ speech synthesis technologies to speak this information to the user. They only capture the plain text from HTML pages and ignore the structural information provided by the tags. Moreover screen readers do not provide the interactive features present in current HTML or VoiceXML pages. James [8] proposed a framework for designing audio interfaces to HTML documents termed *Auditory HTML access system* or the 'AHA'. However, his system is basically an improved screen reader.

Goose et al. [6] proposed an approach for converting HTML to VoXML. VoXML is very similar to VoiceXML and requires an audio browser that is capable of processing VoXML tags and reading out the information contained in VoXML marked-up web page. Since VoXML is a primitive language, current application vendors do not support VoXML or its tags.

Gupta et al. [5] have proposed an approach for translating HTML to VoiceXML. Their approach is based on denotational semantics and logic programming. Even though, the methodology is efficient, it handles only a subset of HTML tags. Our work can be considered as an extension of the approach outlined in [5]. Moreover the translator, developed for a small subset of HTML, is not extensible.

In the rest of this paper we give an overview of the transcoder and its implementation. A more detailed exposition can be found in [9].

## 3 System Model and Architecture

The transcoder has the following components: (i) the lexical scanner, (ii) the parser, (iii) the semantic mapper, and the (iv) interface sheet manger.

The transcoder developed by our approach has two phases: a parsing phase and a translation phase. In the first phase, the input HTML file is parsed and its HTML node tree (similar to a parse tree) obtained. In the second phase, this node tree is passed as input to the semantic translator, which runs a recursive translation algorithm and produces the corresponding VoiceXML file as output.

A prominent component of our transcoder is the *Interface sheet.* It is used as an instruction medium between the system and the user. The model of the Interface sheet is shown in Fig. 1

The Interface sheet is divided into two blocks: the component block and the the tag block. By providing instructions in the attributes and output text section, the user can instruct the system as to how to treat the corresponding components. That is, the user can specify the values of various VoiceXML and voice browser attributes such as the duration of silence (which indicates end of verbal input), duration of time allowed for speaking text that is recorded (similar to a text box in HTML), etc. In the tag block the user can (optionally) specify how certain tags are to be handled. The interface sheet is developed in such way as to allow the definitions for new tags that may get added to HTML in the future. Thus, when a new tag is added to HTML at a later date, the user simply has to include that tag in the interface sheet, and specify the corresponding VoiceXML action/tags. The transcoder will be subsequently able to translate HTML documents marked up with new tags.

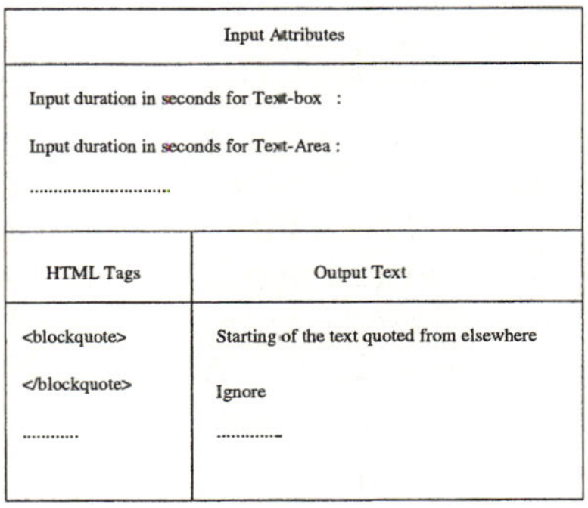


**Fig. 1.** Structure of Interface Sheet

The main component of the transcoder is the *HTML to VoiceXML core semantic converter.* This component contains the transformation logic that needs to be applied to each and every HTML tag. The core converter uses two tables for data storage, the internal data sheet and the external user interface sheet. The internal data sheet contains a list of HTML tags and the corresponding VoiceXML tags which involves complex transformation logic to be applied before obtaining the VoiceXML output. The data contained in this sheet is not provided for the interaction of users, thus these set of HTML tags gets transferred in a standard manner. The external user interface sheet contains HTML tags which are used for text display or appearance of the web-page, etc. These tags adds more value to the web-page only when they are viewed visually. These tags cannot be transferred to audio in a way that would make sense or improve document understanding.
Fig. 1 shows part of an interface sheet. It states that the <blockquote> in the input HTML file will be substituted with the audio comment "Starting of the phrase that is quoted from elsewhere". If the user wishes to change to some other statement, s/he simply has to update the sheet with that statement. The core converter produces VoiceXML statement for every HTML node by referring either to the internal data sheet or to the *external user interface sheet.*

The transcoder developed by our methodology is capable of converting any HTML file to corresponding VoiceXML file, however it has some limitations and restrictions.

- The input HTML file should be a well formed document, in the sense, every opening tag should have a corresponding closing tag. If a closing tag is missing, then the documents has to be preprocessed to automatically insert this missing closing tag (this is accomplished by another module available as freeware called HTML tidy).
- The input file should be error free (i.e., a file which can be viewed through a desktop browser without errors).
- The input file should not have any tags that are not defined in HTML 4.0. When HTML files are viewed through certain browsers, the browser inserts many special tags which may not be found in the HTML specification. However, these tags can be removed by performing some pre-processor operations on the input file. Alternatively, the corresponding VoiceXML actions/tags for such HTML tags should be added in the Interface sheet.

## 4 Transcoder Logic

### 4.1 Parsing Phase

In order to convert any file from one format to another, its syntactic structure has to be understood. The HTML file's structure should be captured by a node tree and then it has to be transfered by identifying the subtrees. The structure of an HTML file can be obtained by parsing the HTML file and obtaining the parse tree in an hierarchical node form. In our application, the HTML parsing is done with the help of wise-system's web-wise package. Web-wise is an HTML template parser which takes in an HTML file and outputs a HTML node tree. An node tree is a tree type data structure of 'HTML nodes'. Each node abstracts an HTML tag. Each of the nodes can have sub-tags and this goes on recursively. The basic structure of a HTML file would start with a root <html> tag having children <head> and <body>

## 4.2 Translation Phase

The second phase of the system does the actual translation. In the translation phase, the output of the parser – the input HTML file's node tree – is traversed in a "left to right depth-first manner" and the corresponding VoiceXML is produced for every visited node. The translation of HTML node to VoiceXML node is not straightforward because the structures of HTML and VoiceXML are entirely different. Browsing a web-page visually differs remarkably when compared to browsing in an audio-only environment. Thus even though a rich multimedia presentation of a web-page cannot be given, our method tries the best possible ways to make the user comfortable with the environment.

**Input HTML file**

```
<html>
  <head> <title> Example 1 </title></head>
  <body>
    <h1> Hello World </h1>
  </body>
</html>
```

**Java Node Tree created by the parser**

```
(htmlRoot = new RootNode())
 .addNode(new PageNode()
    .addNode(new HeadNode()
         .addNode(new TitleNode()
              .addNode(new StringNode().setHtmlData(''Exam
ple 1''))
         ) //end TitleNode
     ) //end HeadNode
     .addNode(new BodyNode()
         .addNode(new H1Node().setAlign(''center'')
              .addNode(new StringNode().setHtmlData(''Hell
llo World''))
         ) // end H1 Node
     ) //end BodyNode
 ) // end PageNode
; // end RootNode
return htmlRoot;
```

**Fig. 2.** HTML Parser - Example conversion

The root node of the input HTML node tree is passed to the translation processor. The translator performs the initial actions that need to be done for the particular HTML node. The initial action may involve producing a VoiceXML tag or setting/resetting of some flags etc. Then the first child of the node is obtained, and is passed to the transcoding processor recursively. If there are no more children nodes then this node is processed, and the final actions are performed. The final actions may be a set of similar actions as the initial action. Then the recursive invoking ends and the control is returned to the parent caller. If the root node does not have any children to process, then the final actions for the root node is performed and the final VoiceXML output file is obtained. Then this file is passed to a VoiceXML syntax checker. This may be any VoiceXML compiler like *tellme, heyanita*, etc. The resulting file is the syntax-free VoiceXML equivalent of the input HTML.

### 4.3 Translation Issues

There are a few basic issues that need to be addressed while converting a HTML file into a VoiceXML file. They are:

1. The transcoder assumes that every open tag (e.g., <form>) would have a corresponding close tag (e.g., </form>). This assumption is very crucial since we would set some flags on the occurrence of some of the open tags and similarly reset the same flags while encountering the close tag.
2. Interacting with a voice browser is not as simple as interacting with a visual browser. Let's assume a user is filling a form which contains many input fields. In the case of a visual browser, he/she can see all the fields at the same time. Thus he/she can check his/her inputs manually before submitting it to the server. But in the case of a voice browser, since the commands are spoken sequentially, it is very difficult to keep track or remember the already filled-in inputs. Thus it becomes necessary that the user's consent has to be obtained before submitting the input items.
3. Since VoiceXML is a derivative of XML, it inherits the nature of being highly structured. Thus, the position of every node or tag in VoiceXML is restricted by a set of possible parents and a set of possible children. So even though a VoiceXML node can be formed with correct syntax, the compiler may throw an error if the node's location (parent or child) is wrong. For example the VoiceXML statement
   ```
   <prompt> It is a beautiful city </prompt>
   ```
   is syntactically correct but the compiler will throw an error if it is used in the following manner
   ```
   <form> <prompt> It is a beautiful city </prompt> </form>
   ```
   The '<prompt>...</prompt>' can appear only within a field or a block, since it is not a child of the '<form>' element.
4. While translating HTML to VoiceXML, in most cases it may so happen that either one HTML tag has to be replaced by two VoiceXML tags or, two HTML tags will map to the same VoiceXML tag. Hence, the translator logic has to be designed in such a way that these features are realized.
   For example, '<h1>' has to be translated to '< prompt> <emp>', since '<prompt>' is for speaking and '<emp>' is for stressing the words.
5. Lastly, it is important to note that every VoiceXML input needs a valid grammar to cross-check against the provided input. In HTML, a text-box input can be defined to accept any text within a limited size, but that cannot be done using VoiceXML. Every input has to have a valid grammar.

### 4.4 Translator Logic

The Translator logic contains the methodology for converting all HTML tags into their VoiceXML counterparts. In this section, we discuss the manner in which some of the more complex HTML tags are handled.

**Form Tags:** form tags are the most important and most complex to deal with during translation. This complexity is due to the interactive feature it provides to the user. The HTML form tag contains the URL of the CGI (Common Gateway Interface) or the web-page to which the form elements have to be submitted and the 'method' used (GET or POST) for submission. The method basically specifies the type of encoding that needs to be used while sending the inputs. The VoiceXML form does not have these two attributes. Instead, it needs to have the *name* attribute since every form has to be identified with a unique name (the form name is used for transition between forms during navigation). In VoiceXML, the URL and 'method' for sending the inputs has to be used only with the 'submit' tag. When the <form> tag is encountered, the 'URL' and the 'method' (GET or POST) is stored in a separate global variable, to be used later along with the 'submit' tag, and a name is automatically generated for the form.

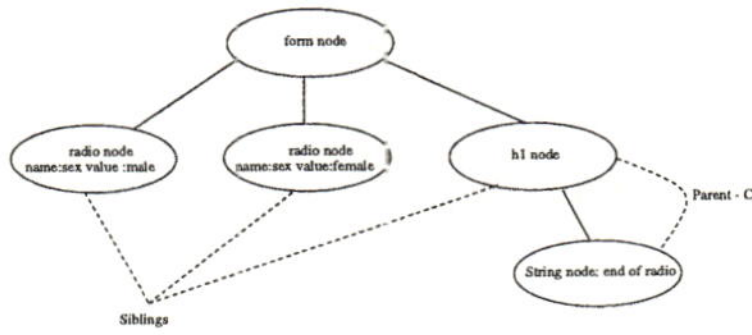


**Fig. 3.** Form Node: Radio Type

**Radio Button:** In HTML, radio buttons are used for providing the user with a list of options from which the user selects exactly one option. In HTML, the radio tags do not have a closing tag. This feature of the radio tag causes problems when it is translated to VoiceXML. Take the following example:

```
<INPUT type = radio name = ''sex'' value = ''male''> Male <br>
<INPUT type = radio name = ''sex'' value = ''female''> Female <br>
```

This creates two check-boxes with the value field besides them. When the user selects one of the check-boxes, the other becomes inactive. Thus only one value of the 'sex' item will be submitted finally. To obtain all these features in VoiceXML, the following logic is employed. When the first radio tag is encountered, the field tag is declared.

The name of this field and the value are stored in a separate structure. The user is also prompted about the presence of options and instructed to select one of the options. The options are read out one after another. Now, the challenge is to recognize the last radio tag of this type and close the field item. For this purpose, the next sibling (nodes in the same level in a tree and having the same parent) is obtained and checked to see whether it is a radio input type and, if so checked whether its of the same type. When it is not the same, the field item is closed.

## 5 Conclusion and Future Work

In this paper we reported on a transcoder that we have developed for translating HTML documents to VoiceXML for aural access. The distinct feature of the transcoder is that it is extensible. As the translation logic is designed with the help of internal data sheet and external user interface sheet, any tags added to HTML in the future can be added to one of the two data sheets, and the corresponding logic for that node can be given by the user. However, the HTML node included should not be a complex node which may require changes in the transcoding logic of other nodes. A trivial text display tag can be added easily to the external user interface sheet. For example in future if a tag "<scatter>" (e.g.,<scatter> text <scatter>) is added to the HTML specification, which displays the enclosed text in a scattered manner, then this tag can be included in our translation logic by adding it to the *external interface sheet.* Future work includes removing some of the current limitations of the browser, e.g., adapting it to more recent versions of HTML, and to XHTML.

## Acknowledgment

We are grateful to Arthur Karshmer of University of S. Florida for discussions and encouragement.

## References

1. World Wide Web Consortium, XSL Transformations (XSLT). Version 1.0 W3C Recommendation November 16, 1999 http://www.w3.org/TR/xslt
2. T. Moertel, 'XSLT, Perl, Haskell & a word on language design', Posted on kuro5hin.org on January 15, 2002. http://www.kuro5hin.org/story/2002/1/15/1562/95011.
3. O. Kiselyov and S. Krishnamurthi, 'SXSLT: Manipulation Language for XML', Proceddings of 5th International Symposium on Practical Aspects of Decalartive Languages (PADL 2003), New Orleans, LA, USA, January 2003, pp. 256-272.
4. W. Keith Edwards and Elizabeth D. Mynatt, "An architecture for transforming graphical interfaces", In *proceedings of the ACM: USIT, 1994*, pp. 39-47. ACM Press.
5. G. Gupta, O. El Khatib, M. F. Noamany, H. Guo, "Building the Tower of Babel: Converting XML Documents to VoiceXML for Accessibility", *Proceedings of the 7th International Conference on Computers helping people with special needs*, pp. 267 - 272, OCG Press (Austria).
6. Goose S, Newman M, Schmidt C and Hue L, "Enhancing web accessibility via the Vox Portal and a web-hosted dynamic HTML to VoxML converter", WWW9/Computer Networks, 33(1-6):583-592, 2000.
7. Hakkinen M, "Issues in Non-Visual Web Browser Design: pwWebSpeak", *Proceedings of the 6th International World Wide Web Conference*, pp. 287-288, June 2001.
8. James F, "Presenting HTML Structure in Audio: User Satisfaction with Audio Hypertext", *Proceedings of the International Conference on Auditory Display(ICAD)*, pp. 97-103, November 1997.
9. N. Annamalai, G. Gupta, B. Prabhakaran. An Extensible Transcoder for mapping HTML to VoiceXML. MS Thesis. 2001.
10. `http://www.voicexml.org/`

# Listener-Controlled Dynamic Navigation of VoiceXML Documents*

Hemambaradara Reddy, Narayan Annamalai, and Gopal Gupta

Department of Computer Science
University of Texas at Dallas

**Abstract.** The next frontier for research on the Web is to make it universally accessible, primarily via audio. Work in this direction includes the development of *voice browsers* and the design of *VoiceXML*, an XML-based standard for marking-up documents to be played on voice browsers. VoiceXML is interactive and allows voice input to be received and processed by a voice browser (i.e., VoiceXML documents can be aurally navigated). Unfortunately, this interaction is completely controlled by the author of the VoiceXML document. Coupled with the sequential nature of audio output, this results in a navigation process that is tedious and not under the listener's control. It also inhibits the development of more advanced applications that require aural navigation. In this paper we develop techniques that put aural navigation under the listener's control. We propose *voice anchors* that allow listeners to aurally tag specific points in the audio document for access via spoken commands later. We discuss a spectrum of techniques for realizing anchors and their implementation. We also introduce *voice-commanded scripting languages* for orally programming aural navigation strategies.

## 1 Introduction

The next frontier for research on the Web is to make it accessible via voice and audio, so that not only it becomes more accessible, it also becomes accessible through other media such as cell-phones, as well as at times when visual medium cannot be used. Considerable work has been done in this direction, which includes the design of VoiceXML [12] and *voice browsers*. VoiceXML is the HTML of the voice web, the open standard markup language for voice applications. Numerous commercial vendors such as IBM [11], TellMe [10] and BeVocal [5] provide voice browsers that can be used to "play" VoiceXML documents. These browsers can be accessed through a microphone and speakers of a computer (e.g., IBM Websphere), or through the phone (e.g., Tellme Studio). The association of these browsers to VoiceXML can be compared to the association of HTML to popular text browsers such as Netscape and Internet Explorer. Though HTML and VoiceXML have similarities such as obtaining user input through "forms",

* Authors are partially supported by grants from the US National Science Foundation, the Department of Education, and the Environmental Protection Agency.

K. Miesenberger et al. (Eds.): ICCHP 2004, LNCS 3118, pp. 347–354, 2004.

and providing dynamic execution of code through server-side CGI, there are a few prominent differences. The foremost of them is the ability of the visual medium to express multiple things at a given time compared to the deficiency of the audio medium to express voice data only sequentially. Thus, the audio data in VoiceXML documents needs to be categorized in modules, or what are called "forms", so that the forms can be played one after another. As a result, the "control of execution" gains utmost importance in VoiceXML documents. Forms are played one after another according to the directions provided by the "⟨goto next=" "⟩" element present at the end of each form. However, this flow of control between dialogs is determined by the writer of the VoiceXML page, and is fixed. This results in the listener having very little control over the document's navigation, resulting in tedium (e.g., if the writer decides that the user must listen to a long dialog, the user has no choice), as well as inhibiting the development of advanced applications of aural navigation.

In this paper, we develop the concept of *voice anchors* and describe techniques for implementing them. Voice anchors permit listeners to have greater interactive control during aural browsing, thus allowing complex interactions to take place through audio/voice. Our research is motivated by our desire to develop aural tools for interactive navigation of mathematical documents by visually impaired students. We started with translating MathML to VoiceXML to make MathML documents accessible through audio. However, we quickly encountered the limitation of current VoiceXML and its browsers in providing dynamic control of navigation to their users. This led us to device *voice anchors* and *voice-commanded scripting languages*. However, our techniques have wide applicability, since VoiceXML is now widely used in the industry for providing information residing in databases & the WEB via audio (e.g., over the phone).

Dynamically navigable VoiceXML will have a significant impact on ease of access to information. Many major airlines and corporations serve information on the phone using VoiceXML. However, these services are limited due to lack of listener-side control. A dynamically navigable and accessible VoiceXML will allow more complex applications. For instance, American Airlines currently provides gate arrival/departure information over the phone through VoiceXML. Given current limitations, anything beyond simply providing information will be too cumbersome for the user. With listener-controlled dynamic navigation, sophisticated VoiceXML applications can be developed. For instance, an audio-based virtual travel agent that allows users to interactively make reservations and book tickets can be built.

VoiceXML extended with voice anchors can be the de facto interface language for assistive technology applications for the blind and visually impaired. We conjecture that just as the visual WEB based on HTML/XML has become the standard interface for all applications that require a visual interface, the aural web based on VoiceXML will become the standard interface for applications that require audio/voice interaction [4]. We assume that the reader is familiar with VoiceXML and Common Gateway Interface (CGI). More details and background can be found in [8].

## 2 Limitations of VoiceXML

VoiceXML restricts the inputs from the listener to a set of predefined phrases called the grammar. This grammar is usually a simple list of words specified in the VoiceXML document. To provide navigation, the developer of the VoiceXML divides the document into a number of forms, gives a name to each, and then prompts the user (via menus) at the end of the document for the name of the form they wish to revisit. Thus, the flow of the VoiceXML document is always controlled by the page author. If the writer fails to anticipate the interaction scenario the listener desires then this interaction pattern is left unspecified in the document, depriving the listener of that particular interaction. These problems are exacerbated by the fact that, unlike visual navigation, aural navigation is necessarily linear in nature. Note that a *grammar* (really a list of words) in a VoiceXML document specifies all the words that the listener may possibly speak while giving the input. Any word spoken outside of this grammar will not be recognized. This is because current voice recognition technology cannot recognize an arbitrary utterance from an arbitrary user[1].

Most of the limitations of VoiceXML stem from this single fact. Figure 1 shows an example VoiceXML document. It contains forms named *chlorine* and *ether*, and another form at the end that allows the user to listen to the information on chlorine or ether again. The data contained in these forms are played by the voice browser one after another. The form *chlorine* is read in full; next, the control shifts to the form *ether* and its contents are read in full (the control has to be explicitly transferred, otherwise the voice-browser will exit the document). Finally, control is transferred to the last form where the user chooses what he wants to hear again. Information is read sequentially in a static manner, until an explicit `'goto'` is encountered, which the document writer includes to provide interactive control. However, there are several flaws in providing interaction in this way. For instance, if the listener chooses to hear information about chlorine, he will be forced to hear information about ether again. More complex control can be designed to avoid this, however, then the page becomes unnecessarily complex. Also, once the browser starts giving out the information on chlorine or ether, there is no way to interrupt it, one has to hear the entire chunk of information, which might be quite large.

```
<vxml>
  <form id = "chlorine">
    <prompt>
     ... information for chlorine ..
    </prompt>
    <goto next ="#ether"/>
  </form>

  <form id ="ether">
      <prompt>
      ... information about ether ...
      </prompt>
      <goto next =" #over"/>
  </form>
  <form id = "over">
   <field name = "choice">
   <grammar > chlorine | ether </grammar>
   <prompt>
   Do you want information for chlorine or ether
   </prompt>
   <filled>
   <if cond = "choice == 'chlorine'"/>
     <goto next = "#chlorine"/>
   <if cond = "choice == 'ether'"/>
     <goto next = "#ether"/>
   </filled>
   <noinput>
     <goto next = "#exit">
   </noinput>
   <nomatch>
     <prompt>
     Wrong input ; please say chlorine
      or ether
     </prompt>
   </nomatch>
  </form>
  <form id = "exit">
  </form>
</vxml>
```

**Fig. 1.** Basic VXML page

---

[1] Arbitrary, free-form utterances can be recognized only after considerable *training* of the software on a *particular* user.

## 3 Listener-Side Control

The focus of our work is to provide greater control to the listener while accessing VoiceXML documents so that users can navigate within a page with a greater degree of freedom. We present a spectrum of solutions and their implementation to improve VoiceXML's interaction. All the approaches follow two basic criteria: (i) The user should have the ability to interrupt or interact at any given time. (ii) The user should have means to hear exactly what they want and skip what they don't want.

A very simple way to provide the listener of a page somewhat more control is to permit them to utter certain pre-defined words (with pre-defined semantics) to move back and forth in the document. For example, uttering `'skip'` should move the control to the next dialog, while uttering `'back'` should move it to the previous one, etc. However, full-fledged dynamic navigation of VoiceXML can become possible only when the listener is granted freedom to *label* a portion of the document with an *audio identifier* of their choice and later return to that *labeled* portion by uttering the identifier. These audio identifiers, termed *voice anchors* by us, are similar to HTML anchors, though HTML anchors are placed by the page's author and not by the user. The various solutions to permit listener-controlled dynamic navigation of VoiceXML, that we discuss in this paper, use voice anchors as their basis.

Current VoiceXML design does not support such dynamic voice anchors or markers. Allowing user defined voice anchor will require supporting grammars in VoiceXML documents that are defined at runtime, i.e., at the time the document is served. It will also require modifications to VoiceXML browsers so that they will support such dynamic grammars. As mentioned earlier, current voice recognition technology cannot recognize an arbitrary utterance spoken by an arbitrary user and convert it to text. Current technology can only recognize arbitrary utterances, as long as the set of such utterances is fixed in advance, as is done in a VoiceXML grammar. Thus, arbitrary voice anchors cannot be supported, however, we outline a number of reasonable solutions to support voice anchors, given this limitation. Ideally, the voice browser should be modified to make these approaches work, however, by dynamically generating new VoiceXML documents through CGI programs called in VoiceXML pages we are able to implement our solutions without having to modify a voice browser. The following section describes various anchor based techniques for supporting listener control dynamic navigation.

Once anchors have been placed in the document, more sophisticated navigation strategies can be specified. This requires the design of voice-commanded scripting languages that are simple enough so that users can verbally state the navigation strategies, yet powerful enough that they serve the users' needs.

## 4 Overall System Architecture

All the above strategies have indeed been implemented in a system that we have designed. Figure 2 shows the overall architecture of our system.

The author of a VoiceXML page can use our system to automatically obtain an enhanced page with extra information added to facilitate dynamic navigation. The author will then post this enhanced page on their site instead of the original document. Alternatively, readers of VoiceXML documents, wishing to navigate them in a dynamic manner, will install our system as a *proxy server* on their computer (Fig. 2). All access to VoiceXML documents will now go through this proxy server, which will retrieve the specified VoiceXML page (that is at another site) and add the requisite code and appropriate CGIs to it. The user will then be able to dynamically navigate this modified page on his/her browser. Since all requests go through the proxy server, the whole process will be transparent to the user. Note that the CGIs invoked during dynamic navigation will reside on a server managed by us. There is no reason why the CGI code for dynamic navigation cannot be executed on the client side, and indeed our eventual goal is to build such functionality into a voice browser. In fact, we are currently beginning to implement such a voice browser that supports listener controlled dynamic navigation as described in this paper.

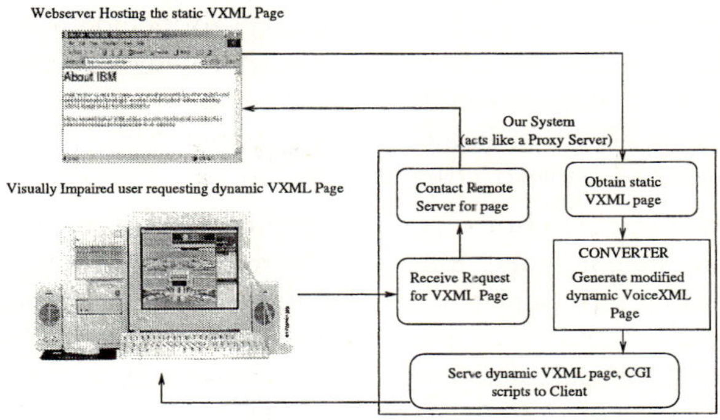


**Fig. 2.** Overall Architecture

We next describe the various anchor-based methods for supporting listener controlled dynamic navigation along with their implementation in more detail.

**Relative Direction Control:** In this approach, a VoiceXML document is extended to allow the user to control the relative direction of navigation, i.e., flow of execution can be controlled by the listener by speaking key words such as 'repeat', 'skip', 'back', 'begin' and `'stop'`, etc. However, a problem with this approach is that control can be shifted only to a restricted scope. The code for interactive control is automatically inserted by our system. Ideally, we would like all VoiceXML browsers to support the above builtin keywords.

**Predefined Anchor Names:** In the predefined anchor approach, each listener will be required to provide a file containing list of anchor names (s)he may use in advance. This list of labels will be used by our system for automatically transforming the VoiceXML page requested so that the words in the file will be recognized as voice anchors. One of the disadvantage to this is that the users may forget what labels they placed in this file. Another approach is to modify the document so that along with each dialog, a possible anchor name will also be read out that the user may select to label that dialog. However, the disadvantage is that navigation time is increased and the user may not be able to remember the label name.

**Domain Specific Grammar Approach:** This approach requires the designer of the document (or a third party) to include all possible words in a particular domain into the grammar for anchor names. Theoretically speaking, the anchor name grammar would be complete only if all the legitimate words in the English language are included in the grammar. Since this is impractical, the words are amassed by restricting the domain.

**Placing Anchors by Spelling:** In this approach the listener is required to *spell* the anchor name. Since each utterance is a letter, it can be easily recognized. The letters can be assembled into an anchor name, and the page appropriately transformed so that next time uttering the anchor name (as a full word) will result in control moving to that corresponding dialog. The most important aspect of this approach is that any name can be chosen for an anchor.

**Obtaining Anchor Inputs and Navigating:** The spelling of an anchor can be easily recognized by a simple grammar which has 26 letters of the alphabet and 10 digits. However, we use the facilities provided in VoiceXML to specify regular expressions since it results in a simpler implementation. These regular expressions can be implemented using one of the several languages designed for this purpose such as GSL (Grammar Specification Language), SRGS (Speech Recognition Grammar Specification) etc. Our system uses GSL to develop the *anchor name* grammar. The grammar is designed in such a way that it can accept alphabets sequentially up to to a finite length. Once the user stops speaking, the grammar concatenates all the alphabets or digits and returns a string as result. Recalling of anchor names can be done by speaking the full word. This is because we add the new anchor name to the grammar every time an anchor is created successfully. Two variables, namely, `'currentName'` and `'nextName'`, are introduced by our system in the beginning of the document when it augments a page for placing of voice anchors. These are declared as document level variables, meaning that their scope is global. These variables get their values updated when the control shifts to a new form. The triplet ⟨`anchorName, currentName, nextName`⟩ is sent to the CGI program in our server. The CGI script stores the triplet in the local memory of the server and generates new VoiceXML document preserving all the information (data, form information, etc.) from the parent document, and puts a new form at the beginning of the document indicating that the navigation should start from the form contained in the variable `'nextName'`. The next step is to allow the user to navigate to these anchors by supplying their names. This is accomplished by invoking the `'recallModule'` by uttering one of the grammar words to recall. The CGI queries the information it saved to find the corresponding form name for the anchor name. A new VoiceXML document is created just in the way described in the previous subsection and the name of the form to start from is provided at the beginning of the document.

**Dynamic Grammar:** The grammar used in our system is developed as a offline grammar and it is stored in the same place as the CGI scripts. Grammar is inserted automatically in a regular VoiceXML document by our system and accepts input spelled *character by character* or entire string at a time. The grammar accepts anchor names only through spelling. But every time the `'anchorModule'` is called, the CGI script appends the new anchor name to this grammar. So after an update, the grammar would be powerful enough to recognize a set of alphabets and numbers plus the newly added anchor name. As a result, the user can speak the anchor names as a whole word when they perform the recall.

**Cumulative Anchors:** The idea of anchors can be generalized to further facilitate navigation. The same anchor name can be associated with multiple forms, so that when that anchor is recalled, all the associated forms are read out. This generalization of anchors is easily implemented in our system by associating multiple form names with each anchor name, instead of associating just one. Cumulative markers thus allow sub-documents to be dynamically created during navigation of the document. Given a large document, one can use cumulative anchors to dynamically build a hierarchy of sub-documents. For example, all dialogs in a chapter that refer to a particular concept can be anchored with the same label. Recalling this label later will result in the sub-document consisting only of the labeled dialogs being read out by the browser.

### 4.1 Verbal Scripting Languages

We can view the VoiceXML document with anchors inserted as consisting of a collection of ⟨`anchor-name, form`⟩ pairs (i.e., a relation between an anchor name and its corresponding form). One can design *voice-commanded scripting languages* – which can be regarded as a query language over this relation – That are simple enough to permit users to pose the queries verbally yet powerful enough to allow them to program complex navigation strategies. For example, if a user wishes to hear the dialog labeled `'chlorine'` repeatedly, he can issue the command `'repeat chlorine until exit'`. Work is in progress to develop such languages.

## 5 Applications

VoiceXML with listener-side control for navigation has vast potential. It makes non-trivial applications of VoiceXML possible. We have applied our work to two major applications: (i)The Aural Web: To make the visual web aurally accessible, Web pages should be automatically translated into VoiceXML. which is dealt by using translators such as the one developed in [9] and the VoiceXML pages should be dynamically navigable by the listener which is dealt with via anchors. Work is in progress to develop such an *aural web.* (ii)MathML is rapidly becoming the mark-up language of choice for Mathematical documents on the WEB. Thus, a simple way of making mathematics accessible to the visually impaired is by translating MathML documents to VoiceXML. However, the static navigational nature of VoiceXML is still in impediment. These impediments can be overcome by using techniques described in this paper. We are currently developing a tool which translates MathML documents into VoiceXML using XSL style sheets. During this translation, different VoiceXML forms are associated with various subexpressions which can then be labeled with voice anchors. The generated VoiceXML document can then be dynamically navigated.

## 6 Conclusions

In this paper we presented the shortcomings of VoiceXML that prevent listeners from having complete control over navigation of audio-based documents. We discussed the possible approaches to overcome these shortcomings. We developed the concept of a *voice-anchor*, namely, audio labels that a user can associate with forms of a VoiceXML document. The user can then access these labeled forms at will by simply recalling the anchor name. The implementation of voice anchoring as well as the working and architecture of the approach adopted to obtain truly dynamically navigable VoiceXML documents was discussed. We also proposed the idea of verbally-commanded scripting languages for orally programming complex navigational strategies. The ideas proposed in this paper are quite novel. The only other work we are aware of is the work on voice-marking by Ramakrishnan et al at SUNY Stony Brook. Voice-marks are audio counterparts of HTML book-marks, and have inspired our work on voice anchors. Voice anchors can be thought of as a generalization of voice-marks. To the best of our knowledge, we are not aware of any other efforts similar to ours. This is perhaps because VoiceXML itself is quite a new technology. There are however, other efforts to provide interactive audio navigation [1–3], however, these are not based on VoiceXML.

**Acknowledgment**

We are grateful to I.V. Ramakrishnan of SUNY at Stony Brook, A. Karshmer of University of S. Florida, and D. Gopal of Logical Software Solutions for discussions.

## References

1. T.V. Raman. Audio System for Technical Readings. Ph.D. Dissertation, Cornell University, 1994.
2. A. Karshmer, G. Gupta, D. Gillan. Architecting an Auditory Browser for Navigating Math Expression. in *ICCHP* 2002. Springer LNCS 2398. pp. 477-486.
3. E. Pontelli, A. Karshmer, G. Gupta, D. Gillan, E. Saad, W. Xiong. Intelligent Non-Visual Navigation of Complex HTML Structures. *International Journal of Universal Access in the Information Society* 2(1):56-69.
4. G. Gupta, Building the Tower of Babel: Converting XML to VoiceXML for Accessibility. Proc. 7th ICCHP00. OCG Press (Austria). pp. 267-272.
5. Bevocal, Inc. http://www.bevocal.com
6. http://eplannews.utdallas.edu/eplan.pdf
7. http://java.sun.com/products/java-media/speech/forDevelopers/JSGF/
8. N. Annamalai, H. Reddy. G. Gupta. Listener-controlled Dynamic Navigation of VoiceXML. UTD Internal Report.
9. N. Annamalai, G. Gupta, B. Prabhakaran. An Extensible Transcoder for mapping HTML to VoiceXML. UTD Technical Report. 2003.
10. Tell Me Studio Voice Solutions http://studio.tellme.com
11. IBM Websphere. ttp://www-3.ibm.com/software/webservers/
12. http://www.voicexml.org/

# Toward User-Centered, Scenario-Based Planning and Evaluation Tools

Paul Bohman and Shane Anderson

WebAIM, Center for Persons with Disabilities, Utah State University,
6807 Old Main Hill, Logan, UT 84322, USA

**Abstract.** Existing Web accessibility evaluation tools are only capable of providing feedback within the context of individual Web pages. This short-sighted approach produces a fractured and fragmentary assessment of the accessibility of the Web site as a whole. A more effective, holistic alternative is to focus on scenarios of user interactions across Web pages, taking into account user characteristics, and focusing on models and patterns.

## 1 Introduction

There are many tools now available to assist Web developers in the process of making their Web content accessible. Though there often seem to be substantial differences between these tools, their functionality is generally limited to two basic purposes: reporting and repairing. Nearly all tools generate some type of report. Some tools also offer repair functionalities, either outside of or within the authoring environment. Both the report and repair functions can be valuable parts of the development process, but the emphasis with both of these functions is on the process of fixing existing code. The approach is reactionary rather than proactive. The end result is that not enough attention is given to the process of planning for accessibility up front.

This paper discusses a framework from which Web accessibility planning and evaluation tools can be developed. This framework can be used to develop anything from a heuristic-based mental checklist to a full-fledged software program with built-in algorithms that customize the planning process based on user input. Throughout all of this, the key is to ground these tools in scenarios, and to center these scenarios in the user experience.

## 2 The Totality of the User Experience

All people experience Web content differently because all users are different. Every individual has a unique set of skills, background knowledge, interests, motivations, and physical abilities. People with disabilities have unique characteristics and methods of accessing Web content that set them apart from other users. In fact, the variability between disability types and even within disability types is also quite pronounced. It is impossible to account for every kind of person with a disability under

K. Miesenberger et al. (Eds.): ICCHP 2004, LNCS 3118, pp. 355–360, 2004.

every type of circumstance, but it is possible to recognize and categorize trends and patterns in the way that people with disabilities experience Web content.

These usage patterns are not limited to patterns within one Web page at a time. People with disabilities, not unlike other users, often navigate through many pages in a Web site and even across different Web sites during a single session. Despite the obviousness of this statement, there are currently no tools for Web accessibility that take this into account. All of the tools currently available focus on analyzing one Web page at a time. These tools look for technical errors, or violations of technical standards, but they do not provide a wider view of the Web site as a whole, or of the user experience as a whole. The result is that the tools give a fragmented picture of the accessibility of a Web site. This fragmentation obfuscates the totality of the user experience, and can cause developers to overlook important accessibility barriers.

### 2.1 Shifting the Focus to Usability

By analyzing the needs, abilities, constraints, and usage patterns of people with disabilities across an entire Web site, it is possible to shift the focus of developers from a "compliance" mentality to a more beneficial focus on the usability of the end product. This kind of shift of focus has been evident in the way that the World Wide Web Consortium (W3C) has approached version 2.0 of its Web Content Accessibility Guidelines (WCAG) [1]. Whereas WCAG 1.0 [2] presented developers with a list of do's and don'ts mostly within the technology of HTML, WCAG 2.0 takes a more holistic approach that spans current and future technologies, with the goal of providing broadly applicable principles, rather than isolated techniques. In the current working draft of WCAG 2.0, there are four broad principles under which all of the more specific guidelines and techniques are subsumed. These principles advocate that content should be:

- Perceivable – the user should be able to "get at" the content.
- Operable – interface elements must be usable.
- Understandable – the content must be organized and presented in a way that makes sense to the user.
- Robust – the content can be used with current and future technologies.

These principles can be applied to single Web pages, but their real power is in their applicability across the Web site as a whole. In broad terms, if only most of the site is designed with accessibility in mind, then people with disabilities will be able to access only most of the site. If key sections of the site are not operable by keyboard, or if these sections are operable but not readily understandable, or if the core principles of WCAG 2.0 are somehow violated, then the overall experience of some users will be unfavorable. They might not be able to do what they wanted to do on the site at all. They will not be able to buy the book they were hoping to buy, or to find the information that they needed to find, or to sign up for the class that they needed to take. Whatever the user's purpose for going to the site, it is the overall scenario – the user's goals, the user's actions, the user's physical constraints – that must be examined in their entirety, otherwise the usability of the site may suffer.

## 2.2 User Characteristics and Constraints

Types of users must also be considered. Characteristics such as age, gender, interest, and disability type are integral to the planning process. Within disability types are a few major categories:

- Visual disabilities (blindness, low vision, color blindness)
- Deafness
- Motor disabilities (slow movement, inability to use a mouse, etc.)
- Cognitive disabilities (reading disorders, attention deficit disorders, etc.)
- Seizure disorders

Each of these types of disabilities affects a person's ability to access Web content in specific ways. For example, a blind person using a screen reader will need alternative text for all non-text content, keyboard access to all functionality, logical linear progression through the page and through the site, etc. It is beyond the scope of this paper to detail all of the specific needs of these disability types, but one point that must be emphasized is that each disability type must be considered within each scenario of Web site functionality. People with the different types of disabilities must be able to proceed through the entirety of the scenarios without obstacles. Ideally, the Web site would also be optimized to make the site not only accessible in a technical sense, but usable in a human sense. User-centered, scenario-based planning makes this possible.

## 2.3 Identifying Patterns in the User Experience

Patterns are important whenever users interact with data. An example of a usability pattern is the "warning" pattern. This pattern occurs when the user is about to perform an irreversible action – whether on purpose or accidentally, and whether the user understands the consequence of that action or not. To protect the user, the solution is to warn the user that the action is irreversible, and then provide the user with the choice to either proceed or cancel the action. This simple feedback can help prevent accidents or misunderstandings.

The concept of identifying patterns in the user experience is hardly a new one. The architect Christopher Alexander applied this approach to the design of buildings in a physical space [3]. Software engineers soon recognized the value in applying this kind of approach to the design of virtual environments. Trygve Reenskaug and others developed the influential Model View Controller (MVC) pattern language while working on SmallTalk-80 at Xerox PARC during the 1970s [4; 5; 6]. Though the idea is not new, it has not yet been fully applied to the realm of accessible Web design.

There are many attempts at creating pattern languages, but the simplicity of MVC allows for a basic discussion of the important ideas without losing sight of their relevance to Web accessibility. The Model View Controller pattern addresses the problem of separating hardware and software into three main areas of functionality. First is the *data model*. Data must have a structure for the computer to work with. Next is the *view*. This label is a bit of a misnomer, especially in the context of disability issues, but the term refers to data as the user perceives it, whether visually on a computer monitor, aurally (by listening) through synthesized voice output, or haptically (by touch) through a refreshable Braille device. What the user perceives and what the computer perceives are oftentimes very different. The last item is the *controller*. The controller manages changes to the data model. Controllers reflect the user's manipulation of the data via input devices such as mouse and trackball devices, keyboards, eye tracking systems, Braille devices, voice recognition software, and so on. By expanding the definition of "view" and "controller" to include a variety of output and input modalities, designers will be able to incorporate these scenarios, or use cases into their thought processes and later into their designs.

## 3 Scenario-Based Planning and Evaluating

Scenario-based planning and evaluation considers the way that different kinds of users will interact with the system as a whole, rather than focusing on single Web pages at a time. The user must be able to start a task, perform all of the necessary intermediary functions, and finish a task. For example, users of an online retail site must be able to search for items, select items, review the selections, enter purchase information, confirm the purchase details, and then submit the purchase. That would be the most fundamental scenario to consider. Other scenarios include checking on order status, submitting site feedback, redeeming virtual coupons, appending orders, submitting product reviews, changing contact information and preferences, etc. The actual scenarios will vary depending on the functionality offered by the site, but the example serves to show that there are several types of possible scenarios for any one site, and many of these scenarios involve several steps. The accessibility of the site must be determined in the context of being able to access every step of the scenarios. Page-by-page analyses, though useful in some ways, shift the focus away from the larger scenario, thus endangering the accessibility of the overall user experience.

Even sites that do not offer advanced user interactivity must consider user scenarios. For instance, a news site must consider the various types of information that users will be searching for. Some users will only want to skim the headlines. This is one scenario. Other users will seek out specific types of news stories, such as technology news stories, entertainment news stories, or political news stories. These scenarios are a bit more complex. Users must be able to find the general category (e.g. politics), select the category, browse the headlines within the category, and read the specific stories that interest the user. Sometimes users will want to access archived news stories. A search scenario must be considered. These and other scenarios must be planned out in advance.

Scenario-base planning includes the use of patterns both on the behind-the-scenes programming side as well as on the interface and design side of Web development. Scenarios provide the larger context for patterns. Patterns alone only address small sections of scenarios. For example, in an e-commerce scenario, the "warning" pattern could be used would be when the user wants to cancel a purchase or when the user is about to submit final payment (e.g. "look over your order and make sure that everything is correct").

### 3.1 User-Based Scenarios within Tools

Within each broad scenario, it is necessary to consider the characteristics of different types of users with disabilities. Using the "warning" pattern again as an example, not all users will benefit from the same type of warning. A deaf user will not benefit from an audible error "buzzer." A blind user will not benefit from an error graphic (unless it has appropriate alternative text). A person with slow muscle movements may not benefit from an error message that requires the user to react within a set amount of time, especially if that amount of time is brief.

The pattern characteristics of most of these user types are at least somewhat predictable, in the sense that developers can anticipate the appropriate sensory modalities, and/or physical constraints of the different categories of disabilities. These characteristics can be programmed into planning and evaluation tools so that the tools can navigate the Web site in ways that replicate both the scenarios and the users' characteristics. In essence, the tools can walk through the site, performing the same functions that real users would perform, and then evaluate the accessibility and usability of each of the steps along the way, from the perspective of users with disabilities. The tools can follow multiple paths within each disability type. For example, in an e-commerce scenario, the tool could:

- Follow an error-free path of selecting the merchandise and proceeding through all of the steps necessary to purchase it
- Enter in mistakes along the way, such as a faulty email address, or incorrect password
- Empty the shopping cart then add more items to it
- Return to shopping several times after entering multiple items into the shopping cart
- Etc.

The tool might be able to recognize and execute some of these patterns automatically, with built-in algorithms that recognize common scenarios in e-commerce situations. The tool could even be designed to "learn" such patterns based upon parameters that the tool users set over time. Where such pattern recognition is not possible, the tool could still be instructed to perform a set of pre-planned actions within a Web site, as defined by the tool users.

### 3.2 Tools for Different Types of Developers

Variations on this basic idea allow for the creation of a conceptual planning tool that anticipates potential problems before any code or HTML is written at all. Planning tools of this nature could be designed for different types of audiences. Programmers could benefit from a tool that worked and acted like a Unified Modeling Language (UML) environment [7]. Designers could benefit from strictly conceptual tool that worked somewhat like an interactive flowchart or even a paper prototype process [8].

## 4 Final Thoughts

It is not enough to say that a Web page passes an accessibility evaluation tool. People with disabilities are not interested in accessibility on a page-by-page basis. They are interested in the accessibility of their entire interaction. People go to Web sites with some sort of purpose in mind. This purpose is what constitutes the scenario. Users of different kinds, with different types of disabilities will likely engage in the same overall types of interactions, or scenarios, so the characteristics of these users must be taken into account. This sort of user-centered, scenario-based planning and evaluation is the key to ensuring that the entirety of the user's experience is taken into account when considering accessibility and usability.

Though they don't exist yet, tools can be created to take advantage of patterns in these scenarios and user characteristics. These tools can be used to plan user interactions that are both usable and accessible. They can also be used to evaluate existing Web content. Only when tool developers concentrate on the user experience as a whole – rather than on individual pages at a time – will these tools reach the level of maturity required to truly transform the Web into an accessible and usable experience for the broadest range of users.

## References

1. W3C: Web Content Accessibility Guidelines 2.0, `http://www.w3.org/WAI/GL/WCAG20/`, W3C internal Working Draft, 14 February 2004, accessed 14 April 2004 (2004)
2. W3C: Web Content Accessibility Guidelines 1.0, `http://www.w3.org/TR/WCAG10/`, accessed 14 April 2004 (1999)
3. Alexander, C., et al.: A Pattern Language. Oxford University Press, New York, (1979)
4. Reenskag, T. M., H.P.: Thing-Model-View-Editor—An Example from a Planning System. Technical note, Xerox PARC, (May 1979)
5. Reenskag, T. M. H.: The Model-View Controller (MVC), Its Past and Present. Paper presented at JavaZone 2003, Oslo, Norway (2003)
6. Buschmann, F.: Pattern-Oriented Software Architecture. Volume 1: A System of Patterns. John Wiley and Sons, Inc., New York, NY (1996)
7. Object Management Group: Unified Modeling Language, version 2.0, `http://www.omg.org/mda/`, accessed April 2004
8. Snyder, C.: Paper Prototyping: The Fast and Easy Way to Design and Refine User Interfaces. Morgan Kaufmann, San Francisco, CA (2003).

# Discovering Structure of Web Pages for Non-visual Navigation: Binding Text to Forms

E. Pontelli and R. Reddy

Dept. Computer Science
New Mexico State University
{epontell,rreddy}@cs.nmsu.edu

## 1 Preliminaries

In recent years we have witnessed an increased effort towards the development of tools and methodologies based on information technology aimed at reducing the communication divide between sighted and blind individuals. In particular, considerable effort has been invested in tackling the complex issue of automatically or semi-automatically providing alternative access modalities to the Web to fit the needs of users with different backgrounds, learning styles, abilities and disabilities. In particular, our focus is on providing access modalities to the Web that are more effective for individuals with severe visual impairment. The existing literature [2, 1] has identified accessibility of tables and use of on-line forms as two of the most challenging problems in this context – since the understanding of tables and forms is directly dependent on knowledge of the spatial layout of the components of the structure, which in turn is an inherently "visual" feature.

In our previous work [5] we presented a framework which makes use of an explicit encoding of the navigational semantics of a Web page; the encoding captures the components of the document, along with the relationships between such components implied by the spatial layout of the document. The explicit representation is then used to assist the user in navigating the document – either offering a roadmap through the document components or offering a formal encoding of the document for reasoning and automated answering of user queries. In particular, in our previous work we explored a successful methodology to automatically recognize the structure of HTML tables, using a combination of syntactic analysis algorithms and machine learning methodologies [5]. In this paper we present a promising methodology to approach the problem of automatically recognizing the structure of HTML forms.

## 2 Problem Description: Understanding HTML Forms

A recognized problem in automatically synthesizing the abstract structure of an HTML document arises from the difficulty of understanding the organization of HTML forms. HTML forms may contain a number of different active components (e.g., textboxes, radio buttons, pull-down menus), each requiring a different presentation methodology. Although it is fairly easy to identify the

K. Miesenberger et al. (Eds.): ICCHP 2004, LNCS 3118, pp. 361–368, 2004.

type of each form component, its direct presentation would be useless without associating the appropriate description of the component – e.g., indicating to the user the presence of a textbox does not make any sense unless we can provide a description of what kind of text is expected in such box. The majority of the forms provide a description of each form's component as English text, spatially located "close" to the component itself. Unfortunately, most existing Web pages do not create explicit connections between active elements and their description (e.g., via the < *label* > element), relying exclusively on spatial location of text elements and form elements. Frequently, the spatial layout is achieved through a complex nesting of forms and tables. These elements make it hard to provide a meaningful aural presentation of forms.

In this paper we describe a novel approach, based on Machine Learning technology (specifically, Inductive Logic Programming and Hidden Markov Models) to the problem of recognizing the structure of HTML forms. The approach is based on the explicit identification of the bindings between text elements and the corresponding form components. Successful recognition of such bindings allows us to extend our explicit representation of document structure (for non-visual presentation) to encompass HTML forms. To the best of our knowledge, no other aural browser provides this sophisticated level of understanding of forms.

## 3 A Machine Learning Approach

In this project, we adopt two different machine learning methodologies to solve the forms binding problem. The first methodology relies on the use of the Progol [4] system, an Inductive Logic programming system, while the second approach relies on algorithms for the construction of Hidden Markov Models. We demonstrate the use of these two methods as effective approaches to bind text and controls in HTML forms. Once trained with sufficient background knowledge and examples, Progol and Hidden Markov Models successfully combine text and controls present in an arbitrary form. The binding of text to a control makes the form navigation easy for a visually impaired user. This report provides an overview of Progol and Hidden Markov Models, followed by an explanation of their applications and the results.

### 3.1 Overview of Inductive Logic Programming and Progol

Progol is a machine learning system based on the formalism of Inductive Logic Programming (ILP). An ILP system develops a declarative knowledge to produce a general rule from a given training set of examples and from some background knowledge. Progol requires the background knowledge and examples to be presented in the form of logical assertions (i.e., Prolog facts and rules). The output, which is a generalized rule that explains the examples in the training set, is also expressed in Prolog syntax. The user must specify the intended structure of the general rule, i.e., the structure of its head and body. This information is given to the system in the form of mode declarations. Mode declarations restrict the predicates which can occur in the generalized rule [6].

There are two types of mode declarations: Header mode declarations restrict the structure of the head in the generalized rule by specifying what predicates can occur in the head; Body mode declarations specify what predicates can occur in the body of the generalized rule.

Progol constructs the generalized rule as follows. It determines the most specific clause that explains the first available example. It then combines the predicates in the most specific clause to make new clauses. Each of these new clauses is tested against the given examples to determine how many they explain. The clause which explains the majority of the examples is declared as the generalized rule [6].

### 3.2 Hidden Markov Models (HMM)

A Hidden Markov Model is a finite set of states, where each state is associated with a probability distribution. State transitions are governed by transition probabilities and the outcome at a particular state depends on the associated probability distribution. In a Hidden Markov model, the state sequence that produces a sequence is hidden, and hence the name. Different state sequences can produce the same sequence of symbols. Even though the state sequence is hidden, it is possible to calculate the probability of states using emission and transition probabilities.

In a HMM, a transition probability is represented as $a_{s,t}$, which is the probability of switching from state 's' to state 't'. The *emission probability*, i.e., the probability of producing symbol $x_i$ when in state $p$, is denoted by $e_p(x_i)$. The joint probability of an observed sequence $x = x_1, \ldots, x_m$ observed on a path $\pi$ can be written as,

$$P(x, \pi) = \prod_{i=1}^{m} (a_{\pi_i, \pi_{i+1}}) \times \prod_{i=1}^{m} (e_{\pi_i}(x_i))$$

Two algorithms can be used to train the HMM, called the forward and backward algorithms [7]. Since the state sequence is hidden, it is not possible to determine the exact state path for a given sequence but we can calculate the most probable state path using the "Viterbi" algorithm [7].

### 3.3 Overview of HTML Forms

HTML forms are used to obtain information from user. A form consists of controls (text field, radio buttons, check boxes etc.) and text explaining the controls. The majority of today's Web pages use HTML tables to format forms. A table can be used in two different ways to format a form. The following structures show the two methods.

- A table is completely inside a form

```
<form> <table> form elements </table> </form>
```

- A form is completely inside a table cell

```
<td> <form> form elements </form> </td>
```

In this project we allow both types of HTML forms.

# 4 Binding Text and Control in Forms: An ILP Approach

The objective is to obtain the most general rule describing how to combine text descriptions and form controls. There are two preliminary steps required before we can use Progol to learn about text and controls in HTML forms. The first step is to transform HTML forms into logical statements (facts). The second step involves providing some basic rules to express the general properties of each element in forms.

## 4.1 Preparing Background Knowledge

*Step1: Transforming a form into Logical Statements (Facts):* A form in HTML is transformed into a set of facts in Prolog, where each fact represents an element in the form. The properties and information about each element are given as arguments to the facts. The prototype of the fact is as follows,

`cell(form_name, tableno, element_type, element_number, rowno, colno)`

Each form in a web page has a unique name and `form_name` provides this name. Table number (`tableno`) is provided because a form can consists of multiple tables. `Element_type` can be either `control` (text field, radio button, check box etc.) or `text`. A serial number is assigned to each element in the form and `element_number` provides this number. `Rowno` and `colno` provide the row and column number of the cell in which the form element is present. The facts are used in the training process to bind text and control present in the form.

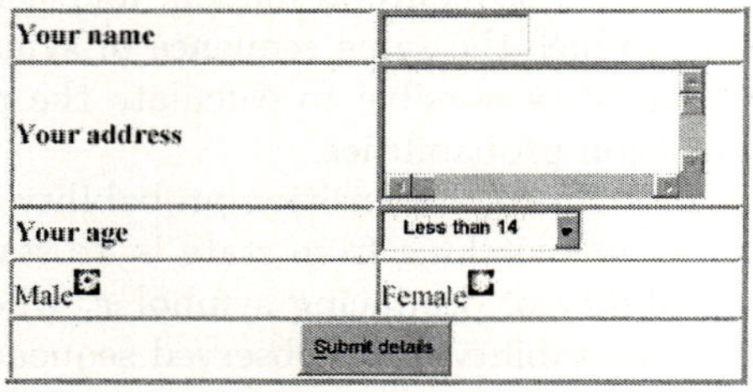


**Fig. 1.** Sample Form

For example, the form in Figure 1 produces the collection of facts listed below:

cell(userdetails, table1, text, 1, 1, 1). cell(userdetails, table1, control, 2, 1, 2).
cell(userdetails, table1, text, 3, 2, 1). cell(userdetails, table1, control, 4, 2, 2).
cell(userdetails, table1, text, 5, 3, 1). cell(userdetails, table1, control, 6, 3, 2).
cell(userdetails, table1, text, 7, 4, 1). cell(userdetails, table1, control, 8, 4, 1).
cell(userdetails, table1, text, 9, 4, 2). cell(userdetails, table1, control, 10, 4, 2).
cell(userdetails, table1, text, 11, 5, 1).

*Step 2: Providing Background Rules:* Progol needs to determine the properties of the individual form elements in the training process. Hence, Progol is provided with some rules to determine the properties and attributes of form elements such as order, positioning etc. The following is an example,

```
nextelement(Form, E1, E2) :-
          cell(Form, Table, _, element1, R, C),
          cell(Form, Table, _, element2, R, C), E3 is (E1+1),  E2 = E3.
```

The facts produced in the first step combined with the rules about element properties in the second step comprise the background knowledge for the application. With this background knowledge and some positive examples, Progol is trained to combine text with controls present in HTML forms.

### 4.2 Training the System

About 20 forms, each having unique structure in terms of number of tables present and placement of controls and text, are selected to train the system. To provide examples, text and controls present in these forms are combined manually. All these combinations are presented as positive examples. For example, the following facts are positive examples for the form given in previous section.

```
controltext(useddetails, 1, 2).  controltext(useddetails, 3, 4).
controltext(useddetails, 5, 6).  controltext(useddetails, 7, 8).
controltext(useddetails, 9, 10).
```

The system is trained with these positive examples and the background knowledge. The trained system is then tested with new forms to estimate the performance. The next section presents the results.

### 4.3 Experimental Results

Every control in the form has a text explaining the control. A control and its corresponding text are considered to be a valid pair. Given a training set, Progol is used to detect such valid pairs in the forms. Fig. 2 lists the details of testing a collection of new forms against the trained system. The benchmark forms have been drawn from a variety of sources, independently from the forms in the training set and in such a way to cover a wide variety of different form structures. The accuracy results, in terms of percentage of correctly identified bindings between text and control, are summarized in Fig. 3.

| S.No | Form Name | No of Pairs | Pairs detected |
|---|---|---|---|
| 1 | IndiaTimes | 3 | 3 |
| 2 | Dev | 43 | 40 |
| 3 | Poll | 3 | 3 |
| 4 | Blind_help | 15 | 15 |
| 5 | Join_rnib | 31 | 31 |
| 6 | Yello_pages1 | 1 | 0 |
| 7 | Yello_pages2 | 4 | 4 |
| 8 | Yello_pages3 | 2 | 2 |
| 9 | Webct | 2 | 2 |
| 10 | Amazon | 4 | 4 |
| 11 | Citybank | 2 | 2 |
| 12 | Ebay | 3 | 2 |
| 13 | Nmsu | 6 | 3 |
| 14 | Pin | 4 | 4 |
| 15 | Yahoo | 1 | 0 |

**Fig. 2.** Experimental Results.

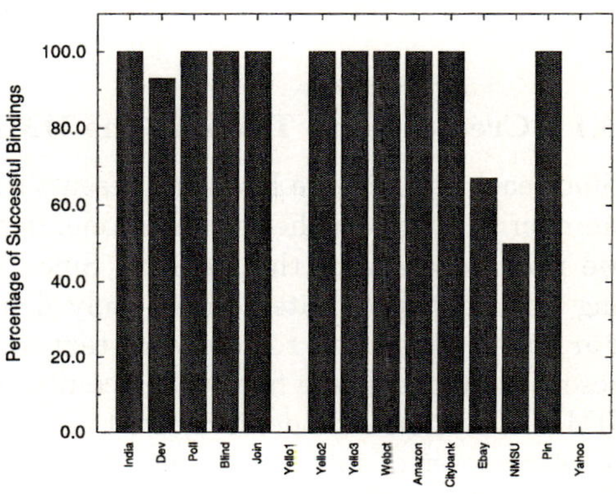


**Fig. 3.** Experimental Results using Progol.

# 5 Binding Text and Control in Forms: HMM

We experimented with HMM using two types of observation sequences: unlabeled and labeled. HMM trained with Labeled data outperforms its unlabeled counterpart, as the former method gives more clues about the structure of the training data. Since obtaining the labeled training data is not difficult in our context (forms), the method proves to be both efficient and easy to implement.

The training data is a file containing a sequence of words followed by their labels, where each word reflects a predominant property of the corresponding HTML form element. These properties are chosen in such a way to help the learning system in associating form elements with proper text. Three properties are considered to represent the text present in the forms, while controls are represented by their names. The properties are the following: `stext`: the text is highlighted using tags such as $< h1 >$, $< title >$ etc.; `lftext`: the text which is label for some control in the form; `text`: simple text; `tb`: text box; `ta`: text area; `rb`: radio button; `cb`: checkb box; `sl`: select list; `sb`: submit button.

The labels given to these words are listed below:

- `for_next`: The text with this label explains the control present next to it
- `for_previous`: The text with this label explains the control which it follows
- `mlt`: Miscellaneous text (group of controls or information about the form)
- `wcontrol`: Control with this label requires some text input
- `scontrol`: Selectable control ( radio button, check box etc..)

The implementation of the HMM algorithms is obtained from Andrew McCallum's website (www.cs.umass.edu/ mccallum/data). The theoretical foundations of creation and training of HMM can be found in [3].

Let us reconsider the form of Figure 1 and show the corresponding encoding as a labeled sequence. The unlabeled observation sequence for this form is:

```
text tb text ta text sl rb text rb text sb
```

and the corresponding labeled observation sequence is:

```
text for_next tb wcontrol text for_next taw control
text for_next sl wcontrol rb scontrol text for_previous
rb scontrol text for_previous sb scontrol
```

## 5.1 Creating and Training the HMM

Since each state in the HMM represents the class a form element belongs to, the number of states in the trained model depends on the number of classifications we need to make of the element. Since we are only concerned about attaching text to appropriate control, only five states are needed: three (`for_next`, `for_previous`, `mlt`) to represent text and two (`scontrol`, `wcontrol`) to represent controls. These five states, combined with start and end states, form the HMM. The initial model is created using Bayesian Model Merging (BMM) with a selected set of forms as input (32 forms have been used). This model forms the basis for further training. The model is then trained with a variety of forms using forward and backward algorithms.

### 5.2 Evaluating the Trained Model

Using the Viterbi algorithm, the most likely state sequence for a given observation sequence (form) can be determined. The following is a sample form tested against the trained model. The input (observation sequence) for this form and the output (most likely state sequence) are also listed.

Consider the example of Figure 4. The input observation sequence is:

```
stext text tb text tb text tb
text sl text cb text cb text
cb text text rb text rb
text text ta text sb sb
```

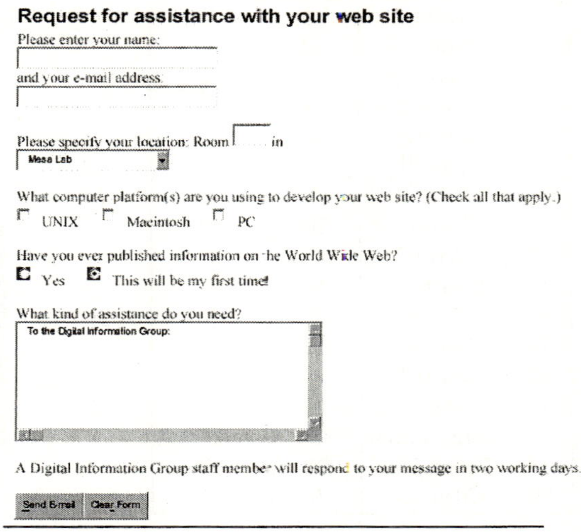


**Fig. 4.** Sample Form

and the corresponding output is:

```
stext mlt text for_next tb wcontrol
text for_next tb wcontrol text
for_next tb wcontrol text for_next sl wcontrol text mlt cb scontrol
text for_previous cb scontrol text for_previous cb scontrol text
for_previous text rb scontrol text for_previous rb scontrol text
for_previous text mlt ta wcontrol text mlt sb mlt sb scontrol
```

where all form elements are properly tagged with their class. Table 5 summarizes the results of testing the model with a variety of different forms, while Figure 6 compares the number of total text bindings in the form with the number of bindings correctly identified.

## 6 Final Considerations

As it is evident from the above tables, the generalized ruled derived using Progol were very successful in binding form controls to the corresponding textual description for regular forms. However, the Progol system still produces poor results in some cases. This can be attributed to the following reasons:

- Form control and corresponding text are present in two different tables
- Form control has corresponding text in the form of a image

Progol also fails to form rules to detect a text explaining group of controls present in the form. Providing some more details about form elements such as color and font size of its text may give good results. Also, varying the background knowledge greatly affects the generalized rule. HMM is considerably more effective in those cases where Progol is lacking, and is capable of balancing out strengths and weaknesses of Progol. HMM is more sensitive to the size of the training set;

| S.no | Form Name | No. of Pairs | Pairs detected |
|---|---|---|---|
| 1 | 2kweb | 11 | 8 |
| 2 | 2kewb2 | 10 | 7 |
| 3 | Devedge | 7 | 6 |
| 4 | lawson | 21 | 21 |
| 5 | Devedge2 | 3 | 3 |
| 6 | Rediff | 19 | 19 |
| 8 | Wdvl | 9 | 9 |
| 9 | Yahoo | 10 | 10 |
| 10 | Wdvl2 | 6 | 6 |
| 11 | Feedback | 16 | 6 |
| 13 | USA | 5 | 5 |
| 14 | Donate | 32 | 31 |
| 15 | Form1 | 13 | 6 |
| 16 | Pizza | 12 | 12 |
| 17 | India Times | 8 | 8 |
| 18 | Example4 | 20 | 19 |
| 20 | Citybank | 5 | 5 |

**Fig. 5.** Experiments using HMM.

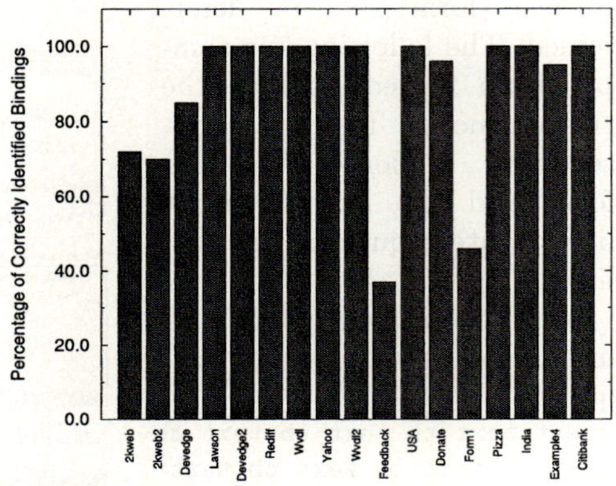


**Fig. 6.** Experiments using HMM.

the training required a considerably larger number of examples before providing models adequate for the effective analysis of other forms. In the future we plan to investigate effective ways to integrate the two methodologies to further improve precision of forms recognition.

## Acknowledgments

This research has been partially supported by NSF grant 9906130.

## References

1. Earl, C. et al.: "A Survey of Windows Screen Reader Users." Journal of Visual Impairment and Blindness, 93(3), 1999.
2. Gunderson, J. et al.: "Usability of Web Browsers by Persons with Visual Impairments." RESNA Conf., 1997.
3. Gusfield, D.: *Algorithms on Strings, Trees, and Sequences: Computer Science and Computational Biology.* Cambridge University Press, 1997.
4. Muggleton, S., Firth, J.: "Cprogol: a tutorial introduction." Dept. Computer Science, Univ. York, 1999.
5. Pontelli, E. et al.: "Towards the Creation of Accessibility Agents for Non-visual Navigation of the Web"', ACM Conference on Universal Usability, 2003.
6. Roberts, S.: "An Introduction to Progol," Department of Computer Science, University of York, January 21, 1997.
7. Seymore, K., McCallum, A. and Rosenfeld, R.: "Learning Hidden Markov Model Structure for Information Extraction," AAAI'99 Workshop on Machine Learning for Information Extraction, 1999.

# Virtual Reality Based Therapy Application for Developmental Disordered Children

Yoshiyuki Takahashi[1], Yuko Ito[2], Takeshi Yamashita[1], Takafumi Terada[3], Kaoru Inoue[2], Yumi Ikeda[2], Keisuke Suzuki[2], Hokyoo Lee[1], and Takashi Komeda[1]

[1] Shibaura Institute of Technology, 307 Fukasaku, Minuma-ku, Saitama-shi, 337-8570 Saitama, Japan
{i0180026,m403187,m702501}@sic.shibaura-it.ac.jp
komeda@se.shibaura-it.ac.jp
http://www.shibaura-it.ac.jp/

[2] Mitsubishi Precision Co. Ltd., 345 Kami-machiya, Kamakura-shi, 247-8505 Kanagawa, Japan
tterada@mpcnet.co.jp
http://www.mpcnet.co.jp

[3] Tokyo Metropolitan University of Health Sciences, 7-2-10 Higashi-Ogu, Arakawa, 116-8551 Tokyo, Japan
{itoyuko,inoue,ikedayum,suzukike}@post.metro-hs.ac.jp
http://www.metro-hs.ac.jp

**Abstract.** We have developed a pen tablet based VR therapy tool for children with develop-mental disabilities. It aims to stimulate visual, audio and haptic sensation. It could be help for sensor integration and cognition treatment. The therapist could edit the task as her/his planed and record the stylus trajectory. It could be help for quantitative therapy and evaluation. The experiment was carried out with normal healthy subjects and confirmed the basic functions of our developed tool.

## 1 Introduction

A developmental disorder is a generic term of disabilities which characterized by a physical, a mental and a emotional impairment in development period. Children with developmental disabilities have developmental delay in sensation, motor skills, cognition, adaptive skill, language, communication and so on. Medical treatment, physical and occupational therapy are required for them to be as independent as possible [1]. Occupational therapy for children with developmental disabilities involves the treatment and evaluation of motor behavior including skilled motor behavior, learning ability, social/emotion ability and basic activity of daily living. Occupational therapy will be carried out through playing with toys and educational tools e.g. bricks, a ball, clay and a puzzle. It can help to obtain a sensor and motor function coordination and learn a general idea which required for study e.g. numbers, colors and shapes. How-

K. Miesenberger et al. (Eds.): ICCHP 2004, LNCS 3118, pp. 369–376, 2004.

ever, it is unreasonable to prepare any type of toys and tools suitable for individuals. Moreover, it needs efforts to keep up children's interest in playing and learning because they may get tired easily. Therapists require the toy and educational tool which can stimulate their sensation effectively and motivate children for playing and learning. In addition, conventional evaluation method of the disability level and the effect of therapy are mostly based on empirical aspect by the therapist. Therapist desires the quantitative evaluation of their treatment.

The objective of our research is to develop a therapy tool which can be used as a toy and educational tool. It attempts to treat sensor integration and cognition ability using visual, audio, haptic sensation stimulation. It also aims to motivate children for therapy and to evaluate the abilities and effect of therapy quantitatively.

## 2 Virtual Reality for Therapy

Virtual Reality (VR) technology can provide various interactions, in visual, audio and haptic. One of the advantages of VR therapy is easily to control the stimulation. If the therapist can change the parameter setting of the program, suitable level of stimulation can be chosen. It could be effective for providing a therapy based on individual ability level and preventing loosing children's motivation. Moreover, computer based VR system can record the behavior of children as numerical data in real-time e.g. position, velocity, angle and reaction time. It could be help for quantitative evaluation of ability and effect of treatment.

The therapeutic system using VR technology to dissipate a phobia of flying, driving, creatures using are under studied. Using VR makes it possible to experience dangerous situation in safe. That is a one of the advantages of VR. The simulator for acrophobia was developed by Hanyang University [2]. The simulator provides 3D scenery using head mounted display. The view from on high allows patient to feel a sense of height and give a clinical treatment. The after stroke rehabilitation systems using VR technology are also developing, MIT-MANUS [3], MIME (Mirror Image Movement Enabler) [4] and Rehabilitation Training System Using ER Actuator [5], use robotic therapy system to recover the motor function. The systems provide a force on to the support of the arm when moving arm in transitively and voluntary. VR - based system using a haptic glove is used for post-stroke hand rehabilitation [6]. Another several research projects related VR therapy for young disabled are on going. VR for pain control of severe burns patient were developed by University of Washington [7]. Patient wears a VR device and can interact VR environment. During interact with VR environment, reducing the pain on the patient was confirmed. A virtual classroom for attention deficit children is developed by University of Southern California [8]. The subject wears VR device and seated in the virtual classroom. The system stimulates the subject and measures the attention level of subject. It aims to use for neuropsychological assessment and rehabilitation.

**Fig. 1.** Haptic Device System.

**Fig. 2.** Pen Tablet Type Therapy System.

## 3 Therapy Tool Applying Virtual Reality

We are trying to develop therapy tools utilizing VR technology. Fig.1 shows a haptic device system which aims to enhance visual and haptic sensation integration and rehabilitation upper limb motor function. The system provides a virtual force on to the grip e.g. spring, viscosity and friction force during moving a grip of the haptic device [9]. Fig.2 shows a pen tablet type therapy system. With this tablet, the user can work directly on the screen using a stylus with watching displayed contents. It is like working with pen and paper. This system could be used for visual perception therapy and evaluation of subject's ability. Finally, both haptic device and pen tablet system will be integrated to provide multi sensory stimulation. In this paper, we describe about this pen tablet system. It was designed and developed based on physical and occupational therapists.

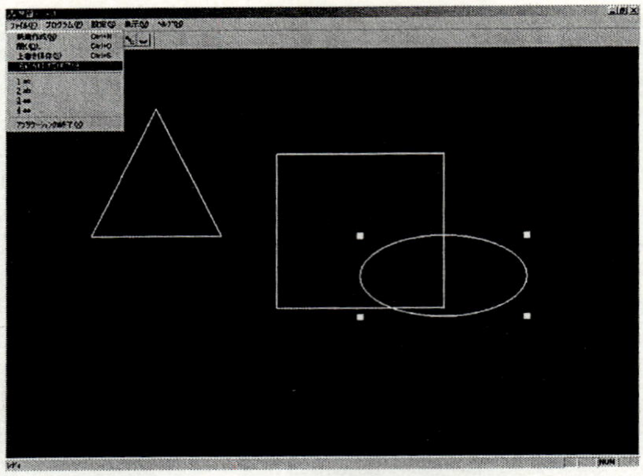

**Fig. 3.** Screenshot of the Symbol Editor.

### 3.1 Hardware

The therapy tool system consists of a computer, a pen display and software for therapy. The computer is equipped with high performance CPU more than PentiumIII and graphic accelerator board to display the visual contents in real-time. CintiQ C1500X(G) tablet (WACOM Co., Ltd) is used for the display. The tilt angle of display can be changed from 22 to 77 deg. The stylus has a pressure sensitive function with 1024 levels and the display can sense the position of the stylus in the area of 304 mm (H) × 228 mm (V) with maximum resolution 0.05 mm with an accuracy of 0.5 mm. The computer can monitor and record the position and the pressure of stylus through universal serial bus (USB).

### 3.2 Software

In the first step, we have developed simple software. Fig.3 shows the screenshot of our developed software. The software allows children to draw a line according to the displayed graphical symbol by using the stylus. The trajectory and pressure of the stylus can be recorded in real-time and store to the data file. After drawing, trajectory can be shown on the display like a VCR. And also, recorded data could be used to compare to the reference data and evaluate the skill of drawing.

Preprogrammed task is a simple drawing program which can draw a line between parallel guidelines. The software does not have only preprogrammed tasks also it can be created original tasks for therapy and diagnosis by the therapist. Primitive symbols e.g. triangle, quadrangle and ellipse (circle) can be chosen from “Draw Symbol Buttons” on the tool bar and set on the screen, move, resize as therapist planed (Fig.4). Created screen image can be saved and loaded again. Visual C++ and OpenGL were used to develop this software.

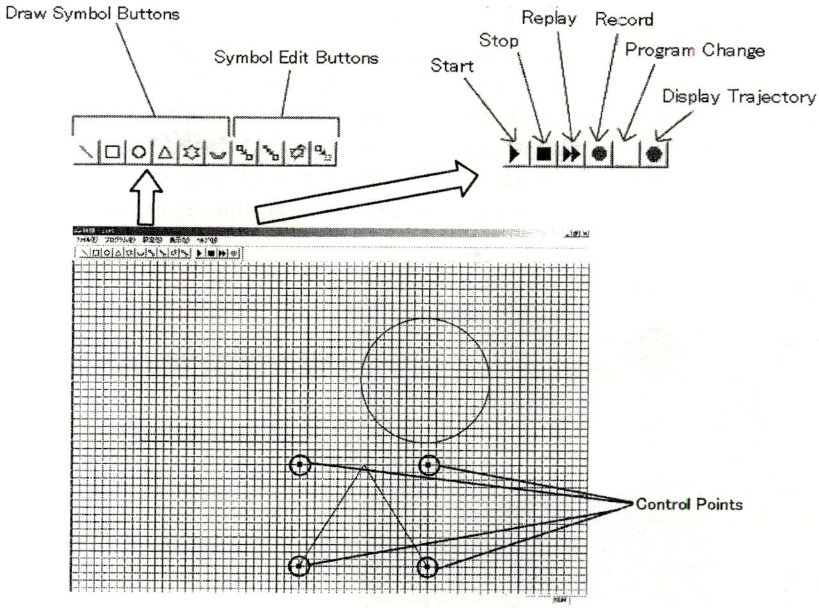


**Fig. 4.** Screenshot of the Symbol Editor.

# 4 Experiment

## 4.1 Materials and Methods

To confirm functions of our developed system and to discuss about future work, experiments were carried out with normal healthy subjects in a nursery school. 19 boys and 14 girls, totally 33 normal healthy subjects were enrolled. The age range was from 4 years and 10 months to 6 years and 9 months. The body height was from 1050 mm to 123 mm (Ave. 113 mm). 30 subjects were right handed and 3 subjects were left handed. The informed consent of this experiment was obtained from all parents of subjects.

Tasks were drawing a line between parallel guidelines using pen-and-paper and pen tablet display. The line was drawn from left side to right side. The guidelines were a lateral straight line and curvature line. The subjects were explained to draw the line fast and accurately as much as possible. When drawing the line, the system records the stylus position and pressure data in real time. In addition, the sceneries of experiments were captured on video to confirm the posture of their trunk and gripping form.

## 4.2 Results

Fig 5 shows the scenery of the experiment in a nursery school and the screen shot of the line drawing task. Fig 6 shows the results of one of subjects. Each graph shows the position, pressure and velocity of the stylus. In Fig 6(a), the origin of the tablet display is set to left bottom and longitudinal axis is Y, lateral axis is X. The width of parallel lines is 13 mm and the center of lines is 109 mm in Y axis. Around 165 mm in X axis, two peaks can be confirmed. Between these peaks, circles indicate on each graph, is related to changing the stylus velocity and tool force. The tool force was started to going up in Fig.6 (b) and the stylus velocity on X axis was reduced in Fig.6 (c). He might change the grip when crossing a median line. It is confirmed on the video.

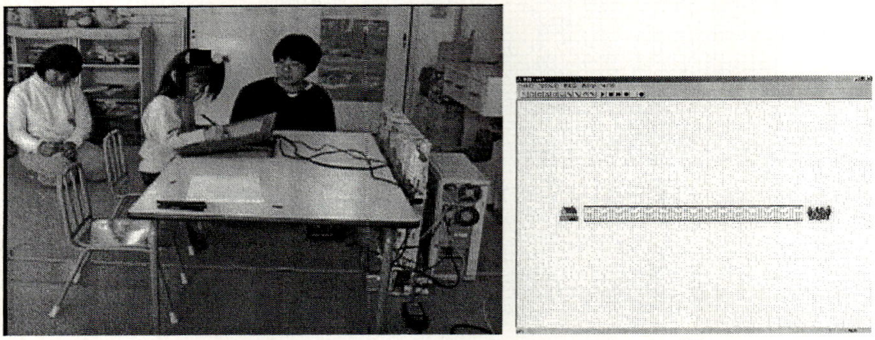

(a) (b)

**Fig. 5.** Experiment in a Nursery School : (a) Scenery of the Experiment, (b) Screenshot of the Line Drawing Task.

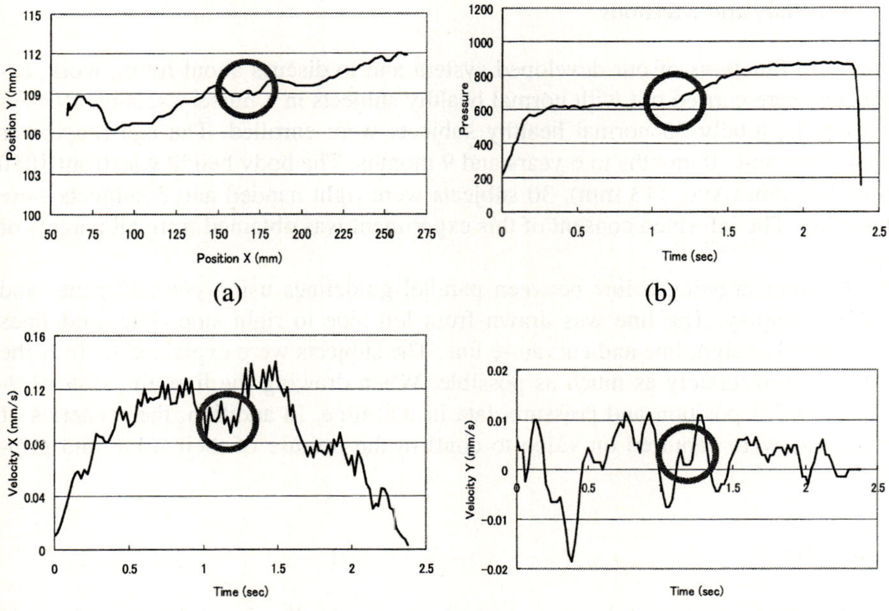


(a) (b) (c) (d)

**Fig. 6.** Results of Drawing Line: (a) Position of the Stylus, (b) Tool pressure of the Stylus, (c) Velocity of the Stylus on X axis, (d) Velocity of the Stylus on Y axis.

### 4.3 Discussions

It was confirmed that all functions worked well as we designed. Handling stylus on the tablet screen was looks difficult comparing with pen-and-paper. It could be caused that the angle of the display was not flat, the friction between tip of stylus and display screen was different, and their ability of hand grasping was immaturity even if they were normal and healthy.

## 5 Conclusions

We have developed a pen tablet based VR therapy tool for children with developmental disabilities. It aims to stimulate visual, audio and haptic sensation. It could be help for sensor integration and cognition treatment. Experiments were carried out with normal healthy subjects and confirmed the basic functions of our developed system. The functions of therapist could edit the task as his planed and record stylus trajectory. It could be help for quantitative therapy and evaluation. In future, more interactive contents, another intricate shaped and varicolored symbol with sound and haptic interaction will be developed. And also, the experiment of children with disability will be carried out and try to compare with healthy subjects quantitatively using corrected behavior data.

## References


1. National Dissemination Center for Children with Disabilities, Disability Information, `http://www.nichcy.org/disabinf.asp` (2003)
2. Dong P.J., Jeong H.K., Young H.C., Brenda K.W., San W.N., In Y.K., and Sun I. K.: Virtual reality as an adjunctive pain control during burn wound care in adolescent patients, IEEE TRANSACTIONSON INFORMATION TECHNOLOGY IN BIOMEDICINE, VOL.6, NO.3 (2003) 213-217
3. H.I. Krebs, N. Hogan, M.L. Aisen, B.T. Volpe: Robot-Aided Neurorehabilitation, IEEE TRANSACTION ON REHABILITATION ENGINEERING, VOL.6, NO.1, (1998) 75-87
4. P.C.Shor, P.S. Lum, C.G. Burgerk, H.F.M. Van der Loos, M. Majmundar, R. Yap: The Effect of Robotic-Aided Therapy on Upper Extremity Joint Passive Range of Motion and Pain, Assistive Technology Research Series, Vol.9, (2001) 79-83
5. M. Sakaguchi, J. Furusho, E. Genda: Basic Study on Development of Rehabilitation Training System Using ER Actuators, Journal of the Robotics Society of Japan, Vol. 19, No.5, (2001) 612-619
6. D. Jack, A. S. Merians, M. Tremaine, G.C. Burdea, V. Adamovich, H. Poizner: Virtual Reality-Enhanced Stroke Rehabilitation, IEEE TRANSACTIONS ON NEURAL SYSTEMS AND REHABILITATION ENGINEERING, VOL.9, NO.3, (2001) 308-318
7. Hunter G. H., Jason N. D., David R. P., Gretchen J. C., Thomas A. F. III: Virtual reality as an adjunctive pain control during burn wound care in adolescent patients, Pain Volume 85, Issues 1-2 (2000) 305-309

8. Albert A R., Todd B., J. Galen Buckwalter, Maria S., Robert M., Cyrus S., Ulrich N., Laehyun K. and Mehdi S.: Virtual Environments for the Assessment of Attention and Memory Processes: The Virtual Classroom and Office, Proceedings of the International Conference on Dis-ability, Virtual Reality and Associated Technology (2002) 3-11
9. Y. Takahashi, T. Terada, K. Inoue, Y. Ito, H. Lee and T. Komeda: Upper-Limb Rehabilitation Exercises Using Haptic Device System, International Journal of Human-friendly Welfare Robotic Systems, Vol.4, No.2 (2003) 18-22

# Real-Time Health-Monitoring Network for Disabled and Elderly People

Yung Bok Kim[1] and Jong Yong Kim[2]

[1] Dept of Computer Engineering, Sejong University,
Gunja-Dong, Gwangjin-Gu, Seoul, Republic of Korea
yungbkim@sejong.ac.kr

[2] Information System Office, Financial Supervisory Service,
27, Yoido-Dong, Youngdeungpo-Gu, Seoul, Republic of Korea
kimscots@fss.or.kr

**Abstract.** The wired Internet has influenced many areas in human society, especially the speed of knowledge and information exchange; the mobile Internet is affecting much more in pervasive computing environment and will introduce many special applications like health-care based on the wireless health-monitoring network. We considered the mobile Internet for the real-time health-monitoring network for the disabled and elderly people as inexpensive and effective system, especially with health-monitoring mobile devices. We studied the Web-based health information network, and discuss the empirical results about performance with emulated model considering the implementation with the real-time information Web server for the disabled and elderly people.

## 1 Introduction

This paper introduces the health monitoring sensor network based on mobile Internet. We will discuss with the results from real implementation of the similar information network using the mobile web page as a WML health-information deck, assuming as the transmission data unit from the watch phone with the health-monitoring sensors. Our main interest is whether the real-time information service is possible with the inexpensive web server and what else should be considered in advance for real implementation of real-time health-monitoring sensor network, especially focusing on the Web server as a role center in the health-monitoring network.

For introduction of background, we considered some related issues for the disabled and elderly people from the previous work done by other researchers. First, we should consider the useful results for the disabled and elderly people after our R&D projects, if possible it's better to introduce the successful products or service for the universal access. Universal access implies the accessibility and usability of Information Society Technologies (IST) by anyone, anywhere, anytime. Research and Development (R&D) in IT (Information Technology) for people with disabilities feels the pressure to bring the results of their projects successfully to the market. R&D in this field, after a pilot period, now must show its impact on practice, on the quality of life of target groups and therefore on related markets [1].

K. Miesenberger et al. (Eds.): ICCHP 2004, LNCS 3118, pp. 377–384, 2004.

To fail to involve consumers in the process of matching person and assistive technology perpetuates a system of service delivery that has not been as effective as it could be from both an outcome achievement and marketplace perspective; this is discussed in the study of assistive technology outcomes in the United States by Scherer [2].

New approaches and related instruments, are needed for capturing human requirements in the new reality. Appropriate architectural framework and development tools will need to be elaborated in the age of disappearing computer [3]. We should consider the milieu of pervasive and ubiquitous computing. The development of highly efficient and effective user interfaces, which are matched to the user needs and abilities, was discussed for the successful application of assistive technology [4]. We are mainly concerning the mobile health-monitoring device and the health-monitoring network in the coming pervasive computing milieu, i.e. the disappearing computer environment; and we can also consider the usage of information with voice interface in the near future. Pervasive healthcare would improve the productivity of healthcare practitioners and greatly facilitate the delivery of a wider range of medical services [5].

The performance of a worldwide web (WWW) server became a central issue in providing ubiquitous, reliable, and efficient information access. The performance issues in the worldwide web servers were studied [6]. We discuss the performance consideration of the health-monitoring network with inexpensive web server for pervasive healthcare of the disabled and elderly people. At first, we discuss the issues about performance of mobile Internet environment considering the real implementation. For the mobile Internet, as one of major protocols, the WAP protocol [7] has been used a lot, especially in Korea and many other countries, and WAP browsers, with WAP 1.0 to WAP 2.0 version, have been implemented in many mobile phone devices; and we consider this mobile Internet technology for the health-monitoring of the disabled and elderly people.

The ubiquitous mobile computing [8] was mentioned in the current environment with a plethora of mobile devices, and introduced several challenges, e.g. authentication, profiles and personalization, performance, etc. The challenged performance is what the bottlenecks in the application architecture or the content path are, and we should try to figure it out and we discuss about performance for the application of the health-monitoring network for the disabled and elderly people.

We need some inexpensive and efficient way for the real-time health-monitoring information network using sensors implemented in the watch, or in the watch phone, or in the wrist PC. We introduce several studies and discussions done by several researchers, especially about the current situation and issues of performance in wired and mobile Internet. We need new performance analysis methodology for the health-monitoring services in the milieu of pervasive and ubiquitous computing.

The sensor network for monitoring health in real-time way using the mobile Internet should be as simple as possible. The performance of the health-monitoring network is important to provide services with cost-effective and inexpensive system solution. Therefore, let's discuss about the performance, constraints and analysis, and consider the requirement for performance in the pervasive computing environment.

The difficulties in simulating the Internet were discussed by Floyd and Faxson [9], and the heterogeneity of the network and the rapid change of the traffic depending upon the new applications, ubiquitous web environment and the stochastic characteristics of the session arrivals and connection sizes, etc. Here, we need to make our traffic behavior to have deterministic characteristics instead of having the heavy tailed distribution of the related random variable, e.g. the arrival rate, transmission time of packet through Internet, processing time in the server, and the size of the contents for health-monitoring information, etc. Barford and Crovella [10] studied the critical path analysis of TCP transactions as follows. Previous work in the performance analysis and improvement of Web transactions falls into two categories: work on servers, and work on networks/protocols, however they studied the effects of file size, server load, network load, path length, and the causes of variability in transfer duration. As conclusion, the server load is the major determiner of transfer time for small files, while network load is the major determiner for large files; in addition the dominant cause of variability in transfer time is packet loss. From the result of this research we can think that to minimize the dependency of the overall performance of the health-monitoring to the network traffic we should use very small sized file as health-monitoring data, i.e. WML web page for mobile Internet and HTML page for wired Internet, and the number of packets for one transaction should be as small as possible. For small sized file or web page, the sever load is the major factor for performance of health-monitoring, therefore the server should be dedicated for single purpose, i.e. only for dedicated health-monitoring Web server.

## 2 Health-Monitoring Sensors and Network

We can consider various type of health monitoring sensors for real application, but here we considered the wrist phone as a future product to measure the health data, e.g. the pulse at wrist, the blood pressure, the strength of pulse, etc. Because the oriental medical science is using this sort of information in the wrist to diagnose the personal health; therefore even though those information may not be perfect for diagnosis of health we considered the real-time health-monitoring network based on mobile Internet.

### 2.1 Health-Monitoring Sensors in Wrist Phone

The following Fig.1 shows health-monitoring sensors in wrist phone at one hand of the disabled and elderly people. The wrist phone is the future product not implemented yet, thus we assume that the sensors for measuring the pulses, the strength of the pulses, and the blood pressure would give the raw data about health of the disabled and elderly people.

Glitho et al. [11] introduced the case study about the mobile agents and their use for information retrieval; the following health-monitoring sensors in wrist phones may be considered as mobile agents even though they are not for same applications.

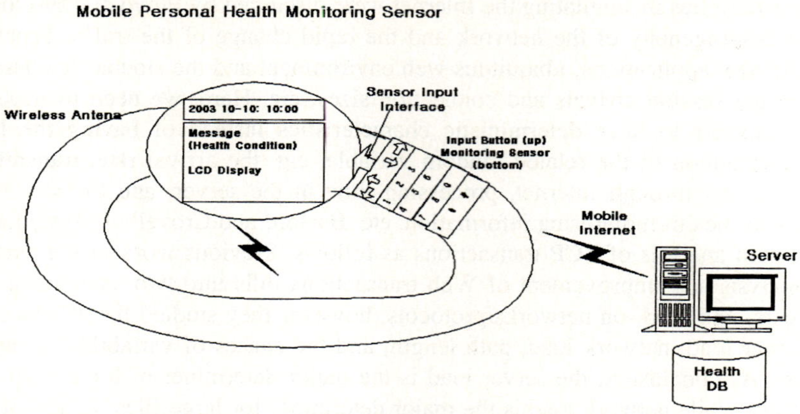


**Fig. 1.** Mobile Health-Monitoring Sensors in Wrist Phone.

Here instead of plain client-server, we need the optimized client server or the mobile agent approach for performance of our health-monitoring sensor network with health Web server.

The performance analysis for real-time health monitoring system may be different from the conventional analysis methodology for non-realtime applications. We should investigate this type of new approach, because the real-time health-monitoring network may be applicable to many new applications for the disabled and elderly people in the pervasive healthcare. We studied the real-time health-monitoring application, getting frequently personal information as well as writing the analyzed information as a response to the request by client or health-monitoring agent in the mobile Internet environment.

## 2.2 Health-Monitoring Network

For the real-time health-monitoring network using mobile Internet, as shown in the following Fig.2, the dominating factor and the standard deviation of that random variable should be bounded within the deterministic response time. To be deterministic for real-time application, the estimation time should be bounded within deterministic time, the interchange of data between the watch phone and the server should be automatic except the requested information by the user, therefore the Web server should be efficient and have high performance for the dedicated application if possible, and the exchanged data and analyzed information should be as simple as possible with simplified and efficient format. If possible, the bandwidth requirement for wireless or mobile Internet should be immune to the network traffic condition; also that will be good in terms of degradation caused by the other rich multimedia contents sharing the same network and server.

The spent time in the Web server may be considered to be immune to the network and server condition, with short packets below 1.5Kbytes that may be upper bound of packet size. In general, the frequency of health monitoring is much more than the frequency of analyzed or diagnosed information from the health Web server.

This system is based on wired or mobile Internet, and the monitored health data from sensors in watch phone can be registered in any time using mobile Internet with the domain name of test Web server, i.e. 'ktrip.net' [12] for wired/mobile Internet. Actually this site has been used for real-time information network server and we considered it as a health-monitoring server, because this server can be used as any Web server for testing.

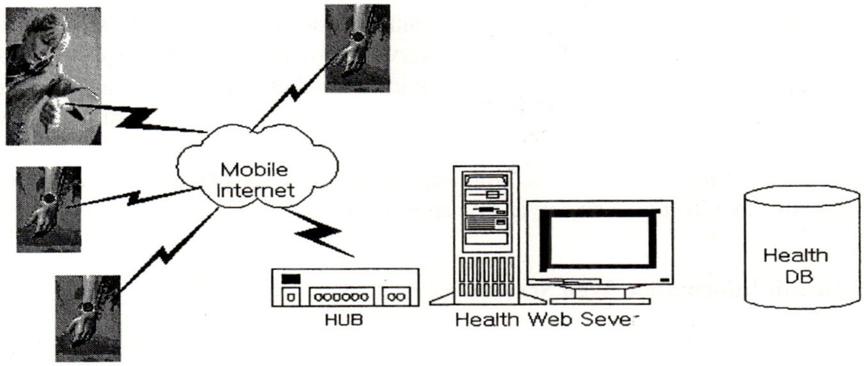


**Fig. 2.** Mobile Health-Monitoring Network.

# 3 Health Information Server

An Information Center designed to meet the various needs of people with disabilities will help them to achieve a higher degree of independence and facilitate their integration into the community; with the following four perspectives, discussed by Kowalik [13], to ensure that a particular disability will not prevent the use of the information system. For a disabled person to fully use the information stored in the information system's database, they have to successfully complete four tasks: 1.connect to the information system; 2.say exactly what information they need; 3.receive the requested information; 4.record it in a way that will allow multiple uses of the information.

For the consistency of health-monitoring information and for the convenient user interface, considering the universal access and universal design for the disabled and elderly people, we need the unified health-monitoring Web server for wired Internet and mobile Internet.

## 3.1 Health Information and Analysis Model

We used single web server as a health information Web server for the simplicity of management and the cost-effectiveness. This method gives the effectiveness and efficiency for real-time health-monitoring network and utilization of resources, e.g. the bandwidth for communication and the size of disk storage of health information Web server for the disabled and elderly people.

We assume that the wrist phone with health-monitoring sensors writes regularly the health information, which should be chosen carefully in further research, to the health information Web server through mobile Internet, and processes the data and analyzes for the request of the results in real-time way. Depending upon the frequency of writing the health information, the workload of the health Web server may change, and the interval of regular writing may be considered as arrival rate in the queuing performance analysis model for health-monitoring. The transmission packet unit for billing by mobile communication service provider is about 0.5 Cent (U.S.); the packet size is 512 Bytes, which is the minimum packet size for charging in Korea. Therefore, if possible, the health-monitoring data for wrist phone to the server through mobile Internet should be below 512 Bytes, and this size is also bounded much below 1.5Kbytes that is one emulated WML deck for performance evaluation of the health-monitoring Web server discussed later.

### 3.2 Health Information Web Server

The health Web server should have the capability of showing the appropriate health contents, i.e. the HTML contents for wired Internet as well as the mobile contents for many different kinds of mobile devices, e.g. WML, mHTML, HDML, etc. For unified service, there are several constraints, compared to the contents for the wired Internet. First of all, we should consider the various kinds of mobile devices as well as the browsers for mobile Internet, and each of those devices may have different capabilities in terms of the image. The environment of the development and application is very different from the existing wired Internet, i.e. mainly based on the almost unified browser, i.e. MS Explorer. Therefore we considered only text-based health-monitoring information from the wrist phone to the heath-monitoring Web server and vice versa, to be immune to any type of Internet traffic load as well as to minimize the mobile communication cost for cost-effective health-monitoring service.

We suggest the minimum requirements as capabilities of health information Web server instead of luxurious capabilities, because of the cost-effectiveness and low cost/performance ratio. To provide the minimum requirement for the wired Internet using PC and for the mobile Internet using the wireless mobile devices, e.g. handheld devices and mobile phones, we can provide the simplest functionality with the less capable mobile Internet phone. Among several constraints with mobile phone, in terms of the contents, the WML deck size should be below around 1.5 Kbyte. We implemented the similar Web server of Information Network for wired Internet with PC as well as for wireless Internet with mobile devices; however we consider the Web server as an emulated health information Web server here. The size of contents is below 1.5Kbyte as a WML deck, which is the transmission packet unit in the WAP environment; and even for the wired Internet we considered the same content with the small size of web page for health information service. This size of 1.5 Kbytes health information will be enough for the real-time monitoring information of health.

### 3.3 Emulated Implementation and Empirical Results

The implemented system is as follows; for the operating system, Windows 2000 server; for wired and mobile Internet web services, IIS5.0 web server and ASP 3.0; for DBMS, MS SQL server; for the mobile markup language, WML mHTML, and HDML. The leased E1 (2.048 Mbps) Internet communication line to a router and the test web server, i.e. the health Web server for both wired and mobile Internet service, is being used. As we discussed already, the size of web page for unified service was considered below 1.5Kbyte for monitored health data and information and 5Kbytes of the almost same analyzed or diagnosed information for wired PC Internet, to minimize the dependency of the overall performance to the shared and stochastically varying network traffic; also the web server is dedicated to minimize the server load, and dedicated for the health-monitoring network.

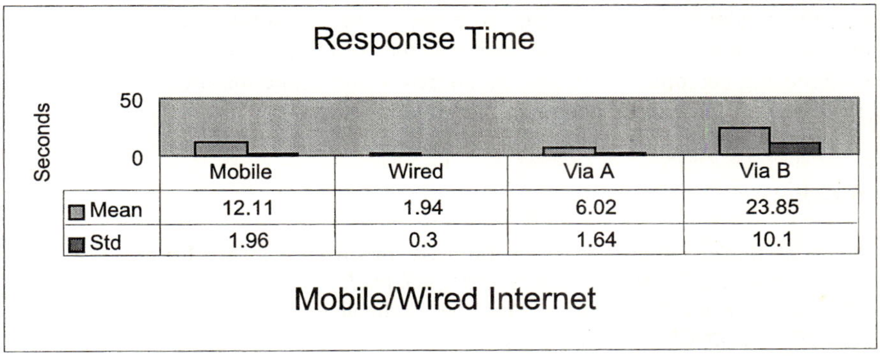


| | Mobile | Wired | Via A | Via B |
|---|---|---|---|---|
| Mean | 12.11 | 1.94 | 6.02 | 23.85 |
| Std | 1.96 | 0.3 | 1.64 | 10.1 |

**Fig. 3.** Response Time (Mean and Standard Deviation).

Fig.3 shows the mean and standard deviation of 100 samples with the emulated health-monitoring Web server, we can observe that the response time at wired PC is fastest and stable with little deviation, the averaged response time with mobile phone Internet is around 12 seconds with about 2 second standard deviation, the other two cases with wired PC via the intermediate server show that depending upon the intermediate server the mean and deviation of the response time become very different. The size of web page for the wired Internet accessed by the domain name ktrip.net is about 5 Kbytes, and the size of the mobile web page is about 1.5Kbytes, that becomes about 1Kbytes after compiling to WAP binary file, that is considered as health information. The mobile 1.5Kbyte content retrieval time with mobile Internet is about 10 seconds longer than the wired (PC) 5Kbyte content retrieval time because of the elapsed time with the gateway and base station etc., and this time should be considered for health-monitoring application with mobile Internet.

Considering the performance of the health-monitoring Web server, we can make the processing time deterministic in the Web server for contents, where the deterministic time is possible with the deterministic size of packet, below around 1.5Kbytes, if possible below 500 Bytes in real implementation. We can consider the health-monitoring server as M/D/1 queuing model, i.e. Markovian arrival rate (M) and with deterministic processing time the departure rate (D), with inexpensive single web server (1) for health-monitoring service, for the disabled and elderly people.

## 4 Conclusions and Future Works

A real-time health-monitoring network for the disabled and elderly people, using the domain name 'ktrip.net', has been studied on the basis of wired and mobile Internet. The results of implementation show that the overhead time in the mobile Internet is not negligible for ubiquitous real-time health-monitoring network. The evaluation of the health-monitoring Web server for the wired and mobile Internet can be applied to efficient investment for worldwide health-monitoring service for the disabled and elderly people with the health-monitoring sensors in the wrist phone. As future works, the availability of the health Web server will be studied for reliability of the health-monitoring sensor network, and also the meaningful parameter for analyzing and diagnosing personal health will be studied for real-time monitoring and diagnosis for the disabled and elderly people in the Silver Society.

## References


1. Christian Buhler: From Research to Business Improving the Take Up of Results of Research Projects. ICCHP 2002, LNCS 2398 (2002) 6-7.
2. Marcia J. Scherer: The Study of Assistive Technology Outcomes in the United States. ICCHP 2002, LNCS 2398 (2002) 764-771.
3. Constantine Stephanidis: The Disappearing Computer: Emerging Opportunities and Challenges for Disables and Elderly People. ICCHP 2002, LNCS 2398 (2002) 41-48.
4. Wolfgang L. Zagler: Matching Typing Person and Intelligent Interfaces. ICCHP 2002, LNCS 2398 (2002) 241-242.
5. Upkar Varshney: Pervasive Healthcare. Computer, December (2003) 138-140.
6. Erich Nahum, Tsipora Barzilai, and Dilip D. Kandlur: Performance Issues in WWW Servers. IEEE/ACM Transactions on Networking, vol. 10, no. 1, February (2002) 2-11.
7. Vijay Kumar, Srinivas Parimi and Dharma P. Agrawal: WAP: Present and Future. IEEE Pervasive Computing, January-March (2003) 79-83.
8. Yih-Farn Robin Chen and Charles Petrie: Ubiquitous Mobile Computing. IEEE Internet Computing, March-April (2003) 16-17.
9. Sally Floyd and Vern Paxson: Difficulties in Simulating the Internet. IEEE/ACM Transactions on Networking, vol.9, no.4, August (2001) 392-403.
10. Paul Barford and Mark Crovella: Critical Path Analysis of TCP Transactions. IEEE/ACM Transactions on Networking, vol.9, no.3, June (2001) 238-248.
11. Roch H. Glitho, Edgar Olougouna and Samuel Pierre: Mobile Agents and Their Use for Information Retrieval: A Brief Overvies and an Elaborate Case Study. IEEE Network, January/February (2002) 34-41.
12. Real-time Information Network site for Health-monitoring Emulation (Mobile/wired Web Site) http://ktrip.net
13. Ryszard Kowalik. Capabilities and Limitations of the Disabled in Remote Access to Information. ICCHP 2002, LNCS 2398 (2002) 707-708.

# A Computer-Based Self-health Monitoring System for the Elderly Living in a Low Income Housing Environment

Judith F. Karshmer[1] and Arthur I. Karshmer[2]

[1] College of Nursing, University of South Florida
Tampa, Florida USA
jkarshme@hsc.usf.edu

[2] Department of Information Technology, University of South Florida
Lakeland, Florida USA
arthur@lklnd.usf.edu

**Abstract.** The aging communities in the United States, and elsewhere, are presenting serious problems for the health delivery systems in many countries. Add to this the problems associated with being poor and having limited access to the health delivery, and the problem becomes one of even greater urgency. One solution to this problem is the distribution of health monitoring equipment to the patient rather than having the patient travel to the equipment. In some cases, this might mean the installation of the health monitoring equipment in the patient's home, while in others it could mean the development of a centralized facility in a housing project that would be easily accessible by the residents. In the current work, the second model was built and tested in a low-income housing environment, the JL Young Center for Elderhealth Primary Care in Tampa.

## 1 Introduction

The JL Young Center for Elderhealth Primary Care was founded in 1991 as a cooperative between the University of South Florida College of Nursing and the City of Tampa Housing Authority to increase access for low-income elderly to quality health care. The center is located in a City of Tampa public housing facility that has 432 units and 497 residents. Over the past ten years services that are easily accessible and cost-effective have been provided to a portion of the housing project residents and the center has provided a multidisciplinary training site for nursing, medical, and social sciences students. However, because of issues related to the mission of the clinic and varying faculty responsibilities and student learning needs, the services that have been provided in the clinic have been somewhat uneven and unpredictable, all too often constrained by the academic calendar. Increasing the consistent availability of health care services to this multicultural, low-income population of elderly has become a high priority for the College of Nursing. One area of particular concern is creating a mechanism that can provide an easy, accessible, accurate, and inexpensive

K. Miesenberger et al. (Eds.): ICCHP 2004, LNCS 3118, pp. 385–391, 2004.

way for patients to monitor and record a number of important health status indicators. The project is designed to use the very latest in information technology to design, implement, and evaluate an innovative method for self-monitoring and self-reporting key health indictors of residents.

## 2 Specific Aims of the Project

### 2.1 Target Population

A number of community assessments of the Tampa Bay area housing projects for the elderly have identified that accessibility to health care services as a major concern for the elderly. The access issue is relevant across a number of areas including cost, distance, and the nature in which the care is provided. Findings of a Prevention for Elderly People II (Ruben, et. al, 1996) risk appraisal project indicated that 90% of the residents in the housing project live on less than $5,000 per year. Up to thirty four percent identified that they had some difficulty with activities of daily living that compromised their ability access health care and more than 70% reported they had some kind of chronic condition. In addition, they indicated that, all too often, when they did access the health care system, the treatment they received was not particularly culturally competent or user-friendly (USF College of Nursing, 1999).

### 2.2 Monitoring Chronic Conditions

The primary goal of the Center for Elderhealth Primary Care is to provide health care services that are accessible, cost effective, and tailor made to the geriatric population. Of particular concern is improved monitoring of the chronic conditions that so often plague the elderly. Nearly 40 percent have a chronic condition that causes morbidity and limits function and seventy percent of all deaths can be attributed to some sort of chronic disease (Adleman & Daly, 2001). The US Centers for Disease Control & Prevention have identified that the most common chronic illnesses among the elderly are hypertension, arthritis, heart disease, vision impairment, and diabetes. To effectively deal with the challenges of managing chronic illness among the elderly, new models of health care delivery must be developed. Key to any approach is assuring that patients are able to take charge of health care decisions and have viable treatment options. Research evaluating the impact of self-care in managing chronic disease has demonstrated that patients who are able to take responsibility for ongoing self assessment fare better than those have limited involvement in their own care (Loring, et al, 1999). When chronic illnesses are effectively monitored, the result can be an increase in life expectancy and improved quality of life (Tetzlaff, 1998).

### 2.3 Community

The Elderhealth Primary Care Center is integrated in the community and represents a coalition between the College of Nursing and a number of community partners. Local hospitals have provided furniture and exam equipment. The YMCA has provided scholarships for an exercise program and assisted with professional expertise. The Senior Companion service provides support to train in-house seniors who in turn provide care for those elderly in need. The City of Tampa Housing Authority provides a four-apartment suite that houses the clinic, pays the utilities, telephone costs, and the salary of the clinic secretary. Solid community support has created the environment that will facilitate expanding the services that are available in the center. The project is one approach to increasing availability of care through a direct, convenient diagnostic reporting mechanism.

### 2.4 The Project

The research is a clinically based, patient-centered project using the very latest in information technology to design, implement and evaluate an innovative method for monitoring and reporting key health indictors of residents.

## 3 Significance

Excellent evidence supports the benefits of early intervention in reducing the morbidity and mortality of many diseases (Adelman & Daly, 2001). Effective, accurate monitoring of signs that are diagnostic of chronic illnesses among the high-risk, economically disadvantaged elderly will provide a strategy for increasing the possibility of timely treatment. Creating a mechanism where by the elderly have control over self-reporting has the potential of maximizing the positive impact of self-care. And, using the latest of information technology as the vehicle will help to bring the, often isolated, elder into the 21$^{st}$ century.

## 4 Data Collected and Collection Method

One of the goals of the project was to collect data in an informal, friendly and convenient manner. The data collection was to be based on the user being able to interact with a system that collected information on a variety of common vital signs and general well-being status. A small lab was created in the housing center so patients could collect their information in a private and convenient location. To accomplish this task we created an automated system that would be simple to use, and non-threatening to the patient. Further, as a large portion of the residents were Spanish speakers, the system had to accommodate users in two languages: English and Spanish.

The system is comprised of two major components. A desktop computer and a CardioTech health-monitoring device which is connected electronically to the computer.

## 4.1 The Desktop Computer

The desktop computer is a Macintosh iMac system with a 15 inch color screen which is fitted with a touch panel. In this way, the patients can enter all information into the system without using the keyboard. Their basic data are first entered into the system after a consultation with a nurse. Part of the information entered in the system includes the patient's social security number and their mother's maiden name. To do regular data collections, the patient is required to enter both of these data items using either the touch screen or the keyboard. All communication from the computer comes in the form of large print on the screen and voice synthesis. A sample screen is shown in Figure 1 below.

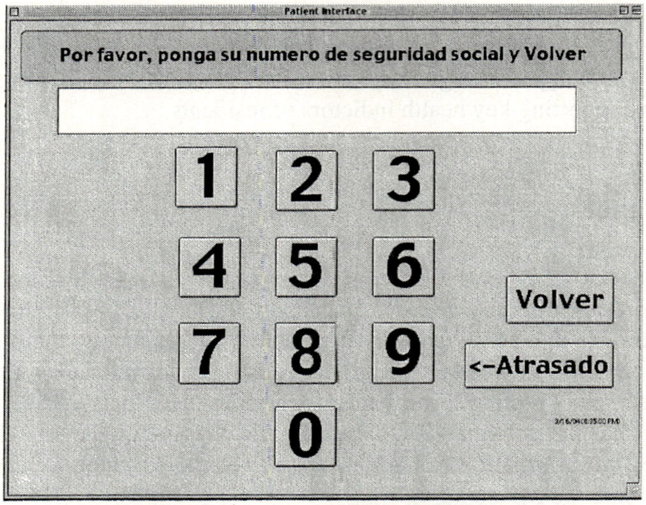


**Fig. 1.** A User Login Screen in Spanish.

After logging into the system, the user is queried concerning a number of issues concerning how they perceive their general health at that moment in time. Figure 2 below shows the screen that queries about these symptoms – in this case the question deals with "headache" in Spanish.

Again, all output includes large print and speech and all input is carried out through the touch sensitive screen.

## 4.2 The Health Monitoring Device

After the basic information is collected, the patient is directed to move to the actual health monitoring device. This device was able to record:

1. Blood pressure
2. Pulse rate
3. Weight

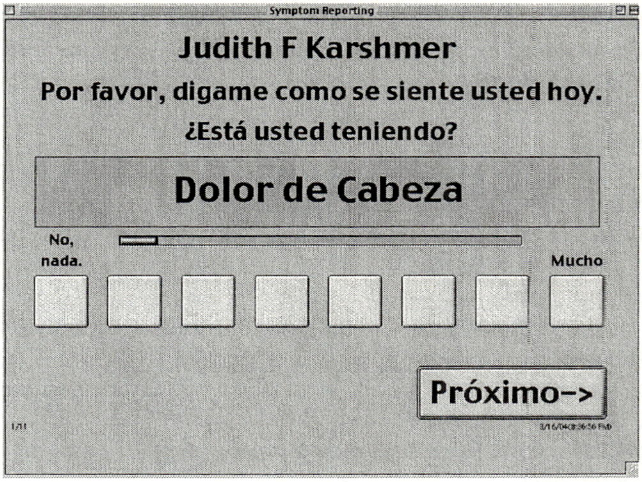


**Fig. 2.** Queries Concerning Current Feeling of Well-Being.

and then transmit these data back to the desktop computer. Devices such as this are commonly found in supermarkets and drug stores in the U.S.

Numerous tests were conducted with the device to verify its accuracy. It was determined that while the device was not as accurate as the medical equipment found in a doctor's office, it was consistent and relatively accurate. It was deemed quite adequate in monitoring changes in the patient's vital signs.

The current data collected are stored in a database for later use and then reports are printed for the patient. The reports fall into two basic categories: the current readings and historical data. The data are presented in the language of choice and included graphical representation of the information. The patient is advised to keep the data print-outs for their next visit to their healthcare provider.

As the database is indexed by both patient, and physician, the system is able to supply reports to both parties. In a future project we plan to automatically send regular reports to the physician.

## 5 Study Findings

The study involved 22 patients and a nurse researcher. The patients used the system on the average of twice a week during a six-week period. The most interesting findings of the project were:

1. The computer was stolen early in the testing period. The project was put on hold until a new system was purchased. While this event has nothing to do with the experiment, it does demonstrate that even the best plans often go awry.
2. The elderly patients found it difficult to stand on the device while vital signs were recorded. Unfortunately, in order to measure the blood pressure / pulse check, the patient was required to stand.

3. While the patients seemed to generally like the anonymity of the process, they preferred spending time with the nurse than with the system. And, indeed were more likely to participate if the nurse was with them during the tests.
4. Patients had difficulty believing the results of the tests. There is no explanation for this finding.
5. Several of the patients actually used the printed reports to make healthier choices dealing with weight or blood pressure medication.
6. Four patients stopped participating because they did not have enough money to purchase their blood pressure medication and didn't want constant reminders of their health problems.
7. Patients had a difficult time mapping their symptom reporting to the actual "hard" data generated by the system.
8. The mastery and use of the system was viewed in a very positive light by the subjects.
9. Three patients reported that the printed reports were of value to their primary health care provider.
10. All participants said that they would like to have continuing access to the system after the project was completed.
11. Part of the study included obtaining information from the actual healthcare providers. Unfortunately none of them responded to our questionnaires.

## 6 Summary

The experiments, while being qualitative in nature, demonstrated that low-income elders were able to use information technology to help monitor their health. Additionally, they reported high satisfaction in using the system and further found the information useful in making health care decisions.

The key finding is that Information Technology and well-designed user interfaces can be a valuable supplement to traditional health care. Further, with growing need for inexpensive, but efficacious care for the elderly, such tools seem to not only useful, but also attractive to the patient.

One can expand the scope of these findings to include a wide variety of people with a variety of disabilities. Testing in this expanded domain could prove to be a boon to less expensive, quality health care to a broad section of our society that find it difficult to currently receive health care monitoring.

## References


1. Adelman, A.W. & Daly, M..P. (2001) *Geriatrics – 20 Common Problems*, New York: McGraw-Hill.
2. Coleman E.A., Grothaus, L.C., Sandhu, N., & Wagner, E.H. (1999) Chronic care clinics; A randomized controlled trial of a new model of primary care for frail older adults. *Journal of the American Geriatric Society 47*, 775-783.

3. Ferguson, T. (2000) Bringing the Patient into the Medical Information Loop: How the New Information Technologies Will Help Us Reconnect Self-Care & Self-Help with Professional Medical Care
4. Karshmer, A., Pontelli, E. & Gupta, G. (1999) Helping visually impaired students in the study of mathematics. *Proceedings of Frontiers in Education-Puerto Rico, November.*
5. Karshmer, A., Pontelli, E. & Gupta, G., (1999) Software technology and computer interfaces for the disabled: non-visual WWW browsing. *Proceedings of the Human/Computer International Conference, Munich, August.*
6. Karshmer, J. & Karshmer, A. (1995) Hand-held computing in the patient care setting: A pilot project. Journal of the American Medical Informatics Association 19, 7 - 11.
7. Lorenzi, N. M. (2000). The cornerstones of medical Informatics. *Journal of the American Medical Informatics Association* 7, 204-204.
8. Lorig, K, Sobel, D.S., Sewart, A.L., et al (1999) Evidence suggesting that a chronic disease management program can improve health status while reducing hospitalization: A randomized trial. *Medical Care 37*, 5-14.
9. Ruben, D.B., Hirsch, S.H., Frank, J.C., Maly, R.C., Schlesinger, M.S., Weintraub, N. & Yancey, S (1996) The prevention for elderly persons (PEP) program: A model of municipal and academic partnership to meet the needs of older persons for preventive services. *Journal of the American Geriatric Society 44,* 1394-1398.
10. Tetzlaff, L. (1998) Consumer informatics in chronic illness. *Journal of the American Medical Informatics Association 5*, 347-356
11. USF College of Nursing Concept Paper: Community Nursing Centers (1999).

# Investigations to Develop a Fully Adjustable Intelligent Toilet for Supporting Old People and Persons with Disabilities – The Friendly Rest Room (FRR) Project

Paul Panek[1], Georg Edelmayer[1], Charlotte Magnusson[2], Peter Mayer[1], Johan F.M. Molenbroek[3], Håkan Neveryd[2], Robert Schlathau[4], and Wolfgang L. Zagler[1]

[1] fortec – Research Group on Rehabilitation Technology
Favoritenstrasse 11/029, A-1040 Vienna, Austria
{panek,edelmayer,mayer,zagler}@fortec.tuwien.ac.at
http://www.fortec.tuwien.ac.at/frr

[2] Certec, Division of Rehabilitation Engineering, Lund University
Box 118, SE-221 00 Lund, Sweden
{charlotte.magnusson,hakan.neveryd}@certec.lth.se

[3] Industrial Design Engineering, Delft University of Technology, Landbergstraat 15
2628CE Delft, The Netherlands
j.f.m.molenbroek@io.tudelft.nl

[4] Multiple Sclerosis Society Austria, Währinger Gürtel 18-20, A-1090 Vienna, Austria
R.Schlathau@viennaairport.com

**Abstract.** The FRR (Friendly Rest Room) project creates and evaluates prototypes of a more user friendly intelligent toilet for old persons and for persons with disabilities. Additionally, applicable knowledge regarding needs and wishes of old and/or disabled persons and their care persons are documented. In this paper the user driven research approach, ethical aspects and the iterative user centred design process are outlined. First results from user tests of lighting, human computer interface and preferred seating heights are described.

## 1 Introduction and Aim

Many of today's toilets in private and public places are not satisfying the specific needs of European citizens who are facing physical and cognitive limitations. The FRR project is carrying out the necessary research and design steps in order to build and test prototypes for a Friendly Rest Room (FRR) for older persons and/or persons with disabilities. All the elements of the FRR will adjust semi-automatically to the individual needs of older persons with functional limitations or persons with disabilities, allowing them to gain greater autonomy, independence, self-esteem, dignity, safety, improved self-care and, therefore, enable them to enjoy a better quality of life. The methods and technologies involved range from contactless smart card technologies with read-write capabilities, voice activated interfaces, motion control and sensor systems and mechanical engineering, as well as ergonomic research, design for all

K. Miesenberger et al. (Eds.): ICCHP 2004, LNCS 3118, pp. 392–399, 2004.

philosophy, gerontechnology and medical and social sciences. The aim of the FRR project is to empower old and/or disabled persons to use public restrooms in Europe even despite an increasing level of disability and to support secondary users by providing an innovative, user-friendly and highly adaptable, smart toilet system.

## 2 Methods

According to a multidisciplinary approach the consortium brings together end-user organisations representing a wide range of European countries, universities, research and rehabilitation centres as well as industrial partners in the area of industrial and public design and the sanitary industry.

### 2.1 Involvement of Users and Collection of User Needs

The project involves broad user driven research to define the user parameters for designing and developing the FRR systems. User involvement takes place in all the stages of the research and problem solving process of the FRR development and testing. Starting from given restrooms [17] ("standard restrooms") it is necessary to find out (a) what older and/or disabled toilet users (primary as well as secondary users) experience as difficult and (b) what they regard as helpful. This is done by applying social research methods (interviews, observations, questionnaires, and secondary statistics) and by referring to given technical/design solutions represented in the different FRR prototypes generations or FRR design specifications. For this reason 3 user test sites have been established in Sweden (Univ. of Lund), in Greece (Univ. of Athens) and in Austria (Vienna Univ. of Technology).

### 2.2 User Test Sites and Ethical Aspects

The three User Test Sites are organised and maintained by the local FRR project partners. At each site independent User Boards consisting of 7-10 expert users, care persons and professionals from therapy, nursing and medicine and user representing organisations have been established. Additionally, each site is equipped with a "physical toilet prototype" in order to run user tests.

The setting-up and carrying out of the user tests is being accompanied by ethical reviewers in order to ensure the protection of the dignity and privacy of test persons and users involved [18]. In addition, to ensure the ethical quality of the on-going work, the reviewers also help to develop new horizons in the design process about the intimate and sensitive aspects of toileting, personal hygiene and public health as a psychological and cultural phenomenon.

### 2.3 Qualitative and Quantitative Research

One of the main tasks of qualitative research in the FRR project are the user tests which are carried out in several cycles with a relatively small group of specifically selected users. The users are asked to use the prototype system and if they have agreed to be observed, the sociologist takes field notes. Technical data are measured by the sensors of the prototype. After the test post-test interviews are conducted. The methodology is based on the "Theoretical Sampling" method and on the "Grounded Theory" by Strauss and Corbin [1]. Additional to the user test cycles, where the users interact with new FRR prototype generations and reflect about interaction during the post test interview (open interviews recorded & transcribed), other methods for collection of qualitative data have been used: Expert knowledge has been gained during expert workshops by conducting exploratory interviews with secondary users and is also continuously provided by user boards.

In 2002 and 2003 FRR questionnaires about the personal situation regarding using one's own toilet were distributed in nearly all regions of the German speaking Europe among members of seniors' organisations by FRR partner Eurag and by the MS-Society of Austria in their members´ journal. Additionally, Greek, English and Dutch versions of the questionnaires have been distributed nationally.

### 2.4 Iterative and User Centred Design

In the FRR project 4-5 cycles of testing and redesigning [12], [16] are foreseen in order to come up with the final FRR system beginning of 2005. Computer Based Interview tools [13], [14] have been developed as a tool to get feedback and response from users, professionals and experts to different design proposals.

The development process of each part in the FRR is based on both literature and own FRR-research and takes place mostly in The Netherlands by the FRR-partners Landmark and TUDelft. Earlier research on anthropometry of 600 elderly in The Netherlands [27] is used as a reference in this FRR design process. The design prototypes have been pre-tested by students of Industrial Design Engineering, partly using an aging simulation kit developed by Loughborough University in the Third Age Suit-project [28]. After the pre-tests the prototypes are sent to the tests sites in order to be evaluated with old people and users with disabilities.

As an example for a basis of the toilet design Fig. 1 illustrates the large variety in two body dimensions within the population of 600 elderly and 150 young people. The popliteal height is the lower leg length and is relevant for the sitting height. The elbow-seat height is relevant for the armrest. The figure shows that there is almost no correlation between these two measurements. This means that the designers are recommended to make the two product dimensions independently adjustable.

## 3 Ongoing Activities and Preliminary Results

Currently the 3rd test cycle has been successfully completed and is being analysed. The specification, design and manufacturing process will come up with the 4th prototype generation to be evaluated by older persons and disabled users in May 2004.

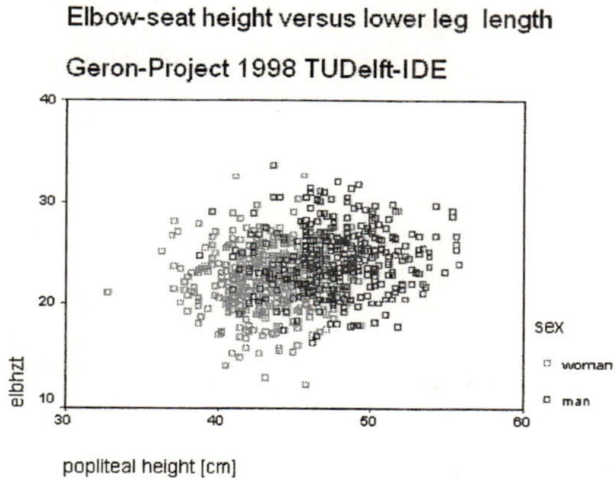


**Fig. 1.** Distribution of popliteal height and elbow-seat height [27].

### 3.1 Design of the Computer Interface

To obtain user input on the design of the computer interface different methods have been used [12], [16]. The process started with an expert user evaluation of a set of scenarios and sketches. This evaluation was performed by expert users both in Lund (Sweden) and in Vienna (Austria). Following this first test, demonstrators of both a voice interface and a hand held control were implemented. The voice interface was based on ASR 3200 (embedded system) from ScanSoft [26]. The hand held control demo interface was implemented on a Pocket PC device (Compaq iPAQ™ 5500) as this type of hardware has a colour screen, is of approximately the right size and allows for the use of images, text and sound. It is important to point out that this device is not intended for the final FRR system, but has been used for obtaining user feedback on different ways to design the computer interface. Preliminary versions of both voice interface and hand held control interface has been tested by groups of expert users both in Lund (Sweden) and in Vienna (Austria). The tests performed so far have confirmed the design approach used.

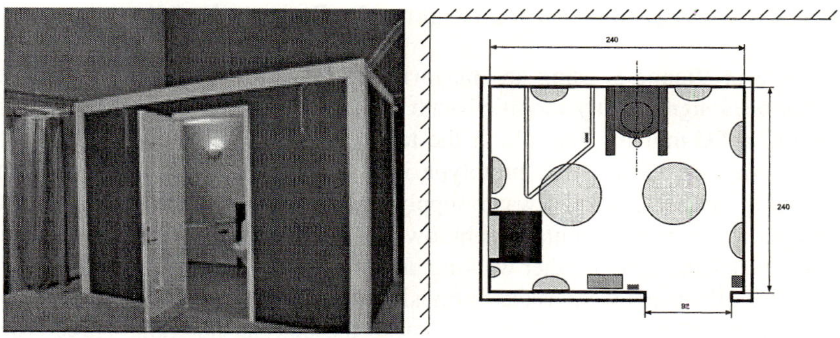


**Fig. 2, 3.** The FRR test room in Lund. Left side (Fig. 2) shows the entrance door, in the background the toilet bowl. Right side (Fig.3) shows site plan with bowl, sink and light sources.

### 3.2 Lighting Tests and Conclusions

Figure 2 and 3 show the test room (usability laboratory) that has been built at the test site in Lund. It was not possible to use a standard usability laboratory because of the privacy aspects involved in toileting. The size of the room was determined by the Swedish standard of 2.40 m x 2.40 m. Illuminance and contrast issues along with the overall impression have been the focus of the tests in Lund. The toilet and sink are connected to the water supply and sewer.

The test room is designed with optimal differences in colour contrast between wall and floor, and between toilet/sink and wall. A blue-painted strip of wood was installed where the floor meets the wall to emphasize the difference in contrast. The NCS (Natural Color System) Lightness Meter [19] was used to measure the difference in contrast. Twelve lamps were installed in the test room:

- Six lighting fixtures on the walls directed upwards.
- Two lighting fixtures with frosted glass mounted in the ceiling.
- Three lights with frosted glass installed around the mirror.
- One spotlight installed directly over the toilet seat.

Frosted glass and lighting fixtures directed upwards were chosen, because many persons with visual impairments prefer indirect lighting. The test set up supplies between 300 and 550 lux when using the maximal effect of the light fixtures. Swedish standards for bathrooms ask for 200 lux, and 300 lux for old persons. From the user tests the following can be concluded:

- Adaptable lighting is necessary
- More work on lighting conditions at the sink (380 lux for sitting users and 416 lux for standing users are not enough for some users with visual impairments).
- One spotlight over the toilet is not enough for the users. If more spots are used, it minimizes the risk that the working area is thrown into the shadow cast by the hands.
- To achieve the optimal lighting solution an extended test time and the possibility for the tester to adapt the lighting on her/his own is required.

### 3.3 Preferences Regarding Sitting Heights – Preliminary Results

The test site in Vienna is using an Hungarian product from Clean Solution Kft [2] which has been significantly modified with additional adjustable grab bars, position sensors and a PC-unit for controlling the toilet and for measuring and logging the users' preferred positions. This prototype is installed in a laboratory environment without being connected to the water supply and sewer. The focus of the user tests has been put on users with limitations in lower parts of the body, meaning users moving with wheelchair, cane or other walking aids.

For the test, the users were asked to transfer to the toilet seat (with clothes on) and to adjust the height and tilt of the toilet seat to the optimal position. Three types of optimal positions were measured: (1) optimal position for sitting down = transferring to the toilet, (2) optimal position for sitting = using the toilet and (3) position for standing up = transferring back to the wheelchair (standing up). Many of the test persons used the test equipment for a time of about 30-60 minutes, therefore several positions were tried and some of them were classified by the test persons as being optimal. The measured values for the sitting height have been transformed using a correction formula in order to become independent from the influences caused by different designs of toilet seats and different tilt angles and different parameters of the used prototypes.

Several test runs were carried out. In the following, the test run in June 2003 is outlined in more details. A height adjustable toilet additionally connected to a PC for steering, measurement and logging purposes was used. The sample consisted of 17 persons (7 male, 10 female) between 15 and 82 years of age (average 53,5), partly older persons (5 persons over 60 years) partly MS (multiple scleroses) patients. The test-persons are partly using wheelchairs, walking aids or sticks.

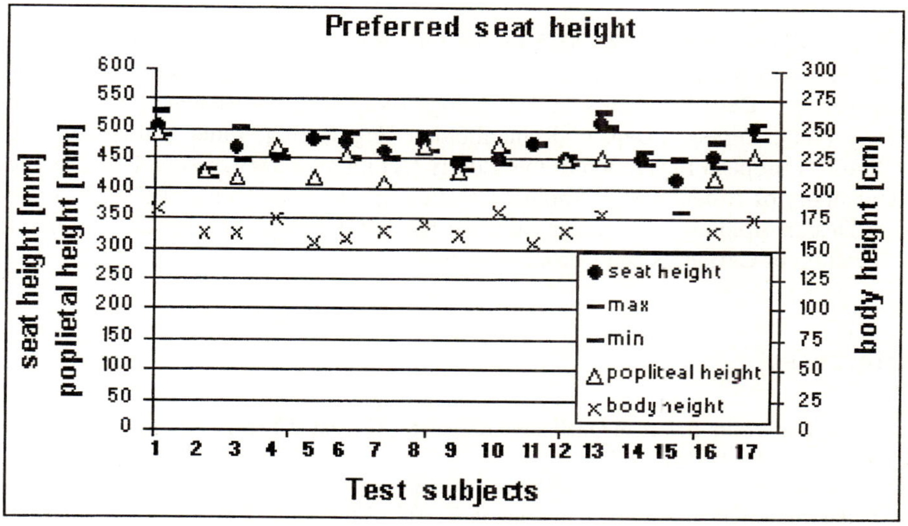


**Fig. 4.** Preferred set heights and basic anthropometric data of 17 test participants in Vienna.

Figure 4 shows measured preferred seat heights for 'position sitting'. Each user has an individual bandwidth of preferred seat heights. The total used range of heights was 364 mm to 529 mm. The popliteal lengths of the test-persons varied between 41 and 49 cm, body height between 183 and 156 cm (average 168.2). There is little correlation between the anthropometric data (popliteal height, body height) and the preferred (average) sitting position. It is obvious, that the different needs of the test-persons need to be covered by the toilet. Preferred seat heights (and also preferred height of supporting bars) cannot necessarily be derived from body parameters but are individual preferences, surely influenced by (remaining) physical abilities. More work on this is currently being done in order to identify important parameters for the future FRR system.

## 4 Discussion and Outlook

The multidisciplinary approach of the FRR project is ensuring a wide horizon to come up with innovative and reasonable approaches which are meeting the users' needs and the economic necessities. An important feature of the FRR project certainly is the strong user involvement which also can be observed in the way the project is structured, especially with the different user test sites and the independent user boards. The 4th prototype is planned to be evaluated in May 2004, the final FRR system will be validated 2004/2005. More information is to be found on the web site of the FRR consortium: `http://www.frr-consortium.org`

## Acknowledgement

FRR is partially funded 2002-2005 by the European Commission as project QLRT-2001-00458 in the Quality of Life program. Project partners are: Industrial Design Engineering – Delft University of Technology (NL), fortec – Vienna Univ. of Technology (AT), Certec – Dep. of Rehabilitation Engineering, Lund University (SE), EURAG - European Federation of the Elderly (AT), Laboratory of Health Informatics – University of Athens (GR), Applied Computing – Dundee University (UK), Landmark Design Holding (NL), Clean Solution Kft (HU), SIVA (IT), HAGG – Hellenic Association of Geriatrics and Gerontology (GR).

## References

1. Strauss, J.Corbin: Basics of Qualitative Research - Grounded Theory Procedures and Techniques, Newbury Park, 1990
2. Clean Solution Kft, Hungary, http://www.cstechnologie.com/
3. F. Aminzadeh, N. Edwards, D. Lockett, R. C. Nair: Utilization of bathroom safety devices, patterns of bathing and toileting, and bathroom falls in a sample of community living older adults, in Technology and Disability 13 (2000), ISSN 1055-4181, IOS Press, pp. 95-103.
4. FRR – Friendly Rest Room Project Web Site: http://www.frr-consortium.org
5. H. Hyppönen: Handbook on Inclusive Design of Telematics Applications, 1999, electronically available on http://www.stakes.fi/include/handbook.htm
6. H. Neveryd, J. Molenbroek, P. Panek: FRR - Friendly Rest Rooms for Elderly and Disabled Persons - A User Centered R&D Project, to be printed in proceedings of Gerontechnology Conf., Miami, U.S., 2002
7. H. Pain, S. Gore, D. L. McLallan: Choosing bathing and showering equipment for people with disabilities, in C. Bühler, H. Knops (Eds.): Proc. of the 5th AAATE Conf., IOS Press, pp. 397-401, 1999.
8. Halkiotis S, Botsis T, Liaskos J, Mantas J. Knowledge Management Approach in the FRR project (poster). In: MIE 2003. CD ROM Proceedings of the Medical Informatics Europe Conference; 2003 May 4-7, Saint Malo, France; 2003.

9. Halkiotis S, Botsis T, Liaskos J, Mantas J. Managing Information and Knowledge gained in the FRR project. In: ICICTH 2003. Proceedings of the 1st International Conference on Information Communication Technologies in Health; 2003 Jul 11-13; Samos Island, Greece; 2003. p. 294-298.
10. INCLUDE Project: INCLUsion of Disabled and Elderly people in telematics, TELEMATICS project 1109, Web Site: http://www.stakes.fi/include/
11. J. A. Sanford: Best Practices in the Design of Toileting and Bathing Facilities for Assisted Transfers – Final Report fro US Access Board, August 2001, http://www.access-board.gov
12. J. Nielsen: Usability Engineering, Academic Press, 1993.
13. Joel S, Alm N, De Campo ME, Gregor P, Hands K, Hine N, Panek P. Eliciting sensitive information about toilet needs using a computer based interview (poster). In: AAATE 2003. CD ROM Proceedings of the 7th European Conference for the Advancement of Assistive Technology; 2003 August 31-September 3, Dublin, Ireland; 2003.
14. K. Hands, P. Gregor, D.R. Peiris, A. F. Newell: A computer-based interviewing tool for usability engineering (UsE-IT), in: CHINS 2001 Consumer Health Informatics Network Scotland, Glasgow, 2001
15. K. Pesola: Bathroom – an important Detail in Designing for Older People, in C. Bühler, H. Knops (Eds.): Proc. of the 5th AAATE Conf., IOS Press, pp. 392-396, 1999.
16. K. T. Ulrich, S. D. Eppinger: Product Design and Development, Second Edition, McGraw-Hill, 2000.
17. Kira, Alexander. The Bathroom, Viking Press, New York, 1976.
18. M. Rauhala, P. Topo: Independent living, technology and ethics. Technology and Disability 15(2003)205-214.
19. NCS - Natural Color System, http://www.ncscolor.com
20. Older adultdata. The handbook of measurements and capabilities of the older adult: data for design safety, Anthropometric and strength data on older people aged 60 and over, publications@dti, Department of Trade and Industry, UK, June 2000
21. P. G. Morasso, L. Baratto, R. Capra, G. Spada: Preventing the risk of falling in elderly patients, in: I. Placenia Porrero and E. Ballabio (Eds.): proc of the 3rd TIDE congress, IOS Press, pp. 101-104, 1998.
22. P. Gregor, A.F. Newell, M. Zajicek: Designing for Dynamic Diversity – Interfaces for Older People, in ASSETS 2002, ACM ISBN 1-58113-464-9-02/07, pp 151-155
23. P. Panek, H. Neveryd, W.L. Zagler: "The FRR Project: Developing a More User Friendly Rest Room"; Presentation: AAATE '03, Dublin; 08-30-2003 - 09-03-2003; in: "Assistive Technology - Shaping the Future"; G. Craddock, L. McCormack, R. Reilly, H. Knops (ed.); IOS Press, Volume 11 (2003), 1 58603 373 5; 678 - 682.
24. R. de Bruin, J. FM Molenbroek, T. Groothuizen, M. van Weeren: On the development of a friendly rest room, proceedings of the INCLUDE conference 2003, Inclusive Design for Society and Business, 2003
25. Sourtzi P, Panek P, Liaskos J, Mantas J. Friendly Rest Room (FRR): Developing the concept and the product. In: Proceedings of the Alzheimer Europe Conference; 2003 June 13-15, Thessaloniki, Greece; 2003.
26. Speech Recognition ASR 3200 from Scan Soft, http://www.scansoft.com
27. Steenbekkers, LPA, J.M. Dirken, C.E.M. van Beijsterveldt, J.F.M. Molenbroek, A.I.M. Voorbij: Design-relevant characteristic of ageing users; background and guidelines for product innovation (Series Ageing and Ergonomics, Volume 1). Delft University Press, Delft (NL), 1998, ISBN: 90-407-1709-5
28. The Third Age Simulation Suit, Taurus, Loughborough University, retrieved from the WWW on March 31st, 2004: http://www.lboro.ac.uk/taurus/simulation.htm

# Tele-surveillance System for Patient at Home: The MEDIVILLE System

Jean-Louis Baldinger[1], Jérôme Boudy[1], Bernadette Dorizzi[1], Jean-Pierre Levrey[1], Rodrigo Andreao[1], Christian Perpère[1], François Delavault[1], François Rocaries[2], Christophe Dietrich[2], and Alain Lacombe[3]

[1] Institut National des Télécommunications – GET F-91011 Evry France
[2] Ecole Supérieure Informatique d'Electronique et Electrotechnique - ESIEE, F-93162 Noisy-le-Grand
[3] Institut Supérieur de Technologie et management, F-93162 Noisy-le-Grand

**Abstract.** This work is concerned with the design and realization of a complete telecare application for remote monitoring of patients at home, including a wireless monitoring portable device held by the patient and a remote central server application located in a surveillance center. Agitation, position and cardiac rate data are used for alarm decision and can be exploited by the central server application. Originality resides in the actimetry and heart rate data combination for alarm decision and in the central server design aiming at offering flexible assistance services for both the surveillance medical team and the practitioner in charge of the patient.

## 1 Introduction and State-of-the-Art in the Telesurveillance Domain

Promoting patient's Home telecare is in France, and more widely in Europe, is today motivated by the fact that generally patients can convalesce at home in their familiar environment by being remotely monitored, and that this also responds to the difficult problem of beds saturation in hospitals. Namely the goals of our telecare system, developed in the frame of the MEDIVILLE project[1] is precisely to offer a technical solution to the Home telesurveillance (i.e. remote monitoring) for elderly persons and cardiac persons who need a constant surveillance in their everyday life. This may also represent an important factor of integration for these persons, young or older, who are susceptible to become insulated from the society due to their illness. Tele-surveillance implementation, and pilot exploitation in certain cases, is growing in North America and in Europe, in particular within the Northern countries such as Norway, Finland but also in Germany. It is expected to spread rapidly in the ten coming years with the population who will become older and older.

Based on a similar alarm-based medical scheme such as found in [1, 2, 4, 5, 6], the MEDIVILLE system is composed of a wireless monitoring portable device hold by

[1] MEDIVILLE project: takes part of the AUTOMOVILLE project funded by the ACI-Ville program of the French Research Office. Started in January 2001 and ended in April 2003. Partnership: ISTM, ESIEE and INT.

K. Miesenberger et al. (Eds.): ICCHP 2004, LNCS 3118, pp. 400–407, 2004.

the patient at home and a remote surveillance server computer located in the surveillance centre (see Fig.1).

The wireless portable device, fixed on the patient's girdle, is connected to several biomedical sensors in contact with the patient's body. When the patient at home is suffering from a malaise, a cardiac attack or makes a fall, the patient's portable device will generate an alarm and immediately transmit it to the surveillance centre where a medical team is looking after the different monitored patients 24 over 24 hours.

For the last decade, several R&D projects (namely European Telematics and IST projects as MOBCARE, TELECARE, CHS...) have been devoted to the remote surveillance of cardiac persons by proposing different concepts such as the intelligent dress with embedded sensors or holter-based systems able to transmit ECG (electrocardiogram) channels to a remote centre; for instance the VTAMN project proposes a medical teleassistance suit ([2, 3]) consisting in several non-intrusive biomedical sensors (complete ECG-leads array, SPO2, sudation, blood pressure, skin temperature...). More recently projects such as AMON[2] and EPI-MEDICS[3] [1] have realised lighter systems often integrated in current devices such as a watch or a light portable box. A most important problem for all these devices, and namely for the ECG signal measurement, is the disturbances generated from the patient movements or the capture of external signal sources interference (electromagnetic, power line,....). On the other side, trying to eliminate these disturbances often means sensors more intrusive for the patient. Most of telecare application for elderly patient at home target fall detection and require a reliable alarm system able to warn a telesurveillance or urgency centre by avoiding false detection: indeed most of urgency cases for elderly people are falls events and several approaches are proposed based on position and inclination measurements and accelerometers sensors such as proposed in [4, 5] showing already satisfactory fall detection results (about 80% good detection). Based on simpler approach similar to [6] (patients'position) the MEDIVILLE system, as developed in section 3, intends to propose an original and simple fusion scheme by combining the patient's position to an agitation measurement and to the heart rate frequency (pulse measurement): indeed the pulse measurement is generally not associated to fall detection schemes as considered as too much unreliable measurement. Namely to make pulse signal acquisition more robust by reducing measurement noise was one of the challenging work targeted by MEDIVILLE. Moreover experience feedback from healthcare professionals were also taken into account and a design methodology, as presented in section 2, was followed by the MEDIVILLE team to design and realise a wireless portable terminal on one hand responding to a trade-off between a minimal invasiveness and a robustness to any kind of interference, on the other hand targeting a simple and low-cost system. The MEDIVILLE portable device, fixed to the patient (section 3), is measuring over a certain time period his activity degree and position status and his heart frequency rate (pulse rate); the whole is being processed and fused to predict an eventual patient's problem and to create an alarm transmitted to the server of the surveillance centre. Section 4 describes the server stage which is based on a quite flexible man-machine interface and communication process based on a VPN protocol (Virtual Private Network): for instance it allows

[2] AMON project: IST program from 2001 till 2003, `http://www.medictouch.net/AMON`

[3] EPI-MEDICS project: IST from 2001 till 2004, `http://www.epi-medics.insa-lyon.fr/` and see also reference [1]

biomedical data exploitation (e.g. history analysis) and access in a quite flexible way for the medical surveillance team and the practitioner to be potentially connected as client to the central server.

## 2 The Methodological Process Implemented to Design the MEDIVILLE System

The methodological process implemented to design the MEDIVILLE prototype was based on five main stages, from the knowledge of the specific area of home telecare to the MEDIVILLE platform realization and its first experimentations:

1 / One stage whose objective was to build the research network and to initialise the collaborative process between partners. During this stage, the project team has defined scientific, medical, sociologic stake of the project, in collaboration with medical and health specialists, local communities representatives and sociologists. The method was essentially based on interviews, workshops or discussions and exchanges during specialised seminars (CATEL, ERGO-IA, BIOMEDSIM 2003).

2 / One stage intended to identify and analyse the context of usage and the needs and constraints in the economical, technological, ethic deontological and regulation fields, taking in account previous research works as such done in the frame of the DHOS CREDES, DREES [7, 8, 9, 10].

3 / One stage of functional analysis and definition based on the "value analysis" methodology[4]. During this phase, we also realised state of the art studies based on technological survey, to identify and choose the different technological hardware and software parts of the system.

4 / One stage of conception and technical realisation and integration built on an iterative process. During this phase, we tried to take into account ergonomic recommendations and to improve the human interface of the different parts of the application (specially on the server part).

5 / One stage devoted to experimentation and test of the demonstrating platform in a simulated environment. At this time we had opportunity to verify the pertinence and reliability of the data delivered by the physiological and motion sensors placed on the patient, and to improve the different algorithms implemented in data processing and transmission. During this phase, we decided to build several scenario of usage (medical emergency, long term medical survey and so on).

The main experience feedback on the project is that acceptability of the products and applications are determinant to deliver efficient homecare services based on information technologies. We believe that it is essential to proceed in an approach implementing simultaneously functional analysis and acceptability evaluation. The track

---

[4] Value analysis is a systematic and creative method to improve competitiveness. It is aimed at satisfying user needs by means of a specific procedure for invention (or modification) which is functional (the purpose of the activity), economic (what it costs) and multidisciplinary (how one does it). This methodology was started in the late 1940's by Lawrence D. Miles while working in the purchasing department at General Electric.

that we wish to explore will seek to adapt the value analysis method in order to take into account, during the stage of functional analysis, acceptability criteria. Beyond the economic value, it is a question of determining the functionalities which can reinforce the practical value of the products and services developed, by taking into account ergonomics and appropriation considerations.

## 3 Home Telesurveillance System

Working in-door and fixed on the patient's girdle, the wireless portable device aims to monitor the patient at home through different biomedical measurements which have been selected from the first stages of the previous methodological process. Hence four sensors were specified accordingly:

- patient's attitude: lied down or standing up/seated
- his activity or agitation
- his cardiac frequency
- urgency call button starting the most recent previous sensors data

All the sensors data are processed within the wireless portable device by using low-consumption electronic components in order to face autonomy problems which are also crucial in that application. The circuit architecture is based on different micro-controllers devoted to acquisition, signal processing and emission.

The portable device is connected by radio to an in-door PC-base station placed in the main room of the patient's house. Continuously receiving the emission signals from the portable device through a VHF radio link, the base station exploits them to detect potential illness situation and, only in that case and after an automatic decision process, it generates an alarm towards the remote server. On the other side the PC-base station is connected to the remote server of the Surveillance centre (Fig. 1) through an IP channel using a VPN protocol (see section 4). The selection of a VHF frequency range for the radio channel has been made to ensure a sufficient emission-reception distance and robustness for a domestic environment such as flat rooms: this was successfully tested in different laboratory rooms separated by metal-composed walls. Nevertheless research are currently been pursued on another radio protocol for in-door home application (e.g. Wi-Fi, UWB...). An important work was devoted to the sensors realisation (activity, attitude and pulse) and signal processing improvement within the micro-controller to make the pulse signal acquisition more robust to patient's movements: an original noise reduction algorithm implemented in the micro-controllers has allowed to lower measurement variance below the 10% required threshold. Errors protection was also implemented for the radio transmission.

## 4 Computer and Communication System Used in the Surveillance Server

### 4.1 Global Design

The overall architecture of the server is based on three separate components:

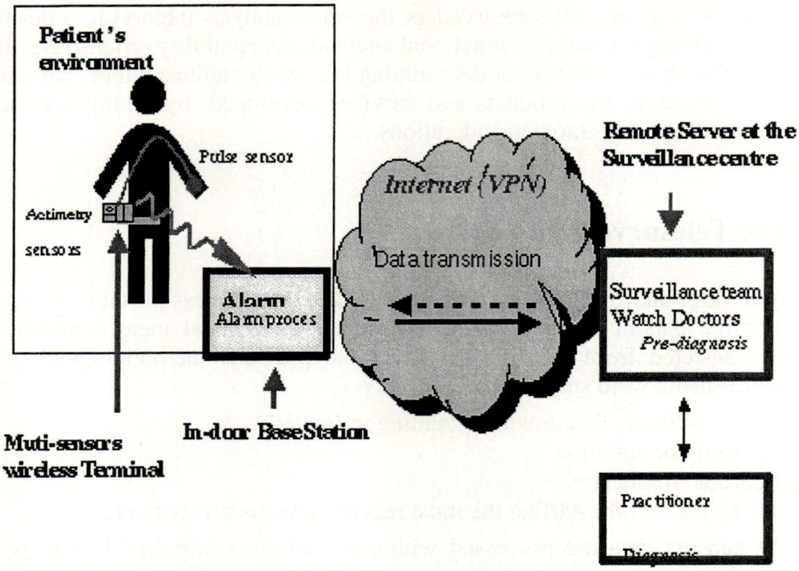


**Fig. 1.** Architecture of the MEDIVILLE system: Patient's environment (wireless terminal with actimetry and pulse sensors + base station) and the Surveillance centre server.

- the patient's system
- the practitioner's system
- the central server

It is linked to the home telesurveillance system by a Virtual Private Network (VPN). The architecture of the proposed prototype is shown in figure 2. Each component is then described in more detail.

The practitioner can be connected to both the main server and the patient's base station either through his cellular phone or his computer.

The main server consists in two main stages: the internet portal and at least one another computer embedding one or more databases as well as the necessary tools for the practitioner.

The central server is the main communication node,managing the following functions:

- The first and most important function is to keep the contact with the patient and insure his security. It receives the alarms from the patient's system and reorients them, according to their seriousness, to the practitioner in charge and, in case of unavailability or absence, to an another emergency system (such as the French SAMU).
- The storage of all the information relative to the patient.
- The security insurance on information storage and the access to this information for authorised users: patient agent, practitioner agent and server manager.
- The provision to the practitioner of all information and aids necessary for taking care of their patients.

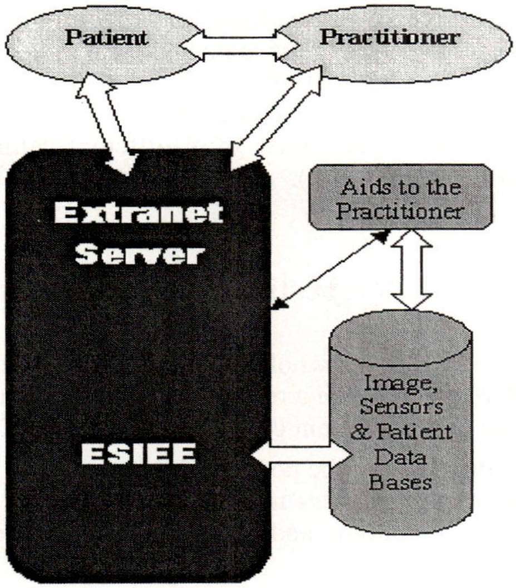


**Fig. 2.** Schematics of the e-health Server prototype: the surveillance server is located in ESIEE.

The importance and complexity of the functions taken over by this server strongly require a reliable and extensive system. The system shall contain a sufficient capacity and redundancy in order to cater for these conditions.

## 4.2 Data Exchange

Data acquired from the patient are stored on the local computer as follows:

- A current file (replaced when a new data set is received)
- A daily file relative to the last 24 hours period.
- Currently, the data exchange performed using an ftp protocol using a VPN.

The transmission system scenario includes the following distinct cases:

1. During normal operation, the local home system is solicited at regular intervals (every 30 seconds) by the central system that transmits the totality of recent sensors data (excepted for a special request such as consulting historical data of the last 24 hours or for the change of data acquisition frequency). Transmission is performed by using a text file with a header specifying the data format and the time stamp followed by the digital data.
2. In an alarm case (generated either automatically by the monitoring system or manually by the patient) the local system takes the initiative to communicate with the central server and transmit (simultaneously to the alarm) the latest available data.
3. The last case corresponds to a direct monitoring requested by the practitioner on a particular patient. Il this case, the central server directly connects the local system to the practitioner who can collect all the necessary data for his intervention.

The normal operation protocol also includes the reliability tests of the communication system and the synchronisation of the main and local systems.

The central system offers other databases facilities such as medical images, medication data and pharmacological models but also assistance tools to access with protection and visualize the set of databases from different cellular terminals (WAP, UMTS) or platforms (PC, laptop, palm).

## 5 Current Results and Perspectives

An iterative validation phase of the whole system has been conducted in laboratory within the second half-year 2003 with a reduced group of experts and testers, leading to following refinements of the different components of the MEDIVILLE prototype:

- the signal processing chain of the portable device has been improved against the patient's movements disturbances namely concerning the pulse signal acquisition; terminal supply autonomy and ergonomic acceptance were also found as very crucial.
- decision strategies combining actimetry and pulse data have been implemented in the in-door PC base station to improve the fall detection and to correlate to heart problems, but still works remain to be done in this area,
- the surveillance server architecture and MMI has been refined to offer more flexibility in the biomedical signals exploitation (signals history and visualizing, acknowledge procedures, multi-agent management) according to the healthcare professionals needs.

Validation and acceptance tests with the collaboration of SAMU (French Medical Urgency Unit) and Toulouse Hospital are planned in course of years 2004 and 2005, in the frame of the TelePat project[5]. This new project consists in the follow-up of MEDIVILLE project focused on usage evaluation and technical re-design of the existing system with the healthcare professionals partners of TelePat project.

## Acknowledgments

The authors would like to thank Ms. J. Andoh and Mr. H.C. Ramara for their contribution to the project, but also Dr. M. Baer and Dr. A. Ozguler from the Urgency unit SAMU of Garches Hospital for their very helpful advises.

## References

1. Rubel, P., Gouaux, F., Fayn, J., Assanelli, D., Cuce, A., Edenbrandt, L., Malossi, C., "Towards Intelligent and Mobile Systems for Early Detection and Interpretation of Cardiological Syndroms", IEEE Conf. On Computers in Cardiology, 2001, pp. 193-196

[5] TelePat is a RNTS project recently started in December 2003 funded by the French Research Office: it is composed of the MEDIVILLE consortium completed with INSERM-Toulouse, SAMU-Garches and MEDIAG (SME manufacturing portable ECG devices).

2. Dittmar, A., Delhomme, G. "Living Tissue Mechanisms and Concepts as Models for Biomedical Microsystems and Devices", 1st Annual International IEEE-EMBS Special Topic Conference on Microthechnologies in Medicine and Biology, Lyon-France, Oct-2000
3. VTAMN Project "Vêtement de Téléassistance Médicale Nomade (Medical Teleassistance Suit)", RNTS-2000 program funded by the French Research Office
4. Kemp, B., Janssen, A., van der Kamp, B. "Body position can be monitored using minitaure accelerometers and earth mangnetic field sensors ", Electroenc. Clin. Neuro., vol.109, 1998
5. Noury, N., Tarmizi, A., Savall, D., Boissy, P., Barralon, P., Virone, G., Rumeau, P., 'A smart sensor for the fall detection in daily routine', SICICA2003, Aveiro, July 2003
6. Williams, G., Dougthy, K., Cameron, K., Bradley, D.A " A Smart Fall and Activity Monitor for Telecare Applications ", 20th IEEE-EMBS conf., October 1998
7. Dhos, Credes, 'Télémédecine et évaluation: aide méthodologique à l 'évaluation de la télémédecine.' Mars 2000
8. Datar-Credes. 'Quel système de santé à l'horizon 2020', Rapport préparatoire au schéma de services collectifs sanitaires,CREDES, octobre 2000
9. Drees, 'Annuaire des statistiques sanitaires et sociales 2000', La documentation Française-Collection Etudes et statistiques
10. Beuscart, R.: Les enjeux de la Société de l'Information dans le domaine de la santé (2000)

# Classification of Infant Crying to Identify Pathologies in Recently Born Babies with ANFIS

Orion F. Reyes-Galaviz[1], Emilio Arch Tirado[2], and Carlos Alberto Reyes-Garcia[3]

[1] Instituto Tecnologico de Apizaco
Apizaco, Tlaxcala, 90400, Mexico
orionfrg@yahoo.com

[2] Instituto Nacional de la Comunicación Humana (INCH)
Mexico, D.F.
arch@infosel.net.mx

[3] Instituto Nacional de Astrofisica Optica y Electronica (INAOE)
Luis E. Erro 1, Tonantzintla, Puebla, 72840, Mexico
kargaxxi@inaoep.mx

**Abstract.** In this work we present the design of an Automatic Infant Cry Recognizer hybrid system, that classifies different kinds of cries, with the objective of identifying some pathologies in recently born babies. These cries are recordings of normal, deaf and asphyxiating infants, of ages from 1 day up to one year old. For its acoustic processing we used a free software tool called Praat [1]. Additionally, we used Matlab to implement the system, based on ANFIS [2], to classify the infant's crying. In the model here presented, we classify the input vectors in three corresponding classes, normal cry, hypo acoustic (deaf) and asphyxiating cries. We have obtained scores up to 96 % in precision on the classification.

## 1 Introduction

Just born babies may be classified as the most handicapped kind of persons in the world. In the first place, they can not even survive without adult's help. Secondly, because they completely lack the ability to communicate, not only their physiological needs, but also their physical and psychological status. The pathological diseases in infants are commonly detected several months, and often times, years, after the infant is born. If any of these diseases would have been detected earlier, they could have been attended and maybe avoided by the opportune application of treatments and therapies. It has been found that the infant's cry has much information on its sound wave. For small infants crying is a form of communication, a very limited one, but similar to the way adults communicate. Given that the crying in babies is a primary communication function, governed directly by the brain, any alteration on the normal functioning of the babies' body is reflected in the cry. Based on the information contained inside the cry's wave, we can determine the infant's physical state; even detect physical pathologies, mainly from the brain, in very early phases [5].

K. Miesenberger et al. (Eds.): ICCHP 2004, LNCS 3118, pp. 408–415, 2004.

## 2 Infant Cry as a Tool for Early Clinical Diagnosis

Neurolinguistics considers the just born baby cry as the first linguistic manifestation. It is the first experience in the sound production, which is followed by propioceptions of laryngeal and oral movements, altogether with the listening capabilities feedback. Which, deliberately, very soon, will be used to the production of phonemes. The acquisition and phoneme selection is achieved through the discrimination between the emissions of a spontaneous vocal activity and its auditory reinforcement. Von Monakow y Morgue [7] in 1928 emphasized the need of innate activities as suction, swallowing, and the crying as a previous stage to the development of language. Late diagnosis of deafness is proven to cause delay in language development. Children with hearing losses identified before 6 months of age have significantly better language development than children whose hearing losses are identified after 6 months of age. Children with normal cognitive development whose hearing losses are identified before six months can develop language at the same or a similar rate to a hearing child [8]. Children identified with a hearing loss between birth and six months old have a receptive language of 200 words and expressive language of 117 words, whereas those identified between ages of seven and 18 months have a receptive language of 86 words and expressive language of 54 words. When tested at 26 months of age, those identified as deaf before six months old have "significantly higher" measures of language growth and personal-social development [9].

In recent studies the subjective auditory analysis of voice and speech, have been replaced by objective spectral-phonographic analysis, with the help of audio taping and computerized analysis. Receiving special attention the spectral-phonographical analysis of the just born baby crying. Preliminary reports are focused in the analysis of full term newborns, premature, with neurological, metabolic, or chromosomal alterations just born babies, as well as those with congenital anomalies among others. The studies suggest an objective variability of the crying related to the health state and the neuropsychological integrity. In the case of the infants who have been through a period of new-born asphyxia, they are exposed to possible changes or neurological level disturbance, depending on the degree of asphyxia that they had suffered. According to the American Academy of Pediatrics (AAP), about 2 to 6 out of 1000 full term newborns present asphyxia, and the incidence is of 60 % in premature newborns with low weight. From them, about 20 to 50 % die during the neonatal period. From the survivors, 25 % develop permanent neurological sequels.

There's a tight relationship between the central nervous system and the efferent ways that involve the phono-articulator apparatus. When this function is not the proper one, changes are produced in a intrinsic laryngeal muscular level so as in the muscles that intervene in the respiratory process, these changes will translate possibly in alterations or modifications in the baby's cry. The cry study importance on the recent born infant during the first months are related with the psychological and neurophysiological information that it provides about the infant, its right interpretation will provide complementary information that could support the different clinical diagnosis.

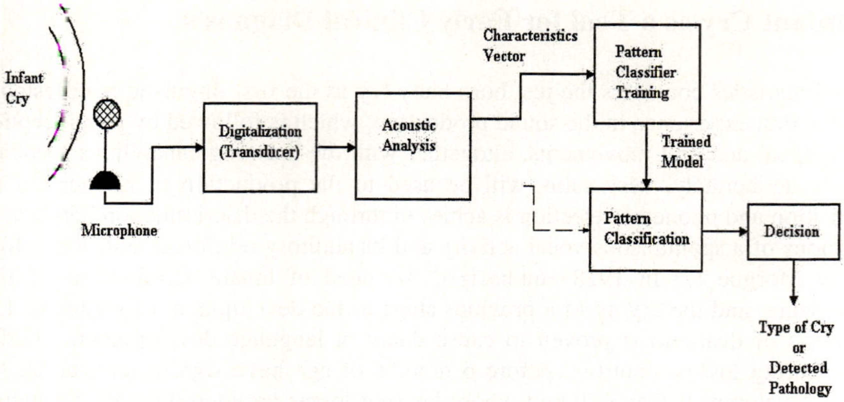


**Fig. 1.** Automatic Infant Cry Recognition Process.

# 3 The Infant Cry Automatic Recognition Process

The infant cry automatic classification process is, in general, a pattern recognition problem, similar to Automatic Speech Recognition (ASR). The goal is to take the wave from the infant's cry as the input pattern, and at the end obtain the kind of cry or pathology detected on the baby [4], [6]. Generally, the process of Automatic Cry Recognition is done in two steps. The first step is known as signal processing, or feature extraction, whereas the second is known as pattern classification. In the acoustical analysis phase, the cry signal is first normalized and cleaned, and then it is analyzed to extract the most important characteristics in function of time. Some of the more used techniques for the processing of the signals are those to extract: linear prediction coefficients, cepstral coefficients, pitch, intensity, spectral analysis, and Mel's filter bank. The set of obtained characteristics is represented by a vector, which, for the process purposes, represents a pattern. The set of all vectors is then used to train the classifier. Later on, a set of unknown feature vectors is compared with the knowledge that the computer has to measure the classification output efficiency. Figure 1 shows the different stages of the described recognition process.

# 4 Acoustic Processing

The acoustic analysis implies the selection and application of normalization and filtering techniques, segmentation of the signal, feature extraction, and data compression. With the application of the selected techniques we try to describe the signal in terms of some of its fundamental components. A cry signal is complex and codifies more information than the one needed to be analyzed and processed in real time applications. For that reason, in our cry recognition system we used an extraction function as a first plane processor. Its input is a cry signal, and its output is a vector of features that characterizes key elements of the cry's sound wave. All the vectors obtained this way are later fed to a recognition model, first to train it, and later to classify the type of cry. We have been experimenting with diverse types of acoustic characteristics, reporting in this work the results obtained with the Mel Frequency Cepstral Coefficients.

### 4.1 MFCC (Mel Frequency Cepstral Coefficients)

The low order cepstral coefficients are sensitive to overall spectral slope and the high-order cepstral coefficients are susceptible to noise. This property of the speech spectrum is captured by the Mel spectrum. The Mel spectrum operates on the basis of selective weighing of the frequencies in the power spectrum. High order frequencies are weighed on a logarithmic scale where as lower order frequencies are weighed on a linear scale. The Mel scale filter bank is a series of $L$ triangular bandpass filters that have been designed to simulate the bandpass filtering believed to occur in the auditory system. This corresponds to series of bandpass filters with constant bandwidth and spacing on a Mel frequency scale . On a linear frequency scale, this spacing is approximately linear up to 1KHz and logarithmic at higher frequencies. Most of the recognition systems are based on the MFCC technique and its first and second order derivative. The derivatives normally approximate trough an adjustment in the line of linear regression towards an adjustable size segment of consecutive information frames. The resolution of time and the smoothness of the estimated derivative depends on the size of the segment.

## 5 Cry Patterns Classification

The set of acoustic characteristics obtained in the extraction stage, is represented generally as a vector, and each vector can be taken as a pattern. These vectors are later are used to make the classification process. There are four basic schools for the solution of the pattern classification problem, those are: a) Pattern comparison (dynamic programming), b) Statistic Models (Hidden Markov Models HMM). c) Knowledge based systems (expert systems) and d) Connectionists Models (neural networks). In recent years, a new strong trend of more robust hybrid classifiers has been emerging. One of the better known hybrid models is the resulting from the combination of the neural and fuzzy approaches [2], [3]. For the development of the present work we'll focus on the description of one of the neuro-fuzzy models, known as Adaptive Neuro-Fuzzy Inference System (ANFIS). We have selected this kind of model, in principle, because of its adaptation, learning and knowledge representation capabilities. Besides, one of its main functions is pattern recognition. Although these kinds of models are still under constant experimentation, their results have been very encouraging.

In a Automatic Infant Cry Classification System, the goal is to identify a model of an unknown pattern obtained after the original sound wave is acoustically analyzed, and its dimensionality reduced. One system with the capability to adjust to changing patterns is ANFIS [2], which also is able to implement a nonlinear mapping from the input to the output space. ANFIS is a neuro-fuzzy system that combines the learning capabilities of neural networks [3], with the functionality of fuzzy inference systems [2].

### 5.1 ANFIS Architecture

ANFIS is a hybrid learning architecture, proposed by Jang [2]. As an adaptive network, the parameters in some ANFIS nodes are adapted during training, in which case the node is called **adaptive** node and it is graphically represented by a square. There are also nodes whose parameters remain unchanged during training, they are called **fixed** nodes and are represented by a circle. The network architecture is composed of five layers. The architecture we used has two inputs, corresponding to each of the principal components previously obtained. We used seven trapezoidal membership functions for each input. The linguistic properties assigned to each membership function, for our purposes, were respectively *Very Low (VL), Low (L), MoreOrLess Low (MLL), Medium (M), MoreOrLess High (MLH), High (H) and Very High (VH)*. During the experiments, we tested different parameter settings, as well as different kinds of fuzzy membership functions. Through a heuristic selective process, we ended up with seven *trapezoidal* membership functions for each of the two input nodes.

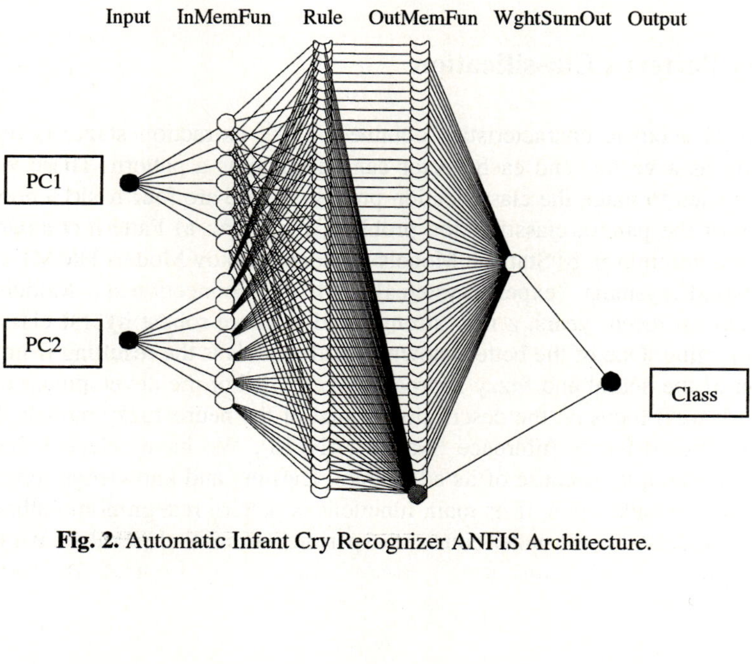


**Fig. 2.** Automatic Infant Cry Recognizer ANFIS Architecture.

## 6 Implementation of the Crying Classification System

A set of 122 samples have been directly recorded from 59 babies by pediatricians, with ICD-67 Sony digital recorders, and then sampled at 8000 Hertz. The same pediatricians, at the end of each recorded sample, do the labeling. The babies selected for recording are from just born up to 6 month old, regardless of gender. The collection of pathological samples is done by a group of doctors specialized in communication disorders, from babies already diagnosed as deaf by them. The corpus collection is still in its initial stage, and will continue for a while. The 116 crying records, from the three categories, were segmented in signals of one second length. In this case, 1376 segmented one second samples were obtained, 157 of them belong to normal cry, and 879 to deaf cry, and 340 with asphyxia. At the following step the samples are processed one by one to extract their MFCC by means of Praat 4.0. The acoustic characteristics are extracted as follows: for every one second sample we extract 16 coefficients from each 50-millisecond frame, generating with this vectors with 304 coefficients by sample. In this situation, the dimension of the input vector is large, but the components of the vectors are highly correlated. In cases like this, and in order to simplify the classifier's architecture, it is useful to reduce the dimension of the input vectors. An effective procedure for performing this operation is the principal component analysis (PCA). This technique has three effects: it orthogonalizes the components of the input vectors; it orders the resulting orthogonal components (Principal Components or PC) so that those with the largest variation come first; and it eliminates those components that contribute the least to the variation in the data set. In the present work, we apply PCA, using Matlab, to the analyzed vectors to obtain reduced vectors with two principal components. The vectors so obtained are the actual input to ANFIS.

The generation of the fuzzy inference system (FIS), as well as the implementation of ANFIS, and the evaluation of the system after training are implemented with the Matlab's Fuzzy Logic Toolbox. The FIS's architecture consists of two nodes at the input layer, each of which is subdivided in 7 membership functions, which generate 49 rules, and at the output layer the cry classes are represented by only one node, as shown in Figure 2. In order to make the training and recognition test, we randomly select 157 samples of each class. The normal cry's sample number available determines this number. From them, 107 samples of each class are randomly selected for training. With these vectors the network is trained. The training is made up to 20 or 30 epochs have been completed. After the network is trained, we test it with the 50 separated samples of each class left from the original 157 samples.

## 7 Experimental Results

The classification accuracy was calculated by taking the number of samples correctly classified, divided by the total number of samples. The detailed results of one of the tests for MFCC, with samples of 1 second, with 16 coefficients for every 50 ms frame, are shown in the confusion matrix shown in Table1.

**Table 1.** Confusion matrix for the classification of Infant Cry with ANFIS.

| Class | Normal | Deaf | Asphyxia |
|---|---|---|---|
| **Normal** | 49 | 1 | 0 |
| **Deaf** | 2 | 48 | 0 |
| **Asphyxia** | 0 | 2 | 48 |

The classification accuracy achieved in this experiment is of 96.67 %. The experimental results still present some variations. Some times the accuracy is higher and some times is lower, although never lower than 93 %. We are working to improve the system s performance.

### 7.1 Comparison with Other Works

In previous experiments performed by ourselves, reported in [10], we used the same set of samples, and the same training approach. The recognition was based on a feed-forward input delay neural network, trained by gradient descent with adaptive learning rate back-propagation. The neural network's architecture consists of 304 neurons on the input layer, a hidden layer with 120 neurons, and one output layer with 3 neurons. The training is made until 500 epochs have been completed or a $1 \times 10^{-6}$ error has been reached. The results obtained are shown in Table 2. As can be noticed, the results in this case are slightly better, but the complexity of the network and the number of epochs needed to be trained are much grater than the system based in ANFIS.

**Table 2.** Confusion Matrix showing a 97.33% efficiency after 296 training epochs using MFCC acoustic characteristics.

| | Normal | Deaf | Asphyxia |
|---|---|---|---|
| Normal | 46 | 4 | 0 |
| Deaf | 0 | 50 | 0 |
| Asphyxia | 0 | 0 | 50 |

## 8 Conclusions

We have shown that the classification of infant cry may be automatically performed. And that, once a robust classification system is developed, its results might be used by pediatricians, nurses or general doctors to identify some kind of pathologies, like deafness or asphyxia, in recently born babies. A system like the one described here, is not intended to substitute the medical specialist, to the contrary, it is thought as a tool to warn doctors of a possible malfunction or pathology present in the baby. An opportune warning on possible pathologies like those will allow placing special attention on the suspicious babies, in order to detect the extent of the pathology as early as possible. The early diagnosis will lead to the application of the adequate therapy, which will avoid learning delays or other future handicapping sequels, and possible death. We also showed that ANFIS is a hybrid model, which offers very acceptable performance in classification tasks. Compared to other classifiers we have tested, ANFIS' accuracy is similar, but it offers some advantages like lower training time and simplicity in its implementation.

## References


1. Boersma, P., Weenink, D. Praat v. 4.0.8. A system for doing phonetics by computer. Institute of Phonetic Sciences of the University of Amsterdam. February, (2002)
2. Jang, J.-S. R., ANFIS: Adaptive Network-based Fuzzy Inference System, in IEEE Transactions on Systems, Man, and Cybernetics, 23(03):665-685, May (1993).
3. Lin Chin-Teng, and George Lee, C.S., Neural Fuzzy System: A Neuro-Fuzzy Synergism to Intelligent Systems, Prentice Hall, Upper Saddle River, NJ, (1996).
4. Sergio D. Cano, Daniel I. Escobedo y Eddy Coello, El Uso de los Mapas Auto-Organizados de Kohonen en la Clasificación de Unidades de Llanto Infantil, Grupo de Procesamiento de Voz, 1er Taller AIRENE, Universidad Catolica del Norte, Chile, (1999), pp 24-29.
5. O. Wasz-Hockert, J. Lind, V. Vuorenkoski, T. Partanen y E. Valanne, El Llanto en el Lactante y su Significación Diagnóstica, Cientifico-Medica, Barcelona, (1970).
6. Ekkel, T. "Neural Network-Based Classification of Cries from Infants Suffering from Hypoxia-Related CNS Damage", Master Thesis. University of Twente, (2002). The Netherlands.
7. Monakow C, Morgue R., Introduction a l'étude de la neurologie et de la psychopathologie. Integration et désintégration de la function, Paris: Alcan (1928).
8. Yoshinaga-Itano 1998, quoted in 'The High Cost Of Hearing Lost; What Our Publics Need to Know', Donald Radcliffe, The Hearing Journal, May (1998), vol 51 no. 5.
9. Yoshinaga-Itano, C. & Appusso, M L., The development of deaf and hard of hearing children identified through the high-risk registry, in The American Annals of the deaf, 143, 416-424. (1998).
10. Reyes-Galaviz, O. F & Reyes-Garcia, C.A, Recognition of Patterns of Infant Cry for the Early Identification of Hypo acoustics and Asphyxia with Neural Networks, in WSEAS Transactions on Acoustics and Music, Issue 1, Vol 1, January (2004), pp 56-61, ISSN 1109-9577.

# Improving Quality of Life and Well-Being for Children and the Elderly through Vibroacoustic Sound Therapy

Phil Ellis

Department of Arts, Design, Media and Culture
University of Sunderland, Bede Tower, Ryhope Road
Sunderland SR2 7SY, United Kingdom
phil.ellis@sunderland.ac.uk

**Abstract.** A particular use of technology in 'open-ended' contexts lies at the heart of the development of Vibroacoustic Sound Therapy, which has been developed in schools for profound and multiply handicapped children and in homes for the long-term care of the elderly and elderly mentally infirm. The therapy uses examples of digital music technology to improve communication skills, motor control and well-being. Three case studies exemplify the effects of this therapy with the client groups.

## 1 Background

The idea of Vibroacoustic Sound Therapy (VAST) has gradually developed over a number of years and is still evolving. It brings together aspects of different worlds which are connected to music but without depending on traditional musical skills or thought processes. In VAST a broad view of music is taken, and we move away from particular ways of organising sound towards the view of sound itself as being the most important element. Therefore, although practitioners of VAST will need to have 'open' ears, traditional musical skills such as the ability to read music notation or play an instrument are not prerequisites.

The initial impetus for developing this therapy came from a visit to a special school in the late 1980s. Initial experiments involved using items of music technology to see if it would be possible to give profoundly handicapped children the possibility for expression, the development of self-awareness and motor control. After some early testing there seemed to be potential for further experimentation and in 1992 a formal research project was begun in a school for profound and multiply handicapped children (PMLD). These are children with no self-help skills who are totally dependent on others for all aspects of daily living. Often they exhibit a range of disabilities and frequently show little or no awareness of the external world.

Over a period of years a non-invasive therapy evolved, and around 45 longitudinal case studies, some extending over five years, offer evidence of progression and development, in some cases involving profoundly handicapped children where previously there had been no success in 'making contact' [1].

In 1997 the therapy was introduced to a home for the long-term care of the elderly for a 30 week-long pilot study. The results were such that a two-year follow-up project was established in three homes for the elderly, one a residential home, and the other two homes for the elderly mentally infirm (EMI). To date more than 35 elderly people have been involved for periods from 20 weeks to more than three years.

K. Miesenberger et al. (Eds.): ICCHP 2004, LNCS 3118, pp. 416–422, 2004.

## 2 Research Methods

### 2.1 Exploratory Methods – Grounded Theory

In such settings the application of methods to analyse the efficiency of the therapy for specific conditions focused on discovery rather than verification. As the research was initially carried out in the environment of a school, aspects of ethnographic research methods were a natural choice and participant observation, case study and video analysis of behaviour were the main tools employed in a programme of grounded theory, [2]. For the work with children and the elderly I devised a longitudinal video-based methodology called Layered Analysis [3]. In this methodology, every session of Sound Therapy is completely recorded. Subsequently, for each individual, significant moments are copied on to separate 'master tapes'. Periodically every example of one aspect from a master tape, a particular arm movement for example, can be copied onto another tape – a 'layers tape' – and an extremely detailed chronological account of behaviour significant to an individual can be assembled for detailed scrutiny. For the purposes of reviews 'summary tapes' can be assembled. These are limited to around 10 minutes in length and so draw perhaps on one example every three months. Rather in the manner of time-lapse photography, where we can view a flower opening in a short space of time, so it is possible to see significant, and frequently very moving, behaviours developing over a period of weeks, months or years. This has been the main research tool for both groups involved in Sound Therapy.

### 2.2 Methods for Measuring the Effectiveness of the Therapy

In order to externally validate the short and long-term effects of Sound Therapy, a small group of EMI residents were involved in a 10 week study conducted by Steven Dennett of STB Consultancy Ltd. Using the Bradford Dementia Group Profiling Scales: Well-being and Ill Being (WAIBS) [4], which form an on-going planning and dementia mapping approach for individuals in residential settings, (see below).

More recently we have begun using the NOSIE (Nurse Observation Scale for Inpatient Evaluation) [5,6]. This provides information on social confidence, social interest, personal neatness, irritability, manifest psychosis and retardation. We have also recently introduced a mood monitoring data collection scale (see below) which is complemented by observation records kept by the therapist, who is also a full-time activities manager within the home.

## 3 Vibroacoustic Sound Therapy

The therapy is essentially non-invasive, with an emphasis placed on the creation of a highly controlled environment in which individuals are able to choose to (re)develop a range of skills through ***aesthetic*** interaction with sound. The essence lies in the internal motivation of the individual; in working from the 'inside-out'. At all times the individual is given the opportunity to take control of the situation as far as possible. It seems that by giving a person absolute control over sound – where even the smallest movement can generate a sound – leads to the development of expression, interaction, physical control and a sense of well-being. Any sound within a session is experienced both as an aural and tactile sensation which reinforces the feedback loop of cause and effect. From the resulting recordings of behaviour, both within and beyond VAST sessions, we can see progression and development in a variety of ways across a range of disabilities.

Three items of (music) technology are central to this therapy, and they lie at the focus of the three divisions of sound therapy sessions:

### 3.1 Interactive Communication Skills

A digital sound processor and microphone era used to (re)develop and/or improve: vocal inflection (expression); enunciation; range of phonemes (vowels, consonants, etc.); enable expressive use of voice; listening skills. This section gives emphasis to vocal interaction, with eye-contact and responsiveness being a focus, encouraging use of the voice and the development of enunciation and expression. The focus given here is on expressive communication through changes in pitch, volume and vocal timbre - non-verbal communication. It is possible that some people who have lost the power of speech are able to (re)develop vocal expressiveness and communication skills by focusing on these elements.

### 3.2 Independent Physical Movement and Control

The Soundbeam [7], can help to (re)develop physical control (typically hand/arm or head, possibly leg); extend/re-energise the listening range (quiet/loud; high/low); awaken curiosity through exploration; enable self-expression. In this section of the therapy session, using the Soundbeam, can lead to the development of expressive ways of controlling sound. It works through the use of an ultrasonic beam. By directing this at a part of the body - the head, an arm or leg, even an eyelid - the smallest movement will result in a sound being heard. Effectively you can move your head and play for example an electronically generated 'harp, 'trombone', 'thunderstorm', or any sound you choose. Perceiving cause and effect and the awareness of control through action seems to be the key to its effectiveness. All the sounds created in these first two parts of the therapy are both heard and also felt as vibration, the Soundchair providing an extra stimulus, reinforcing cause and effect [8].

### 3.3 Relaxation

Here the Soundchair is used to promote a general feeling of physical and mental well-being, and to provide a possible trigger for recollection and reminiscence.This final part of a session is for relaxation. Playing specially recorded tapes which combine gentle classical, or 'relaxing', or 'content-free' music with low frequency sine tones can induce deep relaxation. This in turn can help ameliorate anxiety, stress and depression, as well as muscular aches and pains [9]. Much research has been undertaken concerning vibroacoustic techniques, [10,11]. I have adopted a slightly different approach to others in producing the tapes, mixing sine tones of between 20 – 75Hz with the music, but allowing the music to determine the pitch of the sine tone as well as the timing of its pulsing.

The effects are clear to see with both children and adults. In the environment of the elderly, to date residents with the following conditions have experienced VAST: disaffection, anxiety, paranoia, depression, terminal cancer, possible vCJD, senility, dementia, Alzheimer's and stroke. In an EMI setting, residents are chosen for VAST who seem particularly disaffected, depressed, anxious or have other acute symptoms. Some of the staff in one EMI home now regularly use the chair themselves as this gives them physical and emotional relief.

Within the PMLD school environment the first two sections of the therapy can be very telling, and work in a similar way as with the elderly, the main difference being that the children do not have the rich life experience to draw upon, and often at first cannot communicate directly or indirectly. In the relaxation section, this is most often used as a separate aspect, being called upon when a child becomes particularly agitated or distressed.

## 4 Case Studies

### 4.1 Case Study 1

For PMLD children one case study extending over five years provides an example of the potential for the therapy.

Born in 1986, M has cerebral palsy, epilepsy, hearing impairment, is cortically blind and has gross involuntary movements of the limbs. Initially the suggestion that M might benefit from VAST was a real challenge. Although he could move physically, there was no conscious control of his movements, and similarly there was little apparent response from external stimuli. There were few indications that he might have the cognitive ability to connect his physical spasms to a resulting change in sound, or even that there was the possibility to develop a response to sound itself. Even if he could, would he then be able to develop any control over his physical movements, or develop the ability to know in advance that certain movements would produce certain sounds?

M attended Sound Therapy sessions from September 1994 – December 1999. From the first sessions, although he arrived in a physically agitated state we can see repeatedly a change from agitated muscular spasms to finer, more controlled movements, which are smooth and less frequent and with progressive improvement. This progression continued throughout the first year.

In October 1995 for the first time M produced wonderful smiles. Prior to this his face, although not without expression, had not shown real inner pleasure or delight. From this month onwards there is an increasingly frequent positive expression of delight and joy. He smiles, his face lights up, his eyebrows become raised and his forehead shows, through the production of wrinkles, the development of a positive and enthusiastic outlook.

In March 1996 he began to vocalise (almost sing) as he 'plays' the Soundbeam, a phenomena which repeated frequently thereafter. Often he would arrive at the Sound Therapy room in an agitated state from elsewhere in the school, but almost without exception he would gradually become calm, still, apparently thoughtful, almost contemplative, and reveal real physical control over his movements. He also began to show positive responses, pleasure and delight during each session, and on occasion appeared to 'think' about results before making a physical action, his eyes often 'looking' up towards the ceiling.

Reports from his teacher and classroom assistants indicate that he became more aware of the external world, and sometimes he would smile and sit upright in his wheelchair when certain music was played. Clearly his awareness developed and there was a growing responsiveness and ability to express himself, rather than remain isolated and indifferent to the external world. The head teacher observed that there were tremendous problems in finding a way in with M. He was a 'difficult to get to' child who did not want to know people; any kind of interference or intervention he would repulse rather than accept. Sometimes he would smile, but to see recordings of his Soundbeam activities is described by the head teacher as "just wonderful". Towards the end of the programme he would often be sitting upright rather than flopping, and was also alert. There was real progression and a developing quality of experience and control.

### 4.2 Case Study 2

E, aged 82, had been in a residential home for the long-term care of the elderly for a few years following a mild stroke. Her speech was not impaired, but the left side of her body was weakened and she would not use her left arm. I understood her to be very disaffected with her life in the home, and she was described as somewhat depressed and generally uncooperative.

This video study, taken over a pilot study lasting 30 weeks, shows a developing change in behaviour, interaction, receptiveness and in smiling positive responses. There are moments of fun, delight and energetic interchange with the microphone. When using the Soundbeam we see an increasing ability to interact expressively with sound, and the spontaneous and frequent use of her left arm! The final part of the session reveals a lady deeply moved and involved in listening. During the 30 weeks she received VAST her behaviour in the home gradually changed and she became a member of a small group, with a more positive and out-going demeanour than at the start of the sessions.

### 4.3 Case Study 3

This is located in a home for the long-term care of the Elderly Mentally Infirm. N had been in care for some years and is 57 at the start of this study. He was leading a normal life but suddenly started to become forgetful. Deterioration was rapid and within a few months he needed institutional caring having lost the ability of physical control and apparent cognition. He had lost most, if not all, self-help skills and was unable to walk. The diagnosis was either Alzheimer's or vCJD, but this is not confirmed.

N experienced Sound Therapy initially for a 6 month period. He had cerebral irritation which made him fidgety. He could not sit still and was constantly pulling at himself, never being 'at rest'. During this time the therapist found that he liked a 'droning' sensation produced using the Soundbeam, with some occasional positive responses (vocal, verbal and facially expressive indicators) to his experiences in the therapy. After 6 months there was a gap in the therapy, and it was during this that N suddenly started to walk again. Both his wife, and staff at the home, feel there is a direct link with the Sound Therapy and this change in behaviour. He has again been receiving the therapy for the past 10 months and now he is walking independently around the home and is able to feed himself. According to the therapist he will frequently be somewhat agitated and non-communicative before a session. During sessions he is very responsive to the relaxation tapes. For example, the therapist often records that having put headphones on him he will gradually relax, often smile at her, and become totally still for the next 30 – 40 minutes. On return to the lounge he can often be talkative and smile. His facial expression is often very positive.

## 5 Results

The on-going extended programme in an EMI setting referred to earlier includes a 9 point mood monitoring data collection element. This is, if possible, completed by the resident after their therapy session, but in N's case the therapist has to do this. As she knows him well from working with him for some years, an acceptable level of accuracy has been achieved. Over 16 sessions the mood monitoring data collection scale was used in order to monitor changes in mood before and one hour after the therapy session. The rating scale allows to rate moods from 1 to 9 from negative to positive respectively. The results of a paired t-test showed a significant (.01) change from average 3.93 pre to 5.69 post therapy.

**Table 1.** Results.

| Rating | Pre-therapy | Post-therapy |
|---|---|---|
| Average rating | 3.94 | 5.69 |
| STDV | 1.18 | 1.45 |
| Paired t-test sign | 0.001 | |

The ten week WAIBS study referred to earlier had as its main hypothesis that the participant's total (mean) well-being scores during the hour after the therapy will be greater (therefore showing improved well-being) compared to the hour before the session. With only six residents being involved this can only be seen as indicative, but there was an overall increase in well-being in the hour after sessions for all participants. There was also an unexpected indication of expectation, with residents apparently showing small improvement leading up to the session. A reading of the total scores over the 10 weeks reveals that this positive effect remained high and only dropped off over the following days.

From field observations over five years with the elderly we have seen improvements in mood, level of distress, level of depression, level of aggression, level of anxiety and level of relaxation. After Sound Therapy sessions many of those involved could seem happier and would smile more, with greater awareness of other people. This effect could last overnight and sometimes for some days.

Spanning some 11 years working with PMLD children, as a result of video analysis and notes from a range of observers, the following changes can be seen as indicative of development and progression over time. Children are developing a number of individual ways of performing expressively with sound; clearly listening with care and enjoyment to the sounds they articulate; showing a developing discrimination in the selection and rejection of particular sounds; often making some vocal response as they move in the Soundbeam; developing structures in sound which repeat and grow from week to week; showing 'aesthetic resonance' through most telling facial expressions and body movements; being actively involved for extended periods of time, far in excess of normal activity; developing a greatly increased level of concentration; beginning to discover, explore, give expression to and communicate their own feelings; making significant physical responses - movements and gestures which have not been seen before, or which have not previously been made independently; showing satisfaction and pleasure from their own achievements in structuring sound.

## 6 Conclusion

It seems that the use of this technology in controlled ways as described can effect psychosocial aspects of patients' functioning in many ways. However, the technology itself cannot achieve anything, it is the way in which it is used that is crucial. Supporting intrinsic motivation and giving control to the participants is at the heart of VAST. The ***aesthetic resonation*** which results from this approach is its power.

Current and future plans include the initiation of a project which identifies specific ways of affecting certain conditions such as anxiety, depression, stroke-induced disabilities, dementia etc. and to explore the potential benefits for other groups, such as Parkinson's Disease. We hope to further develop quantitative and qualitative research tools to prove the effectiveness of the therapy for improvement of well-being and quality of life. Six individuals so far have been trained in the techniques of VAST to enable them to independently work in the field. More formal training courses may be established to enable the benefits of VAST to reach out further into the community.

## References


1. Ellis, P.: The Music of Sound: a new approach for children with severe and profound and multiple learning difficulties. In: The British Journal of Music Education, Vol. 14:2. Cambridge University Press (1997) 173 - 186
2. Pidgeon, N.: Grounded Theory: theoretical background. In: Richardson, J. (ed): TheHandbook of Qualitative Research Methods for Psychology and the Social Sciences, BPS Books, U.K. (1996) 75-85
3. Ellis, P.: Layered Analysis: A Video-based qualitative research tool to support the development of a new approach for children with special needs. In: The Bulletin for the Council for Research in Music Education, Vol. 130. University of Illinois at Urbana-Champaign, USA (1996) 65-74
4. Bradford Dementia Group, University of Bradford, School of Health
5. Honigfeld, G., Gillis, R.D. & Klett,.C.J.: Nurse Observation Scales for Inpatient Evaluation. In: The Journal of Clinical Psychology, Vol. 21. (1965) 65-71
6. Honigfeld, G., Gillis, R.D. & Klett,.C.J. Nurses Observation Scale for Inpatient Evaluation: a new scale for measuring improvement in chronic schizophrenia. Noise-30: a treatment sensitive ward behaviour scale. In: Psychological Reports,Vol. 19 (1966) 180-182
7. The Soundbeam Project: www.soundbeam.co.uk
8. Skille, O. and Wigram, T. The Effect of Music, Vocalisation and Vibration on the Brain and Muscle Tissue: Studies in Vibroacoustic Therapy. In: Wigram, T., Saperston, B. and West, R. (eds): The Art & Science of Music Therapy: A Handbook. Harwood Academic Publishers (1995) 23-57
9. Wigram, T. & Dileo, C. (eds): Music Vibration. Jeffrey Books, New Jersey (1997)
10. Skille, O.: Manual of Vibroacoustics. Levanger, Norway: ISVA Publications (1991)
11. Williams, E.: An Introduction to Vibroacoustic Therapy. The Soundbeam Project. Bristol (1997)

# Multimodal Control Centre for Handicapped People

Ana Granados, Víctor Tomico, Eduardo Campos,
Javier Tejedor, and Javier Garrido

Departamento de Ingeniería Informática, E. P. S. Universidad Autónoma de Madrid
Ctra. Colmenar Viejo km15,28049 Madrid, Spain
ana.granados@ii.uam.es

**Abstract.** This system tries to help handicapped people, although it can be used by anybody. It is designed to be used on a PDA, and it provides the following services: have a phone book, make outgoing calls, receive incoming calls, generate manual alarms, generate mobility alarms, locate user, and follow user's condition. The user-friendly interface makes easier the use of these services, and consists of a Macromedia Flash Movie. The system is being proved now by real users and has very good approval in most cases. Now we are thinking of some improvements of the services developed.

## 1 Introduction

This idea emerges with the purpose of assisting those people that, because of their condition, are not able to lead a completely independent life, though their level of disability allows them to lead a normal life with a little external assistance. We are referring to the following communities: old people, brain damaged people, people with Down's syndrome, etc.

The application has to be installed on a device that can be carried by the users wherever they go, therefore it will be installed on a PDA (1). We have chosen this kind of device because PDAs allow full mobility, offering wireless communication and the power and versatility of a computer as well.

This solution is intended to specify and develop an unified assistance centre to old and disabled people. This centre will allow a direct communication with these people, in order to make the user feel under protection the whole time. Our principal purpose is to implement and improve old assistance services for the communities mentioned above, and also offer new services, like locating disabled persons. These location systems are based on wireless terminal communication via GSM (2) /GPRS (3) and GPS (4).

We can not forget that the interface must be user-friendly because we are aware that these new technologies can be difficult to use for handicapped people. We have studied several possibilities in order to make the use of the system easier. The best solution is to use a Macromedia Flash movie as user interface. User only has to click on the screen of the PDA, and the system will do the rest.

This paper is organized into three sections: system architecture, services provided by the system, and conclusions. In the first section, we explain the developed system architecture. In the second section we explain the different services offered by this

K. Miesenberger et al. (Eds.): ICCHP 2004, LNCS 3118, pp. 423–429, 2004.

system. These services are: a phone book, outgoing calls and incoming calls, manual alarms, mobility alarms, locate user, and follow user's condition. In the third section we explain the results we have reached on the tests, the future work, and the limitations of the system as well.

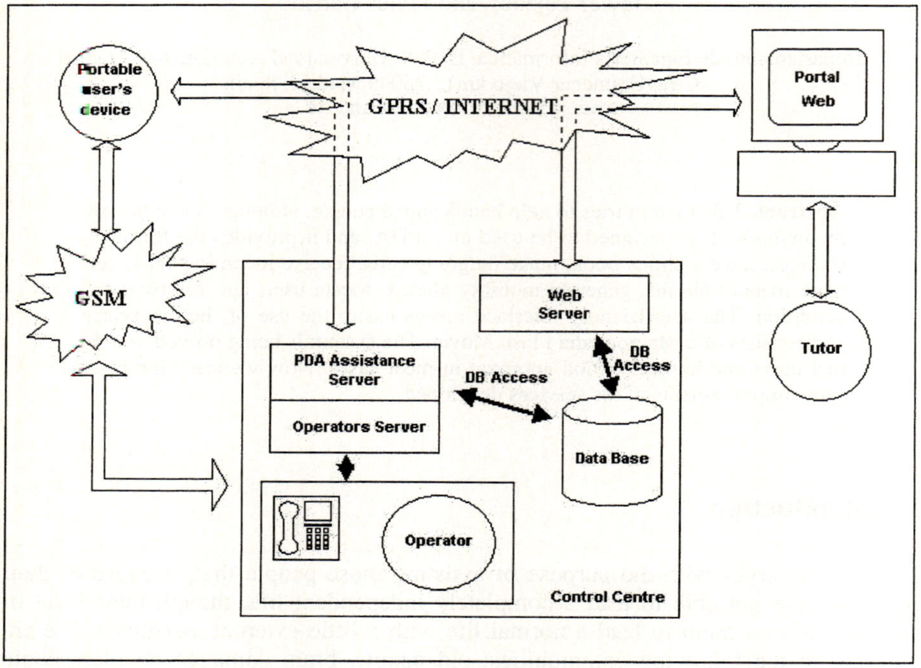


**Fig. 1.** System Architecture.

## 2 System Architecture

The solution is based on a system composed of these modules:

- *Portable user's device:* users carry some kind of portable client device with them, such as a PDA, which is used to communicate with the Control Centre. This device has a communication module (GSM/GPRS) and a SIM card (5). The user interface is a Macromedia Flash movie that would show both phone book data and the emergency button, and that communicates with the C++ Control Program under the XML(6) standard, through a XML socket. The Control Program must communicate with the correspondent servers through GPRS. The C++ program will connect to the Internet, download the appropriate user agenda as well as the jpg files that go with each phone number of the agenda. This program must send the pertinent alarms as well.

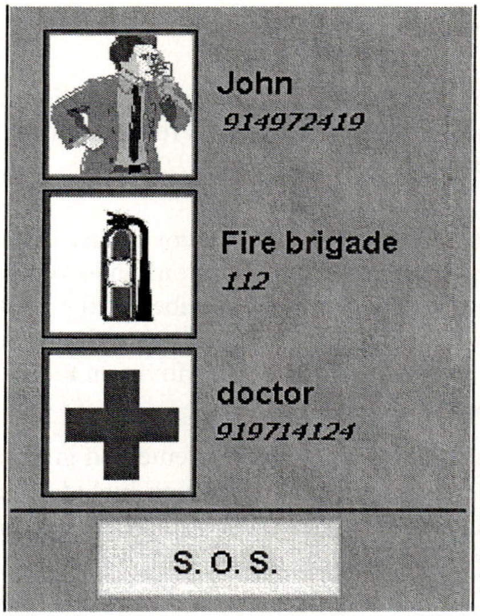


**Fig. 2.** User Interface.

The following figure shows the user interface used in this system.

- *Control Centre:* Set of servers and terminals that offer the appropriate interface of communication with the user and his tutor. It is composed by next modules:
  - *PDA Assistance Server:* This server will communicate with the PDA via TCP/IP through Internet. It will wait for possible messages from the PDA. In case the message was an alarm it will notify the Operators Server of a possible alarm. In case the message was a phone book request, it will do a query to the database to get the phone book of the user and it will send it to the PDA, under XML format.
  - *Operators' Server:* This server will receive the alarm messages from the PDA Assistance Server. Using the identifier of the message, it will do a query to the database to get the data of the user who has asked for help. Those data will be sent to the terminal of a free operator.
  - *Database:* It will store all system data users and also their phone books. Those data will be put in through an Internet portal that will be hosted in the Control Centre.
  - *Web server:* It will contain an access portal that will offer the possibility of adding, modifying or deleting the system user's data into the database.
  - *Operators' Terminal:* Each of the terminals where an operator will be able to see if any alarm message has been sent by any user. User's data are shown on terminal screen. The operator could then make a call from a telephone device to the appropriate user via GSM. The user will receive the call in his PDA.

## 3 Services Provided by the System

Any of the services provided by the system, requires an initialization phase that will be done by the tutor and by the C++ Control Program on the PDA. This phase consists of the following tasks:

User's tutor:

- The phone book is constructed by the tutor of the disabled person on a portal web, placed in the Web Server. The tutor only has to input, for each entry of the phone book, the name and the phone number of the contact, and attach the .jpg file with its image. This information is stored in the Data Base, and will be queried later, in order to construct the Flash Movie on the PDA.

C++ Control Program:

- Connects to Internet, using functions implemented in library "Ras.h".
- Sends a request message for user data, which includes the identification number of the user. The PDA Assistance server will receive it, and will send the data requested to the PDA on a message under XML format.
- Creates a file "data.txt" that only contains the phone book data under a specific format. When the Macromedia flash movie will start, it will read this file to fill the fields on the screen.
- Downloads the necessary images to show the content of the phone book. These files are stored in a FTP Server, therefore the protocol that the program must use to make the request is FTP Protocol.
- Closes the connection to Internet, using functions implemented in library "Ras.h".
- Throws two threads. Server Thread will create a XML socket with the Flash movie, in order to allow the communication between them. Phone Thread will be listening in the modem port, to detect possible incoming calls, and is responsible for managing possible outgoing calls as well.

After these initializations, the system would be ready to offer two kinds of services. Some are focused on answering queries, those can be manual alarms, phone book, user's o orientation. And others are aimed at keeping track of the user's location, those can be mobility alarm, user's localization, user's condition. All these services are explained below:

- *Phone book:* The user has a list of telephone numbers, each one with its respective image, on the screen of the PDA. The phone book is constructed by the tutor of the disabled person on a portal web. The tutor only has to input, for each entry, the name and the phone number of the contact, and attach the .jpg file with the image. When the user turns on the PDA, the application will run, first connecting with the server via GPRS to download the file that contains the phone book's data in XML format, and then connecting with the FTP (7) Server to download the required images. When all this data is on the device, the application will be able to create a new process that runs the Macromedia Flash movie. This clip will be constructed dynamically from the XML data, and will be shown on the screen of the PDA. When user clicks on one of the phone numbers (or its respective image), the device will phone to the person or service required via GSM.

- *User's orientation:* If the user wants to get instructions about the way he must follow to get somewhere, he can ask for this information and he will be assisted. In the current version of the system, this assistance is based on operators. This means that when the user asks for help, the Operator's Server will assign him an Operator, which will make a GSM call to the user in trouble to show him the way. In the future, we want to improve the system by adding map routing. [2] [3]
- *Manual alarm:* The user can inform to the Control Centre when he needs help only by pressing the Alarm Button on the screen of the PDA. Then, the flash movie will send the string "SOS" to the Server Thread, through the socket between them. When this "SOS" string comes in through the socket an alarm message will be constructed and sent, by the C++ Control Program, to the PDA Assistance Server. User's localization, i.e. latitude and longitude, is included in the alarm message in order that he knows it. The PDA Assistance Server will notify the Operators Server this alarm, and then the Operator's Server will assign an Operator, that will make a GSM call to the user in trouble. The C++ Control Program will have a thread listening in the modem port, to detect the incoming call. When it is detected, the C++ Control Program, will inform the Flash Movie, in order that it may change the image shown on the screen of the PDA to a calls interface image and it may begin to sound. This screen contains a "pick up" button, which the user must press if he wants to accept the call.
- *Mobility alarm:* An automatic alarm is generated when the user goes out of the pre-established area. The way we have implemented this functionality is this. Two latitudes and two longitudes are included in the XML message downloaded by the C++ Control Program installed on the PDA. Thus a rectangle is determined by these four values. The main thread of the C++ Control Program on the PDA is always comparing the current localization (latitude and longitude) of the user with these four values. When the user goes out of the pre-established area, a mobility alarm message is sent automatically to PDA Assistance Server. User's localization is included in the alarm message. When a mobility alarm comes in to the PDA Assistance Server, it will inform to the Operators Server, which will assign an Operator, who will make a GSM call to the user.
- *User's localization:* User is located by the control-centre because of a relative's, or a tutor's, call or even in the interest of the centre. This means that the C++ Control Program on the PDA must be able to receive incoming calls. Therefore, it will be a thread listening in the modem port, to detect the incoming calls. When an incoming call is detected, the C++ Control Program will inform to the flash movie, in order that it may change the image shown on the screen of the PDA to a calls interface image and it may begin ringing-beeping. This screen contains a "pick up" button, which the user must press if he wants to accept the call.
- *Studying user's condition:* We can make a data base of user's locations and their length time, and then process them to study the evolution in user's mobility, depending on the medium speed. We need to have another thread on the C++ Control Program, which send this data to the PDA Assistance Server, in order to storage them in the database.

## 4 Conclusions

The system is being tested now by real users, and its use has been widely accepted by the users. The interface has been found quite convenient by the users because it shows images and not only text, so it allows users with sight limitations to enjoy the system. In a similar way, it would not even be necessary that the user is able to read. Among the communities where the tests are being accomplished, we can find people with Down's syndrome and elderly people. It has not been tested with any other kind of disabled people yet.

All the services developed in this system are very useful due to the following reasons. The application allows you to make outgoing calls and receive incoming calls wherever and whenever. It also makes user localization possible. It means that the place where user is can be known in each moment. The application also allows you to receive an alarm when the user is out of the pre-established area. If the user needs some attention he can press alarm button in order to be attended by an operator, via GSM. Therefore, not only the amount of offered services is important but also the facility to access these services. Only a PDA, with a modem and a GPS receptor, is required to enjoy the system.

Nowadays, there are a lot of systems for helping visually impaired people [4][5] or paralytic people, but none of them join PDA, GPS and phoning calls management at the same time. For that very reason, the system described in this paper is so important and original.

Experimental tests have been done with the GPS in open field and no problem of range loss nor sudden failures occurred, but in the city, tests have revealed that sometimes under some buildings GPS has failures due to range losses. A possible solution to this drawback could be to use the localization service that many mobile service providers offer. This localization service is based on studying the power of the signal in the mobile device with several antennas to be able to calculate the position of the mobile device. As GPS is not used, the problem described above will not be such.

Even though special attention has been paid in making the interface user-friendly, different kinds of interfaces should be analysed. Basing the system on the use of PDA devices, a new concept for the interface can be added, based on speech-recognized commands. With this improvement, blind persons could also use the system, and within the other groups any user could use the interface he prefers or finds more convenient.

Due to that mobile phone devices are evolving to have better interfaces (full-coloured and big-sized screens), in a future phase of the project the migration to those devices could be considered and studied. Nevertheless, it should be taken into account that the interface in such devices should not be less user-friendly, or if the interface is slightly worse, it is because in other areas it brings many other advantages.

Now we are thinking about the improvement of this system and we can see that routing maps could replace the actual operator-based orientation system. [2][3]

## Acknowledgements

The system developed belongs to a Spanish project funded by the IMSERSO (Social Services Organization of Spain).

We have counted on several psychologists, with a special help of D. Mª Victoria Fontecha, to design the user interface.

## References

1. "Wireless Local Positioning: Concepts, Solutions, Applications", M. Vossiek, L. Wiebking, J. Wieghardt, C. Hoffmann.
2. "Pervasive Information Acquisition for Mobile AR-Navigation Systems", Wolfgang Narzt, Gustav Pomberger, Alois Ferscha, Dieter Kolb, Reiner Müller, Jan Wieghardt, Horst Hörtner, Christopher Lindinger.
3. "Rendering Effective Route Maps: Improving Usability Through Generalization", Maneesh Agrawala.
4. "Auditory assistive devices for the blind", Robert W. Massof
5. "Accessible GPS for the blind: What are the current and future frontiers?", Michael May
6. "The Cricket Location-Support System", Nissanka B. Priyantha, Anit Chakraborty, and Hari Balakrishnan

## Appendix

1. PDA, Personal Digital Assistant, small portable device, with a big screen.
2. GSM, Global System for Mobile communications, is a cell-based mobile radio system developed using digital technology. In our system, it is used to establish mobile phone calls.
3. GPRS, General Packet Radio Service, is a service in GSM networks. In our system, it is used to send and receive data via TCP/IP.
4. GPS, Global Positioning System, is a satellite-based radio-navigation system that permits users to determine their three-dimensional position (latitude, longitude, altitude).
5. SIM card, Subscriber Identity Module, is a tiny chip card that makes it possible to carry a mobile subscription and data through different types and generations of GSM phone.
6. XML, eXtensible Markup Language, is a metalanguage, it allow you to design your own markup languages, designed to improve the functionality of the Web by providing more flexible and adaptable information identification.
7. FTP, File Transfer Protocol.

# proXimity: Ad-Hoc Networks for Enhanced Mobility

Simon Harper, Stephen Pettitt, and Carole Goble

Information Management Group, Dept of Computer Science,
University of Manchester, Manchester, UK
{sharper,carole}@cs.man.ac.uk
http://augmented.man.ac.uk

**Abstract.** David tries not to use unfamiliar trains and buses, he doesn't travel to places he doesn't know, and he doesn't travel in unusual environments without a companion. David is visually impaired and in such cases he becomes disoriented from a lack of preview, knowledge of the environment, and orientation information and is consequently without the foundations on which to base mobility decisions. While his experiences are not always true for all visually impaired travellers they do represent the majority experience of David's peer user group. proXimity is our attempt to address David's travel problems and is based on our previous work in Hypermedia and Real-World Mobility. By using combined Hypertext and mobility paradigms we move toward a system that will assist David in his travels. The primary goal of proXimity is to augment David's reality by giving hypertext a physical presence in the real world. We analogise the real and virtual, and so aim to provide Nodes (link targets), Links, and Anchors in the real world. Therefore, hypertext information that describes a physical location also has a physical presence and 'local' physical artifacts can be augmented by 'remote' hypertext and semantic information.

## 1 Introduction

We are concerned with the mobility of visually impaired travellers in complex and unfamiliar internal and urban environments. Visually impaired travellers become disoriented in these environments and this is especially the case when airports, bus or train stations, shopping centres, and unfamiliar cities are to be traversed. In such cases the traveller is left without the foundations on which to base mobility decisions due to a lack of information about the environment. However, their journey can be assisted by supplying this 'lost' information and we envisage (and have started to develop) a system that adapts to an individual based on their planned and completed journey, their mobility requirement, and the environment being traversed.

proXimity is our solution to the travel problems of visually impaired pedestrians. proXimity tries to extend the link metaphor from hypermedia into the real world. We try to link the real and virtual so that visually impaired users can access complex travel scenarios and locate physical objects in the real world by links pointed to them in the accessible virtual world.

We perceive inadequacies in the way the real and virtual worlds currently blend, and are particularly concerned by:

K. Miesenberger et al. (Eds.): ICCHP 2004, LNCS 3118, pp. 430–437, 2004.

1. The presumption that ambient devices will always be statically networked either by wire or by wireless means.
2. The conventional wisdom which sites the user-interface (Siren) with the device (Fire Alarm) thereby enforcing a designers view of an individual.
3. The missed opportunity to use an ambient device designed for a specific task (marking a piece of art) to fulfil a different task (like assisting travel and movement).
4. The inability to uniquely identify older artifacts which are not electronic or networked (like a painting).
5. The over reliance on Global Positioning Systems (GPS) to gauge proXimity to virtually marked out areas of interest. These systems are ineffectual because GPS fails to address: artifact mobility, complexity of environments, signal interference and inconsistency in internal and urban environments, and artifact uniqueness.
6. The high cost of – current – networked ambient devices.

Our system aims to solve these problems by using ambient devices and a Personal Digital Assistant in the role of a real-virtual SHIM to conjoin real and virtual worlds and we us the physical traveller (the visually impaired user) to 'walk the links'.

*The Story So Far.* In our previous work we assert that lessons learned in the real-world mobility of visually impaired individuals can also be used to solve their mobility problems when moving around Hypermedia resources. Further, we likened Hypermedia use to travelling in a virtual space, compared it to travelling in a physical space, and introduced the idea of mobility - the ease of travel - as opposed to travel opportunity. Finally, we created a model of mobility that proposed a set of objects, techniques, and principles useful in addressing the travel and mobility issues of visually impaired users [9, **?**]. We have come to realise that visually impaired travellers move around an environment by answering the questions 'where am I?', 'where can I go?', and 'what can I use to help?'. The ease of movement is determined by the complexity of the questions, their sequence, and the returned results ability to inform the formulation of the next question. Previous attempts to answer these questions have used simple markers placed within the environment or on users [1]. These devices have aimed to bridge the gap between visual and audible mobility information and as such have focused on sensory translation. However, our system differs from these in that it uses hypermedia paradigms combined with our mobility models to help us understand the mobility requirements of a user within an environment and to enable those requirements to be fulfilled. In effect the user takes control of their own mobility as opposed to being passive receivers of static information.

*Motivational Example/Problem.* The majority of visually impaired users say that they become disoriented and frustrated when they travel in complex and unfamiliar internal and urban environments [7]. Our scenario focusing on David may seem contrived but it does represent the real life experiences of many blind and visually impaired individuals[1]. It is within this context that we first started to think about helping to solve the mobility problems of visually impaired travellers. Imagine, a traveller running to catch

[1] Used afterward as a general term encompassing the World Health Organisation definition of both profoundly blind and partially sighted individuals.

a flight, who can be directed to his gate based on artifacts encountered on his journey and knowledge of his final destination. Or a visually impaired traveller who can be directed around new environments (which would be previously inaccessible) with ease and confidence.

With the advent of the semantic web and Tim Berners-Lee's desire to describe resources (many of them real world resources) more fully the division between real and virtual will become more of a hindrance. We therefore thought that our system could be extended to other user groups. For example, walking into proXimity of Michelangelo's 'David' could display hypertext information from the local website, unique artifact histories, and other pre-searched information from the web along with annotation services and the like.

*Synopsis.* We provide examples of the current state of mobility with regard to ambient devices concerned with the movement of visually impaired surfers. We briefly review the state of current related work in mobility technology and the concepts of hypermedia and ad-hoc networking. In effect we give a multi-disciplinary background to place the project in a general context. And then address similarities in other projects while highlighting differences with our own. Finally, we describe our initial developments and then give an overview of our system. A system which, automatically and dynamically creates ad-hoc networks from simple imbedded (invisible and embedded) ambient devices by using a Personal Digital Assistant as an egocentric user interface and a network hub. We will show how the system will work and how interconnections with sematic, grid, and web resources will be made. To finish, we will describe our method of using the `HTTP` protocol and stateless network connections to intelligently direct travellers from point to point.

## 2 Background

*ENVIRONMENT – Ambient Devices.* At it's simplest Ambient Computing[2] has the goal of activating the world by providing hundreds of wireless computing devices of all scales everywhere. While the concept of generalised computational devices invisible but situated through an environment is relatively recent the technology to enable the concept is not. Ambient systems work by using infrared, radio, and inductive or electrostatic technologies to transmit information between devices carried by the user and a device fixed within the environment. When the user moves into range either the beacon – within the environment – or the user device can give feedback. Beacons are often placed at strategic points – say on a platform or railway concourse – to augment implicit waypoints or create additional explicit ones, and the pools of mobility information around them are known as 'information islands'. Ambient systems stem from the belief that people live through their practices and tacit knowledge so that the most powerful things are those that are effectively invisible in use. Therefore, the aim is to make as many of these devices as possible 'invisible' to the user, where applicable. In effect making a system 'invisible' really necessitates the device being highly imbedded and fitted so completely into its surroundings that it is used without even thinking about the interaction.

[2] Also known as ubiquitous or pervasive computing.

*USER - Egocentric Universal Access.* Through our work on other projects (TOWEL [6] and POLI [7]) we have become aware that single focus systems exist mainly because the user interface and the functional parts of a device are conjoined such that just one user modality is supported and one system functionality is addressed. Consider the example of a lift, in which a dyslexic user may have difficulty choosing floors and accessing lift functions because the lift user interface (in this case an LCD display) does not support their needs. Or the problem of how to notify a deaf person working in their office that there is a fire when the user interface to a fire alarm is only a siren.

*KNOWLEDGE - Semantic Web.* The Semantic Web is the abstract representation of data on the World Wide Web, based on the RDF standards and other standards to be defined. It is being developed by the W3C, in collaboration with a large number of researchers and industrial partners. It is an extension of the current web in which information is given well-defined meaning, better enabling computers and people to work in cooperation. The development of ontologies will be central to this effort. Ontologies are metadata schemas (built using the OIL / DAML + OIL / OWL languages), providing a controlled vocabulary of terms, each with an explicitly defined and machine processable semantics. By defining shared and common domain theories, ontologies help both people and machines to communicate more effectively. They will therefore have a crucial role in enabling content-based access, interoperability and communication across the Web, providing it with a qualitatively new level of service – the Semantic Web.

## 3 Discussion

We aim to give a real world presence to hypermedia information by electronically marking physical artifacts and groups of artifacts with imbedded non-networked ambient devices. We aim to move descriptions of real-world node functionality, interaction protocols and interface specification, conceptual descriptions and groupings – of nodes – to the virtual world (Web). We propose a connected mobile device (like a PDA or 3G phone) be used as an egocentric user interface and computational hub to control devices and manipulate information structures – stored as HTML and XHTML on the web. In effect we have devices that represent anchors and nodes, and devices that are interfaces - both types follow hypermedia and Web rhetoric.

We expect minimal computational and interface functions to be present on the imbedded device but rather the device and the mobile interface to be used in combination. We aim to bring 'remote' information and control found on the web to the 'local' physical environment, and we expect to use semantic descriptions, disjoint and disparate hypermedia information resources (like the web or Grid), and enhanced searching based on accurate physical proximity to remotely described physically local artifacts.

We connect our imbedded devices to the internet using our mobile hub as the interface therefore we have small infrastructure costs, placement by domain experts is not required, the user-interface is removed from the physical world and is therefore flexible and egocentric, 'remote' hypermedia resources from the web – or other storage paradigms – are constantly searched and presented to the user based on the real world nodes and anchors (and therefore artifacts) encountered which may also be moveable – like books in a library for example.

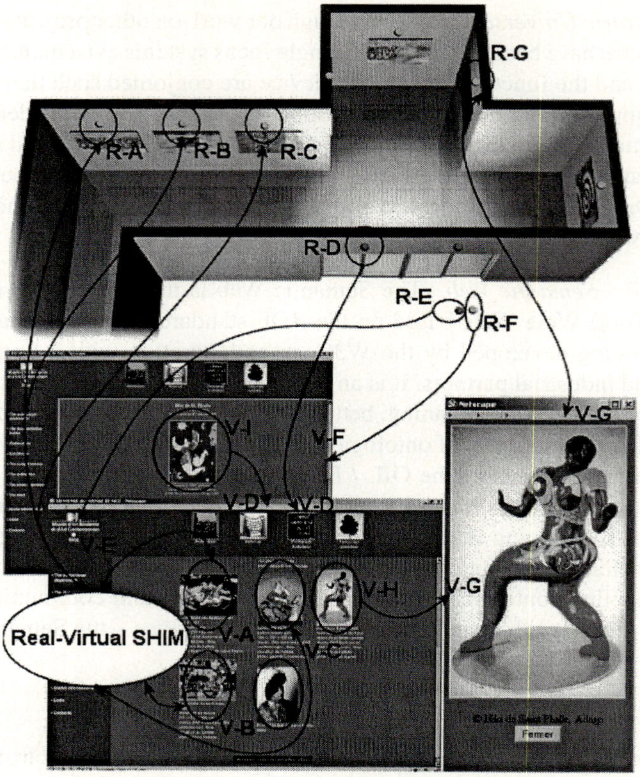


**Fig. 1.** Movement Scenario

There are many possible ways to determine a person's position within a building; camera, infra-red beams, RFID tags, capacitive effect - even prediction might be possible in certain circumstances. However, in our particular application, it was an object carried by the traveller which needed to convey precise location. In fact now that we have contemplated the options we think that infra-red can provide the solution. Consider an infra-red emitting diode, what are its characteristics? Well apart from the output power, the relevant one here is 'beam half-angle' and therein lies the answer. Application notes for various components [12] show that the beam can have a very sharp cut-off, which means that a detector on the person will only respond within a well-defined area. This solves two problems; one of precise location and the other of 'adjacent channel interference'. And this solution has the other advantages of relative cheapness and low power. These emitters may be battery powered and mounted on the ceiling (with the appropriate device chosen according to the required accuracy of the location and the mounted height.

*Hypermedia – Hardware(artifact) Interplay.* proXimity is all about linking the real and the virtual and so the conceptual design of the system is focused on providing this linking (via the Real Virtual SHIM). Figure 1 shows this interlinking in the context of a real world art gallery (depicted at the top of the diagram) with virtual information about that gallery, and the art work within it, shown as a sequence of hypermedia nodes, in this case web pages (depicted at the bottom).

Beacons in the real world locate users to specific hypertext resources by transmitting the address of the location (Fig 1 R-E), in the form of the URI being entered. From this the hypertext start point (home page of the web site – V-F) can be distinguished and shown on a user device. In effect the focus of the interaction has move from the real (R-F) to the virtual (V-F). The hypermedia resource can now be browsed to find the appropriate exhibit (V-I to V-D). Directions to the exhibit area can then be given and focus switches back to the real world (R-D). At this point the user becomes the server and takes the virtual directions to find the real artifact. This is one big real world routing problem and as the artifacts are heterogenous, disparate, and distributed the task can be likened to hypermedia routing requests. Each real world node and anchor doubles as a point on a virtual map and using graph theory [11] the user is directed to the correct artifact location (R-A, R-B, or R-C). Once there the anchor point is activated and hypertext information about the artifact is displayed along with the annotated comments of previous users and a set of links to other related resources (V-A, V-B, or V-C).

## 4 Related Research

*GeoNotes.* Positioning technology is often associated with locating people in geographical space. The GeoNotes system, however, positions pieces of information. GeoNotes allows all users to annotate physical locations with virtual 'notes', which are then pushed to or accessed by other users when in the vicinity. GeoNotes use GPS and DGPS, however this is only good for larger physical areas. Problems also exist with these technologies because they are not accurate enough to react to exact areas (measures suggest only an 18 to 6 metre accuracy level), they seldom work in buildings and internal environments, and are often very inaccurate in complex built up areas like cities [5].

*HP Cooltown - Websigns.* HP Cooltown is a vision of a technology future where people, places, and things are first class citizens of the connected world, wired and wireless - a place where e-services meet the physical world, where humans are mobile, devices and services are federated and context-aware, and everything has a web presence. Cooltown propose that all devices should be connected, we think this creates an infrastructure cost that is static and unmanageable, interfaces and functionality that are inflexible, and information access that is too specific and therefore negates the intention of hypermedia and the web [4]. We also propose that devices in the environment are second class citizens (not first class) and that they cannot be networked without a user device being in range and used as a conduit for device to network communication [2].

*Equator.* The central goal of the Equator Interdisciplinary Research Collaboration (IRC) is to promote the integration of the physical with the digital. In particular, it is concerned with uncovering and supporting the variety of possible relationships between physical and digital worlds [8]. The objective in doing this is to improve the quality of everyday life by building and adapting technologies for a range of user groups and application domains. Our proposed project is relevant to the research agenda of the Equator IRC as it relates the digital and physical worlds. However, projects in the Equator stable like Narrative, City, Artequakt, and AR do not address our key issue of creating a universal real - virtual symbiosis through hypertext information and semantic knowledge [14].

*Auto-ID.* Auto-ID is a project to give everything in the world a unique ID through the Physical Mark-up Language (PML).

> Auto-ID technology will change the way we exchange information and products by merging bits (computers) and atoms (everyday life) in a way that dramatically enhances daily life in the all inclusive global arena of supply and demand-the supply chain.

Auto-ID [3] does not utilise semantic descriptions, does not take account unique artifacts (as opposed to products), and does not take into account ambient device control mechanisms.

*HyperTag.* HyperTag is a system of infrared tags that can be detected by some mobile phones and with the addition of some software to the phone is used to point the onboard browser to a specific web address. It [10] is only used for delivering single page and source hypertext content, it does not address the issues of interface independence, control of ambient devices, Ad-Hoc networking, spatio-temporal searches over hypermedia resources, or semantic descriptions of unique real world artifacts.

## 5 Summary

The research is multi-disciplinary and cross-platform. Primarily the research will be useful to visually impaired pedestrians when travelling within complex and unfamiliar internal and urban environments. However, when complete it may be of use to all users who need mobile, location specific hypermedia information from multiple sources. These could include visitors to public information services, museums, and art galleries. We have a real case study in place, with the collaboration with the Whitworth Art Gallery we intend to demonstrate our system over 3-6 months with real users. proXimity is timely in that it uses new and evolving technologies across the knowledge, environment, and user domains (Semantic Web, Ontologies, IR, Bluetooth, GPRS) to create a novel and unique system [13]. We index physical objects using ambient devices and join the real to the virtual on an Ad-Hoc basis thereby creating large scale physical networks for information and control. In this way we address many of the problems associated with the partiality and transient nature of current and future networks in semantic and physical space. We then deploy a real application over this combined space to demonstrate the feasibility of our ideas.

## Acknowledgments

We would like to thank Julian Tomlin (Curator) and the Whitworth Art Gallery for their assistance in the evaluation of the proXimity project. Further, we would also like to thank Bernard Horan and SUN Microsystems for their continued support.

## References


1. Blenkhorn, P. and Evans, G.: A system for enabling blind people to identify landmarks: the sound buoy. *IEEE Transactions on Rehabilitation Engineering*, 5(3), ISBN 1063-6528 (1997) 276–278
2. Brignone, C., Pradham, S., Grundback, J., McReynolds, A., and Smith, M.: Websign: A looking glass for e-services. In *Proceedings of the Tenth IEEE International Workshops on Enabling Technologies: Infrastructure for Collaborative Enterprises (WET ICE 2001)*, Los Alamitos California, USA. IEEE Computer Society (2001) 311–312
3. A. I. Center: Auto id overview. WWW, Feb 2003. http://www.autoidcenter.com/research.asp.
4. Cooltown: Cooltown overview. WWW, Feb 2003. http://cooltown.hp.com/cooltownhome/.
5. Espinoza, F., Persson, P., Sandin, A., Nyström, H., Cacciatore, E., and Bylund, M.: Geonotes: Social and navigational aspects of location-based information systems. In B. Abowd and Shafer, editors, *Ubicomp 2001: Ubiquitous Computing, International Conference Atlanta, Georgia*, Berlin, Germany, Springer Verlag (2001) 2–17
6. Goble, C., Harper, S., and Stevens, R.: The travails of visually impaired web travellers. In *Proceedings of the Eleventh ACM on Hypertext and hypermedia*, New York, USA. ACM Press (2000) 1–10 Towel Project (`http://towel.man.ac.uk`) - Winner of the Doug Engelbart Award for Best Paper at ACM Hypertext 2000.
7. Green, P. and Harper, S.. An integrating framework for electronic aids to support journeys by visually impaired people. In *International Conference on Computers Helping People with Special Needs*, Germany. OCG Press (2000) 281–288, POLI Project (`http://proximity.man.ac.uk`) - under the auspices of the UNESCO.
8. Greenhalgh, C., Benford, S., Rodden, T., Anastasi, R., Taylor, I., Flintham, M., Izadi, S., Chandler, P., Koleva, B., and Schnädelbach, H.: Augmenting reality through coordinated use of diverse interfaces. Technical Report Equator-01-002.
9. Harper, S. and Green, P.: A travel flow and mobility framework for visually impaired travellers. In *International Conference on Computers Helping People with Special Needs*, Germany, OCG Press. (2000) 289–296, POLI Project (`http://proximity.man.ac.uk`) - under the auspices of the UNESCO.
10. HyperTag: Hypertag overview. WWW, Feb 2003. http://www.hypertag.co.uk.
11. Joest, M. and Stille, W.: A user-aware tour proposal framework using a hybrid optimization approach. In *Proceedings of the tenth ACM international symposium on Advances in geographic information systems* (2002)
12. LiteOn: Optoelectronics databook. WWW, Jan 2004. `http://www.liteon.com.tw/databook/default.htm`.
13. McGinity, M.: Staying Connected: Hibernating During Telecom Winter. *Communications of the ACM*, 46(1), January 2003, 13–15
14. Michaelides, D.T., Millard, D.E., Weal, M.J., and Roure, D.C.D.: Auld leaky: A contextual open hypermedia link server. In *in Proceedings of the 7th Workshop on Open Hypermedia Systems, ACM Hypertext 2001 Conference. Aarhus, Denmark*, Springer Verlag, August 2001, 52–64

# A Context-Aware Locomotion Assistance Device for the Blind

Christophe Jacquet[1,2], Yacine Bellik[2], and Yolaine Bourda[1]

[1] Supélec, Plateau de Moulon, 91192 Gif-sur-Yvette Cedex, France
{Christophe.Jacquet,Yolaine.Bourda}@supelec.fr
[2] LIMSI-CNRS, BP 133, 91403 Orsay Cedex, France
{Christophe.Jacquet,Yacine.Bellik}@limsi.fr

**Abstract.** In this paper, we present a study which aims at designing a locomotion assistance device that can deliver semantic information about its surrounding environment at any time. As a first step towards this goal, we introduce an original model suited for the description of building structure, and we present an algorithm that exploits these descriptions. Then, we explain how it is possible to link semantics to structure. Finally, we expose some research directions for user positioning and human-computer interface design.

## Introduction

Over the past few years, the LIMSI (Laboratoire d'Informatique pour la Mécanique et les Sciences de l'Ingénieur) and the LAC (Laboratoire Aimé Cotton) have been developing the *Teletact* (see Fig. 1), a locomotion assistance device for the blind [1, 2]. The system uses a laser telemeter to measure the distances to obstacles and transforms them into tactile vibrations or musical notes (the higher the tone, the closer the obstacle). A project to improve the system is under way in collaboration with Supélec: we want to give it the ability to provide *symbolic information* about pointed objects.

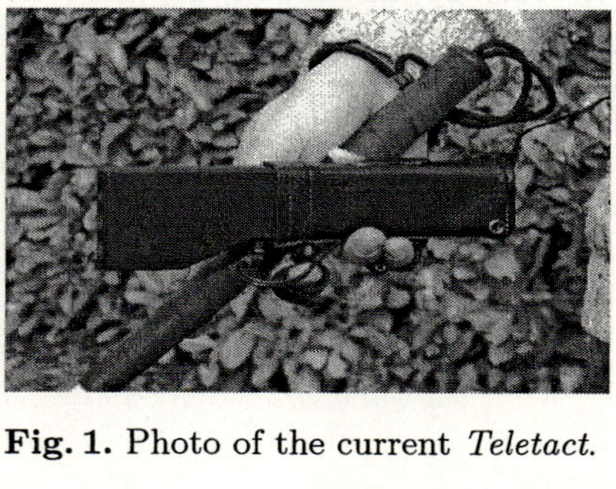

**Fig. 1.** Photo of the current *Teletact*.

After giving a short overview of the system, this paper discusses our preliminary results. We present a model for the description of architectural envi-

K. Miesenberger et al. (Eds.): ICCHP 2004, LNCS 3118, pp. 438–445, 2004.

ronments in buildings. Then, we introduce an algorithm capable of determining which default information is most relevant to the user. Next, we introduce semantic representations, and we show how to link them to building structure descriptions. This represents the work achieved so far. The last part of the paper presents future research directions for user positioning, description acquisition and user interaction.

## 1 System Overview

The system will try to determine its position thanks to a GPS (Global Positioning System) receiver where GPS reception is possible, and otherwise thanks to an inertial unit. The position calculated from these devices will then be matched against structural and semantic information embedded in the environment description retrieved from the ambient network (see section 5.1), so as to increase precision and compensate for positioning errors (see Fig. 2).

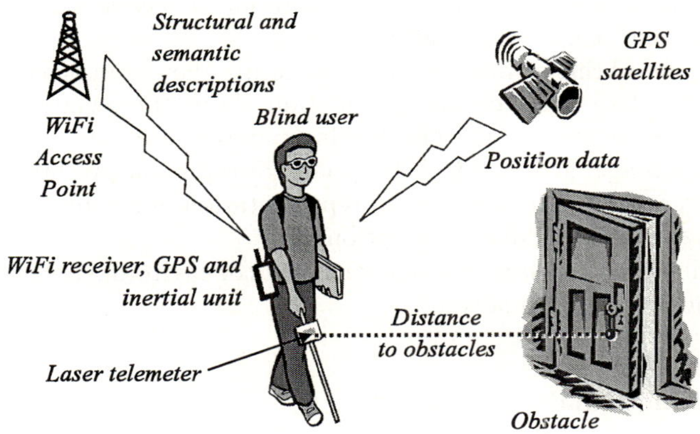


**Fig. 2.** Overview of the system.

Context-awareness will be enhanced thanks to telemeter data (as in existing devices the new system builds upon) and to light sensors that can provide additional information about light sources (sunlight, artificial light).

When the position of users has been determined, the system will give them context-related semantic information. And when they point at some specific object or location, the system will provide them with information *about* this object or location.

For instance, when a user points at their boss' door, current devices are able to tell them that "there is an obstacle three meters ahead". The device we are describing here will be able to add that "this obstacle is a door", and that "this door leads to the boss' office".

In everyday life, such a system can significantly improve blind people's lives, by giving them precise information about their environment.

## 2 Structure Modeling

To build this system, we must be able to model users' environments. To date, we have worked on building descriptions only. But of course, our model will eventually cover the full range of environment descriptions.

### 2.1 Existing Description Formats

Current formats for 3D-scene description (such as VRML [3] or X3D [4]) focus on describing the mere visual *appearance* of environments. Indeed, they target *sighted people* and try to render scenes with as many visual details as possible.

In contrast, we target *blind people* and thus we need to model the *structure* and *semantics* of environments.

The *structure* of architectural environments determines how architectural elements are organized to compose buildings. Structure is either visible (e.g. walls) or invisible (e.g. frontiers dividing a room in several zones, for instance smoking ones and non-smoking ones).

*Symbolic data* bring semantics to the structure they are associated with. For instance, these data may contain information about the owners of rooms in a building, access restriction schemes, fire instructions, etc.

For data storage, geographical databases [5] represent an interesting framework. However, they do not allow the representation of strong structure, so we will not use them for building description.

To describe both the *structure* and *semantics* of environments, we need therefore to define our own formalism.

### 2.2 Modeling Building Structure

**A Three-Tier Model.** We introduce a three-tier approach to describe building architectures:

– *first tier:* we call *lexical elements* the simple (elementary) architectural elements, such as walls, doors, flights of stairs, and so on;
– *second tier:* so-called *syntactic elements* are complex (composed) architectural elements, constituted by putting together several lexical elements. For instance, a room is defined by its walls, a stairway is defined by several flights of stairs and landings, and so on;
– *third tier:* syntactic elements are further aggregated in what we call *aggregation elements.* For instance, several offices can be gathered in a *cluster* called, say, "sales department".

The concepts (or classes) used to build descriptions take place in a concept hierarchy whose main branches correspond to the three families of objects.

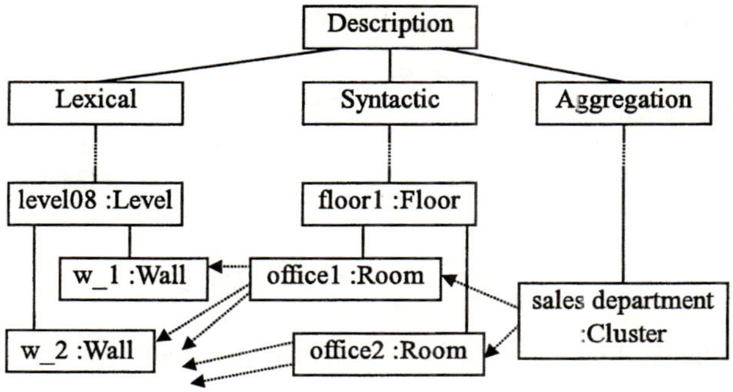


**Fig. 3.** Excerpt of an example description. The *sales department* is composed of two offices, in turn defined by some walls, while being included in a floor.

**Building a Description.** Objects from the three tiers are bound together by two kinds of edges (cf. Fig. 3):

- *inclusion links* (solid lines) represent inclusion between elements within a given tier;
- *composition links* (dotted lines) enable objects of tier $n$ to be composed of elements of tier $n-1$.

## 3 Relevant Information

### 3.1 The Problem

Using these architectural descriptions, the system will be able to determine where the user is, and what object or location he or she points at.

However, we still do not know the *level of detail*, i.e. the *granularity* of information needed by the user.

Indeed, too general information is useless, and too detailed information might not be understandable if the user does not know the associated context. To illustrate this, let us look at an example (see Fig. 4).

### 3.2 Proposed Algorithm

Suppose that the user is located in $u$, on the second floor of the Computer Science (CS) Laboratory. He or she points through the window at $p$, an office on the first floor of another building, the Library building, located next to the CS building. What information shall we return? Information attached to the room, the floor, the building, the campus...?

To solve this problem, we represent the scene as a tree. First, let us find the deepest node that is common to both the path leading from $u$ to the root, and the path leading from $p$ to the root. This node is labeled $c$ on Fig. 4.

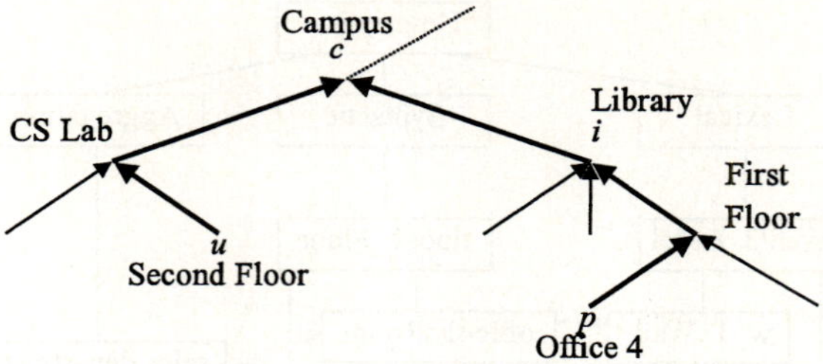


**Fig. 4.** A user points from one building to another one.

What happens if we return information located on $c$ or above? Such information is too general, because it covers $p$ as well as $u$. Thus, it will probably be useless for the user, because being in the CS building they already know that they are on the campus.

In consequence, we should return information located *below* $c$. Therefore, this information will be on the sub-path leading from $p$ to $c$ since it must describe $p$. But it must be within the context of the user, because they could not understand it otherwise.

Therefore, we return information located in $i$, i.e. the most general information on the sub-path leading from $p$ to $c$. This corresponds to a *default granularity level*. However, the user may wish to retrieve information located at another level. For this reason, the final user interface will offer some means of climbing up and down the tree.

## 4 Beyond Structure: Semantics

### 4.1 Motivation

What are we able to do now? When the user points at an architectural element, the system is able to find it in its cartography. For instance, if the user points at a door, the system *knows* that it is a door, and that there is, say, an office behind.

However, our ultimate goal is to provide the user with *semantic* information. In the above example, the system would not only state that the user is pointing at a door leading to an office: it would also return the office owner's name, the office function, and so on.

To do this, we associate semantic information to the structure description. More generally, such information can be used:

- to add *normative* information to the structure, for example in order to tag restricted areas in a building;
- to identify objects, rooms, and zones;
- to represent connexity information;
- to add specific information to certain kinds of objects; for instance information about painters could be associated with sculptures in a museum.

### 4.2 Technical Solutions

To represent semantic information, the Resource Description Framework (RDF), a W3C standard quite close to the theory of conceptual graphs [6], is rapidly becoming commonplace. It allows us to express relationships between objects of interest. These objects are instances of classes that are defined in a class hierarchy expressed in OWL (Web Ontology Language, [7]).

Up to now, we have defined a basic ontology for structure description, that defines:

- object classes, divided in three categories: locations, people and places;
- properties used to specify relations between class instances;

Actually, locations appear both in structure and semantic description. Indeed, they allow semantics descriptions to be *anchored in* the underlying structure. In practice, this is achieved through the use of a common identifier.

## 5 Future Work

### 5.1 Tracking User Position

The whole system depends on its ability to track the position of the user. *Where reception is possible*, GPS will provide a reliable and *absolute* positioning solution. However, in places where GPS reception is unavailable or inaccurate (e.g. inside buildings and in dense urban areas subjected to *canyon effect* [8]), the device will compute its position by means of *dead reckoning* using an embedded inertial unit. This way, new positions are determined in a *relative* fashion, by estimating how far the user has moved since the last GPS-acquired position.

Other systems like the Cyberguide [9] use beacons (infrared beacons, bluetooth devices, etc.) to take over GPS inside buildings, and then compute their position through triangulation. We are not considering this option, because we want our system to work anywhere, not only in specially-equipped places.

Unfortunately, dead reckoning is very much error-prone [10] : computed positions are likely to deviate from real positions because of cumulative errors. To overcome this shortcoming, the *map-matching* method [11] suggests to restrict the movements of people along well-defined paths on a map. Hence, it is possible to reduce deviation errors by computing the most probable position of the user *along a path* and not in every possible direction.

This works well for car drivers that are forced to follow roads, but in case of pedestrians movements are less predictable (especially outside buildings). However, we think that knowledge about the structure and semantics of the environment is likely to help determine users' positions. Therefore, a method of *semantic map-matching* will be further investigated in the future.

### 5.2 Acquisition of Descriptions

Until now, we have assumed that we had environment descriptions at our disposal, but they actually need to be constructed. We have listed three ways of obtaining them:

- to write them from scratch, for example using a graphical editor;
- to perform a conversion from existing description languages, either automatically or semi-automatically;
- to scan environments with the device, and label objects on the fly.

The last method would allow blind people to use their locomotion assistance devices even in places where there is no available description. Visually impaired people would tag the environment when first visiting a new place accompanied by some sighted person (as they usually do). From these data, the system would compute a partial model (cf. *map learning*, [10]) that could be re-used and refined next time. Partial models could even be published for others to use them and improve them in turn.

### 5.3 Navigation Aid

Many navigation aids have already been developed for sighted people: for example, car navigation systems [12] are rapidly becoming commonplace. Thus, it is likely that future locomotion assistance devices for the blind will implement navigation aid functions as well.

If a device knows the structural description of its environment, it can assist users in planning their path to some target. It can list the possible ways, and even find out those with interesting properties, for example: the shortest, the least likely to be crowded, the more secure (from a blind person's point of view), etc.

Thus, a mere topological path planning algorithm will not be sufficient, because the algorithm will have to take into account not just structural information, but also semantic annotations that can influence the choice of a "best" path.

Usually, navigation aid interfaces require graphical output modalities, but since blind people cannot use visual interfaces, the details of user interaction with the device need thinking out, as the interface will determine how the system will be accepted among users.

Indeed, the user interface must remain very simple, but take maximum advantage of available modalities, thus permitting access to the full range of possibilities of the device.

The user interface is likely to use multimodal techniques, combining speech synthesis, musical notes, Braille displays and tactile vibrations.

## Conclusion

Our project builds upon electronic travel aids that have been developed recently. Already useful, these devices are nonetheless capable of only indicating distances to obstacles, and not of giving higher-level information. To achieve our goal of being able to name objects and provide additional information, we have proposed solutions for two critical issues in this paper:

- defining a formalism to model the structure of visited buildings;
- designing a model to represent semantic information associated with the structure. When the system has the ability to constantly know its geographical coordinates, it will be able to determine candidate interesting information.

User position tracking, description acquisition and semantic data presentation will be among the topics of our future research work.

## References


1. Farcy, R., Bellik, Y.: Comparison of various interface modalities for a locomotion assistance device. In Miesenberger, K., Klaus, J., Zagler, W., eds.: Computers Helping People with Special Needs, Springer (2002)
2. Farcy, R., Bellik, Y.: Locomotion assistance for the blind. In Keates, S., Langdom, P., Clarkson, P., Robinson, P., eds.: Universal Access and Assistive Technology, Springer (2002) 277–284
3. Web 3D Consortium: The Virtual Reality Modeling Language International Standard ISO/IEC 14772-1:1997. Technical report, (1997) Available at http://www.web3d.org/technicalinfo/specifications/vrml97/.
4. Web 3D Consortium: Extensible 3D (X3D) International Standard ISO/IEC FCD 19775:200x Final Committee Draft. Technical report, (2003) Available at http://www.web3d.org/fs_specifications.htm.
5. Hadzilacos, T., Tryfona, N.: An extended entity-relationship model for geographic applications. SIGMOD Record **26** (1997) 24–29
6. Sowa, J.F.: Conceptual graphs for a database interface. IBM Journal of Research and Development **20** (1976) 336–357
7. McGuinness, D.L., van Harmelen, F.: OWL web ontology language overview. Technical report, W3C World Wide Web Consortium (2003)
8. Chao, J., Chen, Y., Wu Chen, X.D., Li, Z., Wong, N., Yu, M.: An Experimental Investigation into the Performance of GPS-based Vehicle Positioning in Very Dense Urban Areas. Journal of Geospatial Engineering **3** (2001) 59–66
9. Long, S., Kooper, R., Abowd, G.D., Atkeson, C.G.: Rapid Prototyping of Mobile Context-Aware Applications: The Cyberguide Case Study. In: Mobile Computing and Networking. (1996) 97–107
10. Fusiello, A., Caprile, B.: Synthesis of Indoor Maps in Presence of Uncertainty. Robotics and Autonomous Systems **22** (1997) 103–114
11. Kitazawa, K., Konishi, Y., Shibasaki, R.: A Method of Map Matching For Personal Positioning Systems. In: Proceedings of the Asian Conference on Remote Sensing ACRS 2000, (2000)
12. Philip, O.: Car navigational systems: Futuristic systems. In: 2nd Annual CM316 Conference on Multimedia Systems, Southampton University, UK, (2002)

# Navigator – A Talking GPS Receiver for the Blind

Ryszard Kowalik[1] and Stanislaw Kwasniewski[2]

[1] Gdansk University of Technology, Depatment of Optoelectronic
80-952 Gdansk, Narutowicza 11/12, Poland
kowalik@eti.pg.gda.pl
[2] Migraf 80-268 Gdansk, Chopina 8/3 Poland
stan@migraf.pl

**Abstract.** This paper discusses an new navigation support device based on talking GPS information.

## 1 Introduction

Small and cheap talking navigating GPS receiver for the blind called Navigator was build. Our observations showed that its sensitivity in street canyons was sufficient for practice. Moving around town on their own is difficult for blind people. To do it safely and at a pace not too dissimilar to that of the other pedestrians requires them to continuously concentrate on acoustic, kinaesthetic and sensory feedback. For this reason the operation of the device and the signals it emits must cause the minimum of disruption. Therefore designers equipped Navigator with many easy in use functions. Some of them are automatically triggered following a specific occurrence, the other comprises single key functions. There are ten such functions. E.g.: the parameters of the nearest point along the route, the distance and direction to a selected point and finally, the third group of functions comprising once operated with a few keys. These are used to set Navigator operating modes and modify its operation.

These and other functions that Navigator offers allow the blind person to get around town on their own boosting their self-confidence, improving safety and the convenience of travel.

Especially good situation the disabled have in Gdansk Poland. In this city Computer Information System Gdaskon is designed for people with disabilities and allows them to find their way along city streets safely and on their own. The database of the system stores information about all the things which make travel difficult or easy for the blind, partially sighted, deaf and people with mobility or manual disabilities. Gdaskon generated information is sufficient for people with different disabilities except the blind.

The blind need extra help to navigate because Gdaskon uses names of junctions or tram or bus stops, which the blind are unable to read on their own. To allow blind people to use the system "Gdaskon", Navigator is used.

## 2 User Needs and Functionalities

Our observations of the problems blind people have in finding their way around city streets showed that the positioning accuracy of the widely available GPS is sufficient to solve the majority of the problems [2].

K. Miesenberger et al. (Eds.): ICCHP 2004, LNCS 3118, pp. 446–449, 2004.

It was not our objective to determine how accurate a GPS device is in locating a position on the street and we were happy with the number of System satellites it is in contact with. Instead, our focus was on providing the blind person with an inexpensive and easy to use device to give him supports in difficult situations.

The device called Navigator was designed to specific parameters to reflect the special needs of the user. Those include:

1. blind people specific functions that the GPS is capable of sustaining,
2. the use of the functions bringing into focus the simplicity of use,
3. identifying ways to transmit the results of the functions without too much intrusion.

Navigator has a number of microprocessor controlled electronic parts. To operate, the microprocessor retrieves information from a miniature GPS receiver and tells the blind user the results using verbal messages. The processor also controls the recording and playing back of short messages spoken to the microphone. The messages are heard through an in-built loudspeaker or earphone.

In one-second intervals the navigator receives from the GPS the exact time, geographic co-ordinates of the location and the number of satellites it can track at any one time. The latter is very important because the device needs at least 3 satellites to ensure proper receiver operation.

Moving around town on their own is difficult for blind people. To do it safely and at a pace not too dissimilar to that of the other pedestrians requires them to continuously concentrate on acoustic, kinaesthetic and sensory feedback. For this reason the operation of the device and the signals it emits must cause the minimum of disruption.

Consequently, it was agreed that Navigator would only signal major changes occurring on the blind person's route or at their request, i.e. by pressing a single key. Only some of the functions such as changing the operating mode or recording the next point on the route can be completed using a few keys. Navigator functions are divided into three groups.

Group one comprises functions that are automatically triggered following a specific occurrence. There are three such functions:

1. In the guiding mode a signal is emitted when a previously recorded spot is being approached within a specific distance. The blind person is told the name of the place, how many meters away they are from it and the direction it is in relation to the current route. Other options include automatic notification when the route is deviated from.
2. In the navigation along city streets mode a signal is emitted when a pre-defined spot is being approach within a specific distance. The message includes the name, distance and direction of the point and the angle to turn to reach the next point along the route, its name and distance. Again, other options include automatic notification when the route to the next point is deviated from.
3. When the route is across a bigger area filled with obstacles that the blind person must go round running the risk of losing orientation, Navigator can memorise the desired direction and automatically inform the user every time they deviate from the route by more than 10 degrees.

The second group comprises single key functions. There are ten such functions. Examples include: the number of satellites the device can track at any one time, the parameters of the nearest point along the route, the distance and direction to a selected point. The last function is particularly useful when riding a train, tram or bus and Navigator knows the final stop – that way the blind person knows where to get off.

And finally, the third group comprising functions operated with a few keys. These are used to set Navigator operating modes by changing options, to read additional information or modify its operation.

These and other options that Navigator offers allow the blind person to get around town on their own boosting their self-confidence, improving safety and the convenience of travel.

Especially good situation the disabled have in Gdansk Poland because in this city there is Information centre called "Gdaskon" [1].

The Gdansk Computer Information System Gdaskon is designed for people with disabilities and allows them to find their way along city streets safely and on their own. The system searches its database for a route that best meets the needs of a person with a specific disability. The database of „Gdaskon" stores information about all the things which make travel difficult or easy for the blind, partially sighted, deaf and people with mobility or manual disabilities. The disabled person can input the starting point and the destination one while Gdaskon generates the route along the streets of Gdansk that takes into account the kind of person's disability.

We know from practice that Gdaskon generated information is sufficient for people with different disabilities except the blind [3].

The blind need extra help to navigate because having walked several blocks in an unknown area, blind people do not know where they are.

This is because Gdaskon uses names of junctions or tram or bus stops, which the blind are unable to read on their own. Asking passers-by for information does not always bring the desired results [4].

To allow blind people to use the system "Gdaskon", Navigator is used. It uses GPS signals to:

1. guide the blind person along the Gdaskon generated route from turning point to turning point,
2. inform the user where they are in relation to the entire route.

The definition of the position should include the name of the street section in between two consecutive junctions and the direction in relation to the nearest building, the distance to it and its address.

The street name and address of the nearest building are of particular importance near junctions; that way the nearest building can be positioned as being on a street perpendicular to the one the blind person is walking along.

The blind use it, because the device is small, inexpensive, easy to use and first of all operate in "real time", ensuring that the response is as quick as possible, preferably available within one second. To do it is difficult but possible.

The device's most time consuming operation is finding the place and street nearest to where the GPS receiver is; this takes up the most of the processor's processing time. This is because Gdansk has about 31000 addresses and 12000 street sections. By assigning two byte signatures and dividing the city's area into small squares, the bulk of the processing can be taken care of in the software design and by including a dedicated address database.

There is a record for each square with the signature of its nearest address point and the signature of its nearest street section. Linked with these data is a list of street names.

## References


1. Kowalik, R., Paliswiat, K.: Interfejs miejskiego systemu informacji dla osob niepelnosprawnych. Zeszyty Naukowe Wydzialu ETI PG, Technologie informacyjne seria 1 Nr 1, p. 49-59
2. Kowalik, R.: Psychopsychical Capabilities and Limitations of the Disabled in Remote Access to Information. Proceedings. ICCHP 2002. 8th International Conference. Computers Helping People with Special Needs. Linz, Austria, July 2002. Ed. K. Miesenberger, J. Klaus, W. Zagler. Berlin: Springer**2002 s. 707-708; Lecture Notes in Computer Science vol. 2398. Ed. G. Goos, J. Hartmanis, J. van Leuven
3. Kowalik, R.: The Gdansk Disabled Information Service. TRANSED 2001,9-th Intern.Conf. on Mobility and Transport for Elderly and Disabled People. Warszawa 2001, vol.2, s. 403-406
4. Kowalik, R.: GDASKON - Gdansk System Informacyjny dla Osob Niepelnosprawnych, XII Krajowa konferencja Naukowa Biocybernetyka i Inzynieria Biomedyczna Warszawa, PAN, listopad 2001, tom 2, s.640-644

# Dynamic Lighting Sign System for Way-Finding by People with Low Vision

Junichi Akita[1], Kiyohide Ito[2], Ikuko Gyobu[2], Ken-ichi Kimura[2], Ayumi Mihara[2], Ryo Mizuno[2], Jun-ichi Nakakoji[2], and Keisuke Yanagihara[3]

[1] Dept. of Information & Systems Engineering, Kanazawa University
akita@is.t.kanazawa-u.ac.jp
[2] Dept. of Media Architecture, Future University-Hakodate
[3] Dept. of Complex Systems, Future University-Hakodate

**Abstract.** We developed and proposed a dynamic lighting sign (DLS for short) system for people with poor vision to use to find their way. The DLS system uses a chain of lighting units with LED to indicate the way and is controlled by means of a PC. We implemented the DLS system for helping people to find their way and evaluated it in terms of light-flashing time, spatial interval and colour. We also carried out an experiment to evaluate its effectiveness in helping people find their way.

## 1 Introduction

Intelligibility is a prerequisite for signs indicating a certain route, and over the years many signs have been developed in keeping with this principle. For example, pictograms, because they can be understood at a glance, make it easy for travellers to find their way. Despite their efficiency, pictograms are not always useful for people with poor vision. Firstly, they may have difficulty noticing the signs because they are static. Secondly, they must have knowledge about signs; they are required to make out what the signs mean. And thirdly, some signs are unintelligible due to their small size.

Because the motion of light signs makes them more effective than static signs on the ground, we consider them to be a good alternative. It has been noted that information on the motion of light (referred to as optic flow) is identified intuitively. For instance, James J. Gibson, a pioneer of ecological psychology, noted that when a light sign moves, its motion can provide information that leads people in the same direction as the light[1, 2]. In addition, optic flow attracts the attention of people with poor vision, because the eyes are sensitive to the motion of an object regardless of the their strength of vision. This is also valid for motion that occurs in the peripheral field.

In this paper we will outline our development of a new optical-flow sign system for helping people with poor vision to find their way. We will also show the usefulness of this system.

K. Miesenberger et al. (Eds.): ICCHP 2004, LNCS 3118, pp. 450–453, 2004.

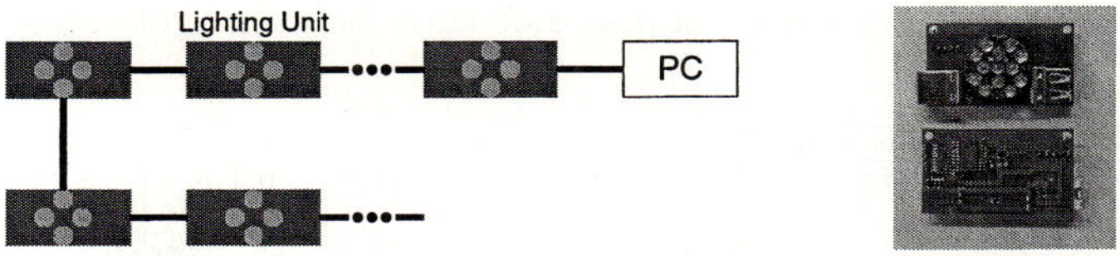


(a) (b)

**Fig. 1.** System structure(a) and lighting unit(b).

## 2 System Structure

The structure of the dynamic lighting sign (DLS) system that we developed is shown in Fig.1(a). The lighting units shown in Fig.1(b) with two coloured LEDs connected in a chain formation so as to form a line of light, and finally connected to the controller PC. Both the colour and the light pattern are controlled by the PC. Each lighting unit has a micro controller (PIC16F627), ID switches, LED module, and driver circuitry, and can be controlled by PC via RS232C.

## 3 Experiments

### 3.1 Time Differences between Light Blinks

We conducted a preliminary experiment to determine the parameters of the DLS system, which enables people with poor vision to be made aware of optic flow by blinking lights. Two males and two females with normal eyesight participated in this experiment. Thirteen stimuli, each consisting of a LED blink, were given to the subjects; starting with 20ms, the time difference between the beginning of two consecutive blinks was increased by increments of 5ms, up to 80ms. The stimuli were given in both ascending (20ms through 80ms) and descending (80ms through 20ms) orders. For the ascending order, the standard stimulus was set to 20ms, and the other 12 stimuli were given for comparison. For the descending order, the standard stimulus was set to 80ms, and the other 12 stimuli were given for comparison. There were two trials for each order of stimuli. Hence, there were 22 trials in one series of stimulus presentation. In addition, two types of lighting stimuli were presented: simultaneous blinks of six LEDs and simultaneous blinks of nine LEDs.

Subjects, wearing Bangerter filter glasses, sat down at a distance of three meters from the DLS system. They were asked to watch the standard stimulus and comparative stimuli sequentially, and to rate each comparative stimulus on a scale of five, from the maximum (Level 5), 'flow of light appears completely', to the minimum (Level 1), 'flow of light never appears'. Table 1 shows a summary of rating averages and standard deviations for the four subjects for both the six-LED and nine-LED stimuli. These results indicated that, on average, all subjects rated the 25ms time difference highest in both series of time differences. Therefore, we determined the parameter of the time difference for both six- and nine-LED conditions of simultaneous lighting stimuli to be 25ms.

**Table 1.** Averages of rating levels in time differences between light blinks experiment.

| time diff. | | 20ms | 25ms | 30ms | 35ms | 40ms | 45ms | 50ms | 55ms | 60ms | 65ms | 70ms | 75ms | 80ms |
|---|---|---|---|---|---|---|---|---|---|---|---|---|---|---|
| 6 LEDs | Avg. | 14.8 | 15.5 | 14.8 | 13.5 | 12.8 | 12.0 | 11.2 | 10.0 | 9.0 | 9.2 | 8.8 | 9.2 | 8.2 |
| | STD | 0.88 | 0.96 | 1.14 | 1.20 | 1.22 | 0.97 | 0.91 | 1.27 | 1.34 | 1.35 | 1.33 | 1.25 | 1.00 |
| 9 LEDs | Avg. | 15.8 | 16.0 | 15.5 | 15.2 | 14.2 | 13.0 | 11.5 | 11.0 | 10.0 | 9.0 | 8.0 | 8.0 | 8.0 |
| | STD | 1.00 | 1.03 | 1.09 | 1.17 | 1.26 | 1.34 | 1.15 | 1.18 | 1.21 | 1.00 | 1.03 | 1.03 | 1.03 |

### 3.2 Inter-LED Spatial Interval

The optic texture gradient may provide a clue for perceiving depth[2]. Based on Gibson's theory, depth perception is thought to be influenced by changes in LED spatial intervals. The aim of this second experiment was to determine the most effective inter-LED interval for perceiving the flow of light.

The subjects of the 'Time differences between light blinks' experiment described above also participated in this experiment. The same experimental setting was used, with two modified conditions. The first of these was the 'normal texture condition', under which equal intervals between LEDs were used. Under this condition, the subjects perceived depth in perspective, thanks to the right texture gradient. The second modified condition, the 'emphasised texture condition' narrowed the intervals between LEDs by degrees, as the distance between the LEDs and the subject increased. Here the virtual depth is magnified by emphasising the texture gradient.

The subjects, wearing the same glasses used for the previous experiment, were asked to watch the two lighting stimuli (same as the previous experiment), and to judge which light stimuli worked better as a dynamic sign for signalling direction. The result of this experiment was that the 'normal texture condition' was more effective than the 'emphasised texture condition' in 88% of the trials.

### 3.3 LED Colour

An experiment for determining the most suitable colour for the blinking LEDs was also carried out. Eight colours of blinking LEDs were used with the same experimental setting. The lighting unit had two colours of LED; red and green, and could control the intensity of each colour over a range of eight levels. Two-colour ratios were set for eight intensities of colour; red:green = 7:0, 6:1, 5:2, ..., and 0:7. (7:0 representing true red, and 0:7 representing true green.)

Three of the four subjects indicated that the ratio of 7:0 was the best colour combination for light, while the other subject indicated that the ratio of 6:1 was the best. According to this result, the most desirable colour of blinking light for the DLS is red.

### 3.4 Evaluation Experiment

**Purpose:** We designed the experiment to evaluate the influence of DLS on way-finding behaviour, with suitable parameters derived from our preliminary experiments.

**Experimental conditions:** We set two experimental conditions and one control condition.

1. Right Direction Condition: The light apparently moved to the right.
2. Left Direction Condition: The light apparently moved to the left.

**Control condition:** In spite of the DLS, only one fire exit sign was turned on.

**Subjects and procedure:** Seven subjects participated in this experiment. Four subjects were assigned experimental conditions: Each experimental condition had two subjects. Another three subjects were assigned the control condition. Each subject was asked to leave the building on foot as fast as possible, wearing Bangerter glasses (PL filters). The way-finding behaviours of each subject were recorded by a video camera, and analysed along with their utterances.

We had expected that the direction of the light's motion would affect the subject's selection of direction to take, but we did not find that it had any effect. Four of the seven subjects took the right direction, whereas the other subjects took the left direction. There was no relationship between the direction they took and the direction of the light's motion. According to utterances made by the subjects under experimental conditions, two of four subjects were aware that the light of the DLS moved, and the other two did not notice the motion. One of them perceived lights that appeared to go on in the right direction.

The light setting was considered to be the clue for him to move in a certain direction. We have not yet come to a conclusion on the efficiency of the DLS for way-finding outside, but it was noted that all subjects in the experimental conditions recognized and walked along the line of lights. This result suggests that DLS can be useful for people with poor vision to find their way to exits. The main reason why many subjects could not notice the movements of the lights was the darkness of the LEDs of the DLS. We are therefore planning to improve the brightness of the DLS.

## 4 Conclusions

We developed and proposed a DLS system to assist people with poor vision in finding their way, and described our preliminary experiments and their results. Our evaluation experiment did not produce a result indicating the efficiency of the DLS system for way-finding because of a lack of LED intensity. We are going to improve and further evaluate the DLS system, and report the results in our future work.

## References

1. Gibson, J.J., Purdy, J., and Lawrence, L.: A method of controlling stimulation for the study of space perception: optical tunnel. Journal of Experimental Psychology (1955) 50, 1-14
2. Gibson, J.J.: The Ecological Approach to Visual Perception. Hillsdale, NJ: Lawrence Erlbaum Associates, Inc. (1979/1986)

# Visual System to Help Blind People to Cross the Street

Joan Aranda and Pere Mares

Automatic Control and Computer Engineering Department
Universitat Politècnica de Catalunya
{joan.aranda,pere.mares}@upc.es

**Abstract.** A system to improve mobility of blind people based on computer vision is presented. It consists of a portable PC endowed with a digital camera and a pair of auriculars. The system is able to detect and to track green and red traffic lights used by the pedestrians without this disability. Colour histogram analysis whereas structural data have been used to recognize these traffic symbols. In order to handle with illumination changes a simple adaptation scheme is proposed. By means of the auriculars, the system inform to the user about semaphore state and also about its pan position in real time.

## 1 Introduction

The development of technological aids to improve the quality of life of handicapped people must be a main objective of the scientific community. In particular, we present a system for the improvement of the mobility of the blind people in our cities, in order to make their displacements easier and safer.

To dispose of proper traffic lights are one of the great fights of blind people that demand the necessity of a safe system to be able to cross the pedestrian crossings on their own. To do it, many of them count on guide dogs, which offer an invaluable aid. Nevertheless all of them do not have access to this solution (due to the expensive acquisition price and maintenance among other factors). The most of them must resort to spontaneous aid of the pedestrians standing near them.

Most of big cities count of fixed acoustic transmitters to solve this problem (at least in their main avenues and downtown). This solution is relatively cheap when semaphores are of new acquisition, but the massive substitution of present semaphores is not affordable for local administrations in a short term. Moreover, the worrisome acoustical contamination that undergoes our cities is increased by these annoying tones, what causes annoyances to the closest neighbours (especially at night). This is the main reason of because in the most of residential areas their installation is discarded, being restricted to the commercial areas or great avenues and only during the day-hours.

Some existing proposals to eliminate this problem consist of the incorporation of a radio or ultrasonic system that connected to a pedestrian traffic light it allows to enable the acoustic signalling in order to indicate to the blind people the free way [1][2]. Its operation is driven by means of a remote control that the blind person activates. With these facilities the acoustic signals are emitted only when the light is green and the blind has activated it with the remote control. On the other hand, this system forces the user to take a transmitter and also needs of more expensive semaphores.

K. Miesenberger et al. (Eds.): ICCHP 2004, LNCS 3118, pp. 454–461, 2004.

Moreover, there is not a standard normalization on frequencies to be used, and different cities use different systems.

Our proposal is the development of a system based on computer vision that allows to learn and to identify such symbols used by the pedestrians without this disability. Such a system permits to increase the mobility of the blind people freeing them from the special facilities provided by different cities or districts. The system is of universal use, what multiplies the possibilities of autonomy of this group of people.

As a first result in this line of applied investigation, we present an autonomous system that learns, detects, identifies and track the state of the semaphores for pedestrians. The use of the standard hardware requirements for the selected solution allows future extensions of the system with the same equipment.

## 2 The Visual System

In this work the task of identify and track traffic lights by means of computer vision is considered. The reliability of the recognition process and execution time both determine the efficiency of an on-line tracking system. Some solutions can reduce the processing time by using expensive computational resources, which reversely limits their generalised application. When standard image acquisition hardware is used, the most important limit is computation time. Colour is a good cue which allows a great reduction in the amount of data needed to be processed with an excellent balance between process time and the lose of robustness in matching the object at every new frame.

In our work, colour histograms have been widely used instead of any other sort of description for colour clusters such as Gaussian distributions or mixtures of them, as can be found in the other works [3][4][5][6][7], due to its simplicity, versatility and speed, all of them features appreciated in tracking applications. Moreover, the use of histograms has been vastly proven helpful in colour object recognition and object indexing [8][9]. Colour histograms have also been used in tracking tasks, as in [10][11].

The most important drawback of using colour information is that of its sensitivity to changes that illumination and relative motion between objects and the visual system carry out on the appraised colour of tracked objects. In general, colour constancy techniques attempt to avoid these misleading effects. For example, in [12] it is developed a correction for the technique of object indexing by colour, as described in [8]. Other colour adaptation scheme can be found in [3][5][7][11], but in this work we only update our histogram description by means of an easy weight rule filter that will be shown later in this paper. In [13] can be found an extension of this technique used in robot tracking tasks.

The goal of this system is to extract the position information of green or red light signals from the image sequence supplied by the wearable camera. We assume that initially the blind is stationary with respect to the scene and we use a model-based approach based on colour histograms to describe the appearance of the icons to detect.

Our visual system has two different main parts: the model learning module and the icon detecting and tracking module. These both modules are fed with images grabbed by the acquisition hardware. With the aid of an operator, first module segments the traffic lights out of the background and learns its colour histogram. The second one relocates a previously identified signal at each new frame.

## 2.1 Object Features

Our model of an object includes two kinds of features describing both appearance of the object and coarse geometry. First, information about how the object looks like, i.e., by the colour histogram of the object. Second, the area and shape of the green or red coloured area, that is first and second moments. Also the localization of the coloured area (up or down) is taken into account.

Be I a colour image and p=(x,y) a colour point, then:

$$H = \{H_{ijk} = \#\{p \mid I(p) \in Bin_{ijk}\}(i,j,k) \in [0,N-1]^3\} \quad (1)$$

is a colour histogram, where $Bin_{ijk}$ is a colour bin and $N$ is the number of bins on each dimension. Then, operations with histograms, such as distance, intersection, union, subtraction, can be defined in an easy way as follows:

$$dist(H,T) = 1 - \sum_{ijk} \min\{H_{ijk}, T_{ijk}\} \quad (2)$$

$$H \cap T = \{\min\{H_{ijk}, T_{ijk}\}, (i,j,k) \in [0,N-1]^3\} \quad (3)$$

$$H \cup T = \{\max\{H_{ijk}, T_{ijk}\}, (i,j,k) \in [0,N-1]^3\} \quad (4)$$

$$H \setminus T = \{H_{ijk}, \text{ if } T_{ijk} = \phi, (i,j,k) \in [0,N-1]^3\} \quad (5)$$

This histograms-based model is used to segment images into traffic lights candidates and background components. The result of the segmentation is employed then to identify and track the traffic sign.

Figure 1 illustrates how a usual histogram of an image window with a red or green traffic light looks like. Only relevant colour bins are showed. They form some colour clusters.

As a first step, the algorithm search for those windows in the image that can contain a traffic light. We call *candidates* to these areas. Instead of applying a colour indexing scheme by means of histogram intersection to find out where the candidates are, as done in [8], the solution we have adopted is very close to the colour histogram backprojection technique in [11]: we binarize an image by deciding for every pixel whether it belongs or not to histogram in the model. In our case, we compute the intersection (3) between a definite neighbourhood $B\varepsilon(I(p))$ of the colour of image pixel p and the model histogram H. If $B\varepsilon(I(p)) \cap H \neq \phi$, this colour belongs to the histogram in the model and, therefore, the pixel p belongs to a candidate.

Figure 2 shows a false candidate area belonging to the tail lights of a car. This is not important because the car will disappear in the next frame. If not, the geometrical analysis about red light surroundings will discriminate the real candidate from the false one.

## 2.2 Model Learning

Any model-based tracking algorithm needs to learn a model of the target that it intends to follow. This learning process can be supervised if the object to track is known before, as in our application, or unsupervised otherwise. In supervised learning, since we a priori know what to track, a ground truth consisting of a fixed model can be established. Then, if the adaptive model goes too far from the ground truth, it is resumed to the fixed one.

**Fig. 1. a)** Example of an identified red traffic light.

**Fig. 1. b)** Colour histogram of the selected window.

**Fig. 1. c)** Example of an identified green traffic light.

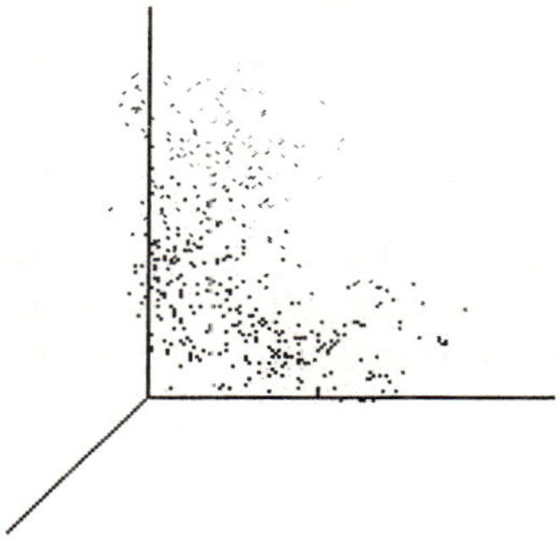

**Fig. 1. d)** Colour histogram of the selected window.

**Fig. 2.** False candidates in the presence of tail lights of a car.

In supervised learning, in order to extract the colour histogram it is necessary to select the image areas where light signals appear. Figure 3 shows some of the patterns used during the learning phase.

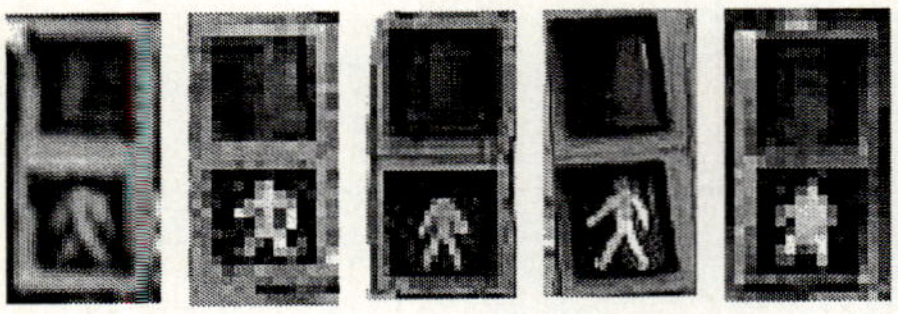

**Fig. 3. (a)** green lights sample patterns.

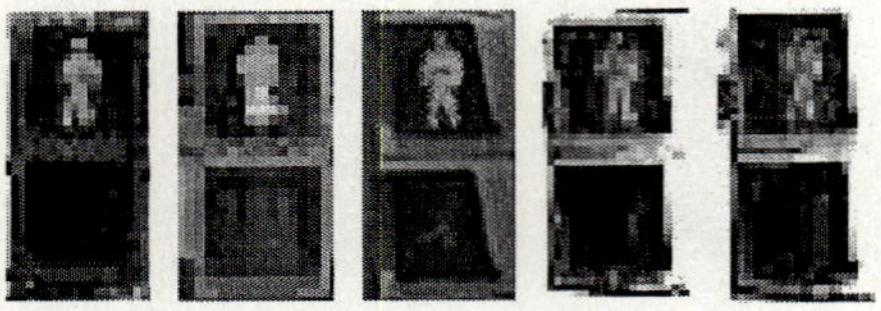

**Fig. 3. (b)** red lights sample patterns.

In our case, we compute the intersection (3) between the definite dilation $D_\varepsilon(G_i)$ of all the colour histograms ( $G_i$ ) of the green lights example patterns, obtaining a histogram model G that contains the common colour identification. The same is valid for red lights, so we can define:

$$G=\{\cap_i\{D_\varepsilon(G_i)\}\ ,\ i\in[0,M-1]\} \tag{6}$$

$$R=\{\cap_i\{D_\varepsilon(R_i)\}\ ,\ i\in[0,M-1]\} \tag{7}$$

From these histograms we extract the common part of their histograms (basically due to black and yellow areas around the lights) in order to get a concise subset of colour bins that identifies the green and red lights:

$$GL=G\backslash R \tag{8}$$

$$RL=R\backslash G \tag{9}$$

The area, shape and position features can be extracted by running a blob analysis over the binarized image obtained by colour histogram backprojection of the pattern (*GL* or *RL*) over the current image window.

## 2.3 Histogram Adaptation

The process of tracking an object has three main steps: object segmentation (colour histogram backprojection), feature extraction (blob analysis) and, finally, histogram adaptation. In this work, we have made use of a very simple adaptation scheme to cope with colour variations based on a weight rule filter:

$$\hat{H}_{ijk}^{t+1}=\beta\cdot\hat{H}_{ijk}^{t}+(1-\beta)\cdot H_{ijk}^{t},\ \beta\in[0,1] \tag{10}$$

where $\hat{H}^{t+1}$ is the updated histogram value for next step $(t+1)$, $\hat{H}^{t}$ is the updated histogram value at step $t$ and $H^t$ is the computed histogram value at step $t$. Histogram adaptation should take into account small and slow colour changes due to relative motion between camera, object and illumination.

## 3 Experimental Results

The overall system on which tests have been made consists of the following parts:

- Camera: Must be mobile and wearable (hands free). We select a pair of glasses with a mini camera integrated because most of blind people already use them (other clothes as hats also can be a good solution to incorporate it). This camera provides digital colour images of 640x480 pixels of 24 bits up to 30 frames/sec. The connection to the PC is by means of a USB port.
- Process unit: Portable PC computer. We propose this standard hardware due to its versatility and existing software tools, standard devices, and standard visual applications (as OCRs). Other cheaper control units (as Pockect PCs or PDAs) can be used with a decrease in the capacities of the system and future extensions.
- Output device: Acoustical signals and voice synthesizer through special stereo auriculars that do not limit outer hearing (main source of information for blind people). Playing with the intensity of the sounds in the left and right channel the horizontal location of semaphores is allowed.

**Fig. 4.** Sequence of a green light tracking performed by the system.

The tracking module supplies with the current pan position of the target in the image. Its output consists of an intensity controlled left/right sound to keep the user informed about the angle position and to lead him/her to the centre position. The error signal to calculate the sound intensity in each channel is defined as the difference between the target image position and the image centre pixel coordinates. Head and camera geometry have been considered to calculate this acoustic signal. This is helpful to maintain the user being always posed facing the signal being tracked, for instance when crossing a wide avenue. In order to avoid unnecessary user shaking, a dead zone is defined around the reference angle.

A video sequence showing the system following a green traffic light while the user is walking on the street is presented in figure 4.

The overall process, including the image processing and visual detection and tracking, are computed in real time (5 Hz). Visual field of the camera can't be nor so wide due to limited resolution neither so narrow because it will be difficult to search the traffic signal. The focal length of the camera has been selected so that with the available resolution we obtain a detection rate of almost 100% for a distance of less than 6 meters, falling until the 60% for distances of about 15 meters (wide avenues). Of course, a higher camera resolution will surpass this effect, but computation time will increase, reducing the feedback rate of the system.

What is important to point out is that the user establishes a feedback relationship with the detection system, so it tries to maintain the target centred in the field of view, helped by the stereo acoustic signal supplied by the own system.

## References


1. Koshi, K., Kani, H., Tadokoro, Y. (1999). Orientation aids for the blind using ultrasonic signpost system. *Proc. 1st.Joint BMES/EMBS Conf. Serving humanity, Advancing technology*. Pag 587.
2. Blenkhorn, P.; Evans, D.G.; A system for enabling blind people to identify landmarks: the sound buoy. *Rehabilitation Engineering, IEEE Transactions on [see also IEEE Trans. on Neural Systems and Rehabilitation]*, Volume:5 . Page(s): 276 –278.
3. Jang, Daesik and Hyung-Il Choi (1998). Moving object tracking using active models. *ICIP'98*, Vol.3: 648 -652.
4. Heisele, B., U. Kressel and W. Ritter (1997). Tracking non-rigid, moving objects based on color cluster flow. *CVPR '97*, pp.253-257.
5. McKenna, S. J. , Y. Raja and Shaogang Gong. (1999). Tracking Colour Objects Using Adaptive Mixture Models, *Image and Vision Computing*, Vol. 17: 225-231.
6. Nakamura, T. and T. Ogasawara (1999). Online visual learning method for color image segmentation and object tracking. *IROS '99*. Vol. 1: 222 –228.
7. Schuster, R. (1994). Color object tracking with adaptive modeling. *Workshop on Visual Behaviors, International Association for Pattern Recognition*: 91-96.
8. Swain, M.J. and D.H. Ballard (1991). Color Indexing. *IJCV*, Vol. 7(1): 11-32.
9. Schiele, B. and J. L. Crowley (1996). Object recognition using multidimensional receptive field histograms. *ECCV'96*, Vol I, pages 610-619.
10. Birchfield, S. (1998). Elliptical Head Tracking Using Intensity and Color Histogram, *CVPR*, pp. 232-237.
11. Chen, Tse Min, R.C. Luo and Tsu Hung Hsiao (1999). Visual tracking using adaptive color histogram model. *IECON '99*, Vol. 3: 1336 -1341.

12. Funt, B.V. and G.D. Finlayson (1995). Color Constant Color Indexing. *IEEE Trans. Pattern Analysis and Machine Intelligence,* Vol. 17(5): 522-529.
13. Vergés J., Aranda J., Sanfeliu A.. Object tracking system using colour histograms. *Spanish Symposium on Pattern Recognition and Image Analysis.* 16-18 . May 2001. ISBN: 84-8021-351-5. Pp. 225-230.
14. Tantribeau,P.;Lee,H.C.; A Stereo Auditory Image-perception Aid For The Blind. *Engineering in Medicine and Biology Society, 1992. Vol.14. Proceedings of the Annual International Conference of the IEEE*, Volume: 4 , Page(s): 1580 -1581

# CyARM – Interactive Device for Environment Recognition Using a Non-visual Modality

Makoto Okamoto[1], Junichi Akita[2], Kiyohide Ito[1], Tetsuo Ono[1], and Tomohito Takagi[3]

[1] Department of Media Architecture, Future University-Hakodate
116-2 Kameda-nakano, Hakodate 041-8655, Japan
{maq,itokiyo,tono}@fun.ac.jp
[2] Dept. of Information and Systems Engineering, Kanazawa University
2-40-20 Kodatsuno, Kanazawa 920-8667, Japan
akita@is.t.kanazawa-u.ac.jp
[3] Human Interface & Design Development, Fuji Xerox Co., Ltd.
Yokohama Business Park East Tower
134 Goudo-cho, Hodogaya-ku,
Yokohama-shi, Kanagawa 240-0005, Japan
friends-history@mail.goo.ne.jp

**Abstract.** The purpose of this research is to develop an interactive device for environment recognition, which uses senses other than vision. At present there is no interactive device with which a person who is visually handicapped can gain an intuitive impression of the external world. Our device, which we have named CyARM, has a mechanism that controls the motion of a visually impaired person's arm according to information about distance gathered by an ultrasonic sensor. We refined the features of CyARM through experimentation. The user can identify not only the existence of an object, but also its form.

## 1 Introduction

The many visual compensation devices for blind people are categorized into two groups from the viewpoint of sensory output. Devices in the first group use audition as the sensory modality of output; information is gathered from the surrounding environment via iconic or sonic sensors and transformed into audible frequencies of sound. Devices in the second group use haptic sense as the output medium; information obtained by sensors is transferred into haptic stimuli (e.g.: vibrations). These types of output can provide blind users with information about distance and direction.

Some commercially available devices convey information about distance change by qualitative or quantitative modification of vibration. Blind users can easily detect a relative change of distance, but it is difficult for them to specify absolute distance. They must therefore improve their cognitive skills such as inference to identify the distance to objects. In other words, those devices can only be used successfully if the user has advanced cognitive skills.

K. Miesenberger et al. (Eds.): ICCHP 2004, LNCS 3118, pp. 462–467, 2004.

In order for blind travelers to move about, it is important for them to obtain information about direction (spatial information). Sound output (e.g. Sonicguide) might be useful for providing spatial information, which is best conveyed by a binaural sound difference. However, artificial sounds generated by devices may mask natural sounds, making it difficult for blind users to hear sounds emitted by surrounding objects.

With the aim of solving the above-mentioned problems, we are designing a new sensory compensation device for the blind, by means of which they can perceive distance and other spatial information directly, with no need for inference.

The unique human-machine interface we are developing is designed to reduce the importance of the cognitive ability of the blind by specifying changes in distance and direction to objects. Consequently, our device is expected to be useful to the visually handicapped.

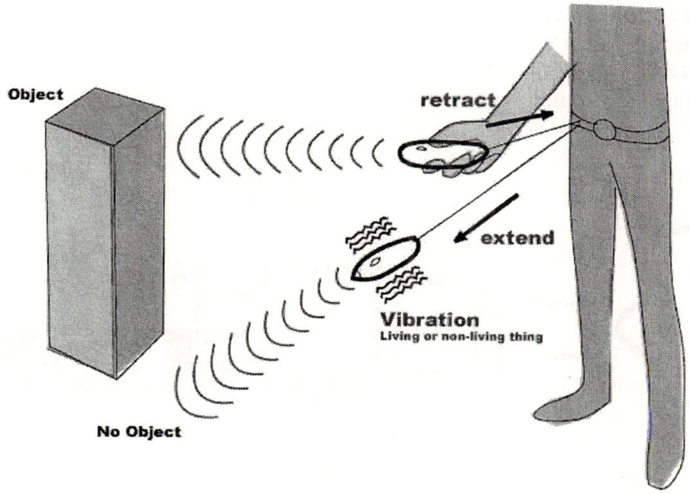


**Fig. 1.** Concept Sketch of CyARM.

## 2 Concept

We propose CyARM, a sensing device with a unique, intuitive interface for assisting blind people with walking.

The user holds CyARM in their hand, and searches the environment by pointing and moving the device. CyARM is connected to the user's body by a wire and transmits ultrasonic waves to measure the distance to the obstacle. The tension of the wire is controlled according to the measured distance to the obstacle. If the obstacle is at a short distance, CyARM pulls the wire tightly so that the user feels that they could touch the obstacle by bending their arm. If the obstacle is at a long distance, CyARM pulls the wire loosely so that the user extends their arm and feels that they cannot touch the obstacle. The user can search for an obstacle in any direction by pointing the device, and this will give them the illusion that their hand is extended to reach the far obstacles. This output interface provides an intuitive interface for the user, who can recognize the environment as if walking around touching things.

# 3 Development of the User Interface

## 3.1 Structure of the Device

We designed the structure of the proposed sensing device, CyARM.

The ultrasonic sensor measures the distance to the obstacle, and the motor is controlled according to the measured distance. The wire position is controlled by PI control. The wire is rewound to the initial position at default, and the rewinding tension is controlled by the measured distance; high tension for short distance, and low tension for long distance. Tension or rewinding of the wire is represented by the P gain in motor control; high motor current for high tension. When the user tries to extend their arm, the device detects a small displacement of the reel caused by the wire tension. The characteristics of the CyARM prototype are as follows.

- Motor: Maxon GP16 (4.5W) with 29:1 gear head and magnetic rotary encoder.
- Motor Driver: iXs iMDs03-CL
- MPU: Renesas H8/3664
- Ultrasonic frequency: 38kHz

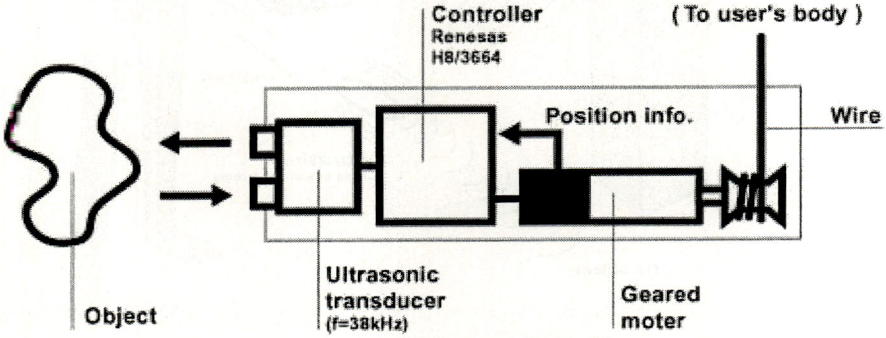


**Fig. 2.** Device Structure.

## 3.2 Package Design

We also designed the package for CyARM. Fig.3 shows the built prototype package. Fig 4 shows a future model sketch of CyARM. The ultrasonic sensor is located at the front of CyARM, parallel to the user's fingers for easy aim at the targeted direction. We are trying to develop smaller, lighter, and easier-to-hold packages for CyARM.

# 4 Evaluation

We conducted two experiments in order to evaluate the usability of CyARM. One evaluates whether the user can identify the existence of an object using CyARM. The other consists of a comparison with another apparatus.

**Fig. 3.** Built Prototype Package.

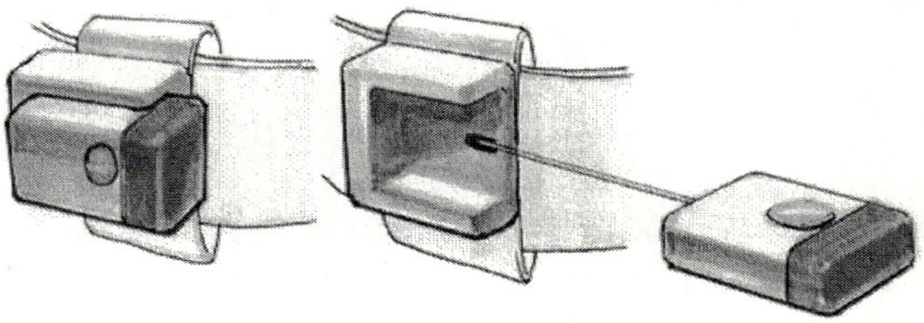

**Fig. 4.** Future Model Sketch.

### 4.1 Experiment on Identification of Object Existence

The first experiment investigated whether a user could identify objective existence. The subjects were five non-visually impaired people and one visually impaired person. The non-visually impaired people wore an eye mask, in order to impede vision, and all subjects wore stereo headphones to prevent them from judging the situation by means of external noise. All subjects had CyARM in hand and stood at a defined position<fig. 5>. A whiteboard was placed at a position 2m ahead of the subject. The subject tried to determine whether or not there was a whiteboard, and it was then removed.

### 4.2 Results of Experiment on Identification of Object Existence

Table 1 summarizes the results of the experiment on identification of object existence. Each subject tried to identify the state in which there was nothing and the state in which there was a whiteboard ten times, respectively. On average, the state in which an object existed was correctly identified 9.17 times out of 10, and the state in which an object did not exist was correctly identified 9.67 times out of 10; thus it was shown that identification is possible. However, it was pointed out in the interview after the experiment that the power to roll round is not enough for comfortable operation.

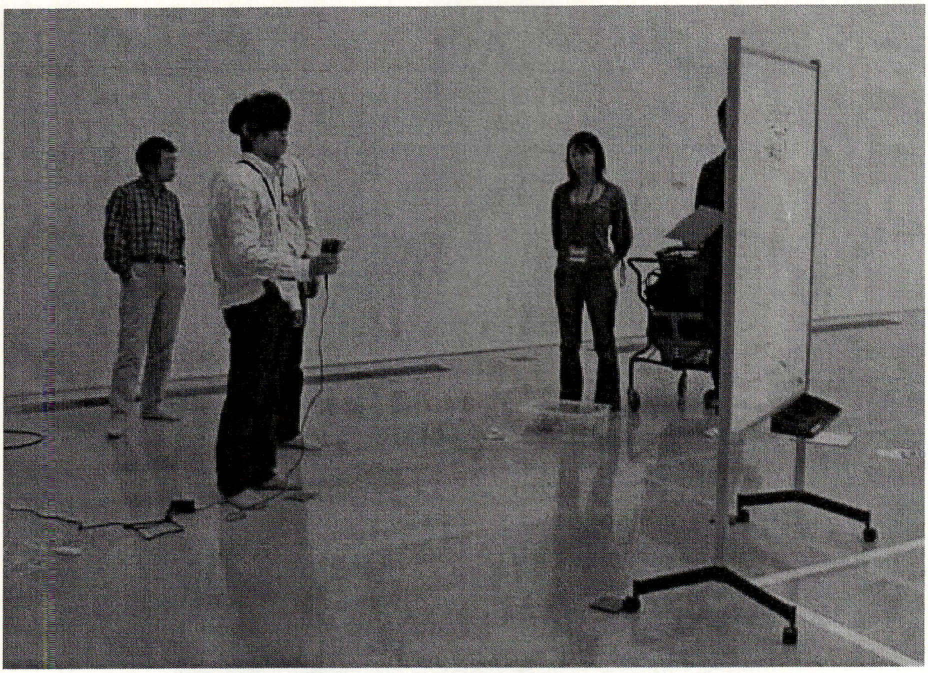

**Fig. 5.** Experiment on Identification of Object Existence.

**Table 1.** Result of Experiment on Identification of Object Existence.

| | Existence (%) | Non existence (%) |
|---|---|---|
| Whiteboard | 91.67 | 8.33 |
| No whiteboard | 3.33 | 96.67 |

### 4.3 Experiment Involving Comparison with Another Device

An evaluation experiment was carried out by four subjects, who used eye masks to impede their vision<Fig. 6>. The subjects were asked to pass between two walls using CyARM and Tri-sensor [1], and to make a comparison based on sound.

### 4.4 Results of Experiment Involving Comparison with Another Device

We investigated issues of usability and user requirements by means of interviews and video analysis. Our experiment showed that the subjects could determine the existence of an obstacle using both devices. It was also shown that CyARM has the advantages of enabling the user to find the end of a wall and the thickness of a wall, and to sense a person who is walking quickly.

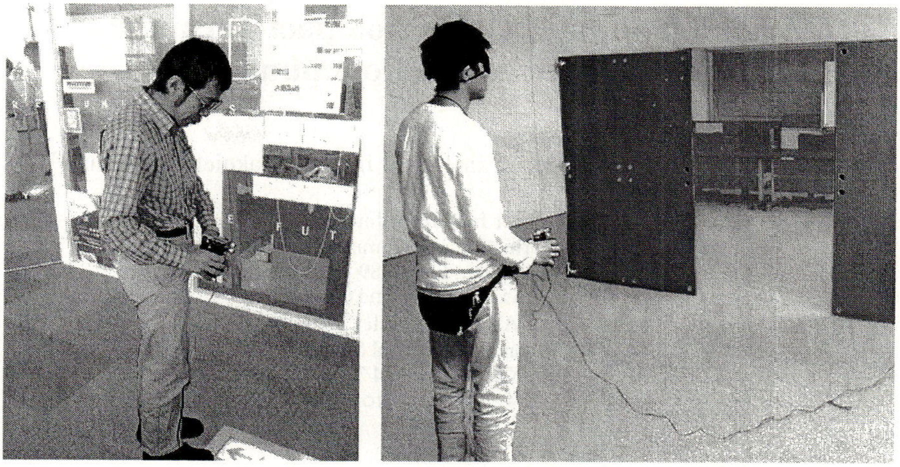

**Fig. 6.** Evaluation Experiment.

## 5 Conclusions and Future Work

We proposed CyARM, a new kind of sensing device for the visually impaired, to assist them in walking and recognizing objects around them. A wire is connected to the user's body, and controlled by CyARM according to the measured distance to the obstacle. This interface gives the user the impression of their arm being extended to an existing obstacle. We also discussed the implementation and package design of CyARM for building the prototype. Future CyARM research will be carried out through the gathering of more information on sensed obstacles, such as their texture (soft or hard, cold or hot) and whether they are living things or man-made objects. Other methods of gathering information will also be used, such as vibration and feeling with the fingers.

These extensions will be discussed in our future work. The device we propose, CyARM, gives new meaning to "sensing the environment". We are also planning to extend our research into joint attention or haptic joint attention feeling, which involves more than two people watching or feeling the same object.

## References


1. Hughes, B.: Active artificial echolocation and nonvisual perception of aperture passability, Human Movement Science 20, pp.371-400, (2001)
2. Takagi, T., Akita, J., Ito, K., Ono, T., Okamoto, M.: CyARM: Intuitive space recognition by Non-Visual Modality, IPSJ Symposium Series Vol. 2004, No.5, pp181-182, (2004)
3. Akita, J., Takagi, T., Okamoto, M.: CyARM: Environment Sensing Device using Non-Visual Modality, CSUN2004 International Conference on Technology And Persons With Disabilities, (2004).

# Walking Support Using Compact Terminals with Infrared Audio Communication

Shinya Oyama[1], Ikuko Eguchi Yairi[1], Seiji Igi[1], and Takuichi Nishimura[2]

[1] Human-Computer Intelligent Interaction Group
National Institute of Information and Communications Technology
3-5 Hikari-dai, Seika, 619-0289 Kyoto, Japan
{oyamas,yairi,igi}@nict.go.jp
[2] Cyber Assist Research Center
National Institute of Advanced Industrial Science and Technology
2-41-6 Aomi, Koto, 135-0064 Tokyo, Japan
taku@ni.aist.go.jp

**Abstract.** We developed a voice guidance system that increases-mobility for visually impaired people. We use infrared communication technology called Compact Battery-less Information Terminals. The user-friendly information terminal of this system provides guidance as well as instructions for the system, which can be installed at various locations. We also developed a bone conduction headphone for the system's information terminal, which helps visually impaired users hear other sounds in the users' surroundings without disturbance by audio information generated by the system. To evaluate the usability of this system, we conducted an experiment in which visually impaired people used the system to be guided to a destination.

## 1 Introduction

Independence of mobility is very important to most people. We try to implement Robotic Communication Terminals, which is a mobility support system for the elderly and disabled people. RCT assists for their impaired elements of mobility -recognition, actuation, and information access [1].

In particular, visually impaired people have problems comprehending their surroundings and acquiring information necessary for mobility equal to that of sighted individuals. We have developed a device that increases the mobility of visually impaired individuals.

To clarify the needs of the visually impaired, we conducted surveys in 1999 and in 2001 and received replies from a total of 788 visually impaired people [2, 3]. From their response we learned that many were unsatisfied with their inability to recognize the surroundings and hoped to gain greater independence of mobility.

Many devices have been developed to provide information for the visually impaired. Most systems require individual terminals or personal computers to process the received signals [4, 5]. Visually impaired or individuals with special needs may find it difficult to use these terminals due to the complexity of their operation.

K. Miesenberger et al. (Eds.): ICCHP 2004, LNCS 3118, pp. 468–475, 2004.

Infrared communication is appropriate for giving directions to the visually impaired because it can transmit signals in a specific direction and direct it at limited range. A system using infrared ray communication called TalkingSign has been developed [6, 7], but this system requires individual terminals and it is rather expensive when combined with the cost of information transmitters.

We considered, therefore, the following points in improving the existing assistance system for the visually impaired: 1)_using infrared communication, 2)_making the terminal user-friendly, 3)_keeping transmitter and terminal cost low. By adopting an infrared communication device called the Compact Battery-less Information Terminal or CoBIT for short, we developed a system which can not only guide users but provide instructions for use [8]. This system works with on user-friendly terminals can be installed at various locations.

## 2 System

### 2.1 System Structure

As shown in Fig. 1, the developed guidance system consists of an infrared transmitter set up near the target location, and a CoBIT, which serves as the audio receiver.

The transmitter amplifies the inputted signal waves and radiates them using infrared LEDs. The solar cell on the CoBIT receives this infrared emission and generates electricity, after which the sound travels through the earphones directly connected to the solar cell. One advantage of using CoBIT is the simplicity of the system's structure. This simplicity lowers the cost of the installation of the system in public places and promotes increased use of the terminals. Since the transmitter includes infrared ray LED arrays, it is capable of easily selecting the proper types, numbers, or the allocation of LED depending on the distance/angles for the signal transmissions. It is desirable to install the transmitter at ceiling height or higher to ensure that people or other objects don't block the transmission, reducing the efficacy of the system.

### 2.2 Bone Conduction Headphone Terminal

The current CoBIT model, however, has a disadvantage because the shape of the earphones prevent users from hearing other sounds in the surroundings when the earphones are outputting audio guidance. Most visually impaired people dislike their hearing ability affected, since the auditory sense is crucial for those who cannot rely on their eyesight.

We improved the CoBIT by developing a terminal adapted for a bone conduction headset with two headphones and placed it on both sides of the headset, which can reliably convey sound information (Fig. 2). The headphones sit just above the ears, leaving the ear canals open and capable of perceiving surrounding sounds. Because the headphone conveys sound while it is tightly attached to the head, it is not susceptible to external sounds. Because of the high electricity consumption rate of the bone conduction headphones, we have not yet been able to develop a battery-free system. As an alternative we have installed a terminal that increases the signals received by the solar cell. This terminal uses one 3-V battery as an outside power source.

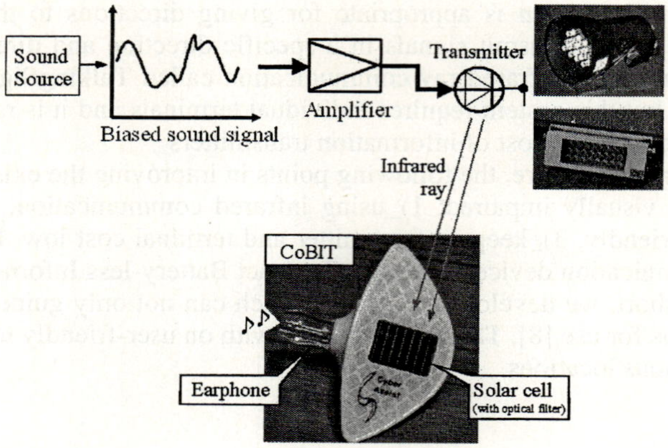


**Fig. 1.** Guidance system.

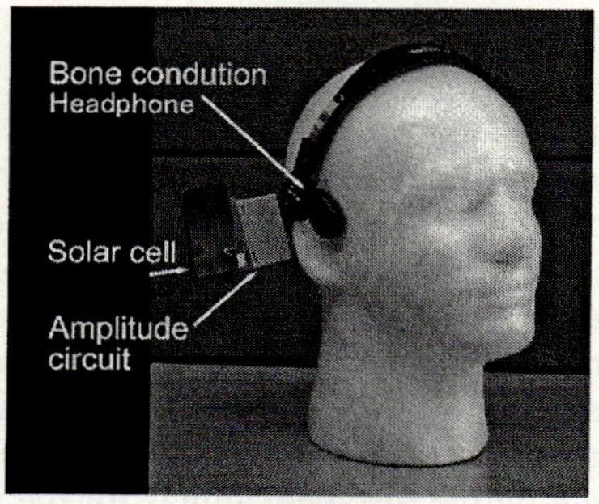


**Fig. 2.** Bone conduction headphone terminal.

The bone conduction headphone terminal can pick up the infrared signals at a distance of about 5 meters from the transmitter and within approximately 20 degrees of the center of the transmitter indoors when there is no noise.

## 3 Testing the System Inside the Building

We tested the viability of the guidance system using the CoBIT system inside the building with the cooperation of visually impaired participants.

### 3.1 Installation

We chose a corridor about 2 meters wide in a common area at our research center as the site of the experiment (Fig. 3). We programmed the system to guide people from the lobby to the elevator, a distance of about 70 meters. There are four turns along the route two left turns and two right turns. There were neither obstacles nor noise, nor were there any tactile tiles for guiding visually impaired people.

Infrared transmitters were installed on the ceiling along the route, and only four instructions were transmitted: "go straight," "turn left," "turn right," and "you have arrived at the destination." We call all of these, except for "go straight," 'location information.'

The transmitters that gave the "go straight" instructions were installed at 10-meter intervals and at a 20-degree angle from the ceiling, so that the participants could hear the instruction at some distance from the transmitter. The transmitters providing location information were installed at an angle of 50 degrees from the ceiling so the participants could hear the instruction when they were only 1 meter away from the corner.

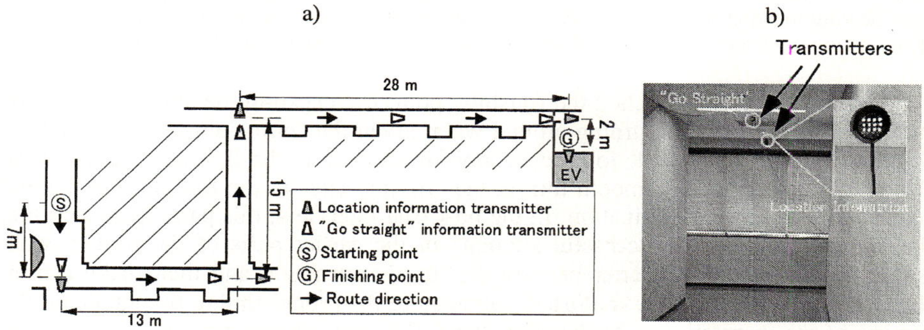


**Fig. 3.** a) Indoors route map. Transmitters were installed on the ceiling as shown in b). Transmitters' tilt angles of the transmitters were adjusted depending on type of sound guidance programmed into them.

### 3.2 Participants and Conditions

Three visually impaired men who use walking sticks in their daily life participated in this experiment. Two of them were are completely blind, and the third can only differentiate between light and darkness. They walked the route twice, using the instructions from the terminal as an aid, once wearing the bone conduction headphone terminal, and once wearing a CoBIT.

None of the participants were familiar with the route or the set-up. Nor were they trained to use this system. If they lost their way, they were taken back to the starting point without retracing their steps to start again from the beginning.

### 3.3 Results

Videotapes of the trials revealed some behaviors that were common to all three participants (Fig. 4)

1. Stopping or slowing down when approaching the corner and hearing the instruction "turn left (or right)."
2. Searching around with the stick after turning to the left (or right).
3. Locating the wall by using the cane, and then walking along the wall in the direction instructed.

**Fig. 4.** Common behaviors in experiments. (1)Stopping or slowing when approaching corner and hearing location instruction, (2)Searching around with stick after turning left or right, and (3)Locating the wall using stick, and then walking along the wall in direction instructed.

All the participants reached the finishing point by repeating the above. One of the three participants, while turning around when given the 'turn right(left)' instruction, hit the wall and was unable to proceed any further both in the first and second trials. Nonetheless, he made a smooth turn at the crossing later in the trial, and in the end managed to reach the destination. In the post-trial interview, this participant said that he learned from the unsuccessful attempts in the earlier parts of the trial to walk straight about one meter after hearing the 'turn' instruction and then make a turn. From this, we may assume that users can acquire the proper timing by practicing the timing of the instructions. On the other hand, the other two participants successfully arrived at the destination although they had never used the system.

Feedback from the participants revealed that the guidance information was easier to hear with the bone conduction headphone than with the CoBIT.

The participants also reported that the presence of the bone conduction headphone did not make them feel uncomfortable as they moved. One participant complained, however, that his temple began to hurt shortly after he began using the headphone. The participants found the CoBIT light, compact, and easy to put on and take off. They also pointed out some shortcomings such as difficulties in securing the earphone in their ear and in hearing the instructions because of low volume. From the above, we concluded that the bone conduction headphone is superior to CoBIT in that the users can hear better. This is a crucial element for the mobility of the visually impaired, since, in order to avoid any potential danger, they must have full access to all surrounding sounds as they move.

## 4 Testing the System Outside the Building

We also tested the system outdoors to evaluate the system's effectiveness in surroundings with traffic noise and sunlight.

### 4.1 Installation

We defined a guide route on the grounds outside our laboratory building (Fig. 5). We programmed the system to guide people from the entrance gate of laboratory to the entrance of the building. The distance was about 80 meters and the width of the path was 3 meters from the starting point to point A (Fig. 5), and 6.5 meters from point A to the destination. There were no obstacles and no tactile tiles.

The transmitters were installed at intervals of 5 meters. They chimed to give the instruction "go straight." Location information transmitters were also installed (points 1-5 in Fig. 5), which gave voice instructions, (1)"cross the street to the right," (2)"cross the street to the left," (3)"there are no curbstones for the next 10 meters," (4)"turn to the right," and(5)"you have arrived at the door." These transmitters were installed on the poles or walls along the route.

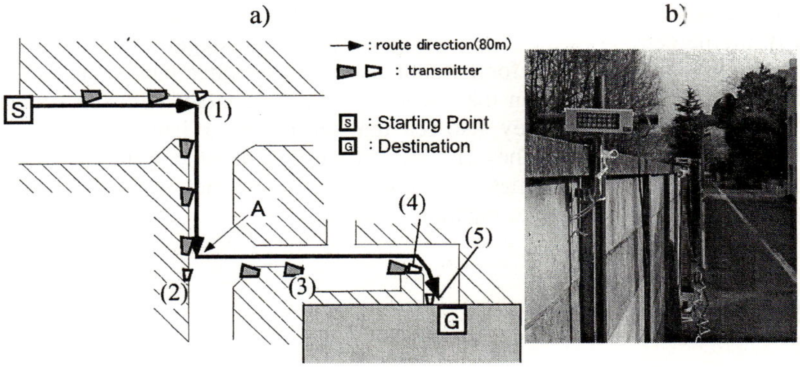


**Fig. 5.** a) Outdoor route map. Numbers indicate transmitter locations on the walls and poles along the path. b) Photograph of route with installation of transmitters.

## 4.2 Participants and Conditions

Four visually impaired people (three men and one woman) who use walking sticks in their daily life participated in this experiment (none had participated in the first one). All of them are completely blind. They walked along the route twice, using the instructions from the terminal as an aid, wearing the bone conduction headphone terminal. As in the indoor experiment, none of the participants were familiar with the route or the set-up. They also were not trained to use this system. If they lost their way, they were taken back to the starting point without retracing their steps, to start again from the beginning.

## 4.3 Results

The participants usually turned at the corners as instructed and searched for places where they could hear the chimes. These actions are similar to those in the indoor experiment. There were, however, fewer clues to finding the route in the outdoor experiment than in the indoor one. Therefore, information from the transmitters was very important in following the route and the directions.

Participants sometimes missed turns and were sometimes disoriented along a straightaway. Failure to receive the directions may be cited as the cause for the participants' inability to walk along the curb stones and the walls. After becoming disoriented and restarting from the beginning several times, the participants eventually reached the destination, aided by the chimes and location information from the transmitter as well as the clues regarding the route learned from previous unsuccessful attempts. It took two of the four participants approximately two and a half and three and a half minutes to reach the destination on the most successful attempt, while it took the other two about nine and nine and a half minutes, significantly longer than the first two. It is noteworthy that the two who arrived at the destination faster frequently go out by themselves on a regular basis, while the other two are usually accompanied by someone else. This may have been the deciding factor in their difference in the moving speed.

It was the general opinion of all the participants that the instructions did not interfere with the perception of the surrounding sounds. This suggests that the bone conduction headphone is suitable for outdoor use. On the other hand, the participants complained that the pressure on their scalp due to the contact with the headphones made them uncomfortable. They also felt that the headgear hanging over the head disturbed their concentration. They also expressed hope that the system could be programmed so the location information is transmitted a few meters ahead of the crossings to allow them longer time to mentally prepare.

## 5 Discussion

In our experiment, the visually impaired participants were able to reach their destination without being familiarized with the route beforehand, which indicates that a simple sound guidance system using infrared rays is quite practical.

The participants in the outdoor experiment, however, were sometimes disoriented. This was mainly because they were unable to hear the instructions due to the narrow transmitter range. The participants' ability to hear the instructions depended on the width of the passage they were traveling on. There is room for further improvements including altering the broadcasting range on the transmitter, or improving the sound quality of the receiver.

The range where users walk freely may be narrowed down to ensure accurate reception of instructions. We plan to solve this problem by combining the infrared communication with a non-directional communication device such as an AM radio. An AM radio can provide rough information within a few meter range such as 'You are approaching a crossing', while the infrared communication system confirms the location of the crosswalk and gives instructions accordingly.

Feedback from the participants in the indoor experiment indicated that the bone conduction speaker was superior to the CoBIT in its ability to pick up sounds but inferior in its ease of use, and that the bone conduction speaker was more effective in ensuring the safety of the visually impaired. Further improvements, though, will have to be made on the sound quality, the wearability, and the design of the terminal.

Although the system proposed here is relatively simple in its construction and does not require highly sophisticated technology, we were able to provide the necessary information for visually impaired people at what seems to be a reasonable installation cost. We are optimistic that improvements can be made, leaving advantages of the infrared communication system intact so that visually impaired people can readily navigate by themselves at any time.

## References


1. Ikuko Eguchi Yairi and Seiji Igi: Robotic Communication Terminals as a Mobility Support System for Elderly and Disabled People(3), Journal of Japanese Society for Artificial Intelligence, Vol.18, No.1, pp.29-35 (2003). (In Japanese)
2. Seiji Igi and Ikuko Eguchi Yairi: Questionnaire and Study on Self-sustaicned Moving Support System for Aged and Disabled, Proc. of Human Interface Symposium 2000, pp.57-60 (2000). (In Japanese)
3. Toshihiko Kashino et al.: A Survey about Daily Problems on Mobility of Elderly and Disabled People, Proc. of Human Interface Symposium 2002 (Japan), pp.647-650 (2002). (In Japanese)
4. Thomas Strothotte et al.: MoBIC: user needs and preliminary design for a mobility aid for blind and elderly travelers, 2nd TIDE congress (1995).
5. Takanori Shimada et al.: Information guidance system for the handicapped in a railway station, Technical report of IEICE, WIT2001-6 pp.29-34 (2001). (In Japanese)
6. William Crandall et al.: Remote infrared signage evaluation for transit stations and intersections, Journal of Rehabilitation Research and Development, Vol.36 No.4, pp.359-368 (1999).
7. Teruyuki Tajima, et al.: Pedestrian Information and communication systems for visually impaired persons, Proc. of CSUN's 16th Annual International Conference "Technology and Persons with Disabilities" (2001).
8. Takuichi Nishimura, et al.: A compact battery-less information terminal system for location-based interactive information support, Journal of Information Processing Society of Japan, Vol.44, No.11, pp.2659-2669 (2003). (In Japanese)

# The Development of Virtual 3D Acoustic Environment for Training 'Perception of Crossability'

Takayuki Shiose[1,2], Kiyohide Ito[3], and Kazuhiko Mamada[4]

[1] Kyoto University, Sakyo-ku, Yoshida-Honmachi, Kyoto, Japan
[2] ATR Network Informatics Laboratories, 2-2-2 Hikaridai, "Keihanna Science City", Kyoto, Japan
[3] Future University-Hakodate, 116-2 Kameda-Nakanocho, Hakodate, Hokkaido, Japan
[4] School for the Visually Impaired, University of Tsukuba, 3-27-6 Mejirodai, Bunkyo-ku,Tokyo 112-8684, Japan

**Abstract.** This study attempted to reveal the role of auditory information in the accurate "perception of crossability" for people with severe visual impairment ('the blind'). We created a 'virtual 3D acoustic environment' in which listeners feel a car passing in front of them to help them cross the street safely. An idea of this acoustic system originated from a previous research that showed that the blind make good use of reflected sounds or reverberations in identifying sources and in specifying distances from objects. The system is useful not only for analyzing critical cues of perception of 'crossability' but also for training the blind how to cross a street. Such auditory information can provide the blind with a safe training system for acquiring such auditory information.

## 1 Background and Goal

Since people with severe visual impairment ('the blind') are forced to make a huge effort to travel independently, they are discouraged from participating in society. On the other hand, some blind people are proficient in navigating for themselves on routes that are not bound to studded paving blocks. They can acquire useful information from perceptual stimuli for traveling independently. Despite its importance, there is little known about their ability to perceive such auditory information in everyday life, let alone training others to develop such skills. Consequently, the blind need time to specify, acquire, and practice such useful information. In reality the danger of crossing the street (referred to as 'perception of crossability') deprives the blind of any chance to practice. This study was held on the assumption that a blind person needs to cross the driveway so as not to contact running cars (see figure 1). Here, the blind are requested to judge their crossability from various accoustic stimuli.

A viewpoint of Ecological Psychology is expected to specify what is the key variable for crossability on the grounds that it has many literatures on 'time-to-contact' or 'time-to-arrival' information. The 'time-to-contact' information of

K. Miesenberger et al. (Eds.): ICCHP 2004, LNCS 3118, pp. 476–483, 2004.

**Fig. 1.** An image of crossing the driveway

an approaching object is specified by the relation of its spatial position to its velocity. It has played an important role in the study of visual control of action. Velocity can be visually perceived either by using the retinal expansion rate or the information provided by motion-sensible neural structures. Lee (1976) showed that the inverse of the relative rate of dilation of an optical angle; he named it $\tau$; specifies the time-to-contact of an observer with an object or surface. Most literatures on ecological psychology have had deep interest in the visual $\tau$ variable; on the other hand, Schiff and Oldak (1990) investigated that a person, sighted and unsighted, could perceive time-to-contact auditorily. Thus, the investigations of acoustic perception of such time-to-contact information contributes to specify when the blind should start to cross the driveway so as not to contact with running cars by using acoustic perception of time-to-contact backward.

In this study we created a 'virtual acoustic environment' in which listeners feel a car passing in front of them to estimate when it is safe to cross. The system is useful not only for analyzing the critical cues to perceive crossability but also training the blind how to estimate when it is safe to cross the street. This paper reported our standpoint and the meaning of paying attention to such a 'virtual accoustic envirionment.'

## 2 Ecological Psychology for the Blind

### 2.1 Acoustic Parameters for Time-to-Contact

Crossing the street safely requires the blind to identify accurately such moving sound sources as cars, footsteps, and so on. Rosenblum (1987) reported that observers use at least three types of acoustic variables to verify that a moving sound source has passed: interaural temporal differences, the Doppler effect, and amplitude change. He pointed out that psychoacoustic literature on localization has been concentrated on fixed sound sources and these variables were presented only in isolation, even if the sound source was assumed to be mobile. Rosenblum emphasized the relative contributions of different tyeps of stimulus variables for a blind person to identify moving sound sources.

Shaw (1991), Schiff and Oldak(1990), and others have taken in an ecological approach to acoustic perception and developed an ecological acoustics. They investigated, for instance, that velocity can be auditory perceived by using the rate of intensity or loudness growth and what acoustic variables can specify 'time-to-contact'; that is acoustic $\tau$. Some researchres built new study area of an ecological acoustics; while others express caution about such a simple analogy between visual $\tau$ and acoustic $\tau$. Conclusion for this controversy needs sufficient evidence to identify the characteristics of acoustic $\tau$.

## 2.2 Previous Research

Noticing the important role played by auditory information when the blind perceive obstacles, Ito; one of autohors; investigated acoustic information for the blind to identify time-to-contact of approaching objects and concluded that such acoustic information as the sound of running cars, footsteps, reflected sounds from objects etc. may also be available to blind pedestrians (Ito, 1997, 1999).

Ito (1999) demonstrated an auditory interceptive pendulum-hitting task by referring to the blind baseball where the player judges the timing of swinging the bat by the sound of the approaching ball on the ground. Ito asked for ten subjects to perform an interceptive Pendulum-hitting task and a judging the arrival time ($T_a$) task in an echoic room using the handcrafted apparatus where the iron ball (38 mm dia.) rolled on the U-shaped trackway (18 x 2700 mm) with a constant velocity. Figure 2(a) shows the front view of the apparatus. In the first task, each subject was requested to intercept the approaching iron ball by swinging a pendulum and, in the second task, to press the switch when s/he thought it was passing in front of her/him.

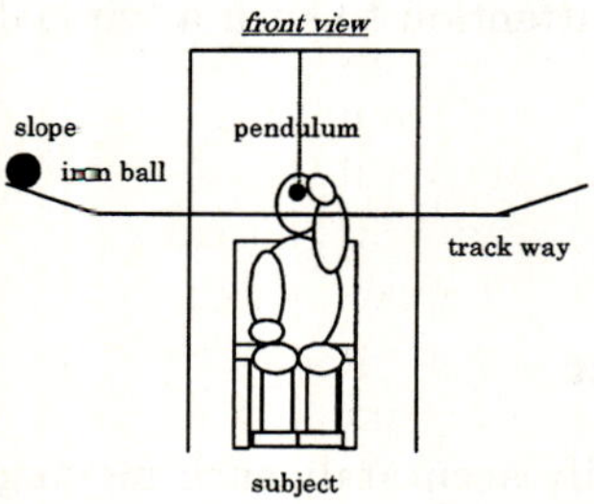


Timing Error in Each Task Under the Two Conditions (n=10)

| | | S Condition | | L Condition | |
|---|---|---|---|---|---|
| | | CE | VE | CE | VE |
| $T_a$ | Mean | 12.26 | 6.81 | 11.61 | 6.00 |
| | Standard Deviation | 4.08 | 1.66 | 3.65 | 2.23 |
| IT | Mean | 20.24 | 11.49 | 18.47 | 12.09 |
| | Standard Deviation | 6.43 | 4.22 | 9.27 | 5.66 |

Note. CE refers to constant timing error, VE to variable timing error (Tresilian, 1994). $T_a$ refers to the judging time-to-arriaval task to press the switch and IT to the interceptive timing task to hit the ball by the pendulum.

**Fig. 2.** (a) A front view of the apparatus (b) A table of timing error in each task (reprinted from Ito (1999))

Interceptive timing errors were defined as the differenve between perceived time and actual time (the time required for the iron ball to reach right in front of the subject). Figure 2(b) indicates that timing error in Pendulum-hitting was about twice as large as that of $T_a$-judging. This is because subjects could not obtain any auditory information on the pendulum except the acoustic information for localizing the moving sound emitted by the iron ball. However, Ito also demonstrated that the accuracy in timing increased after repeating the trials. In this additional experiment, subjects were conjectured to be able to succeed in coupling auditory perception and his/her requested action. Therefore, Ito concluded that familiarity with acoustic environment is considered to play some kind of role in this coupling.

Thus, Ito has cleared various evidences about how the blind can perceive and identify a moving sound sources and has specified reflected sounds or reverberations (see below for further details) of sources as key factors for an ecological acoustic study. In another experiment he ascertained that a periodical change of time delay is more important than pitch or sound pressures, revealing that auditory information was being effectively used at crosswalks for the benefit of the blind. However, no solution has been proposed to give a cue for crossing the street, which is the most dangerous and most necessary hurdle to allow the blind to participate in the society. An explanation of such auditory information can provide the blind with a safe training program to acquire such skills.

## 3 Acoustic Cue Acquisition Training in a Virtual 3D Acoustic Environment

### 3.1 System Architecture of Virtual 3D Acoustic Environment

Since the blind obviously cannot learn timing to cross by trial and error on actual streets, a virtual acoustic environment whose controllable parameters should contain all acoustic factors given in an ecological psychology study on auditory perception is indispensable.

Figure 3 shows the production of sound sources by "audio recorder" (Roland AR-3000) and MIDI sound sources from a PC. The main components of this system are a three-dimensional sound space processor (Roland RSS-10) which, in a virtual 3D sound space, can simulate such acoustic environments as reflected sounds, reverberations, and the Doppler effect. A 'reflected sound' is defined as a sound that emanates from the sound source and is deflected off the floor once; it is a sound that reaches the ears after a short delay or a time lag caused by a long detour. On the other hand, 'reverberations' are defined as sounds that reach the ears again or more than once, as in such a closed space or a room. They are deflected back and forth between the floors, walls, and ceiling.

RSS-10 has four sub-processors: a Binaural Processor, a Distance Processor, a Reverberations Processor, and Delay Mode. RSS10 uses those four subprocessors, based on the Head Related Transfer Functions (HRTFs), which were measured in an anechoic chamber, to enable listeners not only to localize stationary sound sources but also to detect the course of the motion of a sound.

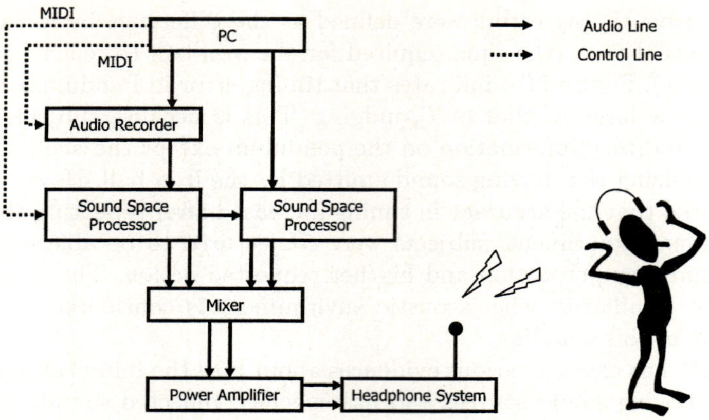


**Fig. 3.** Overview of our system

The experimenter can also design many different trajectories of sound images by using the exclusive software (Roland Creating 3D Sound).

Two "sound space processors" are connected in cascade and linked with the PC (DELL DIMENSION 4500) via the MIDI interface (Roland UM-550). Then, 3D sounds produced by the two RSS-10s are mixed and amplified before reaching the headphones. There are two types of audio output, and this "sound space processor" can produce both of them. Both types of audio output have advantages and disadvantages. For instance, transaural output forces the listener to sit equidistantly from both speakers; on the other hand, binaural output produces invariable 3D sound regardless of listener's head movement. Here, the system's output device is equipped with a digital surround headphone system (SONY MDR-DS8000) with has two unique functions: Digital Infrared Audio Transmission and Head Tracking. This system dissolves both disadvantages at a low price; the headphones perform as an efficient speaker system, using feedback from the movment of the listener's head and by using 3D magnetic track sensors. Figure 4 shows a picture of experimental devices.

In this virtual 3D acoustic environment, sounds processed by two RSS-10s represent motor vehicles. A subject operates a joystick or a mouse to move a stick figure safely across the street. The experimenter can specify and control all sound parameters, facilitating the identification of a listener's acoustic variable specifying time-to-contact while crossing the street. The first aim of using this system is applied for analyzing critical cues of 'perception of crossability.' The second one is applied for training the blind to acquire such cues; especially, theoretical background for cue acquisition training is also based on an ecological psychology as the following.

### 3.2 Cue Acquisition Training Based on Ecological Psychology

The two primary schools of thought in ecological psychology reflect the contributions of two great founders: J. Gibson and E. Brunswik. J. Gibson is famous

**Fig. 4.** Picture of our experimental devices

for his achievements in 'perception' study; on the other hand, E. Brunswik elucidated 'cognitive judgment'. Many researchers have pointed out definitive differences between them, for example, their interpretation of ecological validities; nevertheless, a synthesis of both theories is now being recognized.

Brunswik proposed a lens model wherein relationships between the judgment subject and the environment (distal) were explained by a symmetrical structure that placed cues (proximal) for the judgment at the center. He distinguished "cue utilization validity" from "ecological validity." The former indicates its latent validity in how accurately cues specify the ecological criteria, and the latter indicates its individual validity in how efficiently cues reflect the acting subject's cognitive judgment. The author has developed an interactive skill-transfer system based on Brunswikian Ecological Psychology because it successfully explains the difficulties of skill-transfer (Shiose et al., 2004). Figure 5 shows two judgment versions of the lens model called a triple system design because it analyzes cues from three directions with two judgments and the environment.

Our proposed skill-transfer system regards such processes as an apprenticeship system of 'interpersonal conflict' and 'interpersonal learning' between an expert and an apprentice; that is a collaborative work by using cues in common. Thus, the difficulties of the skill-transfer process are roughly classified into two processes: the difficulty for the expert to externalize his/her personal cues, and the difficulty for the apprentice to embody such acquired cues. This system provides us with the way to acquire judgment cues over the expert's shoulder.

However, one serious problem remains before this skill-transfer model can be immediately applied to acoustic-cue acquisition training programs. This system tacitly postulated that both the expert and the apprentice should notice a common set of cues and recognize their mutual awareness: that is, 'visually joint attention'. Therefore, whether this system is applicable for acoustic cues has not cleared yet. We have not yet proved whether auditory joint attention

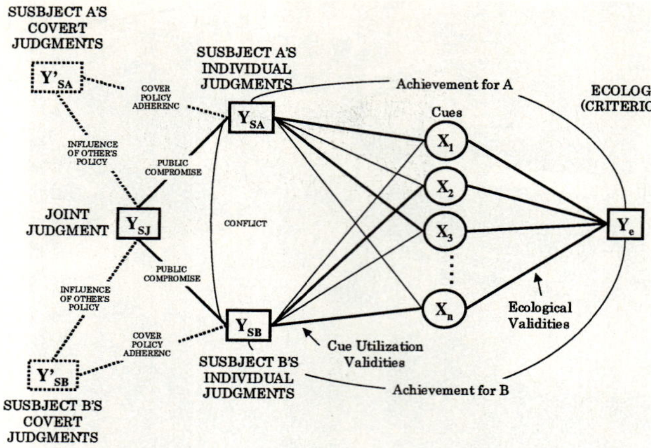


**Fig. 5.** Triple System Design in the Dynamic Interaction of Skill-Transfer

exists and whether it is necessary for skill-transfer. First, we have to specify acoustic cues for the 'perception of crossability' and establish a novel idea for an acoustic-cue training program. Hints for this problem was given by Ito's previous research (Ito, 1999). Ito (1999) demonstrated that repetition of the task trials and familiarity with acoustic environment is important to improve the accuracy of estimating time-to-arrival. Hence, establishment of the virtual acoustic envirnoment is one of the few training system to let the blind acquire acoustic cues for 'perception of crossability'.

## Acknowledgment

This research is supported by the Nissan Science Foundation and by JST CREST Digital City Project.

## References

1. Ashmead, D.H., Davis, D.L., Northington, A.: Contribution of Listeners' Approaching Motion to Auditory Distance Perception, Journal of Experimental Psychology: Human Perception and Performance, **21**(2) (1995) 239–256
2. Brunswik, E.: Perception and the representative design of psychological experiments. Berkeley, CA: University of California Press, (1956)
3. Cooksey, R.W.: JUDGMENT ANALYSIS -Theory, Methods, and Applications-. Academic Press, Inc., (1996)
4. Gibson, J.J.: The ecological approach to visual perception, Hillsdale, NJ: Lawrence Erlbaum Associates, Inc. (1986)
5. Ito, K.: Auditory interceptive timing and familiarity with acoustic environment. Studies in Perception and Action IV, (1997) 83-87
6. Ito, K.: Detection of occluding edges by the use of echolocation. Studies in Perception and Action V, (1999) 52-56

7. Lee, D.N.: A theory of visual control of braking based on information about time-to-collision, Perception, **5** (1976) 437–459
8. Mershon, D.H., Bowers, J.N.: Absolute and relative cues for the auditory perception of egocentric distance, Perception, **8** (1979) 311–322
9. Rosenblum, L.D., Carello, C., Pastore, C.R.: Relative effectiveness of three stimulus variables for locating a moving sound source, Perception, **16** (1987) 175–186
10. Schiff, W., Oldak, R.: Accuracy of judging time to arrival: Effects of modality, trajectory, and gender. Journal of Experimental Psychology: Human Perception and Performance, **16** (1990) 303–316
11. Shaw, B.K., McGowan, R.S., Turvey, M.T.: An Acoustic Variable Specifying Time-to-Contact, ECOLOGICAL PSYCHOLOGY, **3**(3) (1991) 253–261
12. Shiose, T., Sawaragi, T., Nakajima, A., Ishihara, H.: Design of Interactive Skill-Transfer Agent From a Viewpoint of Ecological Psychology, International Journal of Human-Computer Interaction, **17**(1) (2004) 69–86
13. Singleton, J.: Japanese Folkcraft Pottery Apprenticeship: Cultural Patterns of an Educational Institution in Coy ed., (1989)

# Six-In – Braille Input from a QWERTY Keyboard

Paul Blenkhorn and Gareth Evans

Department of Computation, UMIST
PO Box 88, Manchester, M60 1QD, UK
{p.blenkhorn,g.evans}@co.umist.ac.uk

**Abstract.** This paper presents the architecture and operation of a PC-based software program (Six-In) that allows a standard QWERTY keyboard to be used as a Braille keyboard translating the (contracted) Braille to text. It is aimed at people learning Braille and users who prefer to use a Braille rather than a QWERTY keyboard. The system is multilingual (if appropriate Braille-to-text translation tables are constructed for a language). The system works on most PCs, but fails on machines that do not support multiple key rollover.

## 1 Introduction

The traditional method for a blind person to write a Braille document is to *type* the Braille using a brailler. A brailler (for example a Perkins or Mountbatten Brailler) is a mechanical or electro-mechanical device that has around ten keys:

- 6 'dot' keys[1], which correspond directly to each of the 6 dots in a Braille cell;
- a space key, which moves the embossing head one space to the right causing blank Braille cell (a space) to be produced;
- a carriage return key, which positions the embossing head to the left-hand side of the line;
- a line feed key, which moves down one line;
- a backspace key, which moves the embossing head one space to the left.

Braillers are chord keyboards; many Braille characters have multiple raised dots in the Braille cell and hence require between one and six keys to be depressed simultaneously.

Braille keyboards are generally used by blind people in two situations, when they are using a Brailler and as an interface to certain portable electronic devices. When using a brailler, a blind person can directly produce Braille hard copy. Where an electronic copy is required, there are systems that allow a brailler to be connected to a computer, which will translate the Braille to text (see for example [1, 2]). A number of portable electronic devices are provided with Braille keyboards – for example, note takers and personal digital assistants (PDAs) designed for blind users. In this case, the Braille keyboard is effective because it reduces the size of the keyboard needed. If output is to be spoken (rather than displayed on a refreshable Braille display), translation software must exist to translate from Braille to text. Where contracted Braille (for

---

[1] For most of this paper, we confine our discussion to 6-dot Braille.

K. Miesenberger et al. (Eds.): ICCHP 2004, LNCS 3118, pp. 484–489, 2004.

example Grade II English Braille) is used, this is more than a simple character replacement task and quite complex language dependent algorithms have to be used. The issues concerning such translation are described in [3] and revisited later in this paper.

In this paper, we describe a system that allows a user to 'Braille' on a standard QWERTY keyboard, with the result that the Braille is converted into text (represented as the appropriate set of ASCII characters). Where contracted Braille is used, the Braille is decontracted to present a full textual representation. Other systems exist that allow a Braille keyboard to be simulated on a QWERTY keyboard, e.g. Braille 2000 (http://www.c-a-s.com/brl2000/), but these may not decontract the Braille directly into text and route it to an application in the way that Six-In does.

There are two sets of potential users for the system. The first is blind users who find it more convenient to input characters using Braille than a standard QWERTY keyboard. A user will typically choose to do this when he/she finds it faster to type using chord entry. The second set of users is people learning Braille. These will include blind people, where speech output (generally through a screen reader) can be used to reflect the typing, and sighted people where visual output can be used to present the results. It is suggested that for both sets of learners this style of output is more appropriate than producing Braille directly, although in both cases Braille output can be generated by the computer system – in visual form for sighted users if necessary.

## 2 Six-In

### 2.1 Input

Input is via a standard QWERTY keyboard, with the keys S, D, F and J, K & L mapped to the six dot keys in the same layout as a standard Braille keyboard. The space bar, the Enter key and the Backspace key forming the equivalent of a Brailler's space, carriage return/line feed and backspace keys respectively.

### 2.2 Output

Six-In translates the Braille input into appropriate ASCII text. This can be routed to the application that has the current focus. So, for example, a user of Six-In can "type" directly into applications such as Microsoft Word or into a Braille tutor program.

### 2.3 Architecture

Six-In is an application that runs under Microsoft Windows and its architecture is explained in this context. Similar systems could be constructed for other operating systems and the basic architecture remains valid. There are a number of issues that need to be addressed:

- Getting hold of the keystrokes.
- Deleting alphabetic keystrokes that are not part of the input set (S, D, F, J, K, L, Space, Enter, and Backspace).
- Determining when a chord is complete.
- Translating Braille cells to text.
- Routing the text to an application.

The architecture of Six-In is presented in Fig. 1. This figure shows three main sections: the Six-In system itself; the Windows operating system; and the application that receives the text.

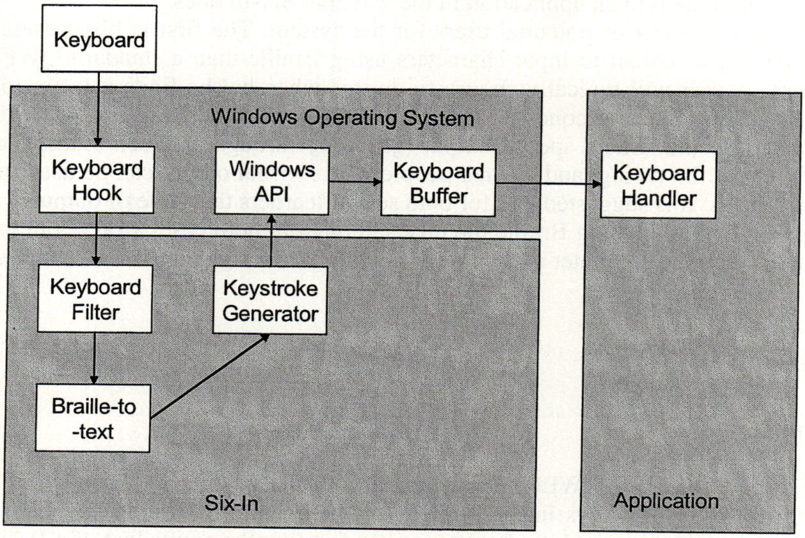


**Fig. 1.** The Architecture of Six-In.

### Keyboard Hook

Keystrokes must be intercepted before they are routed to the application that has the focus. If they were not, the characters would appear in the application. The interception of keystrokes in this way is achieved by using a keyboard hook. A "hook is a mechanism by which a function can intercept events (messages, mouse actions, keystrokes) before they reach an application" [4]. The keyboard hook will provide key down and key up events to the Keyboard Filter. When the keyboard is hooked, keys strokes are removed from the buffer and hence not passed to the application. Of course when Six-In sends keystrokes to the application, these are also hooked. The hook "knows" the difference between "simulated" keyboard input and standard keystrokes and operates appropriated to prevent problems around re-entrancy.

### Keyboard Filter

The Keyboard Hook presents key down and key up events. The filter can simply discard those that are not part of the set of simulated Braille input keys. The filter can also determine when a chord is completed. The filter will receive a sequence of key up and down events. To type the text character 'f' the chord S, D, J must be typed to encode the three dots that make up the character 'f' – see Figure 2. The filter may receive the key down and key up events in any order (for example S down, D down, J down, J up, S up, D up is as likely as J down, S down, D down, S up, D up, J up or any other combination). The filter therefore notes which key down events it has received and then waits until all corresponding key up events occur.

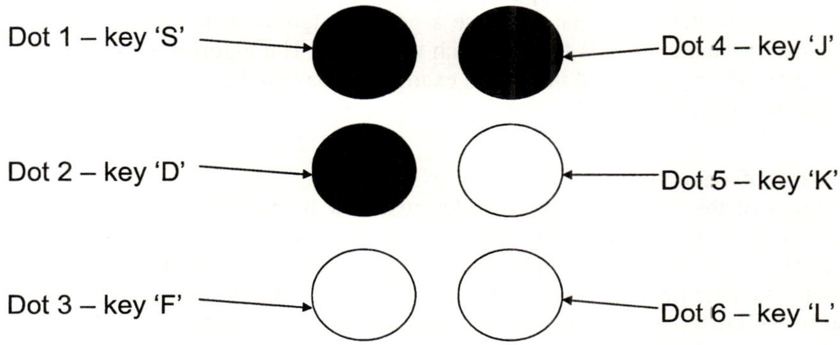


**Fig. 2.** The Braille cell corresponding to the character 'f'.

The filter is now aware of the set of keys used to construct a character. These are then translated into a single character representation that uniquely encodes the Braille cell. American Computer Braille [5] is used for this purpose. It encodes each of the 64 possible combinations of Braille dots (including space) into a unique ASCII character.

**Braille-to-Text**

This module receives a stream of American Computer Braille characters, which must be translated to text. There is no one-to-one translation between Braille cells and text – for example the number '1' is presented as two Braille cells (the number sign cell and the letter 'a' cell – see Fig. 3) – even where uncontracted Braille is used, (e.g. Grade I English Braille). Where contracted Braille (e.g. Grade II English Braille) is

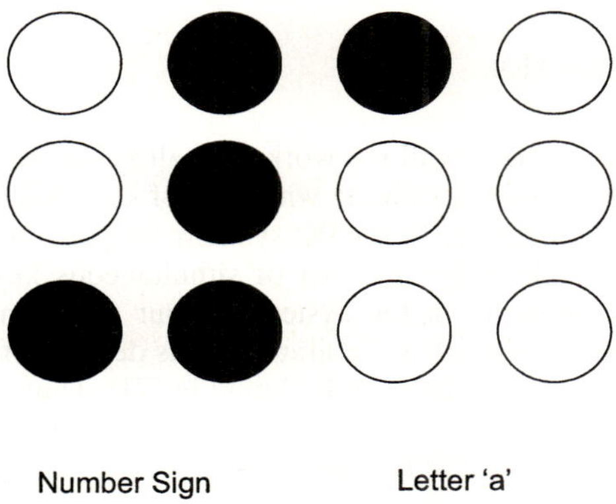


**Fig. 3.** The Braille representation of the number '1' – the number sign cell, followed by the letter 'a'.

used the algorithm becomes more complex, with some single Braille cells being expanded into a number of text characters in a context dependent way. For example, the word 'ab', is the word sign for the word 'about' and must be expanded by the translator. The ACB character '4' (dots 2, 5 and 6) has different expansions depending on its position in a word. At the beginning of a word it represents 'dis', in the middle 'dd' and at the end a period (a full stop).

There are a large number of approaches to Braille translation. Some approaches are multi-lingual in the sense that they use a generic algorithm that is driven by a language-specific table. This is the approach used here. The algorithm and the rules for British English are presented in [3]. An example of developing an additional language (Hungarian) is provided in [6].

**Key Stroke Generation**

The output of the Braille-to-text module must now be routed to the application that has the focus. This is achieved by placing characters back into the Windows keyboard buffer. These are sent to the Windows operating system using the Windows SendKeys function. As noted earlier, the system must be aware of the key strokes that it has added to the buffer so that they are not intercepted by the keyboard hook and subsequently converted to Braille characters.

## 3 8-Dot Braille

8-dot Braille, which is used in specific applications (such as science and mathematics) and in some dialects of Braille languages, can also be supported in a similar way to the way the Six-In supports 6-dot Braille. A program, called Eight-In, has been developed along the same lines as Six-In and uses the 'A' and ';' keys to provide the additional dots. Because 8-dot Braille is fairly specialized it is not necessarily clear which Braille-to-text translation algorithm should be provided. Therefore, Eight-In simply converts the characters to American Computer Braille and places these back into the keyboard buffer. Translation can then be accomplished by an external application.

## 4 Concluding Remarks

One limitation of Six-In is that it will not work with all keyboards. In order for Six-In to work, it must be capable of determining which set of keys (up to six) are held down simultaneously to form the chord. Many PC systems support multiple key rollover – allowing the system to receive any number of simultaneous key presses. However, some systems (most commonly laptop systems in our experience) do not. In such cases, keyboards are designed so that the simultaneous depression of up to 3 keys can be recognised (an explanation of this can be found in [7]). Thus, when a cell requires four or more dots, not all the keys are received by the system. Other than replacing the keyboard, there is no solution to this problem.

## References


1. Spragg, J.: Interfacing a Perkins Brailler to a BBC Micro. Microprocessors and Microsystems, Vol. 8, No. 10, (1984) 524-527
2. Evans, D.G., Pettitt, S., Blenkhorn, P.: A Modified Perkins Brailler for Text Entry into Windows Applications. IEEE Transactions on Neural Systems and Rehabilitation Engineering, Vol. 10, No. 3, (2002) 204-206
3. Blenkhorn, P.: A System for Converting Braille into Print. IEEE Transactions on Rehabilitation Engineering, Vol. 3, No. 2, (1995) 215 – 221
4. Marsh, K.: Win 32 Hooks. Microsoft Developer Network, Microsoft (1993)
5. Sullivan, J.E. Conversion of print format for Braille. 6th Int. Workshop on Computer Applications for the Visually Handicapped, Leuven, (1990) 1 – 14
6. Arato, A., Vaspori, T., Evans, D.G., Blenkhorn, P.: Braille to Text Translation for Hungarian, In K. Miesenberger, J. Klaus, & W. Zagler (Eds.), Computers Helping People with Special Needs, Proc. 8th ICCHP, Lecture Notes in Computer Science, No. 2398, Springer, (2002) 610 - 617
7. Braille 2000: Braille 2000 Keyboard Requirements.
8. `http://www.braille2000.com/brl2000/KeyboardReq.htm`, last accessed 19 Jan (2004)

# A Pair of Wireless Braille-Based Chording Gloves

Sang Sup An[1], Jae Wook Jeon[1], Seongil Lee[2],
Hyuckyeol Choi[3], and Hoo-Gon Choi[2]

[1] School of Information and Communication Engineering, Sungkyunkwan University
300 Chunchundong, Jangan-Gu, Suwon City, Korea 440-746
blue4898@ece.skku.ac.kr, jwjeon@yurim.skku.ac.kr

[2] School of System Management Engineering, Sungkyunkwan University
300 Chunchundong, Jangan-Gu, Suwon City, Korea 440-746
{silee,hgchoi}@yurim.skku.ac.kr

[3] School of Mechanical Engineering, Sungkyunkwan University
300 Chunchundong, Jangan-Gu, Suwon City, Korea 440-746
hrchoi@yurim.skku.ac.kr

**Abstract.** Since input devices for desktop computers are inconvenient to use in a mobile working environment, other small input devices have been proposed. Few of them, however, are for visually impaired people. This paper proposes a pair of wireless Braille-based chording gloves as an input device to use in a mobile working environment for visually impaired people. Its keys are mounted on the fingers and its chording method is similar to that of a Braille keyboard. Since Braille has been efficiently devised to represent many language characters, numbers, and symbols including mathematical and musical notations, the proposed chording gloves will be also used for visually non-impaired people. IrDA (Infrared Data Association) and RF (Radio Frequency) wireless modules are designed and implemented to make the proposed chording gloves wireless.

## 1 Introduction

Keyboards have been used as input devices to computers. In order to improve their performance such as speed, accuracy, typist fatigue, comfort, and muscular strain, several keyboards have been proposed [1]. According to the development of small portable electronic products such as PDAs, cellular phones, and wearable computers, chording keyboards have been proposed as input devices of these small products [2-5]. In chording keyboards, we press a multiple key combination to enter one character instead of using one key for each character in an ordinary keyboard such as the QWERTY keyboard. Though the terminology of a chording keyboard was introduced in the 1960's, Frank H. Hall invented the first Braille writing machine that had a chording keyboard in 1892.

Glove-based devices recognizing hand gestures or contact gestures have been also proposed as input devices to computers [6,7]. These devices are convenient to use in a mobile environment because the gloves can be worn instead of held and are lightweight and take up little space. It is, however, difficult to recognize enough separate

K. Miesenberger et al. (Eds.): ICCHP 2004, LNCS 3118, pp. 490–497, 2004.

gestures to allow useful text input. In [3], a glove-based input device called the chording glove has been proposed in order to combine the portability of a contact glove with the benefits of a chording keyboard. In the chording glove, the keys of a chording keyboard are mounted on the fingers of a glove and the characters associated with all the chords, which is called the keymap, are designed to make fast discrimination reaction time. But it is quite difficult to design a good keymap for a given chording glove. Furthermore, it is not easy to make a new keymap become a standard one for a chording glove.

This paper proposes a pair of wireless Braille-based chording gloves as an input device of a small portable electronic product for visually impaired people. Its keys are mounted on the fingers and its chording method is similar to that of a Braille keyboard. That is, each key at the fingertips of gloves corresponds to each dot in Braille. The characters associated with all the chords in the proposed chording gloves are designed in the same way as in a Braille keyboard, which was already established well. Therefore, visually impaired people using a Braille keyboard can easily use the proposed chording gloves. Furthermore, since Braille is a faster recording medium and has been efficiently devised to represent many language characters, numbers, and symbols including mathematical and musical notations, visually non-impaired people can use the proposed chording gloves after some training required in all chording keyboards. In section 2, a pair of chording gloves is proposed as an input device and its input speed, accuracy, and usability are measured. IrDA and RF modules are used to make the proposed chording gloves wireless. In section 3 and 4, the characteristics of the proposed chording gloves are discussed and the conclusion is described, respectively.

## 2 A Pair of Wireless Braille-Based Chording Gloves

### 2.1 A Pair of Braille-Based Chording Gloves

The proposed chording gloves are shown in Fig. 1 and each glove has twelve keys. Each key consists of conductive silicone ink. When the ground point of thumb touches one key, its corresponding information is detected. A chord keymap is proposed such that four keys at the fingertips of each glove correspond to eight Braille dots [8]. Some keys perform the same function as pressing three keys at the fingertips altogether, the function of the space bar, the function of the backspace bar, and the function of mode change. The other keys are reserved. Therefore, the chording method in the proposed chording gloves is similar to that in a Braille keyboard, which has been already a standard for visually impaired people.

### 2.2 Experiments

Experiments are performed using both the proposed chording gloves and a Braille keyboard to measure the input speed and accuracy for Braille codes [8].

**Subjects.** Ten visually impaired subjects who just start to learn Braille codes participate in the study. None of subjects has used Braille-related input devices. The average age of ten subjects is 28.2 years old.

**Apparatus.** The proposed chording gloves and a Braille keyboard with 7 keys are used as input devices.

**Procedure.** Subjects are trained to use both input devices for Braille inputs that are short pre-defined sentences. The training sessions of each device consist of 3 sessions. Three hours are allotted for each session and therefore a total of 9 hours for each device is devoted to training for one subject. Subjects are asked to learn to enter different sentences during each training session. After training, a new sentence with 58 Braille codes is given in the final test. Input speed in terms of BPM(Braille code Per Minute) and error rate are measured 10 times for each device with the same sentence.

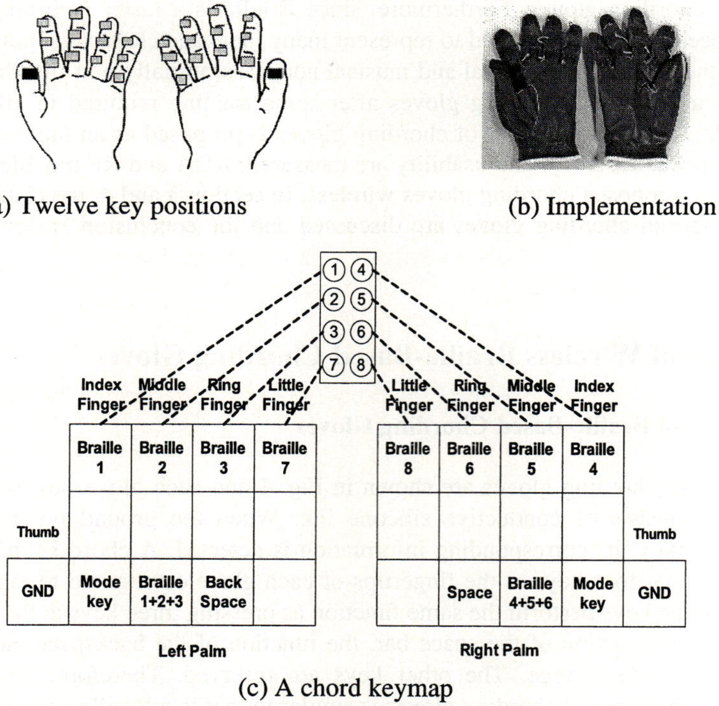


**Fig. 1.** A pair of Braille-based chording gloves.

**Results.** After training, averages of input speed and error rate in each device are calculated and shown in Table 1. No significant difference in input speed could be found between the chording gloves and the Braille keyboard ($p > 0.1$). A marginal difference could be found in error rate. The error rate of the chording gloves is higher than that of the Braille keyboard ($t$= 2.14, $p$< 0.05). Fig. 2 shows the averages of input speed and error rate in training sessions in addition to that of the final test. Averages in training sessions are made during learning hours of 3, 6, and 9. The final test averages are presented at the 12th hour in the x-axis.

### 2.3 Usability Evaluation

Table 2 shows subjects' perceived ratings, which are measured for usability evaluation after the Braille input experiments. On a scale of one to five, subjects rate both input devices in the following categories: portability, learnability, functionality, and overall satisfaction [8].

**Portability.** Subjects rate the portability of the proposed chording gloves as 3.7 and the Braille keyboard as 3.4.

**Learnability and Functionality.** Subjects rate the learnability of both input devices as 3.5 and the functionality of them as 3.5. Since both devices use basically the same keymap and finger combinations for generating Braille codes, there seemed to be no difference in these two categories. As shown in Fig. 2, subjects feel comfortable in using both devices after only 9 hours of learning.

**Overall Satisfaction.** Subjects rate the overall satisfaction of the chording gloves as 3.7 and the Braille keyboard as 3.9. Familiarity must be an important factor to provide overall satisfaction to use. Thus, subjects seem to be more satisfied in using a familiar keyboard type device than in using a glove type device.

### 2.4 Wireless Chording Gloves

In order to make a pair of wireless chording gloves, IrDA and RF modules are designed and implemented.

**Table 1.** Experimental results.

| Device type | Proposed chording gloves | Braille keyboard |
|---|---|---|
| Input speed (BPM) | 121.5 ± 29.8 | 135.9 ± 37.0 |
| Error rate (%) | 5.2 ± 2.7 | 2.8 ± 2.3 |

**IrDA-Based Chording Gloves.** Fig. 3 shows IrDA-based chording gloves that can communicate with a PDA. Since only one communication channel is allowed in IrDA, a single controller for a pair of IrDA-based chording gloves is designed. An 8-bit RISC controller AT90S2313, an infrared controller IR8200IC-H, and a low power infrared transceiver module TFDU6102F are used to implement IrDA-based wireless chording gloves. IR8200IC-H infrared controller is compatible with IrDA 1.0 (SIR) and TFDU6102F transceiver module supports the maximum 4.0 Mbit/s transfer rate [9,10]. The actual transmission rate of the implemented IrDA-based chording gloves is set to 19.2 Kbps. The communication between chording gloves and the PDA is performed with IrCOMM protocol.

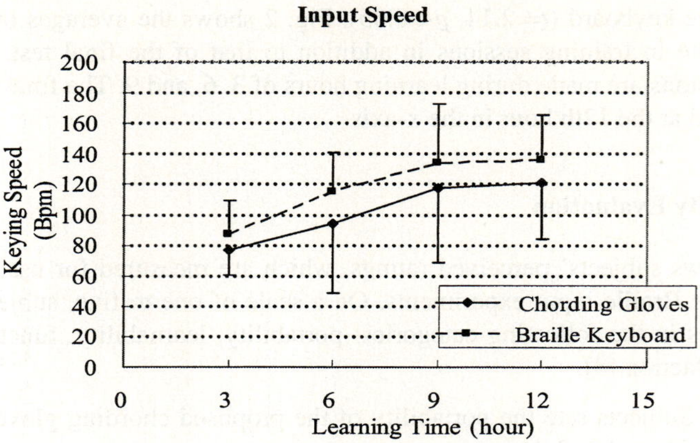


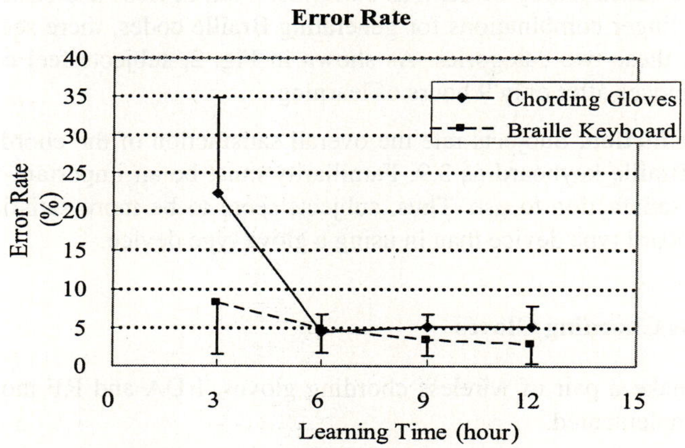


**Fig. 2.** Performance of the chording gloves and the Braille keyboard.

**RF-Based Chording Gloves and Their Communication Module.** Fig. 4 shows RF-based chording gloves and their communication module. The communication module can exchange information with a PDA through an RS-232c serial port and receive information from chording gloves by RF signals. Though each chording glove uses the same frequency band, many chording gloves can communicate with one PDA because each has its own identification code to avoid the frequency interference [11]. As in Fig. 4, an ATMEL 8-bit RISC controller Atmega128L and a RadioMetrix RF module BIM-433 of 433.92MHz are used to implement a communication module [12]. An 8-bit RISC controller AT90S2313 and an RF module BIM-433 are used to implement the controller of each RF-based chording glove. The controller can detect the pressed keys and send the corresponding information to the communication module through the RF module. Due to the antenna optimization problem, the maximum rate that one 8-bit RISC controller can transmit to one RF module BIM-433 without any error is 19.2 Kbps. In order to communicate between two RF modules, each RF module should switch once between transmitting and receiving modes and the stabilization time for switching of 3 msec is needed. Thus, the average rate that two RF modules can communicate is a little bit less than 19.2 Kbps.

**Table 2.** Perceived ratings in usability evaluation.

| Usability aspects | Braille entry input | |
|---|---|---|
| | Proposed chording gloves | Braille keyboard |
| Portability | 3.7 | 3.4 |
| Learnability | 3.5 | 3.5 |
| Functionality | 3.5 | 3.5 |
| Overall satisfaction | 3.7 | 3.9 |

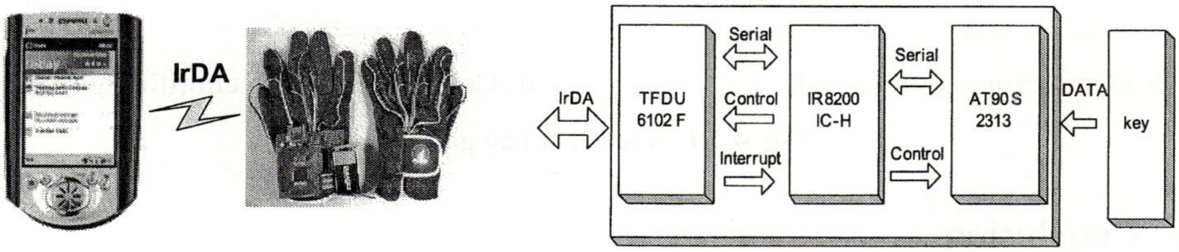


(a) IrDA communication (b) Controller of chording gloves

**Fig. 3.** IrDA-based chording gloves.

## 3 Discussion

Since the proposed chording gloves use two hands to input some characters or numbers instead of using one hand, it has some advantages over one hand chording keyboard, which include fast typing and low error rate [7]. Also, the proposed chording gloves have clear space advantages over an ordinary keyboard and other chording keyboards [8]. In order to develop the keymap for the chording keyboard, either a strong spatial correspondence to the visual shape of the typed character has been used or strong link to a well-built semantic knowledge base has been created [7, 8]. Different from the keymaps as in [7,8], the keymap of the proposed chording gloves is similar to that of a Braille keyboard, which makes visually impaired people who are acquainted with a Braille keyboard use the proposed chording gloves without learning. It may take longer time for visually non-impaired people to learn the keymap of the proposed chording gloves than to do keymaps as in [7, 8]. After learning, however, the input speed of the proposed chording gloves will be much higher than those as in [7, 8] because Braille is a faster recording medium. Since the Braille codes for many language characters, numbers, and special symbols including mathematical and musical notations have been already defined, it does not need to design new keymap for visually non-impaired people. As a result, the proposed chording gloves will help visually impaired and non-impaired people to communicate and understand with each other.

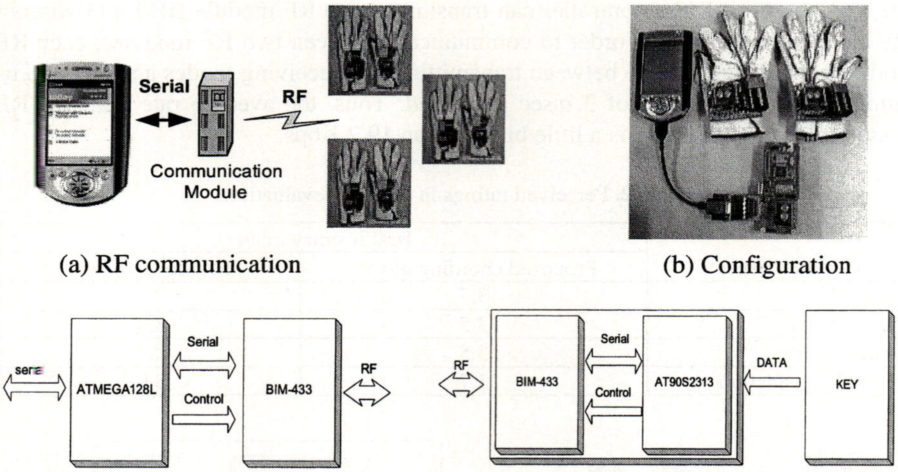


(a) RF communication (b) Configuration

(c) Communication module (d) Controller of each chording glove

**Fig. 4.** RF-based chording gloves.

## 4 Conclusion

This paper proposes a pair of wireless Braille-based chording gloves for visually impaired people to use in a mobile working environment. Since the proposed chording gloves have advantages such as fast typing, low error rate, space saving, and wireless connection, they will be one of good input devices to portable electronic products. Furthermore, since the proposed chording gloves have a similar keymap as in a Braille keyboard, they can be well used for visually impaired people. By designing IrDA and RF modules, the proposed chording gloves can send information to a PDA without wire connections. In RF-based chording gloves, each chording glove can use its own protocol and therefore many pairs of RF-based chording gloves can be used simultaneously as input devices in a mobile working environment.

## Acknowledgement

This research is supported by Grant 2003-s-068 from Advanced Technology Program of Institute of Information Technology Assessment, Daejon, Korea.

## References

1. Porosnak, K. M.: Keys and Keyboards. Handbook of Human Computer Interaction, M. Helander, Ed. New York: Elsevier (1988) 475-494

2. Gopher, D., Raij, D.: Typing With a Two-Hand Chord Keyboard: Will the QWERTY Become Obsolete? IEEE Trans. On Systems, Man, and Cybernetics, Vol. 18, No. 4, (1988) 601-609
3. Rosenberg, R., Slater, M.: The Chording Glove: A Glove-Based Text Input Device. IEEE Trans. On Systems, Man, and Cybernetics – Part C: Applications and Reviews, Vol. 29, No. 2 (1999) 186-191
4. GKOS Keyboard. http://loti.mbnet.fi/~gkos/gkoscom.
5. Bat Chord Keyboard. http://www.nanopac.com.
6. Sturman, D., Zeltzer, D.: A Survey of Glove-based Input. IEEE Computer Graphics & Applications (1994) 30-39
7. Pinch Gloves. Fakespace, http://www.fakespacelabs.com/products/pinch.html
8. Lee, S., Hong, S.H., Jeon, J.W.: Designing a universal keyboard using chording gloves. ACM Conference on Universal Usability 2003(CUU2003), Vancouver, British Columbia, Canada (2003) 142-147
9. IR8200IC-H Specification Manual (2001)
10. TFDU6102F Data Sheet (2002)
11. Park, K., Jeon, J.W.: Wireless Input Devices and Their Communication Module for Computers. Human Computer Interaction Theory and Practice, Vol. 2, No. 1, Crete, Greece (2003) 223-227
12. BIM433 Specification Data sheet. Radiometrix Co., LTD (2001)

# OBOE: Oboe-Like Braille Interface for Outdoor Environment

Tomohiro Amemiya[1], Koichi Hirota[2], and Michitaka Hirose[2]

[1] Graduate School of Information Science and Technology, the University of Tokyo
4-6-1 Komaba, Meguro-ku, Tokyo 153-8904, Japan
rayn@cyber.rcast.u-tokyo.ac.jp
http://www.cyber.rcast.u-tokyo.ac.jp/~rayn/index.html

[2] Research Center for Advanced Science and Technology, the University of Tokyo
4-6-1 Komaba, Meguro-ku, Tokyo 153-8904, Japan
{hirota,hirose}@cyber.rcast.u-tokyo.ac.jp

**Abstract.** In this paper, we propose a wearable interface for textual input designed on the basis of the Braille input method. The device, named OBOE, is shaped like an oboe, which is good for outdoor use, since it can be used while walking. The results of an experiment of learning effect revealed that users who had no experience of Braille input could type Japanese phrases at 35.4 Braille codes per minute, and those who had experience at 112.4 Braille codes per minute. Thus, beginners can master the proposed device and experts can input text very fast using OBOE.

## 1 Introduction

With the sophisticated and miniaturized semiconductor devices available today, we have reached an era of mobile and wearable computers. The input interface, particularly for text entry, is one of the most important research topics in the field of wearable computers, since the miniaturization of a desktop-type input interface is not sufficient for wearable computers. On a keyboard, the major input interface for computers, one key corresponds to one character. The input speed increases with practice. However, the large number of keys is not adaptable to wearable computers because of the device size. As an informational interface that can be used while performing other tasks in the real world for example, it is desired to design such an interface on the basis of concepts different from conventional ones.

In order to decrease the number of keys, many chord keyboards have been proposed. Twiddler is a one-hand chord keyboard with 12 keys [1]. There are also two-hand chord keyboards for wearable computers such as FingeRing [2], which provides a wearable interface using ring-shaped sensors based on accelerometers for inputting 31 different symbols.

Although a Braille typewriter is not a wearable interface, it is a two-hand chord keyboard, whose keys are simultaneously pressed together to input Braille symbols for the Blind. The Braille input method is considered adequate for typing data into wearable computers, since this method is efficient for inputting syllables and is used

K. Miesenberger et al. (Eds.): ICCHP 2004, LNCS 3118, pp. 498–505, 2004.

in almost all languages (e.g., all Japanese characters are expressed by sets of one or two Braille codes.). One example is a pair of Braille-based chord gloves [3], designed on the basis of a Braille input method with polyvinylidene fluoride that generates voltage when it is deformed. However, it is difficult to confirm their input operations, since such sensors do not provide users with tactile feedback. Tactile feedback, such as a key click, is necessary to all users using wearable input interfaces.

In this paper, we propose a wearable interface designed on the basis of the Braille input method for the Blind, and describe our prototype, which is an oboe-like device, and a support for people with disabilities using the device.

## 2 System Structure of OBOE

### 2.1 System Layout

OBOE (Oboe-like Braille interface for Outdoor Environment) is a wearable input interface designed on the basis of the Braille input method. Although portable Braille-based note takers, such as BrailleLite, are now used worldwide, they are designed for use on a desktop. Because they are analogous to musical instruments, they may be called "piano-type" interfaces, which is not good for mobile and outdoor use. In this paper, we propose an "oboe-type" interface, which is good for outdoor-use and capable of being used while walking. Figure 1 shows a prototype system of OBOE. OBOE was designed to be grasped only when necessary; we did not employ a glove-style interface, because the glove prevents the users from experiencing the natural touch due to the covering of fingertips. OBOE is dangled around the user's neck with a strap when not in use.

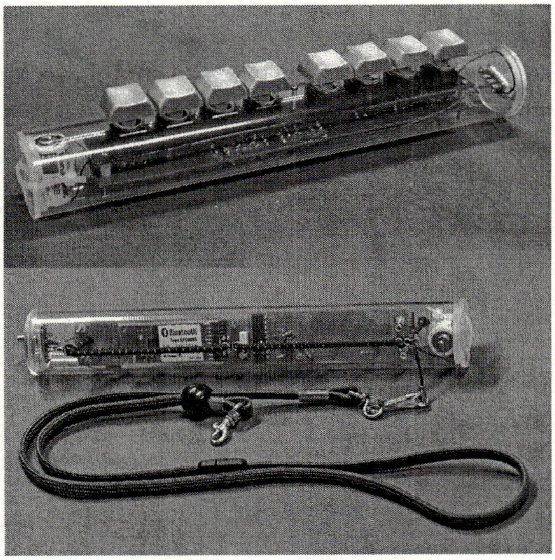

**Fig. 1.** OBOE.

### 2.2 Hardware

The buttons of the proposed device are the same as the mechanical switches used in keyboards for desktop computers (ALPS Electric Co., Ltd., mechanical switch). The key pitch of the switch is approximately 19 mm and the peak of resilient restoring force is approximately 55 g. The top of the key measures 12 mm by 12 mm. The users clearly confirm their input operations by feeling the click, which acceleration sensors and touch sensors lack.

In our prototype system, we fabricated an eight-key device. Six keys are for the six-dot Braille input and two keys are for function keys such as Backspace and Enter. The body of the device is made of an acrylate resin tube with a diameter of 35 mm, a length of approximately 220 mm, and a weight of approximately 150 g.

OBOE has thumb hooks made of rubber band, which enable the user to take a firm grip and prevent the hands from leaving and slipping OBOE.

## 2.3 Input Method

In the Braille input method, a character is determined by the combination of pressed keys. Conventional mechanical Braille keyboards for the Blind were designed to send a Braille code when all fingers released the keys after inputting a chord. The OBOE system adopted this rule. The information encoded by the pressed keys is processed in a microprocessor (PIC16F84A, Microchip Technology Inc.) and is sent to a wearable computer via Bluetooth Ver.1.1, implemented on BlueStick (ADC Technology, Inc.). The system configuration of OBOE with output devices is illustrated in Figure 2. The controllers in OBOE work with a 3V battery.

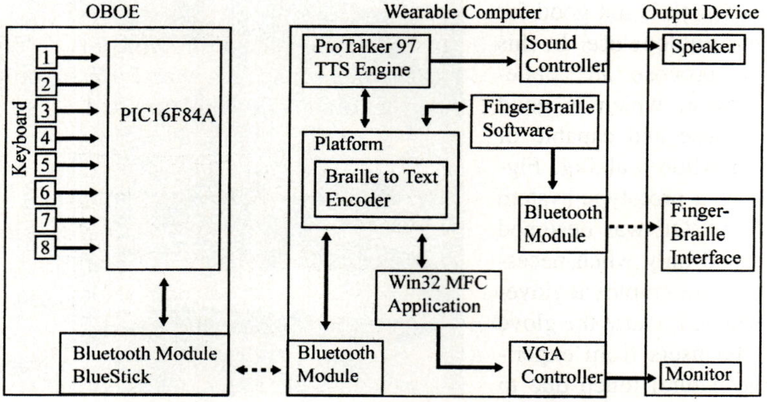


**Fig. 2.** System configuration including output device.

## 2.4 Keymap

Our interface can be used in two different styles: flute, in which the device is held horizontally, and oboe, in which it is held vertically. In order to deal with these styles, the key map can be changed in four styles as shown in Figure 3. The key map of the flute style (a) is identical to that of the traditional Braille keyboard.

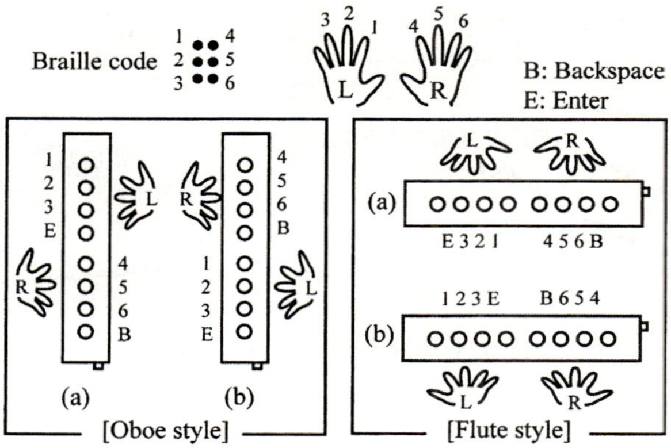


**Fig. 3.** OBOE keymap.

## 3 Experiment

We carried out an experiment to evaluate the device by measuring input speed and error rate. In the experiment, there were five trials to examine the effect of learning.

Four nonblind subjects participated in the experiment. All the subjects were male, right-handed and had no experience using Braille typewriters. The average age of the subjects was 24.0 years.

The experiment was governed by an OBOE and a mobile computer (OS: Windows XP, CPU: PentiumIII 700MHz-M). Bluetooth connection was formed using GW-BH01U (Planex Communications Inc.) for the mobile computer and BlueStick for OBOE.

The experiment consisted of a tutorial session (nonsemantic phrase session) and a semantic phrase session. The tutorial session was a 10-minute trial, followed by a 10-minute semantic phrase session. After each trial, the subjects answered a questionnaire about fatigue, muscle strain, usability, and preference that were rated in a 1 (worst) to 5 (best). In addition, the subjects freely wrote comments about the system. In each session, the subjects were instructed to input as quickly and accurately as possible and not to sacrifice speed for accuracy.

Software used for the experiment was common to both sessions. A screen capture of this software is shown in Figure 4. In this software, the next sample phrase is displayed when the user pressed the Enter key and the input phrase corresponds with the sample phrase.

The subjects were instructed to grip OBOE according to the oboe style throughout the experiment. The subjects could confirm their input through auditory feedback by a text-to-speech (TTS) engine, IBM Protalker97, as well as through visual feedback from a window on the screen.

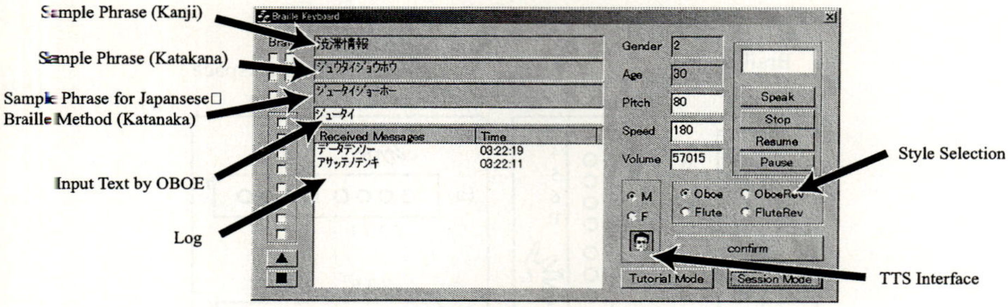


**Fig. 4.** Screen capture of the software.

### 3.1 Tutorial Session

The subjects were initially trained to use the OBOE device by a tutorial session. In this session, the subjects were given a sheet of paper with a list of the Japanese Braille codes and their corresponding characters. The phrases in the tutorial session were nonsemantic phrases that consisted of Japanese characters, numeric characters and alphabet characters such as "abcde".

### 3.2 Semantic Phrase Session

The semantic phrase session consisted of predefined phrases. They were several short phrases, intended to mimic the actual use of the wearable computer, such as "Yes" for answering questions from computers, "Calculate consumed calories" for wearable sensor systems, or "What is today's plan?" for mobile assistants (all written in Japanese). The Japanese Braille has the specific rule that the sentences are written as pronounced. Therefore, we displayed two patterns of the sample phrases during this session, one in the normal Japanese reading and one in the Japanese Braille (see Figure 4).

## 4 Result

### 4.1 Input Speed and Error Rate

The average speed at the fifth trial was 44.1 Braille codes per minute in the nonsemantic session and 35.5 Braille codes per minute in the semantic session. The learning effect in terms of input speed and error rate is shown in Figure 5.

Error rate was calculated by dividing the number of errors by the total number of Braille codes.

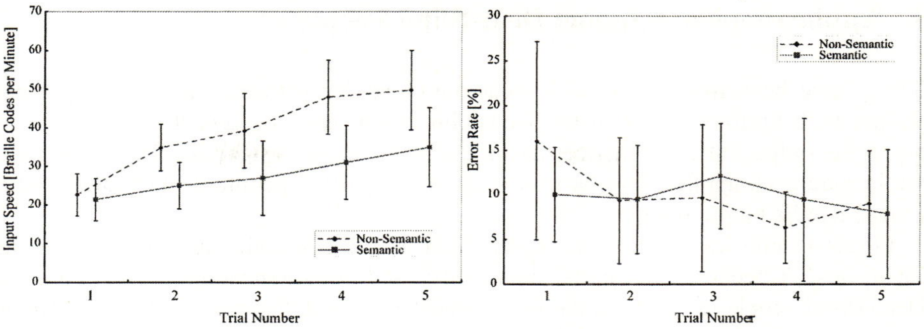


**Fig. 5.** Learning effect in terms of the OBOE. (a)input speed and (b) error rate.

### 4.2 Fatigue and Muscle Strain

The average scores for fatigue were 2.0 at the beginning of the experiment and 3.5 at the end of the experiment. The average scores for muscle strain ranged from 2.5 at the beginning of the experiment to 3.3 at the end. These results suggest the necessity for ergonomic improvements. The average scores for usability were 3.3 and that for preference was 3.3.

### 4.3 Comments

Regarding the comments such as “it is difficult and stressful to find the Braille code in the sheet in the beginning” (two subjects), “I am apt to make a mistake in using the left and right hands particularly when pressing the Enter key and Backspace key” (three subjects), and “some Braille codes can be memorized, but sometimes I made mistakes because I did not look at the sheet for such characters” (two subjects) were expressed.

## 5 Discussion

We carried out another experiment with subjects who had experiences with Japanese-to-Braille transcribing. The transcriber subjects showed a higher input speed of 112.4 Braille codes per minute, and a lower error rate, 4.1 %, than those of the subjects described in Sections 3 and 4, with a little learning in the semantic session. The transcriber subjects commented on the tutorial session that using characters that rarely appear in usual Japanese sentences slowed them down. (e.g., "dya" is almost always replaced by "jya" in a Japanese sentence but the user had to input this character in the tutorial session.).

## 6 Applications to Support Deaf-Blind People

There have been many studies on wearable computer with the view of supporting people with disabilities. From the viewpoint of universal design, it is important to select the output interface devices according to the users' disabilities. In this section, we introduce an application that may support Deaf-Blind people using OBOE and a Finger-Braille output device.

Finger-Braille was invented for Deaf-Blind people to communicate in real time in Japan, and it became one of the commonly used communication methods among Deaf-Blind people in Japan. In the Finger-Braille method, the fingers of a Deaf-Blind person are regarded as keys of a Braille typewriter, and a translator types the six-dot Braille codes on the back of the fingers. We developed a wearable Finger-Braille interface and evaluated the system [4] [5]. The system with OBOE enables Deaf-Blind people who are in remote locations to communicate in real time using the wearable Finger-Braille interface (Figure 6).

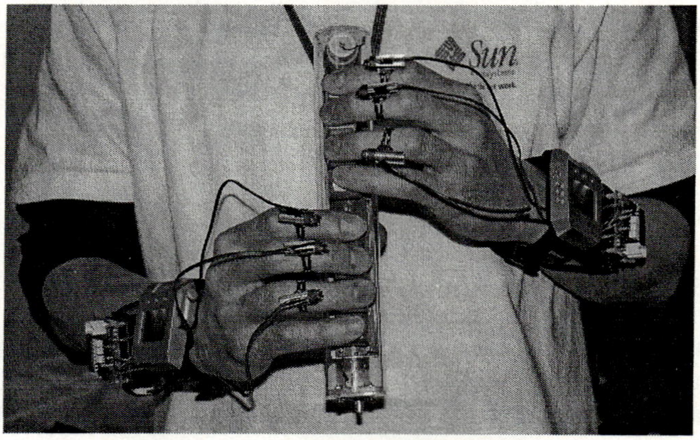


**Fig. 6.** OBOE with Finger-Braille Interface.

## 7 Conclusion

In this paper, we introduced OBOE as a new textual input interface for wearable computers designed on the basis of the Braille input method. The device is shaped like an oboe, which is good for outdoor use. We evaluated the device through an experiment. The results revealed that the users who had no experience using Braille type writers could type Japanese phrases at 35.4 Braille codes per minute, and those who had experience at 112.4 Braille codes per minute.

## 8 Future Works

We are planning to have another experiment with Blind people who have been using a Braille keyboard. Through this experiment, we want to verify the feasibility of the proposed system that may help Blind people to communicate with each other or even with nonblind people who usually do not touch or read Braille.

## Acknowledgements

This research has received support from the CREST project organized by Japan Science and Technology Agency. The authors are grateful to the Barrier-Free Studies Department of the RCAST at the University of Tokyo for assistance and also to all the subjects who participated in the experiments.

## References

1. Twiddler, http://www.handykey.com/
2. Fukumoto, M. and Tonomura, Y.: Body Coupled Fingering: Wireless wearable keyboard. In Proceedings of the ACM Conference on Human Factors in Computing Systems (CHI '97), Atlanta, Georgia (1997) 147–154
3. Cho, M.-C., Park, K.-H., Hong, S.-H., Jeon, J.-W., Lee, S.-I., Choi, H., and Choi, H.-G.: A Pair of Braille-Based Chord Gloves. In Proceedings of the 6th IEEE International Symposium on Wearable Computers (ISWC 2002), Seattle, WA (2002) 154–155
4. Hirose, M. and Amemiya, T.: Wearable Finger-Braille Interface for Navigation of Deaf-Blind in Ubiquitous Barrier-Free Space. In Proceedings of 10th International Conference on Human-Computer Interaction (HCI International 2003), Vol. 4, Crete, Greece (2003) 1417–1421
5. Amemiya, T., Yamashita, J., Hirota, K., and Hirose, M.: Virtual Leading Blocks for the Deaf-Blind: A Real-Time Way-Finder by Verbal-Nonverbal Hybrid Interface and High-Density RFID Tag Space. In Proceedings of IEEE Virtual Reality Conference 2004 (VR 2004), Chicago, IL (2004) 165–172
6. Rosenberg, R., Slater, M.: The Chording Glove: A Glove-Based Text Input Device. IEEE Transactions on Systems, Man, and Cybernetics-Part C, Vol. 29, No. 2 (1999) 186–191

# Java-Powered Braille Slate Talker

A. Arato[1], Z. Juhasz[2,*], P. Blenkhorn[3], G. Evans[3], and G. Evreinov[4]

[1] KFKI RMKI Laboratory of Speech Technology for Rehabilitation
Budapest 114, POBox 49. 1525 Budapest
arato@sunserv.kfki.hu

[2] Dept. of Information Systems, University of Veszprem
Egyetem u 10, Veszprem, 8200, Hungary
juhasz@irt.vein.hu

[3] Dept. of Computation, UMIST
PO Box 88, Sackville St, Manchester, M60 1QD, UK
{p.blenkhorn,g.evans}@co.umist.ac.uk

[4] Dept. of Computer Sciences, University of Tampere, Finland
grse@cs.uta.fi

**Abstract.** A new device, the Braille Slate Talker, is introduced. An ordinary hand held device (a PDA) is used with a fixed layout plastic guide placed over the touch screen to allow Braille input. Contracted Braille is converted to text by a table-driven state machine. Programs are written in Java language to provide full hardware and software platform independence. Future network applications will use Sun's Jini technology.

## 1 Introduction

Recent advances in computing technology and consumer electronics have resulted in the emergence and widespread acceptance of digital devices, such as mobile phones, palm computers, MP3 and similar music players, and dictating machines. These devices, along with traditional computers, are primarily designed to help in carrying out everyday tasks, provide entertainment and communicate with fellow humans.

A key question is whether blind people can take advantage of these devices and if so, to what extent. The current state-of-the-art varies from platform to platform. Traditional computers are typically accessed and operated using a screen reader program (such as e.g. Jaws [4]) that attempts to transform graphical screen content to text which then can be read out to the user with a Text-To-Speech (TTS) program [8]. Creating portable computers and assistants for blind users have typically involved the design and manufacture of custom hardware but recently there is an increased interest in the use of palm computers or Personal Digital Assistants (PDA). These devices are powerful enough to run Windows or Linux operating systems and perform real-time speech synthesis. Since most devices run graphical operating systems, blind people can access information through special purpose screen readers (rare for such devices) or self-voicing applications. The latter is the approach that we discuss in the paper.

---

* Z. Juhasz is also with the Dept. of Computer Science, University of Exeter, UK.

K. Miesenberger et al. (Eds.): ICCHP 2004, LNCS 3118, pp. 506–513, 2004.

Mobile phones and digital devices pose greater problems for blind users as they are normally operated by buttons that often control complex menu systems. These devices very rarely have built-in TTS modules; only the most advanced mobile phones can talk. Not surprisingly, using the very popular short messaging (SMS) technology is an almost impossible task for blind users. There are similar problems when using embedded devices, such as information kiosks, vending and Automatic Teller Machines (ATM).

The aim of our project, as discussed in Section 2, is to look at the accessibility problems of blind users from a different angle and develop a new user interface framework that is platform independent, based on a non-graphical paradigm, and provides a uniform program control and navigation mechanism. In Section 3, we describe the major building blocks of our system, the Braille text input, program navigation and control, the Text-to-Speech module, and their relationship to application programs. Section 4 gives a brief overview of the main application programs we have developed using the new interface framework, and in Section 5 we show how the model can be extended to access and use networked applications and internet services.

## 2 Project Background

Current trends in computing do not favour blind users. The graphical user interface has become the de facto interaction metaphor on desktop computers and continues to spread to emerging, new devices, such as PDAs and smart mobile phones. Non-graphical operating systems are either no longer supported (e.g. DOS) or require special expertise to use (e.g. Linux). Screen reader programs help users to interact with the computer but they have their limitations too: (*i*) most screen reader programs are expensive, (*ii*) they do not solve the primary computer accessibility problems, and (*iii*) applications with heavy visual coding and/or non-textual information content (e.g. browsing typical commercial web pages) represent considerable information mapping difficulties.

In trying to make computers more accessible, various input/output devices have been developed, ranging from special-purpose Braille keyboards, printers and Braille output cells [1]. While these developments appropriately take into account the special needs of visually impaired users, due to their small market segment, they are relatively expensive when compared to standard commercial products. Moreover, most of them can only work with desktop computers, which severely limits the mobility of the blind computer user.

Our main goal was to create a portable, fully accessible, yet inexpensive computing device for blind users that helps them in carrying out everyday tasks without requiring special expertise. Low cost and portability can only be achieved by using commercial, off-the-shelf, mass market computing devices. We have decided on the PDA device as the runtime platform, as this type of device has sufficient computing power and memory to perform the tasks required from a mobile assistant. There were several issues we had to investigate in order to use the PDA, however: providing accessibility without developing or relying on custom peripheral devices; creating a non-graphical user interface and simple navigation capability; and developing a common framework that can be used on other platforms, from desktop systems to phones and embedded devices. In the next section we look at the issues related to accessibility, namely input, output, and program control and navigation.

## 3 System Overview

PDA devices are designed for sighted users. They can start and control programs by clicking (pushing the touch screen with a stylus) on graphical interface elements, such as menu items and buttons. There are alternative methods for text input. Users can use virtual, on-screen keyboards, or the built-in character recognition system, i.e. full handwriting recognition or stylised 'graffiti' writing, or use external keyboards of various types and sizes (including full size keyboards).

These interfaces are clearly inappropriate for blind people. While external keyboards may prove to be usable, they are either cumbersome to carry and most will not support touch typing; furthermore, the program control/navigation problem is not solved. We have developed alternative ways of providing text input, providing feedback and controlling programs. Users are able to type in Braille using the touch screen, receive audio feedback via a TTS and operate programs using the four arrow keys found on every PDA device.

### 3.1 Text Input

The main idea behind the text input mechanism is to use the touch screen as a virtual Braille slate with a fixed screen layout. The user would always have the same arrangement of Braille cells on the screen regardless of the program used. To design the final Braille touch screen, several experiments were carried out.

First, a Windows CE Visual Basic program was developed to test the appropriate number and size of the Braille cells for text input. This prototype had a size of a real Braille slate. Inputting characters via this slate, however – using a touch screen instead of a piece of paper – led to some difficulties. Users with reflex movements of punching the paper with the stylus could easily damage the screen. Also, using small size Braille cells was not accurate enough with the touch screen. Finally, using a stylus for typing is not so convenient.

Based on the results obtained with the first prototype system, a single, large Braille cell was chosen to be displayed on the touch screen, where the Braille dots can be "punched" with fingers. Three more control dots were also introduced beside the enlarged Braille cell, as shown in Figure 1.a. Due to the physical constraints of the touch screen, only one dot at a time can be "punched". The first touch of any of the Braille dots represents a dot "punch", giving an auditory signal at the same time. A second touch on the same dot represents the erasure of the "punched" dot, which is signalled by a different sound. Note that unlike the traditional paper and stylus, our talking Braille slate allows the user to correct the Braille cells during input. Once the Braille cell input is complete, the Cell is Ready (F) control dot has to be pressed. The second control dot acts as a Backspace, while the third one as a Space character.

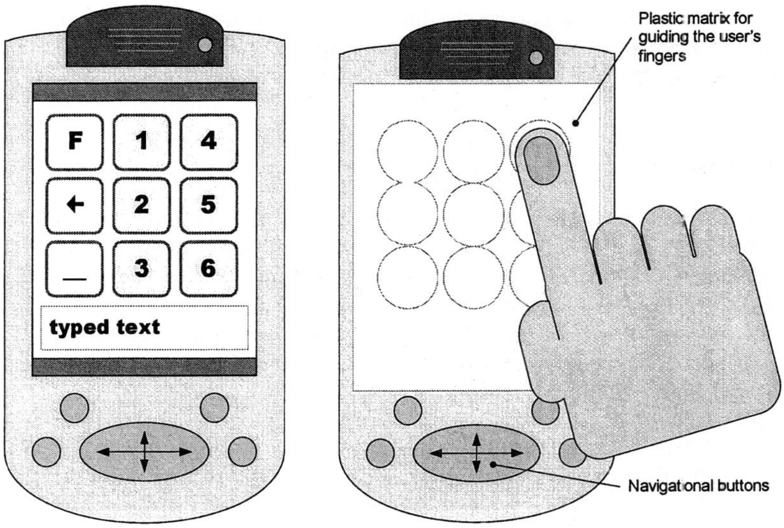


Part a) Part b)

**Fig. 1.** Input with Braille Slate on the touch screen: the virtual Braille keyboard (part a) and the plastic guide in action (part b).

Upon entry each Braille input character is converted to ASCII representation. The first step of the process is to convert the binary dot-representation to Hungarian MetaBraille Code [7]. Then, after pressing the Space control dot, indicating the end of a word, a language-independent, table-driven state machine converts the contracted Braille word into the final ASCII [5],[2]. Every completed Braille cell input is accompanied with MetaBraille Braille cell echo. After converting the full word, the word echo is also played. This three level (dot, cell, word) echo mechanism results in a reliable and fast input approach.

There are two important usability-related characteristics that determine the viability of our approach. The first is whether blind users are able to use the touch screen-based Braille keyboard. The second is typing speed.

We have found that although it is possible to use the touch screen without positional guide, this way of working results in very slow input and high error rate. To orient users, a plastic guide with holes at the dot locations have been designed that can be fitted onto the PDA in a way that it does not touch the screen. The user then only need to find the particular hole for the given screen dot and the hole will guide his or her finger to the correct touch position, as shown in Figure 1.b. The use of this inexpensive guide has speeded up text input and virtually eliminated all user errors.

The theoretical entry speed of the system is app. 300 Braille dot per minute. Based on the relative frequency of the Hungarian alphabet letters, 2.8 Braille dots plus an Accept dot are needed on average for one letter. This results in a top entry speed of app. 80 characters per minute. In reality, users will not be able to achieve this speed; an average speed of 20-40 characters per minute can be expected instead. This may seem slow when compared to professional sighted typists, but if it is compared to sighted users' entry speed using the PDA virtual keyboard, the results are promising.

Several blind users took part in the initial testing of the talking Braille slate. Our system could keep pace with the users' input speed and the resulting ASCII input speed from contracted Braille was close to the one of sighted users.

### 3.2 Program Control

In our system we wanted to create a uniform, unambiguous and non-graphical program control structure. It is based on a virtual menu system – the menu is never visible on the screen, which can be navigated using the four standard arrow keys found in every PDA (see Figure 1.). Two important requirements that have led to this design are: (*i*) the system should be usable by blind people who has very little or no computer experience, (*ii*) the system should provide a very clear and easy to understand mental model for navigation.

The up and down arrows always serve for choosing among possibilities at a given command tree level. The left and right arrows are for moving from one level of the command tree to the next. The left arrow moves the user towards the root of the tree, while the right arrow always travels to the selected submenu or executes the selected menu function.

Upon navigation, each menu item is read out to the user. If the program developer provides recorded sound for the items those are read, otherwise the built-in TTS module will generate the sound feedback to the user. The use of recorded messages is preferable for clarity but there are situations when items are generated dynamically at run-time and consequently no pre-recorded message can be present.

## 4 Implementation Issues

The current system has been implemented in Java [6]. The main advantage of using the Java language and runtime for our system is platform independence. Although this is only true within a particular platform domain (e.g. desktop PC), the major difficulties arose from the fact that most user interface elements in Java, similar to other modern programming languages, are visual. Consequently, many parts of the system had to be developed from scratch, without being able to use available Java classes identical in functionality.

The Braille text input is based on one screen that generates AWT events when a particular dot is pressed. These are then converted using a state machine algorithm. The entered words are passed in to the TTS module as ASCII strings. The current TTS module is the only part of the system that is not implemented in Java. It is a C++ version provided as a DLL that is called via the Java Native Interface mechanism. The reason for not having a Java TTS is lack of time in the project and initial worries about the speed of Java. It is planned to be replaced with a Java version in the near future.

The menu system is custom-designed object tree with application programs and their menus as building nodes. The root of the menu system represents a "desktop" with menus to access programs, settings, task switching. Once the user enters a particular program, the menu system events are forwarded to that program for local menu navigation, hence the user will be able to select functions in the given program. The menu system also allows for the use of complex nodes implementing functionality similar to, for example, visual list, combo box, and selection widgets.

Every application can take advantage of special system classes that provide access to the text input, TTS and menu system functionalities. The programming model is very similar to traditional graphical user interface programming and should not present problems for developers.

The use of Java also enables us to provide the same "look-and-feel" on different platforms. If a user likes the PDA-based Slate Talker, he/she can also run in on a desktop computer and (hopefully soon) on mobile phones as well. Java also allows us to take advantage of many non-graphical classes (e.g. for networking, file access, etc.) to reduce development time, as well as create applications that dynamically download Braille interfaces from remote servers. This we illustrate in Section 5.2.

# 5 Applications

In the project, we have developed a set of stand-alone and networked applications firstly, in order to test the viability of our approach, and secondly to create a PDA-based personal assistant for blind users with the most important applications at hand.

## 5.1 Stand-Alone Applications

The list of stand-alone applications currently includes a word processor, a contacts manager, and a hybrid talking book reader program [3]. Other programs being developed are a calculator, dictating machine, MP3 player, a traditional talking book reader and a mobile phone control program.

The word processor allows our users to conveniently create new or modify existing documents, save them or send them via email. The program does not offer formatting capabilities; it is a basic notepad program. It, however, offers the user the ability to read a document various ways: by words, sentences, paragraphs or in continuous mode. Once a mode is selected, the up/down arrow keys can be used for navigating within the text, similarly to menu navigation.

The hybrid talking book program allows users to read the text and recorded sound of talking books. Users can select which book they would like to read, in what mode (with TTS or recorded voice), set bookmarks and navigate within the book. Books are stored on removable SD memory cards that can store a number of books depending on capacity and book size. This saves the user from storing books on the PDA and can facilitate operation within a library scheme.

## 5.2 Network Applications

The two traditional network applications we have developed are an e-mail client program and a simple web browser. PDAs with network connectivity can take advantage of these programs. Network connectivity is model dependent it can be: a built-in WLAN; a WLAN with adapter and card; or a Bluetooth connection providing Internet sharing on a desktop PC.

The e-mail client allows the user to write e-mails using the standard Braille text input and send the message via an IMAP mail server. Also, the user can download email messages from the server with this program and use the TTS module to read them. If necessary, the user can save – even modify – the message and send a reply.

The web browser is a very simple experimental program providing basic HTML parsing and processing. Our project did not aim to develop a full-blown browser for blind users. The program demonstrates, however, that web pages can be read without screen readers and can be accessed and navigated more easily with our system.

The most exciting and novel set of network applications that our system supports is based on Sun's Jini technology [6]. Jini allows a client to discover network services automatically and download its user interface at run-time if required. We describe the operation and advantages of this approach through a talking book library service we have developed.

Instead of travelling to the library and borrowing a talking book (memory card) personally, the Slate Talker mobile assistant – when on-line – can discover the talking book library service that the user is a member of. The assistant will download the Braille user interface of this service and insert it into the 'network services' menu item in the root menu. Using the arrow keys, the user navigates into the library, logs in, and then browses or searches the book collection. Once the book is found, it can be read either by playing the recorded voice or using the TTS. To avoid delays and excessive memory usage sound is played as a stream. At the same time the user can navigate through the book; if he/she needs to jump to the next section or chapter, he/she uses the arrow keys. In the background, the text data of each read paragraph (or chapter) is downloaded, so if a network error occurs, the user can still read the book by falling back to the TTS operation mode. The text of books can also be downloaded so that a book can be read when the device is not connected to the network.

Jini services are described by their functionality (e.g. library, radio, news), unlike WWW servers that use URLs. This allows us to create a list of different service types of interest at run-time, without using search engines. This framework would allow blind users to access news, radio, educational, entertainment (music, comedy, etc.), and chat services without having to go through difficult-to-read graphical web pages; only by pressing four arrow keys. This version, however, only works on desktop environments at the moment, but we are working on creating a PDA version of the client. In the long term, we envisage various services available in the network, each offering a set of alternative interfaces for users, including graphical ones for sighted users, Braille one for blind users, and other types for people with different disabilities. We also hope that home appliances as well as public facilities (ATMs, vending machines, lift controllers) will be able to provide these downloadable interfaces.

## 6 Conclusions

In this paper we described a PDA-based Braille Slate Talker that acts as a mobile assistant for blind users. The system allows users to type in Braille on a touch screen without expensive devices, have access to a set of useful programs that can be controlled and navigated with a uniform and simple way using four arrow keys. In addition to stand-alone programs, it also enables its users to access the internet from email and web pages as well as for future Jini services. We believe that this system has great potential for individuals and groups in various application areas, such as education (teaching Braille, access to talking textbooks, distance learning), obtaining information (news, on-line libraries), accessing the workplace, entertainment, and using appliances and embedded devices access (heating system, blinds, doors, ATM).

## Acknowledgements

The authors would like to acknowledge the support of the Ministry of Informatics and Telecommunications and the Ministry of Education of Hungary for their joint support under Grant No. IHM-ITEM No. 116. The project could not have been completed without the dedicated work of Vilmos Hevesi and Frigyes Pratser. We are grateful for their contribution.

## References

1. ALVA Mobile Phone Organizer: http://www.alvaBraille.com/mpo/.
2. Arato A.., Vaspori T., Evans G., Blenkhorn P.: Braille to Text Translation for Hungarian. Computers Helping People with Special Needs, Proc. 8th ICCHP, Lecture Notes in Computer Science, No. 2398, Springer Verlag, (2002) 610–617.
3. Arató A.., Barkaszi M., Budai L., Vaspöri T.: Hybrid Books for the Blind - A new form of Talking Books., Proc. 5th International Conference,ICCHP'96, R. Oldenbourg Wien München, 1 (1996). 237–248.
4. JAWS screen reader program. http://www.freedomscientific.com/fs_products/software_jaws.asp.
5. Blenkhorn. P.: A System for Converting Braille into Print. IEEE Trans Rehab Eng, Vol. 3, No. 2, (1995) 215–221.
6. Sun Microsystems, "The Jini Specification", http://www.sun.com/jini "The Java Specification" http://wwws.sun.com/software/java/index.html.
7. Kiss G., Arató A., Lukács J.,Sulyán J., Vaspöri T.: BraiLab, a Full Hungarian Text-to-speech. Microcomputer for the Blind. Proc. World Conference on Phonetics (1987) 1–4.
8. Evans G., Blenkhorn, P.: Architectures of Assistive Software Applications for Windows-based Computers. Journal of Computer and Network Applications, Vol. 26, (2003) 213–228.

# Towards an Integrated Publishing Chain for Accessible Multimodal Documents

Benoît Guillon, Jean-Louis Monteiro, Cédric Checoury, Dominique Archambault, and Dominique Burger

Association BrailleNet, INSERM U483, Université Pierre et Marie Curie
9, quai Saint-Bernard 75252 Paris Cedex 5, France
{benoit.guillon,jean-louis.monteiro,cedric.checoury, Dominique.archambault,Dominique.burger}@snv.jussieu.fr

**Abstract.** Digital techniques have created new and stimulating conditions to provide visually impaired people with a better access to written information. The Helene Server project, started in 2000 by BrailleNet, aims at creating technical solutions to help transcribers to rationalize adapted documents production in France. The first action performed was to create a national repository of adapted documents available to transcription centers. In two years, this repository has gathered more than 1.500 books provided by publishers or transcribers. But the great variety of digital formats used by transcribers now raises the problem of resources normalization. This article presents a production chain of accessible documents based on the dtbook XML format.

## 1 Problem to Be Solved

Since 2000, BrailleNet has developed and maintained the Helene Server [1] (`http://www.serveur-helene.org`), a collaborative Web server to gather files to produce adapted documents for visually impaired people. This national project came as the continuation of a European TIDE project on Secure Document Delivery (SEDODEL [2]). It is currently part of the Vickie European funded project [3].

The Helene Server aims at providing transcription centers with a safe repository for original and adapted files of books under copyright. It offers the common functionalities of a digital library with additional features to manage publishers' authorizations and files versioning. To ensure the access to publishers' files, a secured delivery mechanism based on S/MIME and digital certificates has been set up.

After more than two years of existence, the Helene Server has reached some of its objectives:

- more than 1.500 books are stored, about ¾ of them being under copyright,
- BrailleNet has signed contracts with about 80 French publishers to obtain authorizations and source files,
- 40 transcription centers have been certified and collaborate to produce Braille and large print documents from source files provided by publishers.

These results raise a new problem, related to the great variety of the formats used to store documents. Actually, more than 25 different formats of documents are registered each of them used by transcription centers in different ways for different purposes.

K. Miesenberger et al. (Eds.): ICCHP 2004, LNCS 3118, pp. 514–521, 2004.

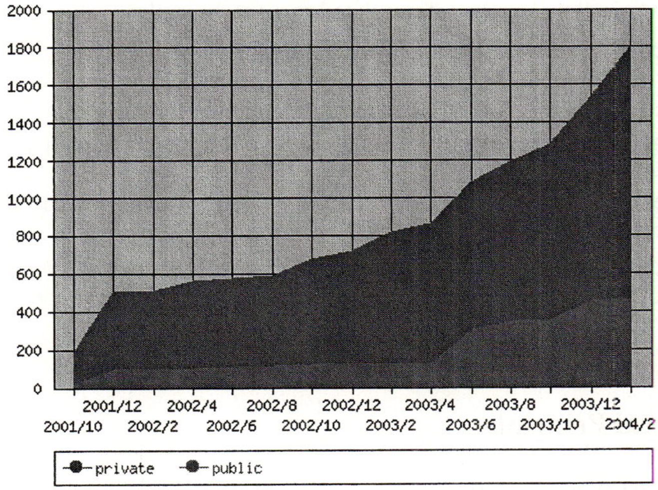


**Fig. 1.** Evolution of books number on the Helene Server since 2001

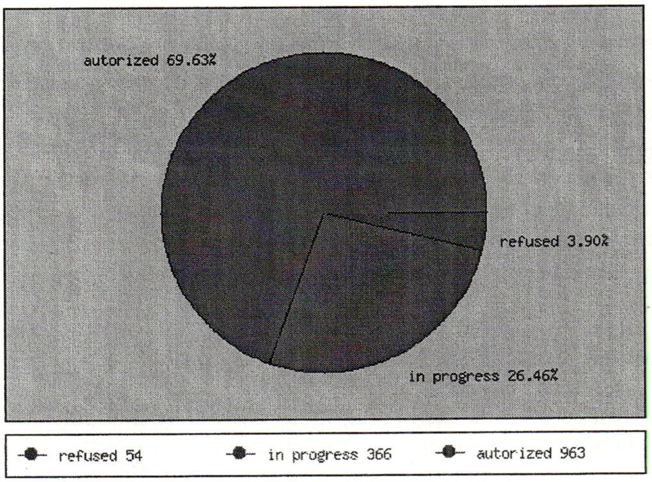


**Fig. 2.** Status of private books' authorizations

This variety of formats raises questions from transcribers, for example:

- "This file was created using another operating system which uses a specific encoding for accentuated characters, how can I recode my file?"
- "This file was adapted for printed Braille using a specific layout format, how can I use it with another software? Can I use it for large print?"
- "I want to adapt this book which contains meaningful images, how can I insert descriptions of these images into the book file for the needs of blind people?"
- "Can I store a mathematical formula in a document so that it will be reused for Braille, large print or audio outputs?"

These few questions can be reformulated more technically:

- How to code structured documents that must be shared between different users in different environments?
- How flexible will this coding be as to be extended in the future?
- How to avoid adapting documents' layout for each output modality (Braille, large print, speech synthesis ...)?
- How to embed content's adaptation in a document so that they can be used selectively according to the modality used?

This article presents a complete solution to create documents in a unique high structured format and to convert them automatically into several specific accessible formats.

## 2 Technical Principles

### 2.1 A Central Representation of Documents Based on Dtbook

The dtbook [3] Document Type Definition (DTD) is part of the NISO Z39.86-2002 standard [4], also known as DAISY 3.0.

We have chosen dtbook as the central representation of documents because:

- it has emerged as a *de facto* XML standard to mark up general documents,
- it improves accessibility to people with print disabilities,
- it facilitates the output of documents in a variety of accessible formats,
- it provides the necessary elements to create semantically rich documents,
- it can be extended with external DTDs, to support specific document types (e.g. MathML for formula, poetry or drama modules ...),
- it can be processed using many existing tools on many platforms.

### 2.2 Collaborative Enrichment Rather Than Adaptation

Adapting a document aims at facilitating its access in any modality. But the adaptation process can not be fully automatic. It requires human expertise. Most of the time this expertise is not concentrated in one center or person. For that reason the document adaptation process has to be collaborative, e.g. flexible and progressive.

In addition, the enrichment of the original document shall be independent of the targeted modality. The final presentation of the document will be parameterized later on when the document will be generated.

To achieve this, some constraints have to be respected in the document coding up stream. For instance:

- The general structure of the document should be marked up as to provide an easy navigation through it. Parts, levels, chapters (...) should be identified.
- The visual pagination should be preserved to allow visually impaired users to share references with sighted users.

- It should be possible to add conditional contents during the adaptation process. These additions may be specific to a modality, like alternative textual description of images, or alternative audio comments …).
- The document shall provide the necessary semantic information for its understanding using any modality (e.g. tables of data should be properly marked up for navigation; in a drama, speakers and speech should be distinguished ...).
- Special contents like mathematical formulas should be coded using a rich description format, as MathML [6].

### 2.3 Automatically Generated Output

The documents, if they were correctly coded and adapted by experts will contain the necessary information to generate automatically:

- Accessible HTML documents following the WAI [7] guidelines about accessibility, including document's logical structure (h1 to h6 elements), short alternative to images (alt attributes) and long descriptions when necessary, appropriate data tables structure for Braille and speech synthesis (thead, tbody, th elements and headers attributes).
- Files ready for Braille embossing, with a double pagination (Braille and original page numbering), navigation features (tables of contents, specific signalization of titles, textual descriptions of illustrations ...),
- a basic large print document including a double pagination and navigation features,
- files used as sources to record narrated books using the DAISY format (human voice or speech synthesis).

## 3 Technical Implementation

To implement the solution proposed above, we have defined a development centered on the dtbook DTD. The objective is to progressively integrate tools into the Helene Server in order to obtain a consistent publishing chain to produce accessible documents. We will consider in this paper three types of tools:

### 3.1 Normalization Tools

A first step in the chain is to rough out the main structure of documents. As the files provided by publishers and transcribers use a great variety of formats, a practical solution is to use a standard word processor, like Microsoft Word, for which most software programs offer exportation filters. Also MS Word is a word processor commonly used by transcribers. We developed a set of Visual Basic macros for MS Word for producing well structured files in RTF format.

These macros make easy:

- To create styles for the main structure elements of dtbook (headings, acknowledgments, bibliography, annex, lists ...)
- To mark-up original page numbers or to convert existing page break marks into page numbers,

- To import files prepared for Braille print into structured RTF files (convert specific ASCII characters into Word styles),
- To convert mathematical formula prepared with MathType [8] into MathML,
- To find bibliographical information on books on the Helene Server, and to fill in automatically the corresponding document metadata,
- To post the enriched document on the Helene Server in RTF.

In addition, the MS Word macro provides transcribers with a set of shortcut keys to markup documents faster.

Once uploaded on the Helene Server, RTF documents are converted into XML following the dtbook DTD using upCast [9] and appropriate XSL stylesheets.

The MS Word Macro can be found at
`http://www.serveur-helene.org/braillenet/helene2/tools/macro/`
The XSL stylesheets to convert upCast XML documents into XML dtbook documents can be found at
`http://dsidtb.sourceforge.net/`

### 3.2 A Document Enrichment Tool

As MS Word does not provide the required functions to create the document structure described above, a more specific tool is necessary to allow transcribers to edit and enrich the structure and the content of dtbook files. This tool may be used on documents obtained with the MS Word macro or on documents outputted by automatic conversions from publishers' XML documents.

This tool should guide transcribers in the adaptation process, by providing them with simplified procedures to enrich documents. It should implement every features of the dtbook document type and hide its complexity to transcribers.

The document enrichment tool functionalities are:

- To apply particular styles to a text selection (Braille specific styles as "do not contract this region", or theatre specific styles as "speaker", "speech" …)
- To mark a text selection as being in a particular language,
- To add production notes to the document and to specify a target modality when necessary,
- To add production notes, short alternatives and captions to images included in the document,
- To markup data tables so that they will be easily understood by blind readers using speech synthesis or Braille displays,
- To create and modify the original pagination of the document and to create more complex numbering schemes.

This tool is currently developed within the Vickie Project.

In addition, we developed a tool to monitor dtbook documents adaptation level. This tool automatically generates a report on the accessibility features contained in a dtbook document. This report includes:

- the table of content of the document,
- the original page numbers,

- the number of images and if they have short alternatives, production notes and captions,
- the number of tables and if they are accessible to blind readers, if they contain a caption and a summary,
- the number of MathML formulas the document contains.

This tool is integrated to the Helene Server and is useful for transcribers to check the quality of dtbook documents before using them.

### 3.3 Output Conversion Tools

The enriched dtbook files can be used for producing:

- accessible HTML documents using customized navigation features (several HTML files linked one to each other using table of contents, navigation links on top and bottom of each file to reach previous or next section), link to particular CSS stylesheets and most of accessibility features recommended by WAI…
- Duxbury files (dollars-code format). Resulting files can imported directly into DBT and then embossed in Braille.
- PDF for large print which may be more specifically adapted to final user's disabilities later on (for instance images size and colors …)
- Text only Daisy 3.0 package: an ncx file for navigation and a smil files for synchronization are automatically generated from a dtbook file. The dtbook file is modified to include references to smil files. Used with an opf file including book's metadata generated by the Helene Server, a full text-only Daisy 3.0 package is built. This package can be read with a Daisy 3.0 player.

We developed XSL stylesheets to convert dtbook files in these different formats. These stylesheets are embedded on the Helene Server and are launched on the fly upon request of the user. The user can customize converters' behavior at generation time so that the output document will be more adapted to the final users needs (font size for large print, contraction or not for Braille, CSS stylesheets to be linked to HTML documents …). Mathematical formulas are translated into Braille notation using MMBT [10].

The stylesheets we developed can be found at
`http://dsidtb.sourceforge.net/`

More specific software may also use these files to produce synthetic audio Daisy 2.02 files, like the software produce by Phoneticom [11].

## 4 Conclusion

The production scheme we exposed provides transcribers with a complete environment to create accessible documents whatever the target modality.

It avoids performing several adaptation works on a same book and helps transcribers to focus more on complex tasks as providing textual alternatives to images for Braille or images adaptation for large print.

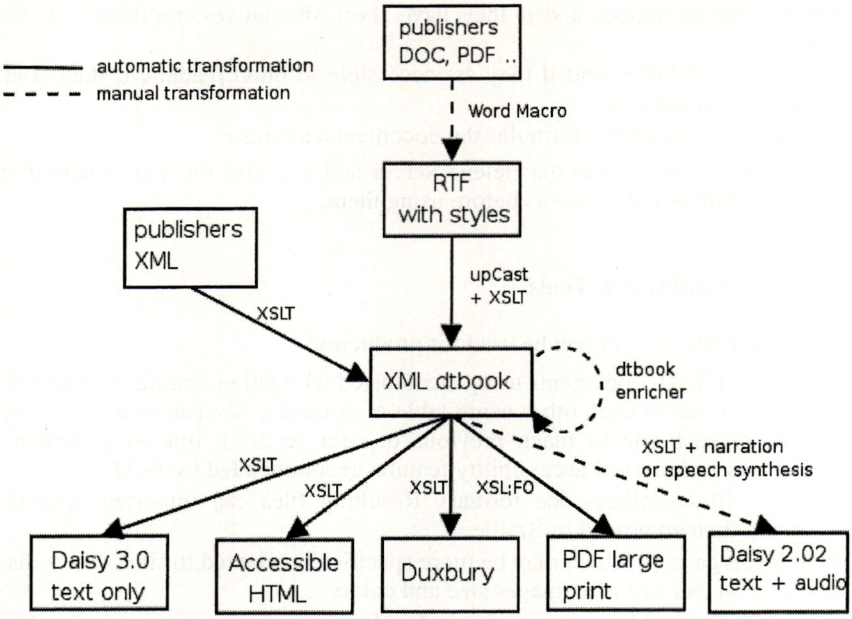


**Fig. 3.** The full production scheme

As the conversion tools are fully integrated to the Helene Server, generating adapted documents is simplified and can be customized to fit the needs of final users.

## Acknowledgment

The Vickie project is funded by the European Commission[1], on the IST (Information Society Technologies) Programme 2001 (FP5-IST-Systems and Services for Citizen/Persons with special needs), under the reference IST-2001-32678.

## References

1. Guillaume du Bourguet, Benoît Guillon, Dominique Burger : Helene: a collaborative server to create and securely deliver documents for the blind, proceedings of AAATE 2003
2. Dominique BURGER, Iain MILLNS, Emmanuel SCHWARZ, Tom WESLEY: SEDODEL: A solution to the copyright barrier to access to information, CSUN 1999
3. Dominique Archambault and Dominique Burger: The Vickie Project, In: Proceedings of the ICCHP 2002 (8th International Conference on Computers Helping People with Special Needs), Linz, Austria, July 2002

[1] The contents of this paper is the sole reponsability of the authors and in no way represents the views of the European Commission or its services.

4. Digital Talking Book Expanded Document Type Definition Documentation for Version V110, http://www.loc.gov/nls/z3986/v100/dtbook110doc.htm
5. Specifications for the Digital Talking Book http://www.niso.org/standards/resources/Z39-86-2002.html
6. W3C MathML, http://www.w3.org/Math/
7. W3C Web Accessibility Initiative, http://www.w3.org/WAI/
8. Design Science MathType, http://www.dessci.com/en/products/mathtype/
9. Infinity-loop UpCast engine, http://www.infinity-loop.de/
10. MMBT : Mathematical Multilanguage Braille Translator, http://sourceforge.net/projects/mmbt/,
Victor Moço, Dominique Archambault: A transcription tool for mathematical Braille proceedings of AAATE 2003, Dublin, Ireland, September 2003
11. Phoneticom, http://www.phoneticom.com/

# Presenting UML Software Engineering Diagrams to Blind People

Alasdair King[1], Paul Blenkhorn[1], David Crombie[2], Sijo Dijkstra[2], Gareth Evans[1], and John Wood[3]

[1] Department of Computation, UMIST, Manchester, M60 1QD, UK
{alasdair.king,plb,dge}@co.umist.ac.uk
[2] Federatie van Nederlandse Blindenbibliotheken
Molenpad 2, 1016 GM, Amsterdam, Netherlands
{DCrombie,SDijkstra}@fnb.nl
[3] The National Council for the Blind, Whitworth Road, Drumcondra, Dublin 9, Ireland
john.wood@ncbi.ie

**Abstract.** The TeDUB system promises to deliver a UML diagram tool accessible to blind software engineers. The system uses a number of different interfaces and representation techniques to overcome the challenges of making diagrams created with the Unified Modeling Language usable for blind people. The system is entirely automated and does not require special preparation of UML diagrams by a sighted user. The results of evaluation of the system with thirty-six users were positive. The system was well-received and the participants were able to complete set UML tasks.

## 1 Context

Computer programming is one field where blind and vision-impaired people have been able to participate in the employment market and in education. Computer code has traditionally been text, and therefore accessible to blind people using assistive technology (i.e. screen readers). In recent years the growth of software engineering has led to an increase in the use of modelling tools that use rich visual presentation to facilitate software development by sighted programmers. These tools are visual languages that aid in the design of software systems. One of these languages is the Unified Modeling Language [5], a graphical modelling standard. It reflects the dominant object-oriented programming paradigm, and is increasingly popular in education and the workforce. UML diagrams consist of nodes and connections between them. This general model allows for twelve types of diagram, two examples of which are shown in Figure 1 and Figure 2.

These two UML diagrams illustrate the problems with presenting UML using conventional accessible solutions, such as tactile diagrams. A great deal of detailed information is contained in UML diagrams, much of it graphically, such as the style of arrow-heads on connecting lines. This imposes practical limits on UML representation in a tactile diagram [1][4]. Users are unlikely to be able to print a UML diagram onto swell paper and create a usable tactile diagram. In addition, UML is designed to be a co-operative modelling tool, a dynamic source of information for a development

K. Miesenberger et al. (Eds.): ICCHP 2004, LNCS 3118, pp. 522–529, 2004.

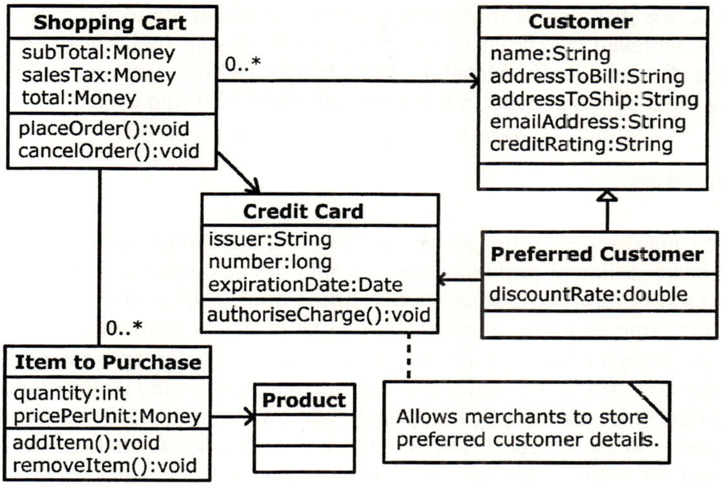


**Fig. 1.** A UML class diagram

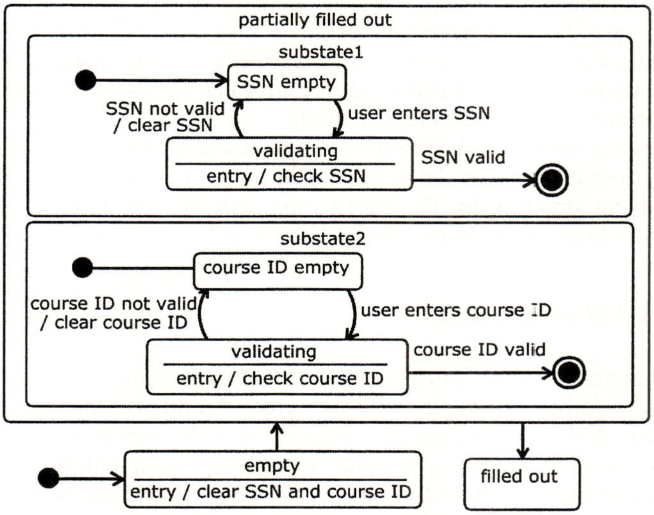


**Fig. 2.** A UML state diagram

team to annotate, amend and change during development. To take advantage of these features interaction with the content is necessary, and the user must be able to access the diagrams autonomously and on demand.

The TeDUB project (Technical Diagram Understanding for the Blind) has been working on access to technical diagrams [3][6]. We have been working on interfaces to structured information, and have now developed a tool to access UML. This is driven by a need to maintain the ability of blind people to compete in the software engineering field. The system is fully automated, so the user can receive a UML diagram and access its contents immediately without the intervention of a sighted mediator. This is achieved by taking the output of UML design tools in a common UML interchange format, XML Metadata Interchange (XMI), and converting and re-presenting the diagram content in a manner suitable for a blind user.

## 2 Difficulties

There are a number of challenges in building a UML design tool for blind people. Some are basic technical problems, for example the inconsistent application of UML standards by different UML design tools. More significant is the problem of how to represent the large quantity of information content that is immediately apparent to a sighted user through UML's graphical presentation. Sighted people can easily identify relationships between items; easily identify the overall structure of the diagram; easily identify different levels of complexity and detail; and move easily between different views or points in the diagram. The fact there is so much information means that the content must be re-presented in such a way as to allow the blind user to process it effectively. Working item by item through the information content in an unstructured linear fashion with a screen reader will not be practical. The advantage of UML is that the information conveyed in UML graphics is explicitly defined in the UML standard, so all of the information content in the diagram is available to be presented to the user. This is very different from non-technical diagrams, where there is no agreed visual vocabulary or grammar, and the user is expected to use visual semantic knowledge to interpret the diagram. Because all the information content is explicitly defined it can be re-presented as required in its entirety.

The challenges therefore relate to how to model and present the UML information. For example, does a simple model consisting of nodes and connections between them provide sufficient structure for the information content, and how is information attached to connections to be represented and accessed?

## 3 The TeDUB Approach

The re-presentation of UML information to blind users must be informed by some analysis of the information source to identify what should be communicated. UML is presented through the visual medium: what visual information is indispensable for understanding the diagram and successfully completing tasks with it?

Information rendered graphically, such as a relationship shown by an arrow, can be re-presented as a text-only equivalent with no loss of factual information. Going further, the absolute layout of the UML diagram does not convey any explicit information that is unavailable should the diagram be distorted. This does not mean that inferential information is not provided by the spatial positioning of nodes in the UML diagram. A clear and rational layout of the contents of a diagram by a sighted user will create a diagram that lends itself to easy analysis and understanding by another sighted user. While two UML diagrams might be informationally equivalent, it does not follow that they are equal in ease of use. This means there is a choice for the TeDUB project: should an attempt should be made to provide the spatial information in a diagram on the grounds that it is useful to sighted people in using the diagram, and therefore should be useful to the blind user? The layout information is likely to be of some value. The blind user may need the spatial information to allow them to co-operate with a sighted user on the same diagram. Against this proposal is the fact that communicating the spatial information (for the system) and building up a spatial mental model of the diagram (for the user) may require more effort than the benefit of gaining the spatial information warrants.

UML diagrams are based upon a connected network of nodes. The type of each node depends on the UML diagram: a node might be a Class in a Class diagram or an Actor in a Use Case diagram. While the spatial layout of nodes may help sighted users, it is the connectivity between nodes that is the important information. The task of communicating spatial information is simplified considerably if one considers that the problem is how to communicate the correct layout of nodes in the network and the connections between them, *not* the absolute spatial position of nodes in the diagram. A further pragmatic consideration is that the modelling of the diagram as a connected network implies *some* layout. The general model for the representation of UML diagrams is therefore a connected network with a layout consistent with the original diagram. However, some UML diagram types cannot be fully modelled in this way. For example, some UML diagrams allow the nesting of diagrams within nodes, such as class diagrams contained within packages. In addition, the problem of the great quantity of information in a UML diagram must be addressed. How can it best be structured?

The TeDUB solution to these two problems is to employ a hierarchical structure that is logically orthogonal to the connected network representation. Generally, all the nodes in a single connected network will be children of a single parent node, which may be a node created to structure the diagram, containing information about the diagram/network it represents such as "Class model of eCommerce system", or a node representing some structure within the UML model itself, for example a package node containing class nodes. A simple class diagram, as shown in Figure 1, might be a shallow two-level hierarchy of class nodes. The state diagram in Figure 2 shows a composite state ("partially filled out") that is composed of two sub states, which would therefore appear in the hierarchy as child nodes of the "partially filled out" node. This is a compositional hierarchy, which serves two roles. First, it provides a way to structure multiple nodes and UML diagrams into one UML model, as required by the UML model specification. Second, and more importantly for blind users, it enables the system to represent compositional bodies and high-level semantic structures in single structural nodes. This is analogous to the sighted user's ability to recognise UML components as parts of a meaningful higher-level whole without needing to painstakingly analyse the function and content of every component. The blind user navigating through the hierarchy from the top root node will encounter, before any atomic UML component like a class node, a structural node that provides summary or context information on the component nodes it contains. If the blind user knows that the set of nodes that are to be encountered next are all children of a "Class model of an E-Commerce system" structural node then they may find it easier to understand the role of each node, or identify that the children are not of interest for task at hand and know to move on to another part of the model. The question arises, of course, of where the semantic information used to create these nodes is obtained. The automated TeDUB system cannot provide meaningful descriptions like a human annotator, but nonetheless the UML model does contain meaningful structural information and text, so these structural nodes are meaningfully titled and typed.

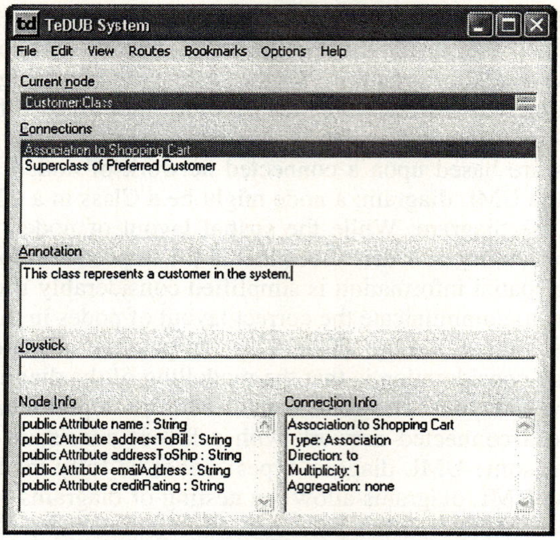


**Fig. 3.** The user interface in action

Finally, although the connected-network and hierarchical models are paramount, to support different tasks and diagram types a number of special functions, views, and rules are also used by the system. These aim to facilitate specific activities, such as identifying all the actors in a use case diagram.

## 4 Styles of Communication

The TeDUB system is intended to provide an accessible interface to the UML diagram content and support four of the twelve UML diagram types (class, use case, sequence and state diagrams) considered to be most useful and commonly used.

The user interface, shown in Figure 3, uses standard Microsoft Windows user interface components, such as text boxes and lists, so as to be screen-reader neutral. This allows the user to employ their usual screen reader. UML users are likely to be skilled computer users and skilled screen reader users, and quite possibly Braille users. Allowing them to use these skills and their screen reader restricts the options available to a self-voicing application (for example, locating speech output around the user) but compensates by leveraging their assumed screen reader abilities. This is combined with a number of alternative interfaces, such as spatialised sound or a tactile device (a force feedback joystick), that allow representation of the spatial information in the diagram, such as the position of nodes or the connections between them. The alternative interfaces use devices that are widely available and low-cost, such as standard sound cards or games joysticks, rather than relatively expensive special purpose devices. The system is intended to be affordable and usable without special equipment by users with their own familiar screen reader. This is important if the system is ever to be used in the real world.

The hierarchical tree structure of nodes is navigated through by the user using a Windows Explorer-style interface controlled by the cursor keys. This approach has been rated very highly in evaluations undertaken by the project [3]. Only the name and type of the current node is immediately available to the user: the user learns which nodes have children or siblings by trying to access them. Context sounds warn the user when no such nodes exist. Navigation commences at the top node of the diagram, which acts as home to the user and can be returned to at a key press if the user becomes lost. The composite structural nodes with semantic meaning are therefore encountered first, so the user can very quickly obtain a high-level understanding of the contents of a model without having to access and explore a single UML component.

A back function enables the user's steps to be retraced in the same way as a web browser. Bookmarks can be set or reset at will and accessed with a key press, so if the user is exploring the relationship between two nodes the user can switch back and forth between them no matter what their location in the hierarchy. All of these features relate to navigation between nodes in the hierarchy: information captured within the nodes, for example connectivity, annotation, and attributes of the node, is all available with a key press and is related to the current node. This helps to structure information so that it is only presented to the user when the user requests it, complying with the principle of "maximum information in minimum time" so useful for screen reader users. Because content is only accessible through the current node the user must change nodes to access different content. This navigation requirement is ameliorated by a find function that searches the entire tree and by a text representation described below.

The second fundamental way to access the diagram contents is related to the representation of the diagram as a connected network. This user still has a current node, but instead of moving around the hierarchy, the user moves to nodes connected to the current node in the diagram network. This can be accomplished by selection of a connection from a list in the main interface or through use of a joystick. If a connected node lies in the direction indicated by the joystick the name of that node is presented. Spatialised sound is used to reinforce the joystick position. This is a simple system, but suffers from one major flaw in that if multiple nodes are connected and located in the same direction then they cannot be discriminated by the joystick direction alone (the system presents the closest node) since it indicates direction only as the crow flies. This means that in large diagrams it may not be possible to access every node through this interface. There might in any case be nodes not connected to any other, not represented in the network (for example top-level nodes) or different diagrams without connections between them. It follows that connection navigation does not necessarily allow the user to access every node in the diagram as the hierarchy navigation does. However, the connection navigation *should* allow the user to access every node connected directly or indirectly to the current node, and the current system cannot guarantee this. For this project diagrams have been selected that avoid this problem. For a real application the some rearrangement of nodes or connection directions would be required, which abandons the consistency between the blind and sighted user's view of the layout of the diagram but retains the simple node-connection model.

Some other functions and views have been added to investigate their potential. One is a function that maps the connected network representation of the diagram (or the currently-connected network, if there are several) onto the joystick area of movement. As the user moves the joystick any node at the position in the diagram corresponding to the position of the joystick is presented to the user. This allows for a quick overview of the diagram, but quickly becomes unusable as the number of items in the diagram increases beyond about twenty. Another approach allows access to the information content of the diagram by representing it as an internally-hyperlinked text-only document, which can be navigated with the cursor keys in the same way as any standard text document. This is effectively a rendering of the diagram as a linear text document, so users can use their text navigation skills and techniques to explore the content, find, cut and paste and access the information directly. There is also a set of functions based on task analysis of the types and uses of the diagrams. For example, a function provided for use case diagrams allows the presentation of only the use cases in the diagram, useful for developers checking the required use cases against implemented functions. A final approach under development is to represent the diagram nodes and connections on a tactile tablet. This is similar to previous work done on software engineering diagrams [2]. This is not a tactile diagram: rather, the nodes and connections of the diagram are accessed through a grid whose vertices along the diagonal correspond to nodes within the diagram. Connections between nodes are represented by the intersection of perpendicular lines drawn from the nodes along the diagonal.

## 5 User Evaluation

The system has been evaluated with 34 blind and partially-sighted users in a first round of evaluation. 11 were students following a computer-related course (one a high-school programmer) and 23 were professional users. Class, use case and state diagrams were evaluated by questionnaire and by assigning the users common tasks for the diagram, such as "To which item or items is 'Hypothesis Buffer' connected?" The results of this evaluation will inform the next round of development (as have previous rounds of development in the project) including support for UML sequence diagrams.

Results of the latest round of evaluation were largely positive: users were comfortable with the interface and completed the tasks set successfully. The simple but varied user interface features, such as the back function, were well-regarded and allowed different users to employ different strategies. A demand for diagram creation and editing functions was strongly expressed. The next stage of evaluation will use larger diagrams, since the diagrams used were small enough for users to 'chunk' or hold in memory entirely, and strategies and outcomes may well be different.

Some interesting results of the evaluation already conducted included the following. Although a consistent alphabetical order of nodes was presented to the users, they requested variable orders more related to the roles of the nodes: for example, in state diagrams, state nodes should be placed in likely order of occurrence. Whilst using the joystick to provide connection information was successful, support will be given to using the number key pad as a replacement. Like the joystick function, this has problems when multiple nodes are in the same direction, but the problem is exacerbated by having fewer directions to discriminate between the connected nodes. The text-only view was received very positively, as might be expected from software engineers accustomed to using computer code. One user referred to the text-only view as the "pseudo code" view.

Further development of the system based on these results are hoped to deliver a useful UML tool for blind people working in software development.

## References


1. Baillie, C., Burmeister, O.K. & Hamlyn-Harris, J. H.: "Web-based Teaching: Communicating Technical Diagrams with the Vision Impaired", *Proceedings of OZeWAI 2003*, Bundoora, Victoria, Australia, December (2003).
2. Blenkhorn, P. & Evans, D.G.: "Using Speech and Touch to Enable Blind People to Access Schematic Diagrams", *Journal of Network and Computer Applications*, ISSN 1084-0845, Vol 21, (1998), pp17–29.
3. Blenkhorn, P., Crombie, D., Dijkstra, S., Evans, D.G., Gallager, B., Hagen, C., Horstmann, M., Ioannidis, G., King, A., Magennis, M., Petrie, H., O'Neil, A., Schlieder, C. & Wood, J.:"Access to Technical Diagrams for Blind People", AAATE, In Craddock, McCormack, Reilly & Knops (Eds.), *Assistive Technology - Shaping the Future (Proc. AAATE 2003)*, (2003),pp 466–470.
4. Levi, J.M. & Amick, N.S.: "Tangible graphics: producers' views" in *Tactual Perception*, editors W. Schiff and E. Foulkes, Cambridge University Press, Cambridge, UK, (1982), pp 417–429.
5. OMG, Object Management Group, OMG website, http://www.omg.org/uml, January( 2004).
6. Petrie, H., Schlieder, C., Blenkhorn, P.,Evans, D.G., King, A., O'Neill, A-M., Ioannidis, G.T., Gallager, B., Crombie, D., Mager, R. & Alafaci, M.: "TeDUB: A System for Presenting and Exploring Technical Drawings for Blind People", In K. Miesenberger, J. Klaus, & W. Zagler (Eds.), *Computers Helping People with Special Needs, Proc. 8th ICCHP, Lecture Notes in Computer Science, No. 2398,* ISSN 0302-9743, Springer, July (2002), pp 537–539.

# Linear Searching in a Non-linear Environment: The Information Seeking Behaviour of Visually Impaired People on the World Wide Web

Jenny Craven

Research Associate
CERLIM, Manchester Metropolitan University
j.craven@mmu.ac.uk

**Abstract.** The information seeking behaviour of visually impaired people was explored in the Non-visual Access to the Digital Library (NoVA) (1) project, undertaken by the Centre for Research in Library and Information Management (CERLIM). The aim of the study was to develop further understanding of user behaviour, with particular reference to people who needed to use assistive technology in order to 'read' or interact with web sites. The findings of the two-year study revealed potential barriers to access, identified from observations of how assistive technologies such as screen readers can force users to search or navigate in a way that is not necessarily reflected in the design of the web page. Recommendations have been made regarding the provision of practical usability guidelines, access to technology, training in the use of assistive technologies, and the importance of universal design.

## 1 Introduction

The development of networked distributed resources enables a wider range of possibilities in the way resources and services are delivered to users. Information is increasingly being provided online and in particular on the world wide web, giving people the opportunity to access information from their preferred point of access and at a time convenient to them.

Access to digital resources is seen as an important factor in combating social exclusion. It provides people with more choice in the way they access information. This includes users who need to use alternative formats and systems in order to read and interact with information on screen. For example, users with a cognitive, audio, motor, or visual impairment. Technology can now provide immediate access to resources that users had to wait a considerable amount of time for in order to be transcribed into a format appropriate to their requirements.

This is a positive move towards widening access for all, however barriers still exist if the content itself has not been structured and displayed in a way that can be 'read' by everyone. For example, a blind or visually impaired person using assistive technology such as a screen reader will only be able to access web-based content that has been structured in a way that enables the assistive technology to interpret it. A classic example is the failure to provide alternative text for graphics in an HTML document, which a screen reader will simply read out as 'graphic', or 'image', or just the file name.

K. Miesenberger et al. (Eds.): ICCHP 2004, LNCS 3118, pp. 530–537, 2004.

To ensure the maximum number of users can access web-based information, people need to become more aware of the importance of designing web pages in an accessible way. This is often referred to as 'universal access' or 'design for all'. Advice and guidelines on the subject of accessible web design are plentiful. A good example is the work of the World Wide Web Consortium Web Accessibility Initiative (2) which looks at all aspects of web accessibility and universal design and provides extensive advice and guidelines. Many organisations base their accessibility policies and guidelines on the work of the W3C/WAI.

A number of other considerations must also be taken into account before a web site truly meets the requirements of universal access. The information seeking behaviour of users can play a significant part in understanding why certain design features work successfully and others leave users confused or frustrated.

Information seeking behaviour and use of the human computer interface is an established field, but it is one that tends to assume visual capabilities which blind and visually impaired people may not possess. An example is the use of frames in a web environment to enable the user to perform complex selections across categories. A sighted person is able to navigate between frames in a random, non-linear manner, but a non-sighted person using audio or Braille output has to navigate linearly within one frame at a time, or through a list of links and headings. The examples below show a non-linear web page (Fig.1) converted to linear navigation (Fig.2):

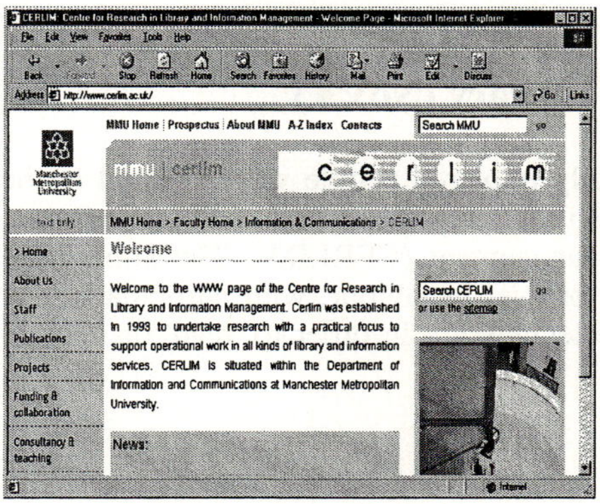


**Fig. 1.** Non-Linear Display

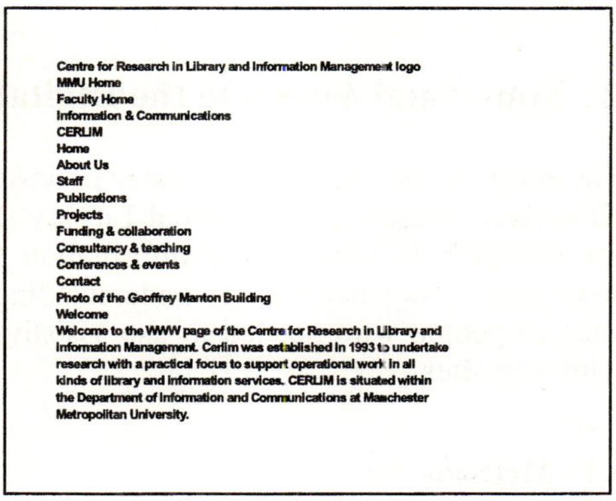

Centre for Research in Library and Information Management logo
MMU Home
Faculty Home
Information & Communications
CERLIM
Home
About Us
Staff
Publications
Projects
Funding & collaboration
Consultancy & teaching
Conferences & events
Contact
Photo of the Geoffrey Manton Building
Welcome
Welcome to the WWW page of the Centre for Research in Library and Information Management. Cerlim was established in 1993 to undertake research with a practical focus to support operational work in all kinds of library and information services. CERLIM is situated within the Department of Information and Communications at Manchester Metropolitan University.

**Fig. 2.** Linear Display

Users navigating in a non-linear way may also have to move back and forth several times in order to reach the desired point. This has implications for the time taken to navigate within a page, particularly if the navigational links are not provided in a logical order.

Despite the availability of good advice relating to usability, such as the work of Nielsen (3), there is still evidence that many web designers do not appear to have taken into account the diverse nature of their potential users and how different information seeking behaviours affect success in navigating their sites. In order to break down barriers to navigation it is necessary for web designers and developers to become more aware, not only of accessibility issues but also usability issues and, in particular, the information seeking behaviour of the users in web-based environments.

In the web environment, studies into usability have identified content organisation and navigation paths as the most important factors to aid the information seeking of visually impaired people. Learning and cognitive styles may also have a bearing on the way visually impaired users approach an information seeking task and how they navigate their way around websites. Research into cognitive styles and their influence on general information seeking behaviour undertaken by Kim (4) suggests that the 'field dependent' and the 'field independent' styles are likely to impact differently on the success of the user searching in a non-linear web environment. Field dependent users tend to navigate in a linear way, moving systematically down a page, whereas field independent users tend to move freely around the system, trying a "higher number of access attempts than field dependents" (4, p.235). Therefore, if a visually impaired user whose natural inclination is to adopt a non-linear (field independent) approach is forced down a linear path (field dependent) by the assistive technology they are using, there is a clear danger of disadvantage.

The aim of this paper is to provide some additional thought to established accessibility and usability advice by considering the information seeking behaviour of blind and visually impaired people in web-based environments. Potential barriers to access will be identified from observations of how assistive technologies such as screen readers can force users to search in a way that is not necessarily reflected in the design of the web page. Comments from users will also be included to illustrate relevant points.

## 2 Non-visual Access to the Digital Library (NoVA)

The information seeking behaviour of visually impaired people was explored in the Non-visual Access to the Digital Library (NoVA) project, undertaken by the Centre for Research in Library and Information Management (CERLIM). The aim of the study was to develop further understanding of user behaviour, with particular reference to people who needed to use assistive technology in order to 'read' or interact with web sites.

### 2.1 Methods

Methods adopted for the study were a combination of observation, talk aloud protocol and interviews. A sample of twenty sighted and twenty visually impaired users undertook the same four information seeking tasks using four web-based resources. For the purpose of the study, 'sighted' users were grouped according to their ability to read a standard (14" or 15") sized computer screen and "visually impaired" were users who needed to use assistive technology or needed to be very close to a standard sized screen in order to read or interpret it.

Four information-seeking tasks were set using four web-based resources: a Search Engine, a library OPAC, an Online shopping site and a Directory of Internet resources. Although each of the chosen resources was accessible (to greater and lesser degrees) they had all been designed in a way that made it easier to search in a non-linear manner. Therefore, comparative analysis could take place between those navigating in a visual way and those navigating using assistive technologies - in particular, screen readers.

As well as observing and logging the information retrieval process, pre and post-task questions were asked in order to gather data of a more qualitative nature. This provided data logs of what the users had done, as well as making it possible to ascertain (to some degree) why they had done it and how they felt about it.

## 2.2 NoVA Project Findings

The NoVA project findings concurred with other usability studies (3) revealing that, unsurprisingly, people who are sighted find searching the web much easier and generally quicker than visually impaired people. On average, it took the visually impaired sample in the NoVA study ten minutes longer to complete the Search Engine task, nine minutes longer to complete the OPAC task, two minutes longer to complete the Directory task and three minutes longer to complete the Online shopping task. Furthermore, the study showed that the users who were visually impaired but possessed enough sight to be able to see part of the screen (either up close or using magnification), found searching the web easier than those whose sight was severely impaired (i.e. those who were either totally blind or had very limited sight) and used screen reading or Braille technology.

The NoVA study showed that not only did the visually impaired users have to spend much more time navigating around a page, but also had to use a greater variety of keystrokes to do so. Step-by-step logging of keystrokes revealed that the sighted sample used the same six keystrokes (or mouse clicks) during each task; these were: clicking on, clicking in, typing in text, clicking back, scrolling up and scrolling down. The visually impaired sample tended to use around sixteen different keystrokes during each task. These included those mentioned above, but also included tabbing up and down pages, using the cursor keys and page up/page down keys, as well as using specific keystrokes relating to the assistive technology they were using (for example, function keys). This meant that the visually impaired sample had to spend more time navigating around the page and also had to remember a greater number of keystrokes. Observations showed that well-placed navigational links had an impact on the success and time spent navigating around a page, therefore in order to provide a better understanding of how different users will have different navigational experiences, it would be useful for designers to test the usability of their pages by navigating using a variety of mouse clicks, tab keys and function keys.

Both samples needed to move from page to page in order to complete the tasks. Although overall the visually impaired sample took more time doing this, the greatest difference between the two samples was when navigating around a page (to type in a search or to browse through a list of links). In total, the sighted sample moved from page to page 201 times and moved around pages a total of 181 times. In comparison, the visually impaired sample moved from page to page a total of 288 times and moved around the page a total of 345 times.

Both samples also needed to spend some time surveying (i.e. reading or listening to) the page before deciding how to proceed. The sighted sample were able to glance at a page, quickly scanning for relevant links, whereas the visually impaired sample had to spend more time deciphering what the page was about - particularly if they had to listen to the information being read out to them line by line. Comments about this included:

*"... you've got a lot of things to get through before you get to the subject matter. I don't like all this http this and http that...." (visually impaired user).*

Although some users were able to listen to screen readers at high speed, others had to spend more time and often had to go back and listen for a second or third time to make sure they had not missed a vital piece of information. The Search Engine page for example had an appropriate link to find the required information, but it was at the bottom of a page with nearly 200 links. Comments about this included:

*"It is a very busy site, there is a load of [rubbish] on it – you know, it's full of adverts really" (visually impaired user).*
*"A lot of it means nothing to me" (visually impaired user).*

Observations and comments showed that the more complex the page, the more time it took the visually impaired sample to find the information they wanted, even if they were looking for something quite trivial, like a weather forecast:

*"A lot of action for something very simple!"(visually impaired user).*

Short cut keys aided navigation when surveying the hypertext links; using the screen reader's 'Links List' could considerably speed up the process, but only if the links were given meaningful titles. For example, searching for a weather forecast was much easier if the relevant link was labelled 'weather forecast' rather than 'click here for the weather forecast' as the user could sort links alphabetically and search for 'W' within the list.

The Search Engine was clearly frustrating to navigate through, and although a search option was provided some users preferred to browse even if it took them a long time:

*"I know I can find things by tabbing through (visually impaired user)".*

Observations of users navigating a site with well-placed navigational links revealed that the visually impaired users were sometimes able to search more efficiently than the sighted sample. This seemed to be because the sighted users became sidetracked by visual distractions. The Directory page, for example, provided clear navigational links along the top (a Search option, an A-Z list etc) which were immediately read out by screen readers:

*"Fairly easy to navigate... brought up some results fairly quickly once it was clear what to do..." (visually impaired user).*

Those using audio or Braille were not aware of visual distractions, such as a group of categories placed prominently in the centre of the page, which lead the sighted users on a less direct route to the information required for the task:

*"Not very easy when you are looking for an area and you are not sure what it comes under" (sighted user).*

This illustrates the need for designers to consider how quickly important information can be reached. Provision of good navigational links is a well-established recommendation, but if these are in placed within a busy layout - even if it is visually pleasing - the user may be distracted and taken down a less direct route to the information.

## 3 Conclusions

Although awareness of web accessibility is increasing, the findings of the NoVA study show that visually impaired users are still faced with usability problems when trying to navigate around web sites. This main problem appears to be that most web sites are not designed to be navigated in a linear way, instead offering a variety of different options within a page. Careful consideration must therefore be given to the layout and navigation of a site and to the different assistive technologies used. The critical issue tends to be the complexity of pages and the logical relationship between areas on the page. Designers must consider the steps needed to navigate within pages since this is the most crucial determinant of accessibility.

Success in navigation can also depend on experience with assistive technology - therefore a greater emphasis needs to be placed on training in the use of assistive technologies - both by users and trainers. To aid the development of user-friendly interfaces and help to produce a culture of 'design for all', designers need to be much more aware of how layout and content affects accessibility, and of the need to incorporate the navigational practices of users into their designs.

## 4 Recommendations

The following recommendations are based on the findings of the NoVA study's observations of navigation and information seeking practice.

### 4.1 Accessibility and Usability Guidance

Observations revealed that accessibility recommendations should include an explanation of why a particular feature should be applied so that designers will have a better understanding of the potential barriers imposed by poor design. A better understand is also needed of how layout can affect navigation - for example how a screen reader navigates through a page of links; and how consistent layout of pages can reduce the cognitive load placed on people. Again, usability recommendations should include explanations and examples of how good layout can considerably enhance usability.

### 4.2 Access to Technology

The NoVA study revealed that users who had access to the most up-to-date software were able to have greater control in the way they navigated through web pages. However, it was apparent that not everyone had access to the most recent versions. For some, this was a decision based on cost, and for others, an older, more familiar version was their preference. Web site developers and designers cannot assume everyone has access to the most up-to-date technology and need to take steps to ensure their site can be accessed using older versions, or at the very least inform visitors to their site that a particular version will perform better than another.

### 4.3 Assistive Technologies

The study revealed that assistive technologies behave in different ways, presenting their own set of problems and solutions regarding web navigation. Users who had received some training were better able to navigate through web pages using the short cuts and command keys provided. However, not all users were aware of the features offered, and those that were aware of them were at times unsure of how to operate them to their full potential. Appropriate assistive technology training is therefore essential for both the user and for anyone who is responsible for providing access to computers with assistive technology.

### 4.4 Universal Design

The study revealed similarities between the two samples. For example, a general dislike of 'cluttered' or 'busy' screens was expressed by both samples. Virtually all said they preferred a simple layout which took them to the information they required in the quickest and most efficient way. This confirms the need for universal design rather than separate systems.

### 4.5 Non-web Alternatives

The NoVA post-task questions revealed that in certain cases users would use non-web alternatives as their preferred choice of resource. Users mentioned printed resources, asking at the local library, visiting a shop, or just turning on the radio (for a weather forecast). This suggests the web will have to be made much more user-friendly to attract more visually impaired people to use it - for many it will still present too many barriers to be an attractive option:

*"At present it is a chore, a struggle and a bore to use the Internet" (visually impaired user).*

This paper has focussed on observations of the user-testing phase undertaken for the NoVA study, with particular reference to linear searching in non-linear web environments. For a more in-depth account of all the findings please visit the project website at: where the final report can be downloaded in Word, HTML or PDF formats: http://www.cerlim.ac.uk/projects/nova/index.php

## References

1. Craven, J. and Brophy, P. Non-visual access to the digital library: the use of digital library interfaces by blind and visually impaired people. Library and Information Commission Research Report 145, Manchester: Centre for Research in Library and Information Management. (2003)
2. Wide Web Consortium Web Content Accessibility Guidelines 1.0. <http://www.w3.org/TR/WCAG10/> (accessed April 2004) (1999).
3. Coyne, K. and Nielsen, J. Beyond ALT text: making the web easy to use for users with disabilities. Fremont, CA: Nielsen Norman Group. (2001).
4. Kim, K.S. Information seeking on the Web: effects of user and task variables. Library and Information Science Research. 23, (2001). pp. 233-255.

# Text Comprehension by Blind People Using Speech Synthesis Systems

Luis González García

Spanish National Organisation of the Blind (ONCE), Psychologist
Gran Vía, 16 – 4th floor, 36203 Vigo, Pontevedra, Spain
lugg@once.es

**Abstract.** This study found that, unlike what happens with reading speed, Braille readers and ink print readers present similar levels of text comprehension. An evolutionary pattern is noted by which reading comprehension evolves slowly in the early years of education, but takes off with Baccalaureate grade, whether the access to the information be by Braille or by a text presented using speech synthesis systems.

## 1 Introduction

Most of the population accesses to information contained in printed texts by means of sight (visual sensory channel). However, the blind people must access to this information using the Braille system (tactile sensory channel), or by using natural voice recordings or speech synthesis systems (auditory sensory channel).

However, as pointed out by Danks and End [1], neither reading nor listening, to which it would be necessary to add the active touching involved in Braille reading, are homogenous processes that work in the same way in all the situation. Therefore, even if the three processes (visual, auditory and tactile) can serve to give us access to information, each one works in a different way, and therefore the capacity to comprehend the information might depend on the channel through which it reaches us.

The reading of texts written in Braille, and the listening to texts recorded by a reader or emitted by a speech synthesis system, and their comprehension, suggest the performance of a complex series of cognitive operations. These operations have many elements in common with reading ink printed texts, but they also necessarily have differences, as the psychological processes that regulate the cognitive operation do not follow a single pattern: different needs and resources cause different neuropsychological processes.

Concerning Braille reading, the origin of the differences between this and print reading lie largely in the sensory system by which the information is collected. Therefore, Lamden [2] affirms that Braille reading is a complex task, which involves intersensory perception and multimodal neurological processing, in addition to tasks of linguistic decoding and comprehension skills.

In this respect, the classical studies by Nolan and Kederis [3] said that reading in Braille came through a collection of sequential information, letter by letter, which supposes a highly specific situation, very different from that given in print reading,

K. Miesenberger et al. (Eds.): ICCHP 2004, LNCS 3118, pp. 538–544, 2004.

where each visual experience simultaneously gathers configurations made up of groups of several letters (the number of which depends on the ability of the reader). Therefore, as Pring and Painter [4] state, people who read Braille must place more stress on processing aimed at decoding the tactile stimuli than on comprehend the texts.

This sequential access to the words of a sentence written in Braille means that the information must be stored in the memory until a sufficient amount is attained to allow the identification of each complete word. The time for identifying a word therefore includes the time needed to perceive each of the letters that make it up plus the time needed to integrate this perception with the information previously stored in the subject's memory. This double processing would explain the low reading speed rates of Braille readers, which Knowlton and Wetzel [5] and Legge, Madison and Mansfield [6], amongst others, place at between 100 and 150 words per minute (wpm) on average in adults, whereas the mean word reading speed for sighted adults is estimated by Foulke [7] at between 200 and 300 wpm.

Despite these differences, the studies recompiled by Hollins [8] would support the thesis that Braille presents profound similarities with other forms of reading in terms of cognitive strategies.

The majority of investigations on Braille have focused on the particularities of the system itself, on its decoding process and on the reading speed rates, with very few, recent ones referring to comprehension. Furthermore, other way of access to information such as those mentioned (recording made by readers and speech synthesis) have not been, as yet, much the object of research. Therefore, in this study we will first analyse the text comprehension performance of Braille readers in comparison with those who can see. Secondly, we will see their output when Braille is replaced with hearing a text recorded using speech synthesis and their respective evolutionary patterns.

## 2 Method

### 2.1 Participants

The study was taken part in by a total of 223 subjects with ages between 10 and 77. Of them, 116 were blind people or had severe visual impairments, and used Braille as reading and writing system, and 107 sighted. Although not all of them were blind, we will use that term hereafter in reference to all the subjects who were blind or had severe visual impairments and took part in the study, as those who are not blind in the strict sense only perceive light. All the subjects had ages in accordance with their educational level except for university graduates, with ages between 28 and 77. All the participants were native Spanish speakers. None had additional disabilities Their distribution by sex and academic level appears in Table 1.

### 2.2 Materials

All the subjects received the reading comprehension test that formed part of the "Batería de Evaluación de los Procesos Lectores en Alumnos del Tercer Ciclo de Educaci6n Primaria y Educaci6n Secundaria Obligatoria [Assessment Battery of

**Table 1.** Sample distribution by sex and academic level

| | | | Blind | Sighted | Total |
|---|---|---|---|---|---|
| Sex | Man | | 62 | 41 | 103 |
| | Woman | | 54 | 66 | 120 |
| Academic level | 3rd cycle Primary Education (PE) | (10-12 years) | 16 | 24 | 40 |
| | 1st cycle Compulsory Secondary Education (CSE) | (12-14 years) | 22 | 25 | 47 |
| | 2nd cycle Compulsory Secondary Education (CSE) | (14-16 years) | 19 | 27 | 46 |
| | Baccalaureate | (16-18 years) | 15 | 31 | 46 |
| | University Degree | (> 18 years) | 44 | --- | 44 |
| Total | | | 116 | 107 | 223 |

Reading Processes in Third Cycle Primary Education and Compulsory Secondary Education Students] – PROLEC-SE" of Ramos and Cuetos [9]. This is a formal test, and is made up of two expository texts. The subjects read each complete text and then, without the text in front of them, they are asked 10 questions on it, half literal and half inferential, in order to determine their comprehension. Each correct reply scores one point.

Blind subjects were given this test right transcripted to Braille, whereas those sighted were given it in its original format.

In addition to PROLEC-SE, a new battery of two texts was used, drawn up especially for this study. These new texts were presented to the subjects using a speech synthesis system, capturing a text with the Job Access With Speech (JAWS) for Windows screen reader. Both the texts and the questions of this new battery were similar to the original PROLEC-SE. The homogeneity of the original and new texts was determined, on the one hand, by analysing their readability statistics, and also by submitting them to the judgement of two psycholinguists.

# 3 Procedure

Before applying the texts comprehension tests, the reading speed of all the subjects was measured in order to control this variable. As a result of the measurement, 7 blind subjects, with a reading speed of 1,2 standard deviations or more below the mean, were eliminated from the study, as it was understood that their Braille decoding process was so slow that it compromised their text comprehension. No sighted subjects had to be rejected for this reason. The final sample is shown in Table 1.

In the first place, all the subjects were given the two text of the PROLEC-SE reading comprehension test. Once the subjects had read each text, the examiner asked questions orally on its content and took textual note of the answers the subject also offered orally. The application was carried out collectively with subjects with sight in terms of academic levels and following the specifications of the technical sheet and the PROLEC-SE rules of application.

In a second phase, involving only blind subjects, they were given the new battery of texts prepared for this study.

The tests were then corrected, and the number of correct answers for each pair of texts was recorded (maximum score: 20 points for pair).

## 4 Results

In the first place, the outputs in terms of speed and reading comprehension of the blind and sighted subjects were determined according to their academic levels. Blind people university degrees were excluded from this phase of the investigation, as the PROLEC-SE is designed for application in subjects in the last cycle of Primary Education and in Compulsory Secondary Education; therefore the sample was reduced to 179 subjects, aged 10 to 18.

Their performance in reading speed and comprehension are reflected in Tables 2 and 3, respectively.

**Table 2.** Reading speed performance (wpm) according to academic level

| Group | Academic level | N | Mean | SD |
|---|---|---|---|---|
| Blind | 3rd cycle PE | 16 | 40,44 | 17,259 |
| | 1st cycle CSE | 22 | 60,32 | 27,861 |
| | 2nd cycle CSE | 19 | 71,47 | 20,525 |
| | Baccalaureate | 15 | 69,87 | 24,853 |
| Sighted | 3rd cycle PE | 24 | 97,42 | 26,195 |
| | 1st cycle CSE | 25 | 145,32 | 29,243 |
| | 2nd cycle CSE | 27 | 166,59 | 28,081 |
| | Baccalaureate | 31 | 199,58 | 40,657 |

An analysis of variance (ANOVA) was performed with these results, taking as factors the groups of subjects (blind and sighted) and their academic levels (3rd cycle Primary Education, 1st cycle Compulsory Secondary Education, 2nd cycle Compulsory Secondary Education and Baccalaureate).

**Table 3.** Reading comprehension performance (correct answers) according to academic level

| Group | Academic level | N | Mean | SD |
|---|---|---|---|---|
| Blind | 3rd cycle PE | 16 | 7,88 | 4,303 |
| | 1st cycle CSE | 22 | 9,55 | 5,378 |
| | 2nd cycle CSE | 19 | 10,32 | 4,204 |
| | Baccalaureate | 15 | 14,80 | 2,704 |
| Sighted | 3rd cycle PE | 24 | 6,67 | 3,761 |
| | 1st cycle CSE | 25 | 11,16 | 3,705 |
| | 2nd cycle CSE | 27 | 12,81 | 3,659 |
| | Baccalaureate | 31 | 14,71 | 2,673 |

In the first place, the reading speed was taken as a dependent variable. This analysis revealed that the differences in reading speed between the blind and sighted subjects were significant ($F (7.171) = 4.521, p < .05$). Later analyses showed that these differences are significant whether the blind subjects are compared with the sighted subjects ($F (1.171) = 424.239, p < .05$) or between all the educational levels analysed ($F (3.171) = 37.372, p < .05$).

Then, reading comprehension was taken as a dependent variable. This analysis also revealed the existence of significant differences ($F (7.171) = 2.525, p < .05$). Later analyses showed that these differences are significant between the different academic levels ($F (3.171) = 25.709, p < .05$), but not if what is compared are the results of the blind with the sighted subjects ($F (1.171) = 1.420, p = .235$).

Later, and only with the group of Braille readers, including university degree subjects (N = 116), their reading comprehension performance was analysed in terms of their form of access to the texts (Braille or speech synthesis systems). In descriptive terms, the results were those appearing in table 4.

**Table 4.** Reading comprehension performance (correct answers) according to the way of access to information

| Academic level | | Braille | Speech synthesis |
|---|---|---|---|
| 3rd cycle Primary Education | Mean | 7,88 | ,00 |
| | SD | 4,303 | ,000 |
| 1st cycle CSE | Mean | 9,55 | 5,55 |
| | SD | 5,378 | 4,032 |
| 2nd cycle CSE | Mean | 10,32 | 6,68 |
| | SD | 4,204 | 2,868 |
| Baccalaureate | Mean | 14,80 | 12,00 |
| | SD | 2,704 | 3,928 |
| University Degree | Mean | 15,57 | 12,66 |
| | SD | 2,609 | 3,497 |

A new ANOVA was performed in order to evaluate the crossed effect of academic level and the way of access to the information. This analysis revealed the existence of significant differences ($F (2.110)= 482.045, p < .05$). A detailed analysis of between which levels and according to which form of text presentation such differences were significant shows us that, in the case of texts presented in Braille, there are no significant differences either between the lower courses (last cycle of Primary Education and the two cycles of Compulsory Secondary Education) or between the highest (Baccalaureate and University Degree), but that there are between both subgroups (the three lowest and the two highest ones).

In the case of texts presented with speech synthesis, significant differences were appreciated between each academic level, except among students of 1st and 2nd cycle of Compulsory Secondary Education and among students of Baccalaureate and on University Degree subjects. The results of these differences are reflected in Table 5.

**Table 5.** Mean differences in reading comprehension by academic level and access to the information channel

| Access to the information channel | (I) Academic level | (J) Academic level | Mean difference (I-J) | Sig. |
|---|---|---|---|---|
| Braille | 1st cycle CSE | 3rd cycle PE | 1,67 | ,667 |
| | 2nd cycle CSE | 3rd cycle PE | 2,44 | ,326 |
| | | 1st cycle CSE | ,77 | ,967 |
| | Baccalaureate | 3rd cycle PE | 6,92(*) | ,000 |
| | | 1st cycle CSE | 5,25(*) | ,001 |
| | | 2nd cycle CSE | 4,48(*) | ,008 |
| | University Degree | 3rd cycle PE | 7,69(*) | ,000 |
| | | 1st cycle CSE | 6,02(*) | ,000 |
| | | 2nd cycle CSE | 5,25(*) | ,000 |
| | | Baccalaureate | ,77 | ,961 |
| Speech synthesis | 1st cycle CSE | 3rd cycle PE | 5,55(*) | ,000 |
| | 2nd cycle CSE | 3rd cycle PE | 6,68(*) | ,000 |
| | | 1st cycle CSE | 1,14 | ,811 |
| | Baccalaureate | 3rd cycle PE | 12,00(*) | ,000 |
| | | 1st cycle CSE | 6,45(*) | ,000 |
| | | 2nd cycle CSE | 5,32(*) | ,000 |
| | University Degree | 3rd cycle PE | 12,66(*) | ,000 |
| | | 1st cycle CSE | 7,11(*) | ,000 |
| | | 2nd cycle CSE | 5,97(*) | ,000 |
| | | Baccalaureate | ,66 | ,964 |

* The mean difference is significant at the ,05 level.

## 5 Discussion

The finding that print readers have a reading speed significantly higher than Braille readers only supports what was already demonstrated by Bertelson, Mousty and d'Alimonte [10], Kilpatrick [11], Mousty and Bertelson [12], among others. As was also expected, the reading speed improves along with the academic level.

As regards text comprehension, it was also expected that there would be significant differences among the academic levels so higher academic level better reading comprehension scores, so we can state that there is a clear evolutionary pattern.

It must be said that, as González García [13] already pointed out, these differences are not significant if we compare the results of Braille readers and print readers, which also agrees with the conclusions of the investigations performed by Gompel and his team [14] referred to children with low vision in ink print reading tasks. Therefore we are able to say that text comprehension levels are independent of the form of access to the information, be it Braille for blind subjects or ink print for sighted subjects.

As for only the blind subjects, it must be said that their texts comprehension is significantly better in Braille than using speech synthesis system. These differences between both ways of access to information decrease when the academic level increase.

Their comprehension levels increase significantly with their academic level. In the case of Braille reading, there is a clear evolutionary pattern by which levels of reading comprehension evolve fairly slowly in the early levels and take off in Baccalaureate. Something similar happens when the form of access to the information is by means of a speech synthesis system, apart from the case of last cycle of Primary Education pupils, who are not used to using such systems, and therefore have negligible comprehension.

The evolutionary leap taken at Baccalaureate is probably due to the fact that only when pupils begin to devote fewer resources to the decoding process can they devote them to text comprehension.

## References


1. Danks, J.H., End, L.J.: Processing Strategies for Reading and Listening. In: Horowitz, R., Samuels, S.J. (eds.): Comprehending Oral and Written Language. Academic Press, London (1987) (271-294)
2. Lamden, S.: Fluency in Braille Reading: A Neuropsychological Approach. [http://www.home.earthlink.net/~slamdem/t560.html]. (1999) [2001, June 20]
3. Nolan, C.Y., Kederis, J.C.: Perceptual Factors in Braille Word Recognition. American Foundation for the Blind, New York, NY (1969)
4. Pring, L., Painter, J.: Recollective Experience in Individuals with a Visual Impairment: The Role of Sensory and Conceptual Processing. The British Journal of Visual Impairment, 20(1) (2002) 24-32
5. Knowlton, M. Wetzel, R.: Braille Reading Rates as A Function of Reading Tasks. Journal of Visual Impairment & Blindness, 90 (1996) 227-235
6. Legge, G.E., Madison, C., Mansfield, J.S.: Measuring Braille Reading Speed with the MNREAD Test. Visual Impairment Research, 1(3) (1999) 131-145
7. Foulke, E.: Reading Braille. In: Schiff, W., Foulke, E. (eds.): Tactual Perception: A Source Book. Cambridge University Press, Cambridge (1982) 168-208
8. Hollins, M.: Vision Impairment and Cognition. In: Silverstone, B., Lang, M.A., Rosenthal, B.P., Faye, E.E, (eds.): The Lighthouse Handbook on Vision Impairment and Vision Rehabilitation. Vol. 1. Oxford University Press, New York, NY (2002) 339-358
9. Ramos, J.L., Cuetos, F.: Batería de Evaluación de los Procesos Lectores en Alumnos del Tercer Ciclo de Educación Primaria y Educación Secundaria Obligatoria [Assessment Battery of Reading Processes in Third Cycle Primary Education and Compulsory Secondary Education Students] – PROLEC-SE. TEA Ediciones, Madrid (1999)
10. Bertelson, P. Mousty, P., d'Alimonte, G. : A Study of Braille Reading, 2: Patterns of Hand Activity in One-Handed and Two-Handed Reading. Quarterly Journal of Experimental Psychology, 37A (1985), 235-256
11. Kilpatrick, J.F.: Perceptual Strategies and the Braille Reading Rate. Unpublished doctoral thesis. University of Louisville, Kentucky (1985)
12. Mousty, P., Bertelson, P.: A Study of Braille Reading, 1: Reading Speed as a Function of Hand Usage and Context. Quarterly Journal of Experimental Psychology, 37A (1985) 217-233
13. González García, L.: Comprensión Lectora en Lectura Braille [Reading Comprehension in Braille Reading] . In: Verdugo, M.A., Jordán de Urríes, F. de B. (eds.): Hacia una Nueva Concepción de la Discapacidad [Toward a New Conception of Disability]. Amarú Ediciones, Salamanca (1999) 593-605
14. Gompel, M., van Bon, W.H.J., Schreuder, R.: Reading by Children with Low Vision. Journal of Visual Impairment & Blindness, 98(2) (2004) 77-89

# Access to Information at Your Own Choice by the Aid of Digital Talking Books

Thomas Kjellberg Christensen

The Danish National Library for the Blind, Teglvaerksgade 37, 2100 Copenhagen
tkc@dbb.dk
www.dbb.dk

**Abstract.** In this paper I shall address the concept and fundamental ideas of the talking book in a digital perspective. There will be a presentation of a possible way to structure a digital production and distribution flow, and I shall discuss how this certain structure influences the end user's access to information. In this connection I shall demonstrate: 'Costumised end user product', 'Book search and generator maschine', and finally 'Server based interactive talking web sites'.

## 1 The Concept of the Digital Talking Book and the Daisy Philosophy

The Daisy consortium was founded in 1996 and has following vision and mission:

### 1.1 Vision

Daisy's vision is that all published information is available to people with print disabilities, at the same time and at no greater cost, in an accessible, feature-rich, navigable format.

### 1.2 Mission

The DAISY Consortium's mission is to develop the International Standard and implementation strategies for the production, exchange, and use of Digital Talking Books in both developed and developing countries, with special attention to integration with mainstream technology, to ensure access to information for people with print disabilities.

The Danish National Library for the Blind (DBB) is a full member of the Daisy Consortium, and produces digital talking books according the international standard: NISO Z39.86 e.g. Daisy 3.0. DBB has played an active role in the development of the Daisy standard.

K. Miesenberger et al. (Eds.): ICCHP 2004, LNCS 3118, pp. 545–551, 2004.

## 2 What Is a DTB?

A traditional talking book is an analog representation of a print publication. A Digital Talking Book (DTB) is a multimedia representation of a print publication. In both instances the rendering of the audio is in human voice.

DAISY DTBs meet talking book reader requirements by providing access to the talking book that has never before been possible with a human voice production of a print book. For instance the reader of the digital talking book can ad his or her own notes to the book in the same way as a seeing person can write small notes to himself in the printed book. In the digital talking book the notes are not added by pen or pencil but either in text format or as an oral comment.

There are six types of DAISY DTBs. Of the six, four of the types offer improved access and human or synthetic voice delivery through links between the digital audio sound files and the marked up text files and/or pictures graphic representations and other sorts of illustrations. It is these links that give the talking book reader access to the structure of the book; these links are the key to a DAISY DTB.

The six categories of DAISY types of DTB are:

1. Full audio with Title element only: This is a DTB without navigable structure. Only the title of the DTB is available as text - the actual content is presented as linear audio only. Direct access to points within the DTB is not possible.
2. Full audio with Navigation Center (NCC or NCX) only: This is a DTB with structure. The structure is two-dimensional, providing both sequential and hierarchical navigation. In many cases, the structure in this type of Daisy DTB resembles the table of contents of its print source. Some of these productions provide page navigation.
3. Full audio with Navigation Center and partial text: This is a DTB with structure as described above, as well as some additional text. The additional text components may occur where keyword searching and direct access to the text would be beneficial, e.g., index, glossary, etc. The audio and existing text components are synchronized.
4. Full audio and full text: This is a DTB with structure and complete text and audio. The audio and the full text are synchronized. This type of production may be used to generate braille.
5. Full text and some audio: This is a DTB with structure, complete text, and limited audio. This type of DTB could be used for a dictionary where only pronunciations are provided in audio form. As in the previous categories, the audio and text are linked.
6. Text and no audio: This is a DTB containing a Navigation Center and marked up/structured electronic text only. No audio is present. This file may be used for the production of braille.

DTBs produced according to the DAISY standard are in and of themselves independent of distribution medium, that is, the digital master file can be archived and may also be distributed on currently available media such as CDs or DVDs. More importantly, as technology advances and digital media distribution methods evolve, these same books can be distributed via the newly developed media or system.

There are currently three ways of listening to a DAISY DTB, either through a special DTB hardware player or through special software programmes on a computer or with an MP3 or a DVD player. In the two latter players you will not be able to use the full structure of the DTB, but you can listen to the DTB and have a very simple and moderate way of jumping forwards or backwards in the book. This may be jumping from paragraph to paragraph. In the process of the Daisy Consortiums' work with developing both the standard for DTBs and production tools for the digital talking book, developers of players has been involved from the very start. This means that to day there is a range of vendors on the market offering accessible players.

Of these various types of players on the market, some are very simple and functions very much like an ordinary old-fashioned cassette player and offers a limited possibility of moving around in the structure of the book. Other players are very sophisticated and make it possible for the user to move to a specific paragraph or page in the book.

## 3 An Overview of the Digital Production Flow at the Danish Library for the Blind (DBB)

Possible concepts and ideas as how best to establish a digital production and distribution environment.

During the last six years DBB has been deeply engaged in developing concepts and systems for production, storage and distribution of digital products. The vision behind these activities is that the end user should be able to choose any title in whichever format he or she wants to read it. It could be an e-book in various formats, it could be a DTB with audio content or the title could be in the Braille format. An essential thought behind the development of the digital flow has been cost efficiency. Also, it has been of major importance that upgrading into future formats can been done as smoothly as possible.

The production flow at DBB takes its offspring in a marked up XML source file. Therefore all material that is produced at DBB is first marked up according to text part of the Daisy standard. This material is either scanned, transformed from a publisher file or grab from direct from the Internet. After the markup process the files are stored in a XML-database. The end-user can then order the material in various formats. The transformation of the source file into the different output formats is done automatically without human interference.

The formats that is offered to the end user is the following: Braille grade 0, Braille grade 1, digital talking books with synthetic speech and for the time being six types of e-books. Digital talking books with human voice and Braille grade two is not part of the automatic production flow, but is produced outside the automatic flow. For both of these types of material a certain amount of human preparation is needed. The production of these two types of material runs simultaneously with the automatic on demand service of other formats of the material. The reason why Danish grade two Braille cannot be generated automatically is that the rules of contractions for Braille

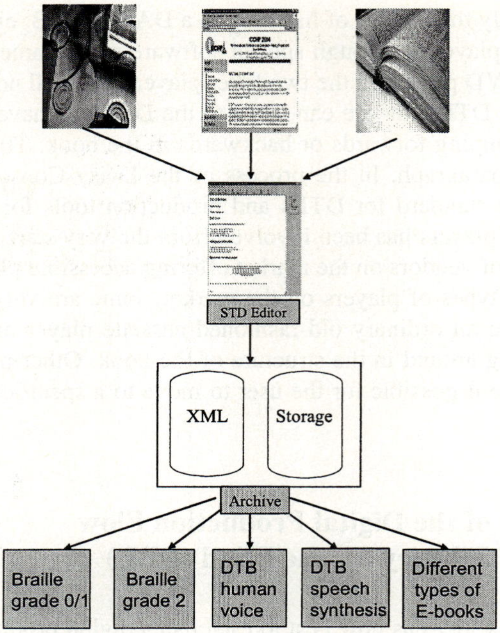


**Fig. 1.** A schematic overview of production flow

are not logical but based on semantic rules. Once the Braille book or the DTB with human speech has been mastered, they are entered into the digital archive and thereby they become part of the automatic end user production flow.

The material is stored on servers and is not actually transformed into a readable media until there is a specific demand for a specific book in a specific format. This means that if there is a need to do encryption or a need to place a watermark in the book this can be done specifically for the individual end user. Thus it is possible to have different forms of encryption or watermarking depending on which kind of material or end user group you serve. There may also be different claims from right holders for different services or different types of material.

## 4 Spin Off Effects and New Possibilities to Gain Access to Information by Digitisation

### 4.1 Customised End User Product

It is possible for the end user to establish a personal profile at his library. This profile describes the lay out and presentations in which the end user wants to receive a given type of material and/or a given type of title from his library. Below is shown an example of some of the choices the user will have when defining his or her personal profile. The user may for instance choose a certain font and a certain background and text color scheme. Furthermore the user can select one or more formats in which he

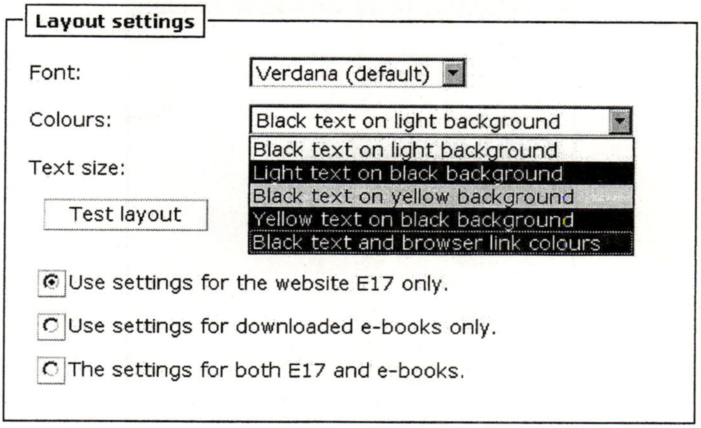


**Fig. 2.** Layout settings

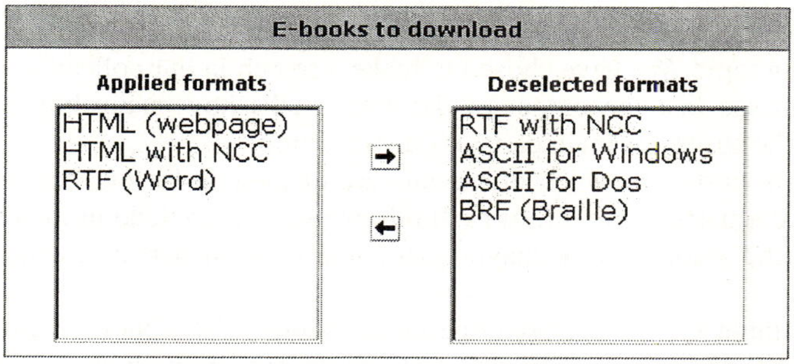


**Fig. 3.** E-books settings for download

prefers to receive his material. In the process of lending out a certain material everything is generated on the fly. This means that the end user can change his profile according to the kind of material he is requesting, thus he may choose to have magazines in one format and literature in another format. It does not cost extra to change among various profiles. The resources spent in generating the material are the same regardless of the chosen profile.

### 4.2 Book Search and Generator Machine

This service offers a scenario in which it will be possible for the end user to generate his/her own customised DTB. The user will be able to construct a compendium from the full collection of different titles. The compendium will be based on the occurrence of particular search words in these texts, and the end user can pick and choose which bits and pieces of texts he wants included in his compendium. And of course the end user will be able to choose his personal format for his compendium.

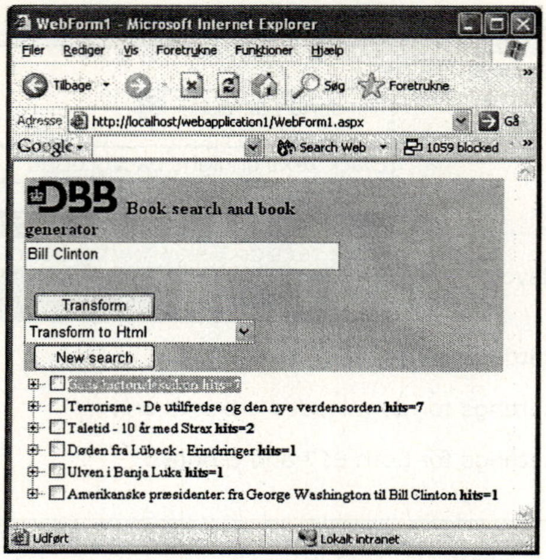


**Fig. 4.** Search for Bill Clinton

Below you will be able to see the various steps in such a search for information about a certain topic. We have chosen to make a search in our collection on Bill Clinton. You will see that the output of the search tells how many hits we got when searching in the structural main parts of our collection.

Next step is to decide which of the hits are of interest for our compendium, and which structural parts, if not all, of each title we want to include in the compendium. Do we want the whole title or maybe just some selected part as chapters or certain sub chapters.

In this example we have chosen one main chapter of the book: 'Terrorisme', and the whole book of the title: 'Taletid' and finally one main chapter from the book: 'Døden fra Lübeck'. Once you have made your selection you press the bottom 'transform' and a request is sent to the XML database, and the various parts of your compendium are selected and transformed into a new compendium and the lay out of the compendium will be done according to your personal profile.

If the end user wants his compendium as a DTB it is also possible to generate this on the fly with aid of synthetic speech for possible parts of the book which has not be mastered with human voice.

### 4.3 Server Based Interactive Talking Web Sites

This service provides the possibility for print handicapped persons to navigate on DBB's web site interactively. The end user can have the web site read aloud without having to invest in his own synthetic speech and screen reader, furthermore the system generates a synthetic speech representation of any generated web page on the fly. This makes it possible for the end user to select and follow a given link on the web page, as it appears in the oral representation.

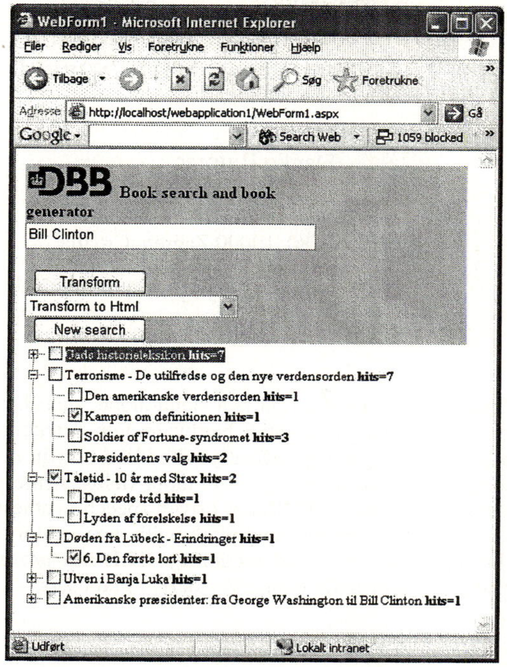


**Fig. 5.** The search result in the collection on Bill Clinton

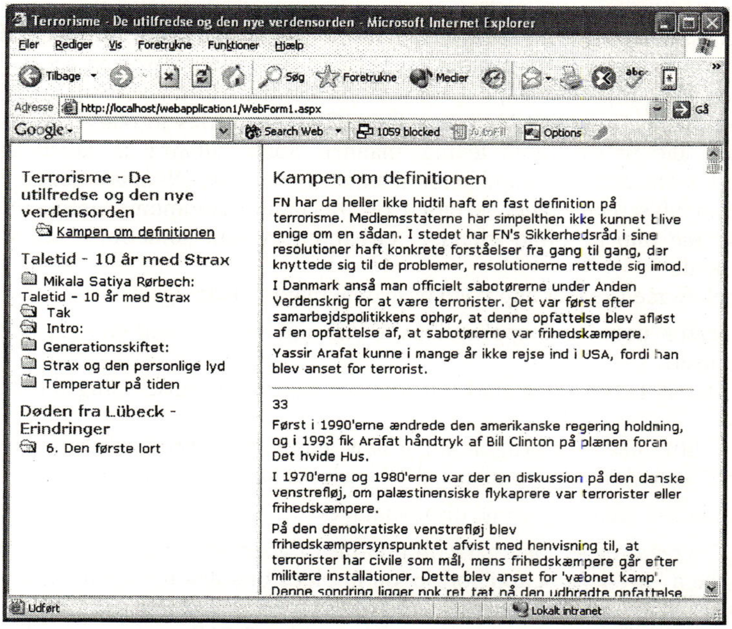


**Fig. 6.** The New DTB is generated

# Talking Linux for the Blind – A CD Distribution with Speech

Danko Butorac

Croatian Association of the Blind,
Draskoviceva 80, 10000 Zagreb, Croatia
danko@ipsis.hr
www.savez-slijepih.hr
www.ipsis.hr/gls

**Abstract.** Talking Linux for the Blind is a stand-alone, speech enabled Linux CD-distribution. It contains all essential hardware auto detection mechanisms and set of applications designed specifically with blind user in mind. TLB gets user input through single keystrokes or text input fields, while presenting information through high quality MBROLA driven speech synthesis. Upon boot users can browse through menus and work with text editor, e-mail, web-browser, file browser, calculator and dictionary. TLB has proven to be most useful for novice users, especially poor and elderly blind users.

## 1 Introduction

Screen access software with speech and Braille is a primary tool for most blind computer users in the world. Most blind users have some kind of screen access software installed on their PCs that helps them read the contents of the screen. Such software sits on top of the Graphical User Interface (GUI), and tries to convey the graphical information and present it in textual manner. Such software is called the screen reader, and is one complex application interacting with the OS and other applications. The concept of screen reader is based on translating commonly used software for sighted people into a "blind-friendly" environment. But sometimes not so "blind-friendly" at all.

Although Screen-reader approach has some major advantages:

1. Blind person uses same applications as the sighted user and can get help from a sighted user.
2. Blind user is better integrated into the community because using the same software.
3. There is little need for programming new applications because users can buy»off the shelf" software that would usually be accessible to some degree.

Screen readers have also some disadvantages:

1. No GUI screen reader can make all options of a software accessible. So there will always be a "mystery button" or option in piece of software when used by a blind person.
2. It's hard for blind user to learn some concepts of GUI such as two-dimensional spatial presentation, popup menus, visual effects, etc.

K. Miesenberger et al. (Eds.): ICCHP 2004, LNCS 3118, pp. 552–559, 2004.

3. Most programs in GUI use redundant information and offer “all-at-once”. All options are available at the same time, which we found to be confusing for a novice user.

So, if a new software for blind persons is to be designed it can go either toward a screen-reader based design or toward (let’s call it) a design-for-the-blind. The major difference between the two approaches is best described by Karl Dahlke [1], author of Jupiter Speech System, when he says: “Think of the application as a conversation between the program and the user. When the user ignores 95% of what the program "says" and selects the relevant 5% by moving his eyes, that conversation must change, in fundamental ways, to be blind friendly. I think most screen programs implement this type of mega-output conversation. That is in fact the screen paradigm. On this basis, I believe most screen programs must be redesigned from scratch to become blind friendly.”

# 2 TLB Design

## 2.1 Design Goals

There were two major ideas behind Talking Linux for the Blind (TLB) interface design. First and most important, we wanted to make a free software that can be used by a novice blind user. Second idea was to make software for blind user and blind user only. We didn’t want to make another screen reader and cope with all mega-output issues it would raise.

Since TLB development was done in Croatia, we also wanted it to speak Croatian in a clean and easy-to-understand synthesized voice. It was also a good idea, and later it also became our goal, to make TLB a multilingual platform for languages other than Croatian. TLB now runs both in English and Croatian mode with single keystroke switching between the two.

To obtain first goal (free software), the logical way was to choose a free operating system such as Linux. And indeed, Linux provided us with some good starting points such as already available speech synthesizers and programming tools. [2] Another great thing about Linux is that in Linux we could easily make TLB as open-source product. This enables any programmer in the world to enhance TLB or customize it for his/her needs. It also enabled us to use some other open-source products such as Lynx (a web browser) or Antiword DOC to TXT converter as part of TLB.

## 2.2 Accessible Linux Software

At the time we started working on TLB (Aug, 2001.), there were also some active Linux accessibility projects. The major ones at that time were EmacsSpeak and BRLTTY projects.

*EmacsSpeak* is an accessible version of a popular editor for Linux called Emacs. But since Emacs is more than an editor, EmacsSpeak offers many useful tools to a blind user. Through EmacsSpeak user can browse web pages, edit programming code, text or web, use spreadsheets and e-mail. The only problem with EmacsSpeak is that it’s rather confusing and hard to learn by a novice user. In words of Mark J. P. Senk [3], EmacsSpeak user: “... it seems that EmacsSpeak users are just gurus and they are way beyond all of this. And they paid all their dues, and they know everything. But for the beginner user, it seems really difficult and arcane."

So, regardless of many options EmacsSpeak gives us, it was not a good option for TLB because TLB needs to be a novice-friendly system. Another trouble with Emacs is that it's written in LISP programming language, and it's hard to find programmers familiar with LISP.

*BRLTTY* is a background process (daemon) which provides access to the Linux console (when in text mode) for a blind person using a refreshable Braille display. It drives the Braille display, and provides complete screen review functionality. Some speech capability has also been incorporated. [4]

For TLB design, BRLTTY was a very interesting concept to consider. It resembles a great communication program between a computer and human. Many will remember something similar from a John Badham movie "War Games" (1983.). In War Games a computer called Joshua "talks" to its users[1]. But when we look beyond this great picture this movie sets, we see that BRLTTY user needs to interact with shell (Linux command line). To do that, BRLTTY uses screen-reader called Screader (one of the first Linux access software), or another screen-reader. Since shell is not something a novice user can easily cope with, we gave up BRLTTY in the beginning.

There are also other Linux projects now active that enable blind user to interact with this great operating system. Some of them are shell screen access software like *Yasr* - a console screen reader, *Speakup* - screen review package for Linux, *Jupiter* and *Screader* - shell access programs. *Gnopernicus* - Gnome screen access software works in X11 Graphical environment for Linux, and provides speech and magnification for applications written for Gnome desktop. Gnopernicus is also a very interesting and advanced project, but goes separate ways from TLB. It uses GUI, and TLB is not a project that aims at GUI users.

More interesting for TLB design, are a stand-alone Linux distribution for the blind. We'll look at two such projects:

- *BRLSPEAK* is a mini Linux distribution (the size of the downloadable ISO image is only 36MB) with two objectives. Firstly, it has been designed in such a way that blind persons can install it without any sighted assistance, and secondly, they should be able to pre-configure and compile the Braille drivers all by themselves. These drivers will be immediately operational upon boot. All stated goals were achieved in November 2001 and BRLSPEAK version 7.0 was released later that month. It was based on Slackware's ZipSlack (hence the inflated version number), which can be installed in a directory on a DOS file system (no hard disk partitioning is necessary) or a ZIP drive.
- *ORALUX* (www.oralux.org) is a recently launched project, first announced in July 2003. Oralux runs directly from a bootable CD and no installation is required. It is based on Knoppix Linux CD distribution, with the usual excellent hardware autodetection and immediate availability after boot. The size of the downloadable ISO image is under 400MB. Upon boot, and after the obligatory hardware detection

[1] In "War Games", Matthew Broderick stars as a teenage computer genius, who hacks into the Pentagon's defence system and sets World War III into motion. When he hacked into the system, Pentagon's computer Joshua greets him in a clear synthesized voice "Greetings professor Folcan". He interacts with the system by typing sentences and computer answers.

and configuration, the user is greeted with the sound of a cockerel, the distribution's official logo, which gives the user an opportunity to adjust speaker volume. The next step is the language selection with English as the only supported language in version 0.04 (courtesy of the Flite synthesis engine), although future releases might include Spanish and German.

One might notice that both BRLSPEAK and ORALUX have been released after we started working on TLB (Aug, 2001.). So, we couldn't use ideas and tools implemented in these two systems. We had to think of our own ideas, and develop our own applications.

### 2.3 Open-Source Technologies Used in TLB

Most of TLB applications are programmed in Python interpreter language. Python was a good choice even though few programmers in Croatia work in Python. This is because programmers who worked in C or C++ could learn Python within first two weeks, and those who worked with JAVA would need less then a month to start contributing to TLB applications. All Python tools and compilers are open-source software.

Some applications are done in C programming language, such as our adaptation of Lynx web browser. Lynx is one of the best text-based web browsers for Linux with large user community. But we needed to change it so that it parses a web site, and gives us information about interactive elements such as links, buttons, forms, etc. TLB web-browser is dependant on Lynx parsing capabilities, but still lets user follow or skip links and fill forms.

For menus and lists we used XML. Python has an integrated XML parser, so it was a pretty easy task to let users navigate menus, and later let people localize them. All TLB menus are easy to navigate. A four-button navigation design (left, right, enter, escape) is implemented throughout the TLB system.

Other open-source products have been used for specific tasks. Fetchmail and sendmail programs have been used to download and send e-mail, mpg123 is used for playing audio, and Antiword is used to convert MSWord documents into text. For hardware detection and support we used: ALSA for sound, CUPS for printers, DHCPD for network, and WvDial for modem support.

## 3 TLB – A Bootable CD

TLB distribution is a bootable CD-ROM that detects all hardware it needs and installs itself on a first available FAT or EXT2 partition. Only requirement for a host PC is a soundcard and a bootable CD-ROM drive. Installation is done by the TLB to speed up future boots and hence the first boot and installation lasts about 2-3 minutes.

TLB makes a folder "GLS" on the computer hard drive where it stores all system and user files. "GLS" stands for "Govorni Linux za Slijepe", Croatian for "Talking Linux for the Blind".

When system is booted next time, TLB CD automatically detects its previous installation on the hard drive, and runs from the hard drive. This speeds up all next boot processes for 1-2 minutes.

TLB does require a CD-ROM inserted into a CD-ROM drive to boot. After boot, a CD can be replaced with a MP3 CD, or CD with user text files, etc. Booting from a CD sometimes requires changing boot sequence in computers BIOS. This may cause a problem for blind user since there is no speech or Braille in BIOS software. Thus we made a TLB boot diskette, which runs a CD-ROM driver, and boots TLB from the CD-ROM without need to change BIOS settings. This is a great option for blind users who wish to run TLB in a public library, university or on any other PC.

During each boot process, TLB searches for a network card and a soundcard. Without a supported soundcard, TLB won't fully boot, and will notify user with series of beeps that it didn't find a soundcard.

## 4 TLB Sounds, Speech and Language

After TLB is successfully started, user will hear a short melody and TLB starts speaking. First words user hears are "Application menu, File browser". This is spoken in Croatian language, but to switch to English and back user can press Ctrl-F4. TLB automatically switches both menus and speech synthesis to another language. Switching languages works only in the main menu (Application menu).

If user wants to switch to another language during the editor, web or e-mail session, it may be done by depressing Ctrl-F3. TLB will switch to another speech synthesizer. This is useful for Croatian users who, for instance, received an e-mail in English, or found an English website.

Croatian speech is generated by MBROLA speech synthesizer created by Belgian Faculte Polytechnique de Mons (`http://tcts.fpms.ac.be/synthesis/`). It's a high quality speech diphone waveform synthesizer (supported by speech synthesizer Festival). MBROLA is freely available, with number of diphone database. Based on Mbrola suggestion, two authors Juraj Bakran and Nikolaj Lazic, at the University of Zagreb, together with the students of phonetics at the Department of phonetics at philosophical Faculty, University of Zagreb, have prepared Croatian diphone database, which everyone can download for non-profit purposes. [5]

For English language we use FLITE speech synthesizer binary that outputs a reasonable quality English speech. FLITE, (festival-lite) is a small, fast run-time synthesis engine developed at Carnegie Mellon University, USA. [6]

Both FLITE and MBROLA are controlled by the TLB. Users can control pitch, speed, volume and level of punctuation for each synthesizer. TLB remembers these settings for each application even if user switches to another language. User settings can also be restored to default at any time in case the speech becomes hard to understand. There is also a "spell mode" in TLB where all text is being spelled out letter-by-letter.

Open-source design of TLB enables a simple localization process for any language with an existing Linux speech synthesizer. All translations can be done by editing simple XML files that define menus and messages.

When entering and exiting application(s), user hears a noticeable sound pattern. All TLB sounds (other than speech) are MP3 samples that are played back by mpg123, an open-source Linux MP3 player. We also use mpg123 to play MP3 files from file browser.

## 5 TLB Applications

Design of TLB applications is menu based – similar to menus of a mobile phone. Through main menu users can access a text-editor, web-browser, calculator, e-mail client, file browser, mp3-player and system control features such as Internet connection control, language settings, printer settings, dictionaries and system shut-down feature. We made a web-demonstration of TLB navigation system in Croatian and English, available at `http://www.ipsis.hr/gls/demo/index.html` [7].

Each application has it's own operation menu accessible through a single keystroke. It also has a help system with manual for each application. TLB offers a keyboard description mode in which every key echoes its function.

- *TLB text editor* is really a simple tool that lets user edit and navigate texts. Users can navigate through text reading character-by-character, word-by-word, line-by-line, or use read-on function. Read-on will read all text after the current cursor position. Through editor's menu, users can open new document, save current document, print current document, or open an existing document. Editor is used by all TLB applications. When user wants to read help file for any application, after depressing F1 editor will open reading a desired help file. Copy-paste, text formatting and other features of modern editors are yet to be implemented.
- *TLB web browser* is actually an adaptation of Lynx web browser for Linux with added speech capabilities. It would read any loaded web page echoing links, buttons and other interactive element. User can stop reading at any time or follow a link by pressing Enter. Navigation is similar as in TLB text editor (word-by-word, letter-by-letter, etc.). User can load a web page from any URL, or local folder. It's also possible to bookmark a page, and use bookmarks list.
- *TLB Calculator* is really a simple tool with basic calculation options such as addition, subtraction, multiplication and division functions. It also has a memory function.
- *E-mail client* lets user browse mail messages in inbox folder, echoing whether current message is read or unread. User can write and send e-mail messages, using a small version of TLB editor within the e-mail program. Attachments, groups, address books, filters and other features common in other e-mail clients are yet to be implemented.
- A *TLB* user can use *file browser* to browse files or run applications. Browser recognizes some file types such as texts, word documents, MP3 and MIDI files, HTML and PDF documents, ... by looking into the structure of the file and determining the type of the file. If user hits enter, file browser will try to open the appropriate application for that file type i.e. Mpg123 to play a MP3 song. To navigate through folders user needs to press left or right arrow, and Enter to open a folder or file. Navigating folders is the same as navigating TLB menus. File browser also lets user copy, move or delete files or folders, and create a new folder. It is recommended that user do all the work inside MyFiles folder, which is open in the browser, by default. If a Windows or other OS is present on a partition where TLB is installed, user can read and write in it's content. Windows system files are no exception.
- For some applications such as e-mail and web browser, *TLB* needs to be *set up* properly. TLB tries to establish a network connection through a LAN (if available), and asks DHCP for an IP address. If no Internet access through LAN is available,

users can connect to the Internet using a serial modem. User is required to enter the necessary username, password and server information for e-mail and Internet access if modem is used. All network settings are available through main menu.
- *TLB* also needs to know the type of *printer* used in order to print texts from the editor. Users can set up printer through "printer settings" menu.
- In Croatian TLB, users can change pronunciation of every word. This is possible through *dictionary* of "mispronounced words". There is also another dictionary for abbreviations and other words that always need to be spelled out.
- When user wants to turn TLB off, he/she chooses *shutdown* from the application menu. TLB opens CD-ROM drive and instructs user to remove any CD's from the drive. Then goes into safe shutdown process.

## 6 TLB and Its Users

In practice, system proved to be a great starting point for persons who never used computers before. Also for elderly people who claimed that computers are "not for them". Mostly because such users find computers to be too complex to use, or they can't understand the language they produce. By using simple TLB menu structure, most users find it to be easy to use within first few minutes. Throughout TLB system, we maintained the function of most keys the same so it's easy to use a new application once user gets comfortable with the menu structure of TLB. We found that learning curve of TLB usage is very steep, and most users are able to learn all features in less than three days. TLB users can easily transfer their knowledge later when using a screen reader or other screen access software of their choice.

Another user pool are those who would never use computer because they could not afford expensive adaptation software and hardware for the blind. TLB gives poor users an easy insight into what a computer can do for them at no cost at all.

Even though TLB has some powerful and advanced features (automatic hardware detection, DOC to TXT conversion, web-site navigation skipping...), we like to think of it as a tool for introducing computers to a novice blind user. Apart from being easy to use, it's also quite easy to understand the high-quality speech in Croatian speech that TLB produces.

TLB is developed in Croatia, but as it is an open-source product, it can be translated to any language. It was introduced in countries where languages similar to Croatian are used such as Bosnia and Hercegovina, Slovenia, Serbia, Macedonia and Montenegro. We found that interest for TLB is growing in these countries.

## 7 Conclusion

TLB is a genuine open-source product, made in Croatia with some nice and exciting features for novice users. So far Linux was an expert system, only for users with good computing background. TLB currently gives limited access to Linux OS, but we strive to increase the number of applications. Up until now TLB project has been financed mostly from Open Society Institute (Soros) and our own resources. In the future, we want to improve TLB by implementing Braille support and console access support. This will also enable TLB users to jump to a higher level, and use powerful features and software available through console. We also wish to give users possibility of playing Daisy publications and if possible scanner support and Optical character recognition. As open-source community becomes more aware about benefits of TLB, we hope to maintain its development and achieve these goals.

## References


1. Dahlke, K.: The Command-Line Interface - Ideal For Blind Users. `http://www.eklhad.net/cli.html`
2. Butorac, D.: Project IPSIS - Web Portal and Linux for the Blind. Lecture Notes in Computer Science, Vol.2398, Springer Verlag, Berlin Heidelberg New York (2002)
3. Senk, M. J. P.: Voices about EmacsSpeak – Give a listen to `http://leb.net/blinux/emacspeak_voices.html`
4. BRLTTY Official home page: `http://www.mielke.cc/brltty/`
5. Papes, Z., Bengez, D., Kirinic-Papes, V.: Understanding Genesis of Cyber Signs and Their States - Designed for the Web - An Example: Development of Speech Synthesis Markup Language, CUC2000, Conference Proceedings, CARNet, Zagreb (2000)
6. Black, A.W., Lenzo, K.A.: Flite: a small fast run-time synthesis engine. 4th ISCA Worskop on Speech Synthesis, Perthshire (2001)
7. Web-demonstration of TLB navigation system in Croatian and English, `http://www.ipsis.hr/gls/demo/index.html`

# Accessing Web Based Documents through a Tree Structural Interface

Esmond Walshe and Barry McMullin

School of Electronic Engineering, Dublin City University
Glasnevin, Dublin 9, Ireland
esmond.walshe2@mail.dcu.ie, barry.mcmullin@dcu.ie
http://eaccess.rince.ie/

**Abstract.** In addition to the intrinsic accessibility difficulties posed by a graphical user interface for blind web users, specific usability penalties arise from the serial nature of blind adapted interfaces (speech, braille). We propose an approach to the design of a browser *tailored* for blind users which may mitigate some of these difficulties. We suggest this may be achieved through maximal exploitation of structural HTML markup to support highly dynamic and interactive user control of content rendering.

## 1 Introduction

The graphical user interface (GUI) has become the predominant mode of human computer interaction in the last decade. The ability to simply point and click on a screen element to perform simple tasks negates the necessity for the (visually enabled) user to learn numerous commands to achieve similar effects. However, adaptation of such interfaces for blind users poses many difficulties [1]. So-called "screen-readers" attempt to lexically analyse the primary visual interface structure to determine relationships between objects, and thereby generate a secondary synthesized speech or braille output. Nonetheless, it is difficult to efficiently convey inherently spatial information in a non-visual manner. Thus, the incorporation of a *primary* non-visual interface has been advocated [2].

This paper proposes a primary non-visual (speech-based) interface for a web browsing application. This is an alternative to current approaches which layer a secondary screen reader interface on top of a generic, primarily GUI-based, browser. We are interested in the user efficiency of primary, non-visual, interfaces. Specifically, if a browser were designed from the bottom up, with a primary optimization for blind users, what would its interface characteristics be? How would they differ from those of present solutions?

It is well known that effective web accessibility for users with disabilities depends on a combination of careful server-side content design with tailored client side browser technology[1]. Unfortunately, relatively few sites currently deliver adequately accessible content [3]. However, it is expected that improved training

[1] `http://www.w3.org/TR/1999/WAI-WEBCONTENT-19990505/`

K. Miesenberger et al. (Eds.): ICCHP 2004, LNCS 3118, pp. 560–563, 2004.

and education of web developers and authors, together with a variety of legal measures, will lead to progressive improvement in this situation. In anticipation of this, we here assume the availability of fully accessible web content and consider the design of a web browser for blind users which would maximally exploit the accessibility features of such content.

## 2 Current Techniques

Human vision supports highly efficient scanning and integration of complex, multi-dimensional, scenes and images. By contrast, audio perceptual channels (such as speech) are one-dimensional or *serial* in nature, and intrinsically less efficient. This imposes a significant performance penalty on access to electronic information for blind users. A variety of ad hoc techniques have emerged in hybrid GUI/screen reader systems which attempt to mitigate this.

One such approach is to supply additional navigational functions based on direct analysis of the structural mark-up of the page (rather than its visual presentation). For example, Jaws for Windows[2] in conjunction with Microsoft Internet Explorer (we'll term this platform `JAWS-IE`), allows the user to directly jump from the current position to the next header element, next hyperlink element, or next interactive control, in a HTML page's underlying structure. Another possibility is to generate alternative views of the page, in conjunction with the main page view. Again, `JAWS-IE` allows the user to create a list of hyperlink elements contained in the page.

Another suggested measure is to analyse the content to automatically create an abridged version – for example, by extracting the sentences containing the most common word trigrams and presenting them as a page summary [4]. The effectiveness of such an approach will necessarily vary depending on the content being analysed.

All of these forms of interaction can signicantly improve efficiency for blind users. However, in current implementations, such functionality is ad hoc and not systematic. Further, the functions may not be well integrated (e.g. co-ordination between multiple "alternative" views is generally complicated).

## 3 Proposed Approach

Instead of statically exposing the entire web page to the user in a linearised form, and/or providing a fixed set of alternative partial views, we propose a single integrated page view which can be dynamically and interactively varied based on the page structure. Specifically, the user would be able to systematically and dynamically hide or expose aspects of the page structure and content. We conjecture that this will allow the user to easily vary the granularity or level of page detail being exposed, and thus to alternate efficiently between scanning and drilling down at any given level of the page's hierarchical structure.

[2] `http://www.freedomscientific.com/`

### 3.1 Tree Structure

XHTML based pages are naturally and necessarily structured in a hierarchical tree-like arrangement, with the higher-level nodes taking on the form of container elements and the lowest level nodes containing the actual textual content.

We suggest that incorporating the facility to directly navigate this tree-like structure should provide the user with a powerful method for establishing a mental model of the page structure and interacting with it[3]. Coupled with this tree-based navigation, we propose the ability to expand or collapse any node in the structure. Expanding the lowest level tree nodes will result in their textual content being exposed. Thus, both the tree structure and the content will be rendered within one single, integrated, but dynamic page view.

Not all XHTML elements are equally useful for tree based navigation; we propose that tree navigation should be limited to the XHTML *block* (as opposed to *inline*) elements.

The page view will thus consist of a combination of tree structural element controls and the textual content from expanded nodes. Prosodic cues and auditory earcons will be used to distinguish block level tree-structure information from inline content, and to indicate the structure of *inline* elements. However, to avoid adding unnecessary complexity to the user interface, the use of such prosodic and auditory cues must be carefully controlled [5]. The more additional cues utilised the higher the expected learning curve placed on the user.

### 3.2 Dynamic Rendering

The ability to expand or collapse all elements at a given level in the tree, or all elements in a given sub-tree is an important piece of the proposed functionality. In this manner, a user can focus in on a specific section whilst ignoring the content contained in the rest of the page.

In addition to this direct, tree-based, expand and collapse functionality, we intend to provide the facility to dynamically hide or display specific element types. This would provide the user with a systematic ability to constrain the page view by specifying their own criteria. For example a view consisting purely of header elements, or one just containing the page's emphasised text. As this would still act though the one single dynamic page view, there should be no problems with synchronization between views.

### 3.3 Multidimensional Elements

While the overall structure of an XHTML page is a tree, certain elements introduce non-hierarchical relationships. These relationships are typically rendered spatially in visual media. Examples are `table` and `form` elements. These have generally posed particular obstacles for blind users.

[3] The w3c's prototype editor/browser `amaya` provides an example of such tree-oriented rendering – however, only in the form of a distinct, alternative, page view. See: `http://www.w3.org/Amaya/`

In the case of tables, it is clearly necessary to be able to navigate directly in two-dimensions – up and down through a column and left or right through a row of cells (cf. the Jaws "table mode"). In addition to this we propose the ability to dynamically hide or expose table content by row or column[4].

### 3.4 Searching

Incremental search within a page is an important alternative navigation strategy. We propose a search mechanism which will automatically interact with the dynamic hiding and exposing of elements; and which will have the ability to explicitly search by structure as well as raw element content – for example, constraining a search for text with hyperlink elements or table cells etc.

## 4 Conclusion

It is hoped that the approaches outlined here to web page navigation and content presentation will demonstrate a noticeable increase in efficiency for blind users. This should be particularly apparent when accessing larger and/or structurally complex pages. Prototype implementation is underway and user-testing will follow.

## References


1. Barnicle K.A.: Evaluation of the interaction between users of screen reading technology and graphical user interface elements. Ph.D. dissertation. Graduate School of Arts and Sciences, Columbia University, New York
2. Savidis, A. and Stephanidis, C.: The HOMER UIMS for dual user interface development: Fusing visual and non-visual interactions. Interacting with Computers, **11**, Issue 2 , 15 December 1998, 173–209
3. McMullin, B.: Users with Disability Need Not Apply? Web Accessibility in Ireland, 2002. First Monday, December 2002. `http://www.firstmonday.dk/issues/issue7_12/mcmullin/index.html`
4. Zajicek, M., Powell, C. and Reeves, C.: Orientation of Blind Users on the World Wide Web. M. Hanson (ed). Contemporary Ergonomics 1998 (Taylor and Francis, London)
5. James, F.: Lessons from Developing Audio HTML Interfaces. Proceedings of the third international ACM conference on Assistive technologies, 1998


[4] As we are restricting our scope to XHTML *basic*, the additional complexity of *nested* tables will not arise. See: `http://www.w3.org/TR/xhtml-basic/`

# Multimedia Medicine Consultant for Visually Impaired People

Javier Tejedor[1], Daniel Bolaños[1], Nicolás Morales[1], Ana Granados[1], José Colás[1], and Santiago Aguilera[2]

[1] Departamento de Ingeniería Informática, E. P. S. Universidad Autónoma de Madrid
Ctra. Colmenar Viejo km15, 28049 Madrid, Spain
javier.tejedor@ii.uam.es
[2] Universidad Politécnica de Madrid, C\Ciudad Universitaria S/N, 28040 Madrid, Spain
aguilera@acacia.die.upm.es

**Abstract.** In this article we present two different ways to use a certain service which is very important as we can see later. The service is based on getting a piece of information about any medicine which exists now using two different ways. With the first way the user sends a SMS and on an outgoing call made by a voice platform, with which the user can access the information he wants. The second one is based on the voice and the user makes an incoming call to get the information that he wants. These two ways have been proved successfully by a lot of laboratories in Madrid (Spain) and by a lot of people and they are very happy with both ways. Now we are working in a solution based on vocal navigation with which a user can get the piece of information of a medicine using the voice in a web page.

## 1 Introduction

The system presented in this document was developed for IMSERSO (Social Services Organization of Spain) in a project named CUSTODYA. The solutions developed in this system are a help for people who have a disability, especially visually impaired people to use a certain service rightly.

Nowadays the medicine is very important in people's life. There are people who have to take some medicines every day. Perhaps many of them don't know how to use them. This can cause a lot of problems in their life.
The system developed tries to avoid these problems. This system, not only can be used by visually impaired people, but also by anyone.

A lot of people often read the information about a medicine before they take it to make sure that they are taking it rightly. This can be a problem for visually impaired people or simply for a person who has not the whole information of a medicine when he needs to take it. The solution based on the web page [1] (which existed before this system) www.viatusalud.com can reduce this problem but it doesn't avoid totally. Using this web page, a person can choose any medicine and can read the information he needs. But it is not sufficient to assure that everybody can access the information rightly. For example, a visually impaired people can't access the information of a web page as a person who does not have this problem. Therefore the new solution developed tries to avoid this problem.

K. Miesenberger et al. (Eds.): ICCHP 2004, LNCS 3118, pp. 564–570, 2004.

In a same way the use of a web page isn't always easy for everybody. In addition to this, a person can't access a web page wherever he is and whenever he wants.

Everybody can access in two different ways the information of the medicines they want with this system developed. In this way visually impaired people (and also everybody) can get the information they want of the medicine they have to take, as well as the counter-indications that this medicine has.

The first way which can use the user is the use of the SMS (short message service). In this way, the user sends a SMS with the name of a medicine of which he wants to get the information and a telephone number (which is optional). After this, a voice platform makes an outgoing call to this indicated telephone number or to the telephone number with which the user sent the SMS if the user only sent the name of the medicine. With this call, the user can get a piece if information about the medicine suitable in the SMS.

The second way is an incoming call towards a telephone number with which the user begins a dialogue with the voice platform to get the information about the medicine he wants.

So, with this system any person can know any piece of information about any medicine he wants wherever he is and whenever he wants. And what is more, the user only needs a telephone with which he can make an incoming call to a voice platform or send a SMS to a SMS platform. That is why the system developed has a very good accessibility.

## 2 The System

The system developed has two different ways with which a person can access the information he wants about a medicine. This information is provided to the user rightly and as quickly as possible. Nowadays two applications exist to provide this two ways. These applications are executed by a voice platform and let the user accesses the information he wants. There is also used a SMS platform to receive the SMS sent for the users in case of the access to the information is via SMS, as well as a web server which is used to get the information about a medicine or when it is necessary to get the medicines available to be enquired.

The information the user can get about a medicine is this: What is the medicine?, How should it be conserved?, How is it used?, What precautions must be taken?, When must not the medicine be used?, What are the counter-indications?, What kind of problems can arise with its use?, Can the medicine be taken during the pregnancy or lactation?, Does the medicine need prescription?, Which are the commercial names?

All these aspects must be known by everybody when he is going to take a medicine to avoid the wrong use. The two applications developed are a solution so as to avoid this wrong use.

The two applications made for the two different ways are explained now:

### 2.1 Solution Sending the Name of the Medicine by Text in a SMS (Short Message Service)

The user has to send a SMS to a number. The SMS is received by the SMS platform. This SMS can have two pieces of information. The first one is compulsory and indicates the name of the medicine of which the user wants to know its information. The second one is optional and is a telephone number which indicates the number to which the voice platform has to make an outgoing call so that the user can get the information. If this parameter doesn't appear, the voice platform makes the outgoing call to the same number used by the user to send the SMS.

When the SMS is received by the SMS platform, it accesses a web server to know if the medicine sent by the user exists. If it exists, the SMS platform accesses a database to insert a new record with three pieces of information: the medicine sent by the user, the telephone number to which the voice platform has to make the outgoing call and a value which indicates that the call has to be made.

By its own, the voice platform is searching in this database if there are some outgoing calls to make, and if so, it makes an outgoing call, beginning a dialogue with the user which lets him know the suitable information using Speech Synthesis and Speech Recognition. Speech Synthesis used lets the user receive the information he wants rightly. In addition to this, the user can listen to this information how many times he wants. This thing is very important to assure that the user has listened to the whole information rightly. And what is more important, thinking about the possible disability of the person, it is the *only* way to assure the information is provided rightly. Speech Recognition is used to get the piece of information that the user wants to know about the medicine and when the user choose, at the end of the dialogue, between two possibilities: to go out of the application or to enquiry another piece of information about the medicine sent by SMS. The voice platform also has to access a web server to get the information requested by the user. When the call finishes the voice platform accesses the outgoing calls database so that this call doesn't repeat changing the value of one attribute in the record suitable.

In case of the medicine sent via SMS by the user belongs to more than one medicine, the voice platform using Speech Synthesis shows him all these medicines and the user has to choose one of them to get the information rightly.

In the next Fig.1 you can see the steps which this solution is based on since the user sends the SMS until the user receives the information about a medicine.

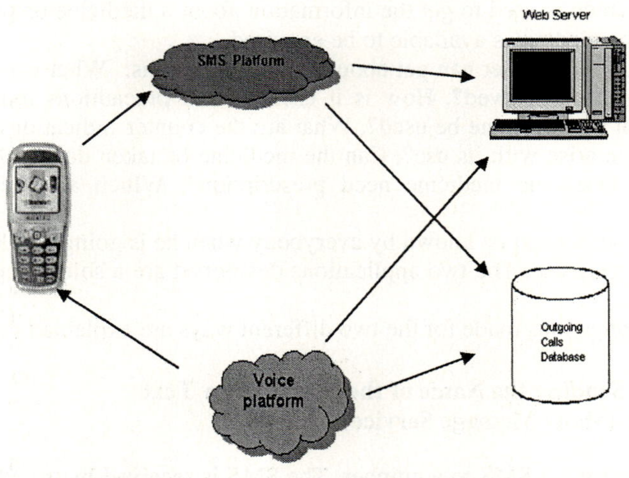


**Fig. 1.** Shows the Steps of the First Solution

Therefore, using this way a user can enquiry any piece of information about any medicine sending a SMS. It's such a very easy thing that anybody can use it.

In this way, any piece of information about any medicine is always available for visually impaired people using the SMS. This solution can be used by this kind of people instead of accessing the web page [1] www.viatusalud.com which can cause a lot of problems for them to get the information rightly.

The application which makes the outgoing call to play the information of the medicine is:

1. Play a welcome message.
2. The voice platform checks if the medicine sent by the user matches one or more different medicines.If the medicine belongs to more than one medicine, the voice platform, using Speech Synthesis, plays the user the different medicines so that he chooses one of them. The user can also listen to this list of medicines as many times as he wants.
3. When the voice platform has the name of the medicine, it plays a message so that the user chooses the piece of information about the medicine that he wants.
4. When the user has chosen the information he wants, the vocal platform accesses via http the web server which contains the web page [1] www.viatusalud.com so as to obtain the suitable information.
5. After that, the information returned by this web page is played to the user using the text to speech. The user can listen to the information as many times as he wants. In this way, the application guarantees that the user has received the information rightly.
6. When the user has received the information, he can enquiry a different piece of information about this medicine. In that case, the voice platform would go back to the step 3. The user can also go out of the application. In that case, the voice platform plays him a goodbye message.

Thinking about the disability of the user, the voice platform always asks for the user a confirmation of which he chooses so as to avoid giving a wrong result.

This solution developed can be used for visually impaired people because with a simple SMS, the user can receive any piece of information about a medicine which he is going to take. The user only needs a mobile phone and nothing else.

So this solution can be used by the user instead of the web page [1] www.viatusalud.com which is not prepared for visually impaired people to get the information he wants.

### 2.2 Solution Sending the Name of the Medicine Using the Voice

This solution was developed as another way apart from the use of the SMS to get a piece of information about a medicine. In this way, the user makes an incoming call to a voice platform. The voice platform asks the user the name of a medicine of which he wants to know a piece of information. The name of the medicine and the piece of information are recognised by the voice platform so that the suitable information can be playing to the user rightly. The dialogue assures that the user receives the information he wants asking for confirmation of the things the user says. The dialogue also lets the user get different pieces of information, as well as he can listen to the information he wants as many times as he wants. This last thing is very useful for people with some disability because perhaps they can't understand the information at once.

In the same way that with the SMS, if the name of a medicine said by the user belongs to more than one medicine, the voice platform using Speech Synthesis, plays the user the different medicines so that he chooses one of them. The Speech Recognition is used to recognise the name of the medicine said by the user, the piece of information the user wants to know about the medicine chosen and the option the user chooses at the end of the dialogue, which can be: enquiry another medicine, enquiry another piece of information about the same medicine or go out of the application.

In the next Fig.2 you can see the steps followed by this application.

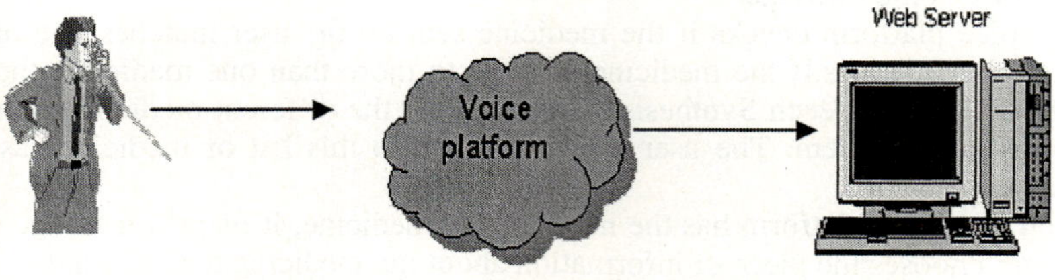


**Fig. 2.** Shows the Steps of the Second Solution

The application that receives the incoming call from the user is:

1. Play a welcome message.
2. The user says the name of the medicine of which he wants to know a piece of information.
3. The voice platform checks if the medicine sent by the user matches one or more different medicines.If the medicine belongs to more than one, the voice platform, using Speech Synthesis, plays the user the different medicines so that he chooses one of them. The user can also listen to this list of medicines as many times as he wants.
4. When the voice platform has the name of the medicine, it plays a message so that the user chooses the piece of information about the medicine that he wants.
5. When the user has chosen the information he wants, the voice platform accesses via http the web server which contains the web page [1] www.viatusalud.com so as to return the suitable information.
6. After that, the information returned by this web page is played to the user using the Speech Synthesis. The user can listen to the information as many times as he wants. In this way, the application guarantees that the user has received the information rightly.
7. When the user has received the information, he can enquiry a different piece of information about this medicine. In that case, the voice platform would go back to the step 4. The user can also enquiry another medicine. In that case, the voice platform would come back to the step 2. The user can also exit the application saying the go out command. In that case, the voice platform plays him a goodbye message.

This application was also developed thinking about people with a disability. That's why the voice platform always asks the user a confirmation in the different things that he chooses, such as the name of the medicine, the piece of information about the medicine and the choice about enquiring a new medicine, a new piece of information about the same medicine, or going out of the application.

This solution is very useful because with a simple incoming call a visually impaired person can know any piece of information about the medicine he is taking. In this way, if a person doesn't know how to use the SMS, he can make an incoming call to get the information he needs to know. In addition to this, the easy use of a telephone is very important to get the information. As the other solution, this second one is better for visually impaired people than the use of the web page [1] www.viatusalud.com which is not prepared rightly for them.

## 3 Voice Platform

The two solutions were developed using a voice platform which has the following modules:

- Dialog Module: It sends the different requests to the servers according to the dialog of the application shown in the two solutions.
- Interface Telephonic Server: It receives the incoming calls from the users and makes the outgoing calls to the users depending on the solution. It also plays files, hangs off the telephone line when an incoming call is received, hangs on the telephone line when the call finishes [2] and recognises the words that the user says [3]. The interface used is a telephonic card named Dialogic, which are made by Intel.
- Synthesis Server: It receives from the Dialog Module the requests of Speech Synthesis [4].
- JavaServer: It sends the different requests to get the information of a medicine when the Dialog Module asks for them. After that, this information is sent to the Dialog Module. It also decides if a medicine belongs to more than one medicine or not or even if the medicine exists or not in case the user makes an incoming call.

## 4 Conclusions and Future Work

Due to there are a lot of people that in their life have to take a lot of medicines continuously, it is necessary that people know whenever they want the information about these medicines. That's why everybody must think about people who have some disability when the information is shown. The access to this information must be clear for everybody. That is why this system was developed and, nowadays, has been proved successfully by a lot of laboratories in Madrid (Spain), as well as for a lot of people who have been making incoming calls or sending SMS to prove the two solutions. Now, a lot of requests have been done by other laboratories to prove this system in a not very far future.

These two solutions, which are been used now, were developed as an alternative to access a piece of information about a medicine to the web page [1] www.viatusalud.com

This system was thought for visually impaired people mainly to get the information that they can't get with this web page rightly. After a lot of people were asking, we could see a very good approval of the two solutions developed.

We thought that the easy way to access both solutions could increase the use of them and we could confirm this fact when we asked a lot of people about these two solutions developed.

Nowadays we are working in a solution based on new *web page* thinking about the possible disability of the person. That is why we have to design a web page which can be accessed by visually impaired people. This web page which is now designing is based on vocal navigation. There is an agent which plays the user the information of the web page in which the user is as well as the possible pages at which the user can access from the page he is in each moment. In this way, the user says a command associated to the web page he wants to access. This command could be the name of the medicine he wants to get, or a command to make an action after he had enquired the first medicine to indicate that he wants to know a piece of information about the same medicine, or about another medicine or simply to indicate that he wants to go out of the application. That will be a good solution for visually impaired people if they want to get the information using a web page. Obviously we have to design the web page thinking on visually impaired people. That's why we have to avoid the use of images if they aren't very necessary (perhaps people can't see them rightly), we have to reduce the possible commands to say in the different pages (perhaps a visually impaired person doesn't remember all of them). We also have to ask confirmation about the things that the user says to avoid giving a wrong result and what is more important, to avoid that a wrong page is shown to the user.
When this web page will be developed, we think that all the ways to access a piece of information about a medicine when a person needs it will be covered.

So a person can choose between three different ways to access the same information (send a SMS, make an incoming call or navigate on a web page).

## Acknowledgements

I have to thanks Ricardo Ribalda and Bruno Caballero who helped me on the communication between the JavaServer of the voice platform and the web server where the web page www.viatusalud.com is to get the information about a medicine and also IMSERSO which was the organization which asked me for the development of this system.

## References

1. Medicine Web Page: www.viatusalud.com
2. Applied Technologies on Language and Speech Documentation: IberVoxDialogic.pdf
3. Dialogic Corporation. Voice Software Reference: Programmer's Guide for Windows.
4. Lernout & Hauspie Speech Products: Telecom RealSpeak Software Development Kit.

# Computer for Persons with Visually Impairment: A Door to Education, Information and Employment

A.H.M. Noman Khan and Sadaf Noori Chowdhury

**Abstract.** There is a general social stigma attached to blindness, which is virtually inescapable. This stereotype affects education and employment opportunities for the visually impaired. As such, employers tend to rely more on sighted employees than visually impaired ones. Contrary to popular belief, it is found that a visually impaired person can perform just as well as a sighted person in the classroom and in the workplace. Simply, they have not been afforded the opportunity to prove so.One way to remedy this nationwide problem is through the utilization of Information Communication Technology (ICT). Using specific computer software, hardware, accessories, and other tools, visually impaired people can advance in both education and employment. Access to such computer technology is essential in promoting positive growth for visually impaired people.The paper reflects the problems encountered, and the future course of action for creating access of visually impaired persons to computer technologies.

## 1 The Situation

In Bangladesh, there are approximately 700,000 adults who report some form of visual impairment. Among the working-age visually impaired, unemployment is rampant. Services that provide specific employment-focused skill development have made great strides in enhancing visually impaired peoples' ability to be competitive in the domestic job market. Furthermore, such programs have pursued a progressive path, which goes beyond employment stability to promote advancement in the workplace.

During the past fifteen years, technology has broadened the job possibilities for people worldwide. Computers have brought about innumerable opportunities for both totally blind and low vision people. In an increasingly interdependent world, information Technology is an essential tool to create, distribute, and exchange knowledge. That said, Bangladesh is not alone in its purpose. In order to be effective in information accumulation, the country must participate in domestic and international information technology exchange. It is vital to sustain open, organized, and cohesive information flows at home and abroad to help facilitate the advancement and empowerment of visually impaired people. Communication and adaptation are crucial in this process.

The barriers for visually impaired people in Bangladesh include lack of computer knowledge, inadequate access to information and insufficient physical access. Throughout the country, provision and support for visually impaired people are not available. Unfortunately, people with visual impairment face many inequities in many aspects of daily living. Most important among them are employment preparation and

K. Miesenberger et al. (Eds.): ICCHP 2004, LNCS 3118, pp. 571–574, 2004.

job acquisition. In fact, the visually impaired people are able to work and contribute in nearly every sector of the Bangladesh economy. They are as likely as any other to use computers and the Internet. This is an indispensable human right.

Visually impaired persons require accommodation in the workplace to successfully perform their job duties. Computers can be used as an intelligent interface between them and the sighted. Information that would otherwise be inaccessible or require manual processing can be automatically transformed into formats better suited for the visually impaired.

## 2 Expected Impact of Computer Access

- **Promoting education at primary and secondary schools:** With the emergence of new IT and Braille equipment, visually impaired people will become more competent and independent, and thus more reliant in society's eye. This will create a positive impact on enhancing the rate of enrollment of visually impaired children in mainstream education.
- **Promoting education at higher secondary and university level:** The high dropout rate of visually impaired students from primary, secondary, integrated, and special education to higher education is a significant barrier to their respective advancement. Reasons for such barriers are limited access to educational materials and the unavailability of an appropriate learning environment in mainstream educational institutions.
  Computer access could widen the scope of the material available, while allowing visually impaired people the ability to take online courses. The Internet has a wealth of information, and visually impaired people deserve the right to educate themselves with this resource.
- **Promoting job opportunities for visually impaired person who completed education:** Only a negligible number of educated, visually impaired people have been employed. Employers prefer to hire one who has vision and have little considerations to the qualities and potentials of visually impaired persons. Computer skills will establish the visual impaired person with focus on their capacity and ability to contribute more in a diverse job market.
- **Establishing visually impaired employees with more competencies in workplace:** The scope for employment for the persons with disabilities in the country is very limited. A few are employed in NGOs that work for persons with disabilities, especially persons with visual impairment. The access of the persons with visual impairment to acquire skills of ICT would build a pool of competent work force of persons with visual impairment.
- **Changing the prevailing negative attitude of common masses on the potentialities of visually impaired persons:** Persons with visual impairment trained on ICT and successfully employed or applying their acquired skills on appropriate sectors and field would provide a strong message to the general masses. This would be the best way to educate people and with more persons with visual impairment included into mainstream development would allow them to interact with people with no visual impairment; ultimately contributing in creating better understanding of the common mass of the abilities and capacities of persons with visual impairment.

- **Promoting self-employment of educated visually impaired person:** The rate of self-employment among the employed persons with visual impairment interviewed in the study is large. Their current level of performance in their line of work is undoubtedly praiseworthy but this can be further enhanced if they can acquire skills on ICT and apply in their line of work. Their access to the 'worldwide information network' would allow further enrichment of their programs and activities.

## 3 Experience from the Interventions

Any interventions must have some impacts either on the society or on individual to bring some changes in the lives of that particular community or person. Various experiences are clearly visible following this interventions in the country.

Some organizations in the country seem to recruit VI people in their ongoing program intervention. These organizations have started engaging VI people in various sector to explore their inner potentialities in order to help them increase a self confidence to move forward. Few of the organizations in the country has set up a remarkable example in recruitment of VI people where they are involved not only in a specific activity rather in multi-sectoral activities.

Interestingly, this intervention has encouraged many organizations in the country to conclude that training is a bottleneck to the HRD plan and thus training in this particular area is a burning necessity. Training must be a desirable approach to recruit them in the most proper area.

Since last decade, awareness and sensitization in this particular issue made people realized about the rights, opportunity and scope of PWDs in the country. VI in the country raised their own voice which has led many organization to create a job opportunity for these people. Many organizations now tend to introduce few quotas for VI people according to their ability and capacity.

A good number of agencies in the country encouraging immensely to introduce Braille in educational setup. VI graduates from universities have shown a keen interest and demand to have introduced Braille in their educational set up. Hence, demand for Braille have gradually been increased.

Some NGOs working with non formal education institutions are trying hard to include disabled children in their educational set up.

## 4 Suggested Interventions

The issue of Information Communication Technology (ICT) for the visually impaired people in the country is new and not very much known to both the consumers and the agencies concerned with promotion of ICT issues in the country. This requires comprehensive planning and execution of interventions at different sectors and levels in the country. The advantage of the issue is the prevailing technology in the neighboring countries with user-friendly devices, which has been proved as an effective mean with options of necessary adaptation. Another notable strength of the issue is the number of NGOs working with the issues of disability who has keen interest to promote ICT for visually impaired persons in the country. Capitalizing all these strengths and advantages, integrated and strategic interventions need to be initiated, focusing on the following broad areas of interventions at different levels:

- Sensitization and Awareness rising at all levels.
- Systematic inclusion in national ICT policy.
- Permanent demonstration of technological devices.
- Introducing ICT in integrated and special schools.
- Introducing ICT in NGOs to decentralize access.
- Initiating human resource development initiatives.
- Ensure maintenance and follow-up of both soft and hardware.
- Research on development needs assessment.

## 5 Conclusion

The benefits of computer accessibility and skills acquisition are numerous and varied, applying to visually impaired people of all ages, educational backgrounds, and employment histories. With these tools, the scope and opportunity for visually impaired people will be improved dramatically. Through demonstrated success in such an endeavor, social stereotypes will recede, and the visually impaired people will acquire a greater sense of motivation, confidence, and independence.

This study is an indispensable resource with respect to visual impairment in Bangladesh, and can contribute to a nationwide policy on ICT development for the visually impaired. It is the suggestion of the study team that action be taken to improve the lives of the visually impaired through the utilization of computers. Development must be just and equal. It must include all citizens, even those with disability.

# Usability of Educational Software for Visual Impairment: A Question of Viewpoint

Silvia Dini[1], Lucia Ferlino[2], and Cristina Martinoli[1]

[1] Istituto David Chiossone onlus, Corso Armellini 11, 16122 Genova, Italy
{dini,martinoli}@chiossone.it

[2] Istituto Tecnologie Didattiche del CNR, Via De Marini 6, 16149 Genova, Italy
ferlino@itd.cnr.it

**Abstract.** The Italian National Research Council's Institute for Educational Technology and the David Chiossone Institute for the Blind have carried out a joint study that seeks to define criteria for evaluating the suitability of educational software in meeting the needs of the visually impaired. This study devotes due consideration to the particular educational context and to the needs of individual students, seen in a positive light as potentialities rather than limits. As a result, we have been able to define a series of characteristics related to analysis and method.

## 1 The Importance of Educational Technology in Learning

Schools, for some time, have recognised the important role that technology, and in particular multimedia educational software, plays as a tool to support teaching and learning. The Italian National Research Council's Institute for Educational Technology in Genoa has supplied interesting contributions to study in this sector, not only through research but also through real contacts with the educational world: training for working teachers, university courses for future supply teachers, articles and publications. In particular, as regards educational software, the following should be highlighted: the reference service at the educational Software Library, and the on line service Essediquadro in collaboration with the Ministry of Education, set up and managed by the Institute. Essediquadro is intended as a database (in Italian) for documentation on over 3000 educational and didactic software products which cover all levels of schooling and all educational subjects, with a section dedicated to software created expressly for the disabled (although, unfortunately, there are few software products on the market which can be used profitably by the visually impaired!). Thanks to the computer and its various programs the teacher can enrich his offerings in class with differentiated courses, for most pupils these could form a learning opportunity, encourage motivation, and allow them to overcome learning difficulties, (even temporary). For disabled pupils, technology in the area of 'General Purpose' programs (word processing, spreadsheets, data archiving) hold an important instrumental role as aids which enable 'to do' independently, revealing themselves essential tools for daily production at home and in class. For the visually impaired pupil, a desktop computer is essential for: helping individual and group production (particu-

K. Miesenberger et al. (Eds.): ICCHP 2004, LNCS 3118, pp. 575–582, 2004.

larly creation of texts); better integration into class activities; at the end, sharing of an individual's work with others. There are many areas of didactic activity where even at daily routine level, the positive influence of Educational Technology (and in particular the use of computers), for the educational integration of disabled pupils, is recognised and certified. However, electronic 'barriers' still exist, which are particularly evident for the visually impaired, especially regarding the use of multi media and interactive material. Our study aims to pinpoint the critical factors which these barriers depend on and the possible environmental and personal variables which can reduce such difficulties. In the educational field it is evidently necessary for teachers to have interactive and multimedia materials available, which are designed for the precise purpose of improving study and learning. As regards access to technical knowledge, all pupils (including the visually impaired) have the same needs, to be able to learn, exploiting their skills at best using stimulating, interesting courses, tailored to their own pace of learning. As well as the instrumental side of technology to compensate operational difficulties connected to visual impairment, (most of all, difficulties in writing, re-reading, and editing a text), education seems to have the same problems for all pupils if technology and any possible hardware/software accessories are able to reduce the 'diversity' relative to 'being able'. This does not exclude, at any level, learning problems or low motivation. Technology can therefore render action, 'doing' less complicated, but 'doing' at school is focused on learning, to access content, to increase knowledge but above all competence. These principles are always valid in teaching and this is exactly the reason why they should not be underestimated in the presence of visually impaired pupils.

## 2 The Visually Impaired's Point of View

Before proceeding it is essential to clarify some concepts necessary to understand the meaning of partial sightedness and visual impairment. Visual impairment is intended as a slight or serious reduction of sensory function resulting from damage suffered to visual organs. Visual function according to the definition and classification of visual impairment by M. Zingirian, E. Gandolfo and F. Gandolfo includes specific perceptive abilities (visual sharpness, field of vision, sensitiveness to contrast, etc) each of which contributes in differing amounts to define the threshold of optimum perceptive functioning. For example, visual sharpness and field of vision are two fundamental parameters according to which a disability is recognised, in a proportionate measure. Visual sharpness means the ability to 'discriminate' in maximum contrast conditions, it is a question of evaluating the individual's ability to perceive the details of an image placed at the centre of his field of vision and in particular an object being looked at, it is measured from a distance and is evaluated with the best correction for each eye. If the eyes are both functioning, there is an improvement of visual sharpness (*visus*) in binocular vision. We can have the minimum visible, that is, the ability to perceive objects without discriminating between them, or the minimum legible; the ability to read words is conditioned by the possibility of simultaneous vision of at least 4 letters in a screenshot. Vision of near or distant objects (near or distant visual sharpness) can be very different: in young people it is often the case that even a partially sighted individual can see nearby almost normally, because his ability to accommodate or focus is normal. On the other hand, visual acuity is always altered in adults over 40 years old because of .presbyopia which arises from the inability to focus on close subjects because of loss of elasticity in the crystalline lens. As regards field of vision, this means the ability to perceive the environment which surrounds the object being looked at, it often happens that we observe a point in front of us and at the same time notice the passing of objects or people that enter at the extremities of our field of vision, whatever enters the field of vision can stimulate the eye to turn the central part of the retina towards this 'intruding' object, with a rapid movement called 'saccade'. Train journeys give us a chance to experience this phenomenon, a person who looks out of the window makes jerky eye movements to follow, for example, the posts which follow one another along the railway line. The most typical alterations are tunnel vision (concentric restriction) and hemianopia following brain damage (both horizontal and vertical, more often vertical). As regards abilities necessary to see the computer screen, these are not the only significant parameters, for example Pursuit phenomena, slow movements following an object, are an essential part of the ability to follow these objects on the screen; to be able to observe and perceive images full of nuances, of half tones, an adequate sensitivity to contrast; is necessary; in oculistic terms this is defined as discriminative ability in reduced contrast conditions, to measure it, it is necessary the appreciate a difference in brightness of the 'target' in the background. Together with sense of colour and brightness, these are all factors which can jeopardise, in functional terms, reading and perception of the computer screen.

## 3 Research Background and Objectives

The Center for Visual Impairment Rehabilitation at the David Chiossone Onlus Institute for the Blind (`http://www.chiossone.it`) has been working for the disabled at national level for many years. The experience gained has confirmed the importance of computer technology for enhancing autonomy. Recognized nationally as a center of excellence in the field of visual impairment, the Center has a number of specialized teams that deal globally with the needs of blind and visually impaired people of all age groups: babies, children, adolescents and adults. For children, the group considered in this study, the center's staff provides specific training in assistive technology, as well as counseling for families, schools and professionals in the field regarding the fundamental issues in visual impairment, methodologies, technologies. The aim is to help visually impaired people achieve smoother, more harmonious integration in their environment.In terms of computer technology, the crucial matters that need to be considered are exactly when to introduce computer use, what assistive devices need to be adopted and what general technical considerations are to be made (LCD monitor, lighting levels, black keyboard with large letters, enlarged font and mouse pointer size, contrast and color choice, etc). Children are expected to acquire at least the basics of computing and to learn how to use any specific assistive devices that might be necessary for their computer use, such as enlarging software and/or text readers. The mouse is not a suitable pointing and control device for all visually impaired computer users; it depends very much on the individual and on the level of impairment. Typing skills are critical and if possible touch typing should be learnt. Over the years the center's staff has been called on by teachers to suggest learning materials and to indicate software that might be suitable for visually impaired users. This has led the Center to forge strong links with another Genoa-based service, the Educational Software Library at the Institute for Educational Technology (ITD). For almost twenty years this publicly-funded library has been collecting, cataloguing and studying educational software published both in Italy and abroad. In that period the service has catered for an increasingly diverse range of users, including teachers, university students, educational and rehabilitation professionals, researchers, parents. In order to meet their varied needs, the considerable body of documentation that the Software Library has produced has been made available via a web site called Essediquadro (`http://sd2.itd.ge.cnr.it`), which has become a focal point for teachers throughout Italy looking for multimedia teaching material. The software catalogued within Essediquadro includes titles produced expressly for visually impaired users but these represent an extremely small proportion of the total and can hardly meet all teaching needs in the various subject areas and at the different school levels. The queries that teachers make to the Essediquadro service reveal that they tend to look for technology and software for: applying what has been learnt, using simulations and virtual laboratories to conduct "scientific experiments"; consolidating knowledge acquisition (drill & practice); developing general skills (problem solving).

These are very immediate, practical needs. Seen in terms of the enormous potential that computer technology offers, they may appear extremely limited but on the other hand they reflect the constraints under which individual teachers operate (work organization, computer availability and access, etc.). In 2003 ITD and the Chiossone Institute for the Blind began a joint study to examine the criteria and methodology for selecting software to be used with students with visual impairment. The scope of the study was limited to material suitable for students from 4 to 12 years of age (chosen from among the Chiossone Institute's user group) who are visually impaired but not blind. This cut off point was determined by the intention to stick to interaction via the visual channel, whether limited through impairment or enhanced by assistive devices. Including blindness would have drastically reduced the material available for study, both because of the technical impossibility of using screen readers and braille bars with multimedia software and the variety of approaches called for by the different graphic interfaces adopted by the majority of educational software titles. We propose to study the very interesting and important area of software for the blind at a later stage. It was chosen to conduct the observations following a natural experimental methodology, respecting the children. It was decided to operate gently, choosing options based on the child and the situation's requirements, as an opportunity to diversify the normal activities carried out by the children with their special needs teachers during the weekly meetings at the Chiossone Rehabilitation Centre. A written record was kept of the observations made by the special needs teachers who used the multimedia and educational to enrich activities, this had a positive effect both on the special needs teachers themselves who acquired knowledge and skills regarding software, on the children who were able to exploit further stimulus during the rehabilitation sessions, and on the teachers, with whom the results were shared.

## 4 Criteria for Analyzing Educational Software

"Looking at" software from the viewpoint of the visually impaired user entails more than merely completing a software analysis grid. More importantly, it means acquiring sensitivity and awareness of aspects related not only to textual content also to the fine processing of images on the part of the student seeking to comprehend the product in question. Anyone can understand that if an image cannot be properly decoded this will harm the development/evolution of comprehension, and it will certainly inhibit memory, categorization and other cognitive processes requiring abstract processing of observable reality. The characteristics we analyse (graphics, user interface, cognitive aspects, technological aspects) are not designed to provide an evaluation of the software *per se*: a tool may prove more or less useful according to the context and the way in which it is used. Hence it is important to recognize these criteria and relate them to the working environment and especially to the needs of the student. Software usability therefore means identifying the elements necessary for reaching an objective, and that objective may not have been contemplated during product design: a game may help the user develop hand-eye co-ordination, conversely an exercise may stimulate interest in a subject through the competitiveness of point scoring.

From an educational viewpoint, the usability of computer technology touches on:

- the possibility to act, where the computer is a compensatory support for attaining a standard level of operability: both for students with sensorial impairments and those without, computers make it possible to respect individual differences, to adapt to different styles and paces of learning, to appreciate the differences that make us all individuals;
- the possibility to learn, to access contents and information, to practice, to consolidate knowledge;
- the ability to act, to apply concepts in a general manner to areas other than the original ones; this is the chief outcome expected of teaching.

At a technical level, software usability largely depends on aspects related to the graphic interface and the mode of user interaction. These comprise:

- Graphics, including font size (suited to user's requirements?, scalable?), colors, contrasts, the text vs. background relationship;
- Interface and mode of interaction, including comprehensibility of interaction mode, reduced spaces, audio feedback, use of keyboard in alternative to the mouse;
- Cognitive aspects, including time restraints, content that is useful and appealing, age group suitability;
- Technological aspects such as compatibility with enlarging software or other support devices (touch screen).
- Usability can be investigated in detail by considering each of these characteristics and for each one identifying a series of discriminating factors for discussion. It is then posible to evaluate the effective usability of a product in different contexts by indicating the relative importance that each factor may assume.

The capacity to exploit educational software depends directly on the elements mentioned above but should be placed in a wider and more complex context which involves all a person's abilities, particularly motivation, interest, previous knowledge, strategies for using residual vision, and environmental conditions that can partially effect them for better or worse. We have drawn up an evaluation table, made up of simple questions which teachers can use to select and offer educational material to partially sighted children, taking account both of the visual characteristics and educational needs. It is a question of examining the educational software normally used, from the point of view of disabled and sighted children.

**Table. 1.** Evaluation criteria to analyse the benefits of educational software

| | | Evaluation | |
|---|---|---|---|
| Analysis criteria and relationship with visual perception | | YES | NO |
| ***Compatibility of the program with enlargement tools*** | | | |
| Does the program work with the assistive technologies used by the child? | Compatibility with the user's enlargement software (if necessary) is the first important 'technical' criteria which can limit the type of educational software available. | | |
| ***Use of space on the screen*** | | | |
| Are the contents of the program shown in the central part of the screen, or, in any case, in a limited area of observation? | According to the type of field of vision and visual acuity, if the working area is reduced this is easier for individuals with a narrow field of vision. | | |
| Is it necessary to move eyes rapidly where looking at the screen? | It could be, related to the rapid movement called saccade (at 30° from the centre of the retina) or Pursuit phonomena, slow following movements, an essential part of following objects on the screen. | | |
| ***Speed of reading/perception*** | | | |
| Are the exercises based on static images and texts? | The ability to read words is conditioned by the possibility of simultaneous vision of at least 4 letters in a screenshot . | | |
| Are the exercises based on slow movements which the user can observe at a relaxed pace? | If what is shown on the screen is static or changes slowly, it allows the user enough time to adopt his own strategies for optimum use of his residual vision. | | |
| Is it necessary to glance and perceive images rapidly | Exercises or games which require glances can be difficult to use for learning (for example reading and memorising a word which stays on the screen only a handful of seconds, but can be used in visual rehabilitation sessions, under the control of specialised staff. | | |

**Table. 1.** (Continued)

| Analysis criteria and relationship with visual perception | | Evaluation YES | Evaluation NO |
|---|---|---|---|
| ***Audio Feedback*** | | | |
| Is the program's interface vocal? | Audio feedback in teaching software has a positive effect because it partly eliminates difficulty in reading and allows the child to concentrate better on what he has to learn or do. | | |
| Are the sounds helpful to highlight and to improve understanding? | | | |
| Are there any sound effects connected to the user's actions? | | | |
| ***Texts*** | | | |
| Are characters well defined and legible? | In relation to visual acuity and sensitiveness to contrast it could be useful to be able to enlarge texts on the screen or change character (with or without serif, normal or bold). This is an important function much appreciated in word processors, but rarely available in multimedia programs. | | |
| Can they be enlarged? | | | |
| ***Contrast and colours*** | | | |
| Are the outlines of the objects well defined with clearly marked lines? | In relation to sensitiveness to contrast | | |
| Are the graphic elements coloured with saturated tones, without texture? | Sense of colour: there are acquired types of colour blindness: blue/yellow and red/green (the most frequent). The individual who shows these alterations does not correctly identify colours, but perceives them as differences in tone.. The request to 'separate the green objects from the red ones' could become a request to distinguish between two different degrees of shading and intensity, but only if the colours which are the same have the same grade of intensity | | |
| Are colours matched in such a way as to allow perception of the difference? | | | |
| Are backgrounds neutral and homogeneous? | To allow the best situation of contrast between the background and the object to be observed or the text to be read. | | |
| Can various contrast combinations be chosen? | The sense of light is the ability to adapt to various brightness conditions in the environment: many partially sighted people are dazzled by a screen with a light background, and prefer to work in negative (dark screen with light writing) | | |
| ***Interaction*** | | | |
| Can other input systems be used, apart from the mouse? | Above all it is helpful to be able to use the keyboard to give commands to the program (for example with arrow keys and short cuts) and to move the cursor, this is needed when using the mouse is difficult because of limited hand to eye co-ordination or in the case of high zoom levels (usually from 6X onwards) | | |

A majority of positive replies would distinguish the software most easily adaptable to use by partially sighted children. This analysis is not enough to guarantee a software's effectiveness, but should be completed with an evaluation of the merit of its contents (relative to context) and the ability to captivate and motivate, two further quality aspects which every teacher applies in the choice of any teaching material. To sum up, it is a question of asking a set of questions about the main aspects of software which can be observed, relative to characteristics of visual perception and the user's motivation. Every positive reply contributes to define an accessibility/usability threshold of the chosen software. All the items are equally important, however a discriminating factor is the enlargement software which the children must use in most cases, to be able to see the PC screen. There are also some aspects, not easily categorised, linked to various types of difficulty which the young user may come across in 'understanding' a program interface, even if it is compatible with the enlargement software. This because he cannot distinguish between images if the screen is too crowded, or cannot interpret the symbols/icons if they are too small (and so if they are enlarged they seem 'out of focus'), or too much hand to eye co-ordination is necessary, for example when the mouse pointer needs to be placed inside very small or poorly defined areas, and in general everything is based exclusively on the reading of icons.

## 5 Conclusions: What Prospects?

Observing and recording the limits of software used by the partially sighted allows us to draw up a sort of guide-line which can be useful for producing the software itself, our research in the near future will be expanded towards improving authors' and editors' awareness. A change in direction, towards greater attention to users with special needs, is proved by, at least in Italy, recent laws regarding accessibility to government bodies' web sites. We hope that in the future, universal design laws are applied in a more widespread way, to have software which is ever more flexible and ever more user orientated.

## References

1. Dini-Mohsen: Postazione informatica personalizzata per lo studio e il lavoro. in Atti del convegno L'Occhio della mente 2002
(online `http://www.chiossone.it >archivio >atti convegno`)
2. Dini-Gettani: Software didattico: risorsa per i ragazzi con disabilità visiva. in Atti del convegno L'Occhio della mente 2003
(online `http://www.chiossone.it >archivio >atti convegno`)
3. Zingirian, M., Calabria, G., Ciurlo, G.: Oftalmologia e qualità della visione. Editoriale I.N.C. Innovation, Roma 1992
4. Zingirian, M., Gandolfo, E.: Ipovisione. Nuova frontiera dell'oftalmologia. SOI-Società Oftalmologica Italiana, Roma 2002

# Use of Bar Code and RFID for the Visually Impaired in Educational Environment

Hisayuki Tatsumi[1], Yasuyuki Murai[2], Masahiro Miyakawa[1], and Shinji Tokumasu[2]

[1] Department of Computer Science, Tsukuba College of Technology
4-12-7 Kasuga, Tsukuba, Ibaraki 305-0821, Japan
{tatsumi,mamiyaka}@cs.k.tsukuba-tech.ac.jp
[2] Department of Information and Computer Sciences
Kanagawa Institute of Technology
1030 Simo-ogino, Atsugi, Kanagawa, 243-0292 Japan
{murai,tokumasu}@ic.kanagawa-it.ac.jp

**Abstract.** Getting information from a bar code or from RFID tags attached to equipments or surroundings is a promising step for building an information ensured area for the visually impaired. For example one can obtain an operation manual (voice version) from the tag attached to some electronic equipment. The purpose of the project we report here is the construction of such information ensured environment in the college life. We present two concrete examples: getting voice access to announcement on the bulletin board by using bar code, and messaging system between students and teacher by using RFID. We show that data-carrier technologies are effective for information ensuring for the visually impaired.

## 1 Introduction

For visually impaired people, information about his surroundings is provided only by strictly limited ways. Braille inscription plate or braille seal (sticker) is widely used for this purpose, but they are too restrictive. On the other hand, there are data carriers such as bar code or RFID (Radio-Frequency Identification) which allow versatile usage. Bar code is well-known. It is read by laser beam. An RFID tag is a device in which IC tip and antenna for radio communications are combined. It emits ID (information) in response to query from a reader (which consists of a radio communication device). Both can be attached to things easily and admit non-contact reading which could be done by the visually impaired (an approximate pointing is required). Simple electronic access to these data carriers yields rich information real time in electronic form. In limited situations where things go routine as in college life, blind students can do access to these data carries as sighted students.

For example, let your pocket computer (PDA: Personal Digital Assistant) read a bar code attached to some electronic equipment. The signal is sent to server and you get an instruction manual (voice version) for using it (this avoids a laborious communication, say, for down-loading, between you and the server

K. Miesenberger et al. (Eds.): ICCHP 2004, LNCS 3118, pp. 583–588, 2004.

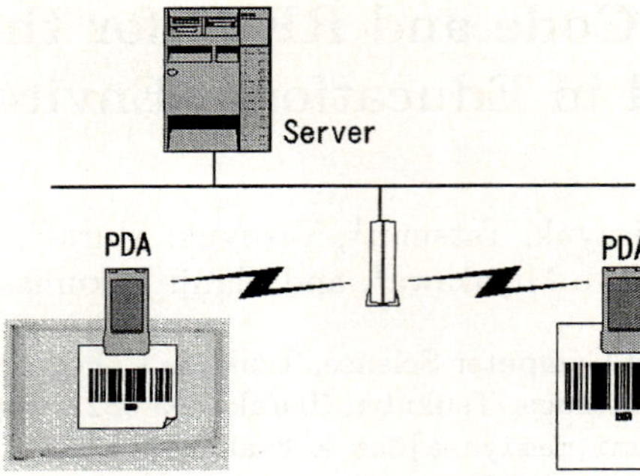


**Fig. 1.** System overview

under voice-environment); or let your PDA read a bar code attached to an announcement on the bulletin board, then the announcement (voice version) is delivered to you by the server (delivering an announcement for visually impaired students is a very complicated task in the college life; currently, printing and its braille translation is placed side by side at the bulletin corner for the students; definitely this is not the best way).

We have started our project first by use of bar code for bulletin system[3]. For bulletining in the college we have alternative ways (for example, we can use Web for this purpose). However, our goal is to provide information ensured environment in which blind students can do the same way as sighted as much as possible. In view of the growing use of RFID, we have extended our information ensuring system to include messaging system using RFID tags. Our preliminary experiments show that reading a bar code by the visually impaired is fairly feasible[3]. And so use of data-carrier system simplifies a complicated interaction and therefore increases accessibility. We expect that our system is useful and promising for constructing information ensured environment for the visually impaired in the college life.

## 2 Bulletin System Using Bar Code

Bar code is a simple data carrier which is used most widely. We use only one-dimensional bar code (two dimensional one is not suited for reading by the visually impaired). Our bulletin system for blind students using bar code functions as follows.

1. A bar code is printed on an announcement (at the left-bottom, Fig. 3) on the bulletin board.
2. Student reads a bar code using PDA with a bar code scanner attached to it.
3. PDA sends the bar code to the server and automatically downloads information from it.
4. Finally, student reads it by using voice reader software.

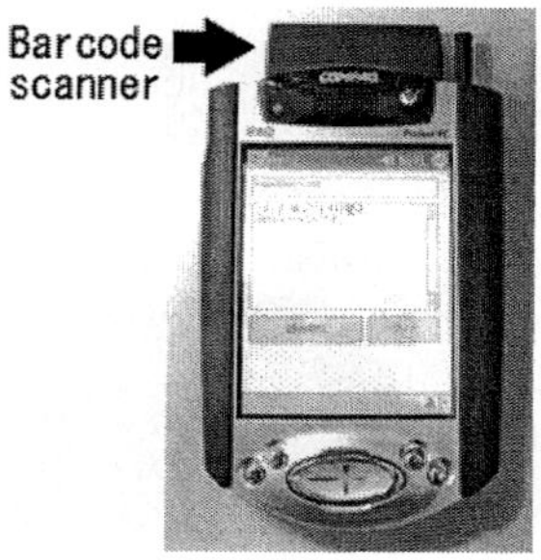


**Fig. 2.** PDA with a bar code scanner attached to it

**Fig. 3.** Bar code printed on an announcement

On Fig. 1 we show our system organization: it consists of the following: 1. Hardware (PDA) with suitably implemented programs, 2. Communication programs, and 3. Database management programs on the server.

For reading a bar code and communicating with the server (downloading) we use a PDA with a bar code scanner attached to it (Fig. 2). A bar code scanner (also called reader) emits laser beam and reads a bar code optically. The detail of our hardware components are as follows.

1. PDA (HP iPAQ Pocket PC h5550 in which wireless LAN is embedded).
2. CF Card style bar code laser scanner (IBS Japan, Pocket Scanner, PLS-5000).
3. A server (PC: personal computer with Windows XP).
4. Access Point for wireless LAN.

On Fig. 2 we show a PDA with a bar code scanner attached to it. On Fig. 3 we show an announcement (it is of a seminar to be held at 13:00 on April 14th at a room on the 5th floor). Corresponding bar code is printed on it (note that it is of elongated shape to provide wider area). On Fig. 4 PDA display after reading is shown (the announcement is shown in the text window).

The program consists of two modules: server module which stores information (text data) in the server and retrieves it from the server and PDA module which reads a bar code on an announcement. Both modules are written in Microsoft Visual Basic.Net on Windows XP and on Windows Mobile 2003 operating system for PDA. For database manipulation we use Microsoft Access and as a communication protocol we use TCP/IP. Bar code scanner is driven by a program under API which works with iSCAN.DLL (delivered together with the scanner device [5]). Test database format consists of three fields: bar code, title and body (text), and here bar code serves as a searching key. Database is registered by Access beforehand in the server.

The server module behaves in the following way.

1. When invoked, the server module is on stand-by for bar code signals.
2. When the bar code is received, searching for the item which has the same key (bar code) is done, and the content (text) is sent back to PDA.

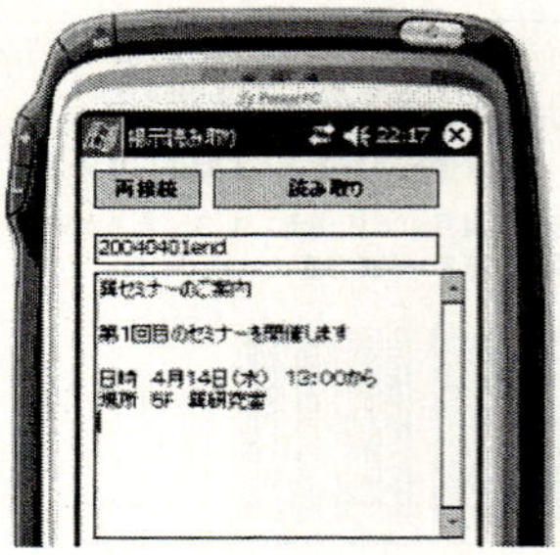


**Fig. 4.** PDA display after reading a bar code

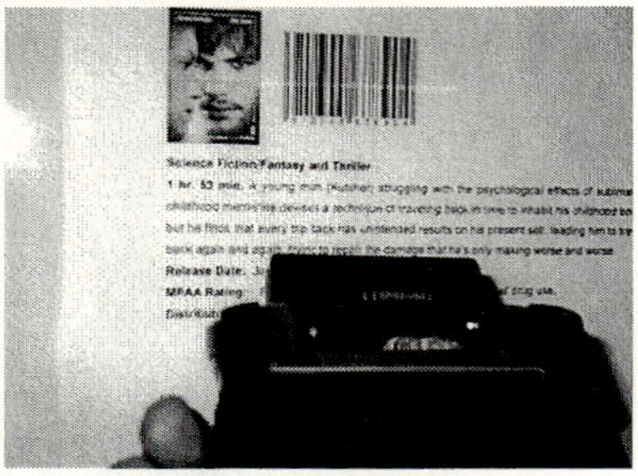

**Fig. 5.** Bar code reading on the bulletin board

The PDA module emits laser beam and reads a bar code on an announcement when a read-in command is initiated. Two different methods are provided for initiating this reading procedure: one is by clicking the software button on the PDA window, and the other is by pressing the hardware button on the PDA equipment (there are four buttons and any of them can be used for this purpose). The latter method is important for the visually impaired. The reply from the server is displayed on the text box of PDA (visually impaired student reads this by voice reader software, but at present time we have no such software implemented on PDA). On Fig. 5 we show a picture of PDA reading a bar code printed on an announcement on the bulletin board.

We have checked the allowance of bar code reading with respect to both the distance between a bar code and the laser diode, and the angle between the normal line to the plane (defined by announcement paper) and the laser beam of PDA [3]. For 32mm x 11mm standard bar code, the allowance of reading is roughly less than 30 cm and less than 50 degrees. Our preliminary experiment shows that blind student can hit a bar code on an announcement provided it is printed in a pre-defined area.

## 3 Messaging System Using RFID

Bar code is a read only memory, while RFID tag contains erasable and repeatedly writable memories in it (the memories are so limited at present that various information is to be stored as simple numbers in coded form), and so one can leave (write) a message on it. Considering these characteristics of RFID we have implemented the following messaging system between students and teacher in the college life.

RFID tag attached to a laboratory door keeps the message from teacher, for example, where he left for (destination) and when he will be back again. Visitor (blind student) can read it and can leave his own message to teacher.

On Fig. 6 we indicate devices used in this experiment. They are an RFID tag (V720-D52P02, OMRON Co.) and a PDA (HP iPAQ Pocket PC h5550,

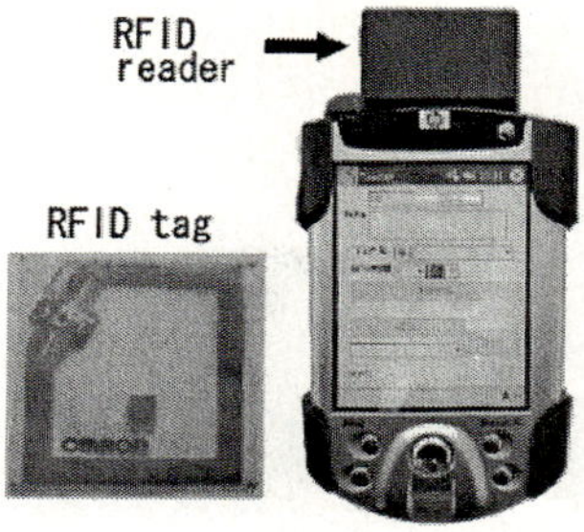


**Fig. 6.** RFID tag and RFID reader

**Fig. 7.** RFID messages (left: for teacher, right: for student)

Hewlett-Packard; the same one which we have used for bar code reading) with a portable RFID reader-writer (CF-card type RFID unit V720-HMF01, OMRON Co.) attached to it. The RFID tag is of the size 5cm x 5cm and has 44 bytes writable memory. Tag and reader communicate with 13.56 MHz electro-magnetic induction wave. As a tag has no electric power supply and reader's electric power is supplied via PDA's battery (which has a very limited capacity), the communication is barely possible only up to (maximum) 5cm distance between them (Fig. 8). However, visually impaired student can establish a communication between the two devices if he knows the rough location of RFID.

We have used the same programming environment as with the bar code system (Section 2). We need ActiveX control (RFIDCom.ocx made by OMRON Co. [6]) for RFID reader-writer together with CFCOM (made by Odyssey Co. [7]) which is needed to operate on .NET Compact Frame. The program consists of two modules. Teacher module inputs teacher's destination and his returning time into RFID and outputs (displays) from it a list of visitors who were there during his absence. The inputting operation is done via display interface by using a stylus pen attached to PDA (we assume that teacher is sighted). Student module displays (reads) teacher's destination from RFID and inputs student name and the time of his visit into RFID. In order to assist his visual impairment we register his name in his PDA beforehand, so that he can input his name into RFID by merely pressing a hardware button of his PDA. On Fig. 7 we indicate respective PDA displays for teacher and for student; for teacher it shows a list of visitors and their visit times and for student it shows teacher's message saying that he is out for lecturing and will be back at 13:30.

On Fig. 8 we show a picture of how we establish a communication between RFID tag (attached near an electronic device) and RFID reader-writer attached to PDA.

## 4 Conclusions

Both bar code reading and RFID reading are preliminarily tested by blind students. Manipulation via hardware button is essential. We have used the bar

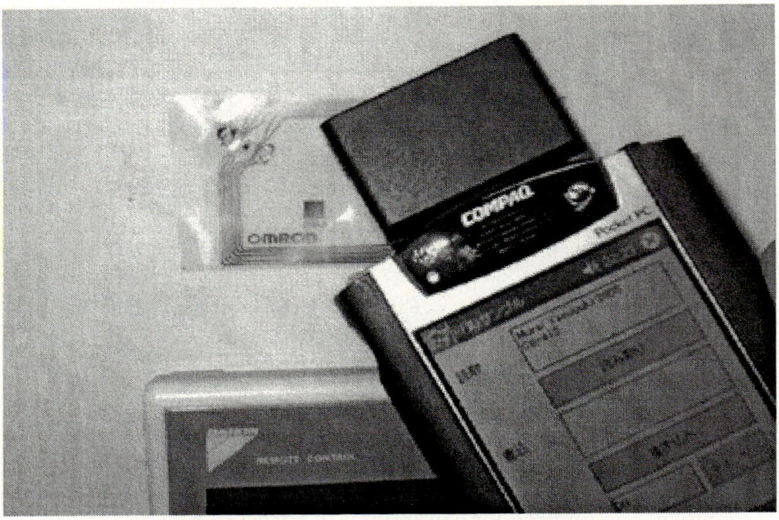


**Fig. 8.** Reading an RFID tag by reader-writer attached to PDA

code scanner attached to PDA and found that this was not always a comfortable choice. Locating a bar code on an announcement is not always reliable. Hardness occurs even though we use a special bar code print in prolonged form (printed by MS Word) and even though we mark its location by a braille seal. So handy scanner or pen type scanner may be more adequate.

We need testing of the systems in real college life for improvement. Some other directions of application we include library and manuals of electronic equipments.

## References


1. Siio, I., Hayasaka, T.: Putting information to things : RFID tags and their applications, IPSJ Magazine, Vol.40, No.8, pp.846-850, Aug. 1999
2. Murakami, M., Kuroda, T., Manabe, Y., Chihara, K.: Shopping support system for blind people using barcode, Proc. Human Interface 2001, No.1412, pp.97-98, Oct. 2001
3. Tatsumi, H., Miyakakawa, M., Kotaka, Y., Murai, Y.: Incorporation of bar code reader system in the education for the visually impaired (Part 1) – Proposal of a prototype, TCT Techno Report, **10**(2), 27-31, 2003.
4. Satoh, I.: Bridging physical and virtual worlds with mobile agents, IPSJ Journal, Vol.44, No.8, pp.2218-2229, Aug. 2003
5. http://www.ibsjapan.com/PocketScannerSDK.htm
6. http://www.omronsoft.co.jp/rfid/index.html
7. http://www.odysseysoftware.com/cfcom_main.html

# Virtual Disability: Simulations as an Aid to Lecturers' Understanding of Disability

Simon Ball[1] and John Rousell[2]

[1] TechDis, The Network Centre, 4 Innovation Close, York YO10 5ZF, UK
[2] Sensory Impairment Service, Sheffield College, Castle Centre, Granville Road Sheffield S2 2RL, UK

**Abstract.** Many organisations and institutions in the education sector are now producing simulations of various disabilities in order to give academic staff an insight into some of the barriers disabled people can face in their education. This short paper will highlight some of the simulations designed by John Rousell of Sheffield College for use in accessibility training of academic staff. The paper shows stills of the original animations which can be found on the internet.

## 1 Introduction

The simulations utilise Flash and Shockwave technology, and therefore are not in themselves accessible to people who are blind or visually impaired. However, as they are designed to give sighted people an impression of what it is like to experience a visual impairment, this is hopefully not too big a problem. The simulations are intended to promote 'enlightened discussion' among academic staff, leading to better understanding of disability issues. The simulations cover four areas of accessibility: visual impairments, dyslexia, autism and hearing.

## 2 Visual Impairment

**Cataracts:** There are a variety of symptoms of cataracts, one of which is a yellowing of the vision. The simulation shows the same picture as seen through five degrees of yellowing.

**Fig. 1.** Simulation of yellowing caused by cataracts.

K. Miesenberger et al. (Eds.): ICCHP 2004, LNCS 3118, pp. 589–596, 2004.

**Colour Contrast:** This is a simple simulation showing a variety of text and background combinations, some of which are easier to read than others!

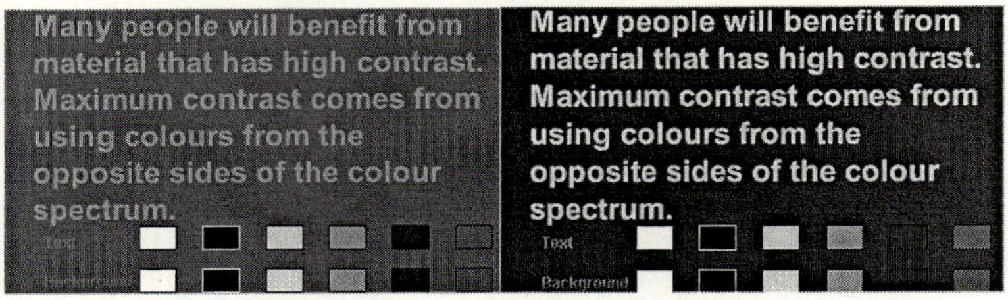


**Fig. 2.** Two combinations of text and background colour from a selection.

**Diabetes:** This simulation shows the effects of a type of diabetic retinopathy, where blood vessels in the retina rupture and form scar tissue, making vision blurred and patchy. The picture shows ducks swimming on a pond.

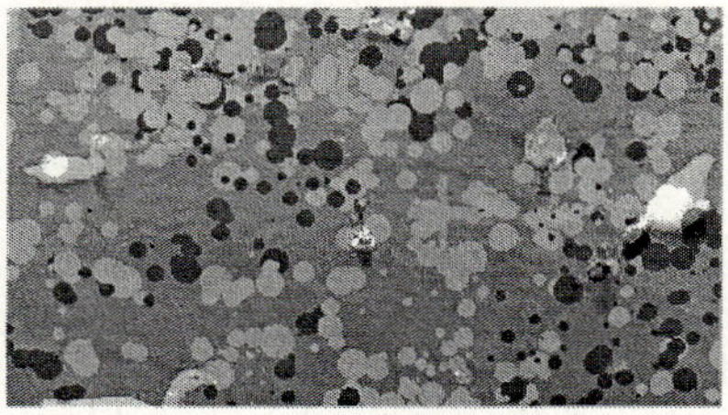

**Fig. 3.** Picture of ducks on a pond simulating diabetic retinopathy.

**Macular Degeneration:** The macular area of the eye enables us to see colour and fine detail. The degeneration of the macular area is a common cause of vision impairment in people over 60 years old. In this simulation the central area of vision has been completely lost.

**Fig. 4.** Simulation of loss of central vision area due to macular degeneration.

Macular degeneration can also cause words to apparently 'run' off the page, like in the example below.

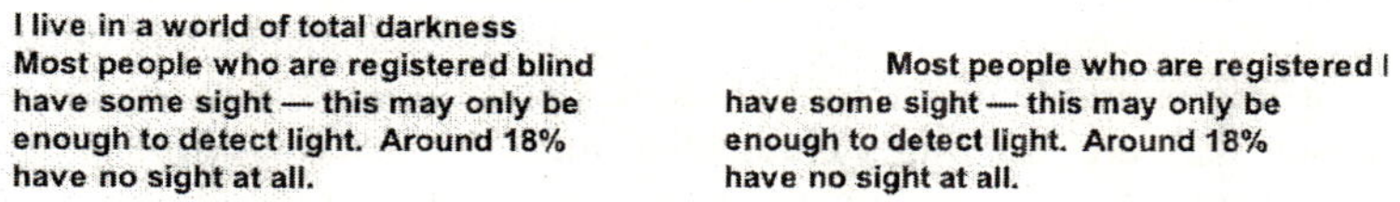


**Fig. 5.** Simulation of words 'running off the page' due to macular degeneration.

**Retinitis Pigmentosa:** This hereditary condition affects the retina, in this case in a way that the rods, which provide peripheral vision, have stopped working, a condition also known as 'tunnel vision'. In this simulation, a road is shown through a moving 'peephole'. To simulate tunnel vision. The user selects when to attempt to cross the road, and must avoid an oncoming vehicle.

**Fig. 6.** Simulation of 'tunnel vision'.

## 3 Deafness / Hard of Hearing

**Background Noise:** Background sounds that are present in many environments can be a great source of distraction for people who are hard of hearing. This may be due to their hearing aid amplifying all sounds. The distraction can lead to difficulties in concentration and lack of performance. Some digital hearing aids amplify sound frequencies around normal speech in an attempt to minimise background noise. The simulation contains background sounds that are likely to be found in most office and educational settings. Much of it would go unnoticed by people with good hearing. In the simulation, if the user clicks upon the lady's pencil she begins to tap it upon the desk, and a click on the clock, computer and printer will add even more background noises to the scenario.

**Intermittent Background Noise:** The simulation contains a background sound that is present in most urban areas – traffic. The opening of a window on a warm day or work outside can introduce this noise to a teaching situation. The simulation shows the difference in clarity between human speech and the same speech in combination with traffic noise.

**Lip Reading:** Lip reading is a common method used by people who are hard of hearing or deaf, either as an additional source of clarifying what is being said or as the only source. The technique involves watching the mouth shapes and position of the tongue. For lip reading to be successful the reader must be able to see the whole face of the person they are 'reading'. Things that make lip reading difficult include poor lighting, beards, and talking with hands or objects in front of the mouth.

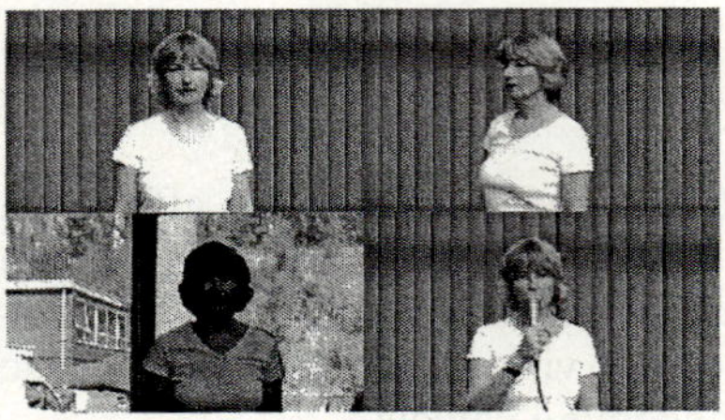

**Fig. 7.** Illustration showing good (top-left) and poor situations for lip-reading.

**Multi-tasking:** In teaching situations students receive information though various channels. Two of the main channels are auditory and visual. Most people are able to take information through these two channels simultaneously. However multiple information in one channel makes little sense. The simulation is based on what a person who is hard of hearing may be faced with if watching a slide show accompanied by a short talk. To access the talk they may use lip reading or follow someone signing, which leaves little or no time to look at the slide show, and greatly increases the cognitive burden. The simulation provides a great deal of information in a variety of forms, which the viewer struggles to take in.

## 4 Dyslexia

**Mirror or Reversal:** Reversal is the confusion of one letter or word with another such as d and b, or p and q. This reversal of letters, sometimes known as backwards or mirror writing is very common in the early stages of writing development among non-dyslexic and dyslexic children alike. In people with dyslexia this confusion may remain. This confusion can be problematic when using a word processor spell checking function. The machine is unable to produce a list of alternatives due to letter reversal in addition to mis-spelling.

**dyslexia affects people in different ways. The way their brains process information may make it difficult for them to interpret text, images and sounds. The difficulties experienced are found in young children acquiring literacy. It is the persistence of these difficulties, which does not coincide with achievements in other areas that indicates dyslexia**

normal

**byslexia affects qeoqle in bifferent ways. The way their drains qrocess information may make it bifficult for them to interqret text, images and sounbs. The bifficulties experienceb are founb in young chilbren acpuiring literacy. It is the qersistence of these bifficulties, which boes not coincibe with achievements in other areas that inbicates byslexia**

d-b and p-q

**Fig. 8.** Example showing reversal of d &b, and p&q.

**Proof Reading:** Proof reading is a very difficult task for many people with dyslexia. We often attempt to make sense of information received by allowing ourselves to be 'fooled' by optical illusions, leading us to 'invent' words in text that are not there in order to give it meaning. This difficulty is exacerbated in some people with dyslexia due to problems decoding the text. If the text has been written by themselves additional deviations from the original meaning may be present making predicting the text or grasping the meaning much more difficult.

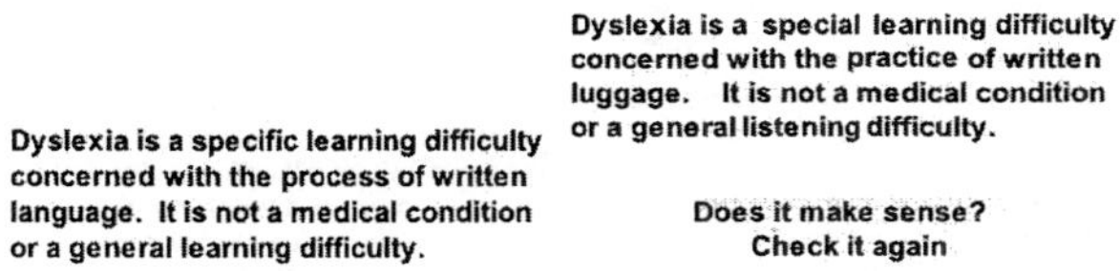


**Fig. 9.** Example showing subtle deviations in meaning by mis-reading.

**Scotopic Sensitivity:** Scotopic sensitivity, also known as Irlen Syndrome is a visual perceptual problem. The problem lies in how the visual information is decoded, it is not a medical eye condition. People with Scotopic Sensitivity 'see' the printed page differently to others and may even be unaware of this. This can lead to slow and inefficient reading, poor comprehension, fatigue and limited attention span. Many people with Scotopic Sensitivity report that the text on the page appears to dither, making reading difficult. Educational psychologist Helen Irlen observed in 1980 that coloured overlays helped students with Scotopic Sensitivity to read with greater ease.

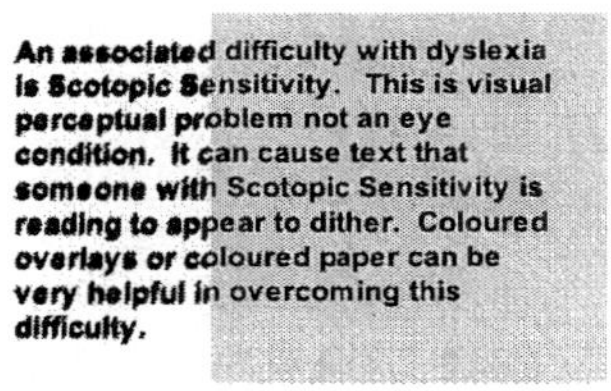


**Fig. 10.** Simulation of text 'dithering' and assistive coloured overlay.

**Shadow:** Some people who have dyslexic tendencies report that when reading text there appears to be a shadow on the text. This may be related to Scotopic Sensitivity difficulties. It may also have a link with the brightness of modern white paper. Room lighting, paper colour, text colour and fatigue are all factors which affect the intensity of the shadow. People seeing a shadow on text are at a disadvantage when reading due to the distraction that this causes. This may have a dramatic effect on reading rates that will fluctuate depending on conditions.

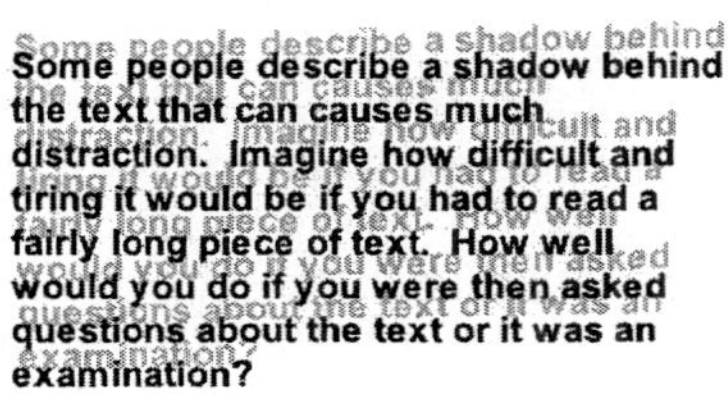


**Fig. 11.** Simulation of text 'shadow'.

**Telescoping:** Telescoping, relating to dyslexia, is a term used to describe words that have been written with sections missing; an example is 'rember' for 'remember'. The words are not always shortened - additional sections can be added; an example is 'begininning' for 'beginning'. It is also common for the ends of words to be missed off completely; an example is 'complet' for 'completely'. This difficulty makes written work produced difficult to understand when read back at a later time. Notes taken in class could be useless as a revision aid or may even be just wrong. Exams where written answers are required would present difficulties.

| | |
|---|---|
| One of the common errors people with dyslexia make is to telescope words and miss endings off. This is done when word processing and when handwriting text. Spellings due to this problem can be so unexpected that the spell checker is unable to make suggestions and rereading the text leaves the errors undetected. | One of the common errors peple with dyslxia make is to telescope words and miss ends off. This is done when word process and when handwring text. Spellings due to this prob can be so unxpected that the spell checker is unable to make suggions and reread the text leaves the errors undeted. |

**Fig. 12.** Simulation of text when 'telescoped' by a dyslexic reader.

**Word Mix:** People with dyslexia can have difficulty due to homophone confusion; an example is using 'there' for 'their' or 'grate' for 'great'. Phonic alternatives may also be a source of difficulty; an example is 'lite' for 'light' or 'ove' for 'of'. Confusion may be experienced in selecting a word from a 'family' of words; an example is 'this, that and the' may be used in place of each other. The substituting of words may not be consistent even within one piece of work. In the simulation below the confusion experienced in selecting words from a word family has been simulated.

| | |
|---|---|
| They set off from the post office where they had picked up a form. They also had picked up different forms for four other friends. When they got back they found some of the forms were not the ones their four friends had asked for, so they set off again with some of their friends so they could get more of the forms for them from another branch of the post office. ① | They set of for the post office where they had picked up a form. They also had picked up different forms of four other friends. When they got back they found some for the forms were not the ones their four friends had asked from, so they set of again with some for their friends so they could get more off the forms from them for another branch from the post office. ④ |

**Fig. 13.** Example of how mixing of similar words can result in altered meaning.

## 5 Autism

**Monitors:** Some people who have autistic spectrum related difficulties report that when working with a computer they can see the screen flashing. The flashing cannot be detected by anyone else in the room and the monitor is probably not faulty. They are observing the screen refreshing itself. A conventional cathode ray tube (CRT) monitor refreshes at a rate of approximately 50 to 80 times per second, most people using the monitor are unaware of the refresh rate and are unable to detect it. It can be observed sometimes when computers are shown on a television broadcast due to the synchronisation of equipment used.

**Overload:** Many designers of printed material want to make their productions as interesting as possible to the target audience. When the audience is young the designers attempt to make things as exiting as they can. This often leads to pictures that are packed with information, much of it additional to the primary message of the material. People who have autism can have great difficulty ignoring the surplus information, so much so that they can miss the message because their attention is being 'grabbed' by the additional information. Pictures that contain bright action images can appear to have movement. Some students complain that certain images contain so much information that they are 'painful' to look at.

**Pixels:** All pictures, text and icons displayed by cathode ray tube (CRT) computer monitors are made up from tiny dots called pixels. The pixels are small and there are a lot of them, around 784 per square centimetre. If you look at a monitor through a magnifying glass you will be able to see them. Most people never notice the pixels as their brains attempt to make sense of whatever is on screen. People with autism may be observing a display of pixels that make very little sense to them. This will be much more pronounced in pictures rather than with text.

**Fig. 14.** Simulation of the pixelation of an image due to autism (please could we increase the size of these pictures a little?).

**Recognition:** There are millions of people in this country yet most people are able to recognise family and friends instantly when they meet them. This is mostly achieved through studying and remembering facial features. Most people have been in the position of being aware that there is something different about a friend, only to discover they have a new hairstyle. One of the defining traits of autism is that people with it may have difficulty reading facial expressions and making eye contact. This can lead to using unconventional methods of recognising individuals. A person with autism would possibly only recognise C as being the same person in the question.

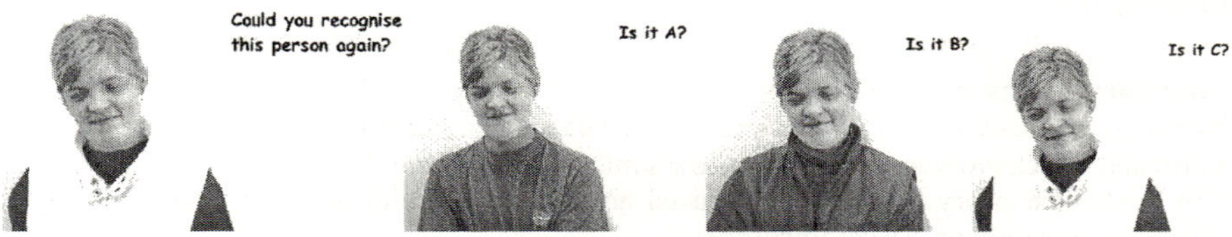


**Fig. 15.** Exercise highlighting the use of features such as clothes in recognition by people with autism.

**Representations:** When representing three-dimensional objects with a two-dimensional medium certain conventions are used. These conventions are used so often that most people require no explanation and are aware of what is being represented. These conventions are used in printed material and on computer monitors. Isometric projection is one of the commonly used conventions for drawing three-dimensional objects. A person with autism may see something quite different to what many others see, seeing only an array of flat shapes (on the right) rather than the three-dimensional shapes most people see (on the left).

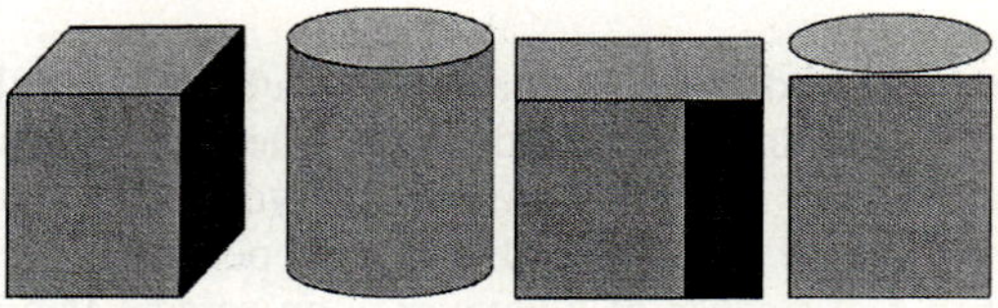

**Fig. 16.** Some autistic people see only flat shapes when most people would see three-dimensional shapes.

**Sounds:** Many working and educational environments contain unwanted background sounds. Most people are able to screen out these sounds to a certain degree. When travelling by plane the engine sound is soon acclimatised to and does not distract the traveller from the onboard entertainment. A person who has autism may be unable to screen out sounds which are barely noticeable to others using the room. The simulation utilised to illustrate this point is the same as the 'Background noise' simulation described earlier.

## 6 Conclusion

Simulations such as these are a useful means of communicating the physical effects of some disabilities to teaching staff who may otherwise be unaware of just how some conditions manifest themselves. They may give an indication to staff of some of the barriers disabled students face when accessing their teaching or learning materials. This in turn may enable staff to make their materials more accessible or inclusive. This is the ultimate goal of these simple simulations.

## References

1. These simulations can be found at:
   `http://members.aol.com/srousell/sim-dis/index.html`,
   Flash and Shockwave are required to view some of the material
2. The Scottish Sensory Centre has produced an extremely useful resource of a similar type which focuses only on Visual Impairment at,
   http://www.ssc.mhie.ac.uk/VI_Video/N_VIDEO/MainIndx.htm

# Multimedia Software Training Tool (MSTT) for Persons with Visual and Mobile Impairments in Four Languages

A. Mousadakou, M. Gemou, and E. Bekiaris

Centre for Research and Technology Hellas / Hellenic Institute of Transport,
6th km. Charilaou-Thermi Road, 57001 Thermi, Greece
{amousa,mgemou,abek}@certh.gr

**Abstract.** This paper presents an innovative, user-friendly multimedia software tool for the training of persons with visual and mobile impairments, to be developed within the TELL-IT European research program. This multimedia software training tool (MSTT) refers to all those persons who are visually and mobility disabled and wish to be trained in order to be employed as help-desk services providers. The MSTT will provide them all the necessary knowledge and training to prepare them for their sufficient tasks performance. The MSTT is a modular training tool, which will be developed in two modes: one for distant, self-learning and another for on-the-job guided training. Both will be translated in four (4) languages (English, French, Greek, Spanish). For both modes, two types of software packages will be developed, one for training and one for testing. It will interface the necessary software and hardware aids, in order to be usable by people with mobility and/or visual impairments.

## 1 Introduction

One of the fastest growing sectors in modern economy is that of services. This sector is creating thousands of jobs Europe-wide annually. A significant part of these jobs are related to service support operations, such as after sales support, public relations and most important of all, helpdesk services. Currently, the employment of PSN in the service sector is far below the average, due to a number of associate difficulties, such as how to reach the office, office adaptations needed, lack of skills required, low level of computer knowledge, etc.

TELL-IT intends, among others, to develop a multimedia, flexible and continuing training program for on-the-job training for people with mobility and/or visual impairments in the service provision sector and more specifically, in helpdesk operations. The developed service will be tested and optimised in Pilots in three EU countries, namely in the helpdesk of a mobile telephone company in Spain, a computer knowledge certification company in Greece, and a disabled training centre in Ireland; all of which belong to pan-European networks.

## 2 MSTT Functional Specifications

### 2.1 MSTT Content and Structure Specifications

The MSTT will be connected to a users performance database, in which the data included in the log files and concerning the trainees performance will be stored. An

K. Miesenberger et al. (Eds.): ICCHP 2004, LNCS 3118, pp. 597–600, 2004.

individual record will correspond to each trainee, which will include, besides the trainees scores, their personal data info.

The MSTT users, who will not attend a guided training course, will be able to register to a remote database themselves and create their own record. In such a case of a new user, the MSTT will request for more personal information than a "user name" and a "password" to login, like in the guided training course case. These will refer to the name/surname of the new user, age, contact info like his/her address, telephone, e-mail address if available, current and previous occupation and finally specific disease/disability (Fig. 1). In this way, the self-learner trainee will be able to continuously monitor his/her performance even if s/he is not attending a course.

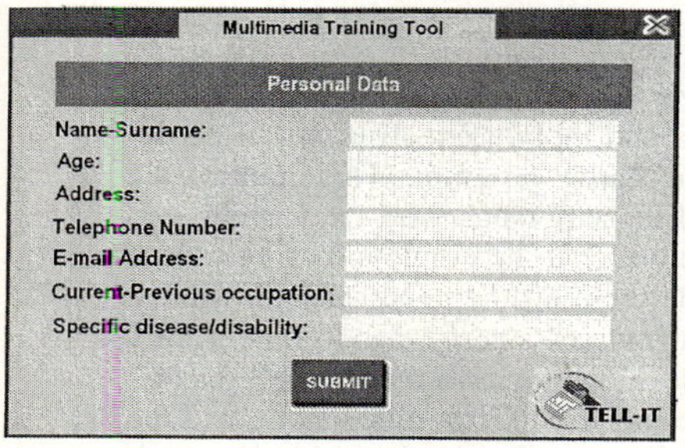


**Fig. 1.** Personal information screenshot.

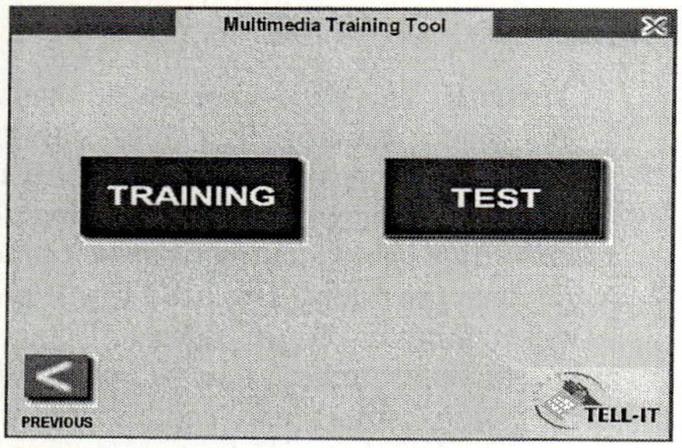


**Fig. 2.** Software package configuration screenshot.

The MSTT consists of two basic modes: the "TRAINING" mode and the "TEST" mode (Fig. 2). The "TRAINING" mode is divided in sessions which consist of scenarios relevant to each other. The critical merging and combination of them lead to the "TEST" mode sessions which are identified according to their corresponding level of difficulty (*LoD*). Three levels of difficulty (LoD) have been proposed. Each section of a level of difficulty will consist of test sessions, the number of which will be the same to the number of the training sessions. At last, three ranking areas are decided for the "CERTIFICATE LEVEL" (LoD 4), which derives from the reprocessing and combination of knowledge acquired from all training scenarios included in the "TRAINING" mode sessions, consists of distinguished exams and aims to classify the trainees according to their performance.

In the training mode, a theoretical and an exercise part for each MSTT scenario determined will be included. The theoretical part will include the description of the task/scenario, the detailed description of the way it should be performed and all the necessary information input, the additional possible responsibilities that might be requested, the content, the aim and objectives of the task described and, finally, in the last part, the references to the aids being applicable to this case for tasks performance for both disability categories.

The training mode will include a series of scenarios distinguished in generic sessions, based on the tasks and the Use Cases determined by TELL-IT Consortium experts. The sessions identified so far are namely, "Answering, routing and prioritizing phone calls" , "Handling correspondence (by post and/or electronically)", "Reading and sending fax messages", "Scheduling, attending and coordinating meetings", "Making travel arrangements", "File keeping and handling (physically, electronically)", "Preparing reports (physically, electronically)", "Preparing list of consumable equipment for purchase", "Handling customers' requests", "Attending to visitors".

Besides the above mentioned tasks, the first session of the training mode will be an explanatory introduction to the help-desk services, including the description of all possible met scenarios of this profession in the market, the main tasks required to be performed, some statistics of the PSN who already work at this area, the relevant laws which are corresponding to the employed PSN in the European Union and some references to the places these persons could seek for job after the training. A short description and useful advice regarding the MSTT use will be also included. Additionally, the last session of the training mode will be devoted to the aids available in the market and their relevance to the main tasks mentioned in the first chapter. The aids use is described analytically and is related to each disability category of the TELL-IT target group and at the same time to each help-desk task. The identified MSTT sessions are depicted in Fig. 3.

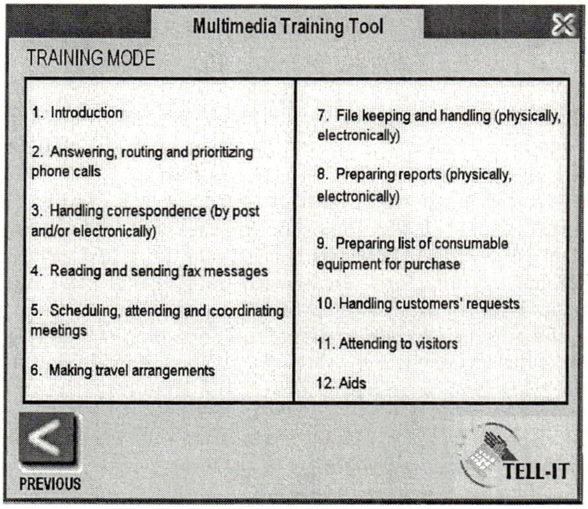


**Fig. 3.** Training mode identified sessions.

For the self-training MSTT, a more extensive introduction including the theory regarding the job's responsibilities, exercises and tests as well as the use and the operation of the self-learning MSTT is included. The self-learning MSTT mode content provides some additional parts in both the theoretical and exercise parts of the training mode scenarios and if it is needed, some additional texts and/or exercises are provided for each disability category in some scenarios.

The exercise part of each scenario of the training mode follows the theoretical part and is closely related to it. The exercise parts of the training mode and the test mode contain tests and exercises of various forms, such as multiple choice questions, simple questions, interactive videos/animations/pictures, correct/wrong questions, matching pairs.

The User Interface accessibility of the MSTT follows all existing standards and the W3C guidelines. The MSTT as well as the Users Performance Database are available in 4 languages: English, French, Spanish, Greek. The MSTT is compatible with the Users Performance Database and the basic PSN aids, and is developed for PC and specifically as a Windows based software.

## 3 Conclusion

The multimedia training software tool (MSTT) to be developed within the TELL-IT project aims at the inclusion of the disabled persons in the production chain, which is significant for the disabled persons autonomy and quality of life as well as for the society as a whole, since the unemployment of those persons and their exclusion from the fundamental social procedures encumber further progress in general. Finally, one of the most encouraging perspectives in the MSTT design is the fact that it allows implementation in other disability categories training besides the mobility and visually disabled, if the corresponding aids are integrated, since its design fills all disabilities requirements, with no further or some slight additional functionalities integration.

## References

1. Morgan, Chilsolm, N., Structured training – A course manual, Morgan A, 1990
2. Bekiaris, E., Panou, M., Knoll, C., Waard, D., User Interface of Interactive Multimedia Tool, TRAINER project, GRD1-1999-10024, April 2003
3. `http://ergo.human.cornell.edu/ahtutorials/interface.html`
4. Istituto "Leonarda Vaccari" (1998). Report of 2nd Transnational meeting at Ferrol (Spain), on the HORIZON Project "H-FORM" (N.H. 1997 - IT 539), ITALY
5. SIPU (The National Institute for Civil Service training and Development, International Division), Handbook for trainers 1991, Sweden.
6. Stephanidis, C., Savidis, A., Akoumianakis, D., Tools for User Interfaces for All, In: The European Context for Assistive Technology, I.Placencia Porrero and R. Ruid de la Bellacasa (eds.), IOS Press, 1995, p. 167-170

# Designing New Technology Based Services to Support Visually Impaired Computer Workers (VICWs)

J. Joyce Beumer, M. Wiethoff, and J. Attema

Delft University of Technology, the Netherlands
Faculty Technology, Policy and Management
Group of Work and Organizational Psychology
The Netherlands
J.J.Beumer@tbm.tudelft.nl

**Abstract.** Audio Supported Application Sharing (ASAS) tool based services design can be used to overcome problems of Visually Impaired Computer Workers (VICWs). ASAS tool services are expected to increase performance of both individuals and organizations. First, the individual performance will be positively influenced because trainers and VICWs will perform tasks in a more efficient way with help of ASAS tools in comparison to the old way of task performance. Second, the organizational performance will be positively influenced because due to the ASAS tool technology the organization can perform their activities in a more efficient way. ASAS tools will contribute significantly to travel time reduction, comfort and reduction of costs on the overall level. Lifelong support will increase the VICW contribution to the working society. Support with ASAS tools will not lead to changes in task time. This paper will describe ASAS tool service design and how the service changes performance.

## 1 Introduction

Visually Impaired Computer Workers (VICWs) are getting new opportunities to work in jobs due to the rapid growth of computer use (Edward, and Levis (1999). More and more computer applications enable VICWs to function where in the past the barriers were impossible to overcome. Astroft (1984, p 108) stated that "Technology is one of the blind person's most powerful allies in overcoming the detrimental effects of blindness." VICWs can work with the same applications as Well Sighted Computer Workers (WSCW's) when using adaptations like speech synthesizers (Arato & Vespori 1982; Blenchorn 1982) and braille displays Dune & Dune 1999). With the introduction of these adaptations, new questions arise (Beumer 2002). VICWs have to learn to work with both new computer adaptations and applications. The rapid growth of new applications and adaptations causes long waiting lists for special computer training at rehabilitation centers. Efficient methods of training should be developed to decrease these long waiting lists. One important solution to help resolving these waiting lists is to present on line help at a distance, so as to enable trainees to receive part of the training at home or to support them after finalizing the traineeship.

Therefore, new services for supporting VICWs with various kinds of computer problems with help at distance were designed in a joint project of Stichting Het Loo

K. Miesenberger et al. (Eds.): ICCHP 2004, LNCS 3118, pp. 601–608, 2004.

Erf and Delft University of Technology[1] This support is given with an Audio Supported Application Sharing (ASAS) tool. Audio support is given via a telephone connection, or via the Internet. Application sharing is mediated by the Internet; it enables cooperation between two persons on a distance by displaying the information appearing on the monitor of one computer also on the monitor of the other computer.

VICWs will be able to shorten their training in a rehabilitation center, if they can finish their rehabilitation at home. Evidently, this would be a considerable advantage for most stakeholders, in particular for the trainees themselves. For the rehabilitation centers, it would allow them to shorten internal rehabilitation periods for individuals and therefore increase their capacity. It also gives them the possibility for more custom-made support, because persons contact the center only if needed. For insurance companies, it would save considerable costs: a day in a rehabilitation center is very expensive, comparable to a hospital day. Furthermore, VICWs would return faster in a paid job because support from a distance can be given. Furthermore, for those situations in which some companies use their own custom made software where it would be virtually impossible to train VICWs outside the buildings of the company, help at a distance would be a solution.

The key question of this paper is:

*What should the functionalities and appearance of a new service based on ASAS tools be, in order to facilitate computer support within the necessary conditions, and how would this tool influence performance?*

By addressing this question, a participatory design approach is adopted. This has a considerable influence on the type and content of the results. Therefore, this article will first discuss the design approach. Second, the functionalities and appearance of the designed services will be presented together with its expected effects. Finally these will be discussed.

## 2 Design Approach EXSE: Early Experiment and Scenario-Based Evaluation

EXSE (Early experiment- and Scenario based Evaluation) is the participatory design approach adopted in this study. It is inspired on ESE (Early Scenario based Evaluation; van den Anker 2003). Basically, the focus is on multiple stakeholder analysis predicting organizational change due to the new ICT applications. Van den Anker defined a conceptual framework for the development of new applications for multimedia communication that fit into mobile work. His statement is that a participatory design approach in which rich scenarios are combined with simulation is needed to evaluate new ICT, already in a very early stage of development. These scenarios are divided in detailed descriptions of the current and future work context in which the new ICT application will function.

EXSE combines multiple stakeholder analysis with end user experiments. Multiple stakeholder analysis will describe the predicted organizational changes due to the new ASAS tool service. End user experiments will be used to pre-test, measuring expecta-

[1] Financed by Dutch Government, Department of Economic Affairs (Min EZ), SENTER.

tions about actual performance, and evaluate the new ASAS tool service. In EXSE, five main steps can be distinguished. The remaining of this section will explain how each step was performed in the design of a new ASAS tool service (see fig. 1).

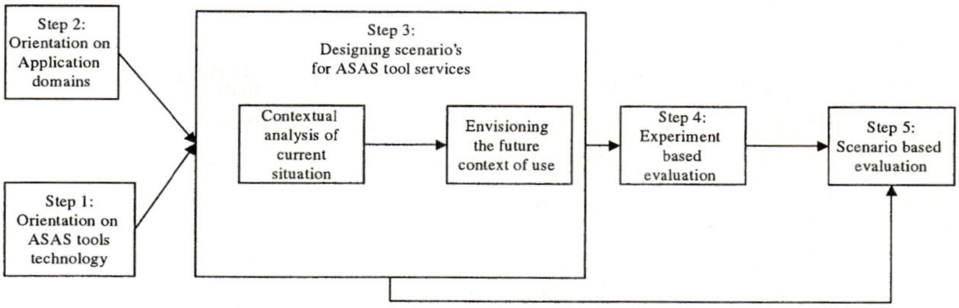


**Fig. 1.** The steps needed to perform EXSE.

Step 1: Orientation on ASAS tool technology consists of a literature review, interviews and presents an overview on tool technology, features and explains the ASAS tool concept such as its generic functions. Preferred features of the ASAS tool are also presented with different tests results. These tests include a systematic analysis of different ASAS tools in combination with different computer aids for VICWs.

Step 2: Orientation on Application domains describes the domain or the (organizational) context in which the ASAS tool may be useful. First, with the help of internal reports, a contextual analysis of the current situation of the organization is performed. In this analysis an insight into the actual new work processes of the organization are envisioned, which contributes to the future context for which the ASAS tool should be designed.

Step 3: Designing scenarios for ASAS tool services. These are designed for the identified organizational context, with the help of internal reports, observations and interviews with different stakeholders at different levels in the organization. In the present study, 9 actors were interviewed individually: 6 came from a national rehabilitation center: 2 members from the management team, 2 computer trainers and 2 management advisors. Furthermore, there were 3 VICWs, from which one was already working in a regular job. Every new interview started with describing the contextual analysis. If necessary, the analysis was completed with a technological enquiry. The corrected and refined analysis was the foundation for an elaborate future work scenario.

Step 4 is the experiment-based evaluation, aimed at evaluating the usability and usefulness empirically of the future ASAS tool service. The experiment setting is based on the developed future ASAS tool service scenarios determined in step 3. The experiment has two functions: first to observe effects in efficiency, effectiveness, satisfaction and content of work of ASAS tool use. Second, it served as an illustration for stakeholders during the scenario-based evaluation phase performed in step 5. In the present study, 3 VICWs rehabilitants performed two hours of their normal computer course with the ASAS tool instead of their normal one. The course was given in two separate rooms; the trainer and the VICW used one. The courses were lessons on how to use the computer adaptation in combination with a Microsoft Office program. Microsoft NetMeeting combined with a telephone represented the ASAS tool. Two Windows 2000 pc's were used. The data together with the speech of the speech synthesizer was sent via the internal network. The internal telephone switchboard was used for sending voice information. Measurements concerned: whether the visual problems are solved with ASAS tools; the understanding of problems; satisfaction of trainer and VICW.

Step 5: The scenario-based evaluation. Here, various stakeholders, such as workers, managers, developers and other relevant stakeholders are involved. The stakeholder evaluation of the future ASAS tool services consists of two parts: first the opinions about performance changes, second the change of opinions throughout the design process. In the present study, 24 actors participated in the workshop. 12 of them came from the national rehabilitation center (1 member from the management team, 4 computer trainers, 3 management advisors and 4 technology experts). The other actors were 2 VICW rehabilitants from the center, 5 people from VICWs special interest groups, 2 trainers from a rehabilitation center concerning labor rehabilitation and two people from a regional center and finally one person from the funding organization SENTER. The workshop first presented the future ASAS tool service scenario followed by the experiment results presented by video fragments of these experiments. The workshop finally ended with a discussion on both the scenario description and the experiment results.

## 3 Results: ASAS Tool Services and Their Effects

**Step 1 Orientation on the ASAS Tool Technology:** The finalized technological enquiry with interview remarks, discussed the preferred ASAS tool features. Choice has been made for as much as possible standard available applications and standard hardware and software to run it on. These were: *ASAS tool*: Microsoft NetMeeting combined with the telephone. *Operating system:* personal computer with Windows 2000 or higher. *Version compute raids:* designed for Windows 2000. *Network:* ISDN, ADSL or faster. *Alternative network*: mobile telephone in combination with a normal telephone connection or cable *Internet connection:* for sending data and sounds of the speech synthesizer.

**Step 2 Orientation on Application Domains:** There are the following specific problems relevant for the case

- *Problems related to limitations of overview and high memory load.*

After VICWs have learned to work with the new aids they have to start to learn a specific application. VICWs will constantly be hindered by their handicap when they learn a new application. They always 'see' only a small portion of the screen at once. In Braille, they see a half to a full line; using a speech synthesizer, they hear all the information in succession, and with a magnification package they again see only a small portion of the screen. This means that VICWs have little or no overview of the screen, so that certain actions are less self-evident than for a well-sighted computer user (Beumer, Jameson, and Waterham, 2000). These problems are increased due to the rapid growth of new applications and adaptations, and the continuous changing process in which a lot of computer workers of an organization – also VICWs - are involved. These changing processes include steps in the career of the VICW, changes in operating systems of the computer, software changes or a new (version) of a computer aid. Sometimes a complete training in a new program or aid is needed; sometimes a single question has to be answered.

- *Problems related to finding support and receiving appropriate support from a helpdesk*

Suppliers of the computer aids, the rehabilitation center, or contact bulletin boards for mutual help have all their restrictions It is difficult for the VICW to see and therefore to communicate the relevant information to get support. Often it is not clear whether it is a technical problem, a usability problem, or a problem with adaptations. Furthermore, when the origin of the question is not clear, it is also not possible to determine in advance who has to pay for this kind of support. Rehabilitation centers do not want to pay for shortcomings in the software, and suppliers do not want to pay for lacks in the knowledge of VICWs. In the meantime special interest groups are struggling to answer the questions of VICWs by stimulating mutual help, bulletin boards and stimulating to contact them via telephone.

**Step 3 Designing ASAS Tool Services Scenario's:** The interviews revealed the following future ASAS tool services for these problems:

*Service: rehabilitation from a distance*

The introduction of ASAS tools will create the possibility of supporting VICWs from a distance, and therefore to go through parts of the computer rehabilitation course at home or at their work place. After the introduction course of the ASAS tool, the decision whether the VICW can finish the training at home, and the contents of the next training, will be based on observation and a questionnaire to be filled out by the VICW. Distance training should be combined with comeback days in which, the trainee has opportunity to receive additional instructions. The following organizations could play a role: 'Stichting Het Loo Erf' for supporting computer rehabilitation related to working situations; the regional rehabilitation centers for supporting the computer training for private situations. Others emphasize that their computer training is strongly influenced by the way in which their (new) computer aids work with the (work specific) software. In the case of specific coordination problems between software and hardware, the software suppliers of the computer aids should give the training.

Part of the additional scenario design will be illustrated with figure 2.Changes made in the scenario development are depicted in italic. Within the process of the scenario design, the initial draft scenarios were developed during the first interview with the project leader. In interviews to follow, these scenarios were enriched and adjusted. The scenarios covered issues like: working processes, roles of involved organizations, problem handling.

See Figure 2 for an example (italics are adjustments after the initial draft).

*Service: national help desk*

Interviewees concluded that a basic ASAS tool functionality would be a possible solution. The use of telephone in combination with an inspection facility in which the helpdesk assistant can share the information on the monitor of the VICW ( 'looking over the shoulder' functionality). Then, the origin of the problem can be determined and the VICW can be supported by the appropriate organization. Also mutual help between users will be stimulated, because the VICWs can see each other's problems and try to find a solution together.

- Jan Smit is 45 year old and worked as staff member at a service desk. One year ago he got a disease which made him blind. Jan went to 'Stichting Het Loo Erf' in which he got training for personal care, learned Braille and got a computer training in which he learned to work with Microsoft Windows *and NetMeeting* in combination with Infofox, a speech module.
- Because Jan wants to go back to his normal life as soon as possible, *the insurance company USZO financed a computer at home with a speech module, an extra speech module at his work, and an ADSL connection with 1000 ours telephone connection with Stichting Het Loo Erf. Also financial support for the mobile technology service of Stichting Het Loo Erf is given for two days to assist by problems with the ASAS tool connection.*
- With these means Jan can continue with his rehabilitation at distance. The courses are at cd-rom which he can follow orally. For problems he can use the ASAS tool: the trainer of Stichting Het Loo Erf will answer his questions immediately *or phones back when he has time*

........

**Fig. 2.** Scenario concerning rehabilitation from a distance.

**Step 4 Experiment Based Evaluation:** The participating trainers and VICWS were enthusiastic about the tool. In all question situations, trainer and VICW had first a telephone connection and then they started Netmeeting (first VICW 3 times, second 5 times and third 2 times). The trainer could give advice about starting NetMeeting directly via telephone. They spent between 3 and 4 minutes to start NetMeeting every time. One VICW was hesitant and had little computer experience. She told over and over that she would have a computer at home when the ASAS tool service would start. Also trainers were enthusiastic. They argued that after VICWs have basic knowledge about computer and adaptation, they can finish computer rehabilitation at home. They argued that every VICW has his own problems and knowledge, and that for every VICW it would be different at which moment during computer trainer they are able to finish their rehabilitation further on distance.Trainers and VICWs were all enthusiastic about help desk facilities with ASAS tools in which single questions could be asked. This service lacks at this moment and hampers a lot of VICWs in working with the computer.

All questions about the computer adaptations and the trained applications could most of the time being answered via ASAS tools. Some exceptions were found: One VICW does not know where she could find the floppy disc of her computer and one VICW does not know how to turn on the cassetterecorder. The trainer needed to show this physically. Another VICW once got a message of the system, which he did not observe. He only observed that he could not work further. When trainer and VICW started NetMeeting, the problem was solved automatically, because the message disappeared. One VICW had once difficulties to explain her problem via telephone, but when the trainer saw her screen after NetMeeting was started, she saw the problem immediately and she could solve it. Once it appeared that the trainer did not know how to solve the problem herself. She herself took over the operating system and with clicking she found the right answer for the VICW.

Three times a problem with Netmeeting occurred. Once a technical problem occurred which could not been solved on distance, because the connection with NetMeeting was not able to show the problems to the trainer. Second, one time the data connection was very slow and this hampered training. Third, there was one complaint about interference between speech of the telephone and the speech module.

Trainers need the same time to answer questions as in the face-to-face situation. Participants reported that VICWs learned better to solve the problem the next time by themselves, because the barriere to ask a teacher is much bigger with ASAS tools than in a face to face meeting. They also discussed that VICWs can easier explain what the trainer should do, which stimulate initiative. One of the VICW asked supplementary questions because he had already ASAS tool contact with the trainer for a question (five times).

**Step 5 Scenario Based Evaluation:** This evaluation showed that the future ASAS tool service is not restricted towards performance effects at the individual level as discussed in the experiment based evaluation The organization has to change different working processes and new organizational goals can be met due to the new technology. An example for a new organizational goal is to give VICWs lifelong support. In the long term this will save labor take over and will therefore save money. In the short term, however, this will cost money, because more VICWs will contact for help. This can be observed in the questionnaires: Although actors were satisfied and enthusiastic about the service, at the end they were negative about ASAS tool efficiency in terms of saving time and support time. The positive effects should be searched beyond.

Other performance effects are caused by some other factors. Actors expected that tasks will increase in amount and complexity. They expect that the amount of clients will increase and their computer skills will vary more, because different groups of users will benefit from ASAS tool use: experienced-, inexperienced- and the more severe their handicap the more they will benefit from the ASAS tool service. They expect that agents will need more skills to answer all questions correctly. They discussed that the organization has to be adjusted towards the new services in which organizational hardware – rooms, infrastructure – should be made equipped as ASAS tool service desk and organizational software – training users and scheduling ASAS tool use – should be adapted towards the new ASAS tool service.

Efficiency and usefulness was also evaluated less positively at the end of the design process. Their less positive ideas about usefulness concerned their thoughts that an ASAS tool will be a help for computer related questions, but can not replace other rehabilitation processes, e.g. emotional reactions and acceptance. Efficiency will be influenced by VICWs who will call with more and more complex questions.

## 4 Discussion and Conclusions

In this study, ASAS tools are designed by the participative design method EXSE. Although it is not possible to show what the final design would be with another design method, it can be shown what the contribution is of each step. Step 1 delivered the ASAS tool features that trainers need to exchange data and speech with VICWs. It would be clear that system requirements are high and this will limit its use. VICWs need a state of the art computer with new adaptations. Step 2 delivered some contexts in which the ASAS tool can be used. This situation overview is applied towards Dutch VICWs support, and has to be generalized towards other countries. Step 3 delivered the future ASAS tool service. Again it should be criticized if all scenario aspects were discussed. Step 4 is the experiment based evaluation. Allthough all participants were enthusiastic, this is only a small group and only tested in a laboratory environment. A real implementation (on small scale) has to test if these results are also obtained in real life. Step 5 is the scenario based evaluation. It showed how stakeholders got a more realistic idea about ASAS tool performance throughout the design; its challenges and its weaknesses. It furthermore specified wich organizational and individual aspects are expected to be influenced due to ASAS tool introduction. It was shown that benefits and cost (both individually and organizationally) are difficult to balance, but that positive effects of ASAS tool introduction are expected.

Evidently, the future ASAS tool service will allow VICWs to perform at least part of the rehabilitation at home instead of the rehabilitation center and it will allow a new way of incidental support. It is difficult, however, to predict the precise performance effects of a future ASAS tool service in advance. More VICWs are expected to call with different questions. The organization has to adapt her services towards question handling via ASAS tools. This will change organizational working processes and goals. The overall expectations of stakeholders and subjects of the experiment are positive.Although support with ASAS tools will not lead to changes in task time, ASAS tools will contribute significantly to travel time reduction, comfort and reduction of costs on the overall level. Lifelong support will increase the VICW contribution to the working society.

## References


1. Anker F.W.G. (2003) Scenarios @ work. Ponsen & Looijen B.V. Wageningen. The Netherlands ISBN 90-6464-973-1.
2. Beumer, J.J. & Jameson, A. & Waterham, R.P. (2000). Screen orientation: a matter of how you look at it: Alternative screen design to improve the computer accessibility for blind persons. *Proceedings of the International Conference on Computers Helping People with Special Needs 2000.* (pp 59-66). Osterreichische Computer Gesellschaft.
3. Arato, A. & Vespori, T. (1982). An intelligent screen reader integrated with synthetic speech for the blind. *Computers for handicapped persons.* Proceedings of the 3rd international conference on computer for handicapped persons, 8-13.
4. Astroft , S. (1984). Research on multimedia access to microcomputer for visually impaired youth. *Education of the Visually Handicapped*, **25**, 109-118.
5. Blenchorn, P.L . (1982). Requirements for screen access software using synthetic speech. *Computers for handicapped persons.* Proceedings of the 3rd international conference on computer for handicapped persons, 31-37.
6. Dune, I.K. & Dune, I. (1999). Instant Print-Braille Compatibility with Cobra. *Journal of Visual Impairment & Blindness,* 140-151.
7. Edward, A.D.N. & Levis, L. (1999). The use of technology in programs for students with visual impairments in Florida. *Journal of Visual Impairment & Blindness,* 302-310.

# Design and Use of Pseudo-electronic Whiteboard for Low-Vision Education

Yasuyuki Murai[1], Hisayuki Tatsumi[2],
Masahiro Miyakawa[2], and Shinji Tokumasu[1]

[1] Department of Information and Computer sciences
Kanagawa Institute of Technology,
1030 Shimoogino, Atsugi, Kanagawa, 243-0292, Japan
{murai,tokumasu}@ic.kanagawa-it.ac.jp
[2] Department of Computer Science, Tsukuba College of Technology,
4-12-7 Kasuga, Tsukuba, Ibaraki, 305-0821, Japan
{tatsumi,mamiyaka}@cs.k.tsukuba-tech.ac.jp

**Abstract.** We have built a pseudo-electronic whiteboard system (prototype) for low-vision education incorporating a commercial capturing system which mimic drawing on a plain whiteboard onto a monitor window (server-window). Moreover the capturing is such that the server window turns into a "super" pseudo-electronic whiteboard (projecting the captured whiteboard onto the whiteboard is essential). We implemented the distribution of the server-window to the class for low-vision education. We have added processing for increasing readability. Additionally the class shares separate window-area for questions and answers. The pseudo-electronic whiteboard system we made makes teacher and low-vision students share classroom education, which had been completely ignored so far.

## 1 Introduction

Education seems to be most influential when it is conducted "face to face". Whiteboard plays a significant role in classroom education; drawing on whiteboard is shared real-time by the whole class and this creates an on-site unity feeling in the class which is important in education. However, for weak-sighted students whiteboard used to be neglected.

In this paper we describe a design and use of a pseudo-electronic whiteboard for low-vision students which is built incorporating a commercial capturing system of whiteboard. The idea is simple: drawing on the whiteboard is captured real time and sent to students simultaneously, where further processing for increasing sight recognizability (basically, enlargement) is added. However, our project is inspired by an important invention incorporated in the capturing system which turns the whiteboard into a "super" pseudo-electronic whiteboard (here a projector is used, see Section 2 for detail). So distributing such a super electronic whiteboard enriches classroom education. Additionally we have implemented a shared area in the window for bidirectional communication between class and teacher. Thus our pseudo-electronic whiteboard system supports

K. Miesenberger et al. (Eds.): ICCHP 2004, LNCS 3118, pp. 609–612, 2004.

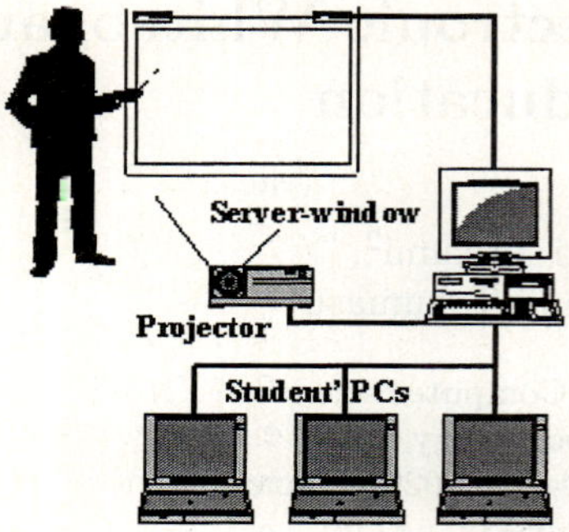


**Fig. 1.** System overview.

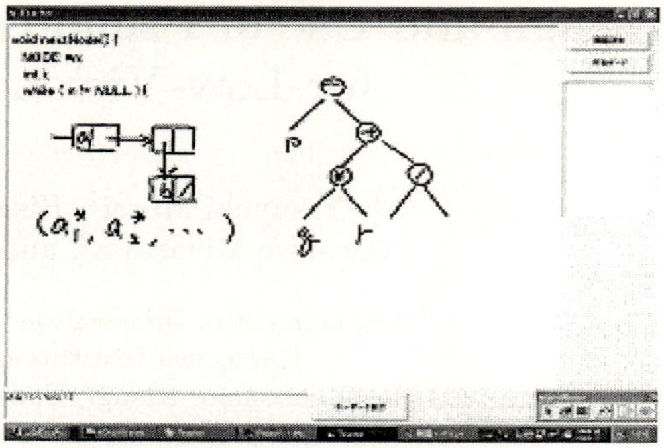

**Fig. 2.** Captured whiteboard.

a usual simultaneous classroom education where low-vision students can share important classroom unity.

## 2 Whiteboard Capturing System

On Fig. 1 we show a general hardware organization: it consists of a whiteboard, a projector and PCs (personal computers) for students and for the server (teacher).

The capturing system of whiteboard we have used is as follows: teacher draws on a usual whiteboard with a special marker called stylus pen which emits signals. Captured signals (i.e. coordinates $x, y$ of the drawing point) are used to mimic drawing on the whiteboard real-time onto a monitor window (the server-window in the sequel). There is a remarkable invention added in this capturing system. The server-window is projected onto the same whiteboard. Now the whiteboard (and the server window) displays a superposition of the teacher's original drawings and the server-window's original content (texts, or figures, see, Fig. 2 for the superposition of drawing and text). Thus the whiteboard and the server-window can contain rich material for teaching. The advantage is not limited to this. By providing a suitable software, the whiteboard turns into a pseudo-electronic whiteboard equipped with the marker playing the role of a mouse; that is, one can manipulate (draw, erase, move and so on) any objects on the whiteboard by the marker, and this manipulation is reflected on the server-window real-time (we call this integrated capturing system simply whiteboard capturing system).

Such a whiteboard capturing system is commercially provided (e.g. it is licensed by Virtual Ink Co. as Mimio and sold by Kokuyo Co. in Japan [3]). Though it is not available in Japan yet and we did not use it, it is announced that a commercial package called classRoom is available for classroom purpose [4]. A plug-in called mimioMouse [3] makes stylus-pen work like a mouse, and the whiteboard turns into a large touch-panel.

## 3 Pseudo-electronic Whiteboard for Low-Vision Education

Incorporating the whiteboard capturing system described in Section 2 we have built a prototype of pseudo-electronic whiteboard system (shortly, e-board system in the sequel) for low-vision education. We have used mimioSoftware and mimioMouse. The remaining part is built by VisualBasic 6.0 on Winsock interface for network programming. We did not use commercial products like classRoom and ZoomText. The reason for this is that we can extend programs for readability for weak-sighted students. Indeed, distributed server windows are processed in the student's PC in order to increase readability and recognizability according to individual sighting. The system consists of teacher module and student module which are to be run separately on respective PCs. The communication between the modules are conducted by UDP (user datagram protocol) using Winsock.

The two modules communicate each other as follows. Teacher's module sends drawings (writings) on the whiteboard to students, receives student's question and display it on the server window. Student module receives and displays drawings (writings) sent by teacher's module and sends questions to teacher's module. It can adjust display according to student's setting so that he can see display comfortably. For text input, teacher can use the screen keyboard (a standard facility attached to MS Windows) displayed on the whiteboard, so he need not leave away from the whiteboard interrupting his explanation. On Fig. 2 we show the server window (teacher's window). Questions with student identifier are displayed in the area at the right end of the window.

Major functions of student module include

1. Change colors of drawings and background.
2. Change sizes of drawings and text.
3. Automatic scrolling of drawings in the window.
4. Input and transmit of student's questions.

In our e-board system student can ask teacher (and class) questions indicating a separate window-region shared by the whole class. When drawing is needed in the discussion, both teacher and student can write shared figures on the special area for drawing. Thus our e-board system provides weak-sighted students classroom education in which students and teacher share feeling of closeness, unity and simultaneousness.

## 4 Conclusions

On Fig. 3 we show a picture of e-board system (server-window and student window with different magnifications and whiteboard in the background, with capture bar attached on the upper-left of the board).

We are given an issue on the current system by low-vision students about automatic scrolling, which sometimes leaves current reading point out of the window abruptly. This is because student window contains relatively small numbers of characters (with a big magnification ratio) and reading takes longer time.

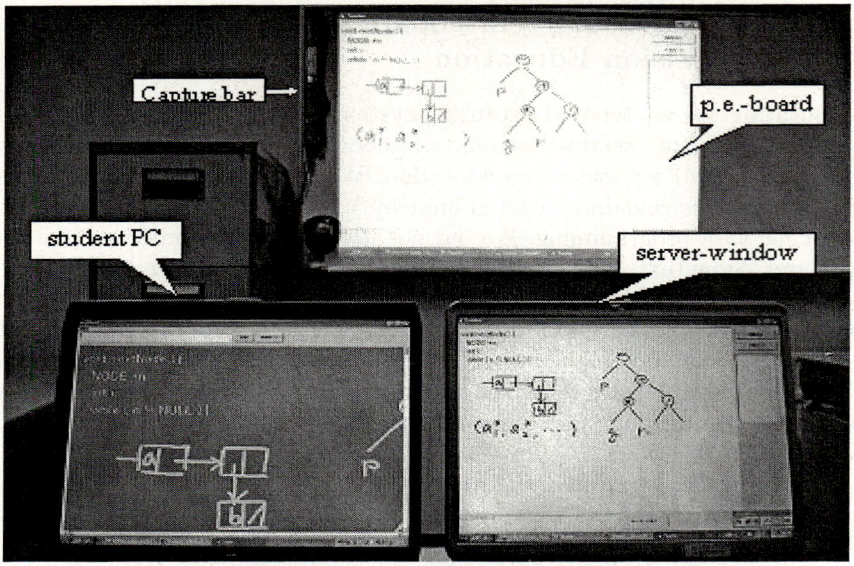


**Fig. 3.** Pseudo-electronic whiteboard system.

We have discussed the e-board system for classes for low-vision students. The same style of classroom education as usual one is feasible for sighted and low vision integrated classes. It is often the case that we need to draw something additionally on the whiteboard. E-board system raises the quality of education and decreases the teacher's load for preparing material. We expect that e-board system can be improved by extensive use and, as a consequence, its better versions could be produced as commercial products.

## Acknowledgment

We thank Nobuyuki Nagai for valuable comments. We thank TCT Educational Improvement 2003 Grant 1546 for partial financial support.

## References

1. H.Bandoh, H.Nemoto, S.Sawada, M.Nakagawa: Educational software on an interactive electronic blackboard, IPSJ Journal, Vol. 42, No. 3, pp.624-632, 2001.
2. Y.Murai, H.Tatsumi, M.Miyakawa, S.Tokumasu: Use of bidirectional electronic whiteboard for low-vision education, Technical Report ET2003-97 of IEICE, Vol.103, No.600, pp.75-80, 2004.
3. http://www.kokuyomimio.com/mimio/products/products.html
4. http://www.mimio.com/meet/classroom/

# Mathematics for Blind People

## *Introduction to the Special Thematic Session*

Arthur I. Karshmer

University of South Florida
Department of Information Technology
Lakeland, FL 33803 USA
arthur@lklnd.usf.edu

**Abstract.** The ability of a blind student to pursue careers in mathematics, engineering, science or technology are severely limited by the students ability to manipulate complex mathematical equations. While there are exceptions to the rule, it has been difficult or impossible for blind members of our society to enter these career domains. The current STS deals with this problem from a broad perspective focusing on what are the best and worst practices in the area of presenting equations to blind math students.

## 1 Introduction

Over the past decade, there have been numerous research projects in North America, Europe and Asia to build computer-based tools to help blind mathematics students in their studies. Early in the process, it was recognized that mathematical equations presented a unique and difficult problem in this domain of assistive technology. Not only are equations complex, but they also use a wide variety of special characters and are two dimensional in nature. To overcome these problems, several research groups designed special equation browsers to simplify the process for the blind student. All of these projects supplied tools that would allow the student to browse equations in an environment that included powerful navigational tools.

In the current STS, a variety of interesting approaches to solve the problems associated with teaching math to blind students are discussed. Each offers some insight to overall problem. Together they point to insights that may, in the future, help so;ve this problem.

K. Miesenberger et al. (Eds.): ICCHP 2004, LNCS 3118, p. 613, 2004.

# The Architecture of a Comprehensive Equation Browser for the Print Impaired

Arthur I. Karshmer, Chris Bledsoe, and Paul B. Stanley

University of South Florida
Department of Information Technology
Lakeland, FL 33803 USA
arthur@lklnd.usf.edu

**Abstract.** Over the past two decades, there have been numerous efforts to design an equation reading system to make the learning of mathematics simpler for the print impaired student. Projects led by MathsPlus Toolbix (Sahyun and Gardner), Aster (Raman), Math Genie (Karshmer) and Maths (Edwards) have all been successful to various degrees in achieving this goal. While each provides some level of support in this endeavor, none of them have been able to deliver a comprehensive tool. Further, none of these tools have been designed to be part of a more general system of delivering math skills and communications to a broad range of visual impairments and users in different countries.

## 1 Introduction

In the current work, the Math Genie project is being integrated into a multi-lingual environment that will allow print impaired users in English, French and German speaking countries to not only learn higher level mathematics, but also to share their knowledge and work with others in these language groups. The design of this environment employs generalized markup languages, which will allow the future inclusion of numerous other national languages and math Braille standards.

The remainder of this paper discusses the issues associated with building an equation browser that both serves the majority of print impaired users (blind, low vision and dyslexic) and also supports numerous natural languages and national Braille codes. This work is part of a larger consortium know as the iGroup UMA (International Group for Universal Mathematical Access), which currently has partners from France, Austria, Ireland and the United States.

## 2 The External Architecture

Figure one, shows an overview of the external architecture of the equation browser In the figure below, we show the external architecture of such an equation browser that is currently running and will be in user testing in the near future. Currently, it includes such features as:

K. Miesenberger et al. (Eds.): ICCHP 2004, LNCS 3118, pp. 614–619, 2004.

1. Automatic input from a high-end visual equation editor
2. Spoken output in a variety of styles which are totally controlled by the user
3. An equation rendering module which allows the browser to present mathematics usable by both low-vision and dyslexic users
4. A simplified set of voice activated commands that can be used to direct the actions of the browser's navigational features.

A refreshable Braille device is also shown in this figure. Its actual implementation is underway and should be available in the near future.

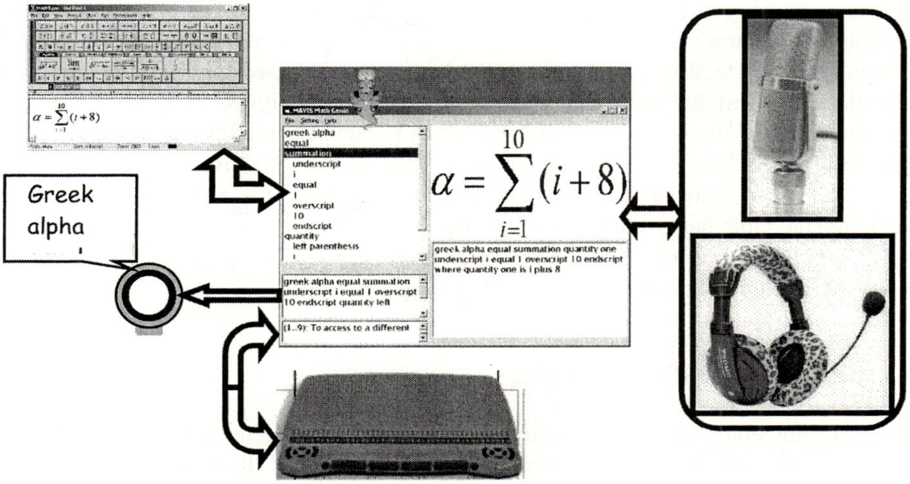


**Fig. 1.** The External Architecture of the Math Genie.

Other features

## 2.1 The Ability to Speak in Virtually Any Natural Language

The primary output mode of the browser is its speech synthesis engine. Once an equation is imported in MathML from the equation editor, or any other source, it forms the internal, hierarchical structure for all browsing. The MathML supplies all needed information concerning the target equation and its logical structure, but it does not directly map into the appropriate language format for reading to the user. In earlier psychological experimentation (Gillan), several aspects associated with successful equation reading were found. These experiments revealed the best way of presenting the overall, and sub structures of an equation.

The ability to clearly present these complex data requires a spoken protocol that both identifies equation "chunks," and allows for the free form navigation of them. In the current version of the browser, we employ the MathSpeak (Nemeth) as it seems best in meeting the requirements uncovered in earlier experiments. The resulting spoken protocol used in conjunction with the MathML seems to serve our needs well. The only problem: the output is restricted to English.

The solution: a language lookup function that translates the MathML text and the MathSpeak language into the target language of the user. A table of math symbols, operators and speech protocol is loaded at start-up. It includes approximately 1,200 entries in their Unicode collating sequence. A second table is also loaded at start-up: the local language table which is determined by requesting the user's language from the operating system. Then, as the MathML is processed in the input phase, the browser's internal representation of the equation is translated into the language of the user, and all browsing is done in the user's native language.

The language tables can be structured in two basic ways depending on the speech synthesis device resident in the user's computer. If the system has tools to properly pronounce the target language, the language table used is composed of words in that language. If this facility is not present, the language table used will include the transliteration of all of the words. The transliterations are designed to force the proper pronunciation of the words. Interestingly, even in our base model which uses American English, we are forced to do the same sort of transliteration. For example the letter "A" is pronounced "ah" by the synthesizer. To force the proper pronunciation, our language table has the letter "ay" for the letter "A".

By employing an advanced lookup algorithm and the corresponding data structures, the lookup process is not noticeable to the user.

## 2.2 Graphical Equation Rendering

As the MathGenie is designed to support a wide range of print impaired users, it is necessary also present some form of graphical rendering of the equation. For example, for low vision and dyslexic users we present both the verbal and graphical representations of the equation. For the low vision user, the browser magnifies the parts of the equation being presenting in auditory form. For dyslexic users, the graphical version of the equation is represented with color highlighting.

The difficult issue is the mapping of the MathML for an addressable graphical representation of the equation. Such renderings are currently under development using a protocol known as Scalable Vector Graphics or SVG (W3C). The rendering process currently requires two steps, translation of the MathML to SVG, and the actual rendering of the SVG file.

Two of the tools available for this process are Custard, for translation, and SVG rendering software (Adobe). While the rendering software seems complete, the same can't be said for the translation software.

SVG files are not particularly complex in structure, but they do contain large volumes of data for each character represented. The problem therefore is designing algorithms and data structure that rapidly maps between the internal representation of the equation and the SVG for the equation. Unfortunately, this mapping must map correctly to the part of the equation currently being browsed – a real-time activity. These are issues currently under study by our group. More information on this subject can be found in a companion paper, also presented at this conference (Stanley). The following SVG segment represents the simple expression "i+8".

<textclass="mi1"x="50.31282279027606"y="32.93521908450705"font-size="10"fill="black">i</text>
<textclass="mo"x="57.64615479027606"y="32.93521908450705"font-size="10"fill="black">+</text>
<textclass="mn"x="64.97948679027606"y="32.93521908450705"font-size="10"fill="black">8</text>

### 2.3 Math Knowledge Base

To aid the print impaired math learner, we have included a basic mathematical knowledge base. At any time during the browsing process, the user can request information about the current section or chunk of the equation. By simply pressing the space bar, the system will query an on-line dictionary of mathematical terms and read the entry to the user. Again, the user will have control of presentation of the spoken material and the knowledge base can be presented in virtually any language.

### 2.4 National Braille Math Codes

Problems associated with mathematics and the print impaired do not end in the educational domain, but are also relevant in the professional domain. Blind mathematicians depend on Braille representations of equations. There are a large number of such representations in the world, and unfortunately, very few are the same. Thus, a mathematician in the U.S. using Nemeth Braille can not easily send his/her work to a colleague in Germany, where Marburg Braille is the standard.

The problem is quite complex and, on a theoretical basis, can't be solved for all cases. The problem is that all national math Braille codes are in the class of context sensitive languages. This class of languages can not be translated to other context sensitive languages with any guarantee of correctness in all cases. These problems are being addressed by other members of our research group. Please see items in the references marked as "Companion Papers," which are also being presented at this meeting. These papers discuss this difficult problem for a variety of national math Braille codes.

Our approach to solving this problem is to use our automated tools to rewrite the users code to an internal format which is "context free." This representation, which is not guaranteed to be perfectly accurate, is then presented through the Math Genie for semantic corrections by the user. Once the user is satisfied, the internal context free representation can then be easily translated to the target national math Braille notation. The use of this interactive technique is the only method of insuring correct translations.

## 3 The Internal Architecture of the Browser

The internal architecture of the Math Genie is shown in Figure 2. It depicts the logical modules of the comprehensive Math Genie and the interaction of these modules. Some of the modules are actually references to external modules and interchange protocols currently under development.

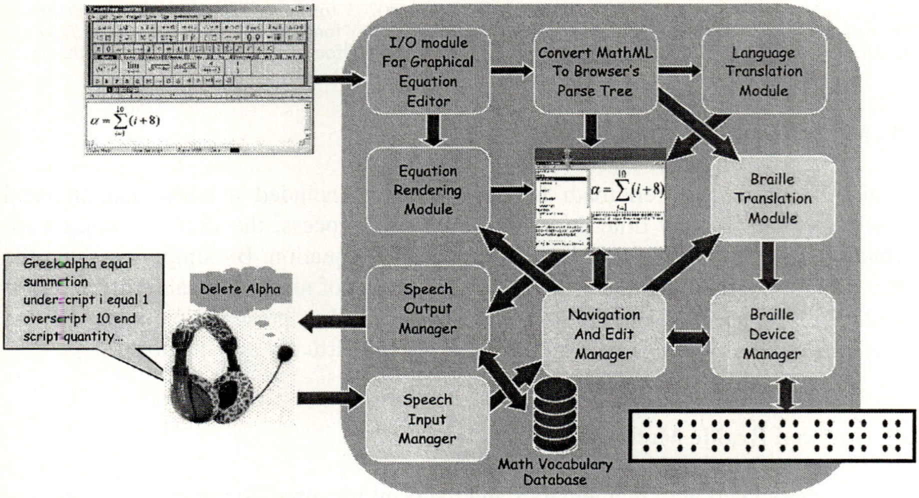


**Fig. 2.** The Internal Structure of the Math Genie.

One of the elements of a math browser is the ability to edit equations interactively as well as hearing them spoken. This is the task of the "Navigation and Edit Module." The Math Genie currently supports basic navigational tools based on the user's speech. Commands such as "Start," "Stop," "Back," "Repeat," etc. But these are only for navigation. What needs to be addressed is speech-based editing commands. Two approaches currently under consideration are speech recognition of MathSpeak commands and the use of VoiceXML.

## 4 Conclusions

The Math Genie is an example of an assistive technology for the print impaired and their interaction with mathematics. It is not complete, and certainly not perfect, but it does deliver a valuable tool for teaching all levels of mathematics to the print impaired. One of its main features is the ability of the math instructor to prepare text with a simple equation editor that can deliverß information to both the sighted and print impaired student. It seems clear that we can not expect math instructors to become familiar with math Braille codes to teach students who are print impaired. With the current work being carried out in the iGroup UMA, we expect to have a math browser with much broader facilities available in the near future.

## References

1. Archambault, Domonique, et al. Towards a Universal Maths Conversion Library, to appear in the Proceedings of ICCHP 2004, Paris, July 2004, Springer-Verlag Publishers **Companion Paper**

2. Edwards, ADN, The TIDE MATHS Project, http://www.cs.york.ac.uk/maths/maths_publications.html
3. Fitzpatrick, Donal, et al., Multi-Modal Mathematics: conveying math using synthetic speech and speech recognition to appear in the Proceedings of ICCHP 2004, Paris, July 2004, Springer-Verlag Publishers **Companion Paper**
4. Gillan, et al., Cognitive Analysis of Equation Reading: Application to the Development of the Math Genie to appear in the Proceedings of ICCHP 2004, Paris, July 2004, Springer-Verlag Publishers **Companion Paper**
5. Karshmer, A., Gupta, G., Annamalai, N., et al., UMA: A System for Universal Mathematics Accessibility, Submitted to the ASSETS Conference, 2004
6. Karshmer, A.I., and Gillan, D., "How well can we Read Equations to Blind Mathematics Students: Some Answers from Psychology ," Proceedings of the 2003 Human Computer Interface International Conference, Crete, Greece, July, 2003.
7. Nemeth, Abraham, MathSpeak, http://www.rit.edu/~easi/easisem/talkmath.htm
8. Miesenberger, Klaus, A Mathematical Working Environment for Blind and Visually Impaired Students, to appear in the Proceedings of ICCHP 2004, Paris, July 2004, Springer-Verlag Publishers **Companion Paper**
9. Moco, Victor, and Archambault, Domonique, Automatic Translations of Mathematical Braille: a survey of main difficulties in different languages, to appear in the Proceedings of ICCHP 2004, Paris, July 2004, Springer-Verlag Publishers **Companion Paper**
10. Pontelli, Enrico and Palmer, Brian, Translating between Formats for Mathematics: Current Approach and an Agenda for Future Developments, to appear in the Proceedings of ICCHP 2004, Paris, July 2004, Springer-Verlag Publishers **Companion Paper**
11. Raman, T.V., 'AsTeR: Audio System For Technical Readings', Information Technology And Disabilities, 1994 http://hegel.lib.ncsu.edu/stacks/serials/itd/itd-v1n04-raman-aster
12. Sahyun, Steve, and Gardner, John, Audio and Haptic Access to Math and Science - Audio graphs, Triangle, the MathPlus Toolbox, and the Tiger printer Proceedings of the 15th IFIP World Computer Congress, Vienna, September 1998.
13. Stanley, Paul, and Karshmer, A.I., Utilizing Scalable Vector Graphics in the Instruction of Mathematics to the Visually Impaired Student, to appear in the Proceedings of ICCHP 2004, Paris, July 2004, Springer-Verlag Publishers **Companion Paper**
14. W3C, Scalable Vector Graphics, http://www.w3.org/Graphics/SVG/

# Translating between Formats for Mathematics: Current Approach and an Agenda for Future Developments

E. Pontelli and B. Palmer

Dept. Computer Science
New Mexico State University
{epontell,bpalmer}@cs.nmsu.edu

**Abstract.** This paper describes the current directions followed in the UMA project to interoperate between different formats for mathematics. We highlight the state-of-the-art along with directions for future development of the project.

## 1 Preliminaries

In recent years we have witnessed an increased effort towards the development of tools and methodologies based on information technology aimed at reducing the communication divide between sighted and blind individuals. An aspect of particular interest is the improvement of accessibility of Mathematical notations. Mathematics represents an international language for the exchange of knowledge, used in a variety of fields. Mathematics is a particular hard notation to be dealt with for blind individuals; this is due mostly to two main reasons:

1. mathematical notation is inherently two dimensional; the correct interpretation of mathematical formulae vitally relies on the knowledge of the spatial layout of its components. Conveying multi-dimensional structure in a non-visual fashion is a notoriously hard problem [4, 3].
2. an incredibly large variety of formats are commonly used to encode mathematics (e.g., digital formats, typesetting formats, Braille formats), and communication between individuals with different capabilities requires the ability to seamlessly interoperate between all these formats.

Over the last two years, an international team of scientists – which includes investigators from the U.S.A., Austria, France, and Ireland – have joined forces to investigate the development of tools to improve non-visual accessibility of Mathematics. The team – called iGroup UMA (international Group for Universal Math Access) – has focused its attention to two central problems in universal accessibility of Math for the visually impaired:

– Interoperation between the multitude of digital, typographical, and Braille formats employed for the encoding of mathematical formulae;
– Interactive Aural Navigation of complex mathematical formulae.

A collection of tools developed from the iGroup UMA activities has been collected and accessible at karshmer.lklnd.usf.edu/~igroupuma.

K. Miesenberger et al. (Eds.): ICCHP 2004, LNCS 3118, pp. 620–625, 2004.

## 2 Interoperation between Formats for Mathematics

The iGroup UMA team at New Mexico State University has focused its efforts in the development of technology to interconvert between digital formats for mathematics (Figure 1).

The emphasis of our approach is on providing an intermediate interchange format along with algorithms to interconvert between known digital formats for mathematics and the interchange format. The interchange format is expected to meet a number of criteria:

- *Expandability:* the wide and dynamic nature of mathematics makes it infeasible to expect a single format to have provision for every aspect of mathematics. The interchange format should be naturally expandable and accommodate for unexpected situations. It should also be expansive for the most common forms of mathematics and mathematical documents.
- *Structure:* the interchange format is expected to be used not only to simplify the translation between formats, but also to drive the navigation process. For this reason, the interchange format should provide a hierarchical structure for mathematical formulae that will facilitate navigation. The mathematical encoding needs to be able to work within an entire document framework so that the non-formula parts of the mathematics are accessible.
- *Semantics Richness:* the interchange format is expected to capture relevant aspects of the semantics of the mathematical formula; semantics can significantly improve the navigation process as well as help in disambiguating formulae during the navigation process.

The selection of the interchange format in the UMA project quickly converged to *OpenMath* [1]. OpenMath meets all the above criteria:

1. OpenMath has a well-defined XML encoding, providing a natural hierarchical decomposition of mathematical formulae.
2. OpenMath has a simple collection of constructs, and the definition of the various operators is modularly provided by *Content Dictionaries (CDs).* Each CD provides formal and informal definitions of semantically related operators (including English and XML encodings of examples). CDs provide also a natural methodology for providing expandability.
3. OpenMath has been explicitly designed to be coherent with MathML (the most commonly used Web format for mathematics).

That said, there are challenges raised by the adoption of OpenMath. OpenMath is very well suited to representing mathematical formulae; it has no provision, however, for representing the textual elements that introduce the context for the mathematical formula. Because OpenMath puts such strong emphasis on meaning, the formulae are still complete and comprehensible; but the relationships throughout a document between the mathematics may be unclear. The OMDoc project is an attempt to represent a document containing OpenMath in a similarly rigorous and structured way, but good navigation and presentation of such a document remains an open problem.

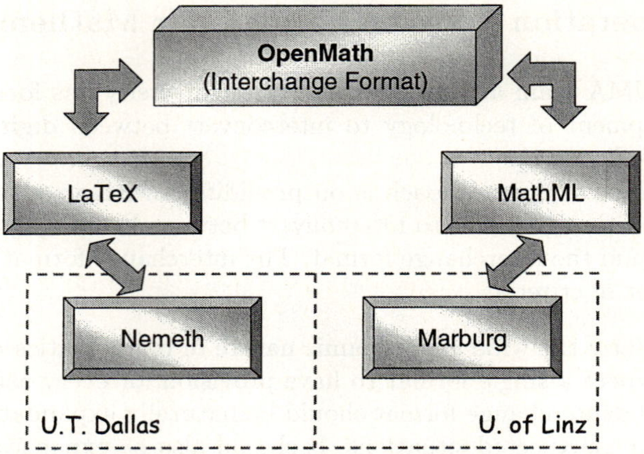


**Fig. 1.** Inter-conversion between formats for mathematics.

Existing Content Dictionaries for OpenMath make a point of associating particular symbols together. For example, set operations are defined in an official CD "set1". However, ad hoc extensions to understand document specific mathematics may not be as comprehensive; operations which, when presented visually, seem clearly associated, may not be defined together, so their exact relationship is uncertain.

Furthermore, while OpenMath provides nice extension capabilities, it shares a fault with many other mathematical systems, as it requires *well-formed* mathematics. This may affect incomplete documents as well as the ability of the user to dynamical create and edit documents.

The NMSU team has completed the development of interchange algorithms between OpenMath, MathML, and LaTeX. In particular,

- MathML Content and OpenMath are easily inter-operable, being both designed to encode the semantic structure of a formula;
- OpenMath is easily used to produce both LaTeX and MathML Presentation;
- Translation from presentation-based formats (LaTeX and MathML Presentation) to OpenMath requires the use of heuristics to resolve ambiguities. User interaction is also employed to solve cases beyond the existing heuristics.

The existing tools are effective for a large number of cases, and the need for user interaction occurs only in complex cases during presentation-to-content translations, or when there is a need to override the chosen heuristics.

## 3 An Agenda to Improve Inter-operation

### 3.1 From Presentation to Content

A number of open problems still exist and limit the applicability of the translation approaches investigated so far in the literature. The literature has highlighted the presence of a deep dichotomy between two classes of formats for mathematics:

- *Presentation Formats:* they emphasize the presentation and "display" properties of the formula. Thus, the main concern of this class of formats is how the formula should be visually presented.
- *Content Formats:* they emphasize the semantic of the formula, in terms of applications of operations to operands and in terms of properties of the operations and values.

LaTeX, MathML Presentation, as well as the most commonly adopted Braille mathematical formats (e.g., Nemeth, Marburg), are all examples of Presentation Formats. MathML Content and OpenMath are examples of Content Formats.

Presentation Formats are highly suitable for visual presentation and for unsupervised and unguided access (e.g., linear access through a Braille refreshable display). Their structure is inherently tied to the visual properties of the formula. As such, a direct aural presentation of these formats to a visually impaired individual might be unclear and potentially misleading.

On the other hand, Content Formats have the advantage of making explicit the semantic structure of the formulae. The explicit knowledge of the semantic of each formula is essential to allow

1. unambiguous and precise translation between formats
2. more meaningful strategies for aural presentation of formulae

Indeed, the importance of Content has been highlighted in other works on universal accessibility [8].

This suggests the need of establishing a more solid bridge between Content and Presentation formats. Knowledge of the semantics of a formula is considered essential to improve formula recognition and translation. The use of heuristics conducted so far at NMSU (to interoperate between OpenMath and MathML Presentation) represents a first step in this direction. A more effective disambiguation and inter-conversion requires the use of more powerful software technology. In this project we propose to make use of machine learning – more specifically Inductive Logic Programming and Hidden Markov Models – to automatically synthesize translation heuristics and guarantee a greater degree of precisions. Machine learning allows us to automatically synthesize translation rules based on a training set – i.e., a collection of sample formulae along with annotations indicating their correct translations. The power of machine learning, within our framework, is its ability of accounting for the context of a formula in aiding its translation. We have conducted preliminary experiments in the use of machine learning methodologies to understand two-dimensional structures (e.g., tables) with very promising results [8].

## 4 Contextual Information

Additional precision in the translation process, and a better connection between Content and Presentation, can be gained by taking advantage of the context in which the formula is used. This opens the problem of:

– Determining ways to represent relevant components of the document containing the formulae; for example, formulae appear as part of definitions, theorems, proofs, examples, etc.
– Determining ways to relate relevant document components to the corresponding formulae.
– Determining ways to relate documents to classes of documents. For example, documents should be related to classes of documents discussing the same topic – e.g., chapters of a back should be related to the topic of the book (e.g., a book on foundations of statistic).

A natural answer to part of this problem comes from the recent work on OMDoc [6], which provides a natural markup framework for the encoding of mathematical concepts (e.g., lemmas, propositions, statements, proofs). On a larger scale, classification and relationships between documents can be captured by bibliographical metadata formats (e.g., the Dublin Core [2]). The current directions investigated are:

– Identification of the relevant document components within presentation formats (e.g., a Braille+Nemeth document) and their explicit representation within OMDoc and additional levels of metadata.
– Use of the knowledge encoded in the OMDoc documents and in the additional levels of metadata to facilitate the translation process. The OMDoc information can be used to provide missing components of the semantics of the formula; e.g., the context provided by OMDoc might determine that the formula is a mathematical logic statement, thus clearly identifying the set of CDs to be used to generate an OpenMath version of the formula.

Observe that the use of OMDoc allows us also to draw knowledge from the existing rich on-line formalizations of mathematics (e.g., as in MBase [7]).

On the other hand, the capabilities of OMDoc are limited to the representation of a single document or part of a document. It lacks the capability to describe global properties of a document – e.g., the topic of a document – or global relationships between components of the document. Even worse, the format does not address the problem of relating between and across different documents. Approaches like those presented in MBase, aimed at the creation of a repository of mathematical facts, is not moving in our desired direction, since they are mostly meant to help automated theorem proving systems and not to directly assist human documents.

This state of things suggests not only the need of better analysis algorithms, but also the need for a high-level markup language that builds on OMDoc and extends its expressive capabilities to the encoding of whole mathematical documents and organized collections of documents. Bibliographical metadata formats (e.g., Dublin Core) can provide some help in this direction, if properly used, but they are more likely to be too general to be highly effective. In this project we propose to explore the design of a specialized content markup to overcome the gap between OpenMath, OMDoc, and general document classification formats.

## 5 Final Considerations

The directions of research highlighted in this paper stress the importance of enriching mathematical formulae with knowledge of their semantics, either drawn directly from the formulae or from the context in which the formulae are used. We expect this knowledge to facilitate the process of interoperation between formats and remove many of the ambiguities encountered in the process of moving from Presentation to Content formats. The knowledge collected regarding the semantics of formulae is also expected to provide guidance during browsing of the formulae. The ideas presented in this work are currently under exploration as part of the UMA project [5] and are expected to be implemented in the near future.

## Acknowledgments

This research has been partially supported by NSF grant 9906130 and by a NIDDR grant from DoEd.

## References

1. O. Caprotti et al. "The OpenMath Standard 1.0", Technical Report, The OpenMath Consortium, 2000.
2. "Dublin Core Metadata Element Set, Version 1.1: Reference Description", `dublincore.org/documents/dces`, 2003.
3. C. Earl et al. "A Survey of Windows Screen Reader Users." Journal of Visual Impairment and Blindness, 93(3), 1999.
4. J. Gunderson et al. "Usability of Web Browsers by Persons with Visual Impairments." RESNA Conf., 1997.
5. A. Karshmer et al. "Towards a Universal Math Conversion Library." In International Conference on Computers Helping People with Special Needs, Springer Verlag, 2004.
6. M. Kohlhase. "OMDoc: Towards an Internet Standard for the Administration, Distribution, and Teaching of Mathematical Knowledge", Artificial Intelligence and Symbolic Computation, Springer Verlag, 2000.
7. M. Kohlhase and A. Franke. "MBase: Representing Knowledge and Context for the Integration of Mathematical Software Systems", Journal of Symbolic Computation, 23:4, 2001.
8. E. Pontelli et al. "Towards the Creation of Accessibility Agents for Non-visual Navigation of the Web", ACM International Conference on Universal Usability, ACM Press, 2003.

# Utilizing Scalable Vector Graphics in the Instruction of Mathematics to the Print Impaired Student*

Paul B. Stanley[1], Chris Bledsoe[2], and Arthur I. Karshmer[3]

[1] MathGenie Project, University of South Florida, USA
pbstanly@lklnd.usf.edu
[2] MathGenie Project, University of South Florida, USA
[3] Department of Information Technology, University of South Florida, USA
arthur@lklnd.usf.edu

**Abstract.** The XML based Scalable Vector Graphics imaging language provides another tool for enhancing the accessibility of mathematics for both the visually impaired and the dyslexic student. SVG possesses two attributes applicable to our purpose. As its name implies an SVG image is scalable, it can be enlarged to fill the viewing area of a computer monitor, then zoomed for further magnification, and do so without sacrificing clarity, thus aiding the visually impaired. An SVG image can also be manipulated in real time. For example, one or more text characters may be highlighted in response to a keyboard or program event. This attribute has potential for the dyslexic student.

## 1 Introduction

Mathematics is a difficult subject for many students. Students who cannot visually perceive a written math statement, are at an even greater disadvantage. Scalable Vector Graphics (SVG) possess two attributes conducive to our goal of teaching mathematics to the visually and learning impaired. As its name implies, an SVG image is scalable, that is the image's size is not intrinsic to the SVG file; its viewing size can expand to fill the entire viewing area of a computer monitor or any portion thereof. In addition to the original sizing, most SVG Viewers include a zoom feature for even greater magnification. More importantly, an SVG image can be enlarged without sacrificing clarity.

Secondly, the ability to manipulate the text in an SVG image in real time combined with a verbal rendering of that same text might be applied to the instruction of the dyslexic student.

## 2 Empowering the Visually Impaired

Anyone with non-correctable reduced vision is visually impaired [3][4]. Visual acuity is determined by the smallest object that can be clearly seen and distinguished at a

* The work reported in this paper was funded through a grant from the U.S. Department of Education, National Institute fro Disability and Rehabilitation Research (NIDRR) under Grant Number H133G010046.

K. Miesenberger et al. (Eds.): ICCHP 2004, LNCS 3118, pp. 626–629, 2004.

specified distance [2]. Hence enlarging the viewed object can assist those with low vision. Historically this has been accomplished by enlarging print media and/or the use of a magnifying glass. Text presented on a computer monitor however is not as cooperative in that it is typically not scalable. The text in a graphic user interface can certainly be magnified. Screen magnifiers, as an assistive technology, do just that, but magnifying pixels on a monitor introduces aliasing, the block-like rendering of images and text characters which may consequently reduce legibility. It should be noted that aliasing is not the fault of screen magnifier technology but is an artifact of making a fixed number of picture elements (pixels) cover a relatively larger area. Stated another way, a particular number of pixels contain a set amount of information. The pixels may be stretched to fit a larger area but the amount of information conferred by the pixels remains constant.

Across the spectrum of persons with low vision, as visual acuity declines, greater magnification is required, but increased magnification results in increased aliasing and a consequent decrease in legibility. This current work proposes that the horizon of visual perception may be expanded to lower categories of visual impairment [4] by combining magnification with text anti-aliasing, i.e. enlarging text while maintaining it's clarity. SVG possesses just such a 'magnification with clarity' capability.

SVG is an XML language for describing two-dimensional graphics for the Web. An SVG image consists of three types of graphic objects: vector graphic shapes (e.g., paths consisting of straight lines and curves), images and text [1]. Most math symbols can be represented as text. Non-character symbols, such as the radical sign, can be drawn with the vector graphic feature. As stated above text is anti-aliased to allow for scalability.

An SVG document is essentially a text file describing what is to be drawn. An SVG viewer is required to render the file into an image. This is analogous to a Web Browser rendering an HTML document, except the SVG viewer operates as a plug-in to a browser.

Some SVG viewers are also available as an ActiveX component for use with Microsoft's ® Visual Basic and Visual C++[5]. Adobe® is one provider of such a component [6]. Implementing the ActiveX component in an application is similar to other components. Drop the SVG Viewer component on a form. Set the viewing area by dragging the edges of the component to the desired dimensions. When called upon to render an SVG document the Viewer fills the pre-set viewing area with the SVG image.

Further magnification is possible with the Viewer's zoom capability. This zoom feature provides greater magnification within the original viewing area. As such it provides even more value. Magnification here refers to redrawing the zoomed image and not merely enlarging a fixed set of pixels. Hence the clarity and resolution is maintained.

Please note that the viewing area for an SVG document displayed on a Web page is set by the author of the page and is not changeable via the Web browser. However the zoom functionality discussed above for the ActiveX component is available. Also note that the zoom feature is implemented by of the specific SVG viewer and that the Viewer utilizes the scaling attribute of SVG. There are no pre-set zoom levels intrinsic to SVG documents.

## 3 Empowering the Learning Impaired

Text is one of the three graphic objects intrinsic to SVG; as such it can be programmatically altered in real time via the SVG Document Object Model. Through the conduit of scripting languages or conventional programming languages, text in an SVG image is made responsive to keyboard or mouse events, permitting the user to interact with the text. Allowing, for example, a student to navigate through a math statement using the arrow keys, accentuating one character at a time, while proceeding at his own pace. The right arrow key employed for forward motion, the left arrow for reversing and returning to a previous segment for reiteration. The above functionality coordinated with a verbal rendering would re-create the multi-sensory effect that is currently used as a reading aid for dyslexic students.

## 4 Scalable Vector Graphics at Work

The attributes of SVG discussed above have been successfully implemented as part of the MathGenie Project conducted at the University of South Florida. Originally the Project focused on creating an application that verbally rendered math statements for blind high school and college students. As an adjunct to that work we've extended our goals to include the visual rendering of math statements for use by both the low vision student and the dyslexic student.

Thus far we've built a prototype application that accepts a user entered math statement; that statement is converted to a MathML document; the MathML document is translated into an SVG file; the SVG file is then rendered and displayed full-screen on a computer monitor. An additional 16x magnification is available through a zooming function implemented by the Adobe SVG Viewer. Image clarity is maintained throughout the rendering process and all magnifications thereafter.

The program also implements keyboard events that change the color of the elements of a math statement in an SVG image. The font color of all elements/characters begins as black. A right arrow key press changes the color of the next character to the right from black to red and the color of the current character from red back to the original black. To the user, the color red appears to move through the math statement one element at a time with each right arrow key press. The same functionality has been assigned to the left arrow key to move the color change to the left. In essence, each element of the math statement is, in its turn, differentiated and accentuated at the discretion of the user.

## 5 Conclusion

The incorporation of Scalable Vector Graphics into the MathGenie Project indicates that SVG possesses attributes applicable to assistive technologies. An SVG graphic of a user-entered math statement has been successfully rendered onto the full screen of a computer monitor, and then magnified 16x, all without loss of clarity. The potential for the low vision student is obvious.

In addition, a program was created that allows manipulation in real time of a math statement rendered as an SVG image. As described above, users accentuate elements of the math statement via keyboard events. This interaction between the user and the text, especially if paired with a coordinated aural rendering, has the potential to extend the benefits of multi-sensory, multimedia applications in assisting the dyslexic student.

The MathGenie Project has produced programs that verbally or visually render a user-entered math statement. The goal of the Project now is to combine and coordinate the visual rendering of a math statement with its associated aural rendering, whereby each element of the statement is simultaneously spoken and accentuated. Movement through the statement, that is the accentuation of each element of the statement in its turn, will be in response to user keystrokes.

## References


1. W3C Recommendation for SVG 1.1. W3C. January 14, 2003. www.w3.org/TR/SVG11/intro.html#AboutSVG
2. The Ophthalmic Assistant: Fundamentals and Clinical Practice, 4th ed. Harold Stein, Bernard Slatt. 1983. The C. V. Mosby Company.
3. Low Vision. American Optometric Association. Web reference retrieved March 29, 2004. www.aoanet.org/eweb/DynamicPage.aspx?site=AOAstage&WebCode=LowVision
4. ICD10 Definition of Low Vision and Blindness. International Classification of Diseases 10th edition (ICD10). Web reference retrieved March 29, 2004. www.who.int/pbd/pbl/img/icd10.gif
5. List of various SVG implementations for various platforms. W3C. Web reference retrieved March 29, 2004. www.w3.org/Graphics/SVG/SVG-Implementations.htm8 - edit
6. Adobe SVG Zone. SVG Viewer download. Adobe Web Site. www.adobe.com/svg/

# Cognitive Analysis of Equation Reading: Application to the Development of the Math Genie

Douglas J. Gillan[1], Paula Barraza[1], Arthur I. Karshmer[2], and Skye Pazuchanics[1]

[1] Department of Psychology, New Mexico State University
Las Cruces, NM 88005, USA
{gillan,pbarraza,spazucha}@nmsu.edu
[2] Department of Information Technology, University of South Florida
Lakeland, FL 33803, USA
arthur@lklnd.usf.edu

**Abstract.** Can information about the perceptual and cognitive processes involved in equation reading be applied in the creation of assistive technology for blind equation readers? The present research used four cognitive/perceptual studies to examine several hypotheses about equation reading: people (1) read equations from left to right, one element at a time, (2) back scan when reading equations, (3) substitute the outcome of a parenthetical expression for the initial elements, and (4) scan the entire equation before element by element reading to create a schematic structure. The process tracing study provided evidence for all of the hypotheses, with three experiments supporting the first three hypotheses, but not the fourth. These results have been implemented in assistive software for visually-impaired users, the Math Genie - an auditory browser.

## 1 Introduction

Equations involve the visual display of a mathematical relation using symbols in a highly structured format. The abilities to read and solve equations accurately are essential to skill in mathematics. Given their degree of visual structure, presenting the information from an equation auditorially would likely increase the difficulty in reading and solving an equation. Thus, visually impaired equation readers would be put at a disadvantage in performing mathematics if they only heard equations. This disadvantage would be acute if the auditory presentation of the equation were strictly linear, as occurs with many browsers for blind equation readers. However, an auditory browser need not be restricted to a strict linear presentation of the alphanumerical elements in an equation. One approach to browser design would be (1) to investigate the perceptual and cognitive processes used in equation reading by sighted people, then (2) to provide the same process capabilities in the auditory channel to blind readers that sighted readers have via the visual channel. We have taken that approach to designing an auditory browser for blind equation readers.

Given that most people have extensive experience reading text and substantially less experience reading equations, it might be reasonable to assume that sighted people read equations in the same way that they read text. People read text letter-by-letter beginning at or near the leftmost symbol in a text line [1]. In addition, readers often engage in backward scans to retrieve information that was previously read. In contrast

K. Miesenberger et al. (Eds.): ICCHP 2004, LNCS 3118, pp. 630–637, 2004.

to the hypothesis that equation reading and text reading are comparable, one might propose that users interact with equations and texts in very different ways – from the goals that motivate the reading to the differences in the structure of equations and texts to differences in the purposes of the – so, readers read equations differently from texts. Specifically, they may engage in an initial scan of the equation to gain information that would allow the reader to set up a schematic representation of the equation structure, followed by an element-by-element reading that fills in the slots in the schema.

## 2 Process Tracing Analysis

We began by observing 15 students as they read equations; we asked them to think aloud as they read the equations. The 14 equations that they read varied in the types and number of operators and in the overall complexity of the equation. The verbal protocols of the participants' thinking aloud were analyzed to determine their cognitive and perceptual processes as they read and solved equations. The analysis suggested the following features of equation reading: (1) reading proceeds largely in a left-to-right direction reading one element at a time, much like reading text; (2) on approximately half of the observed equations, readers performed an initial scan to determine the structure of the problem; (3) readers frequently engaged in backward scanning to previously-read elements; (4) readers chunked together elements of the equation (usually within parentheses) and solved those chunks as separate modules; and (5) as a consequence of chunking, readers solved the equation hierarchically.

Because verbal protocol data may, under some conditions, reflect the participants' expectations concerning their cognitive processes, rather than the actual processes, conclusions drawn from them should be tested by means of true experiments. Accordingly, we conducted a series of experiments to examine these processes of equation reading: (1) an initial scan to determine structure, (2) left-to right, element-by- element reading, (3) solving parts of the equation within parentheses and replacing the elements within the equation with the outcome.

## 3 Experiment 1 – Equation Recall

### 3.1 Method

In Experiment 1, 11 participants read 72 computer-displayed equations varying in complexity (24 low, 24 medium, and 24 high), one at a time. On each trial, the participant first read the equation (for 1, 2, or 4 sec), followed by a distracter screen consisting of dots (with a duration of 1 sec or 8 sec). Then, participants were asked to recall the equation by writing down everything that they could remember from the equation. The dependent variable was recall accuracy of the equation elements (structural elements, e.g., parentheses; arithmetic operators; and the numerical values, i.e., the content of the equation).

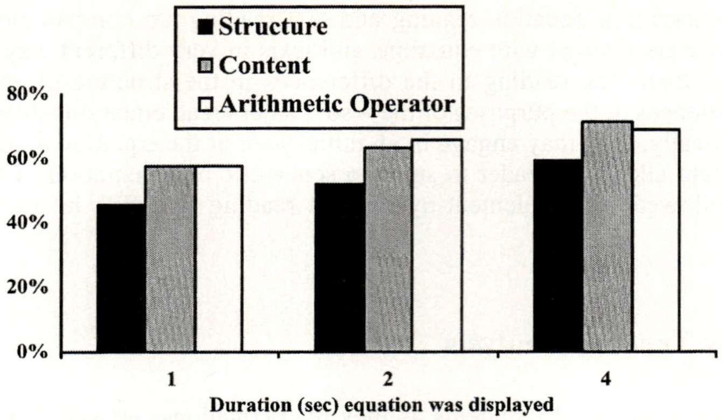


**Fig. 1.** Percent of equation recalled correctly as a function of duration that the equation was displayed and the type of element in the equation.

### 3.2 Results

The results of Experiment 1 (see Figure 1) indicate that content and arithmetic operators were recalled better than structure at all levels of equation duration, Chi-square (2) = 13.4, $p< 05$. This suggests that content and operators may receive more initial processing time compared to structure. This finding does not support the hypothesis that people create a schema focused on structural elements.

A detailed analysis of the equations that participants produced during recall found that they tended to recall equation elements in a connected sequence or block , starting with the leftmost items of the equations (see Figure 2), Chi-square (7) = 142.9, $p<.0001$. This finding is consistent with the hypothesis that people read equations from left to right. Also, in all presentation conditions, participants tended to make more recall errors for the parentheses than for numbers or operators. This finding suggests that parentheses are not processed in the same way as numbers or operators, in that they serve a structural, not a semantic, role. That is to say, parenthesis help the reader navigate through the equation and identify how to organize it, but do not provide meaning. As a consequence, they appear to be easier to forget.

## 4 Experiment 2 – Equation Previews

Experiment 2 further examined the hypothesis that an equation is read with an initial focus on the structure, after which, numerical content elements are filled in. We predicted that if people read the structural and arithmetic operators first in an equation, then a preview of structural and arithmetic operators before the whole equation should result in the shortest reaction time for solving an equation.

### 4.1 Method

Seventeen participants solved 36 computer-displayed equations – nine each with one of four types of previews – no preview, a preview of the entire equation, a preview of the parentheses and arithmetic operators, and a preview of the numbers in their position in the whole equation (see Figure 2). Each preview had a 2-sec duration, followed by the entire equation, which was displayed until the participant responded with the solution to the equation.

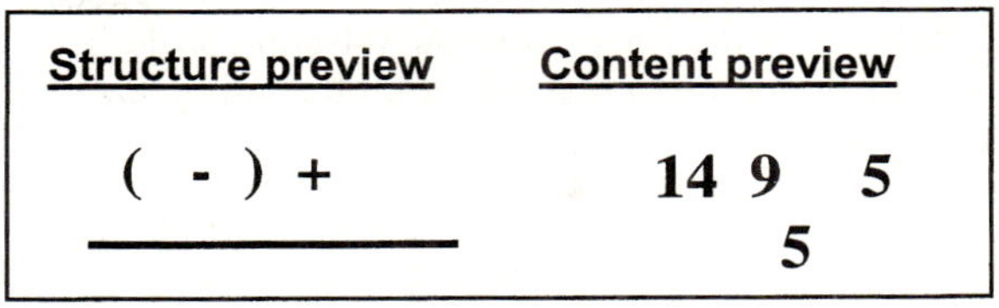


**Fig. 2.** Examples of two of the preview types used in Experiment 2.

### 4.2 Results

The structural preview produced the longest overall solution times (main effect of Preview, $F(3,48) = 6.19$, $p = .0012$). Interestingly, with simple equations, all of the preview types resulted in faster equation solution times than the no preview condition, whereas, with complex equations, the structural preview slowed equation solution times compared to no preview and the other preview types (Preview x Complexity, $F(3,48) = 5.80$, $p = .0018$. The results for Experiment 2 indicate that previewing structural information slowed equation solution, contrary to the prediction from the hypothesis that when people read an equation, they perform an initial scan for structure.

## 5 Experiment 3 – Equation Chunking

Experiment 3 investigated the hypothesis that, when they read an equation, people (1) decompose the equation into chunks defined by expressions contained in parentheses, (2) solve the expression, and (3) store the outcome in memory. We used a recognition task to study this hypothesis – participants read a target equation, then were given different recognition test probes. The probes were either identical to the target equation or differed from the target in terms of the expression within the parentheses or in terms of the equation outside of the expression. In some cases, the changes in elements in the probe resulted in the same solution as the target equation, whereas in other cases the target equation and the probe had different solutions.

### 5.1 Method

Each of 10 participants received a total of 72 trials. The procedure for each trial began with the presentation of a *target* equation and participants solved the equation mentally, at which point, they typed the answer into a response field on the computer screen. Then, a distractor task displayed a randomized starting number (e.g., 187) that was used as a starting point for the participant to mentally count backwards by 3 until the computer made a "beep" sound which signaled the participant to stop counting backwards and type the last number reached into a box on the computer screen. The duration of time from the presentation of the starting number until the computer beeped was a randomized time ranging from 3 to 15 seconds. Following the distractor task, the computer displayed a recognition test probe (an equation). The participant was asked whether the test equation was the same as the earlier target equation or not, and to rate the confidence of their response (on a 4-point scale from not sure to very sure). By combining the recognition response with the rating, each trial resulted in an eight-point response from "No, very sure" (0) to "Yes, very sure" (7).

An R-Index value [2], a bias-free measure of discrimination, was computed from the same/different response and the confidence rating by examining the overlap of the distributions of the 7-point ratings for the Identical condition with the different conditions. Perfect discrimination performance (i.e., no overlap between distributions) would result in an R-Index of 1.00, where as no discrimination (i.e., complete overlap between distributions) would result in an R-Index of .50.

On 36 of the trials, the test probe was identical to the target equation, and on 36 of the trials, the test probe differed from the target, with systematic differences among the probes. Table 1 provides examples of the seven versions of the test probe.

**Table 1.** The versions of the test probe (with differences between the probe and Target equations in italics), the percentage of Yes responses, the Mean recognition score, and the R-Index values for all conditions in Experiment 3.

| Condition | Target Equation | Recognition (test) Probe | % Yes | Mean Score | R-Index |
|---|---|---|---|---|---|
| Identical | 7(8/4)+1-12 = 3 | 7(8/4)+1-12 = 3 | 89 | 5.83 | ----- |
| Different numbers, same outcome in chunk | 3(10/5)+5-8 = 3 | 3(4/2)+5-8 = 3 | 58 | 4.38 | .58 |
| Different numbers, different outcome in chunk | 4(9/3)+6-10= 8 | 4(8/2)+6-10= 12 | 33 | 2.45 | .73 |
| One different number, different outcome in chunk | 6(12/6)+3-5= 10 | 6(12/2)+3-5= 34 | 23 | 2.85 | .79 |
| Different numbers outside of chunk, same outcome | 7(6/2)+4-15= 10 | 5(6/2)+6-11= 10 | 28 | 2.82 | .79 |
| Different numbers outside of chunk, different outcome | 5(8/4)+6-12 = 3 | 3(8/4)+4-6 = 4 | 24 | 1.21 | .80 |
| One different number outside of chunk, different outcome | 3(10/5)+1-2= 5 | 6(10/5)+1-2= 11 | 34 | 2.58 | .78 |

## 5.2 Results

The identical recognition probe had significantly higher recognition scores than all other probe types. The probe that had two changes inside of the parentheses, but the same outcome within the parentheses produced a significantly higher recognition score than any of the other probes that differed from the target (Newman-Keuls, $p$'s<.05). The lower R-Index for the probe with two changes, but the same outcome inside the parentheses, than for all of the other probes that differed from the target indicates that participants did good job discriminating the correct and incorrect probes, except on those trials with the difference in the parentheses.

Table 1 shows the results of Experiment 3. Participants responded that they recognized the test probes with proportions of "yes" responses among the six different probe conditions that differed significantly, Chi Square (5, N = 4500) = 269.5, $p$ <.0001, with recognition scores that differed significantly as a function of the type of recognition probe, $F(6,54) = 20.41$, $p<.0001$, and with R-Indices that differed across the six "different" conditions.

Note that participants had higher recognition scores for that probe than for the probe that had only one different number within the parentheses (Newman-Keuls, $p<.05$). One possibility is that participants simply remembered the outcome of the whole equation and recognized when the outcome differed and when it was the same. However, the probe that had two changes outside of the parentheses with the same outcome also had the same outcome of the whole equation and it produced a proportion of "Yes" responses of only .28, a mean recognition score of -1.82 (significantly lower than both the identical probe and the probe with two differences in the parentheses, same outcome, Newman-Keuls, $p<.05$), and an R-index of .80. Thus, the results support the hypothesis that when people read equations, they substitute the outcome of parenthetical expressions (i.e., chunks of the equation) for the original numbers in the equation.

## 6 The Math Genie: Application

The experiments described above indicate that people (1) read equations from left to right, one element at a time, (2) process operators and numbers more than parentheses, and (3) store the outcome from a parenthetical expression. The process tracing study also suggested that people engage in substantial backtracking when solving an equation. The process tracing study also indicated that people may scan the entire equation to set up a structural schema before they solve the equation, but the experiments failed to support that observation.

The present research provided the following guidance for developing an auditory browser for equation reading: (1) read one element at a time, distinctively, from left to right; (2) permit users to go back to the start of the equation from any point in the equation, (3) permit users to return to self-defined points in the equation from any point in the equation, (4) permit users to substitute (but not completely replace) the expression within parentheses with its outcome, and (5) permit users to scan the equation to provide an overview of the structure of the equation. We believe that, although the fifth guideline is not consistent with all of the data, providing users with this capability would not hurt them, even if it would not necessarily benefit them.

The above guidelines have been implemented in experimental software, the Math Genie [3]. The Math Genie (see Figure 3 for an example screen), uses a hierarchical structure to group subsections of an equation into meaningful units for browsing. The Math Genie also offers refreshable Braille output and specialized video output for low vision users.

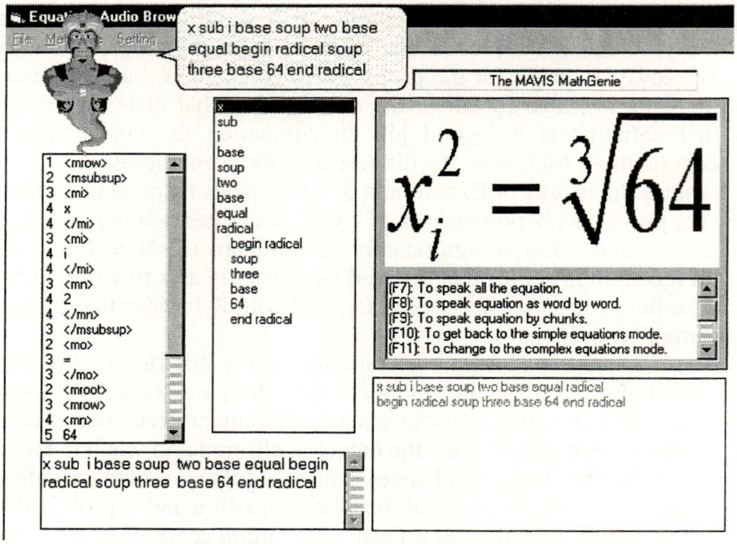


**Fig. 3.** The MAVIS Math Genie.

## 7 Conclusions

The research that is described above has been useful in identifying some of the perceptual and cognitive processes that underlie equation reading by sighted people. We believe that persons with visual disabilities may gain some benefit from having the ability to access the information in equations in the same way that sighted people can, but by no means should visually disabled equation readers be forced to access that information in only one way. Universal access and universal usability as approaches to design should focus on providing users with as much flexibility as possible, while also providing guidance in the use of that flexibility.

The research in this paper, which grew out of the Mathematics Accessible to Visually Impaired Students (MAVIS), and its application in the design of the Math Genie can serve as a model for the ways in which different disciplines can interact in productive ways, while staying true to their disciplinary foci. The cognitive/perceptual psychologists on the project have been able to do research on how people read equations. The results of that research have then been taken up by the computer scientists who have been able to address issues of interest to them. The mathematicians involved in the project will ultimately have tools that will assist in math education. We also hope that, as the products of the research begin to be used, we will receive feedback from the users. That feedback will complete the first iteration in the design cycle and we will begin (1) to formulate new hypotheses about how people read equations, with a greater focus on the unique characteristics of how blind people read equations and (2) to improve on the usability and functionality of the Math Genie.

## Acknowledgement

The work reported in this paper was funded under a grant from the U.S. National Science Foundation (HRD 9800209). The research described in Experiments 1 - 3 were part of the McNair Scholarship Program project of the second author.

## References

1. Smyth, M. M., Collins, A. F., Morris, P. E., and Levy, P. (1994). *Cognition in Action*. Hove: Lawrence Erlbaum Associates Ltd.
2. Brown, J. (1974). Recognition memory assessed by rating and ranking. *British Journal of Psychology*, *65*, 13 - 22.
3. Karshmer, A. Gupta, G., and Gillan, D. J. (2002). Architecting an auditory browser for navigating mathematical expressions. In K. Miesenberger, J. Klaus, and W. L. Zagler (Eds.) *Proceedings of the International Conference on Computers Helping People with Special Needs: Lecture Notes in Computer Science 2398*. (pp. 477 – 485). Berlin: Springer-Verlag.

# Automatic Conversions of Mathematical Braille: A Survey of Main Difficulties in Different Languages

Victor Moço and Dominique Archambault

INSERM U483/INOVA, université Pierre et Marie Curie (Paris 6)
9, quai Saint Bernard, 75252 Paris cedex France
{victor.moco,dominique.archambault}@snv.jussieu.fr

**Abstract.** This article is a general discussion on the automatic mathematical Braille translations. There exist several Braille notations. Each of these Braille notations has particular / specific rules which make the difference between the other notations. Using simple mathematical formulas, we show some particular rules but not all the specific rules. These rules which facilitate the blind reading increase the difficulty of the translation on the side Braille to mainstream notation.

To allow blind people to do mathematics, various Braille specific notations have been created during the last century like Marburg in Germany (1946) and Nemeth code United State (1972) for instance. These notations allow blind people to read and write mathematical formulas. It is still quite difficult to produce mathematical documents for the blind using these very specific notations.

Initially the main aim of automatic translators was then essentially to facilitate the production such documents from mainstream documents. Nowadays the tools used by blind people (computers, speech synthesis, and Braille displays) increase the need of such translators able to convert mainstream notations to Braille as well as Braille to mainstream notations, indeed they allow to display graphically a formula using a MathML rendering tool for instance and to convert it in Braille automatically.

The main problem to face is that mathematical formulas are usually written in two dimensions (in order to reduce the number of signs and to help the reader to understand their meaning) and Braille is one dimensional writing.

This paper will try to summarize the main kind of difficulties encountered while converting between Braille and mainstream Mathematical formats, and to compare the different Braille specific notations in different languages, regarding to the conversion problem.

## 1 Braille Notations

In the middle of the last century, various notations were created to allow blind users to handle more easily mathematical formulas. These notations are usually context-sensitive: they include contextual rules to reduce the size of Braille formulas. Then they are very complex and quite difficult for pupils to learn. It is the case for instance of Marburg, Nemeth, ItalBra, French [1] and British [2] notations.

K. Miesenberger et al. (Eds.): ICCHP 2004, LNCS 3118, pp. 638–643, 2004.

To simplify the automatical translation, the French mathematical Braille notation has changed on 2001. It's a short time to know if the new notation are or not useful for the blind people.

Other countries, like some north European countries for instance, don't use a specific notation but the linear view of formulas as they can always be produced in a mainstream format. The formulas are embossed with Braille characters (for the specific symbols specific Braille tables are used). Using that method, formulas are larger but might be easier for the younger pupils.

Various mathematical Braille notations exist because each of them has his own "philosophy". For instance, in English notation, the space symbol has a signification. Normally the sign '+' is written ' ⠰⠖' (with a space in first position). But, the space symbol in first position is not written when the '+' is included in a complex element, like a superscript. Then in that case, the sign '+' is written with only 2 Braille symbol.

To facilitate automatic transcriptions, two new symbols were created within the new French notation:

- ⠆ for the beginning of a complex element
- ⠰ to close the complex element

These two elements have respectively the same signification as '{' and '}' in Latex for instance.

## 2 Production of Mathematical Braille Documents

The first difficulty for blind people to study mathematics is the small number of mathematical Braille documents. It's difficult to produce these documents because mathematical Braille notations are very complex. Then the documents have to be converted by professional transcribers who have a very good knowledge of mathematical Braille notation. As these professionals are very few, such manual transcription take a long time, it takes a long time for a blind people to have the Braille version of mathematical documents.

Since the 80's, Braille displays allow blind people to read and write electronic files. For mathematical documents, it is still necessary to translate the mathematical part. To accelerate the production of Braille mathematical documents, several projects were launched in the 90's. These projects aim at automatically convert electronic documents containing mathematical formulas into Braille (electronic and format paper). For instance, the LaBradoor [3] project (Latex to Marburg notation) and the MAVIS group [4] (a Latex to Nemeth notation) can be cited.

The main difficulty for these projects is to produce a good Braille formula as short as possible. For instance, numbers are generally represented by the same Braille codes than the ten first letters of the Alphabet, and a special prefix symbol is added to show that this character represents a number. Then, using the English mathematical Braille notation, the formula '1+a' can be translated by:

⠼⠁ ___ ⠰⠖ ⠰⠁ (7 symbols, the space is important)

where ⠁ is the letter 'a', ⠼ the special character for number and ⠰ the special character for 'small Latin letter'. But one of the rules of this Braille code says: « *by default a small Latin letter can be written without the special character* ⠰ *if there is no ambiguity* ». In this case, the formula can be written without the symbol ⠰ and then reduced to only of symbols.

This kind of rules allows to reduce the size of Braille formulas. This example is a very simple formula where the gain is only of one symbol. But on a larger and more complex formula, this kind of rules is very powerful and the size of the formulas can be reduced in a substantial way.

## 3 Mathematical Communication between Sighted and Blind

During the last years, several groups (generally the same as above) started to be interested by conversions in the other way (from Braille contents to mainstream format). Then, several other kinds of difficulties are encountered.

Let us consider for instance the translation of a fraction. Using the Italian or the English mathematical Braille notation, there are 2 different ways to write a fraction whether it is a simple or a complex one. In the case of simple fractions, the writer must use the 'lower number'. The ten first letters have the particularity to be written with only the two first lines of a Braille symbol. A 'lower number' is obtained by shifting these 2 lines to the second and third lines. For instance, ⠁ becomes ⠂ and ⠃ becomes ⠆.

The fraction is translated on the Italian notation by ⠼⠆⠉ and on the English notation ⠼⠃⠒.

For « more complex » fractions, like $\frac{a+b}{2}$, the majority of the mathematical Braille notations use a linear form of the formula: (a+b)/2. This linear form exists also in mainstream, but both linear and bidimensional versions of this fraction have the same representation in Braille. A sighted pupil in school has to learn that the two notations are the same things. If the difference cannot be represented in Braille, all these exercises corresponding to that do not have an interest any more. The following figure illustrates that problem.

The several "context sensitive rules" – like the rule shown on part 2 or the fraction rule for instance – make it difficult to automatically convert Braille formulas to a mainstream notation. Usually the semantics of the formula can be transcripted but not always the writing.

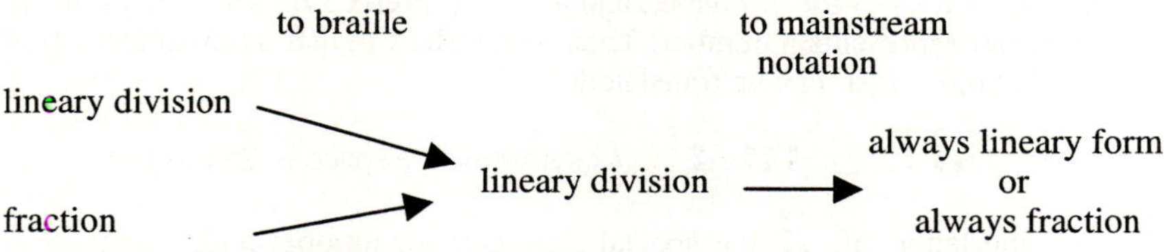


**Fig. 1.** Difficulty to keep the same syntaxic notation after a double transcription.

## 4 Vocal Access

To read electronics document, blind people can use Braille displays or speech synthesis. In the case of speech synthesis, there is an additional kind of difficulty. The mainstream format and the mathematical Braille notations have different semantic levels. On the mainstream mathematical notation, the formula « f(x–1) » is ambiguous. It can represent a function called 'f', to apply to the result of « x+1 » as well as the multiplication of a variable 'f' by the result of « x+1 ». The context and the experience of the reader allow him to decide which case it is.

On the majority of Braille and mainstream formats, this ambiguity is kept. But in MathML [5], the two cases are not written in the same way. This is a problem for translating from any format to MathML. It is very interesting to fix this ambiguity since the vocal output will not be the same in both cases (to have a good vocal output, it's necessary to have a good source code), and it makes MathML a very convenient notation to be used by speech syntheses.

Unfortnaly, it's very difficult to extrapolate this "function semantic" starting from a "poor" input language like Latex or the majority of mathematical Braille notations.

Currently for the vocal access, specific information must be provided manually by a professional transcriber.

## 5 Multi-language Mathematical Braille Translator (MMBT)

Within the framework of the Vickie[1] project [6], we are developing an automatic mathematical Braille conversion tool, called 'mmbt' (Multi-language Mathematical Braille Translator) [7]. This translator aims at being used for production of documents, as part of the different conversion tools that are developed in this project [8], as well as part of the reading software, enabling simultaneous graphical view on the screen and Braille form of the same formula on a Braille device.

It is intended to be convert mathematical formulas from four mathematical Braille notations (2 notations for the French Braille, English and Irish Braille notation) to mainstream notations (LaTeX and MathML) as well as the other way (from Braille to mainstream notation).

MMBT uses a central representation of the formula which goal is to represent – in a tree format- the semantic contents of the mathematical formula. This tree allows the separation between the input and the output format used to write the mathematical formulas. Currently, MMBT can convert algebra formulas (fraction, square root ...), with Latex, MathML and new French Braille notation for input and output format and the old French notation (before September 2001), the English Braille notation and the Italian Braille notation for output format.

The central representation is very important for the conversion. It must be able to express all the information contained in a formula to allow a correct output in another format. Currently, the central representation uses a specific language very close to Braille (see [7] for more details on mmbt).

---

1 Visually Impaired Children Kit for Inclusive Kit.

An online demonstrator is available on:
http://inova.snv.jussieu.fr/maths
mmbt was released as open source software; its source code is available on:
http://sourceforge.net/projects/mmbt/

## 6 Conclusion

Currently, several good automatical translators from mainstream notations to mathematical Braille were developed. The main reason is that – generally – mainstream notations contain more semantic than Braille notations. In that direction, syntactic information can be loosed (see part 3, for the fraction) but the important notion (the semantic of the formula) is saved.

The translation in the opposite direction (from Braille to mainstream notations) is more difficult. When a formula is translated from mainstream to Braille and then again to mainstream (eventually after a modification by the pupil), its syntax may change, which might be a problem.

An international group (iGUMA: international Group for Universal Mathematical Access) was created and aims at harmonizing automatic mathematical Braille translators for various Braille notations. Participants from several countries (Austria, France, Ireland and United State) are involved. Using MathML as a central representation, the various converters will be able to work together, enabling blind mathematicians from different countries to exchange documents containing mathematical formulas. One of the goals of this group is to unify the various converters with the same API [9].

## Acknowledgements

The Vickie project is funded by the European Commission[2], on the IST (Information Society Technologies) Programme 2001 (FP5-IST-Systems and Services for Citizen/Persons with special needs), under the reference IST-2001-32678.

## References

1. Commission Evolution du Braille Français, Notation Mathematique Braille, mise a jour de la notation mathematique de 1971. (2001)
2. Braille Authority of the United Kingdom Mathematics committee, Braille Mathematics notation (1987)
3. Miesenberger K., Batusic M., Stoëger B., (1998), retrieved April 16, 2003 from http://www.jussieu.fr/inova/publi/ntevh/labradoo.htm
4. Karshmer A. I. (2002), Access to mathematics for Blind students retrieved April 16, 2003 from http://www.snv.jussieu.fr/inova/villette2002/res5.htm
5. MathML (Mathematic Markup language): http://www.w3.org/Math

---

[2] The content of this paper is the sole reponsability of the authors and in no way represents the views of the European Commission or its services.

6. Dominique Archambault and Dominique Burger, *The Vickie project* In: Proceedings of the ICCHP 2002 ($8^{th}$ International Conference on Computers Helping People with Special Needs), Linz, Austria, July 2002. " Springer LNCS 2398, K. Miesenberger, J. Klaus, W. Zagler (Eds.).
7. Moço V. and Archambault D.: A transcription tool for mathematical Braille. In Craddock G., McCormack L., Reilly R., Knops H., Eds.: Proc. of the AAATE'03 Conference in Dublin, Ireland. - IOS Press, Amsterdam, The Netherlands (2003) 481 - 485
8. Du Bourguet G. and Burger D.: Conversion Tools for DAISY 3.0 / NISO Z39.86-2002. In Craddock G., McCormack L., Reilly R., Knops H., Eds.: Proc. of the AAATE'03 Conference in Dublin, Ireland. - IOS Press, Amsterdam, The Netherlands (2003) p 446-450
9. Arthur Karshmer, Gopal Gupta, Klaus Miesenberger, Enrico Pontelli, Hei-Feng Guo, The development of a tool to enhance communications between blind and sighted mathematicians, student and teachers : A global translation appliance(2001, HCI conference)

# Multi-modal Mathematics: Conveying Math Using Synthetic Speech and Speech Recognition

D. Fitzpatrick[1] and A.I. Karshmer[2]

[1] School of Computing, Dublin City University,
Glasnevin Dublin 9, Ireland
dfitzpat@computing.dcu.ie,
http://www.computing.dcu.ie/~dfitzpat

[2] Department of Information Technology
University of South Florida, USA
arthur@lklnd.usf.edu

**Abstract.** Over the past decade, the notion of multi-modal access to technology has moved from the realms of science fiction to reality. It is not now unthinkable to communicate with a machine using voice recognition software, and to have the computers' response spoken in a voice comparable in quality to a human.
This paper outlines methodologies for the verbal presentation of mathematical material to a user using prosodically enhanced synthetic speech. We will describe methodologies for generating a prosodic model of the "equation space".

## 1 Introduction

The problem of conveying mathematics to those with a print impairment using non-traditional forms of presentation has challenged researchers for some considerable time. Though Braille affords the reader the facility to use the printed as an "external memory" and hence devote the majority of their effort to understanding and solving equations, its bulky nature, and linear presentation makes it difficult to use. Consequently, an alternative approach must be considered which will afford the reader of mathematics the facility of readily apprehending this form of highly visual material.

One such form of presentation is the use of synthetic speech. However, a drawback with this is the lack of "prosody" [1] which makes the presentation monotonous, and memory intensive. There has been very little work carried out into developing a prosodic model for the conveyance of mathematical material. One such effort can be found in [7].

In order to devise a set of rules to prosodically enhance algebraic utterances, Stevens conducted an experiment involving two experienced subjects, both of whom were native speakers of British English. Each was presented with a random set of 24 equations, and two recordings on high quality tape were made for each speaker. The participants were asked to speak the equations "as if they were addressing a class of sighted students".They were also asked to convey the

K. Miesenberger et al. (Eds.): ICCHP 2004, LNCS 3118, pp. 644–647, 2004.

information in as neutral a manner as possible, that is, not to "...indicate any of the intentions of the mathematical notation" [7]. The recordings were analysed for pitch, timing and amplitude and these three characteristics were related to the syllabic content of the spoken versions. The results provided the designers of the system with the knowledge needed to construct a "simplistic prosodic model" [7] which could be used to convey algebraic notation.

The prosodic model defined by Stevens is, by his own admission, simplistic. However, he formulates the theory that this means of prosodic enhancement could form the basis for a more concrete model. It is pointed out that the range of examples used in his experiment were not wide enough to be certain of the exact nature of the rules required, but maintains that from the data gathered, there should be no problems extending the model to form the basis for a broader set of rules encompassing facets of mathematical content other than algebra. It should also be noted that the model used by Stevens is at odds in important ways with current views of prosodic and intonational phonology, and though it produces reasonable results, it is not the model we are using. For a discussion of appropriate phonological models and their use in synthesis, see [4, 5].

In [3] it is demonstrated through experimental results that the introduction of prosody into the utterance did not dramatically improve the listeners' understanding of the material. However, it should be noted that the readers in these experiments were human and utilised all the vocal characteristics of natural speech. Not all such vocal alterations are feasible when synthetic speech is utilised; causing a markedly different $f_0$ contour. We therefore believe that a standardised, constant prosody introduced by synthetic speech will overcome the inconsistencies demonstrated by natural speech and will assist the listener in understanding and predicting the material.

## 2 Mathematical Prosody

A fundamental feature of prosodic enhancement is the addition of pausing to separate spoken utterances into units. This is particularly true of algebraic, or other syntactically complex material, where the pausing can indicate the grouping within an expression, assisting the listener to more easily understand the verbal presentation. The paradigm on which the spoken mathematical presentation is based, [5] is that of converting a sequence of juxtaposed symbols, delimited by both white space and other visual cues (such as parentheses) into a serially transmitted linguistic approximation. In order to achieve this, a parallel was drawn between the structure found in mathematical expressions and the inherent composition of English sentences [2].

It was decided to render the content by mapping the syntax and semantics of the mathematical material to as close an approximation as possible to an english-like sentence structure. To this end, pausing, rate changes and alterations in both the average pitch and pitch range are employed. Other alterations are made to the accent height, richness and smoothness of the voice however it is beyond the scope of this brief document to outline in depth how the structure and components of formulae are verbalised. It should be stated here that our model is based around the notion of relative rather than absolute changes in the pitch contour. For a more in-depth discussion see [2].

Thus far our work has focussed on providing a model to verbally render the material, and to that end we attempt not to introduce extra lexical cues into the utterance. However, a pilot study of this work described in [2] indicates that illiminating such cues entirely introduces ambiguity into the utterance. To remove any possible ambiguities from the utterance, we are now investigating the incorporation of the lexical cues described in [6] into our model. This will alter the length of the utterance, and will undoubtedly cause modifications to the prosody used, however it is hoped that this will assist in removing those ambiguities thus far observed.

Much of the research effort to date has been directed towards the verbalisation of the mathematical material. It is our intention to use the extralinguistic portions of speech, and the verbal cues described in [6] to enable a print impaired user to enter and edit equations. It is our intention to combine the output of synthetic speech to the input of human speech to provide a truly speech-based equation browser and editor.

## 3 Conclusion

We have described a model for the depiction of mathematics using prosodically enhanced synthetic speech. It is hoped to carry out various impirical studies which will ascertain the efficacy of this form of presentation when synthetic speech is used to deliver the material. From this, it is hoped that a more comprehensive model for the verbal presentation of mathematics can be determined. It is our belief that when synthetic speech is used, the replacement of the monotonous speech signal with an inflected one will aid in the disambiguation and comprehension of the material. We also intend to incorporate speech recognition into the software to enable the user to enter into a two-way communication process entirely based around natural speech.

## References

1. Couper-Kuhlen, E.: *An Introduction To English Prosody.* Edward Arnold Ltd., 1986.
2. Fitzpatrick, D.: *Towards Accessible Technical Documents: Production of Speech and Braille Output from Formatted Documents.* PhD thesis, School of Computer Applications, Dublin City University, 1999.
3. Karshmer, A.I. and Gillan, D.: *How well can we Read Equations to Blind Mathematics Students: Some Answers from Psychology* Proceedings of the 2003 Human Computer Interface International Conference, Crete, Greece, July, 2003.
4. Ladd, D.R.: *Intonational Phonology.* Cambridge: CUP, 1996.
5. Monaghan, A.: *Intonation in a Text-to-Speech Conversion System.* PhD thesis, University of Edinburgh, 1991.

6. Nemeth, A.: *Abraham Nemeth's Anthology on the Unified Braille Code* Available at `http://www.math.virginia.edu/~arm4r/nemeth`
7. Stevens, R.: *Principles for the Design of Auditory Interfaces to Present Complex Information to Blind People.* PhD thesis, Department of Computer Science, January 1996.

# An Integrated OCR Software for Mathematical Documents and Its Output with Accessibility

Masakazu Suzuki[1], Toshihiro Kanahori[2],
Nobuyuki Ohtake[2], and Katsuhito Yamaguchi[3]

[1] Kyushu University, Faculty of Mathematics,
Hakozaki 6-10-1, Higashiku, Fukuoka, 812-8581 Japan
suzuki@math.kyushu-u.ac.jp
http://www.math.kyushu-u.ac.jp/~suzuki/index.html
[2] Research Center on Educational Media, Tsukuba College of Technology,
4-12 Kasuga, Tsukuba-shi, Ibaraki, 305-0821 Japan
{kanaori,ohtake}@k.tsukuba-tech.ac.jp
[3] Nihon University, Junior College Funabashi Campus,
7-24-1, Narashinodai, Funabashi, Chiba 274-8501, Japan
eugene@gaea.jcn.nihon-u.ac.jp

**Abstract.** This paper describes shortly a practical integrated system for scientific documents including mathematical formulae, named 'Infty'. The system consists of three components of applications: an OCR system named 'InftyReader', an editor named 'InftyEditor' and converting tools into various formats. Those applications are linked each other via XML files.

InftyReader recognizes scanned images of clearly printed mathematical documents and outputs the recognition results in a XML format.It recognizes complex mathematical formulae used in various research papers of mathematics including matrices. InftyEditor provides a very efficient interface to correct the recognition results using keyboard. Another feature of InftyEditor is its handwriting interface to input mathematical formulae for users with vision and speech interface for visually impaired uses.

The XML files output by InftyReader/Editor can be converted into various formats: LaTeX, MathML, HTML and Braille Codes; in UBC (Unified Braille Codes) for English texts and in Japanese Braille Codes for Japanese texts.

## 1 Introduction

We presenterd a prototype of mathematical document recognition system in [1] at ICCHP 2000. As a result of the improvements of recognition rates and user interfaces obtained this period, we released the software 'InftyReader' to transcribe printed mathematical documents into digital data with accessibility as a freely usable software by any non-profit users. The purpose of this paper is to describe the outline of the software. A package file of the software can be obtained from the WEB site [7].

K. Miesenberger et al. (Eds.): ICCHP 2004, LNCS 3118, pp. 648–655, 2004.

InftyReader recognizes clearly printed papers, carefully scanned in binary images by either 600 DPI or 400 DPI. The image files have to be prepared in TIFF CCITT-3 or CCITT-4 format. InftyReader segments page images into picture areas, table areas and text areas, and then recognizes text areas including mathematical expressions. To get better recognition results, users are recommended to adjust the binarization threshold of their scanner so that, in scanned page images, the number of the touched or broken characters be less than 1% of the total number of the charactes in each page.

The released version of the software includes an editor of mathematical documents to view and edit the recognition results, named "InftyEditor". InftyEditor is typesetting tool of scientific documents having, in addition to usual keyboard interface by TeX-like command input, a handwriting interface to input mathematical expressions. Users can edit easily the recognition results, and save the results as a LaTeX source file, an HTML file, or in a txt file using a "Human Readable TeX" format for visually impaired persons. The trial version of InftyReader/Editor provides also Braille outputs as well as a speech interface to read and edit mathematical documents for visually impared users. The description of the software below is based on the InftyReader Version 2.4.2 released on April 15, 2004.

The **Fig. 1** below shows a snapshot of a recognition result displayed on the InftyEditor incorporated in InftyReader. Since the Infty system consists of three component applications: an OCR system named 'InftyReader', an editor named 'InftyEditor' and a converter unit of Math-XML into various formats, we shall describe the system in three steps below.

## 2 Optical Recognition of Printed Mathematical Documents

In this section, we shall describe briefly some specification of our software 'InftyReader' to recognize mathematical documents. As for the details about the recognition methodes used and experimental results, see [2], [3] and [4]. Especially, the paper [4] reports a detailed experimental results of InftyReader on 496 page images taken from 25 different volumes of pure mathematical journals and a book from physics, including various levels of scanning quality from good ones to very noisy pages having 20 percent abnormal (touched/broken) characters.

One of the important result of the experiments in [4] and the experiments by the current version of InftyReader is the strong relationship between the total recognition rates of character recognition and the ratio of the number of abnormal (broken/touched) characters included mathematical formulae. There was a remarkable defference on the recognition rates between the scanned images with abnormal (broken/touched) characters less than 1% of the total number of characters in each page and the noisy pages images containing more abnormal (broken/touched) characters in our database. On the other hand, in our experience, usually it is not difficult to reduce the number of abnormal characters less than 1% by carefull scanning, if the document is clearly printed. Almost a half of articles in the test data mentioned above are of this quality.

Note that there is an essential difference between the current version of InftyReader and the version used in the experiments reported in [4]. While the version of InftyReader reported in [4] used a commercial OCR engine for both Japanese characters and alpha-numeric characters in usual text area, the current version of InftyReader makes use of the commercial OCR engine to recognize only Japanese characters[1]. Its English version makes use of no commercial OCR engine and uses originally developed OCR to recognizes alpha-numeric characters and various mathematical symboles. However, as far as in our experiments performed on the same data mentioned above, the total recognition rates of the new version is even better than the old one, by the implementation of a touched character separation method valid both in text area and mathematical formulae areas. The average recognition rate of the new version for 13 articles with with abnormal (broken/touched) characters less than 1% of the total number of characters in the database mentioned above was 99.89% for ordinary text areas and 99.56% including characters and symbols in mathematical formulae.

From each page image obtained by a scanner, InftyReader first cuts out picture areas, table areas and text areas automatically. Mathematical formulae are included in text areas in the first segmentation. As for the tables and the pictures, InftyReader outputs only brief information concerning their positions and their sizes.

From math-text area, InftyReader separates the area into lines and each line into ordinary text parts and the mathematical formulae parts using the recognition results of characters together with their positions and their sizes. In the case of English documents, linguistic information such as fundamental English words dictionary with short spelling, mathematical technical terms dictionary and some morphological analysis are used, in order to improve the accuracy of the recognition of words and the separation of ordinary text parts and mathematical formulae parts.

InftyReader distinguishes more than 500 categories of characters ans symbols, where Roman fonts of Upright, Italic, Caligraphic, Blackboard are classified into different categories. However, it does not distinguish bold fonts with normal fonts at all and the recognition rate of German fraktur or Script Roman fonts still remains very on low level at the current stage of teh development.

As for the recognition of mathematical formulae structure, we introduced a new algorithm to improve the robustness of the recognition against the variation of the styles of printing of the documents, using the spanning tree of minimum cost int the network generated by virtual links of characters [2]. InftyReader some times suceeds to recognize very complex matrices by the implemented algorithm of [3] (see **Fig. 3** below at the end of the paper).

---

[1] We would like to exxpress our thanks to Toshiba coorporation for the supply of the OCR engine.

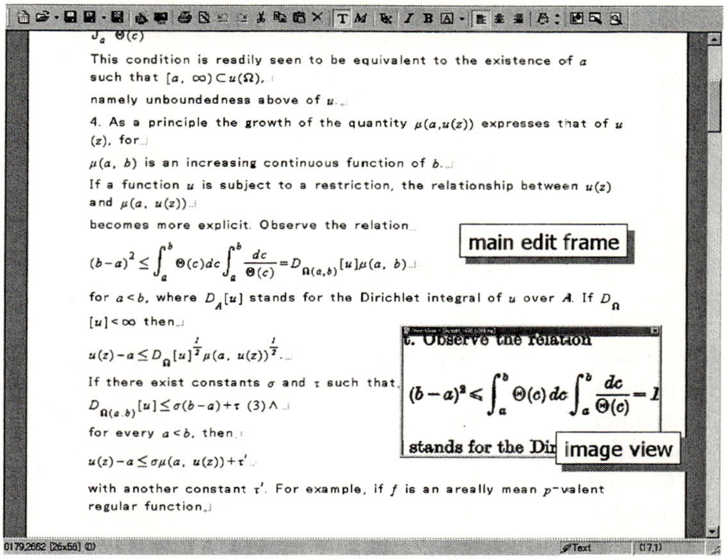


**Fig. 1.** Snapshot of InftyReader

## 3 Editor for Mathematical Documents – InftyEditor

The recognition results of InftyReader are output in a XML object/file and displayed in the main frame of the editor 'InftyEditor' included in the InftyReader package.

### 3.1 Interface for Users with Sight

InftyEditor is typesetting tool of scientific documents having a handwriting interface to input mathematical expressions. in addition to usual keyboard interface by pallete or TeX-like command input. Special edition of InftyEditor incorporated into InftyReader has a special view window to show the original image scanned to compare the recognition results with it (**Fig. 1**).

The displayed texts and mathematical formulae can be edited freely by using ordinary editing operations; cut, copy, paste and delete, and for mathematical symbols, our original front-end processor by LaTeX commands is provided.For example, a fraction '$\frac{1}{x^2+1}$' can be input by a keyboard in the following way;

1. input '`\frac`', then a fractional line is appears and the cursor of InftyEditor moves to the numerator position of the fractional line,
2. input '1', and push an enter key, then the cursor moves to the denominator position,
3. input 'x' and '^', then the cursor moves to the superscript position of '$x$',
4. input '2', then the cursor moves to the right position of '$x^2$',
5. input '+' and '1', and push a enter key, then the cursor moves to the right position of '$\frac{1}{x^2+1}$', and the input is done.

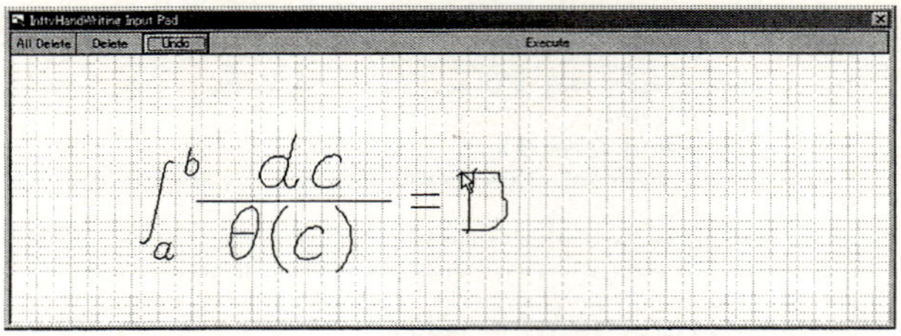


**Fig. 2.** Handwriting Dialog

Another distinctive feature of InftyEditor is that it provides with a handwriting interface to input mathematical formulae (**Fig. 2**). By clicking a button, the dialog to input a pen stroke using a mouse, a data tablet or a pen display opens. The mathematical formulae written by hand in this dialog box is recognized and put into the mathematical text displayed on the main board of InftyEditor, at its cursor position. By this handwriting interface, the system realizes a very easy intuitive methods to edit or correct mathematical formulae, requiring no special skill about, for example, LaTeX notations of mathematical formulae. As for the methods used in our system in order to realize smoother handwriting input of mathematical formulae and other details about this interface, readers are referred to the paper [5].

### 3.2 Interface for Users without Sight

A trial version of InftyEditor is provided with speech interface to read and edit mathematical documents.

As is well known, ordinary screen readers cannot correspond to math editors in which mathematical expressions are usually treated as images. On the other hand, the InftyEditor treats all math expressions as marked-up texts in XML. We, therefore, have a chance to access this editor with speech output.

Actually, we have already developed an interface for the Infty Editor to help visually disabled persons with accessing math expressions by means of speech in Japanese. Since, in Japan, there is no definite or systematic method to convey content of math expressions accurately by speech, we firstly assign manners of aloud-reading in Japanese to all 712 symbols and math structures defined in the Infty Editor: such as a fraction, a subscript, a superscript, a radical and so on. We adopted "95 Reader," the one of popular Japanese screen readers, as a speech output system to read aloud both of bodies of Japanese documents and control menus.

Next, we currently try to extend it so as to correspond to the English version of InftyEditor. In English-speaking countries, contrary to Japanese, it is usually defined properly how to read aloud math expressions. In developing the interface, we are based on that method in principle and assign manners of aloud-reading to all necessary symbols and math structures. We adopt Microsoft speech API and Text-to-Speech engine as a speech output system for bodies of English documents. On the other hand, control menus are supposed to be read by a screen reader itself.

Using this interface, one can accurately understand content of math expressions by means of speech output only. For instance, a fraction is read aloud as follows:

"Frac a plus b over c frac-end."

That is, one can clearly realize where the beginning and the end of the fraction are located, what is the numerator and so on. Furthermore, not only one can access given math expressions, but functions of writing and editing math expressions are also available with a voice guide.

Combining this interface with the OCR technology for math expressions, it is expected that persons with visual disabilities become able to do freely reading and writing of scientific documents for themselves.

## 4 Output Formats

InftyReader outputs the recognition results in our original XML format, called 'KML'. The KML format includes the most detailed information obtained by the recognition results, such as block segmentation information (tag, corrdinates, etc.), line information (type of lines, indentation, centering, display math., equation number etc.), character information (candidates of recognition, coordinate, Math/Text attribute) and link information of the tree structure of mathematical expressions.

When the recognition result is loaded on InftyEditor's display, it is compressed into another XML format, called 'IML' omitting candidates and coordinates etc., information unneccessary to understand the contents of the documents.

The XML files generated by InftyReader (or InftyEditor) can be converted into various formats of mathematical documents; LaTeX, MathML, HTML, and especially for visually impaired, HR-TeX (Human Readable TeX), KAMS (ASCII Mathematics Script) and Braille Codes, in UBC (Unified Braille Codes) for English texts and In Japanese Braille Codes for Japanese texts. The HR-TeXfile is a text file in which mathematical expressions are written in simplified LaTeX notations for convenience to be read by visually impaired people, omitting various commands and simbols unneccessary to understand the meaning. KAMS is a notation of matehmatics developed in the Study Centre for Blind and Partially Sighted Students at the University of Karlsruhe.

There are several Braille notations which express mathematical formulae. Among them, we selected the Unified Braille Code (UBC) proposed by BANA (Braille Authority of North American) to output English mathematical documents. The main reason for this selection is the facility of the transcription. It needs lesser tasks to establish one-to-one correspondence between the printed form and UBC, for mathematical symbols and also in text word level even for the Grade II codes, in UBC.

As for the Japanese texts, the Japanese formal Braille code defines the mathematical notations only for the high school level. The output of our system uses the notations extended by some volunteer but major transcriber groups to adapt it to the notation of the university level mathematics.

As it is described in [1], literal Japanese text is composed of a mixture of Chinese characters (called Kanji in Japanese), two sets of 46 Japanese syllabaries (Hira-gana and Kata-kana) and symbols. Before transcribing Japanese texts into Braille codes, it is neccessary to transform the original text into syllabary text with correct pronunciation and proper punctuation. In our system, EXTRA which is a Japanese Braille transformation software proposed by Jun Ichikawa [6] is used to decode Kanji into syllabaries code.

Although the Braille emboss printer has a `columns` × `lines` restriction (ex. 12-42 characters per line × 10-28 lines per page), there is no automatic line fold function in our system at present. The main reason for it is that our system does not yet recognize the logical structure of the text such as chapters, sections, items, etc., or the mathematical description styles of theorems, definitions, etc.

## 5 Conclusion

The outline of a software called 'Infty' to recognize and transcribe printed matehmatical documents into various digital data with accessibility for visually impaired people is presented. The system consists of three components of applications: an optical recognition system named 'InftyReader', an editor

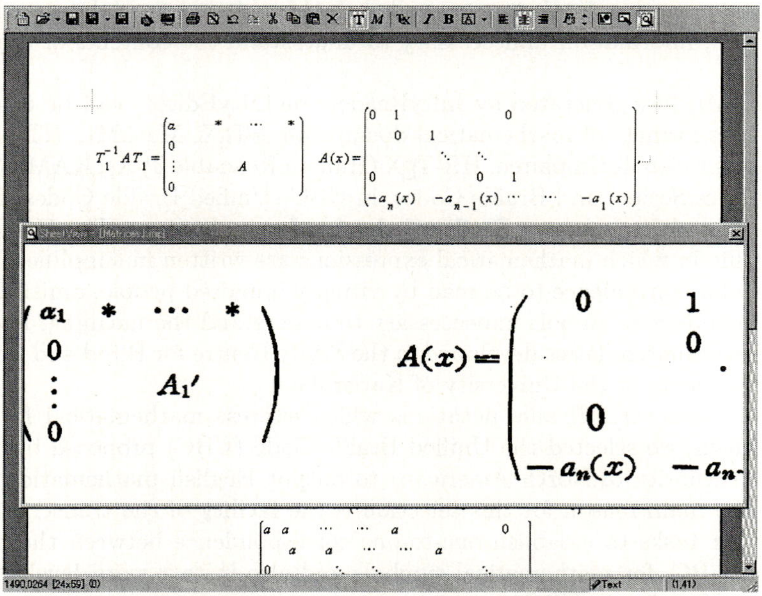

**Fig. 3.** Recognition Results of Matrices by InftyReader on InftyEditor's Display

'InftyEditor' and converting tool unit based on XML technology. InftyReader recognizes carefully scanned in binary images by either 600 DPI or 400 DPI. It recognizes mathematical documents with complex formulae with high accuracy if the noise of scanned images are limited.

The recognized results by InftyReader can be edited easily by InftyEditor incorporated in InftyReader package, including mathematical formulae, and the edited results can be transformed into various data formats: LaTeX, Human Readable TeX, Bralle, etc. Infty Editor is featured with its handwriting interface to input matehmatical formualae for users with sight and a speech interface to edit mathematical notations for users without sight.

Current version of InftyReader does not output the results of logical structure analysis of texts such as section-subsection structure, items, theorem descriptions etc. These subjects are left to future research work, but urgent since the logical structure analysis is inevitable to get correct output of Braille transcription.

To end this paper, we would like to mention the importance of the distinction of bold fonts in mathematical expressions omitted by the current version of InftyReader's output. It is important, since bold fonts are generaly used in mathematical or scientific documents to distinguish vectors and scalar quantities.

## References

1. Fukuda, R., Ohtake, N. and Suzuki, M.: "Optical Recognition and Braille Transcription of Mathematical Documents," *Proc. ICCHP* (2000) 711–718
2. Eto, Y. and Suzuki, M.: "Mathematical formula recognition using virtual link network," *Proc. ICDAR* (2001) 762–767
3. Kanahori, T. and Suzuki, M.: "A recognition method of matrices by using variable block pattern elements generating rectangular area," Graphics Recognition. Algorithms and Applications (Lecture Notes in Computer Science, 2390), Springer-Verlag, 2001
4. Suzuki, M., Tamari, F., Fukuda, R., Uchida, S. and Kanahori, T.: "INFTY – An Integrated OCR System for Mathematical Documents," *Proc. DocEng*, 2003
5. Kanahori, T., Tabata, K., Cong, W., Tamari, F. and Suzuki, M.: "On-Line Recognition of Mathematical Expressions Using Automatic Rewriting Method," *Proc. ICMI*, 394–401, (Lecture Notes in Computer Science, 1948), Springer-Verlag, 2000
6. Ishikawa, J.: *EXTRA for Windows ver. 1.0 users manual*, Amedia Co., Ltd., Tokyo, 2001
7. `http://infty.math.kyushu-u.ac.jp`

# Mathematical Working Environment for the Blind Motivation and Basic Ideas

Bernhard Stöger, Klaus Miesenberger, and Mario Batušić

Universität Linz, Institut "integriert studieren"
Altenbergerstrasse 69
A-4040 Linz, Austria
{bernhard.stoeger,mario.batusic,klaus.miesenberger}@jku.at
http://www.integriert-studieren.jku.at

**Abstract.** The past three decades saw considerable progress in access to information for the group of blind and visually impaired people: Thanks to modern information technology in the mainstream and to very specialized adaptive and assistive technologies, blind and visually impaired people are now able to deal independently and efficiently with almost every piece of information that is composed of pure text. Despite current strong trends towards graphical presentation, text still covers the majority of relevant contents for private and professional life, such that information access for the target group is currently accomplished to a very large extent. Despite intensive research efforts carried out over the last years, blind and visually impaired people are still excluded from an efficient usage and handling of graphical contents. Since Mathematics is presented in a highly graphical way most of the time, this exclusion implies considerable restrictions in access to Mathematics, too. Although "accessibility" is put in place, "usability" and especially support functionalities in "doing" mathematics are very low. This paper analyses the major issues, outlines the existing approaches to a possible solution and describes the current activities at the Johannes Kepler University in Linz, institute "integriert studieren" (Austria) towards a comprehensive software answer to this problem.

## 1 State of the Art

The problems faced by the target group with respect to Mathematics fall into four basic categories:

1. Access to mathematical literature (books, teaching materials, papers etc.)
2. Preparation of mathematical information (presenting school exercises, writing papers etc.)
3. Navigation in mathematical expressions
4. Doing Mathematics (carrying out calculations and computations at all levels, doing formal manipulation, solving exercises)

While the first two problems have been addressed to produce solutions, which are at least satisfactory to some extent, and basic approaches are available to the third problem, almost nothing was achieved by now to support the target group in solving tasks of the last category.

K. Miesenberger et al. (Eds.): ICCHP 2004, LNCS 3118, pp. 656–663, 2004.

The third category, navigation within mathematical contents, deserves attention because it is much more complex than just reading them like ordinary textual information: For sequential reading, as sufficient with text, will not give one the understanding of a complex mathematical expression. To grasp the meaning of a formula, one needs to repeatedly scan passages of it, and to jump over irrelevant portions, which is a heavy challenge if you cannot see. A supportive software environment, which, as a minimum requirement, should furnish collapse and expand functionality, would be needed.

What was said about navigation in formulae is true, but to a much larger extent, for the last category, the task of actually doing Mathematics. Even at secondary school level, formulae tend to deploy to high complexity quite soon within a computation what makes tasks like maintaining an overview, finding relevant spots, minimizing errors in remembering and copying. All these are tasks non-trivial for sighted people, thus still much more challenging for blind and visually impaired students and mathematicians. Even blind people who successfully mastered high-level mathematical courses complain about the cognitive overload, from which it becomes clear that it is a pressing issue for mathematical education of the blind and visually impaired.

The above mentioned software solution for the support of navigation within mathematical expressions needs a substantial extension to support the much more complex task of effectively carrying out computations on all levels for the target group. Such a software suite, which we envisage and which combines the already attained solutions for the first three categories of tasks with new solutions for the latter categories, will be referred to as a Mathematical Working Environment (MaWEn). The following sections shall a) briefly sketch the activities by now undertaken to solve the problems of the first three categories, b) present a concrete example to motivate the need of a software solution addressing the problems of navigation and manipulation, c) list requirements to be fulfilled by a comprehensive Mathematical Working Environment and d) finally sketch a raw draft of modules to be implemented in order to construct such an environment.

## 2 Contributions to Overcome the Problem

For the last 10 years the above mentioned issues were envisaged, and research was started. We developped first a converter from LaTeX into Marburg mathematical Braille Notation – the schoolbook preparation system LaBraDoor[1]. This system is in use in Austria for the schoolbook preparation on all school levels. That project will mainly deliver the know-how for the import module of MaWEn.

As the next step in the overall problem solving process we developed a backtranslator from Marburg Mathematical Notation into MathML[2]. This was accomplished within the framework of the international project UMA (Universal Math Access)[7]. As the most important outcome of this project an international Group for Universal Mathematics Access was initiated. The first common achievment of the Group will be an universal math converter library for interconverting between various standard and braille mathematical formats such as:

- MathML
- LaTeX
- Nemeth Maths Code (USA and Canada)
- Marburg Mathematical Braille Notation (German speaking area)
- French Braille Maths Code

The system allows an easy integration of additional notations.

## 3 Support Functions for Data Manipulation. A Case Study

We would like to use a concrete example to describe the sketched difficulties in formal manipulation faced by blind people. Consider the following simple exercise:

$$(3a - 5b + 6c) \cdot (4a + b - 3c)$$

Let us first describe the process, independently of visual impairment:

1. Each summand of the second parenthesis is multiplied by each summand of the left one, giving a long sum that has to be simplified in a second step. In detail:
   (a) The term $4a$ is multiplied with all the summands of the left parenthesis consecutively, giving the sum:
   $$12a^2 - 20ab + 24ac$$
   (b) The same is done with the expression $+b$, giving:
   $$+3ab - 5b^2 + 6bc$$
   (c) Finally, the term $-3c$ is multiplied against the terms in the left parenthesis, giving
   $$-9ac + 15bc - 18c^2$$
2. The three resulting sums are consticted to the expression
   $$12a^2 - 20ab + 24ac + 3ab - 5b^2 + 6bc - 9ac + 15bc - 18c^2$$
3. The next step is the simplification:
   The sum is scanned from left to right in order to find terms with the same sequence of letters; if found, the terms will be constricted. In detail:
   (a) The term $12a^2$ is not matched by any other term, such that it will be copied "as is" into the final result.
   (b) The term $-20ab$ has to be constricted with $+3ab$ – the addition yields $-17ab$
   (c) The term $+24ac$ unites with $-9ac$ to $+15ac$
   (d) The term $-2b^2$ does not have a counterpart, such that it can be simply appended to the final sum.

(e) The term $+6bc$ adds to $+15bc$ giving $+21bc$
(f) The term $-18c^2$ is a singleton, concluding the sum.
(g) We thus obtain

$$12a^2 - 17ab + 15ac - 5b^2 + 21bc - 18c^2$$

as the simplified final result of the calculation.

When a blind student solves an exercise like this via braille display and computer in the conventional way, one encounters a number of difficulties. In order to understand these problems, let us take a look at the way how a blind student would carry out the steps detailed above. For first one will move the exercise to a free place in a text document, either by manual copying or by cut and paste. One will open a new line, beginning with an equals sign, to enter the first step, namely the factorisation of the two parentheses. Now, the right parenthesis has to be scanned summand by summand. To this end, the student has to direct the braille display to the exercise, to search the second factor, and to find (and remember) its first summand. One will do his/her best to remember that expression well, because it is needed as the reference term to be multiplied against all the summands of the leftmost parenthesis.

Once the first summand is found, the product is calculated and committed to memory, since it needs to be inserted into the interim result after the equals sign. This, in turn, requires a jump to the equals sign.

In order to find the second reference term, another jump into the exercise is needed; furthermore, the student has to know that the first reference term was already processed, which challenges his/her memory: Not within this initial stage where only two reference terms were processed, of course, but in the course of the calculation it can easily happen that the position within the second factor may be forgotten; to synchronize in such an event would mean an investigation of the steps carried out so far, involving a jump to the interim result.

Already with this first step in the calculation – and this is the easier one – two fundamental difficulties become apparent:

1. One has to jump constantly between the exercise and the interim result, namely, for every partial product one jump to the exercise in order to calculate the partial product, and one jump back to the interim result in order to append the partial product. With 9 partial products, as in our example, this sums up to 18 jumps. The jumps into the interim result are simplified by a function of the screen reader that performs a jump to the cursor, because it is expected that, as the interim result develops, the cursor moves along it. However, the jumps into the exercise require navigation with the braille display in any case.
2. Beside the jumps, the task imposes considerable load on the blind student's memory, namely, in two respects:
   (a) One has to well remember the computed partial product to be able to append it to the interim result after having jumped to its end.

(b) In order to compute the next partial product one needs to know what was already processed. This results in the need to remember two positions, one within the left and one within the right factor.

Step 2, the simplification of the computed expanded sum, contains more and greater difficulties: The interim result, which now becomes the exercise, has to be searched summand by summand from left to right and for every summand it has to be checked whether it can be constricted with other members of the sum. This begins with a jump to the exercise, where the first summand $12a^2$ has to be committed to memory. Now the whole long sum has to be scanned and every summand needs to be checked to see whether it is a multiple of $a^2$. In the end the student can determine that this is not the case, such that he/she can append the term $12a^2$ to the final result. A jump to the exercise produces the next reference term $-20ab$. Checking against the whole remaining sum, in whose curse the reference term $-20ab$ has to be constantly remembered, yields that it can be constricted with $+3ab$, which produces the term $-17ab$ to be appended to the result.

Continuing, we get the term $+24ac$ to be constricted with $-9ac$ yielding $+13ac$ for the final result.

With the next term, $+3ab$, an additional problem arises: A scan through the sum to the right does not lead to any summand to be constricted with the term. Rather, the sum now has to be searched to the left of the reference term $+3ab$ in order to see that this term was already processed, namely when it was constricted with $-20ab$.

Continuing in this manner, the simplification of the sum can be completed.

By the above analysis, these difficulties were isolated:

1. Constant jumping between exercise and result
2. necessity to remember the positions within the exercise
3. need to commit reference terms to memory
4. load on memory by partial products that have to be appended to the result
5. requirement to search the exercise in every step bidirectionally, both to the right and to the left of the reference term.

The Mathematical Working Environment, MaWEn shall furnish software tools to support a blind student in tasks like the above. Especially, load on memory should be considerably reduced. Some concrete measures in this direction are listed below:

1. Window oriented navigation:
   every step in a calculation, the exercise, the interim results and the final result, shall be stored in a separate window, probably a multiline edit field. Simple keyboard commands shall navigate between the various windows.
2. No need for manually appending a partial result to a final one:
   Once a partial result is to be computed – multiplication of two factors or joining of two summands in our example – the student can open an edit field that will take the partial result inserted by him/her. Once that field is closed, the partial result is automatically appended to the end of the result and an automatic jump back to the exercise is performed.

3. Controlled jumps:
   The jump back to the exercise shall be performed such that the position from which processing is to be continued becomes apparent: For our example, in step 1, expansion of the product, both the reference term in the right factor and the next term in the left factor to be multiplied by the reference term will be selected.
4. These measures shall largely eliminate the need to remember positions.
5. Parts that have already been processed, like the term $+3ab$ in step 2, are either not displayed at all, or they are marked as "already processed".
6. Direct jumps into the final result during a calculation will be possible, although not necessary:
   For every partial result inserted into the edit field mentioned under 1. shall be automatically appended to the end of the final result.
7. Shortening of expressions as sighted users do by marking already handled expressions.
8. ...

It's quite plain that these and also further supportive functions to be implemented in the MaWEn can be switched on and off. For otherwise a student who is about to learn a particular kind of mathematical exercise would never get into touch with the above outlined difficulties. Rather, the system will be designed more like a "tool box" such that support for a category of tasks of one level of complexity will be offered only if the student is about to learn the next higher level, or at least if she/he has gained a reasonable understanding of the mentioned level of complexity.

## 4 Mathematical Working Environment – MaWEn

"Doing" mathematics as a sighted person is based on a lot of skills and knowledge which is implicit to the visual methods of doing math. MaWEn intends a) to find the implicit skills of doing mathematics which are represented in the visual methods (which you find e.g. described as pathways of doing mathematics in schoolbooks), b) to make them explicit and structure them in functionalities which should c) form the basis of a supporting environment.

Already in 1996 we stated the most important requirements of a future computer aided mathematical working environment for the braille users[6]. These requirements, in addition to those of speech output users which are tackled by our GUMA project partners, didn't lose anything of their actuality. The main requirements of a Braille user in a mathematical working environment can be enumerated as follows:

1. Accessing as many mathematical documents as possible in common formats
2. Ability to present all mathematical constructs in Braille
3. Using a Braille notation of once own choice
4. Parallel Braille and graphical view of the current formula
5. Software support in the concrete data manipulation during a "manual" computational task.

The sections up to now described the available converting tools and gave a detailed insight into the support methods for data manipulation beeing currently developed in a PhD thesis. To round off the presentation of MaWEn we bring a short outline of its specific modules planned so far. We don't refer to the common modules needed in each browser/editor software.

### 4.1 Overall MaWEn Features

It's obvious that MaWEn has to fulfil all software accessibility guidelines to guarantee the best possible ergonomics and efficiency (e.g. keyboard bindings for all functionalities, use of exclusively standard Windows libraries/objects for GUI). All modules are concieved as independent building blocks in DLL format which can be used in other applications.

### 4.2 GUI Module

The GUI module is responsible for the "look and feel" of the main application. Even though the first version of MaWEn should be a MS Windows 2000/XP application, it is planned that all other modules are programmed in such a way that they can interfere also with an alternative GUI module made for an other operating system. A speciality of this module is the "dual presentation mode". It concerns one of the main MaWEn features: displaying the current mathematical formula both in a Braille code and as a 2D visual rendering.

### 4.3 Data Storage Module

Documents processed within MaWEN shall be saved for further reference: As document formats we envisage a flavour of XML or a mathematical standard such as OpenMath or OMDoc. Ordinary text components, as needed, e.g., in school books, shall be imported from and exported to standard word processing formats.

### 4.4 Data Manipulation Support Module

This module contains all support functions and data manipulation rules which can be selectively used. In the section 3 we showed by an example how the functions of this module could be helpful in the editing/calculating process.

As mentioned only now the *help engine* works according to some support rules. An easy-to-use and WYSIWYG tool will be developed to enable users or teachers to design new support rules. For all existing rules the user will have a possibility to set options to enable, disable or to apply them selectively to classes of mathematical expressions. To explain the process of defining support rules would go beyond the scope of this paper. To give roughly a basic understanding of the support rules concept, we can see them somewhat similar to the filtering rules in a mail application. There is an extensible set of appliable actions such as e.g. "hide item, show item, put item in memory (or bookmark item), mark item as finished. A rule defines an action (or a series of actions) to be executed on items/mathematical objects according to the matching conditions.

## Acknowledgement

This work was done in the frame of the project "The Development of a Tool to Enhance Communications between Blind and Sighted Mathematicians, Students and Teachers - a Global Translation Appliance" funded by the US Department for Education. It is expected that future work will be funded by the European Commission, DG IST in the frame of the Micole project (511592).

## References

1. Batušić, M., Miesenberger K., Stöger, B.: LABRADOOR, a contribution to making mathematics accessible for the blind, in: Edwards, A., D., N., Arato, A., Zagler, W., L.: Computers and Assistive Technology - 6th International Conference on Computers Helping People with Special Needs, ICCHP Ý98, Oldenbourg, Wien, München 1998
2. Miesenberger, K., Batušić, M., Stöger, B.: Parser for the Marburg Mathematical Braille Notation, in: Stephanidis, C. (ed.): Universal Access in HCI – Inclusive Design in the Information Society, Volume 4, Lea, Mahwah, 2003
3. Karshmer, A.: Access to Mathematics by Blind Students, Miesenberger, K., Klaus, J., Zagler, W. (eds): Computers Helping People with Special Needs - 8th International Conference, ICCHP, Linz, Austria, July 2002, Proceedings, Springer Heidelberg, 2002
4. Karshmer, A., Gupta, G., Miesenberger, K., Pontelli, E., Guo, H.: The Development of a Tool to enhance communications between blind and sighted mathematicians, students, and teachers: A Global Translation Appliance, in: Stephanidis, C. (ed.): Universal Access In HCI - Towards and Information Society for All, Lawrence Erlbaum, London 2001
5. Guo, H., Karshmer, A., Weaver, C., Mendez, J., Geiger, S.: Computer Processing of Nemeth Braile Math Code, in: Vollmar, R., Wagner, R.: Computers Helping People with Special Needs, ICCHP Ý00, Oldenbourg, Wien, München 2000
6. F. Burger, M. Batušić, K. Miesenberger, B. Stöger: Access to Mathematics for the Blind - Defining HrTEX Standard. Proceedings of the 5th International Conference on Computers Helpling People with Special Needs, ICCHP '96 Linz, Austria, July 1996, pp. 609-616. Oldenbourg Wien München, 1996
7. Project Universal Math Access: http://karshmer.lklnd.usf.edu/
8. http://www.openmath.org
9. http://www.mathweb.org/omdoc

# Towards a Universal Maths Conversion Library

Dominique Archambault[1], Donal Fitzpatrick[2], Gopal Gupta[3], Arthur I. Karshmer[4], Klaus Miesenberger[5], and Enrico Pontelli[6]

[1] Université Pierre et Marie Curie, Inserm U483/INOVA, 9 quai Saint Bernard, 75252 Paris cedex 5, France
[2] Dublin City University, School of Computing, Dublin 9, Ireland
[3] University of Texas at Dallas, Department of Computer Science Box 830688; MS EC31, Richardson, TX 75083-0688, USA
[4] University of South Florida at Lakeland, 3433 Winter Lake Road, Lakeland, Fl 33803, USA
[5] Johannes Kepler Universität Linz, "integriert studieren - integrated study" (i3s3), Altenbergerstrasse 69, A-4040 Linz, Austria
[6] New Mexico State University, Department of Computer Science, Las Cruces, NM 88003-0001, USA

`http://lklnd.usf.edu/iguma`

**Abstract.** The study of Mathematics and Sciences have always been a difficult problem for blind students especially because of the complexity of Braille mathematical notations. Various projects developed converters allowing people to translate a formula from mainstream notations (like LaTeX or MathML) to Braille notations and vice versa. Today a new generation of tools aims at facilitating the understanding of the formulas by blind users, and the communication between sighted and Braille users. The project of Universal Maths Conversion Library is born from the decision of 6 organisations both American and European to join their efforts in that field.

## 1 Braille and Mathematical Formulas

The writing of Mathematical formulas has always been a particular difficulty for Blind pupils and students. The following very simple fraction is usually written with a visual layout (1) that allows a very quick understanding of its semantics. The same formula written in a linear way (2) needs a bit more thought to be understood. Additionally it is written using many more symbols (11 while the first one only necessitates 7).

$$\frac{x+1}{x-1} \tag{1}$$

$$(x+1)/(x-1) \tag{2}$$

Braille is a linear writing system and consequently only the second form is possible. The first "natural" way of writing formulas is then to use this form, using eventually specific Braille characters for specific symbols (like the square

K. Miesenberger et al. (Eds.): ICCHP 2004, LNCS 3118, pp. 664–669, 2004.

root for instance). The problem is that formulas can be very long (the example shown above is quite simple but in the case of complex formulas the number of symbols increases dramatically), and then they are quite difficult to handle by blind students.

In order to reduce the length of these formulas as far as possible several Braille specific notations for Mathematics have been developed in different countries during the last century: Nemeth is used in the United States, Marburg is used in German speaking countries, there are two notations in French (the historical one was deeply revised in 2001), a British notation is used in United Kingdom and in Ireland, ItalBra is used in Italy.

These notations use context sensitive grammars that allow the use of the same symbol strings with different meaning depending on the context. They allow a significant reduction of the length of formulas. In counterpart these notations are quite difficult to learn (and to teach) and it is a fact that they have particular difficulties in the field of Mathematics and more widely in all scientific disciplines. Currently only very profficient Braille users are able to do it, while average mainstream pupils succeed easily. Indeed they have to deal with 2 difficulties: the Mathematical content itself and the Math code which is at least as difficult as the content.

To further complicate things, while the mainstream (visual) math notation is identical in every language, the same is not true for Braille notations. Then a Braille formula written using the Nemeth notation (American notation) is not understandable by a German speaking reader, used to working with the Marburg notation, and so on. This problem is quite important since the number of Braille documents is very small compared to the number of ordinary Maths books.

There exists an alternative way using a "graphical" embosser [1] which enables production of a tactile representation of the formula that is close to the visual layout, using Braille characters only for basic elements (like digits for instance). This method only works for printouts and can hardly be used by students to write formulas.

## 2 Conversion of Mathematical Braille

In the last twenty years, various projects have been developed in the field of Mathematical Braille notations, mainly with the aim of facilitating the written communication between sighted persons and Braille readers in the field of Mathematics (The MATHS Project [2], the LAMBDA project [3]). Various converters have been developed that performs conversions between mainstream mathematical formats like LaTeX and MathML and Braille notations:

**Labradoor** [4] (LAtex to BRAille DOOR) converts a full LaTeX document including Mathematical formulas into Marburg Braille.

**Insight** [5] converts formulas from Nemeth Braille code to LaTeX.

**Bramanet** [6] converts formulas from MathML to French Braille.

**MMBT** [7] (Multi-Language Mathematical Braille Translator) is an opensource project[1] allowing transcriptions from and to LaTeX, MathML, French (historical and new notation), British and Italian Braille notations (MMBT is still under development, some of those conversions are not yet available).

These converters are used for different purposes. One is to facilitate the production of scientifical Braille documents. For instance Labradoor allows a teacher to use a LaTeX document that he/she has prepared for his/her students and to convert it into Braille for a student. In the same way Bramanet produces Braille formulas from documents designed using mainstream Mathematical tools that have a MathML output (like MathType™ for instance).

In the other way (from Braille notations to mainstream formats) they allow sighted teachers or peers to access to formulas written by blind students.

## 3 A New Generation of Tools

Nowadays, the great efforts made around the MathML language and the progress made by rendering programs (like Mozilla for instance) and the equation editing software (like MathType) allow us to develop very useful software that might help the blind users to deal with the intrinsic complexity of Mathematical Braille notations.

### 3.1 MAVIS

MAVIS [8] is a formula browser that allows to navigate in the formula using voice output. It has been designed to convey the structure of the mathematical expression as well as its contents. MAVIS also uses the hierarchical structure of the formula to group subsections of an equation into meaningful "chunks", enabling the user to navigate in this structure.

Studies in psychology allow us to enhance the way voice synthesis reads mathematical formula [9].

### 3.2 The Vickie Project

The Vickie Project[2] [10] aims at facilitating the inclusion of visually impaired pupils and students in mainstream education.

A unified user interface is developed to enable visually impaired pupils and students to access documents using specific devices, while a synchronised graphical display supplies sighted teachers with a view of the same document. This

[1] http://mmbt.sourceforge.net, http://sourceforge.net/projects/mmbt/

[2] The Vickie Project is funded by the European Commission, on the IST (Information Society Technologies) Programme 2001 (FP5/IST/Systems and Services for the Citizen/Persons with special needs), under the reference IST-2001-32678.

interface is an application built on the framework of Mozilla[3]. The interface actually presents 3 views of the same document:

- a graphical view of the document, including images and mathematical formulas. This view is called the teacher's view.
- an adapted view to partially sighted users, with adjustable prints and colours.
- a Braille view. The libbraille library [11] is used to write directly on Braille devices.

The mathematical formulas are stored in documents in the MathML standard, and then can be displayed easily in graphical way thanks to the MathML renderer of Mozilla. This renderer allows to setup the size of print and the colours, for the adapted view.

The formula is automatically converted into Braille in real-time thanks to the MMBT converter [7] (see above). This software will also convert formulas written by the pupil in Braille to MathML in order to be displayed for the teacher.

In the Vickie project all documents are stored on a server [12] using the dtbook DTD format[4]. The mathematical formulas are included in the dtbook documents in MathML, thanks to the module mechanism of the dtbook DTD. Then the MMBT is also used to convert documents from a specific Braille notation that is used in France for printing (BrailleStar). Numerous documents are stored in that format and can then be imported into the Vickie server.

## 4 Next Challenges

The first step will be to allow collaborative work between visually impaired and sighted people, each working on his representation of the same formula. Indeed the current tools allow real time conversions of formulas, enabling a sighted teacher to actually see in his natural way the line written by a pupil but he cannot show a point in this formula, in order to enlight an idea or to explain an error.

Actually doing mathematical calculations is even more difficult than reading and writing formulas. The problems in doing formal manipulations arise from the complex structures that deploy during a calculation: whereas sighted people may organise a computation such that it can be easily surveyed and navigated, blind persons tend to get lost quickly within a formal structure. There is a need for performant editing tools that pupils can use to do calculations more easily.

There is also a tremendous need for tools providing contextual support on the Braille mathematical code and doing calculations. These tools should provide support about the Braille notation itself and not on mathematical contents. The aim is to reduce the gap between blind pupils and their sighted peers induced by the complexity of mathematical Braille notations.

[3] The Mozilla project: http://www.mozilla.org

[4] The dtbook Document Type Definition (DTD) is part of the NISO Z39.86-2002 standard, also known as DAISY 3.0.

## 5 iGroupUMA

To address these challenges, 6 organisations having expertise in the field of Mathematical Braille decided to join their efforts, creating the "International Group for Universal Math Accessibility" (iGroupUMA).

The iGroupUMA members are: University of Texas at Dallas, Dublin City University, University of South Florida at Lakeland, Johannes Kepler University of Linz, New Mexico State University, and University Pierre et Marie Curie in Paris.

## 6 Universal Maths Conversion Library

One of the goals of this group is to produce a programming library encapsulating various converters for various Braille codes in a single library usable through a simple and unique API. This library will be useful as well for transcription tools (from mainstream notations to Braille and vice versa) as for software that need real-time conversions (like formula browsers or editors). It will also make it possible to convert a document from a Braille national notation to another, increasing de facto the number of documents available for students and allowing blind mathematicians from various countries to exchange documents.

To make it possible without growing the complexity, it is necessary to adopt an architecture based on a central representation of the formula, and to develop parsers to generate this central representation from the different input formats, and output generators for each output format [13–15].

The iGroupUMA has decided to use MathML as central language. Input and output independent modules will be designed for each format: LaTeX, Nemeth, Marburg, British notation, the 2 French notations, ItalBra, etc. Those modules can be developed independently by each group. Then they will be integrated in a Universal Maths Conversion Library, that will offer any conversion from and to any formats. The input and output modules API will be published in order to allow other developing teams to create new modules.

## References


1. Gardner, J., al: Simultaneous braille tactile graphics and ink with tiger ink attachment and duxbury. In: Proc. CSUN'04 (19th Annual Conference "Technology and Persons with Disabilities"), Los Angeles, California, USA (2004)
2. Edwards, A.: The Maths Project (2001) [http://www.cs.york.ac.uk/maths/].
3. Nicotra, G.: The LAMBDA Project (2004) [http://www.lambdaproject.org].
4. Batusic, M., Miesenberger, K., Stoeger, B.: Labradoor, a contribution to making mathematics accessible for the blind. In Edwards, A., Arato, A., Zagler, W., eds.: Proc. ICCHP 98 ($6^{th}$ International Conference on Computers Helping People with Special Needs), Oldenbourg, Wien, München (1998)
5. Annamalai, A., Gopal, D., Gupta, G., Guo, H., Karshmer, A.: INSIGHT: a comprehensive system for converting Braille based mathematical documents to Latex. In Stephanidis, C., ed.: Universal Access in HCI – Inclusive Design in the Information Society. Volume 4., Mahwah, New Jersey, USA, Lea (2003) 1245–1249

6. Schwebel, F.: BraMaNet logiciel de traduction des mathématiques en braille (2003) [http://handy.univ-lyon1.fr/projets/bramanet/].
7. Moço, V., Archambault, D.: Automatic translator for mathematical braille. In Stephanidis, C., ed.: Universal Access in HCI – Inclusive Design in the Information Society. Volume 4., Mahwah, New Jersey, USA, Lea (2003) 1335–1339
8. Karshmer, A., Gupta, G., Geiger, S., Weaver, C.: Reading and writing mathematics: The mavis project. Behavior and Information Technology **18** (1998) 2–10
9. Karshmer, A., Gillan, D.: How well can we read equations to blind mathamatics students: some answers from psychology. In Stephanidis, C., ed.: Universal Access in HCI – Inclusive Design in the Information Society. Volume 4., Mahwah, New Jersey, USA, Lea (2003) 1290–1294
10. Archambault, D., Burger, D.: The vickie project. In Miesenberger, K., Klaus, J., Zagler, W., eds.: Proc. ICCHP 2002 (International Conference on Computers Helping People with Special Needs). Volume 2398 of LNCS., Linz, Austria, Springer (2002) 90–97
11. Sablé, S., Archambault, D.: libbraille: a programming library for easy access to Braille displays. In Craddock, G., McCormack, L., Reilly, R., Knops, H., eds.: Assistive Technology – Shaping the future, Proceedings of the AAATE'03 Conference, Dublin, Ireland, Amsterdam, The Netherlands, IOS Press (2003) 435–440
12. an Integrated Publishing Chain for Accessible Multimodal Documents, T.: Benoît guillon and jean-louis monteiro and cédric chécoury and dominique archambault and dominique burger. In Klaus, J., Miesenberger, K., Zagler, W., Burger, D., eds.: Proc. ICCHP 2004 in Paris (International Conference on Computers Helping People with Special Needs). LNCS, Linz, Austria, Springer (2004)
13. Karshmer, A., Gupta, G., Miesenberger, K., Pontelli, E., Guo, H.F.: The development of a tool to enhance communications between blind and sighted mathematicians, students and teachers: A global translation appliance. In Stephanidis, C., ed.: Proceedings of the UAHCI'01 conference – Universal Access in Human-Computer Interaction (joint with 9th International Conference on Human-Computer Interaction) – Towards an Informatino Society for All, New-Orleans, Louisiana, USA, Lawrence Erlbaum Associates (2001) 929–932
14. Batusic, M., Miesenberger, K., Stoeger, B.: Parser for the marburg mathematical braille notation. In Stephanidis, C., ed.: Universal Access in HCI – Inclusive Design in the Information Society. Volume 4., Mahwah, New Jersey, USA, Lea (2003) 1260–1264
15. Palmer, B., Pontelli, E.: Experiments in translating and navigating digital formats for Matematics (a progress report). In Stephanidis, C., ed.: Universal Access in HCI – Inclusive Design in the Information Society. Volume 4., Mahwah, New Jersey, USA, Lea (2003) 1245–1249

# math2braille: Opening Access to Mathematics


David Crombie[1], Roger Lenoir[1], Neil McKenzie[1], and Alison Barker[2]

[1] FNB Netherlands, accessible information for people with a print impairment
Molenpad 2, 1016 GM Amsterdam, The Netherlands
projects@fnb.nl
http://projects.fnb.nl/

[2] University of Glasgow, Department of Electronics & Electrical Engineering
Rankine Building, Oakfield Avenue
Glasgow, G12 8LT, UK
abarker@elec.gla.ac.uk
http://www.elec.gla.ac.uk



**Abstract.** It is clear that Braille has many problems when representing the complex information associated with mathematics. The reliance on linear representation removes much of the structure which aids the sighted user to quickly navigate an equation. A further problem with many accessible education tools is that the teacher must understand the accessible format and this can be both time-consuming and costly. There is little or no real competitor to MathML and the increased development of structural functionalities in the MathML 2.0 specification provides an excellent representation to parse into other formats. In order to improve facilities available in creating accessible solutions, the math2braille Module will soon be made available as an open source module which other developers can incorporate in their own systems.


## 1 Introduction

While building tools for accessible music production (software for producing Talking music, Braille music and Large Print music) [1-6], many concepts were considered relating to understanding musical information in alternative formats. When tackling a similar problem in the mathematical domain it would be sensible to re-visit some of these concepts bearing in mind what we have learned from the musical domain. This paper examines these relationships and provides an overview of the open source accessibility tools we are currently developing for the production of mathematics in alternative formats.

## 2 Existing Approaches

When researching the area of mathematical representations for visually impaired people, it is clear that Braille has many problems when representing the complex


K. Miesenberger et al. (Eds.): ICCHP 2004, LNCS 3118, pp. 670–677, 2004.

information associated with mathematics. The reliance on linear representation removes much of the structure which aids the sighted user quickly to navigate the equation. A further problem with many accessible education tools is that the teacher must understand the accessible format. This can be both time-consuming and costly. The recent widespread uptake of MathML [7] as a standard in most mathematical software allows this process to be made easier. There are now enough ways for teachers to enter and read the mathematics in traditional representations that converter programs between the student and the teacher should allow this relationship to work efficiently. The deeper problems associated with mathematics and Braille as languages are discussed in section three below.

Several research projects have brought some clarity to this field, including: REMathEx (Reader and Editor of the Mathematical Expressions for Blind Students) [8]; LATEX at the University of Applied Sciences Giessen-Friedberg [9]; and the Lambda project [10] funded by the European Union with the objective of creating an integrated system for writing and reading mathematical texts for the use of blind students.

## 3 Key Considerations

When someone has learned to assimilate musical information, scores can become more complex, which increases the motor skills required to play pieces, but there is very little difference in the kind of information associated with a simple piece and a complex piece. We conclude that the most important tool for accessibility within music is a means of offering the level of navigation which a sighted user relies on in order to compute the information within a score, while keeping the actual core of musical representation expandable.

In mathematics, knowledge is built gradually and constantly as new concepts are studied. In all fields of study that use mathematics (but excluding the study of mathematics itself), mathematical knowledge is used as a set of tools which complement the knowledge of the field of study. This set of tools is increased and tailored as and when new concepts require new tools for manipulation and understanding.

While musical information arrives as a time-based dynamic unit, mathematics are static pieces of information. The navigation, while important, does not define the usefulness of the information. The meaning relies heavily on keeping the context contained in the representation.

### 3.1 Meaning in Mathematics

Mathematics at any level is fundamentally a set of symbols that are associated with a set of concepts. Each single concept or symbol carries very little meaning alone. The meaning emerges when these concepts are built into an expression, equation, or any mathematical sentence. The concepts then have a context, which ultimately defines them and can lead to understanding. For example, the number 0 can influence an expression in many ways. If a variable with magnitude zero is added to an expression, its existence in that expression becomes almost meaningless: yet if an expression is divided by the same variable, the more advanced concepts of infinity and divergence become part of the knowledge base required to tackle the particular concept. This is a rudimentary example, but it highlights how symbols are defined by what surrounds them, and it is this which dictates how a user defines them. This has to be kept in mind when designing such a representation system. The surrounding information has to be close at hand (literally in the case of Braille) in order adequately to assimilate the information as it is intended.

This introduces an important concept in building such a representation system; structure. In music-based projects, structure is an essential element in offering navigation in accessible solutions. Indeed, the ability to model in a non-destructive manner could be considered an essential element of any system. The structure in mathematics allows the relationships and interactions to be relayed at different levels of abstraction, ultimately building to relay the meaning of the mathematical phrase or sentence. The meaning is relayed in mathematics through micro-navigation, where each symbol is essential to understanding the concept. Music is based around macro-navigation, where the skills of the player actually dictate how much of the information the player has to actually take in, and how much can be taken from the stored experience (Gestalt) of previous exercises. In mathematics there is also retained knowledge, such as the stages of the integration of a sinusoidal expression in calculus or in arithmetic (e.g. long division), but each element remains as important, because the process is repeatable rather than the information.

The structure of the representation should be such that the above concepts can be adequately perceived. In the case of mathematics, this would require a hierarchical structure that would allow the information to be represented in different output formats, offering the same level of context or meaning no matter which representation medium is required.

### 3.2 Context in Mathematics

Mathematics is a multidisciplinary tool. This ultimately means that mathematics can be ambiguous if it is not known which field of study is being addressed; as with Braille, different units and signs are used for the same concepts across different fields.

If we take, for example, the various ways of measuring energy, there are several units within the world of mathematics which measure similar concepts. Energy is usually introduced at a high school level as being measured in Joules (denoted as E in units of J). Once the study of physics moves on to analysis of electrical systems, the energy is amalgamated with time and is more commonly quoted in watts (Denoted as P(Power) in units of w). Depending on what size of energy is being calculated, ironically as a simplification, higher study will yield further units used to represent energy. Atomic Physicists, who deal with calculations at the atom level, will prefer energy quoted by a unit known as an electron volt (defined as ‘eV’). Atomic chemists are more likely to deal with units of multiple atoms, so prefer to quote a unit of atoms as an arbitrary figure known as Avogadro's Constant. Energy is then quoted per mole, and often Kilocalories per mole. Chemists deal with figures which are extremely small when computation is required and as a result use the atomic Mass unit, defined as one gram per mole of atoms. The famous equation $E= mc^2$ then allows a link back to physics. But which of the above units of energy should we use? The equation certainly becomes less catchy, and this provides four possibilities by changing only one of the symbols for the units.

For anyone who studies two or more of these disciplines, the units used to represent these concepts further complicate the problem. If a mathematician encounters an imaginary number, it is identified by the symbol 'i'. If a physicist performs the same calculation 'j' will be used (remembering that the same physicists will use 'j' to denotes joules of energy).

So, a single symbol in mathematics is of very little use without its context. In order to build accessibility into content, we clearly need to add a certain level of understanding of that content into the process. The meaning of the transformed content will only stay the same if the transcriber owns or is able to access a level of understanding of the content.

## 4 math2braille Module

As highlighted above, the concept and process in converting MathML to Braille take a similar route as the conversion of music to accessible standards. The work is based on recent experience of multimedia modelling techniques and the development of software for producing Braille Music. The intention was to marry this experience to build software which will make mathematics available to a far wider audience of visually impaired people. A great deal of work relating to the presentation of Braille has already been undertaken during the construction of the Braille Music production tools.

### 4.1 Open Source Development Trajectory

In order to improve facilities available in creating accessible solutions, the math2braille Module will be made available as an open source module which other developers can incorporate in their own systems. It was felt that if production protocols and processes were as specialised elsewhere as they are at FNB, the open source development trajectory would provide more opportunities for future development than a generic program. This option also reflected the lack of any general agreement on accessible mathematics output formats and the hope that new guidelines will emerge in future.

### 4.2 MathML

There is little or no real competitor to MathML and with the increased development of structural functionalities in the MathML 2.0 specification, it would appear to be an excellent representation to parse into other formats. The alternative development route would have been to develop a plug-in for an existing leader in Mathematical software which would serve the same purpose. However, the quality of MathML allows the freedom to reach many more users by supporting input from multiple sources. As noted above, this also presents the opportunity to make the material available for the open source community worldwide.

### 4.3 System Overview

The system is based on protocols and procedures which have been developed during the accessible music software project (op. cit.). One advantage in this project is that MathML is already in popular use. Because of the dynamic definition of CWMN (Common Western Music Notation), a decision had to be made as to how the musical information should be entered and represented in the BrailleMusic system. However, in MathML the structure (especially in MathML2.0) and the coverage are very well defined, so we assumed a certain level of mathematical input with a completed vocabulary.

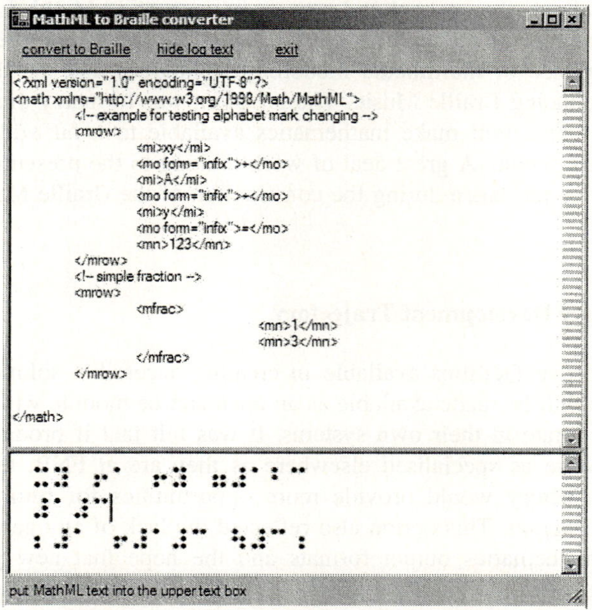


**Fig. 1.** Screenshot of prototype MathML to Braille converter.

Based on best practices a protocol was developed which allows a representation layer to be built that tackles the difference in mathematical representation between the fundamental mathematic equation entered in the MathML input program and the equation as it is seen by the particular Braille decoder being used. The FNB protocols are then implemented using a static configuring structure which communicates with the dynamic processing layer which represents the mathematical information. Such an architecture ensures that the source code remains useful to other developers.

### 4.4 System Components

The architecture of the math2braille application aims to structure the various functionalities in appropriate packages. Low-level objects representing services that are required to achieve a flexible translation process description are collected into components. These components can be seen as the individual phases in the math2braille translation process. Each component is assigned an associated setting object, which collects the available customisable settings for the associated system component.

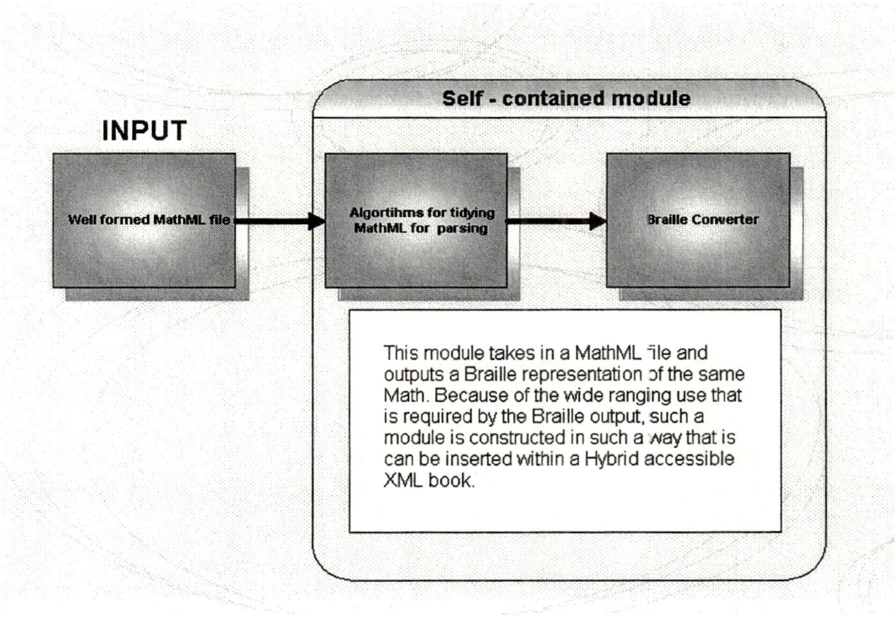


**Fig. 2.** Outline of math2braille Module.

The translation procedure can be split into three phases. Each phase is represented by a package and each package collects the objects and components that are relevant to the associated phase. The input package contains the objects and components relevant to importing Mathematica files. This package defines a specialised class that collects all required behaviour to import a Mathematica file and transform it into a MathDocument that is contained in the representation package.

The input package contains all logic structured into classes and components to import a Mathematica document and convert it into a MathDocument. The extent of these classes includes file access classes, cross-reference classes, collecting relevant external documentations and specifications classes, etc. The representation package creates a dynamic object-based representation of the structure of the MathML document. Compare this with a specialised DOM that captures all relevant aspects of the Math document. Additional objects are used to incorporate specific mathematical knowledge which, if needed, render this specialised domain knowledge accessible. Essentially, this model captures the structure of a MathML document and represents the most important entities of a MathML document as classes. The dynamic model allows addition of higher-level abstractions in a centralised and structured manner. In this representation MathML entities/classes can be associated with program logic.

The setting classes associated with the MathML model contain settings relevant to Math interpretation. It is a central repository that collects all higher level reasoning settings. These settings are accessed by the math2braille interpretation component. A high level of flexible routings can be applied to specific interpretation settings and/or preferences and the mappings of these settings to the Braille domain. The output package collects all logic in classes and components that serialises the BrailleMathDocumentModel into sequences of Braille cells. This last stage involves a selection of various ASCII character tables or replacement of certain escape codes.

The architecture is such that the system has initially been built as a conversion module which can be coupled with whatever system it is required to do so in the future. This level of flexibility is required as output formats are defined and as hybrid multimedia formats emerge.

## 5 Summary

The math2braille project provides a valuable new tool for the accessibility community and it is hoped that by making this tool available as opensource software, further development will be stimulated. The methodologies used in the design of this tool build upon earlier projects as outlined above. In this way knowledge from other research domains and projects is re-used and built upon, creating a sustainable methodology which highlights scalability and adaptability.

## References

1. Crombie, D., Lenoir, R., and McKenzie, N., (2003) Bridging the Gap: Music and Communication, Proceedings Rencontres Internationales des Technologies pour la Musique (Resonances 2003), IRCAM, Paris
2. Crombie, D., Lenoir, R., McKenzie, N., Ng, K. (2003) "Finding the Right Note: Making Multimedia Music Visible" in Proceedings Electronic Arts & Visual Imaging (EVA2003), Institute of Archaeology, London, UK

3. Crombie, D., Lenoir, R., McKenzie, N., (2003) “” in Proceedings Electronic Arts & Visual Imaging (EVA2003), Institute of Archaeology, London, UK
4. Crombie, D., Lenoir, R., McKenzie, N., (2003) “Producing Accessible Multimedia Music” in Proceedings 2nd International Conference on Web Delivering of Music, IEEE
5. Crombie, D, Dijkstra S, Lenoir, R, McKenzie, N, Schut, E, (2002) “Towards Accessible Multimedia Music” in Proceedings 2nd International Conference on Web Delivering of Music, IEEE
6. Crombie, D, Lenoir, R, McKenzie, N, (2002) “Accessible Music: Meeting the needs of the print impaired” in Proceedings 2nd Conference on Assistive Technologies for Vision and Hearing Impairment, University of Glasgow, UK
7. `http://www.w3.org/Math/`
8. Gaura, P., (2002) “REMathEx – Reader and Editor of Mathematical Expressions for Blind Students” Proceedings 8th International Conference, ICCHP, Linz, Austria.
9. Meyer zu Bexten, E., Jung, M., (2002) “LATEX at the University of Applied Aciences Giessen-Friedberg – Experiences at the institute for Visually Impaired Students” Proceedings 8th International Conference, ICCHP, Linz, Austria.
10. Nicotra, G. Fogarolo, F., (2003) "Interfaces for access to music and mathematics by blind persons", Interfaces for accessibility and integration, IST project LAMBDA

# Enhancing the Accessibility of Mathematics for Blind People: The AudioMath Project

Helder Ferreira and Diamantino Freitas

LSS - Laboratory of Signals and Systems
Faculdade de Engenharia da Universidade do Porto, Portugal
{hfilipe,dfreitas}@fe.up.pt
http://lpf-esi.fe.up.pt

**Abstract.** "*How can a blind person surpass the difficulty in reading an on-line document's mathematical expressions? Why wasn't this completely solved yet? Is it not necessary? Is not easy?*" – These questions are only the top of the iceberg of a big problem with accessibility in the Internet. This concerns technical, scientific or even simple documents presented on-line that involve mathematical expressions. Addressing these issues the authors developed the *AudioMath* [1] project at LSS. It can be connected to a text-to-speech engine (TTS), providing speech rendering of the W3C's MathML [2, 3] coded mathematical expressions. The paper intends to present the project methodology as well as the results already obtained. With *AudioMath* we intend to increase the accessibility of, not only, e-learning websites that use MathML, but also general websites. Therefore, *AudioMath* is an accessibility tool that can bring great benefits for visual impaired persons, but not only.

## 1 Introduction: Understanding the Need and the Difficulties

The publication and distribution of scientific papers and articles, as well as e-learning websites, are a desirable way to spread knowledge, promote education and stimulate research and development. The language chosen for these communications is often the *Mathematical Language*, because it is universal and not ambiguous.

However, the mathematical language can be split into 2 parts: the *meaning* and the *notation* [4], i.e., the mathematical concept exists no matter the representation it uses. Nevertheless, a good graphical representation of a mathematical expression leads to a better and fast interpretation of its meaning. Most of the web documents containing mathematical material use images (jpg, gif, png) created by TeX related software or Microsoft Word, to display the mathematical formulae.

Some distribute the documents in pdf, TeX, Postscript, Word or rtf file types. The use of Java applets or plug-ins is also common. This has lead to accessibility problems in the reading of documents containing mathematical expressions for visually impaired persons, and, in particular, for blind persons.

It is also consistent with the idea that the difficulty for blind persons rises and accessibility diminishes as the technical level of documents increase, even if they are

K. Miesenberger et al. (Eds.): ICCHP 2004, LNCS 3118, pp. 678–685, 2004.

already in digital format and using properly equipped computers [5]. The growing concern about accessibility of mathematical expressions on the Internet has taken research groups such as: W3C, OpenMath [6] and AMS [7], to create and develop initiatives in this area, promoting and regulating the accessible publication of mathematical contents over the Internet. One of those initiatives is the creation of the *MathML Mark-up Language* [3] from W3C, which is used in this project.

## 2 The AudioMath Project

The practical interpretation and reading of mathematical formulae is not a simple task. Several challenges have to be overcome, such as:

- Lack of existing knowledge, as well as studies and research on how to read a mathematical expression [8, 9, 10].
- Weak existing implementations in current browsers in support of mark-up languages for mathematical expressions.
- Rather complex parsing and interpretation of mathematical formulae.
- Automatic identification of lexical and non-lexical elements in a text, needing a conversion into plain text. Use of glyphs, characters and fonts from other culture or language in a mathematical expression.
- Hhigh computational performance needed from the conversion module when associated to a TTS engine, in order to provide fast read-out of expressions without too large time lag in the speech output.
- The need of mechanisms to navigate inside mathematical formulae, allowing repetitions or reading of its internal contents in a personalized way.

The main aim of this project is to provide a tool, to work either standalone or integrated with a TTS engine, that converts expressions presently not "understandable" by a regular TTS engine, both in text and in mark-up elements (MathML). The tool is under continuous development and does the parsing, interpretation and conversion into plaintext form and readable by anyone, it is called *AudioMath*. It speaks the mathematical expressions supplied in the *MathML Presentation Mark-up* format.

Applications are many, such as: -teaching or learning how to read mathematical formulae [11]; -reading of technical and scientific documents online for everyone with particular benefit for vision impaired persons; -enhancing general accessibility to computer-based applications, when applied to a TTS engine.

### 2.1 MathML - Mathematical Mark-Up Language

MathML is an XML application developed by W3C (versions on 1998 and 2001). This mark-up language has a simple and concise syntax that currently codes either the notation (*MathML Presentation Mark-up*) or the meaning (*MathML Content Mark-up*) of a mathematical expression. The *AudioMath Project* has chosen MathML for the following reasons:

- It's a mark-up language developed by W3C (organization that issues recommendations about web technologies, that later on become standards through organizations like ISO). The fact that it is a mark-up language allows its parsing, interpretation and conversion to other formats, and consequently a higher accessibility, portability and platform independence.
- Growing development of MathML (already in version 2.0), and the involvement of several relevant organizations associated with the teaching and learning of mathematical contents, such as the *American Mathematical Society* [15] and *The OpenMath Group* [16], and the involvement of software houses like *Design Science*, *Wolfram Research*, *Microsoft*, *IBM* and *HP*.
- Emergence of editors and applications that create and manipulate MathML documents. For example: *Scientific Word*, *Mathematica* and *MathType*.
- Existence of conversion tools between the main publishing formats: TeX/LateX to MathML and vice-versa.

### 2.2 MathML Presentation Mark-Up vs. MathML Content Markup

The representation of mathematical formulae and other mathematical contents is perceived by two distinct concepts: the visual structure or notation of the mathematical expression, and the concept or meaning that it represents [4]. For example: the same concept of "division of a by b" can have the notations:

$$a / b, \frac{a}{b} \text{ or } ab^{-1}. \quad (1)$$

The inverse is also possible; there can be different meanings for the same notation. For instance, the notation "He" can have one of the following meanings: "product between variables H and e" or "chemical symbol of Helium". Therefore the W3C created two sets of MathML mark-up:

- MathML Presentation Mark-up: -Aimed to the visual presentation of a mathematical expression; -Doesn't differentiate the meaning of the mathematical expression; -Not intended to (but possible) audio rendering of mathematics; -The conversion of Presentation Mark-up into Content Mark-up is not advised.
- MathML Content Mark-up: -Aimed to represent the meaning of a mathematical expression; -Used to transfer MathML between applications; -Doesn't differentiate the mathematical notation; -Ideal to audio rendering of mathematical representations; -Can be converted into Presentation Mark-up; -Limited only by the mathematical operators and functions it supports.

Although Content Mark-up is recommended to be used in audio rendering of mathematical expressions [17] (since it preserves the meaning of the formulae) it has some limitations concerning the list of mathematical operators and functions it supports. The OpenMath Group, for example, offers a lot bigger dictionary. Moreover, current editors are WYSIWYG and code the mathematical contents into Presentation Mark-up instead of Content Mark-up. Therefore the online documents that contain MathML expressions are coded in Presentation Mark-up. For these reasons, Audio-

Math uses MathML Presentation Mark-up. The price to pay is that this introduces several difficulties to the interpretation of the formulae.

For instance, consider expression 2. In MathML Presentation Mark-up the indexes "2" and "3" will be coded as "subscript" and "superscript".

$$A_2^3 . \quad (2)$$

This gives no information if the expression refers to the "cubic power of element $A_2$", or "the permutations of 3 elements taken 2 at a time". In conclusion, the use of MathML Presentation Mark-up requires a much bigger effort in the interpretation of mathematical expressions.

### 2.3 The AudioMath Process

**Introduction.** AudioMath has been built in a modular, extensible and configurable architecture, in Perl. Therefore, the support for new languages, the update of dictionaries and the updating of algorithms can be done easily. Currently only the European Portuguese language is supported.

AudioMath contains 6 major conversion modules: Numerals (conversion of several types of numeric forms), Abbreviations (conversion of abbreviations in a text), Acronyms (conversion of acronyms in the document), Network (conversion of IPs, emails and URI/URLs), Mathematical (conversion of MathML expressions) and Auto-Discovery (the "brain" of the operation that recognizes or identifies elements in the document and calls the respective conversion modules). The modules are packed together in the form of one ActiveX DLL.

**Text Analysis.** A technical document can probably come with special characters in Unicode and math glyphs. Therefore the first step is to clean up the text, converting Unicode to Latin1 (in this case to support European Portuguese characters). Next step is an auto-discovery process that recognizes certain types of elements and makes calls to the modules that convert them into a full text form. For example: if "det." is detected, it should be converted into "determinant (of)". To speed up the process the document should be divided into blocks of text, splitting the MathML Mark-up from the rest of the text.

**Parsing MathML.** The MathML Markup is parsed using the Perl module: XML::Parser [18] which acts as a SAX parser type (event-based), supporting Encoding ISO-8859-1 and discarding XML Namespaces.

**MathML Interpretation and Conversion.** Since AudioMath uses MathML Presentation Mark-up, a big effort and computation is needed in the interpretation of the mathematical expression. As the expression is becoming discovered, the conversion process takes place by calling several algorithms as well as Unicode and MathML dictionaries.

*AudioMath* uses two kinds of dictionaries: MathML entities to Unicode and Unicode to European Portuguese full plaintext form. For example: if the "⁢" MathML operator is used, then it is converted into "U+02062"

Unicode element and then into the word "multiplies". The conversion to text form is done according to a database of rules that was built based on a collection of material written by experienced professors. Note that the bigger the expression the more complex the interpretation and conversion process becomes. A solution would be to introduce navigational mechanisms to browse inside the expression.

**Speaking Mathematical Contents.** As already referred in this paper, one of the challenges this project faces is the scarcity of studies or research on how should we read a mathematical expression [8, 9, 10]. The *MathSpeak Project* [9] is one of the proposed methods, consisting of a group of rules to dictate mathematical contents. However it is not a standard and it is intended to serve blind people that want to transcribe their documents into *Nemeth Code* [12], and later into Braille.

Another method comes from the work of *T.V. Raman* [10] the most impressive and recognized study in this area, consisting of a mathematical notation that takes into consideration several audio dimensions that make up the various pieces of the notation. However this only works for TeX related documents. Nevertheless, this work points out several generally useful cues for audio rendering of mathematics.

The objective of automatically speaking mathematical contents has to deal with the non-trivial issues of text generation and phrasing as well as the generation of the prosody to superimpose over the synthetic speech.

Starting with the first one, the main problem is that there are several more or less "common" ways to read a mathematical expression. These "common" ways are used by speakers when the visual form is also present in any way or is known before-hand. We will illustrate the un-definiteness by an example. For instance, consider the simple mathematical expression 3.

$$\sqrt{a^2 + b^2}\ . \qquad (3)$$

This could be rendered more or less ambiguously as:

- Square root of a squared plus b squared, end of radicand.
- Square root of a taken to power two, plus, b taken to power two, end of radicand.

Square root of power base a exponent two, end of power, plus power base b exponent two, end of radicand.

Which of these forms is more correct, not ambiguous and efficient, if any?

Now consider expressions 4 a, b and c. Taking in account the text forms presented before, how should we read these expressions?

One interesting experience is speaking the texts monotonically to persons that have no access to the graphical expression and ask for a written version after the dictation.

The solution of this problem must pass by the adoption of formal ways of text generation that keep the right structure information of the formula. On the other hand this trend considerably complicates the resulting text, by introducing a big overhead of structural words and therefore contributes to decrease the overall efficiency of the spoken communication.

$$\text{(a) } \sqrt{a^{2+b^2}}\ \text{, (b) } \sqrt{(a^{2+b})^2}\ \text{ and (c) } \sqrt{(a^2+b)^2}\ . \qquad (4)$$

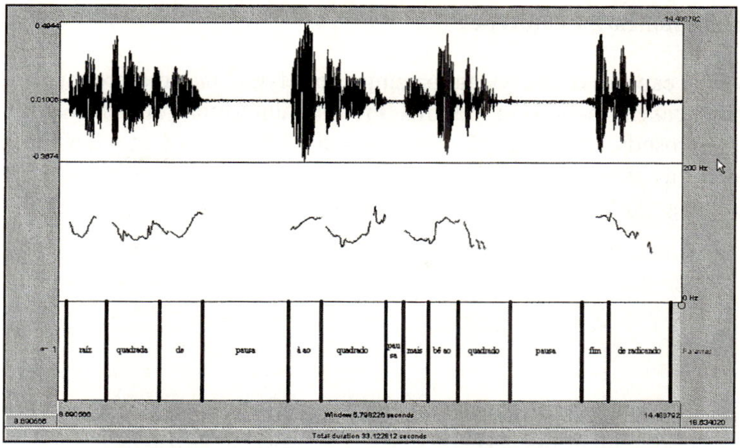

**Fig. 1.** Utterance "Square root of a square plus b square, end of radicand" spoken in European Portuguese.

How do things happen in spoken communication then? Are there specific cues introduced by the speaker in the form of prosodic marks intended to supply the listener boundary and structure information that the text itself does not possess? This topic was investigated and interesting issues resulted as described in the following.

Let's go back to the first example of text rendering of the first expression and consider the sample spoken version, whose waveform, f0 contour (intonation) and text labeling are depicted in figure 1, from top to bottom (the picture was obtained with the PRAAT [19] software).

As can be seen, there are two distinct pauses: one after "Square root of" and another before "End of Radicand". There is also a smaller optional pause between "á ao quadrado" (a squared) and "mais bê ao quadrado" (plus b squared).

Another immediately apparent aspect is the critical use of rising and falling movements of f0 by the speaker to provide classification of the separations introduced by the pauses. A rising tone is used when a lower hierarchical level is starting (see at the end of "quadrada de") and a falling tone is used when this level is ended (see at the end of "bê ao quadrado") while a rising tone associated to a down town are used to classify the smaller separating pause between identical elements, so indicating a continuation. Finally the emphatic falling f0 movement at "fim de radicando" (end of radicand) signals the end of the expression.

The rules already defined in the present development phase of the project are implemented at conversion time by tagging the text with prosodic marks, to command the TTS device in order to produce the required pauses and f0 modulations.

The *AudioMath Project* is continuously studying the prosody of speaking mathematical expressions and is currently working to deepen the knowledge of the use of those common prosodic delimiters and other characteristics inside more complex expressions and their varieties. Although the research is being carried out for European Portuguese, the authors believe that it can be substantially extrapolated to many other languages.

### 2.4 The AudioMath Prototype

*AudioMath* is capable of analysing, parsing, identifying and interpreting several types of mathematical expressions in MathML Presentation format. An especially important issue is the prosody control that is needed as input to the TTS in order for the speech output to be as intelligible and the comprehension as high as possible. Extensive studies of the prosody factors are continuously under way.

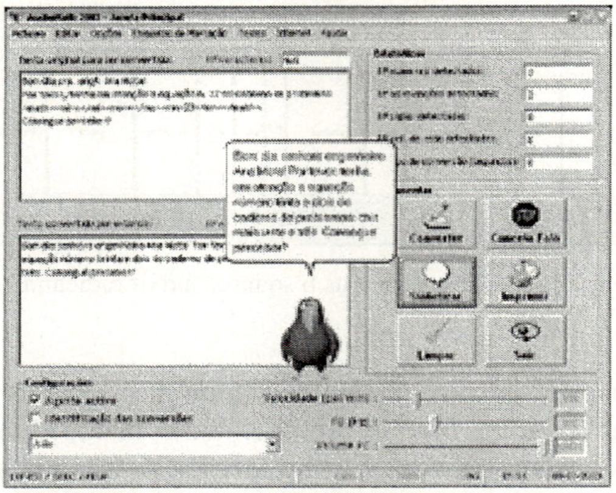

**Fig. 2.** Screenshot from the AudioMath Test and Development Application.

The existing prototype was connected to a European Portuguese TTS engine. However, since it was built in a modular and flexible structure, it is possible to add and change modules that allow conversion and speech output in other languages.

To develop and test the *AudioMath* features, an application has been developed. Through the easy interface (figure 2), text to be read from files or can be entered, or an Internet web page be opened for reading.

## 3 Conclusions and Future Trends of Work

Providing mathematical contents on-line, allows a greater access to information than before. However, problems do exist for blind persons in reading those contents. *AudioMath* is, without doubt for the authors, a valuable contribution to the increase of accessibility in reading on-line documents with mathematical contents.

However it is a work in progress and plenty still needs to be done, such as: -Complete the support to *MathML Presentation Mark-up*; -Add support to *MathML Content Mark-up* [3]; -Further learning how to read mathematical formulae; -Develop modules that support HTML, XHTML, XML [13] and SSML [14]; -Provide mechanisms for navigating inside mathematical formulae; -Adding support for new languages; -Continue to develop the study on the prosody of reading mathematical formulae.

## References


1. AudioMath for European Portuguese – http://lpf-esi.fe.up.pt/~audiomath
2. W3C – World Wide Web Consortium – http://www.w3c.org
3. MathML – Mathematical Mark-up Language – http://www.w3.org/Math
4. Pierce, J., An Introduction to Information Theory. Symbols, Signals and Noise. Dover Publications Inc. New York. 1961
5. Monaghan, A., Fitzpatrick, D. Browsing Technical Documents: Document Modelling And User Interface Design. BULAG 1999
6. The OpenMath Group – http://www.openmath.org/coccon/openmath/index.html
7. AMS – American Mathematical Society – http://www.ams.org
8. Karshmer, Arthur. How Well Can We Read Equations to Blind Mathematic Students? HCII2003 Proceedings. Volume 4
9. MathSpeak - http://www.rit.edu/~easi/easisem/talkmath.htm
10. Raman, T.V., Audio System For Technical Readings. Dissertation to the Faculty of the Graduate School of Cornell University. 1994
11. Freitas, Diamantino. Ferreira, Helder. et al. A prototype application for helping to teach how to read numbers. HCII2003 Proceedings. Volume I
12. Resources to Learn Nemeth Code – http://www.tsbvi.edu/math/math-nemeth.htm
13. Mark-up languages from W3C used to publishing documents in Internet
14. SSML - Speech Synthesis Mark-up Language – http://www.w3.org/TR/speech-synthesis
15. AMS - American Mathematical Society - http://www.ams.org
16. The OpenMath Group – http://www.openmath.org/coccon/openmath/index.html
17. Sandhu, Pavi. The MathML Handbook. Charles River Media. 2002
18. XML::Parser - http://search.cpan.org/dist/XML-Parser/Parser.pm
19. PRAAT: Doing Phonetics by computer, http://www.fon.hum.uva.nl/praat/

# Handwriting Input System of Graphs for Barrier-Free Mathematical Communications

Ryoji Fukuda[1], Masanori Yo[2], and Taichi Kawahara[3]

[1] Faculty of Engineering Oita University, 700 Dannoharu 870-1192 Oita, Japan
[2] Canon Sales Co., Inc., 1-7-2 Nakase Mihamaku 261-8711,Japan
[3] Kyushu Institute of Technology, 680-4 Kawazu 820-8502 Iizuka, Japan

**Abstract.** In this report, we will explain our handwriting input system for mathematical graphs on the $xy$-plane. One can input graphs by hand, and can store them as XML documents. These documents will be available not only for ordinary people but also for people with visual impairment

## 1 Introduction

In mathematical education, as well as other communications using mathematical concepts, we often use graphics. There are often important messages in these graphics, and it is difficult to express them without visual information. The aim of our system is to overcome this difficulty.

The contents underlying graphics vary according to situations. These may depend on knowledge of authors or audiences, and may also depend on topics or categories. Then, to simplify the problem, we limit the situation which the graph used to high school mathematics education, and treat graphs drawn on $xy$-plane only.

For each input curve, our system discriminate the type and find out all cross points and tangent points after user's adjustments of curves. In usual recognition of curves in online or off-line graphics, the recognition is done due to the accuracy of the approximation of the corresponding curve ([1],[2]). However, for our target graphs, we can not expect accuracy to distinguish curve types. Then, according to the tendency of way to write curves, we consider several feature functions by using gradients, curvatures, local minimum or maximum and so on. Each type of estimation function is made by summing up these feature functions by using an idea of Choquet Integral.

The input graph can be stored as an XML document. This document consists of 'Point Elements', 'Curve Elements', and some additional attributions. These concepts can be shared without visual information, and many information can be expressed by using them.

## 2 Outline of the System

A user can input 7 types of curves on the $xy$-plane: 'Straight Line', 'Circle', 'Ellipse', 'Parabola', 'Polynomial(3 -degree)', 'Sin(cos) Curve' and 'Tan curve'.

K. Miesenberger et al. (Eds.): ICCHP 2004, LNCS 3118, pp. 686–689, 2004.

The flow to make an XML document is divided into three aspects, 'Drawing', 'Edit(Correction)' and 'Storing'.

First, a user input a curve or curves using a mouse or a tablet, then the system select the type of the curve after the target curve is clicked on. At the same time, the curve is replaced by a neat curve which match the recognized type and approximates the original one. When the system chooses wrong type, the user select the correct one among the list and the curve is replaced again. When a palabolic curve is recognized as a 3 degree polynomial, for example, the approximation sometimes better than that of proper type. However, the type should be corrected for an adequate document.

A replaced curves is usually different from the curve which the user want to draw. Then, for the input curve, user can give parallel shifts, rotations and scalings ($x$ and $y$ axial direction). Theoretically, any linear translation combined with parallel shift can be realized by combining the above translations.

After deciding the positions and the shapes of all curves, cross points and tangent points are extracted. Then the graphics can be stored as an XML document. We will explain the format in Sect. 4.

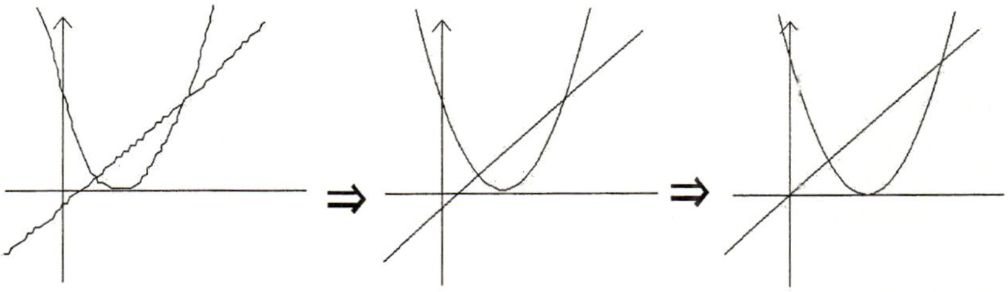

**Fig. 1.** Input of a Curve

## 3 Recognition

We consider 12 functions $f_a(C) \sim f_l(C)$ of a drawn curve $C$. Each function $f_\alpha(C)$ $(\alpha = a, b, \cdots, l)$ takes value in $[0, 1]$ and this takes 1 if the corresponding condition $(\alpha)$ is completely true. We define each condition one by one, $(a)$:$x$ is increasing or decreasing, $(b)$:The start point is near with the end point, something like that.

Set $A = \{a, b, ..., l\}$ and fix one drawn curve $C$. Define a function $F_C : A \to [0, 1]$ by $F_C(\alpha) = f_\alpha(C)$ $(\alpha = a, b, \cdots, l)$. Then our estimation function $\Phi(C)$ is expressed by

$$\Phi(C) = \sum_{\alpha} F(\alpha)\mu_\alpha + \sum_{\alpha,\beta} \min(F(\alpha), F(\beta))\nu_{\alpha,\beta}$$

The parameters $\{\mu_\alpha\}_{\alpha\in A}$, $\{\nu_{\alpha,\beta}\}_{\alpha,\beta\in A}$ are given for each curve type, and $\Phi(C)$ takes large value when the type is correct for the curve $C$. $\Phi(C)$ is expressed by a Choquet Integral $\int F_C d\lambda$ with respect to a certain set function $\lambda$ on $2^A$.

The following table is the result of a recognition test. 19 sample images are given and 4 persons draw each curve once after some training.

**Table 1.** Recognition Ratio

| Closed Curves | | Fuction Curve | |
|---|---|---|---|
| Type | Recog. Ratio | Type | Recog. Ratio |
| Circle | 100.0% | Polynomial(3 digree) | 100.0% |
| Ellipse | 100.0% | sin curve | 100.0% |
| Other | 91.6% | tan curve | 100.0% |
| | | $y = x^3$ | 91.6% |
| | | Streight line | 100.0% |
| | | Parabola | 100.0% |

## 4 XML Documents and Their Translations

We consider that graphical informations cosist of point elements, curve (line) elements, area elements and text elements, and that the first and the second are main elements. Then, as the first version of the system, we describe graphics by these two types of elements and their correlation.

A point element has attributions '$X$' and '$Y$' -coordinate and 'Id' . $(X, Y)$ denotes the display position and 'Id' is the common serial number for all elements. 'Type' is a sub element for a point, not an attribution, since a point can have several meaning at the same time. For example, the peak point of a parabola curve may be a tangent point of this curve and $x$-axio.

The attributions of a curve element are 'Id' ,'Type' and additional properties: ('Radius', 'Oscillation' and something like that). A curve element have point elements as sub elements, and a type element, which is a sub element of some point element, has curve elements as sub elements. For a sub element, 'Id' is replaced by 'RefId' if the element was already described, and the value of RefId is same with Id of the corresponding element. The output document is not user-friendly at all and should be translated to graphics or hypertexts using XSLT or SVG or other technologies. The human acts to obtain graphical information are very active and adequate contents vary depending on situations. On the other hand,

```
<Point X="100" Y="100" Id="1">
   <Type Name="Origin"/>
   <Type Name="Y-Intercept">
       <Curve RefId="7"
         Type="StreightLine"/>
   </Type>
</Point>
..........
```

```
<Curve Id="8" Type ="X-AXIO">
   <Point RefId="2">
       <Type Name="PeakPoint"/>
       <Type Name="TangentPoint"/>
   </Point>
</Curve>
```

**Fig. 2.** An XML Document

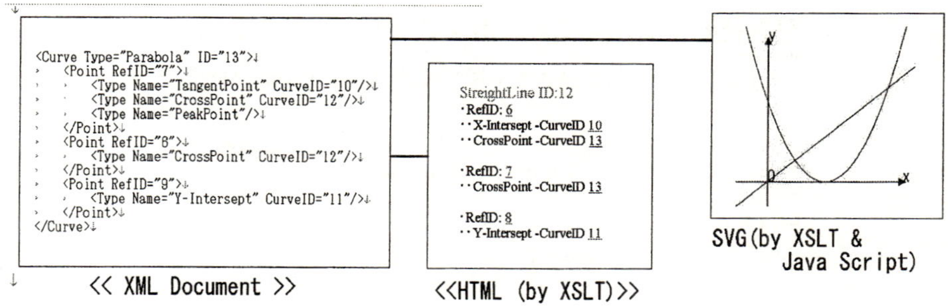


**Fig. 3.** Translation of an XML Document

a hypertext is available without visual information by a voice output system or a Braille display. Then, in the communication without visual information, 'hypertext' is a useful way to express such a document (Fig.3).

## 5 Conclusion

We gave a suggestion for an input and representation method for simple graphs on $xy$-plane. Considering again about the concepts 'point' and 'curve' by which we explain graphics, these are learned in one's early education. Then, they are to be expressed more primitive concepts. This is a future problem beside the improvement of the system performances.

## References

1. Wenyin, L., Qian, W., Xiao, R., Jin, X.: Smart Sketchpad - An On-line Graphics Recognition System. ICDAR 2001 27,EE,2001, 1050–1054
2. Zeleznik, R.C., Herndon, K.P. and Hughes, J.F.: SKETCH: An Interface for Sketching 3D Sciences. In SIGGRAPH 96, New Orleans, 1996, 163–170

# Three Dimensionally Perceived Planar Tactile Illusion Device and Method

Gilbert R. Gonzales

420 Lexington Avenue, Suite 300
New York, NY 10170
ggonzales@essexwoodlands.com

**Abstract.** Described is a method of three dimensional perception of a two dimensional sweeping planar array of sequentially firing vibro-mechanical stimulators vibrating against the skin or other tactile sensitive areas of the body. The vibro-mechanical stimulators are arranged in a substantially two dimensional array over the skin and are triggered in parallel, three or more stimulators at a time, sequentially. A line of three or more parallel stimulators can produce a sense of depth, elevation and contour on the skin by adding or subtracting stimulators. The wearer cognitively perceives the tactual stimulation as a sweeping and moving continuous wave of tactual stimulation that, as it progresses across the skin, produces a non-veridical perception of variable areas of depth, height and contour. This method of three dimensional cutaneous perception using two dimensional arrays could be used, for example, to represent the flat topographical contour of maps to sight impaired persons.

## 1 Introduction and Background

A novel method of non-veridical cutaneous perception of a three dimensional form is described. This method utilizes a sweeping planar array of sequentially firing vibro-mechanical or other stimulators against the skin, mucous membrane or other suitably tactile sensitive area of the body. The vibro-mechanical stimulators are arranged in a substantially two dimensional array over the skin and are triggered in parallel, usually three or more stimulators at a time, sequentially. A parallel line of three or more stimulators produces a sense of depth, elevation and contour on the skin by adding or subtracting individual stimulators. The wearer cognitively perceives the tactual stimulation as a sweeping and moving continuous wave of tactual stimulation that, as it progresses across the skin, produces the non-veridical perception of variable areas of depth, height and contour that can be applied to correspond to a distant veridical three dimensional form.

The ability to perceive or feel three dimensional contour, shape, depth and height on the skin or mucous membrane has only been possible by applying a contoured surface against the skin or by applying the skin surface, such as the fingertip against a surface. By moving the finger across the surface, one is able to determine the shape of an object and its surface characteristics. Described in this paper is a novel method of perceiving three dimensional shapes on the skin or mucous membrane using a two dimensional array of solenoids or other actuators, with lines of these actuators that

K. Miesenberger et al. (Eds.): ICCHP 2004, LNCS 3118, pp. 690–696, 2004.

vibrate sequentially and "sweep" or "scroll" across the skin. These lines of actuators produce a sense or perception of contour on the body surface without moving the finger or other body area that rests against the activated actuator array. No other method is able to produce the non-veridical illusion of three dimensional contour on the surface of the body in fine detail.

There are devices that allow an extremity or a digit to move in space as if moving over a surface, but fine details of the contour of an object are not perceived. In all cases, an extremity or digit must move in space in order to "feel" an object. In addition, a tactile illusion such as the tactile phi phenomenon is not produced.[1, 2] An example of a device described in the literature that gives force feedback but not a phi illusion includes the PHANToM (as defined in the noted website).[3] An excerpt from this site states "A PHANToM is a device which looks rather like a pen which you can slide across a surface in a VR world. You can feel its texture and density. Pushing on the pen sends data representing forces through the Internet which can be interpreted by a PHANToM and therefore felt on the other end. You can not only feel the resulting force, but you can also get a sense of the quality of the object you are feeling, whether it is soft or hard, wood like or fleshy." In addition, a different website describes the limitations of the Thimble Gimble and other similar devices. "The primary limitation of existing devices, such as the Bungee Bat or the recent Thimble Gimble developed at the Massachusetts Institute of Technology, is that they are mounted on some fixed component in the real environment and therefore do not move or rotate with movements of the trainee; to use the device, the trainee must move to it. A trainee-mounted controller may be possible, but may be awkward and may interfere with the training task."[4]

The Tactile Communication Device (TCD) described by Gonzales utilizes actuators in order to produce the illusion of linear continuity motion for the purpose of creating alphanumerics and for position localization (i.e. instrument landing system).[5-8] These devices do not produce the illusion of depth, contour and shape, etc.

Another device described by Gonzales describes a two dimensional array of actuators placed across the torso or elsewhere and tactually received spatial orientation information may incorporate any type of message or position localization desired, as long as the purpose is taught to the wearer.[8] For instance, consider a pilot wearing an array across his or her abdomen or back wherein the array "traces" a straight line across the pilot's torso sequentially using one tactile stimulator at a time. Through training, the pilot knows that when the line is traveling from left to right at about the level of the pilot's umbilicus, the plane is flying upward and level with the horizon. Nose up, nose down or turning inclinations would lend to corresponding changes in the line being "traced". For nose up, the line would move above the pilot's umbilicus and vice versa for nose down. During turns, the line would also bank in the same direction, and to the same degree, as the wings are banked. This system combined with the technique described in reference 5, or the sequential firing of individual actuators that produce a "connect the dots" illusion of symbols could provide the pilot with additional alpha-numerics information such as heading, wind speed, altitude and angle-of-attack. Significant positional information relative to the environment of the pilot and/or the vehicle is presented, but surface, three dimensional information was not possible with these techniques.

## 2 Methods and Results

Microelectrical mechanical systems (MEMS), solenoids, shape memory alloy (SMA), pneumatics, ultrasonic, thermal displacement, piezo-electric ceramic bimorphs and magnetic switches are all methods of actuation that could produce vibration on the skin or mucous membrane at stationary points. The trials in Figures 3 through 5 in this paper were primarily performed using solenoids, but a MEMS device was also used for small arrays especially on the fingertip. Actuator on-time, actuator off-time, number of vibrations and inter-actuator time were settings used and are similar to the settings used in the TCD in some of the references [5-7]. The present device is different in the way it works, compared to the TCD, as follows: an array of actuators is distributed in a planar linear pattern in both the horizontal and vertical axis and rather than a single actuator being activated, a horizontal line of actuators is activated. A line of 3, 4 or 5 actuators, for instance, are simultaneously activated with all actuators in that row and in the entire array having the same settings for actuation (see Figure 1).

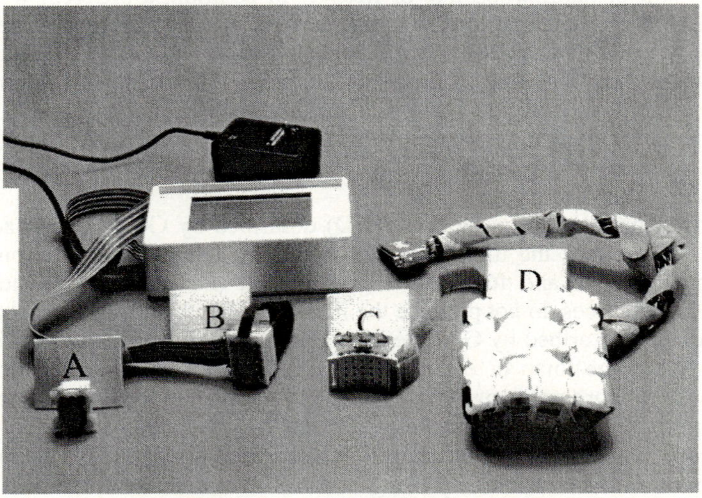


**Fig. 1. A:** Small grouping of solenoids for wrist and palm; **B:** Flat solenoid actuator array for wrist and palm: **C:** Contoured array of 20 actuators for wrist; **D:** Multiple solenoid array for torso

Actuators used include large solenoids, in a 4 by 4 array, grouped together and placed against the chest and abdomen (see Figure 1.D), microsolenoids grouped together in a single carrier and placed against the wrist or palm (see Figure 1, grouping shown in A, B, and C), and a unique piezo and thermal bender clutch actuator array placed against the index fingertip (see Figure 2.A). Twenty actuators or more were used on the wrist and fingertips and as few as 16 actuators were used on the chest. Larger arrays of solenoids were also tested with improved perception by the subjects. Details of some of these devices are described in references 5 and 7. For example, if using a parallel horizontal array of 4 actuators by a vertical array of 5 actuators, settings used may include an on-time of 10 msec, an off-time of 10 msec and 5 vibrations per actuator. An intersolenoid, inter-parallel line time of 10 msec separates the

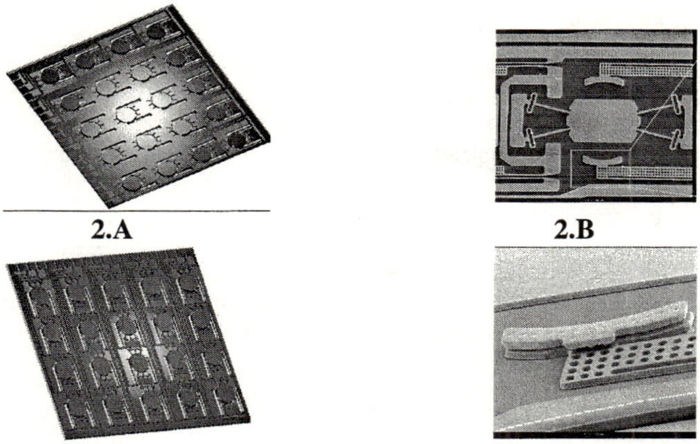


**Fig. 2. A:** Array of 20 switches (top and bottom views); **B:** Magnified view of one of the switching mechanisms with close-up of thermal actuator clutch

activity of the first 4 horizontal actuators in a row and the second 4 horizontal actuators in a row. This continues until the 5$^{th}$ set of 4 vibrators is actuated and then the first set is again actuated in a scrolling fashion after a 250 msec delay. The addition or subtraction (i.e. the activation or lack of activation) of actuators in each parallel line is what creates a more or less dense set of vibrations, as well as a sense of elevation and depth or non-veridical three dimensional perception on the skin. All activated actuators are represented by a horizontal line across the length of the horizontal array of actuators (see Figures 3.A, 4.A, and 5.A).

When the first line of actuators is activated, the subject initially does not have a full sense of non-veridical elevation perception as shown on the first line of 4 dots that represent the first horizontal line of actuators in Figure 3.A. A series of broken horizontal lines that become longer as the lines approach the second string of 4 horizontal dots then converge to form solid horizontal lines that extend from the first dot to the fourth dot in the second horizontal line of dots. This transition represents a perceived sense of more forceful elevation (or sense of displacement) on the cutaneous surface (see Figure 3.B, 4.B and 5.B).

The ability to perceive depth is accomplished by reducing the number of actuators in the horizontal line of actuators, and the duration and perceived length or depth is determined by the number of proximate actuators that are inactive in each line of actuators. Likewise, the perception of elevation is accomplished by adding activated actuators in the horizontal line of actuators. The strength of perceived elevation was determined by the number of proximate actuators that are activated in each line of actuators.

In the above cases a part of the body, such as the pad of a fingertip, may be placed on top of the array of actuators and the fingertip is left immobile upon the array. The vibrators are actuated and the line of vibrators is "scrolled" across the fingertip. Due to the high tactile sensitivity of the fingertip and the two point discrimination of the fingertip, the fingertip can accommodate extremely close approximation of actuators resulting in a greater contour asperity. An objective measure of what the subjects perceived was not possible but a verbal description by 2 subjects led to the composite figures in Figures 3.B, 4.B and 5.B.

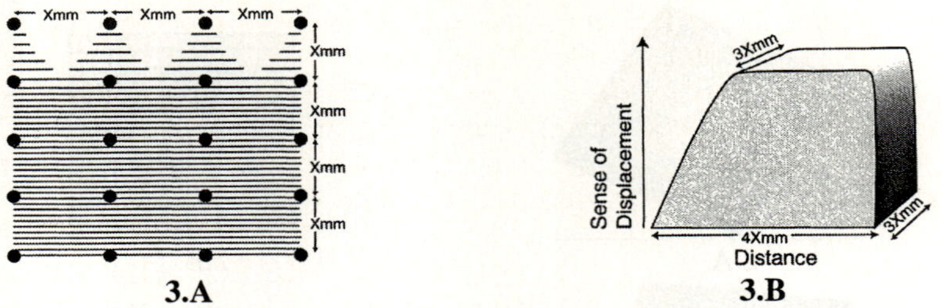


**Fig. 3. A:** Scrolled actuator array on skin (4x5). Black dots represent vibrating actuators; **B:** Representation of sense of displacement perceived and described by subjects based on 3.A

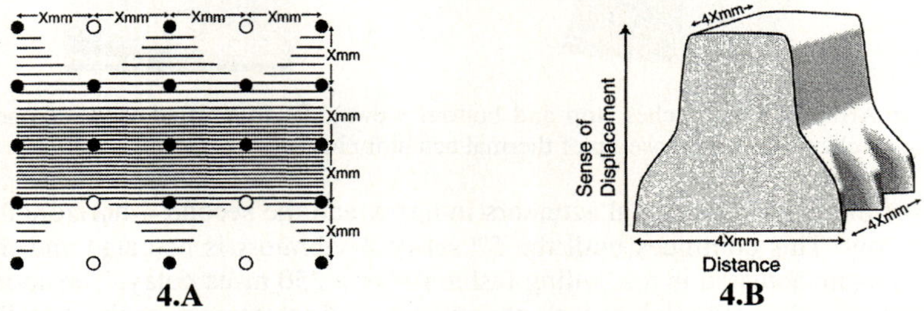


**Fig. 4. A:** Black dots represent vibrating actuators (5x5). Unfilled dots represent non-vibrating actuators; **B:** Representation of sense of displacement perceived and described by subjects based on 4.A

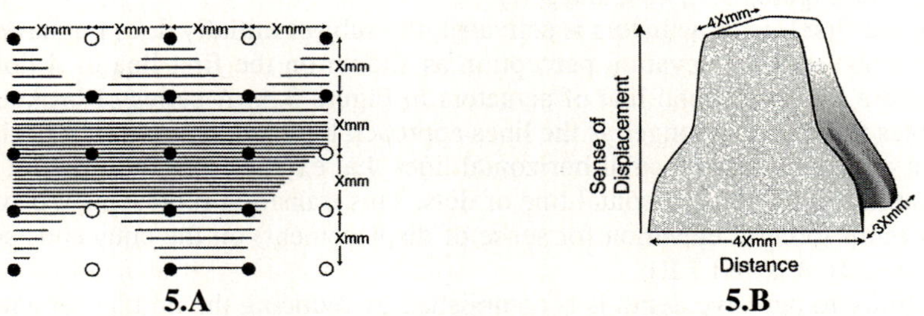


**Fig. 5. A:** Black dots represent vibrating actuators (5x5). Unfilled dots represent non-vibrating actuators; **B:** Representation of sense of displacement perceived and described by subjects based on 5.A

The two dimensional distribution and separation of the actuators can be in the range of 1 mm or less, such that a 20 actuator array of 4 by 5 may fit in a surface area of 7 mm by 9 mm or less to accommodate the fingertip. Vibrators that are piezos or MEMS devices can be distributed in this area or even much smaller areas (see Figure 2.A). A novel combination of piezos that raise a vibrating plate against thermal clutches (see Figure 2.B) was created to be used on the fingertip. This MEMS device has the advantage of approximating the vibration points to within 1 mm or less of each other. While developing these MEMS devices, it was been determined that even more compact arrays than the one produced above can be produced for the most two point discrimination sensitive areas, such as the tip of the tongue.

If the fingertip is slowly moved over a very large array of scrolling or sweeping vibrators (i.e. an area of actuators larger than the area of the fingertip), the area of perception of a represented surface area can be enlarged for the purpose of increasing the total area scanned. In addition increasing an area scanned for depth and elevation can be accomplished by keeping the fingertip stationary on the vibrator array and the scrolling and sweeping of the vibrator area is "moved" to a different area of the desired contour, such as a different part of the contour map.

As indicated above the drawings in Figures 3.B, 4.B and 5.B are idealized composites made by the author of the descriptions by 2 subjects asked to describe what they felt when the 20 solenoid wrist device actuator settings in Figure 3.A and the 25 solenoid torso device in Figure 4.A and Figure 5.A were "scrolled" across the wrist and abdomen, respectively, for periods of up to 2 minutes.

## 3 Discussion

The tactile array described above may be used to represent a surface that is scanned by a distant probe or transducer. Contours that are either stored information or real-time contours measured by ultrasonic or other methods that are transduced to a receiver can be connected to a tactile array for actuation against the skin. Alternatively, the tactile array may be in close approximation to the probe or transducer. A hypothetical example would be a glove of a flight, diving or space suit where a layer of the suit would by necessity separate the outer surface probes or sensors and the inner surface of the glove that would contain the array of vibrators that rest against the fingertip. Alternatively, the tip of the tongue, with its close two point discrimination ability could be placed against an array of closely approximated MEMS vibrators. The tongue would then receive the sensor information regarding a distant contour.

The utility of this technique for blind persons includes the possibility to cutaneously perceive a transmitted, topographical, two dimensional map or other contour descriptions. Contours measured by ultrasound, radiofrequencies or other means and transmitted to a two dimensional array of stimulators could give a real-time perception to the wearer at a distance. In another application, not limited to blind persons, this technique could be useful to "feel" contour of large areas such as geographic topography or small areas such as defects in small blood vessels or other confined but probe- or catheter-approachable areas.

## References


1. Geldard, F.A.: Some Neglected Possibilities of Communication. Science. 1960; 131:1583-1588
2. Sherrick, C.E.: Rogers R. Apparent Haptic Movement. Percept Psychophy. 1966; 1:175-180
3. `http://www.hoise.com/vmw/02/articles/vmw/LV-VM-11-02-35.html`
4. `http://www.ntsc.navy.mil/Programs/Tech/Virtual/VETT/transformations.cfm`
5. Gonzales, G.R.: Symbol Recognition Produced by Points of Tactile Stimulation: The Illusion of Linear Continuity. Mayo Clinic Proc 1996; 71:1039-1046

6. Gonzales, G.R.: Lewis SA, Weaver AL, Paul D. Tactile Illusion-produced Number Perception in Blind and Sighted Persons. Mayo Clinic Proc 1998; 73:1167-1170
7. Gonzales; G.R.: Gust GR, Hughes KE. Fingertip Communication: A Tactile Communication Device for a Glove. American Institute of Physics Proceedings for the Space Technology and Applications International Forum. 2000; 3:154-159
8. Gonzales, G.R.: Tactile Communication Device and Method: Tactile Position Localization Device, Continuation-In-Part. US Patent #6,326,901 B1, December 4, 2001

# Touching Geometry for Blind Pupils

Sophie Rouzier[1], Bernard Hennion[1], Tomás Pérez Segovia[1], and Denis Chêne[2]

[1] France Télécom R&D, DIH/OCF, 28 chemin du Vieux Chêne, 38240 Meylan, France
{defiscience.balg001,bernard.hennion,tomas.perezsegovia}
@rd.francetelecom.com
[2] France Télécom R&D, DIH/UCE, 38-40 av. Général Leclerc,
92794 Issy-les-Moulineaux Cedex 9, France
denis.chene@rd.francetelecom.com

**Abstract.** This paper describes a system based on haptics and sound, to assist teaching planar geometry to blind pupils, and then provides more details on experiments carried out in a school for visually impaired. This system allows to haptically read, measure and construct geometrical figures. Moreover it can help blind pupils to shape a mental representation of geometrical and topological concepts.

## 1 Introduction

Geometry is certainly one of the most difficult subjects to teach to blind pupils [1] and one of the most useful at the same time, as it is necessary for the construction of their mental space representation [4]. This mental representation is essential for education as well as for everyday tasks.

Geometry teaching is based on visual modality: drawings, graphs, lines, curve, etc., all these being unavailable to blind people. We propose to use a haptic device (Sensable's PHANToM) and auditory modality as a substitute for such visuals to teach simple geometric shapes [2].

In the following section we present our system called SALOME. Section 3 details the context, the organization and the results of the first two experiments carried out in a school for visually impaired. Section 4 describes our current work at improving our system taking into account the results of the experiments. Sections 5 and 6 conclude with future work and perspectives.

## 2 System Description

The system is first described from a technological point of view, and then from a functional one.

### 2.1 Technological Description

The basic technology used in SALOME is the haptic force feedback device: Sensable's PHANToM.

K. Miesenberger et al. (Eds.): ICCHP 2004, LNCS 3118, pp. 697–704, 2004.

We developed a software application that uses this haptic device like an active haptic pen, writing with friction on a virtual geometry haptic notebook page.

Geometrical figures are coded as haptic *magnetized rails* that attract the pen towards the different elements of the diagram: points, segments, polygons, circles, lines, etc. At the kilohertz rate, a minimal distance algorithm simulates a virtual spring between the pen and the closest geometrical element thus discovered by the user moving the pen. Each element has also an audio description (synthesizer voice) that enhances the proprioceptive perception of the element. The audio thread is accurately synchronized with the haptic thread to lead the blind user to a consistent and robust mental representation of the geometrical figure. However, less effective than the parallel visual perception, the sequential audio-haptic perception still enables the blind person (even blind from birth) to shape some spatial representation of this figure.

Each geometric element generates a local contribution to an additive 2D force field that controls the device motors. Points generate a centripetal attractive haptic area, leading to a hollow or magnetic point. Straight lines generate a haptic narrow groove in the same way, and circles a circular groove, etc. Two-D haptic textures, soft, smooth or rough, simulate the grain of the paper, allowing nice smooth drawings. The pen runs on a virtual haptic plane and may be pulled or not along each groove, leading to passive or active exploration mode; it may also be kept inside, outside, or on the outline of any closed figure, triangle, circle, etc.

## 2.2 System Functionalities

**Figure Reading.** To understand the figure, visually impaired pupils have to move their *haptic pen* and feel straight lines, points, circles, angles, etc, with it. A synthetic voice module tells the name of the element being touched either at their request (called the *space bar command*), or in a continuous mode. A notion of the relative spatial positions of the different elements is so sequentially built in the blind person's mind.

**Figure Measuring.** The user can quantify the length of segments or the spread of angles. To achieve this haptically, we implemented a graduated ruler with notches every centimetre. The ruler can be automatically snapped along a segment. By pulling the pen along the ruler from one point to the other, the pupil may count the number of centimetres. In the same way, we implemented a haptic circular protractor regularly notched every 30°, the pen being guided along this circle (see Fig.1.).

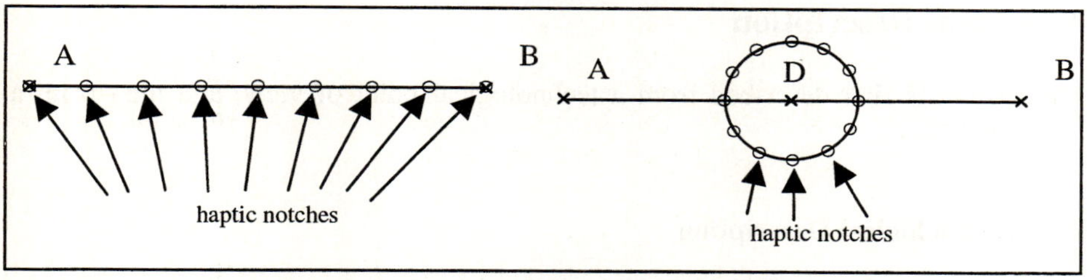


**Fig. 1.** Haptic ruler and haptic protractor.

**Figure Construction.** Lastly the user can make nice and precise drawings, the most difficult task for a blind person. Currently, the following functions are available:

- Place a point anywhere at the current position of the pen;
- Draw a line, given two points;
- Use the haptic ruler and protractor.

Other functions are currently being developed and will soon be available (see section 4).

# 3 Experiments

The context and the organization of the experiments will be described first. Then some results of and observations on these experiments will be given.

## 3.1 Context Presentation

We work in collaboration with the EREADV (*Etablissement Régional d'Enseignement Adapté pour Déficients de la Vue*) of Villeurbanne, a specialized school for the visually impaired near Lyon in France. There are 14 pupils per class at the most. Pupils with amblyopia and blind pupils are mixed. However both groups don't work at the same pace. Their geometry curriculum is the same as for the sighted ones. However the time spent with each blind pupil is much longer!

The main requests of teachers are:

- To reduce the time spent with each pupil, by making the wording of the exercise understandable by all pupils at the same time and by giving the possibility to the pupil to solve it by himself.
- To give the possibility to the visually impaired pupil, as in existing geometrical teaching software for the sighted, to check a conjecture and show invariants by feeling them.

The main request of pupils is to make nice drawings so that they can be proud of their work. Usually, a plastic sheet is used to draw, and all lines, even construction lines, leave so many raised traces that the drawing becomes illegible.

## 3.2 The Organization of the Experiments

We chose to start working with secondary school pupils, as the difficulty level in geometry is not too high yet while not being a starting one. We carried out two experiments in this specialized school with six teenagers and two adults testing SALOME. These experiments are described as follows:

**First Experiment**
The goal of the first experiment is to test the usability both of the haptic device and of our application, observing their difficulty to get used to it and their ability to describe and recognize simple 2D figures.

After a few explanations and a few minutes to get used to the force feedback device, a series of 2D geometrical figures is presented to the blind subject (see Fig.2.). He has to recognize these shapes using the three haptic exploration modes (see section 2.1): *exterior*, *interior* or *contour* mode. He also has to describe them, answering questions such as: which edges are equal? Is it an acute or obtuse angle? Which edges are parallel? What is the smallest edge? …

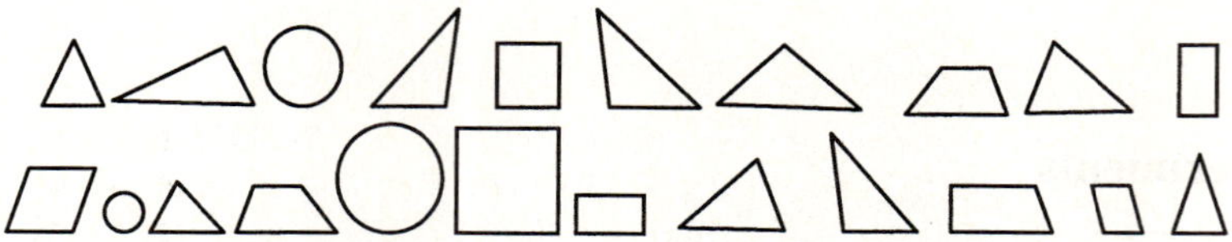

**Fig. 2.** Simple geometrical figures for the first experiment.

**Second Experiment**

The goal of the second experiment is to evaluate the ability of the pupils:

- To describe and recognize more complex 2D figures (composed of several simple figures) with our system;
- To make a simple geometrical construction exercise (draw the perpendicular bisector of a segment) with our system.

Like in the first experiment, the subject starts by getting used to the system, its new *space bar command* and trains on a few simple figures. Then he has to describe and recognize a series of seven figures (see Fig.3.). We particularly pay attention to the following: does he touch every object of the figure? Does he use the naming functionality? Does he check out every characteristic of the figure?

Finally he is asked to draw the perpendicular bisector of an eight-centimetre horizontal segment. To do this, he has two haptic tools at his disposal: a haptic graduated ruler and a haptic protractor (see section 2.2).

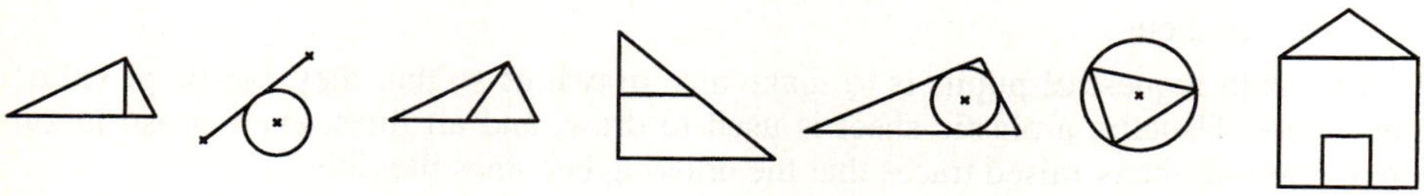

**Fig. 3.** Composed geometrical figures for the second experiment.

## 3.3 Results from Experiments

**First Experiment**

This was the first presentation of our system to visually impaired subjects. The haptic device was accepted very quickly by the children but not as quickly by the two adults. They all were able to discriminate the length of two segments if they differed by more than 20%. The angles were also discriminated within about 15°. During this experiment some perception bias was noticed qualitatively regarding differences in radial vs. tangential perception [5] and the influence of the size and orientation of the shape in the recognition time and rate.

*Contour mode* vs. *interior mode*: No better mode could clearly be distinguished. One person preferred *contour mode* for triangles and *interior mode* for quadrilaterals; another preferred *contour mode* to identify the shapes and *interior mode* to perceive their characteristics. Other points were noticed: when the stylus is held not firmly enough, it vibrates; and when it is held too firmly, the motors get so warm that the overheating protection is activated.

**Second Experiment**

*2D Composed Geometry*

Using *hollow points* enhances angle perception, but may mislead too: one person perceived an angle where there wasn't any. He perceived a quadrilateral instead of a triangle with a point on one of the edges. Another confusing intersection was in the "triangle and inscribed circle" figure (see Fig.4.) where one of the angles ("B") was never reached. The stylus passed from the segment AI to the arc IJ and then to the segment JC, the subject not perceiving the triangle.

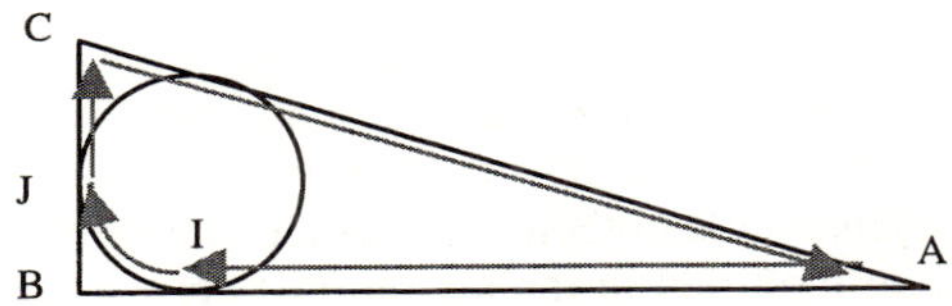


**Fig. 4.** Triangle and inscribed circle (black) and the exploration path (grey).

All the intersections are a problem as it is difficult to express haptically the number of segments and their distribution on the intersection. This difficult problem is still to solve.

*Construction*

The haptic ruler and the haptic protractor were enthusiastically received. In this experiment, we used an *Oz wizard* to type commands (get the ruler, get the protractor, put a point, draw a segment) when necessary. All the subjects were able to get to the end of the job.

**Conclusion**

All of the subjects were enthusiastic about the experiments. We did not notice any kind of rejection and every subject could do what we asked them to. In the simple 2D geometry experiment the results were better than expected in shape, length and angle recognition. Unfortunately we did not make a quantitative evaluation of the shape recognition. In the 2D composed geometry experiment, results were encouraging in spite of a number of pitfalls like the intersections

## 4 Current Work

Following the second experiment, it was decided with the teachers to develop an embryonic haptic editor that would allow a pupil to do a real geometrical exercise by himself. Thus we are currently implementing:

- more commands to create elements with some characteristics (for example, place a point in the middle of a segment, draw a parallel given a line, draw a circle given a centre and a radius, etc)
- the ability to manipulate geometrical objects[1];

The pupil will be able to interact with the application thanks to:

- The haptic device used for touching geometrical figures, and the stylus switch which is used to select or drag-and-drop some geometrical objects of the figure. This last item will make possible to check a conjecture and *feel* invariants.
- A screen reader tool that reads aloud the text of any computer application and also outputs the corresponding text to refreshable Braille displays. This would enable the pupil to navigate on his Windows desktop, to find and launch SALOME, and to navigate in the application's menus and submenus.
- A speech synthesis module that can help the pupil to know where his/her haptic pen is on the geometrical figure at the kilohertz rate (read sound consideration paragraph for more details).

The goal of the next experiment planned in May is to test SALOME in a real teaching situation between a teacher and one pupil. The pupil will have to do a geometric exercise (refer to the details of this exercise in appendix) that corresponds to his geometrical knowledge, with a teacher's help if necessary. We will observe behaviour of the pupil and the teacher, collect their remarks and concentrate on the following questions : what could be modified in the system to improve the interaction between the pupil and the system, the teacher and the system, the pupil and the teacher (through the system)? How could the system integrate the teaching process?

**Sound Consideration**

In order to implement the fusion of the bi-sensorial perception of the elements of the figure, we needed to synchronize the audio perception to the corresponding kilohertz haptic proprio-perception. Without that accurate synchronization, we observed that sounds brought confusion and inconsistency between audio and haptic signals (for instance, the system was playing sound "A" whereas the pen was already at point "B"), and the visually impaired were reticent to use the *space bar command*. Now each element of the figure has its own sound area all around itself (see Fig.5.). A minimum distance test is computed at the kilohertz rate, the result of which being used to decide which element is the closest and thus which sound file must be launched.

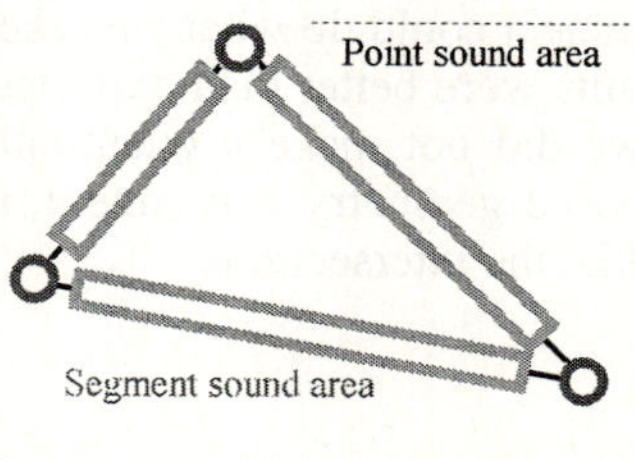


**Fig. 5.** Sound areas for points and segments.

[1] Geometrical object manipulation is particularly useful to teach geometry as it helps highlight geometrical invariants (such as the centre of the circumscribed circle of a triangle is always on the intersection point of the 3 perpendicular bisectors of the triangle for example).

## 5 Future Work

In this section, we present some questions that need further consideration and which, therefore, will be at the focus of our future research.

How could the user be prevented from leaving a figure unless doing it intentionally? Is an auditory or haptically alert a solution?

How to discriminate straight lines from curves? Different sounds could be associated to them, but beware of too much noise in the classroom! How to differentiate different kinds of points like the vertex of a triangle and the intersection of two lines for example? The same problem arises with right angles and other angles, and with construction lines and final ones.

The *ruler tool* is currently a measuring tool for segments only; therefore we have to add a tool for measuring all kind of distances.

One major difficulty is to find out haptically if two lines are parallel because of the single haptic point interaction. What intuitive metaphor could make the parallelism notion tangible?

The stability of the stylus is reduced when it is held not firmly enough or when the arm is extended; a study of its dynamic behaviour when coupled with a hand should lead to a regulation algorithm to reduce oscillations in all conditions.

## 6 Conclusion and Perspectives

The first step was to validate the technological concept. This step has been overcome with success: the visually impaired have received SALOME with enthusiasm, as it helps them achieve some perception of geometrical figures, lengths and angles. The next step is to validate the usability and show the interest of our system in a class during a real teaching situation. The next experiment planned in May will contribute to evaluate it.

Currently our system is aimed at geometry teaching for secondary school pupils. However we plan to study how younger or older pupils could use it. How could this system be useful for basic geometry teaching in primary education when sighted children learn to draw and write? What should be modified or improved to be suited to geometry teaching at university?

Moreover, our system could be extended to other subjects like geography, architecture, handwriting and drawing, and even the perception of postcards, photos or landscapes.

## References


1. Malik, E.: Aprentissage de la représentation multidimensionnelle pour les élèves non-voyants. Rapport de stage de DEA, Laboratoire d'Informatique Théorique et Appliquée, Université de Metz (2001)
2. Roth, P., Petrucci, L., Pun, T.: From Dots to Shape : an auditory haptic game platform for teaching geometry to blind pupils. In ICCHP 2000, International Conference on Computers Helping people with special Needs, Karlsruhe, Germany (2000) 603-610

3. Sjöström, C.: The IT potential of haptics – Touch access for people with disabilities. Thesis, Certec, Lund University, Sweden (1999)
4. Thinus-Blanc, C., Gaunet, F.: Space representations in the blind : vision as a spatial sense ?. Psychological Bulletin, 121 (1997) 20-42
5. Wong, T.: Dynamic properties of radial and tangential movements as determinants of the haptic horizontal-vertical illusion with an L figure. Journal of Experimental Psychology, 3(1), (1977)151–164

## Appendix

Draw an ABC right triangle in A.

Draw two of the three perpendicular bisectors. Call O the intersection point of the two perpendicular bisectors.

Draw the third perpendicular bisector. What can you say?

Draw the circle whose O is the centre and [OB] the radius. What's the name of this circle?

Move point A along the circle. What can you say about the ABC triangle?

# An Indicating, Leading Manipulator as a Good Hand at Teaching Strokes: A Mental-Image-Creation Support System

Yoshihiko Nomura, Haruki Kakehashi, Tokuhiro Sugiura,
Hirokazu Matsui, and Norihiko Kato

School of Engineering, Mie University, Tsu, Mie 514-8507, Japan
nomura@mach.mie-u.ac.jp
http://www.robot.mach.mie-u.ac.jp

**Abstract.** A mental image creation support system was developed. The mechanical device of the system is a 3-DOF manipulator that is composed of a 2-DOF quadrilateral parallel-link manipulator and an arm-end actuator. A couple of servomotors drive a couple of upper links of the 2-DOF manipulator, and they control the arm-end position. The arm-end actuator is attached to the 2-DOF manipulator's arm-end: a servomotor controls the orientation of a knob attached to the servomotor axis. The person is assumed to pinch the knob by his/her fingertips. The position of the knob axis traces the strokes of the presented figures sequentially, and the orientation of the knob is controlled to indicate the orientation of the currently tracing point on the stroke. A couple of preeminent functions are embedded to the process: one is the indicating function, and the other is the leading function. That is, the knob indicates to the person with its orientation to which direction the arm end moves: the direction reflects the orientation of the ongoing stroke. And the translation of the knob leads the person along the strokes. The indicating/leading functions play complementary role. Thus, the person is able to perceive the position and the orientation of the strokes of presented images via somatic sensations of his/her fingertip. It is expected to be a good hand at teaching strokes and to be a visual alternative of the blind persons and a visual aid of lazy eye persons at creating mental images.

## 1 Introduction

Vision is one of the most important sensations for pattern information processing. And, visually impaired peoples suffer inconvenience in daily life and social activity. Therefore, there are great demands on visual alternative of the blind persons and on a visual aid of lazy eye persons. Among various vision relating human brain functions, creating mental images is considered to be one of the important functions. Practical examples of the mental images are such the images as the city maps showing the layout of roads and facilities and the floor plans showing rooms and corridors in the building.

K. Miesenberger et al. (Eds.): ICCHP 2004, LNCS 3118, pp. 705–712, 2004.

There have been reported many devices and studies in the field of mental image creation such as those by audition [1], by tactile sensation [2, 3], and by both audition and tactile sensation [4, 5]. The interactive sound-based color image pattern presentation systems using a pen-tablet [6, 7] and touch-panel display [8] as a man-machine interface were also studied. Regretfully, since those by audition can use market-produced devices, they have advantages in the availability and in cost. However, their performance was substantially low in image perception. And, those by tactile sensation had advantages and disadvantages vise verse.

To improve image perception performance, a novel mental-image-creation support system is developed, which features an ingeniously constituted manipulator, an indicating/leading manipulator. It is expected to be a good hand at teaching strokes to visually impaired persons and to help them creating mental images. This paper presents a method of calibration with the system hardware and some experimental results with the proposed system.

## 2 Methodology

### 2.1 System Description

The proposed mental-image-creation support system features a 3-DOF manipulator. The manipulator-arm end is controlled with a 2-DOF quadrilateral parallel-link manipulator driven by a couple of servomotors. While another servomotor is attached to the manipulator-arm end, and is called the arm-end actuator. And, a knob is attached to the rotating axis of the arm-end actuator. A person is assumed to pinch the knob in use. The position of the knob traces the strokes of the presented images sequentially, and the orientation of the knob always indicates the tangential orientation of the currently tracing point on the stroke. Then, the person is assumed to perceive the position and the orientation of the strokes via his/her somatic sensations of fingertip position and orientation. Concretely, when perceiving the orientation changing, and when perceiving the position stationary, the person can recognize the existence of corners between consecutive strokes. When perceiving the position changing, the person can perceive strokes together with the positions, orientations: if perceiving the orientation stationary, the stroke would be a straight line, and if perceiving the orientation changing, the stroke would be a curved line. In these processes, there are a couple of preeminent functions: one is the indicating function, and the other is the leading function.

*Indicating function*: the knob indicates to the person via its orientation to which direction the arm end moves. The direction reflects the orientation of the ongoing stroke. So it is called the indicating function.

*Leading function*: the translation of the knob leads the person along the strokes. So it is called the leading function.

The couple of functions play complementary role, and help him/her create mental images. Therefore, the manipulator is called an indicating, leading manipulator.

Here, the parallel link mechanism is compared with the serial link mechanism in Table 1. Among various advantages and disadvantages, the advantages in power and stiffness are regarded more important than others. That is, in the parallel link mechanism, its arm end can exert high power even though driving motors are of low power. Then, the parallel link mechanism enables us to employ inexpensive and commercially available servomotors that are used in large quantities such as for radio-controlled models.

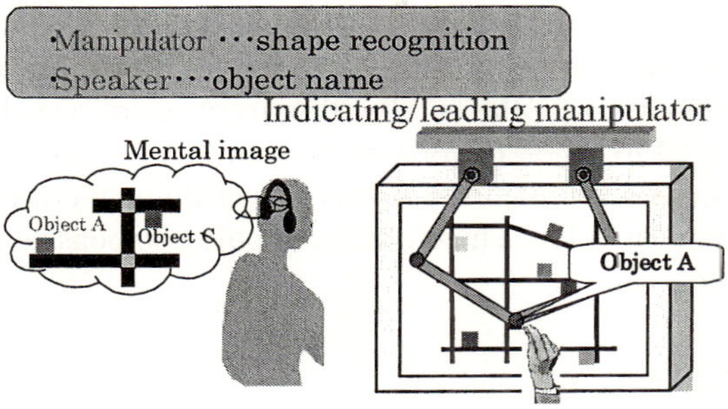


**Fig. 1.** Concept of the indicating/leading manipulator: mental-image-creation support system.

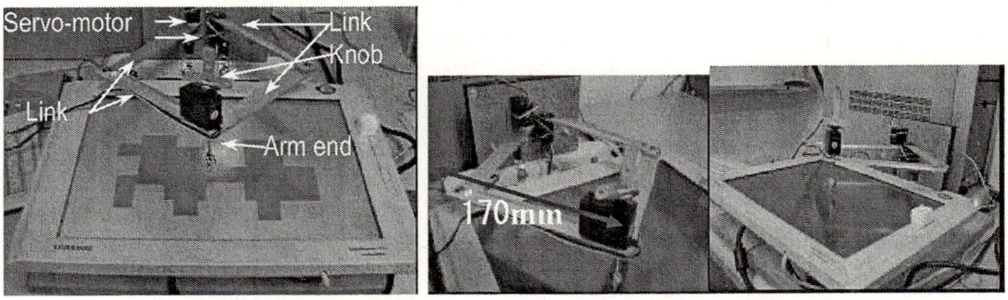


**Fig. 2.** Photograph of the indicating/leading manipulator.

**Table 1.** Comparison between parallel and serial link mechanism.

| Characteristics | Parallel link | Serial link |
|---|---|---|
| Power | Higher | Lower |
| Stiffness | Higher | Lower |
| Movable range | Narrower | Wider |
| Kinematics | More difficult | Easier |
| Inverse kinematics | Easier | More difficult |
| Singular point | More | Less |

## 2.2 Problems to Be Solved

There are many problems to be solved to develop the proposed system:

(1) Design of geometrical specification of the manipulator
(2) Calibration of the geometrical specification of the manipulator
(3) Method of inputting images to be presented
(4) Method of actuating the manipulator, a path planning for the inputted images
(5) Confirmation of effectiveness of the proposed system

In this paper, the way of calibration is presented and the effectiveness of the proposed system is proved by experiments. Although positional errors of the actuators don't increase cumulatively in the parallel link mechanism, we should accept large mount of errors of 10 to 20 % of rotation angle when employing inexpensive and commercially available servomotors. Furthermore, additional errors were involved in manufacturing and in assembly. Therefore, we should compensate the errors with the help of the calibration.

## 2.3 Method of Calibration

Fig. 3 shows the parameters and values to be calibrated: $a_{ul}$ $a_{ur}$ $a_{ll}$ $a_{lr}$ are the lengths of four links, $L$ is the interval of a couple of motors, $k_{l1}$ $k_{r1}$ are the motor angle scales, $k_{l0}$ $k_{r0}$ are the zero shifts of motor, $\phi$ is the rotation angle of touch-panel coordinate systems, $t_x$ $t_y$ are the translations of touch-panel coordinate systems, and $\varepsilon$ is the ratio of vertical to horizontal pixel of touch-panel.

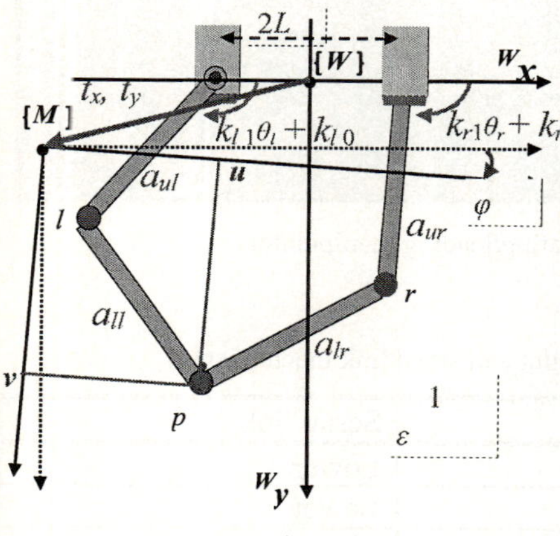


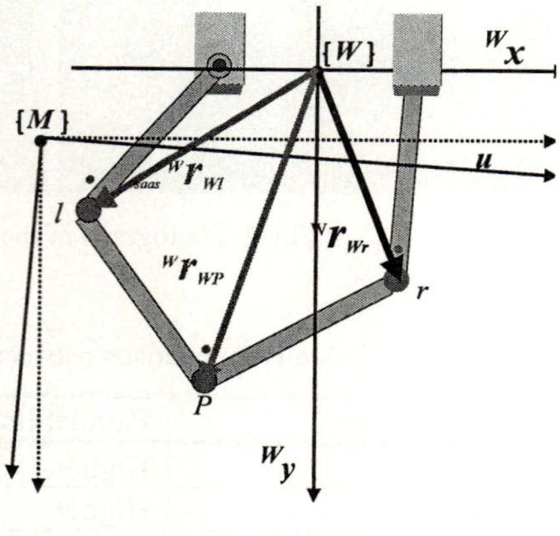


{W}: World coordinates, $[{}^{W}x \ {}^{W}y]^T$ {M}: Moving coordinates (Touch-panel coordinates) $[u \ v]^T$

**Fig. 3.** Parameters and values.

**Fig. 4.** Three positional vectors.

Using the parameters, three positional vectors shown in Fig. 4 are represented as

$$ {}^{W}\boldsymbol{r}_{Wl} = \begin{bmatrix} \cos(k_{l1}\theta_l + k_{l0}) \\ \sin(k_{l1}\theta_l + k_{l0}) \end{bmatrix} + \begin{bmatrix} -L \\ 0 \end{bmatrix}, \quad {}^{W}\boldsymbol{r}_{Wr} = \begin{bmatrix} \cos(k_{r1}\theta_l + k_{r0}) \\ \sin(k_{r1}\theta_l + k_{r0}) \end{bmatrix} + \begin{bmatrix} L \\ 0 \end{bmatrix} $$

$$^{W}r_{WP} = {}^{W}R_M\, {}^{M}r_{MP} + {}^{W}t_M \quad \text{where } {}^{M}r_{MP} = [\, u \quad \varepsilon v\,]^{T}.$$

Using the three positional vectors, the observation equation are constituted by

$$({}^{W}r_{WP} - {}^{W}r_{Wl})^{T}\,({}^{W}r_{WP} - {}^{W}r_{Wl}) = a_{ll}^{2}, \qquad ({}^{W}r_{WP} - {}^{W}r_{Wr})^{T}\,({}^{W}r_{WP} - {}^{W}r_{Wr}) = a_{lr}^{2}$$

The observation equations are to be solved by a non-linear least squares method.

## 3 Experimental Results

### 3.1 Calibration

The positions of the manipulator-arm-end being calculated by un-calibrated initial parameter values are shown by ♦ in Fig. 5 together with the actually observed positions by X. There can be found great difference between them. The standard deviations of the differences in $^{W}x$ direction and in $^{W}y$ direction were 32.7 [pixel] (=9.8mm), and 42.3 [pixel] (=12.7mm), respectively. On the other hand, as shown in Fig. 6, after the calibration, the calculated positions shown by ● match very well with the observed positions. The standard deviations in $^{W}x$ direction and in $^{W}y$ direction were greatly decreased by a fifth part, that is, were improved to 6.7 [pixel] (=2.0mm), and 5.0 [pixel] (=1.5mm), respectively.

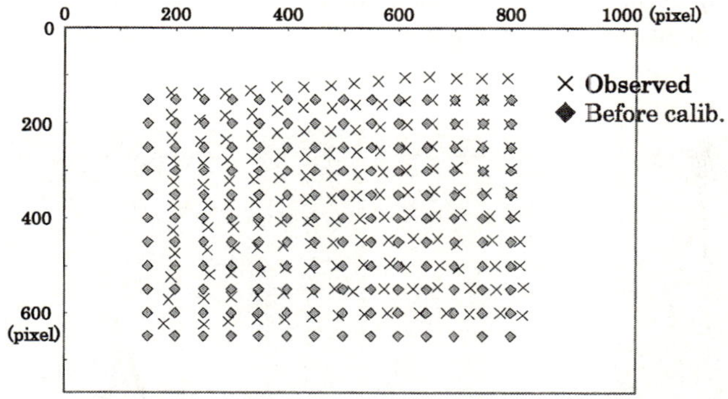


**Fig. 5.** Before-calibration performance.

### 3.2 Mental Image Perception

The proposed mental image creation support system, noted as the indicating/directing manipulator, was compared with the raise writer from the viewpoint of performances with mental image perception. It is assumed that the tactile sense on finger cushions and the somatic sense of fingertip position would be utilized with the raise writer. As for the subjects, four young sighted persons from 22 to 24 years old executed putting on a blindfold. Two of them do first the indicating/directing manipulator, and the rests do first the raise writer. Six image patterns were presented in the random order

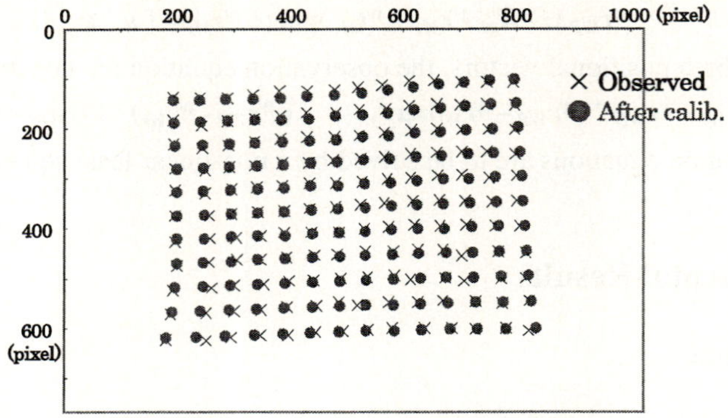


**Fig. 6.** After-calibration performance.

for each of the indicating/directing manipulator and the raise writer, respectively: three patterns are similar to alphabetical characters and the remaining three are deformed as in Fig. 8. The subjects were not informed with the patterns at all.

Experimental results with the consumption time and the correct answer rate are shown in Fig. 9. There is no significant difference between the indicating/directing manipulator and the raise writer. Furthermore, as shown in Fig.10, the consumption time is in proportion to the number of vertices both for the character pattern and the non-character pattern, although the non-character patterns took much longer consumption time than the character patterns. Thus, it was concluded that there have prospects of practicability for the proposed system.

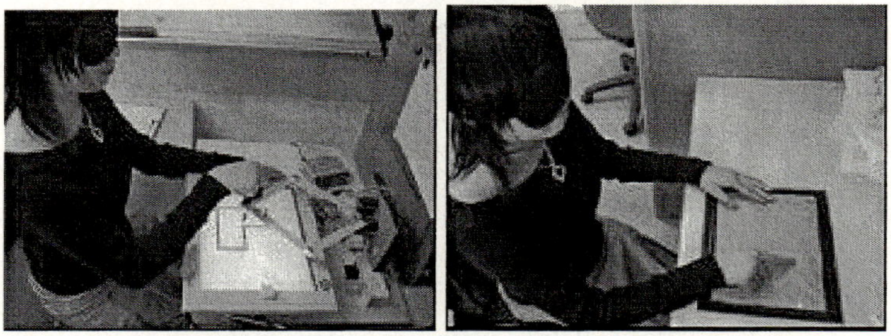

**Fig. 7.** Indicating/directing manipulator (left) and raise writer (right).

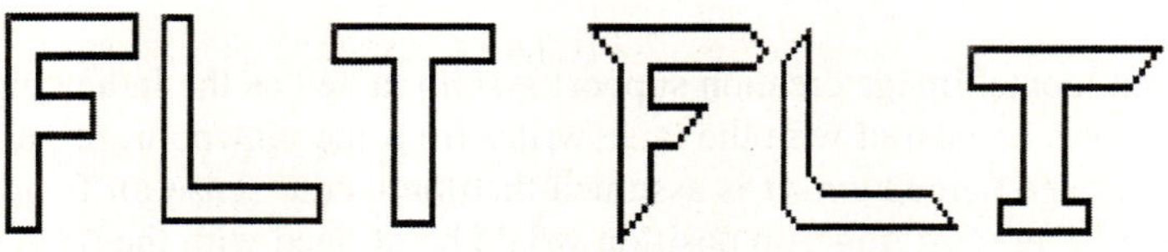

(a) Character pattern (b) Non-character pattern

**Fig. 8.** Presented images.

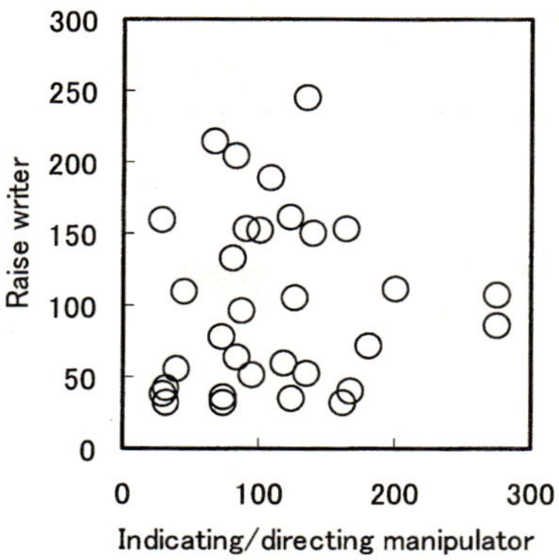


(a) Consumption time

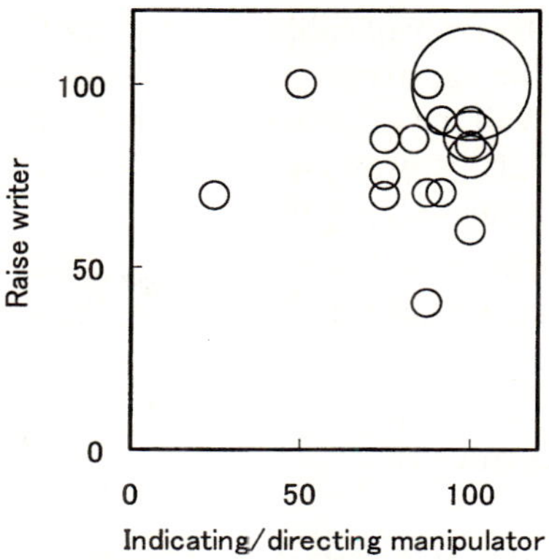


(b) Correct answer rate

**Fig. 9.** Experimental results with the consumption time (left) and the correct answer rate (right).

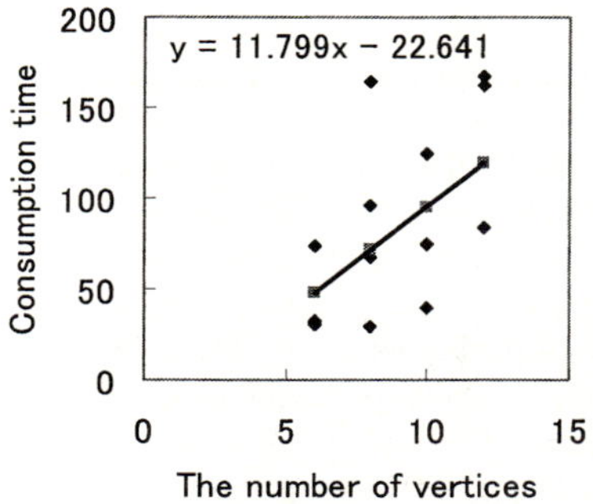


(a) Character pattern

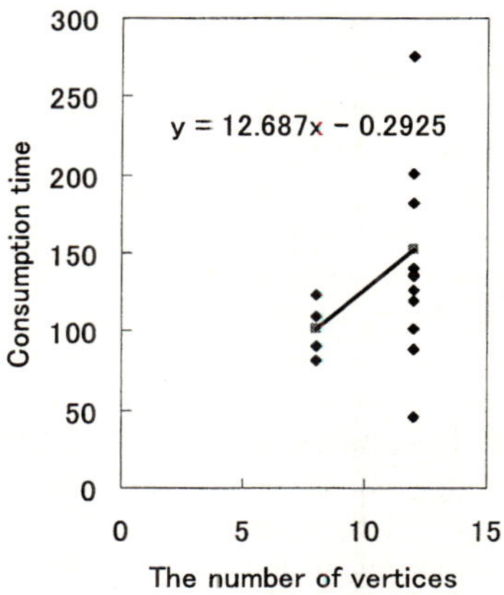


(b) Non-character pattern

**Fig. 10.** Relationships between consumption time and the number of vertices when using indicating/directing manipulator.

## 4 Conclusion

The paper proposed a novel system helping human create mental images. The results are summarized as follows:

(1) A 3-DOF manipulator for teaching strokes of images was developed.

(2) The position of the knob traces the strokes of the figures sequentially, and the orientation of the knob indicates the orientation of the currently tracing point on the stroke. Thus, the indicating function and the leading function are realized.

(3) The way of calibrating geometrical parameters was presented.
(4) Mental image perception performance of the proposed system was compared with the raise writer where the tactile and somatic senses are utilized. As a result, it was confirmed that there have prospects of practicability for the proposed system.

This research is supported financially by The Ministry of Education and Science, Japan: Grant–in-Aid for Scientific Research (B)(1) 13450170.

## References

1. Beddoes, M.P., Suen, C.Y.: Evaluation and a Method of Presentation of the Sound Output From the Lexiphone -A Reading Machine for the Blind. IEEE TRANSACTIONS ON BIO-MEDICAL, Vol.BME-18, No.2 (1971) 85-91
2. Simizu, Y., Saida, S., Shimura, H.: Tactile pattern recognition by graphic display: Importance of 3-D information for haptic perception of familiar objects. Perception & Psychophysics, 53 (1993) 43-48
3. Tang, H., Beebe, D.J.: A Microfabricated Electrostatic Haptic Display for Persons with Visual Impairments. IEEE TRANSACTIONS ON REHABILITATION ENGINEERING, Vol.6, No.3 (1998) 241-248
4. Minagawa, H., Ohnishi, N., Sugie, N.: A Diagram Acquisition and Generation System for Blind Person Using Tactile and Auditory Senses. Trans. Inst. Electronics, Information and communication Engineers, Vol. J77-D-II, No. 3, (1994) 616-624 (in Japanese)
5. Blenkhorn, P., Evans, D.G.: Using speech and touch to enable blind people to access schematic diagrams. Journal of Network and Computer Applications. 21 (1998) 17-29
6. Nomura, Y., Nishihama, S., Ozaki, M., Sugiura, T.: Image Pattern Perception by Interactive Sound Presentation. Proceedings of 23rd Annual International Conference of the IEEE Engineering in Medicine and Biology Society (2001) CD-ROM Paper#369
7. Nomura, Y., Nishihama, S., Sugiura, T., Matsui, H., Kato, N.: Auditory Sensation Aided Image Perception: Integration of Somesthetic Sense of Fingertip Position. Proceedings of 8th Annual International Conference ICCHP 2002, LNCS2398 (2002)448-454
8. Nomura, Y., Kakehashi, H., Sugiura, T., and Kato, N.: Mental Map Creation Support System for Blind Person –Fusion of Verbal Message and Somesthec Sense. Proceedings of HCI International 2003, Vol. 48, (2003) 1315-1319

# The Bigger Picture: Automated Production Tools for Tactile Graphics

David Crombie[1], Roger Lenoir[1], Neil McKenzie[1], and George Ioannidis[2]

[1] FNB Netherlands, accessible information for people with a print impairment,
Molenpad 2, 1016 GM Amsterdam, The Netherlands
projects@fnb.nl
http://projects.fnb.nl/

[2] TZI, Image Processing Department, University of Bremen
gtis@tzi.de
www.tzi.de

**Abstract.** The Graphics to Tactile project (G2T) aimed to provide a semi-automatic image processing tool to enhance the creation of tactile graphics. In attempting to convert graphical and visual information into accessible formats, it is important that the information used for input is sufficiently well defined. Print diagrams and graphics contain information (such as perspective, overlapping lines, and colour) that cannot be represented in a Braille reader. People who are blind therefore cannot access complex formatted text, pictures, graphics or maps. The G2T system makes use of advanced image processing technologies partially to automate the tactile graphic production process and can be used in conjunction with existing drawing tools.

## 1 Introduction

Unsurprisingly, the most difficult set of information to relay to visually impaired people is visual information. If we were able to model the means of exploration (such as tactile or sonic) and provide opportunities to learn the structure of the content this could provide a degree of consistency. Such an ambitious goal would separate content representation and presentation and add other modalities of presentation. The Graphics to Tactile project (G2T) aimed to provide some movement in this general direction by creating a semi-automatic image processing tool to enhance the creation of tactile graphics.

In attempting to convert graphical and visual information into accessible formats, it is important that the information used for input is sufficiently well defined. Print diagrams and graphics contain information (such as perspective, overlapping lines, and colour) that cannot be represented in a Braille reader. People who are blind therefore cannot access complex formatted text, pictures, graphics or maps. Some or all of this information can be vital parallel information. Visual representations provide a further hurdle for visually impaired people in software, where Graphical User Interfaces (GUI) [1] are commonly used. In most cases an alternative navigation method or representation is not provided.

K. Miesenberger et al. (Eds.): ICCHP 2004, LNCS 3118, pp. 713–720, 2004.

## 2 State of the Art

### 2.1 What Is a Tactile Graphic?

There is no generally accepted definition of tactile graphics and it is important to describe what we mean by a tactile graphic. The National Centre for Tactile Drawings in the United Kingdom [2] gives the following definition: *"a tactile diagram is a representation of visual material designed for feeling, rather than looking"*. This definition suggests that for example a sculpture, representing visual material, can be seen as a tactile diagram, and seems very broad [3]. At the 65$^{th}$ IFLA Council [4] the concept of tactile drawings was defined as follows: *"a tactile image is an image scanned with the fingertips; it is executed in relief. A relief can assume many different forms and can be produced by several different techniques"*. This definition does say something about the form and use, but it does not say anything about the content.

The National Federation for the Blind in the USA [5] recently used the following definition and thereby made a distinction between tactile graphics and three-dimensional models: *"tactile graphics are generally understood to be raised images including raised-line diagrams that can be bound into a book (usually a Braille book which includes pages of text), or hung on a wall like a picture. Three-dimensional models are freestanding objects such as model animals, model cars, and those objects that have a substantial Z-axis. Models are often scale models in that they are usually smaller than the actual object....the terms model and three-dimensional model are synonymous and mean a model made to scale and not the exact size of the modelled object"*. In the context of this paper, we would suggest the following definition: *"In general, one can say that any drawing, converted into a tactile two-dimensional relief format without loss of essential information, can be called a tactile graphic"*.

### 2.2 Current Production Techniques

The transcription of the graphics into tactile can be achieved through different approaches and methods. The extended use of Graphical User Interfaces has introduced severe impediments for visually impaired communities who are largely dependent on textual representations. The problem of turning 2-D drawings into raised tactile 2-D drawings with automatic or semi-automatic procedures is still under research. The most common methods used to produce tactile graphics [6] are:

- Thermoform / Vacuum-formed
- Swell Paper / Microcapsule (heat-sensitive paper)
- Embossed (designed on computer then printed on a Braille embosser)
- Tactile-Audio (designed on and used with computer and touch tablet, Nomad Pad [7], Concept Keyboard, Tag Pad)
- Free Hand (With the use of Heat Pen, German Film, Foil)
- Craft (model making, smelly vision, tactile colour)
- Commercial processes (screen printing, signs)

The above solutions vary greatly in cost and effectiveness. Most of these solutions require the intervention of a sighted individual who will access the content and transform it in an appropriate manner. This increases both the time and cost of the system. The human intervention techniques are further compounded by a lack of standardisation. In most of the above methods, the output will vary from one producer to another and possibly even from day to day within producing organisations.

If an automated production method could be created from modern image processing initiatives, the service would be more effective for all involved. Tactile graphic producers would be in a far better position to provide greater volume and quality of information for their clients. The clients themselves would be provided with a much quicker service which could also be cheaper. The process of standardisation for such a system would make the skills required to read such diagrams far easier to develop.

### 2.3 Fundamental Steps in Image Processing

The task of image processing is to extract and retrieve semantics of the image content. In each case a problem image domain is defined where image processing functions should be applied. The fundamental steps [8] in performing these actions are shown in Figure 1 below.

**Image Acquisition.** The first step of the process is *image acquisition.* This requires an imaging sensor and the capability to digitise the signal produced by the sensor. In the G2T Project the imaging sensor is a colour scanner. Ideally, the image should be already available digitally. The sensor itself introduces noise and other distortions into the acquired image due to the process of digitisation and therefore the nature of the sensor is determined very much by the application. It is important to note here that the levels of quality in digital image are as varied as the processes for creating these digital images. Ideally, the input should be of the highest quality that is possible and realistic given the systems processing power.

**Pre-processing.** After obtaining a digital image, the next step deals with *pre-processing* that image. The key function of pre-processing is to improve the image in ways that increase the chances for success of the subsequent processes. Pre-processing usually deals with techniques for enhancing contrast, removing noise, and isolate regions whose texture indicate a likelihood of alphanumeric information. The primary concern at this stage is to create a semi-automatic process which overcomes the most common discrepancies found in image acquisition.

**Segmentation.** The next step of the process deals with *segmentation.* Broadly defined, segmentation partitions an input image into its constituent parts or objects. In general, autonomous segmentation is one of the most difficult tasks in digital image processing. On the one hand, a robust segmentation procedure brings the process near to a successful solution of an imaging problem. On the other hand, weak or erratic segmentation algorithms almost always guarantee eventual failure. Segmentation is directly tied to the compression and storage methods used for the digital file.

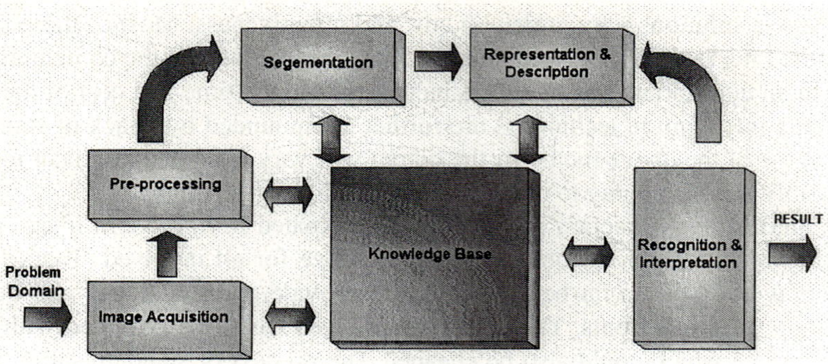


**Fig. 1.** The fundamental steps of Image Processing.

Segmentation methods usually employ homogeneous or discontinuity criteria to extract interesting regions of an image. Homogeneous criterion regions can be built of areas of the same colour and/or texture. The criterion is used to decide whether a point of the image belongs to the region to be segmented or to the background. Often the intensity value in conjunction with a threshold is used as the homogeneity criterion.

More advanced methods involve not only thresholding algorithms but also texture based segmentation and region growing algorithms. The most recent work in this stage is to employ mathematical transforms to move compression from a raster based segmentation to a vector based representation where objects within the image can be vectorised and in later stages compressed in different ways and with different parameters. An example of segmentation is given below.

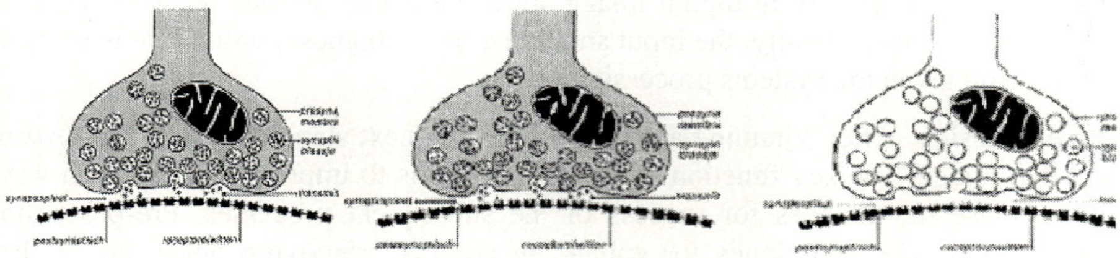

**Fig. 2.** The stages of segmentation; Original image; greyscaling and thresholding.

Segmentation based on the discontinuity criterion uses a two-step procedure: firstly a detection of the discontinuities (edges) that occur in the image and second grouping these points into contour points of objects. Modern approaches for segmentation combine methods based on both the homogeneous criterion and discontinuity criterion using region-based and edge-oriented segmentation methods. The output of the segmentation stage usually is raw pixel data constituting either the boundary of a region or the points in the region itself. In either case, converting the data to a form suitable for computer processing is necessary. Choosing a *representation* is only one part of the solution in transforming raw data into a computer readable form.

## 3 G2T System

Approaches, some of them also patented [9,10], that have been developed in the past to transform graphical information into tactile generally focus on the tactile printing and not on the transformation of the graphic information into tactile information. A tactile image should be in a plain and simple form and can be characterised from lines, texture, plane, volume and also colours. A careful balance between all these characteristics can only result in understandable and accessible drawings, which will contain sufficient amount of information to be comprehensible.

Varying levels of resolution can also give more or less details. The level required to return the necessary information depends on the picture. Figure 3 shows the transformation of an Ebola virus image automatically translated into a tactile form in three different detail stages. The software used is developed in the University of Delaware, at the Department of Electrical and Computer Engineering during a project dedicated to the conversion of real images into tactile drawings, which has engaged both image processing methods and tactile production techniques [11]. The tactile drawing produced can then be xeroxed onto microcapsule paper and fed through the Image Enhancer to produce the raised image [12].

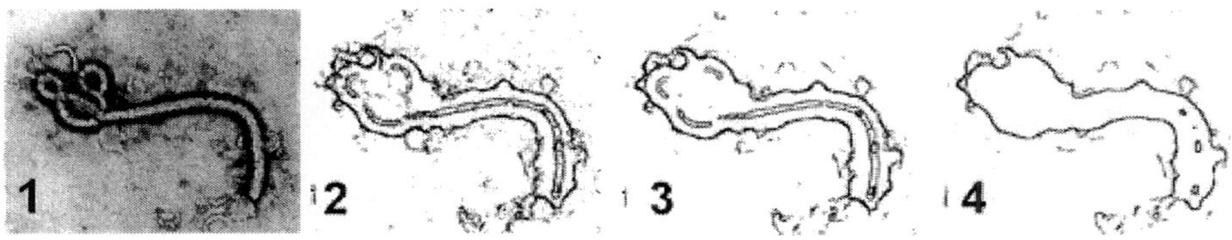


**Fig. 3.** Example of transformation of an Ebola virus image to a tactile drawing at various steps of the process.

Following work done elsewhere, several image processing techniques have been used for the G2T project, including edge detection, blurring, segmentation, negation and median filtering. The sequence of the applied techniques can be decisive for the outcome. Neural network techniques in combination with statistical measures have also been used [13] for the localisation of text regions in images where the document is not aligned on a plane front-parallel to the camera view and the size and greyscale of the text is unknown. An image segmentation method to automatically convert images into tactile form is proposed by Hernandez et. al [14]. This method is based on watershed transformation to interpret the gradient magnitude of an image as a geographical surface, where pixels having the highest gradient values correspond to the watershed lines [15,16]. Under the watershed interpretation, water placed on any pixel central to a common watershed line flows downhill to a common local minimum. All pixels draining to a common minimum form a catchment basin. Thus, catchment basins correspond to segmentation regions and watershed lines form closed region boundaries [17,18]. Although watershed-based methods have shown satisfactory results in several types of grey scale and colour images usually they result in numerous small regions (over-segmentation) which must be merged in order to obtain a meaningful final segmentation.

Intermediate segmentation results may not be as useful as the final results when displaying on tactile devices because boundaries separating light background regions from darker ones will provide wrong information to the tactile device. However, region mean value representations can be adapted to be displayed in the output tactile device. Different textures, representing each grey level in the regions obtained by segmentation, can be printed in microcapsule paper providing the user a way to explore not only the shapes of the main objects contained in the image but also their importance or hierarchy within it. That is, more important regions (objects) will be displayed in the tactile device using a particular texture that the user could associate with regions of high interest, while less important regions will be displayed using different patterns producing for the user the opposite effect.

The supporting idea behind the image processing methods to be used in G2T is to decompose the information that is found on an image into several layers, each of them holding specific part of the information. Those layers will hold information about colour, texture and contours that can be found in the image. By putting one layer on the other, the original image should be restored at the end. Each of the layers should be editable into a graphic application to refine the tactile diagram to be printed at the end by the libraries personnel.

### 3.1 G2T System Architecture

This section gives an overview of the G2T system architecture. The internal image format, the G2T system kernel, is also described and presented. Internally the G2T kernel works on bit planes. Every time the user imports an image, the application converts it to an internal G2T format. A byte array represents here RGB planes of the user's image. The size matches the resolution of a picture. If an image for example has a resolution of:

$$res = width * height$$

then an internal array gets a size s, of:

$$s = width * height * 3.$$

The factor of 3 is due to the fact that RGB images have 3 planes (namely R: Red, G: Green and B: Blue). Every plane gets its own representation for red, green and blue parts of the whole image. Greyscale images require that every colour plane containing the same value as other planes.

The kernel of the G2T system supports three main tasks:

- Handling user's input to select filters and parameters,
- Controlling the internal First-In-First-Out (FIFO) stack and
- Managing the current working image.

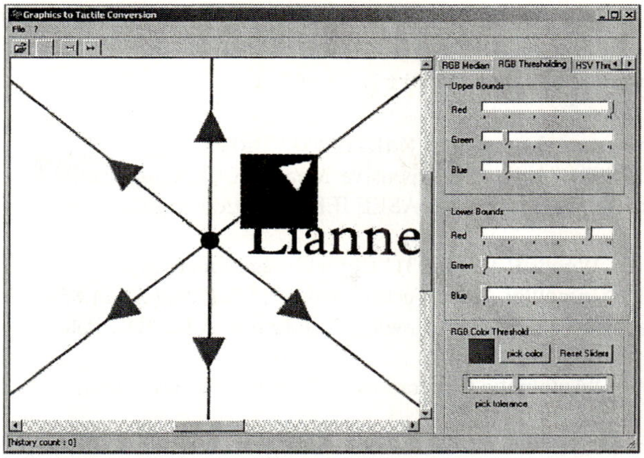


**Fig. 4.** Picture of the G2T user interface.

In the beginning a list of available filters is generated. Every filter is loaded dynamically into memory. The filters are not part of the kernel itself and are delivered as separate Dynamic Linked Libraries (DLLs). The G2T system accesses them with standard Win32 Application Program Interface (API) calls. The kernel then fills the filter list with pointers to every operator. To create input data, the user's image is loaded (I/O) into memory where the kernel applies the selected filters. Every operator needs at least two parameters to work properly:

- The first parameter shows the input data. In this part of the memory every filter can apply the implemented function.
- The second parameter is a parameter that shows where the output data should be written into.

Some of the filters that have been implemented also need additional parameters, which have to be set individually for each of them. The parameters can also be set to their default values (that is the initial status). Additionally, parameters can also be set from the Graphical User Interface through the kernel to selected operators.

## 4 Summary

The G2T system is currently being tested and the results from this evaluation will inform future developments. Full integration with existing production processes is currently underway.

## References

1. Crispien, K., Petrie, H., (1993) "Providing Access to GUI's for Blind People Using a Multimedia System.", 95th Audio Engineering Society, New York
2. http://www.nctd.org.uk/

3. Crombie, D., Lenoir, R, McKenzie, N., (2003) "Eye of the beholder" EVA2003, Institute of Archaeology, London, UK
4. http://www.ifla.org/IV/ifla65/65cp.htm
5. http://www.nfb.org
6. http://www.nctd.org.uk/MakingTG/index.asp
7. Bogess, L., (1999) "A Fast, Inexpensive Means of Creating Tactile Drawings of Graphs and networks for blind students", ASEE IEEE Frontiers in Education Conference, San Juan Puerto Rico
8. Gonzales, R.C., Woods R.E., (1993) "Digital Image Processing", Addison-Wesley.
9. Quzilleau, G., "Computer Aided Tactile Design", US Patent 5,574,830, 12. Nov. 1996
10. Erdos, G., Jankelewitz, E., Yankelewitz, S., Johnson, A.E., "UK Patent Application", GB 2 296 788, A, 10. July 1996
11. Way, T. (1996) "Automatic Generation of Tactile Graphics", Master Thesis, University of Delaware
12. Way, T, Barner K., (1996) "Towards automatic generation of tactile graphics", RESNA
13. Clark, P., Mirmehdi M., (2000) "Finding Text Regions using localised measures" 11th British Machine Vision Conference, BMVA Press
14. Hernandez, S.E., Barner, K.E., (2000) "Tactile-Imaging using Watershed-based Image Segmentation", ASSETS, Airlington, Virginia
15. Beucher, S. and Meyer, F., (1993) "The morphological approach to segmentation", Mathematical Morphology in Image Processing, Rochester, NY.
16. Vincent, L. and Soille, P., (1991), "Watersheds in digital spaces", IEEE Trans. Patn. Anal and Machn. Int
17. Haris, K., Efstratiadis, S.N., Maglaveras, N., Katsaggelos, A.K., (1998) "Hybrid image segmentation using watershed and fast region merging", IEEE Trans. Img. Proc
18. Gauch, J. M., (1999) "Image segmentation and analysis via multiscale gradient watershed hierarchies", IEEE Trans. Img. Proc

# Two Dimension Interactive Voice Browser for the Visually Impaired

Chi-Nung Chu[1,2]

[1] National Taiwan Normal University, Information & Computer Education, 162, Sec. 1, Hoping East Rd., Taipei, 106 Taiwan
[2] Chung Kuo Institute of Technology, Department of Management Information System, 56, Sec. 3, Shinglung Rd., Taipei, 116 Taiwan
nung@mail.ckitc.edu.tw

**Abstract.** Access to the World Wide Web is one of the major problems visually impaired people are confronted with. It is a good way to integrate voice functions into web browser for them to retrieve information on the web aurally. For the time being, most of the voice-driven navigation tools adopt linear strategy to translate each web page contents. That is too time-consuming for the visually impaired to get what they want. To promote the aural retrieving, this paper reports a Two Dimension Interactive Voice Browser design, which simulates the two dimensional reading of web page as sighted people do in a speech output / voice input interactive way. This interactive web browser with voice would supply a new opportunity for the visually impaired to access information through the Internet.

## 1 Introduction

Access to the World Wide Web is one of the major problems visually impaired people are confronted with. There are about half population connected to the Internet in Taiwan [4]. The WWW have become part of our daily life. As a key tool to get into the Internet, the graphic web browser such as Microsoft Internet Explorer and Netscape Communicator is what the most of people use in Taiwan to surf the WWW. However, the aging process will affect an individual's ability to use the standard Graphical User Interface (GUI). It turns using these traditional main stream browsers visually into obstacle for them to read the information from the World Wide Web. The browser with voice which can replace the mouse in most instances to enable hands-free browsing [9].

Sighted people depend upon many visual clues to help them find information on the Web [9]. It is a complex and contextual process developed from the individual's conceptual model. There is a need, therefore, to extract the key factors of web page reading for the design of web browser with voice to provide efficient access to the visually impaired.

This paper describes a preliminary design carried out with a specially modified web browser for the visually impaired. It focuses on improving the reading efficiency of voice browsers used by the visually impaired presently. That means to transcend the limitation of linear manipulation of web page reading. The idea is reduce the aural listening waiting by a two dimension model to support the users' reading strategies

K. Miesenberger et al. (Eds.): ICCHP 2004, LNCS 3118, pp. 721–724, 2004.

with voice interaction. And the existed web site can be read directly by the 2-D voice browser with no reconstruction to meet the visually impaired special needs. As the reading efficiency promoted, the author expects to get the visually impaired people up and get them running with the World Wide Web.

## 2 Related Works

Traditionally, web browsers are designed to interprete HTML file with the actions activated by mouse and keyboard. For the visually impaired, however, the use of alternative voice input and output might prove efficient for them to access the web sites [2]. Presently there are systems which allow voice-driven navigation, some with both voice-in and voice-out, and some allowing telephone-based web access.

The telephone-based web access uses the telephone keypad and voice command as an interface to navigate suitably configured pages. The users can then listen to the information from the handset. Phone-based browser implements the strategy to deploy a specific markup language such VoiceXML for speech rendering [6]. This approach allows the visual impaired people directly to interact with Web sites via spoken commands, and listen to prerecorded speech, music and synthetic speech.

Computer-based voice browsers, such as IBM Home Page Reader [5] and JAWS for Windows, are mainly synchronized with a moving cursor to make reading about web pages. This kind of standard HTML browser usually works in a sequential way. That means scanning from top to bottom and from left to right. Users can hear everything from descriptions of graphics to text in column format. Voice-activated browser also can navigate spoken selection of links within an extra frame with link lists extracted from the active page, such as ConversaWeb and BrookesTalk [1] [8].

However, even telephone-based web sites are built with more powerful voice-activated mechanism. It is intended for proprietary Internet Service Providers. And this new kind of markup language technology is still unfamiliar to lots of webmasters to reconstruct their web sites to meet the special needs of the visually impaired. These are the limitations to the telephoned-based web access for the visually impaired.

Intrinsically computer-based voice browser navigates web page in speech out for the visually impaired in a liner manner. The main distress for the visually impaired comes from waiting the voice browser to get the right place to read out the desired information. That would be a barrier for the visually impaired to access the web sites. Furthermore the voice browsers are mostly designed in English version. That is also a constraint for the non English users to manipulate it.

## 3 Two Dimension Interactive Voice Browser

The design of Two Dimension Interactive Voice Browser (Fig. 1) is based on the Microsoft Internet Explorer engine running on the Windows platform. The IBM ViaVoice Chinese text-to-speech synthesizer is embedded in charge of speaking web-based information aloud just as it is presented on the computer screen. Two Dimension Interactice Voice Browser is integrated into standard graphical browser and installed at the client side so that visually impaired people can work with sighted friends. Thus a range of adaptive interface, such as tool bar position arrangement, voice description for function button and magnifier, should be accommodated at the interface [3].

**Voice Interaction:** In order to provide better web page information access for the visually impaired, the Two Dimension Interactive Voice Browser will first speak out the structure of web page with coded number. The web page structure consists of frame, table and form and the coded number for these structure elements starts from one in increasing sequence with each page. To facilitate voice recognition, the voice commands are driven by speaking number which is selected by the user. Therefore the target area of the web page is focused just like what the sighted people do. The hyperlinks in the focused area are also read out for the user with coded number in the same ordering pattern of web page structure. If users do not choose the hyperlink coded number for further reading, then the browser will finally speak aloud the text content in the selected area for the users.

**2D Vocal Web Page Content Creations:** Normally Two Dimension Interactive Voice Browser is describing web pages to the users via Chinese Text-To-Speech output. The visually impaired could control the Two Dimension Interactive Voice Browser navigation by speaking number just like pressing telephone keypad. However, most web page designers create web pages without considering that the visually impaired might surf them by voice. Therefore much of the responsibility of creating a voice friendly web page relies on the web page designers. The Two Dimension Interactive Voice Browser analyzes the HTML files in accordance with the W3C WAI Guidelines [7]. According to some simple guidelines, the web page designers can often smooth the voice browsing perception for the voice voyagers without substituting the perception for traditional surfing users.

The 2D structure is rendered by analyzing some specific HTML tags and attributes within the tags. In order to make a voice friendly HTML page for the visually impaired to navigate, these tags and attributes would be better not omitted and have to be set up with clear and concise descriptions for the Two Dimension Interactive Voice Browser to generate a speech out dialog. Some key tags and attributes are interpreted by the Two Dimension Interactive Voice Browser as the following:

1. <TITLE>: The TITLE tag displays the title of an HTML document on the browser's title bar. Two Dimension Interactive Voice Browser speaks it out for users as it downloads one page from the web site.
2. Attribute "summary" in <Table>: This attribute provides a summary of the table's purpose and structure for Two Dimension Interactive Voice Browser rendering aural description to the users.
3. Attribute "title" in <Frame>: Two Dimension Interactive Voice Browse reads the frame title to facilitate frame identification and navigation for the users.
4. Attribute "alt" in <IMG>: Two Dimension Interactive Voice Browse reads out image representation of text to the users.

The use of attribute *alt* has been ignoring by the web page developers since it is unseen in the foreground. However, that is extremely important information for the voice browser to speak out for the visually impaired. There are still many other such attributes available in the HTML tags which can be found in the W3C WAI Guidelines for voice browser to interpret.

## 4 Conclusion and Future Work

The goal of this study is to find an efficient solution for the visually impaired to surf the World Wide Web. It is great for them to have opportunity to read the web pages as the sighted people do when they navigate the World Wide Web. The Two Dimension Interactive Voice Browser could decompose the web page structure into directories for the visually impaired to select via speaking number. Spoken number facilitates voice recognition. This is the similar manner to sighted people who select the desired area on the web page to read. Once one target area is selected, the visually impaired could listen to the content or choose the hyperlink with coded number in this area for further reading. With the IBM ViaVoice Chinese Text-To-Speech synthesizer, the visually impaired can read from hearing by themselves. With this approach the web designers have not to reconstruct web pages on the part of server and the visually impaired could listen to the web page efficiently with their own mother tongue.

A new version of Two Dimension Interactive Voice is currently under construction in which the functionality aims at conforming to the requirements of priority 2 and priority 3 initiated in the W3C WAI Guidelines about the visually impaired. As the web page developers get acquainted with W3C WAI Guidelines to construct their web sites. It would be possible for the voice browser to render more friendly and efficient speech out from standard HTML web pages. And the visually impaired can thus benefit from the voice browser to investigate the World Wide Web.

## References


1. Adaptive Technology Center Indiana University – Bloomington `http://www.indiana.edu/~iuadapts/convers2.html`
2. Hemphill, C., Thrift, P., Surfing the Web by Voice. Proceedings of ACM Multimedia, San Francisco, CA, November 7-9, (1995) 215-222
3. Chu, C. N., Chen, M. C., & Li, T. Y. The Design of an Adaptive Web Browser for Young Children with Reading Difficulties. Lecture Notes in Computer Science 2398, (2002) 189-190.
4. Computer Industry Almanac Inc., USA tops 160M Internet Users, `http://www.c-i-a.com/pr1202.htm, December 16 , (2002)`
5. IBM Accessibility Center, `http://www-306.ibm.com/able/`
6. Voice Extensible Markup Language (VoiceXML) Version 2.0. `http://www.w3.org/TR/voicexml20/`
7. Web Content Accessibility Guidelines 1.0, W3C. `http://www.w3.org/TR/WAI-WEBCONTENT/`
8. Speech Project Oxford Brookes University, `http://www.brookes.ac.uk/schools/cms/research/speech/btalk.htm.`
9. Zajicek M., Powell C. and Reeves C. (1998). A Web Navigation Tool for the Blind, In Proc. 3rd ACM/SIGAPH on Assistive Technologies, Los Angeles, USA.

# Exploring Scalable Vector Graphics for Visually Impaired Users

Martin Rotard, Kerstin Otte, and Thomas Ertl

Visualization and Interactive Systems Institute, University of Stuttgart
Universitätsstraße 38, 70569 Stuttgart, Germany
{rotard,ertl}@vis.uni-stuttgart.de
kerstin_otte@gmx.de

**Abstract.** Graphical information is very important in common information publishing. For visually impaired users this information is usually not accessible. Scalable Vector Graphics, a recommendation of the World Wide Web Consortium, describes graphical information in an XML document. We propose a transformation scheme into a tactile representation for this kind of graphics. Navigation modes, filters, and the output of meta information support the exploration of the graphics. Furthermore our software environment can simulate this transformation for all sizes of tactile devices.

## 1 Motivation

Nowadays it is common to have bitmap graphics on web pages. The information presented in images must be accessible to all users. For users with visual disabilities it is necessary to access this information with non-visual devices. Preparing bitmap graphics for visually impaired people in a tactile representation uses techniques like optical character recognition (OCR), because it is not possible to get any meta information like included textual content, shape type, descriptions, stroke width, etc. directly out of the graphics file [8, 10]. Fortunately the next generation of web pages will use vector graphics. The advantages of this kind of graphics are scalability, small file size and the property to store shapes, attributes, and meta information in a well defined way. Our research is based on the Scalable Vector Graphics [11] recommendation of the World Wide Web Consortium (W3C). SVG is an XML application, where shapes and attributes are encoded as plain text.

The main problems in preparing graphics for visually impaired people are the low spatial resolution and the binary mode (pins up or down) of tactile devices. Therefore graphics have to be scaled down and the colors have to be reduced to one foreground color and one background color. The additional information in SVG can be used for transformation, navigation, and filtering. The tactile output in combination with this additional information displayed on the braille line or offered by voice output makes the exploration much easier.

How to create SVG in an accessible way, can be found in guidelines of the Web Accessibility Initiative [7, 12]. Recent publications concerning accessing SVG for visually impaired people focus on specialized areas like extracting meta information [6], visualization of tactile maps [3] and transformation for tactile embosser [5].

K. Miesenberger et al. (Eds.): ICCHP 2004, LNCS 3118, pp. 725–730, 2004.

## 2 Graphics in SVG

In SVG two-dimensional graphics are described using XML. Therefore a set of basic shape elements is defined e.g. lines, rectangles, circles, ellipses, polygons, paths, etc. The position, size, color, etc. of each shape is defined by attributes. Additionally there are special tags to group shapes <g> and reference self-defined symbols <use>. SVG provides a possibility to add alternative descriptions of the content. Therefore each element can include a title and a description tag (<title> and <desc>).

The SVG source code example below describes a series resonance circuit. Each component in the circuit is represented in a group that contains the component itself and the conductor paths. A title and a description of each group, the shape of the component, and the lines of the conductor paths represent this. In SVG 147 color keyword names are defined, e.g. *black* can be written instead of the value "rgb(0, 0, 0)" and *olive* instead of "rgb(128, 128, 0)".

```
<?xml version="1.0"?>
<!DOCTYPE svg PUBLIC "-//W3C//DTD SVG 1.1//EN"
  "http://www.w3.org/Graphics/SVG/1.1/DTD/svg11.dtd">
<svg width="440" height="100">
  <title>Series Resonance Circuit</title>
  <desc>A resistor, capacitor and coil in series</desc>

  <g transform="translate(10,40)"
     stroke="black" stroke-width="2">
    <title>Resistor</title>
    <desc>Graphical symbol of a resistor</desc>

    <line x1="0" y1="30" x2="40" y2="30" />
    <rect x="40" y="20" width="50" height="20"
          fill="none" />
    <line x1="90" y1="30" x2="130" y2="30" />
    <text x="60" y="0" font-family="Arial"
          font-size="24">R</text>
  </g>
 (...)
</svg>
```

An SVG viewer can render the graphical representation of this circuit. Figure 1 shows the graphical output by Squiggle, the SVG viewer of the Apache Batik project [1]. On mouse over Squiggle shows the title and description of a shape or group in a tooltip.

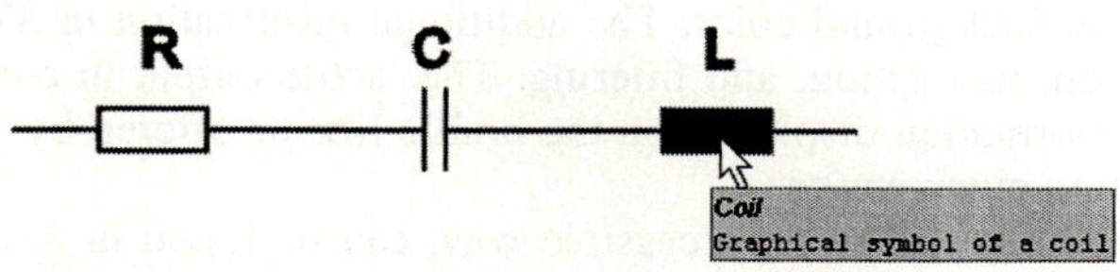


**Fig. 1.** Series resonance circuit in SVG.

## 3 SVG Transformation Scheme for Visually Impaired People

We have developed a software environment for transforming SVG into a representation, which is accessible for visually impaired people. Our environment makes it possible to navigate in the graphics and use filters. We designed our environment to be used directly by the visually impaired users as well as a simulation environment for our development (see Figure 2).

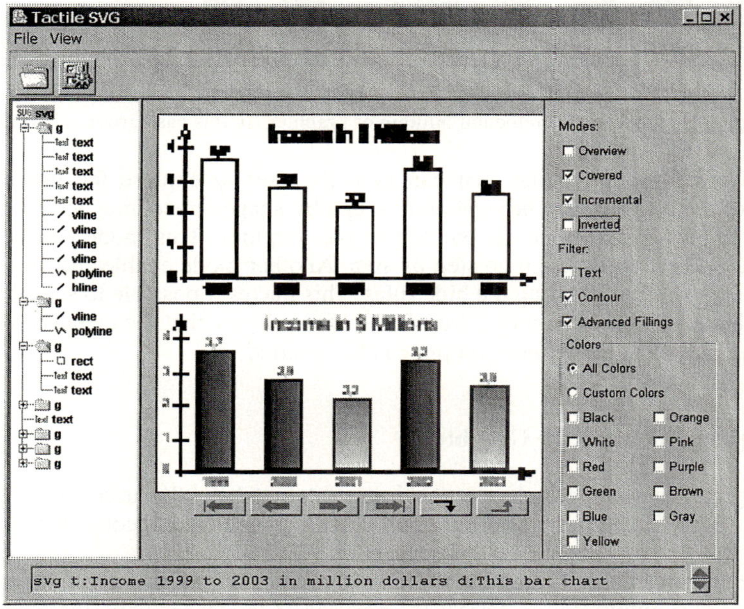


**Fig. 2.** Software simulation environment (scaled original graphics is at the bottom and in this example the outline filtered graphics is at the top).

The down scaled, but original graphics and the color reduced, filtered, shape separated graphics are displayed on the screen. Pins up is displayed in black and pins down in white color. There is also a simulation of a braille line, where meta data of the current shape like textual content, title, description, color, and other parameters are shown. Additionally this information is presented as voice output. For developers the shape hierarchy is displayed in a tree view. The size of the output and the length of the braille line depends on the used devices and can be configured. In our environment it is possible to zoom in/out and scroll the graphics by the user.

### 3.1 Navigation in Graphics

There is a simple concept of navigating through the shapes of a graphics. In our environment the user can navigate to the next/previous shape using the command "show next/previous element". If the current element is a group element, it can be entered and left again. This could be done recursively in each group. There are also commands to view the first or last element in a group. One command shows the whole graphics. This can be useful to get an overview about the position of the current shape in the graphics.

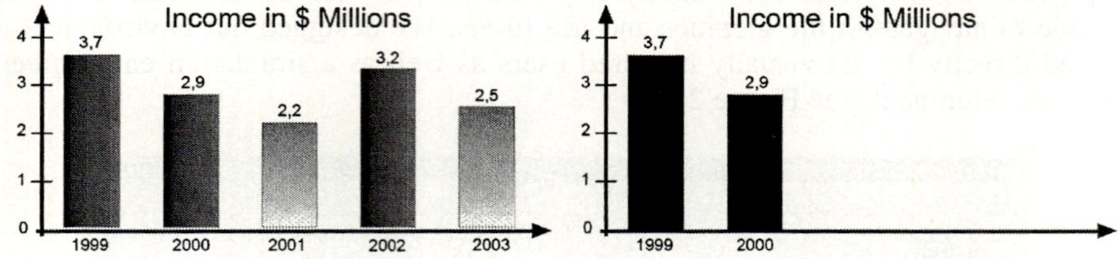


**Fig. 3.** Original and incremental buildup of graphics (in this case group by group).

There are different modes that can help the user to explore the graphics. The buildup of the graphics can be separately shape-by-shape or accumulated incremental. Figure 3 shows the incremental buildup of the graphics. This mode can be used in groups as well, to build them up step by step. Another mode enables the user to view the elements without minding the hide rules. This makes it possible to see a car in one piece, which is partly hidden by a tree. If the user realizes, that the negative version of the output would be better, each output can be inverted.

### 3.2 Appling Filters to the Graphics

We integrated some filters to our environment that help the users to explore the graphics. Each filter can be selected in all situations and can be combined with other filters.

In our transformation scheme SVG text is extracted and presented on the braille line or as voice output. In most cases the position of the text is very important. A text filter extracts the content of text elements and shows their position on the graphics by blinking.

Filtering of colors is necessary because the output on tactile devices is binary (pins up or down). By using color filters it is possible to show just the shapes of a specific color. The color filters can be combined with color filters of an other specific color. This makes it possible to view e.g. just black and red shapes. To have a color filter for every color in the color space is not feasible. In our approach all colors (or SVG color keyword names) are mapped to a limited number of colors. For this color subset we are using the "basic color terms" established by Brent Berlin and Paul Kay [2]. These "basic color terms" consists of the colors white, black, gray, red, pink, yellow, green, blue, purple, brown and orange. We determine the mapped color by the lowest distance in the L*a*b color space [9]. Using color filters will show the suitable shapes with a color similar to the chosen color. If some distances are about the same, the object is shown for all of the corresponding color filters. For additional information the original color value or nearest SVG color keyword name (mentioned above) is printed on the braille line and given by voice output. A color filter of a specific color can only be selected if there is an element in this specific color in the diagram. Figure 4 shows the color filtering result of the original graphics.

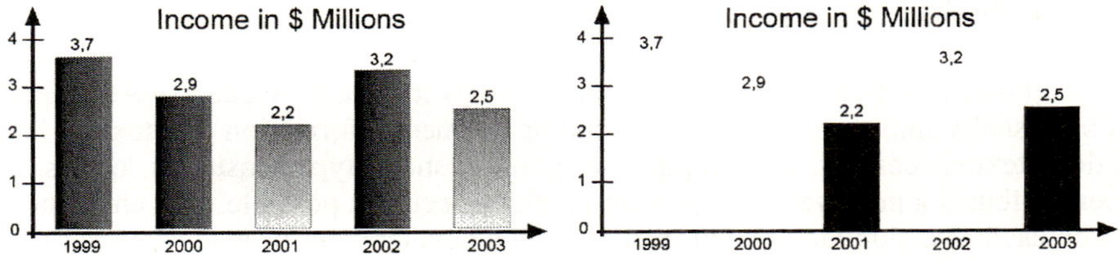


**Fig. 4.** Original and color filtering result (filtered colors are black and green).

Graphics for sighted users are often hard to discretise for tactile devices. Especially gradients and textures of elements are hard to prepare for this usage in a good way. A filter removes the gradients and textures, but keeps the elements. In this case the user is informed that the gradient or texture of the current element is removed. An outline filter draws just the outlines of shapes or groups. In figure 2 the outline filtering result is shown at the top. This filter can be used to get an overview about the whole graphics.

## 4 Preliminary Results

A first evaluation of our software environment by a visually impaired colleague in our group has shown that our approaching is very promising. As equipment we used a tactile device from Metec, which has 120 to 60 tactile pins (see Figure 5). Our software environment was developed in Java. For rasterizing we used the Batik SVG Toolkit [1]. The voice output is based on FreeTTS [4]. Our system has a flexible interface, to which other tactile devices can be integrated easily. Therefore our results are not restricted to this special hardware.

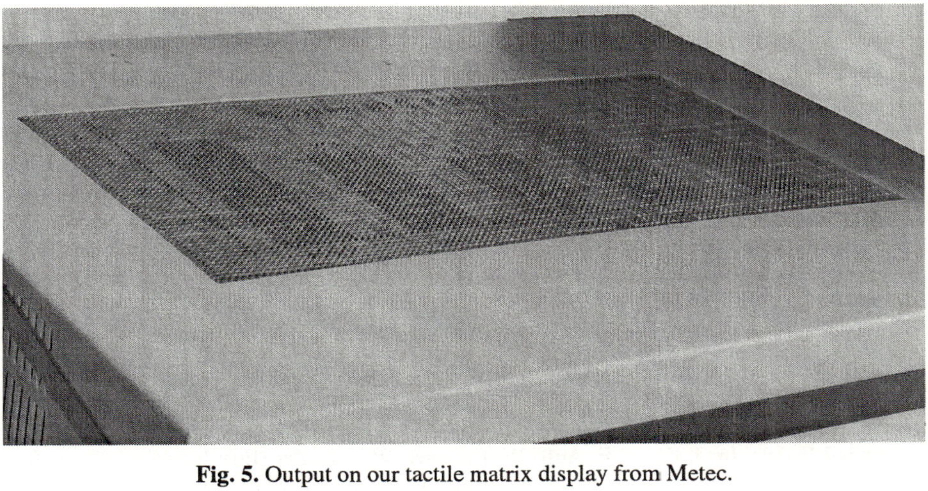

**Fig. 5.** Output on our tactile matrix display from Metec.

## 5 Conclusion

We proposed a software environment and methods to access Scalable Vector Graphics by visually impaired people. By including all meta information like textual information (textual content, titles, and descriptions), shape type, positions, colors, and other attributes a new way of exploring graphics becomes possible. Our environment can be used as a simulation environment for the development of new extended methods in presentation of tactile graphical information.

The next version of our software environment will be able to extract SVG in HTML files. The users will be able to navigate to the next or previous SVG. The color matching in the L*a*b color space can be more effective if we use just the *a* and *b* component and consider the luminance separately. Furthermore it might be useful to integrate the access to bitmap graphics into our system.

## Acknowledgements

We would like to thank Waltraud Schweikhardt, Alfred Werner, Andreas Hub, and Daniel Weiskopf for their help to finish this paper and for the fruitful discussions.

## References

1. Apache XML Project: Batik, http://xml.apache.org/batik/, April 2004
2. Berlin, Brent; Kay, Paul: Basic Color Terms: Their Universality and Evolution. Berkeley and Los Angeles. University of California Press, 1969
3. Campin, Benjamin; Brunet, Louis; McCurdy, William; Siekierska, Eva: SVG Mapping for People with Visual Impairment, SVG Open 2003, http://www.svgopen.net/2003/papers/svgmappingforpeoplewithvisualimpairments/, 2003
4. Kwok, Philip; Lamere, Paul; Schröder, Marc; Vos, David; Walker, Willie: FreeTTS - A speech synthesizer written entirely in the Java programming language, http://freetts.sourceforge.net/, 04.04.2004
5. Gardner, John A.; Bulatov, Vladimir: Smart Figures, SVG, and Accessible Web Graphics, Proceedings of the Technology And Persons With Disabilities Conference, 2001
6. Herman, Ivan; Dardailler, Daniel: SVG Linearization and Accessibility, Proceedings of the SVG Open Conference 2002, http://www.svgopen.net/2002/papers/herman_dardailler_svg_linearization_and_accessibility/, 2002
7. Jackson, Dean: Making Accessible SVG, SVG Open 2003, http://www.svgopen.net/2003/paperAbstracts/making_accessible_svg.html, 2003
8. Kurze, Martin: Giving Visually impaired People Access to Graphics, In: Heinz-Dieter Böcker (Ed.): Proceedings of the Software-Ergonomie '95, Workshop Nicht-visuelle graphische Benutzungsoberflächen, 1995
9. McLaren, K.: The development of the CIE 1976 (L*a*b*) uniform colour space and colour-difference formula, Journal of the Society of Dyers and Colourists 92, 1976
10. Schweikhardt, Waltraud: Interactive Exploring of Printed Documents by Visually impaired People, In: J. Klaus, E. Auff, W. Kremser, W.L. Zagler (Ed): Interdisciplinary Aspects on Computers Helping People with Special Needs, ICCHP96, Linz, Austria, 1996
11. W3C: Scalable Vector Graphics, http://www.w3.org/Graphics/SVG/, April 2004
12. W3C: Web Accessibility Initiative, http://www.w3.org/WAI/, April 2004

# Communication System for the Blind Using Tactile Displays and Ultrasonic Pens – MIMIZU

Makoto Kobayashi[1] and Tetsuya Watanabe[2]

[1] National Universities Corporation Tsukuba College of Technology,
Kasuga 4-12-7, Tsukuba City, Ibaraki, Japan
koba@cs.k.tsukuba-tech.ac.jp
http://www.cs.k.tsukuba-tech.ac.jp/labo/koba/
[2] National Institute of Special Education,
Nobi 5-1-1, Yokosuka City, Kanagawa, Japan
twatanab@nise.go.jp
http://www.nise.go.jp/research/kogaku/twatanab/indexEn.html

**Abstract.** A new Communication system for the blind has been developed. The system, named MIMIZU, is composed of a pair of terminals equipped with refreshable tactile graphic display and ultrasonic pen device. Using the terminal, a blind user can make drawings directly as he likes on the tactile surface with ultrasonic pen. The other blind user can recognize the tactile image appeared on the other terminal by touching it. In this way, the system can support communication between blind users by means of tactile graphics. We describe results of simple experiments in which a subject tried to transmit simple drawings to the other subject. The results show difficulty of transmitting a shape of circle without preliminary information because resolution of the display was not enough. However, it is useful to transmit shapes composed of straight lines. And even if the shape is a circle, the user can recognize it when he has information in advance.

## 1 Introduction

Needless to say, it is important for the blind to read and understand graphical information using tactile sense. To acquire the information, they usually use tangible materials such as embossed pictures or drawings on the swell paper or reliefs of foil. Undoubtedly these tangible materials are available for them to make up spatial information. Early research reported even if the person would have no visual experiment, he could do simple matching task between tangible pictures [1]. On the other hand, it seems that the drawing work is not so common in the daily life of the blind, in spite of they can use graphical information and there are drawing tools for the blind like raised-line drawing kit. We think one of the reasons is that those tools do not allow the user to erase the drawing lines. Therefore, we started a project to develop an "erasable" drawing system for the blind.

TDraw [2], composed of a thermo pen and a swell paper on a digitizer, is one of the systems of drawing tool for the blind. But this system is not erasable because it aims to record how the blind make drawings and analyze a mental model they have, so it is more important to have function of making smooth line than to realize erasable

K. Miesenberger et al. (Eds.): ICCHP 2004, LNCS 3118, pp. 731–738, 2004.

function. Our standing was slightly different from it. We mainly focused on the function of erasing.

After several months, a system composed of refreshable tactile graphic display units and input stylus pen connected with beam arms with angler sensors was developed [3]. We named the system MIMIZU, which means a kind of worm in Japanese, for the motion of the tactile display. When the system runs, it calculates the position of the stylus pen tip from the length of the beam arms and its angle information. Then, the tactile pin under the tip was raised when the user wants to draw, and it was lowered when he wants to erase. We know the dot matrix approximation is not so good to express drawings including several line segments, but there is no choice to realize an erasable tactile display except dot matrix refreshable display by now.

In this paper, we will report improvement of the system. The new version of MIMIZU has more expanded tactile area and convenient stylus pen thanks to an ultrasonic technology. In addition to these improvements, it becomes tactile communication system by connecting a pair of the display terminals through network.

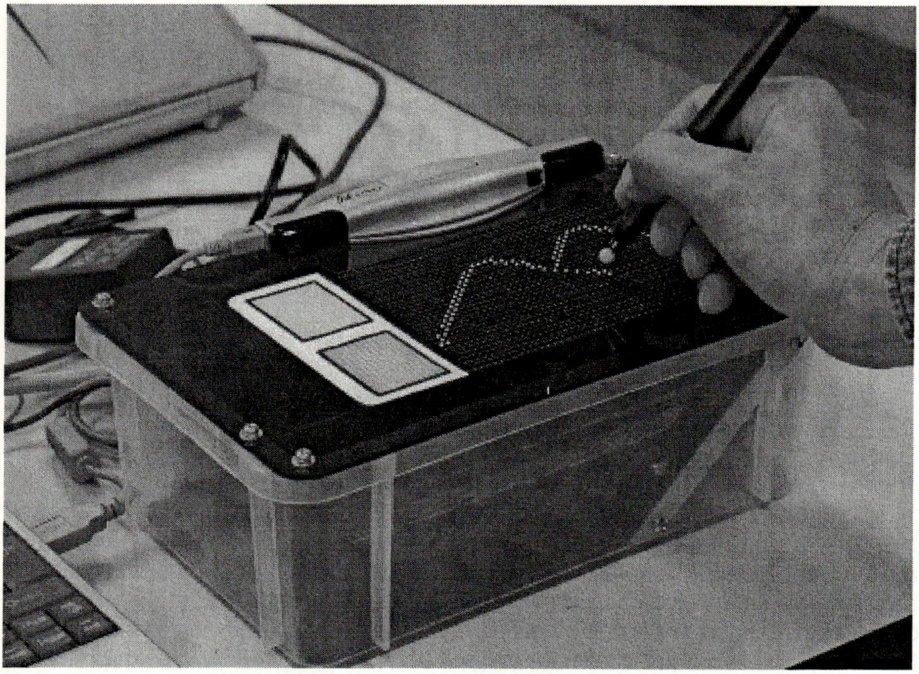

**Fig. 1.** This figure shows an overview of a terminal of MIMIZU. It is composed of ultrasonic stylus pen device, and refreshable tactile graphic display. The user can make a drawing on the display with the stylus and erase it partially. The same drawing appears on the other terminal

## 2 System Constructions

As mentioned above, MIMIZU is basically composed of a refreshable tactile graphic display, an input device, and a computer, which controls those devices. Fig. 1 shows an overview of the terminal of MIMIZU on use. We assembled a pair of terminals and connected the controlling computers via network cables. The detail of the system is explained as below.

## 2.1 Tactile Graphic Display

The area of the tactile graphic display is doubled compared to the first version of MIMIZU. It measures 144mm by 96mm, including 1536 pins arranged in a matrix of 48 pins on columns and 32 pins on rows. The inter-pin spaces are 3 mm, and the pin stroke is 0.7mm. the principle of driving those pins is using piezoelectric actuator, similar to a general Braille display. By adding high voltage electricity, stick-shaped actuator bends to upper the pin. The actuators are controlled by an LSI unit. The LSI receives controlling signal from a computer. Fig. 2 shows an overview and the principle of SC-5, the tactile display unit that we use as a component to make tactile surface.

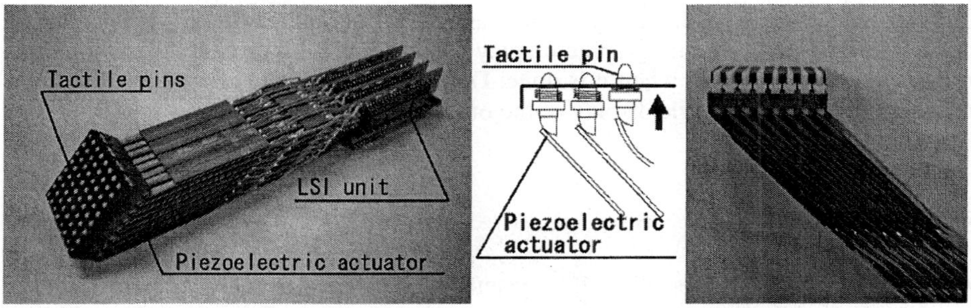


**Fig. 2.** Left figure shows an overview of SC-5, the tactile graphic display unit. Middle figure is the principle of driving pins. Right figure is the side view of SC-5 without top cover

## 2.2 Stylus Pen Utilizing Ultrasonic Technology

Utilizing ultrasonic technology to the stylus pen is the most drastic improvement of the new version of MIMIZU. Its measurement principle is as follows: The pen tip of the stylus has a micro switch and transducers. And a pair of receivers set on the tactile surface. At first, the pen tip emits ultrasonic and infrared signals when the user presses the stylus pen on the surface. Then, the each receiver detects the distance from itself to the pen tip using differences of reaching speed between those two signals. Finally, the receivers lead the position of the pen tip by triangulation method. The advantage of using this device is its flexibility. The stylus pen is not bound to the body of the system any longer. The user can use several terminals (if they are prepared,) without changing the styluses. On the contrary, its disadvantage is that the user has to pay attention not to obstruct the signals from the pen tip to the receivers. In other words, in case the user follows non-dominant fingers to the pen tip for supporting the motion, he has to keep out the fingers between the pen tip and the receivers. Sighted user doesn't need to pay such attention, however, it requires some practices for the blind user to get used to the stylus device.

### 2.3 Functional Scheme

Basically, the system realizes the simple function to draw/erase a drawing on the tactile graphic display. The drawings are shared on each terminal by communicating the drawing data. Also, a function to file the drawings to the hard disk drive is prepared.

When the program runs, the computer waits the user use the stylus pen. If the user moves the stylus pen over the tactile graphic display, the computer calculates the position of the pen tip, and controls the tactile pins under the pen tip. When the running mode is set as "drawing", the computer sends a signal to raise a pin under the pen tip to the tactile display units. On the other hand, when the mode is set as "erasing", the tactile pins under the pen tip will be lowered. Thus, the user can draw and erase an arbitrary part of the drawings by moving the stylus. While the user is making a drawing or erasing it, the computer plays a certain sound file that depends on which running mode is chosen. The sound helps the user to judge which action they are doing at that moment. To change the running mode, the user has to tap a square area prepared by the side of the tactile area (see Fig. 1) with the stylus pen. Also, the user can make all raised pins lower by tapping an area of the other square. i.e., the action causes surface of the tactile graphic display clear. To help to confirm the action, another sound file is played when it is done. During these drawing operations, the same drawing appears on a tactile display of the other terminal.

## 3 Experiment

As described in previous section, this system was designed to make interactive communication for blind users between each other. However, as a first step, we would like to know how correctly the drawing travels from one user to the other user. Therefore, we made a simple experiment like "telephone game" using tactile drawings. One subject who was a sender was required to touch and feel a target picture printed on a swell paper. Then, the sender made a drawing using MIMIZU terminal. The other subject who was a receiver felt a tactile image on the other terminal during the sender is drawing. At last, the receiver made a drawing using raised line drawing kit and a ballpoint pen to express what he/she feels in his/her mind. Through this procedure, it was difficult to remove an effect that comes from each subjects' tactile sensitivity and drawing skill. So the end of a set of the experiment procedure, each subject was required to make drawings, feeling the target pictures on the swell paper. Comparing those drawings made by subject, we made consideration.

### 3.1 Participants

A pair of blind participants was volunteered. Both of them had normal tactile sense and were Braille readers. They usually used tactile materials to get information in studying. Subject A was a male, who has a little light perception on right eye, but could not distinguish the number of the fingers in front of him. Subject B was a female, who is totally, congenitally blind. The age of both subjects is twenty.

### 3.2 Experimental Procedure

At first, they were explained about the MIMIZU system with its function and how to use it. Then, the procedure of the experiment was informed to them exclusive of the kinds of tactile pictures presented. We prepared four types of pictures printed on swell papers. They would be eight types of stimuli by present with upside down. The experiment was composed of two sets.

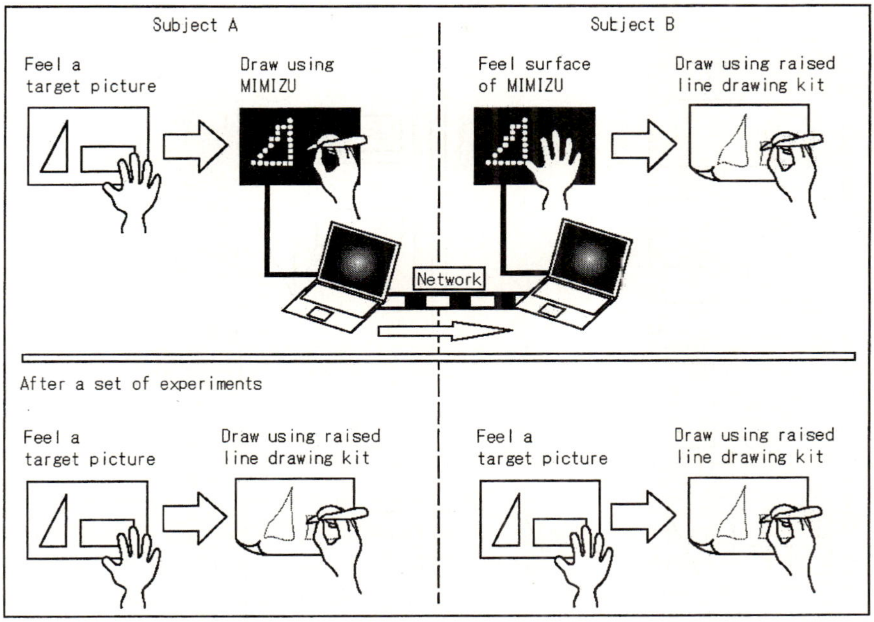


**Fig. 3.** Experimental procedures of the first set are shown in this figure. The main purpose of the experiment is to clear how correctly a picture transmits from one side to the other side. It was designed as a "telephone game" using tactile picture and MIMIZU. After a set of experiment, each subject was required to draw the target picture using raised line drawing kit to subtract the effect of each subject's skill of feeling and drawing

In the first set, Subject A was required to send the target picture to Subject B. Four trials were conducted using four target pictures. After finishing the transmitting experiments, both subjects were required to draw each target picture using raised line drawing kit feeling the original target pictures on the swell papers. A square frame was drawn to the raised line drawing papers in advance. It represents the tactile area. The main flow of the first set is shown in the Fig. 3.

In the second set, the subjects changed their roles. Subject B send the target pictures to Subject A. This time, the four target pictures were set upside down. As same to the first set, they ware required to draw original target pictures after the set was finished. All sequence of the experiment was recorded by two digital video cameras to observe a process of making and touching a drawing.

### 3.3 Results and Consideration

Fig. 4 shows the prepared target pictures printed on swell papers and the drawing answers made by receiver subject using raised line drawing kit. The four cases on the left show the results of the first set. They were transmitted from Subject A to Subject B. The four cases on the right show that of the second set. It was transmitting from Subject B to Subject A. They did not talk to each other about the shapes of drawings, so the results are gained only from tactile information.

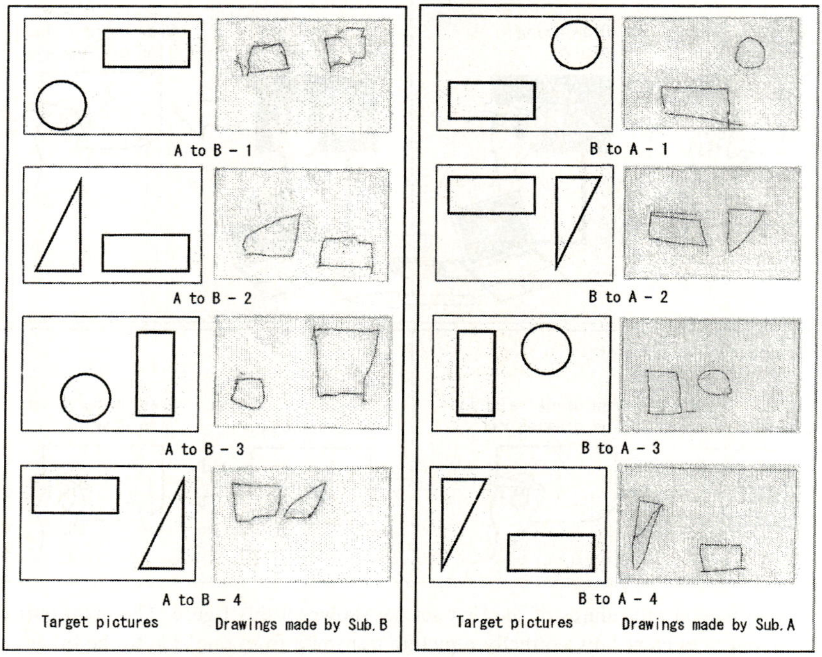


**Fig. 4.** Prepared target pictures printed on swell papers and drawing answers made by each receiver subject. The left four cases are results of the first set, from Subject A to Subject B. The right four cases are those of second set, from Subject B to Subject A

We can simply say that the results in the right four cases, the second set, seem to have correctly reproduced the original target pictures. It is observed that there are some deviances from square frame in those cases, but they were mainly caused by the receiver's haptic sense and drawing skill. It was clear from the fact that receiver made almost same drawings when he touched the target picture directly. On the other hand, the results in the left four cases, the first set of the experiment, seem to have not correctly reproduced the target pictures. The big difference of condition between the first and second set is, "In the second set, the receiver (Subject A) had some knowledge of what kind of pictures would appear in advance." In other words, MIMIZU is available to help to transmit simple images like the target pictures, if the receiver has some knowledge about it.

On the other hand, it is observed that difficulty to transmit the shape of circle from the result of the case of "A to B -1" and the case of "A to B – 3." One of the reasons is that they were not used to the system yet in the first case. Generally, it is said that drawing a circle without visual sense is difficult, as Subject A commented. Furthermore, we think the resolution problem effected strongly. Dot matrix approximation is not appropriate to express a shape with curved lines like a circle. In those two cases, Subject B realized a circle as a small square. She felt the line as straight because the circle that Subject A drew was composed of short straight lines.

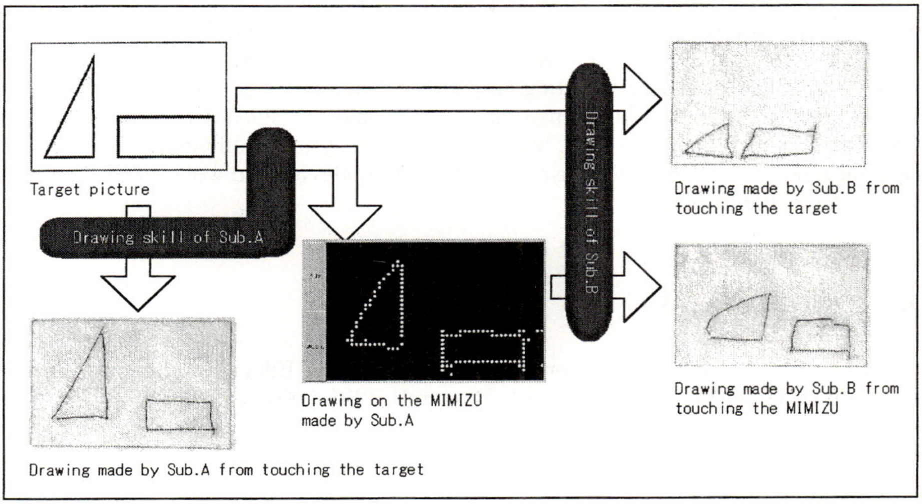


**Fig. 5.** An analyzing chart of the case of "A to B – 2." By comparing drawings made by both subjects, we can consider the effect of each subjects' drawing skill and possibility of MIMIZU to transmit a picture information

To give the first set further consideration, we made an analyzing chart shown in Fig. 5. It is an example of case "A to B – 2" in the Fig. 4. The left upper figure is the target picture. The left lower figure is a drawing made by the sender while touching the target picture. The center figure is a drawing made by Subject A on the tactile surface of MIMIZU. And the same tactile image appears on the terminal in front of the Subject B. The right upper figure is a drawing made by Subject B while touching the target picture. The right lower figure is the answer drawing made by Subject B. The height of the left triangle in her drawing seems lower than the original triangle in the target picture. From the chart, it is clear that the reason was the drawing skill of Subject B. Subject A made relatively correct drawing on the MIMIZU, and Subject B made almost the same drawing even if she touched the original target. However, about upper-side line of the right rectangle, a little bump made by Subject A affected the answer drawing. It means that little bump on the straight line in the dot matrix approximation affects strongly receiver's imagination. Therefore, in the future work, we should make some support function to make straight lines like drawing software for sighted users.

## 4 Conclusions and Future Work

Taking all results into consideration, we can conclude that:

- Some preliminary information is available for the receiver.
- Dot matrix approximation of the present system is not sufficient to express curved line.
- A Little bump on a straight line affects the image the receiver will have.

These conclusions seem not to be so good and are naturally expected. However, we don't take these results pessimistically. We are sure that tangible information is valuable to communication between blind users, even if it is transmitted incorrectly to some extent. The faculty of operating tangible pictures differs greatly from one person to another, so the users should use tangible graphics as subsidiary information to verbal communication. Of course, the usability of the system is important. We have to keep on research to improve the usability of the input device and we need high resolution in the tactile display.

## Acknowledgements

This research was partially supported by the Ministry of Education, Science, Sports and Culture, Grant-in-Aid for Scientific Research, 2003-2004, 15500400.

## References


1. Heller, A.M., Brckett, D.D., and Scroggs, E.: Tangible Picture Matching by People Who Are Visually Impaired. Journal of Visual Impairment & Blindness, May, (2002) 349-353
2. Kurze, M.: TDraw: A Computer-based Tactile Drawing Tool for Blind People. ASSETS'96, Vancouver, (1996) 131-138
3. Kobayashi, M., Watanabe, T.: A Tactile Display System Equipped with a Pointing Device – MIMIZU-. Computers Helping People with Special Needs, 8th ICCHP2002, Springer-Verlag (2002) 527-534

# Directly Accessible Mainstream Graphical Information

John A. Gardner and Vladimir Bulatov

ViewPlus Technologies, Inc.,
1853 SW Airport Avenue, Corvallis,
OR, 97333, USA
FAX: +1 (541) 738 6505
John.Gardner@ViewPlus.com
http://www.ViewPlus.com

## 1 Introduction

Plain text in well-authored electronic documents of nearly any format is accessible to a blind person who knows how to use a computer and screen reader. A great deal of common information is generally not presented as plain text however. Charts, diagrams, and graphs are common in business, scientific, and most professional literature. Maps and geographically-oriented data such as weather maps and complex census information would be virtually impossible to present in words. Until recently it has not been possible for authors of mainstream literature to present graphical information of these kinds in a format that could be accessed directly by blind people. In this paper, a new technology is described that does permit blind people to have direct access to most object-oriented graphical information. This new technology is possible because of two recent developments. One is the emergence of the mainstream SVG (Scalable Vector Graphics) language. The second is the Tiger technology for embossing tactile graphics.

SVG (SVG 2004), is a new XML graphics language recommendation of the World Wide Web Consortium (Jackson 2002; Eisenberg 2002). The SVG format permits graphical objects to have title and description attributes, and these attributes are used to ensure that SVG graphical information can be accessed by people with print disabilities who cannot easily understand the visual representation. These attributes are not visible when the SVG graphic file is displayed in a conventional SVG viewer but can be displayed and, if desired, spoken by users of a new accessible SVG Reader application. The titles are displayed/spoken when selected with the mouse. Blind users can emboss a tactile copy of the SVG graphic, place it on a touch-sensitive pad, and select objects by pressing on the tactile copy.

This technique of enhancing tactile information with additional audio was pioneered by Parkes (Parkes 1988, 1991, 1995, 1998; Parkes and Brull 1997) and used extensively to provide graphical information to blind users (Loetzsch 1994; Loetzsch and Roeder 1996; Landau 2003). Properly used the tactile plus audio information is known to provide excellent access to blind users. Bulatov and Gardner (Bulatov and Gardner 1998; Gardner 2002; Gardner and Bulatov 1998, 2001, 2003, Gardner et al. 1997) have explored the feasibility of using mainstream graphics languages accessed by the tactile/audio method.

K. Miesenberger et al. (Eds.): ICCHP 2004, LNCS 3118, pp. 739–744, 2004.

## 2 Scalable Vector Graphics

SVG development was begun in 1999 as a project of the World Wide Web Consortium (W3C 2004) with major participation by Adobe, Apple, Canon, Corel, Hewlett-Packard, Macromedia, Microsoft, Kodak, Sun and many others. The SVG 1.0 recommendation (SVG 2001) was published in September 2001. Nearly all graphics authoring applications permit authors to export graphics as SVG, and there are numerous SVG-specific applications commercially available.

SVG is a powerful language permitting animation and interactivity, but its most prevalent use is currently as a compact format for conveying static vector graphics on the web and in other electronic media. Its compactness and scalability are the major advantage of SVG over bit maps, currently the most common format for web and other electronic graphics. The inclusion of title and description attributes in the SVG specification along with other features promoting accessibility make SVG a nearly ideal language for creating accessible graphics. Accessibility is not automatic however. An author must include adequate titles for important graphic objects if an SVG file is to be accessible. Some chart or graph creation applications could include all titles and data so that the resulting SVG export could be automatically accessible. At the present time, SVG files can be made accessible only with a ViewPlus SVG file editing application that is scheduled for release in the latter part of 2004.

## 3 Tiger Embossing Technology

The Tiger embossing technology was developed within the Science Access Project (SAP 2004) at Oregon State University (Sahyun et al. 1998a, 1998b) and subsequently expanded and commercialized by ViewPlus (Gardner 2002, Gardner et al. 2002, Walsh and Gardner 2001). Tiger technology is capable of embossing with a resolution of 20 dots per inch or equivalently 400 dots per square inch, and with variable height dots. The ViewPlus embossers utilizing this technology include the Pro (100 Braille characters per second, paper widths to 16 inches), the Max (60 Braille characters per second, paper width to 11.5 inches), the Cub (50 Braille characters per second, paper widths to 8.5 inches), and the Cub Jr. (30 Braille characters per second, paper width to 8.5 inches).

All ViewPlus embossers are accessed by Windows applications through the normal print command just as any Windows printer. Graphics are reproduced normally as height-resolved gray-scale images in which black areas produce high dots, and light gray areas low dots. Text and graphics can co-exist and be embossed. Braille text will be embossed as Braille whereas standard fonts, e.g. Arial, Times Roman, emboss as graphic images.

The variable dot height embossing capability and standard Windows printer interface for ViewPlus embossers permit a blind user to create a tactile copy of most graphic images whose major features are tactually identifiable. This is a critical necessity for blind users to have any chance to access mainstream graphics. Tactual accessibility can be optimized by users through a variety of user commands that presently or in the near future include ability to change contrast and brightness, to emboss outlines only, and to emboss colors as distinctive patterns.

## 4 New ViewPlus Accessible SVG Technology

The first commercial end-user products supporting the accessible SVG technology are a touch-sensitive pad and the accessible ViewPlus SVG Reader Windows software application. The touch-sensitive pad attaches to the user's computer through a USB port and requires no other power. Once installed, the user needs to follow a very simple calibration step to assure that the image on the computer monitor corresponds exactly to the position of the corresponding tactile image on the touch-sensitive pad. The calibration needs to be done only once unless the page setup is changed to print with different margins or to a different paper size. The touch-sensitive pad is optimized for use with A4 or 8.5 x 11 paper.

Once the touch-sensitive pad is installed, a blind user having access to a ViewPlus embosser needs only the accessible SVG file. The user opens the file in the Accessible SVG Reader, prints a copy on the Tiger embosser, and places the copy on the touch-sensitive pad. The user presses on an object and hears the computer speak the name of that object. For example, on a map showing all the countries of Europe, a user can press on a country and hear its name. If the author has included additional information about that country in the optional description field, the user can hear the description. If the user wants to review information, she can switch to a text window and browse anything that has been spoken. This capability makes it possible for authors to include wordy descriptions. All spoken information is also readable in Braille using any common Braille screen reader.

The map of Europe includes large and small countries. While it may be possible to distinguish Germany, France, Spain, Italy, and other large countries on an A4 embossed image, the Benelux countries, Monaco, Andorra, Liechtenstein, and other small countries are nearly impossible to distinguish tactually. Fine details even of large countries are also often not tactually distinguishable. Therefore a user will probably want to zoom the image to enlarge features of interest. There are a number of ways to do this. The SVG Reader permits one to zoom in or out and to pan left, right, up, or down. These are very useful for sighted users and are useful for fine adjustments by blind users. However the two most useful zoom features for blind users are the ability to select an object and zoom it to maximum size. For example, if a user is lucky enough to click on Luxembourg while browsing the full map, she can click on the "fit selection to window" item in the View menu. Alternatively a user may select the "zoom rectangle" menu item, then select two points that define the diagonally-opposite corners of a rectangle that will been zoom to maximum size permitted by the current window. One makes a copy of the zoomed image on the ViewPlus embosser, and then explores the zoomed image. One can always return to the full Europe map with the "fit to window" menu item.

When a user prints an image on the embosser, the computer saves the parameters of that image. If at a later time one wants to return to that particular image, one can place the tactile copy on the touch-sensitive pad, choose the "open from bar code" menu item, and touch a tactile "bar code" on the image to recall the correct file and zoom display to the screen. There are several alternative methods for providing the "bar code" information, eventually including a standard ink bar code.

In some cases, users may need to read graphics files in locations remote from a ViewPlus embosser. In such a case the reader would need the SVG files and embossed copies of all files. If several zoom views are needed, the specially recorded zoom information recalled by the bar code would also be needed. These can be prepared by the user and taken to another remote computer or can be prepared by another person.

Few mainstream graphical documents are made without some text, a title, or labels on some objects, or as scale factors on graphs and bar/column charts. Typical text made for sighted people is far too small for a tactual image to be meaningful without being enlarged by a factor of three or more. Consequently, text in a SVG graphic is usually not even possible to identify as text. Nonetheless, when a text object is pressed, the text is spoken, so a blind user can "read" titles and text labels on graphics. A user option permits one to replace the 20 dpi text images (that are little more than tactual noise) as special "text patterns" that are more readily identifiable. These text and graphics user options provide an experienced blind user with tools that can make almost any image (in accessible SVG format anyhow) usable.

**Fig. 1.** Photograph of young blind woman examining a US map using the ViewPlus SVG Reader computer application and ViewPlus touch pad. The ViewPlus Cub Tiger tactile graphics and braille embosser is on her left. Any graphic on screen can be embossed on the Cub and placed on the touch pad

These end-user products require that the SVG files be made accessible by providing titles for all important graphical objects. ViewPlus will market an SVG Editor software application that provides a user-friendly way to add such titles to existing SVG files. The editing process is very simple if the SVG file has well-defined objects. Common authoring programs such as CorelDraw and Adobe Illustrator can provide good SVG exports if an author is careful in defining the graphical objects. The MS Visio 2003 application, which is a chart/diagram-making program, is particularly well suited for creating excellently organized SVG files. Authors who export SVG files from Visio 2003 can make them fully accessible simply by opening the file in the ViewPlus SVG Editor, opening the title attributes of all important objects, and typing in the names.

## Acknowledgements

The authors are grateful to the National Eye Institute, National Institutes of Health for a SBIR (Small Business Innovation Research) grant supporting development of end user hardware and software. They thank the National Science Foundation for a SBIR grant supporting development of authoring/editing software.

## References

1. Bulatov, V., Gardner, J. (1998) Visualization by People without Vision. Proceedings of the Workshop on Content Visualization and Intermediate Representations, Mont-real, CA, August 15, 1998, pp 103-108
2. Eisenberg, J.D. (2002) SVG Essentials. O'Reilly Media, Inc, ISBN: 0-596-00223-8
3. Gardner, J. (2002) Hands-on Tutorial on Tiger and Win-Triangle. Proceedings of the 2002 CSUN International Conference on Technology and Persons with Disabili-ties, Los Angeles, CA, March 20-23, 2002 http://www.csun.edu/cod/conf/2002/proceedings/300.htm
4. Gardner, J., Bulatov, V. (1998) Non-Visual Access to Non-Textual Information through DotsPlus and Accessible VRML. Computers and Assistive Technology ICCHP'98. Proceedings of the 15th IFIP World Computer Congress, 31 August, -. 4 September 1998, Vienna and Budapest,
5. Edwards, A., Arato, A., Zagler, W. eds, Austrian Com-puter Society on behalf of the IFIP, Vol 118 pp 136-140 Gardner, J., Bulatov V (2001) Smart Figures, SVG, and Accessible Web Graphics. Proceedings of the 2001 CSUN International Conference on Technology and Persons with Disabilities, Los Angeles, CA, March 21-24, 2001 http://www.csun.edu/cod/conf/2001/proceedings/0103gardner.htm
6. Gardner, J., Bulatov, V. (2003) Complete Access to All Paper and Computer Forms, Tables, and Charts. Proceedings of the 2003 CSUN International Conference on Technology and Persons with Disabilities, Los Angeles, CA, March 17-20, 2003 http://www.csun.edu/cod/conf/2004/ proceedings/162.htm
7. Gardner, J., Bargi Rangin, H., Bulatov, V., Kowallik, H., Lundquist, R. (1997) The Problem of Accessing Non-Textual Information On The Web. Proceedings of the 1997 Conference of the W3 Consortium, Santa Clara, CA, April, 1997 (http//dots.physics.orst.edu/publications/www6.html)
8. Gardner, J., Stewart, R., Francioni, J., Smith, A. (2002) Tiger, AGC, and Win-Triangle, Removing the Barrier to Sem Education. Proceedings of the 2002 CSUN Interna-tional Conference on Technology and Persons with Disabilities, Los Angeles, CA, March 20-23, 2002 http://www.csun.edu/cod/conf2002/proceedings/299.htm
9. Jackson, D. (2002) SVG on the Rise. O'Reilly Web DevCenter publication, O'Reilly Media, Inc, http://www.oreillynet.com/pub/a/javascript/2002/06/06/ svg_future.html
10. Landau, S. (2003) Use of the Talking Tactile Tablet in Mathematics Testing. Journal of Visual Impairment and Blindness vol. 97 pp 85-96
11. Loetzsch, J. (1994) Computer-Aided Access to Tactile Graphics for the Blind. Proceedings of the 4th International Conference on Computers Helping People, Vienna 1994, Lecture Notes in Computer Science vol 860, Springer-Verlag pp 575-581
12. Loetzsch, J., Roedig, G. (1996) Interactive Tactile Media in Training Visually Handicapped People. New Technologies in the Education of the Visually Handicapped, Proceedings of the Conference, Paris, June 10-11, 1996, Burger, D. (Ed) INSERM John Libbey 1996, pp 155-160

13. Parkes, D. (1988) Nomad: an Audio-Tactile Tool for the Acquisition, Use and Management of Spatially Distributed Information by Partially Sighted and Blind Persons. eds Tatham AF and Dodds AG, Proceedings of the Second International Symposium on Maps and Graphics for Visually Handicapped People, King's College, University of London, pp. 24-29
14. Parkes, D. (1991) Nomad: Enabling Access to Graphics and Text Based Information for Blind, Visually Impaired and Other Disability Groups. Conference Proceedings, Vol. 5. World congress on Technology 1991, Arlington, Virginia, pp. 690-714
15. Parkes, D. (1995) Access to Complex Environments for Blind People Multi-Media maps, Plans and Virtual Travel. Proceedings of 17th International Cartographic Conference, Barcelona Vol 2. pp 2449-2460
16. Parkes, D. (1998) Tactile Audio Tools for Graphicacy and Mobility. A Circle is either a Circle or it is not a Circle. The British Jurnal of Visual Impairment, Vol 16 pp 98 – 104
17. Parkes, D., Brull, M. (1997) It May Not be Easy, but it is Possible a New Form of Literacy. The World Blind, Journal of The World Blind Union, Vol 14 pp. 48-50
18. Sahyun, S., Bulatov, V., Gardner, J., Preddy, M. (1998a) A How-to Demonstration for Making Tactile Figures and Tactile Formatted Math Using the Tactile Graphics Embosser. Proceedings of the 1998 CSUN International Conference on Technology and Persons with Disabilities, Los Angeles, CA, March 1998 http://www.csun.edu/cod/conf/1998/proceedings/csun98_103.htm
19. Sahyun, S., Gardner, J., Gardner, C. (1998b) Audio and Haptic Access to Math and Science - Audio graphs, Triangle, the MathPlus Toolbox, and the Tiger printer. Computers and Assistive Technology, ICCHP '98, Proceedings of the 15th IFIP World Computer Congress, 31 August - 4 September 1998, Vienna and Budapest, Edwards, A., Arato, A., Zagler, W. eds, Austrian Computer Society on behalf of the IFIP,Vol 118, pp 521-523
20. SAP (2004) Science Access Project web publication overview of project. Oregon State University, http://dots.physics.orst.edu/
21. SVG (2001) SVG Recommendation 1.0. Web reference publication by the W3C, http://www.w3.org/TR/SVG/
22. SVG (2004) Scalable Vector Graphics. Web reference publication by the W3C, http://www.w3.org/Graphics/SVG/
23. Walsh, P., Gardner, J. (2001) Tiger, a New Age of Tactile Text and Graphics. Proceedings of the 2001 CSUN International Conference on Technology and Persons with Disabilities, Los Angeles, CA, March 21-24, 2001 http://www.csun.edu/cod/conf/2001/proceedings/0128walsh.htm
24. W3C (2004) Continually updated web publication describing the work of the World Wide Web Consortium. http://www.w3.org

# Simple Pattern Creation Using a Pen Input Guide and Sound Localization for the Visually Impaired


Masahiko Sugimoto[1,2], Kazunori Itoh[2], and Michio Shimizu[3]

[1] Takushoku University Hokkaido College, Memu 4558
Fukagawa-shi, 074-8585 Japan
sugimoto@takushoku-hc.ac.jp

[2] Faculty of Engineering, Shinshu University, Wakasato 4-17-1
Nagano-shi, 380-8553 Japan
itoh@cs.shinshu-u.ac.jp

[3] Nagano-ken College, Miwa 8-49-7
Nagano-shi, 380-8525 Japan
michio@nagano-kentan.ac.jp



**Abstract.** In this report, we examine whether or not a visually impaired person can make a formal basic figure by himself. The patterns that we treat in this report are restricted to a collection of lines. In order to make formal patterns, we prepared an acrylic pen input guide and put it on a tablet. This guide has a 9 by 9 lattice of holes which correspond to 9 by 9 localized sounds on a 2-dimensional virtual sound screen. Using this guide and a stylus pen, the visually impaired can make a pattern. The input pattern is checked and corrected by hearing the localized sound. Experiments show that the subjects can input simple patterns correctly.


## 1 Introduction

Generally, representing information to a visually impaired person is performed using the senses of hearing and touch. A well known method using the sense of hearing is a so-called screen reader, which reads out text. The way of expressing a figure pattern has also been examined and various methods have been proposed, e.g. [1, 2, 3]. We have tried the sound localization approach [4] which can be used as a computer interface. This method has the advantage of low cost compared with a method using the sense of touch [5] or 3D virtual audio space techniques [6].

We have examined how a visually impaired person can recognize characters, a simple figure, or a layout on a plane using a 2-dimensional virtual sound screen [7], [8]. Through psychological experiments using our system, subjects have correctly recognized simple patterns. Note that these patterns are created by normal sighted people. We also found that our method can support the drawing of handwritten geometric figures such as circles and triangles by a visually impaired person [9].

In this report, we examine whether or not a visually impaired person can make a formal basic figure by himself. The patterns that we treat in this report are restricted to a collection of lines. In order to make a formal pattern, we prepare an acrylic pen input guide and put it on a tablet. This guide has a 9 by 9 lattice of holes which correspond to the 9 by 9 localized sounds on a 2-dimensional virtual sound screen. Using


K. Miesenberger et al. (Eds.): ICCHP 2004, LNCS 3118, pp. 745–752, 2004.

this guide and a stylus pen, a visually impaired person makes a pattern. The input pattern is checked and corrected by hearing the localized sound or a series of sounds. Experiments show that the subjects can input simple patterns correctly.

## 2 Virtual Sound Screen

We have been studying methods to represent positions using sound localization, which use psychological hearing characteristics. Fig.1 illustrates the virtual sound screen. Its vertical axis is audio frequency and its horizontal axis is the interaural level differences between the ears. Its known that high frequency sounds tend to be perceived as an image with a high position, whereas for low frequency sounds the situation is reversed. Sounds that are uniquely characterized by frequency and interaural level difference are called localized sounds.

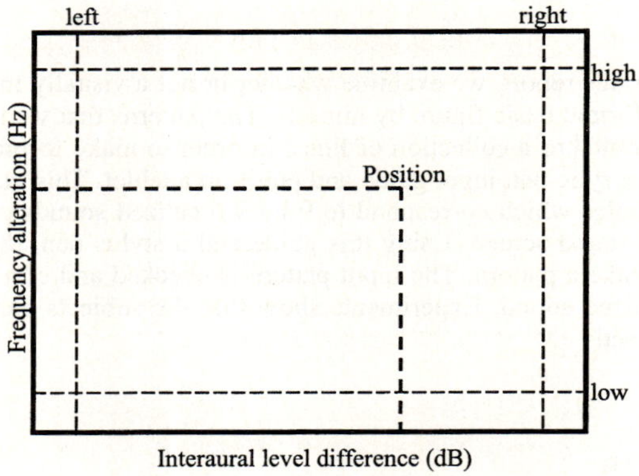


**Fig. 1.** Virtual sound screen.

## 3 Pattern Making System

In order to investigate the possibility of pattern creation, we developed a pattern making system in MS-Windows. Our system consists of a PC, a pen tablet, the pen input guide described previously, the sound board and headphones, and does not use any other special hardware. We examine the possibility that a visually impaired person can make a formal basic figure by himself. The patterns that we treat in this report are restricted to a collection of points and lines. The input tool used is a pen input guide which is put on a tablet (Fig. 2). To make a pattern, a sequence of points is input with this tool. The input pattern can be checked and corrected using a 2-dimensional virtual sound screen.

The pen input guide is made of an acrylic board, which has a matrix of 9 by 9 (=81) holes. The board size is 54 x 54mm with a thickness of 3mm. The hole diameter is 4mm and the hole depth is 1.5mm. There are three function holes above the input guide: DATA-INPUT, DATA-SAVE and SOUND-DISPLAY.

**Fig. 2.** Pen input guide on a tablet.

The 81 holes on the input guide correspond to 81 discrete localized sound positions on the virtual sound screen. Fig. 3 illustrates the discrete localized sound positions. The sounds corresponding to the vertical axis of the screen use different frequencies. Low frequencies correspond to low positions and high frequencies correspond to high positions on the screen.

Each display point is divided logarithmically from 500Hz to 3000Hz. The horizontal axis is expressed by 9 interaural level differences of two adjacent localized sounds set at 5 dB. Frequency alteration is generated by 9 individual wave files. Interaural level difference is generated by the volume control of the left and right channels.

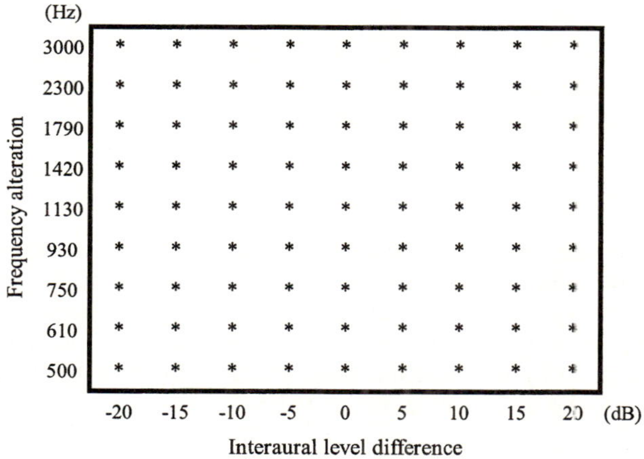


**Fig. 3.** Discrete localized sound positions.

When a visually impaired person points to a hole with a pen and clicks a button on the side of the pen, the coordinate point of the hole is added to a temporary file. If he points to the hole again, a localized sound is outputted so that he may notice that the hole is already registered. If he would like to delete the point, he clicks the side button of the stylus pen. He can input a series of positions and he also can modify the input data. This work may be done mainly through the sense of touch, but the support of sound is also important.

The pattern is displayed by outputting the localized sounds for the input points one after another. A point is displayed for a duration of 30 msec after which a 10 msec silent interval is inserted. If the sounds of two adjacent points output one by one within a short time interval, it can be recognized to be a line by the psychological movement sense of the localized sound [7]. If two points are adjacent, they are displayed for an interval of 250 msec, and if not joined, in a time interval of 2000 msec. The order of the pattern display is the same order of creation. Fig. 4 shows an example of a created pattern.

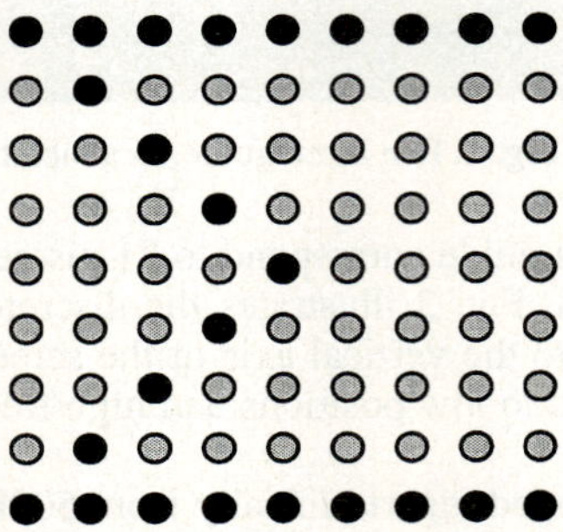

**Fig. 4.** An example of a created pattern.

## 4 Experiments and Results

The possibility that a visually impaired person can create a basic figure using our input tool and sound feedback is examined. The subjects used in the experiments are three sighted persons wearing eye masks.

### 4.1 Point Input

When subjects create the patterns, they have to recognize the starting positions of the patterns. We first tried the experiment to accurately determine the starting positions on the tablet. The total number of input points was 81 and each point position was randomly presented to the subjects by position number (Table 1). Blind subjects can select the input point by touching the holes and they can hear the localized sound by pushing a pen into the desired hole on the tablet.

**Table 1.** The position number of each input point.

Vertical position

| | | | | | | | | |
|---|---|---|---|---|---|---|---|---|
| 80 | 81 | 82 | 83 | 84 | 85 | 86 | 87 | 88 |
| 70 | 71 | 72 | 73 | 74 | 75 | 76 | 77 | 78 |
| 60 | 61 | 62 | 63 | 64 | 65 | 66 | 67 | 68 |
| 50 | 51 | 52 | 53 | 54 | 55 | 56 | 57 | 58 |
| 40 | 41 | 42 | 43 | 44 | 45 | 46 | 47 | 48 |
| 30 | 31 | 32 | 33 | 34 | 35 | 36 | 37 | 38 |
| 20 | 21 | 22 | 23 | 24 | 25 | 26 | 27 | 28 |
| 10 | 11 | 12 | 13 | 14 | 15 | 16 | 17 | 18 |
| 00 | 01 | 02 | 03 | 04 | 05 | 06 | 07 | 08 |

Horizontal position

The characteristics of recognized accuracy and input time for the three subjects are similar, so that the experimental results are shown by the average. The average input time of each point position is shown in Fig. 5. We found that input time was longest for the center position on the tablet and the average input time was about 10 seconds. When a subject wants to select the center hole on the tablet, he does not go directly to this position. At first, he looks a corner. After that he leads the pen to the desired hole in the horizontal and vertical directions.

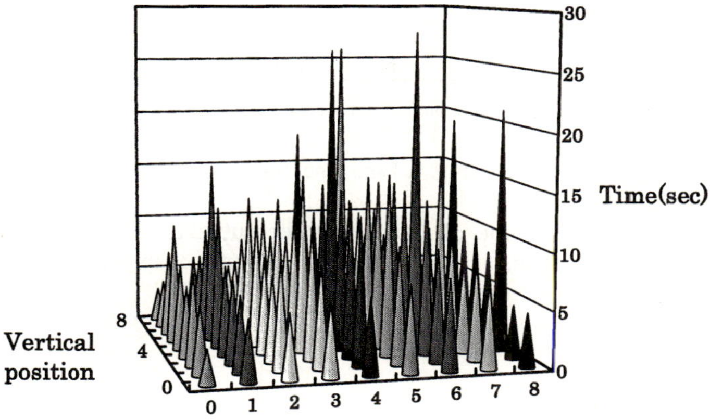


**Fig. 5.** The average of input time in each point.

## 4.2 Line Input

We also experimented with line input. Fig.6 (a), (b) and (c) show the three patterns used in the experiments. Three different types of lines - vertical, horizontal, and diagonal – of made of nine continuous point positions were used. The accuracy and the input time of each line were investigated. Each line was assigned a number and before the tests the subjects were shown the relationship between the corresponding numbers. Randomly selected lines were shown to the subjects. When subjects push the SOUND-DISPLAY hole, they can check the correct line input.

| | | | | | | | | |
|---|---|---|---|---|---|---|---|---|
| **80** | 81 | 82 | 83 | 84 | 85 | 86 | 87 | 88 |
| **70** | 71 | 72 | 73 | 74 | 75 | 76 | 77 | 78 |
| **60** | 61 | 62 | 63 | 64 | 65 | 66 | 67 | 68 |
| **50** | 51 | 52 | 53 | 54 | 55 | 56 | 57 | 58 |
| **40** | 41 | 42 | 43 | 44 | 45 | 46 | 47 | 48 |
| **30** | 31 | 32 | 33 | 34 | 35 | 36 | 37 | 38 |
| **20** | 21 | 22 | 23 | 24 | 25 | 26 | 27 | 28 |
| **10** | 11 | 12 | 13 | 14 | 15 | 16 | 17 | 18 |
| **00** | 01 | 02 | 03 | 04 | 05 | 06 | 07 | 08 |

(a) A vertical line

| | | | | | | | | |
|---|---|---|---|---|---|---|---|---|
| **80** | **81** | **82** | **83** | **84** | **85** | **86** | **87** | **88** |
| 70 | 71 | 72 | 73 | 74 | 75 | 76 | 77 | 78 |
| 60 | 61 | 62 | 63 | 64 | 65 | 66 | 67 | 68 |
| 50 | 51 | 52 | 53 | 54 | 55 | 56 | 57 | 58 |
| 40 | 41 | 42 | 43 | 44 | 45 | 46 | 47 | 48 |
| 30 | 31 | 32 | 33 | 34 | 35 | 36 | 37 | 38 |
| 20 | 21 | 22 | 23 | 24 | 25 | 26 | 27 | 28 |
| 10 | 11 | 12 | 13 | 14 | 15 | 16 | 17 | 18 |
| 00 | 01 | 02 | 03 | 04 | 05 | 06 | 07 | 08 |

(b) A horizontal line

| | | | | | | | | |
|---|---|---|---|---|---|---|---|---|
| 80 | 81 | 82 | 83 | 84 | 85 | 86 | 87 | **88** |
| 70 | 71 | 72 | 73 | 74 | 75 | 76 | **77** | 78 |
| 60 | 61 | 62 | 63 | 64 | 65 | **66** | 67 | 68 |
| 50 | 51 | 52 | 53 | 54 | **55** | 56 | 57 | 58 |
| 40 | 41 | 42 | 43 | **44** | 45 | 46 | 47 | 48 |
| 30 | 31 | 32 | **33** | 34 | 35 | 36 | 37 | 38 |
| 20 | 21 | **22** | 23 | 24 | 25 | 26 | 27 | 28 |
| 10 | **11** | 12 | 13 | 14 | 15 | 16 | 17 | 18 |
| **00** | 01 | 02 | 03 | 04 | 05 | 06 | 07 | 08 |

(c) A diagonal line

**Fig. 6.** Line patterns.

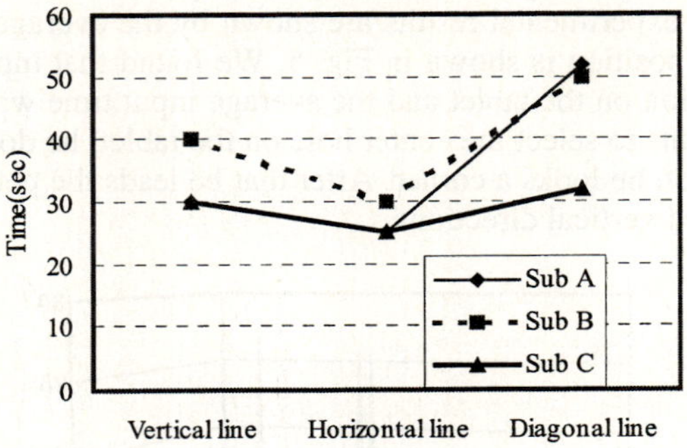


**Fig. 7.** Line input time.

Fig. 7 shows the input time of lines for three subjects. The input time was the shortest for the horizontal lines. Through the results of this experiment, we may conclude that input time and skill operation are fairly related.

### 4.3 Form Input

Since the accuracy of line input was very good, we tested simple figure patterns with similar experiments. Fig. 8 shows 15 form input patterns which consist of several straight lines. We selected these patterns because they are similar. Fig. 9 shows the form pattern input times for three subjects. The input time for simple figure patterns rose from 40 sec to 90 sec for subject C as the number of strokes increased.

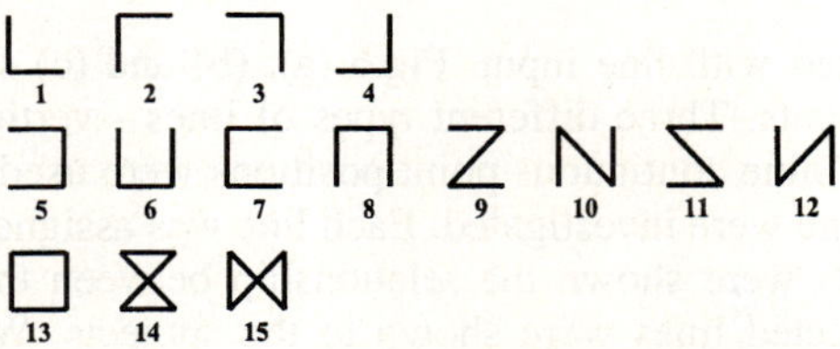


**Fig. 8.** Form patterns.

## 5 Conclusion

We investigated whether or not it is possible for the visually impaired to make a formal figure using a pen input guide and a virtual sound screen. Through psychological experiments using our system, the subjects can input simple formal patterns, which shows that our method can be applied to the pattern making for the visually impaired. In future work, we would like to conduct several experiments upon subjects who are visually impaired. As an application of our method, we would like to investigate the auditory representation of the mini-go game and personal digital assistant usage.

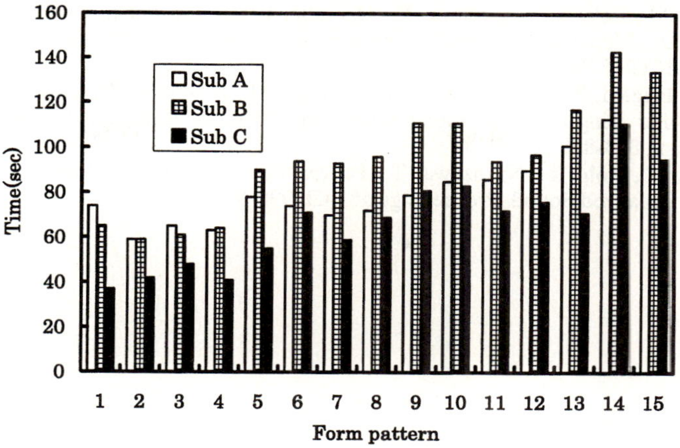


**Fig. 9.** Input time in form patterns.

## Acknowledgment

This work was partly supported by the Grant-in-Aid for Scientific Research No.15500063 (C)(2) from the Ministry of Education, Culture, Sports, Science and Technology in Japan.

## References

1. Kamel, H.M., Roth, P., Shiha, R.R.: Graphics and User's Exploration via Simple Sonics(GUESS): Providing Interrelational Representation of Objects in a Non-visual Environment. Proceedings of the 2001 Inter. Conf. on Auditory Display, 261-266 (2001)
2. Brown, L.M., Brewster, S.A., Ramloll, R., Burton, M., Riedel, B.: Design Guidelines for Audio Presentation of Graphs and Tables. Proceedings of the 2003 International Conference an Auditory Display, Boston, MA, USA, 6-9(2003)
3. Cronly-Dillon, J., Persaud, K., Gregory, R.P.F.: The perception of visual images encoded in musical form: a study in cross-modality information transfer. Proceedings Of The Royal Society Of London Series B-Biological Sciences, 266, 2427-2433(1999)
4. Blauert J.: Spatial Hearing. The psychophysics of Human Sound Localization, MIT Press, Cambridge, MA (1983)
5. Brenner W., Mitic S., Vujanic A., Popovic G.: Micro-Actuation Principles for High-Resolution Graphic Displays. Proceedings of International Conference on Computer Helping People with Special Need, 503-510 (2000)
6. Kawai Y., Kobayashi M., Minagawa, M., Tomita F.: A Support System for Visually Impaired Persons Using Three-Dimensional Virtual Sound. Proceedings of ICCHP2000, 327-334 (2000)
7. Itoh K., Shimizu M., Yonezawa Y.: A Drawing Support System for the Virtually Impaired Computer User using a Virtual Sound Screen. Design of Computing Systems, Elisevier, Amsterdam, 401-404 (1997)

8. Shimizu, M., Itoh, K., Yonezawa, Y.: Operational Helping Function of the GUI for the Visually Disabled using a Virtual Sound Screen. Proceedings of the ifip99 world computer congress(ICCHP '98), 387-394 (1998).
9. Itoh, K., Inagaki, Y., Yonezawa, Y., Hashimoto, M.: A Support System for Handwriting for the Blind using a Virtual Sound Screen, Symbiosis of Human and Artifact, Elisevier, Amsterdam, 803-808 (1995)
10. Shimizu, M., Itoh, K., Nakazawa, T.: Pattern Representation System using Movement Sense of Localized Sound. Proceedings of HCI, 990-994 (1999)

# An Approach for Direct Manipulation by Tactile Modality for Blind Computer Users: Principle and Practice of Detecting Information Generated by Touch Action

Makoto Shimojo[1], Masami Shinohara[3], Michiyo Tanii[2], and Yutaka Shimizu[2]

[1] Univ. of Electro-Communications, Dept. of Mechanical Engineering & Intelligent Systems
182-8585 Chofu, Japan
shimojo@mce.uec.ac.jp
[2] Univ. of Electro-Communications, Dept. of Systems Engineering
182-8585 Chofu, Japan
{satsuki,shimizu}@se.uec.ac.jp
[3] National Institute of Advanced Industrial Science & Technology
305-8566 Tsukuba, Japan
m-shinohara@aist.go.jp

**Abstract.** A basic device combining a tactile display function and a touch position/force direction sensing function is proposed. The trial device consists of two major components, a tactile graphic display and a 6-axis force/torque sensor. The force sensor measures six dynamic values generated by touch action on the display surface and a PC estimates the point based on the data and a simple dynamic principle. Preliminary investigation indicated the validity of this device and its promising capability for HC using tactile modality.

## 1 Introduction

The spread of graphical user interfaces (GUI) made personal computers easier to use. Users can now directly operate their computer through various visual objects in the so-called "WYSIWYG" style. However, although this style of communicating with a PC is convenient for sighted persons, it is inaccessible for blind persons, and so much effort has been made to overcome the difficulty. For example, several application programs that select visual information which can be converted into text form and convey it as synthesized speech or Braille are already on the market. These programs effectively assist blind PC users, but are still insufficient for conveying nonlinguistic information.

The concept of the tactile graphic display was therefore introduced and several devices are on the market now, but they are still a long way from becoming widely used. This must be primarily due to the lack of mature technologies for providing inexpensive devices with sufficient usability.

Most of the tactile display devices developed in the past were only unidirectional communication tools, that is only display devices. If a bidirectional communication function could be provided, graphic information would become more accessible for

K. Miesenberger et al. (Eds.): ICCHP 2004, LNCS 3118, pp. 753–760, 2004.

blind PC users and stimulate their creative activity. The fundamental function for achieving the bidirectional communication is to detect the location where user is touching a tangible surface, so we investigated a new method to detect the finger locus.

## 2 Trial Device

Feasible method of constructing such a device can be roughly classified into two types; adding a detection function to each actuator (such as DMD12060 of METEC), and combining, a display component with a detection component independently. The latter can be sub-classified into several methods but most of them involve complicated wiring. Considering higher independence and simpler wiring, we selected a combination of a tactile display and a force/torque sensor.

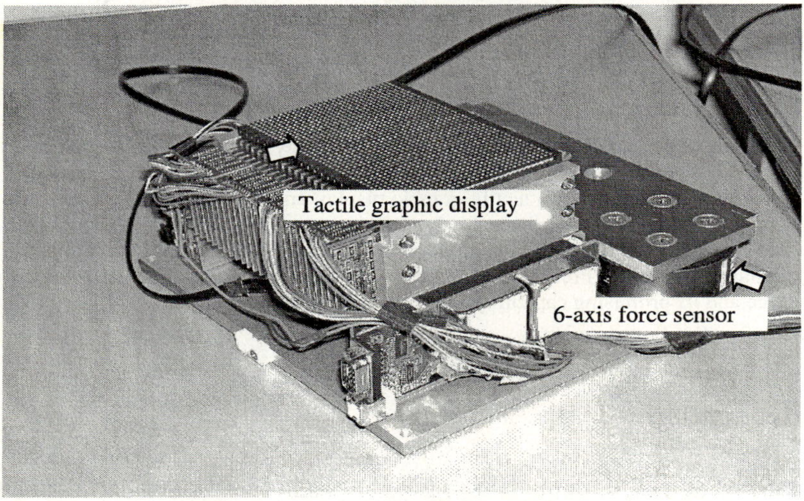


**Photo 1.** An overview of the trial device consisting of two components. The upper is a tactile display and the lower right is a 6-axis force/torque sensor. The tactile display is fixed on a solid plate connected firmly with the force sensor in a cantilever form.

### 2.1 The Tactile Graphic Display

Four bimorph modules (SC-10, provided by KGS Inc.) were used to assemble the tactile graphic display. Each module has a 32x12 arrangement of tactor pins with 2.4mm interspacing. The tactor is 1.3mm in diameter and needs pushing down with a force of at least 10gf in order to the touch surface. The total tactile surface has a 32x48 arrangement activated at a time. The height of the tactor pin when activated by a data signal is 0.7mm. The device interfaces with the host PC through a USB port. The upper part of **Photo 1.** shows the component of the tactile display.

### 2.2 The Force/Torque Sensor

A 6-axis force/torque sensor IFS67M25 and a PCI-board (PCI2184S of NITTA Inc.) were used to detect the touch position and force direction. The sensor measures the force and the force moment generated by touch action, and the touch information is estimated based on the measured data.

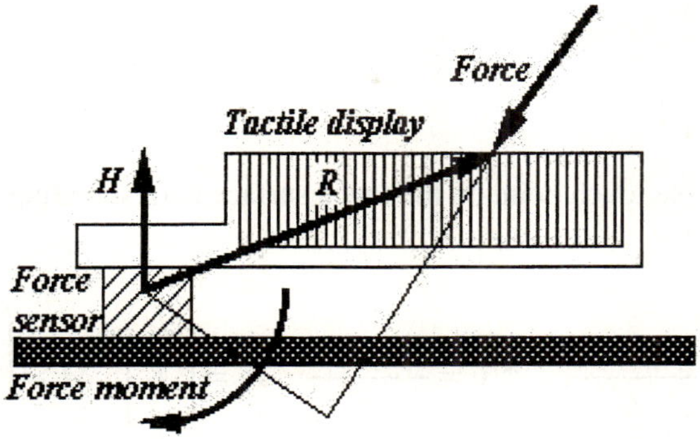


**Fig. 1.** A schematic illustration of the trial device.

### 2.3 Principle of Estimation

The display is fixed on a solid plate connected firmly with the force/torque sensor in a cantilever form as shown in **Photo 1**. When the user touches the display surface, the force sensor detects the six force components (three forces and three force moments) immediately. The touched position, as the center of applied force, is estimated by applying the following equation(1) to the data;

$$M = R \times F \quad \& \quad (H, R - H) = 0 \quad \Rightarrow \quad R = \frac{H \times F + (H, H) F}{(H, F)} \tag{1}$$

Where,
$R$ : touch position vector, $F$ : force vector, $M$ : force moment vector,
$H$ : vector defining the touch surface, $\times$: vector product, and $( \, , \, )$: scalar product
The relationship between these vectors is illustrated in **Fig. 1.**

### 2.4 Coordinate Transformation

The sensor coordinates are three-dimensional, but the touch surface is two-dimensional. Furthermore, the normal vector $H$ may not be parallel with the z-axis of the sensor. Thus, some transformations are needed.

First, we consider coordinate rotation. If $H$ leans against the z-axis, then the touch surface is not parallel with the x-y plane in sensor coordinates. Therefore, coordinate rotation is represented in the following form using Euler angle, in turning $\alpha$

around the z-axis, $\beta$ around the y-axis, and $\gamma$ around the z-axis, and so the following forms are derived.

$$x' = \left({}^{*}x\cos(\alpha+\gamma) + {}^{*}y\sin(\alpha+\gamma)\right)\left(1 - \frac{\beta(f_x \sin\gamma - f_y \cos\gamma)}{f_z}\right) - \beta\cos\alpha\frac{m_z}{f_z} + \beta h \sin\alpha \quad (2)$$

$$y' = \left(-{}^{*}x\sin(\alpha+\gamma) + {}^{*}y\cos(\alpha+\gamma)\right)\left(1 - \frac{\beta(f_x \sin\gamma - f_y \cos\gamma)}{f_z}\right) + \beta\sin\alpha\frac{m_z}{f_z} + \beta h \cos\alpha \quad (3)$$

Here $\begin{pmatrix} x' \\ y' \end{pmatrix}$ is the touch point on the touch surface corresponding to $R = \begin{pmatrix} x \\ y \\ z \end{pmatrix}$,

further ${}^{*}x = \dfrac{hf_x - m_y}{f_z}$, ${}^{*}y = \dfrac{hf_y + m_x}{f_z}$, $F = \begin{pmatrix} f_x \\ f_y \\ f_z \end{pmatrix}$, $M = \begin{pmatrix} m_x \\ m_y \\ m_z \end{pmatrix}$, and

$h = \sqrt{(H, H)}$.

$\beta$ is sufficiently small so that $\sin\beta \to \beta \quad \cos\beta \to 1$.
In general, a small shift must be added to the rotation.

## 3 Laboratory Assessment

Three preliminary investigations were conducted to assess the performance of the trial device. In order to simplify the following discussion, it is assumed that the touch surface is parallel with the x-y plane in the sensor coordinates, in other words $({}^{*}x, {}^{*}y)$ is calculated as a first approximate estimation (in the equation(2) and (3)).

### 3.1 First Investigation: Validity of the Principle for Estimating Touch Position

We first examined whether a touched point on the touch surface is accurately calculated by the algorithm based on the principle. Here, the supporting plate is joined to the force sensor at the outside of the tactile display component (position 1 in **Fig. 4.**) considering freedom of design. Two kinds of stimuli, using an ideal finger and an actual index fingertip, were applied to the surface. The ideal finger, which was a cylinder with a hemispherical tip, acted perpendicularly on the touch surface at 3x3 lattice points with a force of 550gf, whereas the actual index fingertip pushed the center of the surface in five directions. **Fig. 2.** shows the estimated points in comparison with the stimulated points. Each estimated position was the mean of 30 trials. The estimated lattice is considerably distorted to the lower right, seems to be solvable because of the trend of distortion, which may be caused by the setting position of the force sensor or the inclination of the touch surface.

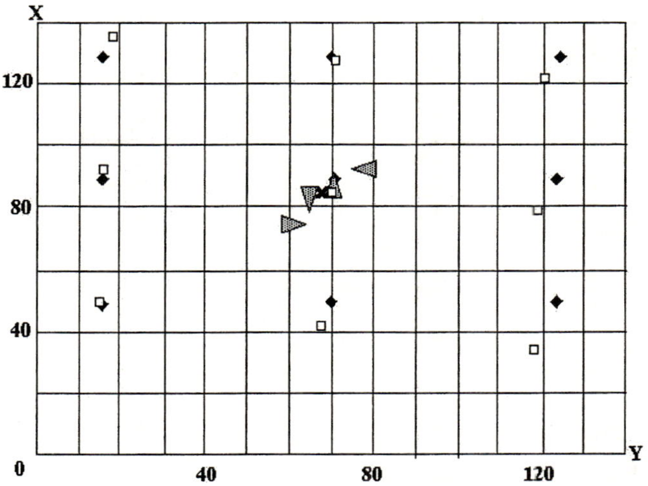


**Fig. 2.** Contrast between the stimulated points and the estimated points in the first investigation. An ideal finger, which is a cylinder with a hemispherical tip, acted perpendicularly on the touch surface at 3x3 lattice points (black diamonds) with a force of 550gf and the corresponding points (white squares) were estimated. On the other hand, an actual index finger pushed the center of the surface in five directions. Each arrow head shows the estimated position and the force direction, and X-mark shows the estimated position corresponding to the perpendicular force.

On the other hand, the estimated finger positions vary widely depending on the direction of the force. This variation seems to be mainly caused by the viscoelastic property of the finger. When the subject pushes the surface down, the contact pressure deforms the shape of the fingertip and so its load center shifts. It is not possible to control the load center through vision. However, as the disparity between the center and the estimated points is not extreme, the results suggests the general validity of the principle.

### 3.2 Second Investigation: Effect of the Sensor Position

The above result suggests that the distortion was caused by the setting position of the force sensor. In practice, the stiffness must be taken into consideration. Thus, three sensor positions as shown in **Fig. 4**, were tested to compare the distortion. The ideal finger pushed the surface down with three different weight values, 100, 200, and 500gf. Each estimated position was the mean of 30 trials.

There was a small discrepancy between three joint positions, suggesting that the optimum or at least optimal point should be reached. The results also suggest that an appropriate load range should be taken into the consideration. The load of 100gf is obviously inappropriate. In the case that the sensor is placed just under the center of the touch display component, the estimation errors are within 4mm without any correction. The trend of the lattice distortion suggests that optimizing the sensor position and some coordinate transformation may keep the estimation errors within a half of the interspacing.

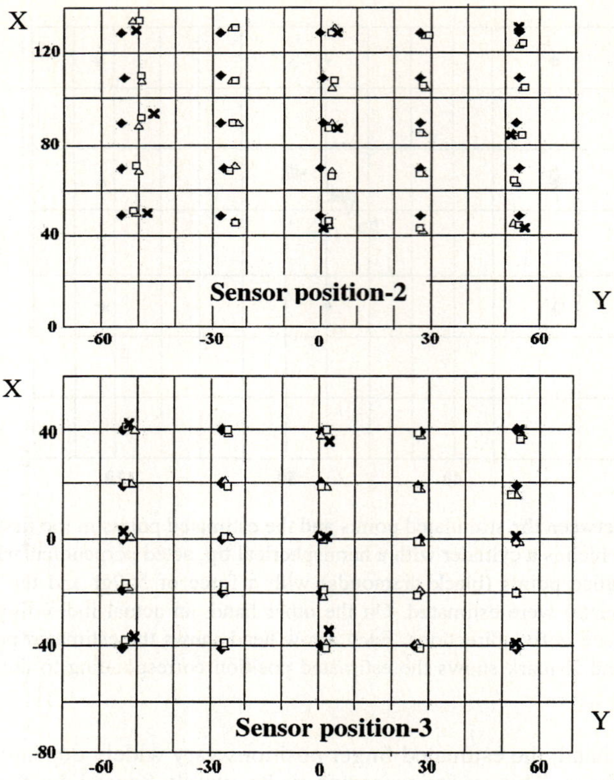


**Fig. 3.** Contrast between the stimulated positions and the estimated positions in the second investigation. An ideal finger acted perpendicularly on the touch surface at 5x5 lattice points (white triangles), and 500gf (white squares). However, in the case of 100gf, 3x3 sub-lattice was used.

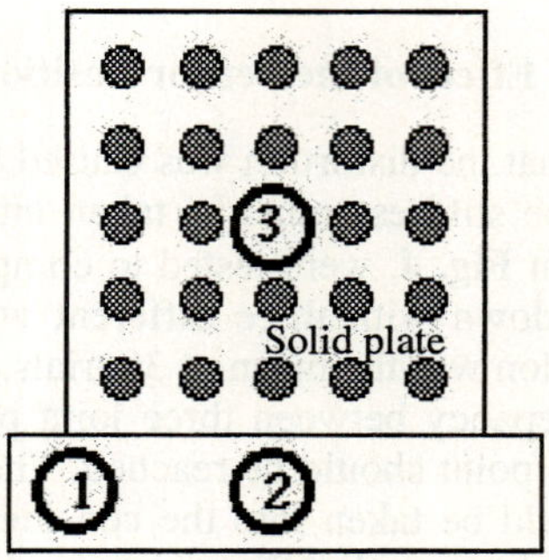


**Fig. 4.** The numbers indicate the force sensor position. (black diamonds) with three forces, of 100g$\bar{}$ (x-marks), 200gf.

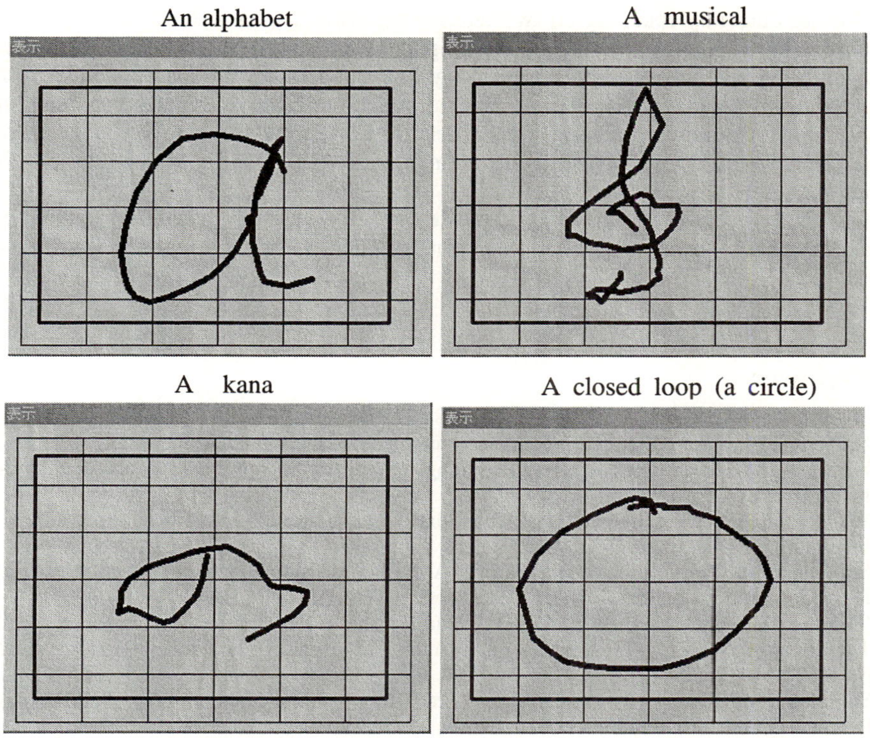


**Fig. 5.** Free finger drawings. The device sampled the six dynamical values changing in response to index finger action and estimated the corresponding position simultaneously. Each locus was recovered as a continuous line image on the VDT.

### 3.3 Third Investigation: Response Speed

If the estimation processing is performed almost in real time, then the device can make graphical information more accessible for the visually impaired. For example, the user can explore, identify, drag, and select the target object on the touch surface via finger action. We examined whether the device can pursue the finger action continuously. The images drawn by an index finger are shown in **Fig. 5.** The results indicate that the device is sufficiently responsive to ordinary finger action and that it may be possible to construct a new HCI method using this system.

## 4 Conclusion

A basic device combining a tactile display function and a force sensing function was proposed. Its promising capability for HCI was roughly shown through three preliminary investigations and the problems to be solved were clarified.

We are currently focusing on two tasks; improving the basic functions in order to minimize the estimation errors, and creating a new HCI method using tactile modality and applying it to several application programs, such as operations described in this paper. Initially, the supporting plate was minimized to remove unnecessary load, and some coordinate transformation algorithms for correcting the estimation error was developed. We are also investigating a finger drawing function and palm scrolling function.

Our final goal is to design an assistive device with which the visually impaired can touch tangible objects and operate them directly, that is, “what you touch is what you get”.

## References


1. Schweikhardt, W., Klöper, K.: Rechnerunterstützte aufbereitung aufbereitung von bildshirmtext-grafiken in eine tastbare darstellung, Institut für Informatik Universität Stuttgart, Institutsbericht, 1-16, 1985.
2. Weber, G.: Modeling interaction of the blind using graphical interfaces. Proceedings of Information Processing’92, 3, 39-46, 1992.
3. Shinohara, M., Shimizu, Y. Mochizuki, A.: A three-dimensional tactile display for the blind. IEEE Transactions on Rehabilitation Engineering, 6(3), 249-256, 1998.
4. Shimojo, M., Shinohara, M., Fukui,Y.: Human Shape Recognition Performance for 3D Tactile Display, IEEE Transaction on Systems, Man and Cybernetics, Part A, Vol.29, No.6,637-644, 1999.
5. Shinohara, M. et al.: An assistive system by tactile and auditory modality for blind PC users. Proceedings of ICCHP2000, 681-688, 2000.
6. Shimizu, Y., Shinohara, M., Nagaoka, H, Yonezawa, Y.: Improvement of user interface for blind PC users. Proceedings of ICCHP2002, 540-542, 2002.

# Remote Eye Gaze Tracking System as a Computer Interface for Persons with Severe Motor Disability

Malek Adjouadi, Anaelis Sesin, Melvin Ayala, and Mercedes Cabrerizo

Department of Electrical & Computer Engineering
Florida International University
10555 W. Flagler Street, Miami FL 33174, USA
{Adjouadi,Anaelis.Sesin,Melvin.Ayala,Mercedes.Cabrerizo}
@fiu.edu
http//www.cate.fiu.edu

**Abstract.** State of the Art human computer interfaces (HCI) for assisting individuals with severe motor disabilities employ remote eye-gaze tracking (EGT) systems which obtain eye coordinates and convert them into mouse-pointer coordinates. The performance of those systems is traditionally affected by mouse-pointer jitter and miscalibration due to head movement. This study addresses this problem and proposes an interface to minimize those errors. The interface allows inspecting and quantifying those errors and collecting the necessary information which is used in real time for training an artificial neural network which improves the coordinate conversion mechanism. The novelty of this study resides in the integration of several procedures, such as: (a) error inspection at system startup, (b) real time improvement of the eye-to-mouse-pointer coordinate conversion mechanism, (c) determination of a practical solution to the mouse click operations, and (d) development of effective means to monitor and evaluate the system performance.

## 1 Introduction

In recent years, remarkable advances have been achieved in the development of universal access tools, in an effort to empower persons with disability at having access to all technological resources so that they will have the same potential at fully harnessing the power of computing. However, with the present scientific and technological breakthroughs, the idea of persons with severe motor disability interacting effectively with a personal computer (PC) still remains a challenging endeavor. A typical modality of such assistive systems consists of the use of an eye gaze tracking system (EGT) which reads and sends the eye coordinates to the stimulus computer, where a conversion into mouse-pointer coordinates occurs. With the advent of such technologies, unwanted collateral effects arise, which considerably restrict and rise doubts about the usage of those systems. In the integration of remote eye gaze tracking systems to computers, the most undesirable effects are the mouse-pointer jitter and the miscalibration due to head movement.

The objective of this study was thus to seek an effective HCI that will allow individuals with severe motor disabilities interact with a computer using only eye movement, with options for practical PC and web browsing, while providing an opportunity to keep jitter and miscalibration to a minimum. Most of the work published to

K. Miesenberger et al. (Eds.): ICCHP 2004, LNCS 3118, pp. 761–769, 2004.

date on the field deals with the improvement and simplification of the eye gaze estimation by means of conventional approaches that are based on the geometry of the cornea. Only a limited number of artificial neural network (ANN) applications can be found on the area of face pose tracking with the purpose of redirecting the camera to the reference eye in case of head movement during working sessions [1, 2]. Very limited research has been conducted so far regarding jitter reduction. Works published in the area of jitter and calibration error reduction for eye gaze tracking systems by means of ANN's have not been found so far, even though that research merits to be conducted. In developing the prototype design, the following important tasks have been performed to ensure accurate cursor displacements:

(1) Enhancement of the data transport mechanism between the eye-gaze system and the host computer, which involved developing a data recovery technique.

(2) Translation of the data into cursor movement using three steps, first the data is converted into monitor coordinates, then to cursor coordinates, and finally calibrated with an improved conversion function (ICF) which uses a trained neural network in order to eliminate the jittering of the mouse pointer.

(3) Experimented with applications involving web browsing, editing and using email with the assistance of an on-screen keyboard that is included in the software interface which is explained in details in [3].

## 2 Eye Gaze Tracking System and Mouse Controller Interface

### 2.1 Interface Components

The Eye Gaze Tracking and Mouse Controller (EGTMC) interface is composed of a CPU for data acquisition, a stimulus CPU, an eye monitor, a stimulus monitor, an eye imaging camera, and an infrared light source (Fig. 1). The CPU for data acquisition is where the eye coordinates are determined with the assistance of the infrared light and the eye camera. It contains three eye-cards (ISCAN RK-726PCI, RK-620PC, RK-464), which are essential to calibrate the system, and the raw eye movement data acquisition software [4]. The RK-726PCI Pupil/Cornel Reflection Tracking System is one-half slot real-time image processor that tracks the center of a subject's pupil and reflection from the corneal surface, and measures the pupil size. The RK-620PC Auto-calibration System is a ¾ slot ISA bus real time computation and display unit used to calculate a subject's point of regard with respect to the viewed scene using the raw eye position data generated by RK-726PCI. The RK-464 Remote Eye Imaging System is an eye imaging system which allows the operator to control the direction, focus, magnification and iris of the eye imaging camera from the control console. The raw eye movement data acquisition software allows the user to control the data collection process. It allows the eye tracking system to be adjusted for any subject. Incoming eye movement and auxiliary data can be seen graphically in real-time, calibrated, and recorded. Calibrated or raw eye movement and auxiliary data can be output in real-time through the serial port. The user interacts directly with the stimulus computer, which is where the software that controls the mouse resides as well as an auxiliary application used to collect data among other task. The eye monitor is used as an assisting devise to locate and focus the subject's left eye. The stimulus monitor is also an auxiliary apparatus, which is connected to the video signal of the stimulus computer. This monitor shows a small cursor that represents the position of the eye.

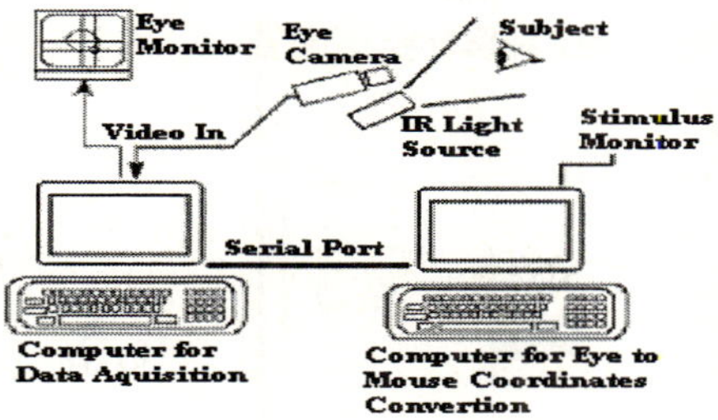


**Fig. 1.** Eye gaze tracking system components

### 2.2 Click Event Implementation

To attain full mouse functionality, the program needs to be able to execute a mouse click as well as move the mouse to any desired position. With this purpose, an investigation was conducted to implement a left click on desired screen areas. When the left eye is closed, the EGT data becomes zeros. Using this information, a left click was defined as closing the eye for a short time interval, which is long enough to differentiate it from a regular blink and short enough to make it as natural as possible. Thus by counting the number of zeros coming into the stimulus computing, the application can differentiate where the action is an eye blink or whether the user wants to trigger a left-click event. Repeated experiments reveal that 20 consecutive zeros are needed to simulate a voluntary left-click.

### 2.3 Software Components

The software interface is composed by two applications: (1) Mouse Control Application (MCA), and (2) Metric Monitoring Application (MMA). The MCA goal is to: (1) read the data coming through the serial port from the EGT, (2) recover the EGT coordinates, (3) convert EGT values to mouse coordinates (4) use the converted values to control the mouse cursor allowing the user to move the mouse pointer as well as to execute a left click event. The MMA application (Fig. 2) is used to: (1) follow the mouse cursor movements and compute a set of indicators, which are needed for jittering and calibration error evaluation and (2) collect data needed to train the ANN.

## 3 Algorithm for Jitter Reduction and Calibration

### 3.1 Algorithm Description

It is relatively difficult to control eye position precisely at all times [6]. Therefore, it would be easier to predict the actual position of the mouse by subdividing its trajectory into smaller sections, which allow the trajectory of the mouse to be described linearly. This is accomplished by taking the x and y ordinates generated by the Mouse Coordinates Generator (MCG) module during $\Delta t$, and using them as inputs to calculate the actual position of the mouse pointer.

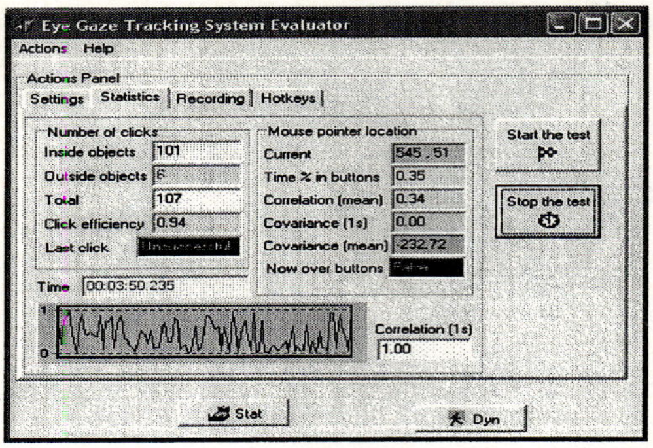


**Fig. 2.** Graphical evaluation application

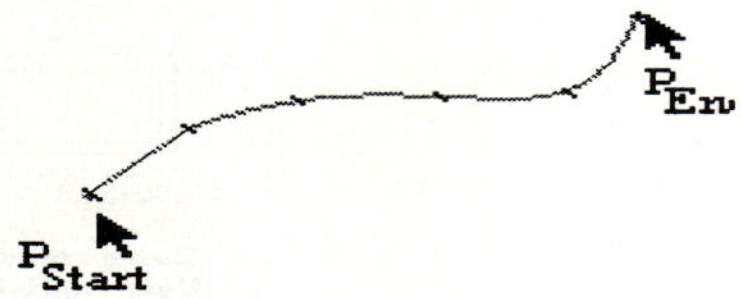


**Fig. 3.** Trajectory is fragmented using a time frame $\Delta t$. $P_{Start}$ and $P_{End}$ are the initial and finalpositions of mouse pointer, respectively

Defining the size of the time frame was a crucial step in determining the number of mouse coordinates that would be used as input to the ANN. Since the EGT data is generated at a frequency of 60 Hz, in order to have an n-to-1 input/output relation, the sampling frequency has to be less than 60 Hz. Simultaneously, the output needs to be generated at a frequency that: (1) still guaranties a smooth mouse pointer movement perception, and (2) permits to have sufficient input data to accurately determine the mouse pointer position. To guarantee a smooth mouse pointer movement, the sampling frequency should not be much less that the physiological frequency of the human eye perception of movement, which is 24 Hz. By choosing a sampling rate of 24 Hz, the number of inputs would be 60/24 = 2.5, which is a very small number of inputs and would cause the jittering to be quite high. Different sampling rates were tested with values less that 24 Hz, and the best results were obtained at a frequency of 10Hz. At this value, the trajectory of the mouse pointer is still relatively smooth, and the size of the sampling window is 60/10 = 6 is an acceptable number of reference points to compute the desired position of the mouse pointer.

### 3.2 Artificial Neural Network Design

The composition of the hidden layers was determined by testing the net using different number of hidden layers and units. The best results were obtained with 1 hidden layer and 20 hidden units with sigmoidal activation functions. Since the outputs of the network are the x and y ordinates, only two output units are needed ($x_{out}$ and $y_{out}$) in the last layer. Training is implemented with 5-fold cross-validation.

### 3.3 Indicators Used for Performance Evaluation

The jittering degree is computed using the relation between the trajectory length and the distance between starting and ending point for each time frame (Fig. 4).

For each set of 6 consecutive mouse pointer locations, the relative percentage between the sum of the consecutive-points distances $d_{ij}$ and the gap between the initial and final points $d_{16}$ is computed as a degree of jittering in that time interval. The jittering can be regarded as a degree or percentage of deviation from the shortest path of movement during a time frame. Equation (1) was used to compute jittering (J). This expression yields values which approach to zero as the mouse trajectory becomes a straight line. In order to estimate the calibration error, the Euclidean distance $D_e$ between the centroid $(x_c, y_c)$ of the mouse pointer and the target button location $(x_b, y_b)$ was calculated for each time frame in each data set (equation 2). The centroid was determined using the six points that fall within the time frame Δt and the target was the position of the moving button at that time.

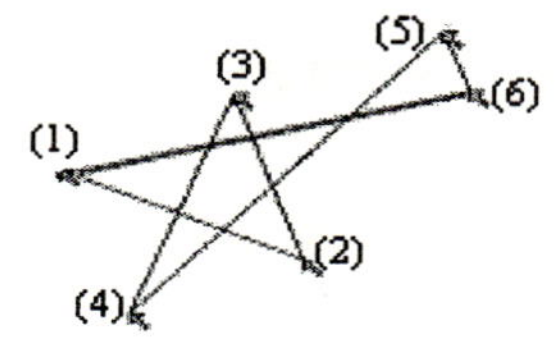


$$J = \frac{\sum_{i=2}^{6} d_{i-1,i} - d_{1,6}}{d_{1,6}} \quad (1)$$

$$D_e = \sqrt{(x_c - x_B)^2 + (y_c - y_B)^2} \quad (2)$$

**Fig. 4.** The jittering degree is computed as a percentage between the trajectory length (sum of the individual distances between consecutive points) and the distance between starting and ending point.

The consistent usage of Equation (1) both before and after employing the ICF tolerates using this expression for evaluating an improvement in the system performance. Additional indicators are used for system evaluation, such as:

- Click efficiency: Is the number of click events effectively triggered when the mouse pointer is over desired locations, with respect to the total number of clicks that are commanded by the user during the whole working session.
- Correlation: Is the correlation degree between the x and y ordinates of the mouse pointer. It is computed in intervals of one second.

### 3.4 Training Pattern Extraction

Before using the ANN to control the mouse pointer, it needs to be trained. This process requires only one minute and requires the compilation of a total of 7200 samples.

$$\frac{60\, points}{\sec} \cdot \frac{60 \sec}{\min} \cdot 1 \min \cdot 2\, features = 7200 \quad (3)$$

Training features are generated from the collected samples and stored in a training table. With a window size of 6 points, 1200 (7200 / 6) training patterns were extracted for each feature (x and y) as illustrated in Fig. 5. Each training pattern consists on screen coordinates collected for each time frame. Furthermore, the target was set to be the average location of a moving button, which the subject is asked to follow with his/her eye during the feature collection procedure. A non overlapping scrolling window is used for data collection, which simplifies the programming code and reduces the training set size. The target value assigned to each sampling window is the average current button position during training. Also, to reduce the complexity of the calculations, the inputs and targets of the network are divided by the screen size (in terms of width and height).

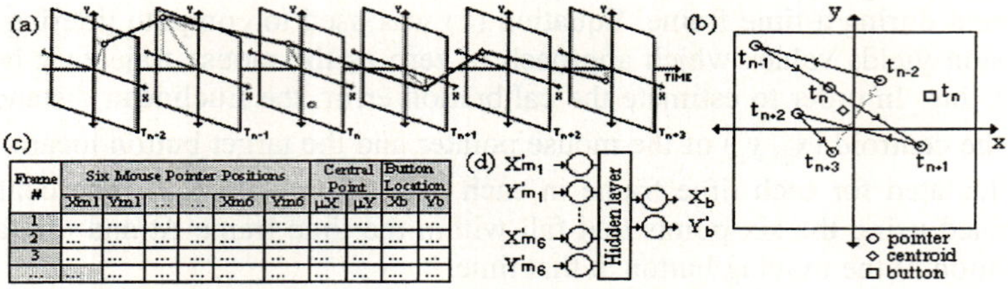


**Fig. 5.** Steps in the data collection procedure and training process to reduce jittering and calibration errors. (a) Eye-gaze point sequence (b) State space diagram, showing mouse pointer locations (c) Raw table as obtained after data collection (d) General ANN configuration using 12 inputs nodes

### 3.5 Working Session Steps

The working session consists of the following steps: (1) EGT system is calibrated, (2) MCA and MMA are loaded in the stimulus computer, (3) serial port connection is opened, (4) data is collected and ANN is trained, (5) user is able to control the mouse with great accuracy with the assistance of the ANN and use any desired computer application, and (6) at the end of the working session, the user can review the performance of the MCA. It is important to point out that the ANN training is performed in real time at the beginning of the working session and not in a separate session. This guarantees that the ANN is trained with data of an individual and takes control of the MCA when the same individual (and not another one) is still using the PC. The flow of the most important working steps can be detailed as follows: When the data collection finishes, for which one minute is required, the evaluation application can be minimized and the user can start interacting with the computer in normal mode, while at the same time, the training process automatically starts in the background (Fig. 6 (a)) and then stops one minute later, totalizing two minutes the time needed for the system to prepare to learn how to cancel future errors. After finishing training, the neural network automatically assumes the role of the eye-to-mouse-pointer coordinate converter. The time dedicated for training can be adjusted at will, thus incrementing the system accuracy the more time the training is executed. The trained ANN learns how the EGT inputs statistically relate to the jittering and calibration errors during a working session in order to provide a mean to reduce as much as possible these effects.

For the data collection, a graphical user interface (GUI) application [5] was developed in which a small button is used as a moving target throughout the screen covering as much screen area as possible. The subject is asked to follow the button with the eyes. As the button moves during a time frame Δt, the EGT data already translated to screen coordinates are taken as the input of the network, while the average of the actual position of the button is considered the target. This process allows the MMA to automatically generate a training table. This information is passed onto a training module, which learns the mapping between the inputs and the jittering on screen, as well as the offset due to the unavoidable calibration error. The weights and bias of the network that will be applied to cancel or reduce the aforementioned negative effects are computed using the backpropagation algorithm. Experiments conducted proved that a time of 1 to 2 minutes is sufficient to train the network with a 5% confidence error.

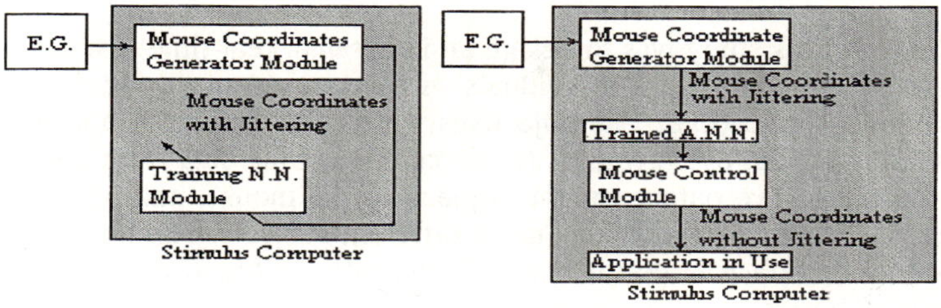


(a) (b)

**Fig. 6.** (a) Employed training logic of the MCA application, (b) Application procedure with trained ANN logic the MCA application

Once the ANN is trained, the screen coordinates generated by the MCG module are no longer used directly to move the mouse pointer. Instead, the output (actual position of the mouse) is passed to the Mouse Control module (Fig. 6 (b)) which shrinks the coordinates and passes them to the trained ANN which in turn outputs a percentage location which is then rescaled in order to obtain the expected mouse position.

## 4 Discussion

An experiment was conducted with six subjects to determine the prospects for jitter and calibration error reduction. For each working session, the system was restarted and new training data was collected with the application shown on Fig. 2 during one minute. Then the user opened a web browser and navigated through the web. The results from all the subjects were averaged and processed using equations 1 and 2 (Table1).

**Table 1.** Jittering and calibration error reduction

| | Without ANN (a) | With ANN (b) | Ratio of Improvement ((a – b) / a) |
|---|---|---|---|
| Jittering degree | 39.31% | 32.94% | 16.20% |
| Calibration error | 62 pixels | 51 pixels | 17.74% |

The more than 15% reduction in both jittering and calibration error was achieved when the EGT is supported with the ANN. This represents a substantial improvement in the use of eye gaze to control the mouse pointer. Experimentation with different control applications showed that the mouse cursor was more stable and easier to control since the trajectory was smoother and could reach the target with a higher degree of accuracy.

## 5 Conclusion

The challenge of this study was to design an integrated, real-time assistive system as an alternate HCI that will allow individuals with severe motor disabilities to use most of the Windows applications. The objectives were (a) to acquire a traceable eye image, (b) to calibrate the eye raw data, (c) to reconstruct the data from the EGT, (d) to translate the use of eye output stream in place of the mouse, and (e) to experiment with different Windows applications using different subjects. The main advantage of the EGT-based interface is that it responds instantly to broad displacements of the user's eye-gaze on the computer screen. Eye gaze interaction gives a subjective feeling of highly responsive system, almost as though the system is executing the user's intentions before the user actually implements them. The results from the conducted experiments reveal that even though the eye is much more than a high-speed cursor positioning tool, eye tracking equipment is still less stable and less accurate than most manual input devices. However, eye-gaze performance can be improved with the use of other supplementary software such as the proposed neural network application as guided by a novel GUI application design. The authors believe that there are no published ANN applications dealing with jitter reduction in eye gaze. Therefore, no comparison with similar methods could be performed. This research endeavor constitutes an effort to redress the problem of jitter and calibration errors that are inherent to EGT systems without recourse to integrating EMG-based systems [7].

## Acknowledgements

The authors gratefully acknowledge the support from the National Science Foundation: EIA-9906600 and HRD-0317692, and the Office of Naval Research: N00014-99-1-0952.

## References

1. Baluja, S., Pomerleau; D. "Non-Intrusive Gaze Tracking Using Artificial Neural Networks," Advances in Neural Information Processing Systems (NIPS) 6, 1994
2. Piratla, N. M., Jayasumana, A. P. “A neural network based real-time gaze tracker,” Journal of Network and Computer Applications, Vol. 25, Issue 3, July 2002, ISSN:1084-8045, Academic Press Ltd. London, UK, pp. 179 – 196
3. Sesin, A., Adjouadi, M., Ayala, M. “A Calibrated, Real-Time Eye Gaze Tracking System as an Assistive System for Persons with Motor Disability,” Proceedings of the 7th World Multiconference on Systemics, Cybernetics and Informatics (SCI 2003), Vol. VI, pp. 399-404, Orlando, Florida, July 27-30, 2003
4. ISCAN INC., Raw Eye Movement Data Acquisition Software, Instruction Manual

5. Ayala, M., Adjouadi, M., "Eye-Gaze Tracking System Evaluator," Programming Tool [Online]. Available: www.cate.fiu.edu/CATEHomePage /Software/index.htm
6. Jacob, R.J.K. "The Use of Eye Movements in Human-Computer Interaction Techniques: What You Look at is What You Get," ACM Transactions on Information System, pp. 152-169, 1991
7. Barreto, A., Scargle, S., Adjouadi, M., "A Practical EMG-Based Human-Computer Interface for Users with Motor Disabilities," Journal of Rehabilitation Research and Development, Vol. 37, No. 1, pp. 53-63, Jan-Feb 2000

# Controlling a PC by Eye Movements: The MEMREC Project

Marcela Fejtová, Jan Fejt, and Lenka Lhotská

The Gerstner Laboratory,
Czech Technical University in Prague, Faculty of Electrical Engineering
Technická 2, 166 27 Prague 6, Czech Republic
fejtovam@k333.felk.cvut.cz
lhotska@fel.cvut.cz
http://cyber.felk.cvut.cz

**Abstract.** In this paper we would like to introduce design of a system for controlling a PC by eye movements. During last ten years the computers have become common tools of work – it is nearly impossible to exist without them in everyday life. We are witnessing the time of revolutionary introduction of computers and information technologies into daily practice. Healthy people use keyboard, mouse, trackball, or touchpad for controlling the PC. However these peripheries are usually not suitable for disabled people. They may have problems using these standard peripheries, for example when they suffer from myopathy, or cannot make moves with hands after an injury. Therefore we are coming with a proposal how to ease the disabled people to control the PC.

## 1 Introduction

Communication between man and technical systems capable of interaction (computers) represents a special category of communication that is acquiring greater importance all the time. Input information from the human is transmitted to the computer using one of the suitable interfaces. However disabled people may have difficulties when controlling a PC by classical peripheries. People with motoric handicap that causes inability to control movements of arms and hands have problems with grasping a mouse, not speaking about fine manipulation with it. Since the computers have become common tools of work and have started to accompany us even in everyday life it is necessary to enable the disabled people easier communication with the computers.

Control of a computer's functionality by eye control has been a practical possibility for several years. Let us describe briefly several existing solutions. The LC Technologies Eyegaze System [1] provides an eye-controlled human-computer interface (HCI), using a video camera mounted below the computer monitor that observes the user's eye and specialised image processing software analyses the video images of the eye and determines the eye's gazepoint on the monitor screen in real time. QualiEye [2], part of QualiWORLD, gives simple, efficient, hands-free control of the

K. Miesenberger et al. (Eds.): ICCHP 2004, LNCS 3118, pp. 770–773, 2004.

PC using a standard USB web cam for tracking eye movements. Electrooculography is used at Boston College in the project called EagleEyes [3] for moving cursor at the computer monitor. Great disadvantage of this method is the necessity of correct sticking the surface electrodes and removal of artefacts originating from eye blinking or movements of face muscles. Another disadvantage is the necessity of special software products that can help a handicapped person to control the PC. At the Cambridge University [4, 5] the project Dasher uses a IR camera that detects the eye position based on the contrast between the light absorbed by the pupil and the reflected light. Each of the presented systems has its advantages and disadvantages. Some of them are already fully developed and commercially available. However, most of these commercially available systems are very expensive, mostly having a single function, namely control of a PC mouse, frequently no head motion is required because the camera is mounted on the PC monitor. That has been the motivation for us. Our goal has been the development of a simple and inexpensive system that is not influenced by head motion and that may provide more functions depending on the software it is equipped with.

## 2 MEMREC Project

In the MEMREC (Mobile Eye Movements RECorder) project currently running at the Gerstner Laboratory, CTU Prague we are designing and developing a simple device for PC control. We cooperate closely with the Neurological Clinic of the 2nd Medical School of the Charles University and Jedlicka´s Institute for Disabled.

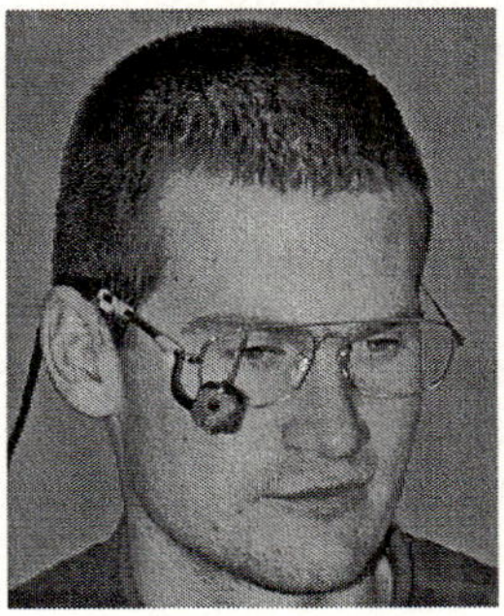

**Fig. 1.** Location of the camera in the MEMREC system

The basic idea is fixing a small camera to the head of a person and recording the eye position in the coordinate system independently on the head movements (evaluation of the eye movements is done based on the deviation from balanced position) (see figure 1). Using this "free" placement of the camera we remove the disadvantage, namely requirement of no head movement. The camera will be connected to the PC using standard communication interface (USB) equipped with corresponding software and enables the handicapped person to control the PC simply by eye movements referred to rest position (view directly ahead). The MEMREC system is designed in such a way that the camera is another input periphery of the PC. The result will be a device that can be linked to any PC and used for control of all programs. In principle the camera would simulate a classical PC mouse extensible by an intelligent keyboard using a special user interface. Using this communication module the problem of compatibility of drivers between individual versions of systems or hardware platforms does not take place. The main requirements laid on the developed system are low price, simple installation and simple control.

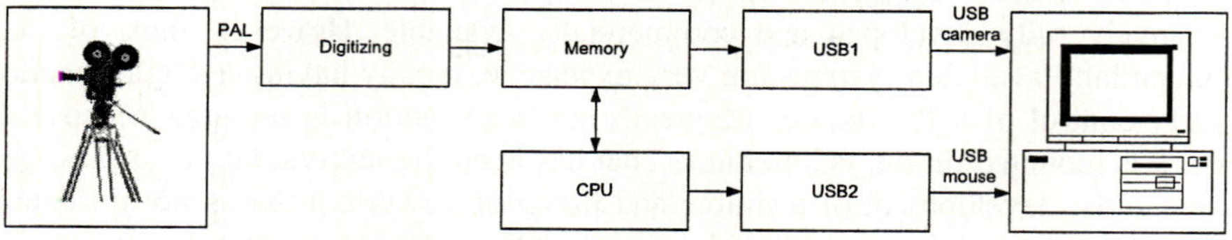


**Fig. 2.** Basic block structure of the MEMREC system

The figure 2 shows the basic block structure of the MEMREC system. The outputs of the system are the x- and y-coordinates of the mouse cursor. The next output is a simple USB camera. The core of the system is black&white PAL camera with a CCD sensor and discrimination 208 x 156 pixels for recording the eye movements. The output of the camera is analog PAL signal that is digitized afterwards. The digitizing block is constituted of an A/D convertor with brightness feedback. Information about position of the pupil is stored to the memory and is evaluated by the CPU (processor) from the digitized PAL signal. In the MEMREC system version 1.0 the SRAM 512 kB memory is used. The processor uses for the detection of pupil position the method of histogram thresholding and other types of filtration (e.g. cubic filter). Mouse click or doubleclick is evaluated when the eye is closed for relatively longer time (it removes influence of spontaneous eye blink). Another task of the processor is to control USB bus ensuring communication with a PC. As it has been mentioned above, the device emulates the computer mouse. From this property it follows that for basic utilization of the MEMREC system there is no necessity to install any special software tool or driver. Neverthless we are designing and developing software applications for utilization of this system in medical diagnostics and therapy.

**Experiments.** We performed a number of experiments with the MEMREC system. The first task was to start individual applications placed on the desktop of the PC. After short training of cursor control, its movement to goal position and clicking, we were able to start the Internet explorer and to go to a favorite URL recorded on the list of favorites. In another experiment we started the software keyboard that is a part of the MS Windows OS. Using this software keyboard we were able to write the URL and we did not have to be relied on the list of favorites. The last experiment performed till now was writing and sending a short e-mail message.

## 3 Conclusion

Simple control of the PC by the designed interface will help people with physical handicap to integrate fully in the society despite their handicap or at least to open the access to the latest information on the Internet. The system will be as miniature as possible so that it disturbs the user at the minimum level. The hardware is based on easily available and financially not demanding off-the-shelf components. It is simple, efficient, fault tolerant. In combination with the software it is flexible and has good resolution. Advantage of this system is its noninvasiveness and the fact that a user of a new computer interface has not to be specially instructed. Using the MEMREC system for control of the cursor, the user acquires certainty and precision after working with the system for some time. The length of this period differs from user to user and depends on his/her abilities to control own eye movements and patience. At present it is possible to control the PC using the MEMREC system similarly to standard PC mouse or keyboard. This type of periphery enables to physically handicapped users to work or study on their own. The device can be used e.g. at patients with decreased ability to express themselves or at patients with cerebral palsy. Recently we have started to perform clinical tests with the MEMREC system at the Jedlicka´s Institute and School for Disabled in Prague at children with different degree of disability.

## Acknowledgement

This paper is based upon work sponsored by the Ministry of Education, Youth and Sports of the Czech Republic (under project No. MSM210000012 "Transdisciplinary Biomedical Engineering Research") and CTU grant No.11-83144 “Complex analysis of eye movements and application to PC control”.

## References

1. http://www.eyegaze.com/doc/cathuniv.htm,cit. 13,Apr.(2004).
2. http://www.qualilife.com, cit. 13.Apr.( 2004).
3. Gips, J., Olivieri, P. EagleEyes: An Eye Control System for Person with Disabilities. In Proceedings 11th International Conference on Technology and Persons with Disabilities, March 1996 Los Angeles, California. Published in Human-Computer Interaction: Applications and Case Studies, M.J. Smith and G. Salvendy (eds.), Elsevier, (1996), pp. 630-635.
4. Cavendish Laboratory, Cambridge: The Dasher Project [online]. Last review 07.Jan. (2004), cit. 20.Jan. ( 2004). http://www.inference.phy.cam.ac.uk/dasher.
5. Ward, D.J. Adaptive Computer Interfaces. Ph.D. thesis. Cambridge: University of Cambridge, Cavendish Laboratory, Inference Group,( 2001). 144 s.

# HeadControl+: A Multi-modal Input Device

Mario Mühlehner[1] and Klaus Miesenberger[2]

[1] Kompetenznetzwerk Informationstechnologie zur Förderung der Integration von Menschen mit Behinderungen (KI-I), IT-Center, Hauptstraße 119, 4232 Hagenberg i.M., Austria
mm@ki-i.at

[2] Institut "integriert studieren – integrated study", University of Linz
Altenbergerstrasse 69, A-4040 Linz, Austria
kmiesenberger@jku.at

**Abstract.** Different groups of people with disabilities, especially those with motor disabilities, have problems in handling the conventional computer mouse and in consequence, as the mouse is a standard component of almost any Human-Computer Interface (HCI), with different systems and applications leading to problems in their educational, vocational and daily life. This paper presents research on a prototype of a laser based, head controlled input device, capable of multiple modes, each representing a different input device emulation. Thus the HeadControl+ system is intended to implement an alternative mouse as well as an alternative keyboard, making use only of off-the-shelve hardware leading to an inexpensive system for different application scenarios.

## 1 State of the Art in Research

A series of projects has dealt with the development of alternative input devices [1]. The majority of these approaches substitutes the hand movements by movements of other parts of the body like e.g. feet, head, eye. Devices using head motion for positioning the mouse cursor and/or operating an alternative keyboard proofed to be very promising for a lot of users with disabilities. [2,3] The technical implementation of measuring the position and movements of the user's head has been solved in various ways. Video/picture analysis as well as different kinds of sensors (e.g. magnetic or infrared) have been used. [4,5]

Previous research [6] has been investigating the application of a laser pointing directly at a computer monitor. The setup consists of a head mounted laser pointer and a web cam, placed immediately in front of the computer screen. The web cam observes parts of the screen or the complete screen, trying to track the movements of the laser navigated by the user. Laser interaction serves two purposes: 1) to operate a simple, custom designed on-screen keyboard and 2) to control the mouse cursor. Both applications require different camera adjustments (in keyboard mode only the lower area of the computer screen containing the keyboard layout is monitored, in mouse mode the web cam captures the complete screen) and therefore are not intended to be used in mutual operation. The setup incorporates rudimentary calibration algorithms,

K. Miesenberger et al. (Eds.): ICCHP 2004, LNCS 3118, pp. 774–781, 2004.

capable of locating the special on-screen keyboard and the entire screen area respectively, considering geometrical distortions resulting from a non-flat computer screen and the special view angle of the observing camera. Unfortunately, reliable laser tracking requires a rather dark display background in order to locate the laser point successfully. Therefore the display settings have been turned to "high contrast" utilizing the "Accessibility Options" offered by the operating system. Interestingly enough there have been no reports on problems caused by the reflection of the laser beam, as witnessed in the early stages of HeadControl [1] research.

Hence, the biggest problems reported by users of such alternative input devices are a) the lack of usability and ergonomics and/or b) the costs of these systems.

## 2 HeadControl+

Based on these results a first prototype of a pointing device making use of a laser was developed. The basic idea is to use a non-expensive off-the-shelve laser to build an affordable, reliable and easy-to-use pointing device. [1]

The first HeadControl prototype was built to find the technical feasibility of the basic idea in terms of the right choice of the image capture device (web cam), the set-up of components, the reasonable overall handling. HeadControl+ now intends to unite various input device emulations - each conceived as a *virtual device* - on top of the laser interaction paradigm.

### 2.1 System Design

HeadControl+ makes use of a PC (desktop or notebook), a web cam and a laser device (e.g. a laser pointer), all of them off-the-shelve products. The software searches for the laser point in the streaming video input and translates the movement of the user's head to movements of the mouse cursor or other input actions. Figure 1 shows the standard setup, installing the web cam to observe the laser navigation area from the same side as the user does.

The user wears the laser device (1) by means of a head set or a head band. The laser device does not point directly on the screen (3), but on the *navigation area* (2) which can be in front of, next to or over the computer display. The laser point hits the center of the navigation area when the user focuses the middle of the screen. The video camera (4) provides a real-time video stream of the navigation area including the laser point. The HeadControl Software running on a PC (5) extracts the coordinates of the laser beam and provides the position to any virtual device emulation, for instance to calculate the movements of the mouse cursor.

Figure 2 represents the "hidden camera" approach where the web cam films the back side of a tablet used as the navigation area. The tablet could be installed on a table of on a wheel chair.

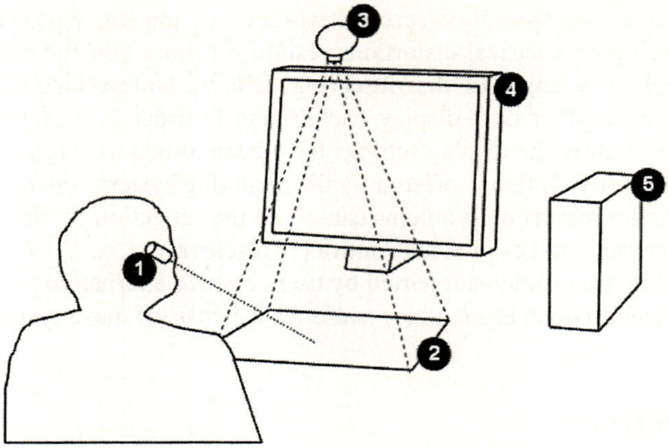


**Fig. 1.** Regular HeadControl+ setup.

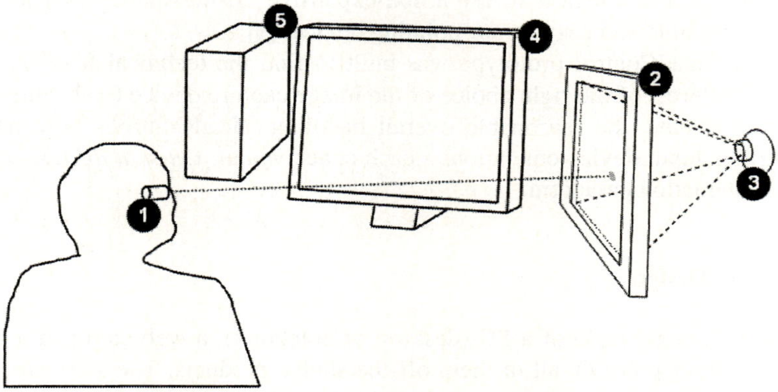


**Fig. 2.** "Hidden camera" setup.

Directing the laser to a separated area was done to avoid unpleasant and in the long run unhealthy blending. In addition, tracking a laser point on a computer screen has not been accomplished in a satisfying and reliable way yet. Therefore our approach to separate the screen area from the navigation area has several positive side effects:

1) Image processing of mainly static images sets considerable less computational demand. Hence, its quite easy to get full-scale, mainly undistorted images of the navigation area.
2) Because the camera is observing the navigation area installing the camera does not lead to conflicts as the camera should be placed near or at the same place as the user when filming the screen.
3) The navigation area may contain any other symbols, enabling extra functionalities (e.g. keys, menu items).Thus an input device can be put in place without minimizing the screen area. In comparison to other approaches like on-screen keyboards or other assistive software tools the screen area is not reduced.

## 2.2 Features and Applications

**Calibration and Adjustment.** The navigation area, whereon the user moves the laser point, contains elements (e.g. border lines) to adjust the camera. The detection of the navigation area during the calibration process has two purposes:

a) Locating the navigation area
To achieve the best image capture resolution, it is necessary to adjust the web cam in such a way, that the captured image frames contain the complete navigation area and its border. Camera settings using only a small part of the captured frame would lead to a waste of spare image capturing resolution anyway.
b) Estimation of camera specific geometrical distortions
Every camera produces individual geometrical distortions depending on its lens. These distortions can lead to serious deviations between the recorded laser point's position in the captured frames and its actual position on the navigation area. Firstly, the position of the laser point has to correlate to the corners of the navigation area in the captured image. Secondly, one must consider the geometrical distortion of the camera, performing a non-linear transition of the actual laser movement. When in mouse mode, these deviations are hardly perceived by the user, because moving the cursor to a desired position is an interactive process where differences between the desired cursor position and its actual one are compensated quite unconsciously. On the other hand, when selecting an item on the navigation area (for instance a key), non-linear movements in the mapping between the selection on the screen and how its perceived in the captured image frame can – although differing only by a few pixels – lead to failures. Thus the mapping error induced by the geometrical distortions has to be compensated.

**Mouse Emulation.** In the mouse emulation mode, the user controls the mouse cursor by moving his head. In its home position the laser point hits the center of the navigation area when the user looks at the middle of the screen. By moving his head sideways and by bowing and raising of his head the user can induce appropriate movements of the laser point within the navigation area.

There are at least two different approaches how to convert the movements of the laser point into movements of the mouse cursor:

1) Direct mapping of the processed laser movement to mouse cursor movement
The regular approach is to map the extracted laser positions after its preprocessing directly to cursor movements. The mouse cursor on the screen performs the same movements as the laser point on the navigation area. This leads to a very convenient and intuitive way to control the cursor because a desired change in the cursor position can be reached in a single motion – without having to figure out, how to steer the current cursor position to the desired destination, like one has to when using a joystick-like input device.
2) Acceleration-driven mouse cursor
The regular approach asks for basic skills in controlling head movements. To support those with less freedom in moving the head an acceleration-driven mouse

mode has been conceived. It works very similar to a joystick The center of the navigation area marks the home position of the imaginary joystick the user operates. Around this center a circle defines the home area which can be adjusted to the individual situation of the user. Whenever the laser point is moved outside the resting circle, the mouse cursor starts to accelerate from its current position taking that direction which is determined by the vector between the home circle center and the actual position of the laser point, just like pushing the joystick towards the new laser point position. The amount of cursor acceleration is calculated as the function of the vector length (the further away the laser point is from the center, the faster accelerates the cursor), or as a function of time (acceleration or speed increases as long as the laser point is outside the resting area). Some users might prefer a cursor with fixed speed, anyway. People with very limited motion control will benefit from this functionality because indicating changes in the cursor's direction might be more convenient than hitting its target position directly.

**Tremor Reduction.** When using the laser interface as a positioning device, tremor can make it difficult to control the mouse cursor, especially when performing fine movements. Although a basic level of tremor is inherent to all human beings, pathological tremor decreases the efficiency of a man-machine interface significantly. González et al [7] present an approach to smoothly input signals through *signal equalization* by diminishing the harmful influence of tremor. Signal equalization also benefits from its ability to adjust to the characteristics of any individual tremor consuming rather low computation resources. As a consequence, deployment of a tremor reduction algorithm is expected to increase the overall handling considerably. This enables us to provide computer access even to users with severe physical limitations.

**Keyboard Emulation.** Refining its original purpose, the navigation area might contain additional symbols, like a *virtual keyboard* (Fig. 3). In keyboard mode the user focuses the keyboard layout and selects a symbol by pointing with the laser on it. After confirming the selection (e.g. using an input switch or staying on the selected item for a certain amount of time) the action associated to the symbol is executed. For instance, when pointing at the 'a' key, the virtual keyboard generates an 'a' keystroke after pushing a confirmation switch (or a sip/puff switch, etc.). Predefined keyboard layouts are part of the HeadControl+ system. A *keyboard layout editor* is under construction enabling the user to draft his own virtual keyboard layouts. Individual preferences might lead to extra large key symbols, to a different set of keys as well as to a different order of symbols, thus supporting the individual requirements of the user.

A virtual keyboard layout can contain conventional key symbols (alphanumeric keys) as well as menu items, which can be linked to various types of actions, like exiting the virtual keyboard, playing a keystroke sequence (macro), launching an application, displaying a popup menu on the screen, etc. The layout of a virtual keyboard defines exactly where each key or menu item is located in the context of the

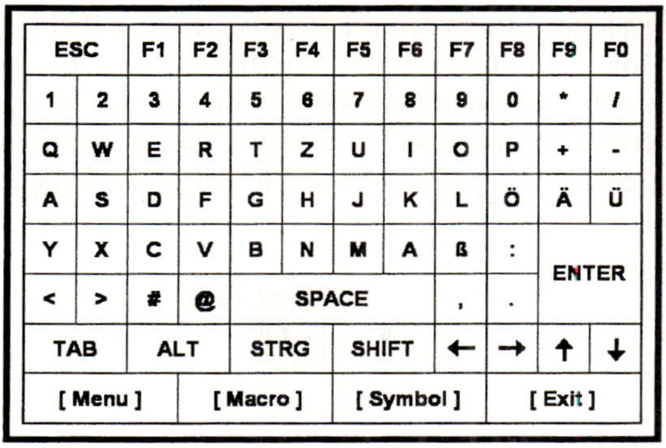


**Fig. 3.** Schematic navigation area layout containing a virtual keyboard.

surrounding navigation area border. Thus it is possible to extract which item was selected from the laser point's position on the navigation area at the moment when the selection has been confirmed. Hence, it is not necessary to detect every key item in the capture image frames in order to figure out where it is. By locating the navigation area border the relative positions of all key items are known.

**SensorBox.** Support of sensor input, enabling the user to integrate her/his assistive devices, is possible by making use of an USB interface [8], called *SensorBox*. This device allows to integrate state-of-the-art sensors (sip/puff switches, buttons, etc.). It is also used to drive the standard laser unit. All attached sensors (currently eight sensors are supported) as well as the laser unit and several LEDs can be monitored by the HeadControl+ software. A wireless connection should be put in place for the SensorBox which is currently connected to the computer via USB cable. This will give more flexibility and increased comfort to the user.

**Training/Rehabilitation Software.** Some algorithms within the HeadControl+ system require certain input tasks from the user, for instance to pursue a moving target with the mouse cursor to investigate his head tremor. We are working on a special training software that adapts to the physical skills of the user. Moving an object through a maze would improve the coordination of head movements. Another application's goal would be to hit static targets. This requires to stabilize the head as long as possible to achieve a maximum hit score – a good exercise to get used to dwelling. There are a lot of other training and exercise scenarios, helping to improve certain skills and therefore hopefully contributing to conventional rehabilitation efforts.

## 3 Outlook

Based on the original HeadControl prototype a professional system will be developed during the next months. Further to the existing features the system should be capable of maintaining various virtual devices (virtual mouse, virtual keyboard, virtual joystick, etc.) enabling the user to switch seamlessly between them. To take full advantage of the SensorBox, configuration tools are planned to allow to integrate external sensors individually. The development work focuses on user centered design; people with disabilities themselves are involved strongly during requirements specification as well as during extensive user tests in order to design different application scenarios.

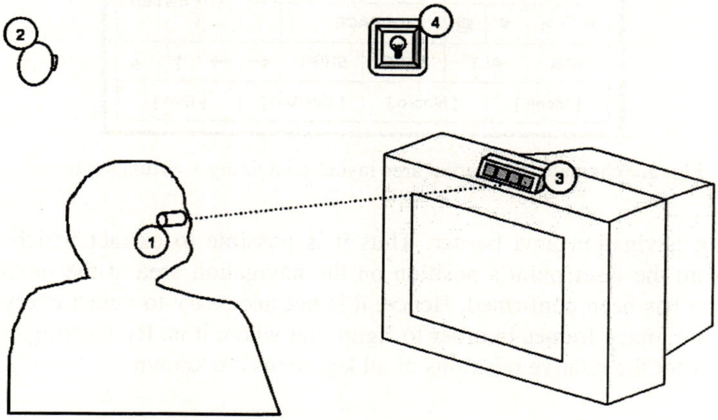


**Fig. 4.** Setups for environment control interfaces.

The latter includes future research in application scenarios to a user interface for environment control systems, offering users the opportunity to control objects by pointing directly at them. Figure 4 shows two reasonable approaches: a) applying his laser unit, the user hits a sensor device (3). The sensor device is dedicated to a certain target device (e.g. TV set) consisting of multiple optical sensors, each assigned to a specific function of the target device. When hitting a particular sensor field with the laser, the sensor device communicates the request to a computer or control device in order to execute the appropriate function. Approach b) in turn integrates a camera (2) observing a broader view of the environment. By selecting objects/regions like a light switch (4) contained in the view, the user can teach the system how to react on laser manipulations of individual objects/regions.

## Acknowledgement

This work is supported by the Regional Government Upper Austria, Department for Social Affaires, and the research Fund of the Austrian National Bank.

## References

1. Mühlehner, M.: „HeadControl – Ein lasergesteuertes Eingabegerät für körperlich beeinträchtigte Computeranwender“, Diploma Thesis, Universität Linz, 2003

2. Wu T., Meng L., Wang H., Wu W., Li T. „Computer Access Assessment for Persons with Physical Disabilities: A Guide to Assistive Technology Interventions“, Pages 204-211 Computers Helping People with Special Needs Conference 2002, ed. Klaus Miesenberger, Joachim Klaus, Wolfgang Zagler, Springer Verlag 2002
3. Bérad, F. 'The perceptual window: Head Motion as a new input stream', Human-Computer Interaction Interact '99, ed. M. Angela Sasse & Chris Johnson, IOS Press, Oxford, 1999
4. Malkewitz, Rainer „Head pointing and speech control as a hands-free interface to desktop computing“ Pages 182-188 ACM SIGCAPH Conference on Assistive Technologies 1998
5. Betke, M., Gips, J., Fleming, P. "The Camera Mouse: Visual Tracking of Body Features to Provide Computer Access For People with Severe Disabilities", Resubmitted to the IEEE Transactions on Rehabilitation Engineering, June 19, 2001
6 Erdem, Í.A. „Vision-based human-computer interaction using laser pointer", thesis submitted to the Graduate School of Natural and Applied Sciences of the Middle East Technical University, 2003
7. González, J., Heredia, E., Rahman, T., Barner, K., Arce, G. "Filtering Involuntary Motion of People with Tremor Disability Using Optimal Equalization", in Proceedings 1995 IEEE International Conference on Systems, Man and Cybernetics, Vancouver, BC, Canada, 1995
8. Schmid H. „Universelle Architektur – Das Programmiermodell des Universal Serial Bus“, S. 180 f in c´t Nr.17, Ausgabe August 2002

# Accessibility through Standard Low Cost Pointing Devices

Barbara Prazak[1], Stefan Mina[1], and Gernot Kronreif[2]

[1] ARC Seibersdorf research GmbH, Rehabilitation & Inclusion Research Group
Viktor Kaplan Str. 2/1, A-2700 Wiener Neustadt
{barbara.prazak,stefan.mina}@arcsmed.at
[2] ARC Seibersdorf research GmbH, Group on Intelligent Robot Systems – GIRO
A-2444 Seibersdorf

**Abstract.** Alternative pointing devices for handling the computer are often needed by people with disabilities. These pointing devices are in most cases not compatible with other aids, which are stand alone devices. This paper points out the development of a converter hardware which allows the use of alternative pointing devices with each aid like talkers, computers etc. In Addition different practical usages with this developed converter hardware are shown.

## 1 Introduction

The growth of the assistive technology industry tends to results in a variety of input devices for people with disabilities. For handling the computer people with disabilities especially people with physical disabilities need very often alternative pointing devices. Usually this pointing device is intended to be used only with a personal computer. The variety of pointing devices enable people with disabilities to find an adequate device however the decision for such a special input device comes often along with a long lasting test phase. The test phase is important to find out which device is most suitable for the individual situation. Afterwards a learning phase is needed where people have to practice the use of this input device in combination with the computer. For regularly usage people with disabilities and their assistants have to configure the input device on individual requirements.

For every day life other additional aids are needed in several cases. Such aids can be for example talker for communication or environmental control devices. These technical aids are in most cases stand alone devices with no possibility to attach the chosen pointing device. In this case the need for a completely new input device arose. The circulation of choosing a new input device starts again and a new training and configuration phase is also necessary [1]. Configuring the new device adequately occupies a lot of time. Beside the fact that additional training and configuration is required there is also the cost factor as the user has to buy additional equipment. For example in Austria it is difficult to get additional funding for a second input device. This often leads to an abandonment of this device and technical aid by people with disabilities.

The idea was to develop converter hardware which allows the use of alternative pointing devices in combination with each aid such as a computer, a talker etc. This

K. Miesenberger et al. (Eds.): ICCHP 2004, LNCS 3118, pp. 782–787, 2004.

paper describes the research project at the ARC Seibersdorf research where such converter hardware was built. The results of this research project for the converter hardware itself will be shown in practical examples. At the end a discussion about advantages and disadvantages of this system will be presented.

## 2 Objectives

The superior aim of this research project was to find a system which allows using one input device especially pointing device for different kinds of technical aids. Thus the availability of such hardware can be increased and additional costs can be greatly reduced for people with disabilities. For the development process the following criteria were significant:

- use of state of the art technology
- an easy handling for end user
- Low costs for the development and the end user

Beyond this, the research project tested the developed hardware for people with physical disabilities in a few examples to evaluate the functionality and the handling. The results will be presented at the end of the paper.

## 3 Methods/Structure of the Project

### 3.1 Available Devices

For using the computer a wide range of various pointing devices are available such as mouse, touchpad, trackball, and in special cases customized switches and alternative pointing devices in combination with mouse emulators [2]. A special pointing device is not always necessary, in certain cases standard pointing devices like trackballs or touchpad can be used by people with physical disabilities. If people with disabilities use pointing devices they would have more possibilities for working with the computer as they would operate with a single switch. Working with a pointing device signified that the user has the potential to move the cursor with no limitation. On the one hand that offers much freedom for the user and on the other hand the users has in special cases to cover a long distance on the screen (e.g. from bottom left corner to upper right corner).

Stand alone devices are in most cases used with various switches or digital joysticks. Most of these technical aids can be used in the scanning mode, which is a necessity for people with severe physical disabilities. However these aids can mostly not be used with a pointing device. At this point people are confronted with the problem that they cannot utilize the same pointing device as the use for the computer.

People with progressive muscular disease can particularly benefit from a converter which allows using pointing devices with stand alone aids. They often have a limited range of motion and low force but with their remaining motion they can operate technical aids with a standard pointing device such as a touchpad. For using an environmental control system (stand alone device) it would be useful to apply this with the chosen pointing device. At the moment they have to use extra input devices.

### 3.2 Feature Extraction of Pointing Device Data

Usually a pointing device changes the position of the mouse cursor on the screen. The whole area of the screen can be seen as Cartesian coordinate system. Each position on the screen can be defined by its absolute X/Y coordinates.

In most cases the pointing devices do not deliver information about the absolute position (except graphic tablets), they only provide information about the relative motion. To move the cursor from point A to point B the pointing devices deliver only the relative ΔX/ΔY coordinates (figure 1).

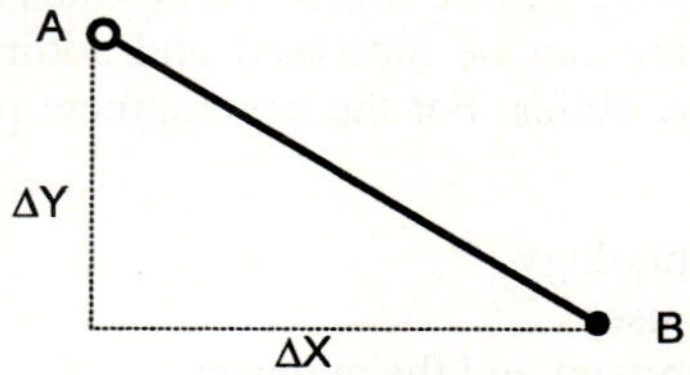


**Fig. 1.** Relative motion from point A to B

This relative motion can be extracted as a feature to actuate an output, e.g. if ΔX reaches a defined positive threshold the output equivalent to 'move right' is actuated. With positive and negative thresholds for the X and the Y axis four direction outputs can be realized. If only a single output is needed the absolute value of ΔX or ΔY reaching the threshold triggers the output.

As an additional feature the speed of the movement can be determined so that the triggering of the output is not only dependent by the relative motion but also by the acceleration.

### 3.3 Converter Hardware Exemplified in Various Applications

The following examples were chosen out of a practical connection. The converter hardware was evaluated in three different settings.

The first application that was tested with this converter is the combination of a mouth-operated input device – the LifeTool IntegraMouse® - and an in-house developed prototype of a toy robot system [3,4]. The toy robot system is an assistant for children with severe physical disabilities for playing with special bricks. The system was developed for the use with a five key input device or a single switch. The four directions and confirmation could be achieved with it. The LifeTool IntegraMouse® enables the user to activate all mouse functions, mouse clicks are slight sucking or blowing.

One of the test people for the toy robot system was a child with a transverse spinal cord syndrome and who could only move her head. This child uses the LifeTool IntegraMouse® as an input device for the computer. Operating with the toy robot system would only be feasible for the child via single switch. Working in the scanning mode results in drawbacks for the child: Training on a new input device and needing more time to move the toy robot than with the established pointing device. With the converter hardware it is possible to control the toy robot system with the LifeTool IntegraMouse® such as with a five key input device.

The hardware converter was tested in a slightly different application by patients suffering from progressive muscle diseases. Due to the limited range of motion and a very low force the patients could only utilize special input devices. Instead of using very expensive sensor devices such as a muscle sensor, a simple touchpad was chosen as interface. With this configuration it was possible to control the environment via a GewaProg III – programmable transmitter - by moving a single finger over the touchpad without the need for an expensive muscle sensor or eye blink switch.

Another interesting application of this converter is the combination of a trackball suitable for children and a simple mains switch box. The converter is set to a direction independent mode, this means that the motion of the pointing device in a certain direction is not associated with triggering the output of the corresponding direction but a motion in any direction causes the activation of one single output.

The appliance connected to the mains via the switch box can be turned on or off by simply pushing the trackball. A threshold can be set to a certain acceleration of the pointing device. Such a simple mode of operation appears suitable for the utilisation of computer software. In this case motion of the pointing device with certain acceleration can invoke an action of the software program. The converter could be connected to an appropriate sensor box to control the software.

To avoid the need of such a sensor box together with special software the same working principle of the converter was implemented as software for the PC.

This program captures mouse cursor movements independent from the used pointing device, converts them into keystrokes or mouse clicks and allows the definition of the mode of operation. The operation modes range from a simple selection if the output is a keystroke or a mouse click to a larger selection if the system distinguishes between different directions.

During the evaluation the software was tested with a trackball as input device and software for single switch use. For example such single switch software provides for example a multimedia photo album which is usually operated by a single mouse click or by pressing the spacebar. With the converter software it was possible to switch between the pictures simply by moving the trackball in any direction without the need of any additional hardware. To allow a similar mode of operation usually an oversized pushbutton and a mouse- or keyboard emulator would be required.

## 4 Results

One of the results of the project is a converter hardware that enables the translation of movement of pointing devices into discrete switch signals.

The core of the system shown in figure 2 and described in the chapters above is an 8 bit microcontroller that manages feature extraction of the pointing device data and threshold detection.

At the moment the attachment of Microsoft mouse compatible devices via a RS-232 serial port is possible. With slight modification of the system it would also be possible to use other RS-232 based devices or even PS/2 compatible equipment.

Since pointing devices with serial port or PS/2 connection seem to disappear from the market it should be thought about USB devices.

The problem with USB is that the converter would have to act as USB host controller (comparable to the function of the PC) which is not as easy as the operation as USB endpoint (comparable to USB peripheral devices).

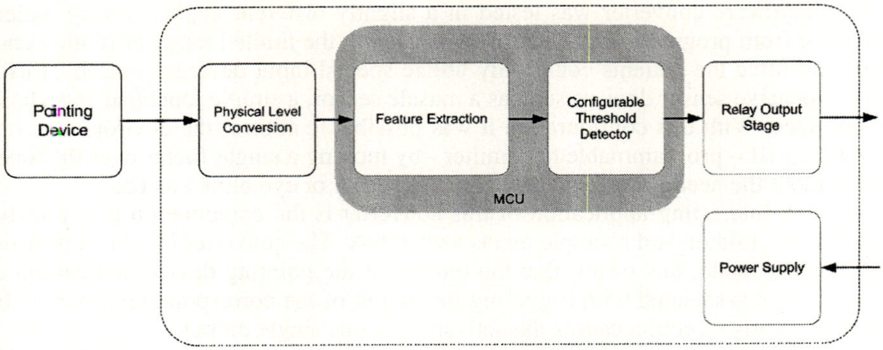


**Fig. 2.** Converter system

The converter hardware was developed with state of the art technology and so costs were reduced. For illustration a cost comparison will be shown now. For example, a person who suffers from muscular disease is working due to her abilities with a touchpad on the computer. In addition the person uses an environmental control system. This technical aid cannot be used with the touchpad, due to her disease a muscle sensor would be a possible input device for this aid. The costs for the muscle sensor averaged out at 530 . By using state of the art technology the developed hardware will cost about 250 . In comparison to the muscle sensor the client will save ca. half of the money. The clients benefit not only from low costs but also because a new training phase with the new input device would be avoided.

## 5 Discussion

The developed converter hardware implicates advantages in certain cases. In cases where the client operates with a pointing device like a mouse, touchpad or a trackball they can benefit from the converter hardware. As mentioned before the developed hardware will be cheaper than an additional input device. But the main argument for taking this converter hardware is that people with disabilities have no additional training phase with the new input device. They can apply their accustomed pointing device.

The converter software can be an additional device to single switches which were used in combination with the computer. It allows fulfilling other motion sequences, for example moving the trackball in any direction to affect actions on the computer.

Another application for the converter software can be the use of it in combination with an onscreen keyboard. Operating with a standard mouse requires free movements and for some people means that they have to strain themselves selecting a field on the onscreen keyboard. To confine the free mouse movements can be a solution for such cases. The converter software can be configured so that only four directions movements are possible and people have to cover a shorter distance on the onscreen keyboard.

## References


1. Cook, A.M., Hussey, S.M.: Assistive Technologies. Principles and Practice. 2nd. Ed., Mosby, St.Louis Missouri (2002)
2. Lazzaro, J.J.:Adapting PCs for disabilities, Addison-Wesley, USA (1995
3. Fugger, E., Asslaber, M., Hochgatterer, A.: Mouth-controlled interface for Human-Machine Interaction in education & training. In: Marincek, . (eds.): Assistive Technology – Added Value to the Quality of Life, Proceedings of the AAATE 2001, IOS Press, Amsterdam (2001) 379-383
4. Prazak, B., Kronreif, G., Hochgatterer, A., Fürst, M.: Robot supported play – new possibilities for physically handicapped children?! In: Assisitive technology – shaping the future, Proceedings of AAATE 2003, IOS Press, Amsterdam (2003) 539-543

# Optimisation of the Selection Set Features for Scanning Text Input

Julio Abascal, Luis Gardeazabal, and Nestor Garay

Laboratory of Human-Computer Interaction for Special Needs
University of the Basque Country-Euskal Herriko Unibertsitatea
Manuel Lardizabal 1, E-20018 Donostia, Spain
{julio.abascal,luisg,nestor}@si.ehu.es

**Abstract.** Scanning is one of the most popular text input methods for people with severe movement restrictions due to diverse kinds of disabilities. It is frequently used to input messages into communication systems, such as text-to-voice translators in order to maintain conversations. Nevertheless, the rate of text production usually obtained is very slow. For this reason, every effort to save time and optimize communication speed is welcome. In this way, this paper presents a study on the influence on the character input rate of diverse parameters related to the matrix that contains the selection set, such as shape, size, number of dimensions and layout of the selectable items. Its purpose is to extract a set of guidelines to design efficient input systems well adapted to the user, based on the scanning of items and its selection by means of one switch or push-button.

## 1 Introduction

In a classical paper [11], Vanderheiden classifies input methods into three types: direct selection, scanning and codification. Direct selection uses *spatial keyboards* (the standard) where selectable items are spatially distributed, mapping each key with an item (character, syllable, word, image, etc.). This kind of keyboard requires a considerable amount of mobility, coordination and strength in the upper limbs required on the user's part. Input by codification also requires coordination and strength in order to press a sequence of keys, usually in a reduced keyboard to compose the code related to each character (e.g. Morse code). However, people with diverse motor impairments that restrict their mobility may use scanning input. This input method is composed of a *temporal keyboard* and an *activation system* benefiting any voluntary residual movement in the user. Temporal keyboards sequence selectable items over the time. That is, the diverse items are sequentially presented to the user until he or she selects one of them by activating any type of switch or push-button. This input method is well described in the literature [1, 2, 3], and the most relevant concepts, such as selection set, control interface, input domain, activation method, etc., are precisely defined by Cook and Hussey [4]. In addition to physical interaction features, other authors have studied the cognitive aspects of interaction using scanning input. For instance, Mizuko et al. [9] considered the effects of selection techniques and array sizes on short-term visual memory.

K. Miesenberger et al. (Eds.): ICCHP 2004, LNCS 3118, pp. 788–795, 2004.

Even if scanning techniques allow people to input texts, the communication rate obtained with temporal keyboards is significantly slower than the one obtained speaking or typing in spatial keyboards. Diverse researches have been conducted to enhance the input rate, producing interesting techniques, such as word prediction [5], and character disambiguation [7]. On the other hand, several authors, such as Lesher [8] and Venkatagiri [12], have shown the influence on the selection rate of various parameters, for instance, the scanning strategies or the matrix layout. In this work, these diverse parameters are jointly studied, simulated and statistically measured. Therefore, this research is aimed at studying the overall influence of the diverse parameters in order to propose clear guidelines for the design of optimal input set configurations, to minimize text input rate using a single push-button.

## 2 Methodology

A number of parameters have been analytically described by means of equations and their influence simulated. For this purpose, we used a simulator that tries to compose sample texts using diverse input sets. This simulator calculates the theoretical number of keystrokes and the lowest time needed to write them. As the user's mistakes in inputting text have a large influence on the real use of the keyboards, the occurrence of errors in text inputting is also modelled in order to study its influence on the input rate.

### 2.1 Variables

The diversity of potential selection sets for each language makes an exhaustive simulation of all the possibilities impossible. In addition, small variations in the number of items that compose the selection set are not relevant for the results. For this reason, in this study we use a selection set[1] composed of 36 items that include 26 characters, a blank, punctuation signs, and a number of commands, such as "erase", "enter", etc. This selection set is easily adaptable to most languages using Latin characters. The variables we can manipulate for the research are the distribution of these elements into a matrix, the number of dimensions of the matrix and its layout.

Therefore, the key question is how to design the matrix containing the input set in order to allow the fastest scanning.

### 2.2 Measurements

In order to be able to compare diverse layouts, we need to calculate the time needed to write a text using them. However, this time cannot be absolutely measured because it depends on the scanning period T that is usually adjusted to the reaction capacity of the user. For this reason, the measurements are given in number of T's.

---

[1] *Selection set* is the items available from which choices are made (Lee and Thomas, 1990). Cited by Cook and Hussey in [4].

Let us consider a selection set distributed in a D-dimensional matrix of [1..n] x [1..m] ... x [1..s] elements (see Figure 1). If the system sequentially scans each dimension, any position may be numbered in order as $X_{i,j...k}$

To select the item in position p = $X_{a,b...d}$, the user needs to wait for a time of **(r-1)*T** seconds, where r = a + b +...+ d. After that, this item becomes selectable for a maximum period of T seconds. The time expended by the user to select the item is called *reaction time* and is assumed T/2, on average. Therefore, the time elapsed to select the item in position p is:

$$t(p) = (r - 1)\,T + T/2 \tag{1}$$

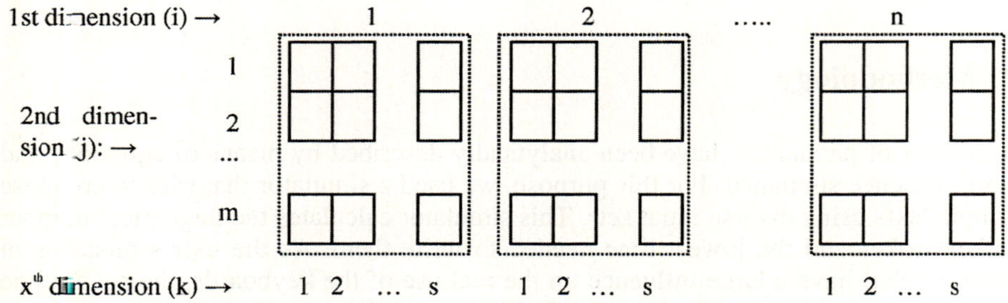


**Fig. 1.** A D-dimensional matrix of [1..n] x [1..m] x... x [1..s] elements

## 3 First Hypothesis: All the Options Have the Same Probability

In order to study the influence of the layout isolated from other influences, the first step is to consider that all the items have the same selection probability. Under this hypothesis, three cases are analysed with the input set distributed in a one-dimension matrix, a two-dimension matrix and a D-dimensions matrix.

From this study, we deduced that the average access time for a D-dimensional matrix with $N_i$ items allocated to each dimension i, is:

$$t = \sum_{i=1}^{D} \frac{N_i}{2} T \tag{2}$$

The selection of an item in a D-dimensions matrix requires D keystrokes. Matrixes having more than two dimensions must be split into blocks of two-dimension matrixes to be displayed correctly. Figure 2 shows, for instance, a three-dimension matrix (2x3x4) containing 24 characters.

In this way, the average access time and the time needed to write a text can be calculated. For instance, using a 4x3x3 matrix for 36 selectable items, the average time is:

$$t_{(3x4x3)} = \frac{3+4+3}{2} T = 5T \tag{3}$$

and the time needed to produce an 80 characters text (with T= 1 s) is:

$$80 \times 5 = 400 \text{ s} \tag{4}$$

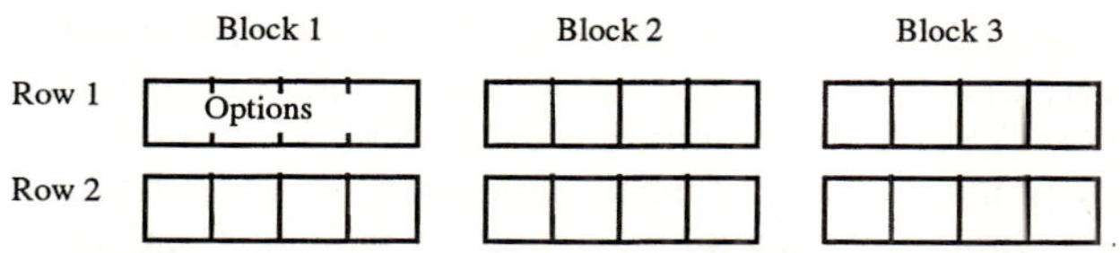


**Fig. 2.** 3-dimension matrix with 2x3x4 distribution

## 4 Second Hypothesis: Distribution of the Items by Frequency of Use

In the previous section, we considered all options equally probable. However, when natural language is used, this is not true. The frequency of each letter is different and, in addition, is heavily dependent on the language. This suggests that the most frequent items should be located in the places requiring the lowest access times. Following this simple procedure, the average access time decreases considerably.

The previously studied three cases are analysed under this hypothesis, with the input set distributed in a one-dimension matrix, a two-dimension matrix or a D-dimensions matrix.

For example, the average access time for a two-dimensional matrix with 36 items sorted by frequency in the Spanish language is:

$$t_{(6x6)} = \sum_{i=1}^{6}\sum_{j=1}^{6} f_{i,j} \times t_{i,j} = 0.1828\times1+0.1126\times2+0.1028\times3+\ldots \cong 3.15T \qquad (5)$$

Using this layout, the average time needed to write 80 characters is

$$T_{(6x6)}(80) = 3.15 \times 1 \times 80 = 252 \text{ s} \qquad (6)$$

As a first conclusion, Table 1 shows the average access times and the average times to write 80 characters for equally probable items and 1-, 2- and 3-dimension distributions, opposed to distributions taking item probabilities into account. Results are given in T units for the average time and seconds for 80 characters.

**Table 1.** Average access times and times to write 80 characters for 1-, 2- and 3-dimensional distributions

| | 1 Dim 36×1 | 2 Dim 6×6 | 3 Dim 3×4×3 | 3×2×6 |
|---|---|---|---|---|
| *Equally probable $T_{m\_a}$* | 18T(1440 s) | 6T (480 s) | 5T (400 s) | 5,5T (440 s) |
| *By frequencies $T_{m\_a}$* | 6,06T (485 s) | 3,15T (252 s) | 3,11T (249 s) | 3,2T (256 s) |

## 5 Modelling User Mistakes

After studying key factors such as the layout and shape of the matrix, it is very convenient to study the influence of the mistakes made by the user and the way they are treated by the system. The aim is to model the type and frequency of errors and to use this model to determine the extra time introduced by their management.

Let us suppose a scanning system that uses a D-dimension matrix. When a user makes a mistake in the selection of the $k^{th}$ dimension, he or she has to wait B scanning cycles in the next dimension without making any selection. Then, the system starts the scanning again by the first dimension.

To start, let us define *error* and *delay* concepts in this environment. An *error* occurs when a selection (a keystroke) different to the one wanted by the user is made. This kind of mistake is frequent when the user is tired or dispersed and when the scanning period T is too small[2]. On the other hand, *Delay* is the time elapsed from the moment a mistake happens until the system recovers the situation before the mistake.

To measure the influence of the delay *e* and $T_{delay}$ parameters are used. *e* is the rate of mistakes in relation to the number of correct selections made by a specific user, and provides an indication of the relative occurrence of errors. In addition, *delay time* is the number of T units needed to carry out a mistaken selection and correct it. That is, the time needed to go back from the wrong selection to the situation in which the user can start the correct selection.

$$\mathbf{T_{delay}} = t_{average\_access} + t_{selection\_abort} \quad (7)$$

$t_{selection\_abort}$ depends on the dimension where the mistake occurred, as the user has to wait B cycles in the next dimension until the system considers the wrong one cancelled. For instance, delay times for a 3-dimension matrix are as follows. If the mistake occurs in the first dimension:

$$t_{delay\_1} = t_{average\_access\_i} + t_{abort\_i} = (½N_1 + B \times N_2)T \quad (8)$$

in the second dimension:

$$t_{delay\_2} = t_{average\_access\_i} + t_{average\_access\_j} + t_{abort\_j} = (½N_1 + ½N_2 + B \times N_3) \times T \quad (9)$$

in the third dimension:

$$t_{delay\_3} = t_{average\_access\_i} + t_{average\_access\_j} + t_{average\_access\_k} + t_{abort\_k} = ½(N_1 + N_2 + N_3)T + t_{abort} \quad (10)$$

$T_{abort}$ depends on the position in the matrix occupied by the abort option. Let us suppose that $T_{abort}$ is equal to the average access time.

$$t_{delay\_3} = (N_1 + N_2 + N_3)\, T \quad (11)$$

2 The scanning period T is a very influencing factor. If this period is too long, the user makes an early selection and the resting time became useless. Since this extra time is included in each scanning steep, the lost time can be considerable. If T is too short, the user has not enough time to react and makes more mistakes. In both cases the time needed to compose a text considerably increases. Most systems include a parameter that allows adjusting this period to each specific user. Nevertheless, the reaction time of each user changes significantly along the day due to factors such as fatigue and attitude. A good solution is to use adaptive systems that dynamically adjust the period T to the user, maintaining a low rate of mistakes. In [7] Gardeazabal presents an adaptive system based on fuzzy logic to continuously fine-tune T.

Generalizing to a D dimensions matrix, the delay time is:

$$t_{delay\_d} = \sum_{i=1}^{d-1} \frac{N_i}{2} T + B \times N_d \times T \qquad \text{with } d < D\text{, and} \tag{12}$$

$$t_{delay\_D} = 2\sum_{i=1}^{D} \frac{N_i}{2} T \qquad \text{with } d = D \tag{13}$$

and the average delay time is:

$$t_{average\_delay} = \frac{\sum_{i=1}^{D} t_{delay\_\dim\_i}}{D} \tag{14}$$

To summarize, Table 2 shows delay times for several layouts.

**Table 2.** Time delays for three matrixes and three different values for B

| | 2 Dim 6×6 | 3 Dim 3×4×3 | 3 Dim 3×2×6 |
|---|---|---|---|
| $T_{delay\_1}$ | (3+6B)T | (1,5+4B)T | (1,5+2B)T |
| $T_{delay\_2}$ | 12T | (3,5+3B)T | (2,5+6B)T |
| $T_{delay\_3}$ | -- | 10T | 11T |
| $T_{average\_delay}$ | (7,5+3B)T | (5+2,3B)T | (5+2,7B)T |
| $T_{average\_delay}$ B=1 | 10,5T | 7,3T | 7,7T |
| $T_{average\_delay}$ B=2 | 13,5T | 9,7T | 10,3T |
| $T_{average\_delay}$ B=3 | 16,5T | 12T | 13T |

To avoid long delays when undesired selections are made, the selection set may contain a special item (represented here by #) to go back without having to wait until the end of the scanning cycle after a mistake. The selection matrix may contain more than one of this kind of cycle-abort item. This procedure speeds up the management of mistakes, but slows down the normal composition of messages. That is due to the fact that the selection set is enlarged by a number of extra characters that must be scanned at each cycle. Therefore, to optimize the message composition speed, the inclusion of cycle-abort items should be conditioned to the average rate of mistakes made by each user. In Figure 3, we show a 3x2x7 distribution with '#' in the 4th position of the last dimension (this is what we call 3x2x7-#4 distribution, being the number after '#' the position where the cycle-abort character is shown).

j=1

| | k=1 | 2 | 3 | 4 | 5 | 6 | 7 |
|---|---|---|---|---|---|---|---|
| i=1 | 1,5 | 2,5 | 3,5 | # | 5,5 | 6,5 | 7,5 |
| 2 | 2,5 | 3,5 | 4,5 | # | 6,5 | 7,5 | 8,5 |
| 3 | 3,5 | 4,5 | 5,5 | # | 7,5 | 8,5 | 9,5 |

2

| | | | | | | |
|---|---|---|---|---|---|---|
| 2,5 | 3,5 | 4,5 | # | 6,5 | 7,5 | 8,5 |
| 3,5 | 4,5 | 5,5 | # | 7,5 | 8,5 | 9,5 |
| 4,5 | 5,5 | 6,5 | # | 8,5 | 9,5 | 10,5 |

**Fig. 3.** Access times for a distribution matrix 3x2x7 with a cycle-abort character in every 4th position (3x2x7-#4 distribution)

In Figure 4, global average times of 3-D distributions, supposing B=2, are summarised. The distributions shown are 3x4x3, 3x2x6, 3x2x7-#4 and 3x2x7-#7.

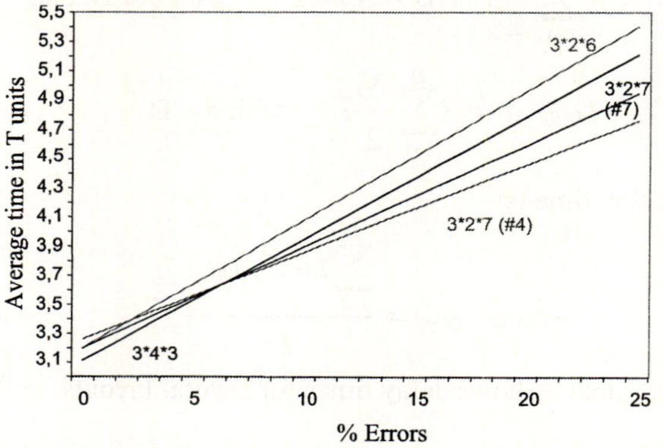


**Fig. 4.** Global average times for 3-D distributions, depending on the user's error rates

## 6 Conclusions

The main contribution of this research is the study of the overall interaction of the diverse factors influencing the performance of input set configurations used in text input rate with a single push-button. These results allow for the proposal of clear guidelines for the design of optimal layouts in order to optimise the input rate. Among our conclusions, we would like to underline the following:

1. Items must be located following their frequency of use. Other dispositions, such as alphabetical order, largely increase access time.
2. The shape of the matrix (number of dimensions) is the second relevant parameter. If a 2-dimensions matrix is used, it should be square: 6x6 is much better than 9x4, for instance.
3. Among the studied layouts, the best results are offered by the ones specified as 3x4x3, 3x2x7-#4, and 3x2x7-#7. The last decision depends on the average number of user errors, his or her preferences, as well as other personal characteristics.

These results for alphabetic characters can be extrapolated to other selection sets containing syllables, words, icons, etc., if their relative frequencies are known.

As these results have been statistically obtained by modelling the user, it is necessary to conduct experiments with real users so as to determine the speed and accuracy that can really be obtained by users (such as the one conducted by Szeto et al. [10]). For this reason, they are being tested with real users to verify usability and accessibility issues. In these experiments aspects such as acceptability, convenience, ease of learning and use, etc., are verified.

## References

1. Abascal J., Gardeazabal L.: Technology to Support Alternative and Augmentative Communication. In: Casals A. (Ed.): Technological Aids for the Disabled, Societat Catalana de Tecnologia-Institut d'Estudis Catalans, Barcelona (1998)

2. Bain B. K., Leger D.: Switches, Control Interfaces, and Access Methods. In: Bain B. K., Leger D. (Eds.): Assistive Technology. An Interdisciplinary Approach. Churchill Livingstone (1997)
3. Barret J. and Herriotts P.: Communication and Access to Computer Technology. The Disability Information Trust, Oxford (1995)
4. Cook A. M., Hussey S. M.: Assistive Technologies: Principles and Practice. Mosby (1.995)
5. Garay N., Abascal G. J.: Intelligent Word-Prediction to Enhance Text Input Rate. In: Moore J. et al. (Eds.): Procs. of the 1.997 Int. Conf. Intel. User Interfaces, ACM (1997) 241-244
6. Gardeazabal L.: Applications of the computer technology to the enhancement of the communication rate in Augmentative and Alternative Communication Systems. Ph. D. Report (in Spanish). University of the Basque Country, San Sebastián (1999). (Published by Servicio Editorial de la UPV-EHU. Leioa (2001)
7. Lesher G. W., Moulton B. J., Higginbotham D. J.: Optimal Character Arrangements for Ambiguous Keyboards. IEEE Trans. on Rehab. Eng., vol. 6, no. 4 (1998) 415-23
8. Lesher G. W. et al.: Techniques for augmenting scanning communication. Augmentative and Alternative Communication, vol. 14 (1998) 81-101
9. Mizuko M., Reichle J., Ratcliff A., Esser J.: Effects of Selection Techniques and Array Sizes on Short-Term Visual Memory. AAC, vol. 10, no. 2 (1994) 237-244
10. Szeto A.Y.J., Allen E.J., Littrell M.C.: Comparison of Speed and Accuracy for Selected Electronic Communication Devices and Input Methods. AAC, vol. 9, no. 4 (1993) 229-242.
11. Vanderheiden G. C.: Augmentative Modes of Communication for the Severely Speech- and Motor-Impaired. Clinical Orthopaedics and Related Research, no. 148 (1980) 70-86
12. Venkatagiri H. S. Efficient Keyboard Layouts for Sequential Access in Augmentative and Alternative Communication, AAC, vol. 15 (1999) 126-134

# FastScanner: An Accessibility Tool for Motor Impaired Users

Stavroula Ntoa[1], Anthony Savidis[1], and Constantine Stephanidis[1,2]

[1] Foundation for Technology and Research – Hellas (FORTH), Institute of Computer Science
Vassilika Vouton, Heraklion, Crete, GR-71110 Greece
cs@ics.forth.gr
[2] University of Crete, Department of Computer Science

**Abstract.** People with motor impairments often face difficulties in accessing interactive applications and services. This paper presents a tool, named FastScanner that enables motor-impaired users to work with any application running in Microsoft Windows, without the need of a posteriori modification, through the use of binary switches as an alternative to traditional input devices. Evaluation of the tool has shown that it facilitates effective and efficient interaction.

## 1 Introduction

People with motor impairments of upper limps often face difficulties in accessing interactive applications and services. Currently available technological solutions may be either too specific or strongly dependent on specific platforms, and, therefore, potentially of limited use.

This paper presents a tool, named FastScanner that enables motor-impaired users to work with any application running in Microsoft Windows, by using only a binary switch as an input device, thus overcoming problems related to the inability to use traditional input devices, such as the keyboard or the mouse. FastScanner employs scanning techniques with dynamic retrieval of the applications' hierarchical structure, making therefore accessible any application in a windows environment. The paper also presents the results of user-based laboratory evaluation of the tool.

## 2 Related Work

Conventional efforts towards the accessibility of interactive applications and services adopt a reactive approach, mainly by adapting commercially available solutions and offering assistive technology add-ons [1]. In particular, regarding people with movement restrictions of upper limps, the most commonly adopted products include speech recognition programs, virtual keyboards, alternative input devices (e.g., special keyboards, switches), word prediction software, voice browsers and applications with embedded scanning. These products, are often too specialized, and therefore of limited use.

Recently, there have been a number of initiatives by mainstream actors (Microsoft, Sun, IBM, Apple, etc) and research consortia to develop technological frameworks

K. Miesenberger et al. (Eds.): ICCHP 2004, LNCS 3118, pp. 796–803, 2004.

that provide more adequate support for accessibility. These efforts aim to provide e-accessibility tools as integral components of mainstream interaction platforms and environments, and include: (i) the accessibility features of an operating system (such as the Sticky Keys, or the Mouse Keys) [3], [4] and, (ii) the open architectures (such as Microsoft Active Accessibility [5] and Java Accessibility [6]) which facilitate software developers in creating more accessible products [2]. Usually, the accessibility features of operating systems are insufficient, whereas open architectures do not directly address the requirements of end users.

Scanning is an interaction method for users with motor impairments of the upper limbs, in which objects are accessed in a predefined order [7]. The user may choose one of the interaction options by using a binary switch as an input device. Until recently, the scanning method could only be embedded in an application by writing the appropriate programming code. As a subsequent step, an augmented library of windows objects supporting scanning was created, providing developers with the opportunity to create applications with scanning by using the augmented library components. However, applications and services developed with these techniques soon became obsolete when the next generation of the Microsoft Windows operating system was introduced.

## 3 A Tool for Alternative Access

Following the proactive approach, a tool, called FastScanner, has been developed in order to provide access to Microsoft Windows applications without recourse to any subsequent modification, through the use of binary switches as an alternative to the traditional input devices (i.e. keyboard, mouse). Sequential access to the interaction elements of a user interface is provided through scanning, while the hierarchical structure of application is dynamically retrieved. For the intended target user group, the use of hierarchical scanning appeared to be the most appropriate interaction method, mainly due to the rapid interaction it ensures compared to simple mouse emulators or on-screen keyboards. Furthermore, the dynamic retrieval of the hierarchical structure of an application ensures that the scanning system will operate with any application in a windows environment. As a result, applications become immediately accessible.

### 3.1 Presentation of the Tool

FastScanner sequentially scans all the interactive interface elements of the application being scanned, providing thus the user with the opportunity to interact with each one of them. There is only one active interface element for each dialogue step, indicated by the coloured border that surrounds it. The user may interact with the indicated element by pressing an appropriate switch. The position of the border indicates the currently interactive element, while the colour of the border indicates the state of the interaction dialogue. There are three types for dialogue states:

- Entry state. It is represented by the green color of the border and indicates that the user is ready to interact with the active object.
- Exit state. It is represented by the red color of the border and indicates that the user is ready to move the dialogue to the next interactive interface element.

- Selection state. It is used only in the case of selection objects, such as the items of a list; it is represented by the orange color of the border and indicates that the user can select the enclosed object.

The user can provide input by pressing one of the two available switches. Each switch corresponds to an input command. The available input commands are "select" and "next". Initiation of the selection action indicated that the user wishes to proceed with the action that the dialogue state indicates. On the other hand, if the user initiates the select action when the dialogue is in exit state, the dialogue will move to the next interactive interface element. Finally, when a next action is initiated, the dialogue state will change to the next available state.

Interface objects have been classified into categories, in order to be able to represent their properties and behaviour appropriately. For each one of these categories a specific diagram has been designed and implemented, in order to represent the user's interaction with it through the FastScanner tool. A general overview of the interaction dialogue for all objects, is presented in Figure 1.

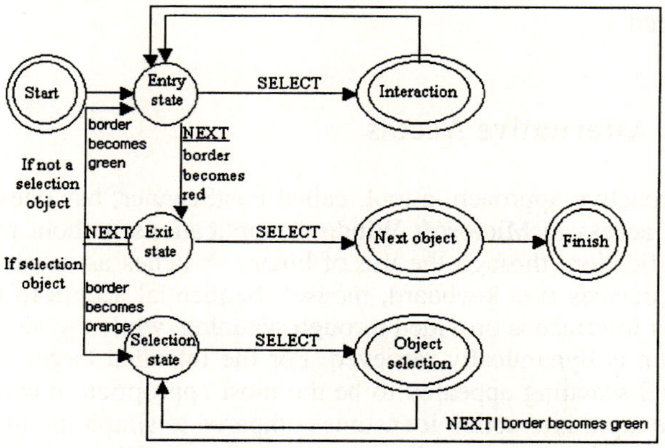


**Fig. 1.** Interaction with an interface element in FastScanner

The possibility for time scanning has been added to FastScanner, in order to help users interact with a Microsoft windows application more efficiently. When working in time-scanning mode, users have to initiate only the "select" actions. The "next" action is automatically initiated by the system when a specific time interval elapses without a user action. This allows for interaction with a single switch.

The graphical interface of the tool is comprised by certain dialogue windows, which allow users to perform actions that are usually carried out with the use of a pointing device, such as moving or resizing a window, as well as to personalise their interaction with the tool.

When the user initiates the FastScanner tool, a window appears presenting all the application windows that are currently open, and asks the user to select the desired application. This dialog is depicted in Figure 2(a). Interaction with the initial dialog of the tool takes place through scanning, and with the use of the binary switches, as described earlier. Once the user selects the "Scan" button, the requested application comes to the foreground and the scanning dialog is transferred to it. It should be mentioned that objects in a window are scanned in a predefined order, from top to bottom and from left to right.

In single switch interaction, one of the two switches is used to initiate the select action, while the other one is used for configuring the size and position of the application window and defining some options, such as the color of the border for each state and the input device settings, by initiating a settings dialog. In the manual scanning mode, the settings dialog window appears when the user presses both switches at the same time. The settings dialog appears in Figure 2(b). The user can move the window of the application by selecting one of the eight buttons of the first two rows, or resize the window by selecting one of the four buttons of the third row. The button with the palette initiates the border settings window, which is displayed in Figure 2(c) and allows the user to set the color for each one of the dialogue states (entry, exit and selection) as well as the width of the border. The button with the input devices in the initial settings window initiates the input device settings window, which is displayed in Figure 2(d) and is used for enabling or disabling the time-scanning mode and specifying the time interval for the automatic triggering of the "next" action. The last two buttons of the initial settings window can be used for pausing and restarting FastScanner and for terminating the operation of the tool.

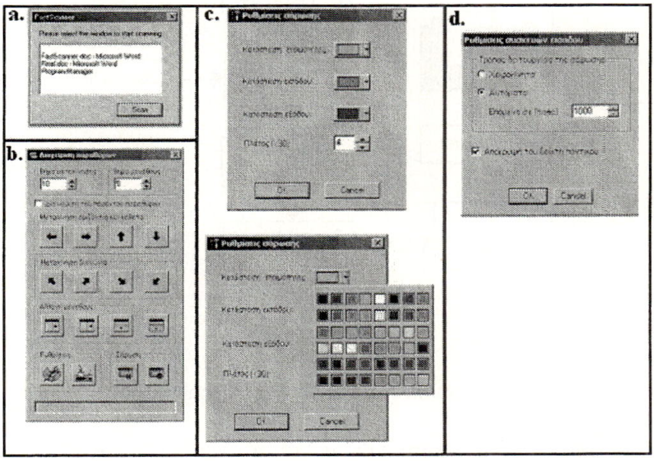


**Fig. 2.** GUI elements of the tool

### 3.2 Architecture of the Tool

FastScanner is mainly comprised of five mutually interacting components, which are presented in Figure 3. The left side of this Figure shows how the Microsoft Active Accessibility platform communicates with the tool and provides information regarding a windows application.

During an initial filtering process, FastScanner analyses the graphical objects that constitute the user interface of an application, and, according to the properties of such objects, determines the final hierarchy of interaction objects to be scanned. The final hierarchy only includes those objects with which the user can interact. For example, a label should not be included in the final hierarchy, since the user cannot interact with it. The root of hierarchical structure is the application window. The hierarchy is recursively built starting from the root. For each node, the number of child objects is determined and a pointer is obtained through Microsoft Active Accessibility. The "Dynamic object retrieval" unit filters the objects, while the hierarchical structure of the objects is created and maintained in the "Dynamic object hierarchy" unit.

The objects participating in the final hierarchy may belong to one of the following categories: *Text entry objects*. These are objects used to enter text, such as text fields. Traditionally, they require the use of a keyboard. *Simple objects*. These are objects related to an action, such as buttons. When using a traditional input device, interaction with these objects takes place by just clicking the left mouse button. *Selection objects*. These are objects that usually belong to a list or a tree structure, and traditionally require selection with the use of the mouse. *Container objects*. These are objects that realise groupings of other objects, such as group boxes. When using a traditional input device, users do not interact with container objects. However, their role is very important when using a binary input device with the scanning method, since they allow the user to indicate whether (s)he wishes to interact with anyone of the contained objects and therefore ensure more efficient interaction.

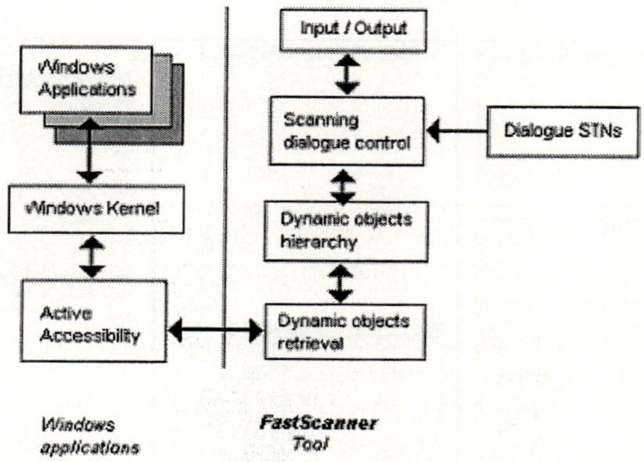


**Fig. 3.** Architecture of the FastScanner tool

The interpretation of input commands as system actions takes place in the "Scanning dialogue control" unit of the FastScanner tool. This unit, which is aware of the current dialogue object, receives a notification regarding the user input, and based on the state transition network diagram of such an object, determines the appropriate system output. For each of the aforementioned categories, a separate state transition network diagram has been modelled to represent the response of the tool to the user interaction with the corresponding objects. Interaction through the select command differs for objects of different types, as follows: *For a text entry object*, selection indicates that the user wishes to enter text, therefore an on-screen keyboard is displayed. *For a simple object*, selection initiates the action to which the object is related. *For a selection object*, selection entails selecting the object and performing the default action to which it is related, and is equivalent to double-clicking an object when using a mouse. *For a container object*, selection entails moving the dialog to the contained objects. Interaction through the "next" command leads the dialogue to the next available state for all objects. For example, if the active element is a container object and the dialogue is in entry state, a "next" action corresponds to the dialogue's transition in exit state and vice versa. However, if the active element is a selection object, the dialogue should move to the selection state, as shown in Figure 1.

In case the user input initiates a modification to the application that is being "scanned", such as, for example, opening a new dialog window, FastScanner receives a notification through the Active Accessibility platform. This notification is processed and when necessary the hierarchical structure of objects is reconstructed. The tool dynamically adapts to the modifications of each application.

## 4 Evaluation

A user-based laboratory usability evaluation of FastScanner was has been performed. The target users of the tool are people with motor impairments (permanent or temporary) of the upper limbs. Ten users participated in the evaluation procedure, five with motor disabilities of upper limbs and five able-bodied simulating a temporary inability to use their hands. Participants were given a background information questionnaire to fill-in, in order to better understand their performance and behaviour during the test. The questionnaire asked questions regarding their age, gender and education, as well as about frequency of computer use, tasks usually carried out when using a computer, attitude towards computers, alternative input devices and special software used.

The evaluation was based on an appropriate scenario of common tasks performed by a typical computer user, such as writing documents, reading and sending e-mail, and navigating in the web. Evaluators were requested to carry out these tasks by using the FastScanner tool in time-scanning mode. The interaction scenario was comprised of two parts. The first part asked the user to compose a short text, using the WordPad application; and in more detail to open an existing file, fill in the required information, save the file and print it. The tasks referring to using an e-mail application and navigating in the web were combined in one scenario part, by employing a web mail application. Therefore, in the second part, the user should log in to the system, customize the layout of the web mail application, sort the received messages by date and read the most recent one, sort the received messages by sender and delete all the messages from a specific sender, compose a new message and attach to it the file that was created in the first part of the scenario, and finally log out of the system and add the login page to the favourite web addresses.

In order to specify how usable FastScanner is, the participants' effectiveness, efficiency and satisfaction was measured. Participants' effectiveness was calculated by studying the metrics shown in Table 1. In order to be able to find out exactly which characteristics of the scanning tool were difficult for users to understand and use, errors were classified in four categories: (A): The dialogue proceeded to a container object, whereas it should not, (B): The dialogue did not proceed to a container object, whereas it should, (C): The user selected to interact with an inappropriate object, (D): The user did not select to interact with the appropriate object. The efficiency metrics that were recorded for each evaluation participant are shown in Table 2. Finally, in order to measure the participants' satisfaction, two widely used IBM satisfaction questionnaires were employed: the IBM After-Scenario Questionnaire (ASQ) and the IBM Computer System Usability Satisfaction Questionnaire (CSUQ) [8].

Analysis of the background information questionnaires indicated that participants were aged from twenty-one to forty-two years old, their education ranged from high school to university degree, their experience in using computers varied from little to high, while in average they had a positive attitude towards computers.

Analysis of the performance results indicated that participants were in general effective in the tasks carried out (see Table 1). In particular, they achieved in both scenarios the majority of requested task goals, and the number of errors was small in average, the majority of which were corrected, while rarely the users asked the observer for help. Comparison among the participants' effectiveness in the two scenarios indicated that they were less efficient in the first one, since the number of errors was greater, while somewhat smaller percentage of errors was corrected. The fact that the majority of errors were of type A and type D indicates that the most serious problem that the users encountered when working with FastScanner was that they sometimes did not press the switch before the predefined interval elapsed and the dialogue moved to the next available state.

**Table 1.** Participants' effectiveness in the first scenario, in the second scenario and overall

| Scenario | Goal achievement (%) | Errors performed | | | | | Corrected errors (%) | Help requested (#) |
|---|---|---|---|---|---|---|---|---|
| | | A | B | C | D | Total | | |
| 1st | 96,6 | 2,9 | 1,8 | 2,1 | 4,2 | 11 | 94,8 | 0,3 |
| 2nd | 96,7 | 2,1 | 1,3 | 1,3 | 2,8 | 7,5 | 98,8 | 0,3 |
| Overall | 96,65 | 5 | 3,1 | 3,4 | 7 | 18,5 | 95,331 | 0,6 |

Furthermore, participants' interaction with the FastScanner application was considered rather efficient, since they did not need a very long time to carry out the requested tasks, and they rarely needed to consult the instruction booklet (see Table 2). Participants turned out to be more efficient in performing the second scenario, since despite the fact that it was approximately twice as large as the first one, they needed in average only few additional minutes to complete it. Participants' increased efficiency in the second scenario may result either from the relative difficulty of the first scenario or from the fact that they were more experienced when carrying out second scenario.

**Table 2.** Participants' efficiency in the first scenario, in the second scenario and overall

| Scenario | Time to complete (min.) | Task achievement efficiency | References to instructions |
|---|---|---|---|
| 1st | 18,74 | 5,49 | 0,4 |
| 2nd | 20,21 | 4,84 | 0 |
| Overall | 38,95 | 2,54 | 0,4 |

Finally, the analysis of the users' responses to the satisfaction questionnaires suggested that they were overall satisfied by the tool. Users' satisfaction could rate from 1 to 7, with 1 being the maximum. Therefore, as shown in Table 3, they were satisfied with the overall usability of the tool, its information and interface quality. However, participants were in average less satisfied during the execution of the first scenario. A detailed inspection of their answers to the questionnaires revealed that they met difficulties in using the virtual keyboard in order to enter text. However, it was noticed that able-bodied users were more dissatisfied than disabled users, probably due to the fact that they are acquainted with a more rapid interaction for entering text.

**Table 3.** Participants' satisfaction

| | ASQ | | CSUQ | | | |
|---|---|---|---|---|---|---|
| | 1st scenario | 2nd scenario | Overall | System Use | Information Quality | Interface Quality |
| **Min.** | 1,33 | 1 | 1,05 | 1,125 | 1 | 1 |
| **Max.** | 3 | 3 | 3,29 | 2,62 | 4 | 4,3 |
| **Average** | 2,04 | 1,82 | 2,11 | 2,02 | 2,24 | 2,11 |

As a conclusion, the analysis of the evaluation results indicated that FastScanner is a useful tool in assisting the interaction of motor impaired users with the Windows environment. However, regarding the participants' efficiency, certain limitations of the tool were identified, since they had to spend quite some time in order to carry out some of the given tasks, especially those involving text writing.

## 5 Ongoing and Future Work

FastScanner enables motor impaired users to have access to interactive applications and services with the use of a binary switch input device. User-based evaluation in the laboratory revealed that the tool was considered a practical and effective solution.

Currently, the functionality of the FastScanner is restricted to providing accessibility for one application at a time. Ongoing work addresses the issue of improving the usability of the tool and providing access to the overall windows environment, by facilitating access to multiple applications concurrently. Furthermore, particular emphasis will be placed in addressing the relative difficulty, revealed during evaluation, associated with the text entry user task.

## References


1. Stephanidis, C., & Emiliani P.L. (1999). Connecting to the Information Society: a European perspective. Technology and Disability Journal, 10, 21-44. Available electronically at: http://www.ics.forth.gr/hci/html/files/TDJ_paper.PDF
2. Stephanidis, C. (Ed.). (2001). User Interfaces for All - Concepts, Methods, and Tools. Mahwah, NJ: Lawrence Erlbaum Associates (ISBN 0-8058-2967-9, 760 pages)
3. http://www.microsoft.com/enable/guides/mobility.htm
4. http://www-3.ibm.com/able/prodsol_mobil.html
5. Corporation, Microsoft Active Accessibility, http://www.microsoft.com/enable/
6. IBM Corporation, Java AccessibilityTM Technology, http://java.sun.com/products/jfc/accessibility/doc
7. Savidis, A., Vernardos, G., & Stephanidis, C. (1997). Augmenting the Windows Object Library with Embedded Scanning Techniques for Motor-Impaired User Access. In Proceedings of the 6th International Conference on Man-Machine Interaction Intelligent Systems in Business (INTERFACES '97), Montpellier, France, 28-30 May (pp. 233-234)
8. Lewis, J.R. (1995) "IBM Computer Usability Satisfaction Questionnaires: Psychometric Evaluation and Instructions for Use" in International Journal of Human-Computer Interaction 7(1), pp. 57 – 78

# A Real-Time Voice Controlled Human Computer Interface to Help Persons with Motor Disability

Malek Adjouadi, Dalila Landestoy, Melvin Ayala, and Walter Tischer

Center for Advanced Technology and Education
Electrical & Computer Engineering Department
Florida International University
10555 W. Flagler Street, Miami FL 33174, USA
{adjouadi,Dalila.Landestoy,Melvin.Ayala}@fiu.edu
waltertischer@yahoo.com
http://www.cate.fiu.edu

**Abstract.** Current speech recognition (SR) systems have evolved technologically to begin having an impact in human computer interface (HCI) designs that can be used by persons with motor disabilities. This study presents a real-time user-friendly programming HCI able to convert voice commands into computer actions. To this end, an interface was developed for facilitating the communication between a *Microsoft* speech (MS) recognition engine and *MS Windows* such that the dictated commands are executed as if they were triggered by mouse or keyboard operations. Experiments were conducted with the mouse functionality commands to statistically establish a confusion matrix to assess the recognition accuracy of the system. Validation results from 15 subjects yielded a performance of 84% of accuracy in command recognition. Unexpected high confusion degrees between unrelated voice commands were experienced and were reported to the developers of this software tool for additional information and for investigating this potential design problem.

## 1 Introduction

The HCI design proposed in this study abides by the design principle "less obvious but powerful", and the notion that people with disabilities should be able to use products and services like everyone else, and if assistive or adaptive technologies are needed, they should be as free of constraints as possible. Therefore, this design approach is one that seeks intelligent software developments that will support our goal for universal access without burdening the users with any aspects of intrusion or overwhelming them with complex control mechanisms that are time consuming and difficult to integrate. The interface of choice is one that would be multimodal in order to address the different constraints imposed by the disability. The proposed voice-based interface is destined however for those individuals with severe motor disability but can still make use of their voice in order to initiate the proper commands. As designed this HCI is augmented with real-time software voice-induced commands for real-time applications, and to facilitate human-computer interaction in a user-friendly manner for web browsing, email, and editing. This is a major undertaking that will result in an alpha prototype that is reliable, accessible, cost effective, and certainly compatible with up to date assistive/adaptive technology based interfaces and with common computer-based platforms.

K. Miesenberger et al. (Eds.): ICCHP 2004, LNCS 3118, pp. 804–812, 2004.

Current speech recognition (SR) systems have evolved technologically to begin having an impact in HCI designs [1, 2, 3] that can be used by disabled individuals to interact with computers. Speech recognition in this case refers to a technology that runs on a personal computer and converts spoken words into text in a word processor [4, 5]. Words are entered into the computer via a microphone which is connected to a sound-card.

Companies devoted to the commercialization of speech recognition systems have become more successful as the technology became more viable. Currently, SR systems are being produced and used by a large number of companies [6]. Inherent problems to these systems continue to be related to the time needed to train the system in order to produce a voice profile that is unique to the user, and in minimizing training errors which result in unrecognized voice commands [7]. Other problems are in the scalability due to increasing vocabulary and in the adaptability of the engine to different users. Modalities such as mouse button operations by voice commands have unfortunately not been widely used to assist motor disabled individuals [8]. The main thrusts for this study are (1) to develop a user friendly speech recognition computer interface for motor disabled persons at low cost, and (2) to test and validate the system on different subjects for a performance evaluation.

## 2 General Design of the System

The proposed application is a combination of several technical resources such as Microsoft Visual Studio .NET [9], User32 libraries, Microsoft Access database [10] and Microsoft Speech Recognition Technology [11]. The main functionality is enclosed in the code implementation using Visual Basic .NET as the programming language, which is the bridge to communicate with the different components used in the development of this application. Its basic structure consists of an on screen-keyboard that receives events from the voice recognition engine as illustrated in Fig. 1.

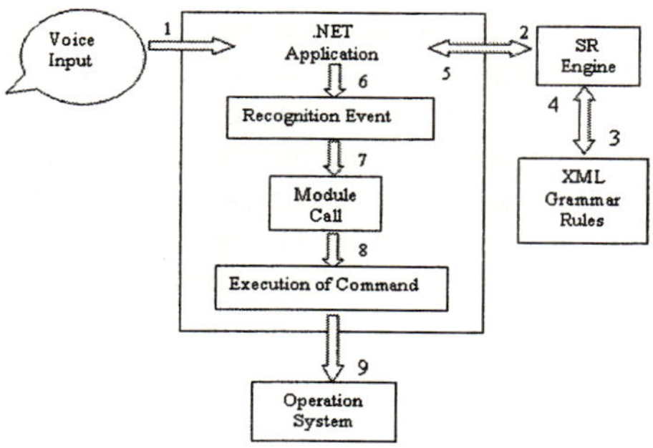


**Fig. 1.** Block diagram of the recognition process

The .NET application is the on-screen keyboard, whose input is a human voice. Once this input is received by the application, the speech recognition engine is initialized, and it loads its grammar rules from the XML file. During that process, the recognition event gets the results obtained from the engine and the result is passed on as an argument to a function call in order to execute the desired command. Finally, the execution of command is passed to the operation system, and the result can be physically seen, for example when the mouse moves to a certain direction.

As an extra feature a word bank of commonly used words was added to facilitate the user to write faster, which is stored in a table made in Access. All three are data components of the Microsoft Visual Studio .NET platform. In this application, two Speech Recognition engines were created. One that reads the grammar rules from an XML file, and the second one is dynamically initialized as the word bank changes its present values. The values vary as the user inputs a letter; consequently the word bank holds words beginning with that letter. If the user inputs another letter the process continues by changing the list in the word bank, which then will contain words beginning with those two letters.

In order to use the software, the user needs to train the computer. This is needed because the engine is not user independent; it will only recognize someone's commands if it was previously trained to this subject's.

## 3 Implementation of the Speech Recognition Engines

### 3.1 Engine for Mouse Cursor Movement Commands (MCMC)

The first SR engine was instantiated and initialized with grammar rules from an XML file, which forms the basis of the SR engine vocabulary. In order to create the recognition engine object, a recognition context, which is the primary means by which an application interacts with a speech application programming interface (SAPI) for speech recognition, was created. Furthermore, an *IspeechRecoGrammar* object was created, which enables applications to manage the words and phrases for the SR engine. After that, the grammar was explicitly created. In this specific application, a command and control grammar is used, which limits a word list by restricting the speaker to a set of words. Moreover, it is necessary to initialize the grammar by loading it from a file. This was achieved by the *CmdLoad FromFile* method. Finally, the grammar is set to active by using the state property. All these previous steps are executed when the form is initially loaded. A SR application has a wide variety of events, of which most are by default active. Once the application receives a recognition event, the *Recognition* code is invoked automatically and immediately. Besides, each event is associated with a particular recognition context. There are two important possible results from a recognition attempt: *Recognition* event and *FalseRecognition* event. Therefore, in the development of this computer interface, these two relevant events were used.

### 3.2 Engine for Dictation

A similar process was used when creating the second recognition engine used in this program. As aforementioned, a second recognition context was declared and created. Moreover, since the purpose this time was to initialize the recognition engine dynamically by getting the current values from the word bank, additional objects were created and new methods were used. This time the grammar was loaded from memory for which a different procedure was implemented. Several objects of IspeechReco-

Grammar class were created to enable applications to manage the words and phrases for the SR engine. In addition, an Object of IspeechGrammarRule, which defines the properties and methods of a speech grammar rule, were also declared. It was necessary to create an object of IspeechGrammarRules to represent a collection of ISpeechPhraseRule objects. In order to present the properties and methods of a speech grammar rule state a IspeechGrammarRuleState object was used, and another object was created to store the contents of the grammar held in memory. The next step was the creation of the grammar for which the previous declared tempGrammar object was used. After that it was necessary to save the collection of grammar rules contained in the RecoGrammar. A new object of IspeechGrammarRule was created in an ISpeechGrammarRules collection by calling the *Add* method. Once the grammar was loaded, it was saved to memory using the CommitAndSave method, which compiles the rules in the rule collection and saves the result. Afterward, the creation of the second grammar was initiated. Then, the CmdLoadFromMemory method was invoked to load the compiled speech grammar from memory. Finally, the rule was set to active using the state property. The CmdSetRuleState method activates or deactivates a rule by its name. This procedure is not only invoked when the form is initially loaded but also within the subroutine of TextChanged since this second speech recognition engine is to changed its present values as the word bank changes.

## 4 XML File

The voice commands are defined in an XML file that is dynamically loaded into the Grammar object at runtime (Table 1). Each command in the file is considered as a grammar rule that is defined with an ID name and value, which is unique and identifies the spoken word that is to be recognized by the SR engine as a voice command. In the tags that define a command, attributes can be set to specify precedence order of a particular word over another. This enables the use of phrases as commands rather than single words. The text grammar format is composed of XML tags, which can be structured to define the phrases that the speech recognition engine recognizes. The formal XML schema for the text grammar format is defined in a separate document. SR engines employ grammar rules to control the elements of sentence construction using the predetermined list of recognized word or phrase choices. This list of recognized words contained in the grammar rules forms the basis of the SR engine vocabulary.

**Table 1.** Commands defined in the XML file

| Voice Command | Resulting Action |
|---|---|
| Mouse Click | A click is simulated at the present cursor position |
| MouseDouble Click | A double click is simulated at the present cursor position |
| Mouse Right Click | A right click is simulated at the present cursor position |
| Mouse Move Left | A move to the left is simulated |
| Mouse Move Right | A move to the right is simulated |
| Mouse Move Down | A move down is simulated |
| Mouse Move Up | A move up is simulated |
| Mouse Drag | A right down click is simulated |
| Mouse Release | A right up is simulated |

The Parent Element of the XML tags is the GRAMMAR tag, which is the container for the entire XML grammar. The GRAMMAR tag is the outermost container for the XML grammar definition. It has two child elements: DEFINE and RULE tags. The DEFINE tag, which is used for declaring a set of string identifiers for numeric values, specifies the constant definitions for the grammar. This tag has a child component, which is the ID. The ID tag is used for declaring a string identifier for numeric values. It has two required attributes: NAME and VAL. The NAME attribute defines the string identifier that will be associated with the constant value, and the VAL attribute defines the constant value that will be associated with the string identifier. The RULE tag, is the core tag for defining which commands are available for recognition. It has several attributes; between them are the ID and TOPLEVEL tags.

## 5 Mouse Functionalities

In this study, the problem of mouse operation was addressed by importing several API (application programming interface) from the User32 libraries in order to communicate directly with the operating system. Most of the functionalities of the mouse were implemented using a combination of API functions and SR technologies. In order to accomplish this, the *mouse_event* function was imported to synthesize mouse events and motion. Its parameters are extremely important since each one of them will provide significant information for implementing desired tasks. The *dwFlags* specifies various aspects of mouse motion and button clicking. Parameter *dx* specifies the mouse's absolute position along the x-axis. Similarly, *dy* specifies the mouse's absolute position along the y-axis. Other important constants were imported in order to be passed as a parameter to the mouse_event function. To implement the mouse click event, a subroutine called *MouseClick* was created. A similar process was used when implementing the mouse double click action. To achieve this, the *MouseClick* subroutine is called twice. Another subroutine was implemented to produce a right click action. In addition, a timer component, which allows the execution of a specific event at a defined interval, models a smooth transition of the cursor position in the specified direction at every 100 microseconds. Since the time interval is very small, the mouse easily navigates through the monitor as if manually executed. To achieve the desired movement in a certain direction, the coordinate parameters (x and y) are passed with different values. By passing the mouse's absolute position equal 1 or -1 in the x and y direction, the mouse will move one pixel at a time. To perform faster movements, a higher number is passed (for example 5 or -5). In order to stop the mouse from moving the *stop* method of the timer component is invoked.

## 6 Experiments and Results

In this study, 15 subjects were used to test the SR interface. A convenient tool for analyzing the results of this system is the *confusion matrix*, which is a matrix containing information about the actual and recognized commands. The confusion matrix was used for finding pairs of commands that were most often confused. For example, C1's *state of confusion* with C2 is given by the amount of C1's commands classified as C2 as a percentage of the amount of C1's classified as either C1 or C2. Similarly, the *overall state* of confusion of a command is its state of confusion with respect to the rest of the commands. The *confusion rate* between two commands is the averaged state of confusion between each other. *The correct classification rate (CCR)* is the proportion of the total number of recognitions that were correct based on the total number of vocalized commands. It is determined using the equation:

$$CCR = \frac{\#\text{ of correct recognitions}}{\#\text{ of given commands}} \quad (1)$$

A confusion matrix tool [12] was used to evaluate the performance of the system. Table 2 shows general confusion rates obtained after integrating the errors of all subjects. It can be observed that the highest confusion rate is 23.16% and corresponds to command C13 (Mouse Drag) and C9 (Mouse Right Click).

**Table 2.** Confusion rates obtained for all subjects during MCMC recognition (rounded values)

| | R1 | R2 | R3 | R4 | R5 | R6 | R7 | R8 | R9 | R10 | R11 | R12 | R13 | R14 | R15 |
|---|---|---|---|---|---|---|---|---|---|---|---|---|---|---|---|
| C1 | - | | | | | | | | | | | | | | |
| C2 | 4.8 | - | | | | | | | | | | | | | |
| C3 | 0 | 0 | - | | | | | | | | | | | | |
| C4 | 0.4 | 5.4 | 0 | - | | | | | | | | | | | |
| C5 | 0 | 0 | 0.4 | 0 | - | | | | | | | | | | |
| C6 | 0 | 0.4 | 0 | 0 | 0 | - | | | | | | | | | |
| C7 | 0 | 0 | 0 | 0 | 0 | 0 | - | | | | | | | | |
| C8 | 0 | 0 | 0 | 0 | 0.5 | 0 | 0 | - | | | | | | | |
| C9 | 0 | 0 | 0 | 0 | 0 | 0 | 0 | 0 | - | | | | | | |
| C10 | 0 | 0 | 0 | 0 | 7.6 | 0 | 0 | 0 | 0 | - | | | | | |
| C11 | 0 | 0 | 0 | 0 | 0 | 0 | 0 | 0 | 0 | 0 | - | | | | |
| C12 | 0 | 0 | 0 | 0 | 0 | 1.3 | 0 | 0 | 0 | 4 | 0 | - | | | |
| C13 | 0.4 | 0 | 0.4 | 0 | 0.5 | 0.4 | 0.4 | 0 | 23 | 0 | 0.4 | 0 | - | | |
| C14 | 0 | 0 | 0.4 | 0.4 | 0 | 0 | 0 | 0 | 0 | 0 | 0 | 0 | 0 | - | |
| C15 | 8.1 | 7 | 2.4 | 3.4 | 6.6 | 6.4 | 2.0 | 4 | 8 | 5.7 | 2.4 | 7 | 0.7 | 2.3 | - |

(Legend: $C_i$: Dictated voice command; $R_i$: Recognized voice command; C1: Mouse Move Left; C2: Mouse Move Up; C3: Mouse Move Right; C4: Mouse Move Down; C5: Mouse Move Left Faster; C6: Mouse Stop; C7: Mouse Double Click; C8: Mouse Move Right Faster; C9: Mouse Right Click; C10: Mouse Move Up Faster; C11: Mouse Click; C12: Mouse Move Down Faster; C13: Mouse Drag; C14: Mouse Release; C15: Unrecognized Command)

Table 3 shows the inter-subject analysis, where column 2 represents the correct classification rate obtained for each subject, and column 3 displays the highest rate of confusion and specifies the corresponding command pair. It is interesting to note that this inter-subject analysis corroborates the aforementioned results shown in table 2, since it reveals that the command pair with the general highest confusion rate coincides with the command pair most confused by half of the subjects. In the general analysis, the highest overall confusion state was found to be command C9 (Mouse Right Click), being follow by command C5 (Mouse Move Left). It can be seen that the rate substantially dropped from 44.58% to 21.67%. Interestingly, although command C9 was highly confused with command C13 (Table 3), this last command was almost always successfully recognized by the speech engine (Fig. 2). In order to evaluate the suitability of the in-place editor, intra- and inter-subject analyses were conducted. To this end, two types of parameters were computed: The character/word misrecognition degree and the misrecognition rate per minute. Table 4 shows the corresponding values for each of the subjects obtained during dictation. The total misrecognition ratio shown in the 4th column was computed by dividing the number of misrecognized characters and words with the total number of voice inputs. During dictation, the average correct recognition degree yielded 83.34 % with an average elapsed time of 12 minutes with 57 seconds. It can be noticed that the average correct classification due to MCMC (83.91%) is almost identical to the average correct classification (83.34%) due to dictation. This yields to an overall performance of the system of 83.63%.

**Table 3.** Confusion rate analysis based on individual subjects

| Subject | CCR (%) | HCR Value (%) | HCR Command |
|---|---|---|---|
| 1 | 81.43 | 25.00 | C5 vs C15 |
| 2 | 92.86 | 25.00 | C9 vs C13 |
| 3 | 88.57 | 11.11 | C9 vs C13 |
| 4 | 92.86 | 30.00 | C5 vs C10 |
| 5 | 89.28 | 11.11 | C10 vs C12 |
| 6 | 81.43 | 38.89 | C12 vs C15 |
| 7 | 83.57 | 18.75 | C9 vs C13 |
| 8 | 77.14 | 38.88 | C9 vs C13 |
| 9 | 65.00 | 50.00 | C1 vs C4 |
| 10 | 80.71 | 50.00 | C5 vs C8 |
| 11 | 86.43 | 25.00 | C9 vs C13 |
| 12 | 88.57 | 40.00 | C9 vs C13 |
| 13 | 82.86 | 25.00 | C5 vs C10 |
| 14 | 79.28 | 40.00 | C9 vs C13 |
| 15 | 88.57 | 15.00 | C2 vs C15 |
| Average | 83.91 | 29.58 | C9 vs C13 |

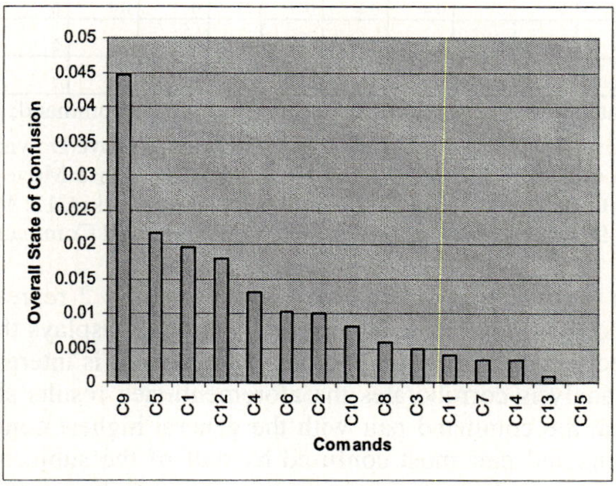


**Fig. 2.** Overall state of confusion of the voice commands sorted in decreasing order

An insight into the results reveals that the recognition degree is higher with words than with characters, and that longer words have a better chance to be correctly recognized. A possible reason may be the fact that, the longer the word, the least likely it is to find a similar word stored in the database. It was also noticed that only three characters have by far the lowest recognition degree, namely characters “d”, “p”, and “u”. Considering the amount of inputs that the SR engine continuously received during the dictation experiment, the average of 1.87 errors per minute can be regarded as an acceptable value.

**Table 4.** Misrecognition ratios obtained during dictation

| Subj. | Chars (%) | Words (%) | Total (%) | errors per min | Subj. | Chars (%) | Words (%) | Total (%) | errors per min |
|---|---|---|---|---|---|---|---|---|---|
| 1 | 15 | 10 | 16.67 | 1.99 | 9 | 16 | 10 | 17.34 | 1.98 |
| 2 | 21 | 11 | 21.34 | 2.43 | 10 | 13 | 12 | 16.67 | 2.23 |
| 3 | 13 | 5 | 12 | 1.29 | 11 | 16 | 9 | 16.67 | 2.05 |
| 4 | 13 | 9 | 14.67 | 1.62 | 12 | 25 | 13 | 25.33 | 2.62 |
| 5 | 11 | 3 | 9.34 | 1.21 | 13 | 8 | 10 | 12 | 1.2 |
| 6 | 11 | 8 | 12 | 1.83 | 14 | 21 | 9 | 20.13 | 2.14 |
| 7 | 9 | 5 | 9.34 | 1.14 | 15 | 17 | 17 | 22.37 | 2.95 |
| 8 | 25 | 12 | 24 | 2.39 | mean | 15.6 | 9.53 | 16.66 | 1.87 |

## 7 Conclusions

This study presented an integrated HCI approach to voice control commands as means to facilitate access and use of computers to persons with motor disabilities. Efforts were extended in the simplification of the user interface for real-time applications with viable performance. The developed application can be easily installed on a home computer, at no additional cost, and trained for later use without major difficulties. The system evaluation yielded what seems to be an internal problem in the MS Speech Recognition Engine, since a pair of commands was repeatedly incorrectly recognized across most of the subjects during the experiments. The authors consider that the results obtained with the 15 subjects are most encouraging for further development of this application as an alpha prototype to serve as a real-time augmentative HCI system to help persons with motor disability. A logical continuation of this study will be the installation of the system in the homes of some motor disabled persons. This study is also intended to be extended to motor disabled patients from Miami Children’s Hospital and will involve a patient follow up for future system enhancements.

## Acknowledgments

The authors gratefully acknowledge the support from the National Science Foundation Grants EIA-906600 and HRD-0317692, and the Office of Naval Research Grant N00014-99-1-0952.

## References


1. Becchetti, C., "Speech Recognition Systems: Theory and C++ Implementation", *Wiley*, 1999.
2. Riverdeep Corp. Website. "Just Speak Naturelly" [Online] Avaiable: http://www.riverdeep.net/current/2000/04/front.060400.speech.jhtml
3. Hideki, H., Yoshifumi N., Yoichi, T.,"Speech Recognition Interface for General Purpose Workstation", IPSJ SIG Notes Human Interface, Abstract No.046 – 003, 2001
4. Holmes, J., Holmes, J. N., Holmes, W., "Speech Synthesis and Recognition", Taylor & Francis, Inc., January 2002
5. Schroeder, M. R., "Computer Speech: Recognition, Compression, Synthesis", *Springer Series in Information Sciences*, 35, Springer Verlag, July 1999
6. Out-Loud. Website, "Computing Out-Load" [Online]. Available: http://www.out-loud.com
7. Ainsworth, W. A. ; and Pratt, S. R., "Feedback Strategies for Error Correction in Speech Recognition Systems", International Journal of Man-Machine Studies 36(6), 833-842, 1992
8. ScanSoft Inc. Website, "QualiLife Selects ScanSoft Speech Technology to Help People with Disabilities Achieve Greater Independence" [Online]. http://www.scansoft.com/news/pressreleases/2002/20020514_qualilife.asp
9. Beamer, G., "Upgrading Microsoft Visual Basic 6.0 to Microsoft Visual Basic .NET" *By Microsoft Press*, July 1, 2002.
10. Howard, T., "The Smalltalk Developer's Guide to VisualWorks",SIGS Books, 1995.
11. Microsoft Corp. Website, "Speech SDK 5.1 for Windows® applications" http://www.microsoft.com/speech/download/sdk51/
12. Ayala M., Adjouadi, M., "NeuralStudio" (A Neural Networks Simulator) [Online]. Available: www.cate.fiu.edu/courses/EEL6991

# First User Test Results with the Predictive Typing System FASTY

C. Beck, G. Seisenbacher, G. Edelmayer, and W.L. Zagler

fortec – Research Group on Rehabilitation Technology
Institute "integrated study", Vienna University of Technology
Favoritenstraße 11/029, A-1040 Vienna, Austria
{beck,seisenbacher,edelmayer,zagler}@fortec.tuwien.ac.at

**Abstract.** This paper gives a brief overview about the partially EU funded project IST-2000-25420 FASTY in the IST program. The objective of FASTY was the creation of a system for increasing the text generation rate of disabled persons by Predictive Typing and dedicated advanced input devices. The system was developed for the Dutch, French, German, and Swedish language, the concept, however, is useable for most European languages. Some results from the user tests with the first prototype during the year 2003 are shown herein and were used to build the second and last prototype. A commercial version of the FASTY software is expected to be available in the second half of 2004.

## 1 Introduction

Motor impairments make the use of standard text input devices to the computer difficult and hence slow. But motor impairment often goes together with articulatory deficiencies. Therefore, communication often relies on slow text-input and that leads to communication disorders and negatively influences the quality of life.

FASTY assists motor, speech, learning and language impaired persons to produce texts faster, with less physical/cognitive load and with better spelling and grammar. FASTY is configurable for different types of disabilities, different communication settings and different European languages. It allows easier access to PC-based office systems, to modern forms of IT communication and a faster usage of text to speech synthesizers for voice communication.

## 2 Aims of the Project

The concrete goal of FASTY was the creation of a system for increasing the text generation rate of disabled persons by so-called predictive typing and dedicated advanced input devices. A prediction system attempts to predict subsequent portions of the text by analyzing the text already entered and using frequency data on the vocabulary of the language. Character-by-character text entry is thus enhanced by the possibility of entering whole words and portions of words as they are proposed by the system. The selection of an alternative should be made by means of a single keystroke. Complementary to the presentation of the suggestions on the screen, they will be read aloud by means of speech synthesis. The success of a system of this kind can be measured in terms of keystrokes that are saved using the predictions as compared to traditional

K. Miesenberger et al. (Eds.): ICCHP 2004, LNCS 3118, pp. 813–819, 2004.

character-by-character input. FASTY aimed at a keystroke saving rate (KSR) above 50%. Laboratory tests with the language part without the user interface showed, that this goal was even exceeded[1]! Additionally, experience gained during the first project year indicates that the linguistic quality of the text will also benefit from using the prediction system.

The FASTY text prediction system currently applies to four languages: Dutch, French, German and Swedish. The future inclusion of additional languages is desired. The multilingual aspect is reflected in the design of the system. Currently, Italian resources are under development[2] and first contacts for Romanian have been established.

An important aspect of the project is the design and development of a dedicated user interface adapted to the needs of the users. The user interface design and the features of the predictor program aimed at a wide coverage of primary users (various disabilities) and secondary users (various roles in supporting the disabled person).

Innovative and ergonomic user interfaces for various existing input methods (standard keyboard, on-screen keyboard, …) were developed together with the predictor (or are incorporated by an open system structure) thus minimizing time and effort for selecting the desired word from a selection list presented on the screen. In addition, a special pressure sensitive switch/keyboard has been developed and will improve the user interface (UI).

## 3 The FASTY System

The FASTY System is divided into a runtime part (for the daily use of the primary user) and an adjustment part, which is used to adjust the system to the needs of the primary user (with or without the help of a care person); additional developer tools are shown in Fig. 1, too.

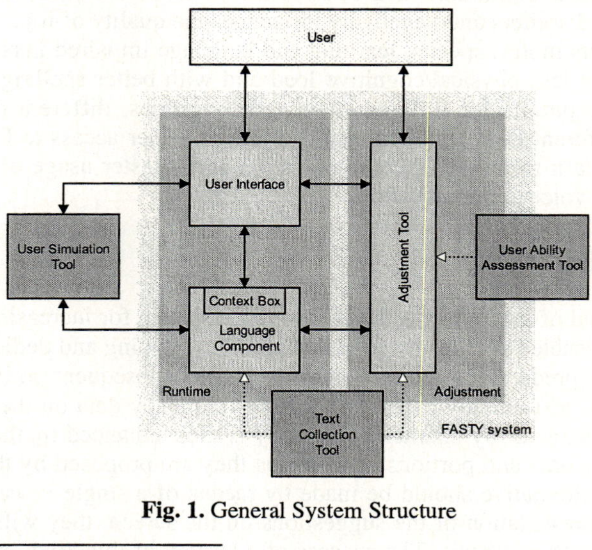


**Fig. 1.** General System Structure

[1] See Fig. 4 and [6] for details.

[2] A first beta version of Italian is already available since April 2004.

The User Interface consists of a modular software package and optional pressure sensitive hardware devices, such as pressure sensitive single switches and some types of pressure sensitive keyboards (see Fig. 2).

**Fig. 2.** Pressure sensitive keyboard

These devices are connected to the computer via a serial connector and an interface box which was also developed (see Fig. 3).

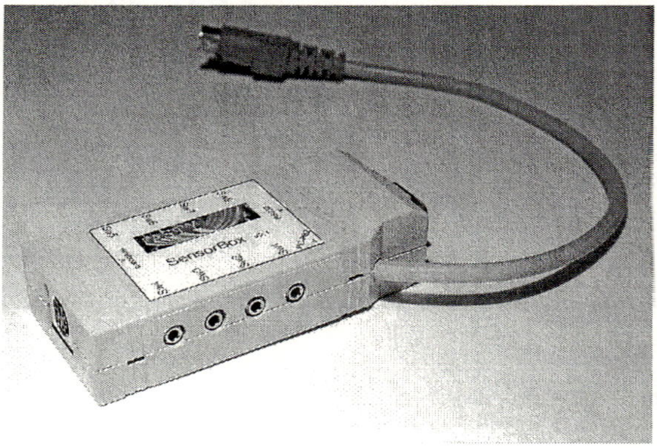


**Fig. 3.** Interface box for pressure sensitive single switches

The Language Component is a modular, nearly complete operating system independent software package, whose functionality is provided by a statistic language model based on word n-grams and part-of-speech tag n-grams in conjunction with one another. Moreover, the possibility to create user specific dictionaries both during a session and on the basis of previously entered texts, serves as a method for further increasing the prediction accuracy. As an example, the results for the German language are shown in Fig. 4. For a detailed description of the complex interaction of the different prediction modules and the structure of the modules themselves, see [1][2][3], for a more detailed view of the results, see [6].

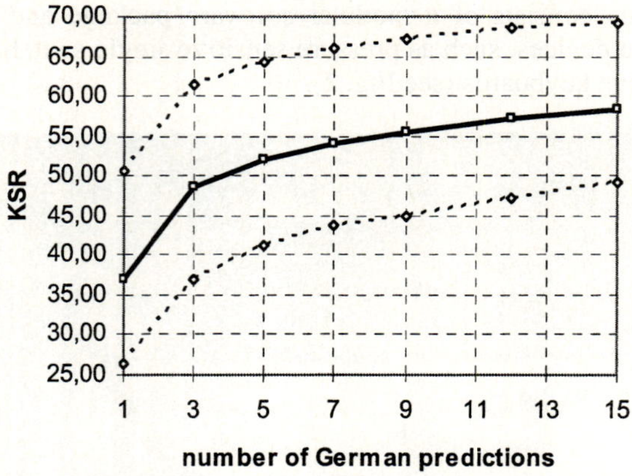


**Fig. 4.** KSR versus shown predictions for the German language during laboratory tests (the solid line shows the average, the dotted lines are the minimum and maximum KSR)

Concerning the development of the FASTY System [4][5][6], the second prototype (see Fig. 5) is ready and the evaluation of the second user test results are nearly done.

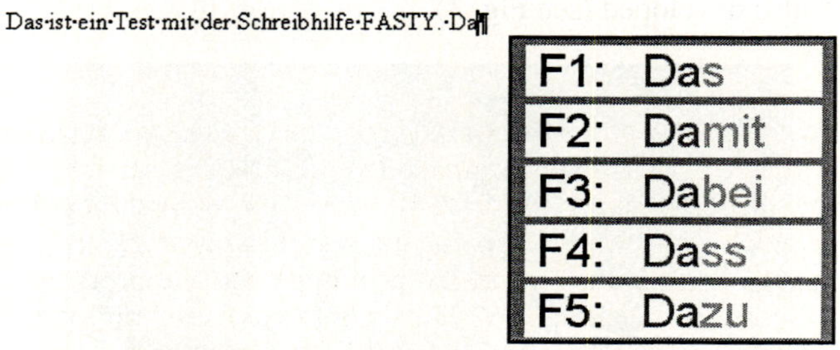


**Fig. 5.** Screenshot of FASTYs prototype 2 user interface during writing German

## 4 Innovations of FASTY

There are a number of word predictors on the market. However, they have, typically, been developed for English, which means that they are not well suited for morphologically rich languages such as Dutch, French, German and Swedish. Simply adapting the English programs to these highly inflecting languages by replacing the English dictionaries usually implies a massive reduction of keystroke saving rate. These effects are due to the simplistic language description that is used for predicting English text and that fails to predict the correct inflectional form of a word as required by inflectional languages. The English language description is, as a rule, limited to frequency data on individual words (unigrams) and sequences of words (bigrams, trigrams). Attempts have been made in research systems for Swedish and Spanish to use a more elaborate language description, including n-grams of word classes and syntactic grammars. The experiences made in these projects are taken into account in the FASTY project. They do not, however, present solutions that will ensure a keystroke saving rate of above 50% for the FASTY languages. An additional problem with most of the FASTY languages is the fact that new compounds can be created on the fly, thus making it hopeless to strive for a complete lexicon. Other methods were employed for coping with dynamic word formation processes. Being able to cope with compounds, even if they are new, is of great importance, since compounds are usually rather long words and failing to predict them can cause a significant drop of the keystroke saving rate. Since no word prediction system currently available is able to handle new compounds, this aspect of the FASTY system is a true innovation.

In particular, the innovative nature of the FASTY system is reflected in the following features:

- prediction of compounds
- prediction of proper inflectional forms based on the use of parsing
- generic algorithms to ensure cross-language portability
- dictionaries based on general language corpora and on the users' own texts
- adaptation of the dictionaries based on actual use of the predictor
- initially supported languages: Dutch, French, German, Swedish
- user interface that is an integral part of the prediction system and
- new input device (such as pressure sensitive switches and pressure sensitive keyboards)

## 5 User Tests Results

The user tests with the first prototype were carried out from April to June 2003 in four countries (Austria, Belgium, Germany and Sweden) testing all four prediction languages. The user feedback was given in form of weekly reports about bugs, problems and highlights, which were summed up and evaluated in reports [7][8].

Most user results dealt with bugs in the prototype and the problems, which arose from them for the users. All in all 262 bugs were discovered and thus, five updates were delivered to the users in the form of small patches within the test phase.

Technical feedback was given in the form of log files (see Fig. 6), which contains statistical data about the prediction process and the interaction of the user with the user interface. Consequently, the predictor and the interaction with the user interface were improved for the second prototype based on this statistical data.

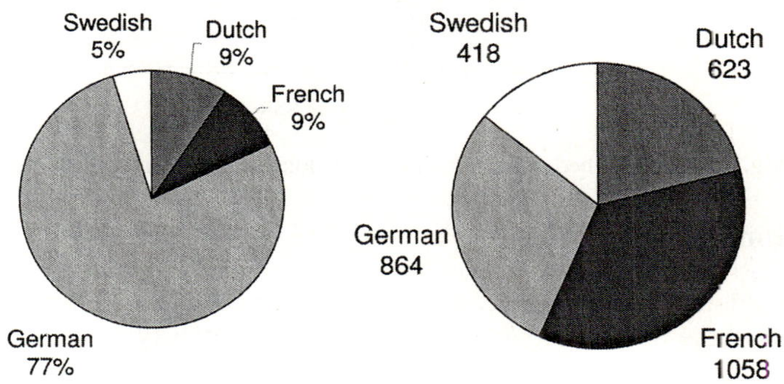


**Fig. 6.** Distribution of log files across language (left), average characters per log file (right)

One of the general results of the user tests was that the users will have to learn to use the system (as described), but this learning process is not as hard as expected. Fig 7 shows the writing speed versus the time of the test. The writing speed increases only slightly within the 5 weeks of testing.

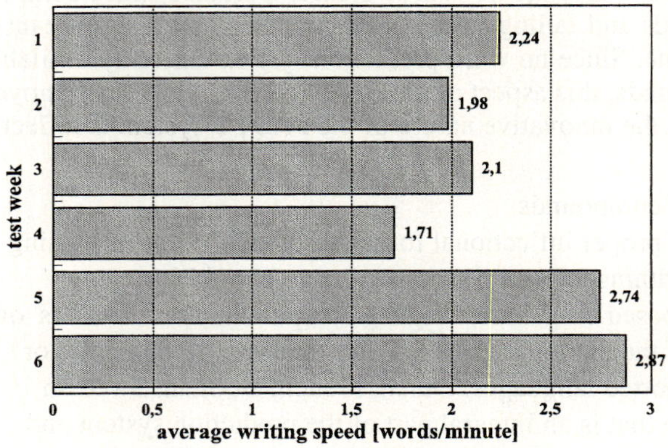


**Fig. 7.** Writing speed (in words/minute) versus time of the tests for German users

The actually reached KSRs of the tests with the first prototype are shown in Fig. 8. They differ from the values from the laboratory tests, because the users had to get used to the system, the users not always chose the available predictions and due to many bugs in the user interface of the first prototype.

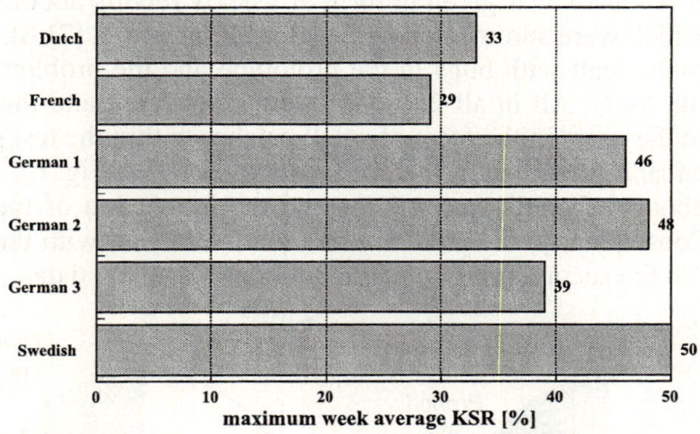


**Fig. 8.** KSRs reached during the user tests done with the first prototype[3]

## 6 Additional Information

More information about the project and the current state of the commercial version can be found on the web at: http://www.fortec.tuwien.ac.at/fasty.

[3] There were three different German user groups in Austria and Germany and they are marked with German 1 to German 3

## Acknowledgements

FASTY was partially funded 2001-2004 by the European Commission as project IST-2000-25420 in the information society technologies (IST) program. The main project partners are:

fortec – Research Group for Rehabilitation Technology, Österreichisches Forschungsinstitut für Artificial Intelligence (ÖFAI), Forschungsinstitut Technologie-Behindertenhilfe der Evangelischen Stiftung Volmarstein, Uppsala University - Department of Linguistics, Multitel ASBL, IGEL Elektronische Kommunikationshilfen GmbH, Seraphisches Liebeswerk für Tirol und Salzburg - Elisabethinum Axams, Ingenieurbüro Jörg-Michael Lindemann, Facultés universitaires Notre-Dame de la Paix.

## References

1. J. Matiasek, M. Baroni and H. Trost, "FASTY – a multilingual approach to text prediction", in Miesenberger K., Klaus J., Zagler W. (eds.): Computers Helping People with Special Needs, 8th International Conference, ICCHP 2002, Linz, Austria, July 15-20, Proceedings, pp. 243-250. Lecture Notes in Computer Science, Vol. 2398, Springer, Berlin-Heidelberg-New York.
2. M. Baroni, J. Matiasek and H. Trost, "Predicting the Components of German Nominal Compounds", in: Harmelen F.van (ed.): Proceedings of the 15th European Conference on Artificial Intelligence (ECAI 2002), IOS Press, Amsterdam, pp. 470-474, 2002.
3. M. Baroni, J. Matiasek and H. Trost, "Wordform- and class-based prediction of the components of the German nominal compounds in an AAC system", in: Proceedings of the 19th International Conference on Computational Linguistics (COLING 2002), Taipei, Taiwan. 2002.
4. FASTY Consortium, "2nd Edited Annual Report – FASTY Project", 2003, http://www.fortec.tuwien.ac.at/fasty
5. C. Beck, W.L. Zagler, "FASTY – Faster Typing for Disabled Persons", European Medical & Biological Engineering Conference (EMBEC 2002), Vienna, 2002
6. W.L. Zagler, C. Beck, G. Seisenbacher: "FASTY - Faster and easier text generation for disabled people"; Presentation: AAATE '03, Dublin; 08-30-2003 - 09-03-2003; in: "Assistive Technology - Shaping the Future"; G. Craddock, L. McCormack, R. Reilly, H. Knops (ed.); IOS Press, Volume 11 (2003), 1 58603 373 5; 964 - 968.
7. FASTY Consortium, "Verification Test Data", 2003, http://www.fortec.tuwien.ac.at/fasty
8. FASTY Consortium, "Review Report and Documentation after Verification", 2003, http://www.fortec.tuwien.ac.at/fasty

# Movement Variability and Speed of Performance Using a Head-Operated Device and Expanded Membrane Cursor Keys

Gilson J. Capilouto

University of Kentucky, Department of Rehabilitation Sciences
900 S. Limestone, Room 120 J, Lexington, Kentucky, USA 40536-0200
gjcapi2@uky.edu

**Abstract.** The performance of computer pointing devices is traditionally measured in terms of speed and accuracy. Such measures are important when comparing input devices for specific users. Although speed and accuracy data verify that performance differences exist, researchers are frequently left to speculate as to the cause. This study explores the value of including data on movement variability in investigations comparing performance of computer input devices for persons with disabilities. Movement variability represents the degree to which recorded sample points vary from the straight-line path between a home location and a target. Analysis of movement variability data provides rehabilitation specialists with clinically valuable information beyond what can be ascertained from measures of speed and accuracy alone.

## 1 Introduction

Scientists in the field of human-computer interaction (HCI) have become increasingly interested in quantifying the movement differences associated with various computer-pointing devices [1-3]. Though the relative performance of input devices is traditionally measured in terms of speed and accuracy [1], HCI researchers agree that such tasks are often ineffective in explaining *why* differences in performance exist [2, 3]. For example, Mackenzie and colleagues found that while a touch pad and trackball performed similarly with respect to speed and accuracy, the two devices differed considerably in terms of their capacity to position the pointer inside a target and remain there [3]; a feature with important implications for both users and device applications. By including measures that focused on the capability of a device to control the cursor's movement path, essential differences in performance were not overlooked. Consequently, measures quantifying the underlying movement associated with a device are now a recommended component of comparative device studies in HCI research [1-3].

The opportunity to quantify movement differences associated with computer pointing devices holds particular promise for users with motor disabilities. For example, little is known about the impact of movement variability on performance parameters such as speed. Since the time required to prepare the motor system increases as a function of the individual movements required to complete a task [4], it seems intuitive that an increase in movement variability would have a negative impact on the

K. Miesenberger et al. (Eds.): ICCHP 2004, LNCS 3118, pp. 820–826, 2004.

time required to capture a target. In fact, a number of researchers have shown that disrupted coordination between muscles and joints associated with neurological pathology may result in trajectories that deviate considerably from the straight-line path and result in increased movement segmentation [5-8]. Consequently, it is possible that computer pointing devices that inherently constrain movement variability could offer an advantage to persons with disabilities.

A previous study comparing the performance of a head-operated device and expanded cursor keys indicated that the head-operated device performed significantly faster in both a target acquisition task and a text-typing task [9]. The devices selected for comparison were designed for persons with disabilities and included one that naturally constrained movement (i.e. expanded membrane cursor keys) and one with infinite movement variability (head-operated device). The purpose of this paper is to analyze the movement variability data collected from the target acquisition task for its clinical relevance. The measures of interest included the time to acquire targets and the standard deviation of movement variability.

## 2 Methods

### 2.1 Subjects

Performance baselines were established using subjects without motor impairments. The use of nondisabled subjects was preferred for a number of reasons. First, consistency of performance was an important factor in this initial phase of investigation and so the use of nondisabled subjects allowed for a focus on performance differences inherent in the devices and their operation rather than variables related to disability status [10]. Moreover, secondary interest in the cognitive processes underlying the operation of each device, as well as group data on learning, also made the selection of nondisabled subjects the initial preference [11].

Subjects were recruited from graduate and undergraduate classes in exercise science at a southeastern university in the United States. Subjects with a history of neurological deficits, motor impairments, and cognitive or sensory deficits were excluded. Twenty-four individuals (five males and 19 females) with an average age of 21 years, 9 months were selected. Twenty-three subjects were right-handed; one was left-handed. Experience using a computer ranged from four to sixteen years with an average use of 10 years. None of the subjects reported experience with a head-operated input device or expanded membrane cursor keys.

### 2.2 Equipment and Software

The experimental task was computer-based. Hardware included a Dell Optiplex GX1 computer with an Intel Pentium II processor. The operating environment was Microsoft Windows 98. The screen was a 15-inch, color SVGA monitor with a resolution of 800 x 600 pixels. The head-operated input device was the Tracker 2000™ (Madentec Limited, Alberta, Canada); this is a hands-free mouse that translates head movements into relative movements of the computer's mouse cursor. The Tracker houses a sensor that tracks a small, reusable dot, placed on the forehead or glasses. When the head moves the cursor moves. The expanded membrane cursor device was the IntelliKeys™ keyboard (Intellitools, Inc., Petaluma, California), a flat, touch-sensitive surface capable of accommodating gross upper extremity movements. The active surface area of the IntelliKeys is 12" wide (30.48 cm) and 8" high (20.32 cm). To complete the target task, a cursor keys overlay was designed which allowed horizontal, vertical and diagonal cursor movements. Operational features for the Tracker and the IntelliKeys (i.e. mode, gain and method of object selection) were set identically to reduce potential bias and confounding.

Participants were tested individually over two sessions as part of a larger study. Positioning relative to the computer was standardized across subjects. Order of presentation of devices and tasks was randomly determined and counterbalanced so each subject completed both tasks and used both devices in each session. Sessions were spaced four to five days apart. At the beginning of the experiment, participants received a brief explanation of the purpose of the study and use of the control devices. The instruction period lasted approximately five minutes and included demonstration by the experimenter and spontaneous practice by the subject. Instruction was followed by the experimental session consisting of a block of target acquisition trials and a block of typing trials [12]. Subjects were instructed to move as quickly and accurately as possible.

A computer-pointing task was developed for the experiment using Visual C++ 6.0. Circular targets representing three widths (0.5 cm, 1 cm and 1.5 cm), three distances (6.2 cm, 3.1 cm and 1.55 cm) and eight radial directions were used (5, 50, 95, 140, 185, 230, 275 and 340 degrees). To begin a trial, the subject moved the cursor arrow tip toward a home target positioned in the center of the screen. When the cursor arrow tip crossed the boundary of the home target, it turned yellow, marking the beginning of a fore period, which varied randomly from 0.5 to 2 seconds. A fore period was included to minimize a subject's anticipation of the appearance of the target, which would have confounded the time results. The fore period was followed by the 'go' signal an auditory beep coupled with a change in color of the home target to green and the simultaneous appearance of the capture target at a random size, distance and angle (Fig. 1). The subject then moved the cursor to the target as rapidly as possible and stopped. To acquire a target, the tip of the cursor arrow had to be maintained inside the target for 500 milliseconds. Subjects completed 6 target acquisition blocks for each device. A block consisted of 72 randomly presented trials representing each target size, target distance and radial combination (3 x 3 x 8) for a total of 432 trials per device, per session.

### 2.3 Data Analysis

Data were analyzed as a mixed factorial design with one random factor (subject) and six fixed factors [device (2); session (2); block (6); target width (3); target distance (3); target angle (8)]. The dependent variables of interest were total time and movement variability. Interactions of interested were device by distance, device by width, and device by angle. Total time was defined as the time elapsed between the appearance of the target and capture. Movement variability was computed from the *x-y* coordinates of the pointer during the target task and represented the degree to which recorded sample points varied from the straight-line path from home location to trial target [3].

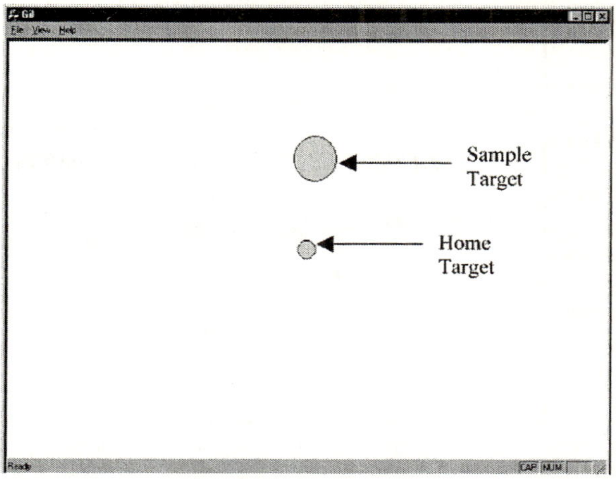


**Fig. 1.** Sample 'go' signal for a target trial included an auditory beep coupled with a change in color of the home target to green and the simultaneous appearance of the capture target at a random size, distance and angle

## 3 Results

Analyses of total time indicated a block by device interaction for the target task ($F_{5,\ 20615} = 12.44$, $p < .0001$)(Fig. 2). Although total time decreased with practice for both devices, the difference in total time for the two devices was not consistent across the blocks. Total time did not change significantly after block four for the head device. Significant differences in total time were detected through block five for the cursor keys; this suggests more practice was required to reach asymptote performance when the cursor keys were used. Computed means from trials occurring after block four are referred to as practiced performance since no significant improvement in total time after the fifth block was observed for either device ($p > .05$).

Analysis of practiced performance indicated that mean total time was significantly faster for the head-operated device ($M$ = 1590 ms, $SD$ = 771 ms) as compared to the expanded cursor keys ($M$ = 2611.99 ms, $SD$ = 1344 ms). Total time was significantly affected by target distance, width and angle, regardless of device. However, the degree to which these parameters affected performance differed for the two devices; the impact of increasing distance and decreasing width had a greater impact on performance time when the expanded cursor keys were used.

Initial analysis of movement variability indicated a significant block by device interaction ($F_{5,\ 20615} = 2.78$, $p = .0164$). Post hoc tests indicated that there was no significant change in movement variability after the third block ($p = .7987$). Consequently, means from trials occurring after block three are referred to as practiced performance. Analysis of practiced performance indicated that movement variability was greater for the head device ($M$ = .1649, $SD$ = .1694) as compared to the membrane cursor keys ($M$ = .1222, $SD$ = .1318). In addition, movement variability decreased in the second session for both devices ($p < .0001$), suggesting that once sub-

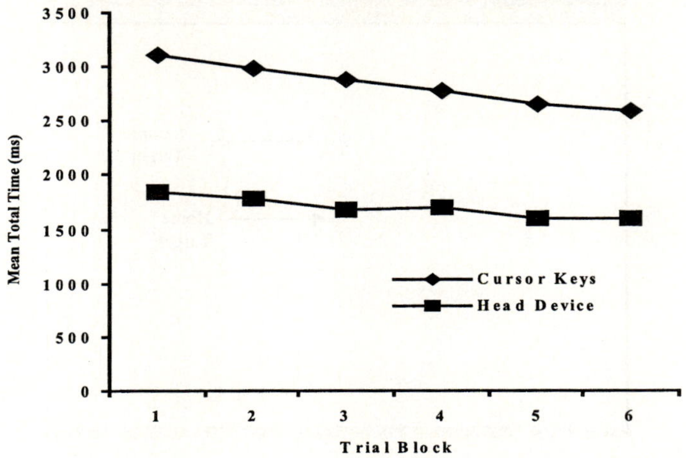


**Fig. 2.** Mean total time of subjects' target trials for the six experimental blocks. Results indicated a block by device interaction where total time did not change significantly after block four for the head device but significant differences in total time were detected through block five for the head/arm device

**Table 1.** Effect size differences of target parameters on movement variability for each device

| | Device | |
|---|---|---|
| **Target Parameter** | Head Device | Cursor Keys |
| Distance | $p < .0001$ | $p < .0001$ |
| Width | $p = .0973$ | $p < .0001$ |
| Angle | $p < .0001$ | $p < .0001$ |

jects became familiar with the operation of the device and the nature of the tasks, movement was more consistent. Results further indicated that movement variability was significantly affected by all of the variables in the model. Analysis of the effect size differences between the two devices is presented in Table 1.

For the head device, target distance ($p < .0001$) and angle ($p < .0001$) had a significant effect on movement variability; there was no effect of target width ($p = .0973$). When the cursor keys were used, movement variability was significantly affected by all target parameters: distance ($p < .0001$), width ($p <$ 0001) and angle ($p < .0001$). As with speed, the degree to which target distance and width and angle affected performance was greater when the expanded cursor keys were used. Pair wise comparisons among target angles revealed no clear pattern for the effect of angle for either device except that there was no significant difference in movement variability between the two devices for the horizontal and vertical targets (Fig. 3).

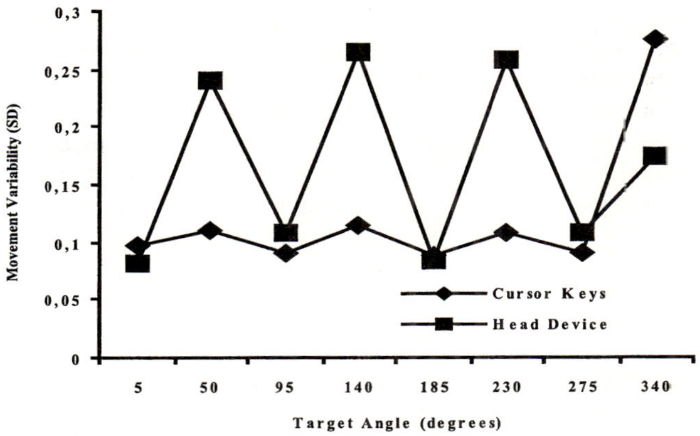


**Fig. 3.** Pair wise comparisons among target angles indicated there was no significant difference in movement variability between the two devices for the horizontal and vertical targets

## 4 Discussion

Previous studies of head-operated devices have shown them to be less effective than other input devices in completing target acquisition tasks [13] and drawing tasks [14]. Results of this investigation do not support that conclusion; rather the data suggest that a head operated device may be an acceptable alternative to particular hand/arm devices for pointing activities. Total time to complete the target acquisition task was significantly faster using the head device.

The head device may have offered an anatomical advantage over the expanded cursor keys in that the stimulus and the response were more naturally linked; subjects moved the head in conjunction with the eyes to map the target location. When using the expanded cursor keys, decisions about where to move were compounded by decisions about how to move since subjects had to consider the cursor arrow combinations needed to acquire a given stimulus. This required greater planning. Together with a required translation from the horizontal cursor keys to the vertical computer screen, the use of the expanded cursor keys may have decreased stimulus-response compatibility resulting in increased total time.

Although the expanded cursor keys took considerably longer than the head device when acquiring a target, its use was associated with significantly less movement variability. Possible contributing factors may include the fact that: (a) the expanded cursor keys provided a stable surface on which to move and (b) movement variability occurred only in response to a change in direction. With respect to the second factor, the constraints naturally imposed by the cursor keys may have actually limited possible movement options leaving it more vulnerable to the effect of target parameters. This would explain why the magnitude of the difference in movement variability in response to increases in target distance was greater for the cursor keys than for the head device and why target width had no affect on movement variability for the head device but was a significant factor when the cursor keys were used.

This study used typical young adults; therefore, questions about the degree of head control necessary to operate the head device cannot be adequately addressed. However, results suggest that increased movement variability does not necessarily result in movement inefficiency; the greater movement variability noted for the head device did not translate to an increase in movement time. In may be that the flexibility offered by the head device served as an advantage over the constraints of the expanded membrane cursor keys by providing movement alternatives that maximized speed.

## References


1. Douglas, S.A., Mithal, A.K.: The Ergonomics of Computer Pointing Devices. In: Paul, R, Thomas, P. (eds.): Advanced Perspectives in Applied Computing. Springer, London (1997)
2. Mithal, A.K., Douglas, S.A.: Differences in Movement Microstructure oof the Mouse and the Finger-Controlled Isometric Joystick. Human Factors in Computing Systems CHI '96 Conference Proceedings. ACM, New York (1996)
3. MacKenzie, I.S., Kauppinen, T., Silfverberg, M.: Accuracy Measures for Evaluating Pointing Devices. Human Factors in Computing Systems CHI 2001 Conference Proceedings. ACM, New York (2001)
4. Christina, R.W.: The 1991 C.H. Mccloy Research Lecture: Unraveling the Mystery of the Response Complexity Effect in Skilled Movement. Research Quarterly for Exercise and Sport, Volume 53 (1992) 218-230.
5. Archambault, P., et al.: Recruitment and Sequencing of Different Degrees of Freedom During Pointing Movements Involving the Trunk in Healthy and Hemiparetic Subjects. Experimental Brain Research, Volume 126. Springer-Verlag, Heidelberg (1999) 55-67
6. Bastian, A.J., et al.: Cerebellar Ataxia Abnormal Control of Interaction Torques Across Multiple Joints. Journal of Neurophysiology, Volume 76. The American Physiological Society, Maryland (1996) 492-509
7. Levin, M.F.: Interjoint Coordingation During Pointing Movements is Disrupted in Spastic Hemiparesis. Brain. Oxford University Press, Oxford (1996) 281-293
8. Teulings, H.L., et al.: Parkinsonism Reduces Coordination of Fingers, Wrist, and Arm in Fine Motor Control. Experimental Neurology, Volume 146. Elsevier, San Diego (1997) 159-170
9. Capilouto, G., et al.: Adapted Computer Access: The Effect of Reducing Degrees of Freedom on Performance. Dissertation Abstracts International, Ann Arbor (2002)
10. Higginbotham, D.J., Bedrosian, J.: Subject Selection in AAC Research: Decision Points. Augmentative & Alternative Communication, Volume 11. Taylor & Francis Group, London (1995)11-13
11. Higginbotham, D.J.: Use of Nondisabled Subjects in AAC Research: Confessions of a Research Infadel. Augmentative & Alternative Communication, Volume 11. Taylor & Francis Group, London (1995) 2-5
12. Capilouto, G., et al.: Performance of Able-Bodied Subjects on a Text-Typing Task Using a Head-Operated Device and Expanded Membrane Cursor Keys. Perceptual and Motor Skills, Volume 98. Missoula (2004)147-162
13. Jagacinski, R.J. and D.L. Monk: Fitts' Law in Two Dimensions with Hand and Head Movements. Journal of Motor Behavior, Volume 17. Heldref Publications, Washington, DC (1985) 77-95
14. Karny, E.M. and D.K. Anson: A Pilot Study Comparing Mouse and Mouse-Emulating Devices for Graphic Input. Assistive Technology, Volume 3. RESNA Publications, Arlington, VA (1991) 50-58

# An Examination about Walking Posture on Gait Training System for Computer-Aided Rehabilitation

Hidetaka Ikeuchi[1], Fumitaka Kamifukumoto[2], Satoshi Arakane[3], Kengo Ohnishi[1], Keiji Imado[1], Hiroomi Miyagawa[1], and Yukio Saito[4]

[1] Oita University, Faculty of Engineering, 700 Dannoharu, Oita-Shi, 870-1192, Japan
{hikeuchi,ohnishi,imado,miyahiro}@cc.oita-u.ac.jp

[2] ASICS Corporation, 1-1, Minatojima-Nakamachi 7-chome, Chuo-ku Kobe 650-8555, Japan

[3] Daihen Technology Institute, 1660-7 Mizoi, Kituki-shi, Oita, 873-0025, Japan
arakane@daihentec.co.jp

[4] Tokyo Denki University, Ishizaka, Hatoyama, Saitama 350-0311, Japan
saito@n.dendai.ac.jp

**Abstract.** Our Gait Training System is a training device that aims to obtain the effect of the walk training in the warm water swimming pool. A trainee is supported by the slinging system while walking on the force plate. Slinging power is controlled on the basis of information instrumented from the force plates. The training effects are evaluated on the basis of the data that obtained from the force plate etc. This system is tested by handicapped person to inspect the function and efficacy. A major problem of deficient body alignment of the walking posture is found from the test. We propose mounting a monitor and the result of improvement is shown. The effect on the walking posture using the Gait Training System is experimented on normal persons. The difference of the posture in normal gait and device-supported gait is shown.

## 1 Introduction

Rehabilitation training is one of the fields where mechatronics systems can provide effective tools for diagnosis. They can also decrease the physical load in the physical therapy treatment. Training for a patient with enfeebled lower limb function often uses parallel bars. This training has the disadvantages of causing pain, and it requires strength in the upper limbs. Training in a heated swimming pool is easy on the trainee's body. However, using a pool has drawbacks which are the scale and maintenance of the facility, as well as the stress on the therapist resulting from the safety in the pool.

We reported the detail of our system[1]. In this report, the test result of a handicapped person using our system is summarized, first. And a problem about walking posture confirmed in this test and a solution is presented. Furthermore, we experiment with normal persons to check the difference with the normal walking and device walking. The difference of the posture with usual and device walking is shown.

K. Miesenberger et al. (Eds.): ICCHP 2004, LNCS 3118, pp. 827–835, 2004.

The main feature of our system is the constant dynamic adjustment of the tension lifting the trainee based on the information of the floor reaction force. The load on the trainee's foot linked to the floor is regularly maintained at a low-burden level; therefore, the load on the foot is similar to the effect of walking in a pool. Another advantage is that the trainee senses the stimulation at the sole and other parts of the body, since he or she is walking on the force plate: a solid surface. This is the difference from a treadmill device. Furthermore, a trainee is able to train in various surface environments by changing the surface, e.g. like a slope, on the force plate.

## 2 Developed System

Fig.1 shows the concept design of the system the system diagram of the signal transmission mechanism. The details are possible to refer to Reference 1.

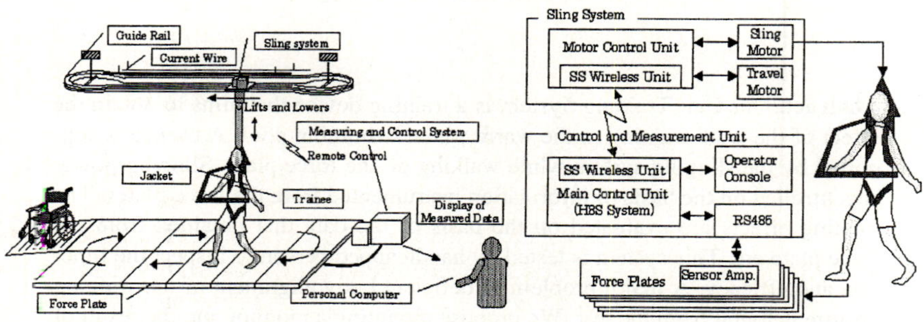


**Fig. 1.** System diagram of the Conceptual Design (left) and System Diagram (right)

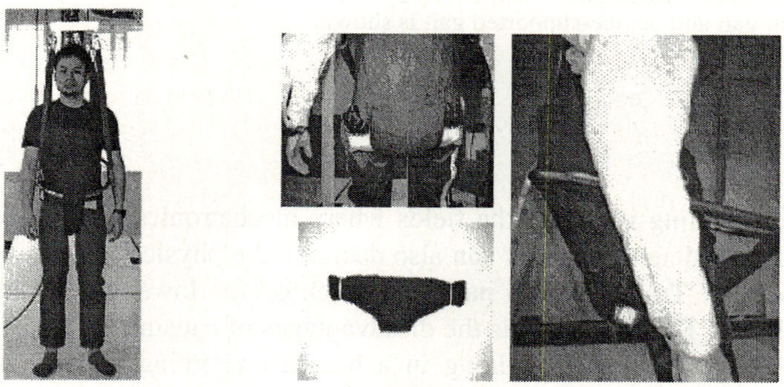

(a) Supporting Vest (b)Load Supported Part. This part at the hipbone eases pain

**Fig. 2.** Supporting Vest

### 2.1 System Overview

The floor area is 7.5*2.9m$^2$, and is covered with aluminum force plates. These plates have 4 force sensors at the bottom that measure the amount of pressure on them, as applied by the subjects. The walking distance on the device is approximately 12m.

Two props support the guide rail that the sling system travels on. The sling system component supports the trainee, and lifts or lowers the person according to the information from the force plates. The information for sling control is sent to the sling system component from the main control unit by Spread Spectrum Wireless Data Communications. Power for the sling system is supplied by a trolley wire; therefore, the trainee can walk without restriction. A touch panel is utilized for system operation. Buttons for setting the load on the foot, walking speed, manual operation of the sling units, and start/stop of training are displayed on the its screen.

### 2.2 Supporting Vest

A supporting vest for the harness device was developed. This device holds and supports the weight of the trainee connected to the slinging unit. Therefore, the comfortableness of this device has a significant influence on the success of the system. We tried a number of off-the-shelf products, but none were durable enough. The device still needs improvements in its functional design, and our goal is to improve it so that it is easy-to-wear, painless, and allows more movement during the gait.

The device in Fig. 2-(a) was developed for this purpose and used in the field test on handicapped person. Denim cloth is mainly used, and the load is sustained mostly the load support part in Fig. 2-(b), while partially supported at the crotch. A frame pipe holds a soft stuffed tube for the crotch in a comfortable manner. Also, this pipe works to lower the mental stress on the trainee by its use as a handle. This type was developed with the chief aim of ease of installation. Several prototypes have been produced through trial and error, and we are continuing to improve on it.

## 3 Field Test on Handicapped Subjects

The successive training on handicapped person was carried out to observe the effect of the system. The subject was a 25-year-old male, who suffered from partial paralysis on his left side caused by a brain tumor. There was also some paralysis on the right. There was no disability in the upper limbs. Therefore, he has used a wheelchair for transportation and has had no gait training in the past 5 years. He could extend both knees and other joints fully, but did not have full control of the lower limbs because of the nervous disorder. Hence, the trainee could maintain a standing position for a short time and had difficulty balancing during gait.

In previous report, we reported the results of first series. In this report, we show the second series.

The subject trained 3 times a week for 28 days. Two 10-minute training sessions were made with a 10-minute break in between. The preset load was set to 200N. Gait speed was set to 11 m/min. The distance of the gait was approximately 110 m/set.

To evaluate the effect of the gait training device, bone density, and lung capacity examinations, blood tests and patient feedback were taken before and after the training for comparison, as in the previous report. The training period, preset load, and gait speed were increased as the subject requested. Verbal feedback was noted each day.

### 3.1 Results

Settings at the last training session exceeded these figures: preset load 200N, gait speed 16 m/min, three-10 minutes training in one day. In the medical check, A little improvement was seen to bone density and lung capacity, and the abnormality was not seen to the blood test. These results are similar to the previous report.

In second series, we try several improvements of the system and collect the subject's opinion. The most important aspect is the walking posture changing considerably by subject's view direction. Next caption shows the detail.

### 3.2 The Effect of Walking Posture Using Display

The stick pictures of the subject's posture in training are shown in Fig.3. These pictures are made from video data recorded in the training. The software used is Frame DIAS II of Co., Ltd. DKH. The posture of Fig.3-(a) is poor because he is looking down on his steps, to alternate the sense of heel contact and foot position with vision. Fig.3-(b) is the stick picture of subject's walking posture when looking forward. This posture is in a straight head-body alignment and obviously ideal than Fig.3-(a).

(a)Walking while Looking Down (b)Walking while Looking Forward

**Fig. 3.** Stick Picture of Walking Posture

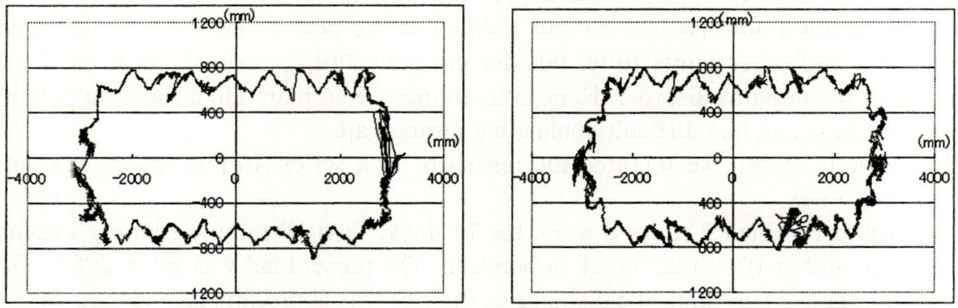


(a)Walking while Looking Down (b)Walking while Looking Forward

**Fig. 4.** COP Trajectory of Training

Fig.4 shows the difference of COP (Center of Pressure of reaction force) between walking while looking down and looking forward. When he is walking looking forward as in Fig.4-(b), COP is unstable and his body is shaken. Additionally, he is feeling uneasy. Fig.4-(a) is the COP of walking while looking down. This COP is more stable than walking looking forward in Fig.4-(b).

The subject cannot sense the heel contact and the foot position because of paralysis. So, he has to depend on visual feedback to stably walk. However, if he looks down to be stable, his spinal is bent and posture becomes inappropriate. In human walking, upright posture is important. To continue the training with misguided posture is disagreeable.

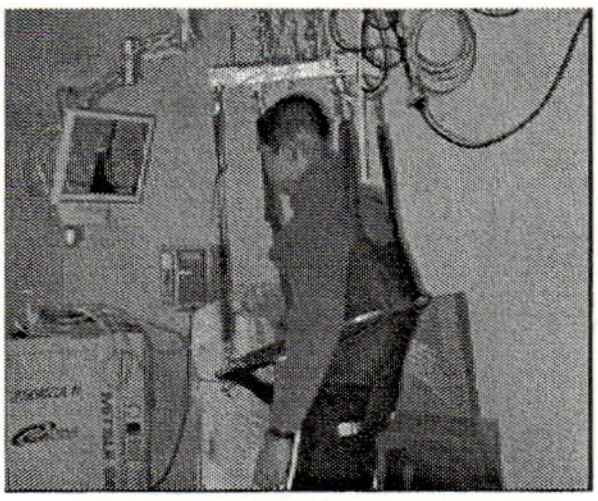

(a) Setting Display

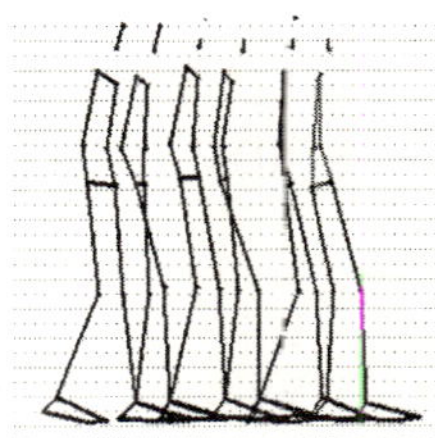

(b) Walking Posture with Display

**Fig. 5.** Improvement for Walking Posture

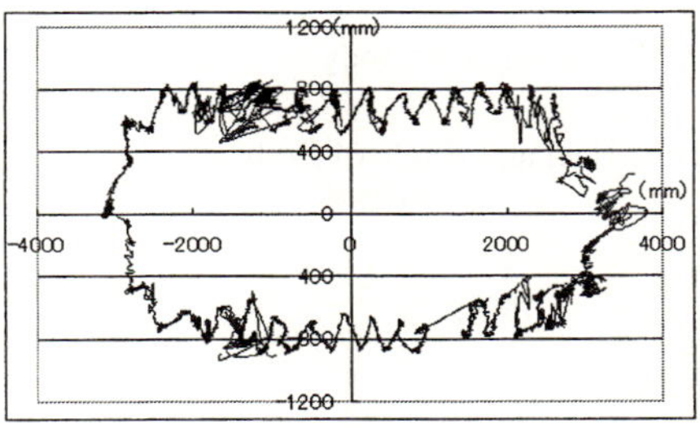


(a) Without Display

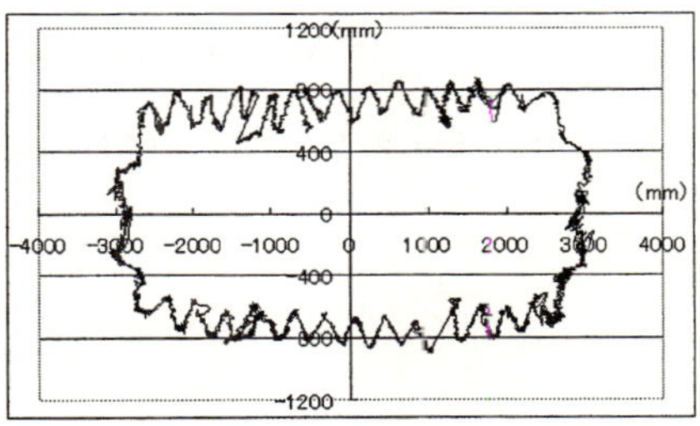


(b) With Display

**Fig. 6.** Trajectory of COP with and without the display

The improvement of good walking posture is shown in Fig.5-(a). We set up the monitor display to display his steps. The CCD camera is installed at the bottom of the display. The camera captures the steps so to watch his steps while looking forward.

The effect of setting the display is shown in Fig.5-(b). This posture is better than Fig.3-(a). Fig.6 is the difference of COP between with and without the display. Trajectory COP with the display is more stable than without thedisplay. Table 1 is the angle of body from vertical axis. This angle is calculated by Frame DIAS II. The angle of With Display is best in this table. The angle of walking with display is smallest.

**Table 1.** Angle of Body from Vertical Axis (rad)

| | Looking Down | Looking Front | With Display |
|---|---|---|---|
| Angle of body | 0.64 | 0.27 | 0.16 |

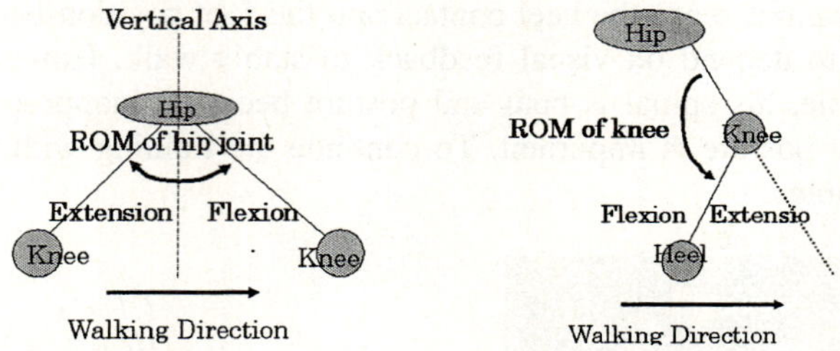


(a) ROM of Hip Joint (b) ROM of Knee Joint

**Fig. 7.** Definition of ROM

(a) Max Height of Heel (b) Angle of Body

**Fig. 8.** Definition of Max Height of Heel and Angle of Body

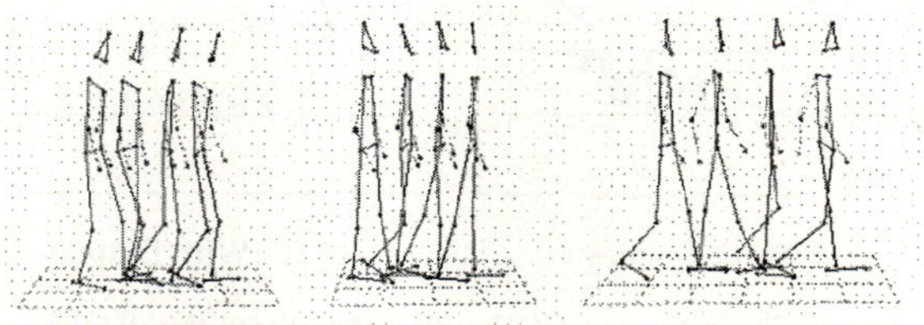

(a) Device Walking (b) Normal-1 (c) Normal-2

**Fig. 9.** Stick Pictures of 3 Type Walking

## 4 The Difference of Walking Posture between Normal/Training

The posture of walking in gait training is very important. But, walking posture may be different from normal walking posture and device walking like previous section. In this section, we consider the difference between normal walking and device walking.

In this experiment, the posture of normal walking and device walking is measured. The posture of walking is measured by a three-dimensional video analysis system, Frame DIAS II. This system consists of 4 video camera recording system and processing software. Markers are fixed to parts of the subjects' body, and the 4 video cameras capture the walk. Walking is 3 types, that is, device walking, normal walking with device speed and normal walking with normal speed. The speed of device walking is slow to fit the lower limb patient use. Human subjects are 5 young people. They are 3 male and 2 female. Each subject performs once in experiment.

We analyze following data; the center of gravity, ROM of hip joint, ROM of knee joint, kicking height of heel, angle of body and step length. Fig.7 and Fig.8 show definition of these values.

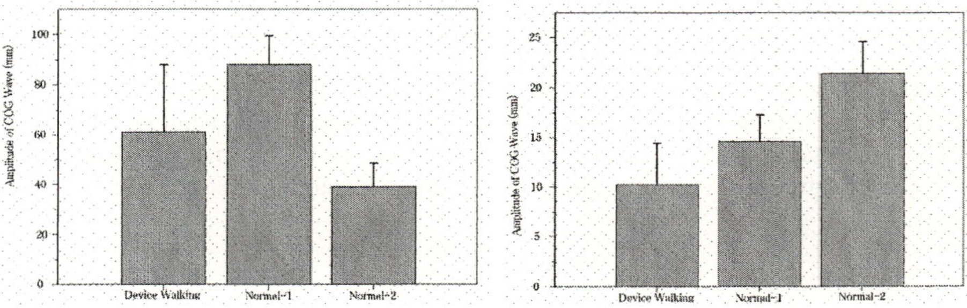


(a) Lateral Direction (b) Vertical Direction

**Fig. 10.** Average of Amplitude of COG(Center of Gravity) Wave

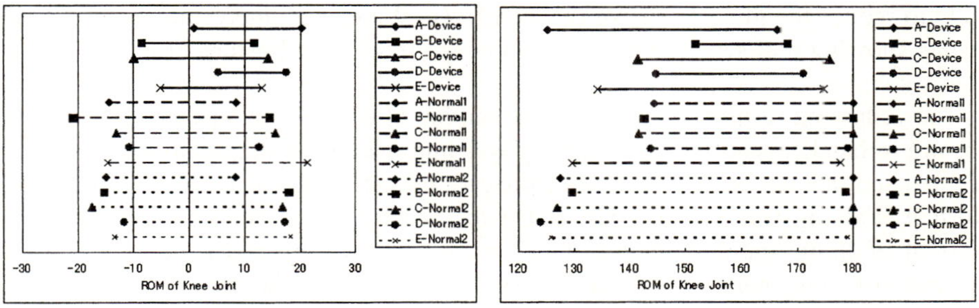


(a) Hip Joint (b) Knee Joint

**Fig. 11.** ROM(Range of Motion) of Hip Joint and Knee Joint

Fig.9 shows the stick pictures of 3 walking types. In Device Walking, it is found that body is inclining; knee joint is not enough straight compared with Normal Walking.

Fig.10 shows the amplitude of COG wave in lateral and vertical direction. Lateral direction amplitude in Device Walking is smaller than Normal-1 and is near the Normal-2. Vertical direction amplitude in Device Walking is smallest. The subject in

Device Walking may be constrained by slinging system. Fig.11 shows ROM of the hip joint and knee joint. Many subject in Device Walking present smaller ROM than Normal Walking. In hip joint, some subject's ROM in Device Walking is always positive.

Table 2 shows body angle of 3 types of walking. Body in Device Walking is inclining forward compared to Normal Walking.

**Table 2.** Average of Angle of Body (Rad)

| | Subject A | Subject B | Subject C | Subject D | Subject E |
|---|---|---|---|---|---|
| Device Walking | 0.072 | 0.264 | -0.038 | -0.037 | -0.080 |
| Normal 1 | -0.017 | 0.007 | -0.044 | -0.148 | -0.084 |
| Normal 2 | -0.005 | 0.000 | -0.028 | -0.126 | -0.091 |

Kicking height of heel in Device Walking is smaller than Normal, but this difference is small. Step length in Device Walking is equal or a little bit small to Normal-1.

The quantitative difference of the Device Walking and Normal Walking is described. We have to develop the support vest and gait training system based on these points.

## 5 Conclusion

A unique gait-training device with a slinging weight support method is presented. The outstanding feature of this system is the control of the tension while holding the body to reduce the impact of floor reaction force. We gained interesting experimental results showing that setting a display improves the walking posture of paralyzed patient's gait.

The following results are obtained; the outline of our system was shown; walking posture in handicapped person's training was improved by setting display to monitor his step and the gait stability was not damaged; the difference of Device Walking and Normal Walking was found; body in Device Walking was inclining compare with Normal Walking; the amplitude of COG wave, ROM of hip and knee joint and the average of kicking height of heel in Device Walking was smaller than Normal.

## Acknowledgement

This work has been supported by a research project entitled "Rehabilitation System for Upper Limb and Lower Limb", an on-going 5-year project founded by NEDO, Japan.

## References

1. Ikeuchi1, H., Arakane, S., Ohnishi1, K., Imado, K., Saito, Y. and Miyagawa, H.: The Development of Gait Training System for Computer-aided Rehabilitation, Coputers Helping People with Special Needs, 8th International Conference, ICCHP 2002 Linz, Austria, July 2002 Proceedings, 2002., 228-235.
2. Gazzani, F., Bernardi, M., Macaluso, A., Coratella, D., Ditunno Jr, JF., Castellano, V., Torre, M., Macellari, V., Marchetti, M.: Ambulation training of neurological patients on the treadmill with a new Walking Assistance and Rehabilitation Device (WARD), Spinal Cord 37 (1999) 336-344
3. Tokyo Denki University: A Study of feedback type gait training system, New Energy and Industrial Development Organization Entrusted R&D Report for FY 1996 (in Japanese)
4. Gazzani, F..Bernardi, M..Macaluso, A..Coratella, D..Ditunno Jr., JF..Castellano, V. et al..Ambulation training of neurological patients on the treadmill with a new Walking Assistance and Rehabilitation Device (WARD).Spinal Cord 1999.37.336-344.
5. Jezernik, S., Clombo, G., Keller, T., Frueh, H., Morari, M., Robotic Orthosis Lokomat: A Rehabilitation and Research Tool, Neuromodulation, Vol.6, No. 2, 2003: 108-115.
6. Arakane, S., Ikeuchi, H., Ohnishi, K., Imado, K., Miyagawa, H. and Saito, Y., The Development and field test of Gait Training System, Proceedings of 6th Japan-France & 4th Asia-Europe Mechatronics Congress, Hatoyama, 2003: 147-152.

# Optimizing Menu Selection Process for Single-Switch Manipulation

Grigori Evreinov and Roope Raisamo

TAUCHI Computer-Human Interaction Unit
Department of Computer Sciences
FIN-33014 University of Tampere, Finland
{grse,rr}@cs.uta.fi
Tel.: +358 3 215 8549

**Abstract.** Single-switch manipulation is considered as a model for optimizing a menu selection task for physically challenged users. We have applied a short-cyclic hierarchical structure with three levels and three alternatives as a basic layout for symbol input and imaging. A user can make use of the triple-stroke or the long-stroke technique when the button is held down for extended period. It allows to jump over one of menu levels or to cut the cycle. We designed algorithm for adaptive scan interval and have applied it for text entry. Long-stroke technique significantly reduces the number of strokes and increases typing speed. The preliminary tests with able-bodied participants showed an average typing speed of more than 20 signs per minute after one-hour training. Adaptive scan interval could be useful for applications that require periodic time correction depending on user performance. Algorithm for adaptive scan interval and the coupled issues are considered in detail.

## 1 Introduction

Assume a person can manipulate only a single button or a functionally similar element. What strategy of behavior is optimal depends on individual opportunities and on the dialogue structure of the interface. Recently diverse versions of the onscreen keyboards with a scanning option were designed to provide alternative access for people who cannot move any pointing device at all [1-5]. Scanning mode is applied with onscreen keyboard to choose highlighted areas by pressing a hot key or using a switch-input device. Cyclicity and hierarchy are two different and opposed parameters which should provide reliable interaction. Cyclicity supposes sequential access to menu items. Herewith, branching with a huge number of alternatives makes difficult not only the navigation itself but the waiting of the moment when a necessary menu item will be accessible.

Real-time manipulations by scan-interval and adjustments of delays have been investigated by Simpson and Koester [5], Lesher et al. [3], and Bourhis [1]. Lesher et al. developed a method for row-column scanning interface based upon quantitative measures of scanning performance. The adjustment scheme optimized scanning delays after approximately 1200 selections (~240 words) starting from 2 s. Bourhis and

K. Miesenberger et al. (Eds.): ICCHP 2004, LNCS 3118, pp. 836–844, 2004.

Pino have built EDITH system based on mathematical model of the operator's behavior and statistical analysis of experimental data.

Several alternatives were considered in development of strategies based on prediction of simple situational behavior and using individual topic-oriented vocabulary. Usually, phrase entry technique uses a complicated asymmetric hierarchical structure with a huge number of branches to specify a phrase category. In eLocutor [4], to type the sentence "what is the date today" took 6 clicks and 13 seconds after the first word was typed. However, before the first word was typed it was necessary to pass 6 levels and make 6 clicks without any mistake. This procedure can take 14 seconds or more depending on a number of alternatives on each level used. The method works when a phrase kit or dictionary is too small, but in such a case, direct text entry with auto-completion, for instance, could also work well.

## 2 Method Design

### 2.1 Method for Menu Selection

The problem of connectivity in complex cyclic menu can be decided via access hierarchy to key-nodes and at using short cycles. It is clear that some menu items are more frequently used and therefore they should have a short length of path from a key-node. A short way should also be provided for such operations as cancel, back step or switching the menu content. However, what exactly is a short way up to menu item?

Suppose we need to enter text. Certainly, typing will be more frequently used than editing or file operations. Herewith, alphabet characters will be used according to Letter Frequency. If a symmetric hierarchical structure with three alternatives and levels will be used in a basic cycle, the length of paths up to each terminal node is measured by the number of clicks and will be equal to three. However, if scan interval equals to 1 s, a choice of the first character in the first line ("E", Fig. 1) will take 3 s and the last character of third line "Z" will take 9 s. The whole matrix of selection times is shown in Fig. 2-a. As it can be seen from Fig. 2-a, only three groups of characters could be achieved within 6 s through a sequence of strokes at scan interval 1 s. The actual values of scan interval are varied in a range 450-800 ms.

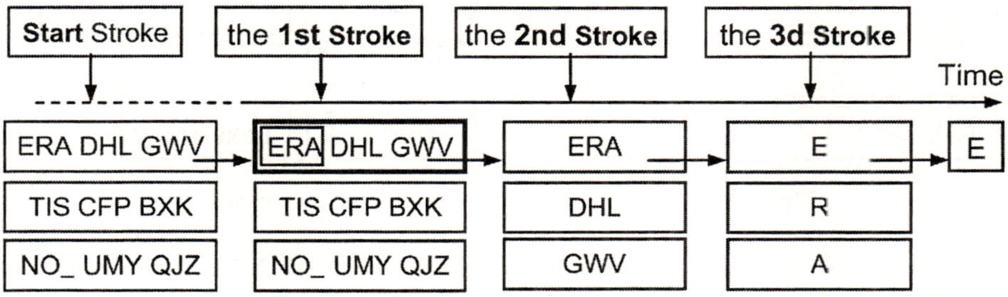


**Fig. 1.** Symmetric hierarchical menu with three alternatives and three levels

The digital button supports two stable states, and “stroke duration” can be used to jump over one of menu levels or to cut the cycle. It could be released when scan interval for one level was elapsed and button remained pressed down (Fig. 3). By applying this technique on the first step of each level, we can decrease typing performance upon 20% for entering, at least, 9 characters (Fig. 2-b). If these characters are more frequently used their portion can achieve 67-70% of entered tokens (English alphabet).

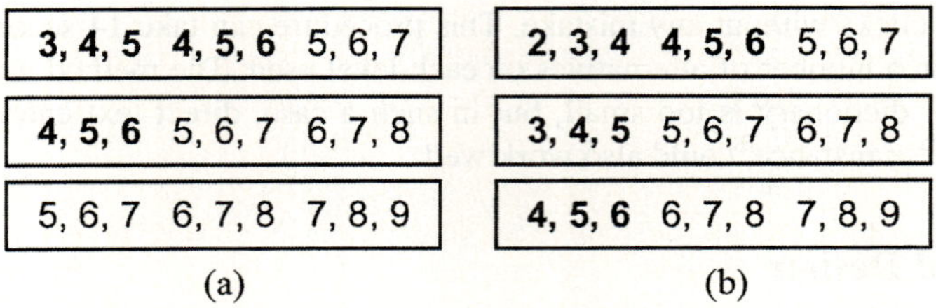


**Fig. 2.** The relative performance in seconds for entering characters with the scan interval of 1 s. The left matrix has 3 strokes per character (SPC) and the right matrix has 2.67 SPC

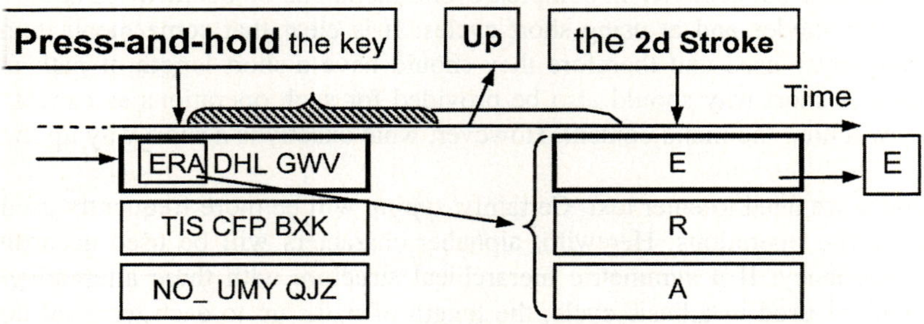


**Fig. 3.** Text entry with long stroke technique

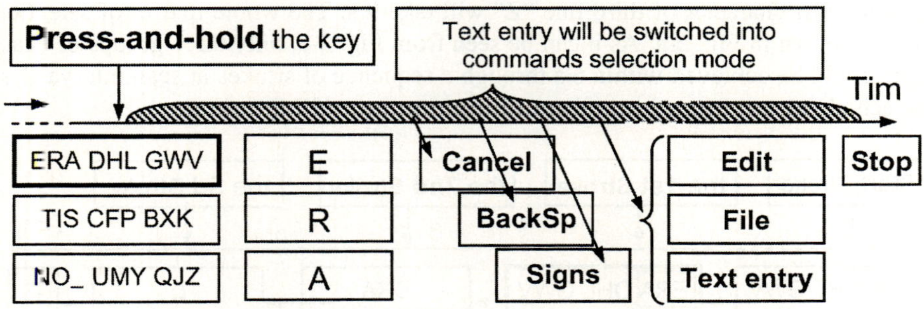


**Fig. 4.** Long stroke technique to choose other commands

The long stroke technique, when a button is held down for 2-7 scan intervals, can be used to provide a transition to the special options, to modify layout inside the cycle (Fig. 4), for instance, to switch to special character mode or to return a layout to its original state (the first level). The entering of the first token after dwelling (E, T, N – the most frequently used characters) does not require long waiting and the duration of sustaining key in a bottom position is not so critical. Besides that, automatism of the choice of the first token (with the coupled stroke) allows to plan the third step directly during implementing the long stroke at the first step.

## 2.2 The Model for Adaptive Scan Interval

Menu pointing and text-input can be considered as temporal processes or stimulus-dependent goal-directed behavior of the user. Herewith, a behavior model includes a particular sequence of actions. On the user side, they are the following: cognitive processing and motor actions. These actions should be synchronized with such procedures as highlighting of a particular alternative within interface. The parameters of the signals may either facilitate synchronization of the interactive process or hinder performance. The physical stimulus starts the motor reaction that could be measured. Based on real-time analysis the visual-motor reaction time (RT), we could also predict or optimize scan interval [1, 3]. The temporal diagram of the algorithm for measuring the user performance through visual-motor reaction time and automatic correction of the scan interval is shown in Fig. 5. Scan interval ($T_{scan}$) consists of three pieces: $T_0$ – the first variable interval, $T_1$ – the second variable interval and $T_2 = T_1$.

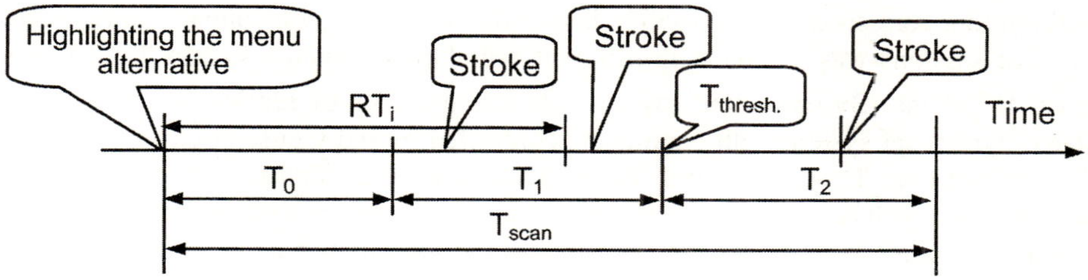


**Fig. 5.** The temporal diagram of the algorithm for adaptive scan interval

Herewith, $T_1$ and $T_2$ present a symmetrical temporal window concerning established dynamical threshold

$$T_{thresh} = T_0 + T_1 \,. \tag{1}$$

Initial conditions could be established from the assumption that 90% of strokes, at an average typing speed, could occur within the field ($T_1 + T_2$), and condition probability when $RT_i \leq T_0$ could be nonsignificant. These data can be excluded from the computation. There is one more important interval $\Delta T$. This magnitude will take part in changing three temporal components of scan interval.

The algorithm works as follows. After each highlighting of menu alternatives, we can record the time of user reply in the keystroke. Besides that, we will record an average magnitude for RT (AveRT) on each 5 realizations. Let us suppose that

$$AveRT < T_{thresh} - \Delta T \tag{2}$$

then we may decrease $T_0$ on $\Delta T$ too. That is, a new scan interval will equal

$$T_{scan} = (T_0 - \Delta T) + 2 \times T_1 \,. \tag{3}$$

Changing scan interval can occur with equal probability in plus and minus side, if user reactions are symmetrical regarding dynamical threshold $T_{thresh}$.

If the user changes typing speed, and after each user action AveRT < $T_{thresh}$, $T_{scan}$ is permanently decreased due to decreasing $T_0$, therefore the time to change $T_{thresh}$. In a kind of criterion could be index of some number of $\Delta T$. For instance, if $T_0$ have changed by ((-3) × $\Delta T$), the magnitude of $T_{thresh}$ may also be decreased, at least, by one half of this magnitude. Then, a new scan interval will equal

$$T_{scan} = (T_0 - 3 \times \Delta T) + 2 \times (T_1 - 3 \times \Delta T /2) \,. \tag{4}$$

Thus, after changing dynamical threshold, probability of user replies in a field $T_2$ will be higher and AveRT > $T_{thresh}$. This situation will lead, or not, to increasing $T_0$. We have built the algorithm prototype and carried out a study of scan interval regulation in dependence on typing speed with a single button.

The test was done with 8 subjects on iPAQ pocket PC. 100 alphabet characters per session were presented in random sequence. The subjects pressed down the key after highlighting corresponding alternative line of the menu with convenient typing speed. Each of sessions was started with different initial conditions of $T_0$ and $T_1$; $\Delta T$ was equal to 20 ms. By excluding low-probable magnitudes of replies, we received a stable dynamical system with parameters controlled by individual visual-motor reactions of the user. It was observed that 40 strokes were enough to replace initial parameters onto individual ones starting from 2 s. That is, one test phrase of eight words could be enough to initialize the system, and the algorithm will automatically keep scan interval near the convenient magnitude with given increment $\Delta T$.

## 3 Pilot Evaluation of the Method for Text Entry

Eight volunteers from staff and students at the University of Tampere were recruited for this study. This group, which was comprised of 3 females and 5 males, covered an age range of 24 to 48. None of the participants had any previous long-term experience with text entry through single-switch manipulation. All of the eight participants were right-handed. None of the subjects had motor or cognitive disorders.

The study was carried out on iPAQ Pocket PC. The test program was written in Microsoft eMbedded Visual Basic 3.0. An external key was connected to serial port. The menu of the software application consisted of three alternatives (Fig. 1), approximately 25 × 5 $mm^2$ in sizes with 10-point Arial capital letters. The key figures such as the mean text entry rate, the number of errors, the number of keystrokes per word, the time per character and the average scan interval were stored for each trial.

The evaluations took place in a usability laboratory. During the first experiment, participants were given one trial to familiarize themselves with text entry method and the features of button manipulation were explained. This trial was important so that the participant could find their comfortable rhythm and behavior strategy: when s/he has a short break and can think or look at test-word, when s/he should fast as possible to strike on the key and how to use long stroke technique at typing.

One trial consisted of entering twenty words, which are randomly selected from a set of 150 words, and displayed one at a time at the top line on the screen. The test words were 6 - 13 characters in length with mean 8.5 and every letter of the alphabet was included, at least several times during the trial. We did not use phrases for retyping to avoid an additional cognitive loading and to check user behavior when temporal window is continuously changed, though that takes place be adaptive. Therefore, the sign "space" ("_", Fig. 1) was not used and the symbol layout is not final for real text entry.

To begin typing each word, the participants had a Start-stroke (Fig. 1). The cyclic mode was started from the upper line ("ERADHLGWV"). By this way, access to all of entered symbols was proportionally close to predicted performance (Fig. 2-b). We also did not admit typing wrong characters; certainly, this influences onto data dispersion but allows detecting other problems dealing with layout. To record the time per character the timer was started after highlighting the first line and stopped when a correct character was entered. When the last character of the word was entered, the word disappeared, the cycle stopped, and the next word to be entered appeared in upper line. At this point, the participant could rest and then, as before, s/he could start typing by doing Start-stroke. Each of the subjects accomplished 20 trials. Fifteen trials were done with long stroke technique and the last ten of them have been taken in further processing of results. In addition, five trials were done with the triple-stroke technique.

## 4 The Results of Pilot Evaluation

Fig. 6 shows average values and dispersion of the times needed to choose any character from the layout used at average scan interval 460 ms (s = 52 ms) regarding predicted values (the left columns). Summarized relative frequency of the characters per one thousand letters used during the test for each group, according to accessibility, is shown in the bottom of the Figure. The correlation of relative frequency of the characters used during the test with English letter frequency was about 0.91. The correlation between predicted time and received was 0.96.

Fig. 7 shows average percentage of errors at the average scan interval 460 ms. The data were collected on one of the participants. The data of other participants have a similar pattern varying in values. As you can see in this sample, the error rate has a big dispersion. Entry of some often-used characters had less errors (E, N, O) than others.

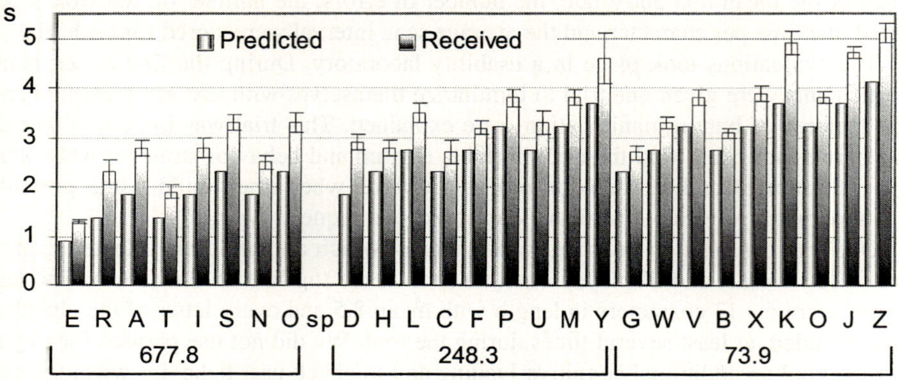


**Fig. 6.** Average times (and standard deviation) needed to choose any character at scan interval 460 ms regarding to predicted values (the left columns)

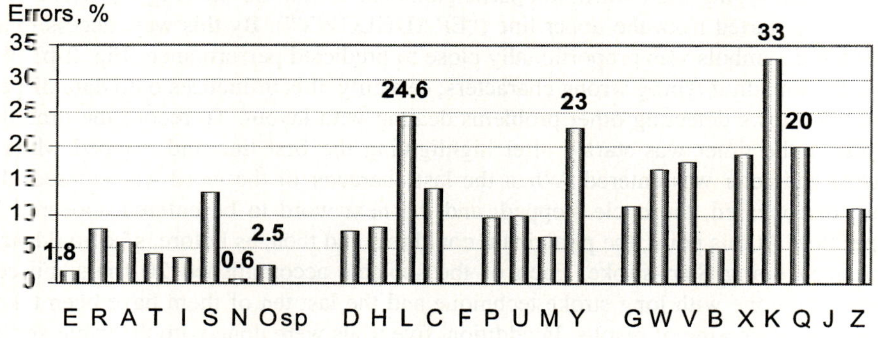


**Fig. 7.** Error rates within tokens groups averaged on 10 trials of the same subject (200 words, 1868 tokens), the average scan interval 460 ms

Rarely used characters (K, Y, Q) have lower frequency of appearing and the percent of error is higher due to the small number of them. The error rate in long stroke arrhythmic typing (~5%) was two times lower than in rhythmic triple-stroke technique (~13.2%). An error could appear when highlighting provoked repetition of long stroke technique in non-suitable moment. For instance, the character "L" often followed after symbols "E", "I" or "O", which were entered with the help of long stroke technique. A desire to apply the same strategy had led of the subject to an error.

We have analysed the process of input for each symbol and the coupled symbol sequences (digrams and trigrams) and found out that proposed layout could be optimised to simplify the user behavior when s/he should continuously change strategy. Long stroke technique essentially decreases the number of strokes with respect to triple strokes technique ($F = 0.16$) and increases typing speed ($F = 0.19$), Fig. 8. Error rate with triple stroke technique was higher as a balance of excitation-inhibition is a very difficult process. It is difficult to break down previously used behavior stereotype, triple-stroke sequence, when two strokes were just made. And vice versa, when strategy is oriented on long stroke, inhibition is facilitated. Most of the participants achieved scan interval 460 ms and typing speed 4.2 wpm after 1 hour training. As it was expected, scan interval varied individually from trial to trial. The average scan interval with triple stroke technique was about 933 ms and average typing speed was lower than 3.5 wpm.

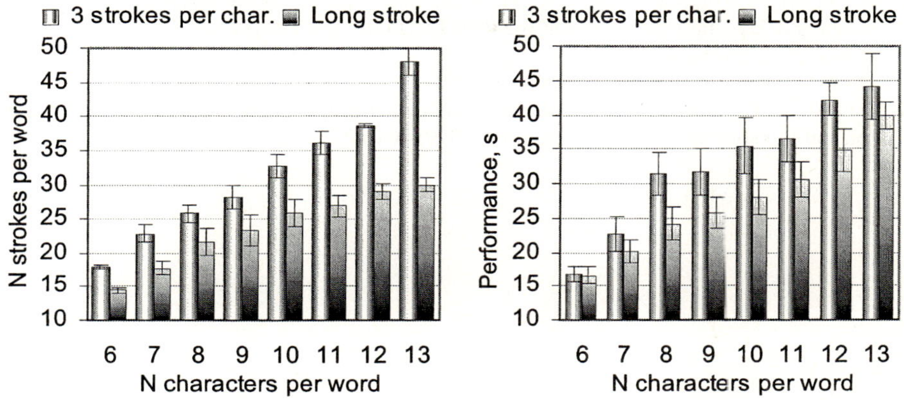


**Fig. 8.** A number of strokes per word (the left chart) and performance (the right chart) averaged on 800 words

## 5 Conclusion

We designed an algorithm for adaptive scan interval and have applied it for text entry through single-switch manipulation. Instead of the switch, any similar signal may be used. To choose any item in the menu, we have applied a short-cyclic hierarchical structure with three levels and three alternatives. A user can use the triple-stroke or the long stroke technique when the button is held down; it allows to jump over one of menu levels or to cut the cycle. Long stroke technique essentially decreases the number of strokes and increases typing speed. In the further development we plan to optimize character layout to facilitate transition from one strategy to another.

## Acknowledgements

This work was financially supported by the Academy of Finland (grant 200761), and by the Nordic Development Centre for Rehabilitation Technology (NUH).

## References

1. Bourhis, G., Pino, P.: Temporal analysis of the use of an augmentative communication device. In: AAATE'03. IOS Press, Netherlands (2003) 294-298
2. Hansen, J.P., Johansen, A.S., Hansen, D.W., Itoh, K., Mashino, S.: Command Without a Click: Dwell Time Typing by Mouse and Gaze Selections. Proc. INTERACT'03. IOS Press, IFIP 2003, (2003) 121-128
3. Lesher, G.W., Higginbotham, D.J., Moulton, B.J.: Techniques for automatically updating scanning delays. In: Proceedings of the RESNA 2000, (2000) 85-87
4. Mehta, A. eLocutor version 2. `http://www.holisticit.com/eLocutor/Elocutorv2.htm`
5. Simpson, R.C., Koester, H.H.: Adaptive one-switch row-column scanning. IEEE Transactions on Rehabilitation Engineering 7(4), (1999) 464-473.

# Designing an Evaluation Method for Computer Accessibility for People with Severe Disabilities

R. Kadouche[1], B. Abdulrazak[1], and M. Mokhtari[1,2]

[1] Handicom Lab GET/INT, Evry, France
[2] INSERM-U483, Université Pierre & Marie Curie, Paris, France
Rachid.Kadouche@int-evry.fr

**Abstract.** This paper presents our research work on the accessibility of assistive technologies dedicated to peoples having severe disabilities. The objective is to provide quantitative and qualitative evaluations methodologies on human-machine interaction while getting access to a computer. We aim to design compensation strategies developed by people having sever motor disabilities in order to use physical input devices to control a computer. The study developed in this paper is based on a quantitative evaluation method when using pointing devices such as mouse, Trackballs, Joysticks, etc. The preliminary results presented corresponds to one month of evaluation with 8 patients mainly having spinal cord injuries and muscular dystrophies from the rehabilitation hospital of Garches and from French Muscular dystrophies Association (AFM).

## 1 Introduction

Most problems encountered by people with disabilities are related to the use of human machine interfaces. Their capabilities in acting on a system can be analyzed with various available peripherals (keyboard, joystick, mouse, etc.). The handling of these peripherals requires a number of degrees of freedom (ddl), a specific movement amplitude and/or a specific strength to control output signals, either continuous (e.g. mouse), or discontinuous (e.g. keyboard). These characteristics condition the various actions which could achievable by each end-user.

In order to adapt existing technical aids, design new ones, and choose the optimal human-machine interface for each specific user, it is necessary to define accurately the users needs, and in particular, their physical abilities. Thus it is important to describe as closely as possible their motor incapability and evaluate their behaviors while using human-machine input devices[1,2].

In this paper we will focus mainly on the analysis of users' strategies when using a computer input device by the development of an evaluation method.

## 2 Evaluation Method

To evaluate users' behavior while using computer input device, we have designed a quantitative evaluation strategy based on the use of newly developed software.

K. Miesenberger et al. (Eds.): ICCHP 2004, LNCS 3118, pp. 845–848, 2004.

Besides the qualitative approach, an ergonomist performed a qualitative evaluation method using a questionnaire to report the mains information about the patient (identity, personal feedback); in addition input device prehension phase was video recorded [4].

The quantitative evaluation method was based on innovative software development for online tracking of users commands when performing a specific task. The main identified parameters recorded were: **Accuracy** of the cursor on the screen which consists on analyzing the trajectories deviations, the **ability** to carry out a simple click, a double click, and drag and drop, and the **time** necessary to performed the task.

The evaluation method that we developed is based on a set of tests which include all possible functions necessary for a computer interface within defined tasks[3]. Two types of analyses were developed: the **user tests** and the calculation of the corresponding **errors** corresponding to each test. We have implemented three tests which evaluate all the operations which can be processed by the device (XY moving of the cursor, simple clicking, double clicking, drag and drop) The duration and the trajectory of the cursor were recorded in a log file: Test 1 consists in connecting two graphical targets by clicking on the first target then, clicking on the second one, it permit to test the accuracy in space, to go from one point to another. Test 2 consist on following a trajectory imposing angles and curves, without having to click. Test 3 is a Drag and Drop test; it allows to maintain the left click down while carrying out a movement, for this test the number of clicks is recorded in the log file.

As shown in the figure bellow, the error analysis is quantified by a surface between the real layout and the ideal layout which is calculated by recursive algorithm, it counts the dots which do not belong to the surface and by deducting the desired surface from total surface.

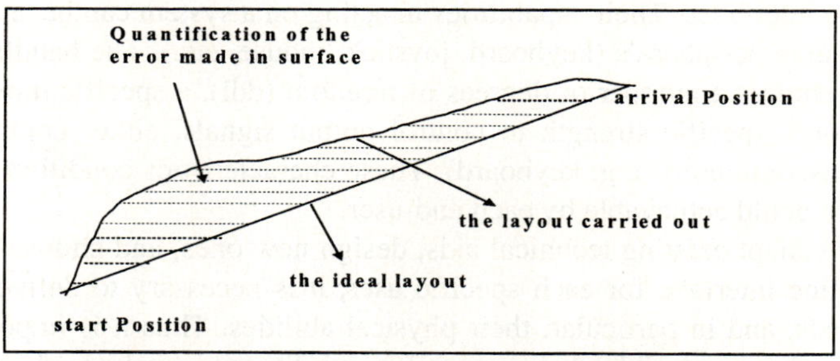


**Fig. 1.** Error calculation based on a recursive graphical algorithm

## 3 Preliminary Results

These preliminary results correspond to one month of evaluation, mainly the average duration of the task is 45minutes, 8 persons took part in our experimentation, 4 quadriplegics patients (Equal1, Equal6, Equal7, and Equal8) from the rehabilitation hospital of Garches, 3 muscular dystrophies patients (Equal2, Equal3, and Equal4) and one person (Equal5) having a degenerative neuromuscular disease from AFM. Three interfaces are tested: mouse, joystick, trackball. Each task was repeated 10 times, where the mean of the time and the error surface are considered. The preliminary results are presented in the three following tables where S represents the error surface (in number of pixels) and T the duration of the task (in tenth of second).

**Table 1.** Error and time duration performed for each test with a mouse

| Mouse | Equal1 | | Equal3 | | Equal4 | | Equal5 | | Equal6 | | Equal7 | | Equal8 | |
|---|---|---|---|---|---|---|---|---|---|---|---|---|---|---|
| | S | T | S | T | S | T | S | T | S | T | S | T | S | T |
| Test1 | 24989 | 40 | 6906 | 43 | 25644 | 24 | 69763 | 376 | 43551 | 89 | 2143 | 135 | 24480 | 60 |
| Test2 | 18419 | 180 | 9005 | 135 | 7265 | 96 | 20746 | 154 | 14089 | 138 | 10121 | 125 | 10004 | 251 |
| Test3 | 0 | 0 | 0 | 0 | 114504 | 15 | 14630 | 16 | 22645 | 76 | 0 | 0 | 58817 | 30 |

In this table we remark that the error surface made by Equal3 for the test1 is the smallest one, so he succeeded the test with a better accuracy compared with other patients. In opposite Equal5 who made the largest error surface with a high duration to perform the test1, because he had difficulties to use the mouse.

**Table 2.** Error and time duration performed for each test with a Trackball

| TrackBall | Equal1 | | Equal2 | | Equal3 | | Equal4 | | Equal6 | | Equal7 | | Equal8 | |
|---|---|---|---|---|---|---|---|---|---|---|---|---|---|---|
| | S | T | S | T | S | T | S | T | S | T | S | T | S | T |
| Test1 | 37990 | 40 | 9537 | 79 | 16177 | 68 | 13327 | 44 | 12337 | 66 | 21108 | 135 | 24016 | 90 |
| Test2 | 0 | 0 | 13670 | 176 | 13919 | 135 | 5673 | 154 | 15523 | 125 | 30673 | 125 | 5615 | 310 |
| Test3 | 0 | 0 | 0 | 0 | 0 | 0 | 29081 | 136 | 0 | 0 | 29152 | 36 | 0 | 0 |

**Table 3.** Error and time duration performed for each test with a Joystick

| Joystick | Equal1 | | Equal5 | | Equal6 | | Equal7 | | Equal8 | |
|---|---|---|---|---|---|---|---|---|---|---|
| | S | T | S | T | S | T | S | T | S | T |
| Test1 | 17104 | 30 | 62626 | 82 | 36637 | 164 | 19951 | 148 | 22527 | 84 |
| Test2 | 19713 | 120 | 48293 | 106 | 19551 | 366 | 114689 | 397 | 13686 | 402 |
| Test3 | 0 | 0 | 114700 | 19 | 68359 | 278 | 42161 | 21 | 25535 | 59 |

We have noticed that:

The absence of the results concerning some users in the tables above ( Equal2 in table1, Equal 5 in Table2, Equal 2, Equal 3, Equal 4 in table3) is due to the non possibility for the patient to use this interface or the fatigability and the rejection to use it, for example Equal5 can't use TrackBall because he has spastic movements.

The value 0 in the tables means that the patient didn't perform the associate test, due to its complexity or to timing.

Peoples with muscular dystrophies had a good results with TrackBall, due to the accuracy of their movements fingers. The results of the quadriplegics patients are not uniform, that is due mainly to different levels of disabilities among the user group. For example Equal1 had better results with the joystick; in opposite to Equal6 who gives better results with trackball. Equal7 and Equal8 had equivalent results for the three interfaces.

We found that, even if the joystick seems not adapted for computer application, it provide a solution for people with shakiness and spastic movements(Equal1, Equal5).

## 4 Conclusion

This work allows us to know the reaction and the behaviors of both populations (peoples with muscular dystrophies and quadriplegics peoples) using the human-machine input device, and to identify the best interface among several. The evaluations highlighted the difficulties to use input devices and proved the ability of the users to compensate their handicap. General conclusions can be validated, so the mouse provide the best scores according to the trackball and the joystick. Actually we are not able to explain this effect, due to the limited number of users. We are aiming for a more significant end-user group and several interfaces to complete this study.

In addition we are working on the modeling of the upper limb posture during the grasping phases to model the description of the residual motor capabilities and evaluate human behavior while using human-machine input devices. Coupling the modeling of residual motor capability with resulted actions on the cursor, should provide a better understanding of the user profile and consequently adapt the human-machine interaction.

## Acknowledgements

The authors would like to thank the users who have participated actively in this research work. This project is funded by the GET and by the industrial foundation Louis Leprince Ringuet.

## References

1. Mokhtari, M.: Interaction Homme-Machine : Application aux aides technologiques pour la réduction du handicap moteur HDR, (Novembre 2002)
2. Kadouche.R.: analyse de l'interaction Homme-Machine dans le cas d'un handicap moteur. Rapport DEA. (2003).
3. Zaefle, M.: Is the trackball a serious alternative to the mouse ? A comparison of trackball and mouse with regard to cursor movement performance in manipulation tacks. Proc HCI'2003, Vol 3. (2003) 158-162
4. Institute of rehabilitation and physical deficiency: http://www.irdpq.qc.ca/index.html

# Computerized Assessment Tool for Mouse Operating Proficiency

Ming-Chung Chen[1], Ling-Fu Meng[2], Cheng-Feng Hsieh[1], Ting-Fang Wu[2], Chi-Nung Chu[3], and Tien-Yu Li[4]

[1] Department of Special Education, National Chiayi University
300 Unoversity Rd., Chiayi, 600 Taiwan, R.O.C.
ming@chen.twmail.cc
n2691431@mail.ncku.edu.tw
[2] Department of Occupational Therapy, Chung Gung University
259 Weng Hwa 1st Rd., Kweishan, 333 Taoyuan , Taiwan, R.O.C.
{ufx53929,tfwu}@mail.cgu.edu.tw
[3] Department of Management Information Systems, Chung Cuo Institute of Technology
56 Sec. 1 Shinglung Rd., 116 Taipei, R.O.C.
nung@mail.ckitc.edu.tw
[4] Department of Information and Computer Education, National Taiwan Normal University
162, Sec. 1, Hoping East Rd., 106 Taipei, R.O.C.
tienyu@webmail.ice.ntnu.edu.tw

**Abstract.** This paper substantiates the process of developing a computerized mouse proficiency assessment tool (CAT-MP), which could be used to measure proficiency of clients in mouse operating skills. Moreover, CAT-MP also helps evaluator to diagnose specific difficulties and provide individual remedies for the persons with limitations to access computer. Based on the results of task analysis of mouse operating, clinical experiences and related literature review, CAT-MP was designed containing four modules responsible for communicating interfaces and databases, organizing test tasks, collecting data and analyzing data respectively. Beside the contents of these modules, the tasks of four sub-tests, the procedure of measurement, and the results of reliability and validity of CAT-MP will be addressed in detail in this paper.

## 1 Introduction

As information and computer technology has grown rapidly and become essential in the educational, vocational, and daily contexts, interacting with computer becomes an important as well as prerequisite skill for individuals. Currently, the major computer operation environment has been accessed through graphic user interface (GUI), within typical users usually manipulate mouse to interact with computer. However, individuals with upper limbs impairments usually experience obstacles when interacting with computer through conventional and suitable input devices because of their restricted movement. They need to be equipped with adequate adaptive pointing and selecting devices, such likes joystick, switch mouse, infrared mouse, and mouse simulator, for the purpose of interacting with computer more effectively.

Through the efforts of the researchers in health, engineer, computer science, and education, the adaptive pointing and selecting devices of mouse system have been

K. Miesenberger et al. (Eds.): ICCHP 2004, LNCS 3118, pp. 849–856, 2004.

developed. Gradually, people with upper limbs impairments could use these alternative devices to interact with computer information technology with fewer barriers. Furthermore, they can participate in the Information Society more equally.

However, it's still difficult for the adaptive computer experts to decide what kind of devices might be appropriate for different individuals; even there are many alternative mouse devices available now. The difficulty partially results from lacking of adequate assessment system to understand clients' mouse operating performance that is important to connect with the adaptive device selecting decision.

Experts need to evaluate the client's proficiency ahead of deciding a suitable item of adaptive devices. Therefore they need related tool to assist them to carry out a proper computer access evaluation. In fact, some assessment tools have been developed for the professionals to execute an adequate assessment, including checklist, flow chart [1], [2], [3], [4]. However, these tools tend to focus on assessment procedure rather than the objective evaluation of task operating capability, besides "The Assessment of Computer Task Performance" which developed by Mazer, Dumont, and Vincent [3].

Test of Mouse Proficiency (TOMP) is a kind of computerized assessment tool [5] which maybe objective. It was developed to assess mouse competency skills in children from preschool to upper elementary school with elaborating on reliability and validity. However TOMP was developed based on the results of mouse competency analysis related to games and educational software. It did not include the indispensable mouse operating skills, such as right side click and double click, mentioned by Mazer et al. [3]. Additionally, clients with poor motor control could not finish even a test task because of the time allowed for accomplishing the task is fixed. For the purpose of identifying the needs of requesting alternative mouse devices, evaluators should acquire more performance information of the clients rather than TOMP could provide. In this regard, researchers develop a more complete and flexible computerized assessment tool for clinical evaluators to perform holistic and objective mouse proficiency assessment and diagnosis.

In this study, CAT-MP was developed through comprehensive literature review [1], [2], [3], [4], [5], task analysis of mouse proficiency skills, and clinical experience of researchers. Finally, content validity and test-retest reliability were conducted to examine the usability of CAT-MP system.

## 2 CAT-MP System

### 2.1 Overview

CAT-MP system was developed to conduct mouse proficiency skills assessment when evaluating computer access difficulties and effect of intervention. CAT-MP system consists of four muddles. They are *main program*, *testing functions database*, *outcome database*, and *outcome analysis program*. As the system executing process shown in Fig. 1, *Main program* communicates the interfaces and the databases. It would organize test tasks by requesting tasks from *testing functions database* based on evaluator's selection on evaluator interface, and presents the test tasks in sequence on evaluatee interface. While executing the tasks through operating the mouse, main program synchronically collects the responses made by evaluatee and writes related information into tables of outcome database. After assessment, evaluator could use the *outcome analysis program* to analyze the evaluatee's performances originated from different testing tasks.

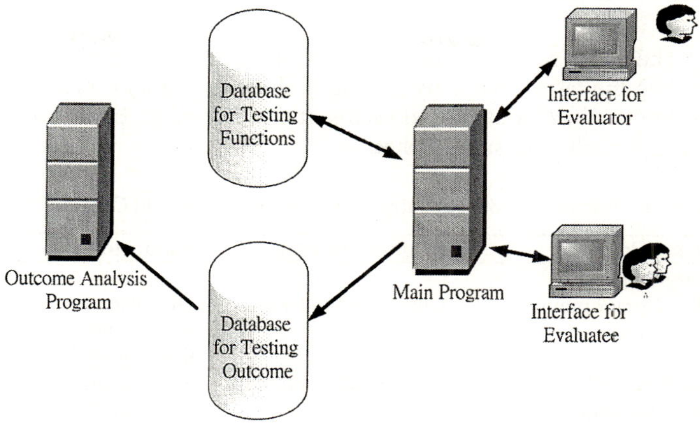


**Fig. 1.** The process of the CAT-MP system executing

## 2.2 Content of Test

CAT-MP system involves four subtests, each consists various mouse-operating skills. Within each subtest, flexible parameters are made to set up target size, target color, targeting distance, and time permitted by evaluator. The four subtests are described below.

**Targeting.** Targeting subtest is concerned with clients' cursor targeting and staying capability. In this subtest, the client is required to move the cursor along a guided line to the indicated target square icon and dwell there for a second. The test tasks vary with the parameters setting depended on assessment need. As the Table 1 indicated, evaluator could set six parameters with combination. Cursor moving distance from starting point to the targeting icon involves 1/5/10/15/20 cm types. Cursor moving directions parameter gives the options chosen by evaluators to indicate where the cursor should move. Target icons vary in size from 0.04 $cm^2$ to 4 $cm^2$ as well as seven types of color for choosing. Time limitation for completing the task could be set from 10 seconds to 100 seconds depended on client's motor control performance. Besides, the amount of each test task, from 1 to 5, could be select if multi tries is needed. Test tasks could be arranged uniquely depended on client's specific situation or purpose of the assessment.

**Stationary Clicking.** The purpose of this subtest is to detect the clients' stationary clicking abilities. In this subtest, evalautee was asked to click the target icon, without moving cursor arrow, by pressing the button of mouse or activating the other selecting devices. Based on the result of clicking skills analysis, single-click on left side, double-click on left side, and single-click on right side are chosen as the essential skills to be evaluated.

**Targeting and Clicking.** This subtest combines the purposes of the aforementioned two subtests. In this subtest, client needs to target the cursor arrow to the objective icon and click it stably. Except cursor moving distance and directions, evaluator could select the other four parameters as well as in subtest one.

**Dragging.** The final subtest aims to assess the clients' dragging skill. Client is required to drag the target image by activating the pointing and selecting devices and drop it into the destined square by disactivating the devices. Evaluator could set the six parameters as well as in subtest one.

**Table 1.** Descirptions of four subtests and their test tasks in CAT-MP system

| Subtests & tasks | Abilities measured | Parameters set |
|---|---|---|
| ■ Targeting<br>● Cursor moving | Cursor moving and staying | Distance, direction, size, color, amount of testing, time for each trail |
| ■ Stationary clicking<br>● Left-side single clicking<br>● Left-side double clicking<br>● Right-side single clicking | Mouse button clicking | Size, color, amount of testing, time for each trail |
| ■ Targeting and clicking<br>● Moving and Left-side single clicking<br>● Moving and Left-side double clicking<br>● Moving and Right-side single clicking | Cursor moving and mouse button clicking | Distance, direction, size, color, amount of testing, time for each trail |
| ◆ Dragging<br>● Moving icon | Mouse button pressing and target moving | Distance, direction, size, color, amount of testing, time for each trail |

## 2.3 Measurement

Speed, accuracy and efficiency are usually regarded as key indicators of motor competency and adopted to assess the mouse operation proficiency [2]. Those indicators are also the three assessment items of CAT-MP system in this present work.

*Speed* means how fast the client could accomplish the single testing item. *Accuracy* is the percentage determined by dividing the amount of correct responses by the total responses in each test task. *Efficiency* defines in term of the stability while moving cursor along guided lines. It could detect the trail and smoothness of path traveling. Detail measuring variables for each subtest were presented on Table 2.

In addition to assess clients' mouse proficiency, CAT-MP system could help the evaluators to identify clients' mouse operating characteristics which could be directly connected to the suitable adaptive solutions for the clients. For example, after diagnosing clients' characteristics in the needed cursor moving distance, cursor moving direction, icon size while clicking, time interval while double clicking, and preferred icon color, the evaluator could use aforementioned information to adapt a suitable human-screen-mouse interaction environment for the clients. Detail variables diagnosed for test tasks of each subtest were presented on Table 2.

**Table 2.** Variables measured and diagnosed for test tasks of each subtest

| Subtests & tasks | Variables diagnosed | Variables measured |
|---|---|---|
| ◆ Targeting | | Speed, accuracy |
| ● Cursor moving | Distance, direction, size, color | |
| ◆ Stationary clicking | | Speed, accuracy, |
| ● Left-side single clicking | Size, color, coordinate | |
| ● Left-side double clicking | Size, color, coordinate interval of double clicking | |
| ● Right-side single clicking | Size, location, color | |
| ◆ Targeting and clicking | | Speed, accuracy, efficiency |
| ● Moving and Left-side single clicking | Distance, direction, size, coordinate, color | |
| ● Moving and Left-side double clicking | Distance, direction, size, coordinate, color, interval of double clicking | |
| ● Moving and Right-side single clicking | Distance, direction, size, coordinate, color | |
| ◆ Dragging | | Speed, accuracy, efficiency |
| ● Moving icon | Distance, direction, size, coordinate, color | |

### 2.4 Procedure of Assessment

After the main program executes, evaluator used interface displays on the screen. Within evaluator chooses (or types) a client's name in advance, and then decides the test tasks and configures each test task. Then the program presents the test tasks on the screen in sequence. The client operates the mouse or alternative mouse device to complete the task on the screen paced by evaluator. The sequence of testing suggested by program was targeting, stationary clicking, targeting and clicking, and dragging. However, evaluators could decide by themselves, or even choose one or two of them to test the client only.

When evaluatee accomplishes the all test tasks, the program will give evaluator a choice to decide whether to terminate the test or to continue another test. If the program was closed, evaluator could open the file of Microsoft's Access to review the data of client's performance or open *outcome analysis program* to review the efficiency of clients' cursor moving performance.

### 2.5 Outcome Analysis Program

Whereas those data collected by Microsoft's Access could be used to analyze the evaluatees' performance quantitatively through some statistical program, such likes Excel, SPSS. *Outcome analysis program* of CAT-MP system was developed specifically to demonstrate the efficiency of their performance. As the Fig. 2 indicated the program could present the track of the cursor moving to show the path and smoothness of cursor moving.

As the examples shown in Fig. two, the path of cursor moving in the upper left picture was direct to the target and the velocity of cursor moving was smooth. The other three tracks demonstrate that the evaluatees had adapted the direction of the cursor continuously on the road to the target icon. The client in the picture of upper right one moved the cursor speedily in the early part of task but slowed down when approaching to the destination. The situation in the lower right picture was similar, however, the client moved and stopped the cursor when targeting. The performance of lower left one was the worst. The client moved the cursor unsmoothly and targeted the icon after missed twice finally.

Besides analyzing the efficiency of each single performance in cursor moving task, evaluator could use this program to compare the efficiency of the performance originated in different situations, such likes various distance of moving or dragging, sizes of the target icons, different pointing and selecting devices, or even different periods of intervention.

## 3 Reliability and Validity

Content validity evaluation was conducted. Two occupation therapists who were professional in computer access evaluation were asked to evaluate the suitability of this CAT-MP system. They both agreed that the testing tasks had presented the necessary skills of mouse operating; meanwhile, they assented to the interface of the CAT-MP designed friendly and clearly.

Test-retest reliability of speed was adopted to evaluate the reliability of CAT-MP system in this study. 31 undergraduates (16 females and 15 males) involved to the evaluation. They are skilled mouse users. Each participant took the same test tasks with same procedure twice at an interval of one week. Spearman's product-moment correlation was used to examine the test-retest reliability of CAT-MP system. As the results shown on Table 3, most of the correlation coefficients are significant. This reveals that the speed of each trail on the same item by the same participant in the two tests was related significantly.

## 4 Conclusions

This paper has described the development of an innovated mouse operating proficiency assessment software. Through the literacy review and task analysis, researchers developed the CAT-MP system to support the experts working in adaptive computer device field to evaluate the client's mouse operating performance whatever pointing and selecting device is used. This tool consists of the full range of tasks needed to manipulate mouse or alternative mouse device while accessing computer. The preliminary validity and reliability studies demonstrated that CAT-MP system is appropriate for measuring purpose. However, additional reliability studies will be still needed in the future by involving individuals with different limitations and their alternative mouse devices.

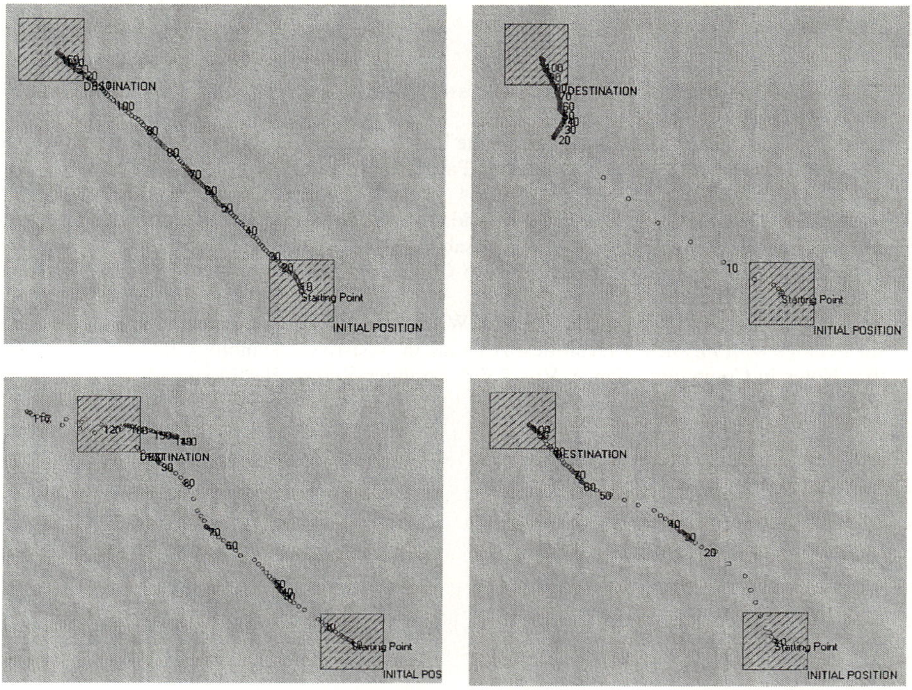


**Fig. 2.** Four examples for track of cursor moving

**Table 3.** Coefficients between test and retest for mal and female

| Test tasks | Male | Female |
|---|---|---|
| Targeting-cursor moving | .63** | .53** |
| Stationary clicking | | |
| Left-single click | .55** | .26* |
| Right-single click | .51** | .66* |
| Left-double click | .27* | .13 |
| Targeting and clicking | | |
| Left-single click | .20 | .49* |
| Right-single click | .04 | .33* |
| Left-double click | .28* | .28* |
| Dragging | .78** | .52** |

Note: * P<.05, ** P<.01


## Acknowledgement

The authors thank Zhi-Wen Wang and Wan-Chi Lin, junior students and part-time research assistants in the Chang Gung University Department of Occupational Therapy (Taoyuan, Taiwan), for their contributions in recruiting subjects, collecting data and running some research related tasks.

## References


1. Anson, D. K.: Alternative Computer Access: A Guide to Selection. F. A. Davis, Philadelphia (1997).
2. Lane. A., & Ziviani. J.: Introduction to the Test of Mouse Proficiency. The Occupational Therapy Journal of Research: Occupation, Participation and Health, Vol. 22(3). (2002) 111-118
3. Mazer, B., Dumont, C., & Vincent, C.: Validation of the Assessment of Computer Task Performance for Children. Technology and Disability, Vol. 15. (2003) 35-43
4. Wright, C., & Nomura, M.: From Toys to Computer: Access for the Physically Disabled Child. Authors, San Jose (1985)
5. Wu, T. F., Meng, L. F., Wang, H.. P., Wu, W.T., & Li, T. Y.: Computer Access Assessment for Persons with Physical Disabilities: A Guide to Assistive Technology Interventions. Lecture Notes in Computer Science, Vol. 2398. Springer-Verlag, Berlin Heidelberg New York (2002) 204-211

# Applications of Computer Access Approach to Persons with Quadriplegics

Ling-Fu Meng[1], Tieng-Yu Li[2], Chi-Nung Chu[3], Ming-Chung Chen[4], Sophie Chien-Huey Chang[5], Arr-Mien Chou[6], Tony Yang[6], Chih Chen Hui[2], Ku Ai Chiao[2], Yun Lung Lin[2], Pei-ting Weng[1], Yu-chen Shih[1], Tsung-ying Lu[3], and Nai-hsien Yeh[1]

[1] Department of Occupational Therapy, Chung Gung University
259 Weng Hwa 1st Rd., Kweishan, 333 Taoyuan , Taiwan
ufx53929@mail.cgu.edu.tw

[2] Department of Information and Computer Education, National Taiwan Normal University
162, Sec. 1, Hoping East Rd., 106 Taipei, Taiwan
tienyu@webmail.ice.ntnu.edu.tw
{genius03,g1h2c3,Harrison}@ice.ntnu.edu.tw

[3] Department of Management Information Systems, Chung Cuo Institute of Technology
56 Sec. 1 Shinglung Rd., 116 Taipei, Taiwan

[4] Department of Special Education, National Chiayi University
300 Unoversity Rd., Chiayi, 600 Taiwan
ming@chen.twmail.cc

[5] Department of Special Education, National Chiayi University
162, Sec. 1, Hoping East Rd., 106 Taipei, Taiwan
chang641@ms27.hinet.net

[6] Taiwan Assistive Technology and Vocational Rehabilitation Association
123, Sec. 1, Neihu Rd., 114 Taipei, Taiwan
o2h@ms62.hinet.net
tonyoung@ms7.hinet.net

**Abstract.** This paper substantiates the process of helping the clients with motor disabilities to operate computer. A team with multiple professionals from different disciplines served eight persons with quadriplegics diagnosed as Charcot-Marie-Tooth Disease, Amyotrophic Lateral Sclerosis (ALS), Athetoid Cerebral Palsy, Cervical Spinal Cord Injury and Muscular Dystrophy respectively. Based on the computer access approach (CAA), the limitations and strengths of motor control, the difficulties of operating computer and the context to support accessibility were evaluated. Furthermore, the evaluation results guided the configuration of computer system to be modified, possibly combined with changing anatomical control site. Finally better accessibility for each person was achieved. It can be concluded that CAA processed by an integrated team can greatly help in solving accessibility problems for quadriplegic.

## 1 Introduction

The persons with quadriplegics need alternative methods to operate computer. Although the alternative methods have been applied, most of those didn't really derived

K. Miesenberger et al. (Eds.): ICCHP 2004, LNCS 3118, pp. 857–864, 2004.

from systematic evaluation to be compatible with individuals' needs. Therefore, sometimes it's difficult to find a really appropriate solution for quadriplegics resulting in insufficient intervention [1, 2]. Based on the purpose of achieving the compatibility between evaluation and intervention in the real life, the concept of *Computer Access Approach (CAA)* with ecological spirit was created by us. Optimistically, persons with quadriplegics or severe hand dysfunctions could access computer through the application of this approach. Basically speaking, CAA equips with the characteristic of dynamic and friendly *person-computer-environment interaction* [3, 4]. Combined with the emphasis on the connection between evaluation and intervention, consequently, professionals can develop their interventions guided by the Professional Computer Adaptation Needs Evaluation (P-CANE).

### 1.1 Professional Computer Adaptation Needs Evaluation (P-CANE)

In terms of evaluation contents, CAA includes the process of evaluating computer access difficulty, motor control performance, computer constraint, and the context to support accessibility. We named the whole evaluation process in CAA as Professional Computer Adaptation Needs Evaluation (P-CANE). P-CANE was synchronously developed with Computer Access Assessment [5]. At this moment, P-CANE was furthermore emphasized on the spirit of dynamic and friendly *person-computer-context interaction*. It is appropriate to be used by professionals who are more familiar with computer access work for physical disabilities since it is not guided by flow-chart style.

The *limitations of computer access*, the *disadvantage of motor control* and the *physical strengths* were identified firstly in the process of evaluation. The purpose of considering the physical strengths is to prepare the possible alternative anatomical control sites that could substitute the original limited control site meanwhile or in the future. Moreover the *constraint of computer* and the context to support accessibility should be explored. In term of computer constraint, it includes hardware and software problems. In addition the *context to support accessibility* contains social support, physical environment, and client's psychological status (ex. motivation to change). And finally the client's needs to independently access computer could be integrated as the basis to guide solutions. Although some literatures have addressed related assessment strategies [1, 2, 3, 4], the characteristic of P-CANE substantiates the interaction among person, computer and context that is much more detailed and sophisticated than those existed assessment.

### 1.2 The Solutions of CAA

After the client's needs to access computer are integrated, the possible ecological solutions can be guided to develop. Derived from the needs mentioned previously, the principles of intervention also focus on resolving the computer constraint problems, positively changing the context to support accessibility, and using client's physical strengths. In term of *overcoming computer constraint*, we usually supply a substitute for standard mouse or keyboard, adjust window access environment, provide hardware and software, and repair computer trouble. While mentioning *changing the context of accessibility*, to adjust the direction and height of digital equipments, to teach client to access web and process word, and to provide psychological support are the examples that could be done. In addition *changing anatomical control site* based on client's physical strengths are also the possible alternative solutions. Through aforementioned solutions integrated, persons with quadriplegics or severe hand dysfunctions can finally access computer without barriers. Team is always important in our previous service [6], papers also supported its influence on the effect of service [5, 6, 7].

## 2 Assessment before Intervention

As the table 1 indicated, we reported eight clients with quadriplegics in this paper. Their diagnosis included Cerebral Palsy ($n$ = 1), Cervical Spinal Cord Injury ($n$ = 2), Amyotrophic Lateral Sclerosis ($n$ = 1), Muscular Dystrophy ($n$ = 2), Charco-Marie-Tooth Disease ($n$ = 1), and Neurofibromatosis ($n$ = 1) respectively. The P-CANE was used to evaluate each client and the results were described as follows.

### 2.1 Motor Control of Upper Extremity

The evaluation of motor control includes distal and proximal control of upper extremity. While concerning the distal part control of both arms (hand and finger movements), the clients with Charco-Marie-Tooth Disease and Spinal Cord Injury (case 2, 3 & 7) didn't show any movement and other clients exhibited limited movements. While addressing the proximal part control, all clients could overcome the pull of gravity and raise their upper arms except the client with ALS (case 4) who only had little movements and couldn't raise his arms against antigravity. The person with athetoid cerebral palsy (case 1) had strong synergy pattern to severely bother both proximal and distal part control although she could elevate upper arms and grasp objects.

### 2.2 Computer Access Difficulty

The details of their performances of computer access are listed in table 2. Four clients (case 5 - 8) were totally unable to operate computer and others were able to use computer but with inefficiency or with assistance. All the clients failed to execute dragging movement except the lady with cerebral palsy (case 1) who was able to perform dragging with right foot.

**Table 1.** Clients' Diagnosis & Their Performances Before Intervention

| Client no. & Diagnosis | Performances Before intervention |
|---|---|
| 1. Athetoid cerebral palsy (CP) – female | 1. She used right foot to type and operate mouse.<br>2. The mouse and keyboard were put on a box with the height equal to the height of her knees. However, that box was too for her to operate efficiently.<br>3. The monitor was on the general table; therefore she had to travel her head and eyes from monitor (higher place) to keyboard (lower place) or from keyboard to monitor. |
| 2. Spinal cord injury (SCI) – female | 1. She used trackball mouse only with right hand. Firstly, her hand palm contacted with trackball. Then through moving upper arm to trigger the motions of hand and trackball together, she could move cursor and click.<br>2. She couldn't perform dragging.<br>3. Because she overused her right arm, the symptoms of shoulder and hand pain existed. |
| 3. Spinal cord injury (SCI) – male | 1. He used hand dorsum to manipulate typical mouse.<br>2. He used metacarpophalangeal joints on hand dorsum to click.<br>3. He could not execute dragging movement. |
| 4. Amyotrophic Lateral Sclerosis (ALS) – male | 1. He was not able to use hand to execute keying, click and dragging.<br>2. Although the imaging system controlled by head was used, the system was not stable. It's very difficult to maintain the cursor in one position for a while (poor stability maintenance of cursor).<br>3. Although the auto-mouse was combined with the imaging system, the cursor often stayed on the non-target figures resulting in going to the wrong web page. He got to spend much energy handle this situation.<br>4. To him, the Window column and square figure were too small to successfully interact with computer. |
| 5. Muscular dystrophy (MD) – male | 1. He was totally not able to use computer. |
| 6. Muscular dystrophy (MD) – male | 1. He was totally not able to use computer. |
| 7. Charco-Marie-Tooth (female) | 1. She was totally not able to use computer. |
| 8. Neurofibromatosis – female | 1. He was totally not able to use computer. |

## 2.3 Computer Constraint

Many computer problems happened to limit our service process. Some clients did not have computer although they really needed. Some computer systems were not compatible with the software of alternative devices and some were not working. Also, the large resistance of ON-OFF button resulted most clients were not able to boot, halt and reboot by themselves because of their insufficient muscle power.

### 2.4 Context to Support Accessibility

Each client had strong motivation to access computer for learning, working or leisure. Therefore, the psycho-context seemed well for them. Two clients (case 1 & 5) living in the public institution were with good social support so that they could receive teaching and assistance. However, for other clients in the private institutions or at home did not have enough social support. The physical environment for each client was not appropriate for accessing computer, such as the inappropriate position of computer equipments and poor seating system.

## 3 Computer Access Intervention

Based on the results of P-CANE, we suggested computer access adaptation interventions for our clients as indicated on table 2. All the clients except case 1 changed anatomical control site (table 2) for the purpose of improving efficiency (case 2~8) and relieve muscle fatigue (case 2 & 7). The control site was decided by the physical strengths of each client, including the dorsum of 2-4 fingers driven by upper arm (case 7), chin and head (case 4), and elbow's ulnar side (case 2). Although case 1 used right foot to type and operate mouse, we finally did not change her control site because of her sufficient performance. The trackball mouse was suggested popularly to compensate the inability to operate standard mouse (case 2,3,5,7,8).

Except case 1 and 5, all clients used external switch as functional as the left button of mouse. We applied Round Press Switch and Stick Switch on six clients. Round Press Switches are prescribed for the clients with cervical spinal cord injury (case 2) and muscular dystrophy (case 7). Stick Switches are prescribed for the client with Charco-Marie-Tooth Disease (case 7), with Amyotrophic Lateral Sclerosis (case 4), with Neurofibromatosis (case 8) and with Cervical Spinal Cord Injury (case 3).

On-screen keyboard was also the important tool for the clients who couldn't use standard keyboard. All clients, except the client with cerebral palsy, had to use on-screen keyboard to resolve their needs of word input. Most clients also needed alternative big trackball mouse to substitute the standard mouse because of their severely limited hand function resulting in the difficulty to operate standard mouse.

We also adjusted the environment of window accessibility to make the toolbar larger for the client with ALS (case 4). Then he could move the cursor to the toolbar and stabilize it on the toolbar or icon and its helpful for him to use window system. We also arranged the research assistants to teach computer skills for some clients (case1, 5, 7, 8). Through the teaching and learning process, these clients could improve their computer skills. During the intervention, we have visited each client many times to resolve the difficulties that the client had. The team kept receiving the information from clients or their caregivers so that we might respond clients' needs faster.

## 4 Effects

Table 2 also indicated the effects of the CAA. Each client got improvement after the intervention. Four clients (case 5~8) could independently operate computer although they totally couldn't access in the initial. Case 4, 5 & 6 were furthermore able to travel on the net and use e-mail system since their living environment equipped with net and web system. We lowered the height of monitor position for the lady with cerebral palsy (case 1) then she did not need travel her head and eyes from monitor to keyboard or in the reverse. Consequently her operating skills improved. Case 2 and 7 used their mouths to hold pen to paint originally, now they could use painting software to paint on the computer.

Excitingly and unexpectedly case 2 relieved her muscle pain on the right shoulder after clicking movement is executed by left arm through triggering external switch. Initially case 2 only used her right hand to engage in moving and clicking resulting in the overloading of her muscles on the right shoulder. Now her left arm divides right arm's partial work to acquire the pain-relief effect. The college student with muscular dystrophy (case 6) in National Taiwan University could type papers and reading lots of information on the web after using IR-track mouse combined with auto-clicking and auto-dragging function.

## 5 Conclusions and Discussions

Generally speaking, all the clients could get improved in accessing computer after applying CAA. A team integrated by different professionals is necessary since health professionals and special educators are not familiar with computer knowledge and the professionals in the computer science do not know much about clients' characteristics [8]. During the intervention or after withdrawing intervention, in addition, to keep contact with clients is also necessary because the clients' physical conditions and environments might change and the computer problems might happen continuously that have to be managed [4]. Teaching assistants are possibly needed to help the clients to learn computer skills and web knowledge, especially for the disadvantaged socio-economic persons [6].

Clients' responses also inspired our thinking. Although auto-clicking is convenient, it's also easily getting trouble. For example, if clients try to return from the non-targeted web page that mistakenly entered before, it would be difficult to handle. The client with ALS had this kind of experience. Auto-clicking function also made the client with muscular dystrophy (case 6, college student) feel that he could not control himself. Therefore, to click by himself was asked by him for the purpose of getting more master feeling (self control) during the accessing process. Since he still could move her both knees toward midline, we arranged an external switch between his knees, as a result he could click by himself.

**Table 2.** Computer Access Intervention and its Effects

| Case | Computer access intervention | Effect |
|---|---|---|
| 1 | 1. made the box surface lower so the client did not have to raise her foot with much effort.<br>2. made trunk more stable while sitting in the wheelchair.<br>3. shifted the monitor on the same surface with the keyboard and mouse. | 1. the efficiency of foot typing improved.<br>2. head and eyes do not have to travel between box and computer table so that the efficiency improved. |
| 2 | 1. used left upper extremity to control external stick switch while right hand operating mouse and moving cursor. | 1. mouse operating proficiency improved and could perform dragging.<br>2. could pain with mouse on the monitor.<br>3. didn't complain shoulder pain anymore. |
| 3 | 1. used joystick to substitute standard mouse (also could use the original way to move cursor).<br>2. used external switch (round pressing switch) to substitute left button of mouse.<br>3. used on-screen keyboard for the purpose of keying. | 1. could draw on the monitor.<br>2. mouse operating proficiency improved and was able to perform dragging.<br>3. could type and writing e-mail to friends. |
| 4 | 1. used chin to control external long stick switch.<br>2. adjusted access environment in the Window to make toolbar lager (the cursor more easily to reach and stabilize on the toolbar area). | 1. could travel to different web pages.<br>2. mouse operating proficiency improved.<br>3. could type and write e-mail to friends. |
| 5 | 1. combined voice input system and trackball mouse. | 1. could type and process e-mail. |
| 6 | 1. used IR track auto-mouse but he wanted click by himself.<br>2. put round press switch between his knees so that he could make both knees move toward inside to press the switch. | 1. could search data on the web for the academic demands.<br>2. could type home assignments required in the class. |
| 7 | 1. used right hand to manipulate trackball for cursor moving.<br>2. used left upper extremity to control external switch for clicking. | 1. performed similarly to case 2. |
| 8 | 1. used trackball mouse.<br>2. used suspension sling to hang on and support both upper arms so that she could move arms to manipulate the trackball mouse. | 1. could play games.<br>2. could learn to type words.<br>3. could learn through traveling on the net. |

Interestingly, the client with ALS (case 4) is an engineer with master degree specialized in computer science. Therefore, he was able to handle the computer issues and provided the team many good ideas to make us also get improve. Now this gentleman is a vice-secretary-general of the ALS association as well as a SOHO worker. Certainly, he continuously helps persons with physical disabilities.

Sometimes, the input devices can be used together to improve efficiency. The client with muscular dystrophy (case 5) in this present study used voice input system to create words on the screen and used trackball mouse to delete the words or letters that were wrongly typed. According to his descriptions, this integrated way can compensate the inconvenience of the voice input system while managing the additional wrong words or letters. However, there was no article to address this issue [1, 2, 3, 4, 7].

## References

1. Anson, D.K.: Alternative Computer Access: A Guide to Selection. F. A. Davis, Philadelphia (1997)
2. Wright, C., Nomura, M.: From Toys to Computer: Access for the Physically Disabled Child. Authors, San Jose (1985)
3. Lazzaro, J.J.: Adapting PCs for diabilities. New York: Addison-Wesley Publishing Company (1995)
4. Alliance for Technology Access.: Computer and web resources for people with disabilities. Alameda, CA: Hunter House (2000)
5. Wu, T.F., Meng, L.F., Wang, H.P., Wu, W.T., Li, T.Y.: Computer Access Assessment for Persons with Physical Disabilities: A Guide to Assistive Technology Interventions. Lecture Notes in Computer Science, 2398, 204-211 (2002)
6. Li, T.Y., Meng, L.F., Chang, C.H.S., Chen, M.C., Chu, C.N., Chou, A.M., Yang, T., Hui, C.C., Ku, A.C., & Lin, Y.L.: The Program for Improving the Working Interfaces and Increasing the Work Competencies of People with Severe Physical Disabilities: The Evaluation Design, and Training of the Adaptive Computer Devices. Lecture notes in computer sciences, 2398, 238-240 (2002)
7. Casali, S.P., & Chase, J.D.: Computer-based system access by persons with disabilities: Differences in the effects of interface design on novice and experienced performance. International Journal of Individual Ergonomics, 15, 237-245 (1995)
8. Bain, B.K. & Leger, D.: Assistive technology: An interdisciplinary approach. New York: Churchill Livingstone (1997)

# Computer Access for Persons with Spinal Cord Injury

Ting-Fang Wu[1], Hwa-Pey Wang[2], Ming-Chung Chen[3], and Wu-Tien Wu[2]

[1] Department of Occupational Therapy, Chang Gung University
259 Wen-Hwa 1st Road, Kwei-Shan, Tao-Yuan, Taiwan, R.O.C.
tfwu@mail.cgu.edu.tw

[2] Department of Special Education, National Taiwan Normal University
162 Hoping E. Road. Sec 1, Taipei, Taiwan, R.O.C.
{e14008,t14004}@cc.ntnu.edu.tw

[3] Department of Special Education, National Chiayi University
300 University Rd., Chiayi, 600 Taiwan, R.O.C.
ming@chen.twmail.cc

**Abstract.** This study investigated the effectiveness of computer input devices on clients with spinal cord injury. Single-subject multiple probe design was used to compare the accuracy and speed of inputs of baseline and intervention phases. Three persons with spinal cord injury participated this study. The participants' levels of the lesion were cervical 3-4, cervical 4-5 and cervical 5-6. In the baseline phase, participants used the regular mouse to move the cursor and click the target. In the intervention phase, the researchers provided participants the computer input devices based on the results of individual assessment. Experimental results indicated that persons with spinal cord injury indeed improved the accuracy and the speed of computer inputs after the assistive equipment provided. Through appropriate input devices, clients with spinal cord injury are able to operate computer effectively.

## 1 Introduction

Computer technology has developed rapidly and become essential for people's daily lives. However, individuals with physical disabilities usually experience obstacles in computer access through conventional input apparatus because of their insufficient motor control. In recent years, computer interface devices have become commercially available to persons with physical disabilities. Computer access training during rehabilitation for persons with physical disabilities increases independence of their daily living [1]. The primary challenge faced by occupational therapists are to choose a proper computer interface devices and to provide appropriate training to fit special needs for individuals with disabilities. Vanderheiden (1987) reported the importance of suitable therapy and training with any selected rehabilitation devices [2]. However, a review of the literature revealed few studies on investigating the effects of applying computer input devices [1, 3, 4]. Therefore, the purpose of this study is to investigate the effect of input devices on persons with cervical spinal cord injury. The speed and accuracy of inputs will be compared with and without input devices. The maintenances of training effects will also be reported.

K. Miesenberger et al. (Eds.): ICCHP 2004, LNCS 3118, pp. 865–872, 2004.

## 2 Methods

### 2.1 Participants

Three participants aged form 24 to 27 years old participated in this study. The participants were recruited from Chang Gung Memorial Hospital in Taiwan. All participants were met the following screening criteria: (a) with a diagnosis of cervical spinal cord injury; (b) with a stable medical status as indicated by onset over 6 months; (c) with a difficulty in accessing computer; (d) with sufficient physical tolerance for sitting upright in a wheelchair more than 1 hour; (e) without significant cognitive, visual, or hearing impairments. Consent forms were obtained prior to the study.

Participant A was a 26-year-old young man who is a victim of a cervical 3-4 level spinal cord injury with limited motor abilities on upper extremities. His right upper extremity was more functional than left side. His right shoulder was able to perform most of the functional movements and right elbow was able to flex. However, the performance of his left upper limb was not satisfied.

Participant B was a 27-year-old man with a diagnosis of cervical 4-5 level spinal cord injury. His two shoulders and elbows were able to execute most of functional movements, but his wrists and hands had limited motor functions.

Participant C was a 24-year-old young man and had spinal cord injury at the cervical 5-6. His two shoulders and elbows were able to perform functional movements and against some resistance given by the therapist. Both wrists were able to extend but not able to against resistance. Both hands' functions were not recovery. Characteristics of three participants were listed in the Table 1.

These three participants were familiar with computer use before their injuries. However, all of them were not able to access computer efficiently after their injuries. According to the participants' therapists, all the participants had not been exposed to any of the specific computer access training in their rehabilitation program. During the study, all the participants continued with their rehabilitation program, which include occupational therapy and physical therapy. The intervention and assessments of this study were done in addition to their regular scheduled physical and occupational therapy sessions.

**Table 1.** Characteristics of the participants

| Participant | Age | Level of lesion | Educational Level | Time after onset |
|---|---|---|---|---|
| A | 26Y11M | Cervical 3-4 | High school | 2 years and 6 months |
| B | 27Y2M | Cervical 4-5 | High school | 1 year and 6 months |
| C | 24Y11M | Cervical 5-6 | College | 6 months |

### 2.2 Instruments

The instruments used in this study include "Computer access assessment for persons with physical disabilities"(CAAPPD) [5] and a self designed computer software program. CAAPPD was used as an assessment tool to identify proper computer interfaces for participants. The computer software was used to record speed and accuracy of computer inputs in this study.

**Computer Access Assessment for Persons with Physical Disabilities(CAAPPD)**
CAAPPD is a convenient tool for rehabilitative professionals to perform a comprehensive assessment when determining appropriate computer interface devices for persons with physical disabilities. CAAPPD consist of the following four major steps: (1) seating and positioning needs, (2) keyboard adaptation needs, (3) potential anatomical control site allocations, and (4) mouse adaptation needs. It was designed as a flowchart. Therapists administrate CAAPPD via following the flowchart by answering several yes-no questions. The answer will lead to the subsequent questions or the final solution of appropriate computer access devices. Advices about special equipment needs will be suggested at the end of the evaluation.

**Computer Software Program**
A computer software program was designed to record the speed and accuracy of computer inputs. Figure 1 illustrates the software screen design. 10 digits from 0 to 9 were allocated to 10 grids. Each grid is 2.5cm*3.6cm. The software program was able to generate a digit randomly from 0 to 9 and show the digit on the screen. The participant was asked to move the mouse 's cursor to the grid corresponded to the digit, and click the left button. The speed and the accuracy of inputs will be recorded.

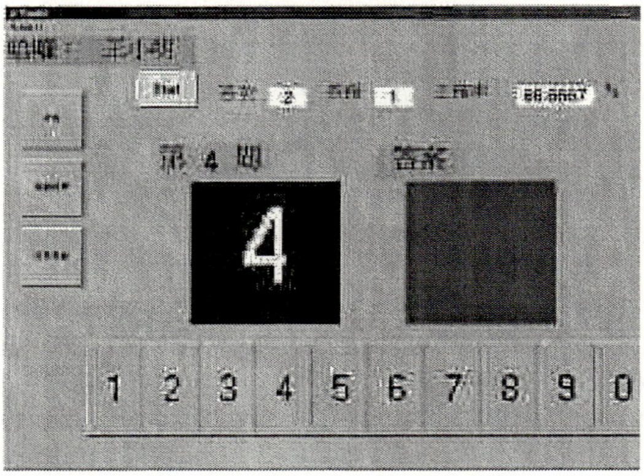


**Fig. 1.** Computer software program used in this study

## 2.3 Experimental Design and Procedures

A single-subject multiple probe design [6] was selected to examine the effectiveness of using computer access devices on increasing speed and accuracy for three persons with spinal cord injury. Use of a single-subject research design allowed for systematic measurements of individual changes in performance following an intervention. Consistent with multiple probe designs, training was sequentially introduced across participant A, participant B, and participant C. The study was conducted in three phases. There were (a) baseline phase, (b) intervention phase, and (c) follow-up phases.

**Baseline Phase.** In the baseline phase, the participants used the standard mouse to move the cursor and click the correct digit shown on the screen. The computer software program generated a digit randomly form 0 to 9. The participants were requested to move the cursor to the right digit grid and click the left button to select. As soon as the participants finish the task, the software will generated the next digit successively for 3 minutes. The speed and accuracy of inputs for using conventional mouse were reported as baseline data. Baseline was ended when participants' performances reach a stable status.

**Intervention Phase.** Followed by the baseline phase, a computer access training program was provided in the intervention phase. The computer access training program consisted of several therapy sessions, and each session lasted 20 minutes. In this phase, the researchers provided participants appropriate computer input devices. The devices provided were based on the results of administrating the CAAPPD. A trackball with an extended single switch was provided to Participant A (refer to fig. 2). Participant A used the trackball to move the mouse cursor to the correct grid, then pressed the single switch to select.

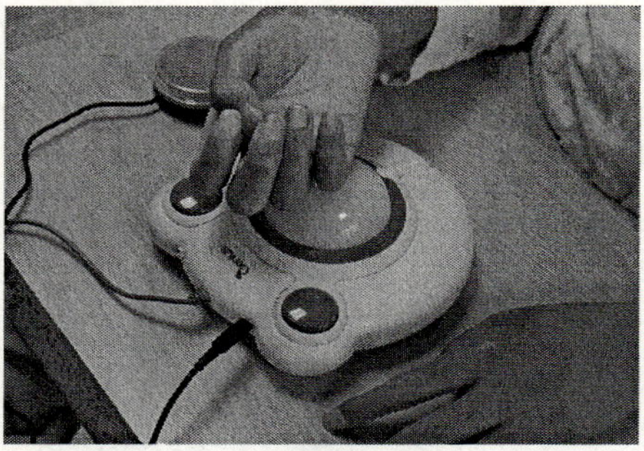

**Fig. 2.** The computer interface devices used by Participant A

For participants B and C, an extended single switch was used to replace the function of a standard mouse' left button (refer to fig. 3). The participants used the standard mouse to move the cursor to the right grid, and pressed the single switch to select the digit. In the intervention phase, the participants practiced how to use the computer interfaces effectively for 15 minutes in each session. Researchers provided physical and verbal cues based on participants' performance. After 15-minutes practice, a 3-minutes assessment will be taken for each session. Both speed and accuracy of inputs for using interface devices were reported. This phase was ended when participants' performances were stable.

**Follow-Up Phase.** Following the intervention phase is the follow-up phase. It starts one week after the intervention phase ended. In the follow-up phase, the maintenance effects of intervention were studied. The participants still used interface devices in this phase, but without any practice used in the intervention phase. Researchers didn't allow provide any physical or verbal prompts according to participants' performance. The participants were asked to take a 3-minutes assessment for 3 sessions. Both speed and accuracy of inputs for using interface devices were reported.

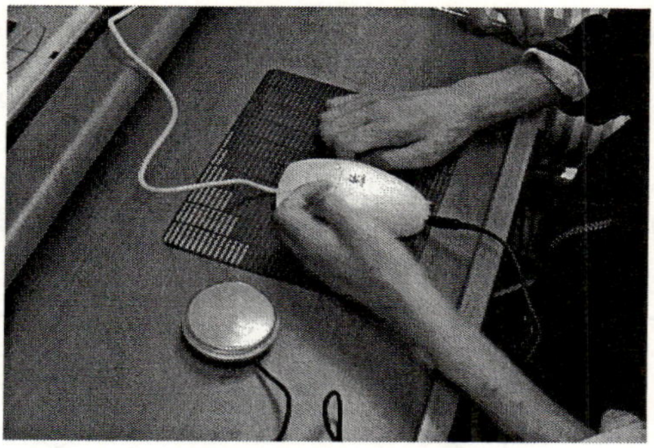

**Fig. 3.** The computer interface devices used by Participant B

### 2.4 Data Analysis

The speed and accuracy of inputs in the three phases were recorded and plotted in the figures 4 and 5. The levels, trends of the data in the three phases were analyzed based on the single subject research design method.

## 3 Results

Experimental results indicated that persons with spinal cord injury indeed improved accuracy and speed of computer inputs after the interface devices provided. Figures 4 and 5 illustrated the three participants' performance in the baseline, intervention and follow-up phases.

### 3.1 Speed

Figure 4 explained the changes of input speed of three participants in the baseline, intervention, and follow-up phases. Participant A was unable to move the standard mouse and click the left button in the baseline phase. The range of the input speed was between 0 and 0.67 (digits/min), and the average of speed was 0.33 (digits/min). In the intervention phase, participant A's input speed increased dramatically with a range from 15.43 to 19.05 (digits/min) and an average of 17.74 (digits/min). In the follow-up stage, the participant A still maintained a high level of input speed with an average of 18.64 (digits/min).

Participant B was incapable to manipulate the standard mouse efficiently in the baseline phase. The most difficult portion for him to manipulate mouse is to click the buttons successfully. The researchers provided a single switch to replace the function of left button in the intervention phase. His performance improved satisfied after that. His speed in the baseline phase was range from 0.67 to 6.59, with a mean of 3 (digits/min). In the intervention phase, the average speed increased to 15.16 (digits/min). In the follow up stage, the mean speed still remained 13.91(digits/min).

Participant C was able to manage the standard mouse to perform the task requested by researchers in the baseline phase, however his performance was unproductively. The mean speed of participant C in the baseline stage was 9.69 (digits/min) with a range form 8.67 to 10.81 (digits/min). The average speed increased to 29.66 (digits/min) in the intervention stage with a range between 27.27 and 32.43 (digits/min). In the follow-up stage, he still maintained a high level of input speed with a mean of 29.50 (digits/min).

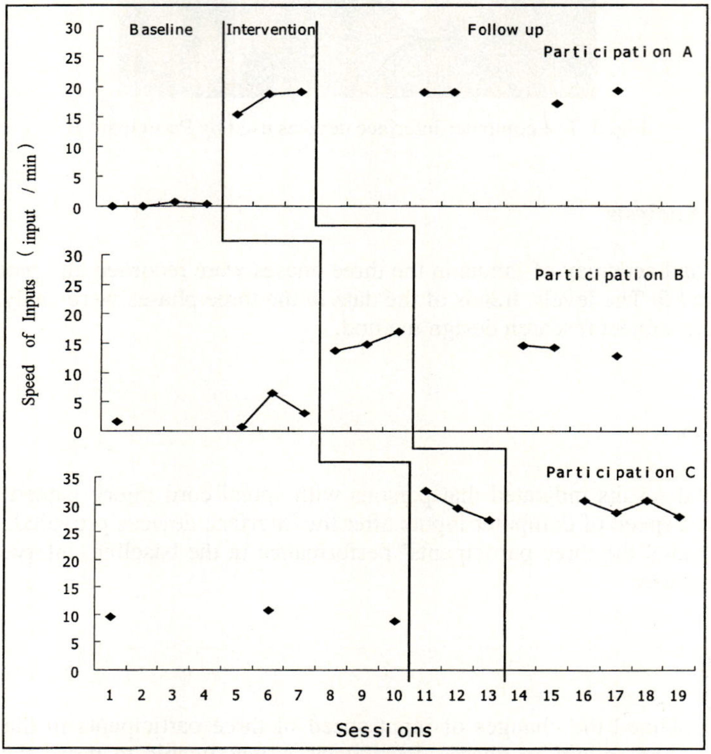


**Fig. 4.** Speed of inputs for 3 participants

### 3.2 Accuracy

Figure 5 elucidated the changes of input accuracy of three participants in the baseline, intervention, and follow-up phases. The input accuracy of participant A ranged vary from 0% to 100% in the baseline phase. The mean of input accuracy of participant A was 50% in baseline phase, was 96.67%in the intervention phase, and was 100% in the follow-up stage. The data displayed that the performance of participant A was unstable in the baseline phase, but the performance progress rapidly after the interface devices was delivered.

The mean of input accuracy for participant B was 78.75% in baseline phase with a range from 50% to 100%, which indicated that the performance of participant B was unstable in the baseline phase. His performance became much better in the intervention phase with a mean of 100% input accuracy rate as well as maintained a high accuracy rate in the follow-up stage with a mean 98.33% and a rage between 95% and 100%. For participant C, the average of input accuracy was 98.33% in the baseline phase, 100% in the intervention phase, and 97.5% in the follow-up stage. His performances of input accuracy were stable across three phases.

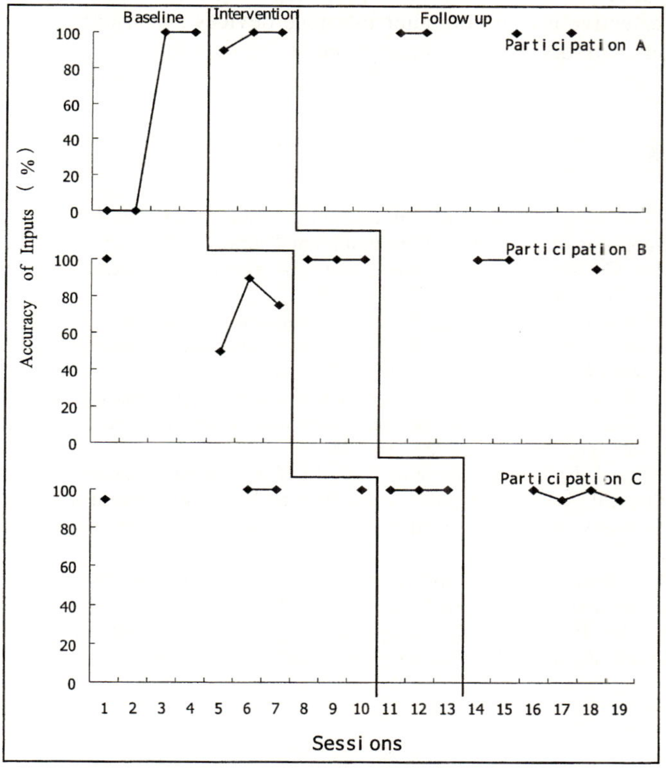


**Fig. 5.** Accuracy of inputs for 3 participants

# 4 Discussion and Conclusions

The purpose of this study was to compare the performances of persons with spinal cord injury with and without computer interface devices. Speed and accuracy of inputs were investigated systematically in this study. The speed enhanced dramatically after delivering the interface devices across the three participants. The input accuracy rate was also improved significantly for participants A and B in the intervention and follow-up phases. The improvement of input accuracy was not significant for participant C was due to the high correct rate in the baseline, however, the speed of participant C enhance significantly in the intervention and follow-up phases. The results of this study elucidated that through appropriate input devices, persons with spinal cord injury are capable to operate computer effectively with speed and accuracy enhanced.

Persons with spinal cord injuries usually have a higher rate of unemployment compared to persons without disabilities [7]. Computer skills can provide persons with spinal cord injuries an opportunity to reach educational and vocational goals that can increase their life satisfaction. A further research on study the effect of computer interface on different disabilities and age groups is needed. In addition, works that validate the effective use of computer interface devices and training in improving of life for persons with disabilities will also need to be developed.

## References

1. Lau, C., O'Leary, S.: Comparison of computer interface devices for persons with sever physical disabilities. American J. of Occupational Therapy, Vol. 47. (1993) 1022-1029
2. Vanderheiden, G.: Service delivery mechanisms in rehabilitation technology. American J. of Occupational Therapy, Vol. 41. (1987) 703-710
3. Hetzel, C., Kallam, M.L., Retting, M.: Touch window versus Powerpad: A comparison of response rates by 3- and 4-year-old handicapped and nonhandicapped children. (1989). (ERIC Document Reproduction Service No. 349116)
4. Casali, S.P., Chase, J.D.: Computer-based system access by persons with disabilities: Differences in the effects of interface design on novice and experienced performance. Int J. of Industrial Ergonomics, Vol. 15. (1995) 237-245
5. Wu, T.F., Meng, L.F., Wang H.P., Wu, W.T., Li, T.Y.: Computer access assessment for persons with physical disability: A guide to assistive technology interventions. Lecture Notes in Computer Sciences, Vol. 2398. Springer-Verlag, Berlin Heidelberg New York (2002) 204-211
6. Horner, R.D., Baer, D.M.: Multiple–probe technique: A variation of the multiple baseline design. J. of Applied Behavior Analysis, Vol. 11. (1978) 189-196
7. Pell, S.D., Gillies, R.M., Carss, M.: Use of technology by people with physical disabilities in Australia. Disability and Rehabilitation, Vol. 21(2). (1999) 56-60

# An Assessment into Touch Screen Input Devices for Cervical Spinal Injured Computer Users

Robert C.C. Chen, Dilys T. Tsai, Li-Chen Chang, and Nick Higgett

Graduate Centre, Faculty of Art and Design, De Montfort University, Leicester, UK

**Abstract.** This study began with interview and contextual observation survey of computer users among SCI including higher-level cervical spinal injured (CSI) subjects for their limitation of human body motion and function during working. Following the findings of the initial surveys, the usability assessments were developed and undertaken in order to understand the limitations and difficulties of SCI and CSI subjects in the use of the research team's input prototype for future design improvement recommendations especially on size/dimensions factors, which can lead to the differences in users' skill performance, productivity, mobility, and cost. A touch screen input device of an appropriate dimension is therefore proposed with the aim of providing a better alternative for people with physical disabilities who are unsuited to the traditional computer keyboard.

## 1 Introduction

Based on ICCP (2003)[1], it is estimated that over 92,000 people globally suffer traumatic Spinal Cord Injury (SCI) annually. The conservative average annual incidence in the West is 14 people per million populations. According to Spinal Injuries Association, (SIA, UK) in 2003 [2], it is estimated that there are currently 40,000 spinal cord injured people in the United Kingdom. Also, in Asian countries, such as Taiwan, 20,000 traumatic SCI discharges were reported by the Institute of Occupational Safety & Health (IOSH, Taiwan) with an averaged increase of 1,000 new cases every year in 2003 [3].

Nowadays, technology plays an even more significant role in the life of individuals with severe disabilities. With the well-accommodated adaptive assistive technology devices (ATDs), many unemployed SCI patients have been successfully returning to their previous jobs after the completion of their rehabilitation i.e. physio-/occupational therapies [2, 4]. Furthermore, lots of computer-based job accommodation cases have also been improving and expanding the opportunities for the disabled employment [5, 6].

For SCI/CSI computer users, only a single finger or/and another part of their body (e.g. head, mouth, or forearm, etc.) can be used to hit the keys or move the pointer. An appropriate assistive technology can accommodate these users and improve their productivity. From this point of view, an integrated prototype of touch-screen-based input device, as showed in Figure 1, was developed by our research team in 2003 to provide those redundant SCI/CSI computer users back to work. However, the size/dimension of the computer input device (i.e. touch screen) will be the main factors which affect the efficiency and accuracy during accessing a computer, and also,

K. Miesenberger et al. (Eds.): ICCHP 2004, LNCS 3118, pp. 873–879, 2004.

from viewpoints of the cost and mobility, it is therefore, very important to choose appropriate dimensions for the computer input touch screen before designing a device.[7]

Recently more and more researches were focused on the disabled users' job and workplace accommodation when designing a special keyboard [8], Yeh & Chen (2001)[9] and Teng & Chen (2003)[10] investigated into two single disability groups (i.e. single upper limb amputees and muscular dystrophy patients). The methods of observation and contextual analysis are used to read the experiences, characteristics and behaviours through their subjects' ATDs assessment. Yeh & Chen also indicated that usability evaluation is a useful method to evaluate an ATD's interface. In this study, the surveys of interviews and contextual observation were selected as the main methodology to not only understand the interactive influence between users and system, but also obtain direct feedback of users for the user-centred interface assessment. Additionally, this study presents a useful guideline that stimulates the thinking of those preparing for the assessment and measurements of ATDs.

**Fig. 1.** Touch-screen-based input device (prototype)

## 2 Aims and Objectives of Research

The purpose of this study is to assess the usability of spinal core injured (SCI) subjects on our new developed prototype of touch screen based computer input device for its appropriate size/dimension design improvement. An integrated prototype of alternative keyboard (touch screen input device) with dimension of 5.7 inches was provided. 28 selected SCI/CSI subjects who can only access computer with single key-in ability. The objectives of this study are as follows.

- To study and identify the limitation of human body motion and function both on normal and disabled subjects.
- To generate surveys of an interview and a contextual observation study for better understanding of the differences of special needs between the normal subjects and those computer users with physical disabilities on hand movement disorders.
- To analyse observed outcomes and formulate a follow-up assessments of efficiency and accuracy from SCI/CSI computer users by using the new developed touch screen input device.
- To evaluate the possibility of applying assessed results for size/dimension of touch screen design.
- To draw conclusions and recommendations for the future development.

## 3 Pilot Surveys (Interview and Observation)

The interview and contextual observation aimed to understand the existing problems of SCI/CSI computer users, who can only access computer by single key-in operation with/out adopted ATDs in accordance with their special needs and difficulties. The protocol of this survey is:

- To collect and analyse data.
- To select the appropriate subjects, contact them and arrange the date and time for observation and interviews.
- To investigate the present practice and special needs of computer use among computer users who suffer CSI.
- To analyse the observed findings.
- To recommend possible solutions.

### 3.1 Subjects Selection

The Taiwanese famous and biggest ATD research association, TATA (Taiwan Assistive Technology and Vocational Rehabilitation Association), provided 28 volunteer SCI/CSI subjects who were experienced computer workers for one year and more, 14 subjects now access the computer only by using single hand, the other 14 subjects need to be supported by higher level ranges of assistive input devices for single key-in operation e.g. head, mouth, or forearm, etc. Figure 2 showed one of CSI subjects was accessing his computer with accommodated input support of assistive mouth-stick. All 28 subjects were wheelchair users (powered or manual).

**Fig. 2.** Assistive mouth-stick input support (CSI subject)

### 3.2 Methodology

This assessment proceeded by using methodologies of observation and interviews. First, as the subjects had only limited motion abilities, there were difficulties in arranging to gather all subjects in a laboratory for assessment. Therefore, their existing workplace, home and/or study/training areas were the first choice of the location for this survey. Second, when accessing their computer, these SCI/CSI subjects were asked to keep all their personal input preference and personal habitual practice.

### 3.3 Summary for Interview and Observation Studies

It was found that the common characteristic of operating a computer involves using only single key-in operation with adoptive assistive devices, such as hand strap for holding the input pencil, wrist and finger orthoses for substitute fingers, or mouth-stick. Furthermore, it was also detected that the dimensions of the computer keyboard created problems for subjects when they use a computer especially the key-in operation. According to observed findings, all 28 subjects both SCI and CSI computer users pointed out that a special support of input device with improved requirements, i.e. easy to use, accuracy, efficiency, and speed, is the first priority for accommodating their jobs.

During designing the touch screen input prototype, the size/dimension was the most difficulty of the main factors which affect the efficiency, accuracy, cost, mobility, and productivity in product/marketing development. It is therefore very important to assess the usability from its target population by choosing suitable dimensions for prototype improvement.

## 4 Usability Assessments

Based on the findings of previous contextual observation, it was found that subjects exhausted their physical strength due to their limited scope of movements and time taken to the existing conventional keyboard. The aims of this study are to assess the usability of SCI/CSI subjects on our new developed prototype of touch screen based computer input device for its appropriate size/dimension design improvement and also to investigate into the influence of changing the size and layout of the displayed keys and letters on the 5.7 inches touch-screen prototype. The stages in this trial assessment can be identified as:

- To contact the selected participants and arrange the assessment.
- To set up the location of assessment and the related ergonomic practices.
- To collect and analyse data with the experimental assessments.
- To draw up conclusions.

### 4.1 Subjects and Equipments Selection

Art and Design, Graduate Centre at De Montfort University provided 20 volunteer subjects, ranging in age from 20 to 45 years, who participated and completed requested actions in a situation (as *Assessment I*) where the arm and elbow were *non-supported* and (as *Assessment II*) where the arm and elbow were ***supported*** in order to simulate the restricted movements as SCI/CSI computer users.

Additionally, the selected computer input device for experimental use, which is an integrated alternative keyboard, which can easily operate a computer, key-in and choose a preferred mode for persons with severe physical disabilities. The developed 5.7 inch-prototype of touch screen input device was provided with an alphabetically arranged layout.

## 4.2 Usability Assessments

According to the standard operating procedure (SOP), the assessor asked the first subject to complete the simulation of requested actions in a situation with arm and elbow supported (i.e. *Assessment I*); collect and record the results; and then complete the simulation of requested actions in a situation without arm and elbow supported (i.e. *Assessment II*); collect and record the results; and then assess the next (the second) subject with the same as previous SOP until 20 subjects were all assessed and the number of errors from each assessed subject was counted and recorded.

The process of requested actions was to access computer with single key-in ability for completing all requested tasks, which was pre-arranged vocabularies, during assessing any input-mistakes were ignored.

## 4.3 Results and Analysis

Following the findings of the former interview and observation survey, computer users who suffer CSI/SCI required for a special support of input device which is able to be easy to use, avoiding too many key-in mistakes, increasing key-in efficacy i.e. accuracy and speed, lessening tiredness when inputting. Additionally, easy to use and accuracy are more essential than speed on accessing a computer for subjects. Consequently, the key-in speed was not been considered in this study. The assessments were conducted on the aims of providing an appropriate dimension of a touch screen input device for people with physical disabilities who are unsuited to the traditional computer keyboard.

Table 1 showed the two different assessed results of on/off arm and elbow supported with 20 volunteer subjects. From the point of view of the accurate rate, it showed that both assessments equally demonstrated the efficacy of subjects when operating a touch screen input device (i.e. *Assessment I* of 96.81% and *Assessment II* of 94.04%). It is also indicated that the provided 5.7-inch touch screen prototype was highly applicable to all subjects.

**Table 1.** The rate of accuracy from usability assessments

| *Assessment I* | | | | *Assessment II* | | | |
|---|---|---|---|---|---|---|---|
| **No** | **Accuracy Rate** | **No** | **Accuracy Rate** | **No** | **Accuracy Rate** | **No** | **Accuracy Rate** |
| 1 | 97.87% | 11 | 100.00% | 1 | 100.00% | 11 | 100.00% |
| 2 | 100.00% | 12 | 95.74% | 2 | 100.00% | 12 | 87.23% |
| 3 | 93.62% | 13 | 97.87% | 3 | 87.23% | 13 | 100.00% |
| 4 | 100.00% | 14 | 95.74% | 4 | 97.87% | 14 | 85.11% |
| 5 | 100.00% | 15 | 91.49% | 5 | 93.62% | 15 | 87.23% |
| 6 | 95.74% | 16 | 95.74% | 6 | 87.23% | 16 | 91.49% |
| 7 | 97.87% | 17 | 100.00% | 7 | 100.00% | 17 | 97.87% |
| 8 | 97.87% | 18 | 100.00% | 8 | 91.49% | 18 | 97.87% |
| 9 | 100.00% | 19 | 85.11% | 9 | 85.11% | 19 | 100.00% |
| 10 | 93.62% | 20 | 97.87% | 10 | 97.87% | 20 | 93.62% |
| **Average : 96.81%** | | | | **Average : 94.04%** | | | |

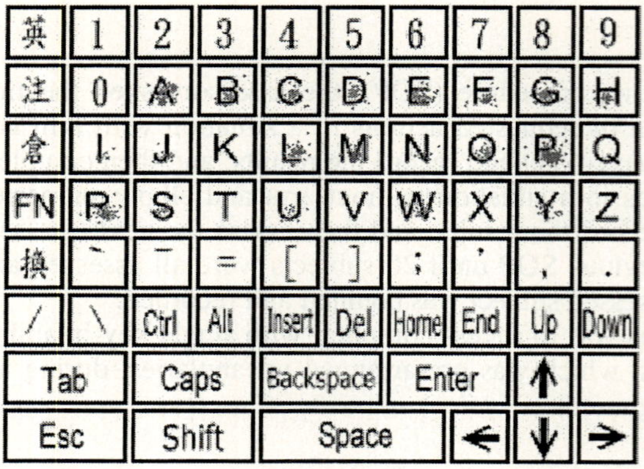


**Fig. 3.** Simulated 5.7 inches touch screen prototype

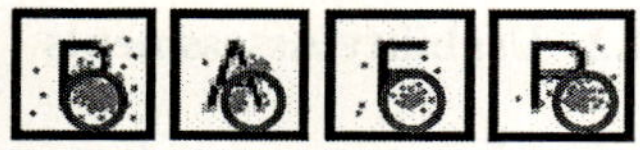

**Fig. 4.** Bottom-right hits

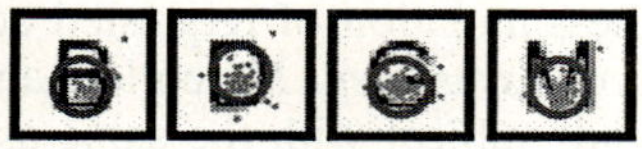

**Fig. 5.** Centred hits

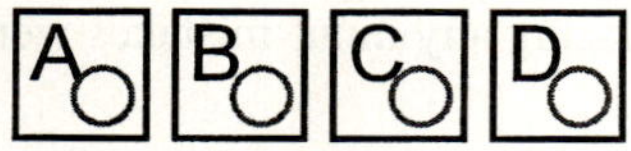


**Fig. 6.** Suggested locations

In addition, it can be seen from the hits record (touched points) of the letters e.g. P, A, F and R, were keyed-in on the *bottom-right* side (as illustrated in figure 3 and 4) when subjects were completed requested key-in actions. Furthermore, some of the letters' shapes were seen to be huge (as illustrated in figure 3 and 5), and most of the hits record were pointed at the *centre* of the keys. It was found that the fonts and sizes of the letters would influence all keyboard users while accessing computer.

Following the outcome of the *Assessment I and II*, we recommended that the printed letters on the keyboard surface should be re-arranged to the *top-left* on each unique key, in order to display the letters clearly on the touch-screen, and the font of letters could also be suggested to downsize appropriately. It is therefore suggested that the letter font/size and its arrangement of print location will be also the main factor for our future prototype improvement (as showed in figure 6).

## 5 Conclusions

An appropriate computer assistive technology can assist persons with disabilities to access the computer more easily. This study drew up the contextual surveys and usability assessments with the purposed understanding of special needs. This research provided an ideal solution for a wide range of users with physical disabilities, in particular of those users with hand movement disorders.

Additionally, the use of a computer input assistive technology device should have long-term guidance, assistance, observation and assessment.

## Acknowledgements

The authors gratefully acknowledge to all my colleagues both in Taiwan Normal University and De Montfort University for their contribution to this research. Thanks also go to Dr. Michael Chou of Taiwan Assistive Technology and Vocational Rehabilitation Association for his arrangement of SCI/CSI subjects.

Special thanks go to the Department of Labour, Taipei City Government, Taiwan for their fully funding support.

## References

1. ICCP, Information Package Version 6.1. 2003, International Campaign for Cures of Spinal Cord Injury Paralysis (ICCP)
2. SIA, Annual report 2002-2003. 2003, Spinal Injuries Association (SIA).
3. IOSH, Introduction into Spinal Cord Injury. 2003, Institute of Occupational Safety & Health (IOSH)
4. Targett, P., Wehman, P.: Successful work supports for persons with spinal cord injury. Official Journal of the American Association of Spinal Cord Injury Psychologists and Social Workers, 2003. **16**(1): p. 6-11
5. Pell, S.D., Gillies, R.M., Carss, M.: Relationship between use of technology and employment rates for people with physical disabilities in Australia: implications for education and training programmes.Disability and Rehabilitation, 1997. **19**(8): p. 332-338
6. Kruse, D., Krueger, A., Drastal, S.: Computer use, computer training and employment. Outcome among people with spinal cord injuries. Spine., 1996. **21**(7): p. 891-896
7. Covington, G.A. Hannah, B., Access by Design. 1996: John Wiley & Sons. p. 1-6
8. Cushman, W.H. and Rosenberg, D.J., Human Factors in Product Design. Series: Advanced in Human Factors/ Ecnomics. 1991, Amsterdan: Elsevier.
9. Yeh, K. and Chen, R.C., A study of the computer input assistive technology design for the single upper limb amputee, in Department of Industrial Design. 2001, National Yunlin University of Science & Technology: YunLin, Taiwan.
10. Teng, Z.C. and Chen, R.C., Designing A Barrier Free Solution for Students with Muscular Dystrophy. in The 10th Annual Meeting Ergonomics Society of Taiwan. 2003. Taiwan: The Ergonomics Society of Taiwan (EST).
11. Tseng, C.C. and Wu, J.G., A study into an integrated alternative keyboard for persons with disabilities, in Graduate Institute of Computer Science and Information Engineering. 2003, National Taiwan Normal University: Taipei, Taiwan.

# Home-Use Upper Limb Rehabilitation Device for Cervical Spinal Cord Injured Patients

Kengo Ohnishi[1], Eri Goto[1], Fumitake Sugiki[2], Keiji Imado[1], Hidetaka Ikeuchi[1], Nobuhiro Kito[2], Hiroomi Miyagawa[1], and Yukio Saito[3]

[1] Oita University, Faculty of Engineering, 700 Dannoharu, Oita
Oita, 870-1192, Japan
{ohnishi,imado,hikeuchi,miyahiro}@cc.oita-u.ac.jp
http://www.hwe.oita-u.ac.jp/mc/eng/
[2] Kawashima Orthopaedic Hospital, 14-1 Miyabu, Nakatsu
Oita, 871-0012, Japan
[3] Tokyo Denki University, School of Science and Engineering, Ishizaka, Hatoyama, Hiki
Saitama, 350-0311, Japan
saito@n.dendai.ac.jp

**Abstract.** This paper presents mechatronics device system to assess and assist the rehabilitation of the palsy arm. The device is developed for assisting the physical and occupational treatment of the patient with cervical spinal cord injury. The system consists of a PC and a joystick-type controller. The controller contains a triaxial load cell to measure the force exerted. With this system, we propose isometric training with biofeedback of visual effects as in video games. The subject is to adjust the force while tracking the target along the trajectory displayed on the screen. For evaluating the performance, accuracy is computed from the recorded training results. Pilot test is carried out on cervical spinal cord injured patients and compared with the senior able-bodied. Results of the pilot test showed that the system is capable of assessing the difference of the individuals.

## 1 Introduction

The age of spinal cord injuries in Japan is reported to have different characteristic than European and American countries [1]. The peaks are formed at the age of twenty and fifty-nine, and the number of cervical spinal cord injuries out numbers the thoracic and lumber spine injured after the age of forty. Furthermore, the rate goes up to 88% for those aged over sixty-five. These statistics shows that Japanese therapists need rehabilitation program for both the aged and young cervical spine injured patients. Additionally, considering the environment of the seniors home nursing care and treatment service provided in Japan, rehabilitation device and service that can be handled at their home or a neighboring medical institutions is needed.

Research has been reported on applying robotics, virtual reality, and haptics technology for rehabilitation purpose [2-7]. However, most researches target stroke pa-

K. Miesenberger et al. (Eds.): ICCHP 2004, LNCS 3118, pp. 880–888, 2004.

tients. The subjects' performances are not equivalent when treating the lesions of the cerebrum and spinal cord. Thus, different system design approaches are required based on their issues.

The problem cervical spinal cord injured patients describe in traditional physical training method are based on the loss of rapid response of muscle fatigue and pain. The loss of physiological signals causes difficulty in subjective self-evaluation of their workout. The critical problem is that patients have difficulty estimating their exercise limitations. They need an aid for gaining information on the magnitude of the output and timekeeping to limit the volume of exercise. Moreover, the loss of sensation decreases satisfaction, which is important to maintain their motivation for continuing the training. Therefore, assistance for recording and evaluating the performance is needed for self-supervised healthcare. Objective and quantitative indices are indispensable to intuitively understand the result.

Our proposal is to augment traditional methods by reconfirming the effect by quantitative methods applying a computer-aided system. The physical training that we propose are: 1) low-burden isometric exercise and 2) repeated workout for adjusting the force in slow-pace. Static training form and gradual response enables patients with contracture deformity or paralysis to exercise safely. The system provides automated recording, storage, computation, and presentation of the information in the rehabilitation progress. Based on these design specifications, a mechatronics system with computer, sensor, software program, and evaluation indices is proposed.

## 2 Upper Limb Training System

Our research suggests that mechatronic devices is capable of providing life supporting technologies with integration of sensors, intelligent systems and other information technologies to augment the traditional rehabilitation programs and enhance the recovery of patient's activities of daily living. Our goal is to develop a computer-aided system that can propose exercise program, automatically measure the performance, and prepare the data to present the effect of the therapy. The specification of the device is as fallows.

### 2.1 Hardware Specification

The system we developed consists of a 15-inch liquid crystal display, a DOS/V PC-AT computer with Microsoft Windows Me OS, interface peripherals, and a joystick-type controller (See Figure 1). The controller consists of a grip, joystick module, buttons and the stage. A tri-axial load cell is developed and installed in the joystick to measure the exerted force. The strain gauge is mounted on the load cell and the amplifier circuit is installed beneath the stage. The joystick is a stiff rod and does not have tilt angle as in video game joystick controllers. The grip, made of thermoplastics and sponge sheets attached inside, gently fits the shape of one's hand. Four buttons are mounted on the stage so that keyboard or mouse operation is not necessary to operate the program.

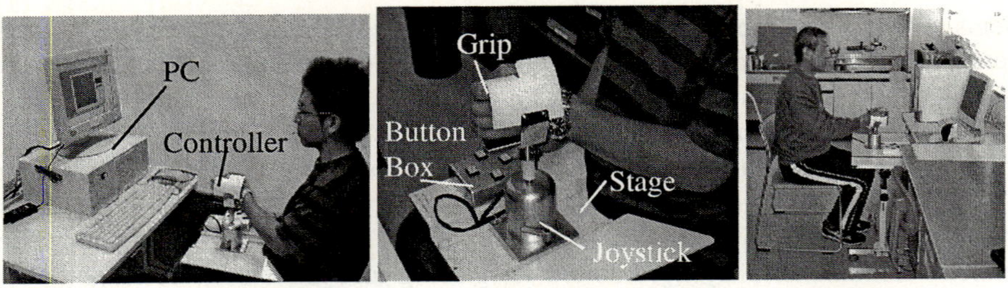


**Fig. 1.** The Upper Limb Rehabilitation System and its components (left and middle) and when the system used on the side table (right)

## 2.2 Signal Processing

Amplified signals from the strain gauges are scanned by 12-bit A-D converter board (Interface PCI-3171A) mounted on the PCI bus in the PC. The sampling frequency is 5kHz. This is conditioned to reduce the rag of marker movements on screen. The instrumentation system is initialized and the initial value of the load cell input signal is computed when first loading the software on screen. The durable error for computing the initial value is smaller than 1% of the measured values. On computing the control signal sampled values dx and dy, first, the signals are smoothed with simple moving-average method with 9 sampling points. Then, the difference from the initial value is computed. Formerly, dx and dy was filtered with a threshold value 9.8N. This was to avert the drift of the marker, but had untoward result of causing a 'lazy control'. The subjects learned to make shortcuts and tapping movements to make up for the dead zone. To modify this, the computed value is assigned to a quadratic function to compute the marker travel distance, dX, dY. The marker travel distance for dZ is processed in proportion to the difference value.

## 2.3 Software and Operation

Figure 2 illustrates the diagram of the system. The computer software is developed with Microsoft Visual Basic platform and consists of 4 main forms: welcoming, database interface, training, result. Circle, zigzag, and flower-patterned are prepared as the training trajectory. Figure 3 displays screen shot of the training and result form for circle trajectory. Sagittal plane is set as the Y-axis on the screen and the frontal plane as the X-axis. The diameter of the circle trajectory is approximately 134mm on the screen. The target on the circle trajectory moves at a constant angular speed counter-clockwise from the initial point on the positive X axis. Scenario of the training is to follow the target, a red circle, which moves along the trajectory with the marker, a green square, and maintain the distance within target's radius.

To operate the system, the trainee sits in front of the PC and places the controller on the lap or side table, as in Figure 1, after the initialization process. Then, selecting the user with the cursor and setting the volume of the training, the hand is placed in the grip. Then, pressing the start button, the program runs automatically to the end of the routine training menu. The target starts to move after a 5-second countdown for each trial. After each trial, the trajectory and score of the result are presented on the screen. The locus of the marker is computed from the control signal data. The data is recorded in a database and organized in a CSV format file at download.

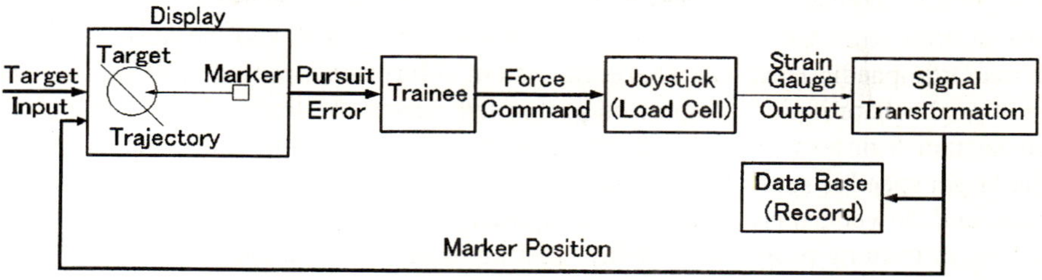


**Fig. 2.** System diagram of the instrumentation system

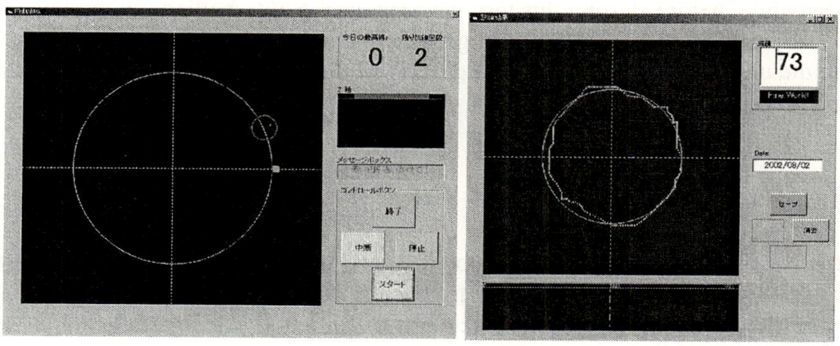


**Fig. 3.** Training form and the result form for the circle trajectory

## 2.4 Evaluation Method

Three assessment indices of the performance are proposed: marker locus, control signal variation, and error distance. The control signal variation is described by plotting the control signal values in X-Y coordinate. The scattering pattern of the signal is evaluated. The marker locus **M** is calculated by summing dX and dY in time sequence and evaluate by plotting the result in X-Y coordinate. The error distance is calculated as the distance of the marker position **M** and the target position **P** as in Equation 2.

$$X_M(t) = \sum_{n=0}^{t} dX(n) + X_0, \quad Y_M(t) = \sum_{n=0}^{t} dY(n) + Y_0 \tag{1}$$

$$E(t) = \sqrt{\{X_T(t) - X_M(t)\}^2 + \{Y_T(t) - Y_M(t)\}^2} \tag{2}$$

$\{M \mid X_M(t), Y_M(t)\}$:Marker position, $\{T \mid X_T(t), Y_T(t)\}$:Target position, E(t) Error distance.

## 3 Experiment

The first pilot test was conducted for 2 weeks to a 47-years-old female cervical spinal cord patient [8]. We are now running a test with a 62-year-old male cervical spinal cord injured patient. The patient is paresis and is capable of walking but have numbness in both arms. Informed consent is given before the test, and therapists of Kawashima Orthopaedic Hospital, where the system is furnished, provide full support. The traditional rehabilitation program is performed during the test and the training with our system followed. Both hands are trained with the system, 2 to 3 times a week. The target speed is set to 1.0 rpm and the system is used on the side table. Each of the circle and flower-pattern trajectory are applied 4 times in sequence, and this is fixed as 1 set of training program per a day. Testing began after the patient understood how to control the marker on the screen through demonstration. Numbness is interviewed as the qualitative measure

Meanwhile, before starting this test, we organized 6 able-bodied senior subjects (3 Male, 3 Female, average age 66.2) to gain comparable data. None had previous history in the upper limb. The program applied is similar to the patient except the trial is set to 3 times.

## 4 Results

The figures of the patient and the senior subjects' performance results for the circle trajectory are shown in Figure 4. The figures are organized from the data of the patient's first day training result. The force exerted on the joystick is set as the vertical axis and time as the lateral axis. The force is computed from the recorded dX, dY, and dZ with the equation gained from the reference test. As seen, the pattern of the 1$^{st}$ trial and the 4$^{th}$ trial of both hands differ. The change in Fx, Fy is made to emphasize a period curve. This periodic curve is seen in the result of the best performing senior subject C and many formerly tested subjects in the 20's. Therefore, we believe that this is the primary feature of evaluating the adjustability of the subject. Forming a smooth periodic curve will be the earliest goal of the training. Furthermore, the error to the curve can be the quantitative measure for the adjustability in this training phase.

The marker locus in Figure 5 shows that, the target is tracked on the circle trajectory except for the first trial of the left hand. This form is necessary to intuitively understand the strategy of the subject.

Figure 6 describes the variation of the Fx and Fy. As seen, the variation of the right hand is wider then the left hand and the senior subjects E's data. Another difference is the space in the center. These may be the next indices for evaluating the performance.

Figure 7 shows the marker-target error. The 1$^{st}$ trial has peaks exceeding the multitude 0.2, whereas, the peaks in the 4$^{th}$ trial are limited to the beginning and end of the trial. This shows that the performance evaluated by this measure rapidly advances with small amount of experience and skill. Therefore, if using this measure for scoring the performance in the competent period or introduction phase of the training, the subject will be gaining better ratting which can motivate the subject to try on new programs.

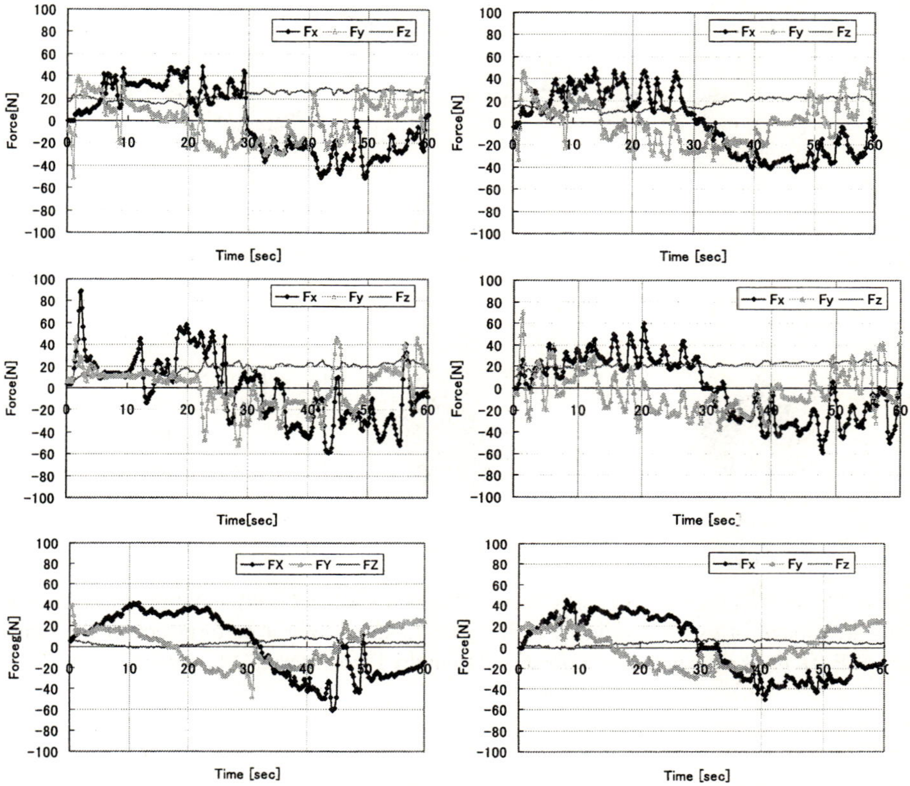


**Fig. 4.** The Fx (*black*), Fy (*light gray*), and Fz (*thin gray line*) control signals are shown in Time Series. Tops and middles are the data from the cervical spinal cord injured patient. The top-left describes the 1st trial and the top-right is the 4th trial of the left hand. The middles are those of the right hand. Bottoms are from senior able-bodied patients C's 1st and 3rd trial of the left hand

## 5 Discussion

Due to the consideration being based on the results of very short and small number of sample, these results should be interpreted with caution. Nevertheless, the results are encouraging. Data gained from previous testing and the current result shows the possibility of using this system for evaluating the performance of the cervical spinal cord injured patient and other patients with disability in the upper limb. And also, senior subjects.

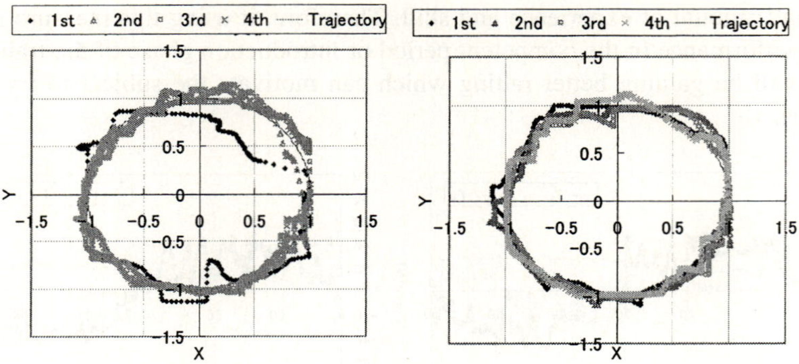


**Fig. 5.** Marker locus of the patient's trial with left hand (*left*) and right hand (*right*) is shown. The data for the sequential 4 trials (*black to light gray*) are plotted with the circle trajectory

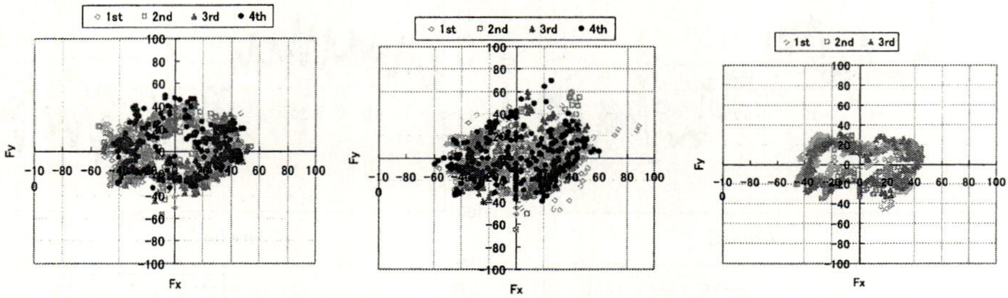


**Fig. 6.** The control signal variation is shown. Patient's left hand (*left*) and right hand (*middle*) trials are plotted in Fx-Fy coordinate as lissajous figure. The best performance of the senior subject E (*right*) is shown. Data are organized from the 1st to last trial in brightness scale

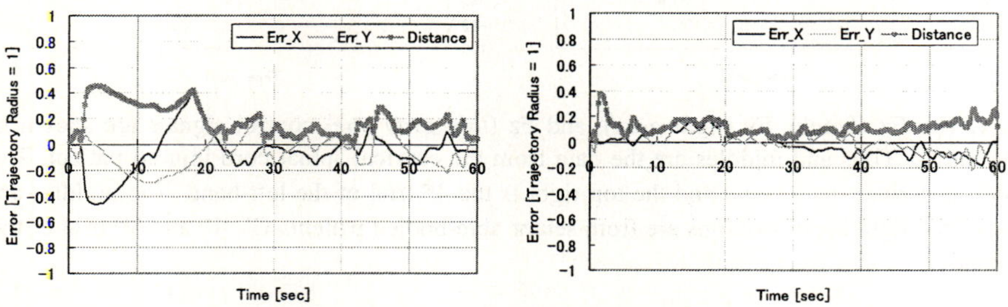


**Fig. 7.** Error of the marker and target position of the cervical spinal cord injured patient is plotted. 1st (*left*) and 4th (*right*) trial of the right hand is shown

The improvement of the feedback control of the arm-eye coordination is verified by the data. Moreover, by analyzing the result in time sequence, the rehabilitation process of the patient can be explained with quantitative evidence. To reinforce this, other sensory or observation system should be used in parallel. Measures that are not influenced by skill should be included. Provided with the position and force data, the therapist will have better insight of the patient's controllability of the arm.

Therapeutic situations, training postures, gripper shapes, parameters in the training software setup and other factors should be considered and confirmed before testing the subjects.

Finally, to bring this system to a practical application, the system should be evaluated in relation to medical indices for assessing the upper limb function. Also, software applications with knowledgebase and other intelligent systems to support the assessment process of the therapist will be important as well. Telediagnosis will be the final step for providing full support to home care and therapy.

## 6 Conclusion

Valid data was gained from a pilot test. Results showed the prospect of the systems use in rehabilitation. The adequacy of the three indices is confirmed. As for future work, single system design experiments are to be planned as well as clinical test with larger pool of patients. Finally, the pilot test revealed some issues, e.g. adjustability of the program settings, on implementing our mechatronics systems in home use and the therapy scene. The modifications will be made and tested in the near future.

## Acknowledgements

This research has been funded by the Cooperation of Innovative Technology and Advanced Research in Evolutional Area (CITY AREA) Project, the Ministry of Education, Culture, Sports, Science and Technology, Japan. The authors would like to especially thank T. Yanase and M. Suzuki at M.E. System Corp. for the production of the device, and the OT staffs and subjects at Kawashima Orthopaedic Hospital for their support, advice, and cooperation to the experiment.

## References

1. Tokioka, T.: Mechanism of cervical cord injury in the elderly. J. of Clinical Rehabilitation, vol.8, no.10 (1999) 921-926 (In Japanese)
2. Krebs, H.I., Hogan, N., Aisen, M.L., Volpe, B.T.: Robot-Aided Neurorehabilitation. IEEE Trans. of Rehab. Eng., vol.6, no.1 (1998) 75-86
3. Kahn, L.E., Averbuch, M., Rymer, W.Z., Reinkensmeyer, D.J.: Comparison of Robot-Assisted Reaching to Free Reaching in Promoting Recovery From Chronic Stroke. Proc. of ICORR 2001 (2001) 39-44
4. Coote, S., Stokes, E., Murphy, B., Harwin, W.: The Effect of GENTLE/s Robot-Mediated Therapy on Upper Extremity Dysfunction Post Stroke. Proc. of the 8th ICORR (2003) 59-61
5. Furusho, J., Koyanagi, K., Ryu, U., Inoue, A., Oda, K.: Development of Rehabilitation Robot System with Functional Fluid Devices for Upper Limbs. Proc. of ICORR 2003 (2003) 31-34

6. Takahashi, Y., Terada, T., Inoue, K., Ito, Y., Lee, H., Komeda, T.: Upper-Limb Rehabilitation Exercises Using Haptic Device System. Proc. of the 8th ICORR (2003) 274-277
7. T.L. Chelette, D.W. Repperger, C.A. Phillips: Enhanced Metrics for Identification of Forearm Rehabilitation. IEEE Trans. of Rehab. Eng., vol.3, no.1 (1995) 122-131
8. Ohnishi, K., Miyagawa, H., Saito, Y.: Rehabilitation System for Arm-Eye Coordination of the Palsy Arm. Proc. of 6th Japan-France Congress on Mechatronics and 4th Asia-Europe Congress on Mechatronics (2003) 117-122

# Smart Environments for All

## *Introduction to the Special Thematic Session*

Gerhard Nussbaum

Kompetenznetzwerk Informationstechnologie zur Förderung der Integration von Menschen mit Behinderungen (KI-I), IT-Center, Hauptstraße 119, 4232 Hagenberg i.M., Austria
Gerhard.Nussbaum@ki-i.at
http://www.ki-i.at

**Abstract.** Smart Environments also called Smart Homes or Smart Houses are often topics of research projects. Some have been and some will be realised. People with disabilities in particular could benefit most from such environments as they offer basic assistive functionalities enabling an increased independence and personal freedom and hence the quality of their life improved.This paper provides a short introduction to the field of "Smart Environments" and to the Special Thematic Session "Smart Environments for All".

## Introduction

"Computer – Light … Computer – Music … Computer – do this … Computer – do that". These words are often said by the Enterprise crew in the TV science fiction series Star Trek. The rooms of the crew are somehow intelligent i.e. smart. A computer recognizes these instructions and executes them. All devices, appliances i.e. functions of the room are somehow controlled by a computer or something like that.

Nowadays this scenario is no longer science fiction and becomes reality. Due to the potential for people with disabilities it becomes one of the most challenging research and development fields. Several projects deal and dealt with such intelligent rooms also called "Smart Environments", "Smart Homes", "Smart Houses", etc.

At a closer look Smart Environments i.e. Smart Homes can be defined as follows: A Smart Home is a home or building which is equipped with special structured wiring to enable occupants to remotely control or program an array of automated home electronic devices by entering a single command. [1] This infrastructure allows an integrated control and monitoring of all linked devices. Furthermore all these devices can also be controlled by a centralized control system. With the help of gateways (e.g. WWW, SMS, ISDN, etc.) these homes can also be controlled externally. (Fig. 1) So the occupant can control his home almost from all over the world.

All the features and infrastructures mentioned above are mostly developed for 'normal' people to raise the comfort and security of their daily life. But improving the independence and personal freedom of the occupant with such a Smart Environment? Why not – such environments can be the ideal home for persons with disabilities and elderly people. Such an environment has the ability to compensate several of the occupant's disabilities. [2] In a Smart Home an occupant with disabilities can control almost every electrical device, appliance and consumer electronics like TV, VCR, etc. independently. Only tasks which need physical interactions like filling or emptying

K. Miesenberger et al. (Eds.): ICCHP 2004, LNCS 3118, pp. 889–890, 2004.

the dish washer or washing machine often cannot be done by occupants with disabilities even if they are in or live in a smart environment. But the things an occupant with disabilities can do in a Smart Environment signify an increased quality of life.

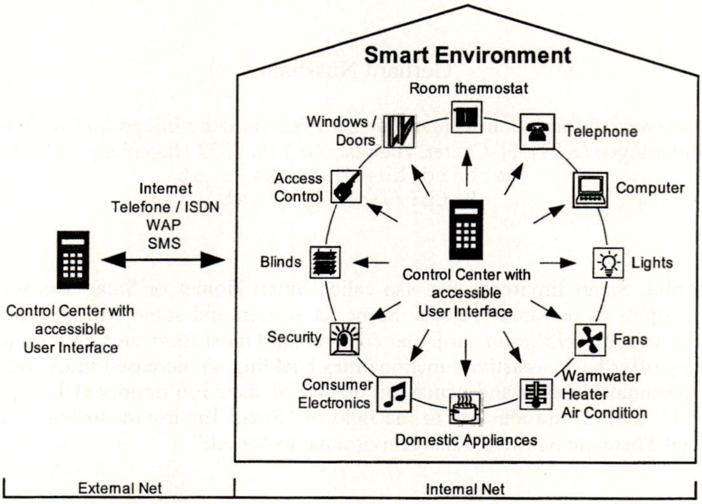


**Fig. 1.** Schematic and functional depiction of a Smart Environment [3]

The features and functions of Smart Environments are not inevitably accessible to and for persons with disabilities. There is at least one important thing a Smart Environment must fulfil before it can be called "for all": The user interface(s) must be accessible to all i.e. there must be the possibility to change the user interface according to the needs of the occupant with disabilities. Usability and user cantered design for Smart Environments have to be supported.

In this special thematic session the topics of the papers cover a broad thematic bandwidth which reaches from theoretic concepts and approaches to technical realisations and descriptions.

It should also not be neglected that Smart Environments have a high potential to increase the quality as well as the efficiency of health care which might increase the demand for research and developments in this field.

It is the aim of this session and of all contributions to help in improving the quality of life of people with disabilities by pushing research and development in the area of Smart Environment forward.

## References

1. Redriksson, V.: Smart Home or Building. A whatis definition. http://whatis.techtarget.com. 2001
2. Dewsbury, G.A., Edge, H.M.: Designing the Home to meet the Needs of Tomorrow … Today: Smart technology, health and well-being. Open House International. Vol26, No2, pp33-42. 2001
3. Aebischer, B., Huser, A.: Vernetzung im Haushalt – Auswirkungen auf den Stromverbrauch. Swiss Federal Office of Energy. November 2000

# The Assistive Home – More than Just Another Approach to Independent Living?

Gerhard Nussbaum[1] and Klaus Miesenberger[2]

[1] Kompetenznetzwerk Informationstechnologie zur Förderung der Integration von Menschen mit Behinderungen (KI-I), IT-Center, Hauptstraße 119, 4232 Hagenberg i.M., Austria
Gerhard.Nussbaum@ki-i.at
http://www.ki-i.at
[2] Institut "integriert studieren – integrated study", University of Linz
Altenbergerstrasse 69, A-4040 Linz, Austria
kmiesenberger@jku.at
http://www.integriert-studieren.jku.at

**Abstract.** The Assistive Home is a new approach to independent living. Other than in Smart Homes, in Smart Environments only important electrical items and appliances are linked together and it is based on market available standard components. The Assistive Home allows the integrated control via a centralized control center or via the electrical items focusing on accessibility and usability for people with disabilities. This paper points out the idea of the Assistive Home and introduces the residential building project "Dauphinestrasse" in Linz, Austria where the apartments will be realized as Assistive Homes. Furthermore the paper points out the advantages and challenges of the project.

## 1 Introduction

*In the 21st century the technology revolution will move into the everyday, the small and the invisible. (Mark Weiser, 1952-1999) [1]*

The technology revolution nowadays (2004) moves into our houses and homes, into the environments of our daily living. Building automation systems, once only used in business buildings and by freaks, get more common in residential building. 'Multimedia apartments' or 'intelligent homes' become more and more a hype. The technical infrastructure of such homes can simplify the daily living in several ways and it enhances the comfort of the occupant. Especially people with disabilities can benefit from such an equipped home. This technical infrastructure has the ability to compensate several disabilities of occupants with disabilities. So the personal freedom and independence of this person group can be enhanced [2].

The research in the field of Smart Homes and Environments is progressing. Several projects have been started with the aim to develop THE Smart Environment or THE House of the Future or THE ... Unfortunately people with disabilities quite often were not taken into consideration in many of these projects. Also techniques, devices and appliances have been developed and used which are currently hardly available for a broad use.

The Assistive Home is a new approach to Smart Environment and Smart Home for occupants with disabilities. The user interfaces of the control centres of these envi-

K. Miesenberger et al. (Eds.): ICCHP 2004, LNCS 3118, pp. 891–897, 2004.

ronments are specially designed for people with disabilities. Ambient and ubiquitous interfaces will be used. Therefore the Smart Home itself becomes an Assistive Technology.

Other than many Smart Homes the Assistive Home is based on "cheap" available and reliable standard components. Almost 'everybody' can allow oneself the luxury of such a home.

The Assistive Home is a concrete conceptual plan. It was designed for a residential building for nine people with disabilities. The architecture, the advantages and the challenges of the Assistive Home will be pointed out in this paper.

## 2 The Assistive Home

A smart home is a home or building which is equipped with special structured wiring to enable occupants to remotely control or program an array of automated home electronic devices by entering a single command [3].

During the last few years several Smart Houses (e.g. Future Life [8], inHaus [9], Wohnhaus Sobek [10]) have been realised. To realise these Houses newest technology was used to link almost all devices, electrical items and appliances together. The result is a Smart Home which has a whole host of features and functions. Unfortunately such Smart Homes currently are far too expensive for social housing.

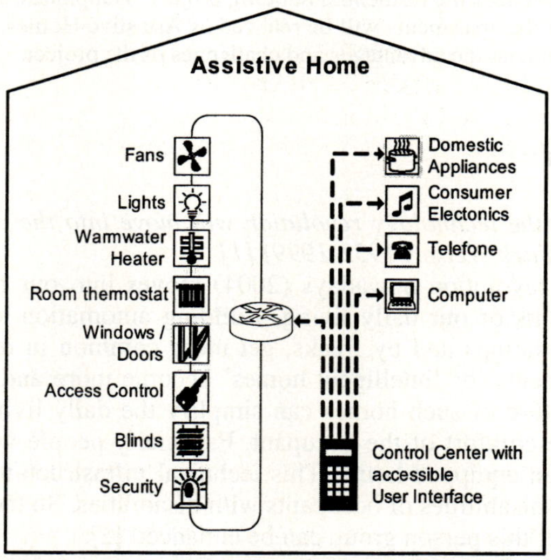


**Fig. 1.** The occupant can control 'all' electrical items and important appliances with a control center i.e. environmental control system

Other than in realised Smart Homes the functions and features of the assistive home are limited to the ones from which the occupant with disabilities benefits in terms of overcoming his functional limitations. This makes the realisation of an Assistive Home cheaper. It can be described and defined as follows:

The Assistive Home is an environment in which 'all' electrical items and important appliances are linked together and which allows the user the integrated control of them. Besides the user interfaces of the items and appliances there is also a central control centre with an accessible user interface based on standard HCI components (Fig. 1). The kind of disability of the occupant determines the user interface of the control centre. In most cases a standard environmental control system (e.g. FST James 2000 [11], SiCare Pilot [12], Proteor Nemo+ [13]) can be used as control centre. But also Tablet PCs and PDAs with special control software (e.g. Autonom [14], SmartX, Pocket Grid [15]) can be used as control centre.

Some of the potential occupants have little or no use for a central control centre. They prefer to use a traditional light switch instead of having a remote controller to do the task for them. This is an acceptable position, as a number of the used systems allow the user to determine how they wish the items and appliances within the home to work. [4]

## 3 Assistive Home "Dauphinestrasse"

In the year 2003 a new residential building for nine people with physical disabilities has been planned in Linz, Austria. To extend the disabled occupant's independence and personal freedom, the apartments were planned as Assistive Homes.

The specification of these apartments and the architecture of the technical infrastructure has been derived from the existing residential building 'Projekt Casa' in Linz. Furthermore the survey "Requirements for Environmental Control" [5] delivered additional input for the conceptual planning.

Every apartment has the following features which can be controlled directly via switches or centralized via an environmental control system:

- Nurse-call system
- Access control system
- Door communication system
- Door, windows, blinds and curtain openers
- Temperature Control of the heating
- Automatic switching off of the stove
- Infrared (IR) interface

Each apartment is equipped with its own home automation system (EIB [17] / Konnex [18]) to link together all electrical items and important appliances. The home automation system of each apartment is additionally equipped with an IR interface which consists of several IR receivers (one in each room) and one IR decoder. So each apartment can be controlled by the use of IR remote controllers.

Furthermore there are four systems i.e. networks which are used in all apartments. These 'global' networks, the nurse-call system, the door communication system, the access control system and the fire alarm systems are independent systems and not based on EIB/Konnex. To use the advantage of the IR interface of the home automation system, the nurse-call system and the door communication system are connected to the home automation system (Fig. 2) via potential-free binary output devices. So the interface of the home automation system is used to control the other systems.

There is only one IR interface to control all these systems instead of several proprietary IR interfaces. Due to the security, the access control system and the fire alarm system are completely stand alone.

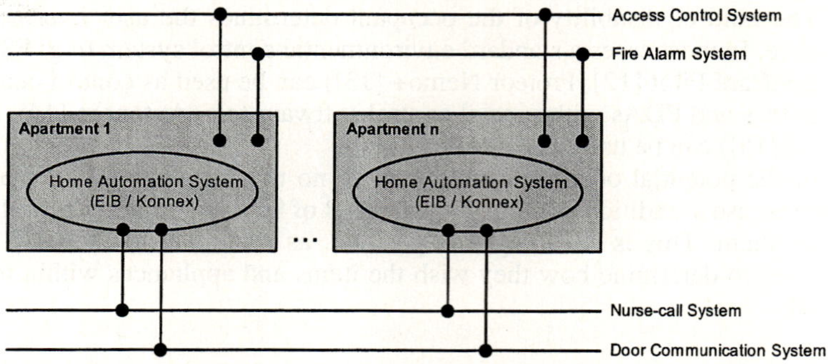


**Fig. 2.** Scheme of the technical infrastructure of the assistive homes 'Dauphinestrasse'

All electrical items of a room like switches for lights or blinds are concentrated in special panels of switches. So the occupant can control all important features of the room from a single place. Additionally special wall mountable IR controllers will be used if necessary. Furthermore, depending on the disabilities of the occupant, an environmental control system (FST James 2000, the SiCare Pilot or the Proteor Nemo+) will be used as control center. So people with severe disabilities are also able to control the Assistive Home.

To increase the occupant's security the stove is interconnected with a Watchdog. If nobody is in the kitchen for more than a definite time span the stove automatically is switched off. So the risk of a fire caused e.g. by hot oil or fat is minimized.

The Access Control System is equipped with contact less readers (reading distance 75cm) and is connected with the door openers. The id carriers can be attached to a wheelchair. For entering the apartment the occupant only has to drive to the door and the door opens. This system is more secure and more reliable than solutions with standard IR- or HF-controllers. The signals of such HF-controllers can be monitored and imitated. So a dishonest person can get access to the house i.e. to an apartment.

To raise the reliability and security and to ensure the operation of all important systems (especially the nurse-call system and the fire alarm system) of the Assistive Home even if power fails these systems are equipped with uninterrupted power supplies. The occupant must be able to raise a nurse-call i.e. emergency-call at any time. All doors with access control are equipped with panic locks.

### 3.1 Advantages

Due to the use of home automation infrastructure and environmental control systems the personal independence of the occupant with disabilities can be enhanced. The occupant is able to control all electrical items and important appliances by himself. Furthermore the occupant is able to open and close specially equipped doors, windows, curtains and blinds.

The occupant has the ability to choose the way of controlling his environment. He can use the standard user interfaces of the electrical items or a centralized control center i.e. environmental control system. Furthermore Computers and Tablet PCs can also be used to control the environment allowing to use the easy adaptable and extendable HCI. This allows an easier integration of Assistive Technology. A blind person e.g. can control his environment with a computer equipped with Assistive Technology like a Braille display. The cognitive overload and the learning demand can be reduced by using a known and stable interface.

The occupants of the residential building 'Dauphinestrasse' might change. Every time when a new occupant moves in the infrastructure has to be adapted. In the worst case electrical items like switches must be moved. In a normal apartment i.e. home such adaptations only can be done with a high technical effort. Due to the used home automation system and its flexibility such adaptations can be made easily. Almost all electrical items in the assistive home could be controlled and automated to work through a control unit or automatically in a way that is determined by the user i.e. occupant or system administrator. [4] A system administrator can change the functions of a switch or can edit properties like timings. With the use of wall mountable IR remote controllers (e.g. Busch-Ferncontrol® IR Wandsender [16]) also the location can be changed easily and no electrical installations have to be done. The occupant decides where the switches should be.

The home automation infrastructure partly makes use of the basic principle of HCI [6]. The content i.e. function of an electrical item is separated from presentation and the handling. So the function of a switch can be changed. The occupant e.g. decides whether a switch activates a light or turns of the fan. A system administrator can change the 'content' i.e. function of the switch quite easily. With the wall mountable IR-controllers also the 'presentation' i.e. the location of the switch is easily changeable.

The infrastructure of the Assisstive Home is open. New technical developments in the field of home automation like intelligent home appliances can easily be integrated. Furthermore the home automation system can be extended with several gateways. Gateways for WLAN, ISDN, SMS, WAP, Internet etc. are already available on market. These gateways open new forms of controlling the home automation system. With the use of such gateways the occupant is able to control his apartment from wherever he is.

A new home automation IR converter now allows consumer electronics and other devices which have an IR receiver to be controlled via the home automation system. This converter can learn the commands of almost every IR remote control of consumer electronics which operates in accordance with the RC5 code [19]. This means that these devices can also be operated from another room. In combination with one of the gateways mentioned before consumer electronics can be controlled and switched even by Internet and mobile phones. This converter can also operate as an IR receiver for EIB/Konnex. [7]

The windows, doors, curtains and blinds are equipped with electric driven openers which are connected to the home automation system. So occupants with sever disabilities can open or close these things by themselves with the control centre. They can leave or enter their apartment every time they want. This increases their personal freedom.

### 3.2 Challenges of the Assistive Home

Due to the usage of building automation infrastructure the assistive home infrastructure can be visualized on computers. With the help of the visualisation the occupant can control and monitor his home. Standard tools are available to create the visualization. Unfortunately the generated visualisations are not as accessible as they could/ should be. With an accessible visualisation also a blind or visually handicapped person can check in an easier way e.g. if lights are turned on/off or if blinds are open/closed and can control the temperature of the heating or air condition.

A (mobile) computer (PC, Tablet PC, PDA) with an accessible visualisation of the Assistive Home and with additional hard and software to control consumer electronics via IR too could be a suitable environmental control system. The realisation of such an environmental control system i.e. accessible visualisation will be done in an additional project.

After the realisation of the project "Dauphinestrasse" a study will be done. This study will examine the sociological and pedagogical aspects of "Living in an Assistive Home". Furthermore a cost-benefit equation will be done and the real additional costs in comparison to a 'normal' residential building will be examined. Aim of the project is to establish Assistive Homes as standard for residential buildings in (Upper) Austria.

## Acknowledgement

This work is done in the framework of projects funded by the Regional Government Upper Austria, Department for Social Affaires.

## References

1. Mattern, F.: Vom Verschwinden des Computers – Die Vision des Ubiquitous Computing. Total Vernetzt. Springer-Verlag (2003) 1-41
2. Dewsbury, G.A., Edge, H.M.: Designing the Home to meet the Needs of Tomorrow … Today: Smart technology, health and well-being. Open House International. Vol26, No2, pp33-42. 2001
3. Redriksson, V.: Smart Home or Building. A whatis definition. http://whatis.techtarget.com. 2001
4. Dewsbury, G.A.: A Smart Home Technology Guide. SMART Thinking. http://www.gdewsbury.ukideas.com. 2001
5. Nussbaum, G.: Smart Environment Control System – User Centred Design, Mensch-Maschine-Interaktion, Authoring- und Konfigurations-Tool „Configurator". Information Technology Enabling Integration at University. Diploma Thesis. Universität Linz. 2003
6. Miesenberger, K.: Applied Computer Science for Blind and Visually Handicapped People. Information Technology Enabling Integration at University. S. 60. Habilitationsschrift. Universität Linz. 2001
7. Gira Giersiepen GmbH & Co. KG: Technical description of Instabus IR converter. http://www.gira.com
8. Steiner, D.: Future Life. http://www.futurelife.ch

9. Impressum Fraunhofer Gesellschaft zur Förderung der angewandten Forschung e.V.: in-Haus - Innovationszentrum Intelligentes Haus Duisburg. http://www.inhaus-duisburg.de/index1.html. 2004
10. Sobek, W.: Wohnhaus Sobek. http://www.baunetz.de/arch/archplus/156/sobek_c.htm. Arch+ 156 Mai 2001.
11. FST – Fondation Suisse Pour Les Téléthèses – Stiftung für Elektronische Hilfsmittel: James 2000. http://www.fst.ch/FST2/CATALOGUE/fiches_produits_details/James2_D.pdf. Oktober 2002
12. Dr. Hein GmbH: SiCare Pilot. http://www.sicare.de/sicarepilot.html. Nürnberg 2002
13. Proteor Group: Nemo+. http://www.proteor.com/proteor/uk/ht/index_cata.htm
14. Flachberger, C., Panek, P., Zagler, W.L.: Autonomy - A Flexible and Easy-to-Use Assistive System to Support the Independence of Handicapped and Elderly Persons, Proc. 4th International Conference on Computers for Handicapped Persons (ICCHP), Vienna, Austria, Sept. 1994, 65 - 75.
15. Sensory Software International Ltd: Pocket Grid. Software for Windows CE Computers. http://www.sensorysoftware.com/software/pocketgrid/index.html
16. Busch-Jaeger Elektro GmbH: Busch-Ferncontrol® IR Wandsender. http://www.busch-jaeger-katalog.de/. 2004
17. EIBA – European Installation Bus Association: EIB. http://www.eiba.org/home.nsf
18. Konnex Association: Konnex. http://www.konnex.org/
19. Bergmans, S.: Philips RC5 Protocol. http://www.xs4all.nl/~sbp/knowledge/ir/rc5.htm. Oisterwijk, Niederlande, 2001.

# Technology Usage for Dependant People: Towards the Right Balance between User Needs and Technology

C. Penaud[1], M. Mokhtari[1,2], and B. Abdulrazak[1,2]

[1] GET-INT, Handicom Lab., 9 rue Charles Fourier, 91011 Evry Cedex, France
celine.penaud@int-evry.fr
[2] INSERM-U483, Pierre & Marie Curie University, 9 Quai Saint Bernard, Paris

**Abstract.** While technology has revolutionised our working and private environment, there is still improvement to be made to allow people with disabilities and senior citizens to live an independent life and take an integral part in the society. The development of the smart home concept allows people with a severe disability to control their home devices using a customised user-interface. Beyond this, the creation of a central system controlling a wide range of daily equipment, unlocks opportunities for the creation of many value-added services or new Usage. In this article, we will present our analysis of the "usage" definition. We will also describe our approach in identifying new technology usages. Although our smart home concept development has followed a user-centred approach throughout the project, taking a step back to analyse its usage has allowed us to expand its potential application scope, and develop an extended investigation of user's needs.

## 1 Introduction

While our research activity in assistive technology have reached a certain maturity in terms of technical development and users needs analysis, we are currently running a "usage" analysis, which enables us to take a step back, and identify what uses will be made of the smart home concept, and ensure that our technological choices allow the widest range of service options.

The word *usage* has been widely used in the last few years, especially in relation to new technologies. We have first attempted to clarify its meaning. A dictionary gives the following definition: 1. the act, manner, or amount of using; use: *the usage of a technical term,* 2. the act or manner of treating: *subjected the car to rough usage.* In recent years, the word usage has been related to how a new and broad-reaching technology has been used: internet usage, mobile telephony usage. In those cases, the word usage has been used to refer to new applications that can be made of a generic tool, but that have been defined subsequently. To understand the context in which the word usage has been used, we have briefly analysed the example of Internet usage. The way people have used the Internet has evolved dramatically, through the apparition of many new services. From its initial use by researchers to today's many dating services, the internet has generated many uses: companies have used it to advertise their products; start-ups have emerged to offer new on-line services such as travel booking. Some parallels can be drawn with the area of assistive technology. On the

K. Miesenberger et al. (Eds.): ICCHP 2004, LNCS 3118, pp. 898–905, 2004.

one hand, many technologies, such as robotics, computing networks, and voice recognition systems have emerged. Their existence opens up solutions for new assistive services and products. On the other hand, people with disabilities and senior people have many unfulfilled needs. This results in a potential for new applications meeting user needs.

## 2 Driving New Usage: Push and Pull Approaches

### 2.1 Technology Push vs. Market Pull

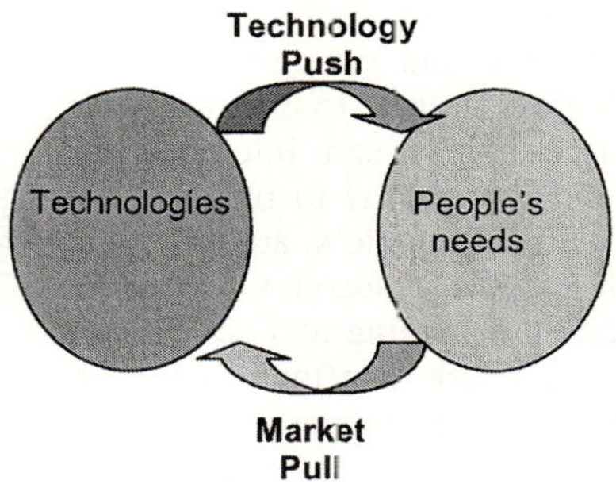


The creation of new services and products can result from two marketing approaches: a technology push method, or a market-pull strategy [Amm 93].
In a technology push approach technologies are developed first and offered to the market, creating new sources of demand. These technology applications respond to needs previously unidentified and generate their own demand. The domain of New Technologies has often followed a Technology- Push approach. The expansion of the internet and the take-up of mobile telephony have both followed this model.

Marketing methods based on a Market-Pull approach result from the apparition of a demand expressed by customers. This identified demand, based on the needs of a target population, results in the creation of services/products which are developed to address this specific demand. This has been the case for electric wheelchairs which have been developed as technical solutions to answer a specific need and compensate a body-function.

### 2.2 Technology Usage: Iterations of Push and Pull

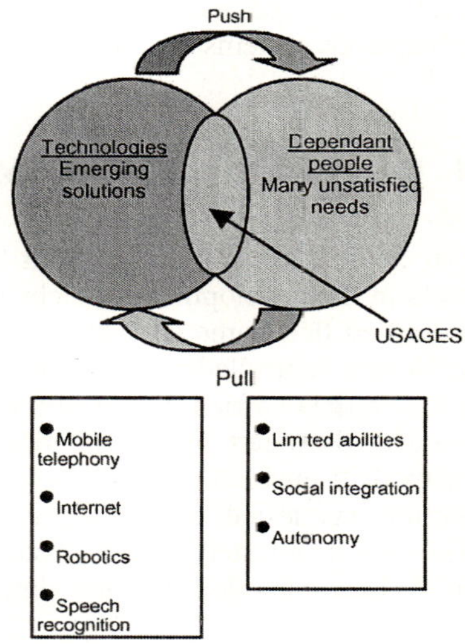


As described above, the word usage has been mostly used in technology-push contexts. Internet usage and mobile telephony usage refer to occurrences when technology has been deployed without clear foresight of their potential demand.

In order to identify the optimal usage that will be made of technologies, it is essential however to pay maximum attention to the users and their needs. A technology usage is indeed at the intersection of emerging technologies and user needs. We have therefore attempted to include, wherever appropriate, elements of a user-centred approach in our research. This has led to mix Push and Pull approaches, in iterative loops. This, we believe, is one of the keys to success to define the most relevant services and products for people with disabilities and elderly people. To achieve this, our solution has been to gather multiple skills within the team, including marketing people to run a user needs analysis, robotics, network and programming experts to develop our systems, as well as ergonomics specialists to design and evaluate our solutions.

## 3 Technology and Usage

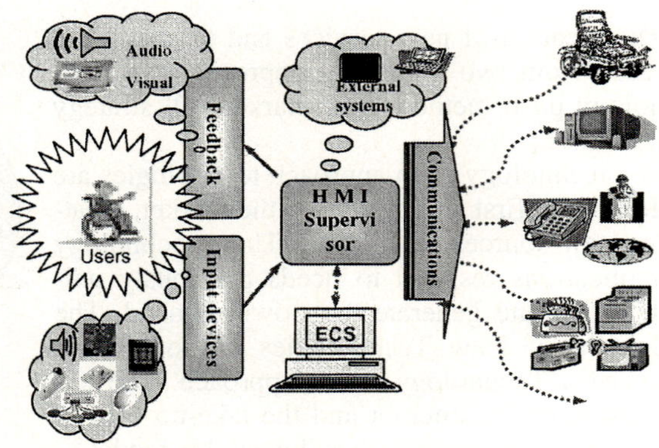


Our project aims at making use of new possibilities offered by existing and emerging technologies, in order to facilitate their accessibility and interoperability. Our goal is to increase dependent people's autonomy at home. Our research work focused on designing and developing a software configuration tool, integrating network and telecommunications technologies, in order to allow people with disabilities to control their home environment comfortably. As shown in the figure above, the software architecture of the smart home concept is built on three main layers: the user interface layer, which include the input/output devices; the HMI Supervisor (Human Machine interaction manager), which could be integrated on a mobile system (portable PC, pocket PC…); and the Communication layer which enable to control home devices via corresponding networking protocols. This architecture allow to separate the user interface, which could be unified and specifically adapted for each end user, from the controlled heterogeneous systems available in user's environment.

## 4 Research Strategy and Methodology

Our approach has included both Push and Pull elements. Our initial idea found its roots in the development of technologies, typical of a technology-push approach. We identified that home appliances and assistive devices could be connected into a network and controlled easily from one central command box, adapted to disabled people. We then carried out an initial user needs' analysis, in order to ensure that users were at the heart of our solution choices. This was an element of a market pull method. It enabled us to identify the type of assistive devices that people with disabilities requested. This analysis led to the design of our smart home architecture. This was then tested through prototypes and demonstrators validated by users' evaluations, in conjunction with the Garches Hospital and the AFM[1]. Beyond this, we have

[1] AFM: French muscular dystrophies association.

decided to run an analysis of the usage of the smart home. This has enabled us to evaluate the relevance of our technical development and identify new applications which will benefit the greatest number of people.

## 5 Process to Identify Technology Usages

In order to clarify the notion of usage within our Smart Home concept, we followed an iterative process.

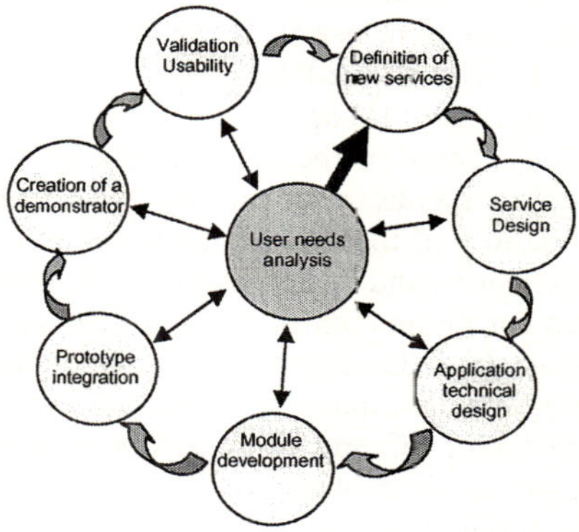


*Above is an illustration of our research process. Is follows an iterative method. At each phase of the process, from the initial conceptual design to the final integration of a demonstrator, we run iterations of evaluations in relation to the initial user needs analysis.*

### 5.1 User Needs Analysis in Terms of Assistive Devices: Survey Results

To assess people's needs in their daily environment, we ran user needs analysis, based on the demand for assistive devices. The study consisted in two phases: a quantitative analysis carried out through questionnaires and a qualitative phase based on open questions. This study aimed at identifying the needs of people with a heavy motor disability, in particular tetraplegics users. The survey was carried out with 30 users and experts (doctors, helpers) and enabled us to identify the assistive devices that they had at their disposal, and their satisfaction level. It also provided some general direction in terms of user needs. Below are some of the findings from our survey:

- Communication tools are used by a vast majority of users, and are considered as very important, they include computers connected to the internet (75% of respondents use one, with an 85% importance rating), a mobile phone (68% use a mobile phone, importance rating: 76%).
- Some tools are considered as important but unsatisfactory. Mobile phones are difficult to use, due to the design of the keypad (buttons are too close together). Voice recognition is considered an important user interface (rate: 3.5/5) but unsatisfactory (rate 2.2/4).
- The tools that are used the most are the ones that belong to "normal" home environment (remote controls are used by 80% of respondents, TV by 93%, mouse by 67%) and they are considered satisfactory and important. "Specialised" aids are less popular. This can be seen with phones with alert systems which are only used by 22% of respondents. Automatic windows are used by less than 4% of respondents.

- This is partly due to the fact that they are "tagged" as handicap tools. Their design should allow them to blend in their environment.
- Overall, a feeling of isolation and lack of autonomy make respondents' life very "heavy".
- There is a difference in attitude towards technical aids whether the person was born with a handicap or whether the disability happened later in life. If the person was injured in an accident, they first look for medical solutions. Acceptability of teachnical aids is greater as time goes.

These initial findings have demonstrated the limitations of existing solutions to help dependent people. Although assistive aids have focused on specific user needs, they have not found the enthusiasm expected. Other factors therefore need to be taken into account. These include psychological factors such as the image people want to convey: some of the aids haven't been adopted because they are too visible signs of people's handicap, or the psychological price users are prepared to pay or indeed the solvability of the users. The initial user needs analysis enabled us to draw some initial conclusions and design our smart home architecture. This design took into account the need for home control devices that were fully customised to users' abilities. Our system enables the use of many adapted user interfaces (trackball, mouse, voice recognition). We also made sure that our system was as ordinary as possible (use of a standard tablet PC and PDA as home interface). This ensured that the system was not tagged as "handicap-only" and that its cost remained within a limited budget. After this initial phase of the project, it has been essential to take a step back from the technology and aids themselves, to try and further identify the potential usage of the smart home. To do this, we tried to understand the needs and priorities of people with disabilities.

## 5.2 User Needs and Usage

The Maslow pyramid model enabled us to structure this analysis [W-Wiki]]. Maslow has identified five categories of needs, which apply to human beings in general, with different levels of priorities. These are in order of priority: 1. Survival, 2. Safety, 3. Social needs, 4. Esteem, 5. Selfactualization. People will first fulfill their needs for survival (eating, sleeping), will then look for situations that keep them safe, before moving up the chain and fulfill their needs to be part of society and achieve things.

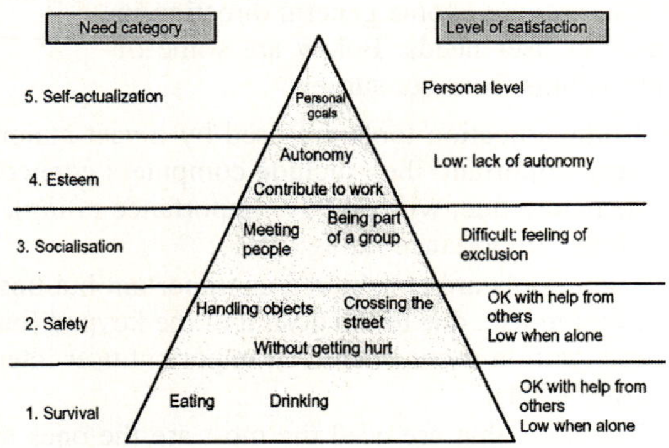


This analysis enabled us to identify many unfulfilled user needs encountered by people with disabilities and senior people. Illustrations of our results include the following. Needs in relation to Safety may be, for a person with visual impairment, to be able to cross the street safely. For a senior person, this might be to get emergency help when falling and not being able to stand up again. Social needs have been when falling and not being able to stand up again. Social needs have been expressed by disabled people as a key element that they would like to develop. Indeed, people with poor hearing suffer from a diminution of their social contacts, people with motor disability also feel excluded from social activities. The third level of the pyramid relates to esteem, both self-esteem and recognition from others. This is often related to the capability of achieving things, contributing to a work activity and being autonomous. Again, people with disabilities and elderly people who are dependent, feel a great need for increased autonomy, and the possibility to demonstrate their worth to themselves and to others through work or other activities.

### 5.3 Design Architecture and Guidelines

The usage and user needs analysis has enabled us to draw some guidelines for the creation of services for dependent people. These apply firstly to the evolution of the service architecture within our system, and secondly to the factors to take into account to create successful services (in terms of usefulness and adoption).

**a. Service Architecture**
Our current system enables the rapid integration, on the one hand of many user interfaces, based on the user's preferences (joystick, trackball, voice recognition, etc) and on the other hand of many controllable devices (phone, TV, radiator). Beyond the stricly home services, our usage analysis suggested that we should expand the scope of the smart homes concept. Indeed, many other potential services can be created by combining the user interfaces and all types of devices (sensors, phone alerts, computer programs). Our architecture must evolve so that any service provider can easily create new services, have access to billing functions, without being necessarily familiar with the actual system. To achieve this, one of the solutions under investigation may be through the implementation of OSGi standard (Open Services Gateway initiative) which should favor service creation using generic tools.

**b. Designing New Services**
Working on usage enabled us to try and understand what utilisation will be made of a technology, i.e. what services will meet users' needs. To design those services, we also need to understand the key factors that will drive people to adopt a service, and integrate it in their daily life. The concept of acceptability must be taken into account [Amm 02]. Acceptability includes four factors, which are the service usefulness (does the service provide the expected functionalities?), its usability (can the user use the service appropriately?), its pleasantness (does the feel that he/she is happy with the service), as well as its cost (is the price acceptable?). Beyond this, the way people will adopt a service may differ from what was originally intended. For instance, tele-alarm was often used by aging people for social interaction, rather than real emergency.

To understand how people will use a service it is important to take into account the context in which they will use it. It is also crucial to understand users' profile, including: their abilities - can they move their lower limb, for instance - as well as their preferences – what are their favourite activities? Traditional marketing segmentation by age, region, purchasing power, have not been found to be relevant factors when it comes to assistive technology. Other factors may be more relevant, such as people's career background, the length of time that they have lost body-abilities, whether they were born with a handicap or has it occurred through an injury or illness. The work that we are carrying out on user profile aims at drawing a detailed picture of these factors.

## 6 Conclusion

Working on the definition of the usage of the smart home has enabled us to focus on a user-centered approach. It has helped us take a step back from technology and understand what type of support people with disabilities needed in their daily life. This has both led us to validate our initial concept and helped us focus on architecture choices which will optimise the usefulness of our development for users. We have also tried to focus our attention on the acceptability of our solutions. To validate our findings, this usage analysis will be taken further through the implementation of limited number of scenarios. These scenarios, which will be based on the implementation of selected services, will help us analyse further the notion of acceptability and technology usage.

From a design perspective, a user-centred approach is necessary in order to ensure that our concept will be useful and indeed used. Ideally, the solution should be useful to all people. To achieve this, we need to integrate "design for all" or "universal design" (respectively European and US terms) elements in our approach. These methods aim at designing products and services which can be used by everybody without specific adaptations. Our research work has aimed to keep this in mind in order to ensure maximum flexibility of use of our concept, so that it can be useful to all users.

## Acknowledgements

Special acknowledgements to:

- All users who have helped with through this project, and have given us their thoughts to design, evaluate our system.
- The GET (Groupe des Ecoles de Télécommunications) and industrial Foundation Louis Leprince-Ringuet for their financial support of this project.
- The AFM (French muscular dystrophies association) for their participation and constant support.
- The ENST Bretagne and Telecom Paris teams for their active participation in the Smart homes project.

## References

[Amm 93] Ammi C., « Le marketing, un outil de décision face à l'incertitude», Editions Ellipses (1993)

[Amm 02] Ammi C., « Domotics and dependence », internal report, INT/GET, (2002)

[Zha 03] Zhang D., Wang X., Leman K., Huang W., « OSGi Based Service Infrastructure for Context Aware Connected Homes » Proc ICOST 2003, 1st International Conference On Smart homes and health Telematics, "Independent living for persons with disabilities and elderly people", Ed. IOS Press, pp.81-88, Paris, (September 2003).

[W-Wiki]] web site wikipedia, free encyclopaedia, « fr.wikipedia.org ».

[Mok 02 b] Mokhtari M., Abdulrazak B. et all,, « Innovative Action: Smart Home : Application Handicap and Dependence », (Del 01) Internal report Groupe des Ecoles des Télécommunications., GET/INT-Evry, (August 2002).

[Soe 03] Soede M., « The Home and Care technology for chronically ill and disabled persons » Proc ICOST 2003, 1st International Conference On Smart homes and health Telematics, "Independent living for persons with disabilities and elderly people", Ed. IOS Press, pp.3-9, Paris, (September 2003).

[Bjo 03] Bjoerneby Sidsel, Duff Petrina, Maki Outi, « Developing Assistive Technologies for people with Dementia – Adaptation of design for all Principles » Proc AAATE 2003, The Association for the Advancement of Assistive Technologies in Europe , Dublin (2003).

[Far 00] Fardeau M. «On a comparative and prospective analysis of the French System to integrate handicapped people; like you, like me, simply » Report to the Employment and Solidarity Ministry and State Secretary for Health, Social Action and Handicaps, (September 2000).

# Coupling Context Awareness and Multimodality in Smart Homes Concept

Mohamed Ali Feki[1], Stéphane Renouard[2], Bessam Abdulrazak[1], Gérard Chollet[2], and Mounir Mokhtari[1]

[1] Handicom Lab, INT/GET, 9 rue Charles Fourier, 91011 Evry, France
{mohamedali.fki,bessam,mounir}@int-evry.fr
http://www.int-evry.fr/handicom

[2] TSI Lab, ENST Paris/GET, 46 rue barrault, 75013 Paris, France
{renouard,chollet}@enst.fr
http://www.enst.fr/tsi

**Abstract.** Development of smart home technologies dedicated to people with disabilities provides a challenge in determining accurate requirements and needs in dynamic situations. In this paper we describe the integration of context awareness and multimodal functionalities in a smart environment. We outline how to optimize user comfort and capabilities. Considering the wide range of user types and preferences and the dynamic system environment created by constant introduction of new product and new context. By taking the environmental information provided by the environment, user profile and preferences, context awareness promises easier interaction and new possibilities such as predictive tasks automatically and adapting new situations to user interface. Multimodality permits in one hand to facilitate accessibility to a wide range of users, and the other hand to offer innovative control method of complex systems. In this paper we present our approach for coupling context awareness and multimodality concepts.

## 1 Introduction

Smart Environment Technologies are an emerging research field due to the potential range of applications. The design of Smart-Home systems dedicated to people with disabilities is still suffering from a gap between user needs and on-the-market solutions. Distinct problems arise through the lack of knowledge of how to transfer needs and data referred to situation and useful context in a reliable and valid manner.

In our approach on designing smart homes systems, user interfaces have to be adapted to the dynamic situation of the environment. Usually most of systems used by people with disabilities (e.g. assistive devices, terminals, equipments, etc) use static models which are non adapted in the mobile environment. Integration of context awareness coupled with multimodality concepts promises easier interactions and new possibilities for applications. Information such as availability of resources, user profile, location, input controls and services can be used to improve the interaction between users and their environments.

K. Miesenberger et al. (Eds.): ICCHP 2004, LNCS 3118, pp. 906–913, 2004.

## 2 Context Awareness Concept

We can define context-awareness as "any information that can be used to characterize the situation of an entity, where an entity can be a person, place, physical or computational object"[1]. According to this definition, three important context-awareness behaviors can be identified as the presentation of information and services to a user, the automatic execution of a service, and the tagging of context to information for later retrieval. These three keys have to be well defined and more adapted for people with disabilities in order to compensate their restrictions.

Context is becoming increasingly important in handheld and ubiquitous computing, where the user's context often changes quickly[2]. But, context isn't limited to handheld and ubiquitous computing and can serve a wide range of other domains. Indeed, context allows users interfaces to be more adapted to new situations into an environment which evolves continuously depending on surrounded parameters. This makes it ideal for our purpose in considering people with disabilities environments as accessible and described in a formalized manner.

Usually, context-aware applications consist on customizing information based on the current location. However, even if location is the most commonly used context data, there is much more parameters to consider such as temperature, time, orientation, affective state, activity, interests, focus of attention, interest/boredom levels, resources available, people nearby, etc. [3].

In case of people with disabilities, each user is a particular case. Our concept aim to be able to describe each user independently as he presents special features, personalized parameters, and specific need. For this reason, we define the context awareness concept into three environment: Sensor environment which is responsible for capturing state of object indoor the home, System environment which is responsible for taking care of application state's, network traffic and equipment managed by the user, and the platform environment which specify features of terminals and related parameters such as capacity and memory. The user environment known as user profile should be an independent module. Information provided from user profile can be useful in case of downloading services related to each user and allow the context awareness concept to adapt environment to a specific user.

To apply our design, we present in section 5 how to implement last definition into a smart home project. Our design is inherited and adapted from standard models working on context topics, mainly we studied the toolkit and Salber model [1, 10].

## 3 Multimodality Concept

Multimodal systems process several combined user input modes( such as speech, touch, manual gestures, gaze, and so on…) in a coordinated manner with multimodal system output. This class of systems represents a new direction for computing, and a paradigm shift away from conventional WIMP interfaces. This new class of interfaces aims to recognize naturally occurring forms of human language and behavior, which incorporate at least one recognition-based technology (e.g., speech, touch, vision). The development of novel multimodal systems has been enabled by the myriad input and output technologies currently becoming available, including new devices and improvements in recognition-based technologies.

The growing interest in multimodal interface design is inspired largely by the goal of supporting more transparent, flexible, efficient, and powerfully expressive means of human-computer interaction. Multimodal interfaces are expected to be easier to learn and use, and are preferred by users for many applications.

In this respect, multimodal interfaces have the potential to accommodate a broader range of users than traditional interfaces in particular people having disabilities including users of different ages, skill levels, native language status, cognitive styles, sensory impairments, and other temporary illnesses or permanent handicaps. For example, a visually impaired user or one with repetitive stress injury may prefer speech input and text-to-speech output. In contrast, a user with a hearing impairment or accented speech may prefer touch or gesture [4].

A mobile multimodal system should provide the adaptability that is needed to accommodate the continuously changing conditions of mobile use. In particular, systems involving speech or touch input are suitable for mobile tasks and, when combined, users can shift among these modalities from moment to moment as environmental conditions change [4, 5]. There is a sense in which mobility can induce a state of temporary disability, such that a person is unable to use a particular input mode for some period of time. A multimodal interface permits the modality choice and switching that is needed during the changing environmental circumstances of actual field and mobile use.

System feedback typically includes multimedia output, which may incorporate text-to-speech and non-speech audio, graphics and animation, and so forth. Application of multimodality concept in the feedback level should provide appropriate output regardless of the physical devices. There are many ways to realize this information processing flow as architecture. One common infrastructure that has been adopted by the multimodal research community involves *multi-agent architectures*, such as the Open Agent Architecture [6, 7], and Adaptive Agent Architecture [8]. Multi-agent architectures provide essential infrastructure for coordinating the many complex modules needed to implement multimodal system processing, and they permit doing so in a distributed manner that is compatible with the trend toward mobile computing.

## 4 Multimodal Context Aware Architecture

Since an application dedicated to the control of the environment running is inherently confronted with a variety of changes it has to adapt itself very quickly in order to deliver the expected results that are, for example, changes on user graphical interface. In order to deliver this level of service, the coupling of information coming from context awareness and multimodality is necessary. Multimodal and context awareness systems differ mainly in the way the information is acquired. Context awareness systems acquire implicit sensing from the environment while multimodal systems use explicit user inputs. Both systems *have got* multiple inputs and outputs. Output in the case of context awareness relates to the control of actuators or the sensors themselves.

As mentioned in [10], context aware and multimodal systems suffer from too much focus on input, and little concern for output.

The WWW consortium (W3C) [15] defined how to handle multiple input and output for multimodality. It distinguishes between three different ways that are *sequential, uncoordinated simultaneous* and *coordinated simultaneous* multimodal input/output (IO). In *sequential IO* there is no requirement that the input modalities are simultaneously active. In *uncoordinated simultaneous IO*, there is more than one input mode available but only input from one modalities is interpreted. The classical example of this is for a secured access, the application says "Enter your name" and the user can either says or enters his name via the keypad. This scenario is more close to what we consider as plurimodality, not multimodality. The last multimodal IO defined is *coordinated simultaneous IO*. In this case, there is more than one input mode and input from multiple modalities is interpreted. The example given is an user in a telephony environment that types 100 on the keypad of his cell phone and says "transfer to checking account". This is clearly what we consider as multimodal.

In order to couple information provided by context aware and multimodal system, data fusion seems to be the key issue [10]. Fusion of data occurs at different level in generic multimodal-context aware application. [11] defined two level of data fusion classified as *early fusion* and *late fusion*. Early fusion means integration of input data at an early stage of processing (typically fusion of data from captors delivering the same information e.g. localization). Late fusion means latest fusion, just before the interpreter, usually at a semantic interpretation level. According to the author, late fusion seems to have attracted more interest than early fusion. For the output, [11] consider *fission* of information, which means the dispatching of single semantic streams to several output channels. Fig. 1 describes a representation of such a generic multimodal-context aware model.

To handle this kind of architecture, especially the fusion part, generic engines have been developed [6, 7, 9]. The Open Agent Architecture [6] seems to be a promising tool to handle such a work, especially for context aware data but the work of investigation for applicability of this concept is still running.

A scenario to illustrate the use of context aware-multimodal system is the possibility to disambiguate situations. This disambiguation is supported by the analysis of context awareness and multimodal information hence leading to more stable and robust overall system performances. One advantage of achieving such a blend is that the resulting process is more robustly than a stand-alone multimodal or context aware system technology, lacking natural complementarities. A good example is the case of the driving situation, where changing location and level of noise is recuperated from context module. It will inform the multimodal module that the use of voice recognition is impossible in such situation.

## 5 Software Platform Requirements

In the framework of the "smart home dedicated to people with disability", we developed a generic modular software architecture to control a domestic environment. The

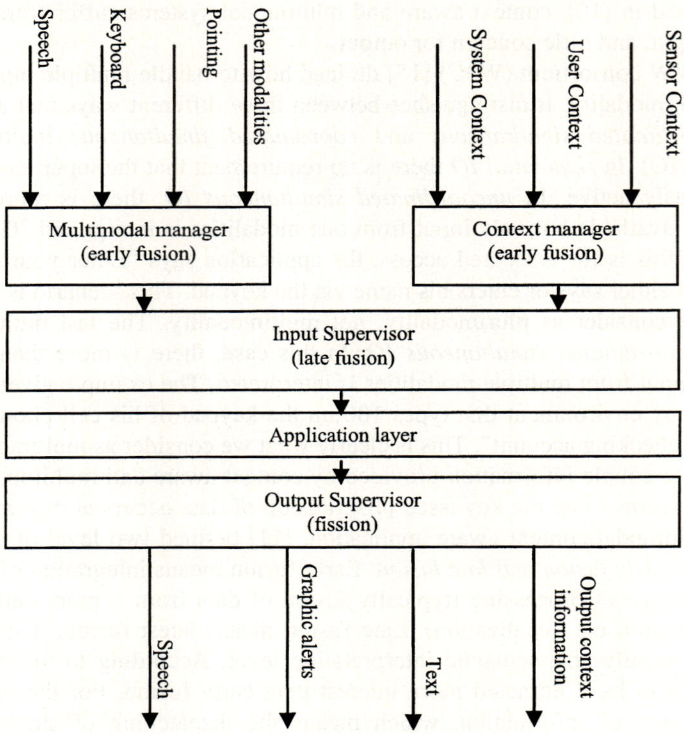


**Fig. 1.** A generic multimodal-context aware architecture

description of the project could be found in [13]. We recently focused our work to move to a service oriented platform based on the integration of OSGi [14]. Context awareness and multimodality appear in our architecture as two distinct modules, which manage data from user and environment as inputs. Each of them is responsible of managing data from both user and environment, as described in figure 1. The HMI layer is responsible for integrating data from both modules.

Our purpose is to be as generic as possible. We want to support interoperability of context applications on heterogeneous platforms. We have to handle devices that are most likely not linked to the same computer running the application. In fact, sensors must be physically scattered and cannot be directly connected to the same machine. This implies that data recuperated are coming from multiple, distributed machines. Our application has to support *context distribution*. The idea is to develop objects responsible for transforming data recuperated from context sources to a unified way using a standard XML and sending output to a smart engine for context analyze and make decision. Figure 2 illustrates these considerations and the separation between five important elements:

- **Sensors:** they represent physical devices responsible for providing data and information by different ways (signals, switch, …)

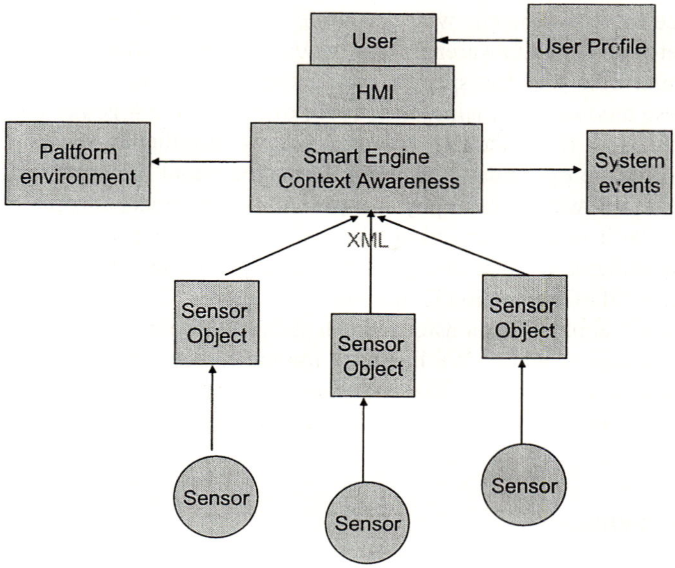


**Fig. 2.** Context model

- **Sensor Object:** Each of them is associated with one or more physical sensors to recuperate raw data and make a unified data representation (standard XML). Models are available to use by high layer applications.
- **System Events:** information related to state of application, state of home, of equipments, and errors generated.
- **Platform Environment:** Context awareness define new decisions to adapt interface downloaded into heterogeneous pervasive computing and handheld devices (PDA, mobile phone...). Platform environment let the context module aware of related functionalities such as size of sceen, memory etc.
- **Smart Engine Context Awareness:** Allow interpreting data on models, interact also with system events and platform parameters, has access to smart rules and take account into user profile to propose new functionalities to integrate at HMI layer.

To present data, XML encode scripts defined by multimodal objects or data collected from context providers. This strategy was used in the same project to make environment models. [13].

## 6 Conclusion

This paper has outlined some features of our vision to integrate both context awareness coupled with multimodality to ensure more efficient update of functionality to user interface in case of people with disabilities. Related work are appeared to distingue more between context awareness and the user profile. In fact, each user is a separated particular case that has specific parameters and attributes. The advantages of coupling those modules are mainly their focus on interacting together and provide the maximum of data. This idea can be improved by introducing the context sharing which will offer the opportunity to gain information about the context of other context aware devices, which are in physical proximity. This mechanism allow to enrich any modules with more information. We say about context which evolves, in the same way multimodality that change and a user profile assistant that update itself through the period of application is running.

Current work aims to demonstrate the feasibility of our architecture indoor and outdoor by a usage scenario. We begin by implementing simple services which are utile for people with disabilities like automats repetitive tasks or predict user position or next task to avoid intervention of user at interface layer.

## Acknowledgement

The authors would like to thank the people who have participated actively in this presented research activities from INSERM U.483, INT and hospital of Garches. Smart Homes project, involving ENST Bretagne from Brest and ENST Paris, is funded by the GET and by the Foundation Louis Leprince Ringuet.

## References

1. Dey, A.K, Abowd, G.D: Toward a better understanding of context and context-awareness., GVU Technical Report GIT-GVU-99-22, College of Computing, Georgia Institute of Technology, 1999
2. Pascoe, J.: Adding generic contextual capabilities to wearable computers. in Proceedings of 2nd International Symposium on Wearable Computers, October 1998, pp. 92-99
3. Schmidt, A., Beigl, M., Gellersen, H.W.: There is more to Context than Location. Proceedings of the International Workshop on Interactive Applications of Mobile Computing (IMC98), November 1998, Rostock, Germany
4. Oviatt, S.L.,"Multimodal System Processing in Mobile Environments," Proceedings of the Thirteenth Annual ACM Symposium on User Interface Software Technology (UIST'2000), 21-30. New York: ACM Press
5. Holzman, T.: Computer-human interface solutions for emergency medical care. Interactions, vol. 6, pp.13-24, 1999
6. Cohen, P.R., Cheyer, A., Wang, M., Baeg, S.C.: An open agent architecture. in Proceedings ofAAA11994 Spring Symposium on Software Agents, pp. 1-8, 1994
7. Martin, D.L., Cheyer, A., Lee, G.L.: Agent development tools for the open agent architecture. In Proceedings of the First International Conference on the Practical Application of Intelligent Agents and Multi-Agent Technology, pages 387#404, Blackpool, Lancashire, UK, April, 1996

8. Kumar, S., Cohen, P.R., Levesque, H.J.: The Adaptive Agent Architecture. Proc. 4th Int'l Conf. Multi-Agent Systems, 159-166, 2000
9. Salber, D., Dey, K., Abowd, G.D.: The Context Toolkit: Aiding the Development of Context-Enabled Applications. In the Proceedings of the 1999 Conference on Human Factors in Computing Systems (CHI '99), Pittsburgh, PA, May 15-20, 1999. pp. 434-441
10. Kvale, K., Warakagoda, N., Knudsen, J.: Speech-Centric Multimodal Interaction With Small Mobile Terminals. Proc. NORSIG 2001 - NORSK SYMPOSIUM I SIGNALBEHANDLING – pp. 12-17, Trondheim, 18. - 20. oktober, 2001
11. Mokhtari, M.: Integration of Rehabilitation Robotics in the Context of Smart Homes: Application to Assistive Robotics. Proceedings of the ICORR 2003 (The Eighth International Conference on Rehabilitation Robotics), 23-25 April 2003
12. Feki, M.A., Abdulrazak, B., Mokhtari, M.: XML Modelisation of Smart home envirement. Proc ICOST 2003, 1st International Conference On Smart homes and health Telematics, Ed. IOS Press, pp.55-60, Paris, September 2003
13. http://www.osgi.org
14. http://www.W3C.org/TR/multimodal-reqs

# On the Design of Ambient Intelligent Systems in the Context of Assistive Technologies

J.L. Sevillano[1], J. Falcó[2], J. Abascal[3], A. Civit-Balcells[1], G. Jiménez[1], S. Vicente[1], and R. Casas[4]

[1] ETSI Informática, Universidad de Sevilla, Av. Reina Mercedes, s/n, 41012, Sevilla, Spain
{sevi,civit,gaji,satur}@atc.us.es

[2] CPS, Edificio A, Universidad de Zaragoza, María de Luna, 3. 50015, Zaragoza, Spain
jfalco@unizar.es

[3] LIPCNE. EHU-UPV, Manuel Lardizabal 1, 20018 Donostia-San Sebastián, Spain
julio.abascal@si.ehu.es

[4] DEE-UPC, Av. del Canal Olímpic, s/n, E-08860 Castelldefels, Spain
Roberto.Casas@upc.es

**Abstract.** The design of Ambient Intelligent Systems (*AISs*) is discussed in the context of assistive technologies. The main issues include ubiquitous communications, context awareness, natural interactions and heterogeneity, which are analyzed using some examples. A layered architecture is proposed for heterogeneous sub-systems integration with three levels of interactions that may be used as a framework to design assistive AISs.

## 1 Ambient Intelligence

The concept of *Ambient Intelligence* (AmI) is one of the main guiding principles for the Future Information Society [1]. It defines a set of properties of a responsive and proactive environment to enable individuals and devices to interact easily. There are a number of key research areas in the development of AISs [2], including components related to ambience (smart materials, sensor and embedded systems technologies, ubiquitous communications, adaptive software, etc.) and intelligence (natural interactions, context awareness, emotional computing, etc.). Efforts should also be made to integrate and converge these specific components.

A new challenge is the development of complex distributed systems that integrate many heterogeneous digital devices and services and their networks into everyday environments [2,3]. In this paper, we consider how existing and future devices and subsystems could be integrated to design AISs in the context of assistive technologies. First we identify the key components of an AIS [4]:

- *Ubiquitous communications:* access at anytime and from any place or (mobile) device. In this case, mobile does not only mean that it is carried by the user, but that it is actually "on the move". Guaranteeing ubiquitous access is the most important infrastructure to support AmI. Wireless connections now permit low-cost commercial solutions for this type of communication.

K. Miesenberger et al. (Eds.): ICCHP 2004, LNCS 3118, pp. 914–921, 2004.

- *Context awareness:* defined as the *use* of information to characterize the *situation* of an *entity* (person, place, object) [5]. The *situation* may have several "dimensions" [6]:
  - o Location awareness (the most studied issue); adaptation to changing geographical positions, location-based services, etc.
  - o Temporal awareness; including time schedule of events.
  - o Personal awareness; dynamic adaptation to user needs, abilities or preferences.
  - o Other dimensions; device (processing power, battery) or physical environment (noise).

  Finally, the correct *use* of this information involves taking the appropriate actions autonomously [7], although current systems fall short. The problem is probably that AmI requires common sense decisions about everyday situations, but this apparently modest reasoning is the most difficult to emulate [8]. On the other hand, several experimental studies have reported that users are willing to be active [6]. These two considerations suggest that in some cases a simpler solution would be to let the users provide context information (location, personal) and configure or select the most appropriate service. Furthermore, the information provided by one user may be useful for another with similar characteristics or abilities. So, we could develop useful AISs with a limited intelligence.
- *Natural interactions*: AISs should be based on a user centered approach (the user is *the* single master device) instead of a device centered approach. This is a somewhat more technological version of the ISTAG *holistic citizen-centered* view, which also includes other factors like culture and business [2]. Obviously, the approach is especially important in the context of assistive technologies. Smooth integration between user and all subsystems requires natural languages (speech, gestures, etc.), reduced learning effort and services that are easy to find and use.
- *Heterogeneity:* A major problem with AIS design is the integration and interaction among heterogeneous subsystems. A common channel is needed to communicate all subsystems, the latter were probably not designed to interact with each other. Services and information from a given subsystem should be described using common languages and media formats to be accessible to other subsystems. This issue also affects previously described components. For example, interaction between context-aware subsystems requires common context representations that are independent of the applications. But it is not just a simple problem of using a common *format*. Further issues are how this context information is interchanged among subsystems, how services are discovered or offered, and how they are integrated in user interfaces.

Other research issues like smart materials and device and sensor technologies are more related to individual "components" than to the integration of components into AISs. Advances in these individual technologies (mainly related to "ambience" rather than to "intelligence") would improve some aspects of these systems, providing smaller, cheaper and more powerful devices, but may not represent significant achievements towards real AISs.

## 2 AISS and Assistive Technologies

### 2.1 Ubiquitous Access

Ambient intelligence requires ubiquitous access when the user is the master and main element of the system. Generally speaking, ubiquitous communication allows access to services that are not restricted by the location of resources/users. This is particularly well suited for people with mobility restrictions, but it may also be useful for the handicapped who want to access assistive services through personalized interfaces in unfamiliar environments. For instance, a visually impaired mobile user should be able to access audio descriptions ubiquitously or alternatives to semaphores or warning light signals. Moreover, support is greatly improved if the user can access services from different locations. One example is a common remote control for TV, answering the phone from a wheelchair, turning lights on or off and opening the door. More advanced systems include monitoring user location in terms of safety (falls), support or comfort, or informing about tasks to be performed at a certain time due to cognitive disabilities. All of these require ubiquitous access.

### 2.2 Context Awareness

For systems that adapt their function in terms of the environment, the first aspect that seems to be taken into account is physical position. Location awareness requires external inputs regarding the geographical (absolute/relative) position of the user, which is particularly useful in special situations (e.g. unfamiliar environments). Typical applications track user location, including assisted navigation (e.g. semi-automatically guided wheelchairs in structured environments: hospitals, airports, etc.), care for people who may get lost (e.g. elderly residences [9]), etc. Another situation is location based services [6] where the definition of user location is less accurate and the question is what services are offered at specific locations. For instance, visitor guides and information at the entrance of hospitals or residences or facilities for wheelchair users. For a mobile user, these services may change and, more importantly, the infrastructure and even the positioning system may vary when users move from one place to another.

With personal awareness, services and information can be adapted to user needs, abilities, preferences, privileges and state. This is especially useful for people with limited physical and/or cognitive abilities. For example, the timing of automatic doors may depend on user mobility restrictions or a tourist guidance system may propose alternative routes for wheelchair users. In this context, one of the main issues is a generic and universal description of personal abilities and characteristics.

Personal parameters may be *static* or *dynamic*. Static parameters include abilities and limitations, special needs, type of interface and personal preferences. The system could memorize user-preferred options for frequently visited locations to propose a default (room temperature, music, light level). Dynamic parameters include mood or anxiety levels that are sensed or inferred from user response. Depending on the system intelligence, it could learn from user behavior (e.g. infer voluntary movements from uncontrolled tremor) and adapt these dynamic parameters. Once the system has learned to detect the situations, it can take palliative actions, such as playing relaxing music.

Other aspects of context awareness include time of the day or week, special dates, sequencing of events (e.g. time orientation for the mentally disabled), technological awareness (bandwidth, display resolution, battery capacity, computational power), and environmental (weather conditions), building or outside conditions (restricted areas, crowded areas).

All of these context dimensions should be used together. For example personal location-based services and information (e.g. audio environmental description for visually impaired people) can be combined with avoiding useless content (e.g. alternative wheelchair routes for a non-wheelchair user). On the other hand, personal preferences or privileges depend on location. Available location or personal information may be time dependent, e.g. if the user wants to plan his/her subsequent activities when privileges or available services are time-limited.

### 2.3 Natural Interactions

In AmI, technology should be enabled by simple and effortless interactions [3]. Current research focuses on so called *Natural* interactions through speech, gestures and facial expressions. These general advancements can benefit assistive technologies provided that accessible human-machine interfaces are designed following the Design-for-All policy [10]. Since these new technologies may present accessibility problems, user interfaces should be able to cope with diversity, including the disabled. A mixed approach can be used to guarantee universal access while considering specific interaction devices for people with special needs [11]. Another problem with AISs is that interactions between the user and the rest of elements usually occur with little or no advance planning. In other words, there is a need for spontaneous and occasional use [6]. Therefore, natural interactions are not only a problem of using advanced/accessible interfaces, but also of interfacing devices or services without *a priori* knowledge of what type of device we may encounter.

### 2.4 Support for Heterogeneous Subsystems and Service Interaction

The whole system should be able to support the interaction of heterogeneous networks, services and applications. Assistive technologies are very heterogeneous when attending needs due to individual and temporal variations. Moreover, devices were designed by different manufacturers using different technologies for heterogeneous applications [14]. The Design-for-All concept considers the lack of simplification usually made when considering a standard user. At the same time, this lack of standardization and individual diversity and variability increases heterogeneity in subsystem development, both in terms of applications and services, in a kind of vicious circle.

## 3 Layered Architecture for Sub-system Interactions

Here we consider the integration/interaction of heterogeneous sub-systems, and propose a layered architecture.

In previous studies, the term *interoperability* refers to mean interactions among systems at higher levels [2,12,13,14,15]. Usually, a reduced version of the OSI standard of layers is used, sometimes including non-OSI levels like *Internetworking* (including the routing and internetworking components) and *Middleware*, which could be defined as an interface among applications and the network operating system, equivalent to session and presentation levels of OSI [16]. However, from the point of view of subsystem interactions, a three level definition may be more useful, including the *Application level* (the classical one defined in OSI model), the *Middleware level*, and the *Internetworking level*, with all the lower level functions in our model (transport, network, data link and physical layer).

The systems to be connected are also distributed. The three levels help to model the interaction among systems with different types of interactions depending on the level. The interactions are named *Interconnectivity*, *Interoperability* and *Interfunctionality* at the Internetworking, Middleware and Application levels, respectively. In the next section we revise and reformulate these concepts.

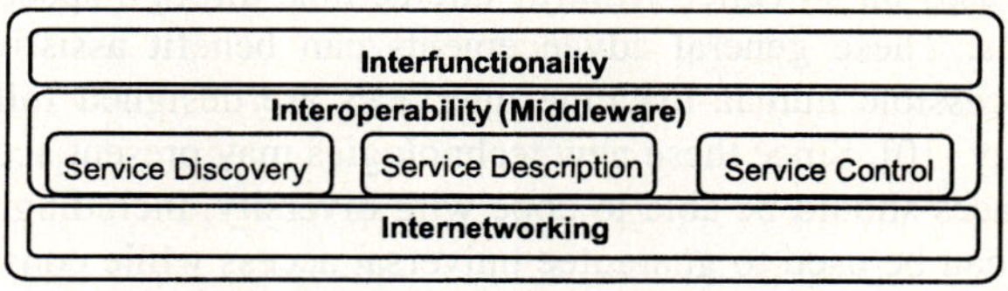


**Fig. 1.** Layered architecture for sub-system interactions

### 3.1 Interconnectivity

The *interconnectivity* between heterogeneous systems is defined as the ability to interact at the internetworking level. A good example is the Internet, which has a robust and contrasted solution based on the IP protocol [14], and other advantages such as direct Internet access in *home automation* through *Residential Gateways* [17]. This configuration permits environmental control in a remote mode via a web page [18,19,20]. Other solutions for interconnection include HAVi, most domotic systems and the *Simple Control Protocol (SCP)*. None of them are based on IP, but they all involve the interaction of devices in somewhat homogeneous environments. In some cases a combination of these two approaches is the best solution. Most devices can be connected through IP networks while secondary (maybe simpler devices like sensors), are connected using non-IP communications. In this case a gateway is used to interconnect IP and non-IP subnetworks.

There are two options regarding the gateway development to link different media, depending on the context. A centralized system can be used for interconnectivity [13], such as in home automation where the *residential gateway* interconnects all heterogeneous networks at home and supports Internet access [15,17]. In other contexts a system of several interconnected gateways could be used, as in large buildings (airports, hotels). But more problems remain, such as finding the most adequate access point or handoff for mobile systems [21].

### 3.2 Interoperability

The concept of interoperability is widely used to describe interaction among devices at all levels [14], including control, configuration and information sharing in different formats [15]. To distinguish this term from *interconnectivity*, we consider *interoperability* related to the sharing services at the middleware level, such as import/export services [13]. Interoperability can provide a set of services to all elements. In the literature there is a general agreement about the functions that should be related with interoperability ([16, 22]), including dynamic service discovering (periodically or triggered by determined events [17]), service description (including actions that may be performed, properties that may be useful, even devices for which connection was not planned), and service control (actions and modifications of state or attributes of a service in a sub-network from another device connected to a different sub-network). The usefulness of this interoperability will be greater for mobile devices, changing environments and pervasive computing.

A number of architectures can support these functions (Jini, UPnP), but not all of them are useful in the environments and applications for Ambient Intelligence. There are three basic issues to take into account in systems with several heterogeneous networks that include mobile devices with wireless connections [16]:

- Mobile devices usually have limited resources (computing power, bandwidth, memory). The complexity needed or desired for some functions should be placed in fixed systems.
- Interconnectivity cannot be guaranteed at any time. Wireless connections may suffer frequent connection losses, that forces *asynchronous* communications.
- Mobility and environmental variability in systems that require *context dependent computation* (which is central to the Ambient Intelligence concept, see above).

### 3.3 Interfunctionality

There is an interaction among subsystems at the interoperability level. As a result, the services can be discovered and shared as a *syntactic* interaction, without considering their "meaning". We propose a higher level of *semantic* interactions, similar to those described in the literature for other fields [10,23,24]. Obviously the usefulness of the service and its applicability should be described in more detail. Several languages have been proposed, such as RDF (Resource Description Language) [25] and future work will address the issue of which language best suits AmI applications.

Interfunctionality would add two main values for subsystem interactions. First, the semantic descriptions allow us to pre-select the services previewed as useful for the applications of a particular subsystem. This allows a selection for limited resource subsystems when entering environments with higher richness of services or high complexity. Thus, the system can have a set of available services, and every subsystem can choose the most useful or manageable via semantic interaction. Although users may be active (selecting and configuring the most useful and appropriate services), pre-selection is often desirable to offer adapted assistive services to the right people. Excess or useless contents must be avoided because the users will reject them [6].

Second, interfunctionality can be used to adapt or empower the functionality of existing applications according to new services. The new applications may become available based on the new services. One example is a wheelchair user with an assisted navigation application who enters a building with a positioning and location system. Under user supervision, the navigation system can ask for information about the path to follow to reach the desired destination, and then incorporate the positioning service to follow it. The functionality of navigation assistance has improved greatly due to the new services and involve more than just avoiding bumping into objects and helping when passing doors.

## 4 Conclusions

In this paper, the design of Ambient Intelligent Systems (*AISs*) is discussed in the context of assistive technologies. AISs include several devices and sub-systems that should provide support for ubiquitous communications, context awareness and natural interactions, and also deal with heterogeneity. As a kind of higher layer, interaction among these sub-systems is identified as a key issue. We identify three levels of interactions, including a higher, semantic interaction that would extend the usefulness of future AISs.

## Acknowledgements

This work was supported by the Spanish MCyT project TIC2001-1868-C03.

## References

1. ISTAG (Information Society Technologies Advisory Group) report: "Strategic Orientations & Priorities for IST in FP6". 2002. http://www.cordis.lu/ist/istag.htm.
2. ISTAG Draft Consolidated Report: "Ambient Intelligence: from vision to reality". Sept. 2003. http://www.cordis.lu/ist/istag.htm.

3. M. Lindwer *et al.*, "Ambient Intelligence Visions and Achievements: Linking Abstract Ideas to Real-World Concepts". Proc. DATE'03. pp. 10-15, March 2003.
4. J.L. Sevillano, "Smart Homes: Ambient Intelligence". 1st French-Spanish Workshop Assist. Techs. http://www.ifrath.univ-metz.fr/article.php3?id_article=57
5. A.K. Dey, "Understanding and Using Context". Pers. Ubiquit. Comput. 5(2001)20-24.
6. E. Kaasinen, "User Needs for Location-aware Mobile Services". Pers. Ubiquit. Comput. 7:(2003)70-79.
7. T. Erickson, "Some Problems with the Notion of Context-Aware Computing". Communications of the ACM 45(2002)102-104.
8. A.A. Hopgood, "Artificial Intelligence: Hype or Reality?". Computer 36-5 (2003) 24-28.
9. J. Falcó, "Assistive Technology for old adults and mental disability". 1st French-Spanish Workshop Assist. Techs. http://www.ifrath.univ-metz.fr/article.php3?id_article=57
10. Stephanidis C., Savidis A. "Universal Access in the Information Society: Methods, Tools, and Interaction Technologies". Universal Access in the Information Society. 1(2001)40-55.
11. J. Abascal, "Accessibility to Information and Communication Technology". 1st French-Spanish Workshop Assist. Techs. http://www.ifrath.univ-metz.fr/article.php3?id_article=57.
12. J.H. Jahnke, M. D'Entremont, J. Stier, "Facilitating the Programming of the Smart Home". IEEE Wireless Communications (2002) 70-76.
13. Cho S.Y., "Framework for the Composition and Interoperation of the Home Appliances based on Heterogeneous Middleware in Residential Networks". IEEE Trans. Consumer Electronics 48-3. (2002) 484-489.
14. Carpenter B. E.: "Interoperability among Heterogeneous Communications Networks- an IETF Perspective". Computer Standards & Interfaces 20(1998)147-149
15. Rasheed Y., Edwards J., Tai C., "Home Interoperability Framework for the Digital Home". Intel Technology Journal 6 (2002) 5-16.
16. Mascolo C., Capra L., Emmerich W.: "Mobile Computing Middleware". Tutorial in IEEE MWCN'02. Stockholm, Sweden. Sep. 2002.
17. Wils A. et al.: "Device Discovery via Residential Gateways". IEEE Trans. Consumer Electronics, 48-3(2002)478-483
18. Saif U., Gordon D., Greaves D.: "Internet Access to a Home Area Network". IEEE Internet Computing 5-1(2001) 54-63.
19. Corcoran P.M., Desnonnet J., Biogioi P., Lupu I.: "Home Network Infrastructure for Handheld/Wearable Appliances". IEEE Trans. Consumer Electronics, 48-3(2002) 490-495.
20. Nakajima T. et al.: "A Virtual Overlay Network for Integrating Home Appliances". Proc. 2002 Symp. Applications and the Internet. Nara, Japan. Jan. 2002. Pp. 246-253.
21. Pahlavan K. et al.: "Handoff in Hybrid Mobile Data Networks". IEEE Personal Communications (2000) 34-47.
22. Miller B. A., Nixon T., Tai C., Wood M.D.: "Home Networking with Universal Plug and Play". IEEE Communications Magazine 39 (2001) 104-109.
23. Paolucci, M.; Sycara, K.; "Autonomous Semantic Web services". IEEE Internet Computing, 7-5(2003) 34 -41.
24. Special issue on "Web Services". Computer, vol.36, Oct. 2003.
25. S. Decker, P. Mitra, S. Melnik, "Framework for the Semantic Web: An RDF Tutorial". IEEE Internet Computing 4-3(2000) 68-73.

# PACS: Communication and Environment Control System for Disabled

Vidas Lauruska

Siauliai University, Faculty of Technology
141 Vilniaus Str., LT-5400, Siauliai, Lithuania
vidas.lauruska@tf.su.lt

**Abstract.** There are a lot of disabled people in the world. In many cases persons with severe disabilities who can't move or speak are isolated. These persons at least have one primitive way to communicate with others (it could be head movements, eye blink, voice intonations, mimics and others). The usage of electronics can help to transform it into understandable communication signs for others or into control signals for devices. Electronics means improve self-sufficiency of disabled people and enable communication with others. We have created communication and environment control system for physically disabled persons with speech and language impairments. A very important feature of this system is that it is controlled by one on/off type switch. Alternative input devices as head pointer, eye blink registrar, person's capacity registrar, suck-blow tube, etc, can be used instead of the similar switch.

## 1 Introduction

There are a lot of communication and control equipment designed for the disabled. Most of them are either very primitive, like cards with pictures, or very complex and expensive computer systems [1].

The aim of PACS project is further improvement of communication and environment control for disabled people. The major tasks of project are as follows [2]:

- Providing environment control (it includes lighting, heating, shutters, motorised doors and windows). These functions are available by using EIB network. Also the system can control home equipments such as TV, VCR, Audio systems via IR transmitter;
- Providing communication (telephone, e-mail, SMS, voice intercom). These functions are available on PC by using a special software and an internal PC hardware – the voice modem on the server and the sound cards on both PC's – server and client;
- Providing security (watching the outer, alarm for detection of intruders, safety alarms: gas, fire, smoke detection). A standard security system can be used with RS232 or EIB network to enable communication with the PC and a standard video camera for watching the outer.

The two main user's requirements were identified:

- The system should be simple to operate and entirely controllable through one single switch.
- It should support simple communication and control mode.

K. Miesenberger et al. (Eds.): ICCHP 2004, LNCS 3118, pp. 922–925, 2004.

This project is also useful for other applications (such as games or mechanical assistant) where the user's hands are occupied and applications dictate the use of auxiliary 'hands-free' input. It can also be used as a signalization or control device in hospitals for people in postoperative period.

## 2 Methods

The principle of the system's user interface is based on scanning OS MS Windows (9x, NT, XP) control elements (mostly buttons) on virtual menu (button menu), and waiting for control signal at the same time. The virtual button is activated on the screen for a short timeout and this timeout interval is set up programmably. The next button is focused if there is no control signal, etc. The user activates the focused button by ON-OFF switch. The simplest switch can be a separate key which is connected parallel to the standard keyboard's "enter" or "space" keys. The main function of the P is to scan Windows menus with control and communication options. When the user presses the switch, the PC sends appropriate data to EIB network or infrared transmitter depending on data type. We used EIB Falcon run-time components to enable the full bus access from a Windows application [3]. When EIB device gets a telegram, it executes an action given by the telegram and after the finishing action, it sends a response telegram to the PC informing whether action is successful or not. According to the response telegram PC displays an appropriate message to user. So the user is always being informed about the current state of controlled device. In the same way he knows if another user controls any device on EIB network.

Graphical user interface can be design as 3 levels dialogue structure with buttons: 1st level – selection of available rooms in the flat or house; 2nd level – selection of available controlled objects (lights, door, window, etc) in the selected room; 3rd level – selection of available functions (commands) in the selected object. (For example: my room -> window -> open). The view of this user's interface is shown in figure 1. The next realization of graphical user's interface may be a 3D room drawing with all available controlled objects presented in the drawing.

Communication mode is realized by using an alternative text typing way and virtual keyboard. The button in virtual keyboard is selected by scanning buttons in the keyboard. The keyboard must be with minimum of "x" letters, "x" is the number of letters in language. The maximum of keyboard's size is limited by the seeking time of element in keyboard. The seeking time increases when we use more buttons. So we need to find the most optimal way between keyboard's possibilities and the increase time of reaching the element in keyboard.

The second step is to choose the layout of the keyboard. We must know the absolute frequency of the letters' repeating in the language if we use non-predictive typing. Mostly used letter must be in position that we can reach in the shortest time and the seldom-used letter must be in position that we can reach in the longest time. We must know the absolute frequency of the first letters in the word if we use predictive typing. Letters must be arranged in the same way as in non-predictive typing.

We must design the algorithm of prediction if we use predictive typing. There are a few possibilities. First of all we can predict letters. It is the simplest way. Next type of prediction – prediction of words after typing the first letter or after typing the first two letters. Also other types of prediction can be used. We select the word prediction after two letters are typed.

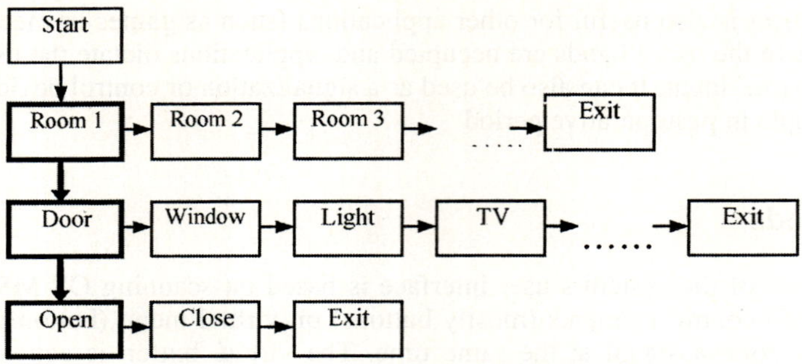


**Fig. 1.** The view of user's interface

The last step is to choose the scanning method. There are three main scanning methods: serial scanning, rejecting half of keyboards elements scanning [4], column-raw scanning [5]. Serial scanning is very slow; rejecting half of elements scanning is useful when the keyboard elements' (letters or symbols) frequency of appearing in the word do not have a big difference. Column-raw scanning is more useful when the keyboard elements' (letters or symbols) frequency of appearing in the word have a big difference. In the Lithuanian language the difference of frequency of appearing letters in the word between the most popular letter and the most unpopular letter is 60 times.

## 3 Results

We have found that for the Lithuanian virtual keyboard the most suitable scanning method is column-row method.

The description of the experiment: every user have got 10 statements and one minute for typing of each statement, scanning speed was 4/3 step per second (waiting time for user's reaction is 750ms).

An experiment shows that it is difficult to reach high typing speed using scanning method and one ON-OFF type switch. The achieved typing speed is 16 symbols per minute. It is about 3 times slower than typing using eye gaze, and 40 times slower than speaking speed.

For environment control we used a Smart home (or Domotics) technology. Domotics technology is dedicated for command, control and supervision of home environment. Mostly it includes safety alarms, HVAC but excludes telecommunication and entertainment events. Smart home devices are connected to a network (bus). The type of the network is different from telecommunications networks.

Several types of domotics are available and we selected EIB [3] due to its advantages and EIB was used for distribution of control and command signals.

The designed system allows the integration of the functions that a disabled user should like to use. This includes not only home environment control (lighting, heating, shutters, motorized door and windows) but also entertainment equipments (TV, VCR, DVD and Audio systems), communication (e-mail, SMS) and security (alarm for detection of intruders, safety alarms). A PC must be connected with a universal infrared transmitter for communication and entertainment equipment control. A PC is also used for user's interface implementation.

## 4 Conclusion

We have used modular structure in our system's software and hardware. It allows more flexible adaptation to individual abilities and needs of a user. Also there is a possibility of easy system upgrade by changing or adding new home environmental equipments and communication events when necessary. The usage of standard and certified devices shows the system's reliability, flexibility and safety.

## Acknowledgements

This research was carried out during the project PACS of the Eureka program with the co-financing of the Lithuanian State Science and Studies Foundation.

## References

1. Lauruska, V., Musteikis, T.: Developing Predictive Communication System for the Physically Disabled People. In: Miesenberger, K., Klaus, J.,Zagler, W. (eds): ICCHP 2002. Lecture Notes in Computer Science, Vol . 2398. Springer-Verlag, Berlin Heidelberg New York (2002) 267-270
2. Serafinavicius, P., Lauruska, V.: Adaptive Smart Home System. Human-Computer Interaction. Theory and practice (Part II). (Volume 2). LEA Publishers (2003) 133-137
3. European Installation Bus Association. `http://www.eiba.com`
4. Vera, J., Jiménez, M., Roca, J.: Case Study. EIB Bus as a Key Technology for Integrating People with Disabilities, EIB event 2000, scientific conference and technology workshop. `http://www.dteupct.es/personal/manuel.jimenez/investigacion/congresos/pdfs/EIB2000.pdf`
5. Kubilinskas, E., Lauruska, V.: Smart Home System for Physically Disabled Persons with Verbal Communication Difficulties. Assistive Technology – Added Value to the Quality of Life. AAATE'01. IOS Press (2001) 300-304.

# Performance Analysis of User Interface for the Disabled in Real-Time Ubiquitous Information Network

Yung Bok Kim[1] and Jong Yong Kim[2]

[1] Department of Computer Engineering, Sejong University
KunJa-Dong, Kwang-jin-ku, Seoul, 143-747, Korea
yungbkim@sejong.ac.kr

[2] Information System Office, Financial Supervisory Service
27, Yoido-Dong, Youngdeungpo-Gu, Seoul, Korea
kimscots@fss.or.kr

**Abstract.** Beyond the computer networking, the wired Internet and mobile Internet penetrate deeply in all kinds of information processing systems and applications. Web-based services with wired Internet and mobile Internet should be considered for convenient user interface for the disabled and elderly people without any gap of the Digital Divide. The Web server for knowledge and information should be unified as a center for real-time information network in the milieu of ubiquitous computing. We studied the performance analysis of user interface for the disabled in real-time ubiquitous information network based on wired and mobile Internet.

## 1 Introduction

The wireless, mobile Web promises to provide users with anytime, anywhere access to the same information; ubiquitous Web access should also facilitate greater acceptance of new services that are specialized for mobile use [1].

We studied new performance analysis methodology for ubiquitous information network, based on the user's perspective for the disabled, i.e. at the customer's viewpoint about the services and contents for information processing in this ubiquitous computing environment. We introduce the new performance analysis for real-time unified portal for worldwide information network based on wired and mobile Internet, especially about user interface at the customer's perspective for the disabled.

We will discuss the user interface with the results from real implementation of a unified portal for the disabled in real-time ubiquitous information network, e.g. Korean information network as an example of a ubiquitous information network using PCs as well as handheld phones. With the proliferation of new Information Technologies, we need to consider convenient way for the disabled to overcome the Digital Divide. We need to provide the simple user interface for the disabled and elderly people, considering the performance analysis of user interface.

## 2 Real-Time Mobile User Interface and Performance Analysis

In many countries, a better access to Web services and Web administration is becoming an important issue; and a few action lines of improvement for the Web Content

K. Miesenberger et al. (Eds.): ICCHP 2004, LNCS 3118, pp. 926–929, 2004.

Accessibility Guidelines are suggested [2]. For user interface in the real-time information network, even the input of characters becomes important for retrieval of information or registration of information, especially with keypad in the mobile phone for the disabled. To access the unified portal ubiquitously, the user interface for the disabled and elderly in the Silver Society should be as convenient as possible even for typing-in the domain names or URLs, or information.

We studied the important performance metric, delay, at the user's perspective for the disabled as well as normal users to prevent the gap of the Digital Divide. For example, for the mobile user, let's assume that the random variables, the round-trip response time for user's single interaction in a session, from user to the contents in DB through wired/mobile Internet before next interaction, with mobile phone is $r_m$, which is composed of the preparation time for the disabled to get mobile device (e.g. handheld phone, etc) in his hand is $U$; the time spent by the disabled with mobile phone to do appropriate action for service is $D$; the aggregate time to the web Server after the mobile device through wired/mobile Internet for mobile service is $S$ (the conventional network time is embedded here); the time depending upon mobile contents is $C$.

The session time may be dependent on this content retrieval or registration, and there may be several back and forth iterations. However we simply use the aggregate time instead of breaking them down, then

$$r_m = r'_m + r_{mback} = U + D + S + C + r_{mback} \tag{1}$$

The returning round trip time, from the content retrieval time to the requesting user through Web server and wired/mobile Internet using mobile device, is $r_{mback}$.

Among the above random variables without subscript for mobile, i.e. the performance metrics, ($U$, $D$, $S$, $C$) for mobile user and PC user, the most dominating factor, i.e. the random variable, may be different from person to person. We can order the dominating random variables, after estimation with an implementation for information network with the unified server, http://ktrip.net [3].

For the real-time application using wired Internet and mobile Internet, the dominating factor and the variance of that random variable should be bounded within the deterministic response time. To be deterministic for real-time application, the user should be skilled, the user interface of device should be convenient, the network should be stable if possible, the server should be efficient and have high performance for the dedicated application, and finally the contents for information processing should be simple as possible with simplified and efficient format.

We also considered the packet size to be independent from the network traffic condition as well as the simple service in the web server to be independent from the load of the web server. The bandwidth requirement for wireless or mobile Internet, should be as little as possible to be immune to the network traffic condition; also that will be good in terms of degradation caused by the other rich multimedia contents for information processing. The user's preparation time $U$ will be shortened depending upon the proliferation of ubiquitous devices for the disabled, e.g. special mobile Internet devices for the disabled and handicapped users.

Let's consider the average time with mobile devices and this is related to the device time $D$. For writing the information in real-time way, the user's handling speed of mobile devices is one of important performance factors in any mobile Internet services for the disabled with the mobile phone. We studied to order the dominating factors in the overall performance at the user's perspective for the disabled and handicapped users. We found that there were some difference between the relationship for wired Internet with PC ($U > D > C > S$) and the relationship for mobile Internet with mobile phone ($U > D > S > C$). Therefore the user interface design for the disabled with the mobile device in the ubiquitous computing environment (i.e. $U$ becomes smaller as the ubiquity increases.) is most important to decrease the time $D$, that is heavily related to the mobile user interface for the disabled and handicapped users.

## 3 Implementation and Empirical Results

The implemented system is as follows; for the operating system, Windows 2000 server; for wired and mobile Internet web services, IIS 5.0 web server and ASP 3.0; for DBMS, MS SQL server; for the mobile markup language, WML, mHTML and HDML. The E1 (2.048 Mbps) Internet communication line to the web server, i.e. the unified portal, for both wired and mobile Internet service, is being used.

We could get the relationship between $S$ and $C$. Firstly, with the PC using wired Internet, the time $S$ may be considered rather short period (around 5~30 msec with Ping, which is related to the $S$; but with 5Kbytes web page for PC the response time is around 2~3 seconds, which is related to the $S$ and $C$, here $C$ is much larger than $S$); and with PC, for larger contents (over 20Kbytes, in our case), the server time is longer than the shorter packet (below 5Kbytes). Secondly, with recent mobile phone using mobile Internet (for short packets below 1.5Kbytes and even around 5Kbytes), the response time is around 12 seconds with little deviation through the WAP gateway; therefore the time $S$ is longer than $C$, where $S$ includes the elapsed time at the gateway in the mobile Internet. We need to try continuously to decrease the times $U$ and $D$ for the disabled and handicapped people. We can also consider speech technology to decrease the time $D$. Even though they are not mainly focusing on the mobile applications, there are some examples of the speech applications as follow.

The maturity of speech technologies represents a great opportunity for people working with other or/and with a piece of information through Interactive Voice Systems; and the research with the Voice XML technology was considered for the universal access paradigm by speech for the new generation of interactive systems [4]. With the comparison between Voice XML approach and structural approach, Raynal and Serrurier [5] studied an HTML browser for visually impaired people. For the disabled and handicapped people, the ubiquity and mobile user interface should be studied for each handicapped case, with the metrics $U$ and $D$, respectively; those will be studied in our further research.

## 4 Conclusions

The performance analysis of user interface for the disabled in real-time ubiquitous information network with the wired and mobile Internet, considering the effective response time with efficient investment was studied for unified information service to the disabled and elderly people in the ubiquitous information network. For more future works, the voice application for the disabled and elderly people in the ubiquitous information network will be added for the real-time retrieval of information as well as for real-time registration of information or advertisement to reduce the dominating times, i.e. the discussed user time and device time; and the case study for each handicapped people will be done in further research with the dominating metrics.

## References

1. Pashtan, A., Kollipara, S. and Pearce, M.: Adapting Content for Wireless Web Services. IEEE Internet Computing. September-October 2003. (2003) 79-85
2. Duchateau, S., Boulay, D., Tchang-Ayo, C. and Burger, D.: A Strategy to Achieve the Accessability of Public Web Sites. ICCHP 2002, LNCS 2398 (2002) 58-60
3. Ubiquitous Information Network Site (test site), Korean Information Network Web site: http://ktrip.net
4. Privat, R., Vigouroux, N., Truillet, P. and Oriola, B.: Accessibility and Affordance for Voice Interactive Systems with VoiceXML Technology. ICCHP 2002, LNCS 2398, 61-63
5. Raynal, M. and Serrurier, M.: CYNTHIA: An HTML Browser for Visually Handicapped People. ICCHP 2002, LNCS 2398 (2002) 353-359

# The HM2PH Project: A Database to Help Prescription of Assistive Technologies

Jérôme Leloup[1], Pierre Gaucher[1], and Sybille Pellieux[2]

[1] Computer Science Laboratory of the University of Tours
Computer Science Department of Polytech'Tours
64 avenue J. Portalis, 37200 Tours, France
{Jerome.Leloup,Pierre.Gaucher}@univ-tours.fr
[2] Hospital Doctor, Service of Physical Medicine and Rehabilitation, CHU Trousseau
37000 Tours, France
S.Pellieux@chu-tours.fr

**Abstract.** The aim of the HM2PH (Habitat Modulaire et Mobile pour Personnes Handicapées) project is to specify the functionalities of a movable, opened and adapted living area, enabling a better autonomy by means of appropriate assistive technologies, home automation and electronic devices, linked by a home network. Moreover, it should be able to be inserted in a strongly medicalized facility, as well as in a familial area. To design the interior layout of this adapted living area in a minimal time, we propose a software tool that will allow making the layouts taking the constraints, needs and wills of the resident into account. After a short presentation of the software (see *http://www.hant.li.univ-tours.f/webhant/HM2PH* for further details), this paper describes the databases used in our tool.

## 1 Introduction

According to the last statistics, the rate of disabled and elderly people is constantly increasing. This induces several problems, including that of finding the best way to take care of them and overall the way to keep them at home. The aim of the HM2PH project (initially CNHL [5] then HMPH [3]) is to specify the functionalities of a movable, connected and adapted living area, enabling a better autonomy by means of appropriated assistive technologies, home automation and electronic devices, linked by a home network. Moreover, this house should be able to fit into a strongly medicalized facility as well as in a familial area and should give disabled and elderly people the possibility to live at home as long as possible with an increased autonomy. The same kind of research is presented in [1]. The design of such an adapted area calls for skills such as architecture, occupational therapy, home automation... According to [2], this leads to important design times (about 2 to 3 months) and costs. The use of a specific software environment, which will help during the conception, will tend to reduce these two points. This software will enable the design of the layouts of the HM2PH, taking into account the constraints linked to the disabilities (architecture, home automation, furniture, circulation...) and those linked to the needs and wills of the future resident. Moreover, the software includes an analysis step in order to understand the disabilities of the future inhabitant and to help an occupational therapist to

K. Miesenberger et al. (Eds.): ICCHP 2004, LNCS 3118, pp. 930–936, 2004.

prescript the better devices. Using software to design such an adapted area has been tested in [4] and should lead to significant results. This paper presents the software, and particularly focuses on the databases that help the prescription. It ends with a conclusion on the work done and the prospects of the project.

## 2 The Software

### 2.1 Presentation

The aim of the software is to create several layouts for a HM2PH taking several constraints into account: the constraints linked to the construction of a building for disabled people, those linked to basic architecture, and finally those linked to the wishes of the inhabitant. Indeed, the software gives the possibility to create own constraints, for example the orientations of the rooms, the number of bedrooms...

The first step of the software is an analysis of the disabilities of the future resident. With a few forms, it proposes a list of devices that could be included in the living area in order to give him a better autonomy. This step, which could be seen as a way to bypass the work of an occupational therapist, is in fact a way to help him perform his prescription. We found very interesting to include such a help in order to provide the user a tool that quickly retrieve lots of useful information about assistive technologies. It's indeed almost impossible to know all the devices that compensate a disability, and this could lead to the oversight of effective assistive technologies. Moreover, this tool gives a list of producer and suppliers, the dimensions and the price of each device, which significantly saves time.

We now describe the software and its architecture, and we'll focus on the databases and the analysis step. Further information about the other parts (the virtual tour and the automatic creation of the layouts) can be found in [3].

### 2.2 The Software That Helps the Creation of Layouts for the HM2PH

As previously said, we chose to create this software in order to reduce the times and costs needed to draw the layouts of an HM2PH. The software has three main modules, as shown on figure 1. The first module is composed by two databases, which enable the analysis of the future resident's disabilities. The second module is the Automatic Layout Generation Engine (ALGE), which actually computes the layouts of the HM2PH taking the several constraints into account. The last module is the Real Time Virtual Tour, which enables to move in real time into a 3D living area created from the 2D layouts given by the ALGE. The aim of this tour is to provide a way to assess the configuration and the equipments of the living area, and later to interact with the different devices in the scene. We'll now explain the module with the databases, how it works and how it can be used to analyze the disabilities of the resident and thus retrieve a list of devices that should give him a better autonomy in his house.

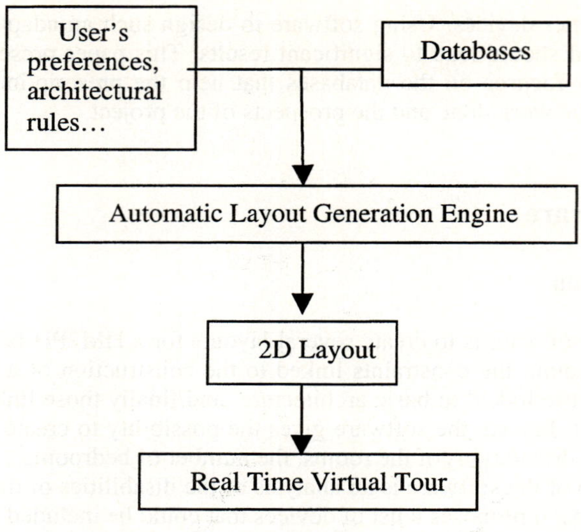


**Fig. 1.** The synoptic of the software

## 2.3 The Module of Analysis

This module is composed by two databases. The first database describes the different rooms that can be put into the living area. It thus gives information about the minimal dimensions and whether or not the room needs water drainage. This precision is used by the ALGE to reduce conception cost by putting all rooms needing water drainage in order to reduce the canalization length. The minimal dimensions used are those advised by the standards for buildings that accommodate disabled people, but the user has the possibility to create rules in order to make the ALGE create layouts with larger rooms.

The second database is the one that enable the actual analysis. It gives several information about each device: a description, the dimensions, the price and a list of producers and vendors for this device. Moreover, this database includes an analysis engine, consisting of a suite of simple forms, which enable to help the user do his prescription for the future resident. To schematize, the database associate:

- A room with several assistive technologies,
- A device with several producer and suppliers,
- A disability with several categories of devices,
- A category of devices with several disabilities that avoid the use of devices in this category.

The main idea of the analysis is to associate the devices with a relation between an action and a disability. For example, it associates a magnifying glass with the couple difficulty to read / short-sighted. There are a lot of databases of assistive technologies, and they are often available for consultation on the Internet. The following table presents the most important databases available on the Internet, and how the research can be performed (legend for search modes: 1=keywords, 2 = activity, 3 = trademark, 4 = supplier, 5 = type of product, 6 = iso code, 7 = relation activity/abilities-disabilities).

**Table 1.** Main databases available on the Internet

| Name | Address | Search modes |
|---|---|---|
| AbleData | http://www.abledata.com | 1, 3, 4, 5 |
| Assistive Technology & Software Database Search | http://www.pattan.k12.pa.us:591/atdevices/ device_search.html | 1, 2, 4 |
| AssistiveTech | http://www.assistivetech.net | 1, 2, 4, 5 |
| Autonomia | http://fm01.nic.be/autonomia | 3, 4, 6 |
| Central Remedial Clinic | http://www.crc.ie/atdb/ | 1, 2, 3, 4, 6 |
| Fondation Suisse pour les Téléthèses | http://www.fst.ch/ | 7 |
| Independant Living Center | http://www.ilc.asn.au/home.php | 1, 2, 5 |
| The Boulevard | http://www.blvd.com/ | 2, 5 |

Those databases offer different types of research, but the user have to previously know what he's looking for. They don't act as an actual help for the prescription, and it's necessary to have a lot of time to retrieve a list of devices that could help in a particular case. The only one that should be put apart is the database from the Fondation Suisse pour les Téléthèses. Indeed, this database allows retrieving the devices that should fit a situation after having answered several questions about the person to help. Our database is made on the same principle: a good way to find the best device is to consider the relation between the action to perform and the disabilities and abilities of the person.

To understand how our database works and to use our different forms, we propose to follow an example. The first form to fill asks for the type of disabilities concerning the resident. You can check visual impairments, earring impairments or motor disabilities (see figure 2).

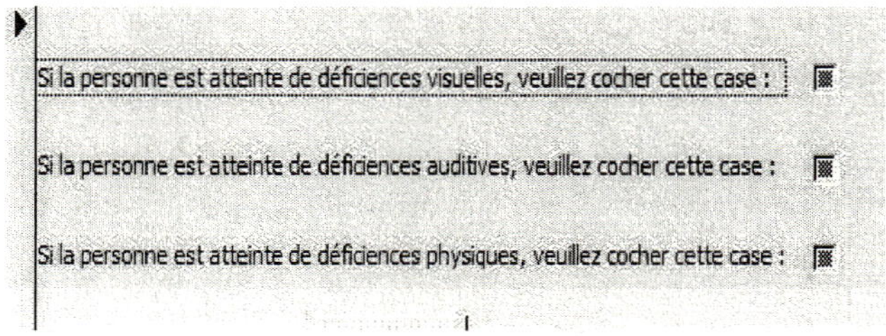


**Fig. 2.** Type of disabilities

After this step, there is a first form with a list of difficulties that may concern the resident. Those difficulties are classified in 6 groups: communication, personal care, home care, chores, mobility and home control of the environment. In the following figure (cf. figure 3), you have for example difficulty to read, difficulty to talk or difficulty to use a computer classified in the category communication.

The user picks several difficulties from the lists. But it's not enough to conclude on the type of devices to use. We have to know the reason that causes the trouble. For example, if the user chose "difficulty to read", we must know whether it's caused by a bad sight, shakings, or the impossibility to turn the pages of the book. So the software opens another form to ask precisions about the selected difficulties (see figure 4).

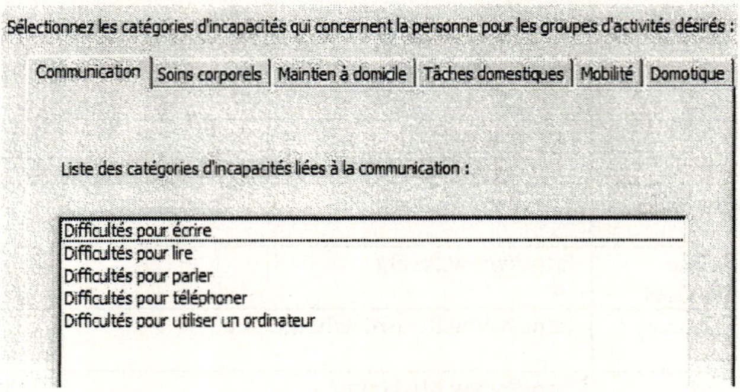


**Fig. 3.** First difficulties the user has to select

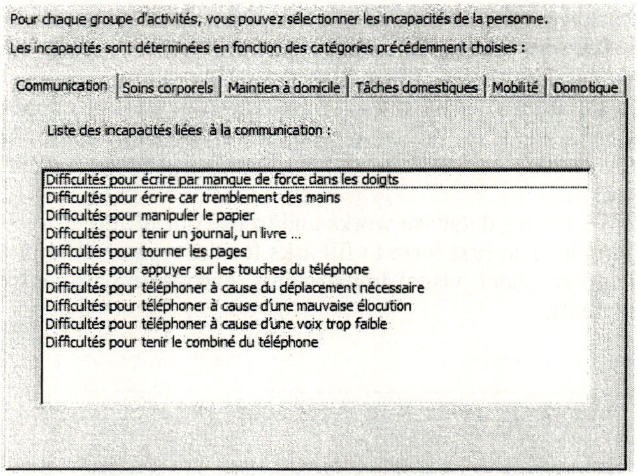


**Fig. 4.** Possible origins of each difficulty previously selected

The possible origins of the difficulties that were selected before are also classified in the same six categories. The user can now select why the resident have the difficulties, and the software will here be able to select the correct devices into the database. It's important to precise that selecting some origins of disabilities will automatically avoid the use of some devices. We previously selected that the user has difficulties to read. The form allows for example the selection of the reason "a lack of strength to hold the book" for this difficulty. The software will thus propose devices that can help the resident to hold the books (desk…). But it will also remove from the list of the potential devices the ones that require the same strength needed to read.

The results of the analysis are given in three lists of devices. The first list presents the devices in alphabetic order. This list only gives the name of each device, and allows selecting those chosen by the user. The second list presents the devices in alphabetic order but with more precisions about each device. It gives descriptions of the device, its dimensions, its price, and a list of manufacturers and suppliers for this device (see figure 5). This list is very useful for the user, and allows making an estimate for the whole living area. The third list gives the devices ordered according to the rooms where it should be set (see figure 6). It's very important for the ALGE which will use this list to draw the complete layouts of each room. Moreover, all selected devices will be included in the real time virtual tour in order to give a very realistic view of the living area.

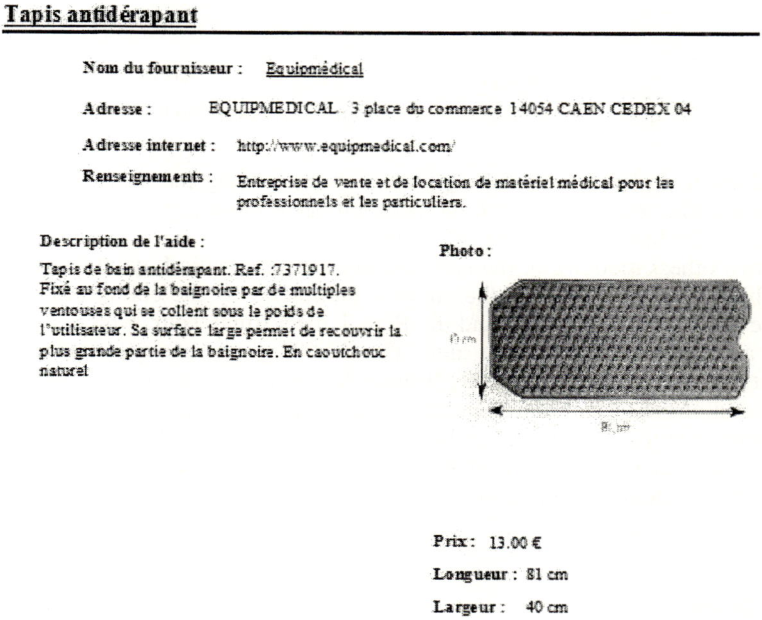


**Fig. 5.** Complete description of each device

## 3 Conclusion and Prospects

During our work on the HM2PH project, we have created a database that allows the analysis of the disabilities of the person who might live in our adapted living area. The aim of this database is to assist a professional (e.g. an occupational therapist) in the prescription of assistive technologies. We think that this database could be a powerful tool and could save precious time.

At the moment the several tests with the database seems convicting, but we are in a phase of assessment with the help of professionals, and we'll be able to conclude accurately after this phase. According to the occupational therapists that we met, the method of analysis which puts in relation the activity and the disabilities (and of course abilities) of the person should lead to a good first prescription. Moreover, the

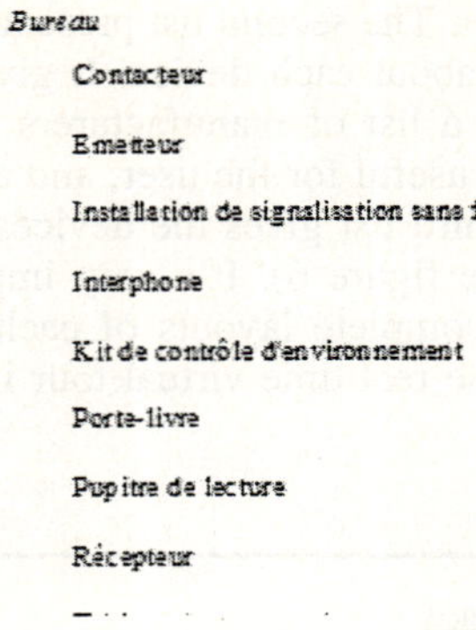


**Fig. 6.** Devices ordered by the rooms where they should be set

information given by the lists of devices allow estimating the costs of the different equipments. The tests done at the moment will give more accurate results about the relevance of the lists given by the software.

The two others modules in the software are the Automatic Layout Generation Engine, which uses the results of the analysis completes by the choices of the user to draw the layouts of each room, and the Real Time Virtual Tour, which allow assessing the architecture of the living area. The ALGE gives relevant results to set the different rooms (see [3]), and the algorithms that will equip each room are in hand. A new version of the virtual tour is in hand too. At the end of the project, we'd like the virtual tour to allow the interaction between the user and the virtual living area. This could be a way to assess the different devices set in each room. We invite you to visit the project website at http://hant.li.univ-tours.fr/webhant/HM2PH for further information.

## References


1. Dewsbury, G., Edge, M.: Designing the Home to Meet the Needs of Tomorrow…Today: Deconstructing and Rebuilding the Home for Life, ENHR 2000 conference, Gavle 26-30 (2000).
2. Kruse, C.: Examples of state funded home modification projects for people with physical disabilities, Technology and Persons with Disabilities conference, March 20-25 (2000).
3. Leloup, J., Gaucher, P., Garcia, J., Siffert, J.: HMPH – "Habitat Mobile pour Personnes Handicapées" – software for the design of an adapted living area, 7th conference of the Association for the Advancement of Assistive Technology in Europe (AAATE), University College of Dublin (Ireland), August 31st – 3rd September (2003).
4. Martins Ferreira, J.M., Amaral, T., Santos, D., Agiannidis, A., Edge, M.: The CUSTODIAN Tool: Simple Design of Home Automation Systems for People with Special Needs, EIB Scientific Conference, Munich Oct (2000).
5. Richard, P, Gaucher, P., Maurel, D.: Projet CNHL : Chambre Nomade pour Handicapés Lourds, Colloque Handicap 2000 – Nouvelles Technologies : assistance technique aux handicapés moteur et sensoriel, Paris 15-16 juinv (2000), pp 101-107.

# Networking and Communication in Smart Home for People with Disabilities

Mahmoud Ghorbel[1], Maria-Teresa Segarra[2], Jérome Kerdreux[2],
Ronan Keryell[2], Andre Thepaut[2], Mounir Mokhtari[1]

[1] Handicom Lab, GET/INT, 9 rue Charles Fourier, 91011 Evry, France
mahmoud.ghorbel@int-evry.fr
[2] GET/ENST Bretagne, Technopôle Brest-Iroise - BP 832 - 29285 Brest Cedex, France
mt.segarra@enst-bretagne.fr

**Abstract.** People with disabilities need several assistive technical aids to increase their autonomy and perform daily living tasks. This paper describes the role of networking and communication in the smart home concept which allows people with disabilities and elderly people to retain a certain level of independence within their daily environment, such as at home, work, school, outside and so on. The purpose of our research activity is to explore the difficulties by determining the most suitable approach to federate the different communication protocols available indoor and outdoor environments. In this paper we are presenting our main concept in the design of the smart home architecture. We also describe our approach to design an open software environment adapted to people with disabilities. This approach is based on the service discovery protocol UPnP (Universal Plan and Play) to discover devices in smart home. It is based also on wireless technologies and protocols (Wifi, Bluetooth, etc.) to enhance mobility and dependency. Some solutions are adapted to favor integration of new modules and devices, and to improve the communication between the different layers of our software architecture.

## 1 Introduction

In order to enhance their quality of life, people with disabilities and elderly people need to be independent and autonomic in their environment. That implies a freedom of moving using wheelchairs, a compensation of upper arm impairments using robots, environmental control systems for home appliances, and so on, without the intervention of another person. Our work does not lie in this last point only, but also in the federation of all these assistive helps within the framework of an intelligent environment defined as the smart homes concept.

Smart homes is the term commonly used to define a residence that uses a home controller to integrate various automation systems (controlling devices together). Integration of the home systems allows communication with one another through the home controller. This enable single button and voice control of various home systems simultaneously, in pre-programmed scenarios or in operating modes.

Several research projects investigated this domain by using multi-agents systems in order to design the smart home architecture [1, 2]. This solution can resolve some problems of communication between existing modules, but seems complex and does

K. Miesenberger et al. (Eds.): ICCHP 2004, LNCS 3118, pp. 937–944, 2004.

not solve the problem of accessibility and multimodality. Our solution is based on a multi-layer architecture, which improves accessibility and supports multimodality with a software configuration tool and a voice recognition module [3]. The Human Machine Interface (HMI) represents an essential layer in our architecture that allows interaction between user, external events, and the system [4]. Interaction with physical devices is ensured by the COM layer (COMmunication) through a particular module called Ametsa (UPnP gateway), able to send commands via IP-enabled, infrared (RC5), and power-lined controlled devices [5]; or through the industrial CAN protocol (Controller Area Network) when it deals with a robot manipulator called MANUS robot. Below, we detail our running designed prototype and how networking technologies are used to cope with communication needs.

## 2 Software Architecture of the Smart Home: A Layered Structure

The Smart Homes concept is composed of modular software components [7]. This architecture is based on our experience on controlling the Manus assistive robot [6]. The concept has been adapted to the smart environment to control various heterogeneous systems corresponding to different networking protocols. This modular software architecture offers several advantages to the developers and consequently to the users:

- Adding or developing any input device driver does not require high background of the controlled system since each action has a user oriented description in XML [4].
- Remote maintenance of any device through the Internet is facilitated through a Tele-maintenance Unit (TMU). This module was designed for robotic purpose, but has not been developed yet.
- An HMI supervisor allows coupling modalities to control any appliance. For example, coupling voice recognition for device selection and shin control to perform the corresponding movement the wheelchair.

This software architecture is decomposed in three main layers (figure 1):

### 2.1 User Layer

**Input Devices:** Manage user interfaces events according to any input device (keypad, joystick, voice recognition, etc.) selected and configured with the ECS (Environment Configuration System) software according to each end user.

**Feedback:** Gives user information about status of his environment (ex. input and output devices states) via visual representation (text, icons and images) or via audio feedback (sound). This module allows using direct pointing devices (Mouse, Trackball, etc.)

### 2.2 HMI Layer

This layer supervises the whole system: it converts user events into actions according to selected output devices (Manus, TV, VCR, etc.), transmit the information to the feedback module, manage multimodal aspects, manage errors situations, manage the synchronization of modules, etc.

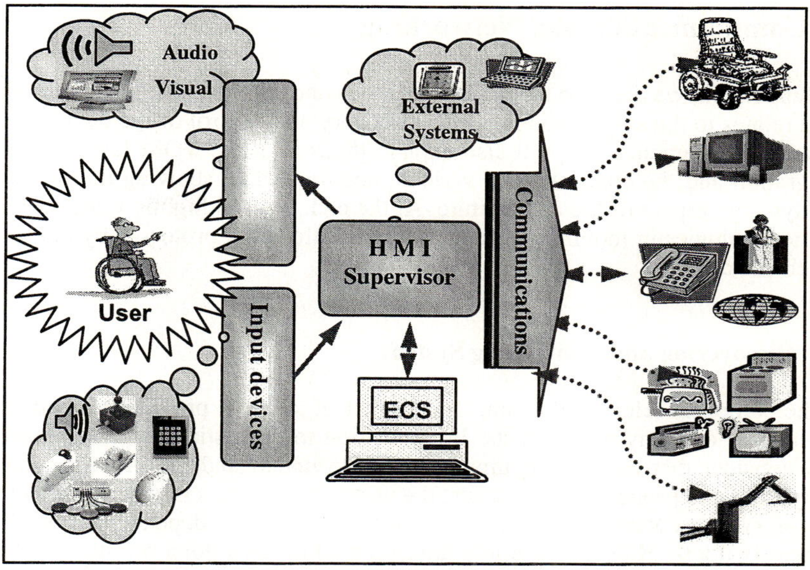


**Fig. 1.** Modular software architecture

## 2.3 Communication Layer

Deals with specific characteristics of any output device according to its communication protocol (CAN, infrared, radio protocol, etc.). Indeed, traditional home services are proposed by home devices manufacturers by means of a proprietary control device which may be accessed either directly or from the phone network. Services allowing the (remote) control over lights, heating or shutters are usually proposed and implemented by proprietary means. On the other hand, home services are gaining more and more interest in the computer science community. In particular, several service discovery systems have been proposed that use open and standard Internet communication protocols in order to discover available devices and to send commands to them. Although these solutions are independent from device manufacturers, the lack of home devices understanding Internet protocols has restricted the proliferation of home appliances of such systems, which still restricted to computer applications.

Home services take profit of new technological developments in communication networks. These services are not only dedicated to a large public of users but also to specific users such as dependent people (persons with disabilities and elderly people). These services aim at improving their ability to evolutes in their indoor environments and compensate their handicap. Today, as a consequence, many products are available on the market allowing the control of the heating, lightning or automatic shutter systems at home through wired and wireless communication networks. Occasionally, it is possible to access the control panel from outside, mainly through the telephone network (DSL). This allows setting up adapted services, such as remote monitoring.

# 3 Communication and Networking

In this section, we describe the various methods and solution adapted to our approach. That relates to the solution adopted for discovery and control of the devices available in user environments. We will also explain the role of the COM layer, enabling the integration and the connection of various modules, while showing its implication to the dynamic aspect of the architecture. At the end, we will highlight the role of wireless technologies in mobility through WiFi and Bluetooth protocols by the use of the handhelds devices.

## 3.1 Discovering and Controlling System

In the computer sciences domain, the concept of services provided in houses raised the interest of many protagonists. In opposition to domestic devices manufacturers, they consider that domestic equipments able to understand the Internet protocol already exist and propose tools to assist the user in the process of discovery and utilization of systems. Such opened and standard systems are independent from domestic devices builders. However, the low development of such domestic devices has slow down the development of home controlling applications. This situation limits the use of such systems to computers.

In order to ensure the independence from home devices manufacturers, the COM layer is mainly based on the Ametsa service which offers a generic interface allowing clients to be aware of the arrival/removal of devices to/from the network and to send specific commands to devices. Ametsa uses a service discovery system based on UPnP [8]. UPnP functionalities are used to be aware of arrival or removal of devices and to send or receive commands to/from available devices. As many home devices are not able to manage Internet protocols, we have developed gateways which translate UPnP protocols on the corresponding (proprietary) protocol of devices.

As shown in figure 2, UPnP communication protocols are used by a control application, called Ametsa Core, that supervise all available devices and allows sending commands, via UPnP protocol, to physical devices represented as Gateway devices, based on X10 and X2D power lines protocols, infrared RC5 protocol, etc.

Moreover, in order to allow non IP devices management, we developed a gateway framework that translates UPnP protocols used by Ametsa to the corresponding protocol.

Control commands are sent by the use of the CORBA API offered by Ametsa [9]. These calls are translated into UPnP messages which are sent to the concerned UPnP protocol stack.

Ametsa uses an UPnP Stack in order to be informed of the arrival/removal of devices to send corresponding control actions. Gateways use UPnP protocols to inform Ametsa on their arrival/removal status, their resulted actions processed, and on the corresponding effective communication protocol.

All these functionalities are actually running on a common prototype which should be installed in the Rehabilitation hospital of Garches for validation with implication of users having four limbs impairments.

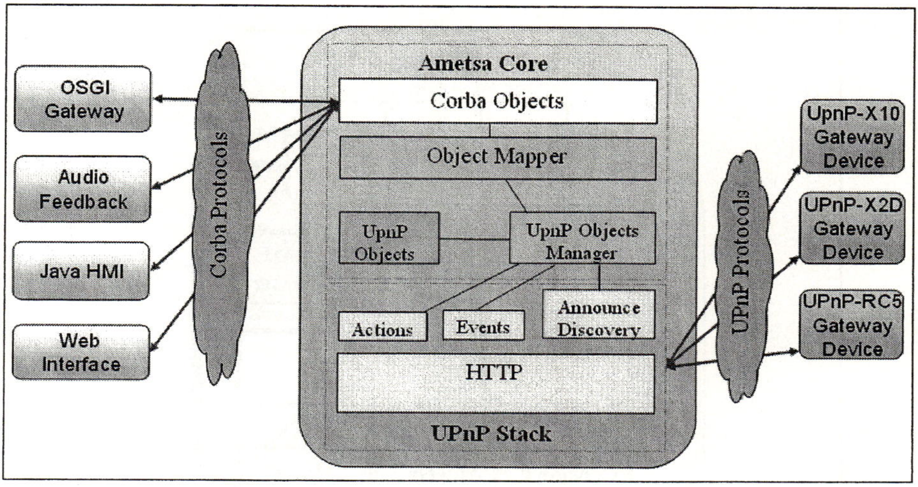


**Fig. 2.** Architecture of the devices discovery and control system

### 3.2 Generic Communication System

Above, we saw the conceptual architecture of smart environment and we attempted to outline the networking design of heterogeneous communication objects in user's environment. The HMI allows the interaction between the user events, the external events and the system. The problem of devices discovering is resolved with the UPNP protocol as described above mainly dedicated for indoor environmental systems. However it is also necessary to control devices outdoor, such as control of Manus robot mounted on user electrical wheelchair, and other devices directly (e.g. control TV, telephone, etc.) through a unified user interface used as remote controller (e.g. portable PC, tablet PC, Pocket PC, etc.).

In order to ensure networking interconnection between all these modules, we have developed an open communication platform called "COM layer" (Fig.3). This layer offers two services: Scan and Control functionalities. Scan function allows scanning of all kind of devices which can exit in the home (robot, wheelchair, devices controlled by Ametsa, etc.). The description of these devices and all their possible actions and services is based on a standard description with XML. The XML output file resulting of the scan operation is at the disposal of ECS configuration tool in order to configure and adapt the user interface. This file is built in a way which allows the HMI using it dynamically and displays the corresponding graphical user interface and enabling available input modalities.

The Control function treats the command, sent by the HMI, in order to convey it with the selected module through the suitable interaction output (e.g. Manus Slave, Ametsa Slave, etc.). The structure of the order is selected in a way that a table of correspondence is avoided. An add/remove device event cause the reuse of the scan service by the dynamic module in order to inform the user about this event and refresh the user interface.

The interaction with the Manus robot is made through Manus slave using sockets. Currently, we are studying the evolution of this connection towards the use of

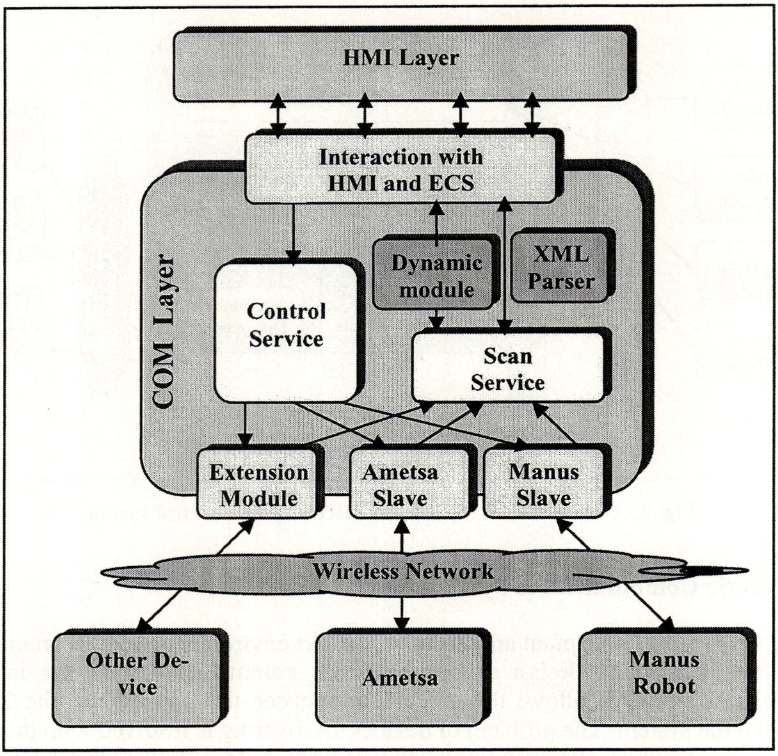


**Fig. 3.** Open communication layer architecture

CORBA communication bus, aiming to add more flexibility and safety to this connection. The COM layer uses CORBA API to connect with Ametsa gateway and control available devices. We also planned to integrate other gateways, such as Bluetooth and infrared IrDa to discover and control wireless devices. All communications and interconnections are independent of the physical layer of the networks. That's why we could adapt and introduce easily available and emerging wireless protocols in the future to fit with our smart homes concept, such as 802.11x, 2G and 3G technologies.

### 3.3 Mobility and Portability

Wireless networking improves both communication and mobility, which are two common limitations amongst people with disabilities. This technology permits greater mobility for these people; there is no need for the installation of cables which would cause troubles if the household is fully arranged and which is therefore disturbing for these people. It avoids an over wired environment especially in the user movement field. Moreover, a wireless medium allows a high flexibility of the module or the device being connected.

On the other hand, the handhelds and wireless devices expand rapidly and support a wide range of applications and services. Besides their simple and comfort use, they become today indispensable tools for a broad spectrum of end-users ranging from the new-age teenager to the corporate road warrior. In this issue, we believe that our concept should be generic and deployed in various kinds of handhelds and wireless devices (PDA, cell phone…), thus involve a portability problem.

To validate this step, we choose Java technology for the development of majority of our modules considering its benefits on portability on several operating systems and its benefits on wireless applications. We chose the Wifi (802.11g) technology as a wireless protocol ensuring the transition and connection between some modules inside the home and we tried to deploy our application on PDA, running on a Linux platform, to control the environment. This work is under development and it should also integrate the control of the environment, not only indoor, but also outdoor, based on 2G and 3G generation of mobile communication, with an "indoor/outdoor continuing services concept" we are designing.

## 4 Conclusion

This paper described our research activity on the integration of networking and communication technologies in the smart homes concept dedicated to people with disabilities. In this context, we outlined the importance of an open communication platform describing our architecture. The developed prototype is based on the UPnP protocol to discover and control devices indoor. It uses wireless technologies to enhance mobility. Its importance resides in managing different protocol and ensuring internetworking and communication between environment's devices.

The limits of our work reside on a security problem coming from the use of wireless technologies and diversity of communication protocols. For that reason, our team are investigating the OSGI framework (Open Services Gateway initiative) [11] which can be deployed to bridge the internet, the home networking, and the devices. This framework, which is compatible with UPnP protocol, is based on services oriented infrastructure that provides a managed and extensible framework to connect various devices indoor and outdoor environments.

## Acknowledgement

The authors would like to thank the people who have participated actively in this presented research activities from INSERM U.483, INT and hospital of Garches. Smart Home project, involving ENST Bretagne from Brest and ENST Paris, is funded by the GET and by the Foundation Louis Leprince Ringuet.

## References

1. Park, K. H., Bien, Z. Z.: Intelligent Sweet Home for Assisting the Elderly and the Handicapped. . ICOST proceedings, ISBN 1 58603 380 8, (2003) 151-158
2. Michael H. Coen: Design Principles for Intelligent Environnent. MIT Artificial Intelligence Lab Proceedings of the 1998 National Conference on Artificial Intelligence (AAAI-98)

3. Renouard, S., Charbit, M., Chollet, G.: Vocal interface with a speech memory for dependent people. ICOST proceedings, ISBN 1 58603 380 8, (2003) 15-21
4. Feki, M.A., Mokhtari, M., Abdulrazak, B.: XML Modelisation of Smart Home environment. ICOST proceedings, ISBN 1 58603 380 8 (IOS Press), France (September 2003) 55-60
5. Segarra, M.T., Thépaut, A., Keryell, R., Poichet, J., Plazaola, A., Peccate, B.: Ametsa a Generic Home Control System Based on UPnP. ICOST proceedings, ISBN 158603 380 8 (IOS Press), France (September 2003) 73-80
6. Abdulrazak, B., Mokhtari, M., Grandjean, B.: Toward a New High Level Controller for Manus Robot: The Commanus Project. ICORR proceedings, ISBN 1 58603 171 6 (IOS Press), France (April 2001) 221-226
7. Mokhtari, M., Fki, M.A., Abdulrazak, B.:Human-smart environment interaction in case of severe disability. HCI proceedings, Greece (June 2003)
8. Truche, C., Mokhtari, M, Vallet, C.: TeleContribution to the development of open software architecture for the robotic Manus arm. AAATE proceedings, IOS Press, Germany (November 1999) 302-307
9. UPnP Forum. Home Page. www.upnp.org
10. Object Management Group. "CORBA Basics". www.omg.org/gettingstarted/corbafaq.htm
11. Open Services Gateway Initiative. "Specification Overview". www.osgi.org

# SmartX – Enabling Traditional Environmental Control to Use Standard HCI

Gerhard Nussbaum[1] and Klaus Miesenberger[2]

[1] Kompetenznetzwerk Informationstechnologie zur Förderung der Integration von Menschen mit Behinderungen (KI-I), IT-Center, Hauptstraße 119, 4232 Hagenberg i.M., Austria
Gerhard.Nussbaum@ki-i.at
http://www.ki-i.at
[2] Institut "integriert studieren – integrated study", University of Linz
Altenbergerstrasse 69, A-4040 Linz, Austria
kmiesenberger@jku.at
http://www.integriert-studieren.jku.at

**Abstract.** Traditional Environmental Control (EC) systems mostly make use of remote control units. Due to that traditional Ecs

a) are often stand alone products which are inflexible and hardly extendible
b) can not use the flexibility and adaptability power of modern Human Computer Interfaces (HCI) what leads to accessibility and usability problems
c) can not easily integrate functionalities like communication, context awareness, pervasive computing…

In the project SmartX the functionalities of a traditional EC have been ported to a standard HCI interface. The purpose of this approach is to build the system on a stable and well known working environment to increase acceptance, usability, flexibility and adaptability and to integrate new functionalities mentioned above.
In this paper the SmartX prototype will be presented. Actual work and future steps to improve the application of EC by improving its usability, by integrating it into other features of standard devices will be discussed.

## 1 Introduction and Background

People with physical disabilities often have problems to use a TV-set, a video cassette recorder, … Nowadays, most of these devices are serially equipped with interfaces which allow the user to remotely control them.

Unfortunately, persons with disabilities often have problems with remote control units, too. They simply cannot use the interface as they can not see or feel it, handle the buttons, …. Because of non-standardized interfaces, almost every consumer electronic device has its own remote control produced by different manufacturers. This aggravates the problem of the user with disabilities.

A couple of years ago, EC units were developed to overcome this. The idea is to use one universal remote control which "learns" the commands of the proprietary remote control units of each device and which is accessible for persons with disabilities, in particular those with physical disabilities. EC enables to handle all devices in the nearer environment (e.g. apartment) which have an IR receiver with a single unit.

K. Miesenberger et al. (Eds.): ICCHP 2004, LNCS 3118, pp. 945–952, 2004.

The EC unit might be adapted according to the needs of individual users. Most of today's EC units on the market follow this principle. Most of them are again proprietary hardware devices making them expensive, inflexible and hardly adaptable to different groups of users. The possibilities to change or adapt the user interface are very restricted. Systems offering more adaptable user interfaces are often quite large, unhandy and not mobile. [1]

The ideal EC is easily adaptable to the user, flexible, multifunctional and does not restrict the user in mobility. Furthermore this EC has communication functionality (e.g. GSM telephony).

## 2 The Idea SmartX

Based on the analysis above possibilities of implementing a small, mobile and multifunctional EC system, which is easily adaptable to the user needs, were studied. EC should make use of the basic principle of HCI that

- content/function
- presentation
- handling

are separated and can be adapted according to users needs and situation of usage. In standard remote control units as well as in traditional EC systems the operation of a function is dependent on a certain presentation and style of handling. HCI opens more freedom to the user in accessing and handling a certain function. [2] It became obvious that a modern EC system should make use of standard devices running a standard HCI to benefit from

- adaptability and usability
- extendibility, modularisation and combination of functionalities
- consistency of interaction principles over different applications
- accessibility and integration of Assistive Technology (AT)
- cost effectiveness by using off-the-shelve products and concentrating on software development

PDAs (or other emerging handheld devices like smart phones, Tablet PCs, etc.) which integrate functionalities of modern HCI and are capable of using ambient technologies and ubiquitous/pervasive computing functionalities can be seen as an ideal infrastructure for research on modern EC and systems like SmartX. A PDA's graphical user interface can easily and individually be adapted. Also more and more AT for PDAs becomes available. PDAs are quite small and mobile.

EC therefore could be integrated into a system providing further functionality like Email-Client, Web browser, Pocket Word, navigation support, telephone ... As the same environment and the same principles of the HCI can be used for all applications more acceptance and usability of EC can be reached.

With the use of communication technologies like GSM, GPRS or WLAN also remote maintenance and support will be realized. Remote maintenance reduces the service costs and also the time the EC cannot be used. Furthermore a WYSIWIG configuration program to configure SmartX is realized.

**Table 1.** Comparison between SmartX and the state of the art devices (tbd = to be done – planned feature in next release)

| Feature | SmartX | FST James II | GEWA Access | Sicare Pilot | Sicare Light | PROTOS | Proteor Nemo | Autonom | The Grid |
|---|---|---|---|---|---|---|---|---|---|
| IR-Control | ✓ | ✓ | ✓ | ✓ | ✓ | ✓ | ✓ | ✓ | ✓ |
| Support of Bluetooth and WLAN | tbd | – | – | – | – | – | – | – | – |
| Support of communication technologies like GSM | tbd | – | – | – | – | – | – | – | – |
| AAC | tbd | – | – | – | – | – | – | ✓ | ✓ |
| Internet connection | tbd | – | – | – | – | – | – | – | ✓ |
| Alternative input device | ✓ | ✓ | ✓ | ✓ | – | ✓ | ✓ | ✓ | ✓ |
| Alternative user interfaces (ambient, ubiquitous) | tbd | – | – | – | – | – | – | – | – |
| Speech recognition / Speech output | tbd | – | – | ✓ | ✓ | – | ✓ | – | – |
| User can configure the ECS | ✓ | ✓ | ✓ | ✓ | – | ✓ | ✓ | ✓ | ✓ |
| WYSIWYG-configuration at the device | ✓ | – | – | – | – | – | – | ✓ | ✓ |
| Configuration via PC | tbd | ✓ | ✓ | ✓ | – | ✓ | – | ✓ | ✓ |
| Remote-Support / Remote-Maintenance | tbd | – | – | – | – | – | – | ✓ | – |
| Configuration sharing | tbd | ✓ | ✓ | ✓ | – | – | – | ✓ | ✓ |
| User / Device profiles | tbd | – | – | – | – | – | – | – | – |
| Visual Feedback (Scanning, etc.) | ✓ | ✓ | ✓ | ✓ | ✓ | ✓ | ✓ | ✓ | ✓ |
| Audio-Feedback (Scanning, etc.) | ✓ | ✓ | ✓ | ✓ | ✓ | ✓ | ✓ | ✓ | ✓ |
| Context Awareness | tbd | – | – | – | – | – | – | – | – |
| Location Awareness | tbd | – | – | – | – | – | – | – | – |
| Modular – Extendable via PlugIns | tbd | – | – | – | – | – | – | – | – |
| Mobile | ✓ | ✓ | ✓ | ✓ | ✓ | ✓ | ✓ | – | ✓ |

## 3 The SmartX Prototype

A prototype of the SmartX system has been implemented as a feasibility study which is the basis for further research and development.

SmartX is developed using Microsoft's .Net technology and so also versions for PCs, Handhelds and Tablet PCs will be available with the next release.

SmartX is component oriented and its architecture bases on three layers (Fig. 1) – the hardware integration layer, the application logic layer and the presentation logic layer. The result is an architecture which can be extended and adapted very easily and which is quite flexible. The next release of SmartX will be extendable via software PlugIns. Every user only gets the components and PlugIns for the functionalities he needs or wants.

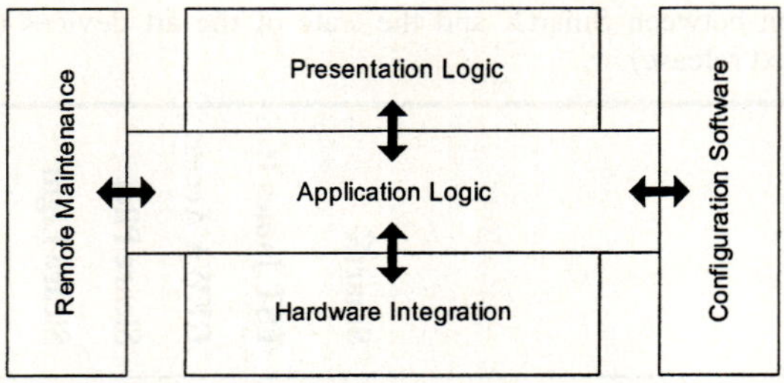


**Fig. 1.** Scheme of the architecture of the SmartX prototype

The configuration software "Configurator" and the remote maintenance software are separate applications and use components like the GUIs and the database of the core system.

### 3.1 User Interface – Presentation

The presentation of a SmartX item corresponds to the classic graphical user interface (GUI). SmartX uses the multimodal, bidirectional Icons (at SmartX named items) (Fig. 2) which are defined in [3] in a modified way. The presentation of a SmartX item is multimodal i.e. aural as well as visual. Users with sensory as well as cognitive problems benefit from this.

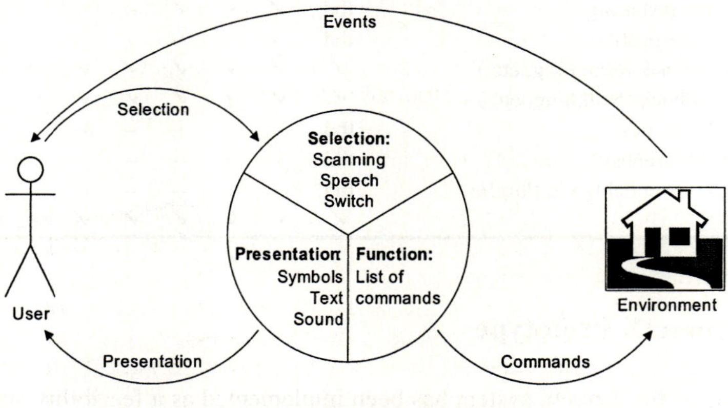


**Fig. 2.** SmartX Interface scheme

The visual as well as the aural presentation of a SmartX item can be changed. The standard symbols of the SmartX items are derived from well known symbols which are used at standard remote controls. It is also possible to use the symbols of a symbol language like Bliss, PCS or Picto to raise the usability for persons with mental and multiple disabilities [1].

In the current version of SmartX the graphical user interfaces can be changed easily. In the GUIs ListView and IconView (Fig. 2) the items are organised in a matrix which is quite often used in switch controlled software [4]. The dimension of the matrices can be changed. On PDAs with 240x320 Pixel displays 4x4 or 4x5 matrices have proved themselves.

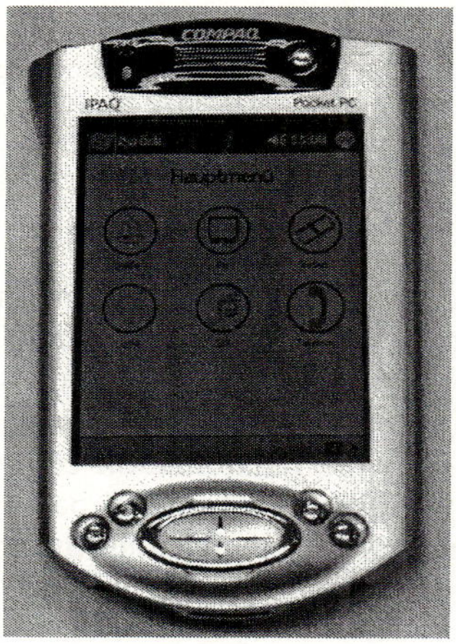


**Fig. 3.** SmartX running on an iPAQ PDA

## 3.2 User Interface – Handling

Since the items of SmartX are organized in form of a matrix several ways of activating an item are available. The ways depend on the number of installed keys or sensors. In SmartX an automatic scan (col/row and linear) and a manual scan are implemented. It is also possible to activate an item by using the touch screen. Voice input is planned for release 2.

With the current available hardware up to five switches can be connected to SmartX. These switches can be configured individually.

## 3.3 Functionality of SmartX

SmartX at the moment is a flexible EC system able to integrate any device using an IR or HF based remote control unit. Depending on the sampler used devices with IR and HF interfaces can be controlled.

SmartX can be configured with the authoring and configuration tool "Configurator". With this tool the whole menu can be built and changed. Also the IR commands can be scanned i.e. learned and the functionality of the hardware device can be integrated into the system. Furthermore the configuration of the scan modes and the functionality of the switches can be done.

The contents of a SmartX item can consist of 1..n functions which can be changed. The contents e.g. of the on/off key of the hands free function from a telephone can also consist of several functions. At turning on: switching the TV-set and/or the HiFi system mute; activating the hands free function. At turning off: deactivating the hands free function; switching the TV-set and/or the HiFi system loud [1].

## 3.4 Technical Requirements for SmartX

In the current release SmartX runs on standard PDAs (with at least 64 MB RAM) based on Microsoft's Pocket PC operating system with installed .Net Compact Framework 1.0 Redistributable Package.

For connecting switches and sensors to the PDA or PC a sensorbox for the RS232 port is necessary. To send and receive IR commands an IR sampler is necessary. Both the sensorbox and IR sampler are standard products.

### 3.5 User Centred Design

To meet all requirements and needs of the future users, the development of the Smart Environment Control System follows the principles of "User Centred Design". To get to know the requirements of the potential users a survey was carried out.

To get feedback the GUI prototypes IconView and ListView were tried out with potential users in a field test in the rehabilitation centre "Bad Häring" in Austria. Seven persons with physical disabilities (Table 2) participated in the field test. The test persons had to do several tasks like changing the menus or activating an item. After a short introduction all test persons were able to do the test tasks.

**Table 2.** Data of the test persons and results

| Name | Age | Disability | Preferred GUI | Problems with | |
|---|---|---|---|---|---|
| | | | | IconView | ListView |
| A | 27 | Tetraplegia C1 | IconView | no | no |
| B | 28 | Tetraplegia C4 | ListView | yes | yes |
| C | 25 | Tetraplegia C4 | IconView | yes | yes |
| D | 61 | Tetraplegia C4 | IconView | no | no |
| E | 68 | Tetraplegia C6 | IconView | yes | no |
| F | 14 | Paraplegia TH3-4 | ListView | no | no |
| G | 11 | Cleft Spina | ListView | yes | yes |

Some persons had problems with items of the GUI IconView which only had an icon and no further description. They could not allocate specific functions to some icons. If the item had both an icon and a description text these problems did not arise. The problems with the GUI ListView affected the very small item size (60 items in one menu) and the texts. Some used words (e.g. Rewind) in the items were unknown.

Persons who preferred the IconView described it as 'more intuitive', as 'clearer' and as 'more concise and appealing'. Persons who preferred the ListView said that it is easier to understand and that icons are not needed.

In SmartX both GUIs, the ListView and the IconView are included. The font size is adjustable and the number of items i.e. the dimension of the matrices are definable during the creation process of the menus. The third GUI TreeView failed in the survey and was not implemented in release 1. There are additional UIs planned for the next release. These interfaces will also be accessible for blind and visually handicapped persons.

## 4 Future Research and Implementation Work

Future research and implementation work will include among others:

- Feasibility study and further usability studies: Some of these planned features never have been realised on other platforms than PCs. So these features will first be implemented as prototypes for feasibility studies. After the implementation of the new features a new user test will be done. The feedback of these tests will play a significant role in the further development of SmartX.
- User profiling: Different users often need different settings in SmartX. These settings, the menus and commands, etc. will be stored in a user profile. If the user has to change his PDA with SmartX he can copy this profile to the new one. Furthermore standard profiles for user groups will be provided in order to ease the configuration process of SmartX.
- Device profiling: To make use of Context Awareness device profiles have to be implemented. Every device gets a profile where IR commands and further properties are stored. So SmartX can recognise the device and can display it.
- Support of TV set top boxes: TV set top boxes become more and more popular. Many people are used to the handling of TV sets. With a set top box the TV gets more intelligent and can provide services like Internet (WWW, Email) and electronic program guides. With the help of such boxes these services can be provided.
- Speech In- / Output: Speech driven in- and output was charged to be the most popular User Interface in the survey [1]. Speech interface have a high potential to reduce the cognitive and learning demand of the interface.
- Developer/Adaptation/Device Integration functionalities "Lego for EC": A set of components and PlugIns will be developed. With this set SmartX can be adapted to the individual needs of users. Every user gets only the components he needs. So costs can be reduced.
- Context/Location Awareness: To improve the usability of SmartX also Context and Location Awareness will be realised. E.g.: Every time the user enters a new room with SmartX it will recognize all remote controllable devices and will display corresponding menus for them.
- AAC: SmartX will integrate Augmentative and Alternative Communication (AAC) functionalities. Persons with multiple disabilities can control their environment and do 'conversation' i.e. AAC with one single device. The users must only get used to one single HCI.
- Integration of communication technologies like WLAN, Bluetooth and GSM/GPRS: To use SmartX as a communication device GSM/GPRS will be integrated. WLAN and Bluetooth will be used for data communication. It is possible that sampler and sensorbox will communicate with SmartX via wireless technologies. So the usability of SmartX can be additionally improved. Furthermore WLAN can be used for communication between SmartX and home automation systems like Konnex [5].
- IR code database: The learning process of new IR codes is sometimes quite tricky and not every IR code can be learned. So a database of IR codes for 'all important and common' consumer electronics devices will be developed. When a user gets a new device he can download the IR codes from this database and use them with SmartX.

## Acknowledgements

SmartX is currently being developed by a research team of KI-I and "integriert studieren" including, beside both authors, Markus Alexander, Stefan Parker and Klemens Stelzmueller.

The project is sponsored by the company OMV Agrolinz Melamin GmbH and by the Johannes Kepler University of Linz.

## References

1. Nussbaum G.: „Smart Environment Control System – User Centred Design, Mensch-Maschine-Interaktion, Authoring- und Konfigurations-Tool „Configurator“, Information Technology Enabling Integration at University, Diplomarbeit, Universität Linz, 2001
2. Miesenberger K.: „Applied Computer Science for Blind and Visually Handicapped People“; Information Technology Enabling Integration at University, S. 60, Habilitationsschrift, Universität Linz, 2001
3. Flachberger C., Panek P., Zagler W.: „Das Technische Assistenzsystem – Unterstützung der Selbständigkeit bewegungs- und mehrfachbehinderter Personen“; it+ti – Informationstechnik und Technische Informatik 39 (1997) 2; R. Oldenbourg Verlag
4. Colven D., Dethridge T.: „A Common Terminology for Switch Controlled Software”; ACE Centre, Ormerod School; Oxford 1990
5. Konnex Association: Konnex. http://www.konnex.org/

# Indoors Pervasive Computing and Outdoors Mobile Computing for Cognitive Assistance and Telemonitoring

Sylvain Giroux, Hélène Pigot, and André Mayers

Department of ComputerScience, Université de Sherbrooke
2500 boul. Université, Sherbrooke, Canada J1K 2R1
{Sylvain.Giroux,Helene.Pigot,Andre.Mayers}@USherbrooke.ca
http://www.dmi.usherb.ca/~sgiroux/domus/

**Abstract.** People suffering from cognitive deficits – Alzheimer disease, schizophrenia, brain injuries – are often obliged to live in medical institutions. Pervasive computing and mobile applications are key technology that may help them to stay at home. They can be at the root of information systems as cognitive assistance and telemonitoring. Inside a smart house, cognitive assistance could alleviate cognitive impairments by giving personalized environmental cues. Besides telemonitoring could inform relatives and medical staff of the disease evolution and could alert them in case of emergency. But cognitively impaired people must not be confined in their home. Cognitive assistance and telemonitoring must be available outdoors too. This paper sketches an infrastructure and prototypes making the most of indoor pervasive computing and outdoor mobile computing to achieve cognitive assistance and telemonitoring.

## 1 Introduction

People suffering from cognitive impairments – Alzheimer disease, schizophrenia, brain injuries... – often have no choice other than living in medical institutions. Smart houses [10] and mobile applications, e.g. activity compass [5], can play a central role in keeping them at home. Inside a smart house, cognitive assistance could alleviate cognitive impairments by giving personalized environmental cues to assist cognitively impaired people in their activities of daily living (ADL). Besides a smart house could inform relatives and medical staff of the evolution of the disease and could alert them in case of emergency. But cognitively impaired people must not be confined in their home. Cognitive assistance and telemonitoring must be available outdoors too.

The required pervasive and mobile infrastructure for indoors and outdoors ADLs calls for specialized middleware and frameworks for managing distributed systems, dynamic generation of personalized user interfaces for heterogeneous devices, algorithms based on artificial intelligence techniques, localization and geo-referenced information. Though goals and means are different for indoor and outdoor cognitive assistance, both need to rely on common models and a similar infrastructure (Fig. 1).

K. Miesenberger et al. (Eds.): ICCHP 2004, LNCS 3118, pp. 953–960, 2004.

This paper first sketches the distributed layered architecture we developed (§2). Application layer is then described using two prototypes for indoors (§3) and one prototype for outdoors (§4). It completes with hardware and middleware layers (§5).

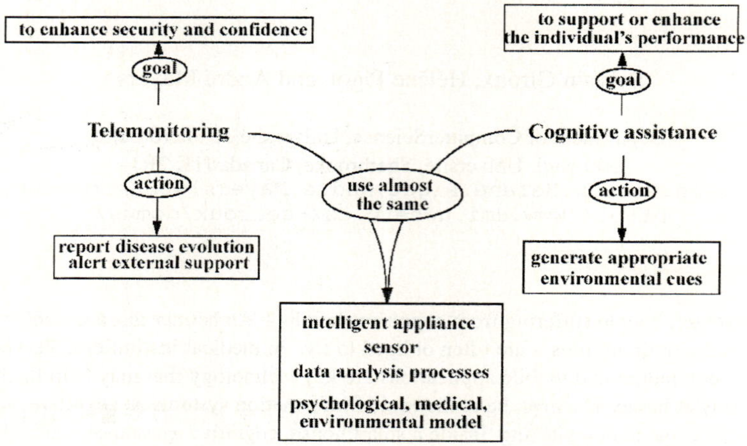


**Fig. 1.** Cognitive assistance and telemonitoring share the infrastructure and similar models.

## 2 A Layered Distributed Architecture

The distributed architecture (Fig. 2) is logically organized in three layers: hardware, middleware and application [7, 8]. The application layer offers services like cognitive assistance and telemonitoring, as well as supporting services like plan recognition and user modeling. The hardware layer deals with hardware and low-level software: sensors, devices, domestic appliances, wireless networks... The middleware layer copes with hardware heterogeneity through dedicated middleware and frameworks. Middleware enables to link the application layer services to the hardware. Frameworks are a structuring set of tools and software components that help to develop mobile and pervasive services. Since indoors and outdoors services face similar issues, a common generic part has been identified and extracted into the middleware and frameworks.

## 3 Indoors Assisted Cognition

Building and deploying information systems for assisted cognition and telemonitoring offer more options inside a house than outside. We gain more control over the devices installed and we can expect to collect more accurate, redundant and rich information. In addition we may have richer means of interactions with people. At the same time, heterogeneity and multiplicity of devices and networks raise challenging issues. Security and fault tolerance calls for highly distributed and redundant systems.

Pervasive computing [12] seemed the right approach. Thus to explore pervasive computing and to put the base of the infrastructure, two prototypes have been designed. The first prototype (§3.1) focus on distributed computing, code migration, and spontaneous networks. It also shows how to coordinate and intertwine heterogeneous networks and protocols to personalize the environment and to deliver the information wherever the user is and whatever the device is. The second prototype (§3.2) concentrates on structure and deployment of distributed computations to provide for local decisions and feedbacks whilst global perspectives and decisions are also occurring.

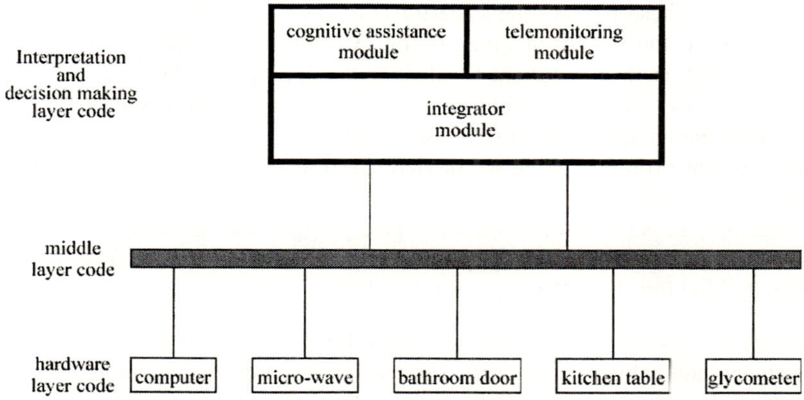


**Fig. 2.** A three layers architecture. In practice, the overall infrastructure is highly distributed and any device may host pieces of code belonging to each layer at the same time.

## 4 Indoors Assisted Cognition

Building and deploying information systems for assisted cognition and telemonitoring offers more potential inside a house than outside. We got more control over the devices installed and we can expect to collect more precise, redundant, and complex information. We could also hope to get richer means of interactions with people. At the same time, heterogeneity and multiplicity of devices and networks raise challenging issues. Security and fault tolerance calls for highly distributed and redundant systems. Pervasive computing [12] seemed the right approach. Thus two prototypes have been designed and implemented to explore pervasive computing and to put the base of the infrastructure. The first prototype (§4.1) focus on distributed computing, code migration, and spontaneous networks. It also shows how to coordinate and intertwine heterogeneous networks and protocols to personalize the environment and to deliver the information wherever the user is and whatever the device she uses. The second prototype (§4.2) concentrates on structure and deployment of distributed computations. The aim was to provide for local decisions and feedbacks whilst supporting global perspectives and global decisions.

### 4.1 Communication with the User in a Pervasive Home

In a smart home, a patient can move from room to room. Each room may contain a wide variety of fixed or mobile devices. Some devices may serve to interact with the patient while other may solely collect low-level information, e.g. sensors. To be effective a cognitive assistant must know the patient position, at least in which room she stands, the devices she can use, the devices features, the information they provide. Finally code may need to migrate to be delivered on specific devices since devices may join or leave the room. We thus designed and implemented a pervasive system that investigates these points. The system has to keep a list of messages and appointments to send to the patient at given times. At appropriate time, the system has to localize in which room the patient is, identify the appropriate devices, and "display" the message to the patient. It could then serve as a basis for a cognitive assistant to recall to a patient an appointment or a task to perform.

In the current prototype (Fig. 4), devices used are Ethernet-based PCs, Wifi and Bluetooth enabled PDAs, a Bluetooth enabled printer, a WiFi router, wireless movement detectors, an X10[1] infrared (IR) receptor plugged into the house electrical system, an X10 decoder / encoder plugged into a wall electrical outlet. The information system is divided into five cooperating subsystems:

- *Jini*: Jini [1] provides http servers to deploy Java classes and services, Phoenix for persistence and robustness, a lease service for resource management, and service discovery. Jini also makes available spontaneous networking facilities.
- *the Domus federation*: the Domus federation contains services and Java code specific to the applications deployed inside the house. It relies on Jini.
- *messaging services*: messaging services allow to deliver a message to somebody and to receive an acknowledge. For telemonitoring, a nurse may use it to et a confirmation an action has been done by a patient. For assisted cognition, an agenda containing monitored tasks may use it to recall a patient to take her medication. The lifecycle of message is summarized as follows
  - a request to send a message to a given user is issued to the message server;
  - the message server searches in the Domus federation the client devices able to display the message, and forwards the message to them;
  - when an acknowledge is received or when the message becomes meaningless (for instance if outdated), the message is withdrawn from the Domus federation. In any case, messages are always garbage collected.
- *X10 service*: this service acts as bridges between the electrical system used as a network and other devices. A part of this service is connected through a serial port to the X10 interface device. The other part makes available X10 signals to other Domus services. This server enables reading and writing X10 message on the electrical wires. The decoder linked to the server can write X10 signal to the electrical wires to control X10 devices, for instance lights. Domus services only need to reg-

---

[1] X10 is a communications "language" that allows compatible products to talk to each other using the existing electrical wiring in the home [2].

ister and to specify the X10 codes that are relevant for them. They will be notified whenever corresponding X10 messages are transmitted over the electrical system.

- *localization services*: Wireless movement detectors are used to infer the room in which a user is located. These movement detectors generate X10 signals. They communicate their states via infrared (IR) to an X10 receptor plugged into the house electrical system. This receptor transmits the signals through the house electrical system. States of movement detectors can then be analyzed to determine wether the patient is entering or exiting a room.
- *the agenda service*: this service is a pervasive application that keep sessions alive from device to device. It acts in collaboration with messaging services. It keeps track of appointments or tasks to do. For instance it can be used to specify the ADLs a patient has to perform — taking pills, breakfast, diner, etc. The agenda will remind them to the patient as the day proceeds.

Order of connection of services is not an issue. Services and devices can join and leave the system in any order. The system is fully decentralized and used on cheap commercially available devices. When necessary, services, e.g. the agenda system, can migrate from device to device preserving the state of the user session.

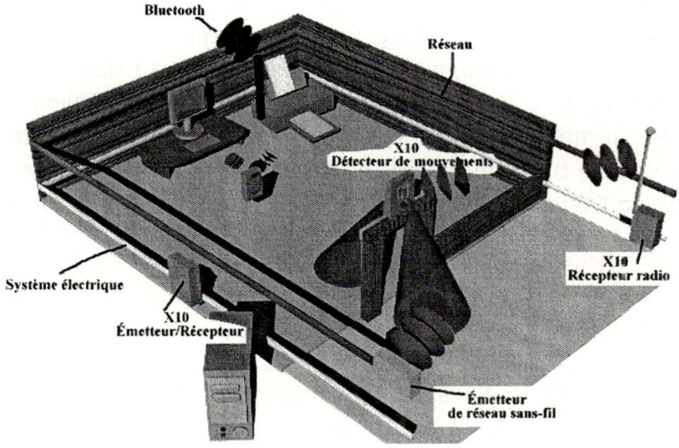


**Fig. 3.** Current prototype implementation of the pervasive agenda system.

### 4.2 A Distributed Infrastructure for Plan Recognition

Once the home pervasive information systems can interact with the user and collect information from sensors, plan recognition [11] is the next issue to tackle. Plan recognition is compulsory to achieve cognitive assistance or telemonitoring. Indeed the system must assess what the patient is doing, what she intends to do, what she has done, how she did it. Hence the second prototype focuses on distributed plan recognition for maintaining and updating a patient model. Distributed plan recognition is driven by predefined scripts. The prototype is based on Epitalk [6].

Plan to recognize are represented as task graphs. These graphs describe epiphyte[2] hierarchical multi-agent systems. For each node there is a matching agent. Agents of the plan recognition system are distributed across the devices of the house, their host. The agents choose the devices to graft onto according to generic descriptions of devices owned by the environment model, e.g. sensor type. As an activity proceeds, isolated events are detected by sensors. Events are captured by the low-level agents grafted on sensors. These events feed the reasoning process. Each node may have a rule base implemented in JESS[3]. Each node/agent has a local view on the current situation and owns part of the user model. When enough, relevant or synthetic information is available, the agent sent it to its hierarchical superior node. As information goes upward, higher-level agents get a broader view on what is going on. As data is percolating up, local decisions are taken and ADLs scripts are inferred. When a handicap situation occurs, personalized cues are generated. In case of risk, the telemonitoring system sends messages to the medical staff and the relatives. So at each node, reasoning can generate pieces of advice for cognitive assistance or can inform medical staff for telemonitoring. Thus if a failure occurs, the system will continue to operate partially. Information is also kept in a remote database a doctor may consult.

Apart localized cues, we use plan recognition for assessment of illness evolution based on the global deterioration scale for assessment of primary degenerative dementia.[9]. Since our plan recognition systems enables to detect loss of memory, trouble in performing task in the proper order... it can infer when there is a level change in the deterioration scale. When this occurs, an email is sent to medical staff. This prototype will be integrated with the pervasive messaging systems to build the sought for common framework for cognitive assistance and telemonitoring.

## 5 Outdoors

For obvious reasons, patients must not be constrained to stay at home. However outdoors offer a completely different environment for cognitive assistance and telemonitoring. Much less control is possible over devices available. Much fewer devices and sources of information can help than in an indoors controlled setting as is patient's home. Nonetheless monitoring tools are as well helpful when the patient is not at home. Mobile computing can provide the adequate answers. A prototype is currently under development for the monitoring of people suffering of schizophrenia (Fig. 5). For them such tools can make the difference between being obliged to stay in the hospital or being allowed to go outside. The prototype system comprises a PDA, a GPS and a CDMA network card. It has two purposes: 1) gather ecological data, and 2) anticipate and help during crisis.

Schizophrenic people usually see their psychiatrist once a month. Often answers of the patient are vague or not representative of the true situation. Furthermore medica-

[2] Epiphyte plants, as ivy, are plants that grow on to other plants, called hosts.

[3] JESS is a rule engine and scripting environment for the Java platform.

tion has often harsh side-effects, and doses must be fine-tuned with care. Our prototype enables a patient to note facts valuable for a better cure, e.g. occurrence of symptoms and their intensity... So the psychiatrist will have real ecological values when he meets the patient. In the prototype, data are also uploaded to a database thanks to wireless networking, so the psychiatrist can adjust the dose of medication according to the observation and the intensity of side-effects.

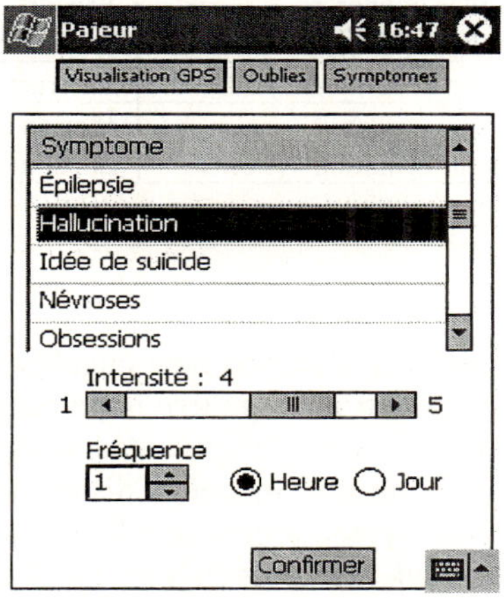


**Fig. 4.** The PDA interface for gathering ecological data for schizophrenic people.

When they are in crisis, patients tend to follow characteristic paths or to stay in front of specific locations, for instance churches. The GPS connected to the PDA enables to follow the patient movements and to detect crisis. Since we know at that moment the patient location, we somebody can go there and help her. A messaging service and task monitoring has also been implemented to help staff monitor patients ADLs. Doctors and nurses are notified when precise tasks (medication, meals, etc.) have been or not performed. If the task has not been performed, medical staff can send a message.

## 6 Hardware, Middleware, and Frameworks

Hardware involved in indoors pervasive systems and outdoors mobile systems is truly different in nature and processing power (Table 1). Fortunately there are languages, middleware and frameworks useful in both cases. First we used Java as a basis, in particular for mobile code. Mobile code enables algorithms to move from device to device. At low-level, communication through networks use Ethernet, Wifi, Bluetooth and X10. At a higher level, spontaneous networking is managed by Jini. Finally Epitalk is used for distributed plan recognition and to structure distributed reasoning and assistance for adequate deployment on this distributed infrastructure. In the near future, we will integrate relevant parts of E-mate [3] and MORE [4]. E-mate lies over

Jini and supplies generic solutions for the deployment of mobile personalized geo-referenced services. E-mate also supports the core of the personalization process. MORE dynamically generates user interfaces on fat, thin or web-based clients.

**Table 1.** Some differences between indoors and outdoors hardware and systems.

| | **Outdoors** | **Indoors** |
|---|---|---|
| **Devices** | PDAs cellular phones…<br>Small number of devices | Sensors, Digital TV…<br>High number of devices |
| **Network** | Not available or low-bandwidth | Ethernet;Bluetooth,WiFi,RF;X10; |
| **Localization** | GPS;<br>geographic information systems | Motion detectors;<br>Localization systems; |

## 7 Conclusion

We presented three prototypes that sketched how cognitive assistance and telemonitoring can assist people suffering from cognitive impairments and lessen the burden on caregivers. Apposite interventions are generated using a model describing the person, the ADLs and the environment. Indoors a distributed architecture is processing data acquired from sensors spread around the house. Data are percolating up to the distributed cognitive assistant. Outdoors cognitive assistance relies on small portable device and GPS-based localization. Pervasive computing and mobile computing provided the basis of the architecture of the information systems.

## References


1. Arnold, K., ed., *The Jini Specifications*, Addison-Wesley, 2nd Edition, 2000.
2. Boone, K, *Using X10 for Home Automation*, http://www.kevinboone.com/x10.html.
3. Carboni, D. et al., *e-MATE: An open architecture to support mobility of users*, Fifth Intn'l Baltic Conf. on Databases and Information Systems, June 3-6th, 2002 Tallinn, Estonia.
4. Carboni, D., et al., *Interactions Model and Code Generation for J2ME Applications*, 4th Int. Symp. on Human Computer Interaction with Mobile Devices Mobile, HCI 2002, Italy.
5. Kautz, H. et al. *An Overview of the Assisted Cognition Project*, AAAI 2002, workshop.
6. Paquette, G., et al., *EpiTalk, generating advisor agents for existing information systems*, J. of AI in Education, AIED Society, AACE, vol. 7, no 3-4, 1996.
7. Pigot H., et al., *The role of intelligent habitats in upholding elders in residence. 5th Intl Conf. on Simulations in Biomedicine*, 2003, Slovenia. WIT Press.
8. H. Pigot, et al., *The intelligent habitat and everyday life activity support. 5th international conference on Simulations in Biomedicine*, Slovenia, April 2003.
9. Reisberg B, et al. *The Global Deterioration Scale for Assessment of Primary Degenerative Dementia.* Am J Psychiatry 1982; 139: 1136–1139.
10. Rialle .V, et al. *An experimental Health Smart Home and its distributed Internet-based Information and Communication System. MEDINFO 2001,* IOPress. pp. 1479-1483.
11. Schmidt, C. F.; et al.. *The plan recognition problem: an intersection of psychology and artificial intelligence*. Artificial Intelligence 1978. 11:45–83.
12. Weiser, Mark, *The Computer for the 21st Century*, Scientific American, 1991.

# Computer Use for People with Learning Difficulties: Basic Needs

Paul Tréhin

trehinp@aol.com

*In memory of Jean-Claude Gabus who always knew how to concentrate his work on the fundamental needs of people with disabilities. We miss you Jean-Claude.*

**Abstract.** My main area of interest and competences is autism, and in that domain quite a few research programs have been proposed over these years. However many of the needs for educational programs that I will develop here are applicable to learning difficulties in general.
The main idea being that such program development should start from the needs of the people with disabilities rather than from the available technology. The case of programs for people with autism will illustrate some of the specific needs that should be satisfied.

## 1 Introduction

Early on, computer assisted education thinking was done by computer specialists. We still have examples of such views in recent developments. "*Unfortunately, many decisions about applications of technology in special education are 'device driven'.*" (Blackhurst 2001)

This is understandable; computer technology is a fascinating domain, and university teams need to work on advanced technologies. However, as responsible advocate of the needs of children with autism and aware of the priorities in a limited resource world, I feel that there is still a need for basic programs.

A few psychologists were interested very early on by the potential of computer based teaching, even considering the limited functionalities of the IT technology in the fifties and sixties. The concept of Computer Assisted Instruction (CAI) was still viewed in a mechanical way(Skinner 1959). Some of the first "programmed teaching" systems were even implemented in the form of books (Austwick 1964). But whether being supported by a book or by a computer, the idea was to have a well defined course with a student path using "If Then Else" branching upon answers to questions.

In the mid seventies, researchers like Seymour Papert and Jim Howe, reacted to mechanical teaching systems (Papert 1980).

Most programs available for special education though are coming from the domain of drill and practice. Actually, for most basic skill acquisition these programs can be very efficient. They tend to address mainly the domain of procedural knowledge, which is knowledge that enables a person to behave appropriately in local situations where knowledge of how things work is not necessary to make them work.

Some programs, called tutorials, attempt at teaching conceptual knowledge: how things work, enabling people to adapt their procedural knowledge to other environments that the local one.

K. Miesenberger et al. (Eds.): ICCHP 2004, LNCS 3118, pp. 961–968, 2004.

## 2 Behaviourism in Computer Teaching Systems

From the first article I presented at a conference in The Hague (Trehin 1985) and ever since, I have put the needs of the people with learning difficulties upfront. This means first having a current understanding of the specificities of each learning disability that is being addressed by an educational program, having information on strategies that have proved to be efficient, propose a new education strategy, building upon all this knowledge, and finally being in a position to implement this education strategy on advanced technology devices. Obviously such a strategy requires teamwork since it is unlikely than an individual program designer would master all the variety of knowledge necessary to complete such an endeavour.

### 2.1 Understanding Autism and the Needs of People with Autism

One doesn't go without the other; a general knowledge of the current understanding of autism will lead to a better understanding of individual people with autism and to better education programs

**Understanding Autism.** Here is a short description that gives in a nutshell some of the most important features of autism:

*<<In depths investigations and brain explorations have made it possible to single out anomalies within "sub networks", the function of which is to collect information coming from the environment, to decode it and to react appropriately. And indeed, the brain functioning of a child with autism is peculiar, and this, even for simple operations such as understanding a signal or imitating a movement. On the one side, he appears overwhelmed by the environmental "cacophony". On the other side, his gestures lack in fluidity. It is evident that the child with autism can neither decode the messages that reach him nor address clearly his own messages to the people surrounding him. These difficulties are disturbing him a lot, as his sensitivity is of the "skin deep" kind.>>*

*Professeur Gilbert Lelord, "L'exploration de l'autisme", Grasset, Paris 1998*

Signals tend to be perceived with equal intensity, regardless of their pertinence to the context. Detail elements are perceived with the same strength as the overall picture. Under such conditions, language acquisition and generalisation of concepts will be most difficult. The response to the environment is inappropriate; or rather we, Neuro Typical (NT[1]), think it is because we don't perceive the situation like autistic children do. This is the biggest challenge that we have to face when designing education programs for these children. Some more fundamental skills tend to be also impaired such as imitation, hand eye coordination, joint attention.

"Theory of Mind (ToM) deficit" describes the difficulty that people with autism have to appreciate the state of mind of other people(Frith 1997). People with autism will have difficulties to understand when we are serious or if we are just being funny. They may tell us something not taking into account that we don't have the same view as they have and they won't understand why we don't understand them...

---

[1] NT : Neuro Typical. This is the expression autistic self advocates call people who are not autistic or Asperger syndrome. Self advocates think that we behave strangely.

Sensory anomalies can trigger unexpected reactions. These could be sensory overloads, sometimes with sensory signals that NT would consider innocuous (Grandin 1991). In designing computer software, sounds and colour intensities should be modifiable. Beyond intensity, it should also be possible to choose colour or musical pitch of sounds, many people with autism have perfect pitch (Heaton).

**Understanding the Person's Needs.** Parents, people with autism and professionals may not (and perhaps shouldn't) express their need in computer terms. They would limit themselves to what they know about computers or dream about some extraordinary possibilities that are far beyond current technologies capabilities. These needs are similar to those of other children, they may appear at a later age. Some basic needs are so easily satisfied through the normal development of children, often without specific teaching, that we may have difficulties understanding that, for children with autism, a specific educational program will often be necessary…

### 2.2 Assessment of Learning Capabilities

Even though assessing learning capabilities of children with autism could be extremely interesting domains of research for computer application, this is not the object of this text. I mention this aspect here primarily to insist upon the lack of proper indication of the developmental age for which educational programs and or computer games have been designed. Ideally, user's manuals should provide the developmental age, gross and fine motor capabilities, language and social skills required to use the program or the game. Teachers so far rely upon trial and error to select educational programs and games.

### 2.3 The Education Strategy

On the basis of the assessment of the child learning capabilities, teachers will put together a strategy which may call for several computer programs. This will most likely entail using several vendor products elements in the sequence of teaching. The teacher will have to switch in real time from one interface to another. Actually even in single provider situations it is often hard to build smooth teaching sequences that follow the strategy selected by the teachers.

This is one of the biggest challenges for educational program designers. It would be useful here to have a "meta" authoring system which teachers could use to combine several drills in a seamless education sequence.

### 2.4 Can a Computer Be Useful to That Strategy?

Computers have characteristics which could benefit the education of an autistic child (Tréhin 1985). The ideas expressed then are still valid with minor updates.

**1/ A computer does not react like a person:** many of the difficulties of the autistic child with persons and animals lies in their unpredictable behaviour. A computer has very consistent reactions to the same actions. It doesn't mean that the goal is to provide a cold, mechanical interface to the child for ever. On the contrary, it is just to ease early interventions and sense of agency. It isn't hence necessary to be trying to provide an environment that imitates human behaviour, at least for the early phases of education. Later on it may be important to introduce some controlled "unpredictability" that will make the program react more like a person…

**2/ A computer can be programmed to create very stable pictures** of simple objects, people or situations, and respond consistently to the child interactions.

Once the basic concept has been acquired, the next step will be to try progressively building a more complex categorisation of objects by introducing small variations on the objects images and a more complex context.

**3/ A computer can be programmed to create very stable sounds.** The use of a speech synthesiser permits a similar strategy for teaching verbal language. The words for the same simple objects would be pronounced by the synthesiser in a very stable auditory stimulus in simultaneity with the picture. Once the acquisition of a concept is definitive, variations in the voice can be introduced in the pitch, in the speed, in the intensity, in the various parameters that differentiate speaker's voices.

In point 2 and 3, **stability of visual and auditory stimuli** is not an end in itself. The end goal is to teach the child to live in an ordinary context. People with autism have a very fine capability to spot small details out of a complex situation (Happé 1994). It is hence necessary to take into account that such a "normal context" may prove to be far too complex for the child with autism, entail frustrations and possibly severe behaviour problems (Laxer Tréhin 2001). The programs should be designed to preserve stimuli sensory stability, unless teachers decide the child is ready to accept some variations.

**4/ A computer provides a wealth of input/output devices** that can be used will enable interactions adapted to the progress of the child:

- Touch sensitive screen or a touch sensitive pad for sensory motor acquisitions interactions (as in the step 2)
- CD-ROM of a DVD for more accurate images of objects as the child progresses in object complexity.
- Printer or plotter for the production of a durable output
- I already mentioned the speech synthesiser
- Some voice input can be already envisioned as for example the one used in the programs for deaf children developed by I.B.M. France Scientific Centre
- Voice recognition is still very experimental but would of course be key in language development (improvements here have been important since 1985 but not up to the needs of educational programs for children with autism)
- A scanner or a Digital camera to capture still pictures or videos

All these devices can provide a great link between the classroom environment and the open environment. It is nevertheless important that product designers keep in mind the ease of use of such devices, including "default options" that will provide a result, even if it isn't perfect, for users who aren't experts. Fortunately the predictability of computer programming makes the use of I/O devices by people with autism, some of the most handicapped manage to learn rather complex sequences.

**5/** The computer has one very specific quality that is not often mentioned: **the computer is a mean of communication**. For some of the children who will not develop spoken language, this possibility constitutes a realistic alternative. One can think of portable devices, but also about home computer networks enabling a very rich communication. The overwhelming success of internet use by people with autism (Trehin 2001) has gone beyond my own most optimistic expectations. Unlike face to face meetings or phone conversations, internet is a "connexion less" communication interface, that isn't as intrusive as a conversation, it gives autistic people time to think about what was written on the messages and time to answer[2]. Recent developments allow picture based communication over the internet (see ALDICT[3] project).

**All these seem to be leading to fairly straight forward requirements:**
The main concerns in all these educational requirements, once expressed in computer programming terms, turns out to be **adaptability** to individual learning styles and a **progressive integration of context complexity**.

Assume we have determined that learning to recognise and name colours is a useful educational module[4]. There are of course hundreds of such modules available on the market. But what specific constraints should be applied if we want to develop it for children with autism?

For the very first levels, for the more severely handicapped children, the colours should be presented in a completely context free setting. The same voice should be used in naming the colour. The goal is to make sure that it is indeed the colour that is recognised and not a small context detail associated to each colour. Progressively, various shapes and order positioning in the presentation of colours can be introduced, more context added, the voice calling the colour names can be changed, this should be monitored by the teacher according to the evolution of the child. Note that the starting point will also depend from the assessment of each individual learning capabilities.

For each item, the teacher should be in a position to determine the difficulty of the task according to the attention span of the child: number of colours presented on a single frame, duration of the frame presentation before prompting again for an answer, number of frames in the whole exercise.

After several steps, when recognition of colours in context being acquired, it is then necessary that this acquisition be assessed in other drills which are no longer destined to teach colours, but where colours play a role in the exercise. This tests the generalisation of the acquisition of the knowledge of colours when outside the direct environment of colour learning drill. In case of error at this level, the program should send a message to the teacher "*This child may not have completely mastered colours*". What I am addressing here is the interactivity between modules (This concept of incidental testing is valid for other basic learnings : sounds, numbers, letters, etc.)

Adaptability to various learning styles also means to have the possibility to go progressively from a very concrete representation of objects, living subjects and situations to more abstract representations. At the lowest level of teaching techniques, it may be necessary to work with physical objects, pictures of the object may be too abstract for a severely autistic person. Computer technology can provide a support, providing a stable vocal stimuli: BaBar, developed by Jean Claude Gabus at the FST

[2] Note that this is equally applicable to people with learning difficulties.

[3] http://www.siwadam.com/hmm/euae.htm

[4] Strategies for teaching colours may have to start at a far lower level, for example differentiating colours, pairing colours which means that "same" and "different" have also been acquired, even if not verbally.

(Swiss Foundation for Rehabilitation Technology), permits this by placing a code bar sticker on objects and using a hand held code bar reader and speech synthesizer which translates the code bar on the object in a pre-recorded word naming the object.

These programs should then progressively move on to more abstract representations: photographic pictures, realistic colour drawings, realistic line drawings, schematic drawings, iconic drawings and possibly printed words as the child makes progress in symbolic representations.

**This again may seem very natural so why insist on it?** People with autism not only differ from one another but a same person there may be extreme variations in various cognitive domains (Schopler Mesibov 1988): Verbal comprehension may be low while hand eye coordination may be "normal". Adaptability of educational program must take into account these skills discrepancies.

To give a concrete example, "*ordering a sequence of events*" exercises should be adaptable: a complex sequence could be illustrated by photographic pictures for one person and a very simple sequence illustrated by symbolic pictures for another person. In most programs available on the market, such fine adaptability is not factored in.

This example leads us to one major basic application of computer education: simulation of social situations. In this domain the principles of adaptability remain valid. It would be essential to be able to fine tune the presentation of the drills: the level of complexity of the situations and of the contexts, coupled with the level of capability for abstract representations. Some multimedia programs have been designed for social simulations but most miss the adaptability that would make them really usable with people with autism, even though that was the initial goal.

Some research was done about Virtual Reality (Strickland 1997) proving that children with autism could adapt to a virtual environment. One limit in the present state of technology remains the cost and cumbersome aspect of VR helmets. But also the scarcity of content…

## 3 Constructivist Educational Programs

The constructivist approach, aims at providing a learning space rather than a teaching program, "*a deficit in learning to be replaced by one of a difference in learning*"(Gay 1996) . This second approach has been less developed in special education than the first one.

In the case of autism, specific difficulties exist with such an approach where "the learner rather than the teacher develops or constructs knowledge and that opportunities created for such construction are more important than instruction that originates from the teacher" (Diaz 2001). Children with autism have difficulties to learn by experience, they tend either not to generalise or to over generalise. They also tend to see the details rather than the whole (Happe 1996).

LOGO programming is one of such learning environments. Sylvia Weir (1976) was among the first to use the Logo system to teach autistic children various communication and interaction skills. The Logo programming language is still being used in special education for teaching spatial relations and orientation.

A research program was developed in the mid eighties at the IBM Yorktown Heights Research lab, using a constructivist strategy. It was designed to enable children to program animated scenarios, first building virtual objects, animals or people (house, dog, stickman, robot, plane); then using simple "verbs" (move, shake, tilt, etc.) and attributes (left, right, up, down, in front of, behind, etc.) and with a simple syntax, allowed children to build and tell animated story : “CALL ROBOT” ; “MOVE ROBOT LEFT IN FRONT OF HOUSE” ; “SHAKE ROBOT”. This created a superb learning space with infinite combinations.

There is likely to be a broad area of research to be explored in this domain. A wealth of literature has been published on the constructivist teaching, see for example Willey (1999). Making programs adaptable, to use appropriate levels of representations according to the cognitive abilities of each child.

The AURORA Projects for children with autism is another example of constructivist programs where a learning space is provided rather than a teaching system. It is based upon robots interacting with children (Dautenhahn).

**Promising projects are starting to show up:** The specific features of autistic reasoning are analyzed to design software tools for diagnosis and training of the children with autism (Galitsky 2000). A lot of teachers do practice such constructivist approaches with children when using peripheral devices like digital camera, for example to let children tell stories. The use of picture editing software adapted to a young man with autism, in particular during leisure time, was presented at the World Autism Organisation Melbourne Congress (Noyes 2002).

Applications of computers for Leisure time would justify by themselves another full paper… Computers could help freeing some of the special talents, existing in some people with autism (Hermelin 2001).

## 4 Conclusions

Children with autism need to learn the same things as other children, in a sense they don’t have “special needs”, but they need to be taught things that other children learn so naturally and these may be the hardest thing to teach… There will always be the need for programs that help teach basic things: colours, shapes, relations between objects, sameness, difference, spatial relations (under above, next to, in, out of, etc…) later on social skills and general knowledge.

Children with autism will require special means for learning, enabling teachers to really fine tune exercises to each individual child. A lot of the programs for children education could very well be used for their content, providing the teachers could adapt the presentation to each individual child. I also spoke of the need to be able to prepare for the child seamless combinations of exercises taken from various vendors.

There is finally the whole area of constructivist educational programs which opens up a vast domain of research and development. These may prove to be quite challenging for research programs in the future…

## References


1. Austwick K. "*Teaching Machines and Programming* ", Pergamon Press, Oxford (1964).
2. Blackhurst A.E. “*Perspectives on Technology in Special Education*”, Council for exceptional children,http://www.cec.sped.org/bk/aprtec.html, (2001).

3. Dautenhahn K. "*The AURORA Project: Using Mobile Robots in Autism Therapy*", http://www.aurora-project.com/.
4. Diaz M. "*Computer-Assisted Instruction/Programmed Instruction*". http://informatics.buffalo.edu/faculty/ellison/Syllabi/519Complete/formats/programmedinstr/program.html.
5. Frith U. "*Autism: Explaining the Enigma*", Blackwell, Oxford (1991), vastly revised edition (2003).
6. Gabus J.C. "*The B.A.Bar Project, To Stimulate and Improve Speech and Communication*", FST (Fondation Suisse pour les Téléthèses), June (2002) http://www.fst.ch/FST2/IMAGES_GLOBALES/photos_contenu/photos_publications/-E101.pdf.
7. Galitsky B. "Simulating autistic patients as agents with corrupted reasoning about mental states", American Association for Artificial Intelligence, http://www.dcs.bbk.ac.uk/~galitsky/pdf/galitskyFSS00.pdf.
8. *Gay G. "Technologies for Remediation and Compensation of Learnin Disabilities*", Ontario Institute for Studies in Education,( 1996), http://snow.utoronto.ca/prof_dev/ict/adaptive/week3/literacy8.html.
9. Grandin T. " *Sensory Problems in Autism*", Proceedings, Conference of the Autism Society of America,( 1991).
10. Happé F. "*Autism, an introduction to psychological theory*", UCL Press, London (1994).
11. Happé F. "Studying weak central coherence at low levels: children with autism do not succumb to visual illusions. A research note", J Child Psychol Psychiatry. (1996) Oct; 37(7):873-7.
12. Heaton P. et al, "*Autism and pitch processing: a precursor for savant musical ability*", Music Perception, 15,(1998), pp 291-305 .
13. Hermelin B. "*Bright Splinters of the Mind. A personal story of research with Autistic Savants* ", Jessica Kinsley Publishers, London (2001).
14. Jordan R. "*Education of Children and young people with autism* ", Guides for Special Needs Education number 10, UNESCO, Paris (1997 ).
15. Laxer G. Tréhin P. "*Les Troubles du comportement associés à l'autisme et aux autres handicaps mentaux*", AFD, Mougins (2001).
16. Noyes P. "*Iconic Solutions – how a multi media package engaged a young autistic man & changed his family's life*", World Autism Orgnisation Congres, Melbourne Nov. (2002).
17. Papert S. "*Mindstorms Children, Computers, And Powerful Ideas*", Basic Books, NY (1980).
18. Schopler E. Mesibov G. "*Diagnostic and assessment in Autism*", Plenum press (1988).
19. Skinner B.F. "*The Programming of Verbal Knowledge* ", in E. Galanter ed. "*Automatic Teaching : the State of the art* ", John Wiley& Sons, NY (1959).
20. D. Strickland, "*Virtual Reality for the Treatment of Autism*", In G. RIVA (Ed.), "*Virtual Reality in Neuro-Psycho-Physiology*",©.Ios Press: Amsterdam, Netherlands (1997), (1998).
21. Trehin P. "CAI for children with learning difficulties", Proceedings of IBM Internal symposium for people with disabilities, (1985 ).
22. Trehin P. "*Pratique de l'internet par des personnes atteintes d'autisme*", Journées d'échange "ADAPT", CNEFEI, Suresne 2-3 mai 2000, CNEFEI Suresnes (2001).
23. Wiley D., "*Learning objects and the new CAI: So what do I do with a learning object?*" (1999). http://wiley.ed.usu.edu/docs/instruct-arch.pdf
24. Weir S. Emanuel R "*Using Logo to catalyse communication in an autistic child*". DAI Research Report No. 15, University of Edinburgh. (1976).

# Using 'Ambient Intelligence' for Compensating Intellectual Difficulties of People with Severe Learning Difficulties and/or Autistic Spectrum Disorders

Gerardo Herrera[1], Amparo Plasencia[1], Gabriel Labajo[2], Rita Jordan[3], and Cristina de Pablo[4]

[1] Autism and Learning Difficulties Group, Robotics Institute
University of Valencia, P.O.Box 2085, 46071 Valencia, Spain
Gerardo.Herrera@uv.es
http://robotica.uv.es

[2] Diagnostic and Intervention Centre, Montes y Martín Baró, 3-9
47007, Valladolid, Spain
Gabriel.Labajo@terra.es

[3] School of Education, University of Birmingham, Edgbaston
Birmingham B15 2TT, UK
R.R.Jordan@bham.ac.uk

[4] Autismo Burgos Association, Valdenuñez, 8, 09001 Burgos, Spain
http://www.autismoburgos.org

**Abstract.** This paper describes a set of services and software created so that what is called 'ambient intelligence' would compensate for the 'intellectual difficulties' that people from this collective have. Existing concepts and standards of ambient intelligence are strongly reinforced through the use of the exact current user's position as a key factor to calculate how the 'digital home' or any 'digital environment' behaves at every moment. This will be obtained using both Wi-Fi personal locators (embedded in necklaces or bracelets) and Wi-Fi communication from the PDA. This mix, together with individual capabilities and preferences, makes the development of a wide range of services possible when combined with the multimedia capabilities of new technology devices.

## 1 Introduction

Many of the behaviour problems that are shown by the more severely affected people with autism and/or learning difficulties, have their origin in the lack of comprehension of the codes and rules that govern the environment where they live which in turn causes a lack of predictability in their lives. In addition to their very well- known expressive communication difficulties, they have problems in the receptive plane of their communication and they seem to get very anxious when trying to cope with the most basic daily activities because of his/her non-comprehension of what happens, when it happens and for how long it will happen. They need, like everybody, predictability in their lives.

K. Miesenberger et al. (Eds.): ICCHP 2004, LNCS 3118, pp. 969–975, 2004.

When the person doesn't know or doesn't understand the set of cultural and social rules that govern the environment where he/she lives, then he/she can't predict what will happen in the next moment, he has no "predictability":

"... predictability means having an idea or a mental image about 'where' and 'when'. The answer to the question 'How long?' is also very important... Moreover, we want that information in a language we can understand... " [1].

But it is not necessary to use complex and very technical psychological explanations to be in the same boat as someone without predictability. We can say that it would be as if, for example, someone travelled to a foreign country with a different language and alphabet such as Japan, without having received any previous educational support. This person will probably also get very anxious and nervous when trying to cope with the most basic daily activities because of his/her non-comprehension of what happens, when it happens and for how long it will happen. The continuous experience of many people with autism and /or mental retardation may be like this, with the additional feature that they don't even have a reference or a prediction about how the information they receive should be, because their development was, since their first infancy, different to typical.

## 2 Matching Individual Needs: User Profile

One of the key factors when addressing the needs of someone with a disorder classified within the Autism Spectrum is to take into account the very high diversity among this population by finding flexible solutions which match their heterogeneity.

'Individual abilities', together with 'current time' and 'location' are the basic data entries our system uses to calculate the relevant information that must be provided to the user with autism (Figure1). The information is always audiovisual and it is provided through a set of devices distributed by the environment, such as information murals, personal PDAs, tablet PCs and others, always with a very intuitive interface or even with automatic functioning when appropriate.

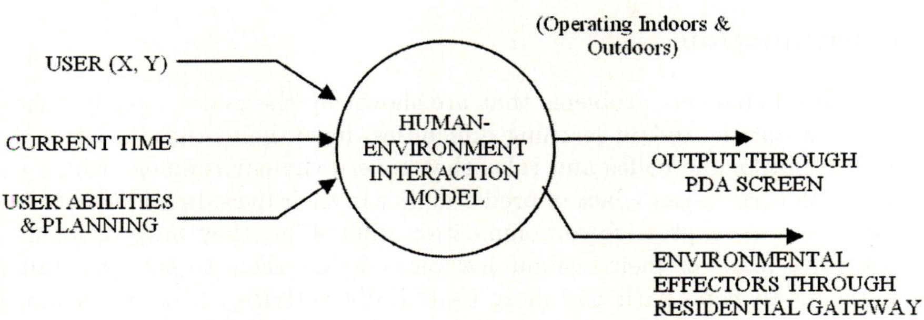


**Fig. 1.** New Services for People with Autism

Autism is defined by a triad of impairments in communication, socialisation and a reduced set of interests and a tendency to routine. As part of a set of individual characteristics that must be taken into account to construct the 'user profile', we can find the degree of those impairments, general intellectual abilities and also other variable issues such as the mood or predisposition of the user on a given day.

The user profile will also define the format in which activities and information are shown and the extent to which the technology will be inserted into his or her environment. There are lots of issues that will be different depending on each individual:

- Temporal Range covered by the notebook (task, day, week, month, year).
- Alternatives of the selection repertoire. The 'alternative activities' group will be a set associated with a given user, and a subset of this one will be associated to a given period of time. For example, we couldn't include 'going to play with class companions' when the user is at home with his/her parents. It would be possible to manipulate this set to add or eliminate alternatives when adapting it to a given period of time.
- The level of complexity of the interface: with issues such as having pictures, pictograms or written words, and also the type of menus, with it being possible to have single-level menus (restricted) or to have multiple level foldable menus.
- The environments that can be considered hazardous and those which are safe.
- Level of autonomy in carrying out the tasks.
- Elements of the Expressive Communication Repertoire: photographs, pictograms, pre-recorded sentences, pre-recorded manual signs, etc. A number of objects, actions and expressions will be included for every activity of the user planning. Within the repertoire of things to communicate, together with objects and actions there will also be included expressions (visually or verbally, that are heard when they touch the screen, together with visual messages for the deaf). For example: 'I want to stop doing this', 'I want to rest', 'Wait', 'Give me more time', 'I don't understand', 'I don't know', 'I am nervous', 'I am happy/sad/angry', etc.
- Format for time representation: decreasing time bars / standard clock. The aim here is to represent time in a way that the user understands that the current activity has a beginning, a period of validity and an end. So, when an activity is ending, the user must know that there is a change to another activity. For doing so, we will use a decreasing bar with different colours, that will be blue at the beginning and red during the last seconds of a task, finally beeping when the time has expired. Here it is important to remember that when training on new tasks, there will not be a time limit, and that these kinds of visual indications will be provided as a support only once an activity has been mastered. It is equally important to start using it with very short tasks (with a very short period of associated time). If the time is too long, the user would lose his/her confidence in obtaining any prize.

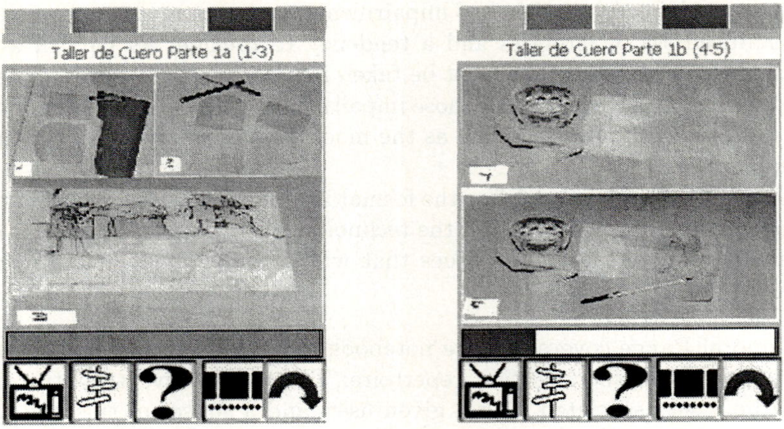


**Fig. 2.** Decreasing Time Bar indicators for showing the time passing by

- History of learning in relation to the notebook: it is expected that the user progresses in the management of the notebook as time goes by, due to the parallel teaching he/she will receive over relevant issues and also due to his/her familiarisation with the device. It is considered that data about this process will also be part of the 'user profile' and that this data will consist of different views of the user configuration at different times within the process of using the notebook.
- Planning elaboration: the possibility exists for the teacher to create the user planning and it can also be done by the user him/herself, doing it from the Data Management System and from the Information Point.

With these ideas in mind, we intend to compensate individual limitations on each functional area providing greater or lower support within them. Another aim when adapting the system individually is to be able to follow a process throughout which we introduce support (visual, acoustic, etc) gradually and then, once the desired level of self-management is reached, to retire it gradually in order to have more autonomy.

## 3 New Services

By doing this, these new technologies can reinforce the information flow that goes from the environment to the person, automatically reading the environment's information, translating it, and finally showing it to the person in a format he/she can understand. Appropriate information can be provided according to the situation and location of the individual at any given time.

The services we are developing will make the environment more understandable, more predictable and manageable. Thus, technology will be used: to show the time passing by in a format they can understand (decreasing time-bars, Figure 2); to alert them and their carers about environmental risks (when near to balconies, roads, etc.); to make the understanding of how to cope with the environment easier; to make some devices function automatically (such as lights, blinds, etc.) depending on user location and other semi-automatic devices (microwaves, fridges, etc.); to provide more structuring (Figure 3) to the environment and to time through a very intuitive audiovisual schedule shown on information points as well as on the PDA.

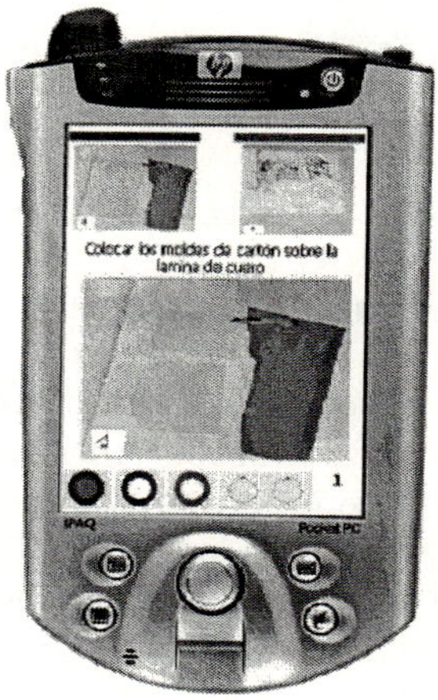

**Fig. 3.** Snapshot of our software on a step by step structured activity

All of the above have the constant possibility of giving audiovisual feedback to the handicapped user so that he can gain control over the environment by means of his/her own moves and interaction with other people, with information points, with PDA's, with electrical household appliances or even objects (in the near future when Auto-ID technology has already spread).

The connection among the set of devices is as follows:

Following the philosophy we have revealed above over the 'user profile', we would obtain very different services depending on each individual profile. For example, if we have an individual in mind with what is called 'High Functioning Autism', with good general intellectual abilities but with all the impairments of the autism triad, we can imagine that he would use the notebook for creating his own plan or agenda for the weekend, for allowing his parents to track his position when going out autonomously or for alerting them automatically when he or she is in unsafe locations, etc. All of these can be very different when thinking about other individuals with lower abilities and autonomy. For example, a user with a profile like that would know the remaining time for a given task throughout the 'decreasing time bar' that represents it. He would also obtain help to carry out a step by step activity or he would communicate his current feelings to others through the images included in the repertoire for expressive communication.

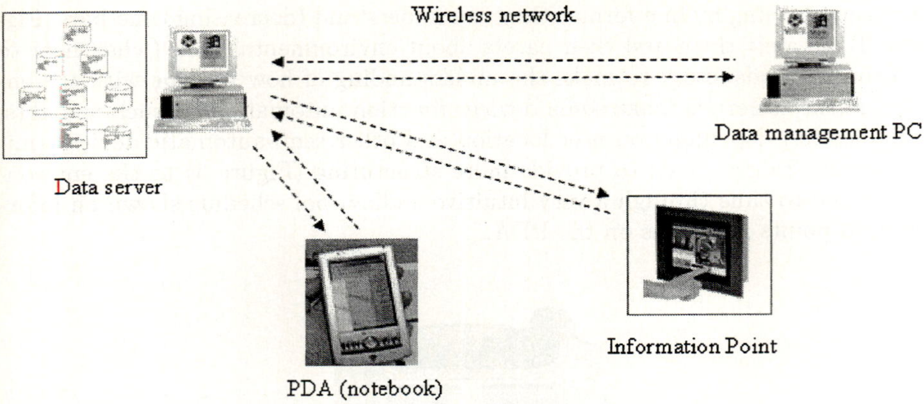


**Fig. 4.** Basic elements and infrastructure

## 4 Conclusions and Future Work

The services described above have just been developed and prepared for a group of adults with severe autism that attend the 'Autismo Burgos' Day Centre. They are currently starting to use these tools and we are defining ways of assessing it objectively. For doing so, we will assess individual time understanding and time perception, individual's level of communication (receptive and expressive) and individual's global autonomy and on-task autonomy. However, before assessing those long-term desired benefits, we should assess whether or not they are using it correctly. Interaction details are being represented in a states graph where 'states' represent the information shown to the user and 'flows' are user actions such us interacting with the PDA or moving from one room to another, etc. Laboratory tasks as well as daily ones are being prepared to assess this, with and without help from professionals.

In order to reinforce the practical nature of the results we pursue with this project, the imminent convergence of PDA's and mobile phones will be very important, together with the creation of Wi-Fi infrastructure everywhere. In order to be able to respond to the new possibilities that will emerge from this technological progress, our team is also working on expanding these services towards other collectives.

All the ideas above only make sense if used appropriately for people with Autism and/or Learning Difficulties, at all times being respectful towards their rights as humans, especially regarding self-determination and personal autonomy. This will be guaranteed by continuously assessing if an adequate balance has been reached between supports provided and level of independence, and with deep reflection and definition of the ethics of the project.

Despite the fact that our objective is to develop services for the more severely affected, and in spite of the advance that we would have obtained towards this extreme of the spectrum, a considerable range of people would remain outside the scope of these services. We hope to be able to progress towards them in the near future.

## Acknowledgments

The project within which we are carrying out this research, named ACIERTA [2], [3], is funded by the Spanish Ministry of Science of Technology and is in its last year of development.

## References

1. Peeters, T.: El autismo y los problemas para comprender y utilizar símbolos. 'El tratamiento del autismo: nuevas perspectivas'. Angel Riviere y Juan Martos (Comp.). Spanish Ministry of Social Affairs (1997). Madrid.
2. Herrera, G.: New Information Services for providing predictability to the environment of the more severely affected people with mental retardation. Presented at the 126th Annual Meeting of the American Association on Mental Retardation. Orlando, Florida. May 28 - June 1, 2002. Part of the Session 'From Research to Practice'.
3. Herrera, G., Plasencia, A., Labajo, G., Blanquer, A., Arnáiz, J., Cuesta, J.L., de Pablo, C., Jordan, R., León, E.: New Information Services for providing predictability to the environment of people with autism. Presented at the 6th Autism Europe International Congress. Lisbon, November 2003.

# Assessing B.A.Bar Device as a Tool for Supporting Labour Integration of a Severely Affected Person with Autism Who Carries Out Classifying Tasks

Gerardo Herrera[1,2] and Gabriel Labajo[3]

[1] Autism and Learning Difficulties Group. Robotics Institute
University of Valencia P.O.Box 2085. 46071 Valencia, Spain
Gerardo.Herrera@uv.es
http://robotica.uv.es

[2] Autismo Avila Association, Spain
http://www.autismoavila.org

[3] Diagnostic and Intervention Centre, Valladolid, Spain
Gabriel.Labajo@terra.es

**Abstract.** This paper describes the case research carried out to demonstrate the utility of a specific technical aid (adapted bar code reader) to train an adult with severe autism in the performance of a work task of classifying products in a shop. The individual with autism who participated in this research has a combination of difficulties (degree of 76 percent of disability and unable to learn to read and write) and abilities (being able to follow single verbal instructions). Positive results are expounded together with considerations about the desirable features of future products that would overcome the mere training process and also be useful for the final and real task in any working environment where bar codes are present. This paper also provides a preview of what work this group will face in the future in order to progress in the development of this more general and standard aid.

## 1 Problem Statement

This research has been carried out to demonstrate the usability of the B.A.Bar device (Adapted Bar Code Reader, from the Swiss Foundation for Rehabilitation Technology FST) when used for preparing an adult with autism for the labour market. The rationale of the research is that a given person (N=1) with a specific combination of abilities and difficulties can take great advantage of using this device to carry out classifying work tasks autonomously, thus obtaining her labour market integration. Her specific and individual profile of abilities and difficulties is as follows:

K. Miesenberger et al. (Eds.): ICCHP 2004, LNCS 3118, pp. 976–982, 2004.

### 1.1 Difficulties

The subject who participated in this research was a 24 year old girl with an Autistic Spectrum Disorder (ASD) with severe learning difficulties and a certified degree of disability of 76 percent.

### 1.2 Abilities

Her more relevant abilities were that, although she wasn't able to learn to read and write, she was able to follow single verbal instructions related to colours and to identify those colours in different places. She was also able to follow single instructions related to objects and easy actions within her repertoire. These abilities were complemented with a technological aid (B.A.Bar) to allow this person to carry out the classifying task autonomously.

## 2 Method

All the products in a wide set of shops came with Bar Codes. Bar Codes provide information about the product that can be related to several issues, included the shelf where it should be stored. But this information, as occurs with other tags and words we can find in the product box, does not mean anything for our adult with autism.

Our particular focus to resolve this problem is to use a B.A.Bar device in such a way that it translates Bar Code Information into some instructions in a format that our adult could understand, such as 'Put this object on the red shelf'. We illustrate this idea with the following picture:

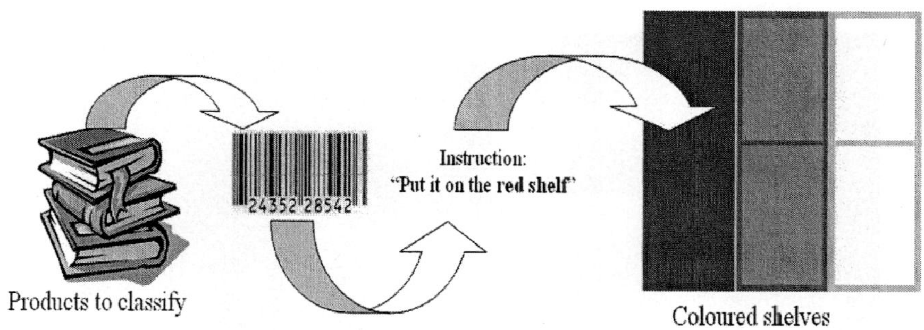


**Fig. 1.** Classifying process

When putting the Bar Code reader in front of the Bar Code, it automatically reproduces a pre-recorded audio message with the verbal instruction about where to put this product.

As it can be seen, the idea exposed above for the training stage is very simple but useful. Nevertheless, as far as the authors know, no one has had any previous experience of using this kind of device for this purpose.

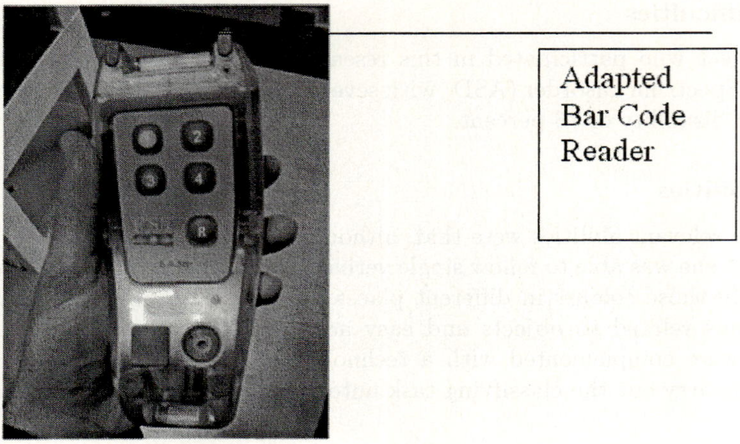


**Fig. 2.** B.A.Bar Device

## 2.1 Approach Stage

Before starting with the training process itself, there was a previous approach stage. This stage started by using coloured recipients and small pieces of plastic to train the individual with autism in the underlying task of classification following the colour criterion (Figure 3).

In a later step of this approach stage, this material has been substituted by books and shelves, both covered with coloured paper. In these previous stages, we found some initial difficulties that were more related to the motivation of the

**Fig. 3.** Approach task

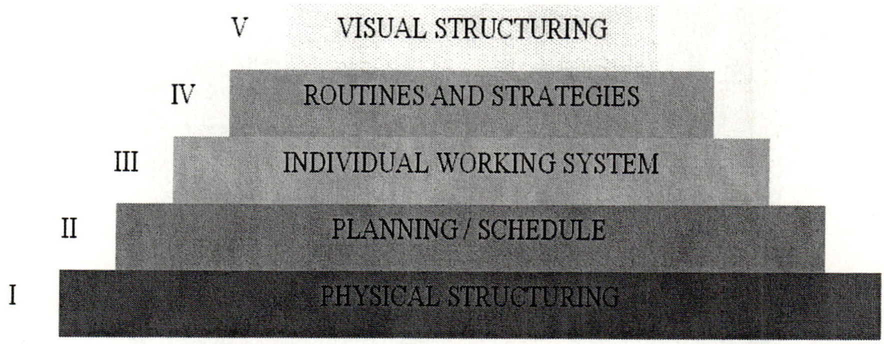


**Fig. 4.** TEACCH Levels

participant doing the task without continuous eliciting from the preparer, than on the task itself.

The colour criterion is not a necessary one for this kind of task, as other visual elements can be used for the process of matching a product with a shelf, such as very well known characters with, for example, the instruction 'put it in the Mickey Mouse shelf'. This criterion can be chosen according to the abilities and preferences of the given individual with autism.

### 2.2 Structuring

Both approaching and training stages have been planned within a global framework of environment and time visual structuring, for providing this user with autism the predictability and structuring she needs. For doing that we have followed TEACCH Method[1], from North Carolina University (USA), implementing visual structuring at different levels (Figure 4 and 5).

## 3 Results

### 3.1 Usability

As we have indicated above, the B.A.Bar was assessed in terms of its usability (composed measure of effectiveness, efficiency and satisfaction):

*EFFECTIVENESS:*

- Functional: we have checked that the B.A.Bar serves as it was intended, allowing the association of Bar Codes to products and to record audio messages for any of these codes. These Audio Messages are automatically played by the device whenever it is in front of the associated Bar Code,
- Resistance: one of the relevant issues of this device for this training stage was its resistance to impacts. In this sense we haven't found any difficulty,

**Fig. 5.** Approach task designed, using coloured books and shelves

– Easy to manage: the management of this device has been found to be very easy, making possible for it to be used by people with severe learning difficulties.

*EFFICIENCY:*

– Complete: it doesn't need other tools. The use of any other Bar Code reader would imply a specific and strong software development to reach the desired functionality.
– Wireless: it can be easily moved from one place to another, also with the possibility of being shared by several people.
– Long Bar Codes: this device comes with a set of long Bar Codes that are easier to read than those we normally find in the market. The only one difficulty we found is that those Codes aren't standardised.

*SATISFACTION:*

– People with autism normally have preference to single and mechanical tasks as the proposed one. This, together with the simplicity of management, resulted in a very gratifying task for our subject with autism.

### 3.2 Results Analysis

General results found after this training are positive, as the individual with autism participating has finally learnt to do the classifying task autonomously. However, some difficulties have been found during the process.

Associating visual and acoustic stimuli, such us hearing the instruction 'put this box on the red shelf' and the act of finding this shelf, is not always an easy thing for someone with autism. Perhaps, this is the reason for the main difficulty we found, that was at the last stage of the process when visual cues (colour) were retired from the products to be classified and non-neutral covers with different colours started to be used, with it being necessary to only pay attention to the auditory stimuli provided by the device.

If we analyse the task of classifying as defined in the approaching stage in detail, it is necessary for the pre-worker with autism to look for the recipient which has the same colour as the product she has in her hands, with both the product and the recipient cues being visual. However, in the final stage of the process, the product cue is no longer visual but auditory. The fact that the products have embedded coloured elements in the cover represents a visual distraction that creates confusion as to where to put the product. For example, if the instruction is 'put it on the red shelf' but the product has small portions of green colour on its cover, then our user would find difficulties in deciding whether the right stimulus is auditory (as trained in the last stage) or visual (as trained in the approach stage).

To overcome this difficulty, we temporally added some coloured cards as a complementary reinforcement to the auditory aid in order to avoid the distractive elements of the product cover. However, in any replication of this experimental process with other individuals, it would be appropriate to try not to use the colour criterion as a visual cue but only as an auditory one, without this colour being visually present in the origin of information (the product) that the worker receives as regards where to put the product. This can be obtained with a higher and more intense amount of help from the preparer and it is necessary that the individual with autism only pays attention to the verbal instructions provided.

## 4 Conclusions and Future Work

The specific technical aid used in this research has been found to be tremendously useful for the proposed training. However, taking into account that this device is not compatible with standard barcodes, and with the aim of spreading this possibility to any adult with autism with a similar profile to the one participating here, this research group has initiated contact with several European-wide companies with software products in this field of the market (software for boutiques, shoe shops, sport shops, perfume shops, superstores and retail stores).

It is intended that the new versions of the existing software include an additional module that, connected with the existing database, provide auditory and/or visual instructions about where to put products through the use of a standard barcode reader. By doing it this way a future or occasional migration to electromagnetic tags (i.e. Electronic Product Cards EPC[2]) will also be guaranteed once barcodes have disappeared.

The extension that this will mean will also make it possible to advance from the current case study to a more complete group research, being then possible to gain more general results.

## Acknowledgments

This Project has been funded by the Spanish Ministry of Social Affairs and by the ONCE Foundation (Spanish Foundation for the Blind). It has also been possible thanks to the gentle provision of this device from the Swiss Foundation for Rehabilitation Technology (FST)[3].

## References

1. Treatment and Education of Autistic and related Communication Handicapped Children `http://www.teacch.com/teacch.htm`
2. Electronic Product Card Global `http://www.epcglobalinc.org/`
3. Swiss Foundation for Rehabilitation Technology (FST) `http://www.fst.ch/`

# An Adaptive and Predictive Environment to Support Augmentative and Alternative Communication

Nicola Gatti, Matteo Matteucci, and Licia Sbattella

Dipartimento di Elettronica e Informazione
Politecnico di Milano
Piazza Leonardo da Vinci 32, I-20133 Milano, Italy
{ngatti,matteucci,sbattella}@elet.polimi.it

**Abstract.** In this paper we describe BLISS2003, an Information and Communication Technology (ICT) aid for verbal impaired people supporting the use of Augmentative and Alternative Communication (AAC) languages. BLISS2003 allows to compose messages in Bliss and other AAC languages (i.e. PCS, PIC, etc.), to translate them in natural language, to send and receive them via email, or to vocally synthetize them. BLISS2003 is characterized by a predictive module that allows for a more efficient selection of graphical symbols and more natural sessions of communication by adapting a model of the user language behavior.

## 1 Introduction

Communication represents the main way in which man can live his sociality; in fact, only by communication, man can express thought, emotions, and ideas. Communication plays an important role in everyday life; by communicating man can express necessities, feelings, request for information and aid. Nowadays, millions of verbal impaired people live currently in the world [1]; their communication capabilities are permanently or temporarily corrupted and, for this reason, most of them suffer a condition of social exclusion.

To help verbal impaired people, ad-hoc alternative languages have been developed by the International Society for Augmentative and Alternative Communication (ISAAC) established in 1983 in USA [2]. Among the currently most adopted AAC languages [3] we can cite: Bliss, PCS, PIC, PICSYMB, CORE, Rebus. Each of them is based on a peculiar dictionary of words represented by pictures or symbols, and specific composition rules simple enough to be learnt and used by disabled people [4].

ICT, especially in cases of verbal impaired people, has been widely used to develop effective tools for rehabilitation. BLISS2003, developed from APBLISS [5], is an adaptive and predictive environment for AAC developed to provide people during the communicative process with a personal table of Bliss symbols and a set of intelligent tools. BLISS2003 can translate the composed messages to natural language making use of a syntactic/semantic analyzer, vocally synthetize

K. Miesenberger et al. (Eds.): ICCHP 2004, LNCS 3118, pp. 983–990, 2004.

them, and exchange them via email. With respect to traditional AAC software aids, BLISS2003 addresses a set of novel features: an innovative predictive composition assistant based on a discrete implementation of auto-regressive hidden Markov model [6] called DAR-HMM, the simultaneous support of several AAC languages, and the adoption of a graphical interface designed on purpose for impaired users. BLISS2003 has been registered by the Blissymbolics Communication International (BCI) center of Toronto and has been adopted for hundreds hours of experimental validation by several Italian clinics for verbal impaired people. In the following section we introduce the BLISS2003 environment and in Section 3 we describe its the main novelty: the predictive composition assistant. A case study, taken from the validation activity of the tool, is presented in Section 4.

## 2 The Bliss2003 Graphical Environment

The collaboration of a psychologist expert on graphic trace helped us to design a specific graphical interface that improves usability in order to reduce the difficulties a verbal impaired person can undertake interacting with graphical applications [7]. The main issues we have taken into account regard the iconographic style, the graphical structure of the windows, their place, the number of buttons and their function as well. The whole iconographic collection has been drawn by a web-designer with the requirements of a simple and clear interface, intuitive and unambiguous, with well-blended colors and uniform strokes to assist visual difficulties while supporting content decoding (see Figure 1).

BLISS2003 is organized in seven environments to facilitate the user concentration by reducing buttons, functions and information that the user can simultaneously find on the screen. This environment-based structure has been designed to facilitate users since they express an higher concentration in specific environments than in a general environment that requires to discriminate among many choices. Environments are also related to the capabilities of the user and the adoption of a specific one should be accomplished in collaboration with a therapist.

Since the universality of Bliss language, Bliss messages can be synthesized in any natural language. The user can set more speech features such as male or female voice, tonality, volume, emphasis and so on. The vocal synthesis makes easier the interaction with other people. In addition the verbal impaired user can operate a syntactic concordance, using a syntactic/semantic analyzer, of a Bliss message into natural language according to grammar rules for verb, personal ending using gender concordance and prepositions in order to achieve a sentence syntactically correct. The transposition of messages makes more comprehensible a sentence for people that do not know Bliss language.

Similarly to other AAC communication software application, BLISS2003 is focused on the symbols table. In particular, BLISS2003 provides a *master table* composed of all Bliss symbols – about 2000 – and a *personal table* composed of just the symbols used by the user. Through the symbol editor environment

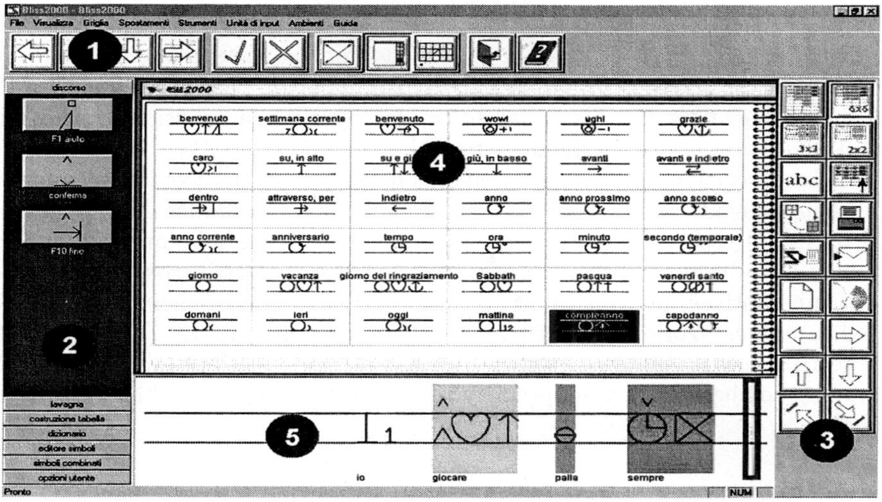


**Fig. 1.** BLISS2003 graphical user interface. The underlined spots refer to the *Main Command Bar* (1), the *Environment Option Bar* (2), the *Environment Command Bar* (3), the *Data Zone* (4), and the *Temporary Processing Zone* (5).

therapists can load PCS, PIC, or Rebus collection, so that BLISS2003 could be employed as a generic software for alternative communication and could be used as a multiuser system (in clinic, with people who communicate using different alternative codes). The provision of multi-language support evidenced extreme utility in rehabilitative processes. Furthermore BLISS2003 interface supports devices other then classical mouse and keyboard, in order to overcome motor disabilities in the user (e.g., joystick, touch sensor, switch buttons, graphic tables, etc.).

## 3 Predictive Composition Assistant

The BLISS2003 environment provides a predictive composition assistant, named CABA$^2$L [8], which supports disables in composing sentences, by speeding up the symbols selection process, reducing the strain and the composition time, while increasing their self esteem. Literature about AAC languages application is rich of works concerning alphabetical prediction systems [9], but it is almost completely lack of systems performing symbols prediction [10]. To overcome this issue we have designed an innovative prediction system for Bliss language. CABA$^2$L is a prediction system able to suggest the user a set of Bliss symbols as next probable choice for his/her sentence according to the last symbol selected and the history of sentences previously composed. In other word, when a symbol is selected from the table, CABA$^2$L shows a list of symbols that it considers as most probable ones – with respect to its model of the user language behavior – to continue his/her text. For instance, in the sentence "I want to eat" the next symbol will probably be some kind of food, so the assistant should suggest "pizza", "pasta", "bread", "cake", on the basis of last selected symbol and user characteristics. CABA$^2$L proposes a limited number of symbols defined by the therapist depending disable capabilities and operates a scansion of them by adopting an adaptive rate similarly to [11].

The composition assistant is based on a novel auto-regressive Hidden Markov Model implementation, called Discrete Auto-Regressive Hidden Markov Model (DAR-HMM) that we have developed specifically for symbolic prediction. Bliss symbols have been divided in six grammatic categories (adverbs, verbs, adjectives, substantives, persons, punctuation), and each one of them has been divided in sub-categories using semantic network formalism [12] (about 30 sub-categories). In the following, we give a brief formal description of DAR-HMM according to the notation adopted by Rabiner in [6] to specify hidden Markov models:

- $S \triangleq \{s_i\}$, (sub)categories set with $N = |S|$;
- $V \triangleq \{v_j\}$, predictable symbols set with $M = |V|$;
- $V^{(i)} = \{v_k^{(i)}\}$, set of symbols predictable in (sub)category $i$
- $O(t) \in V$, observed symbol at time $t$;
- $Q(t) \in S$, (sub)category at time $t$;
- $\pi_i(t) = P(Q(t) = s_i)$, probability of $s_i$ being (sub)category at time $t$;
- $a_{ii'} = P(Q(t+1) = s_i | Q(t) = s_{i'})$, transition probability $s_{i'} \to s_i$;
- $b_k^i = P(O(0) = v_k^{(i)} | Q(0) = s_i)$, probability of observing $v_k^{(i)}$ from (sub)category $s_i$ at $t = 0$;
- $b_{kk'}^{ii'} = P(O(t) = v_k^{(i)} | Q(t) = s_i, O(t-1) = v_{k'}^{(i')})$, probability of observing $v_k^{(i)}$ from the subcategory $s_i$ having just observed $v_{k'}^{(i')}$.

Given $\lambda =< \Pi^0 = \{\pi_i(0)\}, A = \{a_{ii'}\}, B = \{b_{kk'}^{ii'}\} >$ the vector of parameters describing a specific language behavior model, we can predict the first observed symbol as the most probable one at time $t = 0$:

$$\begin{aligned}\hat{O}(0) &= \arg\max_{v_k^{(i)}} \left(P(O(0) = v_k^{(i)} | \lambda)\right) \\ &= \arg\max_{v_k^{(i)}} \left(P(O(0)|Q(0), \lambda) P(Q(0))\right) \\ &= \arg\max_{v_k^{(i)}} \left(b_k^i \cdot \pi_i(0)\right).\end{aligned}$$

Then, using the DAR-HMM generative model described in Figure 2, to predict the $t^{th}$ symbol of a sentence we want to maximize the symbol probability in the present (hidden) state given the last observed symbol:

$$P(O(t) = v_k^{(i)}, Q(t) = s_i | O(t-1) = v_{k'}^{(i')}, \lambda).$$

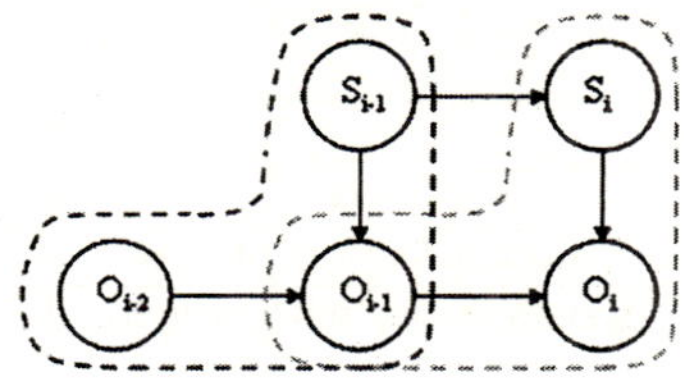

**Fig. 2.** Symbols emission in DAR-HMM; $S_i$ is the $i^{th}$ state (Bliss subcategory), $O_j$ is the $j^{th}$ observed symbol.

Recalling that we can compute the probability of the current (hidden) state as

$$P(Q(t)) = \sum^{N} P(Q(t)|Q(t-1))P(Q(t-1)) =$$
$$= \sum_{i'=1}^{N} \pi_{i'}(t-1)a_{ii'} = \pi_i(t),$$

we obtain the a recursive form for symbol prediction at time $t$ :

$$\hat{O}(t) = \arg\max_{v_k^{(i)}} \left( b_{kk'}^{ii'} \cdot \sum_{i'=1}^{N} \pi_{i'}(t-1)a_{ii'} \right).$$

In CABA$^2$L, the probability tables on $\lambda$ vector are computer using a data set of Bliss sentences from the user and can adapt their values according to the evolution of the composition capabilities of the disable. In doing this, we have adopted a variation of the Baum-Welch algorithm, an iterative algorithm based on the Expectation-Maximization method [6], adapting this technique to the specific case of DAR-HMM. This feature is particularly relevant in the rehabilitation cases where, during the rehabilitation, the dictionary of the disable increases and his/her linguistic capabilities improve (an interested reader can retrieved a deeper analysis of CABA$^2$L in [8]).

## 4 Tool Validation

According to recent studies [13], 37% of impaired people dismiss to use the rehabilitation tool mainly because of lack of a real match to their needs. For this reason, in the development of BLISS2003, we have collaborated with two Italian clinical centers operating on verbal impairment – PoloH and SNPI of Crema (Italy) – to focus on an extensive experimentation of the new tool. Among the users who collaborated with us we have chosen to report the case study we consider as the most significant: "Elisa" an eighteen-year-old girl, who has been communicating with Bliss language for ten years.

From a disable perspective the most significant reason for assessing effectiveness is to assure that his/her problem has been solved. The effectiveness of an

**Table 1.** IPPA interviews comparison.

| Problem | Imp | D1 | D2 |
|---|---|---|---|
| speeding up communication | 5 | 4 | 2 |
| aiding the symbol selection process | 5 | 4 | 2 |
| compose Bliss message with much autonomy | 5 | 4 | 1 |
| performing the social integration making easier communication with non-Bliss interlocutor | 5 | 5 | 3 |
| exploiting communicative found | 5 | 4 | 2 |
| increasing user's attention degree | 4 | 4 | 2 |
| making powerful learning | 4 | 4 | 3 |
| **Total score** | | **137** | **70** |

assistive technology provision, in its most basic form, can thus be defined as the degree to which the problem is actually solved in relation to its intended aim. We dealt with this by using two international ad-hoc protocols: IPPA [14] and MPT [15]. In the following we report the results we have obtained using IPPA and MPT protocols introducing an overall evaluation of BLISS2003 (we do not describe the evaluation of each single components, such as composition assistant or multi-language adoption).

### 4.1 IPPA (Individually Prioritized Problem Assessment)

IPPA is a protocol centered on the verbal impaired user, in particular on the evaluation of the difficulties the disable undertakes interacting with the aid. The user is asked to identify a set of problems that he/she experiences in daily life and that he/she hopes to eliminate or decrease. This is done at the very beginning during the service delivery process so that the user is not influenced by service provider. The evaluation consists in the comparison of interviews regarding the use of different aids, and reporting the difficulties that the user undertakes in the accomplishment of the problems previously identified. The identification process is an interactive process and we take care to designate problems on the basis of user's concrete activities. Table 1 reports the problems identified by Elisa.

A first interview has been accomplished before the use of BLISS2003 and refers to an AAC communication software previously adopted by Elisa at SNPI; Elisa with her parents and clinical staff assigned scores (on a five-grades scale) to the tool both with respect to the importance (Imp) of the problem and the level of difficulty of performing the specific activity (D1). During the follow-up interview, a few months after Elisa has started using BLISS2003, she had assigned a new difficulty score for the same activities (D2). The total score for each interview is calculated summing each difficulty score weighted by relative importance factor. The difference between the total IPPA score before and after the provision of BLISS2003 represents an index of the aid effectiveness. The data reported in Table 1 evidence that the difficulty score is decreased in all identified

**Table 2.** SOTU questionnaire comparison.

| Interview | Positive | Indifferent | Negative |
|---|---|---|---|
| 1[a] | 10 | 12 | 9 |
| 2[a] | 22 | 6 | 3 |

**Table 3.** ATD PA questionnaire comparison.

| Area | Scores $1^{st}$ int. | Scores $2^{nd}$ int. |
|---|---|---|
| Disability | 1.214 | 3.28 |
| Aid | 4.3 | 4.6 |
| Environment | 3.571 | 3.71 |
| Character | 4.027 | 4.25 |

problems while the total score is almost cut by half. Similarly to the Elisa case of study the interviews obtained from other disables evidence a lower difficulty score in comparison with the previously adopted AAC communication software.

### 4.2 MPT (Matching Person and Technology)

MPT is a validation protocol founded on active dialogue between the disable and the assistive technology expert. It allows to identify disables needs and their point of view on assistive technology aids so that we can develop a software to prevent assistive technology abandonment. In particular we have used three MPT instruments:

- *MPT working sheet*: to define targets and guidelines with possible information technology solutions;
- *SOTU questionnaire*: to analyze user's personal and social characteristics;
- *ATD PA questionnaire*: to analyze the features of assistive technology aid and its applicative domain.

These instruments are structured as questions with closed answer which have been compiled by Elisa parents, her clinical staff and us as information technology experts, according to two session: before using Bliss2003 and a few months after using it.

Comparing the first interview score with the second one about SOTU questionnaire (shown in Table 2) the negative answers decrease in the light of the progress on the social and communicative integration. Taking into account the ATD PA questionnaire results (shown in Table 3) the score is higher thus indicating that Bliss2003 has improved Elisa's communication capabilities.

## 5 Conclusions

In this paper we have introduced Bliss2003 an adaptive and predictive environment to support augmentative and alternative communication. In particular we described its overall architecture, its innovative predictive composition assistant and the experimental activity we did to validate the tool.

## References


1. Bloomberg, K., Johnson, H.: A statewide demographic survey of people with severe communication impairments. Augmentative and Alternative Communication **6** (1990) 50–60
2. ISAAC: International society for augmentative and alternative communication. http://www.isaac-online.org (1983) Last accessed October 1st, 2003.
3. Gava, M.: ...e se manca la parola, quale comunicazione e quale linguaggio ? AAC: una risposta nell'ambito delle disabilità verbali. Riabilitazione Oggi **16** (1999) 8–42
4. Shane, B.: Augmentative Communication: an introduction. Blackstone, Toronto, Canada (1981)
5. Somalvico, M., Gava, M., Squillace, M., Stefanato, M.: APBliss per Windows. In: Convegno Nazionale di Informatica Didattica e Disabilità, Napoli (1995)
6. Rabiner, L.: A tutorial on hidden markov models and selected applications in speech recognition. In: Proc. of the IEEE. 77, IEEE Computer Society Press (1989) 257–286
7. Taylor, A., Arnott, J., Alm, N.: Visualisation to assist non-speaking users of augmentative communication systems. In: Proc. of the Int. Conf. of the IEEE on Inf. Vis., London, UK (2001) 251–256
8. Gatti, N., Matteucci, M.: CABA$^2$L a Bliss predictive composition assistant for verbal impaired people. In: Proceedings of ICEIS 2004. Volume 5. (2004) 89–96
9. Simpson, R.C., Koester, H.H.: Adaptive one-switch row-column scanning. IEEE Trans. on Rehabilitation Engineering **7** (1999) 464–473
10. Higginbotham, D.J., Lesher, G.W., Moulton, B.J.: Techniques for aumenting scanning communication. Augmentative and Alternative Communication **14** (1998) 81–101
11. Cronk, S., Schubert, R.: Development of a real time expert system for automatic adaptation of scanning rates. In: Proc. of the Conf. on Rehabilitation Technology, RESNA. Volume 7., Washington, DC, USA (1987) 109–111
12. Quillian, M.: Semantic memory. In: Minsky ed. Semantic Information Processing. MIT Press, Cambridge (1968)
13. S.I.V.A.: Assistive technology research and information center. http://www.siva.it (1980) Last accessed October 1st, 2003.
14. Andrich, R., deWitte, L., Ferrario, M., Lorentsen, O., Oberg, B., Oortwijn, W., Persson, J., VanBeekum, T., Wessels, R.: IPPA, a user-centred approach to assess effectiveness of assistive technology provision. Technology and Disability **13** (2000) 105–116
15. Scherer, M.J.: MPT: Matching person & technology. Technical report, Fond. Don Gnocchi IRCCS-ONLUS, SIVA, Milan, Italy (1999)

# Intelligent Model for Rating Cognitive Capability for Computer Access of People with Disabilities

Thomas A. Pushchak[1] and Sreela Sasi[2]

[1] Community Resources for Independence, Inc.
Erie, Pennsylvania, USA
tom@crinet.org
[2] Gannon University
Erie, Pennsylvania, USA
sasi@gannon.edu

**Abstract.** People with cognitive disabilities often have difficulty in the cognitive dimensions of executive function, memory, orientation and attention, visual-spatial processing, sensory-motor processing, language, and emotions. They can gain independence in performing many daily living activities with the help of computer technology. However, a standard computer system does not provide them with the appropriate support they may need. A comprehensive person-centered evaluation is required to assess an individual's cognitive ability to determine the most appropriate combination of user interface hardware and software. This paper presents a novel architecture for a fuzzy rule-based expert system that can rate cognitive capability of an individual with a cognitive disability for computer access using the WAIS-III intelligence quotient test model.

## 1 Introduction

A cognitive disability can be broadly defined as any deficit or impairment in performing perceptual and/or memory mental processes. As of the year 2000, there are 12.4 million people in the United States (4.8% of the population) that have a physical, mental, or emotional condition that causes difficulty in learning, remembering, or concentrating [1], and this number is expected to increase as medical advances enable people born with disabilities or who sustain severe injuries to live well into middle-age and older. The latest revision of the Rancho Los Amigos scale can be used to determine the level of cognitive functioning. These levels range from "Level 1 – No Response" to "Level 10 – Purposeful, Appropriate: Modified Independent" [2]. This research focuses on adults functioning at levels 7 through 10. These individuals may have several types of cognitive disabilities which include dyslexia, dysgraphia, dyscalculia, and dyspraxia.

Cognitive disabilities interfere with "thinking" activities. Cole and Dehdashti have categorized these cognitive processing activities into six major dimensions: executive function, memory, orientation and attention, visual-spatial processing, sensory-motor processing, and emotions [3]. People with cognitive disabilities can regain independence in performing many daily living activities with the help of computer technology in the areas of advocacy, communication, daily living, educational, medically related,

K. Miesenberger et al. (Eds.): ICCHP 2004, LNCS 3118, pp. 991–994, 2004.

recreation, self-education, self-improvement, and vocational. However, a standard computer system does not provide the appropriate support they may need. Inappropriate or unsuitable selections of computer interface devices can lead to the nonuse or abandonment of the technology [4]. A comprehensive person-centered evaluation is required to assess an individual's cognitive ability to determine the most appropriate combination of user interface hardware and software.

## 2 Computer Access Assessment Techniques

The need for successful computer access strategies has long been an interesting area of study ever since the advancement of computer technology. A process for evaluating computer access can include the following sequence of activities: analyzing background information, observing the user's environment, assessing the user's skills, investigating, proposing and personalizing the access system, training the user, implementing the system, and monitoring and providing follow-up services [5]. Rule-based expert systems for automating this process for users with special needs are given in [6] and [7]. The capability of a person with a cognitive disability to use a computer can be hard to measure precisely. A variety of assessment models have been developed to address this issue [8], [9].

This paper presents a novel architecture for a fuzzy rule-based expert system that can rate cognitive capability of an individual with a cognitive disability for computer access using the WAIS-III intelligence quotient test model. This cognitive capability rating can be used for making recommendations for an appropriate combination of user interface hardware and software. These assistive supports for using a computer system will increase their independence, enable a more active integration into the community, and improve their quality of life.

## 3 Intelligent Cognitive Capability Rating Model

The main purpose for assessing an individual's level of intellectual functioning is to measure cognitive potential and to obtain clinically relevant information [10]. This information is essential for clinicians to identify neurological dysfunction, make educational and vocational placement decisions, and help guide an individual with cognitive disabilities to reach their intellectual functional potential. The WAIS-III has emerged as the most frequently used test for measuring cognitive ability [11]. The WAIS-III provides a measure of verbal, nonverbal, and general intelligence for adults ranging in age from 16 to 89 years.

Determining the capability of a user to access computers by analyzing the results of these assessments can be difficult due to the vagueness in precisely measuring how close a particular class of hardware or software meets the access needs of the user. This ambiguity necessitates the application of fuzzy logic techniques to deal with these uncertainties and to attain a more suitable solution to these issues [12]. An intelligent model consisting of four hierarchical levels for rating the cognitive capability for computer access of a person with a cognitive disability is shown in Figure 1.

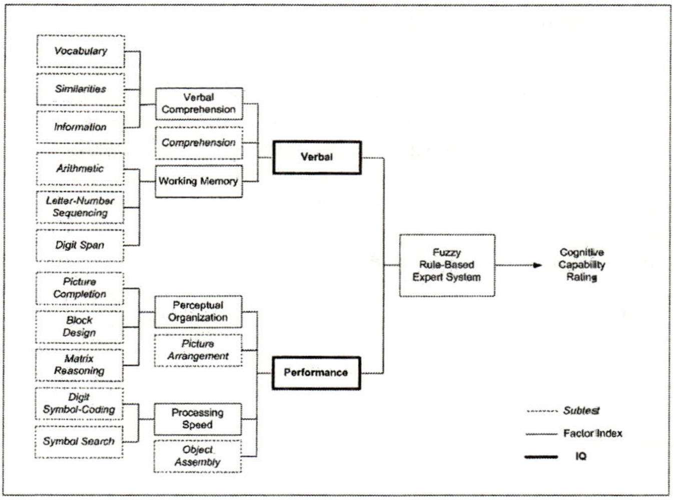


**Fig. 1.** Intelligent Model for Rating Cognitive Capability

## 4 Simulation

The cognitive rating consists of verbal IQ and performance IQ. The verbal IQ is based on the verbal comprehension index, the comprehension subtest, and the working memory index. The verbal comprehension index is based on the information, similarities and vocabulary subtests. The working memory index is based on the arithmetic, digit-span, and letter-numbering sequencing subtests. The performance IQ is based on the perceptual organization index, the picture arrangement subtest, the processing speed index, and the object assembly subtest. The perceptual organization index is based on the block design, matrix reasoning, and picture completion subtests. The processing speed index is based on the digit-symbol coding and symbol search subtests. A fuzzy rule-based expert system is simulated for cognitive capability rating using rules formulated by combining verbal IQ and performance IQ. The fuzzy inference engine consists of a number of if-then rules combining inputs and outputs with the linguistic terms 'low', 'medium', and 'high' using Bell-shaped membership functions. The fuzzy inference engine for this cognitive capability rating is implemented using the Fuzzy Logic Toolbox component of MATLAB version 6.5 from The MathWorks. Four-tier architecture shown in Figure 1 is used for formulating the inference engine. A few of the fuzzy rules used for rating verbal comprehension index and working memory index are given below.

*IF Vocabulary is High AND Similarities is High AND Information is High THEN Verbal Comprehension Index is High*

*IF Arithmetic is Medium AND Digit Span is Medium AND Letter-Number Sequencing is Medium THEN Working Memory Index is Medium*

## 5 Conclusion and Future Work

This paper presents a novel architecture for a fuzzy rule-based expert system that can rate cognitive capability of an individual with a cognitive disability for computer access using the WAIS-III intelligence quotient test model. Fuzzy logic techniques resolve the issue of dealing with the imprecise definition of the capability of a person with a cognitive disability to access a computer. This paper is a part of major research on developing an intelligent computer access assessment system for people with disabilities which includes ratings for cognitive capability, physical functionality, speech, and vision. This intelligent system will recommend a suitable combination of user interface hardware and software to enable people with disabilities to live more independently.

## References

1. Waldrop, J., Stern, S.: Disability Status: 2000. U. S. Census Bureau. Census 2000 Brief. (2003) 1-12
2. Revised Rancho Los Amigos Assessment Scale. http://www.neuroskills.com/tbi/rancho.html
3. Cole, E., Dehdashti P.: Computer-based Cognitive Prosthetics: Assistive Technology for the Treatment of Cognitive Disabilities. Proceedings of the Third International ACM Conference on Assistive Technologies. (1998) 11-18
4. Reimer-Riess, M., Wacker R.: Factors Associated with Assistive Technology Discontinuance among Individuals with Disabilities. Journal of Rehabilitation. 66 (2000) 44-50
5. Lee K., Thomas D.: Control of Computer-based Technology for People with Physical Disabilities: An Assessment Manual. University of Toronto Press, Toronto Canada (1990)
6. McMillian, W., Wisniewski L., Zeiger, M.: A Rule-Based System that Suggests Computer Adaptations for Users with Special Needs. Proceedings of the First Annual ACM Conference on Assistive Technologies (1994) 129-135
7. Pushchak, T., Sasi, S.: Fuzzy Rule-Based Computer Access Assessment System (CAAS) for People with Disabilities. Proceedings of 2003 International Conference on Artificial Intelligence (2003) 400-403
8. Nisbet, P. Poon, P.: Special Access Technology. University of Edinburgh (1998)
9. Glennen, S. DeCoste, D.: Handbook of Augmentative and Alternative Communication. Singular Publishing Group San Diego (1997)
10. Harrison, P., Kaufman, A., Hickman, J., Kaufman, N.: A Survey of Tests Used for Adult Assessment. Journal of Psychoeducational Assessment 6 (1988) 188-198
11. Kaufman, A., Lichtenberger, E.: Essentials of WAIS-III Assessment. John Wiley & Sons New York (1999)
12. Langari, R. Yen, J.: Fuzzy Logic: Intelligence, Control and Information. Prentice-Hall UpperSaddle River New Jersey (1999)

# Automatic Modification of Text for People with Learning Disabilities Using Internet Services

Gabriele Nordbrock, Henrike Gappa, Yehya Mohamad, and Carlos A. Velasco

Fraunhofer-Institut für Angewandte Informationstechnik (FIT), Schloss Birlinghoven, D53757 Sankt Augustin, Germany
{Gaby.Nordbrock,Henrike.Gappa,Yehya.Mohamad,Carlos.Velasco}@fit.fraunhofer.de

**Abstract.** The paper presents the results of a user study that investigates the applicability of automatic text modifications to support learning disabled people in text comprehension while browsing the Internet. It presents some results that contradict traditional beliefs in regard to better support reading in this target group by providing them with screen readers.

## 1 Introduction

Browsing the Internet and using the information found presents a particular problem for people with learning disabilities, because the comprehension of text material is inhibited by complex sentence constructions and abstract wording. People with learning disabilities have difficulties to extract important information, especially out of continuous text that burdens the reading process. To avoid exclusion of this user group from the Information Society, guidelines have been issued that include recommendations on how to present information in the Web appropriately to them [2,3,5,6]. In the present working draft of the Web Content Accessibility Guidelines 2.0 (WCAG 2.0), there are also success criteria and best practice examples listed that may facilitate the creation of understandable text materials for people with a learning disability [1].

However, not much implementation of the published recommendations can be seen yet in the Web, particularly when continuous text is presented. This is partly due to the fact that these guidelines are not widely known yet, but above all, techniques and tools are missing that support Web authors in writing text that is easy to understand, by warning them about abstract words or passive voice constructions, for example. Until such tools are developed, methods must be found that allow for automatic modification of continuous text considering the mentioned guidelines. The text modifications must be achieved automatically – that means without human intervention – so they can be offered on-demand. In this approach, the content level cannot be touched by these modifications, because reliable semantic analysis of text is not possible yet, which would be very important to this user group. To investigate whether text modifications on the structural level as opposed to the content level can support learning disabled people in text comprehension, a user study was conducted with 13 learning disabled people. As part of the user study, a test group utilizing a screen reader was

K. Miesenberger et al. (Eds.): ICCHP 2004, LNCS 3118, pp. 995–998, 2004.

also established, so the test participants did not need to read the text themselves, which is also a recommendation to facilitate text comprehension. The user study was carried out in course of a larger user study dealing with other issues of barrier-free Web design in the scope of the IRIS project[1].

## 2 Methodology

It was the purpose of this study to gather qualitative rather than quantitative data, because the individual opinion and experience of each test participant was considered very valuable when judging the feasibility of the taken approach to modify text. Thus, the data were analyzed by parameter-free descriptive statistics, and a sample size of 6 test participants was considered sufficient to give validity to the results [4].

Questionnaires and protocols served as main tools for data collection. In the beginning of the test scenario, a questionnaire was presented to all test participants gathering data about their personal, educational and professional background. It also assessed the Internet expertise of the test participants by inquiring how long, how often and since when they are using the Internet. The type of Internet application accessed by the test participants was also considered to determine their Internet expertise. Test participants were then asked to fulfill a standard task (read a text) followed up by a second questionnaire researching possible problems they had with the text and how comprehension of text on a Web page could be facilitated for this user group.

For the standard task, test participants were first asked to read a text. The test group utilizing a screen reader was asked to listen to a text. Afterwards, they were asked several questions about the text in order to assess their comprehension. The chosen text for the standard task was carefully selected so it contained only a limited amount of jargon and abstract words, yet it was representative of text information as typically presented in the Web. A glossary was provided including easy-to-understand explanations of jargon or terms that could not be assumed to be part of everyday knowledge.

The test participants were subdivided in three test groups: group one (3 test participants) was confronted with the text in the original version, group two (4 test participants) used a screen reader in order to have the text read to them while the text was shown on the screen in its original layout, and group three (6 test participants) was confronted with the modified text version (see figure 1). The text was modified in the following way:

- punctuation was separated from the word before by inserting an extra space and showing it in bold type face,
- dashes were replaced by commas,
- written numbers were transferred in digits,
- after every comma, a line break was inserted and the following text was indented,
- after every "and", a line break was inserted and the following text was indented, and
- after every period, a line break and a blank line was inserted.

---

[1] Incorporating Requirements of People with Special Needs or Impairments in Internet-based Services (IST-2000-26211): `http://www.iris-design4all.org/`

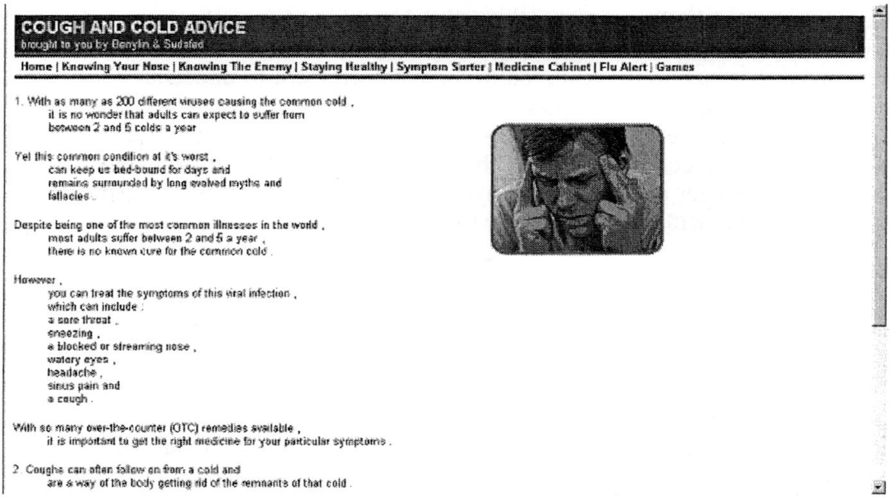


**Fig. 1.** Modified text version.

## 3 Results

Since it was the goal of this user study to investigate whether the proposed text modifications will support learning disabled people in text comprehension, the error rate in text understanding of test groups one and two (7 test participants) working with the original version of the text was compared against the results of test group three (6 test participants) testing the modified version. An error rate of 11 % appeared in group one and two (group one 9%, group two 13%), while in group three, 8% of all given answers were incorrect. However, we must consider that the degree of text comprehension required to answer the questions correctly was different. The questionnaire was designed like that to ensure that some questions could be answered by every test participant to avoid frustration. For interpretation of test results though, it is very important to analyze the error rate of questions demanding a high level of text comprehension. The error rate in this regard varied a great deal among the test groups from 60% for groups one and two (group one 50%, group two 70%) as opposed to 30% in group three. In summary, the test group working with the modified text version showed the lowest error rate in all instances. This is an encouraging result to pursue the taken approach in text modification. It must be considered however, that modifying text in this manner causes text to be split in many bullets which results in an unusual layout and presents a confusing appearance as it was also mentioned by some of the test participants. Furthermore, for people with good reading skills, text presented in this way will probably inhibit the reading process, so text modifications as suggested should only be offered on-demand.

A surprising result of the study can be seen in the highest error rate of test group two utilizing a screen reader to facilitate the reading process in overall (13%) as well as when questions were asked demanding a higher level of text comprehension (70%). Unintelligibility of the screen reader, which could have accounted for this test result, was investigated in the questionnaire following the reading task. All test participants reported that they could understand the speech of the screen reader very well. They also noted that having the text read to them helped them to understand the text. The reasons accounting for the highest error rate in this test group can be manifold, e.g., having to read the text oneself supports focusing and processing of text information. Since it is often recommended in Web design guidelines for learning disabled people that a screen reader should be employed in order to facilitate text comprehension, a larger user study will be conducted by the authors to investigate this issue further.

## Acknowledgements

Parts of this work have been undertaken in the framework of the project IRIS IST-2000-26211, which is partly funded by the European Commission. The authors would like to acknowledge the contributions of their colleagues from European Dynamics S.A., the University of the Aegean, the University of the Basque Country and ISdAC (Information Society disAbilities Challenge) International Association.

## References

1. Caldwell, B., Chisholm, W., Vanderheiden, G., White, J. (eds) (2002). Web Content Accessibility Guidelines 2.0, W3C Working Draft 11 March 2004. World Wide Web Consortium. Available at: `http://www.w3.org/TR/WCAG20/`
2. Brown, D J, Lawton, J (2001). Design Guidelines and Issues for Web Site Production for Use by People with a Learning Disability. Available at: `http://www.learningdisabilities.org.uk/html/content/webdesign.pdf`
3. Jiwani, K (2001). Designing for Users with Cognitive Disabilities. Available at: `http://www.otal.umd.edu/UUPractice/cognition/`
4. Maguire, M C , Heim, J, Endestad, T, Skjetne, J H, Vereker, N (1998). Requirements Specification and Evaluation for User Groups with Special Needs. Telematics Application Project TE 2010 "Requirements Engineering and Specification in Telematics (RESPECT)". Available at: `http://www.ejeisa.com/nectar/respect/6.2/index.htm`
5. Mencap (2003). Am I Making Myself Clear? Mencap's Guidelines for Accessible Writing. Available at:`http://www.mcu.org.uk/articles/makingsitesaccessible/design.html`
6. Rainger, P (2003). A Dyslexic Perspective on e-Content Accessibility. Available at: `http://www.techdis.ac.uk/seven/papers/`

# Soft Keyboard for the Disabled

Paul Gnanayutham[1], Chris Bloor[2], and Gilbert Cockton[2]

[1] Department of Computer Science and Software Engineering, University of Portsmouth, Buckingham Building, Lion Terrace, Portsmouth, PO1 3HE, United Kingdom
Paul.Gnanayutham@port.ac.uk
+44 (0) 23 9284 6404

[2] School of Computing and Technology, University of Sunderland, The David Goldman Centre, St Peter's Way, Sunderland, SR6 0DD, United Kingdom
{Chris.Bloor,Gilbert.Cockton}@sunderland.ac.uk
+44 (0) 191 515 2000

**Abstract.** This paper discusses an investigation carried out in designing and evaluating a neurorehabiliatory communication interfaces for nonverbal Quadriplegic and other clinically brain injured persons. Research was conducted where brain-injured persons communicated using a brain-body interface and a computer program with simple text such as Yes, No, Thanks etc. This research was further developed into a soft keyboard, which gave a brain-injured person an interface to create simple sentences. The users used the soft keyboard with a brain body interface. This paper reports on the soft keyboard developed and the experimental results of this research.

## 1 Introduction

This study collected the information from neurologically disabled persons by conducting simple non-invasive communication tasks and created interfaces for communicating with the outside world for the very first time, after a brain injury. Soft keyboards have been designed and implemented for disabled users in the past but this study covers the new area of soft keyboards for the brain-injured. This group of non-verbal, quadriplegic users will manipulate the keys using a brain body interface. As medical technology not only extends our natural life span but also leads to increased survival from illness and accidents, the number of people with disabilities is constantly increasing. World estimates show that there are more than 500 million people who are disabled as a consequence of mental, physical or sensory impairment. This makes people with disabilities one of the world's largest minorities [1]. Approximately 5.3 million people, currently live with disabilities resulting from brain injury [12]. It is estimated that there are 2.2 annual hospital admissions for traumatic brain injury for every 1000 people of the population in the Western World [12]. A certain percentage of these brain-injured people cannot communicate, recreate, or control their environment due to severe motor impairment. At the 52nd meeting of the Third Committee, on 29 November 2001, the representative of Mexico introduced a draft resolution on an international convention on the rights of persons with disabilities and was adopted on 19 Dec. 2001.

K. Miesenberger et al. (Eds.): ICCHP 2004, LNCS 3118, pp. 999–1002, 2004.

## 2 Assistive Technology

Assistive technologies fall into various categories [11]. The research reported here only concentrated on communications for the brain injured, hence dealt with the electric signals emanating from brain waves, muscle contraction, eye movement or some combination thereof [9]. Having considered various assistive devices, we chose the Cyberlink™ as the ideal device for the brain injured non-verbal participants [2–5][7]. Cyberlink™ consists of three electrodes (non invasive) in a headband wired to an instrument that magnifies brain waves 500,000 times. Through biofeedback techniques and slight facial movements, patients can use the Cyberlink™ to communicate via a computer interface. The signals for communications are obtained by attaching a probe on the forehead of the patients. Basically it is 3 silver/silver chloride contact electrodes (non-invasive), which are placed on a headband and pick up EEG (brain waves), EMG (Facial Muscles) and EOG (eye movements) signals. These are then fed into an amplifier and then to the mouse port, so the computer just sees the device as a mouse, which controls the cursor [5][9].

## 3 Past Research

Past research involved using the Cyberlink™ with appropriate communicating interfaces. The design process went through various stages of development. It started with a simple interface written in Visual Basic, which gave the opportunity for this group of disabled people to say yes or no for simple questions [7][8]. This research proved beyond any doubt, that every disabled person regardless of having a particular type of disability was still an individual with his or her own characteristics. Hence each one needed an individual profile not a group profile. The next design problem encountered was the unintentional movements of the cursor when a brain-body interface is used. This identified a need for better control over the cursor. This was done by splitting the computer screen into tiles and configuring the time spent on each tile, size of tile, gap between tiles, time to reach a target etc to suit each individual user. Now this research has been taken a step further by changing the targets into a soft keyboard that uses cursor control and audio feedback to help participants make simple sentences.

## 4 The Soft Keyboard

A soft keyboard (Fig.1) is made up of alphanumeric keys (shown in blue), control keys (shown in green) and configuration keys (shown in grey). This is an on-screen keyboard that can be configured to suit and individual user. The keyboard can be used in two modes: normal and scan mode. In normal mode, the user moves the cursor to a key and keeps the cursor on a key for a pre-defined time. This will display the alphanumeric character, read the key in an audible voice and jump to the middle of the Starting Area. This will be repeated for each character. This is to cater for brain-injured users who can move the cursor but cannot perform a click. In the scan mode

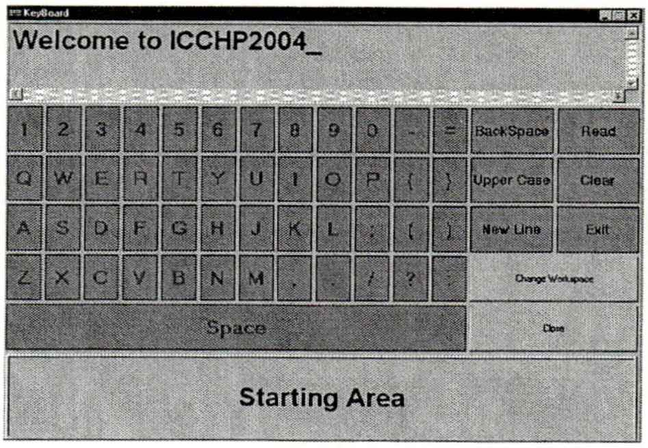


Fig. 1

the keys will be scanned row by row and the user need to perform a click and choose the key. This will display the alphanumeric character, read the key in an audible voice and continue scanning. The control keys perform Backspace, Caps Lock, New Line (or enter), Read (reads what the user has written in the display window), Clear (clears everything in the display window) and Exit. There are two grey configuration buttons, "Close" and "Change Workspace". These two buttons are for the exclusive use of the carer. "Close" button is to close the application. When you click on the "Change Workspace" button, it will open into window shown in Fig.2. This window enables the carer to change the following parameters of the keyboard:

- Key Height/Key Gap
- Keyboard Layout
- Text Window Height
- Stating Area Window Height
- Wait time on a Key
- Wait time on the starting area
- Font
- Enable/Disable Sound

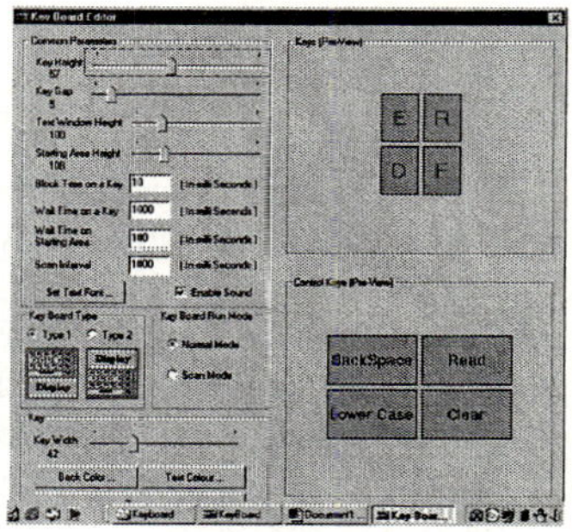


Fig. 2

## 5 Experimental Results

The ethics boards at each institution approved this research, using Cyberlink™ as an assistive technology. It should be noted that the investigator obtained all permissions and informed consents from the institutions, participants and/or their guardians before research began. When it came to this research, there was no previous methodology so a new methodology was developed. The approach used was one of developing a prototype interface using non-disabled people as test subjects, then evaluating the interface with brain-injured participants. This allowed better feedback at the development stage and faster development. Many versions of the programme were developed to get the appropriate individual interface. The keyboard was tested with ten able participants for refining the prototype. Having designed the prototype, the keyboard was tested with five brain-injured participants. Two of the disabled participants (39yrs, 60yrs male), were able to make simple sentences e.g. "I am hot", "I am tired", "I can understand", "thank you" etc. There were carers who believed these two patients did have the capacity to understand but until this study there was no evidence to prove this. The next two participants (32 yrs, 43yrs, male) gave inconsistent results and one disabled participant (61yrs, female) was unable to use it at all.

## 6 Conclusions

This keyboard was evaluated with Cyberlink™ but can be used with any mouse or switch; hence the researcher hopes other users with motor sensory deficiencies will consider it [6]. The most powerful feature of this keyboard was the "Change Workspace" which offered configuration facilities for this keyboard to set individual preferences according to the level of disability.

## Acknowledgements

To Mr. Wishwa Weerasinghe and to the following institutes Holy Cross Hospital Surrey and Castel Froma, Leamington spa.

## References

1. Agarwal, V. (2001), Disability India Journal
2. Doherty E.P, Cockton G., Bloor C. & Benigno, D., "Mixing Oil and Water: Transcending Method Boundaries in Assistive Technology for Traumatic Brain Injury," in Conf. on Universal Usability, eds. J. Sholtz and J. Thomas, ACM, pp 110-117, 2000.
3. Doherty E.P, Cockton G., Bloor C. & Benigno, D., "Improving the Performance of the Cyberlink Mental Interface with the Yes/No Program," in Proc. CHI 2001 Conference, Eds.
4. Doherty E.P, Cockton G., Bloor C., Rizzo J. and Blondina, B., "Yes/No or Maybe – Further Evaluation of an Interface for Brain-Injured Individuals," in Interacting with Computers, 14(4), 341-358, 2002.
5. Doherty, E, Bloor, C., Cockton, G., Engel, W., Rizzo, J., Berg, C., (1999a) Cyberlink – An Interface for Quadriplegic and Non – Verbal People, Pages 237-249, Conference Proceedings, CT99 3rd International Cognitive Technology, Aug 11-14,1999 in San Francisco, Proceedings Available at http://www.cogtech.org/CT99, Published by M.I.N.D. Lab, Michigan State University
6. Evreinov, G and Raisamo, R., Cyclic Input of Characters through a Single Button Manipulation – July 2002, ICCHP 2002, Linz.
7. Gnanayutham, P., Bloor, C and Cockton, P., AI to enhance a brain computer interface – June 2003, HCI International 2003, Crete.
8. Gnanayutham, P., Bloor, C., Cockton, G. Robotics for the brain injured: An interface for the brain injured person to operate a robotic arm – October 2001, ICCIT'2001, New York.
9. Metz, S., Hoffman, B. (1997), Mind Operated Devices, Cognitive Technology, Vol. 2 Issue 1,Spring1997, Indiana State University, Terra Haute Indiana, pages 69-74
10. Polak, M., Kostov, A., (1997),"Development Of Brain-Computer Interface: Preliminary Results", Proceedings – 19th International Conference – IEEE/EMBS Oct. 30,1997 – Nov. 2,1997, Chicago, Illinois, p1543 – 6
11. Schmiedl, T and Dyser, S. L., Taking Assistive Technology to the Highest Degree - July 2002, ICCHP 2002, Linz.
12. Falconer, J. A., http://www.bisociety.org/about.cfm, visited 14th April 2004.

# A Talking Word Processor and Web Browser

Gareth Evans, Miltos Kritikos, Alasdair King, and Paul Blenkhorn

Department of Computation, UMIST
PO Box 88, Manchester, M60 1QD, UK
{g.evans,a.king,p.blenkhorn}@co.umist.ac.uk
miltiadis.kritikos@postgrad.umist.ac.uk

**Abstract.** This paper presents a talking word processor and a talking web browser aimed at cognitively impaired individuals. Both the word processor and the web browser can display information and text and/or symbols. EdWord provides the user with a simple word-processor in which all objects, including menu items and tool tips are spoken. Microsoft Active Accessibility (MSAA) is used to implement this level of speech access; a feature which is unusual in simple word-processors. EdWeb uses a web browser component that linearises a web page into a single linear document. This style of interface has proved successful with a range of novice web users. Both EdWord and EdWeb are freely available.

## 1 Introduction

The software described in this paper was designed to provide deaf-blind people with access to a simple word processor and web browser. In doing so, it has to be acknowledged that many potential users have some functional vision and/or functional hearing, so the provision of a talking application that provides large clear print and/or graphics is appropriate to the needs of many of the user group. Many such users have cognitive impairments that also significantly affect their fluency with print, so support for symbols is desirable. Finally, the great variation in individual user needs demands that the program be easily configured to their needs by the user or by a support worker.

### 1.1 EdWord and EdWeb

There are a number of widely used symbol systems (e.g. Rebus, PCS, Makaton, Bliss[1]) for people with cognitive difficulties, and also a wide variety of simple symbol-based, talking word processors that are aimed at a similar client group – i.e. users with a combination of sensory, cognitive and/or learning disabilities. These include Writing with Symbols, Clicker and Inclusive Writer[1]. These systems typically have simple text word processing capabilities that are augmented by symbols. One symbol generally corresponds to a single word; although some symbols represent a phrase of up to five words. These systems are primarily designed and used by people with good functional vision but with difficulties in literacy. Therefore, speech is often provided

---

[1] This list is certainly not exhaustive, and nothing is implied by the set of products/systems selected/omitted.

K. Miesenberger et al. (Eds.): ICCHP 2004, LNCS 3118, pp. 1003–1008, 2004.

to support the writing and reading back of text. However, speech is not extended to support more general word processing operations, for example use of the program menu and dialog boxes. The user is expected to handle these without speech support.

The main motivation for the development of our systems – in spite of the existence of these products – was, for our target user group, that all operations should be speech enabled, supported by symbols, and have a simple user interface that could be tailored to the needs of the user. In addition, at the time of our work, there were no web browsers that both supported symbol users and talked. (Since the development of EdWeb two symbol-based web browsers have been developed, a commercial example that became available at the end of 2003 [1] and a research prototype has also been developed. [2, 3]) A further goal was to make a system that was available at no cost as both an executable and as source code to potential users and developers.

In summary, EdWord is a talking word processor that can display text as symbols and EdWeb is a talking web browser that can also use symbols. In this paper, we discuss the some of the characteristics of these tools and their design.

## 2 EdWord

### 2.1 User Interface

A screenshot of EdWord is shown in Fig. 1. As shown it has toolbars containing items for creating a new document, opening, saving and printing documents setting the font attributes (bold, italic and underline), the text alignment (left, centre, right and justified), the font (Times New Roman, Arial or Courier) and the text size. It also presents File, Edit, Format and Settings menus that provide the same functionality. These functions handle the majority of word processing tasks for the inexpert user and allow for considerable scope in document creation, making EdWord a useful program.

Everything in EdWord talks. So, for example, when the mouse dwells over a tool bar item the tool tip is not only displayed but is also spoken. The menu items also speak, so the entire application presents itself through speech.

Because different users have different needs, EdWord is highly configurable, in the sense that the interface can be configured to suit the user's preferences. One aspect of configuration is control over the complexity of the interface. As shown in Fig. 1 the EdWord interface is at its most complex but simpler interfaces can be presented that reduce the tool bar to a single item (New) and the menu to a file item. This configuration can be accomplished by the user or by a support worker with a simple built-in interface. EdWord can thus be configured to meet the characteristics of a particular user. Control is provided over a number of features including:

- The set of user interface options presented to the user, including: the set of menu and toolbar options; access to clipboard operations (cut, copy and paste); and access to control colour and speech settings.
- The default colours (foreground and background), font, and font size presented to the user.
- The size and font of the menu items.
- The characteristics of the speech, for example, whether the speech should echo each letter, each word or both. The last option is useful for blind people learning to type.

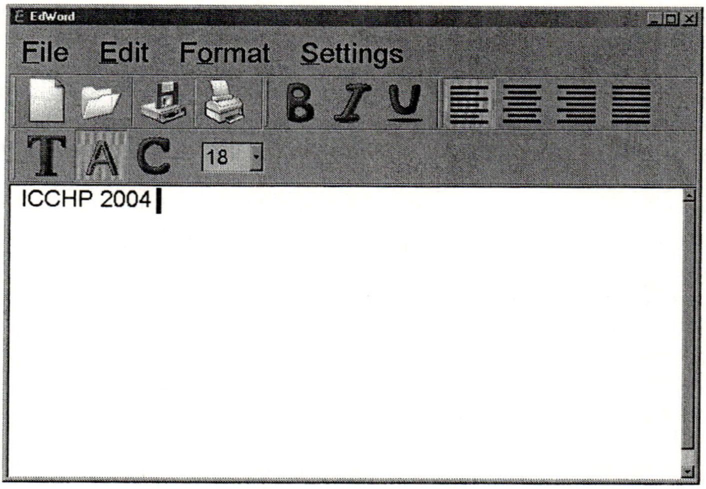


**Fig. 1.** A screen shot of EdWord

User profiles are used to store user preferences and, when a user is logged into EdWord (by selecting the user's name from a list), his/her default settings are restored.

EdWord can translate words to symbols so that when a word is typed by the user the appropriate symbol is shown above it. Text files opened in EdWord are processed to present the appropriate symbols. EdWord supports a variety of symbol types and provides a utility to access symbol sets already installed on the computer, so it can work with a preferred existing symbol set.

EdWord can also be used with a (talking) grid to support switch users. EdWord is supplied with a simple grid creation/editing program so the default grid provided in the program can be customised to suit the needs of a particular user.

## 2.2 EdWord Design Considerations

EdWord uses a commercially available text control (TX Text Control – `http://www.textcontrol.com/`) to present the text and, when appropriate, symbols.

Custom menus have been used so that the font size and associated symbols are controllable. All of the menus can therefore be changed to suit the user.

A major difficulty in the design of the system was making these menus and mouse-activated tool tips talk. Making the menus talk has been achieved using Microsoft Active Accessibility (MSAA). MSAA "allows applications to effectively cooperate with accessibility aids, providing information about what they are doing and the contents of the screen" [4]. MSAA provides EdWord with the ability to detect when the program focus moves to a different object, e.g. menu item, controls on a dialog box, and speak appropriately. Tool tips are spoken by capturing mouse movement and noting when the pointer hovers over a button. When this occurs, the button's "key" property is spoken. The key property of the button and the tool tip are set up to hold the same text, so what is shown on the screen is the same as that spoken by EdWord.

## 3 EdWeb

EdWeb extends EdWord to create a simplified web browser. It inherits much from EdWord including a similar set of configuration options (indeed both EdWord and EdWeb use common user profiles so that the preferences saved for a user in one tool are reflected in another).

EdWeb embeds an application called WebbIE[2] [5], which was originally designed as a simplified interface to a web browser for blind people using a screen reader. The key attribute of WebbIE is that it linearises a web page (all text is presented in a single window in a linear form so that the document can be read top to bottom). WebbIE has been quite successful for screen reader users (particularly novices) who find that a linear re-presentation of the page together with a moveable cursor provides a relatively easy means of navigating within a web page. It is interesting to note that WebbIE is also used by users who have some functional vision. The linear presentation of the page with clearly marked large text can provide, for some users, a more effective interface than using a standard web browser with a screen magnifier, because it greatly reduces the complexity of handling a web page. Based upon this experience it seems that this style of interface may be very appropriate for the user group identified in this paper.

The user interface of EdWeb is shown in Fig. 2. It consists of a small number of control buttons (back, forward, home, refresh and stop) together with a text box for the URL and a presentation of the web page content in text and symbols.

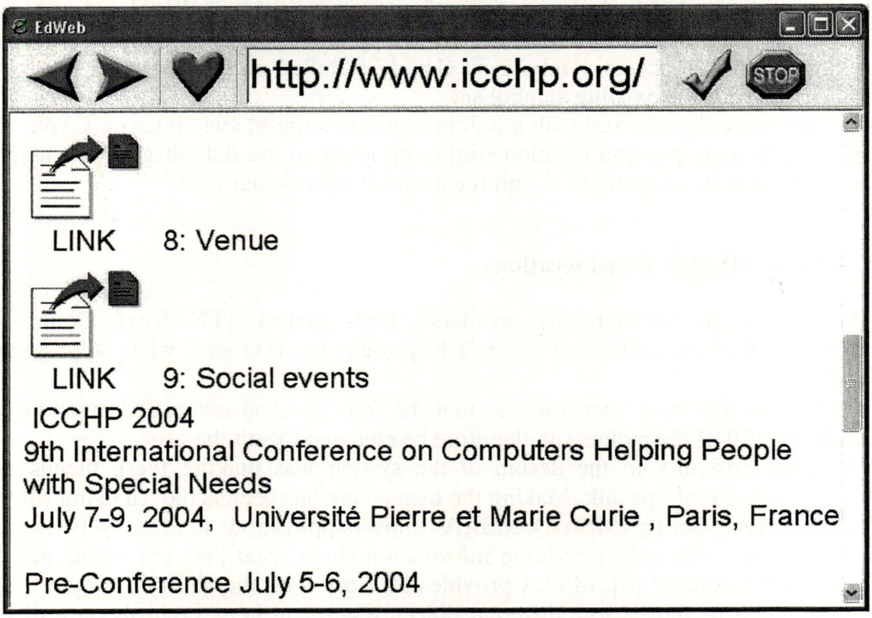


**Fig. 2.** Screen Shot of EdWeb

---

[2] Webbie can be downloaded from `http://www.webbie.org.uk`

EdWeb presents a web page as linear text and/or symbols. Special items such as links and text boxes are marked with text and symbols (see Fig. 2) or by symbols. Links can be followed by moving the cursor to the link and pressing enter. The text of the web page can be presented as text-and-symbols in the same way that EdWord translates text to symbols. EdWeb inherits from WebbIE a number of user commands that can be used to help the user navigate within and between web pages and to find information within a page. For example, links can be suppressed so that only the text is presented and long sequences of links (which are often indicative of a navigation bar) can be skipped by the user with one key press. These simple user functions are intended to increase the usability of web pages without requiring advanced knowledge or ability of the user.

In order to access the Web, EdWeb's WebbIE component accesses Microsoft Internet Explorer (IE) through Object Linking and Embedding (OLE). This gives Webbie access to the W3C HTML document object model (DOM), which provides access to all the elements of the web page. IE can therefore be left to handle the complexities of webpage parsing, and WebbIE need only handle the re-presentation of the webpage as a linear text document.

## 4 Availability

EdWord and EdWeb are free and can be downloaded from www.sense.org.uk/NOF. Source code is available from the authors and will published on the web shortly.

## 5 Concluding Remarks

EdWeb and EdWord require further evaluation with a range of user groups. There are a number of issues to be investigated. For example, EdWeb translates web pages to symbols, but no evaluation has yet been done to determine the level of benefit that this gives to symbol users.

EdWeb and EdWord can also be further extended so that they match the needs of a wider set of client groups. For example, interest has been expressed in using tools such as EdWord with dyslexic people and older people. However, the tools need to be configured to their needs. Care has been taken to provide useful default configurations and options but this is no replacement for personalisation to a particular user or new development to address a specific user group.

## Acknowledgements

This work was conducted as part of a project undertaken by Sense to provide a Community Grid for Learning for deaf-blind people in the United Kingdom. The work was funded by the New Opportunities fund. The authors wish to thank Sense, and especially Andy Partington-Uttley, for their contribution to the project.

## References

1. Widgit Software Ltd, "Communicate: Webwise", http://www.widgit.com/products/webwise/browser.htm
2. Poulson, D., Nicolle, C.: Improving Access to the Internet Within the AAC Community. Assistive Technology – Shaping the Future, Proc AAATE '03, Eds. Craddock, McCormack, Reilly, Knops, IOS Press, (2003) 263-266
3. Nicolle, C., Black, K., Lysley, A., Puolson, D., Hekstra D.: An AAC-Enabled Internet: From User Requirements to Guidelines. In A More Inclusive World, Eds. Keates, Clarkson, Landgon, Robinson, Springer Verlag, (2004) 72 - 80
4. Microsoft, www.microsoft.com/Windows/platform/Innovate/Marketbulls/msaakybull.asp, current 7 Dec (1999)
5. King, A., Evans, G., Blenkhorn, P.: WebbIE, a web browser for visually impaired people. Proceedings 2nd Cambridge Workshop on Universal Access and Assistive Technology, 22-24 March (2004), 71-80

# Sibyl: AAC System Using NLP Techniques

Igor Schadle

Valoria EA2593, University of South Brittany, BP 573,
56017 Vannes Cedex, France
igor.schadle@univ-ubs.fr

**Abstract.** This paper presents Sibyl, a new AAC (Augmentative and Alternative Communication) computer system, that aims at improving text typing for persons with sever speech and motor impairments. Typical AAC systems display virtual keyboard on screen which enables key selection via a few switches device. However, text typing is cumbersome. Sibyl aims at allowing faster typing by means of two predictive modules SibyLetter and SibyWord. SibyLetter facilitates key selection through a dynamic keyboard by predicting next letter. It takes advantage of a n-gram statistical model applied on letters. SibyWord allows keystroke saving by word completion. It predicts next word using natural language processing techniques. A robust chunk parsing (non-recursive constituent) is achieved and prediction is based on the last chunk heads occurrences. Best predictions are displayed in a word list. This paper presents the two predictive modules and the Sibyl software used in the Kerpape French rehabilitation center.

## 1 Introduction

This paper presents Sibyl, a new French AAC (Augmentative and Alternative Communication) computer system for persons with speech and motion impairments. When disabilities aim with sever impairments, most of common interaction modalities are unavailable and the communication capabilities are limited. AAC is the field of research concerned with providing techniques to (partially) restore the communicative abilities of handicapped people. A typical computer based AAC system consists of four components (Fig. 1).

The first one is the physical input interface (command by breath, command by eye-tracking, joystick, pushbutton …) that replaces the real keyboard, unsuited device for much of disabled people. An important point is the degree of freedom for interacting with the computer. The choice of the input depends on the user's abilities. The second part is the virtual keyboard displayed on screen and driven by the input device. It allows the user to select items of vocabulary (letters and words in Sibyl, but icons or a phonetic alphabet in other systems) to compose sentences. In the case of single switch device, the key selection is achieved by scanning. In linear scanning, a cursor highlights successively each key. The user hits when reaching the desired key. In the faster row-column scanning, the selection takes two steps, first the row and then the key in the row; however, it takes two hits, source of errors. The last two components are a text editor, which shows the message and a speech synthesis to pronounce the final text.

K. Miesenberger et al. (Eds.): ICCHP 2004, LNCS 3118, pp. 1009–1015, 2004.

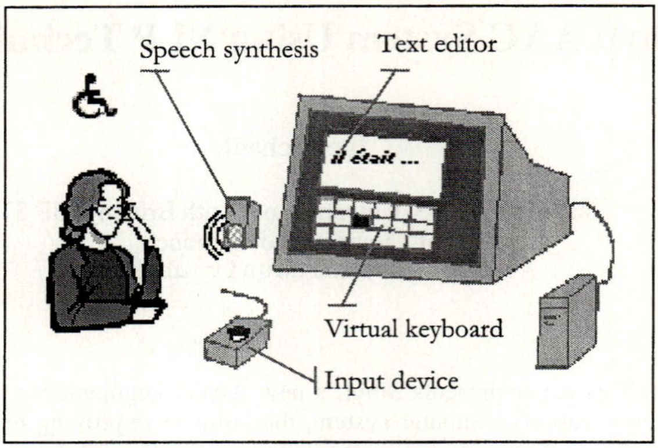


**Fig. 1.** Computer based AAC system

The main problem in such AAC system is the speed of text input because typing is very slow and time consuming. To allow faster typing, two additional approaches are available: fast key selection and keystroke saving. The aim of the first approach is to reduce the number of steps to reach the correct key, when scanning. Faster key selection can be achieved with appropriate scanning (e.g. row-column scanning vs. linear scanning), by arranging keys in an efficient order to facilitate access to the most used keys [3], or with letter prediction like SibyLetter of our Sibyl system [8]. Nowadays, research for communication aids focuses on methods for keystroke saving. The recall of pre-stored phrases is useful for common phrases or urgency communication. Some systems make use of abbreviations [7]. Finally, a growing number of systems, including Sibyl with SibyWord, allow automatic word completion by displaying a list of predicted words: Profet [4], HandiAS [6]. The use of Natural Language Processing (NLP) techniques increases the accuracy of the predictions.

In spite of significant advances, communication aids can be still improved. The research in assistive communication technologies is especially dynamic and tends towards a pluridisciplinary approach with psychologists, linguists, ergonomists, computer scientists, like, for example, the universities of Dundee (Scotland), Stanford and Delaware (USA), the Royal Institute KTH (Sweden) and the LIM, IRIT French laboratories.

In this paper we present the Sibyl project. Part 2 describes the interface of the Sibyl software, its main characteristics and the principle of our *dynamic keyboard*. The next two sections are dedicated to the predictive modules, part 3 for SibyLetter and SibyWord in part 4. In both cases, we present model, results and the evaluation in the French rehabilitation center of Kerpape with children with cerebral palsy.

## 2 Interface of Sibyl

### 2.1 Presentation

The Interface of Sibyl (Fig. 2) is especially designed for single switch input device. It consists of a text editor, a virtual keyboard and used linear or row-column scanning. The inputs with word prediction are in light gray.

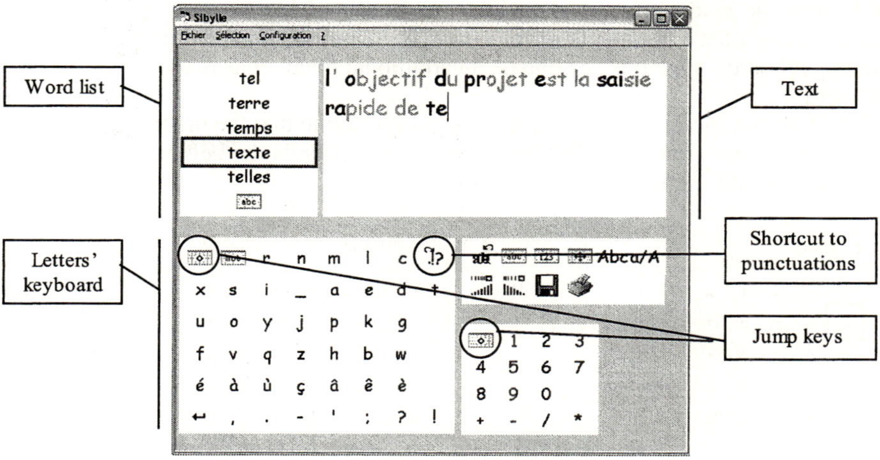


**Fig. 2.** Display of Sibyl

The keyboard is a set of keypads (called keyboards), this split reducing the number of steps to reach key in scan mode. *Jump keys* provide moves between keyboards; these are usually in the first keys of keyboard. The picture of the key specifies the target keyboard. On same principle, a shortcut key (at the end of the first row of the keyboard of letters) facilitates, in linear scanning, access to punctuation marks (on the last row).

## 2.2 Text Input

Let us now give a sample of text input on the sentence "comme chaque…" (like every…). When starting, there's no context, the word list displays the most common words at a beginning of a sentence (determiners, conjunctions, prepositions) and the letters keyboard the most common letters starting a word ("d, l, p…" in French). The word "comme" doesn't appear in the word list, letter "c" must be typed. The cursor moves from the first key of the letters keyboard (initial position) to key "c" (Fig. 3).

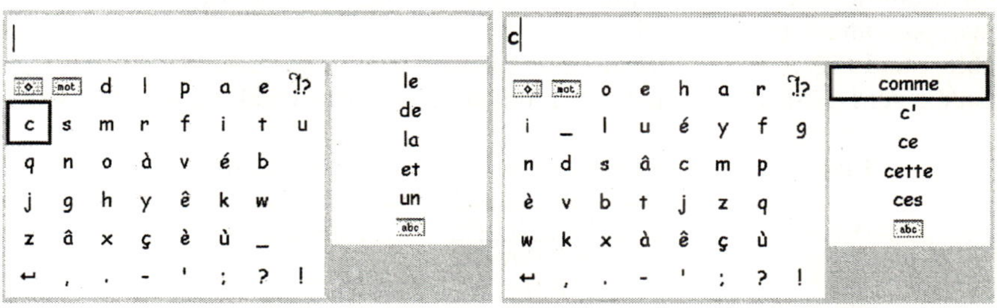


**Fig. 3.** Input of word *comme* (*like*)

After hit, display is refreshed: cursor goes back to the initial position, the ordering of the letters and the words in the list take new context into account. A short time is let to read the words, word *comme* appears. For word input, two steps are required: access to word list and then word selection. The "jump key" to words is the second of letters keyboard. After typing *comme*, an additional blank char is written at the end of the word.

Fig. 4 shows the input of the next word *chaque*. Note that the ordering of the letters is the same as previous (the context of letters prediction is the beginning of the word) but words are different.

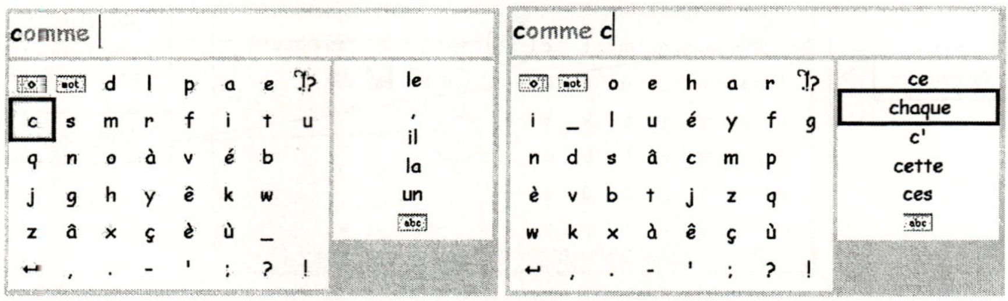


**Fig. 4.** Input of word *chaque* (*every*)

## 2.3 Dynamic Keyboard

As we've just seen, the ordering of letters is changing while typing, giving the letters keyboard its name of dynamic keyboard. Basic idea is to arrange letters so that most frequently letters are positioned on first keys and hence, facilitating their access in scan mode. For example, in *qwerty* keyboard, the most frequently hit key, the *space bar*, is improperly located because in last row. Some new virtual keyboards have taken this problem into account and sort letters by frequency. But the probability of letters differ with the context and the aim of the dynamic keyboard is to reflect this changing order.

After each input, the current context (the first letters of the current word) are given to the letters prediction module, SibyLetter (see Part 3). This one returns the letters sorted by an estimation of their probability to appear. An *end of word* letter (the blank char) is added to prediction. The keyboard is refreshed, the next input can start. The dynamic keyboard uses linear scanning, because as the keys are moving, the row-column scanning became unsuitable (during searching the desiderate letter, row scanning can pass above the row of the letter).

Table 1 and Fig. 5 present the input of each letter of word "comme". Table 1 gives the context sent to SibyLetter, the first propositions returned and the letter to type.

**Table 1.** Context and first propositions when typing word *comme*

| Context | Propositions | Letter |
|---|---|---|
| ∅ | D L P A E C ... | C |
| C | O E H ... | O |
| CO | N M U ... | M |
| COM | M P B ... | M |
| COMM | E... | E |
| COMME | _... | _ |

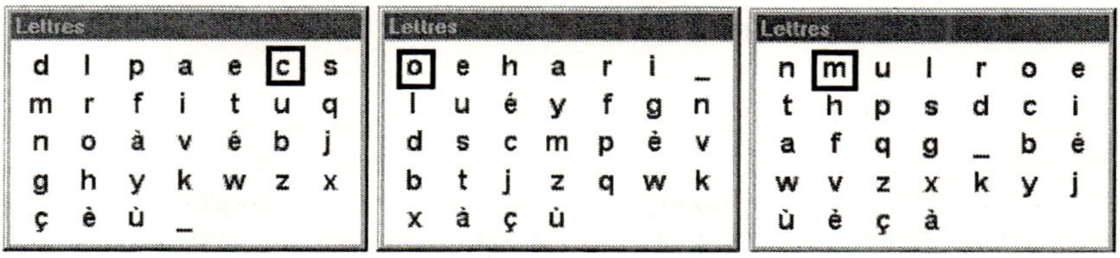


**Fig. 5.** Dynamic keyboard when typing COM …

The efficiency of letters prediction and dynamic keyboard will be discussed in the next part on SibyLetter.

## 3 SibyLetter

In Sibyl, the prediction of letters is based on the statistical model N-gram [5]. This one makes it possible to estimate the probability of an event (here of the letters) according to the n-1 last events (according to the 4 last letters of the word in Sibyl). The estimate of the parameters of the model was carried out on the "Le Monde" newspaper (more than one hundred million words).

The theoretical evaluation shows, that on average, the desired letter appears at row 2,9. On the same corpora of training and test, we also calculated the performances of three other modes of selection:

1. row-column scanning on a AZERTY keyboard organized in 3 x 10 ("traditional" keyboards),
2. linear scanning on a keyboard whose keys are classified according to their frequency of use without context ("frequential" keyboard),
3. row-column scanning on the same keyboard as previously.

Table 3 gives the performances obtained in number of steps to reach the desired letter (by taking account only letters).

**Table 2.** Performances of various modes of selection

| Keyboard | Scanning | Steps (average) |
|---|---|---|
| AZERTY | row-column | 7,3 |
| frequential | linear | 7,1 |
| frequential | row-column | 4,3 |
| Sibyl | linear | 2,9 |

The results show a significant saving of access time with Sibyl compared to the other modes of selection. This gain is all the more appreciable as the selection of a letter is done into 1 click contrary to the modes of selection using the row-column scanning which require two validations.

The improvement of the effectiveness given by the prediction of letters was confirmed during the evaluation by ten children with cerebral palsy (CP) in the French rehabilitation center of Kerpape [8]. Moreover, this evaluation (without the prediction of words) shows a fall of the typing errors (thanks to the linear scanning) and a fall of the spelling mistakes (necessary in the school context in Kerpape). However, the dynamic aspect can be awkward and we note the failure of the use of Sibyl with one person.

## 4 SibyWord

For the prediction of words, Sibyl uses an advanced language model [9] with a robust *chunk* parsing (non-recursive constituent [1]. The prediction is carried out in two stages: a preliminary stage of analysis of the sentence then a stage of prediction. The stage of analysis determines for each word their grammatical category (noun, adjective, verb, ...), their inflection (gender, number, person, tense). The sentence is then parsed in *chunks* :

l'année du dragon

↓

[l' (article, singular) année (noun, feminine singular)] Nominal Group
[du (preposition, masculine singular) dragon (noun, masculine singular)] Prepositional Group

**Fig. 6.** Example of sentence analysis on « l'année du dragon » (the year of the dragon)

In the second stage, the system delivers the estimate of the probability of each word of its lexicon (50 000 entries). The predictions are based on the last words and the last heads of the chunks (the main words of the chunks). The model allows a partial management of the grammatical agreements and also a presentation of words in relation to the context. On the previous example, the verbs suggested are "to start, finish", (in relation with "year"), at the third person of the singular and firstly in the present indicative.

The model was evaluated on a test corpus of 50 000 words (from the "Le Monde" newspaper) after a training on two million words. The results of the experimentation show, for a list of 5 words, a rate of keystroke saving of 57 %.

Some commercial systems propose already a list of words. However, the proposals are established without context. The interest to adopt a language model is thus double:

1. It makes it possible to increase the performance of the system in keystroke saving. For example, during the evaluation, we measured a rate of only 43 % with a prediction without context,
2. As mentions [2], the presentation of incoherent words with the sentence disturbs the user.

The integration of the words prediction in the Sibyl application is relatively recent and the evaluation by the users of Kerpape is in hand.

At the present time, the predictions of Sibyl do not adapt to the vocabulary of the user, the proposals are based only on the training of the newspaper "Le Monde". Thus, the rate of keystroke saving expected is lower than that estimated in a theoretical way. The adaptation to the user is one of the prospects for Sibyl.

## 5 Conclusion

In this article we presented the Sibyl AAC system. The aim of this system is to restore partially the communication function for people with severe motor impairments. We propose to integrate linguistic knowledge to increase the input speed. One of the originality of Sibyl is the dynamic keyboard, tested successfully at Kerpape. Now the evaluation continues for the prediction of words and by the addition of a black box to collect quantitative information.

## References


1. Abney, S.: Parsing by chunks. In R. Berwick, S. Abney, and C. Tenny (Eds.), Principle based parsing. Kluwer Academic (1991)
2. Boissière, Ph., Dours, D.: VITIPI : Versatile Interpretation of Text Input by Persons with Impairments. In 5th national Conference on Computers for Handicapped Persons, Linz (1996) 165–172
3. Cantegrit, B., Toulotte, J.-M.: Réflexions sur l'aide à la communication des personnes présentant un handicap moteur. Proc. TALN'01, Tours, vol 2 (2001) 193–202
4. Carlberger, A.: Profet, a new generation of word prediction: an evaluation study. In: Proceedings of the ACL workshop on Natural Language Processing for Communication Aids, Madrid (1997) 23–28
5. Jelinek, F.: Self-organized language modeling for speech recognition. Readings in Speech Recognition, Waibel and Lee (Editors). Morgan Kaufmann (1989)
6. Maurel, D., Le Pévédic, B.: The syntactic prediction with Token Automata: Application to HandiAS system. Theoretical Computer Science, vol. 267 (2001) 121–129
7. Mc Coy, K. F., Demasco, P.: Some applications of natural language processing to the field of augmentative and alternative communication. In Proceedings of the IJCAI'95 Workshop on Developing AI Applications for Disabled People, Montreal, Canada (1995) 97–112
8. Schadle, I., Antoine, J.-Y., Le Pévédic, B., Poirier, F. SibyLettre : système de prédiction de lettre pour la communication assistée. RIHM, Revue d'Interaction Homme Machine, vol 3, n°2 (2002) 115–134
9. Schadle, I. Sibylle : Système linguistique d'aide à la communication pour les personnes handicapées. Thèse de doctorat, Université de Bretagne Sud, (2003)

# Mobile Devices Converted into a Speaking Communication Aid

Bálint Tóth, Géza Németh, and Géza Kiss

Department of Telecommunications and Media Informatics
Budapest University of Technology and Economics
1117 Budapest, Magyar tudósok krt. 2, Hungary
toth.b@alpha.tmit.bme.hu, {nemeth,kgeza}@tmit.bme.hu

**Abstract.** The goal of the present study is to introduce a speaking interface of mobile devices for speech impaired people. The latest devices (including PDAs with integrated telephone, Smartphones, Tablet PCs) possess numerous favorable features: small size, portability, considerably fast processor speed, increased storage size, telephony, large display and convenient development environment. The majority of vocally handicapped users are elderly people who are often not familiar with computers. Many of them have other disorder(s) (e.g. motor) and/or impaired vision. The paper reports the design and implementation aspects of converting standard devices into a mobile speaking aid for face-to-face and telephone conversations. The device can be controlled and text is input by touch-screen and the output is generated by a text-to-speech system. The interface is configurable (screen colors and text size, speaking options, etc.) according to the users' personal preferences.

## 1 Introduction

The estimated number of severely speech impaired people living in the European Union is two million[1]. Speech impaired people have many difficulties both in face-to-face and in telephone conversations. The problem is more severe if the loss of speaking ability has just developed – the recently disabled person has difficulties making him/herself understood which may induce anxiety, frustration, even depression. Consequently "talking machines" can solve not only communicational, but also psychological and social problems.

Furthermore impaired speech can often cause uncomfortable situations (e.g. difficulties in asking for a glass of water, food, telling the need to go to the toilette, etc.) and unfortunately the lack of vocal communication can result in fatal events as well (e.g. people can't phone when they feel the symptoms of a heart attack).

With the intensive development of technology the desire of disabled people - to approach the conditions of a fully abled person as much as possible - can be more and more fulfilled. Nowadays there are several devices with audio capability and telephony. But which would be the best for such a purpose? We had to consider the fact that

[1] Telephone users with disabilities – the numbers, http://www.tiresias.org/phoneability/telephones/user_numbers.htm

K. Miesenberger et al. (Eds.): ICCHP 2004, LNCS 3118, pp. 1016–1023, 2004.

the majority of vocally handicapped users are rarely familiar with computers. Many of them are mentally retarded [1], have other disorder(s) (e.g. motor) and/or impaired vision. Furthermore for everyday use the size of the device must be as small as possible with a rather large display panel. There are difficulties even with a laptop computer (especially for elderly people). For example if a speech impaired person would like to do shopping, s/he has to pack the laptop computer at home and carry it (it is rather large and heavy). If s/he would like to use it then the laptop has to be taken out of its bag and at the end of the conversation it has to be put back. The whole process is uncomfortable. In case of smaller devices the process is much easier. In addition the integrated telephone is often necessary and the device must have a considerably fast processor.

## 2 Problem Statement

Considering the aspects given above we had to face the problem that an interface for a small, portable device should be developed for speech impaired people who are rarely familiar with computers, and probably have vision, motor or/and mental disabilities. Therefore the decision was not easy. The choice of the device is significant because with an inappropriate hardware even the best software fails easily.

### 2.1 Related Work

We examined several devices and systems to take advantage of their features, design concept and effects on users to avoid the imperfections they had. In this study we did not examine the old mechanical machines [2], only the newer devices and interfaces. Let us have a look at the most important systems:

1. The example of a Swedish speech impaired teenager is very instructive [3]. He used a Swedish text-to-speech (TTS) system as a communication aid first in 1978. This instance demonstrated the social, psychological help of a speaking machine.
2. Bliss symbols based talking machines (Blisstalk, 1981) [3] and computer programs (e.g. Blissvox, 1994) [4] are significant communication aids. These systems use Blissymbolics [5] to communicate. In general each symbol refers to one word. The input is the symbols, the output is synthetic voice. We can conclude that in some cases it is worth compressing the text into shorter, previously stored units. This idea [6] is developed in newer systems (*see 2.3*).
3. The Multi-Talk system was a real communication aid (Galyas and Rosengren, 1989) [3]; this was portable and had several important services. We considered useful many of these features (stored messages, repeatable last word, sentence, configurable display, etc.) though telephony is not supported and developing software on Multi-Talk is difficult for third parties.
4. In the early 90s laptop computers became increasingly accessible for average users. One of the beneficial speaking applications is VOXAID (Gábor Olaszy and Géza Németh, 1993) [7]. The usefulness of the system is proved among others by an elderly non-speaking woman who used this system for about ten years. With the help of an adaptor the system is able to make phone calls. There are disadvantages of

the system as well: the everyday usage of a laptop is uncomfortable and VOXAID is black and white what can often make difficulties for visually impaired people. (Configurable text and background color results in better visibility.) In our application we inherited some features (free text input, previously fixed text) and improved many (better telephony) from VOXAID.

### 2.2 Analysis

Summarizing the observations we considered free and fixed text input and telephony beneficial from the former systems. We also applied new features in the software according to the needs of speech impaired users. User requirements have been kept in mind during the whole development process.

### 2.3 Approach

Considering the facts, that we need a small, portable device with rather large memory, built-in sound module, telephony and reasonable processor performance we chose the nowadays popular mobile devices, including Pocket PC based Personal Digital Assistants (PDAs) with integrated telephone, Tablet PCs, Smartphones and Symbian based mobile phones. Each device has its own special profile: mobile phones are the best for telephone conversations, Tablet PCs for face-to-face conversation, and PDAs for both, with some compromises. Currently the PDA version of the software is ready. We are just implementing the application on the other platforms as well.

In our point of view choosing mobile devices was the best choice as the first step of creating a scaleable speaking interface, though we had to make compromises. These devices have several deficiencies (*see 4.2*) but can satisfy our purpose even so by solving the most critical problems with a smart speaking interface.

Some augmentative communication aids already exist on PDAs. WinSpeak[2] and IconSpeak[3] are very similar to each other – they displays icons on the screen, every icon means a word, and the user can make sentences from them by clicking on the icons. These software enable fast communication [6], but they are rather rigid, not suitable for wide range of utilization, because speech impaired people cannot adapt them for their needs and the software do not provide text input, only a fixed vocabulary. There are some multifunctional speaking applications for PDAs as well (like Polyana[4]), but they are able to speak only the language that the application was written for. Namely, no standardized speech I/O has been developed yet on these mobile systems. Furthermore these systems are expensive ones – not only the hardware, but the software too [1]. Consequently there was no doubt we had to develop our own, customizable, multifunctional speaking application.

---

[2] Pocket Winspeak - Symbol based communication aid program for Pocket PC, http://www.zygo-usa.com/pokspeak.html

[3] IconSpeak Palm PC software augmentative communications aid for people with impaired speech, http://www.bostock.com/ IconSpeakInternational.htm

[4] Polyana 3 with Persona - an augmentative communication Pocket Windows device, http://www.zygo-usa.com/polyana.html

## 3 Interface Description

Our concept was to create an intuitive interface the basic usage of which can be easily learned by a non-computer user in a few hours with the help of the documentation. We included many partly hidden functions which make communication faster (see below: *3.4, 3.5*). The name of the application is "*SayIt*".

### 3.1 Main Functions

There are three main functional parts of the program, called "*Free Text*", "*Fixed Text*" and "*Partly-fixed Text*". In **Free Text** mode one can enter any text. The program may read a line (Fig 1., "*Hello ICCHP!*"), a selection (Fig 1., "*king*") or the whole content of the text field. The text can be saved, loaded and erased anytime. The content of the text field remains the same if the mode is changed to Partly-fixed or to Fixed Text. Cut/Copy/Paste/Clear commands are also supported. In **Fixed Text** mode the user can choose from a set of categorized sentences (Fig. 1.). The categories may have subcategories, and the subcategories may have further subcategories, and so on. For example the category "*The way you feel*" has subcategories like "*common*", "*pain*", etc. These categories have sentences like "*I'm sick.*", "*I have headache.*", "*I am afraid.*", etc. The number, the length and the depth of the categories and sentences are not limited. The selected sentence can be read by clicking on it, or on the *Say* icon/menu item. The selected sentence can also be copied to Free Text for additional changes. The **Partly-fixed Text** is very similar to Fixed Text mode. The difference is manifested when the user selects a category item.

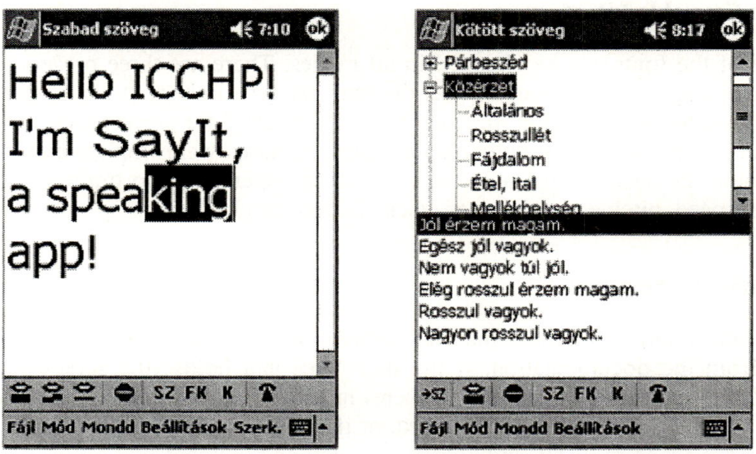


**Fig. 1.** Free text (left) and fixed text (right)

The selected sentence(s) appear(s) in a new text field (Fig. 2.), and only some predefined parts of the sentence(s) are editable. Clicking on a non-editable area the cursor jumps to the nearest editable text. One can move along the editable texts by the two arrows ("<", ">"). The whole text, a line or a selected area can be read by the

**Fig. 2.** Partly-fixed text

software. For example we have the "*Meet at <time> in <place>*." sentence. The user can edit only the <time> and <place> field, and the predefined sentence can be easily and swiftly changed to "*Meet at 6 p.m. in the ICCHP conference room.*". Furthermore the sentences can be copied to the Free Text for additional changes. This mode enables fast and flexible communication.

These are the main function blocks of the program. One can change between modes by the icons or by *Mode* menu.

### 3.2 Telephony

One of the most important features is the possibility of phone calls. Nowadays there are many PDAs with integrated telephone modules (e.g. Siemens SX45, Qtek 1010, T-Mobile, etc.). On these devices speech impaired people can make phone calls. No external accessories are required in contrast with PCs or laptops. Making or receiving phone calls can be easily accomplished by the default phone software.

### 3.3 Configurable Interface

The size of the fonts can be changed in all modes. There are three presets (normal, large, extra large), and one can also set the font size by numbers. It is also possible to change the color of the background and font. There are eight presets according to the basic mix of the RGB color components. These features were implemented - taking into account the needs of the users of our former system [7] - to improve visibility. The type, speed, pitch and volume of voice can also be changed.

### 3.4 Enhanced Features

There is an important function that has no icon or menu item. Users can know this feature from the documentation: if the user 'taps and holds' the screen (e.g. puts his/her finger on the screen and lets it there) in any mode, the most obvious text will be read. In Free Text mode the whole text, or if text is selected then only the selection is said by the program. If tap and hold is executed on the upper part of the screen, the selected category will be read. If tap and hold is done on the lower part of the screen, the selected sentence will be read in Fixed and Partly-fixed Text mode. The same method works after selecting a sentence in Partly-fixed Text (Fig. 2.) mode. This feature was also applied following the request of the users of our former system [7]. It helps users with motor disorders, because it is much easier to tap-n-hold a 32 pt large letter instead of a small icon.

### 3.5 Administrator Functions

The software has an external component, an administrator interface for Fixed and Partly-fixed Text. This is an executable program separate from the main application. With this software Fixed and Partly-fixed categories, subcategories and sentences can be added/edited/deleted. In addition the fixed parts of the Partly-fixed sentences can be defined. We recommend the administration only for expert users. We did not integrate this interface into the main program, because we did not want average users (e.g. elderly, non-computer users) to have an opportunity to spoil the databases. Of course, with the help of the documentation and with some practice anyone can easily learn to use the administrator tool.

### 3.6 Technology

The software was developed with eMbedded Visual C++ (eVC). The application is object-oriented, based on Microsoft Foundation Class (MFC). The Document-View architecture was not applied, the application is dialog based to save resources. The Pocket PC 2000 and Pocket PC 2002 emulation environments and some PDAs (including Siemens SX45, HP Jornada, Qtek 1010, T-Mobile) have been used during the development and tests. *SayIt* uses the MULTIVOX TTS engine developed by the Department of Telecommunications and Media Informatics, Budapest University of Technology and Economics cooperating with Phonetics Laboratory of the Hungarian Academy of Sciences. At the time of writing (January 2004) the source code is approximately 4200 lines long.

## 4 Evaluation Results

### 4.1 Technical Tests

When the software was ready for tests both objective and subjective measurements have been carried out. The program was tested on four devices: T-Mobil, HP Jornada, Qtek 1010, Siemens SX45. As the tables shows below, Qtek 1010 proved to be the best regarding the needs we wanted to fulfill.

**Speed.** The unit of text-to-speech is a sentence. We measured the elapsed time from the start of the text synthesis till the end of it with different sentences of different length (60 sentence / device). The average values can be found in Table 1.: in the third case we had to wait about 3.7 seconds for speech output after the synthesis started. This is acceptable. Consequently it is worth to use 75 word long or shorter sentences on the newer devices. On older ones it is better to use shorter sentences.

**Display, Volume.** The visibility of the display and the volume level are very important for everyday usage. We made the tests indoor and outdoor. The results can be found in Table 2. (Notation: 1 - poor, 2 - average, 3 - good)

### 4.2 Occurrent Problems

As mentioned above choosing PDAs for the software implementation we had to compromise. There are several problems – from the one hand technological, from the other hand financial.

**Technological Problems.** Our work was stopped for days as a consequence of the poor documentation of the PDAs and their operating system. Furthermore there is no standardized speech I/O on the Pocket PC. The speed of the device is not satisfying as well. It takes too much time to synthesize a complex sentence. During a phone call it's not good to wait for the answer for a long time. We made several tests to find out the limit of the maximum text length, where the delay is small enough. In the future we would like to solve this problem by optimizing the speech synthesizer for mobile usage. There are problems with the volume level of some devices also. In sunshine the visibility of the display is also a problem. The fragility of the devices is a relevant matter (there are PDA armors[5], but they affect usability).

**Financial Problems.** Besides the technological difficulties the financial problems are also very significant. In Central-Eastern Europe the price of PDAs is too high for average people. The government does not support speech impaired people appropriately. Furthermore the penetration of PDAs in Hungary is rather low, therefore companies do not sponsor the development for these devices.

**Table 1.** Results of the speed tests (average). (1) - T-Mobile, HP Jornada, Qtek 1010; (2) – Siemens SX45

| Num. of chars | Length of synthesis[s] | | Relative speed [char/s] | |
|---|---|---|---|---|
| | (1) | (2) | (1) | (2) |
| 242 | 12.4 | 21.1 | 19.56 | 11.49 |
| 138.8 | 7.4 | 12.4 | 18.71 | 11.18 |
| 74.85 | 3.7 | 6.6 | 20.8 | 11.4 |

**Table 2.** Results of the volume and display tests

| | T-Mobile | HP Jornada | Qtek 1010 | Siemens SX 45 |
|---|---|---|---|---|
| Display | 2 | 3 | 3 | 1 |
| Volume | 2 | 2 | 3 | 1 |

### 4.3 Future Plans

Our final goal is to create a scaleable communication aid platform for speech impaired people. Many features of the application already developed and the applications under development are defined by the users of our former system [7] which assures the user-centered design of the speaking interface. Moreover, when the application is ready on all platforms (PDA, Smartphone, Tablet PC) we will develop alter-

[5] Mobile Planet Product: Heavy Armor 3600 PDA Case, http://www.mobileplanet.com/private/pocketpc/product.asp?cat%5Fid=203&cat%5Fname=Accessorize&pf%5Fid=MP289629&dept%5Fid=3716&listing=1

native applications and apply several user tests to solve the occurrent problems and to reveal the usefulness of the systems in combinations and separately.

In the framework of the Microsoft Junior Research Group Contest this project has received access to a Smartphone Development Kit and a Tablet PC. As a result we are able to implement our software – with additional changes – for these mobile devices as well. In the near past the multilingual, pre-release version of *SayIt for Smartphone* won the Hungarian round of the Imagine Cup[6] software design competition.

## 5 Conclusion

*SayIt* is ready for use on Pocket PC powered devices. This is the first software on PDA for speech impaired people in Hungary. Its' functions make it unique compared to other speech applications (*see above*). Implementation to other languages can be easily solved with the appropriate TTS engine.

We hope that *SayIt* will be a really useful communication aid for many people.

## References


1. Bauer, S.M., Drenchek, J.A., Fossa, J.L., Panchura, C.A., Higginbotham, D.J.: Industry profile on augmentative and alternative communication. Rehabilitation Engineering Research Center on Technology Transfer, On-Line Publication (2001) (http://cosmos.buffalo.edu/t2rerc/dissemination/t2rerc-materials/industry-profiles/aac.pdf)
2. Lemmetty, S.: Review of Speech Synthesis Technology. Master's Thesis, Department of Electrical and Communications Engineering, Helsinki University of Technology (1999) 4-10
3. Hunnicutt, S.: The development of text-to-speech technology for use in communication aids. In: Syrdal, A., Bennett, R., Greenspan, S. (eds.): Applied Speech Technology. CRC Press, Inc., (1995) 547-563
4. Olaszi, P., Koutny, Y., Kálmán, S.L.: From Bliss Symbols to Grammatically Correct Voice Output: a Communication Tool for People with Disabilities. International Journal of Speech Technology, Vol. 5, (2002) 49-56
5. Bliss, C.: Semantography. Semantography Publications, Sidney (1965)
6. Agate, T., Dougherty, A.: Iconic encoding with picture communication symbols. Technology And Persons With Disabilities Conference On-Line Proceedings (2001) (http://www.csun.edu/cod/conf/2001/proceedings/csun01.htm)
7. Olaszy, G., Németh, G.: VOXAID: An Interactive Speaking Communication Aid Software for the Speech Impaired. Proc. Eurospeech '93, Vol. 3 (1993) 1821-1824


---

[6] http://www.imaginecup.com

# SOCRATES: Barrier Free Communities of Aphasics on the Internet

Marc Spaniol[1,2], Luise Springer[1,3], Ralf Klamma[1,2], and Matthias Jarke[1,2,4]

[1] Forschungskolleg "Medien und kulturelle Kommunikation", Universität zu Köln, Bernhard-Feilchenfeld-Str. 11, D-50969, Germany

[2] RWTH Aachen, Informatik V, Ahornstr. 55, D-52056 Aachen, Germany
{mspaniol,klamma}@cs.rwth-aachen.de

[3] Universitätsklinikum Aachen, Lehranstalt für Logopädie, Pauwelstr. 30, D-52074 Aachen, Germany
lspringer@ukaachen.de

[4] Fraunhofer FIT, Schloss Birlinghoven, D-53754 Sankt Augustin, Germany
jarke@fit.fraunhofer.de

**Abstract.** The barrier free internet is one of the greatest challenges for computer science in the future. While in the last years the growth of the internet was exponential, still many potential user communities can not use internet technology for their communication needs because of inappropriate tools and narrowly designed communication processes. These problems become obvious when transferring applications to communities of people with special needs. Many people suffering from aphasia are not able to interact with current chat tools while need for money for therapists could be eased by such virtual self-help groups in a geographically distributed setting. This is because massive word finding problems can sum up typing a simple sentence up to several minutes. We have designed, implemented and preliminary evaluated a new chat tool for such groups. By using the tool aphasics can constantly monitor their communication behavior and in case of difficulties switch to a synchronous talk mode where up to four people can monitor typing letter by letter. Proposal for phrases can be generated by the community to help their member. Therapists and linguistic researchers can also monitor online and offline conversations from automatically generated transcripts.

## 1 Introduction

Universal access to information society technologies is an important topic in the new research framework of the HCI community and the European Community [6]. Recent work focuses on new design of input assistance as well as automatic prediction of the user input or adaptive content presentation. Input assistance has made good progress due to the utilization of touch pads for handicapped or elderly people as in [4], but is still bound to costly and sensitive equipment. Other attempts try to increase usability by voice assistance, but are still to be improved since the rate of misrecognition is still very high and depends heavily on the pronunciation [8]. An alternative is research that aims at transforming the

K. Miesenberger et al. (Eds.): ICCHP 2004, LNCS 3118, pp. 1024–1031, 2004.

content to fit the user's needs by increasing the readability [2], but usability of those approaches is limited in interactive systems, since input is not supported. That is what predictive and abbreviation systems try to cover, but as well as auditory user interfaces, those systems now lack up detection reliability as well [5, 14].

Nevertheless, this work focuses on individuals only. It neglects the observation that many communication barriers are best overcome in cooperative learning communities with people facing similar problems. Our research in the collaborative research center on "Media and cultural communication" aims at analyzing and evaluating the impact of difficulties in new media applications [10, 11] (http://www.uni-koeln.de/inter-fak/fk-427/). In this paper we present a cooperative web-learning environment called SOCRATES (Simulation of Oral Communication Research Analysis and Transcription Engineering System) to overcome difficulties in new media usage. SOCRATES supports a learning community comprising patients suffering from aphasia (aphasics) [3], therapists, researchers on linguistics, and system developers.

## 2 Difficulties in Virtual Community Media Usage

Digital media has improved lifestyle and abilities to communicate for most of us. Nevertheless, communities of people with special needs sometimes face unexpected problems when using new media. These problems are not only restricted to misdesigned user interfaces, but commonly arise in the medium of conversation. Obviously, troubles appear and we have to make them productive. So, we are trying to find media mixes that allow us to overcome these problems, by combining media to increase their benefits by simultaneously reducing their deficits. When designing community software, it is necessary to analyze the nature of difficulties and to distinguish whether they are caused by media specific or user specific influences. In addition, we have to adjust the repair strategies with respect to the difficulty.

The design of community systems depends on a tight interplay between the organization of knowledge and communicative processes within the communities of practice [13]. To increase usability it is necessary to analyze the kind of difficulty taking part in a conversation. Basically, we distinguish the following influences on difficulties:

- *Media specific:* influences that depend on the medium itself.
- *User specific:* effects, caused by the user's deficits.

Usually, a mixture of both kinds of difficulties can be recognized. In case of an aphasics community it is obvious that problems emerge due to word finding, comprehension and spelling problems of users. Those problems are common in other communities, too. However, in combination with media specific difficulties, the situation becomes worse. Since aphasics face spelling and word finding problems, communication via an asynchronous chat-board is of danger in breaking down. Due to the delays in between of letters of words to be spelled, other participants in a chat system might believe that a user has left the community system. Indeed, this effect might happen in conventional chat boards, too, but in communities of people with special needs, visibility is interesting to indicate problems in digital media. Difficulties of aphasics in digital media depend on the communication structures simulating synchronousity of conversation. Because of word finding and spelling problems conversation gets asynchronous, since delays and line based inputs may sum up to minutes in comparison to reference conversations of non-handicapped people, which take seconds.

## 3 SOCRATES

SOCRATES is a community system combining digital media to make difficulties in single media usage accessible to repairs by the community members. To support this community initiated communication process, SOCRATES has been developed as a community system enabling aphasic communities to make use of distant communication in specially designed chat boards. On the one hand we are creating a meeting point for aphasics and on the other hand therapists and researchers can also use the system for a further analysis on conversation structures. Research on oral aphasic communities is still in its infancy and this is even more true for simulated orality as in chat boards. For linguistic research and therapy development, one of the most interesting features is the automatic recording of time delays between pressed keys because this might indicate the grade of disability.

SOCRATES is similar to Internet Relay Chat (IRC) [7], which offers a good possibility for a real-time text-based communication in communities. An IRC Server relays all incoming messages to the other participants taking part in the same conversation. Our relay servers are used to coordinate conversations and to enrich them with additional metadata, which is necessary for further computation. In the case of SOCRATES, especially time delays between letters to be spelled are captured. The digital community media are being captured in XML trace files to be placed in the SOCRATES conversation repository.

Access to SOCRATES is granted by a login procedure. By making the system exclusive to those persons suffering from aphasia, their therapists and researchers, members are being protected from people that might molest or make fun of the aphasic's stories. Only those who share a common value are allowed to participate. Passwords are only provided to those that are known to persons active in the self-help groups.

### 3.1 Community Centered Repairs in (Re-)Combined Digital Media

Obviously, spelling of words takes some time, and aphasics might be disadvantaged in a single media system based on a chat board. Hence, we are implementing community initiated repair strategies in digital media. Regarding conventional chat board communication, repair strategies are limited to line based messages. Nevertheless, little can be done, since users are restricted to the information given by the line-based inputs of the aphasic. Therefore, we are analyzing the impact of (re-)combined digital media in aphasics' community software.

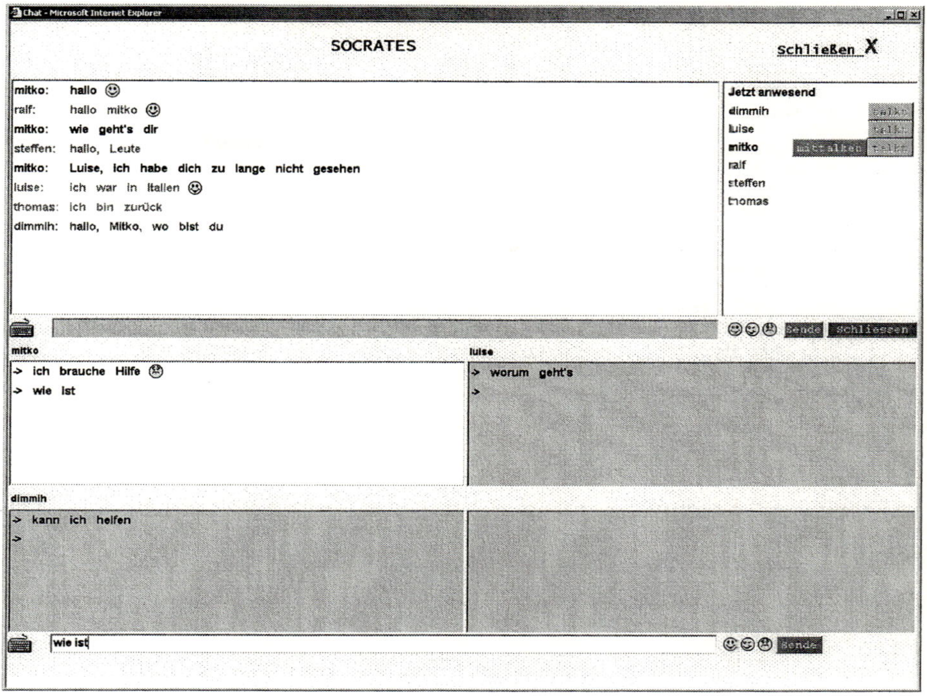


**Fig. 1.** SOCRATES: Combining chat and multi-user talk (in German)

Figure 1 shows a user initiated repair process in a SOCRATES Java applet. The design is similar to conventional chat boards, but has been adapted to the community's needs, which have been assessed in workshops together with the aphasic community. To keep transparency, each user has its own color to distinguish his inputs from those of others. The new approach to overcome the word finding and spelling problems of aphasics is a button on the right hand side of the applet that starts a self-initiated transcription process. By pushing the button "Talkrunde" (eng. multi-user talk), an aphasic might indicate the need for a decoupled conversation with only a restricted number of participants. Then, a multi-user talk is being activated, and on the bottom of the client Java applet a screen becomes visible which allows a synchronous talk conversation between up to four persons. For keeping focus on the user's own window, the chat windows of participants are colored bluish. The command line is automatically set to the lower section on the screen, allowing input for the multi-user talk. All other participants in the chat get the information that somebody has initiated a multi-user talk by highlighting an orange colored sign behind the aphasic's name. Those persons, who are willing to help, click on the sign to activate their help modus which automatically displays a yellow button behind their name, indicating their participation in a multi-user talk. Due to the synchronization of multi-user talk conversations, community members can now directly see the

```
Id:      1644
Typ:     TALKRUNDE
Server:  RS1
Start:   2004-03-16 11:00:32.0
Ende:    2004-03-16 11:06:22.0
Dauer:   00:05:50

Teilnehmer:
1. mitko
2. luise
3. dimmih


TRANSCRIPT

                00:00:00                                                        00:00:37
<mitko  #1> ¤                 i(18.51)ch·brauche·hilfe<<<<<Hilfe·§:-(§(1.53)
<luise  #1>                                                               w(27.18)p<p<oru
<dimmih #1>

                00:00:37                                                        00:01:06
<mitko  #1>
<luise  #1> m·g(1.05)eh+<t's¶(24.66)
<dimmih #1>

                00:01:11                                                        00:01:41
<mitko  #1>
<luise  #2>
<dimmih #1> k(59.51)ann·ich·H(20.33)ei<<<helfen¶(5.79)

                00:01:54                                                        00:01:54
<mitko  #1> ¶(86.56)
<luise  #2>
<dimmih #2>

                00:01:56                                                        00:05:50
<mitko  #2> w(1.55)ie·isr<t          ¤(230.01)
<luise  #2>                                     ¤(283.05)
<dimmih #2>                ¤(195.01)
```

**Fig. 2.** pdf transcript of a SOCRATES multi-user talk (in German)

problems in the aphasic's spelling process. They are able to guess the word that causes the trouble for the aphasic by proposing different words. The aphasic is now able to take over the word or even sentence by clicking on it, so that the words can be posted on the chat board.

### 3.2 Therapy and Research Assistance Offered by SOCRATES

Data in SOCRATES is based on XML. The data captures all necessary information needed to cover the context of a conversation, which are participants, global time, delays and the conversation itself. By keeping compatibility to XML, SOCRATES data can be easily interpreted by applications compliant to the standard. Automatic processing of the files is backed by their hierarchical structure. Hence, queries can be used to access selected elements of a document via XPath/XQuery [1].

SOCRATES offers the transcription of conversations into various output media. This allows therapists to adapt a therapy individually to the user's needs. To personalize the information as good as possible, the generated transcripts offer lavish information on the conversation process. The generated transcripts

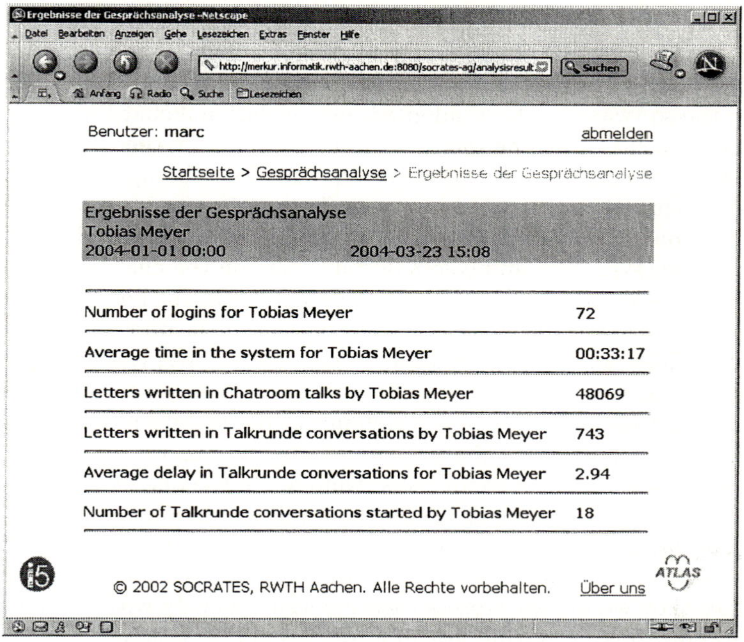


**Fig. 3.** Statistical information about SOCRATES usage (name changed)

are - apart from the replay function - based on the discourse analysis standard in linguistics GAT [9] and modified for written text pool [12]. The transcript covers writing delays of more than one second, time of conversation, corrections and the nicknames of the participants in addition to the spelled words (cf. figure 2). Deletions, corrections, delays, and other typing operations are marked for every line of conversation type in our chat system. To (re-)experience the discourse situation even an offline therapist can replay the whole transcript in SOCRATES based on the XML transcript. Researchers can manually or semi-automatically extract discourse features like recurring patterns of spelling problems. In addition, via the webinterface therapists and researchers are able to access the statistical information about the overall system or an individual community member. In figure 3 the evaluation of Tobias Meyer's activities (name changed) within a period of about the last three months is being displayed. By comparing these information with those spanning other time intervals therapists can gain worthful evidence whether results of the therapy indicate improvements of the disease pattern.

## 4 Conclusions and Outlook

We are working together with logopedics from the clinical center of the University of Aachen (RWTH Aachen) and psychologists from the German Unterfranken aphasia self-help center (http://www.aphasie-unterfranken.de). Aphasics are coming mostly from Unterfranken, Cologne, and Aachen, all located in Germany. SOCRATES usage and feedback of aphasics' communities is very promising. Since we have created an access authorized community system, localization of the software has been adopted on conventional chat board systems to fit the requirements of an aphasics community. Therefore, the user interface has been designed in cooperation with aphasics and their therapists. Reducing the user interface functionalities to a minimum is one of the results of the cooperative design process. This shall avoid that aphasics get lost in SOCRATES due to information overload. Size and colors of the letters on the chat board have been adapted to the aphasics needs. Also, the naming of buttons has been adapted to the community's interests. For instance the button "Talkrunde" (eng. multi-user talk) was initially named "Hilfsgespräch" (eng. help conversation), which led to unsatisfying usage by members, since most participants were embarrassed to push it. Another improvement of the system was derived from the workshops we arranged together with the aphasics community by integrating smiley buttons in the system. The reason therefore was twofold. On the one hand side, aphasics with a minor degree of disability liked to use smiley symbols they frequently use in mails for fun. On the other hand, aphasics still suffering of a higher degree of aphasia wished to have the buttons integrated into the system for a more serious reason since they wanted to express their emotions quickly without writing long sentences and probably getting lost in a too fast conversation.

An important aspect of introducing a new system to aphasics communities is personal support. In the beginning, support was needed to promote the system and for troubleshooting of technical aspects in particular (like the installation of a browser) since aphasics have a tendency to give up quickly in case of any malfunction. Now, SOCRATES is self-promoted by the members of the community as their system and giving support in case others encouter problems using it. In the meantime, SOCRATES has become very popular in the aphasics community enabling them to communicate freely with others without being afraid that they might get lost in rapid conversation. Since they have the option to indicate their need for a conversation in a smaller circle, other community members get aware of their media dependent difficulties. Participants are now able to meet others over spatial distances while protecting their privacy in an insular virtual community. By integrating other self-help groups of aphasics nationwide into SOCRATES, we hope to support even more aphasics in the near future.

The usage of XML has been applied successfully, since it is able to cover versatile information for further computation. The automatically generated transcripts of SOCRATES conversations are of great importance for therapists. Therapists are now able to adapt therapies due to the SOCRATES transcripts. Our colleagues from logopedia and linguistics are currently carrying out a controlled study with a group of about 50 aphasics frequently using SOCRATES. Analysis of human computer interaction that had been done manually before can now be computed automatically saving time and money in a steadily reduced budget of therapists and researchers.

**Acknowledgements**

This work was supported by German National Science Foundation (DFG) within the collaborative research centers SFB/FK 427 "Media and cultural communication" and SFB 476 "IMPROVE". We'd like to thank our colleagues for the inspiring discussions.

## References

1. Berglund, A., Boag, S., Chamberlin, D., Fernandez, M.F., Kay, M., Robie, J., and Siméon, J.: XML Path Language (XPath) 2.0. *http://www.w3.org/TR/xpath20/* (2002)
2. Chene, D. and Hoel, M.: Web site accessibility auditing tool for visually deficient persons OCAWA. *Miesenberger, K., Klaus, J., and Zagler, W. (eds.): Proceedings of ICCHP 2002, Linz, Austria* (2002) 27-32
3. Damasio, A.R.: The nature of aphasia: Signs and syndromes. *Martha Taylor Sarno (ed.): Acquired Aphasia, New York, Academic Press* (1981) 51-64
4. Holzinger, A.: User-Centered interface design for disabled and elderly people: First experiences with designing a patient communication system (PACOSY). *Miesenberger, K., Klaus, J., and Zagler, W. (eds.): Proceedings of ICCHP 2002, Linz, Austria* (2002) 33-41
5. Lauruska, V. and Musteikis, T.: Developing of predictive communication system for the physically disabled people. *Miesenberger, K., Klaus, J., and Zagler, W. (eds.): Proceedings of ICCHP 2002, Linz, Austria* (2002) 267-270
6. Miesenberger, K., Klaus, J., and Zagler, W. (eds.): Proceedings of the 8th International Conference on Computer Helping People with Special Needs. *ICCHP 2002, Linz, Austria, July 15-20* (2002)
7. Oikarinen, J. and Reed., D.: Rfc1459 - internet relay chat protocol (1993).
8. Privat, R., Vigouroux, N., Truillet, P., and Oriola, B.: Accessibility and affordance for voice interactive systems with the voicexml technology. *Miesenberger, K., Klaus, J., and Zagler, W. (eds.): Proceedings of ICCHP 2002, Linz, Austria* (2002) 61 63
9. Selting, M. et al.: Gesprächsanalytisches Transkriptionssystem (GAT). *Linguistische Berichte, 173* (1998) 91-122
10. Spaniol, M., Klamma, R., and Jarke, M.: Semantic processing of multimedia data by MPEG-7 for capacious knowledge management. *B. Grosky (ed.): Proceedings of SOFSEM 2002 Workshop on Multimedia Semantics, Milovy, Czech Republic* (2002) 56-65
11. Spaniol, M., Klamma, R., Jarke, M.: Data integration for multimedia e-learning environments with XML and MPEG-7. *Karagiannis, D., Reimer, U. (eds.): Proceedings of PAKM 2002, Dec 2-3, Vienna, Austria, Springer-Verlag, Berlin Heidelberg, LNCS/LNAI 2569* (2002) 244-255
12. Springer, L. 2004: Mediendifferenz und Sprachverwendung - Eine emprirische Studie zur medienspezifischen Prozessierung des Sprachwissens bei Agrammatikern und Sprachgesunden. *Jäger L. and Linz E. (eds.): Medialität und Mentalität - Theoretische und empirische Studien zum Verhältnis von Sprache, Subjektivität und Kognition, Fink-Verlag, München* (2004) in print
13. Wenger, E.: Communities of Practice - learning, Meaning, and Identity. *Cambridge University Press, Cambridge, UK* (1998)
14. Willis, T., Pain, H., Trewin, S., and Clark, S.: Informing flexible abbreviation expansion for users with motor disabilities. *Miesenberger, K., Klaus, J., and Zagler, W. (eds.): Proceedings of ICCHP 2002, Linz, Austria* (2002) 251-258

# Evaluations of an Information and Communication Technology (ICT) Training Programme for Persons with Intellectual Disabilities

Cecilia W.P. Li-Tsang[1], Chetwyn C.H. Chan[1], Chow S. Lam[2], Christina Hui-Chan[1], and Siu-sze Yeung[1]

[1] Department of Rehabilitation Sciences, The Hong Kong Polytechnic University, Hung Hom, Hong Kong
rscecili@inet.polyu.edu.hk
[2] Institute of Psychology, Illinois Institute of Technology, 3101 South Dearborn Street, Suite 252, Chicago, Illinois 60616-3793
psychology@iit.edu

**Abstract.** 106 persons with intellectual disabilities were recruited for the evaluation of an information and communication technology (ICT) training programme (77 in the experimental and 29 in the control group). The main features of the programme were a specially designed training curriculum with software designed in appropriate language and appropriate levels for people with intellectual disabilities. In the training programme, participants were taught about the operations of mouse and keyboard and browsing the Internet using Internet Explorer (IE). Participants in the control group underwent equal number of hours of ICT training by the staff working in their centers. All participants were assessed on ICT competence at pre- and post-training and one month follow up using a skill-based checklist. Results from repeated measure ANOVA and *t*-tests showed that participants acquired a higher level of computer competence after training and retained skills within one-month follow-up period, [$F(75) = 70.06$, $p=.000$]. For the control group, there was no statistically significant difference in the score on sub-tasks of use of mouse and keyboard [$t(28)=1.51$, $p>.05$], the sub-task of internet browsing [$t(28)=1.00$, $p>.05$] and the overall score [$t(28)=.90$, $p>.05$]. Results indicated that persons with intellectual disabilities have the capacity to learn ICT skills in a structured group with appropriate learning assistance and appropriate training tools.

## 1 Introduction

In the past, persons with intellectual disabilities have been segregated in many ways from the mainstream of life. The computer-mediated communication of cyberspace offers these individuals the potential of access to social, educational, and vocational recourses and interactions [1]. In advocating the use of technology for individuals with intellectual disabilities, Siegel pointed out that obviously technology would not cure intellectual disability or even fully compensate for the difficulties encountered by persons with intellectual disabilities [2]. Information and communication technology (ICT) can, however, improve their abilities to better integrate into the technology world. In addressing the impact of technology on the lives of persons with intellectual disabilities, Franklin noted that the technology explosion "has redefined their abilities

K. Miesenberger et al. (Eds.): ICCHP 2004, LNCS 3118, pp. 1032–1038, 2004.

to successfully learn, work, live, and play in their communities" (p.6) [3]. As ICT become more available, less expensive and user friendly, persons with intellectual disabilities could learn to utilize this valuable tool in modern societies.

Bremer and Beresin found that the use of information through Internet allows persons with intellectual disabilities to have better access for information and become educated consumers [4]. In the same vein, the advantages of using computer technology including minimizing the effect of a disability, enhancing training and skill development, increasing social participation and improving quality of life for persons with intellectual disabilities were reported elsewhere in the literature [5]. Before they could learn through this valuable tool in the modern societies, basic ICT skills such as the operations of the mouse, the keyboard and the internet browser are essential.

Technology can change the way a person learns. Every person, regardless of his/her functioning level, deserves access to this valuable media so that he/she can expand their horizons and opportunities now and into the future. The present study was an initial endeavor to explore the effectiveness of ICT training programme for persons with intellectual disabilities in groups which has not been quantitatively evaluated in the past literature.

### 1.1 Aims and Objectives

The purpose of the present study was to systematically evaluate an ICT training programme for people with intellectual disabilities. A total of two intensive training sessions (three-hour session) were conducted. Persons with intellectual disabilities were taught about the mouse and keyboard usage, and browsing the Internet using the Internet Explorer (IE). Specially designed software was incorporated into the ICT training program to facilitate the learning of the skills. Assessments on the basic ICT skills were completed on each participant pre-, post- and one month after training. It was hypothesized that the ICT competence of participants would be increased after training. A one-month follow-up assessment was conducted on the participants to test the sustained effect of the training. A delayed waiting list controlled group was also incorporated into this study for comparison of the effectiveness of the training programme. For the control group, there was no systematic ICT training provided but participants had the opportunities to undergo 2-4 hours per week ICT training at their centers under the supervision of the staff there. After the evaluation period (one month), participants in the control group were placed back to the training program.

## 2 Method

### 2.1 Participants

106 persons with intellectual disabilities were recruited for the study using a randomized sampling method from a group of 1100 persons with intellectual disabilities who had joined the training programme. A follow-up assessment was done one-month after the training programme. There were 42 (54.5%) male and 35 (45.5%) female participants in the experimental group and the mean age is 23.17 (SD=10.07) years. For participants in the control group, 18 (62.1%) of them were male, and 11 (37.9%) of them were female. The mean age is 27.65 (SD=10.05) years.

## 2.2 The Training Program

*Training Format.* Two 3-hour sessions of group training on ICT skills were provided. The size of the training group ranged from 15 to 30 people depending on the levels of intellectual functioning of the participants. An instructor was assigned to each training group. He/She must have prior experiences in teaching persons with intellectual disabilities and was given a three-hour training workshop before being an instructor. During the training session, the instructors would provide the instructions and training to the whole group and four to ten tutors were assigned to provide individual help to each participant where necessary. Similar to the instructors, the tutors were given a three-hour training workshop before. The tutor-trainee ratio for all groups regardless of the size of the group was around 1:3 in each group. Each trainee was given a training manual on the tasks learned in each session.

*Training Materials.* The participants were taught on the use of the mouse (Single Click, Double Click, and Dragging) and the use of the keyboard (Pressing keys), and function keys on the keyboard (ENTER, SPACE BAR, ARROW KEYS, BACKSPACE), and Internet browsing using IE.

Three pieces of software, written in language appropriate to the participants, were developed by the project team to enhance the interests in learning. The software was developed according to participants' intellectual levels. They are easy to operate (simple steps) and with visual and verbal feedback incorporated into the programme. The language used was appropriate to participants' intellectual levels.

## 2.3 Control Group

For those who were assigned to control group, there was no systematic training provided to participants but they were given equal number of hours to undergo ICT training at their center, supervised by the staff there. For ethical consideration, they were given the ICT training one month after the evaluation was completed.

## 2.4 Instrumentation

A skill-based checklist was developed to evaluate the effectiveness of the training programme based on the task analysis of computer operation. The main tasks identified were namely, use of mouse and keyboard, and Internet browsing using IE. There are altogether eight items in the subtasks of use of mouse and keyboard. Each participant would be assessed on how well they could edit a pre-set Microsoft Word document by using the mouse and the keyboard to perform single click, double click, dragging, and pressing the specified keys on the keyboard. There are 9 sub-tasks on Internet browsing. Each participant was asked to use the web browser-Internet Explorer to browse a specified webpage, typing in a web address, bookmark, and retrieve a bookmark.

For each item, participants were given standardized instructions to perform the designated computer task. One mark would be given to those who could successfully perform the specified behavioral descriptions. Zero mark would be given to those who failed to complete the task within 30 seconds. The overall score was calculated by summation of the marks obtained from each item. The assessors were given a session of training to conduct the assessment prior to the actual evaluation of subjects.

*Content Validity and Test-retest reliability.* The items were reviewed by five professionals working for people with intellectual disabilities to ensure satisfactory content validity. The professionals had agreed that the checklist taps on the essential IT skills. Some minor changes were made in the instruction manual based on the feedback of professionals. Inter-rater-reliability was calculated by means of intra-class correlation (ICC). Two raters conducted the checklist on ten participants independently. The reliability analysis showed that the checklist had high inter-rater reliability (ICC (3, 1) = 0.98).

## 3 Results

In the pre and post assessment of the experimental group, the mean score for the sub-task of use of mouse and keyboard was 1.83 out of 7 (SD=1.74) before training and 4.04 (SD=2.54) after training. For the sub-task of Internet browsing, the mean score before training was 2.56 (SD=2.63) and after training was 5.53 (SD=3.19), the full score was 8. The overall assessment score before and after training were 4.39 (SD=3.96) and 9.57 (SD=5.23) respectively. Significant differences were shown on sub-task of use of mouse and keyboard, $t$ (76) =9.34, p<.00, the sub-task of internet browsing, $t$ (76) =10.54, p<.00 and the overall score, p (76) =11.73, p<.00. These results indicated that participants obtained significantly higher scores on the skill-based checklist after training, which indicated that the ICT group training programme were able to increase participants' level of ICT competence (See Table 1).

For the control group, the mean score for the sub-task of use of mouse and keyboard was 1.41 (SD=2.47) before training and 1.72 (SD=2.64) after training. For the sub-task of internet browsing, the mean score before training was 1.79 (SD=2.81) and after training was 1.65 (SD=2.83), the full score was 8. The overall assessment score before and after training were 3.21 (SD=5.19) and 3.41 (SD=5.42) respectively. No significant difference was shown on sub-task of use of mouse and keyboard, $t$ (28) =1.51, p>.05, the sub-task of internet browsing, $t$ (28) =1.00, p>.05 and the overall score, $t$ (28) =.90, p>.05. These results indicated that participants obtained no significantly difference in scores on the computer-skills (See Table 1). Results from the repeated-measure ANOVA and t-tests indicated no significant difference for pre-assessment between the experimental and control group (ps>.05) but significant difference was found for post-assessment between two groups on both the two sub-tasks, use of mouse and keyboard [$t$ (104) =4.06, p<.00] and internet browsing [t (104) =3.75, p<.00], and the total score [t (104) =5.35, p<.00].

### 3.1 Follow-up Assessment

Follow-up assessments were conducted on all the participants in the experimental group one month after the completion of the training in order to measure the retention of learnt skills. The scores obtained from the checklist at different times were pre-

**Table 1.** Mean Scores (N=106) in computer- skills checklist before and after training

| Task | | Before Training Mean (SD) | After Training Mean (SD) | *t* | *p* |
|---|---|---|---|---|---|
| Use of mouse and keyboard | Experimental group | 1.83 (1.74) | 4.04 (2.54) | 9.34 | .000 |
| | Control group | 1.41 (2.47) | 1.72 (2.64) | 1.51 | .142 |
| Internet Browsing | Experimental group | 2.56 (2.63) | 5.53 (3.19) | 10.54 | .000 |
| | Control group | 1.79 (2.81) | 1.66 (2.83) | 1.00 | .326 |
| Total | Experimental group | 4.39 (3.96) | 9.57 (5.23) | 11.73 | .000 |
| | Control group | 3.21 (5.17) | 3.41 (5.42) | .90 | .375 |

sented in Figure 1. The scores showed that the participants lost some of the learnt skills as the scores were lower than that obtained after training. Yet, their ICT competence was still higher than their initial level before training.

Significant effects were shown from the repeated measure ANOVA for the two sub-task, use of mouse and keyboard, [F (75) =39.46, p<.00], and internet browsing, [F (75) =59.18, p<.00] as well as for the total score, [F (75) =70.06, p<.00]. *t*-tests were conducted to reveal the mean differences between levels of computer competence immediately after training and at the follow-up period. No significant differences were found on the subtask of use of mouse and keyboard, *t* (78) =1.33, p>.05 and internet browsing, *t* (78) =1.53, p>.05 as well as the overall score, *t* (78) =1.67, p>.05. These results seemingly indicated that participants were able to retain what they have learnt after a one-month period. The ICT training programme successfully enhanced the basic ICT competence among the participants though the level of achievements was slightly deteriorated in one month's time.

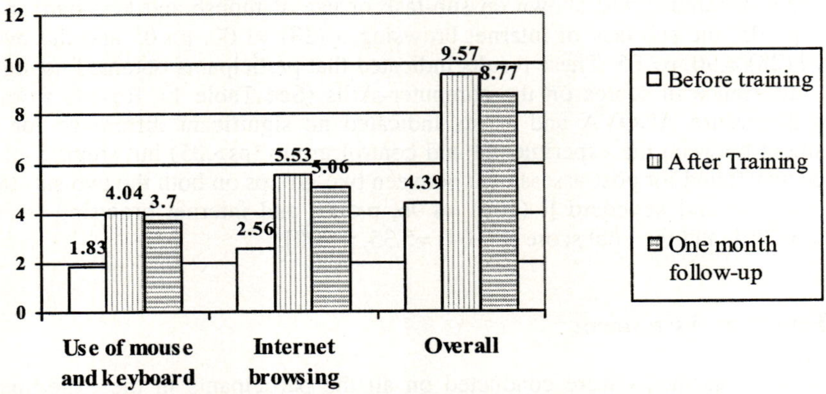


**Fig. 1.** Mean scores from skill-based checklist before training, after training, and at one month follow-up

## 4 Discussion

Information and communication technology (ICT) skills and access to technology are becoming an indispensable aspect of life of people growing up in 21$^{st}$ century. These skills are vital to the social and economic standing. As mentioned before, the value of ICT in enhancing the quality of life and employment opportunities for persons with intellectual disabilities has been well-established.

ICT has a significant impact on every aspect of one's daily life. The "digital divide", the gap between people who have access and training to computers and internet and those who do not, could significantly impede persons with intellectual disabilities the opportunities for success and chance for full integration to society. With sufficient assistance, people with intellectual disabilities, as shown in the present study, are able to learn ICT skills. The digital divide among this group of people in general could be reduced if sufficient training opportunities are available.

The main features of the present ICT training programme are that the trainer-trainee ratio is low and that specially designed curriculum and training software are used. Low trainer-trainee ratio is important to ensure effective learning as people with intellectual disabilities were found to have low attention span [6],[7] and low ability in following instructions [8].

The specially designed training content might be another important feature that contributed to the success of the training programme. The curriculum used in the present study was designed to breakdown the complex ICT skills into simple steps to suit the needs of the participants. Past studies indicated that persons with intellectual disabilities could acquire different skills through step-by-step training [9], [10].

The software was found appropriate to their level of understanding, and allow them to learn complex skills through a number of simple steps. The training software, unlike the commercially available training software, is more user friendly, easier to understand and the language is commonly used by the participants. This perhaps has aroused their interests in learning ICT skills, and present strong reinforcements for them to keep practicing and sustain their attention. Though some software were developed in previous studies for persons with intellectual disabilities to train up daily life skills, such as vocational skills [11] and time management skills [12], so far there is no software specifically developed for training IT skills and enhancing computer competence.

Follow-up study gave us positive indications and encouraging results that participants could retain some of the trained skills after one-month period. Persons with intellectual disabilities have been shown to have weak retention over the learnt skills [13]. It is suggested that follow-up training should be given to enhance the learning through home training or new programme.

Favorable feedback was given from parents and caregivers of the participants to the present training programme. They indicated that the training pace was appropriate and sufficient assistance was given to the participants during the training session. They were particularly impressed by the specially designed training software which aroused those participants' interests to computer and could assist them to learn the IT skills through a step-by-step way.

### 4.1 Conclusion

This is an initial endeavor to provide a systematic, structured and group ICT training for people with intellectual disabilities. The training programme was found to be effective to increase the level of ICT competence among persons with intellectual disabilities. The training sessions, though short, was shown to be effective the training programme was delivered in groups and that the instructor-tutor training program might help to remediate the short attention span and difficulties in learning complex skills among persons with intellectual disabilities. The likely shortfall that we perceived are the need to continue the training to reinforce learning and to develop more advanced ICT training software and programme so that people with intellectual disabilities could further advance their ICT skills. This will eventually minimize the prevalent digital divide for them.

## References


1. Borchert, G. D: The Challenge of Cyberspace: Internet Access and Persons with Disabilities. In Ebo, B. et al. (eds.): Cyberghetto or cybertopia?: Race, class, and gender on the Internet. Praeger Publisher/Greenwood Publishing Group, Inc, Westport, CT (1998) 50-63.
2. Siegel, J.: Utilizing Technology for the Inclusion of Individuals with Mental Retardation. In: Retish, P., Reiter, S. et al. (eds): Adults with Disabilities: International Perspectives in the Community. Lawerence Erlbaum Associates, Inc, Mahwah, NJ (1999) 287-308.
3. Frankin, K. S.: Assistive Technology: Where Are We? Where Are We Going? Journal of Vocational Rehabilitation. 1(2) (1991) 6-7.
4. Bremer, J., Beresin, E. V.: Computers in Psychiatry Today. Academic Psychiatry, 24(3) (2000) 168-172.
5. Shimizu H., Twyman J. S., Yamamoto J. I.: Computer Based Sorting-to- Matching in Identity Matching for Young Children with Developmental Disabilities. Research in Developmental Disabilities 24(3) (2003) 183-194.
6. Fuller, P. W.: Attention and the EEG Alpha Rhythm in Learning Disabled Children. Journal of Learning Disabilities 11(5) (1978) 303-312.
7. Huguenin, N. H.: Employing Computer Technology to Assess Visual Attention in Young Children and Adolescents with Severe Mental Retardation. Journal of Experimental Child Psychology 65(2) (1997) 141-170.
8. Hughson, E. A., Brown, R. I.: Some Effects of Verbal Instructions on Learning by Developmentally Handicapped Adults. Australia and New Zealand Journal of Developmental Disabilities 9(3) (1983) 107-115.
9. Hartwick, J., Yuen, H. K.: A Compensatory Counting System: Academic Skill Training. American Journal of Occupational Therapy 50(9) (1996) 740-746.
10. McCarl, J. J., Svobodny, L, Beare, P. L.: Self-recording in a Classroom for Students with Mild to Moderate Mental Handicaps: Effects on Productivity and On-task Behavior. Education and Training in Mental Retardation 26(1) (1991) 79-88.
11. Davis, D. K., Stock, S. E., Wehmeyer, M. L.: Enhancing Independent Internet Access for Individual with Mental Retardation through Use of a Specialized Web Browser: A Pilot Study. Education and Training in Mental Retardation and Developmental Disabilities 36(1) (2001) 107-113.
12. Davis, D. K., Stock, S. E., Wehmeyer, M. L.: Enhancing Independent Task Performance for Individuals with Mental Retardation through the Use of a Handheld Self-directed Visual and Audio Prompting System. Education and Training in Mental Retardation and Developmental Disabilities 37(2) (2002) 209-218.
13. Garcia, E. E., DeHaven, E. D.: Teaching Generalized Speech: Reestablishing a Previously Trained Repertoire of Functional Speech in a Profoundly Retarded Adolescent. Behavior Research of Severe Developmental Disabilities 1(2) (1980) 147-160.

# Effect of Dynamic Features on Diagnostic Testing for Dyspraxia

M.A. Razian, M.C. Fairhurst, and S. Hoque

Department of Electronics, University of Kent,
Canterbury, CT2 7NT, UK
M.C.Fairhurst@kent.ac.uk

**Abstract.** In the analysis of shape-based drawing assessment of neurological dysfunction or motor-perceptual functioning, there is a growing awareness of the need to simultaneously measure static and dynamic parameters for diagnosis and therapy-directed assessment of patients suffering or being at risk from such impairments. This is especially the case in evaluating and determining the degree of functional impairment in children exhibiting developmental irregularities such as dyspraxia. The aims of this paper are first, to describe the extraction and investigation of various dynamic features from the standard Visual Motor Integration (VMI) drawing test and determine the most effective features in clustering between three groups of children utilising feature ranking techniques. The second aim is to explore the possibility of reducing the number of geometrical shapes of the VMI test used by clinicians and occupational therapists in conventional evaluation, utilising the most effective dynamic features in diagnosing dyspraxic patients. The third aim is to analyse the effectiveness of static scoring in determining the mental age equivalent when dynamic features are considered by comparing patients of age equivalent similar to the biological age of control subjects.

## 1 Introduction

The measurement of mechanical dynamic features in fine motor skill such as velocity, acceleration, pen pressure, hesitation and execution time provide scientific researchers with a rich source of information regarding children's learning disabilities. These features have been investigated with respect to handwriting [1] and it is possible to evaluate children's developmental maturity by acquiring and analysing some of these dynamic parameters of shape drawing tests [2].

### 1.1 Dyspraxia or Developmental Co-ordination Disorder

Dyspraxia is generally defined as 'difficulty in planning and carrying out complex movements'. It is also known as Developmental Co-ordination Disorder. According to research studies it affects up to one in twenty children. It would therefore seem rea-

K. Miesenberger et al. (Eds.): ICCHP 2004, LNCS 3118, pp. 1039–1046, 2004.

sonable to assume that there is at least one sufferer in each class at school with extreme emotional and behavioural difficulties [3]. Children with dyspraxia may demonstrate various different types of symptoms, examples of which include:

- poor fine motor skills (e.g. pencil grip and use of scissors),
- immature drawings / poor copying skills,
- undecided as to which hand is dominant,
- very emotional with associated temper,
- barely legible handwriting,
- tantrums,
- prefer adult company,
- slower response time,
- problems with comprehension.

### 1.2 VMI Drawing Test

In the Visual Motor Integration test [4] the participants are asked to copy a series of geometrical shapes (24 shapes in total) in an increasing order of complexity. Performance is not time-limited. The general scoring system of this test is to convert raw scores (number of acceptable copies) to standardized scores and than to mental age-equivalent. The higher the scores by the predefined criteria, the more competent is the performance. Figure 1 illustrates the first 15 shapes used in the VMI tests. In this study the first 15 shapes were analysed as all the patients reached shape 15 but many did not exceed this.

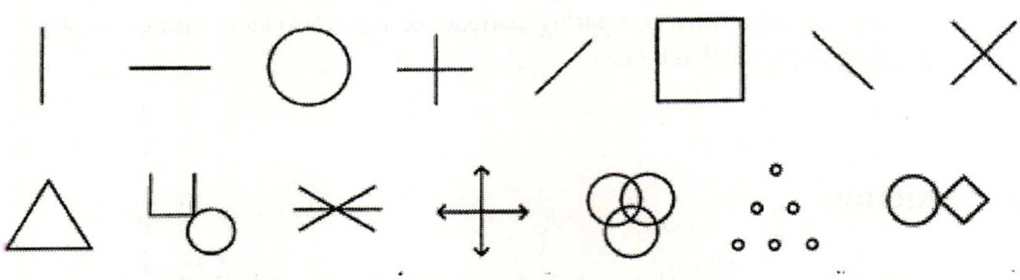

**Fig. 1.** The first 15 VMI shapes from the developmental test of Visual-Motor Integration VMI (shape 1- top-left, shape 15 - bottom-right).

## 2 Participants and Comparison Group

Two main populations of patients and control subjects participated in the study. The patient population is divided into two further groups of 16 children of 7 years of biological-age and 15 children whose age-equivalent is 7 years as determined through the VMI test (biological-age range from 8-11 years) with confirmed dyspraxia. The control group is from a local primary school and consists of 16 children of 7 years of age without any known neurological impairment.

## 3 Data Collection

The VMI test protocol was implemented by fixing the test sheets to a graphics tablet (interfaced to a computer). The child was asked to sit comfortably and copy the VMI shapes in sequence with no feedback of performance measures given during the test. No erasing were allowed during the test. Pen-tip displacements were recorded by tracking pen movements on the tablet. The frequency and spatial resolution of the system were 100Hz and $10^6/cm^2$ respectively. Figure 2 illustrates a block diagram of the overall VMI shape analysis system.

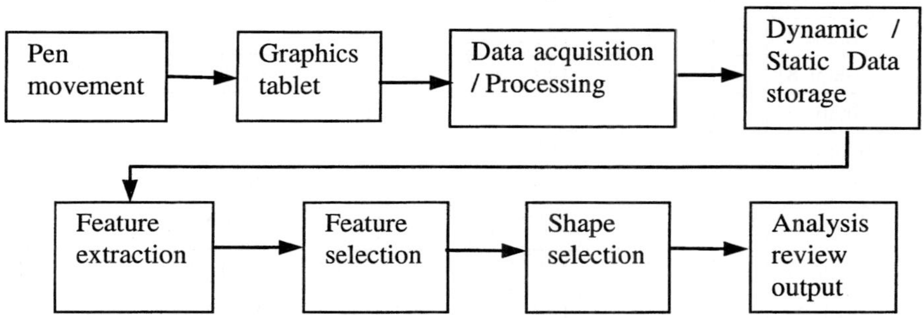


**Fig. 2.** Schematic block diagram of dynamic data process and analysis.

## 4 Data Analysis

The available parameters such as pen pressure, pen position and movement (x and y coordinates) and time were recorded. From these data more than 20 different features such as average pressure, peak pressure, time to peak pressure, average velocity and acceleration, number of strokes, pen down and pen up time, pen movement time, total execution time, shapes height and width etc. were extracted.

A ranking scheme [5] is then adopted to find the most discriminatory of the dynamic features being extracted. The scheme generated real values for each of the features for a given shape, a higher value indicating superiority in rank over others. Features from all the individual shapes are thus ranked independently. Different shapes lead to different features as most suitable and the five features covering all the shapes are retained. These five features are then ranked again against all the shapes in order to determine the best 'shape-feature' pair that can best cluster the control, patients and age equivalent populations. Table 1 shows the feature ranking for the 15 shapes illustrating the 'best' five features with its corresponding ranking scores. The features within the table are numbered e.g. 1= average pressure, 2= maximum pressure, 7= velocity, 8= no.of strokes, 14= total time, 15= pen movement time.

**Table 1.** Features and corresponding rank scores

| Shape No. | Feature No. / Rank score | | | | |
|---|---|---|---|---|---|
| | 1st | 2nd | 3rd | 4th | 5th |
| Shape 1 | 15 / 2.12 | 9 / 1.90 | 14 / 1.54 | 6 / 0.96 | 7 / 0.89 |
| Shape 2 | 15 / 4.63 | 9 / 4.40 | 7 / 2.18 | 4 / 2.03 | 11 / 1.86 |
| Shape 3 | 15 / 3.72 | 9 / 3.59 | 4 / 2.24 | 7 / 2.22 | 14 / 2.10 |
| Shape 4 | 15 / 2.16 | 14 / 2.01 | 9 / 1.97 | 10 / 1.79 | 18 / 1.79 |
| Shape 5 | 15 / 2.67 | 9 / 2.55 | 7 /1.81 | 4 / 1.45 | 6 / 1.25 |
| Shape 6 | 14 / 3.36 | 15 / 3.36 | 9 / 3.27 | 8 / 2.81 | 7 / 2.49 |
| Shape 7 | 15 / 1.55 | 19 / 1.16 | 9 / 1.09 | 7 / 1.08 | 2 / 0.87 |
| Shape 8 | 10 / 3.05 | 14 / 2.95 | 15 / 2.65 | 9 / 2.60 | 7 / 1.59 |
| Shape 9 | 15 / 3.58 | 9 / 3.14 | 14 / 2.81 | 6 / 2.76 | 7 / 1.93 |
| Shape 10 | 15 / 3.31 | 9 / 2.61 | 6 / 2.30 | 14 / 2.27 | 7 / 1.96 |
| Shape 11 | 15 / 1.98 | 12 / 1.73 | 7 / 1.49 | 19 / 1.23 | 9 / 1.19 |
| Shape 12 | 2 / 2.14 | 3 / 2.14 | 1 / 1.56 | 7 / 1.49 | 6 / 1.46 |
| Shape 13 | 15 / 2.25 | 9 / 2.00 | 13 / 1.68 | 14 / 1.65 | 6 / 1.31 |
| Shape 14 | 7 / 1.92 | 19 / 1.51 | 15 / 1.18 | 9 / 0.86 | 16 / 0.83 |
| Shape 15 | 15 / 2.98 | 19 / 2.25 | 7 / 2.02 | 16 / 1.96 | 18 / 1.96 |

## 5 Results

The following discussion illustrates the three important and dominating features for clustering between controls and patients, which are pen movement time, maximum pressure and mean velocity with pen movement time (feature 15) being the most dominant. Figure 3(a) shows the average pen movement time of the three groups while drawing shapes 1 to 15. It illustrates that the average pen movement time of the control subjects is the highest for all shapes and shape 2 is the best in the rank (table 1) and with one of the lowest standard deviation values. Therefore the feature 'pen movement time' of shape 2 was used in clustering individual groups of the three populations and is illustrated in Figure 3(b). According to static scoring the age equivalent subjects were expected to have a similar profile to those of control subjects but the results show that for dynamic parameters these subjects behave in a similar way to the patient population.

Pen Pressure is also an important factor in the study of drawing dynamics of children with visuo-motor dysfunction which has up to now received relatively little attention. Initial findings are shown in Figure 4(a) which illustrates the average values of maximum pen pressure applied within individual populations. It reveals that the patient population tend to apply higher pressure than the other two groups. However in ranking, shape 12 was of highest order for this feature. Therefore pen pressure of shape 12 was used in clustering of the three populations and is illustrated in Figure

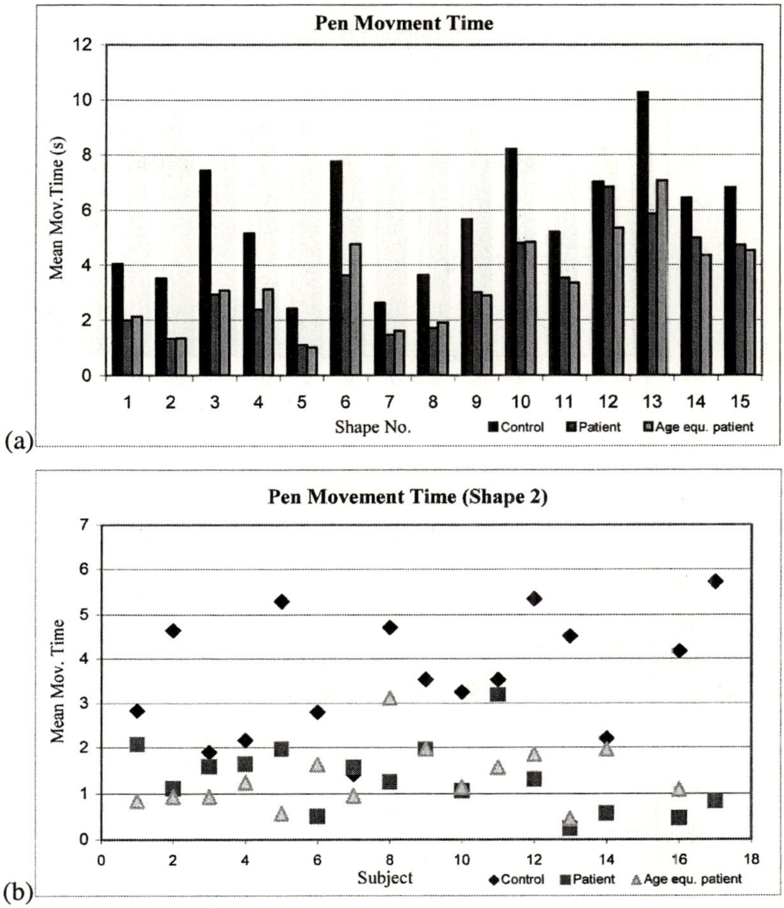


**Fig. 3. (a)** Mean pen movement time for individual shapes for the three groups of control patients and age equivalent. **(b)** Mean pen movement time for drawing shape 2 for the three groups of control patients and age equivalent.

4(b). The age equivalent subjects were again expected to have a similar profile to those of control subjects but it is found that these subjects generally have values in a range between that for controls and patients.

A further important feature is pen velocity. Figures 5(a) and 5(b) show that the mean pen velocity and standard deviation of the patients and age equivalent subjects is higher than controls for all shapes.

These initial results indicate that there is considerable potential for restricting the figure-copying test such that fewer shapes are required to be drawn by subjects for superior clustering between relevant groups when dynamic features are considered. It is also clear that some of the dynamic features measurable using this method of on-line data capture can reveal important information about dyspraxic patients not otherwise available, and can provide the basis for identifying relevant sub-groupings.

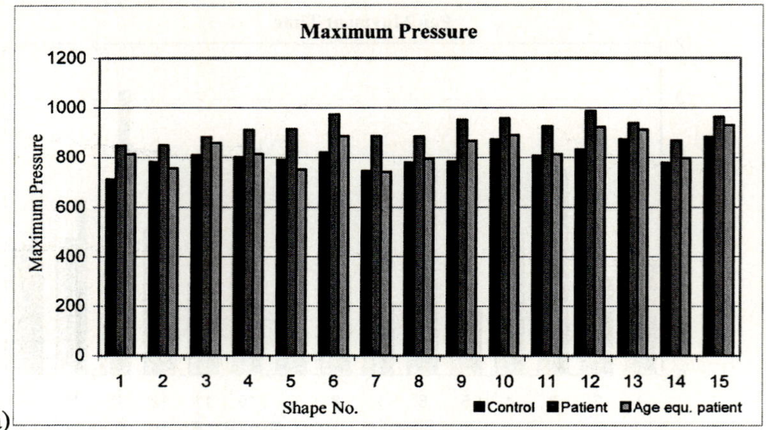


(a)

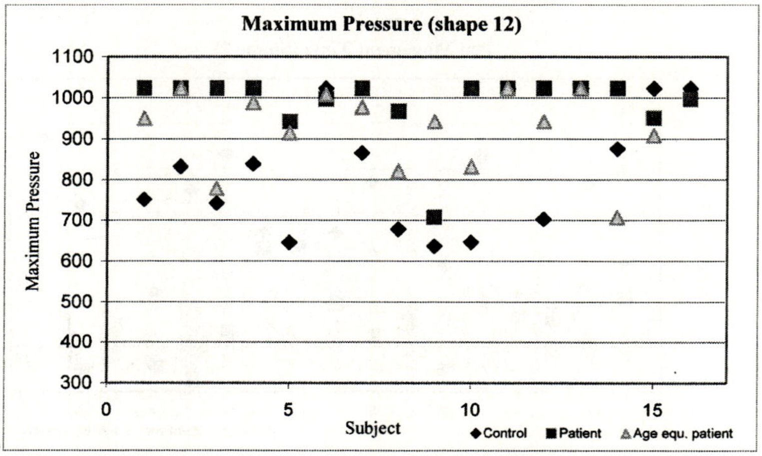


(b)

**Fig. 4. (a)** Maximum pressure applied during the drawing of individual shapes for the three groups of control patients and age equivalent. **(b)** Maximum pressure applied during the drawing of shape 12 for the three groups of control patients and age equivalent.

## 6 Conclusion

This paper has reported some preliminary findings of a study which is using the extraction of dynamic characteristics of drawing ability (especially in figure copying tasks) to create a profile of behavioural traits in dyspraxic patients. This can support the enhancement of diagnostic and rehabilitation scenarios and underlines an important finding in the analysis of visuo-motor drawing tests, that extracting dynamic features from a single shape can facilitate the clustering between different populations of patients and controls.

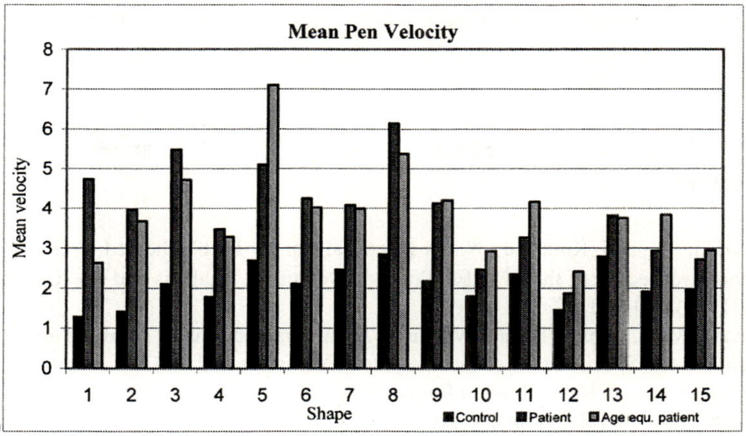


(a)

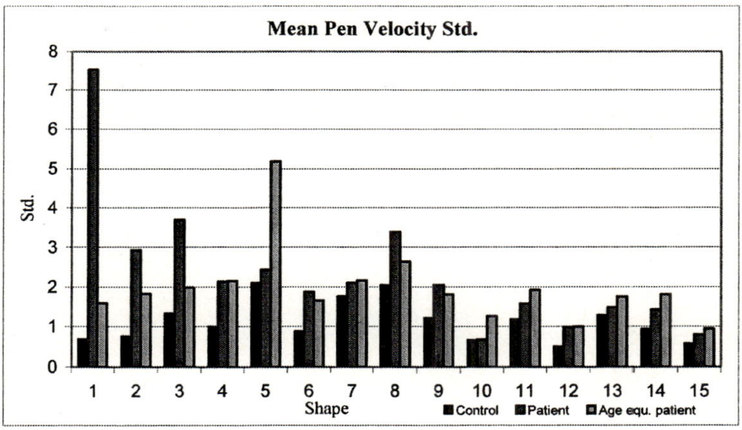


(b)

**Fig. 5. (a)** Mean pen velocity during the drawing of individual shapes for the three groups of control patients and age equivalent. **(b)** Standard deviations of pen mean velocity of the drawing of individual shapes for the three groups of control patients and age equivalent.

The analysis of dynamic features and parameters show more differences between patients, age equivalent patients and controls than static analysis alone would have shown. For example, the study reveals that patients still apply a higher pen pressure than controls even in cases where age equivalent measures suggest comparable performance characteristics.

The results reported here clearly demonstrate the potential of this type of analysis, and will inform on-going studies.

## Acknowledgement

The authors gratefully acknowledge the support of the UK Engineering and Physical Sciences Research Council. We also acknowledge the work of Wendy Clarke, Marian

Bond and Roger Bradford in collecting and interpreting of the results. Thanks are also expressed to members of staff, parents and children of Vernon Holme and Blean Primary School for their participation.

## References

1. Yamazaki, Y. and Komatsu, N.: A Proposal for a Text-Indicated Writer Verification Method, Proceeding of the 4th IEEE Conf. on Document Analysis and Recognition (ICDAR '97), (1997) 709-713
2. Fairhurst, M.C., Smith, L. and Mitchell, J.: Automated Image Analysis in Visuo-Motor Testing for the Specification of an Integrated Evaluative and therapy support tool for rehabilitation, Trans. on Rehabilitation Engineering, (March 1995) Vol. 3, No. 1, 103-111
3. Portwood, M.: Developmental Dyspraxia: Identification and Intervention: A Manual for Parents and Professionals, David Fulton Publishers, (1999)
4. Beery, K.: The VMI- Dev. Test of Visual Motor Integration, 4th Rev. Parsippany, NJ: Modern Curr. Press, (1997)
5. Michaek, M. and Lin, W. Experimental Study of Information Measure and Inter-Intra Class Distance Ratios on Feature Selection and Orderings. IEEE Trans. on Sys., Man and Cybernetics. 3(2), (1973)

# Feature Selection Optimisation in an Automated Diagnostic Cancellation Task

S. Chindaro[1], R.M. Guest[1], M.C. Fairhurst[1], M.A. Razian[1], and J.M. Potter[2]

[1] Department of Electronics, University of Kent, Canterbury, UK
r.m.guest@kent.ac.uk
[2] Kent and Canterbury Hospital, Canterbury, Kent, UK

**Abstract.** This paper describes an investigation into feature selection and classification in the automation of a standard target cancellation task for the diagnosis of visuo-spatial neglect. Alongside a conventional assessment based on the number of targets cancelled, a series of time-based *dynamic* features have been algorithmically defined which can be extracted by capturing the test subject's response on a graphics tablet connected to a computer. We identify the diagnostic capabilities of the individual features and show that dynamic data contains important indicators for neglect detection. Furthermore, employing standard pattern recognition techniques, we establish the optimum feature vector size and classifier for a multi-feature analysis of a test attempt and show that an improvement in diagnostic error rate is achievable over any single individual feature.

## 1 Introduction

Visuo-spatial neglect relates to a dysfunction caused by brain damage, especially as a result of stroke, the main effect of which is to cause subjects to fail to respond to stimuli in the visual field on the opposite side to the location of the lesion [1]. Conventional assessment techniques for the condition usually include a number of simple "pencil-and-paper" based tests such as line bisection (location and marking of a line midpoint) and shape and image copying (usually geometric shapes or familiar symmetrical objects) [2].

Cancellation tasks have a long history in the study and detection of visuo-spatial neglect [3]. They require that a set of visual "targets" are located and cancelled using a single pen stroke through the target. The targets are usually either multiple lines (such as in the Albert's cancellation task – Figure 1) or letters/shapes arranged in a uniform, random or pseudo-random formation. Performance assessment is measured by counting the number of targets successfully cancelled. It has been shown, however, that alongside such a *static* performance measure, assessing the 'outcome' of the task, constructional (or *dynamic*) features detailing the strategy of the task execution also contain important diagnostic indicators [4]. Due to the nature of the neglect condition, it is also appropriate to measure the differential between the performance in the left and right sides of the visual field and, for additional information, on a quadrant basis.

K. Miesenberger et al. (Eds.): ICCHP 2004, LNCS 3118, pp. 1047–1053, 2004.

**Fig. 1.** Configuration of Albert's Cancellation Task.

To enable the analysis of 'dynamic' constructional features we have implemented a computer-based assessment system which captures pen responses in real-time using a standard graphics table. Having defined a series of generic performance features which can be extracted from a test response file, the results reported in this paper detail experiments relating to feature selection and improvement of diagnostic sensitivity through the combination of features. The experiments aim to identify those features which are able to best discriminate between neglect and non-neglect subject groupings, determine whether a combination of features increases diagnostic accuracy over that obtained by any one individual feature and identify the optimum number of performance features to be included in a vector to produce the best diagnostic classification.

## 2 Experimental Infrastructure

In our implementation, we use the standard Albert's task [5] which contains 40 lines arranged in varying orientations printed on an A4 sized (29.7 x 21 cm) paper overlay (Figure 1). The cancellation tasks were completed by the test subject with the overlay positioned and fixed on a graphic digitization tablet (Wacom Intuos2) connected to a PC. Figure 2 shows the experimental infrastructure.

As the test subject marks the overlay, the co-ordinates of a cordless pen are transmitted to the computer. The spatial coordinate data along with other pen position data (such as pressure and $x$ and $y$ tilt values) are time-stamped with an offset from the start of data capture (in ms) and stored in a separate data response file on the computer. The main benefits of this storage method (as opposed to real time processing of the data) are twofold. First, complex feature extraction routines can be used on the data without the need to buffer the real-time data stream from the graphics tablet, and second, responses can be re-analyzed at any time such that new features can be defined and extracted without the need for re-testing.

**Fig. 2.** Experimental Infrastructure.

A total of 30 neglect subjects were included in the trial, with data collected over a four-year period. These subjects were identified using standard clinical assessments and expert clinical diagnosis. A group of 57 stroke subjects without neglect were used as the stroke control group.

## 3 Features

The following 44 features are automatically extracted from each cancellation task response file by the computer-based test system. They can be identified as belonging to one of four groupings: Timing, Cancellation, Regression and Sequence.

### Timings (30 Dynamic Features)

Two global features, *Execution Time* – time between first and last cancellation and *Time per Cancellation* – task execution time divided by the number of cancellations, provide an indication of overall performance.

A series of features measuring timings between cancellations strokes were also defined. These features enabled the analysis of motor aspects of construction (drawing and movement times) and cognitive 'planning' aspects. *Movement Time* was defined as the time between the pen leaving its previous target and start of the next cancellation, *Planning Time* as the duration in which the pen remained stationary after the completion of a cancellation before the next movement began and *Drawing Time* as the time from beginning to end of each cancellation stroke. The sum of these form an *Intercancellation Time* between individual target cancellations. A mean of each of these timings was calculated globally (4 features), within each quadrant in the overlay (16 features) and within each side (left and right) of the overlay (8 features) enabling the effects of target location to be investigated.

**Regressions (4 Dynamic Features)**

The timings described above are calculated independently for each cancellation made during task execution. The values throughout the cancellation sequence are used in a regression calculation which indicates whether the test subject had increased or decreased in speed for each feature. A slope of a regression is calculated for *Intercancellation, Movement, Planning* and *Drawing* times.

**Cancellation (5 Static Features)**

Alongside *Total Cancellations* – the number of targets on the overlay that have been cancelled - an analysis was conducted into the number of cancellations made in each quadrant of the task overlay. These features automated the process by which cancellation tasks are conventionally assessed.

**Sequencing (5 Dynamic Features)**

The sequence in which the cancellation targets were visited is assessed by matching against a series of templates containing anticipated sequences. Sequence Number is the sequence ID with the best match against the drawn sequence. Matches is the number of direct matches with one of the model sequences. Shift indicates the number of sequence positions the best match sequence had to be shifted to find the maximum number of matches. *Start* indicates the starting cancellation point in the test subject's drawn sequence. The number of *Path Crossings* (the number of times the cancellation path crosses over itself indicating a disorganisation within the strategy) were also computed.

Full details of the sequencing and path crossing features can be found in [6].

## 4 Feature and Classification Performance

Two commonly used classifiers, the k-nearest neighbour classifier (knnc) and a decision tree classifier (treec) were trained and assessed in the experiments. The classifiers were implemented using the PRTools toolbox for MATLAB. Details of these standard classifiers used can be found in [7]. By training multiple classifiers on the same data we are able to identify the optimum classifier to achieve maximum performance.

The leave-one-out technique [8] was employed to estimate classifier error rates in the experiments. For a sample size, $n$, a classifier is generated using ($n$ - 1) cases and tested on the single remaining case. This is repeated $n$ times, each time designing a classifier by leaving-one-out. The error rate is the number of errors on the single test cases divided by $n$. Evidence for the superiority of the leaving-one-out approach is well documented [9]. The leave-one-out error rate estimator is an almost unbiased estimator of the true error rate of a classifier. This means that over many different sample sets of size n, the leaving-one-out estimate will average out to the true error rate.

Many methods exist for feature selection within a larger feature vector, and a number of algorithms are presented in [10]. An aim of the experiments is to investigate the composition of a feature subset that is necessary and sufficient to accurately enable discrimination between neglect and stroke control patients. From the large feature set available (44 features), some features may be partially or completely irrelevant/redundant to the final classification. Reducing the number of these features reduces the running time of a learning algorithm and, in many cases, improves learning. The motivation for doing this is to improve classification performance through a more stable representation and removal of redundant or irrelevant information.

The composition of an optimal subset is determined by using an evaluation function which measures the discrimination ability of a single feature or subset vector to distinguish the different class labels. Although a number of evaluation functions exist, for our investigations we used a classifier error rate measure and a stepwise search known as forward feature selection. The one-nearest-neighbour leave-one-out classification performance measure was used as an evaluation tool for feature subset selection in the implementation described in this paper.

## 5 Results

As an initial experiment, all 44 features were ranked using the forward feature selection method as the basis of their diagnostic classification performance (that is distinguishing between neglect and control subject responses). At this stage the classification error rate for each individual feature was also calculated. Table 1 shows the best 10 features identified by this method. The top ranking feature, the number of cancellations in the top right quadrant, has an individual error rate of 0.05% which forms a performance benchmark for any multi-feature classifier system to improve upon. It is also interesting to note that 7 out of the top 10 features are dynamic in nature, confirming the importance of extracting these novel data.

**Table 1.** Top 10 features in terms of diagnostic ability and classification error rate.

| Rank | Feature |
|---|---|
| 1 | Top Right Cancellations |
| 2 | Bottom Right Cancellations |
| 3 | Time Per Cancellation |
| 4 | Top Left Movement Time |
| 5 | Mean Left Intercancellation Time |
| 6 | Execution Time |
| 7 | Top Left Cancellations |
| 8 | Top Left Intercancellation Time |
| 9 | Sequence Matches |
| 10 | Intercancellation Time on L/R Movements |

The second experiment was to establish the optimum classifier and size of feature vector. Feature vectors of size *n* were constructed based on the top *n* features from the ranking list. These vectors were used to train the two standard classifiers within the leave-one-out evaluation framework. Figure 3 shows the error rates produced from the various vector sizes (with *n* varying between 2 and 40). It can be seen that a vector containing the top 5 features using the decision tree classified produced the lowest error rate of 0.02%, improving on the error rate of the best single feature. Diagnostic performance deteriorates as the number of features within the vector increases.

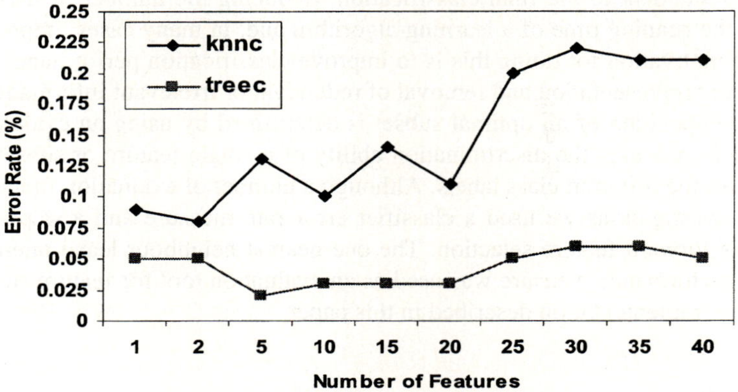


**Fig. 3.** Error rates with varying size feature sets.

## 6 Conclusions

In this paper we have identified the features from a standard cancellation task for visuo-spatial neglect that provide the best diagnostic indicators of the condition. Importantly, we have introduced a series of novel time-based 'dynamic' features, unmeasureable using conventional assessment techniques which have been shown to be as effective as the static 'target cancelled' measures as well as establishing objectivity in their algorithmic definition. Our experiments in combining features have shown that only a subset of the entire feature set is necessary for the best diagnostic results and that an improvement in diagnostic error rate is achieved when classifying using the top 5 features with a decision tree classifier. We can conclude from this analysis that an effective approach to improving diagnosis may lie in a multiple-feature approach that takes into account the strengths and weaknesses of the various diagnostic features and exploits the complementary information in them. This approach has been shown here to improve the results obtained by using a single feature.

## Acknowledgement

The authors acknowledge the support of the UK Engineering and Physical Sciences Research Council for this work.

## References


1. Halligan, P.W., Marshall, J.C., Wade, D.T., Visuospatial neglect - underlying factors and test sensitivity, The Lancet, Vol. II, (1989), pp. 908-911.
2. Ericsson, K., Forrsell, L.G., Holmen K., Viitanen, M., Copying and handwriting ability in the screening of cognitive dysfunction in old age, Archives of Gerontology and Geriatrics, 22, (1996), pp. 103-121.
3. Bradshaw, J. L. and Mattingley, J. B., Clinical Neuropsychology, Academic Press, (1996.)
4. Remi, C., Frelicot, C., Courtellemont, P., Automatic analysis of the structuring of children's drawing and writing, Pattern Recognition, 35, (2002), pp. 1059-1069.
5. Albert, M. L., A simple test of neglect. Neurology, 23, (1973), pp. 658-64.
6. Donnelly, N., Guest, R., Fairhurst, M., Potter, J., Deighton, A., Patel, M., Developing algorithms to enhance the sensitivity of cancellation test of visuo-spatial neglect, N. Donnelly, Behavior Research Methods, Instruments and Computers, 31 (4), (1999), pp. 668-673.
7. Duin, R.P.W., PRTools - A Matlab Toolbox for Pattern Recognition, Delft University of Technology, (2000).
8. John, G.H, Kohavi R., Pfleger, K., Irrelevant features and the subset selection problem, Proceedings of the 11th International Conference on Machine Learning, (1994), pp. 121-129.
9. Goutte, C., Note on Free Lunches and Cross-Validation, Neural Computation, 9, (1997), pp. 1211-1215.
10. Dash, M., Feature Selection For Classification, Intelligent Data Analysis, 1, (1997), pp. 131-156.

# Minus-Two: Multimedia, Sound Spatialization and 3D Representation for Cognitively Impaired Children

Thimoty Barbieri, Antonio Bianchi, and Licia Sbattella

Dipartimento di Elettronica e Informazione, Politecnico di Milano
{thimoty.barbieri,licia.sbattella}@polimi.it
abianchi@sonic.it

**Abstract:** Multimedia and Hypermedia technologies can be successfully used in education and rehabilitation for cognitively disabled persons. In particular, storytelling has always proved successfully in creating imaginary worlds that could both protect the child from the difficulties of the outer world and create the conditions to feed new stimuli without causing discomfort. However, traditional storytelling techniques (paper, pencil, the voice of the teacher) sometimes might be vastly improved by using multimedia and hypermedia technologies. The possibility to play different music, to explore spatialized sounds, to record sounds and voices, and the opportunity to play with 3D images within a 3D space using devices as simple as touch screens, may ensure an enhanced level of attention from the children and may give to the teacher new and powerful tools to convey his/her message through the common activity. In this paper we motivate the use of hypermedia educational techniques with cognitively impaired children, outlining the general requirements of an educational framework that might be provided to teachers. We then describe the functioning of a prototype we developed following these requirements, MINUS-TWO: a storytelling environment mainly characterized by a strict cooperation between the child and the teacher or the therapist, by multimodal interaction, sound spatialization and 3D representation. The paper also presents the results we obtained by using these techniques with more than twenty cognitively impaired children.

## 1 Foreword and Motivations: Storytelling as an Activity towards Autonomy

Marc Augè [1], in his book published in 1993, has introduced the concept of *non-lieu* (non-place), defining it as "*a space in which who passes through cannot read anything about his identity, nor about the relation with himself, the relations with others, or more generally, about relations among ones and others, or a fortiori about their common background*". This article, in agreement with a rich literature, proposes narration as affirmative answer to *non-lieu*: the place of the meeting, where a person can perceive his origins and his possible developments. The main motivation for the storyteller framework described in this paper is the following: narration is a fundamental opportunity for a human being to develop and maintain his personal identity. An opportunity which cannot be overlooked especially in cases of cognitive disability, even when language or relational competencies are strongly compromised (as in autistic syndromes). A person in situation of disability risks to be overwhelmed by his

K. Miesenberger et al. (Eds.): ICCHP 2004, LNCS 3118, pp. 1054–1061, 2004.

immediate needs, a condition which compromises his harmonious development. A story organizes the human space in different ways; creating complex time sequences it allows to explore different situations, and to face them with more flexibility. A dramatization may be useful to let the students understand a situation by playing it, moving it to a different plane, retrieving only in a second moment its details connected to reality. Building a tale as a background creates a sort of perceptive structure. It is at the same time a recognition of a given reality, it is a given "data" from which the single actor may receive support and stimuli. We can think of a storyteller framework as a rehabilitation tool too, in the sense it offers stimuli directed to the sphere of attention, memory, problem solving, both from a logical-deductive and relational point of view.

Situations characterized by joy, sadness, anxiety, may be faced in an interactive way cooperating with the tutor in known contexts, under his supervision. The literature describes different storytelling activities involving persons with different kind of problems (e.g. Alzheimer…). Pedagogy and traditional rehabilitation often use objects such as dolls, toys and books to support narration or encourage children to draw using paper and colored pencils. Why then using an information technology framework for storytelling? It is very difficult to involve in a storytelling activity children who don't speak and do not draw, who feel this kind of relationship really uncomfortable. We think that 3D spaces, sounds and music may improve opportunities contributing to stimulate attention and to make the experience more vivid. Beside this, it gives the important possibility to introduce variations, to create new scenarios, to support different views on narration, to allow the listener to interact with the story as it gets unfold, and with the description of characters as they present themselves, as a further step in stimulating the child to an autonomous elaboration of information and messages proposed by the teacher. Within a 3D scene, the sound acquires a spatial dimension, and is perceived as directly linked to particular objects. Navigating in the space, it is possible to listen to how sounds change in direction and intensity, adding the possibility to explore the objects even from this point of view. The possibility to interact with the environment in different ways - using traditional interface devices, touch screens, voice or real musical instruments – gives more opportunities to involve children with cognitive, expressive or relational disabilities, as shown by the use of our prototype with more then twenty cognitively impaired and autistic children.

## 2 Requirements of a Multimedia Interactive Storytelling Framework

Before implementing a working prototype that could prove the effectiveness of semi-immersive 3D graphics and spatial sound for the aforementioned purposes, we tried to outline its main requirements. We refer here to three different figures of possible users: the *Disabled Person*, the *Tutor* and the *Scene Designer*, that of course may be the tutor himself. As general, conceptual, goals we wanted our storyteller to be *extendible*, *metaphoric*, *cooperative*, *multimedia-capable*, *recordable*.

*Extendible*: the Storytelling Framework should present itself in an open form: it should be possible to extend functionalities at different levels, operating at different levels of competence.

*Metaphoric*: metaphors are often useful*: if something seems totally new in one of our descriptive worlds, it's possible that, translated into another world's language, begins to look like something already known* [2]. The Storyteller should be a framework to build a story as a sequence of scenes. The scene is the place inside which interactions occur among who are writing the story and the events that constitute the story itself.

*Cooperative*: a significant feature of a storyteller is its support for a cooperative way of working and learning, which results effective both on a cognitive and formative planes. From a formative point of view, self-esteem may develop among peers participating in the story, as well as a growing feeling dignity deriving by the fact to be able to help another person.

*Multimedia*: The storyteller should activate meaningful and alternative channels of communication through the of *text*, *graphics* and *sounds*. The interaction with the environment is mediated by a representation that doesn't need to fill the gap with the real world; the use of fictitious settings encourage drifting away from reality, an aspect that proves to be fundamental when a direct interaction with the real world is refused or conflictual.

*Recordable*: the sharing of the creative act continues in sharing of the result; the story as it gets unfold with the participation of the children may be recorded and subsequently re-played, or printed in a sequence of pictures. This impressive possibility to produce a meaningful product, both in the form and in the content, *appears to be very motivating* for students and teachers alike.

With these goals in mind, we have chosen the following as the most important requirements for a tutor using the multimedia educational framework, to be implemented in the first or subsequent versions of our storytelling prototype:

- The possibility to display multiple 3D scenes, which can be viewed in sequence, forward or backwards. This allows the teacher to choose the best scenarios, suited to the context he/she wants to set for his/her narration.
- Tools for inserting or removing objects, available from a predefined library. It may be possible to enable or disable particular properties (making them interactive), and to link sounds or recorded voices to them.
- The possibility to modify the parameters of each single object, like for example the volume or the pitch of the sound linked to a particular object, in order to create different stimuli, that the teacher may exploit during the telling of the storytelling activity.
- The possibility to record the teacher's vocal comments, or the child's one, which may characterize the game and the story. Alternatively, the possibility to note these comments down in some textual form, as notes to be attached to the objects themselves.

The requirements on the disabled person's side focus on the possibility to interact with the educational tool in the following ways:

- Navigate and explore the 3D scene, performing movements in various directions of the virtual space, by means of a simplified keyboard or a trackball.
- Interact with the objects, by touching them with a switch button, or by directly pointing the finger on them with a touch screen (making them moving or playing).
- Pay a particular attention to the "sonorous dimension" of the environment. Use some objects within the scene to listen back to one's own voice, modifying it in re-

lation to the event or the context of the story, putting it in context along with the other "voices" of the story. In this way it is possible to reach a stronger level of motivation, because the child, with his voice or sound, gets more involved and more in tune with the other elements of the story.
- Have the occasion to articulate, contain and modulate complex sequences of events along the temporal dimension. In this way it is possible to increase the self esteem, the flexibility of the relational behavior, and the emotional control which allow to expose ourselves respecting the role of others.

The tutor needs to be able to modify the features of the scene as the story gets told: therefore the tool has to offer advanced configuration features, which ideally should allow to build, element by element, the scenes, assigning to their different components a predefined set of behaviors and sounds. Object shapes, sounds, and behaviors could be picked from a library. It is thus necessary to define requirements, for the third actor, the *Scene Designer*, as stated before. The requirements for the Scene Designer might be the following:

- Choose or draw the 3D geometries to use as "scene background". Link this scenes together to create a navigational sequence.
- Assign to each scene a musical theme, or a narrating voice.
- Pick the objects which should be present in the story. Arrange them in each scene.
- Assign to each object a predefined behavior (or program a new one, by writing a script which implements the behavior interface), and a predefined sound.

Starting from these requirements, the general framework of the storytelling tool should be composed by three main elements, contained in a general structure, which we named The Application Canvas:

- Procedures for loading the story configuration
- Presentation of the run-time control options to alter the properties of the scenes and the objects, as defined by the designer (a sort of "control panel" which allows to the teacher to control how the story progresses)
- The rendering space of the 3D scene, with functionalities for exploring and navigation

To ensure the needed level of configurability during the storytelling activity, the 3D scene must be composed by Elements. The Elements are geometrical entities which contain a 3D shape description, and one or more behavior and sound links. In this way, the scene and the objects which populate them can be described with the same data structure, and can share the same base properties and actions.

The Scene elements may link to each other to form a sequence, with the roles of Previous Scene and Following Scene. The Object Elements may be arranged within the scenes before or during the narration. Another important requirement is related to the possibility to add new capabilities to different categories of objects defining several subclasses of objects. As for the behaviors, they might also be represented by classes, and they all should support two different callback invocation methods: a callback to be automatically invoked every predefined period of time, and when the object is on a idle state. These general principles, and in particular the callback principle for event handling, are at the foundation of several 3D APIs, like VRML [3, 4], or Java3D [5].

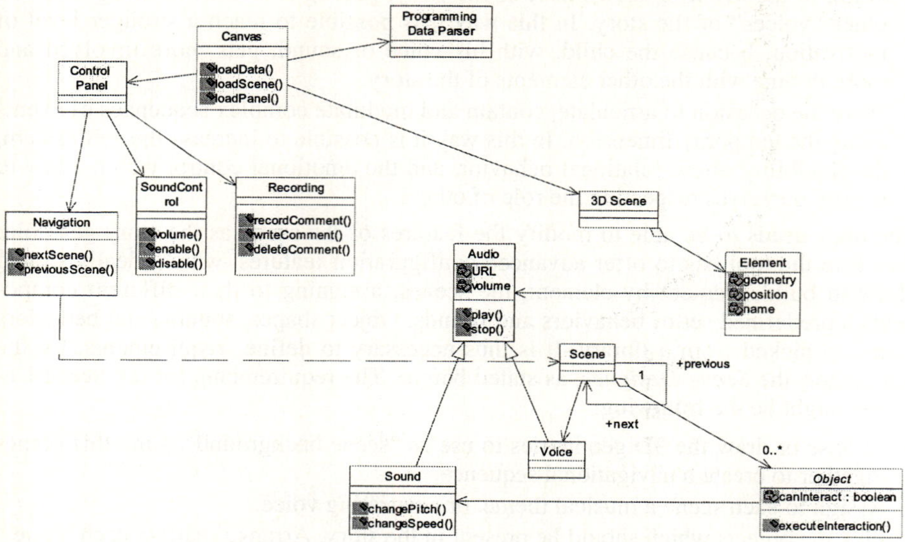


**Fig. 1.** The general architectural scheme of the Storytelling Prototype.

## 3 Minus-Two: A Prototype for a StoryTeller Application Based on VRML

Another main goal in implementing the first version of our storytelling prototype, called MINUS-TWO, was to create a tool which had low technological barriers, easy to install on normal personal computer, and at the same time flexible enough to allow the creation and editing of the 3D objects within the scene.

The use of VRML and of a framework based on HTML web pages allows to access the contents of the interactive story using a common browser with the VRML plug-in, with a broadband internet access to download the graphical and sound resources related to the objects. Moreover, the structure of VRML is very similar to the conceptual structure of application architecture and behavior handling we previously sketched. The coordination between the VRML scene and the sounds is implemented using JavaScript, linked to the appropriate VRML nodes. The page loads with the VRML plug-in and a controlling Java Applet, which allows the teacher to select the musical backgrounds and the characters of the story that he wants to load. The communication between the controlling Applet and the VRML plug-in is made possible through the EAI API [4], a commonly used intercommunication layer between the browser and the 3D scene. VRML gives the possibility to spatialize the sound: in this way, by moving nearer to the different characters it is possible to listen to the sounds coming from different parts of the scene. Switch buttons and a touch screen are used to manipulate the 3D object, as programmed within the VRML nodes using specific VRML syntax.

## 4 Using Minus-Two: Description and Results

As a case study and example for interactive 3D storytelling, to emphasize the importance of the sonorous dimension of an interactive environment, we referred to the symphonic fairytale "Peter and the Wolf", by Sergej Prokofiev.

This tale is well suited to be told via MINUS-TWO, thanks to the strong characterization of the characters involved through the musical themes and sound, and it allows the teacher to create occasions of interaction and exploration with the child during the storytelling sessions.

The story gets told in different scenes, one for each main episode of the tale. It is possible to navigate from one scene to the other, following the HTML links. Each scene is completed with a recorded voice telling the story, and the animation of the different characters, which can be taken and manipulated by the user. Each character has assigned the famous themes written by Prokofiev.

At any time it is possible to stop the recorded voice telling the story, and interact and play with each character, manipulating its shape and its sounds, or using other objects in the scene to produce new sounds, or to play along the background music. Each scene provides a set of virtual drums, linked to suitable switch buttons, and a small piano keyboard. Working on the switch buttons or on the virtual keys of the piano, it is possible to play the virtual instruments. Navigating and moving through the virtual space, both the sound and the voices of the scene and of the objects can be perceived in various ways in a spatialized effect. Different types of musical backgrounds are used within the scenes: the symphonic original background allows to listen to the original musical work, while moving at the same time the characters in the scene (or just looking at the characters while they are moving following the music). The other type provides only a piano part, to allow the teacher and the children to enrich and orchestrate the background music with original parts obtained using the interactive sound objects (marking the rhythm, modulating dynamics, changing the global timbre through the drums or the piano keyboard). It is also possible to vary the pitch of the sounds linked to the various objects, creating variations from a very low to a very high pitch, to obtain stimuli of different intensity, and train the child to distinguish different sound and intensities.

Minus-Two was used with 15 children aged 6-8 and 10 youngsters aged 17-22. Twelve of these suffered from an autistic syndrome (problems of shared attention, lack of communication capabilities, eight of them presented serious cognitive retardation); eight had language problems and congenital cognitive retardation, five had sensorial problems (two with hypacusia, three with hypovision). Each one was involved in six working sessions of one hour. In four sessions tutor and student cooperated together; in the following two a small group (three students, two teachers) participated in the activity. In each session, Minus-Two was used in conjunction and before other computer programs designed for storytelling (using 2D representation).

Each of them really enjoyed using our storytelling prototype, remaining engaged for a long period, if compared with traditional interactive sessions. The most important results refer to the following points:

*Exploration*: the colorful and rich 3D scene, and the animation of the characters engaged the students and created lively and intense working sessions, stimulating a dialogue even with autistic subjects. The possibility to move the characters within the scene, shifting the point of view, and listen to the sounds was appreciated and commented verbally and non-verbally. Many students proposed their own suggestions to enrich the possibilities of exploration. Several wanted to enter grandpa's house and explore it (see fig. 2), a possibility we didn't think about until the students pointed it out.

*Sounds and Music*: music and sounds played an important part during these sessions. We could experience several targeted and conditioned ways to listen to the orchestra and the piano. The students contributed in a pertinent way to the sounds, using the virtual instruments, also for subjects with communication problems or with limited shared attention abilities.

*Computer Interface*: we tried to clear the way from difficulties of interfacing to the computer, using special devices (trackballs and special mice), using bigger buttons within the windows, and using touch screens or tablet PCs. Using the stylus of the tablet PC instead of the mouse was very helpful for small children.

*Cooperation and Communication*: The richfulness of the environment was motivating to overcome the initial difficulties presented by the novelty of the tool. Each student was engaged in working sessions which became increasingly complex and long. The possibility to cooperate and communicate for an entire hour even with the most problematic children created a wave of enthusiasm and opened the way to the use of other programs which require good skills of attention and memory. It was evident that the tool offers the possibility to work with continuity and enjoyment within a session, even on a typical issue of autistic syndromes, the ability of shared attention. Students and teachers requested new stories, new sounds, and new interaction devices (real MIDI instruments, data glove, voice recognition control).

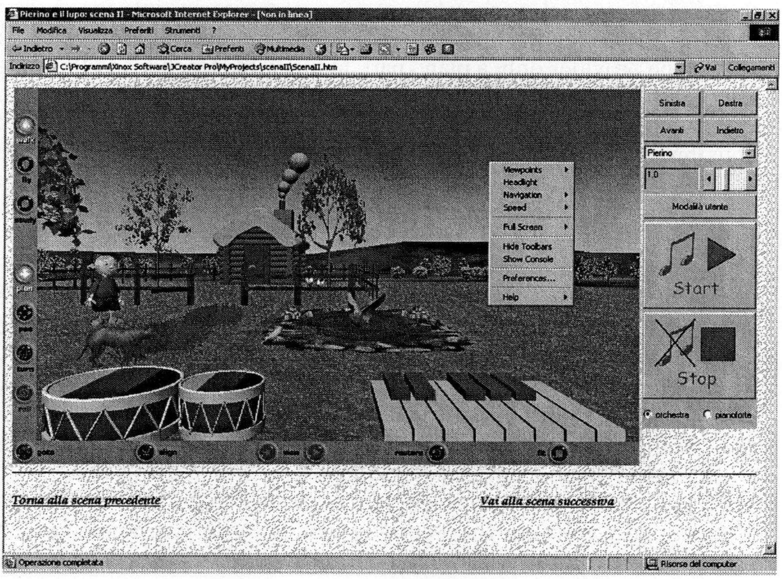


**Fig. 2.** This scene shows Peter, the wolf, the duck and the little singing bird. It is possible to explore the Grandpa's house. The two virtual instruments are controlled via switch buttons and keyboard, and allow to participate with sound stimuli to the music or the narration. On the right is visible a small console containing the story's controls dedicated to the Teacher: it is possible to vary the sound pitch, modify the positioning of the objects, and so forth.

## 5 Conclusions

The clear success we had using our prototype with children and teachers alike, is clearly indicated by the length and the liveliness of the working sessions which took place. This encourages us in exploring deeper the importance represented by all aspects related to sound and music, when they allow to perform an active role within the session, and the possibility of multimodal expression (gesturing, writing or uttering a word, acting, interacting, perceiving...). In the future we will enhance our prototype and delve even further in possible applications of 3D interaction and spatialization, exploring virtual exercises and training, role playing, and enhanced storytelling.

A musician who wants to express him/herself at the higher level buys a "Minus-One Concert": a recording of an orchestral performance where his/her instrumental part is missing so that he/she can play enriching the global execution. We thought of a "Minus-Two" environment to offer to the child and to his/her teacher or therapist the best occasion to express themselves in a story ... "a quattro mani".

## References


1. Augé, M.: Introduction à une anthropologie de la surmodernité, Éditions du Seuil, Paris, 1992
2. Minsky, M.: The society of mind. Simon & Schuster, New York, 1986
3. Web 3D Consortium VRML Specifications `http://www.web3d.org/x3d/specifications/vrml/`
4. VRML 97 External Authoring Interface specification, ISO/IEC 14772-2:2002 `http://www.web3d.org/x3d/specifications/vrml/ISO_IEC_14772-All/index.html`
5. Barbieri, T.: Networked Virtual Environments for the Web: The WebTalk-I and WebTalk-II. Architectures, in Proceedings IEEE for Computer Multimedia & Expo 2000 (ICME), New York, USA, Luglio 2000
6. Barbieri, T., Sbattella, L.: Virtual Sounds and Virtual Spaces to support Persons with Cognitive and Physical Disabilities during Information Retrieval, Rehabilitation and Learning. Proceedings of AAATE'03, Dublin (Ireland), 2003
7. Heyn, P.: Functional Exercises for Alzheimer's Disease Based on Storytelling. Proceedings of 130$^{th}$ American Public Health Association Meeting `http://apha.confex.com/apha/130am/techprogram/paper_41790.htm`
8. Swingler, T.: Electronic Music Interfaces for people with disabilities: do they lead anywhere?. Proceedings of AAATE'03, Dublin (Ireland), 2003
9. Antonin, H., Pashler, E.: The Psychology of Attention. MIT Press, 1998
10. Oatley, K., Jenkins, J.M.: Understanding Emotions. Blackwell Publishers, 1996
11. Siegel, D.J.: The Developing Mind. The Guilford Press Inc, 1999

# Neuropsychological Function for Accessibility of Computer Program for People with Mental Retardation

Alex W.W. Wong[1], Chetwyn C.H. Chan[1], Cecilia W.P. Li-Tsang[2], and Chow S. Lam[3]

[1] Ergonomics and Human Performance Laboratory, Department of Rehabilitation Sciences, The Hong Kong Polytechnic University, Hong Kong
{alex.wk.wong,rschchan}@polyu.edu.hk

[2] Department of Rehabilitation Sciences, The Hong Kong Polytechnic University, Hong Kong
rscecili@polyu.edu.hk

[3] Institute of Psychology, Illinois Institute of Technology, Chicago, Illinois, USA
lam@iit.edu

**Abstract.** The extent to which people with mental retardation are benefit from the modern information technology is not well explored. A better understanding on ways that the existing human-computer interface would challenge people with mental retardation would shed light on this issue. This study was investigated the neuropsychological functions which are important for enhancing the competence of people with mental retardation to operate on the Internet Explorer (IE) program. Sixty-two participants with mental retardation were invited to conduct a set of neuropsychological tests. Their computer performance was also evaluated. Resulted indicated that some specific neuropsychological functions including attention and visual scanning, psychomotor and language were predictive of their overall computer competence. The implication on ways to improve the design for computer programs for this population was discussed.

## 1 Introduction

Access to computing technology has become important in our lives. The contribution of information technology has increased people with mental retardation successful integration into community [1]. However, the design of existing information technology remains underutilized by people with mental retardation. Some studies suggested that the cognitive demands to operate these computer systems were not accommodated the needs of the people with mental retardation which in turn interfere their use and learn most of existing computer systems [2].

The theoretical model of human information processing for human-computer interaction is used as a basis from which to make prediction about participants' computer performance and investigate which cognitive processes are importantly involved when they interact with the computer [3]. The central theme of this model is that human is like an active information processor in which the human performance, from displayed information to response, is a function of several processing stages including stimulus identification, response selection and response execution. Interacting with

K. Miesenberger et al. (Eds.): ICCHP 2004, LNCS 3118, pp. 1062–1068, 2004.

the web browser and operating system required the user to identify displayed information e.g. menus, scrollbars, or icons (stimulus identification), to select responses based on the displayed information (response selection), and to executive those response e.g. clicking the icon via mouse button (response execution). These processes when the user interacts with the computer required to devote different extent of cognitive resources. For example, the user must search the displayed information and attend to the appropriate aspects of it. The user must also recall the commands, remember information specific to the task that is being performed, and make decisions and solve problems during the process [4]. These task demands seemed not to fit the lower neuropsychological profiles of people with mental retardation. The promise of technological design should be explicitly considered the cognitive compatibility of ultimate users [5]. In order to design a user-centered interface which is matched with the user's information processing capabilities, it is worthwhile to explore how neuropsychological functions to attribute people with mental retardation to operate IE program. The purpose of this study sought to determine the relative importance of neuropsychological functions in predicting the computer competence in the people with mental retardation. It will also shed light on ways to improve the design of the computer technologies to fit the profiles of this population.

## 2 Method

### 2.1 Participants

Total 62 participants with mental retardation were available for this study. They were recruited from those who enrolled computer training program designed for people with mental handicapped held in The Hong Kong Polytechnic University. To reduce any training effect of this program, they were invited to participate in this study before the training program was started. As part of their participations in our institutions, ethical approval was obtained and informed written consent was obtained from all their guardians. All the subjects were selected from the following criteria: 1) an ability to follow instructions; 2) an absence of identified organic etiology or secondary diagnoses; and 3) an non-verbal intelligence quotient score from the Test of Non-verbal Intelligence (TONI-3) ranged from 55 to 80. They were then classified into high (n=33) and low (n=29) IQ groups (cut-off score= 70). Demographic characteristics for the two groups are presented in Table 1. They were youths and only 29% of them were adults (18 years of age or older). They averaged about 17.37 years of age and had used computers, on average, for about 4.1 years on the time of this study.

**Table 1.** Demographic characteristics of participants.

| | Mean | SD |
|---|---|---|
| Age (years) | 17.37 | 5.98 |
| Education (years) | 7.44 | 1.78 |
| Computer usage (hrs/wk) | 4.10 | 2.83 |
| Gender | | |
| Male | 40 | |
| Female | 22 | |

## 2.2 Experimental Materials and Procedures

**IE Competence Test.** The demographic characteristics of participants were gathered and TONI-3 was conducted before the commencement of IE competence test. The IE competence test consisted of 16 IE-related tasks which was validated by an expert panel consisted of 9 professionals working in mental retardation field with a mean of 7.1 years (SD= 4.41). These tasks constituted a total of 161 subtasks which are used as the test items for assessing the computer competence on using IE. The reliability of these tasks was from moderate to good in which the ICC values ranged from 0.69 to 0.99. The discriminative method of this test based on two of 16 tasks (Use customized bookmark & General motor function) for differentiating people with mental retardation into three competence groups was also produced [6]. The participants were instructed to sit in front of the computer running with Window XP operating system and Microsoft's Internet Explorer 6.0 for the IE competence test. The tasks were administered in random sequence for each participant. Standardized instructions and ultimate goals on each of the sixteen tasks were given by the first author before the participants performed each of the tasks. The participants' performance on each of the test items was observed and rated on a four-point scale with "1" indicated "complete assistance", "2" indicated "performance with verbal and physical prompts", "3" indicated "performance with verbal prompts" and "4" indicated "competent performance". It took approximately 40-60 min per subject to complete.

**Neuropsychological Testing.** After the IE competence test, the neuropsychological assessments were conducted. Six cognitive domains including attention, visual-spatial, language, memory/ working memory, reasoning/ executive function, and psychomotor functions were selected. All subjects were administered the neuropsychological tests in a random order. All assessments were administered by the first author who was trained on the administration and scoring criteria of both tests by a certified neuropsychologist. The standardized instructions were given throughout the tests. The time to complete all tests is around 2 hours per subject. The following is the tests with regard to primary cognitive domains:

*Attention.* Digit Span Forward (DSF) (span & sequence scores), Part A of Trail Making Test (TMT) (total time), Sustained Attention to Response Task (SART) (commission error), Digit Vigilance Test (DVT) (omission error) & Symbol Digit Modalities Test (SDMT) (total score).

*Visual-Spatial.* Judgment of Line Orientation (JLO) (correct score), Chinese version of Neurobehavioral Cognitive Status Examination (Cognistat) (Construction subtest score), and Hooper Visual Organization Test (HVOT) (total score).

*Language.* Cognistat (Comprehension, Repetitive, and Naming subtests scores), and Chinese Characters Test (CCT) (total score).

*Memory/Working Memory.* Cognistat (Memory subtest score) and Digit Span Backward (DSB) (span & sequence scores).

*Reasoning/Executive Function.* Cognistat (Similarities and Judgment subtests scores), TMT (interference time score) and Chinese version of the Stroop Color-Word Test (Victoria Version) (CST) (interference time score).

*Psychomotor.* McCarron Assessment of Neuromuscular Development (MAND) (fine motor & gross motor scores), Development Test of Visual-Motor Integration (VMI) (total score) and Purdue Pegboard (PP) (dominant hand, nondominant hand, both hands, & assembly scores).

## 3 Statistical Analysis and Results

The mean task score of the 16 IE competence test was computed. These 16 IE task scores were then summated to derive the global IE competence score. Possible scores of global IE competence range from a minimum of 0 to a maximum of 644, with higher scores reflecting higher overall competence in computer utilization. A series of stepwise multiple regression analyses were conducted to examine the overall IE competence as dependent variable and the neuropsychological test scores in each of the cognitive domains as predictors in the sample with mental retardation.

To determine the relative importance of neuropsychological domains in predicting IE competence, separate multiple regression analyses in each of the six domains on the global IE competence score were conducted. For attention domain, the SDMT was first entered. This was followed by the DSF-Span, the SART and the DVT. All predictors in the equation were significant [total $R^2$ = .609, Model $F(4, 57) = 22.196$, $p<.001$], but SDMT alone was contributed 49.7% of the variance accounted for by the prediction equation. For visual-spatial domain, the JLO test score was only found to be significant predictor on the global IE competence [total $R^2$ = .27, Model $F(1, 60) = 22.213$, $p<.001$]. For language domain, the CCT test score was entered first and was followed by the Cognistat comprehension test score. These two predictors in equation were significant [total $R^2$ = 461, Model $F(2, 59) = 25.183$, $p<.001$], in which CCT score was uniquely accounted for 35.7% variance of the global IE competence. For the memory/working memory domain, the DSB-Span test score was found to be significant predictor on the global IE competence [total $R^2$ = .304, Model $F(1, 60) = 26.150$, $p<.001$]. For reasoning/ executive function, the Cognistat judgment metric score was the only significant predictor [total $R^2$ = .205, Model $F(1, 60) = 15.454$, $p<.001$]. For psychomotor domain, the MAND fine motor (FM) test score was entered first and was followed by the MAND gross motor (GM) test score. All two predictors were found to be significant [total $R^2$ = .461, Model $F(2, 59) = 20.977$, $p<.001$], in which the MAND FM score alone contributed 37.4% of the variance. Finally, the regression analysis of the global IE competence was conducted by entering the best predictors in each of the domains for the final regression equation. Entering these six predicted task scores in a stepwise fashion, the overall model was significant [total $R^2$ = .586, Model $F(3, 58) = 27.399$, $p<.001$] in which three test scores: SDMT ($R^2$ = 49.7%), MAND FM ($R^2$ = 5.8%) and CCT ($R^2$ = 3.2%) were found to be significant on predicting the global IE competence score (see Table 2).

**Table 2.** Regression analysis on IE task competence by the predicted task scores in six neuropsychological domains.

| Variables | Variables in the equation | | | | |
|---|---|---|---|---|---|
| | B | SE | Beta | *t* | p |
| Constant | 380.908 | 25.294 | | 15.059 | < .001 |
| SDMT | 2.843 | .854 | .402 | 3.328 | .002 |
| MAND FM | .290 | .113 | .272 | 2.576 | .013 |
| CCT | .389 | .184 | .229 | 2.12 | .038 |

# 4 Discussion

The results of this study indicated that attention with visual scanning (SDMT), psychomotor (MAND) and language processing (CCT) were found to be significant predictors on the global computer competence among people with mental retardation. Previous studies indicated that users' neuropsychological or cognitive functions were the prerequisites for their access on the computer interface [7]. A content analysis of these tasks would provide us with more insight into the neuropsychological demands imposed by these IE tasks and how these functions modulate people with mental retardation to operate computer program successfully. It would also provide some interface design recommendations for software developers whose products might have potential users with cognitive disabilities, such as those with mental retardation.

Analysis on the SDMT test tasks indicated that the subjects appeared to sustain attention for holding the geometric design and digit, and simultaneously visually search for a series of nine meaningless geometric designs [8]. The high correlations between the SDMT task and operation of IE tasks suggested that operating the web browser required the users to sustain attention to hold the theme or keywords in mind and, at the same time, to browse the information and visually search for target icons or links. In order to enhance the web access for people with mental retardation, the IE interface design should limit the target items free from distraction and minimize the need for visual tracking of target items in screen because the excessive information displayed in the interface would reduce user's cognitive resources for processing the target information and thus cause user's cognitive overload [9]. Therefore, the modification of IE interface should explicitly consider the presentation content such as to reduce the visual complexity of the output display, to make the target objects salient [10], and to display important information at a prominent place [11].

Analysis on the MAND FM tasks, these tasks demand precise eye-hand coordination and movement [12]. Further examination on the psychomotor demands on the operation of IE tasks, it has indicated that operating IE appeared to require the user to grasp the mouse, to click on the mouse buttons, and to slide the mouse to locate the icon. These movements particular using mouse would demand complex visual-motor coordination [13]. Some guidelines on the accessibility suggested that these psychomotor impairments would be minimized by providing some alternative actions or enlarging the buttons for pressing so that the requirement on fine motor control is not as critical [14].

Further analysis of CCT task revealed that this task taps on the ability to read the Chinese characters and comprehend its meaning. The correlation between CCT task and IE tasks suggested that operation of IE required the user to recognize and understand the Chinese characters or words in icons or menu options. In order to enable our participants to operate IE, some solutions from previous studies suggested that the accessible design for people with language limited would provide simple language, use concept-based visual icon to enhance the lexical retrieval [15], match the instructions to their linguistic levels and provide voice output to reduce reliance on reading [16]. It is important to note that the recommendations made here, though in general, have special meaning for people with mental retardation since these techniques may assist such participants to use their compensatory mechanisms to accommodate the cognitive demands of the IE tasks.

The results of this study revealed that people with mental retardation have problems using IE. Though these problems may vary from one to another, they are strongly associated with the neuropsychological abilities. Since people with mental retardation are characterized by general lower neuropsychological abilities compared with normal counterparts, the existing person-computer interface of the IE program is considered not to fit their capabilities. Our findings may form a good basis for software developers to design more user-friendly programs that cater for the specific needs of people with mental retardation. Future research should investigate the mechanisms by which attention and visual scanning, psychomotor and Chinese language processing deficits contribute to the competence of people with mental retardation in using a person-computer interface. The enhanced IE prototype based on strategies suggested in this study would be developed and evaluated its usability for people with mental retardation.

## References

1. Davies, D. K., Stock, S. E., Wehmeyer, M. L.: Enhancing Independent Internet Access for Individuals with Mental Retardation through Use of a Specialized Web Browser: A Pilot Study. Education and Training in Mental Retardation and Developmental Disabilities. 36 (2001) 107-113
2. Wehmeyer, M. L.: National Survey of the Use of Assistive Technology by Adults with Mental Retardation. Mental Retardation. 36 (1998) 44-51
3. Preece, J., Rogers, Y., Sharp, H.: Understanding and Conceptualizing Interaction. In: Preece, J., Rogers, Y., Sharp H. (eds.): Interactive Design: Beyond Human-Computer Interaction. John Wiley & Sons, New York (2002) 35-71
4. Proctor, R. W., Vu, K. P. L.: Human Information Processing: An overview for Human-Computer Interaction. In: Jacko, J. A., Sears, A. (eds.): The Human-Computer Interaction Handbook: Fundamentals, Evolving Technologies and Emerging Applications. Lawrence Erlbaum Associates, Mahwah New York (2003) 35-51
5. Chignell, M., Hancock, P. A., Takeshita, H.: Human-Computer Interaction: The Psychology of Augmented Human Behavior. In: Hancock P. A. (eds.): Human Performance and Ergonomics (eds.). Academic Press, San Diego California (1999) 291-329
6. Wong, A. W. K., Chan C. C H., Li-Tsang, C. W. P., Lam, C. S.: A Classification Method on Computer Competence for People with Mental Handicap. In: The Occupational Therapy Symposium. Hong Kong SAR (2003) 30
7. Cress, C. J.: The Development of Computer Control Skills in Children with Mental Retardation. Unpublished Doctoral Dissertation. University of Wisconsin-Madison (1993)
8. Lezak, M. D.: Neuropsychological Assessment. 3rd edn. Oxford University Press, New York (1995)

9. Dalal, N. P., Quible, Z. Wyatt, K.: Cognitive Design of Home Pages: An Experimental Study of Comprehension on the World Wide Web. Information Processing and Management. 36 (2000) 607-621
10. Sutcliffe, A., Fickas, S., Sohlberg, M. M., Ehlhardt, L. A.: Investigating the Usability of Assistive User Interfaces. Interacting with Computers. 15 (2003) 577-602
11. Preece, J., Rogers, Y., Benyon, D., Hollard, S., & Carey, T.: Human-Computer Interaction. edn. Addison-Wesley, Singapore (1994)
12. McCarron, L. T.: McCarron Assessment of Neuromuscular Development: Fine and Gross Motor Abilities. McCarron-Dial Systems, Dallas Texas (1997)
13. Lane, A., Ziviani, J.: Children's Computer Access: Analysis of the Visual-Motor Demands of Software Designed for Children. British Journal of Occupational Therapy. 62 (1999) 19-25
14. Petrie, H.: Accessibility and Usability Requirements for ICTs for Disabled and Elderly People: A Functional Classification Approach. In: Nicolle, C., Abascal, J.: Inclusive Design Guideline for HCI. Taylor & Francis, New York (2001) 29-60
15. Singh, S.: Designing Intelligent Interfaces for Users with Memory and Language Limitations. Aphasiology. 14 (2000) 157-177
16. Cress, C. J., Goltz, C. C.: Cognitive Factors Affecting Accessibility of Computers and Electronic Devices. In: 12th Annual Conference of the Association for the Advancement of Rehabilitation and Assistive Technology. RESNA Press, Washington (1989)

# Accessible Digital Media and Sign Language

## *Introduction to the Special Thematic Session*

Deborah Fels

Ryerson University, 350 Victoria St., Toronto
M5B 2K3, Canada
dfels@ryerson.ca

Digital media and the World Wide Web (WWW) are providing unprecedented opportunities for global access to and distribution of information, products, business, and services such as education. In addition, these technologies are providing opportunities for individuals to form new communities, and create and transmit information themselves within a global context.

For people with disabilities these new technologies have presented many opportunities. Indeed, access to WWW content and interactive structures for people with disabilities has been advocated and legislated for some time [1, 2]. However, it has also erected many barriers particularly as new information presentation methods and mechanisms have been developed without the associated accessible equivalent or without consideration of the impact on people with disabilities. Access solutions are often considered retroactively rather than as part of the design or development process. Considering accessibility in design practices is one of the pillars of universal design. One paper in this session reports on experiences with designing accessible public kiosks as an example of using universal design principles.

The WWW has, until very recently, been a mostly visual medium comprised of text and graphics. Although, this presents potential difficulties for people with low literacy or for people with low vision or who are blind, there are numerous solutions for providing accessibility. One paper in this session presents an innovative solution using tactile displays for graphics.

As high bandwidth networks become more widely deployed, it is becoming common design practice to incorporate animation, video, audio, and high quality graphics on the web. This presents many challenges for people with disabilities, particularly those with sensory disabilities such as people who are blind or deaf. In addition, online communities and services are being formed and used at rapid rates through the use of high bandwidth applications such as video conferencing, chat (text and audio), videos, and e-commerce which can present even more barriers to people with disabilities. Providing access to these types of applications becomes much more complicated and involved compared with text and simple graphics. The W3C through the WAI initiative [1] makes an attempt at providing guidelines for web accessibility. However, the industry seems slow at adopting and incorporating these guidelines into design practices, particularly for rich digital media such as video and audio.

K. Miesenberger et al. (Eds.): ICCHP 2004, LNCS 3118, pp. 1069–1070, 2004.

This new, high speed web, however, has also opened exciting possibilities for visual language users. It is now feasible to interpret/present/transmit sign language communication using video and/or high quality animation on the WWW. They also allow multiple display channels to be used for presentation alternatives such as captioning, video description, multiple text channels for low literacy or additional language displays. On-line communities of sign language speakers can now develop communities based on sign language rather than on text (at best a second language for sign language users). Two papers in this session explore some of the issues of expressing sign language in animated form, and two papers examine computer-based interpretation of physical sign language. A third set of two papers explore the use and development of sign language webs as unique from text based webs. A seventh paper presents the issues of teaching sign language using on-line video materials and a final paper considers the use of camera-based video to track sign language speakers.

As seen by the diversity of papers in this session, researchers and practioners are exploiting the opportunities digital media and the WWW offers for people with disabilities in innovative and creative ways.

## References

1. W3C. Web Accessibility Initiative. http://www.w3.org/WAI/. retrieved Oct. 3, 2003. (2003)
2. US Department of Justice. ADA home page. http://www.usdoj.gov/crt/ada/adahom1.htm. retrieved Oct. 3, 2003. (2003)

# Integration of Signage Information into the Web Environment

Rashad Aouf[1] and Steve Hansen[2]

[1] University of Western Sydney,
School of Computing and Information Technology,
Sydney, Australia
r.aouf@uws.edu.au

[2] University of Western Sydney,
School of Computing and Information Technology,
Sydney, Australia
s.hansen@uws.edu.au

**Abstract.** This paper outlines an ongoing initiative in broadening accessibility issues of the "deaf community" into the web environment. From a brief overview of the deaf culture this paper goes on to support the viewpoint of cultural interchange rather than "disability". In addition this paper puts forward that there are many aspects arising from signage parsing and display that have direct applications in generic multi-representational user interfaces, such as in multiple language or limited-language-skills interfaces. The paper outlines a current research initiative that is exploring the use of appropriate XML/SMIL-based "wrapping" methodologies to incorporate "intermediate" signage objects such as gesture, speech action, facial emotion (and others) along with other objects such as text, audio, video and "style".

## 1 Introduction

"The power of the Web is in its universality. Access by everyone regardless of disability is an essential aspect." – Tim Berners-Lee, W3C (World Wide Web Consortium) Director and inventor of the World Wide Web [3].

In its wide use of the Web by millions of people every day, there is a requirement to cater for differing languages, cultures, technical and social environments, "abilities" and "disabilities" [6].

Accordingly, accessibility (and the development of multiple representations of content), both in general and in specific instances is a current issue in the web environment. A consideration of the need for global access is highlighted by the growth rate of usage by people with "disabilities" being twice that of the "non-disabled" [12].

Arising from these issues, the W3C has proposed and is currently developing initiatives into web accessibility WAI (Web Accessibility Initiative) [3]. Coming from this have been various activities such as the accessibility guidelines (with e.g. Web Content [4], Authoring Tool, User Agent and XML [6]) and Web services [8] that can assist in lowering the barriers for people with "disabilities" [13].

K. Miesenberger et al. (Eds.): ICCHP 2004, LNCS 3118, pp. 1071–1078, 2004.

The W3C has also dedicated initiatives to include a high degree of usability for those people with recognized "disabilities" [1] , as can be seen in their generation of "impairments" scenarios in web interactions [2].

This paper focuses in addressing the accessibility needs arising from the hearing-impaired arena, with particular emphasis in integrating web components (i.e. multi-media or audio) with appropriate non-audio technologies. In order to handle the "hearing impairment" or "loss", the WAI specifies an approach based on captions for audio content [2] whereas as most of multimedia or audio events, at the present, do not contain captioning [6]. However, studies in the deaf community and their culture indicate that a number of deaf people have difficulties in reading and writing [16]. For example, a study by Dawson et al [5], has findings that a significant proportion of the deaf in the UK do not read print at all. This is covered in more detail in a short discussion of the deaf community and culture in section 2. This is followed, in section 3, by a short review of some current implementations of machine generation of signage and its relationship to web. Sections 4 and 5 cover the approach being taken at the University of Western Sydney in developing an integration of signage information with web objects. This covers the nature of the "intermediate objects" and the requirement for the XML wrapping. Section 5 presents various conclusions and gives a summary and indications of future directions.

## 2 Overview of the Deaf Community and Culture

Community and Culture are two related words to describe grouping of people together, that have their own language (or shared languages), shared experiences, norms and behaviors, common interests and traditions [14]. People born deaf or having lost their hearing at a very young age are classified as belonging to the deaf community and culture. The Deaf culture has characteristics identifiable to that of other subcultures [18] in relation with society [10]. Their culture is built on shared experiences and language [18] and these people are called "Culturally Deaf People" [15]. In particular, they rely on sign language as their first language. However, the term "Hearing-Impaired" is the generic term used to describe this disability [15]. Many "Hard of Hearing" individuals prefer "Deaf Culture" over "Hearing Culture" and vice-versa [14]. The cultural development in the Deaf community takes place parallel to that of society [10]. As there are readily available statistics on the American Deaf community, an overview is given in the following section. From current discussions of the authors, with various representatives of the Australian deaf community, there are strong parallels between the American and Australian experiences.

### 2.1 American Deaf Community

The American deaf community [14] is based on cultural principles, communicated by ASL (American Sign Language) that gives each individual his /her unique valuable identity. Because there is a community with its own language and culture, this provides a cultural frame in which "to be deaf" is not to be considered "disabled".

Aspects of the "deaf" cultures may appear in different norms, such in marriage and in education. For example, in marriage, there maybe a preference (or stronger) for both partners to be from the deaf community. It is estimated [14] that 9 out of 10 in the American deaf community marry other members of their cultural group and wish for deaf children. Education for some of these deaf communities is in separate "deaf community" residential schools. These schools provide the deaf culture and language environment for children develop their social skills and entertainments (such as sports) [14].

### 2.2 Sign Language

Sign Language is used extensively along with "lip-reading" in the deaf community [19] [20]. It is different from country to country. It is also different in form from spoken languages with a differing grammatical structure, incorporation of spatial elements (some of these maybe in expressions in parallel rather than the strict sequential nature of speech), and in emotive components such as from hand motions and facial expressions along with local variations [20]. It is a sequence of gestures with gestures being a sequence of postures. In addition to the signage languages such as ASL and AUSLAN (the Australian variety), there are a variety of associated signage methods using a single or two handed symbolic alphabet for literal character by character translation of text (called "signed English"). This is commonly used in assisting the deaf community in their initial learning of spoken languages from the text form and makes use of a double translation process. Namely the characters of text translated to a visual representation, followed by translation of these symbols to the "reader's" actual signage language and gram-mar. This is a slow process and as indicated above, a process many in the deaf community do not enjoy and resulting in the low literacy rates in this community.

Finally, the ability to "lip-read" is varied and is usually combined with other forms of translation, on its own having typically no more than 70% accuracy in the well trained.

## 3 Generation and Display of Signage (Web Environment)

This section gives a summary of current work in providing or incorporating signage related information into the web environment. This falls into two categories, namely as display of the actual signage as a video display or as a reconstructed signage image using some form of animated figure. The former method may involve various forms of signal processing to reduce the bandwidth, while the latter form usually works from a machine translation of the transmitted textual message.

This work of translating text into signage falls into two categories, either the generation of single or double handed "literal" character by character gestures into a signed English or by full animation into the actual signage language. The first method, as outlined in section 2.1 is not preferred and has little advantage over displaying the actual text, as text is as good a visual representation as a handed gesture representing it. The second method may make use of a combination of gestures (as in or use these in combination with various forms of "lip-sync" or "talking heads" [8],[9] where morphing of the face or head and presenting facial expressions associated with emotional state are synchronized to the speaking out of text with the signage. There are a number of development of toolkits that enable real-time animation of virtual 3D talking head from inputted text.

As mentioned previously, there are a number of people with sign language as their first language who prefer not to read and others who may have problems in reading-comprehension. This concern and other accessibility issues raise particular problems in integration of signage information into the web environment. As indicated in an online survey in America conducted by the NAD (National Association of the Deaf) there is a high level of interest from deaf or hard of hearing people in using internet services (instant message and email) [17] even though signage services are still immature.

In considering the incorporation of signage into the web, this paper supports the proposition as outlined in the previous sections that for many who have little or no hearing sense, this is not viewed as a disability rather as a differing culture.

As such, in terms of web usage and accessibility, many of the issues arising in the interaction of the deaf and hearing cultures and their respective web accessibility can be viewed in cultural terms, with text in particular viewed in terms of a "second language". This paper supports the premise that many of these issues will also be of assistance in other accessibility environments. In particular, in differing language environments; in online education with users of varying capacities of text and other comprehensions; in reduced display environments such as in mobile phone and PDAs; or in intermittent or slow data flows.

In addition, this paper puts forward that there is a wealth of information in the "intermediate objects" in parsing signage into text such as the visualization symbolism, emotional associations such as in facial expressions, and gesture symbolism [20] that can be incorporated into generic accessibility and generic web-user-interface interactions.

In surveying the extent that signage representation has impacted into the web, an examination of the main international news websites such as CNN, BBC , Le Monde and ABC (Australian) along with their representative government sites do not at this stage, provide any "signage streaming" or similar, nor are there any provisions in their accessibility legislation for any provision for the deaf culture. In fact, as of the time of writing, the authors have found no web sites at all that provide as the main or alternate representation any form of signage. There are sites that demonstrate or give dictionary lookups of signage, and lists of links to signage resources, but none of these viewed by the authors made use of alternative signage representation of the sites content.

From organizations such as the W3C have come a number of Web Accessibility Guidelines to assist site web usage and there are now a number of multimedia technologies and methodologies including SMIL and MPEG-4 which can be used in synchronization of multiple representations.

Finally, in terms of the integration of signage into the web and its implications for use not only by the deaf community but in applications for those with special language or learning needs, as quoted from Judy Heumann in [7], for "for people without disabilities, technology makes things convenient, whereas for people with disabilities, it makes things possible".

## 4 Integration of Signage into the Web Environment

This section outlines a current project at the University of Western Sydney Australia, in incorporating signage information into web operation. This project is based on making use of signage information both to provide increased accessibility for the deaf community and in generic web enhancement. The generic web enhancement having applications into e-learning, ESL (English as a Second Language) browser clients, and in generic web design. For example, from the "emotive, facial gesture" aspect of a signage message, to be able make use of this with other web objects such as style, content or navigation. As another example, from a specific emotional gesture, to invoke a change of style such as changes of colour, size, backgrounds, other multi-media objects and even aspects of audio for the hearing. Further, there could be the change or augmenting of existing text by the visualization content in the signage parsing to assist its understanding and comprehension .

The focus of this project is in the identification of useful objects that maybe generated in the process of capturing signage, and in then developing appropriate methodologies and protocols for their inclusion into web interface interactions. This inclusion giving flexibility to give static relationships that are time independent, such as a visualization or emotion state associated with a static web object, or in a dynamic sense as in synchronized streaming of corresponding multi-media representations, or in an interactive sense that supplies event-driven object-components. Although the web environment is the prime environment, this project is also looking at the generic multi-representation of the signage objects into the mobile technologies and is complimenting an associated project on 2, 2.5 and 3G mobile devices (such as the later generation mobile phones and to an extent PDAs).

In terms of the incorporation of signage into the web environment, the signage aspect is in relationship to a number of factors. These include development of the content and the corresponding server-browser interaction. In this, the browser side is considered in terms of the "cultural mix" of the users. The "target" being the deaf, non-deaf or others with specific presentation needs.

In this project at its current stage, the various parsing objects are being generated by "live" rather than machine methods. The original "scene" is broken up into a time series of message blocks. With each block a set of attributes is then assigned. These attributes being as follows.

### 4.1 Plain Text and Captioned Text

Plain text is a translation of any spoken dialog. As in any translation process between languages, the text translation is only a measure of the original. The grammar and vocabulary may be quite different from one translation to another. The captioned text is for use in describing the scene.

### 4.2 Audio Including Speech and Other Sounds

There maybe a variety of sounds either in vocalizations or in associated movements that can be captured in a signed conversation (many deaf sing and sense through non auditory means various vibrations). These objects may be of use in the generic interface to the non-deaf. The audio object is considered either as a "streamed" object covering a stream of the communication or as an associated property of a segment of the signage.

### 4.3 Gesturing Attributes

A facial (or other) gesture associated with a unit of the signage message can be typically represented as an emotional comment or an indication of "depth". This project defines these two attributes as "emotion content" categorized by a set of labels such as happy, sad, perplexed, anxious, worried (and the like) and the other attribute as "depth" categorized by labels such as quick, slow, large, small. These attributes can be used to provide inputs into a number of web display objects. The project is investigating using these in interactions with style, voice intonation, cartoon-like heads/ "talking head" displays.

### 4.4 Speech Acts

Speech acts is a classification of a dialogue (speech also includes signage) into "acts" such as "assertive", "directive", "commissive", "declarational", and "expressive" [21]. Their use being as given in the section above.

### 4.5 Object Interaction and Communication

This project is developing a suitable XML based protocol for "wrapping" of the signage objects. For the gesturing object, the protocol will draw on SiGML (Signed Gesture Mark-up Language) as proposed by the ViSiCAST project [8]. This representation being suitable for interaction to animation technologies for signage display. However a separate protocol is being developed for the facial gestures/emotive object. The requirements of this object being to interact with style, talking heads, and text to speech (to give various emphasis) components.

In addition, an XML protocol is being developed to wrap the translated text to be compliant with the other web objects. The project is making use of this XML environment in general, for the generation of a generic set of signage information. This being used as an intermediate digital object for the communication between objects (sign language and web objects). XML is sufficiently flexible in describing data [10] and enabling the exchange of a wide variety of data between applications on the Web [11], [3]. The proposed development of the interaction and communication is divided into three levels. Level-1 is based on the creation of an XML object (i.e. digital form) from the signage information as input, this object being wrapped by different layers for signage information processing such as signage parsing. Level-2, is the incorporation of the text. This text will be wrapped by several XML documents of data description such signage and context description. Finally at level-3 is the user or browser side where the object is "unwrapped" for display and for interaction with other web objects such as text, audio and video (i.e. animation).

There is also an alternative communication of the signage as part of a multimedia stream. This project proposed that for flexibility and the movement of processing off the client end that effective streaming can be achieved by suitable synchronizing of the signage with other associated multi-media such as other video, audio and voice with a SMIL or MPEG-4 protocol at the server side.

## 5 Summary and Conclusion

This paper gives an overview of a current project in utilizing signage information into the web environment. This utilization being useful for addressing accessibility issues and requirements of the deaf community in web access and also being of use in generic terms as part of the design of multi-representational content. From a discussion of the current research into parsing signage into textual forms and the reverse of generation of signage from text, the paper brings out the of intermediate objects such as facial expression The paper puts forward that these objects, through the development of appropriate markup methodologies and in conjunction when appropriate with synchronizing methodologies as from SMIL or MPEG-4, can be used to interact with both content and style

## References

1. Brewer, J., About Web Accessibility Initiative. (2000).http://www.w3.org/WAI/about.html
2. Brewer, J., How People with Disabilities Use the Web. (2001). http://www.w3.org/WAI/EO/Drafts/PWD-Use-Web/
3. Brewer, J., Web Accessibility Initiative WAI. 2003. http://www.w3.org/WAI/
4. Cladwell, B., Vandeheiden, G., White, J., and Chisholm, W., Web Content Accessibility Guidelines 2.0. (2003). http://www.w3.org/TR/2003/WD-WCAG20-20030429/
5. Dawson, D., Weisen, M., and Poole, N., NOF-Digitise Technical Advisory Service. (2003). http://www.ukoln.ac.uk/nof/support/help/papers/writing-web/

6. Dardailler, D., The Web Accessibility Initiative (WAI). (1999). http://www.exploit-lib.org/issue3/wai/
7. Disability Resource Center, Adaptive Technology Center. Sacramento City College, (2003). http://www.scc.losrios.edu/~drc/atc.html
8. Elliott, R.,Glauert, J.,Kennaway,J., Marshall,I The Development of Language Processing Support for the ViSiCAST Project, Proceedings of the Fourth International ACM Conference on Assistive Technologies, (Virginia, USA, 2000) 101-108
9. Famous3D, About Famous3D. 2003. http://www.famous3d.com/company/aboutus.html
10. Fredang, P., "Deaf Sign Language Users. Identity changes in the Swedish Deaf community." (Doctoral Dissertation, UPPSALA University, 2003). http://www.soc.uu.se/publications/doktabst/2003-3_a.html
11. Haas, H., Web Services Activity. (2003). http://www.w3.org/2002/ws/
12. Hendershot, G., Internet Use By People with Disabilities Grows at Twice the Rate of Non-Disabled, Yet Still Lags Significantly Behind. National Organization on disability (NOD), (2001). http://www.nod.org/content.cfm?id=682
13. Jacobs, I., Web Accessibility Initiative Resources. (2003). http://www.w3.org/WAI/Resources/
14. Padden, C., Introduction to Deaf culture. ICan News Service, (2002). http://www.ican.com/news/fullpage.cfm/articleid/4B2CFD88-8882-48AB-B94C394ADFEAA706/cx/news.opinion/article.cfm
15. Palmer, S. B., McCathieNevile, C., and Dardailler, D., XML Accessibility Guidelines. 2002. http://www.w3.org/TR/xag.html
16. Siverston, C., and Sivertson, L., Who's Who in the Deaf Community. (2003). http://www.hearinglossweb.com/Issues/Identity/who's_who.htm
17. Szczesny, A. L., and Ericsson, A., Deaf People with Multiple Disabilities. 5th European Conference, 2nd World conference, (Copenhagen 18th-22nd of October 2000).
18. The National Association of the Deaf, How Deaf and Hard of Hearing Americans are Using Instant Messaging and E-mail at Home and at Work. (2002). http://www.nad.org/infocenter/newsroom/nadnews/surveyresults.html
19. Torsi, Deaf Culture and Community. (2001). http://home.inreach.com/torsi/culture.html
20. University of Sheffield, Teaching Deaf and Hearing Impaired Students. (2003). http://www.shef.ac.uk/disability/teaching/hearing/5_strategies.html
21. Vanderveken, D. Meaning and Speech Acts. Cambridge, UK: Cambridge University Press (1990)

# Progress in Automated Computer Recognition of Sign Language*

Barbara L. Loeding[1], Sudeep Sarkar[2], Ayush Parashar[2], and Arthur I. Karshmer[3]

[1] Department of Special Education, University of South Florida, Lakeland, Florida
Barbara@lklnd.usf.edu

[2] Computer Science and Engineering, University of South Florida, Tampa, Florida
sarkar@csee.usf.edu

[3] Department of Information Technology, University of South Florida, Lakeland, Florida

**Abstract.** This paper reviews the extensive state of the art in automated recognition of continuous signs, from different languages, based on the data sets used, features computed, technique used, and recognition rates achieved. We find that, in the past, most work has been done in finger-spelled words and isolated sign recognition, however recently, there has been significant progress in the recognition of signs embedded in short continuous sentences. We also find that researchers are starting to address the important problem of extracting and integrating non-manual information that is present in face and head movement. We present results from our own experiments integrating non-manual features.

## 1 Introduction

Human computer interaction is gradually moving towards a modality where speech recognition is playing a major role because of the advances in automated speech understanding and synthesis. This shift to speech-based I/O devices is likely to present a barrier in the near future for people with disabilities. In particular, it may be next to impossible for people who rely on sign language for communication to access state of the art technology unless these devices also incorporate automated recognition of sign language into speech and vice-versa. Research in speech-to-sign translation using a computer-generated signer has progressed to the level of being potentially useful, public, or commercial applications in various countries [1–3]. However, development of end-to-end products in automated recognition of sign language have proceeded at a slower pace. We could find information about only two kiosks [4, 5] that recognize a limited number of individual signs or sentences made by people wearing special gloves.

Many natural sign languages throughout the world incorporate a manual alphabet with 26-40 hand shapes or letters that allows people to spell out a word. This process is called finger spelling. To allow a deaf person to communicate proper names and concepts for which there is no readily known manual sign, a translation system needs to incorporate recognition of continuous finger spelling also. Since 1990, researchers have focused on automated recognition of isolated hand shapes (some are actual letters in manual alphabets) and individual signs. Representative examples of this work

* This material is based upon work supported by the National Science Foundation under Grant No. IIS 0312993.

K. Miesenberger et al. (Eds.): ICCHP 2004, LNCS 3118, pp. 1079–1087, 2004.

include [6–14]. Fortunately, in the last ten years, researchers around the world are gradually moving beyond isolated recognition to work on automated recognition of continuous letters, i.e., finger spelling [15–17]) and sentences of continuous signs, e.g., signs without intentional pauses between them [18–25]. Due to space limitations, we review only work in continuous signs in this paper. Table 1 compares data sets, features, technique(s) used by different research groups working on continuous sign language recognition and indicates the recognition rates reported in the literature. From this review, we make the following observations about the state of the art.

## 2 Input Data

Researchers are using a variety of input devices to collect sign data ranging from data gloves such as Cybergloves, to magnetic markers and 3SPACE position trackers, combinations of the above or vision-based systems that have no special input devices at all. Wearable devices bypass the segmentation problem by directly conveying location features but are unnatural and cumbersome. Number of cameras used also varies from one to three yielding 2D and 3D images. In some studies, the background has been uniform, signers wear dark clothes and/or colored gloves to make it easier for the computer algorithms to segment the hand and face regions.

## 3 Recognition Approach

Most groups up through the year 2000 used a Hidden Markov Models (HMMs) approach with one HMM per sign to automate the process of sign recognition [26, 19, 18, 27–32], with Taiwan also using a word segmentation approach and Japan using word segmentation and minCost approach. These HMM-based models have problems in scaling with the vocabulary. Many groups seem to have abandoned this model and adopted a parallel HMM model or a model where each HMM models a phoneme or subunit of a sign although different groups have different techniques for defining a subunit (movement-hold [21, 33], fenones [34]) An excellent example is the Chinese system [24] that uses a large hierarchical decision tree and state tying HMMs at three levels for 2400 basic phonemes of Chinese signs. They also have a model for distinguishing transitional movements that signers make between signs.

## 4 Databases

In terms of databases, typically, researchers have created their own video recordings of gestures, signs and sentences. The test data sets vary with one group focusing on continuous sentence recognition based on a sign vocabulary of 5 [35] to China's 5113-sign lexicon [24]. Three articles [19, 25, 35] report sentences composed from a sign vocabulary of 10 or less signs. Ten articles reporting a vocabulary of 22-49 [18, 20, 26, 36, 28, 37, 38, 33, 39, 22] and six report vocabulary of 52-250 [21, 27, 30–32, 40]. Most groups have attempted to recognize a set of 10 to 196 sign sentences of 2-12 signs in each sentence with recognition rates varying from 58% - 95.8%. A few groups have tested between 400 and 1000 sentences [26, 36–38, 33, 41, 24] and report recognition rates of 52.8% - 90+%.

Large, common, datasets are rare. One such database is SignStream, an annotated video database tool for analysis of ASL linguistic data [42]. Linguists continue to study how the grammar of ASL differs from that of English. A recent boon for ASL researchers is availability of an extensive video database of ASL motions, handshapes, words and sentences created by Purdue University [43].

## 5 Recognition Performance

Most groups measure recognition rates for isolated signs and continuous signs, with some groups choosing to look at other variables such as context independent and context dependent; short vs. long sentences; with rule-based grammar and colored gloves vs. with no grammar and colored gloves and with grammar and skin tone compared to no grammar and skin tone. Reported recognition rates for continuous sign recognition vary from 58% [44] to 99% [36]. Although less useful, rates for recognizing isolated signs range much higher (91% -99%).

We advocate a need to build consensus regarding meaningful measures of performance from a communication point of view rather than reporting signal-based accuracies. Some researchers report total number of words (actually they mean signs) in all sentences that were correctly recognized and/or percentage of words (signs) within all signed sentences correctly recognized by their system. We propose that a more meaningful performance measure is the percentage of sentences that were correctly translated or recognized. Just word level recognition rates are not good indicators of communication performance. Some signs in a sentence are more important to recognize than others. So, instead of categorizing errors as insertion, deletion or substitution, perhaps judging to what degree an error affected the meaning of the sentence or assigning weights to errors would be preferable.

## 6 Non-manual Features

In addition to conveying meaning through manual signs, signers also convey information non-manually through their facial expressions and body movements. Facial expressions can include movements of the eyebrows, lips and head. Different groups have now started to tackle the issue of feature extraction related to non manual features such as head motion (Xu *et al.* [45], Erdem & Scarloff [46]), facial expression and lip movement (Canzler & Dziurzyk [47]). None of these groups have yet published combination strategies for manual and non-manual information and the impact of non-manual features on sign language recognition. At the University of South Florida, we have explored one possible strategy for extracting, representing, and integrating non-manual aspects such as facial expression and head movement into the recognition process [39].

To date, it has been difficult to directly use the facial information because of the following reasons. Manual information is not necessarily synchronized with non-manual information. For example, the same facial expressions are not present at the same temporal position with respect to the manual in two instances of the same sentence. Another problem has to do with not being able to extract facial expression information in every frame of a sequence. If there is presence of a strong non-manual indicating 'Assertion' or 'Negation' in the sentence, the facial expressions, as registered in the images, are totally swamped by the face movements which are indicated by 'head shakes' or 'head nods'. For these two reasons, we employ a sequential integration approach where the non-manual information is used to prune the list of word hypotheses generated by manual information. We show that the additional use of non-manual information increases the accuracy of recognition of continuous words from 88% to 92%, which is a significant difference. We were also able to detect 'Negation' in sentences based on simple motion trajectory based features 27 out of 30 times.

## 7 Multiple Signers and Background

Other issues that are important has to do with being to able to handle multiple signers and multiple backgrounds. From what we can discern from published reports, a number of groups have utilized more than one signer but only a few groups are working on signer independent systems [24, 25]. There does not seem to be any group working on pure video based systems that can handle complex backgrounds.

## 8 Conclusion

To summarize, we have compared and contrasted different approaches to producing continuous sign language recognition in terms of the reliance on gloves vs bare hand, recognition method, database used for testing, performance achieved, use of non-manual information, and the ability to handle multiple signers. Recognition of continuous signs has progressed to a point where we are starting to see the emergence of the design for some future commercial systems [5, 49]. Among the research challenges that remain as excellent future research directions are: (i) signer independent recognition, (ii) development of bi-directional systems for each sign language, (iii) use of non-manual information to enhance recognition, (iv) development of communication based performance measures to quantify progress in sentence level recognition, and (v) development of non-glove based systems that scale up to a large vocabulary and handles different backgrounds. One of the long term inter-modality integrative efforts include the use of wide-area, high bandwidth networks and wireless communication technologies to provide "modality translation and assistance services" so that a variety of remote services such as instant text transcription or sign language interpretation on demand would be available anywhere anytime [50]. Second, the W3C now has published the first working draft of EMMA (Extended MultiModal Annotation markup language) which takes user-supplied information from speech recognizers, handwriting recognizers, keyboard and mouse device drivers and converts it into an EMMA representation [51]. It is advisable for researchers working on automated sign recognition and translation to communicate with W3C so that EMMA will also be able to utilize information supplied from "sign translators and sign recognizers".

**Table 1.** Automated Continuous Sign Recognition, i,e. Signs Embedded in Sentences

| Citation | Type | Data Set, Accuracy Rate, Input Device, Technique Used |
|---|---|---|
| 1995 Starner [26] and Starner & Pentland [36] | ASL | 400 sentences based on 40 signs about 4 signs each 95% w colored gloves 90% w/o colored gloves w strict grammar 99%, camera-based, HMM |
| 1996 Braffort [19] | French | 7 signs, 44 sentences, 92-96%, HMMs, Data-glove |
| 1996 Starner & Pentland [18] | ASL | 40 signs, constrained sentence structure, no gloves-92%, gloves 99%, 1 camera, HMM |
| 1997 Vogler & Metaxas [27] | ASL | 53 signs 97 sentences widely varied sentence structure HMMS modeling 3 video cameras 3D movement parameters better than context dependent HMMs 92.1-95.8% |
| 1997 Starner, Weaver & Pentland [28] | ASL | continuous, real time, sentence level, 40 sign lexicon, no gloves 92%, camera in cap 98%, (97% unrestricted grammar) |
| 1998 Assan & Grobel [29] | Netherlands | 26 signs, 14 sentences of 3-5 signs, 72.8%, signer dependent, HMMs |
| 1998 Liang & Ouhyoung [21] | Taiwanese | 71-250 signs, HMMs with explicit segmentation Movement-Hold, 1 Dataglove, signer dependent, real time, Long sentences 4-5 signs each recognition better than short sentences (2-3 signs ea), overall average rate is 80.4%, rate decreases as size of sign vocabulary increased |
| 1998 Vogler & Metaxas [30] | ASL | 53 signs, unconstrained sentence structure, HMM and 3D motion analysis |
| 1999 Hienz, Bauer & Kraiss [31] | German | 52 signs, signer dependent, sentences with 2-9 signs each, single camera, HMMs, Stochastic grammar language model, 95% bigram model |
| 1999 Vogler & Metaxas [38, 37] | ASL | 22 words, 499 sentences of diff lengths, 3 experiments, word accuracy 91.82%, phoneme level with local features 88.36%, Phoneme level with global features 91.19%, HMM recognized phonemes not whole signs |
| 2000 Bauer, Hienz & Kraiss [32] and Bauer & Hienz [40] | German | Sentences based on 52 signs, 94%, sentences based on 97 signs, 93.2%, with bigram model, 1 HMM per sign |
| 2000 Sagawa & Takeuchi [44, 5] | Japanese | 10 sentences, 1 and 2 handed signs, 200 samples, 58% |
| 2000 Vogler, Sun & Metaxas [33] | ASL | 99 test and 400 training sentences over 22 signs, parallel HMMs each HMM based on single phoneme Movement Hold, 84.9% sentence level, 94.2% sign level |

**Table 1.** (Continued)

| Citation | Type | Data Set, Accuracy Rate, Input Device, Technique Used | Non-Manual |
|---|---|---|---|
| 2001 Vogler & Metaxas [41] | ASL | 400 training, 99 test sentences, 22 signs, phoneme level, Parallel HMMs | |
| 2001 Xu [45] | Japanese | 11 head motions, "good recognition", real time 2 video cameras | Head motions |
| 2002 Erdem & Sclaroff [46] | ASL | 10 ASL video sequences, 3D head tracker, no sign recognition results | Head Shakes |
| 2002 Canzler and Dziurzyk [47] | German | Nonmanuals facial features, 24 persons, 30 images, no sign recognition results | Face |
| 2002 Yuan *et al.* [48] | Chinese | 40 signs, upto 4 sign sentences, 2 gloves and 3 trackers, 70%, HMMs (strong/weak connections) | |
| 2003 Brashear *et al.* [35] | ASL | 5 signs, 72 sentences, 90.48%, accelerometer | |
| 2003 Chen [24] | Chinese | 5113 signs, 1000 sentences, 6 signers, signer independent, 87.58%, decision tree, fuzzy VQ | |
| 2003 Kapuscinski & Wysocki [25] | Polish | 10 signs, 12 sentences, 2-4 sign each, for 1 signer recognition rate of 82.5-86.7%, 3 signers results in 81.3% - 86.4%, PaHMM + bigram = best, Camera Long sleeves, No gloves | |
| 2003 Parashar [39] | ASL | 39 signs 25 sentences, with 1-5 signs each, 2 cameras, bottom up approach using relational features, 88% sign recognition, 92% with nonmanual info | Face, Head nods |
| 2004 Vogler & Metaxas [22] | ASL | 22 signs 99 test sentences, 88.89%, movement channel, handshape channel, Parallel HMM | |

## References


1. Cox, S., Lincoln, M., Tryggvason, J., Nakisa, M., Wells, M., Tutt, M., Abbott, S.: TESSA, a system to aid communication with deaf people. In: Proceedings of the fifth international ACM conference on Assistive technologies, ACM Press (2002) 205–212
2. Phelps, K.: Signing avatar characters become virtual tutors. In: Virtual Voice. (2002)
3. Toro, J., *et al.*: An improved graphical environment for transcription and display of American Sign Language. Information **4** (2001) 533–539
4. Akyol, S., Canzler, U.: An information terminal using vision based sign language recognition. In: ITEA Workshop on Virtual Home Environments. (2002) 61–68
5. Sagawa, H., Takeuchi, M.: Development of an information kiosk with a sign language recognition system. In: Conference on Universal Usability. (149–150) 2000

6. Kramer, J., Leifer, L.: The talking glove: An expressive and receptive 'verbal' communication aid for the deaf, deaf-blind and nonvocal. In: Conference on Computer Technology, Special Education, and Rehabilitation. (1987)
7. Murakami, K., Taguchi, H.: Gesture recognition using recurrent neural networks. In: SIGCHI Conference Proceedings. (237–242) 1991
8. Charayaphan, C., Marble, A.: Image processing system for interpreting motion in American Sign Language. Journal of Biomedical Engineering **14** (1992) 419–425
9. Waldron, M., Kim, S.: Isolated ASL recognition system for deaf persons. IEEE Transactions on Rehabilitation Engineering **3** (1995) 261
10. Kadous, M.W.: Machine translation of AUSLAN signs using powergloves: Towards large lexicon-recognition of sign language. In: Workshop on the integration of Gesture in Language and Speech. (1996) 165–174
11. Vamplew, P.: Recognition of Sign Language Using Neural Networks. PhD thesis, Department of Computer Science, University of Tasmania (1996)
12. Lee, C., Xu, Y.: Online, interactive learning of gestures for human robot interfaces. In: IEEE International Conference on Robotics and Automation. (1996) 2982–2987
13. Al-Jarrah, O., Halawani, A.: Recognition of gestures in Arabic sign language using neuro-fuzzy systems. Artificial Intelligence **133** (2001) 117–138
14. Fang, G., Gao, W., Zhao, D.: Large sign vocabulary sign recognition based on hierarchical decision tree. In: International Conference on Multimodal Interfaces. (2003) 125–131
15. Messing, L., Erenshteyn, R., Foulds, R., Galuska, S., Stern, G.: American Sign Language computer recognition: Its present and its promise. In: ISAAC Conference. (1994)
16. Hernandez-Rebollar, J.L., Lindeman, R.W., Kyriakopoulos, N.: A multi-class pattern recognition system for practical finger spelling translation. In: The 4th IEEE International Conference on Multimodal Interfaces. (2002) 185
17. Vassilia, P.N., Konstantinos, M.G.: Towards an assistive tool for Greek Sign Language communication. In: IEEE International Conference on Advanced Learning Technologies (ICALT'03). (125) 2003
18. Starner, T., Pentland, A.: Computer-based visual recognition of American Sign Language. In: International Conference on Theoretical Issues in Sign Language Research. (1996)
19. Braffort, A.: ARGo: An architecture for sign language recognition and interpretation. In: Progress in Gestural Interaction. (1996) 17–30
20. Grobel, K., Assan, M.: Isolated sign language recognition using Hidden Markov Models. In: International Conference System: Man and Cybernetics. (1996) 162–167
21. Liang, R., M.Ouhyoung.: A real-time continuous gesture recognition system for sign language. In: International Conference on Automatic Face and Gesture Recognition. (1998) 558–565
22. Vogler, C., Metaxas, D.: Handshapes and movements: Multiple-channel ASL recognition. In: Lecture Notes in Artificial Intelligence 2915. (2004) 247–258
23. Ma, J., Gao, W., Wang, C., Wu, J.: A continuous Chinese Sign Language recognition system. In: International Conference on Automatic Face and Gesture Recognition. (2000) 428–433
24. Chen, Y.: Chinese Sign Language recognition and synthesis. In: IEEE International Workshop on Analysis and Modeling of Faces and Gestures. (2003)
25. Kapuscinski, T., Wysocki, M.: Vision-based recognition of Polish Sign Language. In: Methods in Artificial Intelligence. (2003)
26. Starner, T.: Visual recognition of American Sign Language using Hidden Markov Models. Master's thesis, MIT, Media Lab. (1995)
27. Vogler, C., Metaxas, D.: Adapting Hidden Markov Models for ASL recognition by using three-dimensional computer vision methods. In: International Conference Systems on Man and Cybernetics. (1997) 156–161

28. Starner, T., Weaver, J., Pentland, A.: A wearable computer based American Sign Language recognizer. In: International Symposium on Wearable Computers. (1997) 130–137
29. Assan, M., Grobel, K.: Video-based sign language recognition using Hidden Markov Models. In: International Gesture Workshop: Gesture and Sign Language in Human-Computer Interaction. (1998) 97–109
30. Vogler, C., Metaxas, D.: ASL recognition based on a coupling between HMMs and 3D motion analysis. In: International Conference on Computer Vision. (363–369) 1998
31. Hienz, K., Bauer, B., Kraiss, K.: HMM-based continuous sign language recognition using stochastic grammars. In: Gesture Workshop. (1999)
32. Bauer, B., Hienz, H., Kraiss, K.F.: Video-based continuous sign language recognition using statistical methods. In: International Conference on Pattern Recognition. (2000) 463–466
33. Vogler, C., Sun, H., Metaxas, D.: A framework for motion recognition with application to American Sign Language and gait recognition. In: Workshop on Human Motion. (2000) 33–38
34. Bauer, B., Kraiss, K.F.: Towards an automatic sign language recognition system using subunits. In: International Gesture Workshop: Gesture and Sign Language in Human-Computer Interaction. (2002) 64–75
35. Brashear, H., Starner, T., Lukowicz, P., Junker, H.: Using multiple sensors for mobile sign language recognition. In: IEEE International Symposium on Wearable Computers. (2003)
36. Starner, T., Pentland, A.P.: Real-time American Sign Language recognition from video using Hidden Markov Models. In: Symposium on Computer Vision. (1995) 265–270
37. Vogler, C., Metaxas, D.: Toward scalability in ASL recognition: Breaking down signs into phonemes. In: Gesture-Based Communication in Human-Computer Interaction. (211-224) 1999
38. Vogler, C., Metaxas, D.: Parallel Hidden Markov Models for American Sign Language recognition. In: International Conference on Computer Vision. (116–122) 1999
39. Parashar, A.: Representation and interpretation of manual and non-manual information for automated American Sign Language Recognition. Master's thesis, University of South Florida (2003)
40. Bauer, B., Hienz, H.: Relevant features for video-based continuous sign language recognition. In: International Conference on Automatic Face and Gesture Recognition. (2000) 440–445
41. Vogler, C., Metaxas, D.: A framework of recognizing the simultaneous aspects of American Sign Language. Computer Vision and Image Understanding **81** (2001) 358–384
42. Neidle, C., MacLaughlin, D., Bahan, B., G., L.R., Kegl, J.: The SignStream project. In: American Sign Language Linguistic Research Project, Report 5 Boston University. (1997)
43. Martinez, A.M., Wilbur, R.R., Shay, R., Kak, A.: Purdue RVL-SLLL ASL database for automatic recognition of American Sign Language. In: International Conference on Multimodal Interfaces. (2002)
44. Sagawa, H., Takeuchi, M.: A method for recognizing a sequence of sign language words represented in a Japanese Sign Language sentence. In: International Conference on Automatic Face and Gesture Recognition. (434–439) 2000
45. Xu, M.: A vision-based method for recognizing non-manual information in Japanese Sign Language. In: International Conference on Advances in multimodal interfaces. (2000) 572–581
46. Erdem, U., Sclaroff, S.: Automatic detection of relevant head gestures in American Sign Language communication. In: International Conference on Pattern Recognition. (2002) I: 460–463
47. Canzler, U., Dziurzyk, T.: Extraction of non manual features for videobased sign language recognition. In: Proceedings of IAPR Workshop on Machine Vision Applications. (2002) 318–321

48. Yuan, Q., Gao, W., Yao, H., Wang, C.: Recognition of strong and weak connection models in continuous sign language. In: International Conference on Pattern Recognition. (2002) 10075
49. Clendenin, M.: Chinese lab hopes to commercialize sign-language recognition platform. In: http://www.eetimes.com/article/showArticle.jhtml?articleId=10801270. (March 2003)
50. Zimmerman, G., Vanderheiden, G.: Modality translation and assistance services: A challenge for artificial intelligence. Journal of the Australian Society of Artificial Intelligence **20** (2001)
51. Larson, J.A.: EMMA: W3C's extended multimodal annotation markup language. Speech Technology Magazine **8** (2003) http://www.w3.org/TR/emma/

# Creating Sign Language Web Pages

Daniel G. Lee[1], Jan Richards[2], Jim Hardman[3], Sima Soudain[1], and Deborah Fels[1]

[1] Ryerson University, Toronto, M5B 2K3, Canada
{d1lee,s3soudia,dfels}@ryerson.ca
[2] University of Toronto, Toronto, Canada M5S 1A5
jan.richards@utoronto.ca
[3] Canadian Hearing Society, Toronto, Canada M5R 2V3
jhardman@chs.ca

**Abstract.** For many people the World Wide Web has become an indispensable tool for work and entertainment. However, for people using sign languages, which convey meaning by gestures moving in time and space, the primarily static and textual nature of the WWW medium has, until now, posed an important challenge. Signing linguistic communities should be able to develop their own signing Webs that include hyperlinks based on moving gestures and signs instead of using static images or text for links. We present a mechanism, signlinks, and a content authoring tool, SignEd., that can facilitate development of such Webs, without requiring any degree of bilingualism with a written language by the user. Preliminary evaluations indicate the users are able to understand and create signlinks for video content. Four major design modifications were made as a result of these evaluations and are presented in this paper.

## 1 Introduction

The World Wide Web is evolving towards being an interactive multimedia environment. However, in comparison to a richer multimedia experience (e.g. video games), the majority of websites are still primarily composed of text and static images. This is usually a positive feature for Web accessibility, since textual information can be transformed by assistive technologies into other forms (e.g. text-to-speech, separating presentation from content, etc.). In fact, the Web Content Accessibility Guidelines [1] include text equivalents as one of the highest priority recommendations.

Access to WWW content and interactive structures for people with disabilities has been advocated and indeed legislated for some time [1, 2]. However, for deaf and hard of hearing users, often access to rich media involves conversion of spoken language and sounds into text. For many deaf users, communicating primarily in a signed language (e.g. American Sign Language (ASL)), print-based material such as closed captions is experienced as a second language, posing potential literacy barriers. In addition, even for those signers without literacy challenges in a print-based language, the prospect of experiencing Web content in their preferred mode of communication naturally have benefits.

K. Miesenberger et al. (Eds.): ICCHP 2004, LNCS 3118, pp. 1088–1095, 2004.

ASL, like other sign languages, is a visual-spatial language with few grammatical similarities to English [3]. Vocabulary and semantics in ASL are expressed using a series of hand and facial gestures such as eyebrow motion and lip-mouth movements, and body movements that change in time and space. A series of gestures cannot easily be represented by a single written or spoken word, or static image equivalent.

Some Web sites do provide sign language content (see [4]) although these sites are often language dictionaries or text-based information sites. If there are sign language videos used on these sites (e.g., ASLQuest [4]), they are usually surrounded by navigation mechanisms and supplemental content provided exclusively in a textual language (e.g. English, French, etc.). Signing users must therefore continually switch between their language of choice and a second language, which in some case may present a literacy barrier. In fact, it may be most fitting to describe this signed content as being "on" the Web, rather than "of" the Web.

At a high level, the WWW may be considered to be a collection of sub-webs, each created by a particular linguistic community (e.g., "English Web", or "Chinese Web"). Signed content will only be "of" the Web when Signing Webs that are similar in nature to other sub-webs have begun to form. A Signing Web would be a collection of Web pages created by a particular signing community (e.g., "ASL Web" or "LSQ Web") and bound together by sign language based connections.

While this may be an overly simplistic view of the complex nature of the WWW and individual web page design strategies contained within it, the foundation of the WWW is the concept of non-linear navigation and connection between content pages though hyperlinking [5]. Users are able to traverse a series of content pages by accessing links located on those pages. Most static elements such as text and static images on a Web page can become a hyperlink. However, elements that are time-based such as video, animation and sound do not normally contain hyperlinks. In creating new Webs or participating in existing ones linking functionality must be preserved at the root of each design. Otherwise, there is no Web or grouping but only a series of unconnected content artifacts.

This paper describes two design iterations and evaluation of a prototype providing hyperlinks within video specifically for sign language-based, text optional web environments.

## 2 Signing Web Design

In order to effectively create Signing Webs we require a mechanism that allows linking within moving images such as video or animation to accommodate time-based, gestural languages that cannot easily be expressed using static elements. Such a mechanism, called signlinking, has been developed to allow hyperlinking within time-based media, such as video and animation rather than text. Each link is an authored defined amount of time within the video clip. When the video reaches a signlink, a link indicator (a red icon appearing in the top left corner of the video) appears to notify the user. This is similar to the blue underline for indicating text-based links. At this point the user can click and follow the link or continue playing the content. In addition, all the signlinks are displayed in the link density bar as well as thumbnails just below the main video window, where they can be accessed at anytime. Further description of the elements can also be found in Richards, et. al [6].

## 3 Authoring Signlinked Pages

One of the most important features of the Web is its public and participatory nature. A range of authoring tools, including tools that conceal technical details, allow authors to generate and publish Web content. In order to facilitate Web page development for people who want to author in a sign language using the signlink mechanism, we have developed an authoring environment, SignEd., which requires no knowledge of the technical aspects of authoring for the Web (e.g., HTML, and JavaScript).

SignEd allows the user to import existing videos or to capture new video from any QuickTime compliant video input device. An author can perform basic video editing operations such as cut, copy, paste, and insert basic transitions to produce a final video. Once the video is edited, authors can add signlinks and, if the user wishes, add optional text content within the authoring environment. Authors can add hyperlinks to the text by selecting from the list of currently defined signlinks. The SignEd editing interface is built to look similar in appearance and layout to the Signing Web format so that users would only need to learn one interface design strategy.

Signlinks are added by selecting the Add button on the main screen. This action takes the user to a separate signlink window where the user can define and edit the signlink's properties (see Figure 1). The length of the new signlink is 3 seconds by default. However, it can be adjusted using the video in and out markers as seen in Figure 1. The density bar below the main video shows the number of signlinks, their distribution and length. Once a new signlink is added, it appears in the density bar and as a thumbnail image along with a play-link button. The link being edited appears in red while the others are blue.

When authoring a signlink, users can change the appearance of the thumbnail by manipulating a red rectangle representing that image in the main video. The maximum size of the rectangle is the entire 320 x 240 pixel video frame and the minimum size is 14 x 10 pixels. The rectangle size can be altered using the arrow handles in the top left, and bottom right corners of the box as seen in Figure 1. When resizing the box, the aspect ratio remains the same. Clicking and dragging anywhere inside the rectangle allows it to be moved anywhere within the movie frame.

The authoring tool also includes a novel help feature: ASL tool tips. Throughout the authoring interface, small "help" icons are provided. When the user clicks on a help icon, an ASL video appears in a separate window and provides a short context sensitive explanation of the specific function.

## 4 Evaluation of Signlink Authoring Tool

### 4.1 Method

Eight deaf ASL speaking youth (age range 18 – 30) participated in a study to evaluate the usability and functionality of the SignEd. Seven of the eight participants were community college students, and one was a university level student. All participants used the Internet daily. However, 50% of participants had never used a video player on their computer. Four of the eight participants rated their English proficiency at around a grade 4 level. Three participants rated their English proficiency at around a grade 11 level and one at advanced. Five participants thought that text information on websites was difficult to understand. Most participants (75%) rated tabs as their most or second most preferred navigation style, followed by buttons such as next and previous, table of contents and hyperlinks.

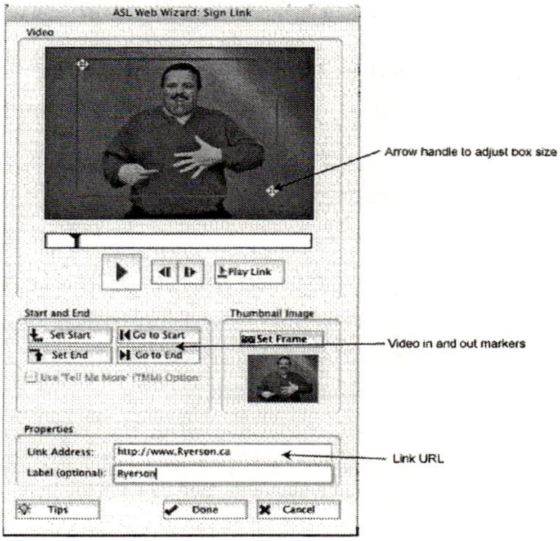


**Fig. 1.** Screen used to edit link's properties

The study tasks consisted of using the editor to create signlinks in a set of nine test videos that detailed one person's trip through the eastern United States. To begin, participants were shown a video tutorial and then hands-on examples of completed signlink pages. As reinforcement training, they were allowed to become familiar with the editing interface by creating signlinks for a prerecorded test video. Participants were then asked to create two new signlinks. Participants spent approximately 1 hour performing all of the study tasks.

Data were collected using the Gestural Talk Aloud Protocol [4] with simultaneous verbal translation, notetaking and pre/post study questionnaires (note: questionnaires were administered using sign language). ASL communication was recorded with one video camera while the participant's screen activities and any verbal translation of ASL were captured with a second camera. The data from the notes and pre/post questionnaires are reported in this paper. The detailed video data are not reported.

## 5 Results and Discussion of Evaluation

There were some important results in this study that confirmed some design decisions made during development and illustrated some critical user difficulties.

### 5.1 Data from Observation Notes

Five of eight participants had considerable difficulty using "Set Start" and "Set End" buttons. Five of eight participants were confused with the actions of the buttons performed, and did not notice the relationship between button presses and the change in current time indicator of the video.

There was considerable confusion with moving and resizing the red rectangle that appears on the main video. Five of eight participants thought that the Set Frame button would allow them to manipulate this rectangle. One participant was able to resize the rectangle, but did not know how to position it. Participants were mistakenly using the resize handles to move the box.

Three of five people were noted to have difficulty with the Macintosh operating system interface and needed assistance with manipulating files and applications.

### 5.2 Results from Post Study Questionnaire

Ease of learning and use for the tasks of creating signlinks, specifically manipulating the link properties (e.g., start and end times, URL) were the primary data collected through the post study. Participants were also asked to provide open-ended comments on likes, dislikes and improvements of SignEd. Post questionnaire data for only five participants are available and reported in this paper.

There was mixed response to the ease of learning of SignEd.; three participants rated SignEd. as very easy to use and two people rated it as difficult. A majority of participants (three of five) found SignEd. easy to use and two reported that inserting a signlink was difficult the first time.

Four participants rated adding a signlink task as very easy or easy, and one as difficult. All five participants rated setting the size and position of a signlink as easy or very easy. This finding is in conflict with the observation notes taken. Three people found that adjusting the start and end times for the signlink was easy and two found it not difficult or easy. This result is also in conflict with the observation notes taken.

Participants were also asked to provide feedback on their likes and dislikes of SignEd., on any specific problems, and on suggestions for improvements as opened ended questions. Most participants reported liking the interface (three of five). Only one person reported any dislikes.

There were a range of specific problems that participants reported having but there was little consensus. Two people of five reported experiencing no problems. There were a range of suggestions for improvement with some consensus on two suggestions; three people suggested changing the interface colours and three suggested changing the layout including the text box sizing/layout.

### 5.3 Discussion

In general, participants were able to successfully create signlinks using SignEd. and considered SignEd. easy to use even though important difficulties were observed particularly during first time use.

There appears to be discrepancies between some of the questionnaire data and the observation notes. It was observed that all five participants had difficulty adjusting the signlink time while none reported that this task was difficult in the post study questionnaire. In addition, the majority of participants had difficulty adjusting the size and position of the rectangle although none reported this difficulty, and in fact all participants reported in the post study questionnaire that this task was easy or very easy to accomplish. There are several possible explanations for these conflicts.

One explanation for these discrepancies is that the notetaking activities focused on recording difficulties. Many of the difficulties experienced by subjects occurred during their first attempt at adding a signlink to the video content. Three of five participants commented in the post study questionnaire that SignEd was difficult to use during their first attempt at adding a signlink. However, there are no observational notes or indication from the post study questionnaire of the signlink creation task becoming an easier process for the second signlink although three of the five participants did indicate that SignEd. was easy to use and three indicated it was easy to learn. The video data may provide verbal or time evidence of ease of use differences between the first and second attempts at creating signlinks.

A second explanation could be that participants believed that they should provide positive questionnaire responses in order to show support for the development effort. This could also explain the dearth of comments on problems with and dislikes of the system/interface. However, a number of suggestions for improvements were made, and even some convergence on two main suggestions indicating that participants were willing to provide feedback. One of these suggestions, the need to change the layout specifically the size of the text entry box, did correspond with the observational notes.

The purpose of the usability study is to identify difficulties with using SignEd. regardless of how these difficulties are identified. As a result, difficulties that are observed directly such as problems using the signlink time settings and adjusting the size and position of the rectangle are considered important regardless of post study reports. As SignEd. is a new approach to web page design it is highly likely that most users would encounter it as a new experience. We want the system to be easy to use for first time users so that they will be encouraged to continue using it. In addition, we anticipate that there will be a considerable number of deaf users with little web development experience trying to create sign language web pages. We must therefore attempt to make the process of creating signlinks simple and obvious to first time or naïve users.

## 6 SignEd. II

As a result of the issues identified in the first usability study there were four main interface design changes made to the original design of SignEd. In addition, a Windows and Macintosh version of SignEd was made available.

During the initial evaluation, participants identified that the text field size was too large. In response to this issue, the size of the text field was reduced. The space gained from this reduction allowed the signlink viewing area to be increased to five signlinks from the original three that could be displayed simultaneously.

The signlink authoring interface was redesigned to simplify the process of adding/designing a signlink. Using a tab navigation strategy, the interface is divided into three sections: Link Address, Timing, and Image tabs. The Link Address tab allows users to assign the URL for the link location. This step in the process of creating a signlink is the most important, and therefore it appears first in the tab order. The URL can be entered directly by the user or selected from a list of previously used links. The option of assigning a text label to the signlink is also available under this tab.

The Timing tab allows the user to set the start and end times of the signlink (length of video play used for signlink). This replaces the set start time and end time buttons used in the original design. As seen in Figure 2 the user can directly manipulate the start and end positions by dragging the sliders located on the timeline. Adjusting the signlink playing time is optional for users as a default timing value of two seconds is used (by default two seconds of the video will play as the signlink).

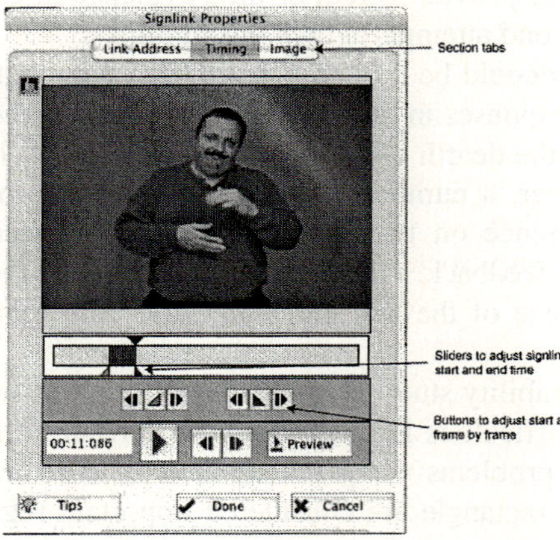


**Fig. 2.** Screen used to edit link's start and end time. The green slider is used to adjust the start time and the red slider is used to adjust the end time

The Image tab allows the user to change the size, location and frame of the thumbnail image using a framing box. Users experienced difficulties positioning and sizing this box in the original design. To overcome this, we attempted to design a simpler manipulation strategy. The user can click on and drag the top of the box moving the entire box (a technique commonly found in a windowed user interface). Clicking and dragging the bottom right corner of the box changes its size. A video frame selector has also been added so that any video frame within the signlink can appear as the thumbnail image in the signlink viewing area. The image appearance is set for the signlink when the user selects "Done" in the image tab. Default size and position for the framing box and location of the video frame have default settings so that adjusting these settings is optional.

## 7 Conclusion

We have only just begun to explore the tools by which authors will create text-optional sign language-based web content. At the foundation of this exploration is the need to implement and author video-based hyperlinking. We have advanced signlinking as one mechanism for achieving video-based hyperlinking for sign language video material, and in this paper we have described two design iterations of an authoring tool, SignEd, that can produce signlinked content. Although important interface design issues were raised for the first iteration of SignEd, signing web authors were still able to create signlinked web pages without the need for sophisticated technical knowledge or skills. Changes in the interface to address these issues were made in the second design iteration. This new design will be submitted to wide scale evaluations to determine if the difficulties with the original interface have been resolved. With this usable tool now available, the development of a signing component of the WWW can finally begin.

## Acknowledgments

Funding for this project is provided by the Applied Research in Interactive Media program of CANARIE, grant # CP13. The authors also wish to gratefully acknowledge The Canadian Hearing Society, the University of Toronto, marblemedia, and Ryerson University.

## References

1. W3C. Web Accessibility Initiative. `http://www.w3.org/WAI/`. retrieved Oct. 3, 2003. (2003)
2. US Department of Justice. ADA home page `http://www.usdoj.gov/crt/ada/adahom1.htm`. retrieved Oct. 3, 2003. (2003)
3. Stokeo, W.C.: The Study and use of sign language. Sign Language Studies 1.4. (2001) 369-406
4. ASL Quest. `http://www.aslquest.com/mainatt.htm`. retrieved Oct. 1, 2003. (2003)
5. Pilgram, P., My concerns about a future internet. retrieved Jan. 22, 2004 from `http://www.xenonsoft.demon.co.uk/internetii2.html` (2000)
6. Richards, J., Hardman, J., Soudian, S., Silverman, C., Fels, D.I.: The Signing Web. CSUN 2004. (2004)
7. Roberts, V., Fels, D., Methods for inclusion: employing think aloud protocol with individuals who are deaf. In Miesenberger, K., Claus, J. & Zagler, W. (Eds.), Computers Helping People With Special Needs: 8th Annual Conference Proceedings/ICCHP 2002: Springer, New York. (2002) 284-291

# Sign Language Communication Support at the Class for Hearing Impaired Using a Control Camera

Hiroki Minagawa

Department of Information Science, Tsukuba College of Technology
4-3-15, Amakubo, Tsukuba, Ibaraki 305-0005 Japan
minagawa@a.tsukuba-tech.ac.jp
http://www.tsukuba-tech.ac.jp/

**Abstract.** Sign language is a visual language, which is difficult to share the information without their view. In the class of Tsukuba College of Technology and the other school for the deaf, there are many efforts to share the sign language presented by a deaf student with other participants. So we attempted a new method to share the sign language by using a camera and a monitor screen. We got some results as "a lecturer and a student can be simultaneously put into a view", "there are few mental and physical loads". However, some problems were left such as the camera control and the way to take and show the sign language video.

## 1 Introduction

About 150 hearing impaired students are studying in the Division for the Hearing Impaired of Tsukuba College of Technology in Japan. About ten students study in each class. Since sign language is a visual language, it is necessary that the sign language of the lecturer and other students is visible to each individual student. Therefore, we sometimes arrange students' desks in a circle so that students can see each other's sign language. However, when the number of students reaches 20 or more, satisfactory communication by this method becomes impossible. An alternative method is that a student stands and speaks in front of the other students. However, it is difficult to have a smooth discussion using this method. Therefore, we propose a new method in which a camera and a large monitor are placed in front of students, and a camera image of a student is displayed on the monitor. We realized a system that supports communication using sign language by this method. Furthermore, we attempted to use the system in an actual class.

## 2 Communication Support Using Video Camera

The system consists of a camera, a monitor, and a camera controller. The camera can be adjusted vertically and horizontally in order to capture the image of the student speaker properly. Furthermore, it is also possible to zoom in and out. The shooting position of the camera can be pre-programmed with every student's seat position. Therefore, when a student asks a question, the lecturer can turn the camera to the student using just one button.

K. Miesenberger et al. (Eds.): ICCHP 2004, LNCS 3118, pp. 1096–1098, 2004.

## 3 Evaluation

In order to evaluate the performance of sign language communication through the camera, we compared and examined various methods.

Method 1: The method that a student speaker moves in front of the class (Fig. 1)
Method 2: The method using desks placed in a circle (Fig. 2)
Method 3: The method using the camera (Fig. 3)

The above three methods were compared in the class of the Division for the Hearing Impaired of Tsukuba College of Technology. Afterwards, we asked the students for an evaluation of performance. The points evaluated were as follows.

- Visibility of the lecturer from each seated position
- Visibility of the speaking student from each seated position
- Visibility of both the lecturer and the speaking student simultaneously from each seated position
- Ease of asking a question from each seated position
- Little of the mental load
- Little of the physical load

Evaluation by questionnaire was obtained from ten students who attended the class.

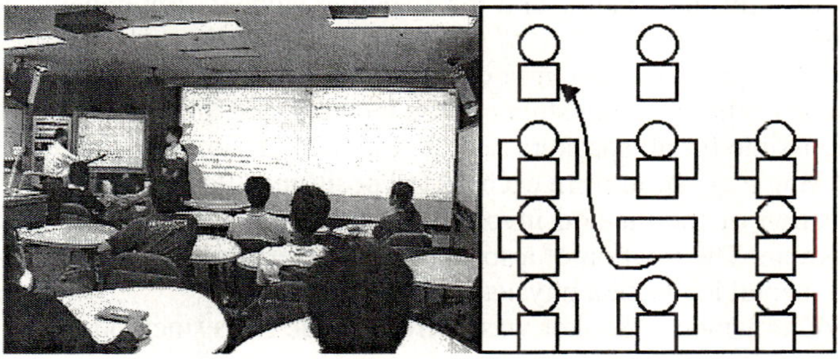

**Fig. 1.** Method 1: The method that a student speaker moves in front of the class

**Fig. 2.** Method 2: The method using desks placed in a circle

**Fig. 3.** Method 3: The method using the camera

## 4 Result

1. Visibility of the lecturer from each seated position
   The method of placing desks in a circle (method 2) had a large variation in evaluation. There were some very uncomfortable seat positions that required the students to turn their heads 90 degrees to look at the lecturer.
2. Visibility of the speaking student from each seated position
   Evaluation of the method using the camera (method 3) was rather poor. Information loss caused by delay in camera operation occurred.
3. Visibility of both the lecturer and the speaking student simultaneously from each seated position
   The method of placing desks in a circle (method 2) received a poor evaluation. If the positions of the speaking students, the lecturer, and the other students were bad, it was impossible for all speakers to be in the field of view simultaneously.
4. Ease of asking a question from each seated position
   The evaluation of the method involving placing desks in a circle (method 2) was quite favorable. The rotation of a speaker can be performed smoothly.
5. Little of a mental load and a physical load
   The method in which a speaker was in front of the class (method 1) has large mental and physical load.

## 5 Discussion

Since camera control was not adequate to catch a student's speech, the beginning of the speech was sometimes missed. The way each student pushed the button and turned the camera to him/herself was also considered. It is also necessary to evaluate and examine these methods.

It is also necessary to make a rule, such as "do not speak until the camera moves" etc.

In order to have a smooth discussion between two students, a method using two cameras should be researched.

## References

1. Minagawa, H., Naito, I., Kato, N., Murakami, H., Ishihara, Y.: The User Interface Design for the Sign Language Translator in a Remote Sign Language Interpretation System, Proceedings of 8th International Conference on Computers Helping People with Special Needs, ICCHP2002, pp. 164-165, Linz, Austria, July 2002

# CD-ROM on Austrian Sign Language: Course OEGS 1, Lesson 1–6

Marlene Hilzensauer

Centre for Sign Language and Deaf Communication, University of Klagenfurt, Universitaetsstrasse 65-67, 9020 Klagenfurt, Austria
marlene.hilzensauer@uni-klu.ac.at

**Abstract.** Sign language is a visual language for deaf people, using hands, facial expressions and body movements. The Centre for Sign Language and Deaf Communication (ZGH) at the University of Klagenfurt produced a multimedia CD-ROM as a companion to the Beginners' Course in Austrian Sign Language (OEGS) for hearing students. This CD-ROM is the first available electronic course of Austrian Sign Language. It contains dialogues, exercises and games as well as explanations on sign language grammar and hints on Deaf culture, covering more than the first semester of sign language instruction. It is not intended for self-study, but should rather be used as a study tool in connection with a presence course. Special features are its flexible programming, which allows the reuse of the structure for other products, a small authoring tool called "Lesson Manager", and the variety of exercise types.

## 1 Introduction

Sign language is a language of deaf or hard-of-hearing people that uses the visual mode. Instead of speaking, the signers use their hands and their body to express meaning. Facial expressions play an important role as well. It is not an auxiliary language, but the mother tongue of many deaf people. There are different national sign languages, which are split into different dialects, similar to spoken languages.

Although Austrian Sign Language (OEGS) is still not an officially recognized minority language, the demand for sign language courses has been steadily rising over the last few years. The Centre for Sign Language and Deaf Communication at the University of Klagenfurt is one of the two academic institutions in Austria that are concerned with sign language and sign language research. Sign language courses for hearing students are offered every semester, held exclusively by our deaf collaborators. As we adhere to the theory of learning languages by immersion, the courses are in sign language only (i.e. without any spoken language at all; an interpreter is only present during the first lesson).

In spite of their enthusiasm, the students found it difficult to remember the signs and the grammar they had learned over a longer period of time. They requested some study tool that could be used at home. Books are relatively unsuitable for sign language, because two-dimensional representations (pictures, line-drawings) cannot really capture the movement of a sign, even if they are annotated with small arrows. We tried videotapes some years ago, but it was not a comfortable solution: The users had to keep rewinding the tape in order to watch signs or a part of a dialogue again. Modern multimedia technology was ideal for our purposes. When we received fund-

K. Miesenberger et al. (Eds.): ICCHP 2004, LNCS 3118, pp. 1099–1106, 2004.

ing from the Austrian Federal Ministry for Education, Science and Culture three years ago, we started work on the first course of Austrian Sign Language on CD-ROM. We tried to adhere to the original course "Oesterreichische Gebaerdensprache (OEGS) Kurs I" [1] as closely as possible, but included some new ideas as well.

It soon turned out that there was too much material to fit onto a single CD-ROM. Therefore we decided to split the course into two parts: Part 1, i.e. Lesson 1-6 (which corresponds to more than the first semester of instruction), is completed. Work on the second part has already begun.

As the CD-ROM is intended primarily for students at the University of Klagenfurt who are learning the Carinthian variant of OEGS, its focus is on Carinthian Sign Language (KGS). Beginners have more than enough to do with remembering the Carinthian signs, without worrying about those in other provinces of Austria. Nevertheless some references to other Austrian variants can be found. Lesson 7-12 on the next set of CD-ROMs will include more information about Austrian Sign Language dialects. Signs from these dialects can also be found in the steadily growing online lexicon at www.sign-it.at.

The CD-ROM is not intended as a stand-alone course, but should be used in connection with a presence course held by a native signer. We also recommend as much contact with native signers as possible, because they can correct the students in ways that a computer program will never be able to.

## 2 Technical Concept

The ZGH teamed up with an Austrian software company, Ailec IT, which handled the actual programming while we provided the linguistic input. The development environment is a Visual Basic 6.0 front-end application. The used components in Visual Basic are Windows Media Player and OCX standard components. Videos, glosses and the references to signer and sentence are connected via a relational MS Access database. The program accesses the database with OLEDB.

Because the CD-ROM was programmed without static parameters, its framework could be used for other courses as well. For instance, it could be relatively easily adapted for other Austrian Sign Language dialects, other sign languages or even spoken languages, simply by inserting different videos or exchanging some of the data.

### 2.1 The Lesson Manager

A special feature is the so-called "Lesson Manager". This is a special tool, developed to link dialogue videos to their written translations.

First, the person using the tool has to link the video to the program. The video can then be manually split into small parts, e.g. a single signed sentence. Afterwards, the user types in the name of the respective signer, a translation of the sentence into German and a translation into glosses[1].

[1] A very simple and not completely exact "translation" of a sign, used in transcribing signed texts. Glosses are always written in capital letters. For instance, the gloss CAT would be used to write down the sign for a cat. Glosses are only a convenience for sign language researchers who are familiar with the signs, because they do not tell the reader anything about what the corresponding sign looks like and how it is produced.

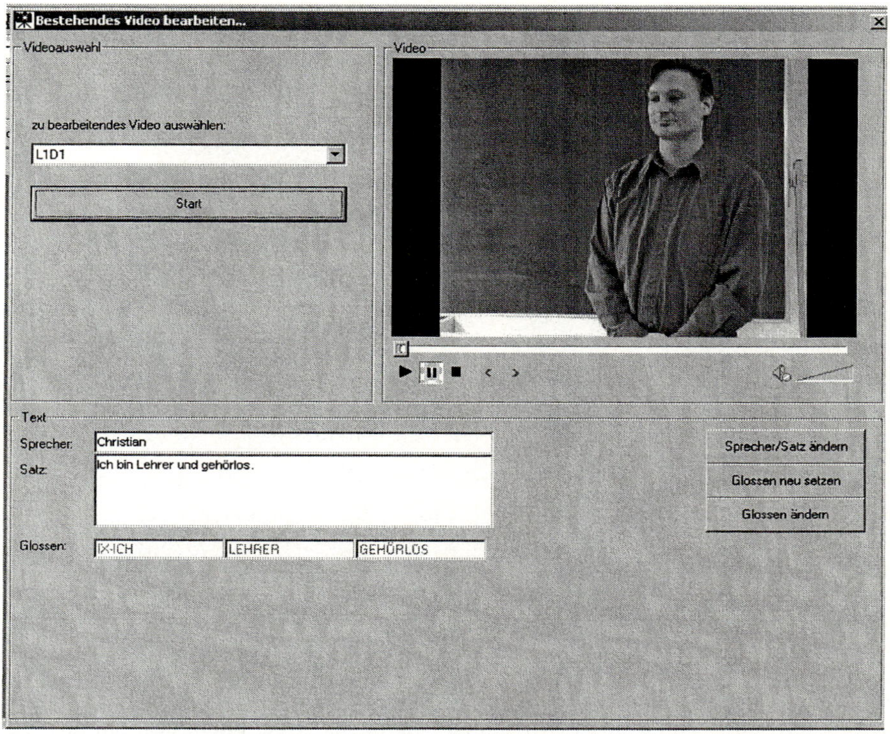


**Fig. 1.** Example for connecting a video with translations with the Lesson Manager

## 3 Structure of the CD-ROM

Navigation within the CD-ROM is free; there is no compulsory order in which the user has to work through the lessons. The lessons become increasingly complex, however. All of the lessons are structured in the same way:

- Dialogues
- Exercises
- Games
- Sign Language Grammar Section
- Deaf Culture Section

In addition, the first three lessons include videos teaching the (one-handed) Austrian manual alphabet[2] and respective exercises. At the end of each lesson, there is a vocabulary list.

[2] A certain handshape is assigned to each letter of the alphabet so that words can be spelled out by producing the respective handshapes one after the other. The manual alphabet is used by the Austrian deaf mainly to spell out foreign words and proper names.

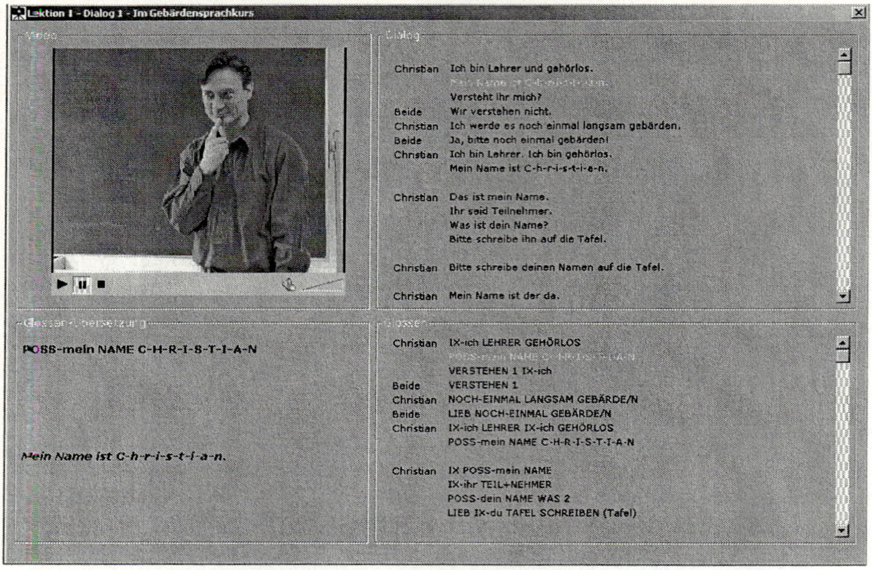


**Fig. 2.** Lesson 1: Dialogue 1 – In the Sign Language Course

### 3.1 Dialogues

Each lesson starts with at least two signed "dialogues" (real dialogues, but also conversations between several persons or a virtual "conversation" between the computer and the user), introducing the main topic(s).

To the right of the video window, a German translation of the full text and the full text in glosses are available. The current position in the video is marked in yellow. By clicking on them, sentences can also be activated individually, i.e. the video starts from this point. Below the video window, users can activate or deactivate the current (part of the) sentence in German and in glosses, according to their wishes[3].

### 3.2 Exercises and Games

The grammar topics and the vocabulary of the introductory dialogues reappear in a variety of exercises and "games".

There are various kinds of exercises, e.g. understanding signed statements, matching videos of questions and answers, matching videos and pictures or answering questions in sign language. As the computer cannot check what the user signs, we used a compromise: Many exercises require the user to arrange glosses in the correct order (e.g. in the order in which they would be signed), thus checking at least the user's grasp of sign language grammar. These exercises use the "drag-and-drop"-method; wrong glosses revert instantly to their original position.

---

[3] When developing the dialogue window, we kept to the design of the German Sign Language CD-ROM "Die Firma" [3].

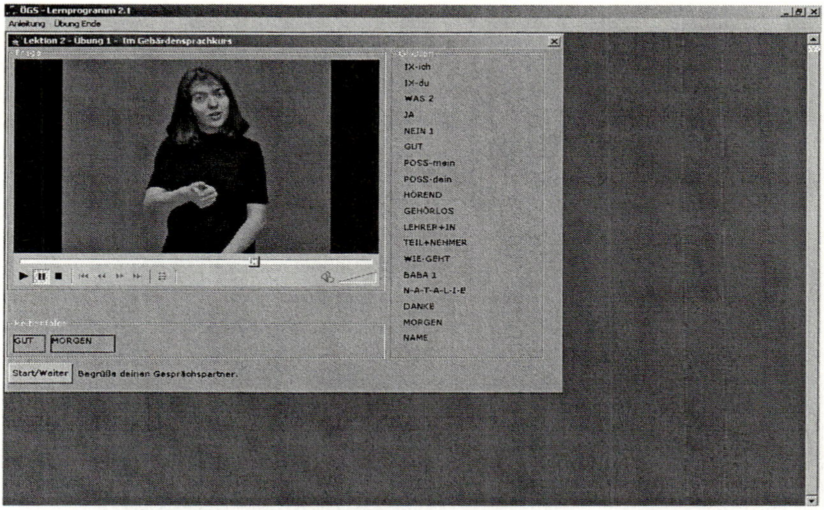


**Fig. 3.** Lesson 2: Exercise 1 – In the Sign Language Course

Some of the exercises focus on facial expressions, because hearing people usually have difficulties learning and recognizing the fine nuances used in sign language. For instance, special expressions are used for very small, thin or large objects. In the exercises, the users have to match facial expressions with the corresponding pictures (e.g. various geometric objects) or descriptions of certain situations.

There is no ongoing assessment from Lesson 1 to Lesson 6, i.e. each exercise is assessed on its own. We also tried to make the assessment as unobtrusive as possible. Sometimes, correct and wrong answers are counted; at other times correct answers are marked with a hook, wrong answers with an "X". Most of the time, however, the users get a feedback video (with various signed equivalents of "right" or "wrong") or they simply cannot finish the exercise until they have given the correct answer (with drag & drop, for instance, only the correct gloss will stay in the blank space). We decided on this method because we did not want to feel the users as if they had to sit a test. Mistakes should be brought to their attention, but not highlighted.

Games include real games, e.g. Tic Tac Toe, which teaches you how to sign directions, but they also allow the users to learn new signs or to repeat the content of other exercises in an entertaining way.

### 3.3 Sign Language Grammar Section

Each lesson includes a grammar section, explaining the main grammar topics of the dialogues. Each grammar entry consists of a short text based on our grammar book "Grammatik der Oesterreichischen Gebaerdensprache 1" [2] and illustrative sentences on video.

**Fig. 4.** Lesson 3: Game 1 – Tic Tac Toe

### 3.4 Deaf Culture Section

The entries for Deaf culture do not only deal with facets hearing people are probably unfamiliar with, but also give advice on how to avoid various faux pas, e.g. abruptly turning away from the deaf person you are signing with because the phone rings. Lesson 6 also includes signed interviews on Deaf culture (with subtitles) so that students will get used to longer texts in sign language.

### 3.5 Vocabulary Section

Signs can be looked up for each lesson separately or in an alphabetical list combining the signs of all the lessons. A search function allows to find certain signs in the complete list by entering one or more letters of its gloss.

### 3.6 Manual Alphabet

The manual alphabet is introduced with videos of each letter of the alphabet. The user may choose between a view of the hand only or of the whole upper body. There are two basic types of exercises: Understanding signed words (e.g. watching a video and typing in the correct German word) and "producing" fingerspelled words.

In order to produce a word, the users must be able to recognize the different handshapes from photos of the "letters" of the manual alphabet. They have to choose the correct handshape and to arrange the photos via drag & drop in the correct order for the word they want to spell out.

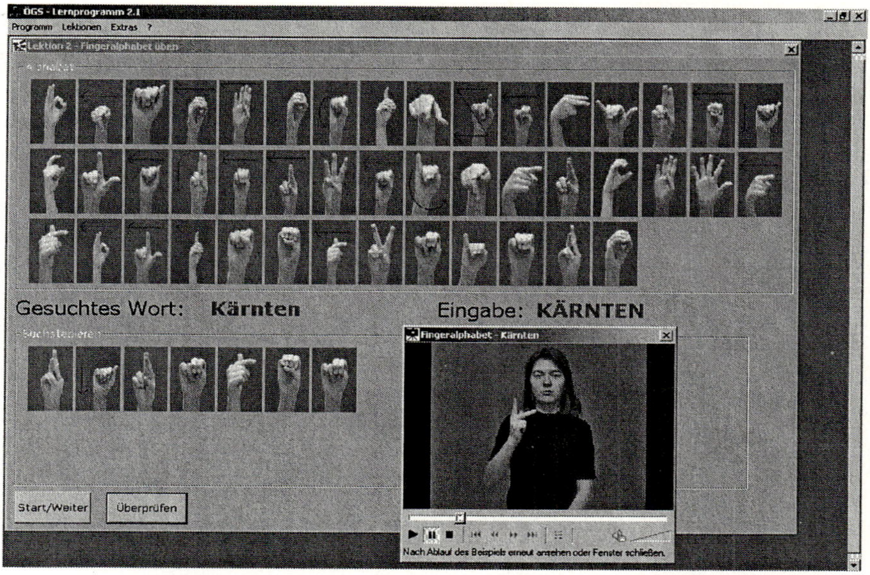


**Fig. 5.** Lesson 2: Manual Alphabet 2 – Practising the Manual Alphabet

## 4 Benefits to the Users

The CD-ROM format allows students to repeat the material at their own pace; they can watch a video as often as they want to, until they have grasped every nuance of the sign. It also provides the user with comfortable navigation as opposed to video tapes.

We used different signers in the videos, so that students would get used to small individual differences in signing and also to avoid boredom. All of the signers are deaf and competent in Austrian Sign Language. Some of them are tutors from the OEGS courses at the University of Klagenfurt, but there are others as well, both male and female. We did not ask our collaborators to sign any texts that were prepared in advance, but explained to them what we needed and asked them to use their own creativity. They developed the scripts for the videos on their own, drawing on their knowledge of their native language, thereby guaranteeing authenticity.

With the aid of this CD-ROM, students without personal access to deaf signers can experience longer texts, where signing flows naturally, in contrast to the single signs or phrases featured in most sign language dictionaries.

The flexible navigation of the CD-ROM as well as the minimum of assessment emphasize the free choice and the individual responsibility of the users. Although some students might prefer a rigid structure, we believe that the users should do an exercise or work through a dialogue because they want to do so, not because they are forced to do it.

Most of the exercises and games were programmed with a random generator, so that they remain a challenge. For instance, pictures used in an exercise are chosen randomly or will at least appear in a different order each time.

We hope that this CD-ROM will help even more people to learn Austrian Sign Language, thereby promoting a better understanding between hearing and deaf people.

## References

1. Okorn, I.: Oesterreichische Gebaerdensprache (OEGS) Kurs I. Version 2.0. (1998)
2. Skant, A., Dotter, F., Bergmeister, E., Hilzensauer, M., Hobel, M., Krammer, K., Okorn, I., Orasche, C., Orter, R., Unterberger, N.: Grammatik der Oesterreichischen Gebaerdensprache 1. Veroeffentlichungen des Forschungszentrums fuer Gebaerdensprache und Hoergeschaedigtenkommunikation, Vol. 4. (2002)
3. Metzger, C., Schulmeister, R., Zienert, H.: Die Firma. Deutsche Gebaerdensprache do it yourself. CD-ROM. Signum Verlag, Hamburg (2000)

# Developing an e-Learning Platform for the Greek Sign Language

E. Efthimiou[1], G. Sapountzaki[1], K. Karpouzis[2], and S.-E. Fotinea[1]

[1] Institute for Language and Speech processing (ILSP)
eleni_e@ilsp.gr
Tel: 0030-210-6875300
[2] Image, Video and Multimedia Systems Laboratory,
National Technical University of Athens, Greece
kkarpou@softlab.ece.ntua.gr
Tel: 0030-210-7723037

**Abstract**. In this paper we introduce the characteristics of the educational platform that is being developed within the SYNENNOESE project. The platform integrates avatar and animation technologies, exploiting electronic linguistic resources of the Greek Sign Language (GSL), in order to provide a Greek-to-GSL conversion tool that allows to construct, store and maintain educational material in GSL. Besides reference to tool development in the context of a specific application, emphasis is placed on the adaptability of the Greek-to-GSL converter as a tool in line with the requirement for Universal Access and the Design for All principles in the context of Information Society.

## 1 Introduction

The work to be presented here is being developed in the framework of the national project SYNENNOESE, which in Greek means 'mutual understanding' and is addressed to the population of deaf Greek pupils of primary schools. The aim is to set up an educational platform with animated signing in Greek Sign Language by a virtual human tutor (avatar). The test bed learning procedure concerns teaching of GSL grammar to early primary school pupils, whereas the platform also incorporates a subsystem that allows approach by the deaf learner to material available only in written Greek form by means of a signed summary. The requirement for translation of educational content to GSL, follows the official -recently reformed- guidelines for the teaching of Greek language in primary schools for the deaf. According to the aforementioned guidelines, GSL is the first language of Greek deaf students by law (Act 2817/2002), and consequently it should be their primary means of education. Moreover, according to EU principles for accessibility to information in special education (see also COM(2000) 284 final [1]), all Greek schools have been provided with suitable equipment for unrestricted Internet access, so any e-learning platform supporting GSL can be readily applicable to real life school routine.

K. Miesenberger et al. (Eds.): ICCHP 2004, LNCS 3118, pp. 1107–1113, 2004.

## 2 GSL Linguistic Analysis – The Background

Greek Sign Language (GSL) is a natural visual language used by the members of the Greek Deaf Community with several thousands of native or non-native signers. Research on the grammar of GSL per se is limited; till mid '90s mostly fragmentary work had been done, whereas recent studies mainly focus on individual aspects of its syntax (negation, morphology, auxiliary verbs), as well as on applied and educational linguistics (GSL acquisition and onomatopoeia). Systematic analysis and creation of linguistic resources for the language has been strongly connected with the maturing of technologies, which enabled the 3D representation of its linguistic content. As a consequence, in the recent past there have also been some serious attempts in the domain of lexicography (*NOEMA: a Multimedia Dictionary of GSL Basic Vocabulary* and *a Children Dictionary of GSL*) mainly with educational scope.

The actual linguistic data of the current study are based on basic research on GSL analysis undertook since 1999, as well as on experience gained by projects NOEMA and PROKLISI [2]. The data consist of digitised language productions of Deaf native GSL signers, triangulated with the participation of Deaf GSL signers in focus group discussions. The project follows methodological principles on data collection and analysis suitable to the minority status of GSL. Wherever the status of individual GSL signs is in consideration, the Greek Federation of the Deaf is advised upon, too.

In this respect, SYNENNOESE offers a great challenge for in-depth work on both directions, lexicography and linguistic analysis of GSL; for the first time research goes beyond mere collection of glosses, into the domain of productive lexicon, i.e. the possibility of building new GSL glosses following structural rules. From a linguistic point of view the resulting database of glosses, rules and tendencies of GSL will be a significant by-product of the project, of great value to future applications.

In the area of signed languages there have been some similar projects (VISICAST [3], Thetos, SignSynth and eSIGN among them) that SYNENNOESE uses as background (relevant sites include:

http://www.leidenuniv.nl/hil/sign-lang/sl-sites.html#technical,
http://www.sign-lang.uni-hamburg.de/Quellen/default.html,
http://www.fhs-hagenberg.ac.at/mtd/projekte/FFF/3dSign/bookmarks.html).

The linguistic part of the project is based on overall assumptions for the adequacy of signed languages as by Stokoe [4], [5], Kyle & Woll [6], Valli & Lucas [7] and Sutton-Spence & Woll [8] among many. Greek sign language is analysed to its linear and non-linear (simultaneous) components, and each sign in GSL is described as to its handshape, location, movement, orientation, number of hands and use of any obligatory non-manually articulated elements (e.g. mouth patterns, head and shoulder movements etc). In the project it was considered essential that the output is as close to native GSL as used in the Greek deaf community. In this respect, forms of 'signed Greek' or other manual codes for the teaching of Greek were excluded and the two languages (GSL and Greek) were treated as the first and second language respectively for the users of the platform, quite as other bilingual platforms may function outside the domain of special education. However, although the target of the project is to decode and automatically translate full texts of written Greek into natural Greek Sign Language, it is accepted that in the current 18-month-long project phase, only simpler syntactic patterns can be successfully recognised and presented in natural GSL.

## 3 Animation Applications for the Representation of Sign Languages

In general, integrated sign synthesis architecture consists of the following transformations:

1. from natural language text to semantic representation
2. from semantic representation to sign language morphological representation
3. from sign language (SL) morphological representation to a sign notation language and
4. from this notation language to the animation of a virtual actor

This sequential process is illustrated in figure 1.

Animating a virtual actor brings up a number of interesting issues that are not necessarily dealt with in the same manner in every application. More specifically, research and development in this area are usually concerned with full-body and coarse gestures, such as those found in a computer game, while in the case of signing, one would utilize more detailed animation, both for the hands and the torso. Besides this, signing is not constrained to hand gesturing but also includes concepts communicated via the signer's body stance or general movement or even facial expression, as is the case with questions; the ability to utilize these notions must be abundant in a sign synthesis system.

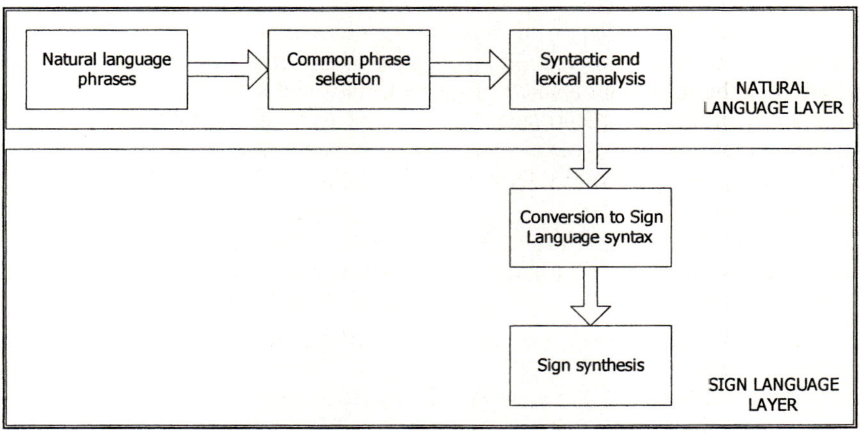


**Fig. 1.** Data flow sequence for sign synthesis

An interesting parameter of a virtual signer is the ability to sign letters of the written alphabet (finger spelling). This technique is useful in cases of proper nouns, acronyms, terminology or even general terms for which no specific sign exists. As a general rule, a sign synthesis system should support the concept of modularity as much as possible, so as to give the opportunity to the content design to build sequences from individual signs, using them as building blocks.

## 4 Adopted 3D Technologies

For the content designer to interact with an avatar, a scripting language is required. In our implementation, we chose the STEP language (Scripting Technology for Embodied Persona) as the intermediate level between the end user and the virtual actor [9]. A major advantage of languages such as STEP is that one can separate the description of the individual gestures and signs from the definition of the geometry and hierarchy of the avatar; as a result, one may alter the definition of any action, without the need to re-model the virtual actor. The avatars that are utilized here are compliant with the h-anim standard, so one can use any of the readily available or model a new one.

An integrated system based on STEP is usually deployed in a usual HTML page, in order to maximize interoperability and be accessible to as many users as possible. This page includes an embedded VRML object, which represents the avatar and includes references to the STEP engine and the related JavaScript interface. From this setup, one may choose to create their own script, for sign representation, and execute them independently, or embed them as JavaScript code, for maximized extensibility. The common VRML viewing plug-ins offer the possibility to select the required viewpoint at run-time, so it is possible for the user to experience the signing from any desired point of view [10], [11], [12]. As an example, a frame of the signing sequence for "radio" is presented in figure 2.

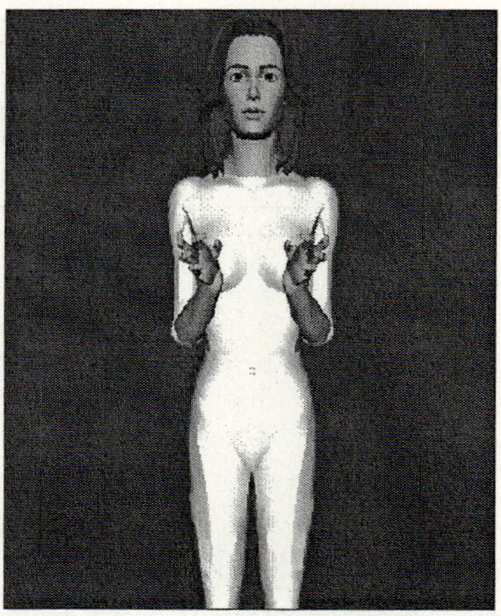

**Fig. 2.** The virtual signer signing "radio" in GSL

In SYNENNOESE, the input is written Greek text which is then transformed into GSL and appears animated on screen. A syntactic parser decodes the structural patterns of written Greek and matches them into the equivalents in GSL, and these resulting patterns are signed by a virtual human (avatar).

Tools for transcription and notation of GSL include HamNoSys, a pictographic notation system developed by the University of Hamburg for the description of the phonology of signs, and ELAN language annotator developed by the Max-Planck Institute of Psycholinguistics in Nijmegen, the Netherlands. In the ELAN glossing process the classic Stokoe model is used, including one tier with written Greek words of harsh semantic equivalents of utterances. It is an aim of the project to transcribe and synthesize GSL signs with high accuracy and include non-manual features of linguistic importance as soon as the first stage of synthesis is successfully completed.

## 5 Linguistic Knowledge of the System

The knowledge of the system in respect to GSL grammar includes both lexical and syntactic aspects of information. Given the features of sign formation, a basic distinction is made between single-sign and multi-sign units. In respect to single-sign units, a further differentiation holds, between free and bound signs; the latter, in principle, correspond to the notions of free and bound morpheme of spoken language. Free signs are included as independent parts of the lexicon knowledge of the system. Bound signs are included as sign building blocks that feed sign generation in combination with other signs.

It is important to notice that, along with lexical signs, the system incorporates a library of phonological features of sign formation that include:

- The list of handshapes of GSL
- Locations of sign formation
- Palm orientations and
- Hand movements

as the set of independent structural units for the formation of grammatical GSL signs at the phonological level.

This set is further enhanced to incorporate features for mouth patterns, facial expressions and body movement, used especially for the indication of phonetically (stress) or syntactically uttered (focus position in sentence) elements of the linguistic message in spoken languages.

Multi-sing units may be composed of a) free signs or b) combinations of free and bound signs, in order to create sign sequences, according to the rules of either inflectional or derivational morphology, or in order to construct sign phrases.

Lexical resources include the whole of vocabulary to be used in the e-learning application, annotated according to HamNoSys. Linguistic resources also include a computational grammar of the core structure rules of GSL. The combination of lexical items and structure rules allows generation of infinite sign phrases. The GSL grammar descriptions are matched against the output of the ILSP parser for Greek [13], [14], [15], so that structure equivalences between input written text and output signed streams are defined.

## 6 Greek-to-GSL Converter as a Universal Access Tool

The above described linguistic knowledge allows for robust conversion from written Greek text to GSL signing, a tool which, in our case, is combined with an e-learning educational platform that exploits standard e-learning techniques. In this way, the e-learning system architecture is enriched to accommodate access to e-content by a special user group at the early stage of system design. Irrespective of the selected application, the development of the Greek-to-GSL converter is in line with the main principles of Universal Access and Design for All. Under current definition, Universal Access is becoming predominantly an aspect of design that is raised to a critical quality target in the context of the Information Society [16], [17]. In this respect, the notion of accessibility crucially differs from the original interpretation of the term as concerning modification of already developed systems so as to meet the requirements that would allow their use by groups of users with disabilities [18], [19].

Accordingly, the development of the Greek-to-GSL converter constitutes, in principle, a tool independent of application environment, that supports access by deaf users to e-content in the context of Information Society Technology.

## 7 Extensibility Perspectives

The Greek-to-GSL converter is a fully extensible tool, in respect to both quality of performance and dynamic content.

- The tool's library that feeds the linguistic knowledge of the system, will be enriched so as to include non-manual structural components that will support signing performance of the avatar closer to natural signing.
- Enrichment of the system's linguistic knowledge will also allow for improvement of its generative capacity.
- New written texts can be launched, so the e-learning platform may receive unlimited educational content besides primary school grammar units.
- Greek-to-GSL conversion may be extended to apply to different environments, such as Greek language teaching to deaf students of higher grades, GSL teaching for hearing students, Greek for specific purposes etc.
- A database with the bulk of GSL utterances, described as to their features from the phonological up to the pragmatic level, will improve knowledge of GSL grammar and create reusable resources.
- The Greek-to-GSL conversion tool will be applicable to a number of systems, other than the e-learning platform under development. As an independent tool, it may support accessibility of content in environments of text generation, information retrieval, summarisation, etc.
- From a socio-economic point of view, the existence of a Greek-to-GSL conversion tool will greatly contribute towards ensuring equal opportunities for the deaf population in Greece.

## Acknowledgements

This work is partially supported by the national project SYNENNOESE (GSRT: e-Learning 44), the consortium comprising the Institute for Language and Speech Processing (ILSP), Systema Technologies S.A. and the Institute of Communication and Computer Systems (ICCS). The Hellenic Federation of the Deaf (HFD) participates as the project's user.

## References


1. COM(2000) 284 final: Towards a Barrier Free Europe for People with Disabilities. Communication from the Commission to the Council, the European Parliament, the Economic and Social Committee and the Committee of the Regions, Brussels, May (2000)
2. Efthimiou, E., Vacalopoulou, A., Fotinea, S-E., Steinhauer, G.: Multipurpose Design and Creation of GSL Dictionaries. In: Proc. of the Workshop on the Representation and Processing of Sign Languages "From SignWriting to Image Processing. Information techniques and their implications for teaching, documentation and communication", LREC-2004 Conference, 30 May 2004, Lisbon, Portugal (2004) in print
3. Bangham, J.A., Cox, S.J., Elliott, R., Glauert, J.R.W., Marshall, I., Rankov, S., Wells, M.: Virtual Signing: Capture, Animation, Storage and Transmission - An Overview of the ViSiCAST Project. IEE Seminar on "Speech and language processing for disabled and elderly people" London (2000)
4. Stokoe, W.: Sign Language Structure, monograph. Gallaudet University (1960)
5. Stokoe, W.: Sign Language Structure. (Revised Ed.) Silver Spring, MD: Linstok (1978)
6. Kyle, J. G. and Woll, B.: Sign Language: the study of deaf people and their language. Cambridge University Press (1985)
7. Valli, C., and Lucas, C.: Linguistics of American Sign Language. 2nd ed. Washington D.C. Gallaudet University Press (1995)
8. Sutton-Spence, R. and Woll, B.: The Linguistics of British Sign Language; an Introduction. Cambridge University Press (1999)
9. Huang, Z., Eliens, A., and Visser, C.: STEP: A Scripting Language for Embodied Agents. In Proc. of the Workshop on Lifelike Animated Agents (2002)
10. Kennaway, R.: Synthetic Animation of Deaf Signing Gestures. In: Proc of the International Gesture Workshop. City University, London (2001)
11. Kennaway, R.: Experience with, and Requirements for, a Gesture Description Language for Synthetic Animation. In: Proc. of the 5th International Workshop on Gesture and Sign Language based Humman-Computer Interaction. Genova (2003)
12. Verlinden, M., Tijsseling, C., Frowein, H.: A Signing Avatar on the WWW. In: Proc. of the International Gesture Workshop 2001. City University, London, (2001)
13. Boutsis, S., Prokopidis, P., Giouli, V., Piperidis, S.: A Robust Parser for Unrestricted Greek Text. In: Proc. of the 2nd Language Resources and Evaluation Conference (2000) 467-474
14. Elliott, R., Glauert, J.R.W., Kennaway, J.R., Marshall, I.: The Development of Language Processing Support for the ViSiCAST Project. In: Proc. of the 4th International ACM SIGCAPH Conference on Assistive Technologies (ASSETS 2000). Washington, (2000)
15. Safar, E. and Marshall, I.: The Architecture of an English-Text-to-Sign-Languages Translation System. In: G. Angelova et al (ed): Recent Advances in Natural Language Processing (RANLP). Tzigov Chark Bulgaria, (2001) 223-228
16. Stephanidis, C.: Editorial. International Journal of Universal Access in the Information Society. Vol. 1/1, (2001) 1-3
17. Stephanidis, C., Savidis, A.: Universal Access in the Information Society: Methods, Tools, and Interaction Technologies. International Journal of Universal Access in the Information Society. Vol. 1/1, (2001) 40-55
18. Story, MF: Maximising usability: the principles of universal design. Assistive Technol. Vol. 10 (1998) 4-12
19. Vanderheiden, G.: Universal design and assistive technology in communication and information technologies: alternatives or compliments?. Assistive Technol. Vol. 10(1) (1998) 29-36

# Design of Computer Animation of Japanese Sign Language for Hearing-Impaired People in Stomach X-Ray Inspection

Kazunari Morimoto, Takao Kurokawa, Norifumi Isobe, and Junichi Miyashita

Graduate School of Engineering and Science, Kyoto Institute of Technology
Hashigami-cho, Matsugasaki, Sakyo-ku, Kyoto 606-85858, Japan
{morix,Kurotak,n-iso03,miyaj03}@ipc.kit.ac.jp
http://media.kit.ac.jp

**Abstract.** The aim of this paper is to examine the effects of JSL (Japanese Sign Language) animation for hearing-impaired people in stomach X-ray inspection, and to improve the system. Evaluation tests were carried out on JSL animation improved based upon referring to the movement of a signer. Results showed that the improved animation has obtained very high ratio in comprehensibility and some important factors for designing JSL animation were indicated to develop the sign animation.

## 1 Introduction

Sign language is very important to make fruitful interaction among hearing-impaired people. On the other hand they can hardly convey their feelings to the person who cannot use the sign language. Especially it is problem that the communication between medical doctors and hearing-impaired patients is highly difficult, and the failure of the communication may cause infinite damage of their life (Taoda, 2003).

To communicate each other, they need a sign interpreter who always practices the sigh language in a academy for sign training. However, a few sign interpreters engaged in a hospital, so that the deaf patients refused to knock the door of the doctors for doing diagnosis. Unfortunately absence of sign interpreter inclines the patients to anxiety (Kitahara, 1999). Furthermore professional sign interpreters were very few in Japan. Therefor they always have to work hard, and become strongly utter pain of their shoulders and hands.

To overcome the communication barrier between deaf patients and doctors we have developing a bi-directional translating system from Japanese Sign Language (JSL) into Japanese and vice versa (Kurokawa, 1993). Sign animation system has being developed by many researchers, because this system would be greatly contribute to many hearing-impaired people in any interaction scene (Nagashima, 1996).

In this paper, we demonstrate the method for representing JSL animation on screen in stomach X-ray inspection. The purpose of this paper is to evaluate the comprehensibility of JSL animation developed for hearing-impaired people.

K. Miesenberger et al. (Eds.): ICCHP 2004, LNCS 3118, pp. 1114–1120, 2004.

## 2 JSL Machine Translation System

### 2.1 Components of JSL Machine Translation System

The prototype of JSL translation system is composed of four parts that are sign word recognition, sign word procession, reproduction of sign images, and sign dictionary. In the searching part a sign word corresponds to the word inputted from keyboard is selected from sign dictionary, and is changed in sign-word codes. In the word processing part sign words is adequately arranged as JSL. In the image representation part, sign animation by virtual-human frame model is displayed on screen following a rule composition on code of sign words.

### 2.2 Some Issues of JSL Animation of Our System

The translation system takes a sentence to words, and makes the sign words in accordance to the sign dictionary. Then the words are ranged about Japanese sentence, and the sign animation is represented. Sign animation of our JSL translation system can reproduce the movement of the hands and fingers on screen. In addition we can change or control the shape of eyelid and mouth, motion of head and eyebrows, and the direction of eyesight and body.

To improving our sign animation we thoroughly analyzed the movement of hands and fingers of the sign animation and video images of professional sign translator who make a translation of an instruction in X-ray inspection into JSL (Morimoto 2000). Then we caught some issues on naturalness in representation of sign animation, and the following differences between the sign animation and the interpreter were revealed. The locus of hand in sign animation was different from sign translator, and the speed of the hand in the animation was faster than in the translator. The pose between sign words wasn't clear in sign animation. Face expression of animation was hardly put without the movement of eyes. Moreover we can indicate that the sign animation was constructed with a few factors about the situation in stomach X-ray.

### 2.3 Improvement on JSL Animation

The sign animation was changed for better about following five points.

1. The speed of the sign animation is performed as the same as a sign translator.
2. The pose between sign words was sufficiently taken to make contrast on movement of hands.
3. To include the situation of stomach X-ray, sign animation was changed into sign language expression that used in the stomach X-ray inspection.
4. Face expressions such as the nod, the blink, motion of the neck and motion of the eyebrows were added to the conventional animation.

Finally, the color of the hands and the lip were changed to enhance legibility of the motion of fingers and mouth. Figure 1 represents an example of improved images of sign animation based on those items.

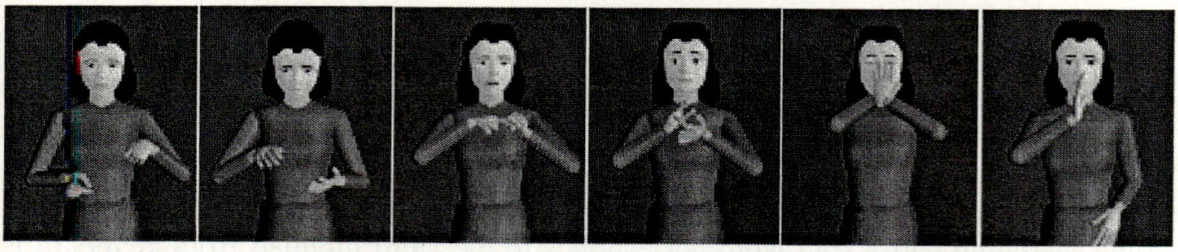


**Fig. 1.** An example images of sign animation improved. Instruction: Take this medicine that puff out your stomach.

## 3 Method

### 3.1 Instructions from Technical Stuffs of a Hospital to Patient in X-Ray Inspection

To arrange the instructions for making the sign animation to inspect stomach by X-ray, we investigated the instructions that were used in the X-ray inspection from technical stuff to a hearing-impaired person on the inspection bed. Twenty-seven sentences were selected as the instructions in Table 1. At least, sign animation of these sentences has to be reproduced by sign words in the sentences. Sign animation of the other sentences used for instruction to the patient would be made by replace other sign words instead of the sign words of these sentences.

**Table 1.** Instructions demonstrated by sign animation.

| No. | Contents of instruction | No. | Contents of instruction |
|---|---|---|---|
| 1 | Take this medicine that puff out your stomach. | 15 | Relax. |
| 2 | Do not burp. | 16 | Stretch your legs, and touch the stand of the bed. |
| 3 | Take all of the medicine. | 17 | Your bed raises up. |
| 4 | Hold the both side bars hard. | 18 | A rod touches your body on stomach. |
| 5 | Your bed inclines to backward. | 19 | Raise your right shoulder a little. |
| 6 | Lower your hands. | 20 | Hold the cup by left hand. |
| 7 | Relax your grip on the bar. | 21 | Swallow the medicine a little. |
| 8 | Lift up your waist from right side. | 22 | Wash it down at a given signal. |
| 9 | Replace slowly your waist. | 23 | Yes, wash it down. |
| 10 | Lie on your stomach turning from right side. | 24 | Lift slightly your jaw. |
| 11 | Turn your face toward left side. | 25 | Your bed shortly swings. |
| 12 | Lie slowly face up. | 26 | Turn the right, and fall forward. |
| 13 | Breath a little. | 27 | All is finished. |
| 14 | Puff your stomach, and choke steadily your breath. | | |

### 3.2 Comprehensibility Test of JSL of Sign Animation and Signer

The experiment on comprehensibility of our sign animation was carried out to reveal the effects of the improvements above on sign animation. The comprehensibility of JSL was compared among pre-improved sign animation (Nakata, 1998), improved sign animation and the sign by professional sign translator who engaged in a hospital.

**Fig. 2.** Typical situation of the experiment on comprehensibility of sign animation.

Sign animation of all sentences made by computer system was converted into video images. As shown in figure 2, the subjects looked at every sentence on video screen, and wrote down the contents of sign animation or signer. Before starting the experiment, we explained to the subjects that the contents of these signs were used in X-ray inspection of the human stomach using photos of X-ray inspection apparatus. Moreover, questionnaire survey with five-point scaling method was carried out about every sentence on five evaluation items; easiness to catch the meaning of the signs, the facial expression and the pose position of sign words, the aptness of speed of hands and naturalness of sign expressions. Twenty-seven signers participated in this evaluation were made up a nine some. These subjects of each group evaluated the comprehensibility by one sentence on JSL of the sign animation or signer.

## 4 Results

### 4.1 Comprehensibility of Sign Animation Improved

The percentages of correct answers in meaning of sign animation and signer were calculated about each sign sentence. Figure 3 showed that many sign animations improved were higher ratio than the conventional animations. The rates of correct answer rose more than 30 percentages due to above improvements in sign animations

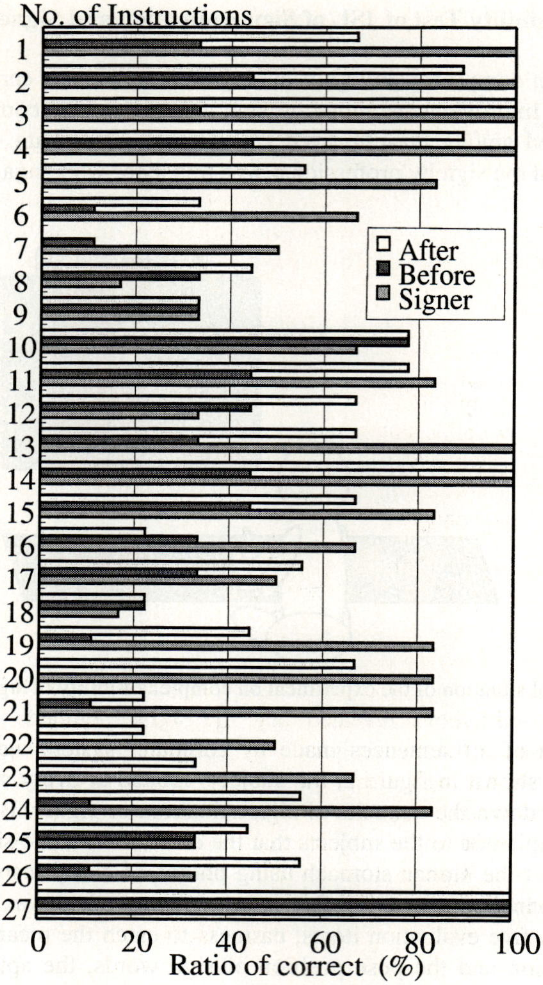


**Fig. 3.** Ratio of correctness in sign animations and sign translator.

for the number of 5, 20, 23, 24 and 26 sentences. The rates of these sentences before improvement animation were less than 10 percentages. The average ratio of all sentences in sign language translator was 69 percentages that was highest score in three groups. The comprehensibility of sign animation after improvement was increased considerably. However, the correct ratio of the sign animations was lower than that of a signer in 18 sentences. The average ratio of before and after sign animations improved were relatively 56 and 30 percentages. However, the ratio of two sentences of 7 and 16 were declined through the improvement.

### 4.2 Subjective Rating Value of Sign Animation

Subjective rating values of the sign language animations were increased in many sign sentences by improvement. Mean rating values of improved animation were higher than conventional sign animations as shown in Table 2. However the rating values of signer were highest in all evaluation items. The rating values of the sentences 11 and 13 were high in all evaluation items. On the other hand, many subjects indicated that some animation after the improvement was hard to take in the correct meaning of the instruction number of 4, 7, 10, 12, 16 and 18.

**Table 2.** Mean rating values.

| | Before | After | Signer |
|---|---|---|---|
| Readability of sign | 2.2 | 3.2 | 4.4 |
| Facial expression | 1.8 | 3.1 | 4.4 |
| Naturalness | 2.1 | 3.2 | 4.4 |
| Pose of sign words | 2.4 | 3.5 | 4.5 |
| Speed of sign | 2.9 | 3.6 | 4.5 |

## 5 Discussions

The sign animations improved that took higher value of comprehensibility than the conventional sign animations revealed that the signs included gesture of actual movement in the part of the instructions. This indicates that it is significantly important to represent not only sigh words but also a situation of inspection. Furthermore subjective rating values on comprehensibility of a facial expression, gap between the sign words and the speed of animation ascended by setting up nod expression and pose between the words. On the other hand, the sign animations that rating values did not rise were different from signer's movement of the whole body and of sign words looked up in our sign dictionary for interpreting from Japanese words to sign words. For instance, in the instruction sentence 18, the meaning of the movement of sign animation was hard to understand if a subject was not on the X-ray inspection bed and did not look the stick for touching his/her stomach. Moreover it is difficult to know the meaning of sign animations including a delicate movement.

The sign animations developed could not represent slight movement of shoulders according to contents of sign words. Therefor, for instance, it is impossible to express the shoulder for rising and taking down in the instruction 7. It was greatly difficult to convey the meaning of sign animation of the instruction 10 and 12, because subjects who had not been experienced the stomach inspection could hardly understand the situation of turning their body on the bed. In case of No. 6 and 21, the comprehensibility of signer was superior to the sign animation improved because the animation needs delicate movement of hands and mouth, and it is difficult to represent exactly. This movement and facial expressions of the sign animation aren't usually familiar and are unnatural in comparison with the sign language translator who is a human being. We consider that the sign animations were hard to read. Some subject gave us valuable opinion that it is better to use gesture instead of sign words that have constraint to express the non-verbal information.

## 6 Conclusions

We examined the effectiveness of the sign animation in the stomach X-ray inspection system for the hearing-impaired people who would not want to go to a hospital, because there is not a sign translator. Results showed that improvement of the proposed sign language animation had many effects on communication. However, sign animation improved was satisfied less than sign translator. Moreover, we knew that the sign animation could not express delicate movement and lacked facial expression.

There are still many problems to make up effective sign animation. For instance,

1) To create sign animation that has fine expression.
   We have to enhance the power of facial expression and body movement of the animation.
2) To introduce natural and more comprehensive expressions into sign animation.

We have to create new sign animation that takes account of the situation of stomach X-ray inspection for hearing-impaired people.

## Acknowledgments

We thank all subjects for their cooperation in the experiment. This research was partly supported by the MESCJ under Grants-in Aid No. 14370122.

## References

1. Kitahara, T., Taoda, K., Watanabe, S., Sato S. and Nishiyama K. 1999. Are Deaf People inhibited from seeking medical services. – Surveys on Deaf People and a Hospital Due to Lack of Sign Language Interpreters-, Bullet. Social Medicine, 14, 103-107 (1999) (in jpn)
2. Kurokawa, T., Morichi, T., and Watanabe, S.: Bidirectional translation between sign language and Japanese for communication with deaf-mute people, Human Computer Interaction: Software and Hardware Interface, Elsevier, 1109-1114 (1993)
3. Nakata, Y., Morimoto, K., Kurokawa, K., Kitahara, T., Taoda. K. et al.:The Proposal of Stomach X-ray System with Sign Language Animation for Deaf People, Proceedings of Kansai-Branch Conference in Ergonomic Society of Japan, pp.109-112 (1998) (in jpn)
4. Morimoto, K., Uchikawa, K., Ogawa, K., Kurokawa, K. et al.: Evaluation of Japanese Sign Language Animation for Hearing-Impaired People in Stomach X-ray Inspection, Human Interface, 2(5), 174-179(2000) (in jpn)

# Basic Study of a Communication Device for the Deaf-Blind Using a Finger and a Palm – Measurement of Finger Speed and Pressure

Chikamune Wada and Yasuhiro Wada

Graduate School of Life Science and Systems Engineering, Kyushu Institute of Technology
Hibikino 2-4, Wakamatsu-ku, Kitakyushu 808-0196, Japan
wada@life.kyutech.ac.jp
http://www.life.kyutech.ac.jp/~wada

**Abstract.** We proposed a device which used palms and fingers as both a transmitter and a receiver of communication for the deaf-blind. Our device would be set on the palm of a deaf-blind person. The movement of the finger would then be detected by the device and sent to a computer. Next, the letters written on the palm would be displayed on a computer screen where non-disabled people could receive the message. For the opposite case, when the deaf-blind received messages from non-disabled people, the letters would be formed on their palms through the use of tactile stimulation. First of all, we attempted to determine which presentation condition most facilitated the correct recognition of Japanese letter. The results are summarized as follows. The optimal pressure could not be determined. Regarding speed, it was postulated that each subject's own speed was optimal, within the range of 4-11cm/s.

## 1 Background and Purpose

Since the deaf-blind suffer from both visual and auditory impairments, it is easy to imagine their difficulty in communicating with others. The deaf-blind can roughly be divided into two categories - Type A and Type B. In the case of Type A, the visual sense has been damaged prior to the auditory sense; whereas in Type B, the auditory impairment has preceded the visual.

Those who are Type A deaf-blind use Braille at school in Japan. According to the finger Braille method, six fingers – 3 from each hand – correspond to the six dots used in standard Braille. Naturally, learning finger Braille is easy if one has already learned standard Braille. Therefore, having lost their auditory sense after first losing their visual sense, such Type A people can still communicate with others through finger Braille. The concept of a device which supports the use of finger Braille has been studied in Japan. More specifically, if such a device were successfully developed, it would facilitate communication between the deaf-blind and the non-disabled, even when the latter had not learned finger Braille.

Conversely, the Type B deaf-blind have already learned sign language. Thus, fingerspelling is one useful method of communication for them as a sign language which can be perceived by the hands. In short, they can still communicate through fingerspelling despite having lost their visual sense. Although a five-fingered robotic hand has actually been developed for fingerspelling, it is not practical to carry around due to its considerable weight.

K. Miesenberger et al. (Eds.): ICCHP 2004, LNCS 3118, pp. 1121–1128, 2004.

Japan has experienced an increase in the number of elderly people who have lost their vision as a result of diabetes mellitus. When such elderly citizens lose their sight, some of them learn standard Braille and finger Braille. Others, however, use sign language or fingerspelling without learning Braille. Unfortunately, not all people in our society can use sign language or fingerspelling. In view of this, consideration should be given to other methods of communication that could serve as an aid to the elderly Type B deaf-blind.

Since schools throughout Japan teach students to write phonetic symbols, known as 'kana', even the deaf-blind are familiar with this standard Japanese writing system. Most people can write letters on their palms with their own fingers while keeping their eyes closed. Consequently, it should also be possible for the deaf-blind to use their palms and fingers as both a transmitter and a receiver of communication.

## 2 An Outline for the Conceptualization of Such a Device

Figure 1 shows a block diagram of our communication device. The device would be set on the palm of a deaf-blind person. The movement of the finger would then be detected by the device and sent to a computer. Next, the letters written on the palm would be displayed on a computer screen where non-disabled people could receive the message.

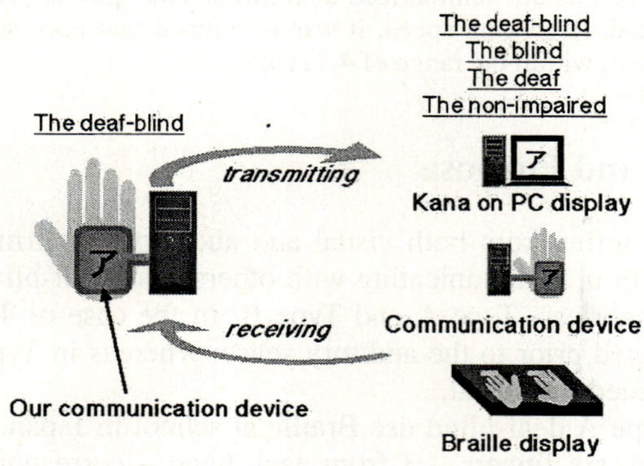


**Fig. 1.** Block diagram of our communication device

For the opposite case, when the deaf-blind received messages from non-disabled people, the letters would be formed on their palms through the use of tactile stimulation. In particular, by combining various tactile stimuli, such tactile stimulation could give a deaf-blind person the sensation of someone forming letters on their palm with their fingertips. Although the sending and receiving of such messages would be somewhat time-consuming, no training period would be necessary, since all Japanese have learned this writing method in primary school. In summary, the purpose of this study would be to obtain guidelines for the design of such a device. At this time, we would like to report on our investigation of the optimal pressure and speed to be used when the kana characters are written.

# 3 Measurement of Finger Pressure and Speed

Our measurements showed that finger temperature did not influence the correct answer rate under four presentation conditions (shape of the character, temperature, pressure, and speed) when the character was written on the palm [1]. We also measured the finger pressure and speed when the shapes of the characters were held constant.

## 3.1 Experimental Setup and Method

Figure 2 shows the experimental setup. The experimental setup was composed of three parts – the template to make the shape of the character constant, the pressure sensor and a three dimensional positioning sensor. Data from the positioning sensor and the pressure sensor were digitalized and input into a computer. The written characters included 46 Japanese kana, which is a standard Japanese writing system (shown in appendix). Eight non-impaired subjects were temporarily deafened and blinded by using stopples and eyeshades. All subjects filled the two roles – writing kana on other subjects' palms and answering which kana were written on their palms.

One of 46 kana was written randomly and the subjects were asked to indicate which kana had been written. Subjective regular force, speed and tracks, corresponded to the force, speed and tracks which the subjects used to write Japanese kana in their daily lives.

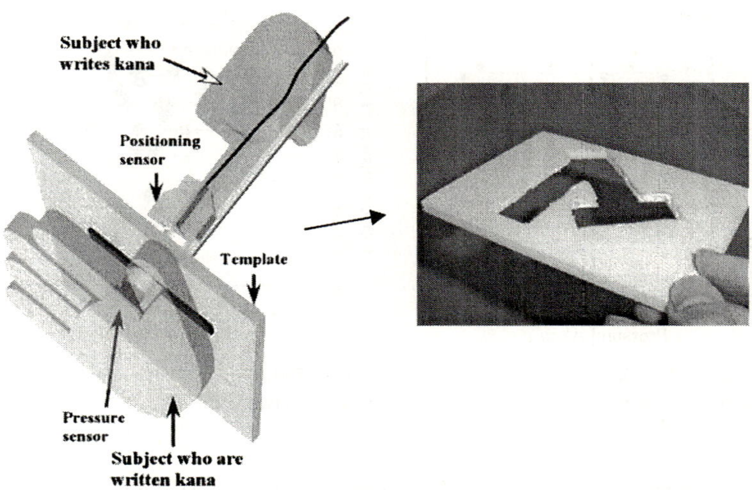


**Fig. 2.** Experimental setup

## 3.2 Results and Discussion

The results for finger pressure are shown in Figure 3, while the results for finger speed are shown in Figure 4. Figure 3 indicates the frequency of each $5gf/cm^2$. In

Figure 4, the frequency of each 0.5cm/s is shown. Moreover, the relation between the correct answer rate and pressure is shown in Figure 5, while the relation between the correct answer rate and the speed is shown in Figure 6.

As can be seen in Figure 3, it was found that the frequency was high for 30-60gf/cm$^2$, and the correct answer rate was comparatively high for 30-60gf/cm$^2$ (shown by the dotted line in figure 5). Therefore, we considered the optimal pressure to be roughly between 30-60 gf/cm$^2$. On the other hand, it was found that the frequency was high for 4-11cm/s (figure 4), including one case (figure 6) where the correct answer rate was relatively high at 4-11cm/s. Therefore, we considered a suitable range of the speed to be about 4-11cm/s.

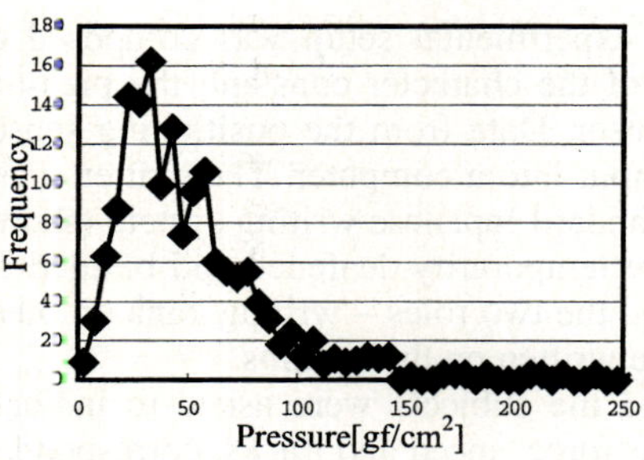


**Fig. 3.** Relationship between finger pressure and frequency

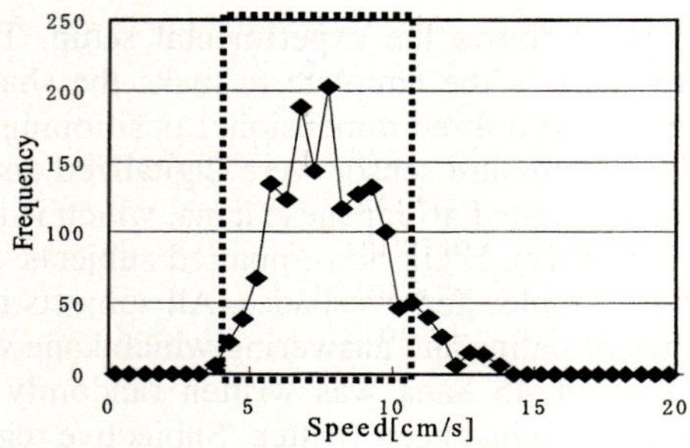


**Fig. 4.** Relationship between finger speed and frequency

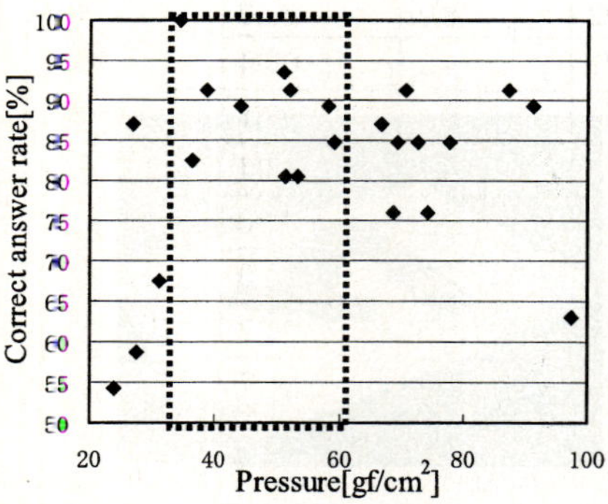


**Fig. 5.** Relationship between finger pressure and correct answer rate

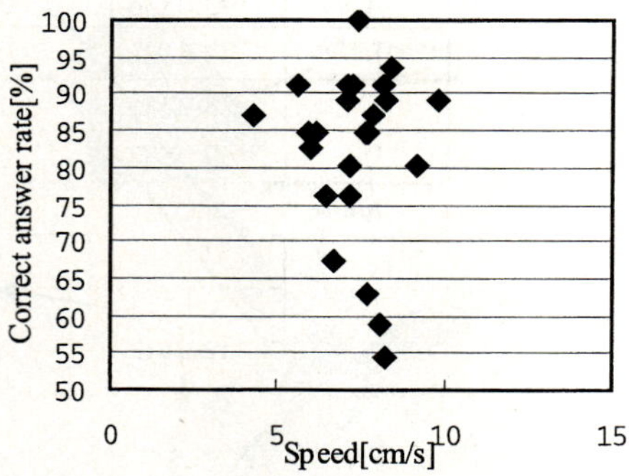


**Fig. 6.** Relationship between finger speed and correct answer rate

## 4 Measurements of Finger Movement when Subjects Wrote Kana on Their Own Palms by Using Their Own Fingers

When the subjects used their own fingers to write kana on their palms, needless to say, they knew which kana should be written beforehand. Therefore, we supposed that finger pressure and speed might be optimal when kana was written by subjects using their own fingers. During this activity, we measured the speed and pressure which the subjects used and compared those findings to the results in chapter 3.

### 4.1 Experimental Setup and Method

The experimental setup was the same as in chapter 3. However, because the shape of the characters should not be constant, a template was not used. For the written characters, 46 Japanese kana were used. Eight non-impaired subjects were temporarily deafened and blinded by using stopples and eyeshades and all subjects were the same as in the experiment described in chapter 3.

### 4.2 Results and Discussion

Pressure, speed, and the standard deviation are shown in Table 1. In chapter 3, the correct answer rate was high when the range of the finger pressure was between 30gf/cm$^2$ to 60gf/cm$^2$. However, table 1 indicates that subjects did not write their own kana by using finger pressure in the 30 to 60 gf/cm$^2$ range. This can be explained by the fact that even when the subjects did not apply their fingers to their palms, the finger position could still be perceived merely because the subjects were moving their own fingers. Therefore, we surmised that they did not pay any attention to finger pressure while writing kana by themselves. Actually, some results were even obtained when the pressure on a subject's palm was 0.

**Table 1.** Pressure and speed for all subjects

| Subjects | Pressure [gf/cm$^2$] | Pressure S.D. | Speed [cm/s] | Speed S.D. |
|---|---|---|---|---|
| A | 93.0336 | 37.92 | 8.7 | 2.62 |
| B | 72.6422 | 22.01 | 4.1 | 0.94 |
| C | 23.7245 | 12.03 | 6.4 | 1.51 |
| D | 59.9527 | 16.35 | 10.1 | 3.04 |
| E | 36.8178 | 14.97 | 4.2 | 0.90 |
| F | 26.2756 | 14.63 | 11.7 | 2.90 |
| G | 18.9404 | 4.66 | 10.5 | 2.72 |
| H | 29.365 | 5.84 | 5.4 | 0.87 |

Next, optimal speed was considered by comparing the results of chapter 3 and chapter 4. The results for subject D were chosen as an example. Figure 7 shows the finger speed when subjects wrote kana by themselves, when others wrote kana and the correct answer rate. The correct answer rate tended to be higher if the speed that others wrote kana approached the speed at which subjects wrote kana by themselves, as shown by the square in Figure 7. In particular, we wondered if the correct answer rate would rise when the mean speed fell in the range of the standard deviation. This supposition is indicated by a black oval. The mean speeds, shown as a black triangle and a black square, fell within the large square frame, meaning that they were within the range of the standard deviation. In contrast, we supposed that the correct answer rate would be low if the mean speed was outside of the standard deviation. This supposition is shown by a gray oval. The mean speed, indicated by a black diamond, was not within the standard deviation, as can be seen by its location outside of the large square frame.

The frequency at which the mean speed fell within or outside of the range of the standard deviation can be seen in Figure 8. Figure 8 shows the results for all subjects. In the case of a high correct answer rate, it is possible that there were more cases when the mean speed was within the range of the standard deviation (indicated by a black bar graph) than in the opposite case (indicated by a gray bar).

We surmised that the correct answer rate rose if the finger speed of other people was close to a subject's own finger speed. In that case, we assumed the optimal speed to be the subject's own writing speed.

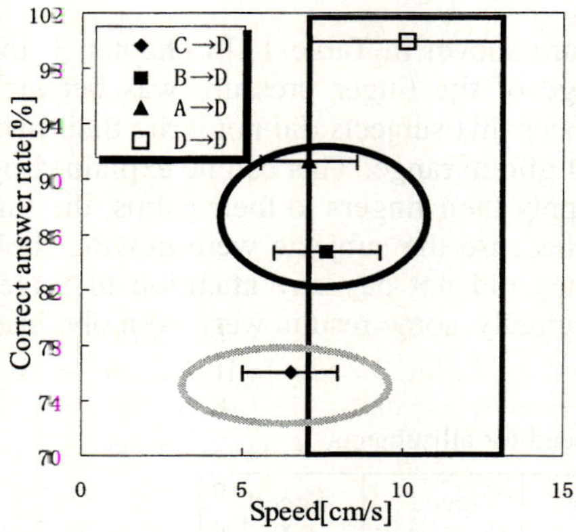


**Fig. 7.** Relationship between speed and correct answer rate in the case of subject D

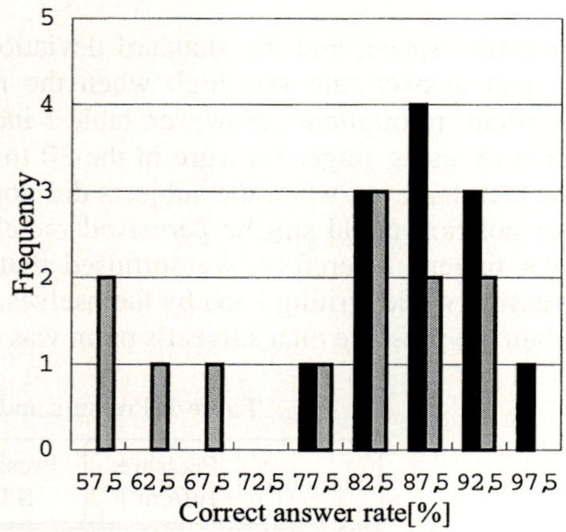


**Fig. 8.** Relationship between correct answer rate and frequency for all subjects

## 5 Demonstration of Optimal Finger Speed

Here, we examined the hypothesis stated in chapter 4. The correct answer rate was measured when kana was written on the palm by using the subject's own finger speed which had been previously measured in chapter 4.

### 5.1 Experimental Setup and Method

A device, made by using two pulse motors, was able to move a pointer two-dimensionally across a palm, as shown in Figure 9. This device could write kana on the palm at the same speed which had been measured in chapter 4. Six non-impaired subjects were deafened and blinded temporarily by using stopples and eyeshades, and all subjects had undergone the experiments described in chapter 4. After writing one of 46 kana on a subject's palm, each subject was asked to determine which kana had been written.

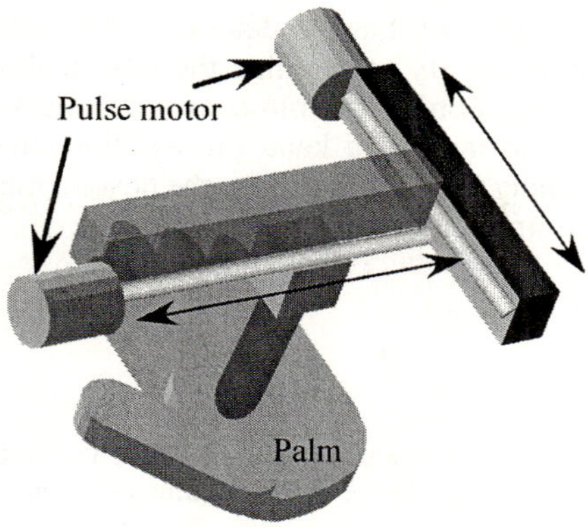


**Fig. 9.** Demonstration device

### 5.2 Results and Discussion

Table 2 shows the correct answer rate for each subject. Table 2 also shows the highest correct answer rate when kana was written by others in chapter 3. It was found that most of the correct answer rates in this experiment were higher than the rates obtained when others wrote kana. In view of this, we surmised that the subject's own speed was optimal for writing kana on the palm. Incidentally, it was also found that the kana which all of the subjects misunderstood were the same kana. Therefore, we supposed that the particular features of each kana had to be emphasized in order to discriminate the kana easily.

**Table 2.** Comparison of correct answer rate between this experiment and experiment in chapter 3

| | This experiment | Experiment in chapter 3 |
|---|---|---|
| | Correct answer[%] | |
| A | 84.78 | 84.78 |
| B | 93.48 | 91.30 |
| D | 67.39 | 91.30 |
| E | 80.43 | 63.04 |
| G | 97.83 | 91.30 |
| H | 95.65 | 93.48 |

## 6 Summary and Problems to Be Resolved

We attempted to determine which presentation condition most facilitated the correct recognition of written kana. The results are summarized as follows:

- The optimal pressure could not be determined.
- Regarding speed, it was postulated that each subject's own speed was optimal, within the range of 4-11cm/s.

To begin with, future studies will have to determine the optimal pressure for writing kana. Next, it will be necessary to examine the best method of emphasizing the unique features of each kana in order to avoid confusion over kana whose shapes are similar. Once we succeed in making a kana presentation device which meets our goals, we would hope to apply that technology to the development of a comprehensive system that will improve communication for the deaf-blind.

## References

1. Wada, C., Wada, Y.: A proposal for a communication device with a finger and a palm for the deaf-blind. Proc.10th International Conference on Human Computer Interaction, volume 4 (2003) 281-285

## Appendix

The list of kana (a standard Japanese writing system).

**Consonant**

**Vowel**

| | | /k/ | /s/ | /t/ | /n/ | /h/ | /m/ | /y/ | /r/ | /w/ |
|---|---|---|---|---|---|---|---|---|---|---|
| /a/ | ア | カ | サ | タ | ナ | ハ | マ | ヤ | ラ | ワ |
| /i/ | イ | キ | シ | チ | ニ | ヒ | ミ | | リ | |
| /u/ | ウ | ク | ス | ツ | ヌ | フ | ム | ユ | ル | |
| /e/ | エ | ケ | セ | テ | ネ | ヘ | メ | | レ | |
| /o/ | オ | コ | ソ | ト | ノ | ホ | モ | ヨ | ロ | ヲ |

| /nn/ |
|---|
| ン |

# A Tactile Display System in the Use of a PC for Individuals Who Are Deaf-Blind

Masatsugu Sakajiri[1,4], Shinich Okada[1], Kazuyuki Ito[2], Atsushi Sadakane[3], Naoki Sugiyama[3], Hideo Tomita[3], and Tohru Ifukube[4]

[1] National Institute of Vocational Rehabilitation, Japan
[2] Research Institute National Rehabilitation Center for people with Disabilities, Japan
[3] College of Science and Engineering, Tokyo Denki University, Japan
[4] Research Center for Advanced Science and Technology, University of Tokyo, Japan

**Abstract.** A purpose of this study is to develop a sensory aid system for totally deaf-blind persons who are not Braille users. We developed a tactile display system and also designed special font style for the display. In this paper, we evaluated the font style as well as the tactile display from a viewpoint of the character identification test. It is found that the percent correct answer was more than 90% when ninety-three characters were presented onto the display. This result suggests that it is enough to enable the deaf-blind to understand the presented characters using our tactile display system instead of the Braille display.

## 1 Introduction

Although sign languages, finger-spelling method, a print-on-palm method, a tadoma method, and a finger Braille have been used as the deaf-blind communication tools, it is restricted and difficult for the deaf-blind without an interpreter. Furthermore, the acquired deaf-blind are likely to only choose a print-on-palm method because it is difficult for them to master the other communication skills. Therefore, it was almost impossible for these persons to access communication tools such as an Internet, an e-mail, and a printed Braille. The communication aids for these people have been expected to be designed using advanced information technologies. Though there were some preceded studies (1), (2) regarding the tactile display for the blind, there was no device for the deaf-blind PC-users respect a Braille display. We have designed a tactile display system that can present Japanese kana-characters instead of Braille. In this paper, we described the tactile display system and evaluated the font style designed for the display from a viewpoint of a character recognition test by the deaf-blind.

## 2 Tactile Display System

Figure 1 shows the tactile display system that we proposed. This system consists of a tactile display unit, a mobile phone type switch and a cursor key, all of which are connected to a PC as shown in Figure 2. The tactile display is constructed by ten tactile display modules (Graphic cell SC5) developed by KGS Corporation in Japan.

K. Miesenberger et al. (Eds.): ICCHP 2004, LNCS 3118, pp. 1129–1136, 2004.

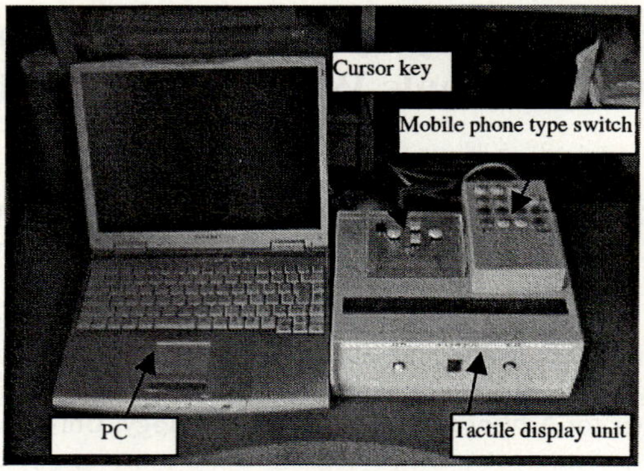


**Fig. 1.** The tactile display system. This system consists of a tactile display unit, a mobile phone type switch and a cursor key, all of which are connected to a PC as shown in Figure 2. The display has 8 x 80 pins arranged at 3 mm intervals in a matrix.

Each module contains 8 x 8 pins arranged at 3mm intervals so that the hole pins are arranged at 3 mm intervals in a matrix (8 x 80). Since 8 x 8 dots are used for each character presented on the display, it can simultaneously present ten characters.

The tactile display shown in Figure 2 is presenting characters "DISPLAY". An underline of "S" represents a cursor, and the end of character on the display represents a space. The details of the fonts displayed on the tactile fonts are described in the chapter 3 and 4. Although the mobile phone type switch was designed in different way of a keyboard, it is useful to write or to edit sentences. How to use this switch to input the characters is as follows. When you press a "2" key, "2" is shown on the tactile display When you press the 2 key again, "A" is shown on it instead of "2". When you press the 2 key again, "B" is shown on it. When you press the 2 key again, "C" is shown on it. When you press the 2 key again, "2" is shown on it again. When the character that

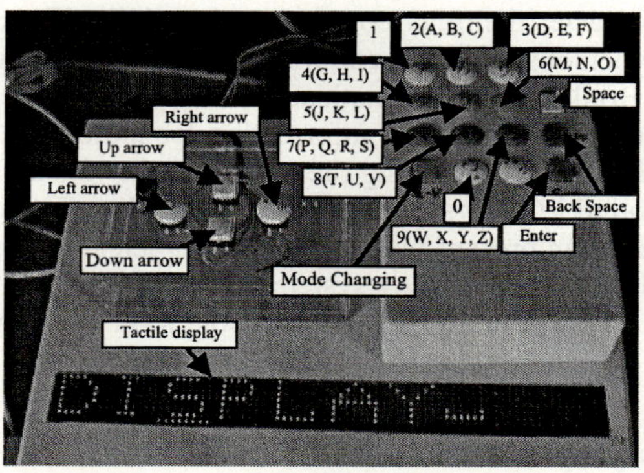


**Fig. 2.** The tactile display unit, the mobile phone type switch and the cursor key. The tactile display has 8 x 80 pins arranged at 3 mm intervals in a matrix. Since a character shown on the display uses 8 x 8 dots, it is able to show ten characters on it. The tactile display in this figure shows "DISPLAY". A under bar under "S" is a cursor, and the last character shown on the tactile display illustrates a space.

you would like to settle is shown on it, you have to press an Enter key to settle. Then the character is inputted on the word processing software in the PC and is shown on it. Before you press the Enter key, any letter is not settled.

How to input “DIS” is as follows. On inputting “D”, you press a 3 key twice. Then “D” is shown on it. Since you press the Enter key to settle, “D” is inputted as shown on the first character of the tactile display in Figure2. To input “I”, you press a 4 key four times. Then “I” is shown on it. You press the Enter key to settle, then “I” is inputted after “D”. On inputting “S”, you press a 7 key four times. Then “S” is shown on it. You press the Enter key, then “S” is inputted after “I”. From these operations, “DIS” is inputted on the word processing soft wear in the PC and is shown on the tactile display. In the same way, you are able to input “PLAY” which is the rest of the characters shown on the tactile display in figure 2.

A line under “S” on it is a mark of the cursor. You can move the cursor by pressing a Right Arrow key or a Left Arrow key. When you press a Back Space key, the character before the cursor is deleted. A symbol that is the end of “DISPLAY” on it is the mark of a space. When you press a Space key, a space is inputted. The mobile phone type switch has three inputting modes that are the Japanese kana-characters, the Arabic numeric (including the alphabet) and the symbols. The Japanese kana-characters is a kind of Japanese phonogram. The symbols are ASCII•American Standard Code for Information Interchange• characters which do not include the Arabic numeric and the alphabet. You can change these three modes by pressing the Mode Changing key. All keys on the PC are also available. Since one of Japanese screen reading software which name was WinVoice was improved to connect this system, the display is able to show characters on the tactile display. You can use the PC in full keyboard by using this tactile display system instead of the Braille display.

## 3 Designs of Fonts

We designed the fonts of ASCII code (JIS X 0201 Roman standardized in Japan). The characters in this standard consist of the Japanese kana-characters, the alphabet, Arabic numerals and the other characters for example a dot, an asterisk, round brackets, and a tilde and so on.

The tactile display was designed 8 x 80 dots in a matrix to present ten characters on it. Though a character can use 8 x 8 dots in a matrix, we designed a font in 7 x 7 dots in a matrix. The two reasons are as follows. First, since the under cursor which is shown in Figure 2 is used on the tactile display; the lowest line is occupied to present it. Second, spaces both side of a character are needed to distinguish adjacent characters.

All designed fonts are illustrated in Figure A-1 and Figure A-2 in the appendix. Figure A-1 illustrates “A”, “B”, “C”, “D”, “E”, “F”, “G”, “H”, “I”, “J”, “K”, “L”, “M”, “N”, “O”, “P”, “Q”, “R”, “S”, “T”, “U”, “V”, “W”, “X”, “Y”, “Z”, “0”, “1”, “2”, “3”, “4”, “5”, “6”, “7”, “8” and “9”. Figure A-2 illustrates the symbols which are “!”, “#”, “$”, “%”, “&”, “(“, “)”, “*”, “,”, “.”, “-”, “/”, “:”, “;”, “?”, “@”, “[“, “]”, “^”, “_”, “{“, “|”, “}”, “~”, “’”, “””, “<”, “>”, “+”, “=” and “\”. The fonts of the Japanese kana-characters and another character standardized only in Japan are not mentioned in this paper. The small letters of the alphabet are omitted due to limitation of space.

## 4 Evaluations of Fonts

### 4.1 Subjects and Methods

Subjects are three males whose ages are from twenty-two to twenty-four years old. They have no difficulty in their tactile sense.

The tactile display system was used as an experiment device to present the font sets. The four font sets that are used in this evaluation are as follows:

(1) The capital alphabets: twenty-six characters shown in Figure A-1
(2) Arabic numerals: ten characters shown in Figure A-1
(3) The symbols standardized in ASCII code: thirty-one characters shown in Figure A-2
(4) Above three font sets and the small alphabet: ninety-three characters in total

Processes of an evaluation are as follows:

(1) The subject put on the eye mask.
(2) All characters of the font set were presented to subject once. The tester told the subject the correct name of the character to let the subject know all characters of the font set.
(3) All characters of the font set were presented to subject at random. The subject answered the name of the font. The time from presenting the font until the subject replying the answer was measured. The tester let the subject know the correct answer after the subject replied the answer.
(4) Above process was repeated five times.

All answers of the subjects were recorded and all the time required to answer was measured. Since the subjects were not instructed how to touch the tactile display, they were able to use any fingers.

### 4.2 Results and Discussion

Figure 3 shows the evaluation results of the font recognition in the case of capital alphabets. As shown in the figure, the percent correct answer of the both subjects is more than ninety percent. However, the average time required to answer showed about two times longer in the subject A than the subject B.

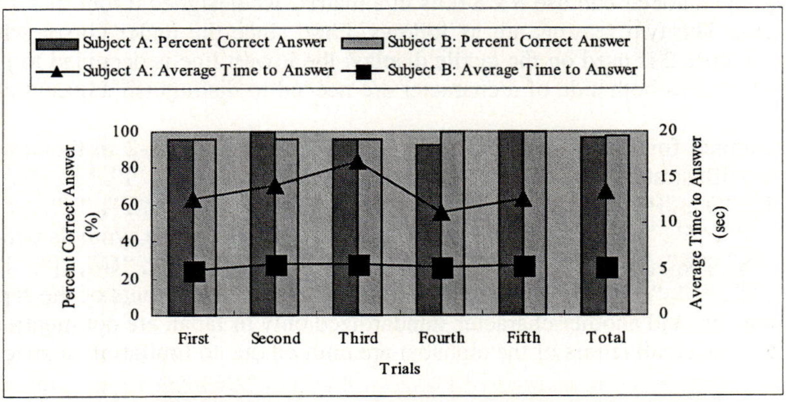


**Fig. 3.** Evaluation Results of the Font Recognition in the Capital Alphabet.

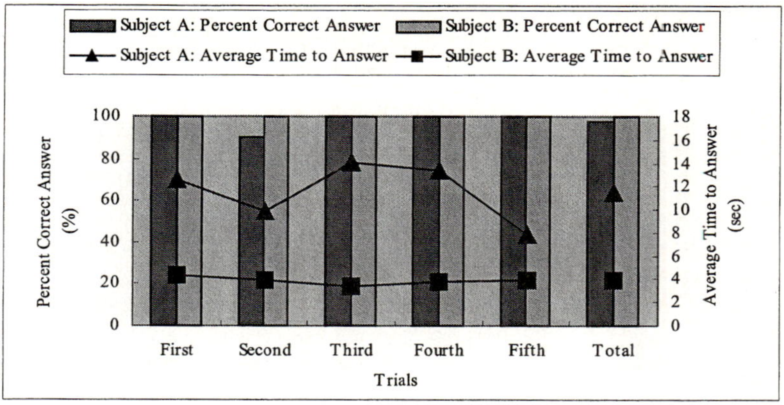


**Fig. 4.** Evaluation Results of the Font Recognition in Arabic Numerals.

Figure 4 shows the evaluation results of the font recognition in the case of Arabic numerals. The percent correct answer of the both subjects is almost 100%.

Figure 5 shows the evaluation results of the font recognition in the case of symbols. The percent correct answer of the subject B is close to 100%. On the other hand, that of the subject C is under 90% in average. With the regard to the contents of the mistakes, subject C tended to confuse in brackets, for example he mistook the square bracket for the round bracket twice. He also mistook the round bracket for the angle bracket. These mistakes of subject C occupy 41% of all mistakes.

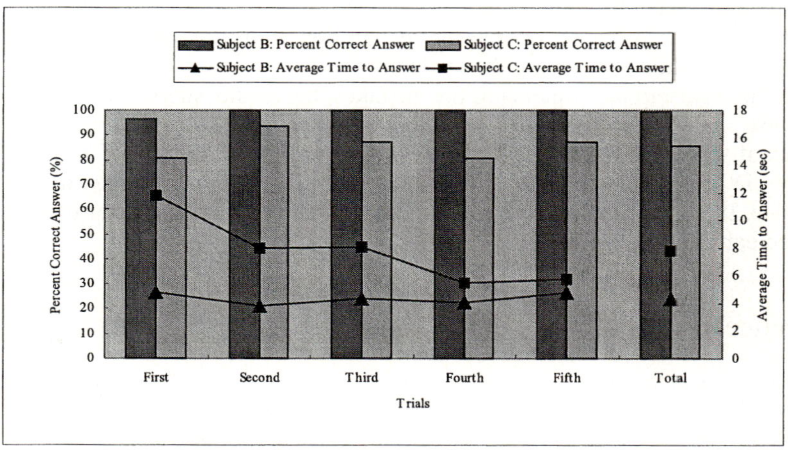


**Fig. 5.** Evaluation Results of the Font Recognition in Symbols.

Figure 6 shows the evaluation results of the font recognition in the case of all characters. Though the number of all characters is ninety-three, the percent correct answer in total is more than 90% for both in subject B and in subject C. This result shows that it is enough to understand the displayed characters using our tactile display system. However, some researchers reported that the function of the tactile sense deteriorates

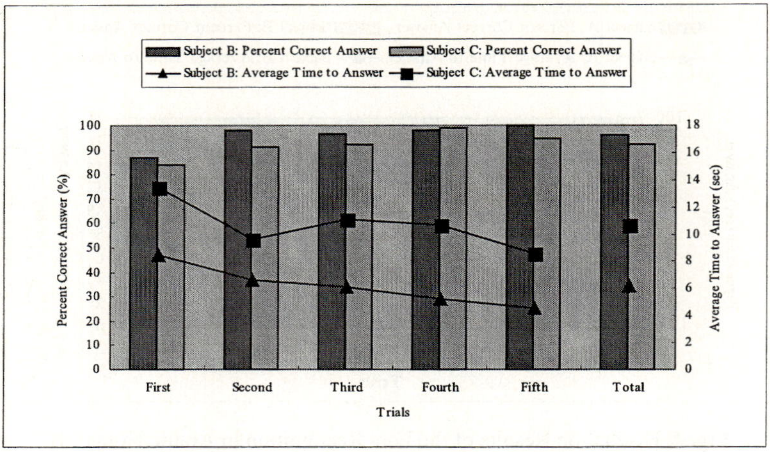


**Fig. 6.** Evaluation Results of the Font Recognition in All Characters.

with aging (3), (4). Our previous study also shows that the recognition ability of the tactile fonts of the elderly is lower than that of the young. It also shows the learning effect of the elderly is lower than that of the young (5). Since the subjects in this report include the elderly, other measurements including a special training program will be needed.

The reason why the correct answer of subject C shown in Figure 6 is higher than that of Figure 5 is seemed to be because Subject C has had a few experiences before this evaluation tests. The other subjects were also able to confirm the correct answer on each process. It is suggested that the recognition ability of subject C increased by learning effect while performing the evaluation tests.

With the regard to the contents of the mistakes, the results show as follows. Subject B mistook "B" for "8" twice. Subject B also mistook "D" for "0" twice. The other mistakes of subject B were once. Subject C mistook "5" for "S" twice. Subject C also mistook "D" for "O" twice and "O" for "c" twice. The other mistakes of subject C were once. It is supposed that we need to improve the design of several fonts that are observed conspicuous mistakes.

## References


1. T. Watanabe and M. Kobayashi: Prototypes of the electronic tactile drawing system for blind persons, TVRSJ, Vol.7, No.1, pp.87-94, 2002. (In Japanese)
2. M. Shinohara, Y. Shimizu and A. Mochizuki: Three-dimensional tactile display for the blind, IEEE Transactions Rehabilitation Engineering, Vol.6, No.3, pp.249-256, 1998.
3. D. Kenshalo: Somesthetic sensitivity in young and elderly humans, Journal of Gerontology, Vol.41, No.6, pp.732-742, 1986.
4. J. Stevens: Aging and spatial acuity of touch, Journal of Gerontology, Vol.47, No.1, pp.35-40, 1992.
5. M. Sakajiri, K. Ito, S. Okada, H. Tomita and T. Ifukube: A development of the tactile display system to show the characters for individuals who are deaf-blind, Journal of Human Interface Society, Vol.5, No.4, pp.455-464, 2003. (In Japanese)

# Appendix

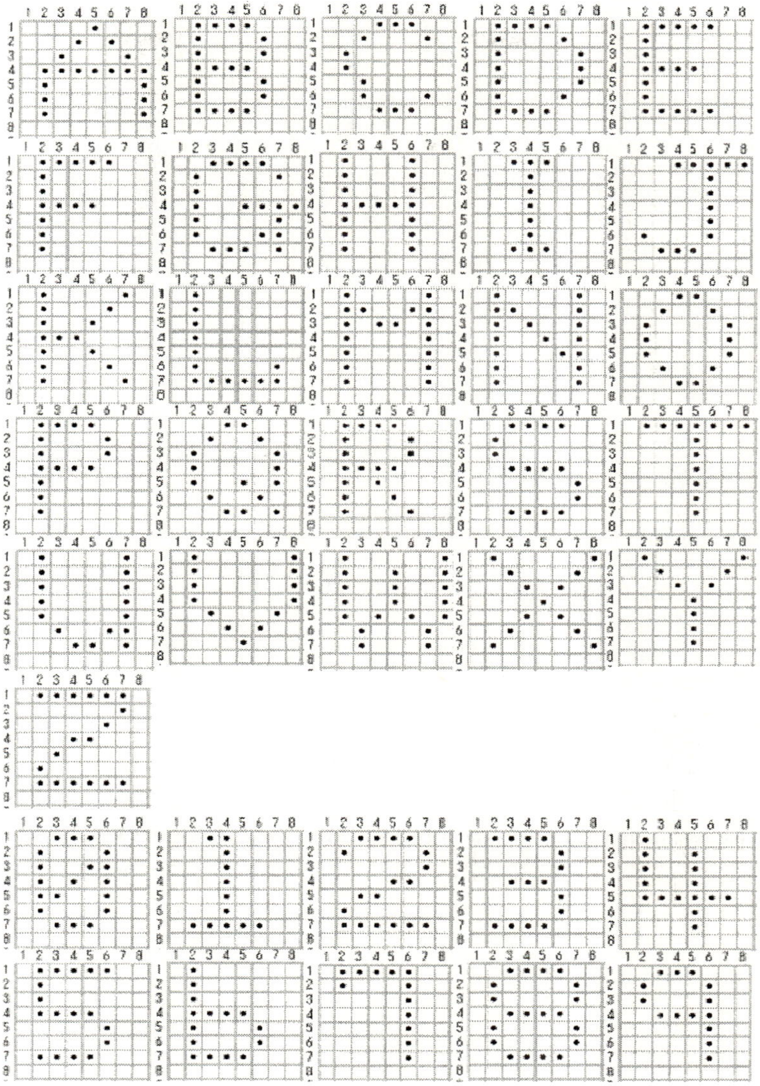

**Fig. A-1.** This figure illustrates "A", "B", "C", "D", "E", "F", "G", "H", "I", "J", "K", "L", "M", "N", "O", "P", "Q", "R", "S", "T", "U", "V", "W", "X", "Y", "Z", "0", "1", "2", "3", "4", "5", "6", "7", "8" and "9".

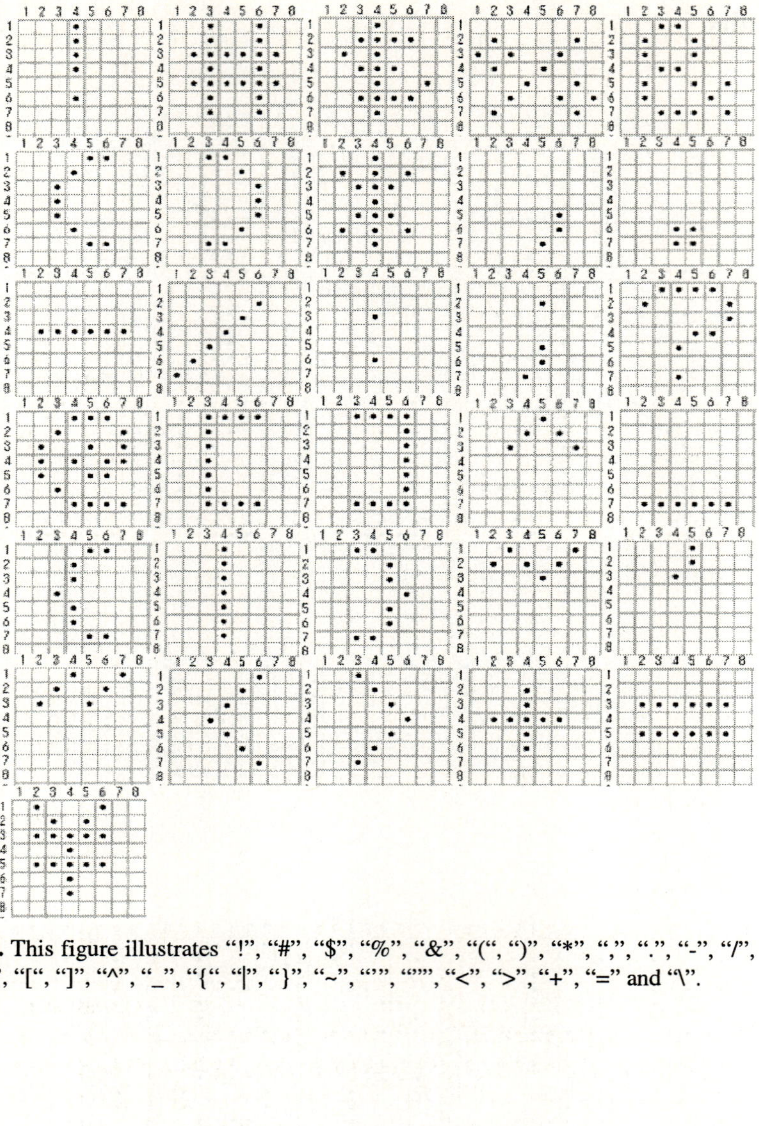

**Fig. A-2.** This figure illustrates “!”, “#”, “$”, “%”, “&”, “(“, “)”, “*”, “,”, “.”, “-”, “/”, “:”, “;”, “?”, “@”, “[“, “]”, “^”, “_”, “{“, “|”, “}”, “~”, “’”, “””, “<”, “>”, “+”, “=” and “\”.

# Approaches to Using a Wireless Mobile Terminal to Help Severely Hearing Impaired People

Sangman Moh

Dept. of Internet Engineering, Chosun University
375 Seoseok-dong, Dong-gu, Gwangju, 501-759, Korea
smmoh@chosun.ac.kr

**Abstract.** In this paper, new technology-adaptive approaches to using a wireless mobile terminal are presented in order to help severely hearing impaired people, which are remote human translation, remote server translation, and mobile terminal translation. The three step-by-step approaches are to adapt the evolution and feasibility of advanced computer and communication technologies. The first approach can be easily implemented but requires the involvement of human interpreters. The second and third approaches require not only speaker-independent voice recognition but also hand-writing text and sign language recognition. In particular, for the mobile terminal translation scheme, a light-weight, low-power, high-performance, small-sized mobile terminal should be provided to process the computing-centric voice, hand-writing text and sign language recognition on real-time basis. Even though this work is currently at the startup phase, as technology evolves, it will be possible to provide severely hearing impaired people with the context-aware mobile terminals that interpret voice, hand-writing text and sign language on the real-time basis.

## 1 Introduction

In general, severely hearing impaired people communicate with each other by sign languages. Inevitably, however, they have difficulties to communicate with others without visual aids. In order to help them, in recent years, there have been active research activities [1-10]. In order to empower hearing impaired people to benefit from modern technology, hearing improvement devices [5-9] such as a telecommunication adapter between phone and hearing aids have been studied. On the other hand, a remote sign language interpretation system associated with the related sign language translator was introduced with its graphical user interface [10].

In this paper, as a startup phase, we explore new approaches to using a wireless mobile terminal to help the severely hearing impaired people. To adapt the evolution and feasibility of technology, this paper considers three step-by-step approaches: remote human translation, remote server translation, and mobile terminal translation. In the remote human translation, human interpreters at the interpretation center translate the voice and hand-writing text/sign language transmitted from mobile terminals into text/sign language and voice, respectively, and then the translated results are transmitted back to the mobile terminal. In the remote server translation, the overall

K. Miesenberger et al. (Eds.): ICCHP 2004, LNCS 3118, pp. 1137–1143, 2004.

procedure is the same as in the remote human translation scheme except that computer-based machine translation is used instead of human interpreters. In the mobile terminal translation, the wireless mobile terminal itself performs the computing-centric function of automatic machine translation, enabling real-time recognition and translation of voice, hand-writing text and sign language. The first approach can be easily implemented but requires the involvement of human interpreters resulting in financial burden. On the other hand, the mobile terminal translation scheme is currently an implementation challenge in terms of technological complexity and cost.

Notice that mobile camera phones and PDA (Personal Digital Assistant) phones with a camera can be effectively used for the wireless mobile terminals. Fig. 1(a) and 1(b) show a mobile camera phone and a PDA phone with a camera, respectively, which are currently available in the market [11]. The PDA phone shown in Fig. 1(b) supports CDMA-2000 1x (IS-95C) communication. Note here that most of the cameras are rotatable. Nowadays the mobile camera phones are popular in some countries. The PDA phones are sometimes called pocket PC phones by some vendors, and can have wireless LAN interface as well. Even now, the qualified service of real-time video transmission is not guaranteed due to the limited bandwidth but will be possible in the near future (in a few years in some countries).

(a) Camera phone

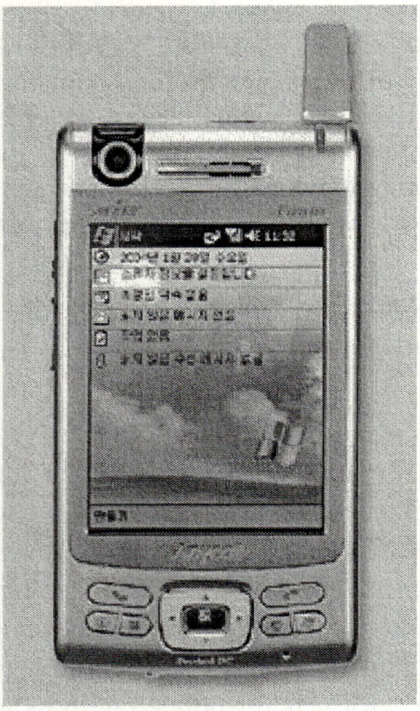

(b) PDA phone with a camera

**Fig. 1.** Wireless mobile terminals available in the market.

The rest of the paper is organized as follows: The remote human translation scheme and its operational procedure are introduced with conceptual figures. Section 3 discusses the remote server translation scheme in terms of major technical issues. The mobile terminal translation scheme and its implementation challenge are presented in Section 4. Finally, conclusion is covered in Section 5.

## 2 Remote Human Translation

The remote human translation involves wireless mobile terminals that severely hearing impaired people use, a remote interpretation system where human interpreters translate the voice and hand-writing text/sign language transmitted from the mobile terminals into text/sign language and voice, respectively, and wireless communication channels. A mobile communication network or a wireless LAN can be used for the wireless communication channels, and a mobile camera phone or a PDA phone with a camera can be used as a wireless mobile terminal.

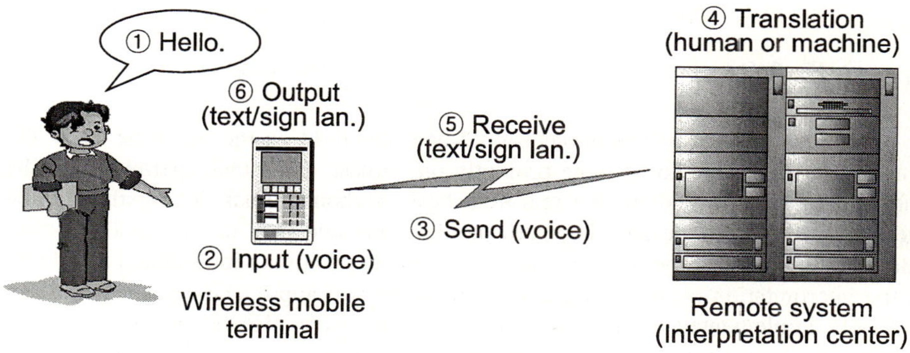


**Fig. 2.** Operational procedure from a person to a severely impaired person.

Fig. 2 shows the consecutive procedure that a severely hearing impaired person with a wireless mobile terminal recognizes the voice a person says. As Fig. 2 reveals, when a person says "Hello," the voice is input to the mobile terminal that the severely hearing impaired person has. The mobile terminal then sends the voice (in fact, electrical signals) to the remote interpretation center where a human interpreter translates the voice into text (ASCII characters) or sign language. Subsequently, the mobile terminal receives the hand-writing text or sign language from the remote system and displays it on the screen.

Fig. 3 shows the reverse case of Fig. 2, where a person recognizes the hand-writing text or sign language that a severely hearing impaired person writes or gestures. When a severely hearing impaired person writes on the touch screen (most PDA phones support the touch screen with a stylus pen), the hand-writing text is input to the mobile terminal as an image. On the other hand, while a severely hearing impaired person gestures, it is required for the partner to take hold of the wireless mobile terminal, and then the sign language is input to the mobile terminal via the attached camera as a video clip. The mobile terminal then sends the video clip consisting of the hand-writing text or sign language to the remote interpretation center where a human interpreter translates the hand-writing text or sign language into voice. Subsequently, the mobile terminal receives the voice from the remote system and speaks it out via its speaker.

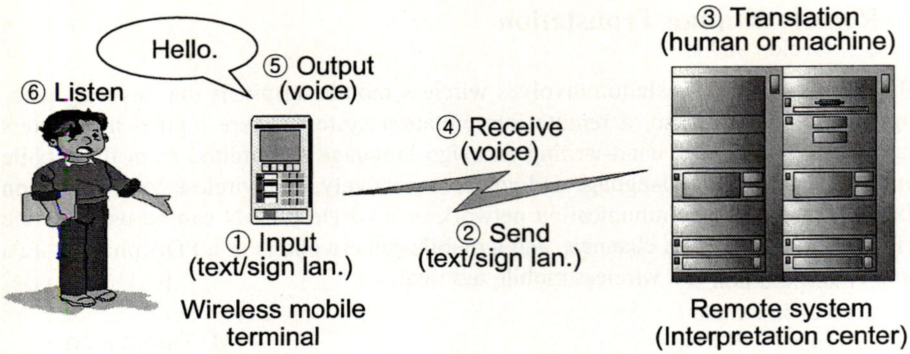


**Fig. 3.** Operational procedure from a severely impaired person to a person.

Since such a series of operations should be carried out on the real-time basis, the human translation has to be done promptly on request. The other operations can be automatically performed on the real-time basis without human involvement. Sine there might be many hearing impaired mobile users and they can request real-time interpretation at the same time, a reasonable number of human interpreters should be in the interpretation center. Compared to the other two approaches, this scheme can be easily implemented in terms of technical complexity. However, this approach requires the involvement of human interpreters resulting in financial burden.

## 3 Remote Server Translation

Like the remote human translation, the remote server translation involves wireless mobile terminals, a remote interpretation system, and wireless communication channels. However, instead of human interpreters, computer-based machine translation is used in the remote interpretation center. In other words, a speaker-independent voice recognizer, a hand-writing text recognizer, and a sign language (gesture) recognizer are used.

When a severely hearing impaired person recognizes the voice a person says as shown in Fig. 2, this approach requires a fancy speaker-independent voice recognizer for translating the voice into text (ASCII characters) or sign language. Noise filtering techniques should be included in the voice recognizer. When a person recognizes the hand-writing text a severely hearing impaired person writes as shown in Fig. 3, a hand-writing text recognizer is required for translating the hand-writing text into voice. On the other hand, when a person recognizes the sign language a severely hearing impaired person gestures as shown in Fig. 3, a sign language (gesture) recognizer is required for translating the sign language into voice.

For real-time service, the computer-based machine translation has to be done promptly on request. Of the three approaches, this scheme can be regarded as intermediate solution in terms of technological complexity. In order to provide severely hearing impaired people with this kind of service, however, it is highly required to further develop and tune novel voice, hand-writing text and sign language recognition systems.

## 4 Mobile Terminal Translation

Unlike other two approaches, the mobile terminal translation does not involve a remote interpretation system. It consists of wireless mobile terminals and wireless communication channels. Strictly speaking, the wireless communication channels are not required in this scheme, but they are used for usual telecommunication. Hence, the translation functions should be performed within the wireless mobile terminal without any remote assistance. In other words, the mobile terminal has to perform the functions of voice recognition, hand-writing text recognition and sign language recognition on the real-time basis. Fig. 4 shows the operational procedures between a severely impaired person and a person in the mobile terminal translation scheme.

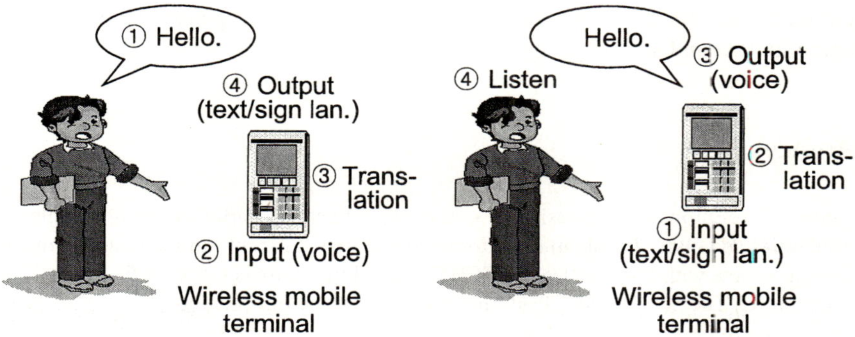


(a) From a person to a severely impaired person

(b) From a severely impaired person to a person

**Fig. 4.** Operational procedure between a severely impaired person and a person.

In the mobile terminal translation, the wireless mobile terminal itself performs the computing-centric function of automatic machine translation, enabling the real-time recognition and translation of voice, hand-writing text and sign language. Therefore, in order to process the computing-centric voice, hand-writing text and sign language recognition on the real-time basis, a light-weight, low-power, high-performance, small-sized mobile terminal should be provided in the mobile terminal translation scheme. This fact makes the mobile terminal translation scheme an implementation challenge with respect to technological complexity and cost. As a matter of fact, at this time the qualified service of real-time video transmission is not guaranteed due to the limited bandwidth but will be possible in the near future (in a few years in some countries).

## 5 Conclusion

In this paper, in order to help severely hearing impaired people, new technology-adaptive approaches to using a wireless mobile terminal have been presented. To adapt the evolution and feasibility of advanced computer and communication technologies, the three step-by-step approaches of remote human translation, remote server translation, and mobile terminal translation have been proposed as a startup phase. While the first approach is easily implemented but requires the involvement of human interpreters resulting in financial burden, the second and third approaches require not only speaker-independent voice recognition but also hand-writing text and sign language recognition. In particular, in order to process the computing-centric voice, hand-writing text and sign language recognition on the real-time basis, a light-weight, low-power, high-performance, small-sized mobile terminal should be provided in the mobile terminal translation scheme.

Even though this work is currently at the startup phase, we believe that it will be a feasible and adaptable solution for severely hearing impaired people. In the near future, as technology evolves, it will be possible to provide severely hearing impaired people with the context-aware mobile terminals that intelligently interpret voice, hand-writing text and sign language on the real-time basis.

## References

1. Buhler, C.: eEurope – eAccessibility – User Participation: Participation of People with Disabilities and Older People in the Information Society. Proc. of 8th Int. Conf. Computers Helping People with Special Needs (ICCHP-2002). Linz, Austria (2002) 3-5
2. Nishioka, T.: The See-through Head Mount Display as the Information Offering Device for the Hearing Impaired Students. Proc. of 8th Int. Conf. Computers Helping People with Special Needs (ICCHP-2002). Linz, Austria (2002) 166-167
3. Solina, F., et al.: Multimedia Dictionary and Synthesis of Sign Language. Added Value to the Quality of Life (Proc. of AAATE). IOS Press (2001) 472-476
4. Oliveira, F., Kobayashi, I., Sugawara, M.: A Multimedia Based Software for Non-Japanese to Learn Japanese Sign Language. Proc. of 8th Int. Conf. Computers Helping People with Special Needs (ICCHP-2002). Linz, Austria (2002) 162-163
5. Bauer, D., Plinge, A., Finke, M.: Towards a Wearable Friction Transposer for Severely Hearing Impaired Persons. Added Value to the Quality of Life (Proc. of AAATE). IOS Press (2001)
6. Plinge, A., Bauer, D., Finke, M.: Intelligibility Enhancement of Human Speech for Severely Hearing Impaired Persons by Dedicated Digital Processing. Added Value to the Quality of Life (Proc. of AAATE). IOS Press (2001)
7. Finke, M., Bauer, D., Plinge, A.: Telecommunication Adapter for Hearing Aid Wearers – with Extensions. Added Value to the Quality of Life (Proc. of AAATE). IOS Press (2001)
8. Bauer, D., Plinge, A., Finke, M.: Selective Phoneme Spotting for Realization of an /s, z, C, t/ Transposer. Proc. of 8th Int. Conf. Computers Helping People with Special Needs (ICCHP-2002). Linz, Austria (2002) 153-161

9. Bauer, D., Plinge, A., Finke, M.: Digital Speech Signal Processing to Compensate Severe Sensory Hearing Deficits: The /s, z, C, t/ Transposer Module in Simulation – An Overview and Examples. Proc. of 8th Int. Conf. Computers Helping People with Special Needs (ICCHP-2002). Linz, Austria (2002) 168-169
10. Minagawa, H., Naito, I., Kato, N., Murakami, H., Ishihara, Y.: The User Interface Design for the Sign Language Translator in a Remote Sign Language Interpretation System. Proc. of 8th Int. Conf. on Computers Helping People with Special Needs (ICCHP-2002). Linz, Austria (2002) 164-165
11. Samsung's digital world, `http://www.samsung.com/` (also at `http://www.anycall.com/`), Apr. 2004.

# A Preparatory Study for Designing Web-Based Educational Materials for the Hearing-Impaired

Miki Namatame[1], Muneo Kitajima[2],
Tomoyuki Nishioka[1], and Fumihiko Fukamauchi[1]

[1] Tsukuba College of Technology, 4-3-15 Amakubo Tsukuba Ibaraki 305-0005 Japan
{miki,nishioka,fhiko}@a.tsukuba-tech.ac.jp
http://www.tsukuba-tech.ac.jp/

[2] National Institute of Advanced Industrial Science and Technology (AIST), 1-1-1 Higashi Tsukuba Ibaraki 305-8566 Japan
kitajima@ni.aist.go.jp
http://staff.aist.go.jp/kitajima.muneo/

**Abstract.** Our aim is to design web-based interactive educational materials for the hearing-impaired based on their interaction style. We describe the results of an eye-tracking experiment that demonstrates behavioral differences between hearing-impaired and hearing persons when using web-based materials. We found that the hearing-impaired exhibited a smaller strategic scan pattern, and shallower and more intuitive text processing. These findings suggest that the design of web-based educational materials, which currently only consider textual or image substitutes for auditory information, is insufficient for the hearing-impaired.

## 1 Introduction

Traditionally, the primary focus of computer-based support for the hearing-impaired relied on computer-generated images of sign language and real-time text annotation. These are the primary means for the hearing-impaired to access auditory information. Examples of such studies include Jensema et al. [3][4] who investigated the use of TV captions for the hearing-impaired. However, we believe that this approach has limited utility considering that only a small portion of the hearing-impaired, 10 to 20%, can use mother-tongue sign language, and the understanding level of textual information of the hearing-impaired is inferior to that of a hearing person's. We have supporting evidence for this claim from our experience in using traditional class materials.

Recently, computer-based support for the hearing-impaired has expanded with the development of a web-based interaction environment. For example, Barman et al. [1] initiated a web-based science program for deaf students called the "SOAR-HIGH Project." The web is a more promising medium for designing educational materials for the hearing-impaired than traditional, less interactive educational media since it allows us to control content presentation. However, our experience in using traditional class materials suggests that the hearing-impaired

K. Miesenberger et al. (Eds.): ICCHP 2004, LNCS 3118, pp. 1144–1151, 2004.

would interact differently with web-based materials than hearing persons. Currently, the issue of how the hearing-impaired interact with the web is inadequately studied. We believe computer-based support for the hearing-impaired will improve when we better understand their interaction with computer-based educational materials. Our study began with detailed observations of how the hearing-impaired use the web by tracking eye movement and hyperlink selections and comparing the results with those of hearing persons.

## 2 Eye-Tracking Experiment

We plan to develop web-based educational materials that will incorporate similar tasks currently performed on the web, including on-line shopping, browsing, information searching, and manipulating objects. Web-based tasks are performed interactively, requiring comprehension of information provided on the computer screen as it relates to the task goal, and the selection of an appropriate action, typically clicking on a link to another page. We suggest that the hearing-impaired would perform these processes differently from hearing persons. In this section, we describe a preparatory study aimed at understanding web-interaction processes of the hearing-impaired by observing their eye movement while performing web-based tasks.

### 2.1 Subjects and Procedure

Three hearing-impaired persons (two males, one female), and three hearing persons (two males, one female) participated in the experiment. Their ages ranged from 18 to 24 years old. All subjects were regular Internet users. None had viewed the web pages used in the study prior to their participation.

Each subject was asked to accomplish a task that included an information search and object manipulation on an experimental web site. At the beginning of each session, the eye-tracking equipment was calibrated. Instructions for the task were relayed to the hearing-impaired subjects using sign language and an A4-size board, and to the hearing subjects using voice and an A4-size board. The tasks were performed on a PC by clicking links on the pages. Subjects' eye movements were measured using a head-mounted eye-tracking system, EMR-HM8 of NAC Inc.

### 2.2 Task

The task was to locate a page that described car model Z4, and to choose a favorite color for it. The subjects were given the following instruction: "*Please choose your favorite color for the car model Z4.*"

The task was performed on an experimental web site modified from an actual automobile web site. Figure 1 illustrates the top page that consisted of five columns, four content columns and one news column, and a field at the bottom of the page. Content columns had a *heading* at the top, a *picture with promotional*

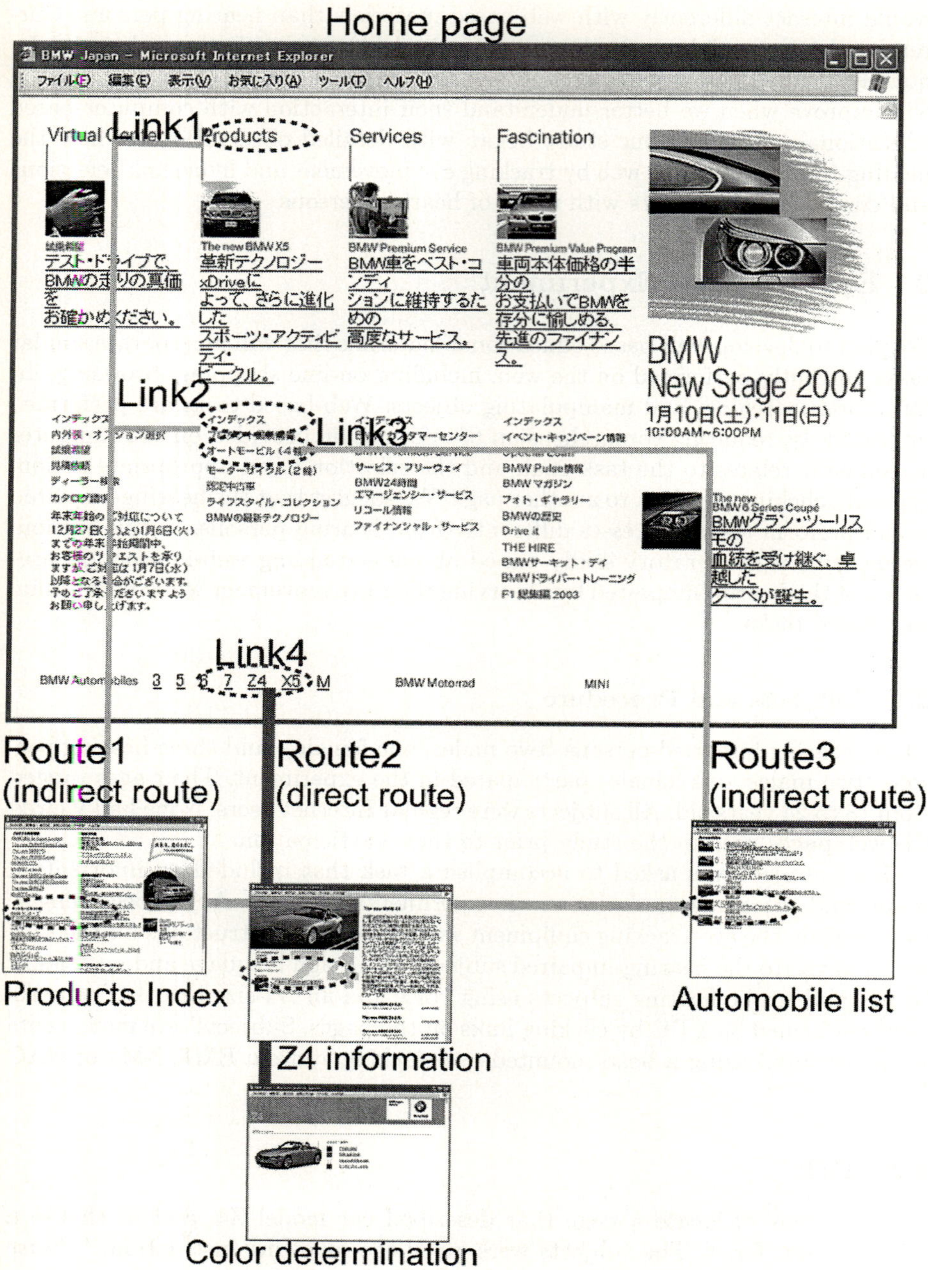


**Fig. 1.** Experiment task and routes to the "Color Determination page".

*text* in the middle, and a *list of topics* at the bottom. An important feature of this specific page was that the contents were organized vertically. Successful task performance required correct understanding of the page layout since the column boundaries were not clearly defined.

To reach the color determination page, the subjects should follow one of three routes. When the subject selected a wrong link, however, an error page was returned and they were forced to press the "Back" button of the browser (or the back button on the page) to begin again.

**Route 1** consisted of selecting either Link 1, which is the heading of the second column labeled Products or selecting Link 2 in the topic list labeled by Index under the Products heading, both of which lead to the correct intermediate page, **Products Index**. This route is considered an indirect route because it requires comprehension of the meaning of the label to select on the top page. To select one of these links, the subject must infer that the term *Products* or *Index* under the *Products* heading implies *car model*, which is part of the task description. The subject should then select the BMW Z4 on the **Products Index** page to open the **Z4 Information** page where the color combination is to be selected to accomplish the subtask. These two selections, selecting BMW Z4 and color combination, are trivial because both are part of the task description.

**Route 2** consists of selecting Link 4 in *the model-name field* labeled by Z4, which leads to the **Z4 Information** page. This route is considered a direct route because there is no inference required of the subjects to select the link.

**Route 3** is an indirect route, consisting of selection of Link 3 labeled by automobile in the topic list under the Products heading, followed by selection of the BMW Z4 link on the **Automobile List** page. This follows the **Z4 Information** page.

## 3 Results

Table 1 displays trial number, time to select a link, and the property of the selected item for the hearing-impaired (Subjects A, B, and C) and the hearing (Subjects D, E, and F). Figure 2 identifies the order of link selections. From these we derive the following results.

- Subject A (hearing-impaired): The time required to complete the task was 3'15" with 16 errors. Most of the selection times were short; of 17 selections, 13 took less than 10 seconds. The order of selection looked horizontal, suggesting that the subject didn't understand the structure of the page. The subject finally selected Link 4, the direct **Route 2**.
- Subjects B and C (hearing-impaired): Both subjects took the direct route. The times required to complete the task were 2'18" and 3'10", with 9 and 3 errors, respectively.
- Subjects D, E and F ( hearing): The times required to complete the task were 53", 1'26", and 1'14", with 0, 2, and 1 errors, respectively. These results were consistently better than those of the hearing-impaired. Subject D took the direct route, while the other subjects took the indirect routes.

**Table 1.** Results of link selections. Subjects A, B, and C are hearing-impaired. Subjects D, E, and F are hearing persons.

| | Time | Selected Item | | Time | Selected Item | | Time | Selected Item |
|---|---|---|---|---|---|---|---|---|
| | Subject A | | | Subject B | | | Subject C | |
| 1 | 0:16:32 | Picture | 1 | 0:41:28 | Picture | 1 | 0:56:40 | Content |
| 2 | 0:03:17 | Picture | 2 | 0:17:48 | Topic Index | 2 | 0:14:24 | Picture |
| 3 | 0:05:21 | Picture | 3 | 0:08:24 | Topic | 3 | 0:40:10 | Heading |
| 4 | 0:07:05 | Topic | 4 | 0:14:10 | Topic | 4 | 1:09:38 | **Link4:Z4** |
| 5 | 0:03:23 | Topic | 5 | 0:22:32 | Picture | | | |
| 6 | 0:04:16 | Picture | 6 | 0:01:36 | Picture | | Subject D | |
| 7 | 0:05:04 | Topic | 7 | 0:00:34 | Picture | 1 | 0:53:56 | **Link4:Z4** |
| 8 | 0:05:40 | Topic | 8 | 0:03:14 | Topic | | Subject E | |
| 9 | 0:02:51 | Picture | 9 | 0:02:10 | Topic | 1 | 0:38:38 | Topic |
| 10 | 0:03:58 | Topic | 10 | 0:06:24 | **Link4:Z4** | 2 | 0:35:24 | Picture |
| 11 | 0:03:09 | Topic | | | | 3 | 0:05:23 | **Link1:Heading** |
| 12 | 0:28:17 | Topic | | | | | Subject F | |
| 13 | 0:38:04 | Heading | | | | 1 | 1:05:50 | Heading |
| 14 | 0:04:33 | Topic | | | | 2 | 0:04:10 | **Link2:Topic Index** |
| 15 | 0:08:14 | Topic | | | | | | |
| 16 | 0:15:11 | Topic Index | | | | | | |
| 17 | 0:07:11 | **Link4:Z4** | | | | | | |

Compared to the hearing, the hearing-impaired were more error prone, spent less time per link selection, and consistently chose the direct route to the goal.

Next, we present the results concerning eye-fixation patterns. Figure 3 displays eye-fixation patterns from two of the six subjects. The left figure plots Subject A's eye fixations and the right plots Subject D's. The circles correspond to the positions on which the subjects' eyes fixated. The circle size is proportional to the duration of fixation. By observing the figures, we found the following features:

- Subject D's fixation times were significantly longer than those of Subject A. A distribution of fixation times revealed about 75% of Subject A's fixations were shorter than 200 msec and about 40% of Subject D's fixations were between 200 and 400 msec.
- Subject D's scanning paths looked vertical, but those of Subject A didn't show a coherent pattern.

From the analysis of the eye movement and link selection data described above, we suggest that there are two aspects where the performance of the hearing-impaired significantly differed from that of the hearing subjects. First, scan paths of the hearing-impaired were not as strategic as those of the hearing. Second, the level of textual information used by the hearing-impaired was shallower than that used by the hearing subjects. In other words, they seemed to understand the textual information intuitively, rather than with the deep knowledge associated with the textual information.

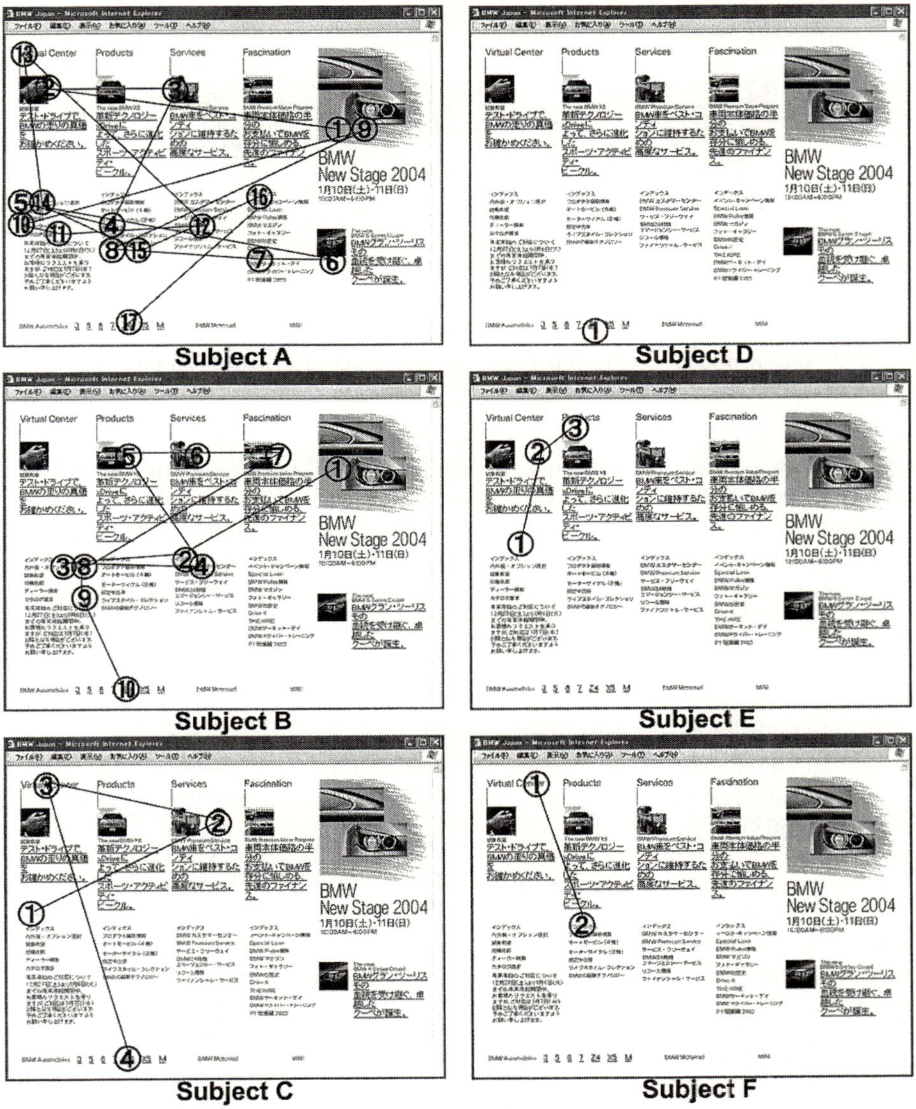


**Fig. 2.** Order of link selections. Left column: Hearing-impaired. Right column: Hearing.

## 4 Issues in Designing Web-Based Educational Materials for the Hearing-Impaired

Designers of web-based educational materials for the hearing-impaired should refer to web design guidelines from W3C's WAI and the US Government. W3C's WAI recommends that the web should provide equivalent alternatives to auditory

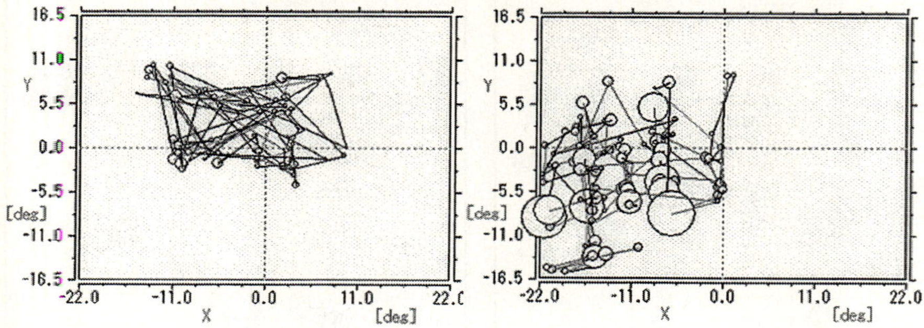


**Fig. 3.** Fixation points on the top page. Left: Subject A (Hearing-impaired). Right: Subject D (Hearing).

and visual content for the hearing-impaired by describing the sound of auditory content and providing non-text equivalents of text. The US Government, Section 508, suggests that the web should attach synchronized captions for hearing-impaired people, such as audio, video, and multimedia material.

These guidelines suggest that providing alternative information to audio is the key for web accessibility for the hearing-impaired [5]:

- Provide equivalent alternatives to auditory and visual content (W3C).
- Describe the sound of auditory content (W3C).
- Provide non-text equivalents of text (W3C).
- Attach the synchronized caption for hearing-impaired people in the case of audio material, video material, and multimedia material (US Government Section 508).

Another criteria useful for designing good web pages is suggested by Ivory et al.[2] Guidelines for operationalizing web design are unclear, so the methodology to derive statistical models from expert-rated empirical data has developed. However, these criteria would have limited utility when designing web pages for the hearing-impaired because they have nothing to do with special needs of the hearing-impaired. Rather, these are supposed to be dealt with by the superordinate guidelines.

Our experiments clearly demonstrate that the hearing-impaired interaction style differs from that of hearing persons, thus the current use of guidelines for the hearing-impaired is seriously limited. Specific guidelines that also consider behavioral characteristics for the hearing-impaired are warranted. If new guidelines are established, they should have applicability for those with similar behavioral characteristics as the hearing-impaired. The currently used guidelines only concern one aspect of web-based interaction, namely, substitution of audio information. Our results suggest this is not sufficient. Guidelines for the hearing-impaired that consider their behavioral characteristics is warranted, and, if established, should have applicability for those with similar behavioral characteristics as the hearing-impaired.

## 5 Conclusions

1. *Scan paths of the hearing-impaired were not as strategic as those of the hearing subjects.*
   The strategic movements that searched for the desired information were conducted by viewing the category titles on a page in order, and seeing the characters in category groups sequentially from the top. Many strategic movements were observed in the hearing subjects, but not in the hearing-impaired subjects.
2. *The hearing-impaired had lower text comprehension than the hearing subjects.*
   Most of the hearing subjects used category information, but all of the hearing-impaired used direct information.

The preliminary eye-tracking experiment confirmed that the hearing-impaired interact with the web differently than the hearing persons. More thorough study with an increased number of subjects and wider range of web-based tasks will be needed to derive useful guidelines for the hearing-impaired.

## References

1. Barman, C.R., and Stockton, J.D., "An Evaluation of the SOAR-HIGH Project: A Web-Based Science Program for Deaf Students", *American Annals of Deaf*, **147**, pp. 5–10 (2002).
2. Ivory, M.Y., Sinha, R.R., and Hearst, M.A., "Empirically validated web page design metrics", *Proceedings of the SIGCHI conference on Human factors in computing systems*, pp. 53–60 (2001).
3. Jensema, C.J., Sharkawy, S.E., Danturthi, R.S., Burch, R., and Hsu, D., "Eye Movement Patterns of Captioned Television Viewers", *American Annals of Deaf*, **145**, pp. 275–285 (2000).
4. Jensema, C.J., Danturthi, R.S., and Burch, R., "Time Spent Viewing Captions on Television Programs", *American Annals of Deaf*, **145**, pp. 464–468 (2000).
5. Paciello, M.G., "Web Accessibility for People with Disabilities", CMP Books (2000).

# FLIPPS: Fingertip Stimulation for Improved Speechreading

Hans-Heinrich Bothe, Ali F. Mohamad, and Martin R. Jensen

Technical University of Denmark, Oersted-DTU, Bygning 348,
DK-2800 Kgs. Lyngby, Denmark
hhb@oersted.dtu.dk

**Abstract.** FLIPPS is a new hand-hold tactile stimulation device developed for the improvement of speechreading conversation with or amongst hearing-impaired persons. It makes additional speech information available through multiple fingertip stimulation using power-balanced frequency bands for the vibrator stimulation. FLIPPS is battery-powered, so that it may be used in daily life conversation. The small size allows for pocket use. First field tests indicate the applicability of the device. At the moment, a prototype hardware realization is at hand, which allows for parameter optimization and for further field tests.

## 1 Introduction

Hearing-impaired people use *speechreading* or lip-reading, as it is commonly known, for better communication with each other or with people having normal hearing abilities. The goal is to read and to understand visible articulatory movements of a communication partner such as the movements of lips and tongue including recognition of gestural cues, facial expressions and body postures. The worse the impairment becomes, the more they need to understand visual signals in order to compensate for their hearing-disability. Hearing-impaired also miss out information through the visual modality. A thumb rule proposed by hearing-impaired communities states that only approximately 30% of the speech signal can be recovered by this process, whereas the rest must be guessed from the speech context. The reasons for this are the ambiguity of visual articulatory movements in combination with a large number of guttural or post-guttural articulatory movements that are only vaguely visible in the speaker's face. The articulation of phonemes such as /p/, /b/, or /m/ creates similar visual sensations yielding to the same perception, and phonemes such as /g/, /k/ or /h/ do not significantly change the facial movements of a speaker at all. Furthermore, detailed knowledge of the language and of articulatory movements is important for good speechreading results.

The intelligibility of speech signals is in general increased when several senses are simultaneously stimulated. Multimodal perceptual phenomena are well known, and they have been described by a variety of scientific disciplines, such as cognitive science, perceptual psychology, or neurology. It is, for instance, regular though subcon-

K. Miesenberger et al. (Eds.): ICCHP 2004, LNCS 3118, pp. 1152–1159, 2004.

scious behaviour to turn the head towards a speaker's face when background noise dominates an acoustic speech signal. The auditory perception of the noisy speech signal improves by observing the facial movements. Such phenomena have impressively been explained by neurophysiologists, who investigated single neuron responses in various parts of animal brains to uni- or multimodal stimulation (e.g., [1]). When stimuli from different modalities are combined, multimodal enhancement of the neuron activities results in a response that often far exceeds the sum of the activities evoked by the individual stimuli.

These results support heuristic investigations on assistive tactile aids, which can significantly improve visual speech perception when the auditory modality fails. It is necessary to control such devices by suitable acoustic features and to present tactile stimuli to the receiving person in a way, which allows for a reasonably good distinction by training a respective auditory-tactile substitution.

## 2 Tactile Stimulation

The idea to support the process of speechreading with the help of a tactile assistive aid is motivated by the success of the Tadoma method of speechreading [2, 3]. Tadoma is a natural vibro-tactile method. It is mainly used for the communication with deaf-blind persons, who perceive articulatory movements and actions that occur during the production of speech with the help of their fingers and hand by touching the speakers face and neck. The great success of Tadoma has initiated different technical tactile aids, which are able to convey certain information about a speech signal or the acoustic environment to the user.

At present, there are diverse tactile aids commercially available, which support speechreading by providing extra information that is visually not available. Examples are the Tactaid 2 and 7 [4], the MiniVib4 [5] or the Mini-Fonator [6] devices, which consist of vibrator arrays or bands attached to the body (e.g., to the chest). Fixed attachments to the body or large areas of stimulation make these devices relatively unpractical to use in daily life situations. Output of a typical research project in the area is the OSCAR hand-held vibro-tactile aid [7, 8], which presents features of the acoustic signal through two vibrators to the user.

Tactile communication aids usually use a signal processing device that manipulates the acoustic signal coming from a microphone, sending selected sound features to the tactile stimulators. Electro-tactile aids produce sensations on the user's skin by electrical stimulation of the nerves, other non-vibratory aids like Braille arrays stimulate the skin with complex mechanical patterns, and vibro-tactile aids deliver signals by one or more vibrators. The information flow is generally too low to convey sufficient information for a fluent speech message to be understood. Therefore, tactile aids are used as assistive devices rather than as stand-alone solutions.

The sensitivity of parts of the body surface to mechanical or electrical stimulation is varying with respect to location. Touching a particular location on the skin creates an activation of related neurons in the somatosensory cortex of the brain. Reversely, neurons in the somatosensory cortex are associated to specific tactile *receptive fields* on the skin, within which stimulation activates related neurons.

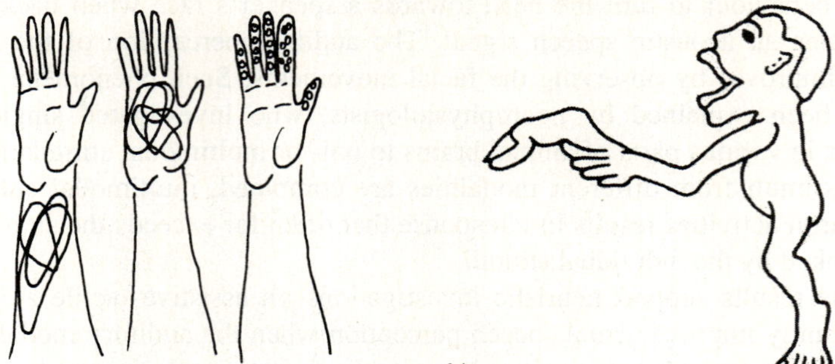


**Fig. 1.** a) Examples of receptive fields on the forearm, in the palm of the hand, and on the fingers. High density and small diameters indicate a high tactile sensitivity and a high differentiability for evoked tactile stimulation, b) sensitivity-distorted surface proportions of a human body

Examples of such tactile receptive fields are shown in figure 1a. Areas on the skin with a large density of receptive fields, as found on the fingers, indicate a high tactile sensitivity, and small receptive fields indicate a large ability to distinguish between neighbouring locations of a complex stimulation pattern, yielding better masking properties.

Other parts of the body often used in evoked tactile stimulation experiments (e.g., the back or the arms) show larger and fewer tactile receptive fields than hands or arms. Figure 1b illustrates the sensitivity of the human body with the help of distorted surface proportions. Large proportions represent high and small proportions low sensitivity. Figure 1b shows that the fingers are disproportionately sensitive and that the rest of the body but the mouth is underrepresented. Size and density of tactile receptive fields in figure 1a as well as the surface proportions in figure 1b indicate that high sensitivity and good abilities to distinguish between tactile patterns can be expected from the tip of the fingers. We thus decided to develop a hand-held tactile communication aid.

## 3 Functionality of the Assistive Device

FLIPPS is a hand-held vibro-tactile assistive speechreading aid. It allows for touching or relinquishing the vibrators at any time, and it nevertheless consists of a relatively large number of five actuators, one for each finger tip. A photo of the device is shown in figure 2. The body consists of voluptuous to touch, lightweight foam surrounding the electronics and the battery. Five vibrators are placed on the body at natural finger tip positions. Either internal or external microphones can be used.

The hand-held device needs to be small, handsome, inexpensive and equipped with a long-lasting battery in order to be accepted by the community of hearing-impaired people as a valuable additional aid.

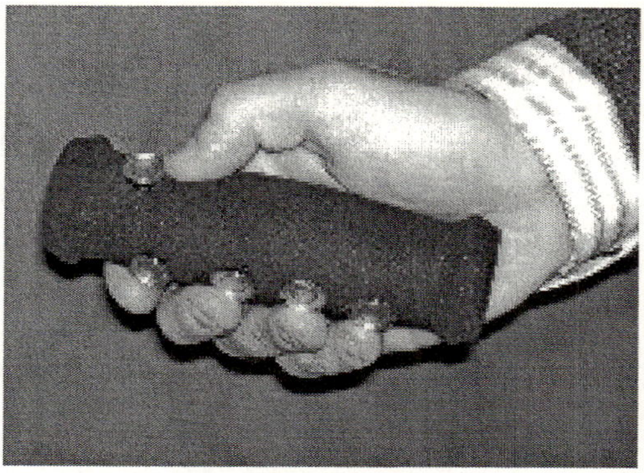

**Fig. 2.** Photo of a right-hand vibro-tactile speechreading aid FLIPPS. The body consists of voluptuous to touch, lightweight foam surrounding the electronics and the battery. The vibrators are arranged at natural finger tip positions. Either internal or external microphones can be used

The first points are questions of a proper design, which will be essential for a commercial product. From a technical point of view, the functionality and the energy consumption of the vibrators are important. In order to minimize the energy consumption, we decided to use pulse-stream signals with a small duty cycle or a short pulse-width, respectively. The parameters of this signal were optimized with respect to the vibratory perception.

As vibrators, ø14 [mm] miniature speakers are used with an impedance of 32 [$\Omega$], a maximum power of 70 [mW] and a sensitivity of 85 [dB]. By re-arranging the positions of the vibrators, right-hand or left-hand aids can be designed.

### 3.1 Vibrator Control

The electronic circuitry for vibrator control and for signal processing is built with discrete analogue devices, placed on a small printed board fitting into the body. A schematic block diagram is shown in figure 3.

$S_1$ and $S_2$ are arrays of analogue switches, which are connected in series with the vibrators $V_{1\text{-}5}$. The switches of $S_1$ are synchronously controlled by a pulse generator

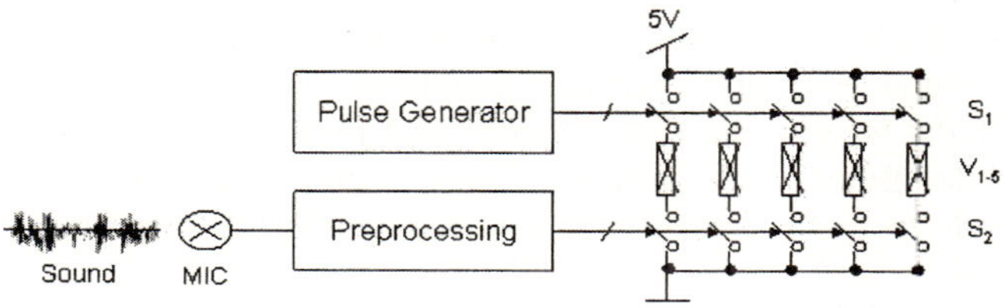


**Fig. 3.** Schematic diagram of the electronics forvibrator control and signal processing; $S_1$, $S_2$ are analogue switches, $V_{1\text{-}5}$ are the vibrators

with constant amplitude *a*, pulse frequency *f*, and duty cycle or pulse width $\tau$, respectively. A pre-processing unit converts the microphone input into a time-series of low-frequency pulses on five different control lines, each of which triggering a separate switch of $S_2$. The pulse frequency of the generator is far higher than that of the pre-processing unit. Thus, a vibrator $V_i$ is set 'on' with a vibration frequency *f* if the related switch (i) of $S_2$ is on. The reason for using a set of static parameters *f*, *a*, and $\tau$ is that in preceding experiments, dynamic modulation of these parameters was difficult to determine and to judge by the test persons. The static parameter settings of *f* and $\tau$ were heuristically optimized while keeping the energy consumption of the vibrators at a constant level. A subjective sensibility value *s* between [0, 10] was assigned to each parameter set (f, $\tau$), resulting in the distribution shown in table 1. The values were determined by a single person who repeated the experiment several times.

**Table 1.** Sensibility of vibrator stimulation with different pulse frequencies *f* and duty cycles $\tau$. The values are chosen from an interval [0, 10] with '5' as an intermediate reference, by definition related to the parameter set f=100 [Hz], $\tau$=2 [%]. The crosses *x* indicate pairs that were not considered

| | **f [Hz]** | | | | | | | | | |
|---|---|---|---|---|---|---|---|---|---|---|
| | | **17** | **20** | **40** | **80** | **100** | **160** | **200** | **400** | **800** |
| $\tau$ [%] | **2** | 3 | 4 | 4 | 5 | 5 | 5 | 4 | 3 | 2 |
| | **5** | 4 | 5 | 6 | 7 | 7 | 6 | 6 | 5 | 4 |
| | **10** | 6 | 6 | 7 | 7 | 8 | 6 | 7 | 6 | 5 |
| | **20** | 6 | 5 | 6 | 5 | 8 | 6 | 7 | 7 | x |
| | **50** | 5 | 6 | 7 | 7 | 7 | 6 | 8 | x | x |

The distribution of the sensitivity values is caused by the complex electronic impedance of the vibrators in combination with the perception of different vibrating frequencies. For the actual implementation, we chose the parameter set f=100 [Hz], $\tau$=10 [%] in order to keep the duty cycle as small as reasonably feasible.

### 3.2 Processing of the Sound Signal

A block diagram of the signal pathway from the microphone to the five switches of $S_2$ in figure 3 is shown in figure 4. At first, the sound signal is fed into an automatic gain control circuit (AGC) in order to reduce the dependency of the performance on slowly varying sound levels and on distances to the sound source(s).

The AGC output is split into five channels, one for each finger tip. A filter bank with five $2^{nd}$-order Butterworth bandpass filters is used. The output signal of each filter corresponds to the smoothed signal power within the respective filter bandwidth.

The design goal is to have only two or less vibrators switched 'on' at a time and thus, keeping the complexity of the possible vibratory patterns reasonably low. Therefore, two circuits $Max_1$ and $Max_2$ are used to calculate the largest and the sec-

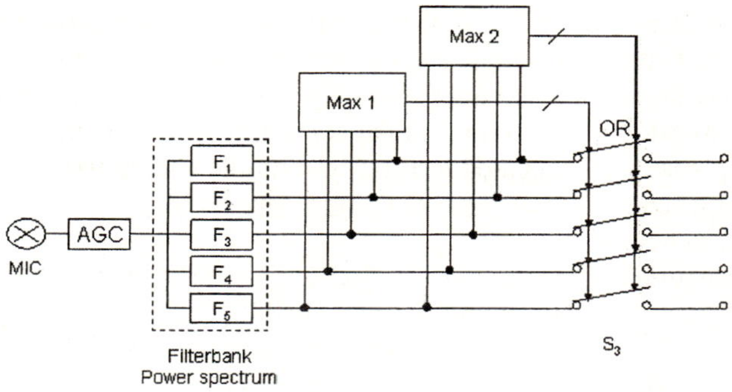


**Fig. 4.** Block diagram of the pre-processing pathway and of the feature extraction from the sound signal

ond largest filter output. These values control the switches of array $S_3$. Both $Max_1$ and $Max_2$ have a threshold circuit integrated, which allows positive output only for power levels above pre-given thresholds. They each guarantee that only one or none switch is 'on', so that each vibratory pattern consists in total of a maximum of two vibrators 'on'.

The cut-off frequencies of the filters were calculated and fixed in a preceding experiment. For this purpose, a speech utterance with a certain background noise of 40 [sec] lengths was examined with the help of a Matlab program. The outer cut-off frequencies of the filter bank are set to 75 [Hz] and 5 [kHz]. Then, the average energy $<E_{tot}>$ within this bandwidth is calculated for the complete speech utterance and divided by five. The four missing cut-off frequencies are then fixed so that the energies $<E_1>,\ldots,<E_5>$ in the five single bands yield $<E_1>=\ldots=<E_5>=<E_{tot}>/5$.

## 4 First Results from Short-Term Field Tests

We initiated short-term field studies with the FLIPPS prototype system. The goal of these studies is to demonstrate that multiplicative multimodal perception can occur already after a few hours of training. For this purpose, CVC sequences, one-syllable words, or short speech utterances were presented to persons with normal hearing abilities. In later tests, hearing-impaired persons should be integrated.

Some of the results are presently at hand. The respective test corpus consists of 89 CVC permutations, ordered in 12 categories. Each category covers 2-4 vowels embedded in alternating voiced-unvoiced consonants of the same or similar articulatory position. Examples of such consonant groups are {/p/, /b/, /m/}, {/g/, /k/, /ng/}, or {/d/, /t/}, or {/th/, /dt/}.

The test sequences were recorded on digital video with a speaking face on the screen in an anechoic room. During the later tests, the FLIPPS system was connected to the line-out of the sound card of the computer instead of having any microphone input, and three different modalities of the utterances were presented to the test persons: i) sound + face + vibration, ii) face + vibration, iii) face only. Test i) was used in a training lap of the test persons, instantaneously followed by the recognition tests ii) and iii). The test persons had approximately one hour time for 'playing' with the system and for developing a 'feeling' of the correlation sound + face + vibration. The tests ii) and iii) were then executed in form of multiple choice tests. The comparison of the results of ii) and iii) determines the improvements of the test persons due to the assistive vibratory system.

In several categories of the test corpus significant improvements of the hitting rates are visible. The best results occurred in group {[p], [b], [m]}/{[o], [u], [a]}, where we found in average of 4 hits out of 14 possibilities with the device disconnected and 8 out of 14 with the device connected. The improvement is 100%. In this group, the confusions with the vibrations 'on' occurred for each, voiced or unvoiced consonant pairs, which naturally look very similar. On the other hand, there are also categories in which the speechreading results became worse with the vibrator connected. An example is group {/th/, /dh/}+{/a/, /o/, /i/}. Probably, there was some kind of attentional mismatch between the distinctive visual cues of the corpus and the respective vibratory patterns.

In general it can be stated that after a short one-hour training period there is a small overall improvement of the ability to speechread short utterances. To determine the real value of the vibratory device as an assistive speechreading aid, more complex field tests with long utterances as, for example, complete sentences with balanced test corpora must be evaluated. This is planned to be one of the next steps in the development of the FLIPPS system.

## 5 Conclusions and Future Perspectives

The paper describes the design of the FLIPPS assistive, hand-held, vibro-tactile communication aid, designed to increase the speechreading effort of hearing-impaired persons. Short term studies with people with normal hearing show that the ability to speechread can increase significantly when using the system or, at least, they show that the test persons can improve their ability to memorize short visual sequences. The results may be explained by the advantages of multimodal stimulation against unimodal visual stimulation. Long-term field studies are intended to follow the optimization of the FLIPPS system.

## References

1. Meredith, M.A., Nemitz, J.W., Stein, B.E.: Determinants of Multisensory Integration in Superior Colliculus Neurons. I. Temporal Factors. J. Neuroscience, 10 (1987) 3215-3229
2. Alcorn, S.: The Tadoma Method. Volta Rev. 34 (1932) 195-198.
3. Reed, C.M., Durlach, N.L., Braida, L.D., Schultz, M.C.: Analytic Study of the Tadoma Method: Effects of Hand Position on Segmental Speech Perception. J. Speech Hearing 32 (1989) 921-929

4. Tactaid 2 and 7: Audiological Engineering Cooperation, 35 Medford Street, Somerville, MA 02143-9925, U.S.A.
5. MiniVib4: Special Instruments Development, Box 3050, SE-18103 Lidingö, Sweden
6 Mini-Fonator: Siemens Hearing Instruments Inc., 10 Costitution Ave, PO Box 1397, Piscataway, NJ 08855-1397
7. Spens, K.E., Huss, C., Dahlqvist, M., Agelfors, e.: A Hand-held Two-channel Vibro-tactile Speech Communication Aid for the Deaf: Characteristics and Results. Scandinavian Audiology, Suppl. 47 (1997) 5-13
8. Faulkner, A.: The TIDE project OSCAR. Scandinavian Audiology Suppl. 47 (1997) 38-44

# A New Mobile Text Telephony System Based on GPRS Communications

Santiago Aguilera[3], Sergio Jiménez[1], Daniel Bolaños[1], Mari-Satur Torre[3], and José Colás[1]

[1] Departamento de Ingeniería Informática, E. P. S. Universidad Autónoma de Madrid
colas@ii.uam.es
[2] Fundación Vodafone España
mari-satur.torre@vodafone.om
[3] Universidad Politécnica de Madrid, Ciudad Universitaria S/N, 28040 Madrid, Spain
aguilera@acacia.die.upm

**Abstract**. Deaf people have had many difficulties to enjoy the advantages of modern telephone technology up to early days. Since Alexandre Graham Bell invented the telephone in 1876, the first text telephones have needed almost a century to appear in the market and to allow deaf people to communicate with others at long distances. In the same way, the design and development of new text telephones using mobile telephony networks have needed time. Nevertheless, nowadays deaf people suffer from a great economical discrimination due to the telephone call cost in many countries. We must consider that a text conversation need much more time if it is compared with voice one and the service rates depended on connection time and not on transmitted data only.
The system we present is based on GPRS (2.5 G) data mobile communications which considers only the transmitted information for billing and in the text conversations case, this amount of data is very limited and independent of telephone call duration. The terminals used are PDA (Personal Digital Assistant) with Pocket PC or Palm operative system. All the system has been designed using Internet technology (TCP/IP protocol), so it is possible to communicate with several terminals like mobile telephones with TCP/IP stack or PC. In the last case, a client text telephone program has been implemented. In the first case, a WAP text telephone client has been developed by the Spanish Vodafone Foundation which is able to communicate with the PDA text telephone client.

## 1 Introduction

The telephone invented by Alexandre Graham Bell in 1876 supposed a great advance in the telecommunications history because it allowed the instantaneous communication by voice among two speakers independently the distance between them. This invent did not be enjoyed for deaf people during almost a century up to the apparition of text telephones in USA, in the sixties. Germany was the first European country in producing and selling these products at the middle of seventies (1) (2).

The main problems of current text telephony are:

- The using of specific terminals for this application, with reduced production volumes. So, the production costs are higher than the most of usual telecommunications products.

K. Miesenberger et al. (Eds.): ICCHP 2004, LNCS 3118, pp. 1160–1166, 2004.

- The text communication speed is slower than voice one. To exchange the same amount of information is necessary much more time with the first way. Like the telephone rates depend on call duration (time), the cost of text calls is bigger than voice calls. So, deaf people have had to pay great telephone bills.
- Every country uses incompatible text telephones with its neighbourhoods, so deaf people have difficulties to establish international calls.

## 2 Previous Work

In 1998, we developed a project with the interest of supplying deaf people the same movements freedom than no deaf people based on mobile telephony. To get it, we looked for a solution implemented on a commercial terminal to reduce the production costs and increase the project viability.

After an exhaustive search we founded the Nokia 9110 mobile terminal (see Fig. 1) like the most convenient: the hardware adapted perfectly to our needs and we would must develop the appropriated software. In those days, this and other programmable terminals used specific compilers for specific operative systems, so the reduced experience and information to work with them were great difficulties. Beside, the developed programs did not be portable. Nevertheless, our application worked without problems (1).

**Fig. 1.** Nokia Communicator working as text telephone

This text telephone has had a great acceptation among deaf community. The proof is the more than 5000 terminals which are being currently used in Spain. It is important to indicate that this project has been nominated by European Union like a good example of the concept "Design for Everybody" in the communication barriers elimination.

In the moment we developed this system, two difficulties did not have solution at the end of nineties:

- Deaf people, using text, need much more time than no deaf people, using voice, to transmit the same information amount and the only existing GSM telephony at that date, considers the call duration like the factor to bill the conversation.
- By the other side, the existed few programmable mobile terminals at the end of nineties, used property operative systems, doing non portable the developed software for them. This was the case of the selected Nokia terminal, which integrated GEOS operative system, with a little diffusion.

## 3 Text Telephone Based on GPRS Mobile Communications

The objective of present project was applying the new technological solutions appeared in the last years to solve the previously mentioned problems: calls cost and no portable software (dependence of mobile terminal).

To solve the first aspect we have designed an application based on 2.5 mobile generation (2.5 G) with the possibility of GPRS data communication (5) (6), which allows to bill for transmitted information amount (very reduced in the text telephony case) in comparison with the traditional based on calls temporal duration.

The solution for the second problem (dependence of the terminal or no portability), we have programmed the software (application) in C/C++ for the three mobile terminals families which cover almost the 100 % of programmable terminals used, currently, by the most of people: PDA with Pocket PC (7) (8) or Palm OS (3) (4) and PC with Windows OS.

### 3.1 System Components

The system is based in a client / server architecture. Although the client terminal could be a PDA (Personal Digital Assistant) or a PC, like we commented before; in the following we refer to PDA like the only clients.

### 3.2 The Software for PDA Client

The software for PDA client terminal has been designed to allow the language change. Currently, we offer three versions for Spanish, English and Portuguese. Its main functions are:

1. To access GPRS network for its connection and getting of one IP address for its identification like IP client in Internet. This IP address is dynamically provided by the GPRS network to the different devices connected to it.
2. To register itself (client terminal) in the text telephone server, communicating it the obtained IP address in the previous step.
3. To allow the user to make a call to other registered PDA.
4. To inform the user of the calls reception proceeding from other terminals. To be able to inform people with audition problems, the indication (event signal) is visual (blanking the screen terminal) and tactile (activating the vibrator included in the terminal).
5. To register in the user PDA terminal the non attended calls (lost calls).
6. The last and most important function is to offer the possibility of an instantaneous, in real-time, telephone conversation between two users.

### 3.3 Server Software

The server software, running in a remote server computer connected to Internet, carries out the following functions:

1. To allow the registration of the PDA client terminals to be able to communicate among them. This process supposes an information storage which identifies each PDA (user): telephone number and IP address assigned by GPRS network.

2. To detect the communication requests from a PDA (caller) when it wants to communicate with other PDA (called). If the called PDA is not registered (connected to the server), the server will inform that this conversation is not possible. In the other case (PDA registered), if the called PDA is not busy, the server will inform to it about the intention of other PDA (caller) to establish a text conversation with it.
3. When a call is accepted by the called PDA and the communication channel is on, the server drives the information traffic between them.

### 3.4 Description of the Communication Process

The PDA application (software) is, basically, a program with a "always-on" philosophy from a GPRS network connection point of view. When this program starts, the first it does is the PPP connection to the GPRS network and the petition of a dynamically assigned IP address (see Fig. 2) to identify itself in the Internet network. In a second step, the PDA client sends this IP address to the server for its registration (new user) in the text telephony service (see Fig. 3). The server will allow the text conversation between any text telephones previously registered (connected to the server).

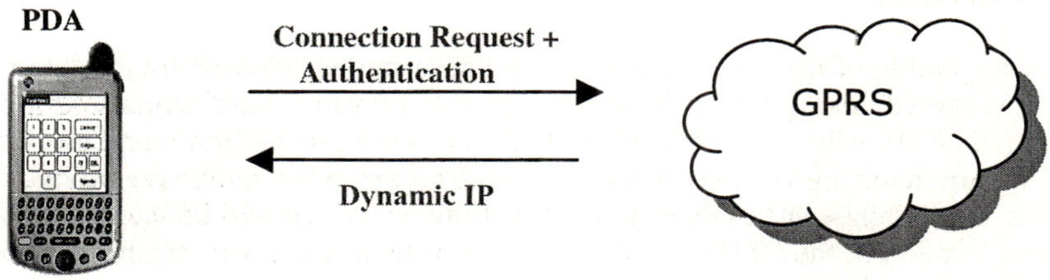


**Fig. 2.** Details of PDA connection with GPRS network. Dynamic IP assignation by the GPRS network. IP is fixed while connection is on

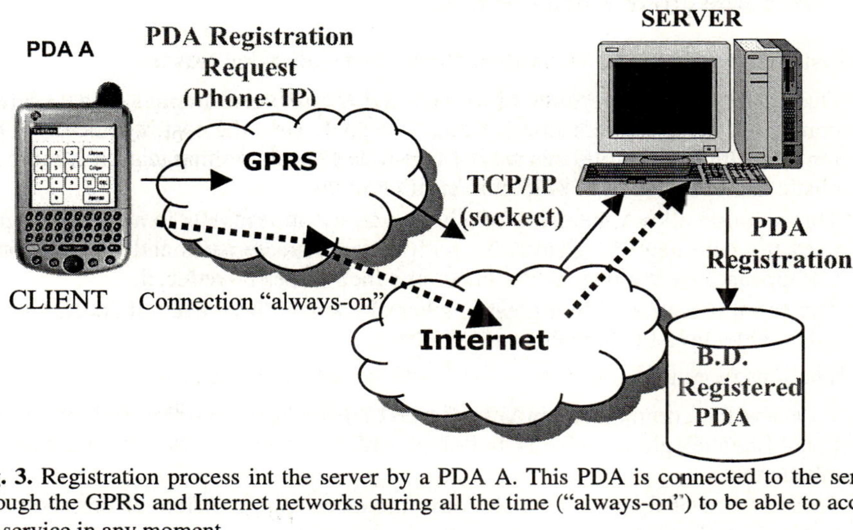


**Fig. 3.** Registration process int the server by a PDA A. This PDA is connected to the server through the GPRS and Internet networks during all the time ("always-on") to be able to access the service in any moment.

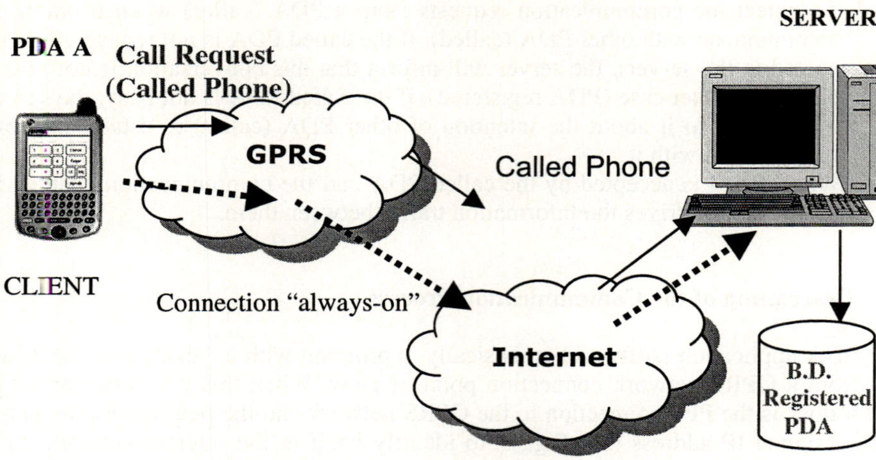


**Fig. 4.** Call request to the server from a registered PDA A.

## 4 Evaluation

At the beginning of this year, an evaluation phase started. Around 60 PDA terminals were distributed among deaf users belonging to the Spanish Deaf Organization Foundation (FCNSE), which is collaborating in the project from the first moments. With its help, we are detecting working problems which appear when a massive product using is done. Beside, they are analysing new functionality which will be interesting to add to a new version of the GPRS text telephone. This evaluation is in the middle and will finish in the next June month.

## 5 Conclusions and Future Works

The system is proving to be very efficient due to the following reasons:

- Due to the data traffic rates based on, and the reduced amount of data which comprises a text conversation between two deaf users, the cost of the calls is being very limited. Beside, this way of real-time textual communication is more realistic and effective than SMS conversation based on.
- This solution allows the using of a great variety of terminals in a very changing market where new PDA terminals with better characteristics and functionalities are appears in a fast way, at the same time their prices be reduced.
- The communication with a great number of users without need of special terminals, only with a PC in their house or office.

The functions more useful which we must consider in a near future are:

- To allow the communication with the text telephones connected to the conventional fixed telephone network building a gateway which carries out the protocol translation
- To add a lot of functions which conventional telephony offers at this moment: voice mail, telephone agenda, party calls, and so on.

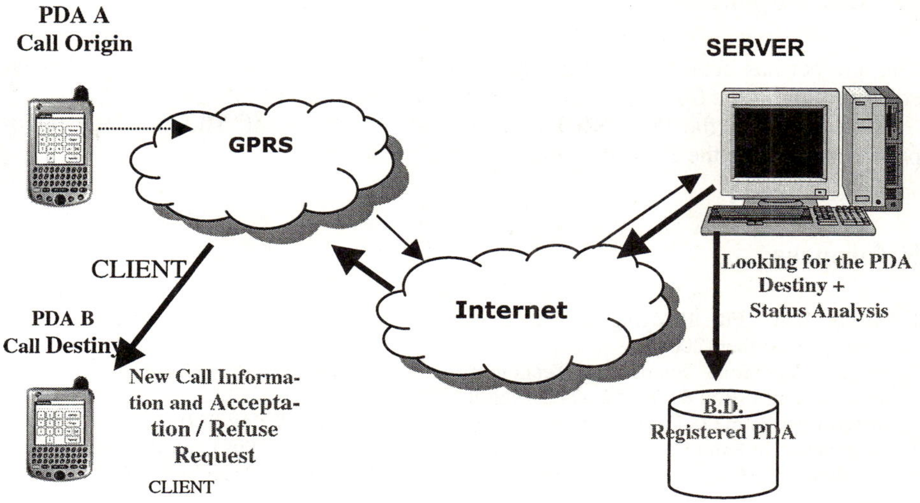


**Fig. 5.** Localization of PDA B (Call Destiny ) and analysis of its status (no connected / busy / free) by the PDA A (Call Origin), through the server

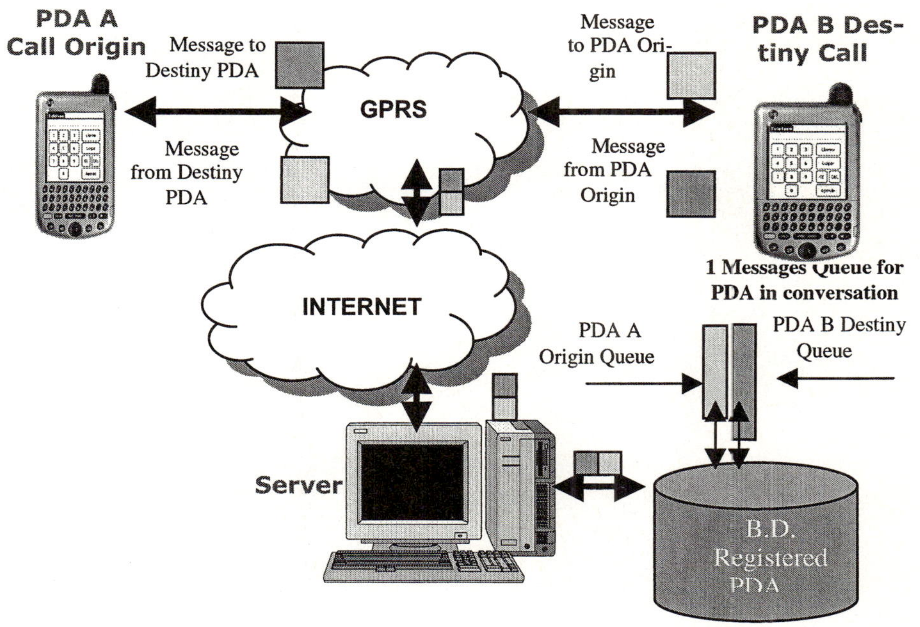


**Fig. 6.** Details of the process in the server during an established conversation between a PDA A and a PDA B.

## Acknowledgements

This project has been financed by the Spanish Vodafone Foundation with a intense collaboration of the Spanish Deaf Association Foundation (FCNSE).

It has received the IMSERSO Infanta Cristina 2003 grant. This is a prestigious prize conceded by the Spanish Social and Work Ministry.

## References

1. Patrick, R.W. (Ed): Bridging the Gap?. Access to telecommunications for all people. Cost 219bis, November (2001).
2. Spanish Vodafone Fundation: Tecnologías de la Información y Comunicaciones y Discapacidad ISBN: 84-932521-7-9, Madrid (2003).
3. Foster, L.R: Palm OS Programming Bible 2nd Edition, (2002). Wiley (Ed).
4. Bachmann, G.: Palm Programming The Authoritative Solution , (1999), SAMS (Ed).
5. Andersson, C.: GPRS and 3G Wireless Applications: Professional Developer's Guide, Wiley (Ed).
6. Heine, G., Sagkpb, H.: GPRS: Gateway to Third Generation Mobile Networks, Mobile Communications Series (Ed).
7. Makofsky, S.: Pocket PC Network Programming, Wiley (Ed).
8. Bruce E., Ph.D. Krell, Pocket PC Developer's Guide, Mc Graw-Hill (Ed)

# Head Mounted Display as a Information Guarantee Device for Hearing Impaired Students

Tomoyuki Nishioka

Division for the Hearing Impaired
Tsukuba College of Technology
4-3-15 Amakubo, Tsukuba, Ibaraki 305-0005 Japan
nishioka@a.tsukuba-tech.ac.jp
http://www.tsukuba-tech.ac.jp/info/staff/nishioka

**Abstract.** Augmented reality(AR), which extends human cognition, is also useful in providing equal accessibility for disabled. Recently, Head Mounted Displays, which is key device of AR technology, become consumer products and easy to obtain. In this paper, feasibility of these products for guaranteeing information for hearing impared students at lecture in college is examined.

## 1 Introduction

Augmented reality (or Mixed reality) is a natural extension of virtual reality. At the case of augmented reality(AR for short), computer generated information is not virtual but based on physical world. Information about the physical world is collected by external sensors and processed by a computer, and is then displayed, overlapping the physical world.

The technology not only extends human cognition of the real world but also has the possibility of offering equal accessibility for people with disabilities. From this point of view, we are interested in information guarantee using augmented reality technologies. In the typical case of guaranteeing information for the hearing impaired, assistive information such as textual captions or movies of sign language interpreters is displayed separately from what the user wants to see. The viewpoint of the user may drifts. Using head mounted display(HMD), assistive information is displayed in users field of view. The user may not need to change viewpoint so frequently. Moreover, assistive information stay in users field of view whenever the user moves his head.

In previous paper in ICCHP'02[1], we examined the see-through style head mounted display, and got result that the display can not work well at the case of lecture in a classroom because of low brightness of the device. In this paper, we evaluate another(non see-through) types of head mounted display at the same context.

K. Miesenberger et al. (Eds.): ICCHP 2004, LNCS 3118, pp. 1167–1171, 2004.

## 2 Guaranteeing Information Using HMD

From viewpoint of equal accessibility, hearing impaired have a privilege to access same information as the others. But it is hard for hearing impaired to aquire acoustic information including verbal information. *Information guarantee* fill this information gap.

For example, at the case of small meeting or lecture in college, hearing impaired may lost information if there are no special effort. So information guarantee activity like notetaking or computer assisted notetaking(CAN) or interpreting sign language is needed. In typical situation, a sign language interpreter stands just beside of a lecturer. There may be an another material like Powerpoint presentation. In this case, the subjects frequently had to change their viewpoint between lecturer, interpreter, and their notebook.

Using HMD to display powerpoint materials or movie of a interpreter, the subjects could see the lecturer and the image of the interpreter simultaneously. It also helps making attention from student by flushing display. (This is very easy for student of normal hearing - lecturer simply say 'hey', but not so easy for hearing impaired students.)

When HMD is used as an information guarantee device in a lecture, the user may wear HMD continuously through the lecture. Under such long(an hour or two) duration of wearing, comfortability of the device becomes important. Lightweightness of the display and way to hold the device on users head make a large contribution to this comfortability. An appearance of the display should be considered when it is used in a public space. It is not desirable that the device lets the user stand out.

## 3 HMD Device

In the context of augmented reality, computer processed information is typically provided as visual information using a head mount display. To offer computer generated information with real world vision simultaneously, there are two methods[2]: video see-through, and optical see-through.

Video see-through captures images of the real world using a video camera. The image is electrically combined with a computer-generated image and is provided to the user by a small video display just in front of the eyes. Whole the field of view is covered by this video display. In this method, the smallness of the display narrows the users field of view. Visual image losts depth due to flat display panel. The weight of the display is heavy because of the external video camera and position sensors which forms part of it.

In the case of the optical see-through, a computer-generated image is provided on a transparent display. The user receives images of the real world directly. The images are combined at the user's pupils. The combination is very sensitive for time. The display device is lightweight and interferes less with the user's field of view.

Correctness of position and time on combining image is very important in most AR applications. From this point of view, video see-through has a advan-

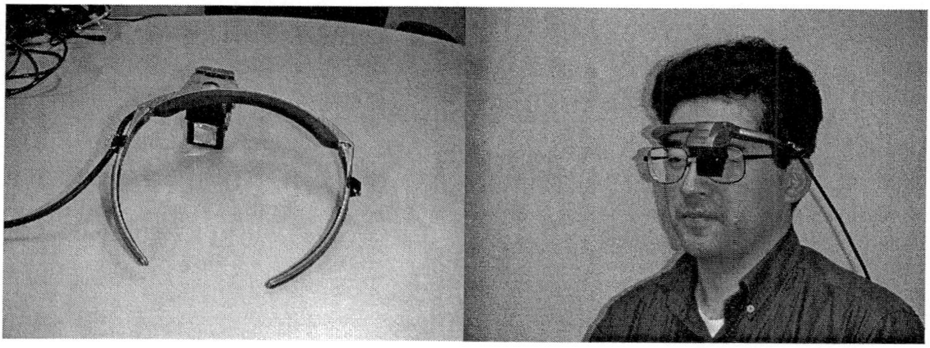

**Fig. 1.** DataGlass 2/A(Shimadzu Corp.)

tage. However, in our context of guaranteeing information, lightweightness and width of the field of view are more valuable than correctness of combination. For this reason, we choose the optical see-through HMD(ST-HMD) as an information guarantee device.

We examine following two HMDs. Both of them are monocular displays.

1. Dataglass 2/A(Shimadzu Corp.)(Fig.1)

The resolution of the display is 800x600(SVGA), 18bit depth of color. It is half see-through, 15% transmissivity. The size of the image is just the same as a 13 inch computer display 60 centimeter away. The weight of the display is 80 grams. The display is mounted on forehead of user by half-ring frame. It can be mounted with eyeglass. The display unit places just front of eyes. It covers most field of view. The position of the unit is easy to replace. So the HMD can be used on either the left or right eye. Input signal comes from analog RGB(HD-Sub15). It can be work under USB bus powered. no AC adaptor is needed.

2. Eyetop(Ingineo SAS)(Fig.2)

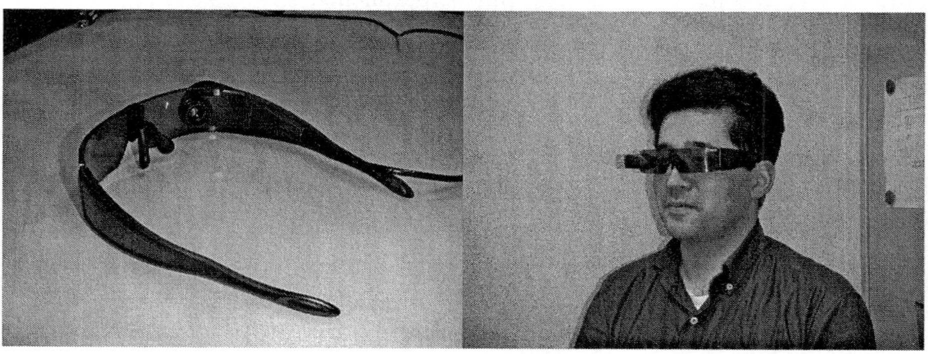

**Fig. 2.** EyeTop(Ingineo SAS)

The resolution of the display is 320x240(QVGA), 16bit depth of color. The display unit places not just front of eyeball but 20 degree offset from center of eyeball. The placement of the display ensure that the subjects field of view never be interfered by display unit. The weight of the display is 60 grams. The display looks like sporty sunglass. Due to its rounded shape, the frame of the display conflicts eyeglasses. Changing the position of the display is possible, but you have to exchange assembly to alter the position. Input signal is video composite(RCA plug). Powersupply of the display are 4 AA batteries, which are mounted on control unit. The weight of the control unit is 180 grams(without batteries).

## 4 Preliminary Experiments

We evaluated the device under the situation of lecture in a classroom. The subjects were hearing-impaired students of Tsukuba College of Technology.

We use two different materials; a textual caption and a movie of a sign language interpreter. The caption is generated by IPTalk(CAN software). Source of the movie of a sign language interpreter is MPEG-2, and played by Windows Media Player. Both displays are connected to a computer using VGA connector(DataGlass 2/A) or NTSC Video output(Eyetop).

At the case of Dataglass 2/A, the images of assistive information is very clear. The textual caption is easy to read and the images of the sign language interpreter is easy to understand. One of the subject reports that half see-through feature make the display less bright. The placement of display unit causes discomfort of the subjects. Some subjects report that they are very tired because the field of view of an eye is almost covered by display unit.

At the case of Eyetop, the textual caption is rather difficult to read. It comes from offset placement of display. The subjects need to change their viewpoint explicitly and concentrate to watch the images. This breaks continuity of real world to assistive information. It is hard to keep viewpoint to display contineously although its sunglass like form ensure comfortability of wearing the device. So the subjects feel uncomfortable in long time experiments.

## 5 Discussions

The results show that the devices do not have capability to serve rich contents like movie of sign language interpreter or textual caption in a context of information guarantee at long duration lecture in a college. Rather, simple contents like signaling to make attention are appropriate. Compare with eyeglass type display[1], visibility of assistive information itself gets high evaluation than before. There are no advantage on comfortability of wearing the device.

In this paper we examine at the case of lecture. Direction of the communication is fixed from a lecturer to students. More interactive situation like dialogue or meeting may suitable for those HMDs.

## Acknowledgement

This work was supported by Grant-in-Aid(No. 15700389) for Young Scientists (B) from Ministry of Education, Culture, Sports, Science and Technology (MEXT), Japan.

## References

1. Nishioka, T. : The See-through Head Mount Display as the Information Offering Device for the Hearing Impaired Students, LNCS **2398** (2002) 166–167, Springer-Verlag
2. Ohta, Y. and Tamura, H. (Eds): Mixed Reality (1999), Springer-Verlag.

# Facial and Head Movements of a Sign Interpreter and Their Application to Japanese Sign Animation

Sumihiro Kawano[1] and Takao Kurokawa[2]

[1] Tsukuba College of Technology, 4-3-15 Amakubo, Tsukuba, Ibaraki 300-0005 Japan
kawano@a.tsukuba-tech.ac.jp

[2] Kyoto Institute of Technology, Matsugasaki Sakyo-ku, Kyoto 606-8585 Japan
kurotak@ipc.kit.ac.jp

**Abstract.** In order to improve communication environments among the hearing impaired and the hearing people, the authors are developing a system translating Japanese into Japanese Sign Language (JSL) and vice versa. We represent the results of translation from Japanese by sign animations. Although JSL is multimodal, the roles of non-manual actions such as facial and head movements are not well known. We analyzed non-manual gestures spoken by a female sign interpreter, and we concluded that facial and head movements conveyed linguistic information on JSL. We carried out an experiment for evaluation of facial and head movements introduced into sign animations. The facial and head movements introduced into the animations had positive effects on recognition of JSL words.

## 1 Introduction

Japanese Sign Language (JSL) is a native language for the hearing impaired in Japan. JSL is highly multimodal, and is spoken with abundance of non-manual gestures that include actions of the head, trunk and eyes, and facial expressions, as well as manual gestures. The hearing impaired cannot communicate with most of hearing people without support of JSL interpreters, because it is difficult for hearing people to master JSL. Besides, they cannot enjoy computer-supported communication environments because sign languages are not fully processed by a computer. In order to solve these situations, the authors are developing a system that digitally processes JSL and translates Japanese into it and vice versa[1]. The immediate objective of our project is, however, presenting information such as news, weather forecasts and notices with the system. It displays the resultant JSL sentences of translation from Japanese ones in the form of animation where a human model talks by signs[2].

Although the model human should make a free use of various kinds of non-manual expressions, at present it lacks natural facial and bodily actions. This is partly caused by functional imperfection of the model, but the main reason for it is that syntax and semantics of JSL non-manual actions have not yet been well known, especially in the intermediate type JSL treated in our system. The intermediate type JSL (IJSL) is widely used by people from native JSL speakers to sign interpreters and in broadcasting. IJSL has been being influenced by both the traditional JSL and spoken Japanese:

K. Miesenberger et al. (Eds.): ICCHP 2004, LNCS 3118, pp. 1172–1177, 2004.

its words were borrowed from JSL and its word sequences resemble to those of Japanese sentences. Although it does not have the standard, IJSL used in signed TV news is constructing the standard position of IJSL. The grammar of IJSL is a little known [3]. The authors and their colleagues are exploring syntactic and semantic rules of IJSL using a signed news corpus [4,5]. In order to utilize the results of this analysis for Japanese-into-JSL machine interpretation, the obtained rules are described as a case grammar. In order to heighten the quality of translation we need to iterate the process of (1) analyzing non-manual expressions with actual JSL utterances, (2) synthesizing animations that adopt the non-manual actions extracted in (1), and (3) evaluating them from the standpoint of naturalness and understandability.

In the previous study, we focused on nodding, blinking and eye movements produced by a female sign interpreter in JSL TV news, and found some of their roles in conveying linguistic information on JSL. The introduction of them into animations has been confirmed to improve recognition rate of animated JSL and understandability of the structure of JSL sentences by the hearing disabled [6,7]. In addition, her facial expressions by eyes and eyebrows were analyzed and it was found that they conveyed emotional information on objective impression about the news contents. They also had positive effects on recognition rate of JSL words [8].

In this paper, we will advance our process to the further stage by exploring facial and head movements incidental to individual JSL words, adopting movements proper to each specific word as the morphemes that compose the word and showing that those movements produced by the human model are effective for understanding the meaning of the word. The previous results are confirmed and their precision and reliability are increased.

## 2 Facial and Head Movements in Signed News

What we call facial and head movements include nodding, blinking, gaze direction, eye opening, eyebrow actions. The material for analysis was a corpus of videotaped 153 JSL TV news sentences simultaneously accompanied with Japanese speech. The signer was the interpreter mentioned in 1. It contained 1824 sign words. Every time she produced one of the above actions, its magnitudes and the location where it appeared were measured on a monitor screen.

All nodding and blinking occurred at the boundary of words except two blinks in the corpus. There were 522 noddings observed in the material; 20 of them occurred at the beginning of words, and 502 occurred at the end of words. Besides, 325 blinks were observed in it; 40 of them occurred at the beginning of words, and 283 of them occurred at the end of words. Figure 1 shows the results on nodding and blinking. Nodding was omitted if the head was shaken or turned to another direction by a syntactic or semantic reason and a blink was also omitted if the eyes needed to be closed when it might occur. When these omissions are included, we can say that nodding occurred at the beginning and at the end of sentences, and it tended to be produced at the subject boundaries and at punctuations (as judged from simultaneous speech). Occurrence probability of nodding was 100.0 % at the end of sentences, 93.8 % at punctuations, 71.4 % at the beginning of topics, and 76.9 % at the end of subjective parts. Blinking was also produced at the locations where nodding occurred, but its frequency was lower than nodding except at punctuations. Occurrence probability of blinking was 77.8 % at the end of sentences, 68.8 % at punctuations, 72.1 % at the beginning of topics and 57.7 % at the end of subjective parts. Therefore, we can conclude that both nodding and blinking convey syntactic information of JSL sentences.

Among the 257 observed changes of gaze direction, she watched her signing hand(s) in 89.1% and in the remainder she gazed at other direction as if there had been an interesting object in that direction. Generally speaking, to gaze at the signing hand(s) clarified or stressed the word. However, when she watched other than the signing hand(s), gaze direction supplemented the meaning of the ongoing sign, as seen in the word "rain" where she looked up at the sky. In addition, head movements have functions clarifying the meaning of the sentence. When the head was directed to the opposite point of the signing hand(s) or was shaken a few times, it expressed a negative meaning.

The eyes and eyebrows were strongly related to the impression that specific words conveyed. The eyes were fully opened when words had a meaning such as "surprising", "bright" and "pleasurable". They were half opened with words having a difficult, gloomy or hard impression as "rain". The closed eyes expressed a dark, sad or miserable impression, or pictographically illustrated a meaning of words such as "night", "think" and "sleep". The eyebrows were lowered with words which gave a dark or sad impression. On the other hand, they were raised when words had a bright impression.

Lastly, we analyzed whether there was strong relation or not between sentence impression and facial expression appearing in words which belonged to the sentence. All the news sentences were classified into three categories according to the impression conveyed by them; good, neutral and bad. Then one of the three facial expressions, bright, neutral and gloomy, was assigned to each of sign words composing the sentences according to the actions of eyes and eyebrows that characterized the words. For every category of sentences, the number of words that had each facial expression was acquired. The results showed high correlation between sentence impression and the frequency of each of the three facial expressions in the sentences as seen in Fig. 2.

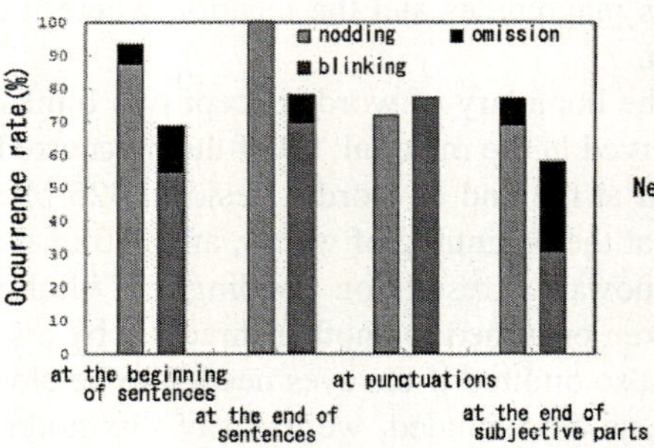


**Fig. 1.** Occurrence and omission of nodding and blinking in JSL TV news.

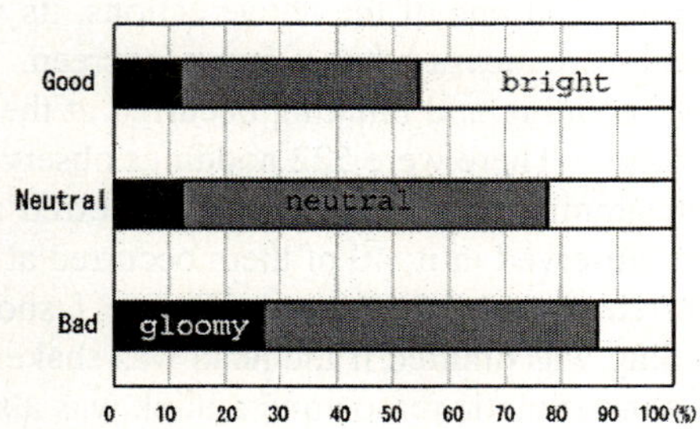


**Fig. 2.** Ratio of words with bright, neutral or gloomy facial expression in three kinds of news sentences.

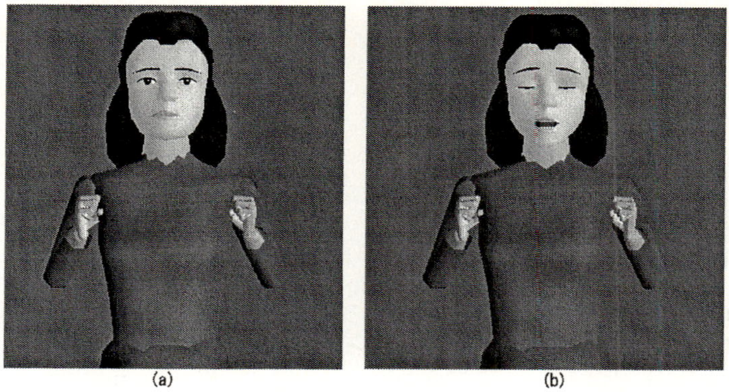

Fig. 3. The model human presented in the experiment.

# 3 Effects of Facial and Head Movements by Human Model on News Recognition

## 3.1 Method

In order to confirm the results in **2.** and in order to introduce them into animations, we carried out an experiment in which synthesized sign animations and a part of the corpus were evaluated. For this aim ten sentences were chosen from the corpus stated in **2.**, and used in the experiment. We synthesized two sorts of JSL animation for the chosen sentences: in one the model human talked only with manual gestures (Fig.3(a)) and in the other it talked with facial and head movements as well as with manual and mouth action (Fig.3(b)). These two were video-recorded in Tape A and Tape B, respectively. For control, the original sentences from the corpus were prepared in Tape C. In order to synthesize the animation for Tape B, special rules were derived based on the results of JSL sentence analysis:

- Nodding and blinking were inserted at the end of sentences, punctuations and the end of subjective parts,
- They were also produced at the beginning of topics[8]
- Eye direction, eye opening, eyebrow action, head shaking and mouth imitated those of the sign news interpreter.

24 subjects, who used JSL in everyday life or could understand it, participated in the experiment; 16 were hearing impaired and 8 could hear. In the experiment, to every subject was presented ten sentences in the same order, but each sentence was taken at random from the three tapes. The frequencies of the source tapes used to present each sentence were balanced over the subjects. They were instructed to write down the words in Japanese that they recognized after watching each sentence twice. Moreover, they were required to evaluate naturalness, friendliness and understandability of animated representation for each sentence.

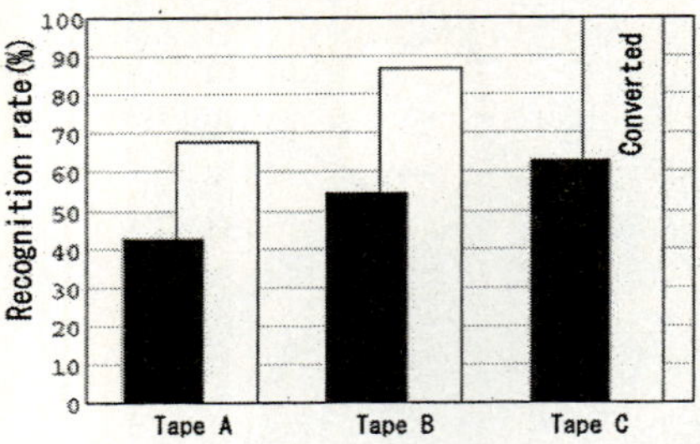


**Fig.4.** Rate of correct recognition of JSL words for three tapes.

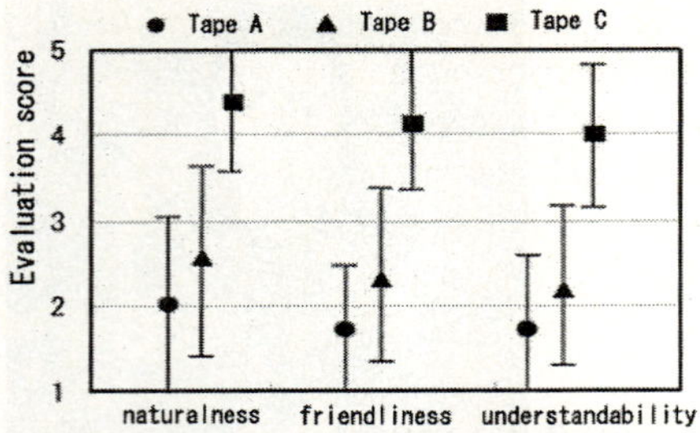


**Fig.5.** Means and s.d. of evaluation scores for the three tapes.

### 3.2 Results and Discussions

Fig. 4 shows rate of correct recognition of words for three tapes; 42.6% for Tape A, 54.8% for Tape B and 62.9% for Tape C. There is significant difference between Tapes A and B ($p < 0.05$). It can be said that there are positive effects of facial and head movements on understanding animated words. Evaluation for Tape C is significantly higher than that for Tapes A and B ($p < 0.05$). Recognition rate of about 63% in Tape C suggests that for the subjects the news sentences were difficult to understand. This is because it included comparatively many news terms that do not be used in daily life. Besides, in the actual news they know the meaning of unrecognized words by means of subtitles simultaneously presented in Japanese.

The correctly recognized words in Tapes A and B were included in those in tape C. If the correct recognition rate in Tape C is assumed to be 100%, then those in Tapes A and B are converted to 67.7% and 87.1%, respectively. Compared to the subjective evaluation of quality of the animations, the rate of 87% in Tape B is not low.

The results of subjective evaluation are shown in Fig.5. The means of the evaluation value were 2.00 (Tape A), 2.58 (Tape B) and 4.38 (Tape C) for naturalness, 1.71 (Tape A), 2.53 (Tape B) and 4.13 (Tape C) for friendliness and 1.71 (Tape A), 2.17 (Tape B) and 4.00 (Tape C) for understandability. Evaluation for Tape C is significantly higher than that for Tapes A and B ($p < 0.05$). These results suggest that there is ample room for improvement in sign animation. Some subjects commented on the quality of sign animation: it was difficult for them to recognize finger and lip actions, and facial expression because of unfamiliarity of the words used.

## 4 Conclusions

We analyzed non-manual gestures in JSL TV news and carried out an experiment for evaluation to establish the rules of facial and head movements in JSL animation. Some functions of non-manual gestures were found. Nodding and blinking conveyed information about the structure of JSL sentences. Gaze and head movements functioned as signals of conveying meanings of JSL words and sentences. Facial expression with each word had correlative with impressions of JSL sentences.

We synthesized JSL animation based on rules given from the results of the analysis and carried out an experiment for evaluation. As the results, facial and head movements introduced into sign animation had positive effects on recognition of JSL words. Subjective evaluation showed that quality of JSL animations was lower than original video in any item. Our next studies will be to solve exploring other non-manual actions and improving the human model.

## Acknowledgement

We thank Ms. Nakano of NHK for her permission of recording her image during talking in sign language. We also thank Mr. Itou, a graduate student of Kyoto Institute of Technology, Mr. Sakai of Kyoto Prefectural School for the Deaf and Ms Mitsuya of Kyoto Deaf Center for their cooperation in the experiment.

## References

1. Kurokawa, T., Morichi, T. and Watanabe, S.: Bidirectional translation between sign language and Japanese for communication with deaf-mute people, Advances in Human Factors/Ergonomics, 19B (1993) 1109-1114.
2. Watanabe, S., Izuchi, T., Fujishige, E. and Kurokawa, T.: Sign language animation using a synthesis-by-rule method, Proc. 9th Symp. on Human Interface (1993) 385-390
3. Adachi, H., Yosizawa, S., Fujita, M., Matsumoto, T. and Kamata, K.: Analysis of news sentences with sign language and sign translation processing, Rept. of JIPS Technical Meeting, 92, 24, NLC92-5 (1992) 17-24
4. Demura, T., Itou, T., Fujishige, E. and Kurokawa, T.: Building a database of Japanese Sign Language sentences and Its application to analysis of JSL grammar, Proc. of the Human Interface Symp. 2000 (2000a) 185-188
5. Demura, T., Itou, T., Fujishige, E. and Kurokawa, T.: Analysis of Deictics in Japanese Sign Language by using a database of JSL sentences, Rept. of 3rd IEICE Technical Meeting for Sign Language Informatics (2000b) 37-40
6. Kawano, S., Takahashi, Y. and Kurokawa, T.: An analysis of blinking, gazing, nodding and their meanings in sign language interpretation of TV news, Human Interface News and Report, 11 (1996) 435-440
7. Kurokawa, T., Senba, K. and Kawano, S.: Synthesis of facial movement images for sign language animation and their effects, Advances in Human Factors/Ergonomics, 21(1997)5-8
8. Kawano, S. and Kurokawa, T.: The effects of facial expression on understanding Japanese sign language animation, Human-Computer Interaction, 1 (1999) 783-787

# SYNFACE – A Talking Head Telephone for the Hearing-Impaired

Jonas Beskow[1,*], Inger Karlsson[1], Jo Kewley[2], and Giampiero Salvi[1]

[1] Kungl Tekniska Högskolan (KTH), Dept of Speech, Music and Hearing, SE-100 44 Stockholm, Sweden

[2] Royal National Institute for Deaf People (RNID), London EC1Y 8SL, UK

**Abstract.** SYNFACE is a telephone aid for hearing-impaired people that shows the lip movements of the speaker at the other telephone synchronised with the speech. The SYNFACE system consists of a speech recogniser that recognises the incoming speech and a synthetic talking head. The output from the recogniser is used to control the articulatory movements of the synthetic head. SYNFACE prototype systems exist for three languages: Dutch, English and Swedish and the first user trials have just started.

## 1 Introduction

For a hearing-impaired person it is often necessary to be able to lip-read as well as hear the person they are talking with to communicate successfully. This is particularly relevant for telephone communication, where the hearing-impaired user is at a distinct disadvantage. It has been shown that the videophone can be a valuable form of communication for hearing-impaired people, providing essential visual speech information. However, videophones require expensive equipment at both ends and high bandwidth. In this paper a different solution is presented where the hearing-impaired telephone user is supplied with a system that is connected to the ordinary telephone. This system, SYNFACE [1], shows the lip movements of the speaker at the other end synchronised with the speech. SYNFACE has the distinct advantage that only the user on the receiving end needs special equipment. The SYNFACE technology has its background in the Teleface project [2, 3], which demonstrated that synthesised facial movements driven by an automatic speech recogniser can provide phonetic information that is not available in the auditory signal to a hearing-impaired user. In the SYNFACE project this has been further developed into a multilingual synthetic talking face, Fig. 1. A phoneme recogniser that works with very low latency has been developed as it is crucial in conversations that the visual and auditory speech signals are delayed relative to each other.

The key technological task for the SYNFACE system is to control a 3-D model of a talking face so as to generate, in real-time, prominent information-bearing oral movements derived from arbitrary acoustic speech signals. While

* Authors in alphabetical order.

K. Miesenberger et al. (Eds.): ICCHP 2004, LNCS 3118, pp. 1178–1185, 2004.

current technology is able to synchronise lip movements with arbitrary speech, the result is neither very natural nor does the visual information carry substantial phonetic information. Thus there are two main research areas that have been addressed in the SYNFACE project. The visual speech information requirements of auditory-visual communication have been defined, and techniques to derive this information from the acoustic speech signal in near real time have been developed. A multilingual prototype of the SYNFACE system has developed for Dutch, English and Swedish. This prototype will be evaluated by hearing-impaired users during this year. The user trials are about to start at three sites: RNID in the UK, Viataal in The Netherlands and KTH in Sweden. During the coming year the use of SYNFACE for two further languages, Finnish and Italian, will be demonstrated. The different parts of the SYNFACE system and the planned user trials are described in detail in this paper.

**Fig. 1.** The SYNFACE system

## 2 The SYNFACE Recogniser

The conditions faced by a speech recogniser for SYNFACE are adverse in many respects. The system is required to be speaker independent as the identity of the caller is not known in advance, task independent as the conversation is not restricted to any particular domain, narrow band as the conversation is supposed to happen across the telephone line, low latency as very short delay is allowed between the incoming speech and the lip movements, if the turn taking mechanism in the telephonic conversation is to be preserved. Furthermore the system is to be developed for three different languages.

Task independence can be achieved either by very large dictionary word recognition, or by avoiding decoding the speech signal at the lexical level, e.g. with phone recognition. The last was chosen here as the task of mapping acoustic to visual articulatory movements is independent of the higher levels of speech understanding. The speech signal is thus first classified into phonetic classes. The rule-based system described later in this paper is then used to generate the visual parameters from the phonetic sequence.

The task could in principle be considered as one of regression rather than classification, and the visual parameter trajectories could be directly estimated from the acoustic signal avoiding any phonetical representation. This solution, even if appealing from the research point of view, was abandoned, due to earlier experience [4], and the constraint of building a fully working system, imposed by the project plan.

The system is based on a hybrid of recurrent neural networks (RNNs) and hidden Markov models (HMMs) [5, 6]. The RNNs are used as frame-by-frame posterior probability estimators given the acoustic evidence. Probabilities are then fed into the HMMs that bear a model of time evolution. A Viterbi-like decoding scheme is employed in order to obtain the best phonetic sequence for a given speech segment. The latency constraints are met by approximating the Viterbi solution with a limited look-ahead length. This reduces the effectiveness of the time dependent information contained in the HMM. As shown in [5], this degradation is limited by the ability of the RNNs to learn their internal representation of time evolving problems. The interaction of these factors is thoroughly examined in [6].

The system was trained on the SpeechDat databases for Swedish, English and Flemish (Dutch). These databases are suitable for this application as they contain recordings of a large number of speakers (speaker independence) over telephone lines. Moreover they are available in over 20 different European languages, allowing easy development for other languages.

## 3 Synthetic Talking Head

The visual signal generation is based on 3D polygon models, which are parametrically articulated and deformed. The facial models are parameterised using weighted geometric transformations (translation, scaling and rotation) of the vertices. This is a generalised version of the scheme proposed by Parke [7] see [8] for details. The control parameter set used for the synthetic face articulation is chosen to reflect the articulatory phonetic features often used to describe speech production, and most parameters are defined in terms of articulatory targets rather than general geometric measures. The most important articulatory control parameters are jaw rotation, lip rounding, lip protrusion, mouth width, bilabial closure, labiodental closure and apex (tongue tip elevation).

### 3.1 Articulatory Control Models

To animate the movements of the talking head, an articulatory control model is used, that takes time-stamped phonetic symbols as input and produces articulatory control parameter trajectories to drive the face model. One of the problems that a control model has to deal with is coarticulation. Coarticulation refers to the way in which the realisation of a phonetic segment is influenced by neighbouring segments. It is the result of articulatory planning, inertia in the biomechanical structures of the vocal tract, and economy of production [9]. But coarticulation also serves a communicative purpose in making the speech signal more robust to noise by introducing redundancies, since the phonetic information is spread out over time. Backward, or carry-over coarticulation, refers to the way in which articulation at some point in time is affected by the articulation at some previous point in time. Forward, or anticipatory coarticulation, on the other hand, is a term used to describe how articulation at some point in time is affected by articulation of segments not yet realised. This means that a model that accounts for anticipatory coarticulation will need to look at future segments to calculate movements at the current point in time. In the SYNFACE scenario, this poses a problem, since the control model has to react with very short delay to the phonemes received from the speech recogniser.

A talking head that does not account for coarticulation will seem jerky and unnatural in its articulation. In the SYNFACE project, we have investigated several alternative articulatory control models, both rule-based and data-driven. In the rule-based model [10], each phoneme is assigned a target vector of articulatory control parameters. To allow the targets to be influenced by coarticulation, the target vector may be under-specified, i.e. some parameter values can be left undefined. If a target is left undefined, the value is inferred from context using interpolation, followed by smoothing of the resulting trajectory. As an example, consider the lip rounding parameter in the word "askew": an unrounded vowel, followed by a consonant cluster and a final rounded vowel. In this case, lip rounding would be unspecified for the consonants /s/ and /k/, leaving these targets to be determined from the leading and trailing vowel context by linear interpolation from the unrounded vowel /a/, across the consonant cluster, to the rounded /ew/. Definition of the targets in the rule-based control model is a manual labour, based on comparisons between animation and video recordings. For the prototype SYNFACE system, the articulatory targets for the synthetic talking face has been adapted to Dutch and English, in addition to Swedish [11]. In addition, a special real-time version of the rule-based control model has been developed, that uses a finite time-window of articulatory anticipation, as opposed to the original model of [10] that required access to the full utterance prior to synthesis. The current prototype uses a look-ahead window of 200 ms.

As an alternative to the rule-based control model, we have investigated several data-driven (trainable) methods of generating articulatory parameter trajectories to control the face model [12]. The data-driven models are trained on a corpus of articulatory movements recorded from a human speaker, and learn to reproduce the articulatory patterns. We have recorded audio-visual speech databases with articulation movement tracking for the three project languages. The optical motion tracking is done using a Qualisys system with four IR cameras (`http://www.qualisys.se`). The system tracks about 30 small reflectors (4 mm diameter) glued to the subject's jaw, cheeks, lips, nose and eyebrows and a pair of spectacles (to serve as reference for head movements) and calculates their 3D-coordinates at a rate of 60 frames per second. The procedure is described more fully in [13]. In the comparison study, four different data-driven models were trained on the same data (Swedish only). Two of the models are based on coarticulation models from speech production theory, that have previously been employed for visual speech synthesis [14, 15] and two of them are based on artificial neural networks (ANNs). The models are trained by estimating the free parameters, to minimise the error between predicted and measured parameter trajectories over a training set of 200 sentences. The models have been evaluated objectively (by comparing RMS error and correlation between target and prediction) over a set of sentences not part of the training material. The evaluation showed a small advantage for one of the speech production theory-based models [14]. In addition, an audiovisual sentence intelligibility test with 25 normal-hearing subjects was conducted, where the four data-driven models were compared against the rule-based model as well as a no-face condition. This evaluation showed that all models provide significantly increased intelligibility over the audio alone case, and the rule-based model produced the most intelligible articulation. One possible explanation why the rule-based model outperformed the data-driven ones is that the rule-based model was developed with clear articulation and high intelligibility as the primary goal, and as such it almost tends to hyper-articulate. The data-driven models on the other hand, are trained to mimic the speaking style of the target speaker, who could be characterised as having a rather relaxed pronunciation. On the basis of these experiments, the rule-based control model has been chosen for the current version of the prototype. However, work to improve the intelligibility of the data-driven models by re-training on data from a more intelligible speaker is underway.

### 3.2 Intelligibility Experiments

Intelligibility testing has been performed during the development of the prototype system based on the rule-based control model. Sentence intelligibility measures have been obtained for Dutch, English and Swedish from normal listeners using filtered speech, and from a group of English and Swedish hearing-impaired listeners [16]. Additionally, visual consonant confusion data have been collected from English normal listeners to identify weaknesses in the consonant synthesis rules. Some intelligibility test will also be included in the final user tests of the complete SYNFACE system with hearing-impaired users.

In the sentence intelligibility tests the filtered auditory signal was presented either alone, with the synthetic face or with a video of the original talker. Normal-hearing listeners heard noise-vocoded speech. Hearing-impaired listeners heard speech that was unprocessed but telephone-band limited. 12 native speakers for each language took part along with 10 hearing-impaired English listeners (average hearing loss of 86 dB). 24 Swedish hearing-impaired listeners (average hearing loss 86 dB) had performed a similar test earlier [3]. The speech material consisted of lists of everyday sentences in Swedish, Dutch and English designed to test speech perception ability. Subjects were seated in front of a computer screen and a loudspeaker or headphones, were presented with sentences in their native language, and were then asked to repeat what they perceived. The test leader noted the subjects' response. The number of correctly perceived keywords was counted. Scores are expressed as percent of keywords correct. Intelligibility scores for the normal-hearing subjects are shown in Fig. 2 a). Both for normal and hearing-impaired listeners, intelligibility with the added synthetic face was always significantly higher than for audio alone. The average improvement in intelligibility was 22% for both hearing-impaired and normal listeners. Except for the Swedish normal listeners, the addition of the natural face gave significantly higher intelligibility than did the synthetic face. There was a considerable spread of scores in the hearing-impaired group, especially in the sound alone and synthetic face conditions, reflecting a wide range of auditory abilities and of usefulness of the synthetic face. The subjects not being used to synthetic faces could to a part explain this. There was no clear relation between hearing loss and either auditory alone performance or the advantage gained from the addition of the synthetic face. However, as Fig. 2 b) shows, the synthetic face was generally more effective for those hearing-impaired listeners with poorer auditory-alone scores, although listeners with virtually zero auditory-alone scores showed around 10% intelligibility gain when the synthetic face was added.

For the VCV intelligibility tests video recordings from two female native British English talkers were used in addition to the synthetic face. 24 different British English consonants were produced in left and right /i/, /a/ and /u/ contexts. Five male and five female native speakers were shown a silent movie of the VCV productions and were asked to indicate the correct consonant in a forced choice task. Accuracy was low overall with 13.6% for the synthetic face and 23.4% for the natural faces. The difference between intelligibility was small for bilabial and labiodental articulations. For back articulations the synthetic face tended to give a large proportion of /l/ responses compared to the natural faces. This indicates that the production rules for tongue movements in the synthetic face need to be improved.

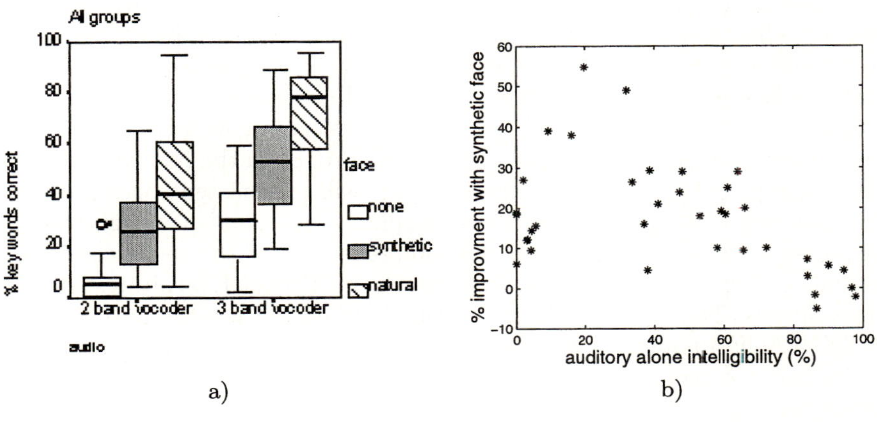


**Fig. 2.** a) Sentence intelligibility for degraded speech with synthetic and natural visual speech. Results from all languages and normal-hearing subjects. b) Intelligibility gain with synthetic face compared to auditory-alone scores for hearing-impaired listeners

## 4 SYNFACE Prototype

The present prototype is implemented on a portable Windows PC connected to a standard telephone via off-the-shelf hardware. The remote and local talkers voices are fed into the line-in of a USB sound card. In order to facilitate programmatically controlled delay of the incoming speech, the ear-piece/loudspeaker of the telephone is connected to the line-out of the USB sound card. The prototype system software consists of three distinct modules: the recogniser (that is also responsible for input and delayed output of audio), the articulatory control model, and the facial rendering engine. To facilitate system integration and promote rapid prototype development, we use a scripting language (Tcl/Tk [17]). The recogniser, the articulatory control model and the facial rendering engine are implemented in C/C++ as compiled extensions to the Tcl interpreter.

## 5 User Trials

User trials will be carried out in the UK, Sweden and the Netherlands to evaluate the usability, effectiveness and perceived value of the SYNFACE prototype. In the UK about 40 users will participate in the trials while in Sweden and the Netherlands about 10 subjects will test the system.

In the UK, trials will initially be carried out in the lab with hearing impaired users discussing set topics/scenarios with an experimenter, using SYNFACE. To gain an greater understanding of the potential uses of SYNFACE and to illustrating the speech recognition aspects of the system, users will also be shown a video of SYNFACE being used for a conversation, and will then watch several short stories and sentences that have been pre-recorded. Information on the usability, effectiveness and perceived value of SYNFACE will be gathered using a questionnaire, as well as a de-briefing interview. From the users that complete these UK lab-based trials, a number of users will be asked to use the SYNFACE in their home or workplace for 2-3 weeks to investigate how users attitudes and experiences change with prolonged use of SYNFACE. In the Netherlands, trials will be comprised of two parts. The first part will present sentences to users in three different ways - SYNFACE, Video telephony and sound only. This will allow comparisons to be made between the comprehension of the sentences for each method of display, and reveal the extent to which SYNFACE facilitates telephone conversations. The second part of the Dutch trials will get the participants to use SYNFACE for spontaneous conversation. In Sweden, it is planned that trials will include a perception test on sentences and then the system will be left with participants to use for one day in their homes, to call friends and relatives.

To allow comparisons to be made between the findings of trials in each country, the same questionnaires will be used in all trials. The trials will start during May this year, some preliminary results will be presented at the conference.

## Acknowledgements

The SYNFACE project is financed by the European Union (EU) under the FP5 IST Key Action I Programme: Systems and Services for the Citizen. The project also benefits from an equipment donation within the HP VoiceWeb Initiative.

The authors would like to thank B. Lyberg at Linköping University who allowed us use their equipment for recording the audiovisual speech databases.

We would also like to thank the other project members at KTH and Babel-Infovox, Sweden, UCL and RNID, the UK, Viataal the Netherlands.

## References

1. (http://www.speech.kth.se/synface)
2. Beskow, J., Dahlquist, M., Granström, B., Lundeberg, M., K-E.Spens, Öhman, T.: The teleface project: Multimodal speech communication for the hearing impaired. In: Proc. of Eurospeech, Rhodes (1997) 1651–1654
3. Agelfors, E., Beskow, J., Dahlquist, M., Granström, B., Lundeberg, M., Spens, K.E., Öhman, T.: Synthetic faces as a lip-reading support. In: Proc. of ICSLP, Sydney, Australia (1998)
4. Öhman, T., Salvi, G.: using HMMs and ANNs for mapping acoustic to visual speech. TMH-QPSR **1-2** (1999)
5. Salvi, G.: Truncation error and dynamics in very low latency phonetic recognition. In: ISCA workshop on Non-linear Speech Processing. (2003)
6. Salvi, G.: Dynamic behaviour of connectionist speech recognition with strong latency constraints. Speech Communication (submitted)
7. Parke, F.: Parametrized models for facial animation. ieee computer graphics. IEEE Computer Graphics **2** (1982) 61–68
8. Beskow, J.: Animation of talking agents. In: Proc. of AVSP'97, Rhodes (1997)
9. Lindblom, B.: Economy of speech gestures. In: The production of speech. P. MacNeilage, New York: Springer-Verlag (1983) 217–245
10. Beskow, J.: Rule-based visual speech synthesis. In: Proc. of Eurospeech, Madrid, Spain (1995) 299–302
11. Karlsson, I., Faulkner, A., Salvi, G.: SYNFACE a talking face telephone. In: Proc. of EuroSpeech. (2003) 1297–1300
12. Beskow, J.: Trainable articulatory control models for visual speech synthesis. Journal of Speech Technology (in press)
13. Beskow, J., Engwall, O., Granström, B.: Resynthesis of facial and intraoral articulation from simultaneous measurements. In: Proc. of ICPhS. (2003) 431–434
14. Cohen, M., Massaro, D.: Modelling Coarticulation in Synthetic Visual Speech. In: Models and Techniques in Computer Animation. Springer Verlag, Tokyo (1993) 139–156
15. Reveret, L., Bailly, G., Badin, P.: Mother: a new generation of talking heads providing a flexible articulatory control for video-realistic speech animation. In: Proc. of ICSLP, Bejing, China (2000) 755–758
16. Siciliano, C., Williams, G., Beskow, J., Faulkner, A.: Evaluation of a multilingual synthetic talking face as a communication aid for the hearing impaired. In: Proc. of ICPhS. (2003) 131–134
17. Ousterhout, J.: Tcl and the Tk Toolkit. Addison Wesley (1994)

# Author Index

# Lecture Notes in Computer Science

For information about Vols. 1–3019

please contact your bookseller or Springer-Verlag

Vol. 3125: D. Kozen (Ed.), Mathematics of Program Construction. X, 401 pages. 2004.

Vol. 3123: A. Belz, R. Evans, P. Piwek (Eds.), Natural Language Generation. X, 219 pages. 2004. (Subseries LNAI).

Vol. 3120: J. Shawe-Taylor, Y. Singer (Eds.), Learning Theory. X, 648 pages. 2004. (Subseries LNAI).

Vol. 3118: K. Miesenberger, J. Klaus, W. Zagler, D. Burger (Eds.), Computer Helping People with Special Needs. XXIII, 1191 pages. 2004.

Vol. 3116: C. Rattray, S. Maharaj, C. Shankland (Eds.), Algebraic Methodology and Software Technology. XI, 569 pages. 2004.

Vol. 3114: R. Alur, D.A. Peled (Eds.), Computer Aided Verification. XII, 536 pages. 2004.

Vol. 3113: J. Karhumäki, H. Maurer, G. Paun, G. Rozenberg (Eds.), Theory Is Forever. X, 283 pages. 2004.

Vol. 3112: H. Williams, L. MacKinnon (Eds.), New Horizons in Information Management. XII, 265 pages. 2004.

Vol. 3111: T. Hagerup, J. Katajainen (Eds.), Algorithm Theory - SWAT 2004. XI, 506 pages. 2004.

Vol. 3109: S.C. Sahinalp, S. Muthukrishnan, U. Dogrusoz (Eds.), Combinatorial Pattern Matching. XII, 486 pages. 2004.

Vol. 3105: S. Göbel, U. Spierling, A. Hoffmann, I. Iurgel, O. Schneider, J. Dechau, A. Feix (Eds.), Technologies for Interactive Digital Storytelling and Entertainment. XVI, 304 pages. 2004.

Vol. 3104: R. Kralovic, O. Sykora (Eds.), Structural Information and Communication Complexity. X, 303 pages. 2004.

Vol. 3103: K. Deb (Ed.), Genetic and Evolutionary Computation - GECCO 2004. XLIX, 1439 pages. 2004.

Vol. 3102: K. Deb (Ed.), Genetic and Evolutionary Computation - GECCO 2004. L, 1445 pages. 2004.

Vol. 3101: M. Masoodian, S. Jones, B. Rogers (Eds.), Computer Human Interaction. XIV, 694 pages. 2004.

Vol. 3099: J. Cortadella, W. Reisig (Eds.), Applications and Theory of Petri Nets 2004. XI, 505 pages. 2004.

Vol. 3098: J. Desel, W. Reisig, G. Rozenberg (Eds.), Lectures on Concurrency and Petri Nets. VIII, 849 pages. 2004.

Vol. 3097: D. Basin, M. Rusinowitch (Eds.), Automated Reasoning. XII, 493 pages. 2004. (Subseries LNAI).

Vol. 3096: G. Melnik, H. Holz (Eds.), Advances in Learning Software Organizations. X, 173 pages. 2004.

Vol. 3094: A. Nürnberger, M. Detyniecki (Eds.), Adaptive Multimedia Retrieval. VIII, 229 pages. 2004.

Vol. 3093: S.K. Katsikas, S. Gritzalis, J. Lopez (Eds.), Public Key Infrastructure. XIII, 380 pages. 2004.

Vol. 3092: J. Eckstein, H. Baumeister (Eds.), Extreme Programming and Agile Processes in Software Engineering. XVI, 358 pages. 2004.

Vol. 3091: V. van Oostrom (Ed.), Rewriting Techniques and Applications. X, 313 pages. 2004.

Vol. 3089: M. Jakobsson, M. Yung, J. Zhou (Eds.), Applied Cryptography and Network Security. XIV, 510 pages. 2004.

Vol. 3086: M. Odersky (Ed.), ECOOP 2004 – Object-Oriented Programming. XIII, 611 pages. 2004.

Vol. 3085: S. Berardi, M. Coppo, F. Damiani (Eds.), Types for Proofs and Programs. X, 409 pages. 2004.

Vol. 3084: A. Persson, J. Stirna (Eds.), Advanced Information Systems Engineering. XIV, 596 pages. 2004.

Vol. 3083: W. Emmerich, A.L. Wolf (Eds.), Component Deployment. X, 249 pages. 2004.

Vol. 3080: J. Desel, B. Pernici, M. Weske (Eds.), Business Process Management. X, 307 pages. 2004.

Vol. 3079: Z. Mammeri, P. Lorenz (Eds.), High Speed Networks and Multimedia Communications. XVIII, 1103 pages. 2004.

Vol. 3078: S. Cotin, D.N. Metaxas (Eds.), Medical Simulation. XVI, 296 pages. 2004.

Vol. 3077: F. Roli, J. Kittler, T. Windeatt (Eds.), Multiple Classifier Systems. XII, 386 pages. 2004.

Vol. 3076: D. Buell (Ed.), Algorithmic Number Theory. XI, 451 pages. 2004.

Vol. 3074: B. Kuijpers, P. Revesz (Eds.), Constraint Databases and Applications. XII, 181 pages. 2004.

Vol. 3073: H. Chen, R. Moore, D.D. Zeng, J. Leavitt (Eds.), Intelligence and Security Informatics. XV, 536 pages. 2004.

Vol. 3072: D. Zhang, A.K. Jain (Eds.), Biometric Authentication. XVII, 800 pages. 2004.

Vol. 3070: L. Rutkowski, J. Siekmann, R. Tadeusiewicz, L.A. Zadeh (Eds.), Artificial Intelligence and Soft Computing - ICAISC 2004. XXV, 1208 pages. 2004. (Subseries LNAI).

Vol. 3068: E. André, L. Dybkjær, W. Minker, P. Heisterkamp (Eds.), Affective Dialogue Systems. XII, 324 pages. 2004. (Subseries LNAI).

Vol. 3067: M. Dastani, J. Dix, A. El Fallah-Seghrouchni (Eds.), Programming Multi-Agent Systems. X, 221 pages. 2004. (Subseries LNAI).

Vol. 3066: S. Tsumoto, R. S lowiński, J. Komorowski, J.W. Grzymala-Busse (Eds.), Rough Sets and Current Trends in Computing. XX, 853 pages. 2004. (Subseries LNAI).

Vol. 3065: A. Lomuscio, D. Nute (Eds.), Deontic Logic in Computer Science. X, 275 pages. 2004. (Subseries LNAI).

Vol. 3064: D. Bienstock, G. Nemhauser (Eds.), Integer Programming and Combinatorial Optimization. XI, 445 pages. 2004.

Vol. 3063: A. Llamosí, A. Strohmeier (Eds.), Reliable Software Technologies - Ada-Europe 2004. XIII, 333 pages. 2004.

Vol. 3062: J.L. Pfaltz, M. Nagl, B. Böhlen (Eds.), Applications of Graph Transformations with Industrial Relevance. XV, 500 pages. 2004.

Vol. 3061: F.F. Ramas, H. Unger, V. Larios (Eds.), Advanced Distributed Systems. VIII, 285 pages. 2004.

Vol. 3060: A.Y. Tawfik, S.D. Goodwin (Eds.), Advances in Artificial Intelligence. XIII, 582 pages. 2004. (Subseries LNAI).

Vol. 3059: C.C. Ribeiro, S.L. Martins (Eds.), Experimental and Efficient Algorithms. X, 586 pages. 2004.

Vol. 3058: N. Sebe, M.S. Lew, T.S. Huang (Eds.), Computer Vision in Human-Computer Interaction. X, 233 pages. 2004.

Vol. 3057: B. Jayaraman (Ed.), Practical Aspects of Declarative Languages. VIII, 255 pages. 2004.

Vol. 3056: H. Dai, R. Srikant, C. Zhang (Eds.), Advances in Knowledge Discovery and Data Mining. XIX, 713 pages. 2004. (Subseries LNAI).

Vol. 3055: H. Christiansen, M.-S. Hacid, T. Andreasen, H.L. Larsen (Eds.), Flexible Query Answering Systems. X, 500 pages. 2004. (Subseries LNAI).

Vol. 3054: I. Crnkovic, J.A. Stafford, H.W. Schmidt, K. Wallnau (Eds.), Component-Based Software Engineering. XI, 311 pages. 2004.

Vol. 3053: C. Bussler, J. Davies, D. Fensel, R. Studer (Eds.), The Semantic Web: Research and Applications. XIII, 490 pages. 2004.

Vol. 3052: W. Zimmermann, B. Thalheim (Eds.), Abstract State Machines 2004. Advances in Theory and Practice. XII, 235 pages. 2004.

Vol. 3051: R. Berghammer, B. Möller, G. Struth (Eds.), Relational and Kleene-Algebraic Methods in Computer Science. X, 279 pages. 2004.

Vol. 3050: J. Domingo-Ferrer, V. Torra (Eds.), Privacy in Statistical Databases. IX, 367 pages. 2004.

Vol. 3049: M. Bruynooghe, K.-K. Lau (Eds.), Program Development in Computational Logic. VIII, 539 pages. 2004.

Vol. 3047: F. Oquendo, B. Warboys, R. Morrison (Eds.), Software Architecture. X, 279 pages. 2004.

Vol. 3046: A. Laganà, M.L. Gavrilova, V. Kumar, Y. Mun, C.J.K. Tan, O. Gervasi (Eds.), Computational Science and Its Applications – ICCSA 2004. LIII, 1016 pages. 2004.

Vol. 3045: A. Laganà, M.L. Gavrilova, V. Kumar, Y. Mun, C.J.K. Tan, O. Gervasi (Eds.), Computational Science and Its Applications – ICCSA 2004. LIII, 1040 pages. 2004.

Vol. 3044: A. Laganà, M.L. Gavrilova, V. Kumar, Y. Mun, C.J.K. Tan, O. Gervasi (Eds.), Computational Science and Its Applications – ICCSA 2004. LIII, 1140 pages. 2004.

Vol. 3043: A. Laganà, M.L. Gavrilova, V. Kumar, Y. Mun, C.J.K. Tan, O. Gervasi (Eds.), Computational Science and Its Applications – ICCSA 2004. LIII, 1180 pages. 2004.

Vol. 3042: N. Mitrou, K. Kontovasilis, G.N. Rouskas, I. Iliadis, L. Merakos (Eds.), NETWORKING 2004, Networking Technologies, Services, and Protocols; Performance of Computer and Communication Networks; Mobile and Wireless Communications. XXXIII, 1519 pages. 2004.

Vol. 3040: R. Conejo, M. Urretavizcaya, J.-L. Pérez-de-la-Cruz (Eds.), Current Topics in Artificial Intelligence. XIV, 689 pages. 2004. (Subseries LNAI).

Vol. 3039: M. Bubak, G.D.v. Albada, P.M.A. Sloot, J.J. Dongarra (Eds.), Computational Science - ICCS 2004. LXVI, 1271 pages. 2004.

Vol. 3038: M. Bubak, G.D.v. Albada, P.M.A. Sloot, J.J. Dongarra (Eds.), Computational Science - ICCS 2004. LXVI, 1311 pages. 2004.

Vol. 3037: M. Bubak, G.D.v. Albada, P.M.A. Sloot, J.J. Dongarra (Eds.), Computational Science - ICCS 2004. LXVI, 745 pages. 2004.

Vol. 3036: M. Bubak, G.D.v. Albada, P.M.A. Sloot, J.J. Dongarra (Eds.), Computational Science - ICCS 2004. LXVI, 713 pages. 2004.

Vol. 3035: M.A. Wimmer (Ed.), Knowledge Management in Electronic Government. XII, 326 pages. 2004. (Subseries LNAI).

Vol. 3034: J. Favela, E. Menasalvas, E. Chávez (Eds.), Advances in Web Intelligence. XIII, 227 pages. 2004. (Subseries LNAI).

Vol. 3033: M. Li, X.-H. Sun, Q. Deng, J. Ni (Eds.), Grid and Cooperative Computing. XXXVIII, 1076 pages. 2004.

Vol. 3032: M. Li, X.-H. Sun, Q. Deng, J. Ni (Eds.), Grid and Cooperative Computing. XXXVII, 1112 pages. 2004.

Vol. 3031: A. Butz, A. Krüger, P. Olivier (Eds.), Smart Graphics. X, 165 pages. 2004.

Vol. 3030: P. Giorgini, B. Henderson-Sellers, M. Winikoff (Eds.), Agent-Oriented Information Systems. XIV, 207 pages. 2004. (Subseries LNAI).

Vol. 3029: B. Orchard, C. Yang, M. Ali (Eds.), Innovations in Applied Artificial Intelligence. XXI, 1272 pages. 2004. (Subseries LNAI).

Vol. 3028: D. Neuenschwander, Probabilistic and Statistical Methods in Cryptology. X, 158 pages. 2004.

Vol. 3027: C. Cachin, J. Camenisch (Eds.), Advances in Cryptology - EUROCRYPT 2004. XI, 628 pages. 2004.

Vol. 3026: C.V. Ramamoorthy, R. Lee, K.W. Lee (Eds.), Software Engineering Research and Applications. XV, 377 pages. 2004.

Vol. 3025: G.A. Vouros, T. Panayiotopoulos (Eds.), Methods and Applications of Artificial Intelligence. XV, 546 pages. 2004. (Subseries LNAI).

Vol. 3024: T. Pajdla, J. Matas (Eds.), Computer Vision - ECCV 2004. XXVIII, 621 pages. 2004.

Vol. 3023: T. Pajdla, J. Matas (Eds.), Computer Vision - ECCV 2004. XXVIII, 611 pages. 2004.

Vol. 3022: T. Pajdla, J. Matas (Eds.), Computer Vision - ECCV 2004. XXVIII, 621 pages. 2004.

Vol. 3021: T. Pajdla, J. Matas (Eds.), Computer Vision - ECCV 2004. XXVIII, 633 pages. 2004.